Street by Street

HAMPS

C000125084

Enlarged areas ALDERSHOT, ANDOVER, BASINGSTOKE, BOURNEMOUTH, FAREHAM, GOSPORT, HAVANT, NEWBURY, PORTSMOUTH, SOUTHAMPTON, WINCHESTER
Plus Canford Heath, Christchurch, Farnham, Ferndown, Haslemere, North Tidworth, Poole, Sandhurst, Verwood, Wimborne Minster

2nd edition June 2005
© Automobile Association Developments Limited 2005

Original edition printed May 2001

Ordnance Survey® This product includes map data licensed from Ordnance Survey® with the permission of the Controller of Her Majesty's Stationery Office. © Crown copyright 2005. All rights reserved. Licence number 399221.

Published by AA Publishing, a trading name of Automobile Association Developments Limited, whose registered office (from 1st October 2005) will be Fanum House, Basing View, Basingstoke, Hampshire RG21 4EA.
Registered number 1878835.

Mapping produced by the Cartography Department of The Automobile Association. (A02256)

A CIP Catalogue record for this book is available from the British Library.

Printed by Oriental Press in Dubai

Ref: ML011z

Key to map pages	ii-iii
Key to map symbols	iv-1
Enlarged map pages	2-23
Main map pages	24-339
Index – towns & villages	340-342
Index – streets	343-392
Index – featured places	392-400
Acknowledgements	400

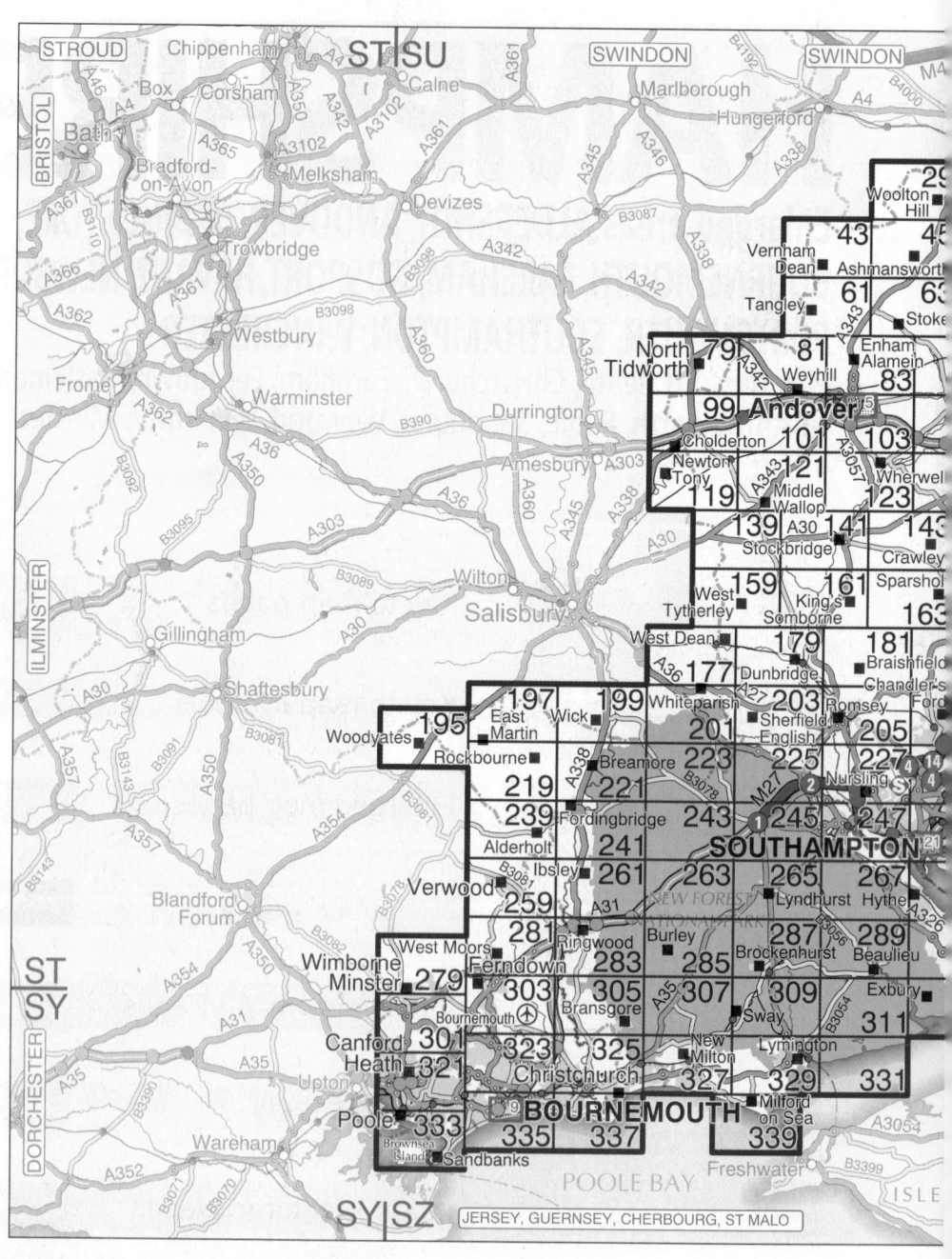

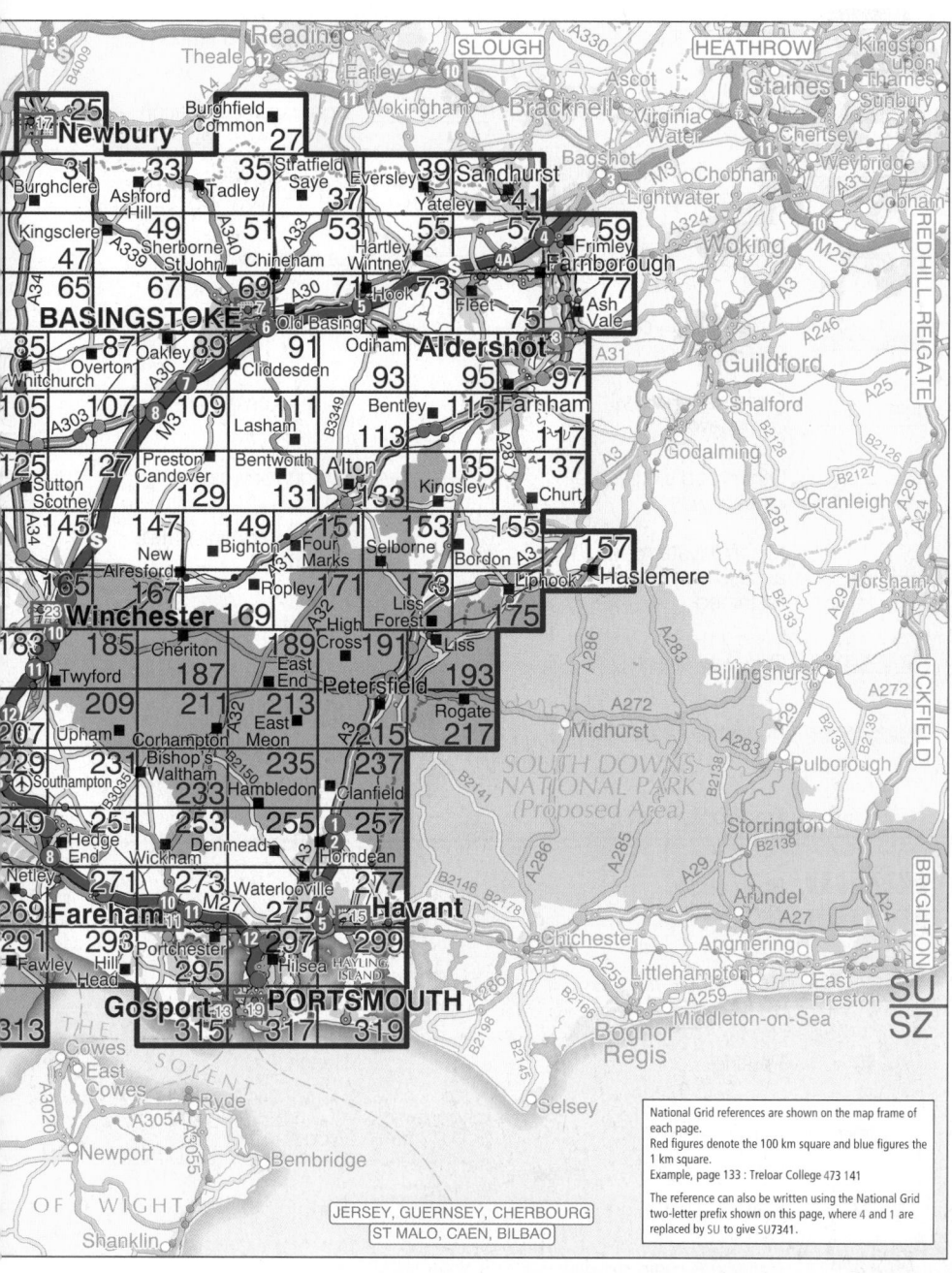

National Grid references are shown on the map frame of each page.
Red figures denote the 100 km square and blue figures the 1 km square.
Example, page 133 : Treloar College 473 141

The reference can also be written using the National Grid two-letter prefix shown on this page, where 4 and 1 are replaced by SU to give SU7341.

JERSEY, GUERNSEY, CHERBOURG
ST MALO, CAEN, BILBAO

2.5 inches to 1 mile   **Scale of main map pages 1:25,000**

Junction 9	Motorway & junction	⊖	Underground station
Services	Motorway service area	⊖	Light railway & station
	Primary road single/dual carriageway	+++++++++	Preserved private railway
Services	Primary road service area	LC	Level crossing
	A road single/dual carriageway	●—●—●—●	Tramway
	B road single/dual carriageway	------------	Ferry route
	Other road single/dual carriageway	··················	Airport runway
	Minor/private road, access may be restricted	— · — · — · —	County, administrative boundary
← ←	One-way street	▼▼▼▼▼▼▼▼▼	Mounds
	Pedestrian area	**47**	Page continuation 1:25,000
============	Track or footpath	**3**	Page continuation to enlarged scale 1:10,000
	Road under construction		River/canal, lake
⊏ - - - - ⊐	Road tunnel		Aqueduct, lock, weir
P	Parking	465 ▲ Winter Hill	Peak (with height in metres)
P+🚌	Park & Ride		Beach
🚌	Bus/coach station		Woodland
	Railway & main railway station		Park
	Railway & minor railway station	✝ ✝ ✝	Cemetery
			Built-up area

Featured building

City wall

A&E Hospital with 24-hour A&E department

PO Post Office

Public library

Tourist Information Centre

Seasonal Tourist Information Centre

Petrol station, 24-hour
Major suppliers only

Church/chapel

Public toilets

Toilet with disabled facilities

PH Public house
AA recommended

Restaurant
AA inspected

Madeira Hotel Hotel
AA inspected

Theatre or performing arts centre

Cinema

Golf course

Camping
AA inspected

Caravan site
AA inspected

Camping & caravan site
AA inspected

Theme park

Abbey, cathedral or priory

Castle

Historic house or building

Wakehurst Place NT National Trust property

Museum or art gallery

Roman antiquity

Ancient site, battlefield or monument

Industrial interest

Garden

Garden Centre
Garden Centre Association Member

Garden Centre
Wyevale Garden Centre

Arboretum

Farm or animal centre

Zoological or wildlife collection

Bird collection

Nature reserve

Aquarium

Visitor or heritage centre

Country park

Cave

Windmill

Distillery, brewery or vineyard

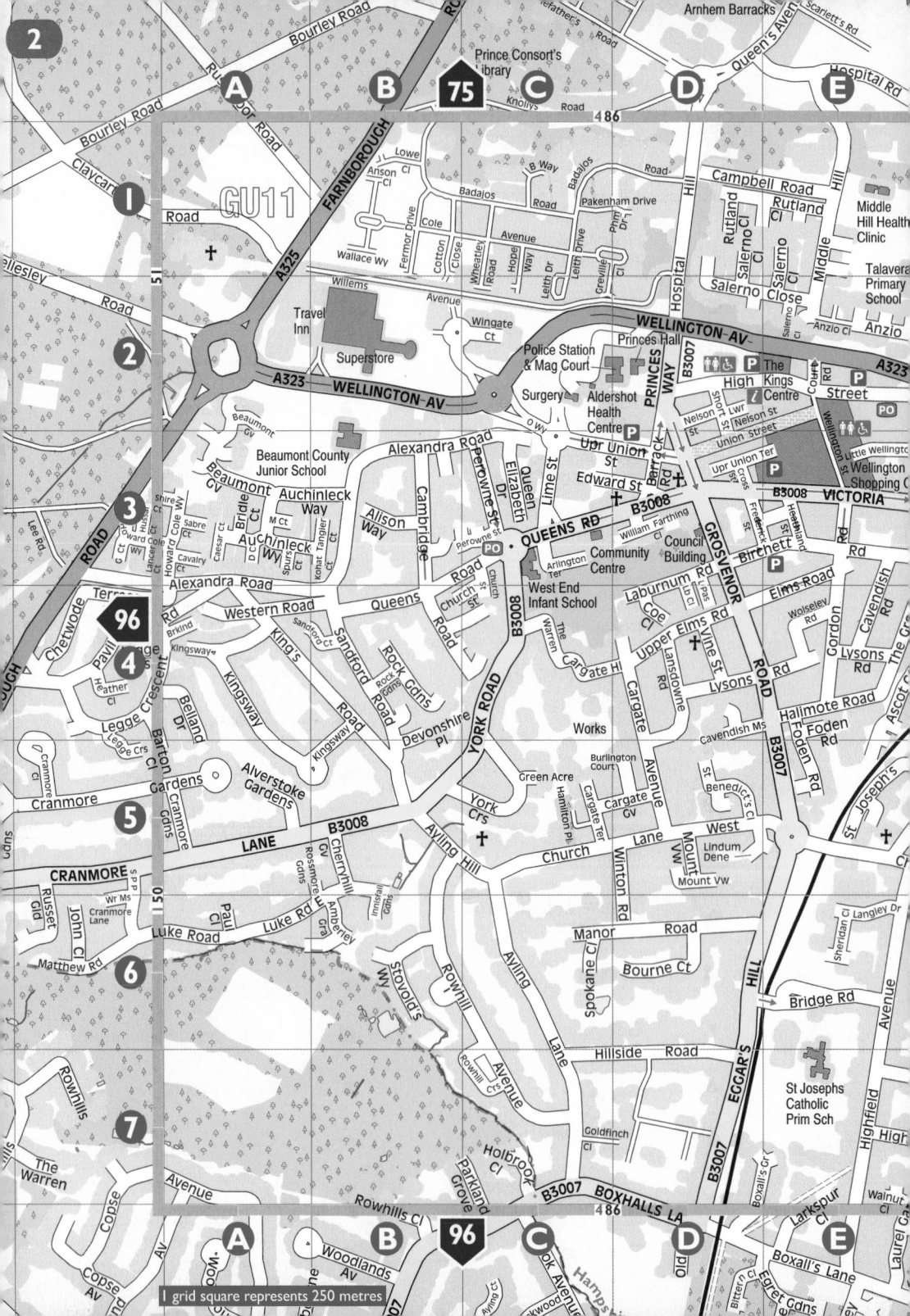

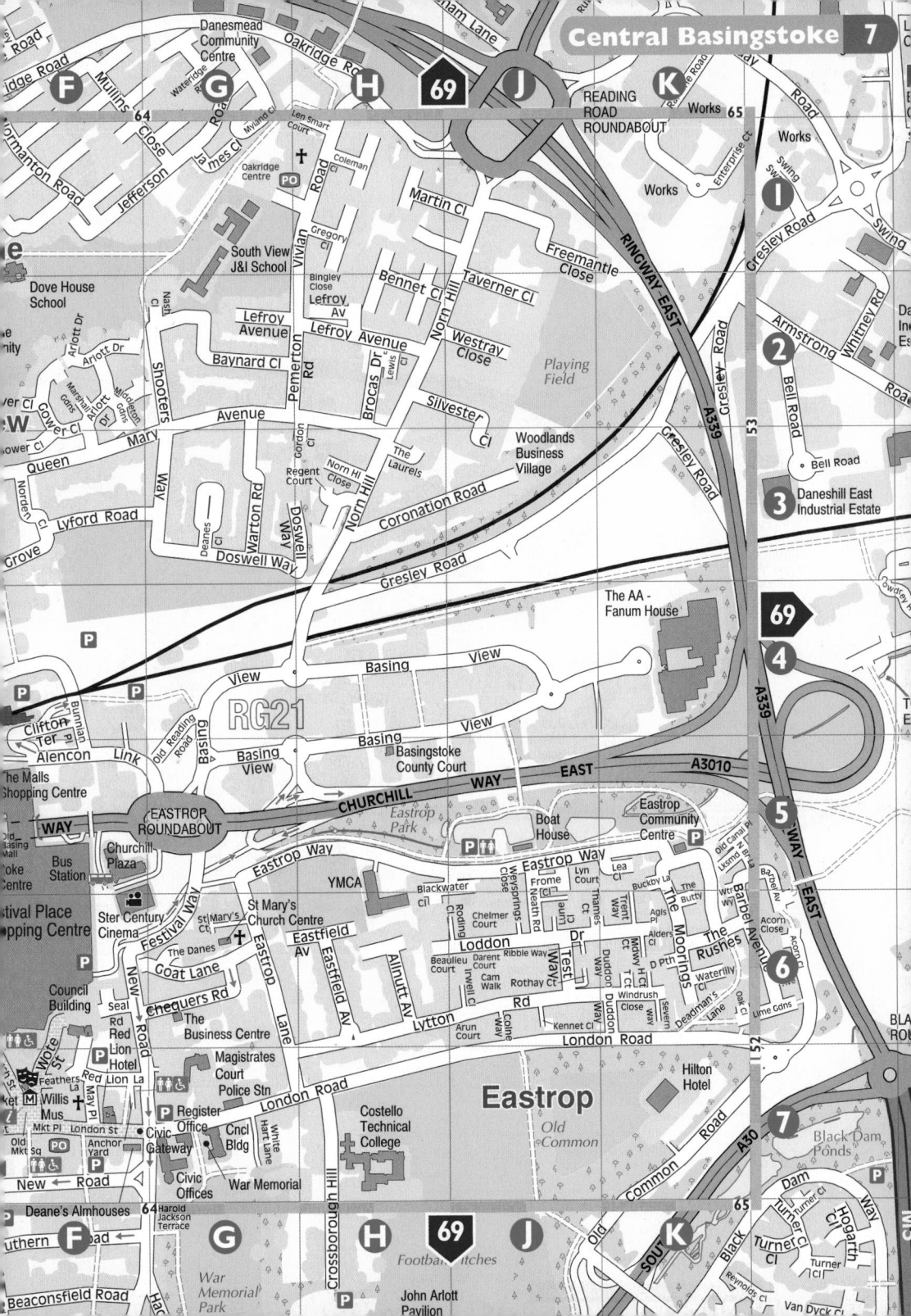

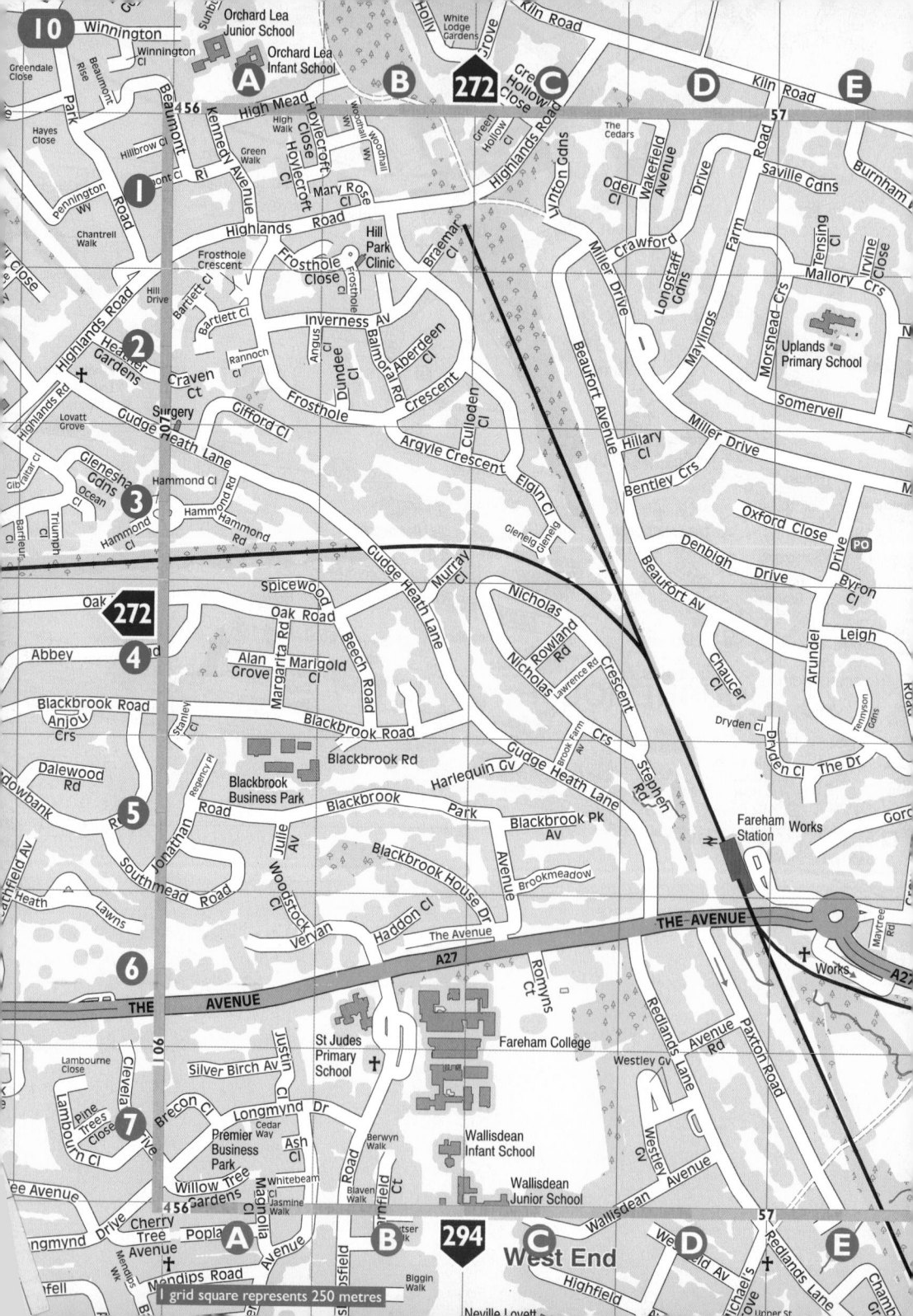

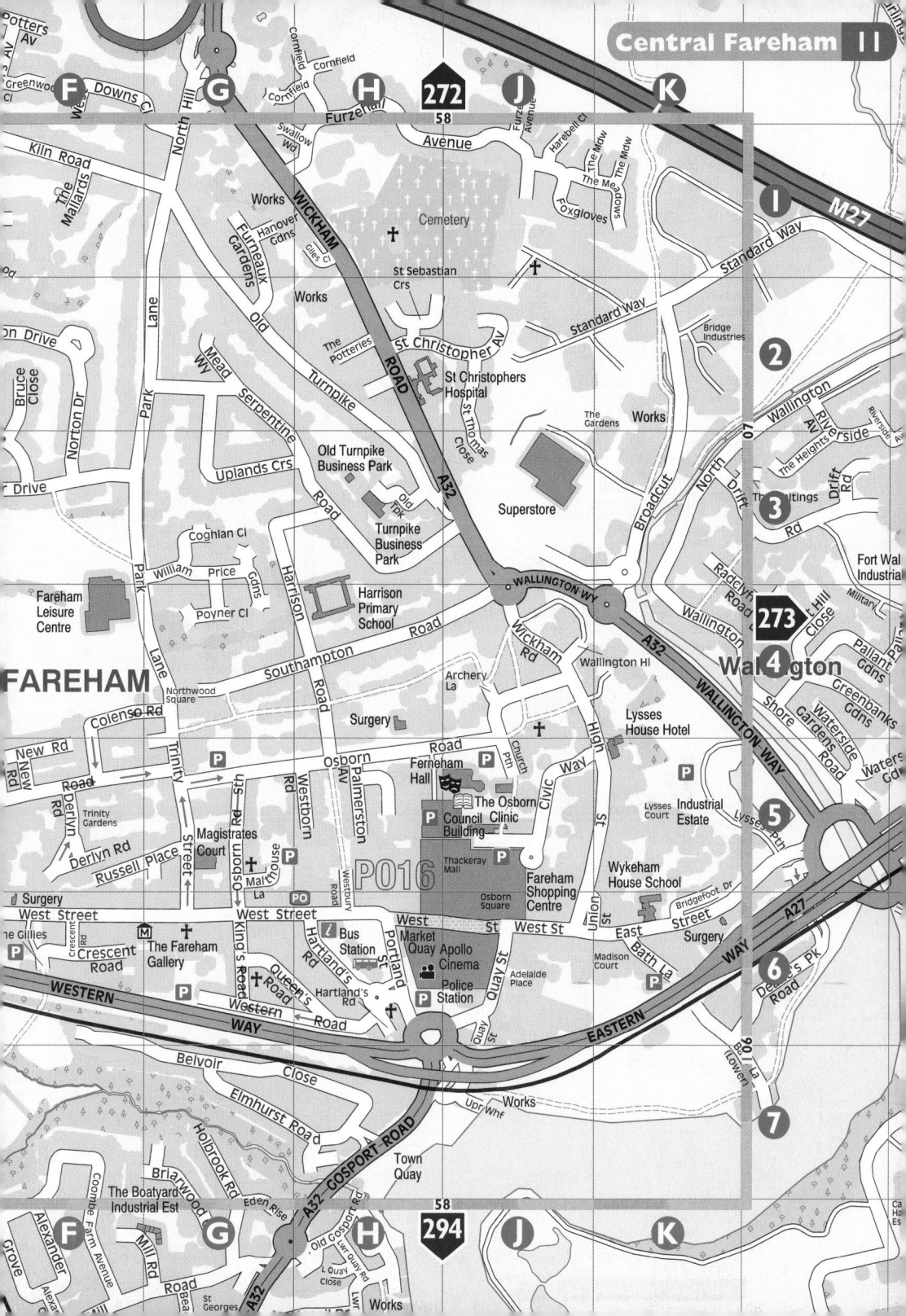

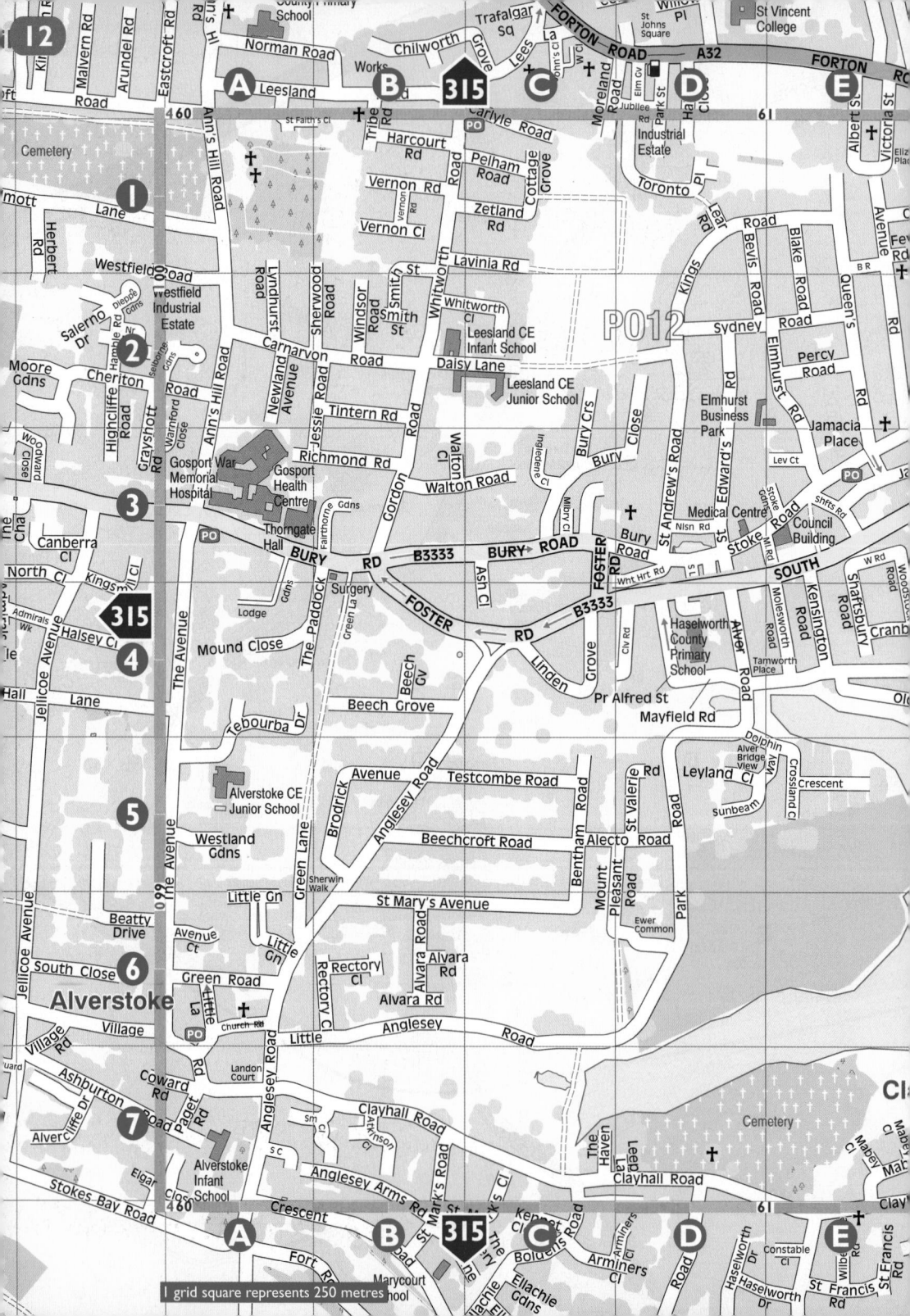

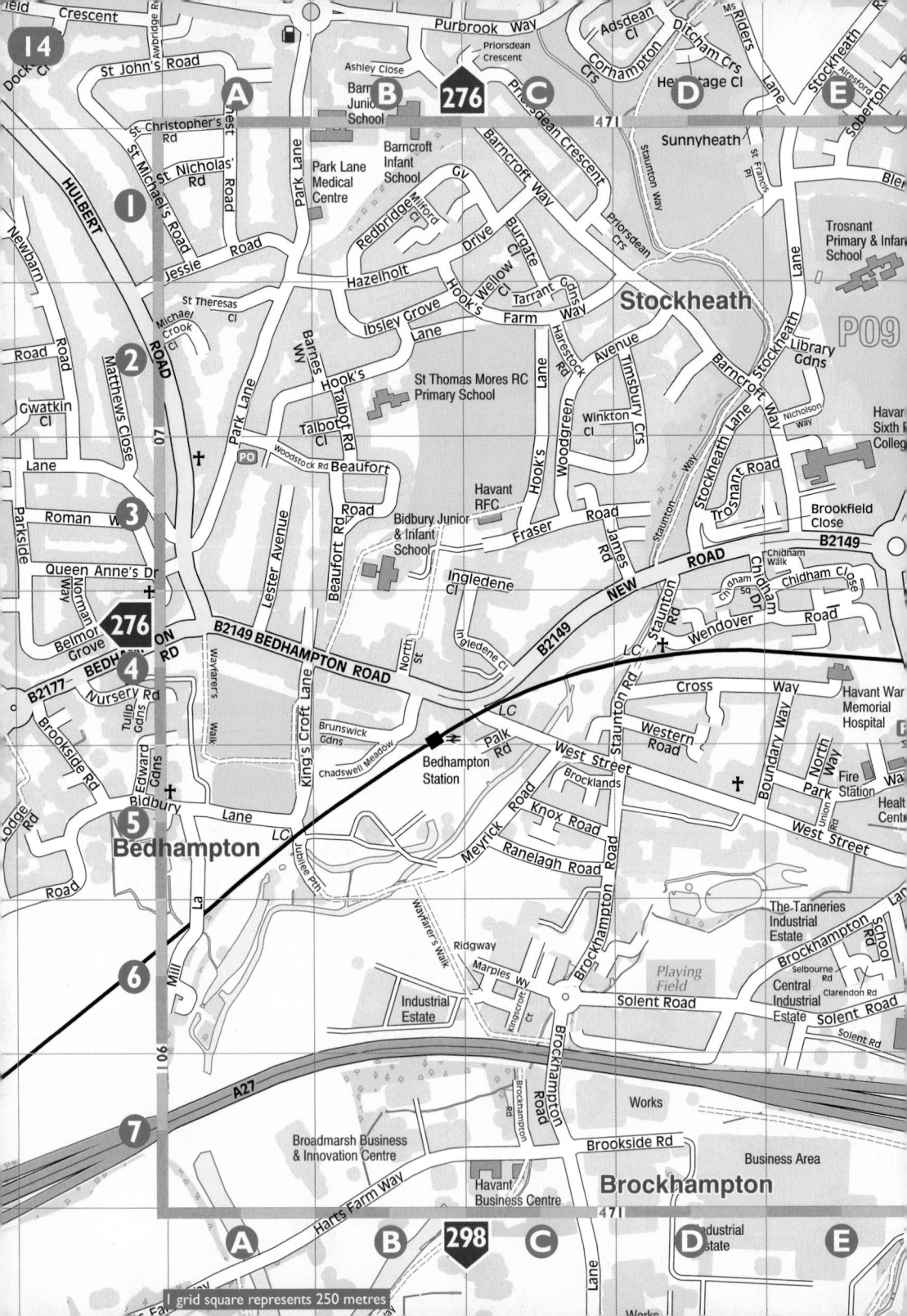

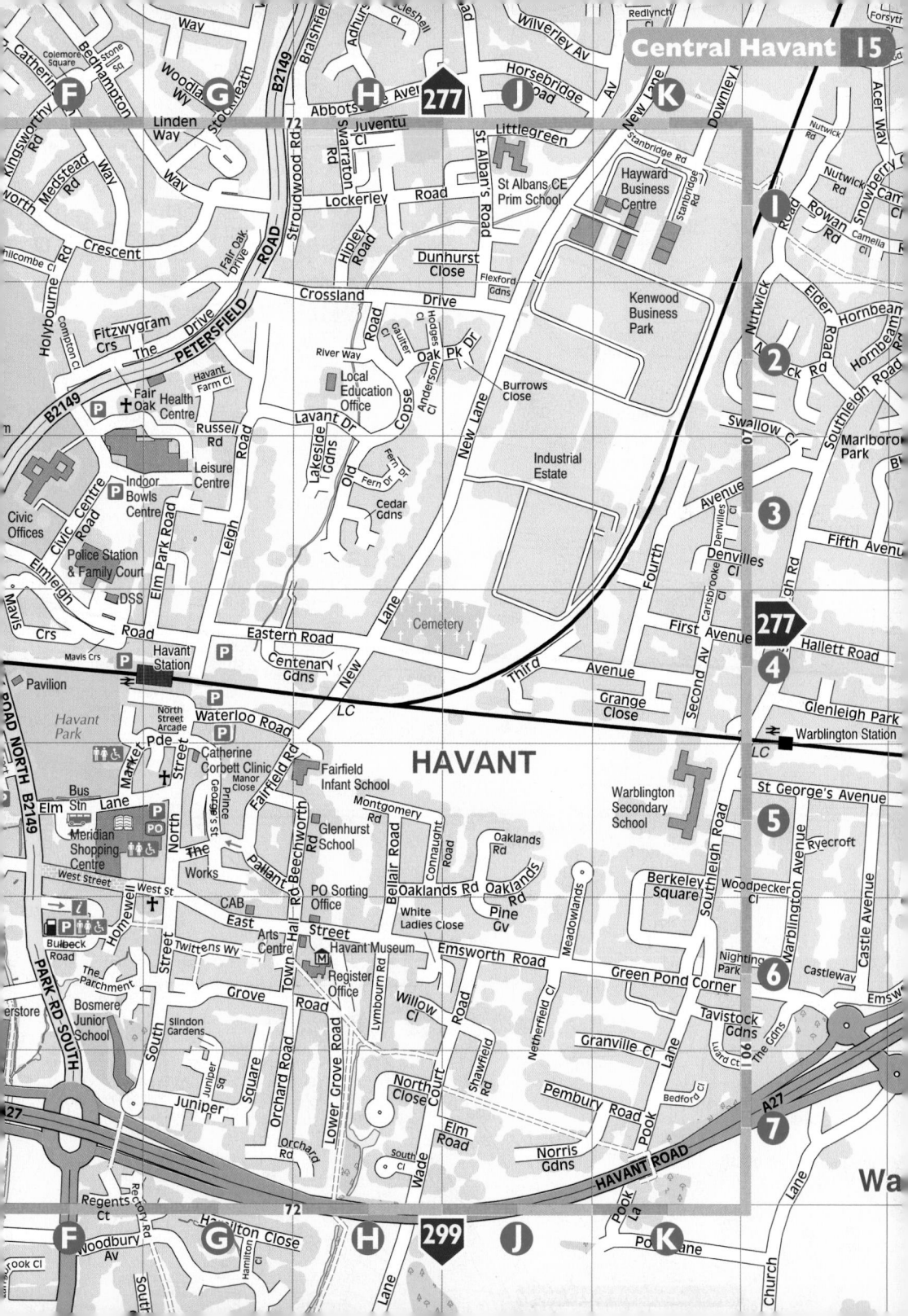

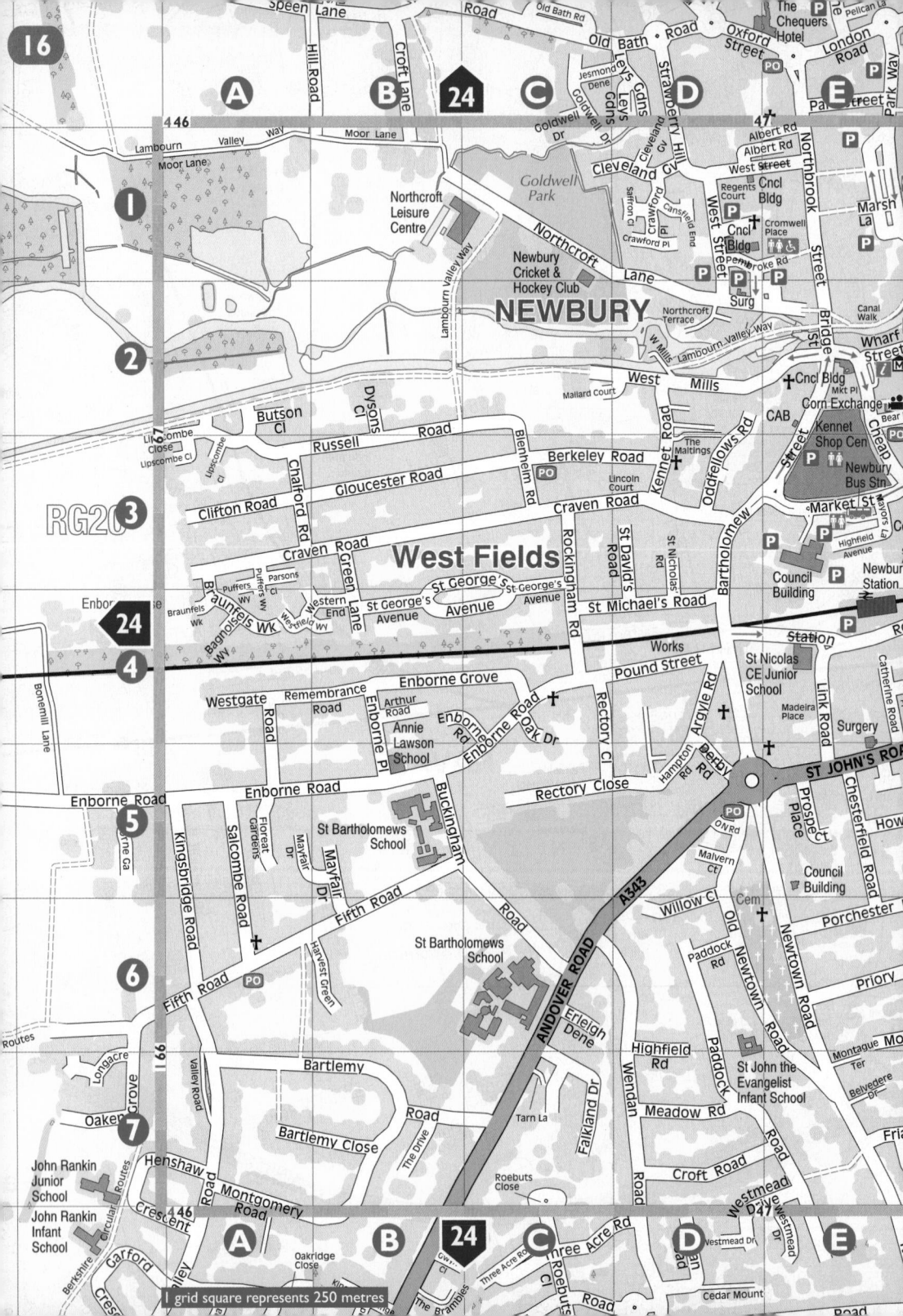

16

A   B   **24**   C   D   E

446

1

Speen Lane   Old Bath Rd   The Chequers Hotel   Oxford Street   London Road

Hill Road   Croft Lane   Goldwell Dr   Old Bath Road   Strawberry Hill   Northbrook Street   Park Street

Lambourn Valley Way   Moor Lane   Jesmond Dene   Leys Gdns   Cleveland   Albert Rd   Albert Rd   West Street   Marsh La

Moor Lane   Goldwell Park   Cleveland   Regents Court   Cncl Bldg   Cromwell Place   PO

Northcroft Leisure Centre   Saffron Cl   Crawford End   Cncl Bldg   Pembroke Rd

2   Newbury Cricket & Hockey Club   Northcroft Lane   Crawford Pl   Surg   Canal Walk

NEWBURY   Northcroft Terrace   W Mills   Cncl Bldg   Wharf Street

W Mills   Lambourn Valley Way   Mkt Pl   Corn Exchange   Bear L

West   Mills   Mallard Court   CAB   Kennet Shop Cen

Butson Cl   Dysons Cl   Russell   Road   Berkeley Road   The Maltings   Newbury Bus Stn   Cheap

Lipscombe Close   Russell   Blenheim Rd   PO   Lincoln Court   Market St

Clifton Road   Chalford Road   Gloucester Road   Craven Road   St David's Road   St Nicholas' Rd   Highfield Avenue   Newbury Station

RG20 3   Craven Road   Green Lane   St George's Avenue   St George's Avenue   Rockingham Rd   St Michael's Road   Council Building

West Fields   Braunfels Wk   Puffers   Parsons   Western End   Works   Station

24 4   Bagnols Wk   Westfield Wy   Enborne Rd   Pound Street   St Nicolas CE Junior School   Madeira Place   Surgery

Enbor...   Braunfels   Puffers Wy   St David's Road   Bartholomew   Catherine Road

Bonemill Lane   Westgate Road   Remembrance Road   Arthur Road   Enborne Rd   Oak Dr   Rectory Cl   Hampton Rd   Argyle Rd   Derby Rd   ST JOHN'S   Prospect Pl   How

Annie Lawson School   Enborne Road   Rectory Close   PO   Council Building   Chesterfield Road

5   Enborne Road   Buckingham Road   ON Rd   Malvern Ct   Willow Cl   Porchester Road

Byrne Ga   Kingsbridge Road   Salcombe Road   St Bartholomews School   Mayfair Dr   Fifth Road   A343   Cem   Priory

Floreat Gardens   Harvest Green   St Bartholomews School   ANDOVER ROAD   Paddock Rd   Old Newtown Rd   Newtown Road   Montague Mo

6   Fifth Road   PO   Highfield Rd   St John the Evangelist Infant School   Belvedere

Longacre   Oaken Grove   Valley Road   Bartlemy   Erleigh Dene   Wendan   Meadow Rd   Paddock Rd

7   Bartlemy Close   The Drive   Tarn La   Falkland Dr   Roebuts Close   Croft Road   Westmead Drive   D47

Routes   Henshaw Road   Montgomery Road   Oakridge Close   Gwn   Three Acre Rd   Westmead Dr

John Rankin Junior School   Crescent   446   The Brambles   Roebuts Road   Cedar Mount   Fri

John Rankin Infant School   Carford   Berkshire Circular Routes   Cresc   Valley

A   B   **24**   C   D   E

Kin

1 grid square represents 250 metres

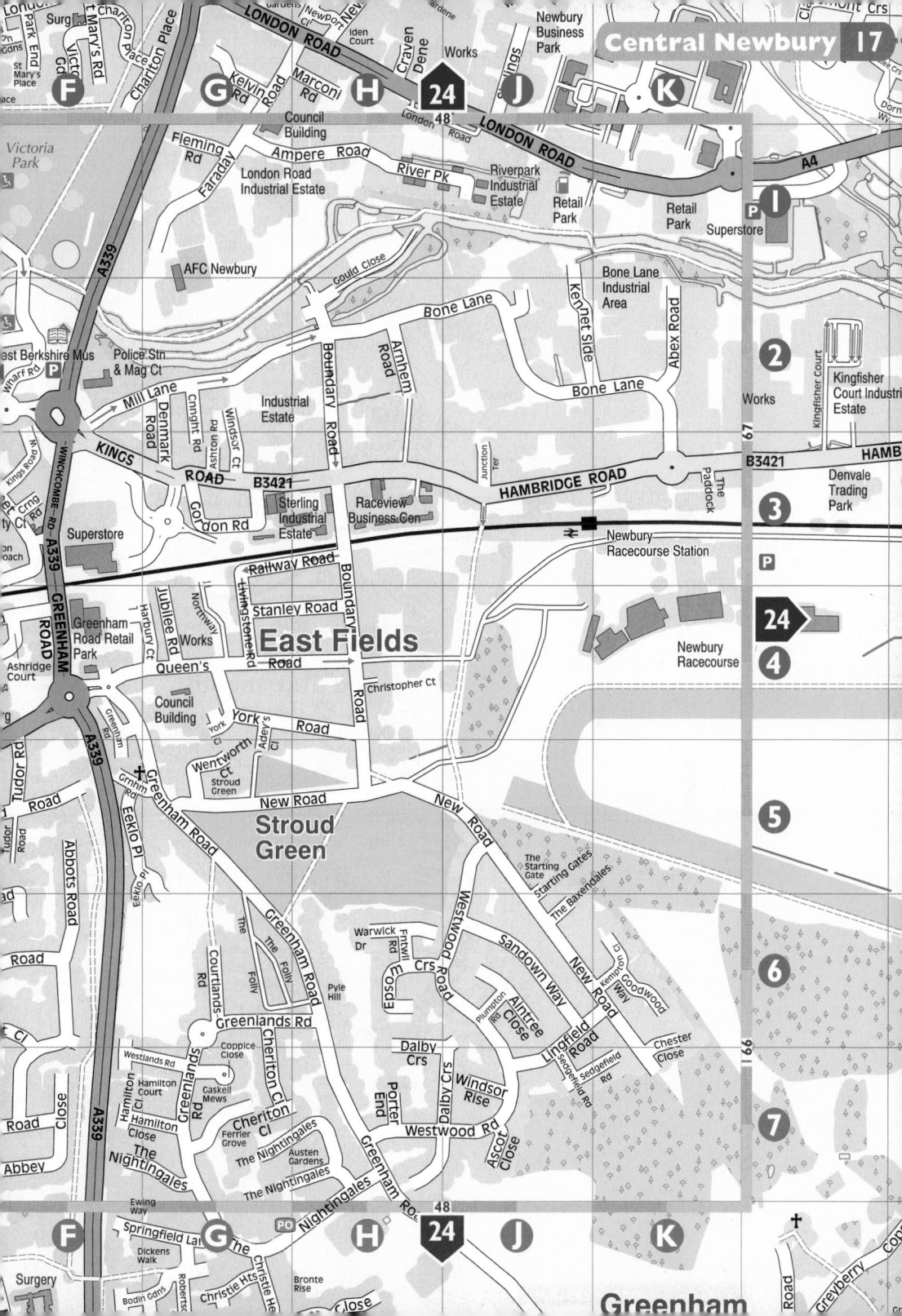

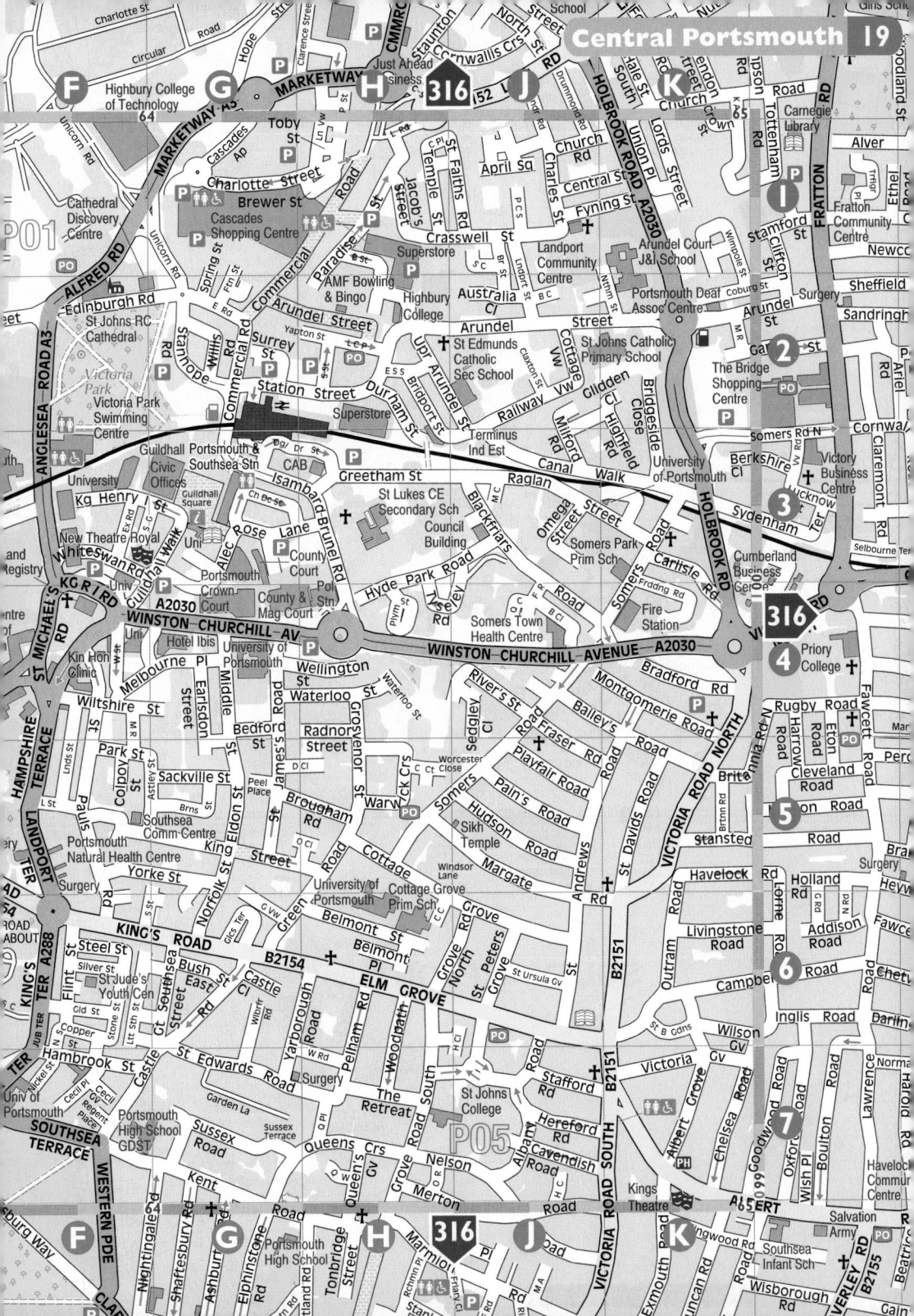

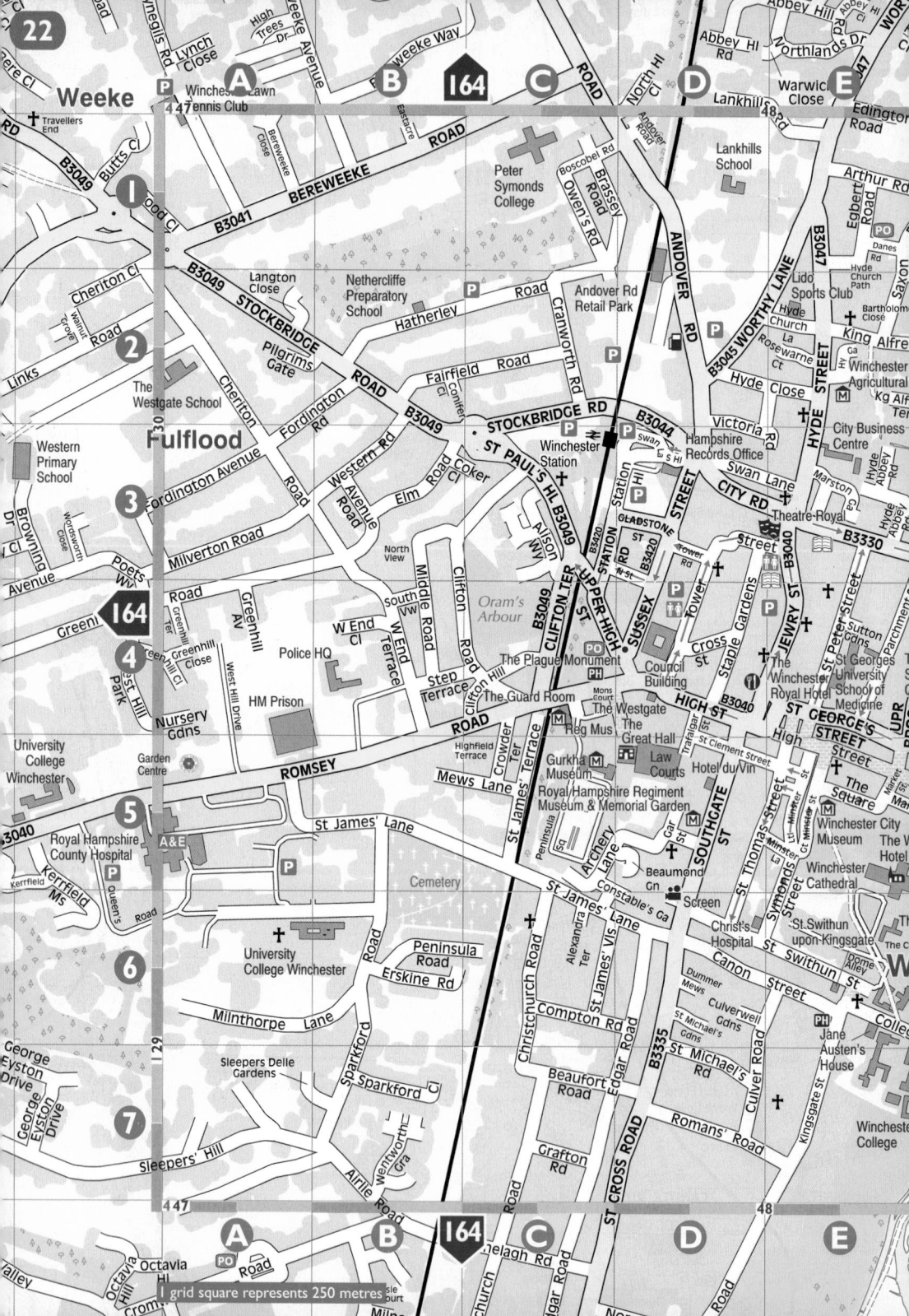

Weeke

Fulflood

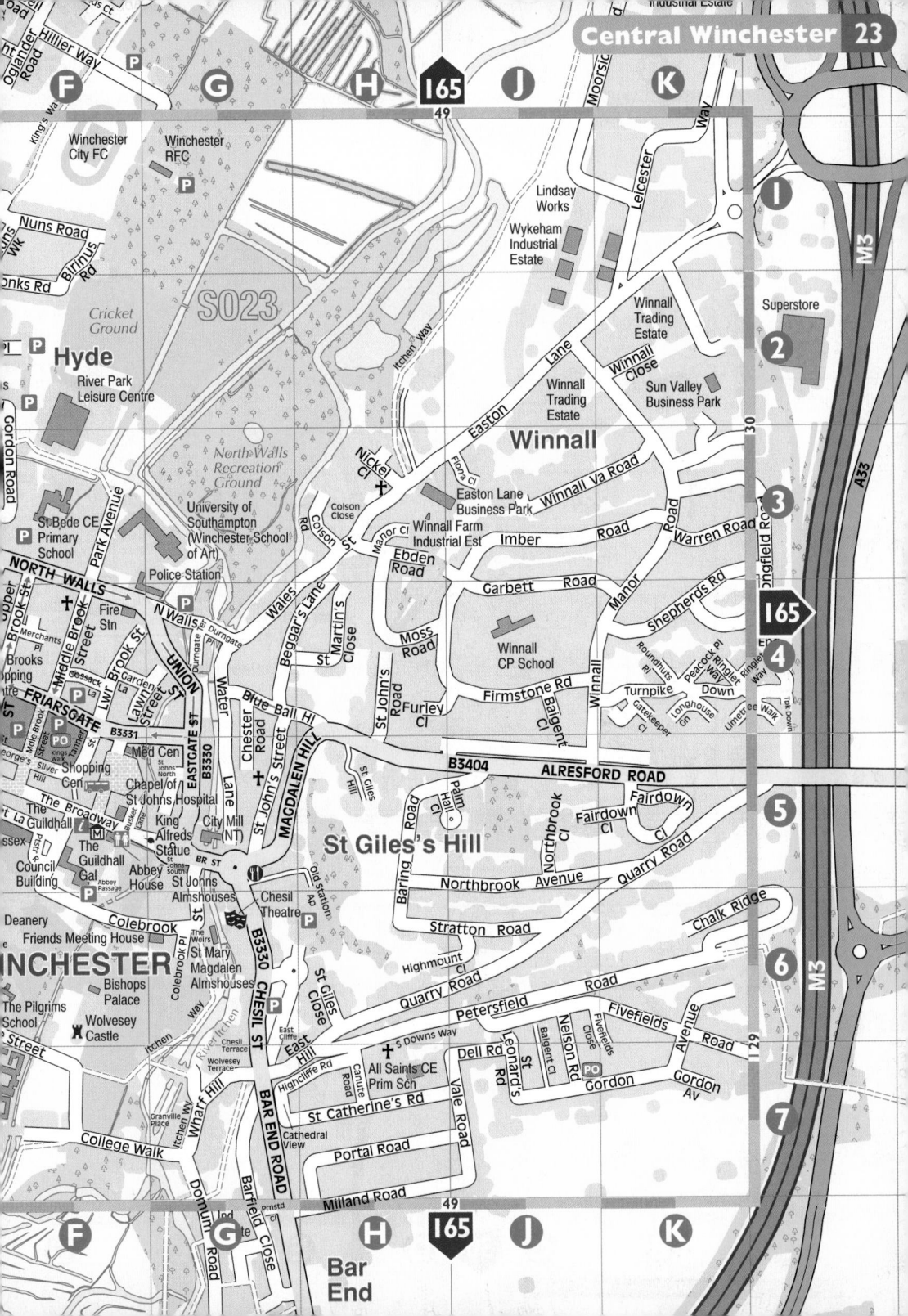

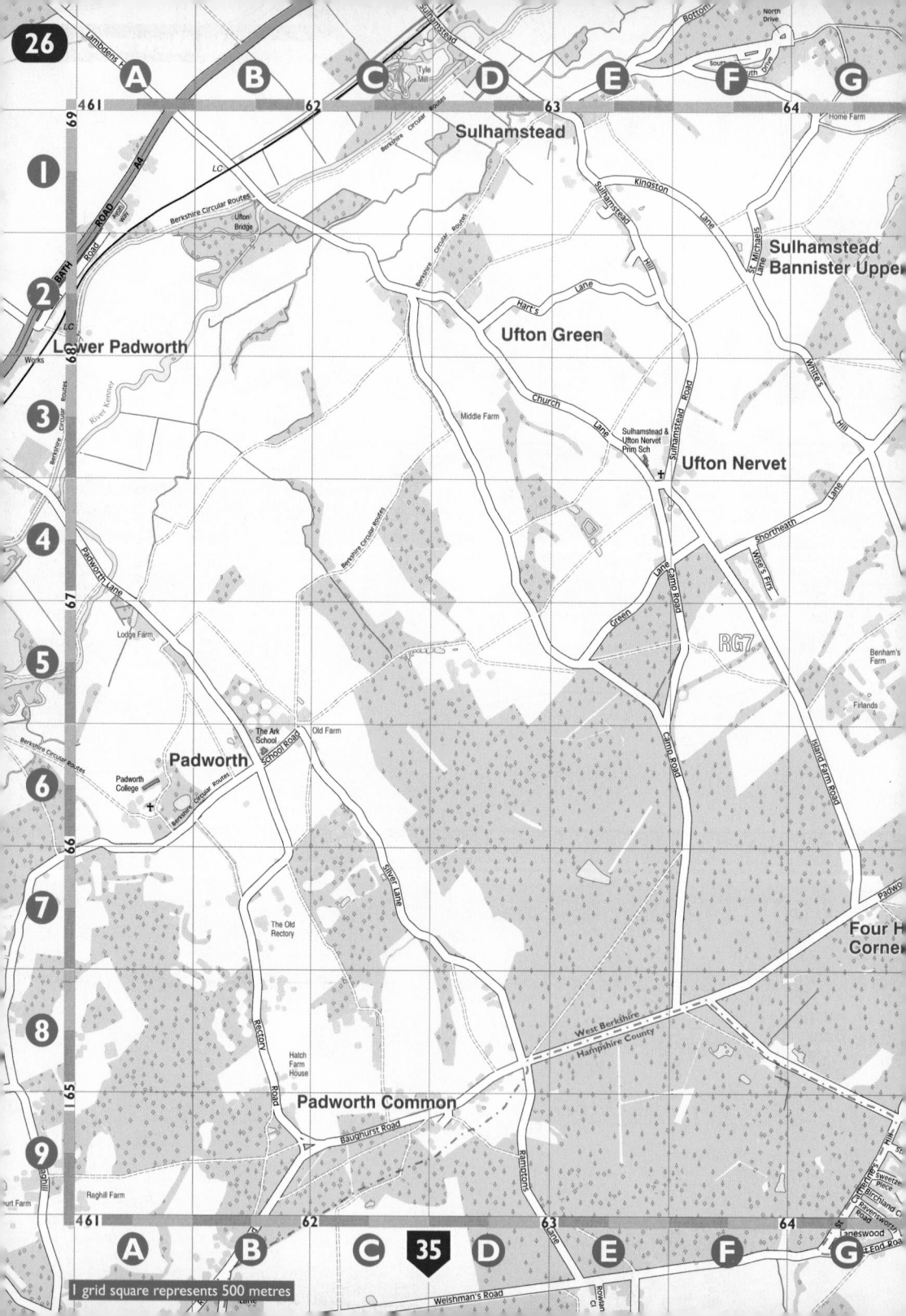

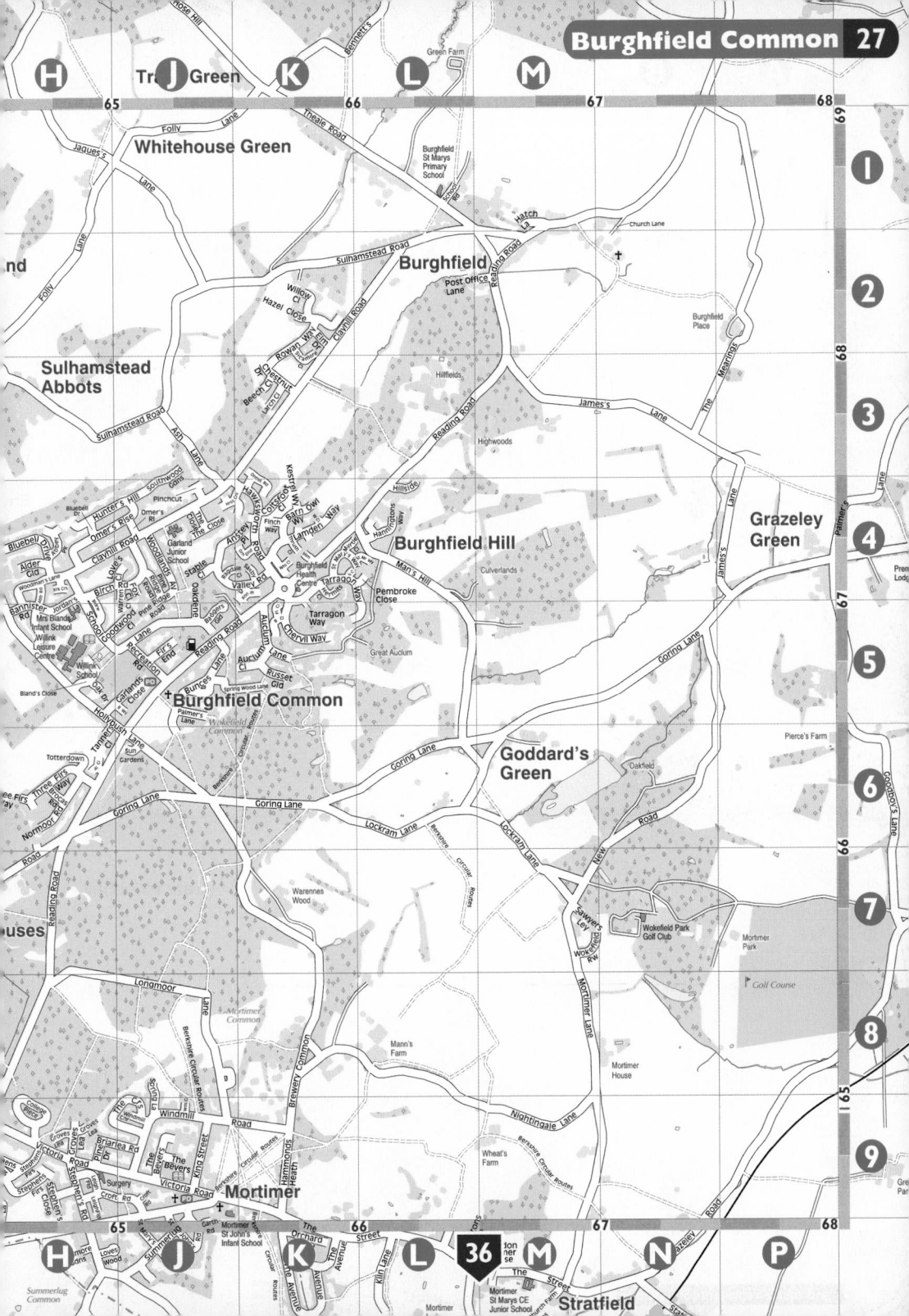

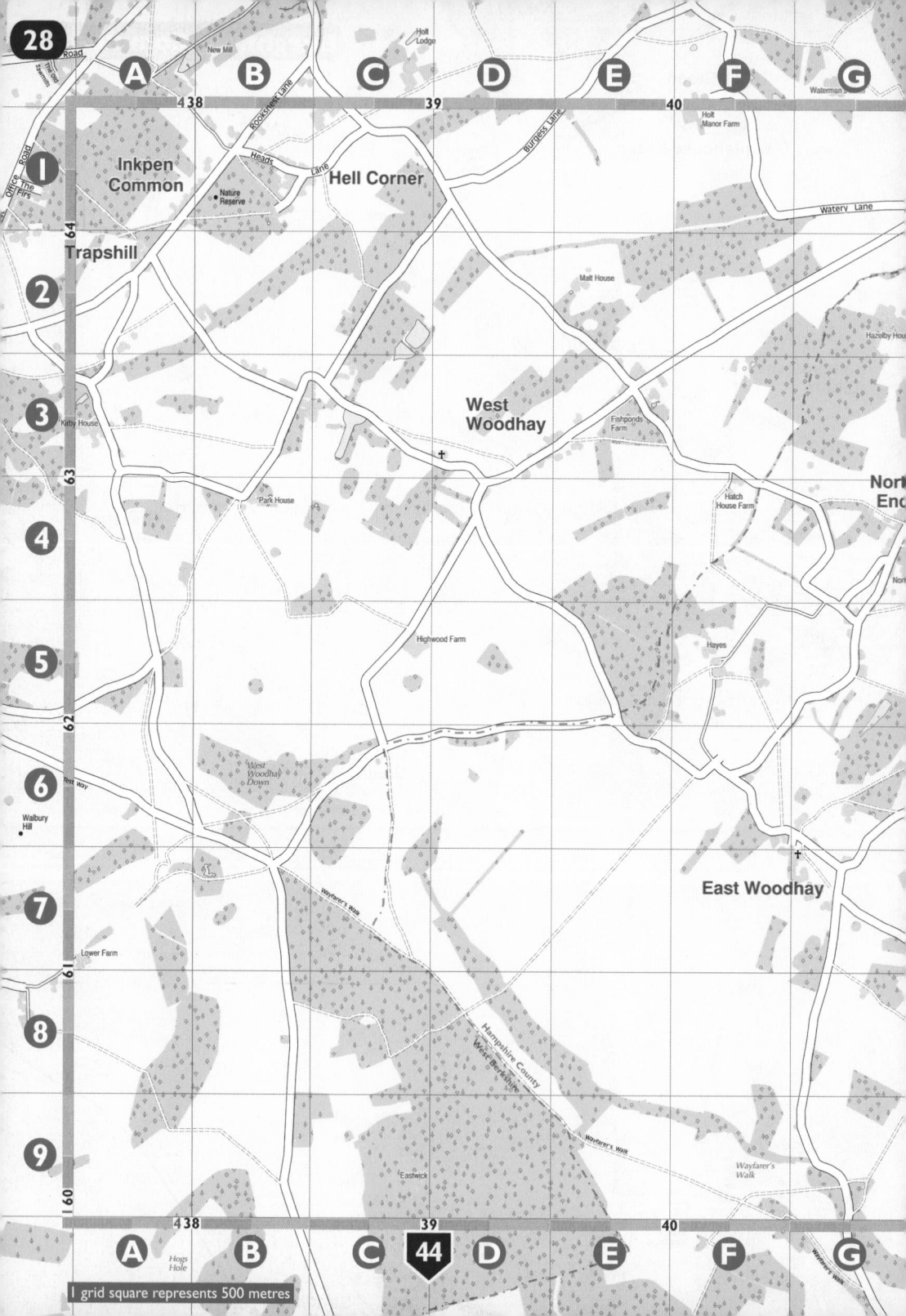

H J K L **25** M N

8 49 50 51

Greenham Common

Goldfinch Bottom

I

RG

Warehouse Road
Seventh St
Apron Road
Lindemann Way
Firth St
Mercury Road
Keynell
First St E
New Greenham Park
New Greenham Park Leisure Centre
Murdoch Road

64

A339

Thornford Road

2

River Enborne

A339

63

3

Adbury House

Aldern Bridge House

Sydmonton Common

Bishop's Green

Ash Rd
Beech Rd
Ash Rd
Willow Rd
Fabric Road

Knightsbridge House

Knightsbridge Dr

Works

Brooksfield

Works

4

wn

on

Adbury Farm

Adbury Park

North Sydmonton House

Hyde Lane

Headley Stud

62

5

North Echinswell Farm

32

6

School

Frith Copse

Brock's Green

Hyde Farm

7

Whitehouse Farm

Hyde Lane

61

Strattons

8

Palmers Yard

Kisby's Farm

160

9

Woodside Farm

A339

8 49 50 51

Cowhouse Farm

Ecchinswell

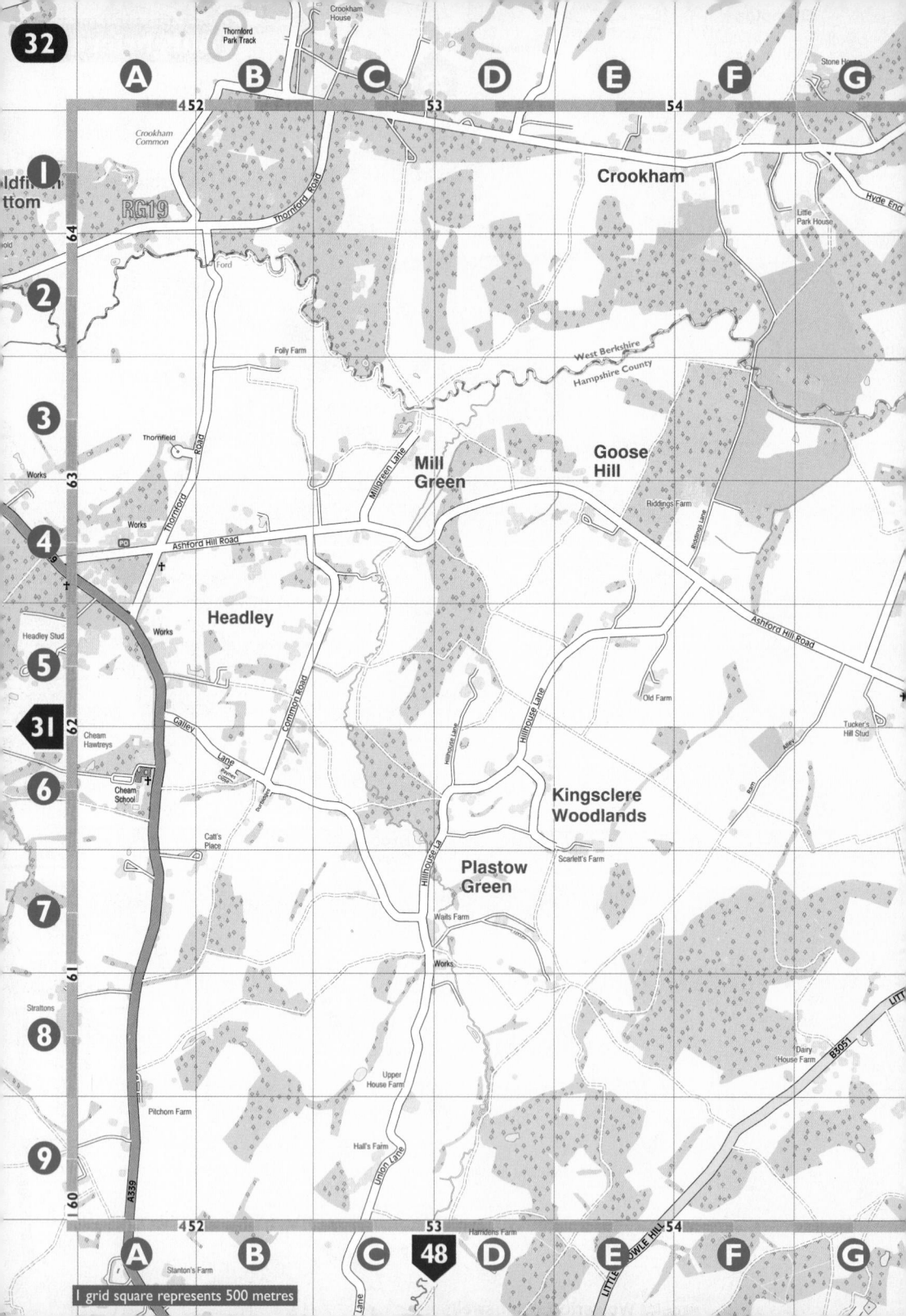

Brimton

H · J · K · L · M · N

5 · 56 · 57 · 58

Shalford Farm

The Business Centre

Brimpton CE Primary School

Wasing Park

Wasing

I

Wasing Farm

64

Oak Cott

Hyde End

2

Boot Farm

Back Lane

Wasing Wood

3

A340

63

Woodhouse Lane

Hockford Lane

Blacknest Farm

Brimpton Lane

Brimpton Common

B3051

4

Plantation Rd

Woodhouse Farm

Firtree Cnr · Conifer Cl

Birch Road

The Hurst Community College

Playing Field

John Cl

Woodlands Road

Pinks La

O' Bee Gardens

Old Lane

B3051

Ashford Hill

Ashford Hill Primary School

Chapel La

Hollycroft

Morton's Lane

Inhurst Lane

Stokes Lane

Hurst Leisure Centre

Portway

Shyshack

62

34

ath d

Wi Ro

Haughurst Hill

Haughurst Hill

Bishopsw

The Hawthorns

5

6

The Holt

Heathrow La

Poplar Close

Inhurst

Wolverton Road

Holt Cottages

Baughurst Road

7

Inhurst Farm

Fair Oak

Wolverton Road

Axmansford

Baughurst

KNOWLE HILL

Violet Lane

Little Ham Farm

Shaw La

61

Wheat Hold

Hook Lane

8

Oak Hous

Ham Lane

9

Wolverton Road

60

Frith Farm

Baughurst Road

Hillside

5 · 55 · 56 · 57 · 58

Ham Farm Hou

H · J · K · 49 · L · M · N · P

Chapel Road

Holt Lane

Wolverton

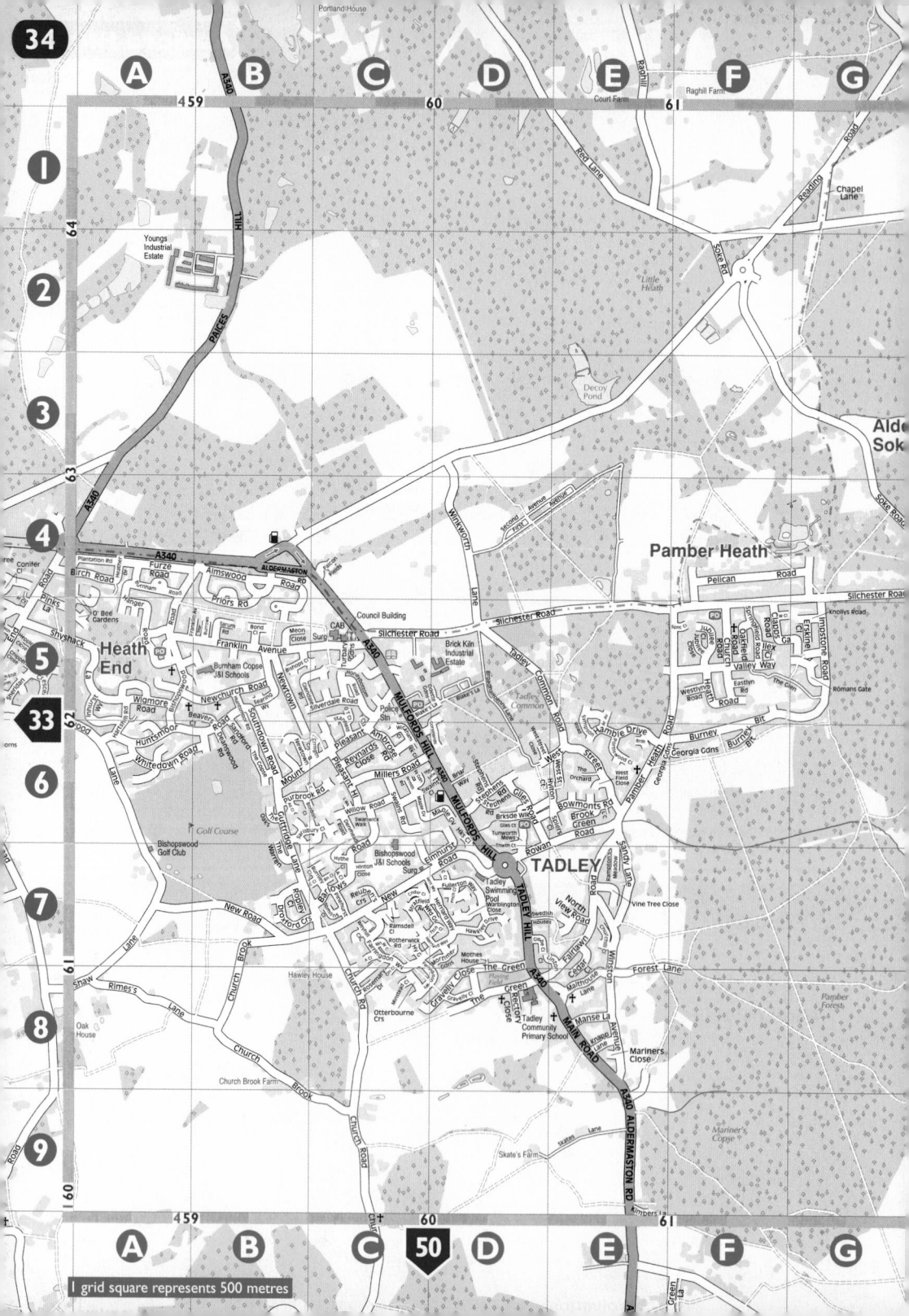

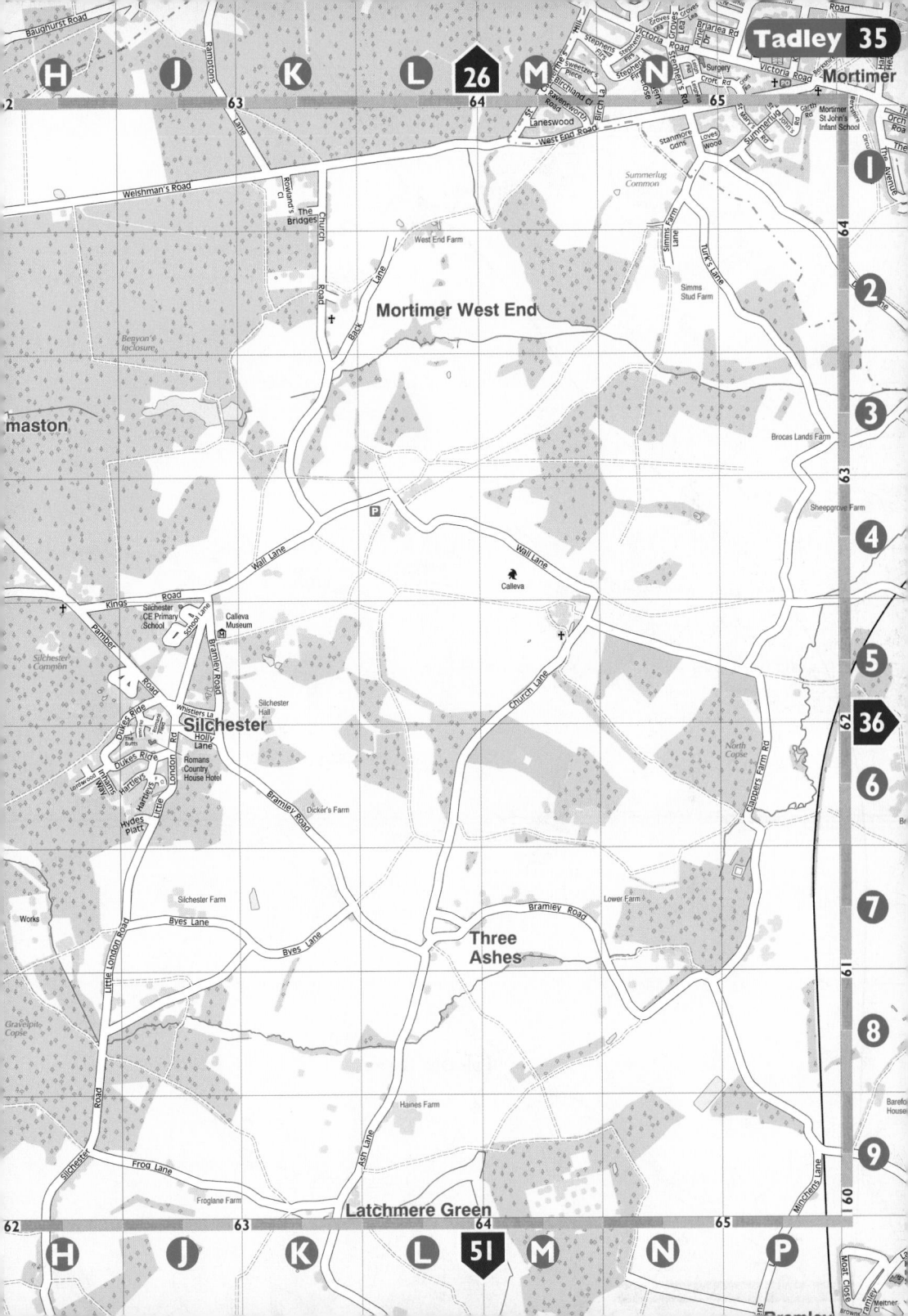

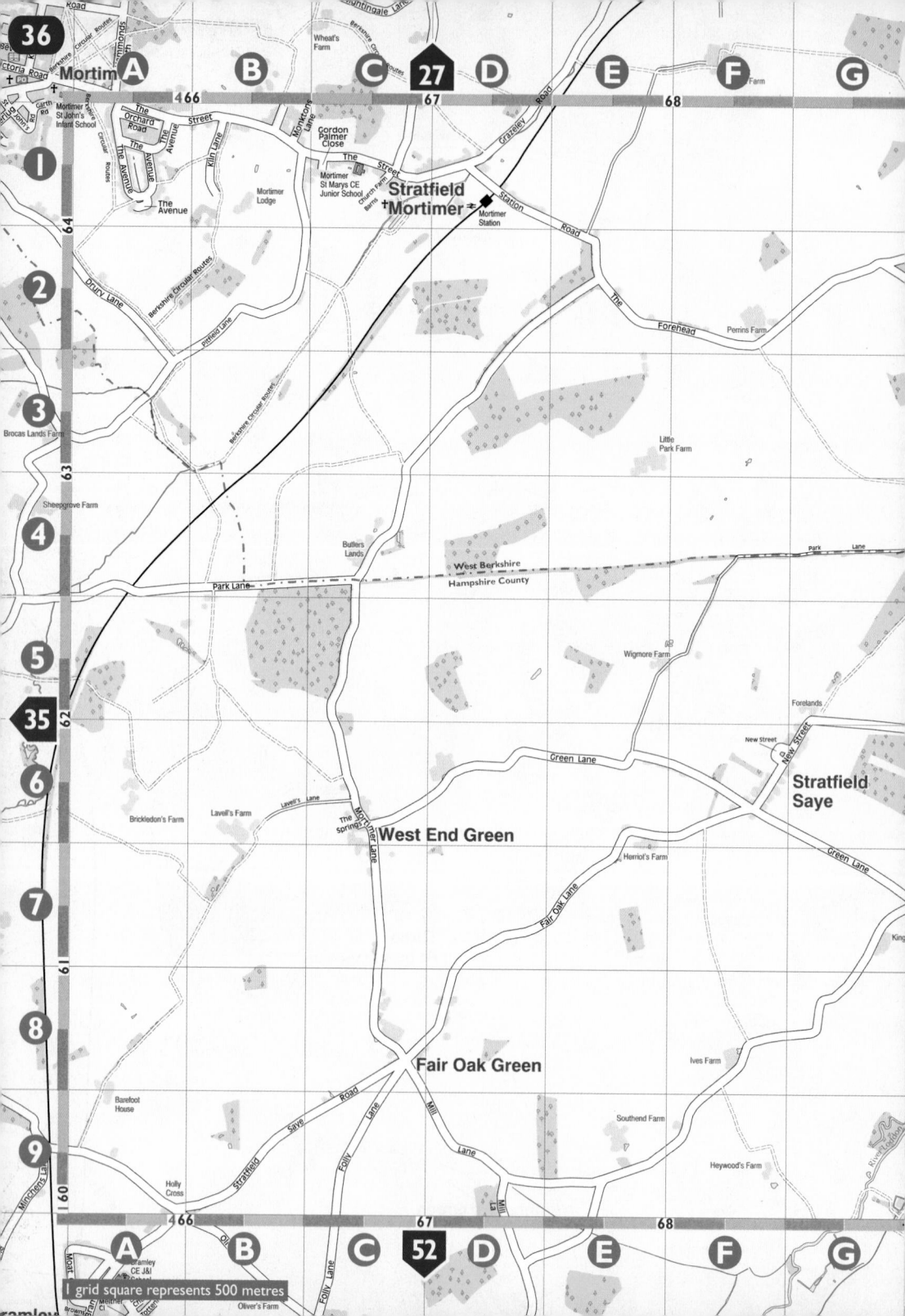

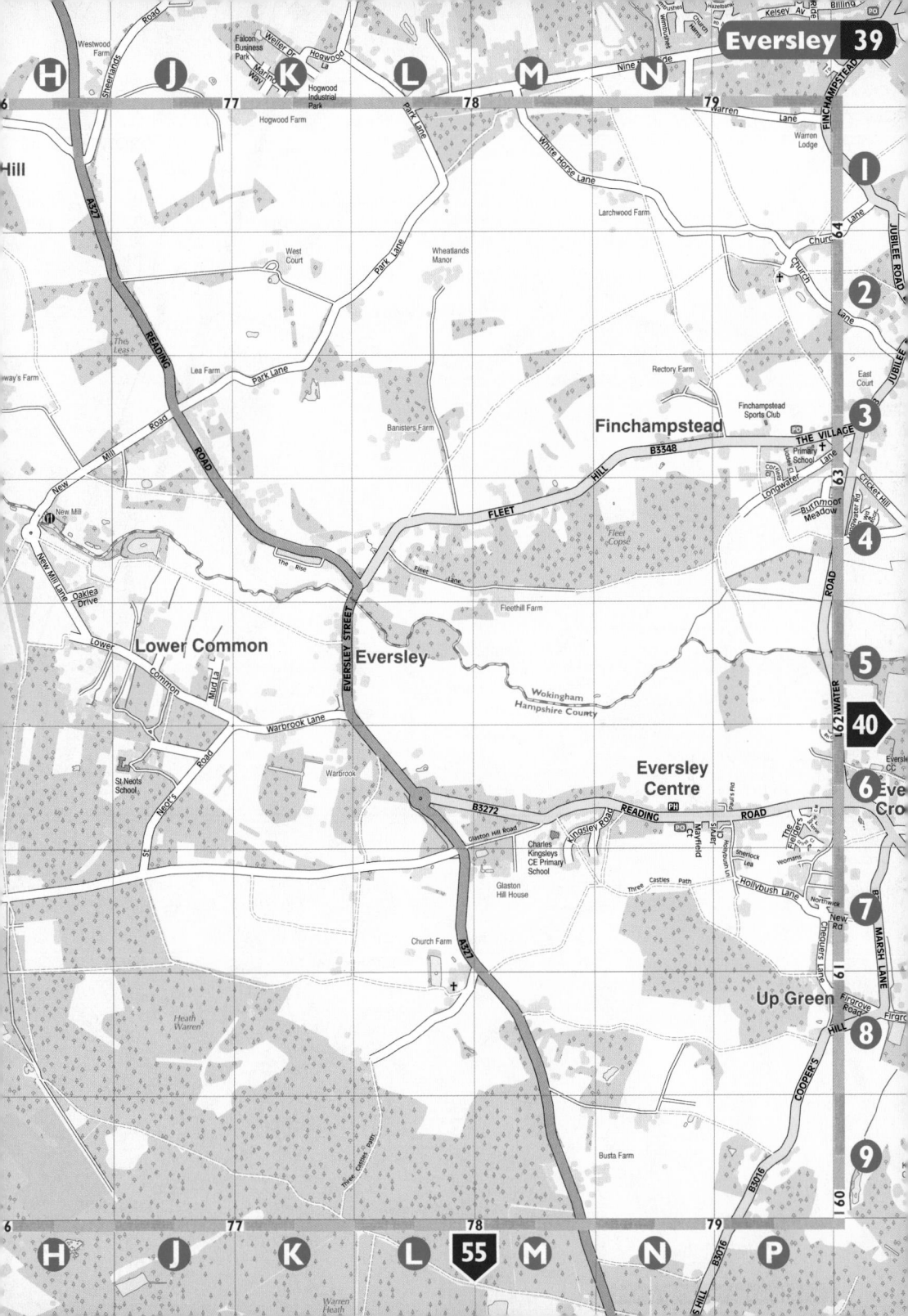

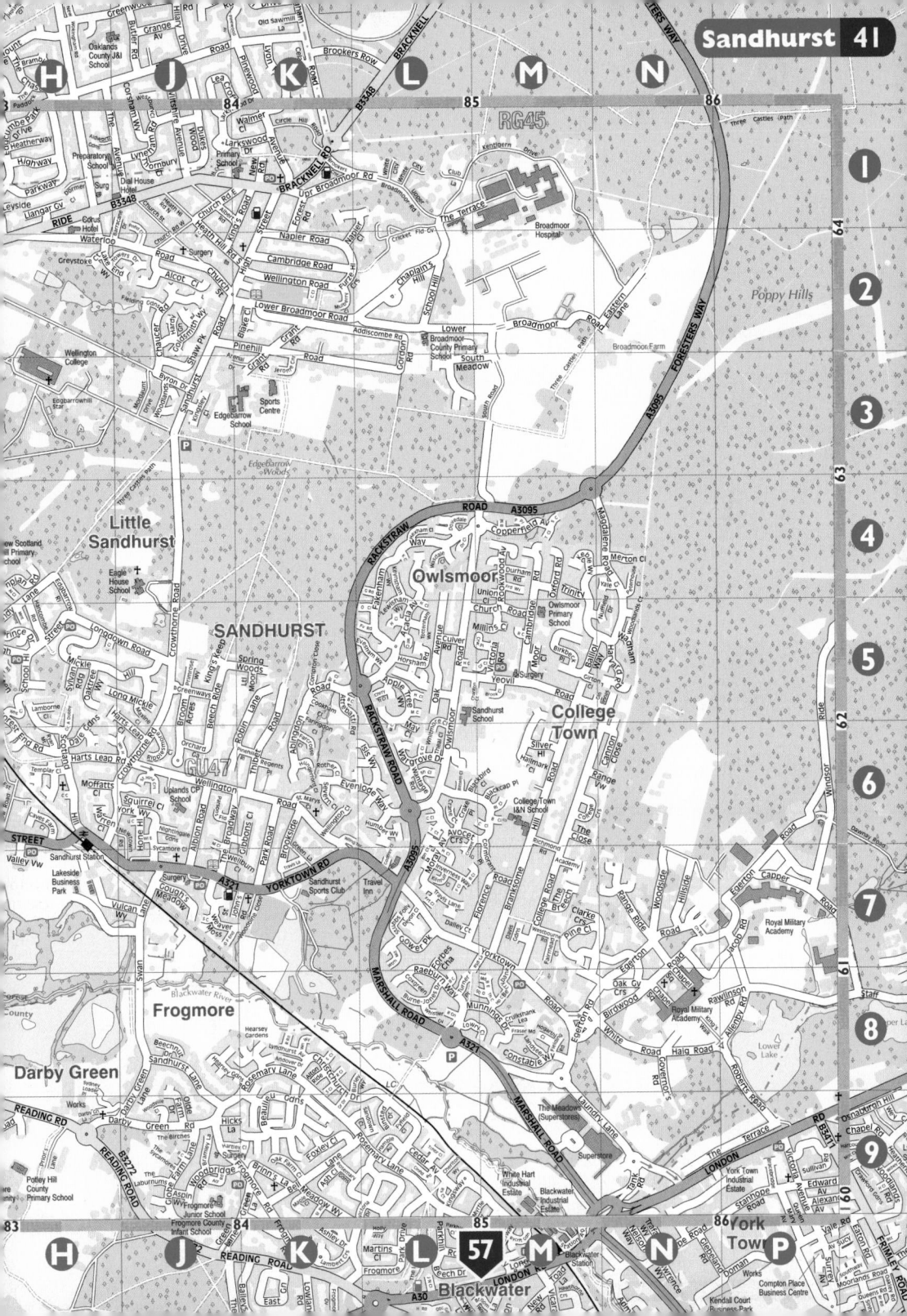

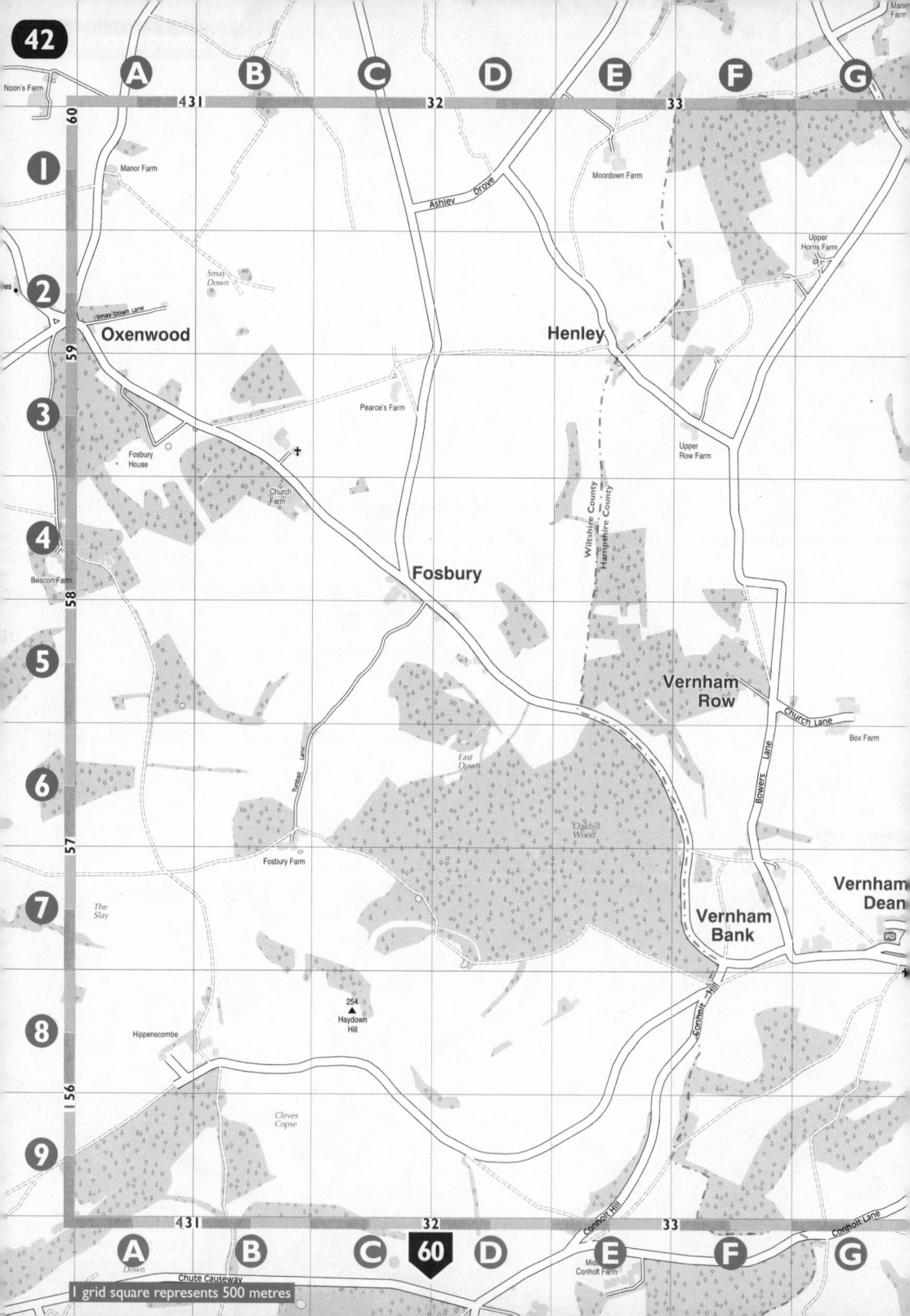

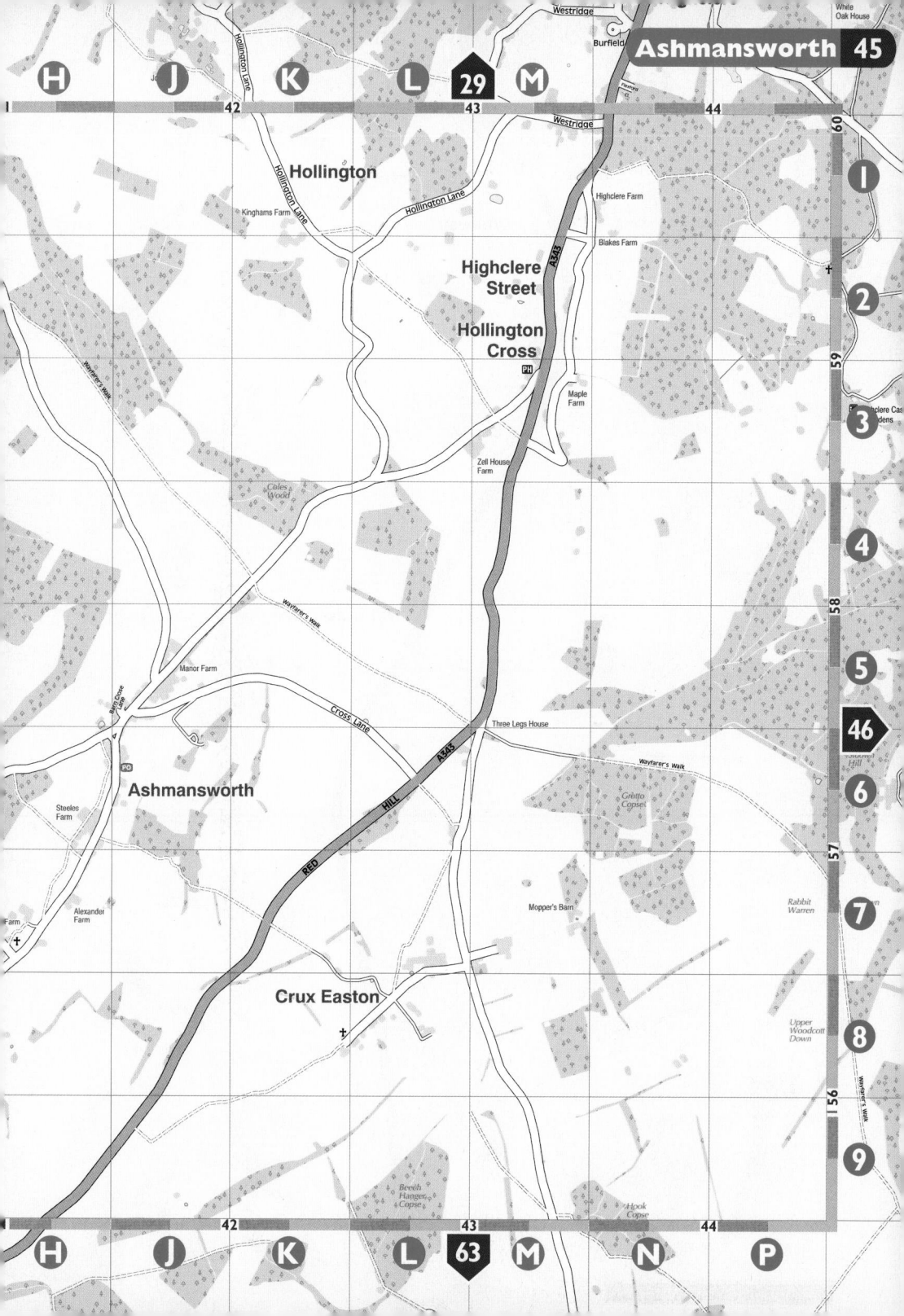

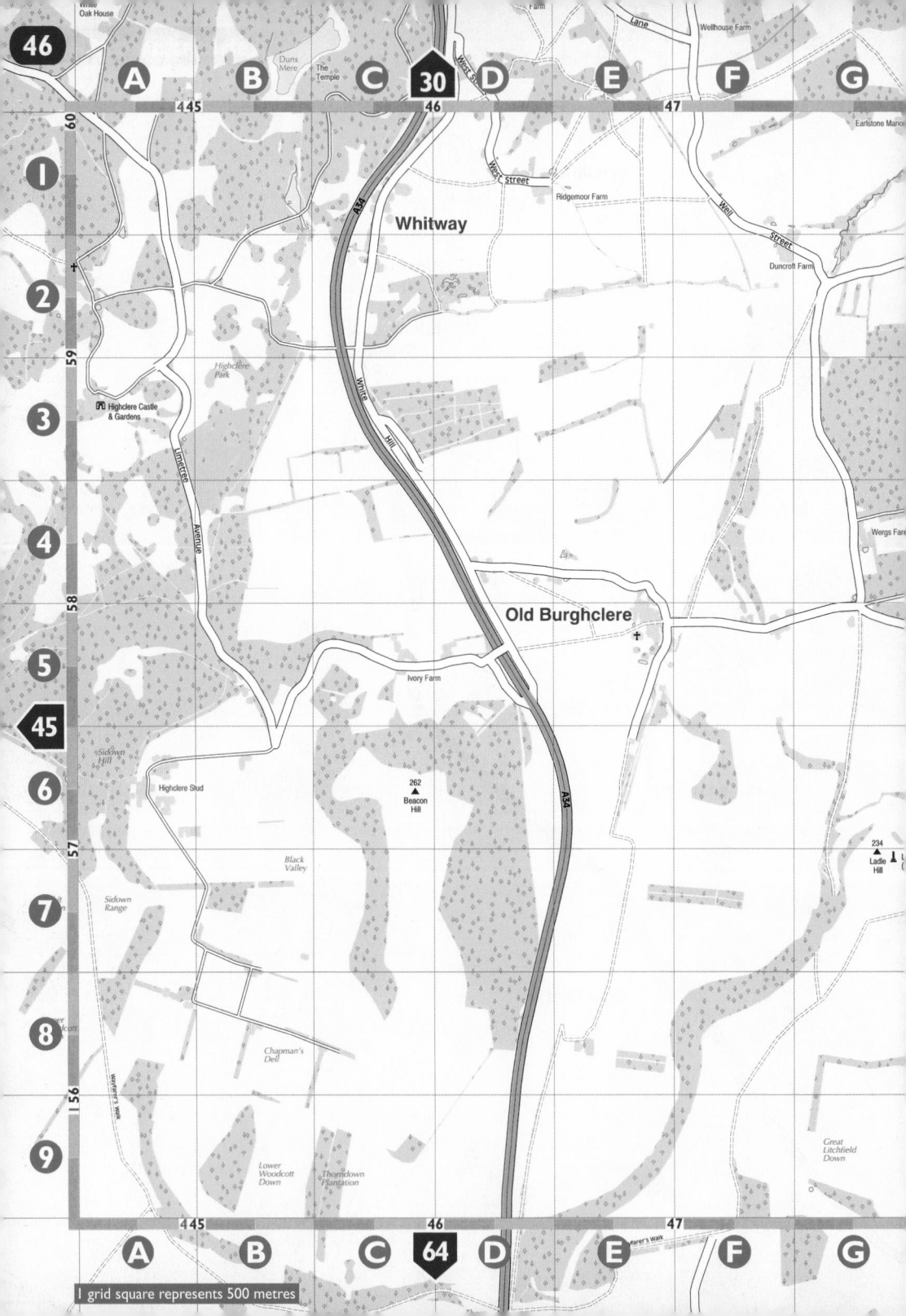

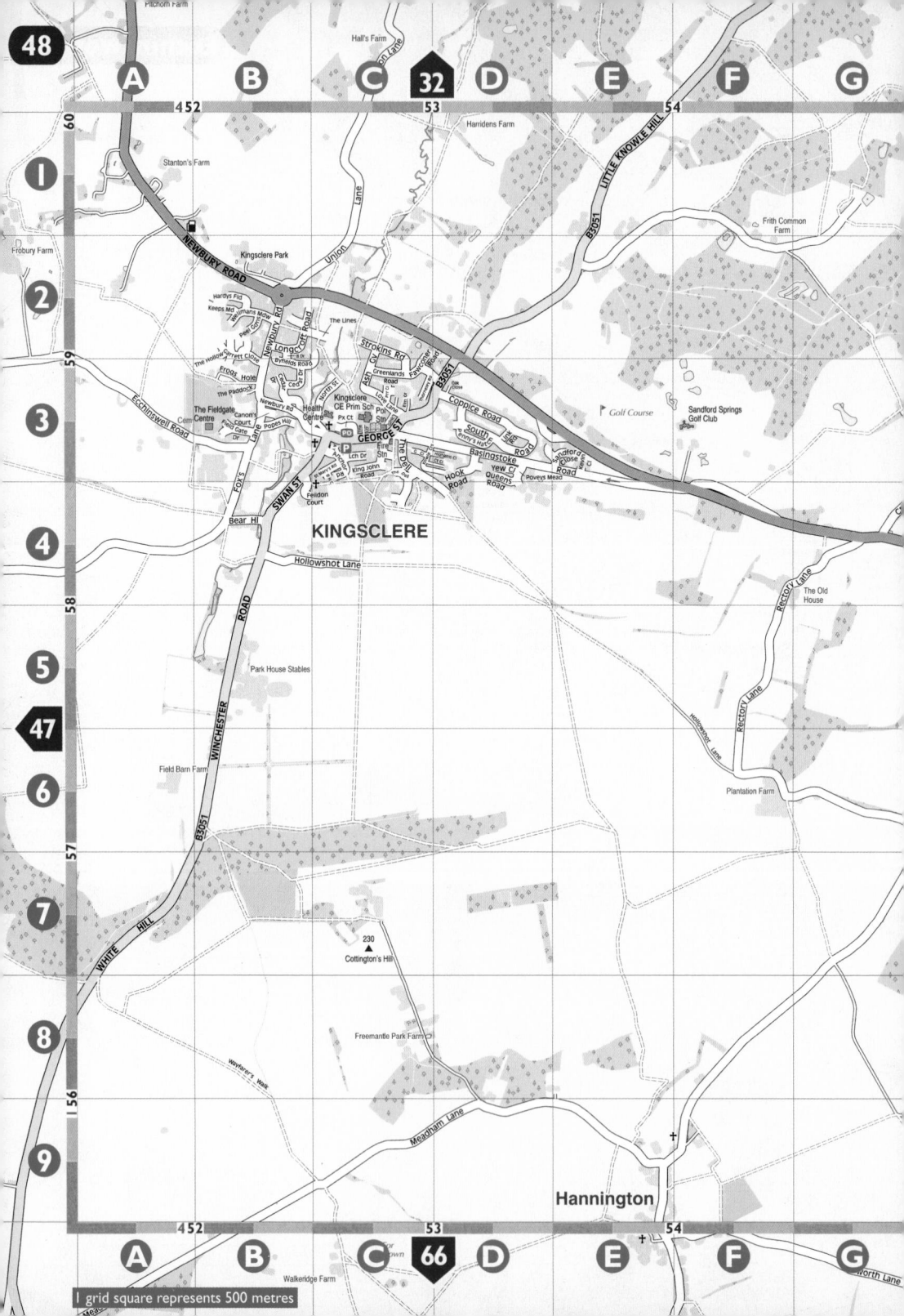

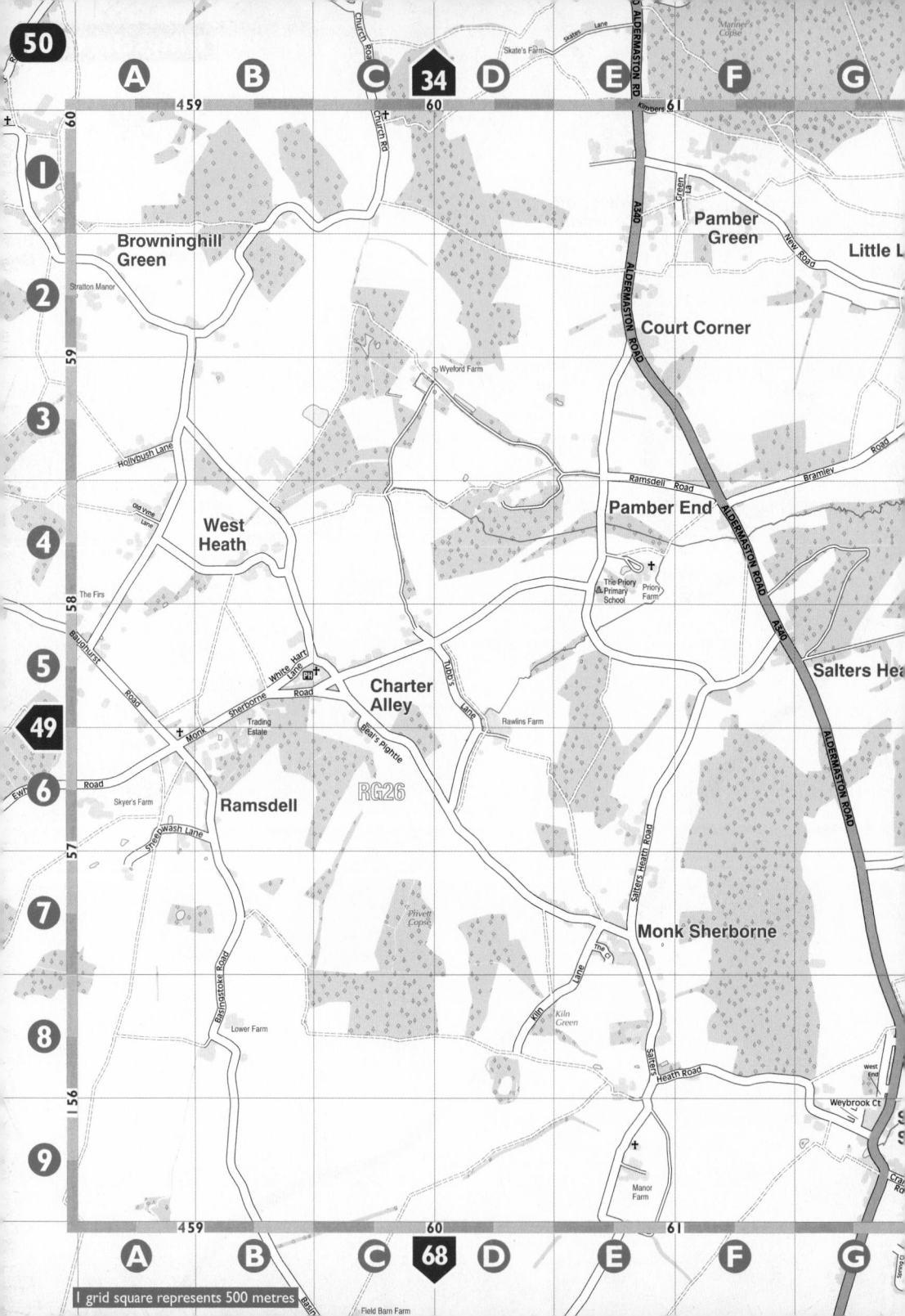

A   B   C   34   D   E   F   G

459   60   Kimbers   61

1

Browninghill
Green

Stratton Manor

2

59

3

Hollybush Lane

Old Vyne
Lane

4

West
Heath

The Firs

58

5

White Hart
Lane

Sherborne
Road

Charter
Alley

49

Monk
Road

Trading
Estate

6

Ewhurst
Road

Skyer's Farm

Ramsdell

57

Sheep Wash Lane

RG26

Beal's Pightle

Rawlins Farm

7

Privett
Copse

Basingstoke Road

8

56

Lower Farm

9

Church Rd

Skate's Farm

Skate's
Lane

Wyeford Farm

Pamber
Green

Green La

New Road

Little L

Court Corner

A340

ALDERMASTON ROAD

Ramsdell   Road

Bramley

Pamber End

The Priory
Primary
School

Priory
Farm

Tubb's
Lane

Salters Hea

ALDERMASTON ROAD

A340

Percy Heath James

Monk Sherborne

Kiln
Lane

The C

Kiln
Green

Salters
Heath Road

West
End

Weybrook Ct

Manor
Farm

Craw Rd

A340

459   60   61

1 grid square represents 500 metres

Field Barn Farm

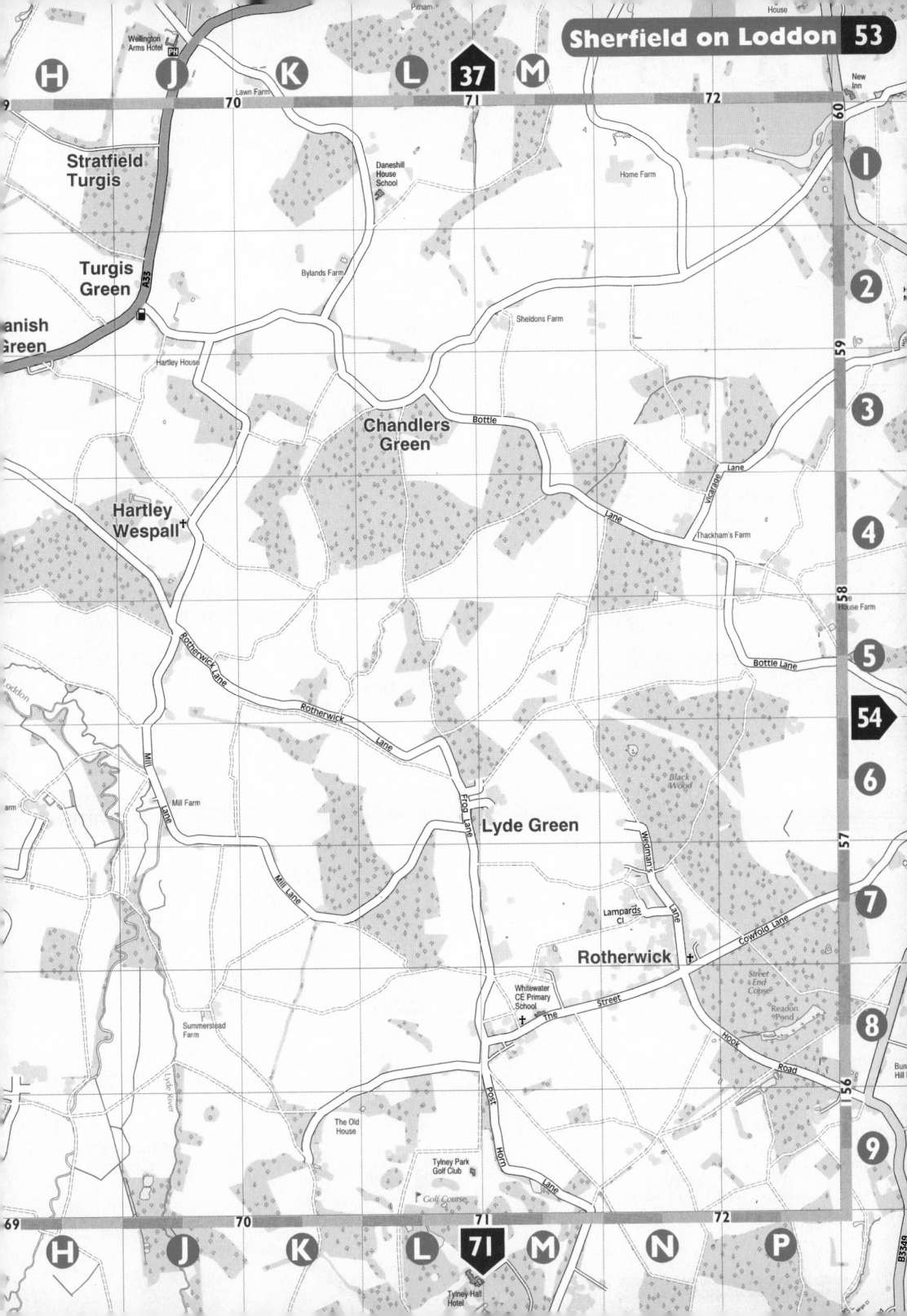

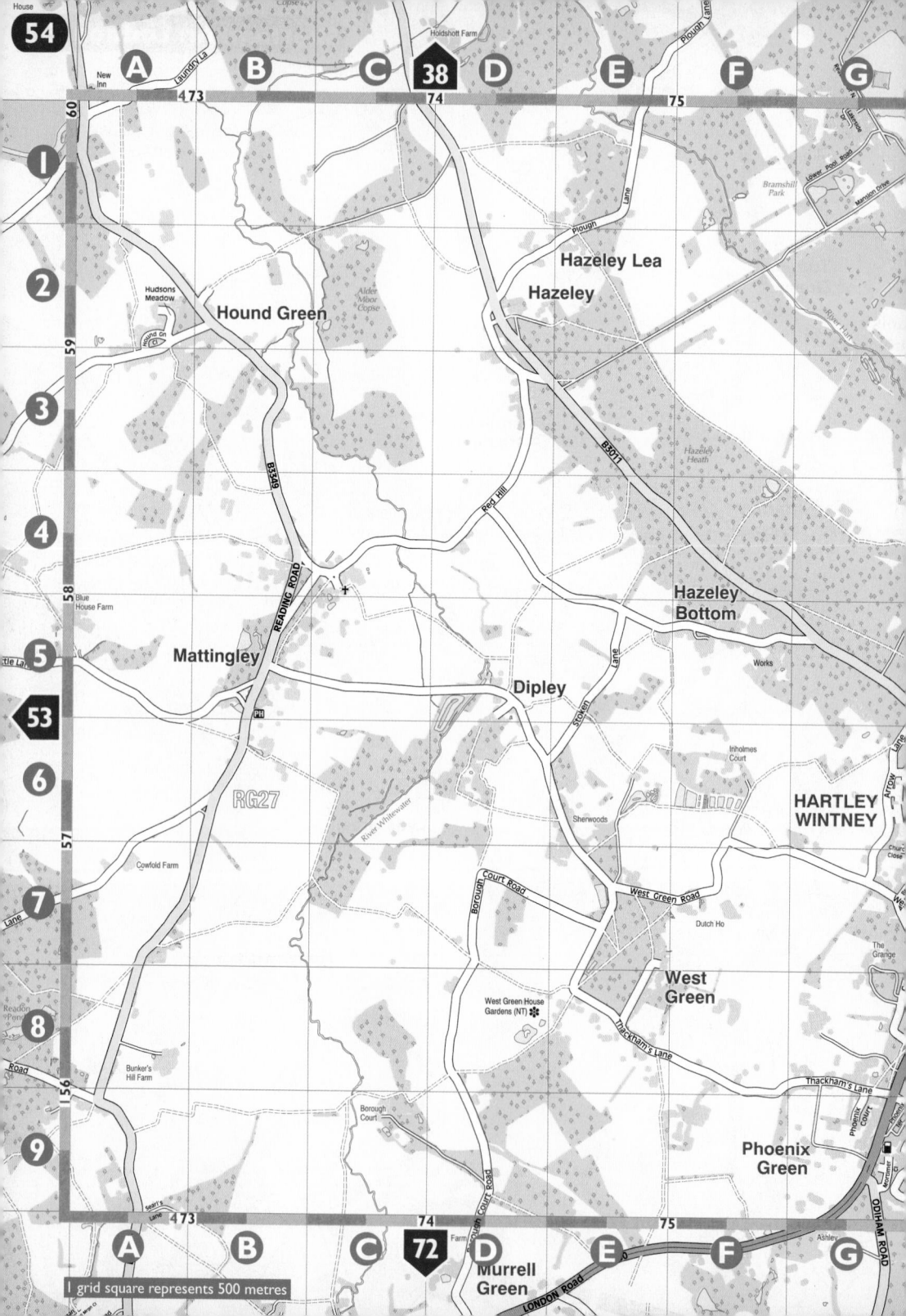

A B C **38** D E F G

473 74 75

House

New Inn

Laundry La

Holdshott Farm

Plough Lane

I 60

Lower Pool Road

Marston Drive

Bramshill Park

2 Hudsons Meadow

Hound Green

Alder Moor Copse

59

Plough Lane

Hazeley Lea

Hazeley

River Hart

3

B3349

Hazeley Heath

B3011

4

Blue House Farm

58

Reading Road

+

Hazeley Bottom

5 **Mattingley**

Dipley

Stroxen Lane

Lane

Works

ttle La

PH

53

RG27

Inholmes Court

HARTLEY WINTNEY

Arrow Lane

6

57

River Whitewater

Sherwoods

Church Close

7 Cowfold Farm

Borough Court Road

West Green Road

Dutch Ho

The Grange

Lane

8 Readon Penn

Road

56

Bunker's Hill Farm

West Green House Gardens (NT)

West Green

Thackham's Lane

Thackham's Lane

Phoenix Court

9

Borough Court

Phoenix Green

ODIHAM ROAD

Ashley

Sear's Lane

A B C **72** D E F G

473 74 75

Murrell Green

LONDON ROAD

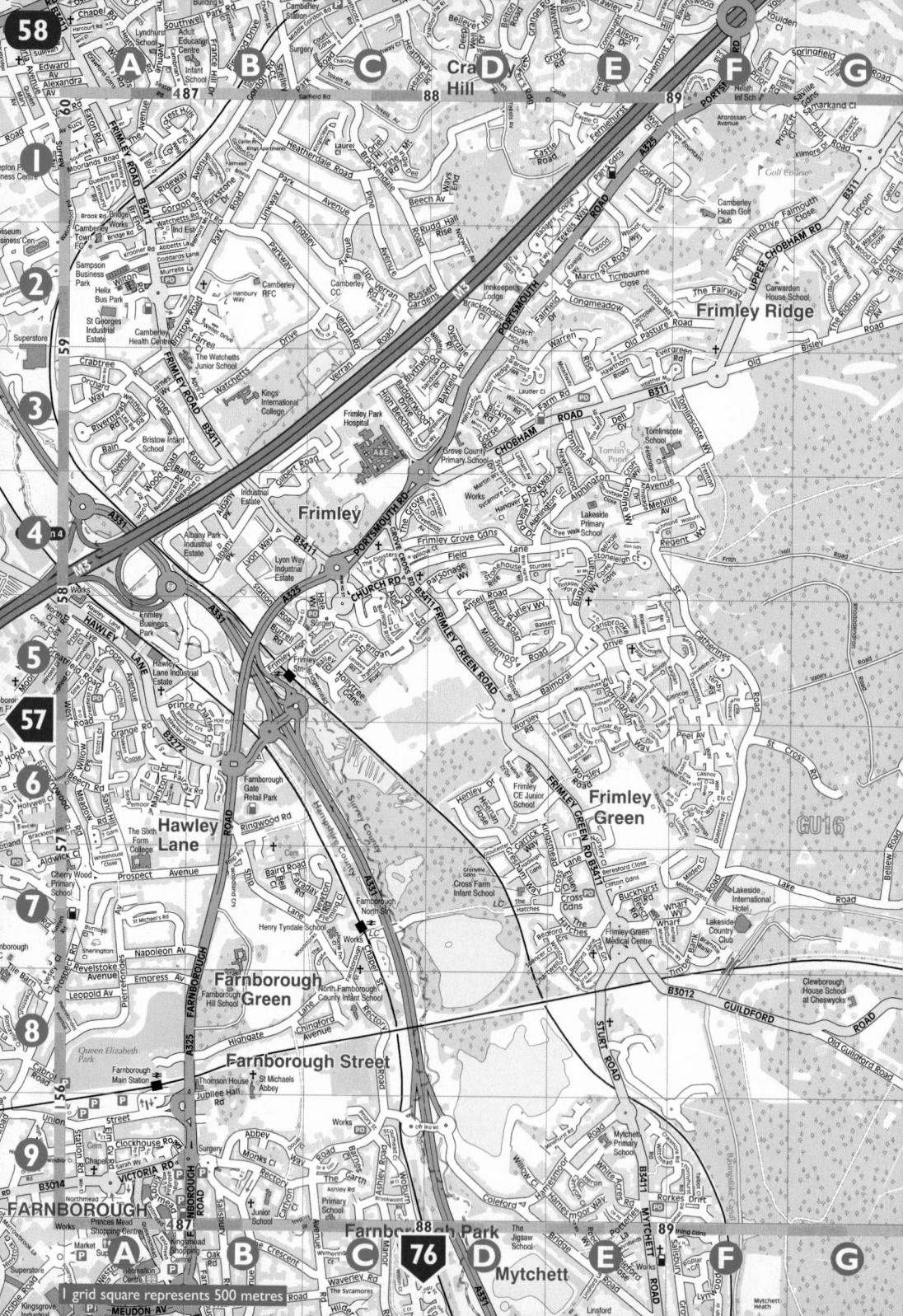

A B C **42** D E F G

431 32 33

I Little Down
Chute Causeway
Conholt Hill
Middle Conholt Farm
Conholt Lane

55

2
Du... Lane
Conholt Park
Conholt House

3

54

Standen House
Breach La
Chute Standen
Hampshire Gate
Cathanger Wood
Wiltshire County
Hampshire County

4
Dummer Lane
Chute Cadley
Holt Lane
Dowlands Farm

Chute Cadley

5
Lower Chute
Tangley Bottom

53

6
Forest House
Jolly's Farm
Clark Lane
Tangley

Hungerford Lane

7

52
Lodge Lane
Ipswich Road

8
Coach Hill
Chute Lodge
PH

51

9
Lodge Lane
...tom F

431 32 33

A B C **81** D E F G

Redhouse Farm
Roundaway Lane
Roundaway Farm

I grid square represents 500 metres

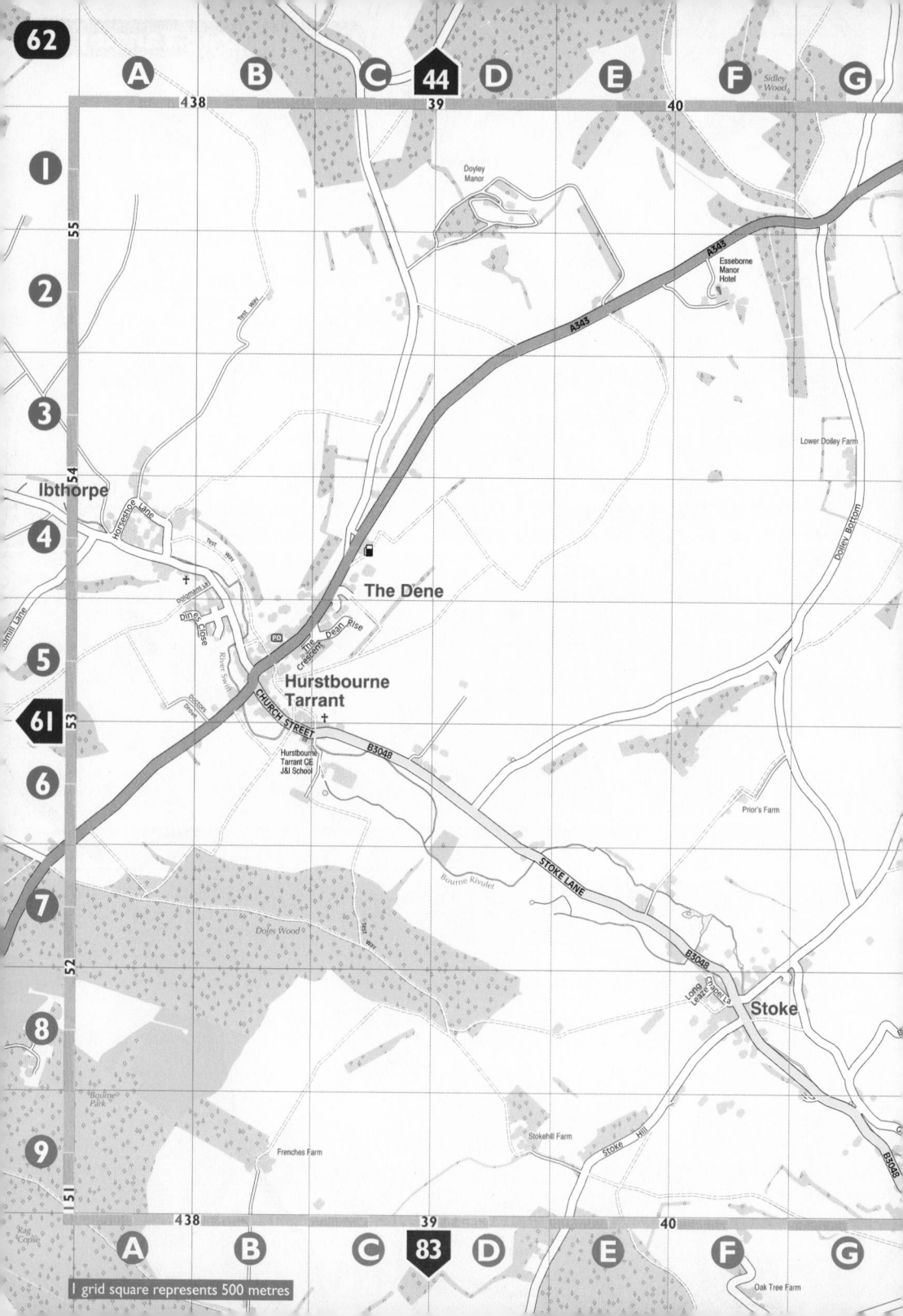

H J K L 45 M

I

Woodcott

55

Lower Woodcott

2

Lye Farm

Easton
Park
Wood

Sladen
Green

Woodcott House

3

Stubb's
Copse

Suggeraston
Copse

54

Highfield House

'Pad's
Copse

Buckets Down Farm

4

Binley

Hollyerott
Copse

5

Wadwick
House

64

53

Wadwick

6

Egbury
Farm

Egbury

Slade Bottom Farm

Elm Farm

7

Binley Bottom

Wadwick Bottom

Downhams Farm

52

8

Egbury Castle Farm

Cold Harbour

9

Wakeswood

51

Swampton

H J K L 84 M N P

41 42 Spring Hill Lane Hill Road 43 44

St Mary Bourne

Newham

64

A　B　Thornydown　C　**46**　D　E　F　G
Lower　Plantation
Woodcott
Down

Great
Litchfield
Down

I

4 45　46　47

Wayfarer's Walk

55

Thorn
Down

2
Lower Woodcott Farm

Shell's
Copse

A34

3
Woodc...

Old Orchard
Copse

Suggeaston
Copse

+

Down Farm

Little
Down

4
...kets Do...

Dunley
Manor

The
Village

Litchfield

Litchfield
Down

Wormley
Copse

Dunley

5

63　**53**

Angledown
Copse

Roman Road

Streatley
Copse

Furze
Copse

6

7

Bradley Wood Farm

Clap Gate

52

Bradley
Wood

8

9

Cooper's in the
Wood Farm

Cole Henley
Manor Farm

Peak House
Farm

51

**Cole
Henley**

A　B　4 45　C　**46**　**85**　D　Larks　E　F　G
Cole Henley
Farm
BATTON

1 grid square represents 500 metres

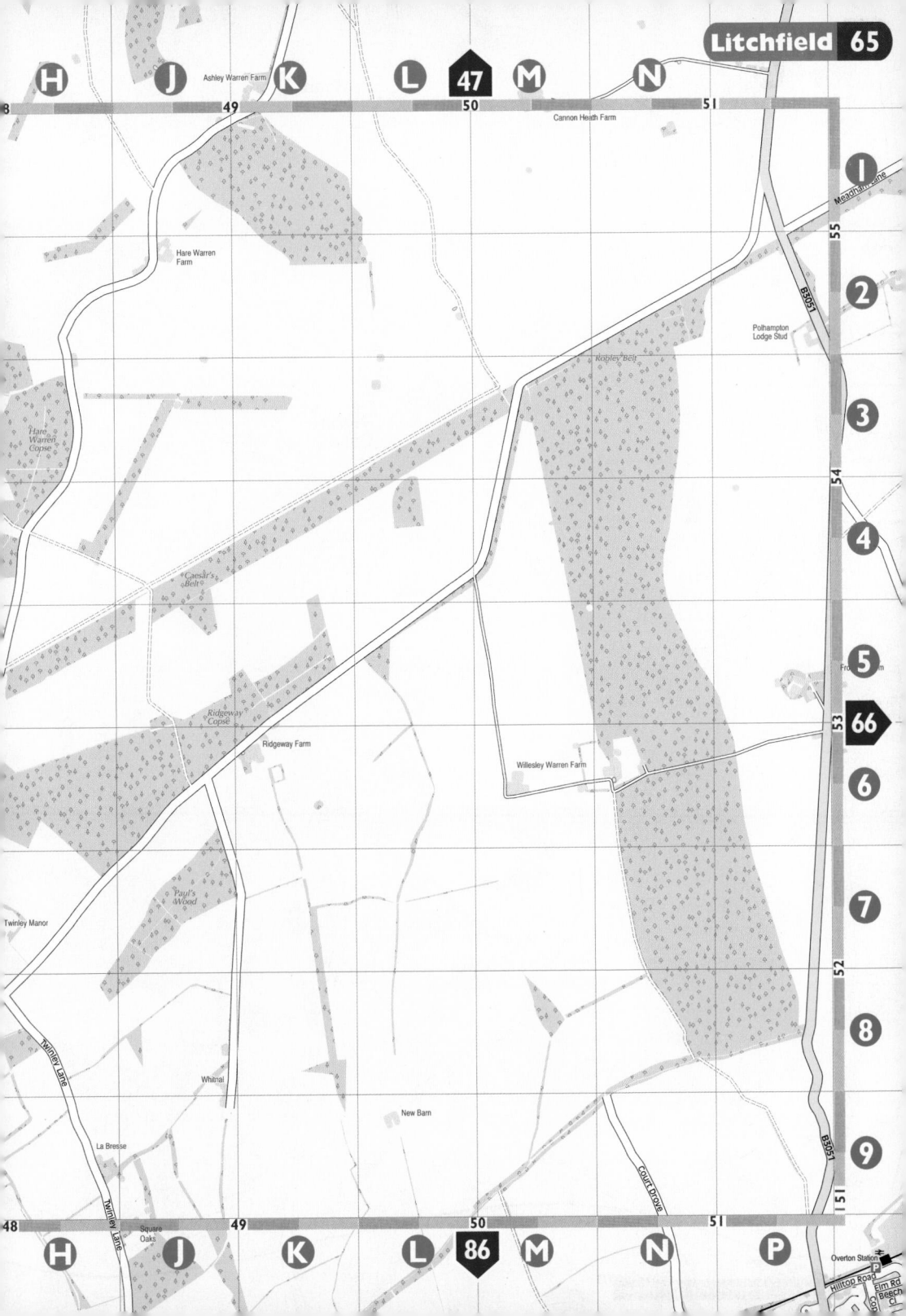

H J K L 47 M N

49 50 51

I 55

B3051

2

Maadie Bourne

3 54

4

5

53 66

6

7 52

8

B3051

9 51

48 49 50 86 51

H J K L M N P

Ashley Warren Farm

Cannon Heath Farm

Hare Warren Farm

Polhampton Lodge Stud

Hare Warren Copse

Ropley Belt

Caesar's Belt

Ridgeway Copse

Ridgeway Farm

Willesley Warren Farm

Paul's Wood

Twinley Manor

Twinley Lane

Whitnal

New Barn

La Bresse

Square Oaks

Overton Station

Hilltop Road

Elm Rd

Beech

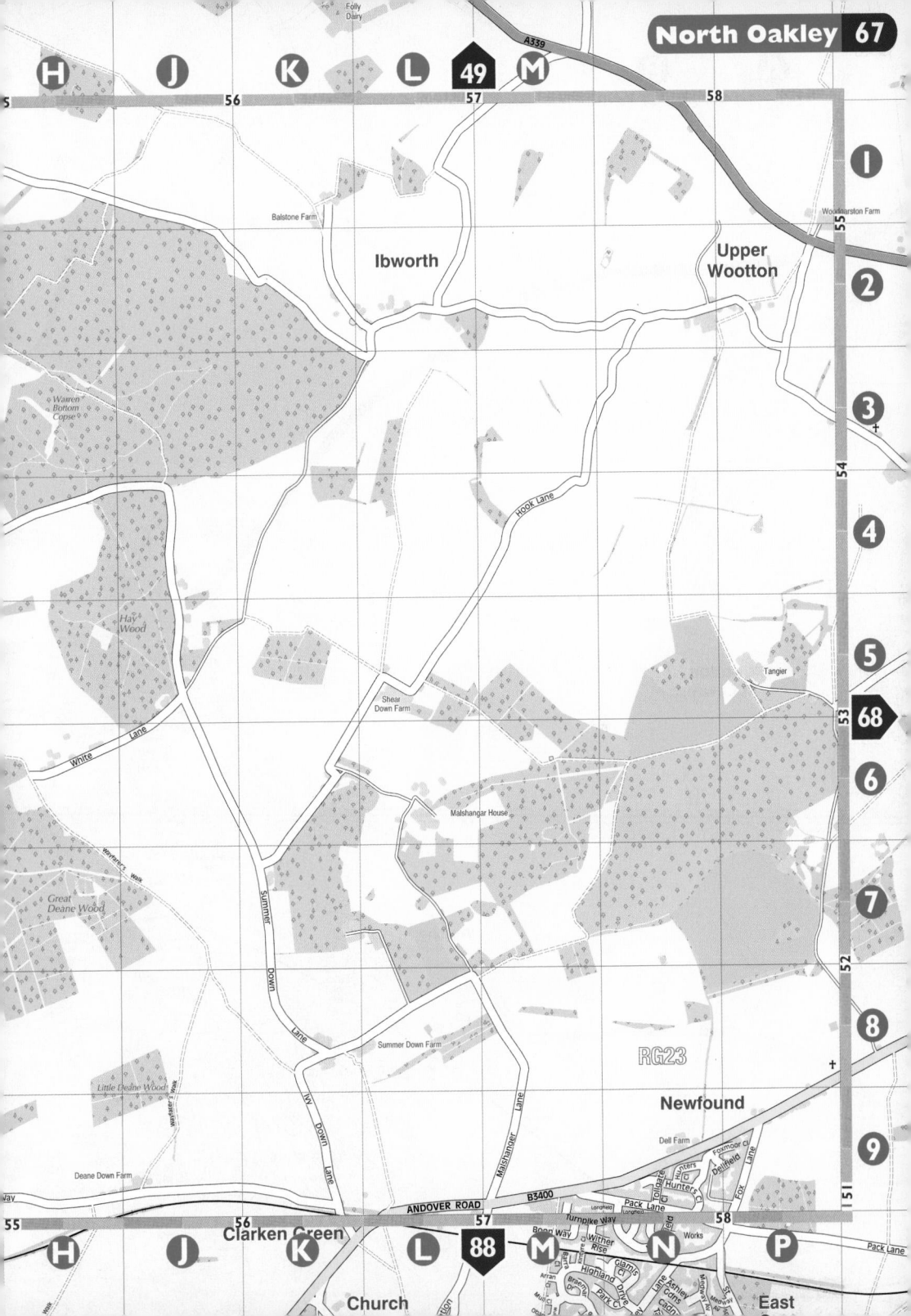

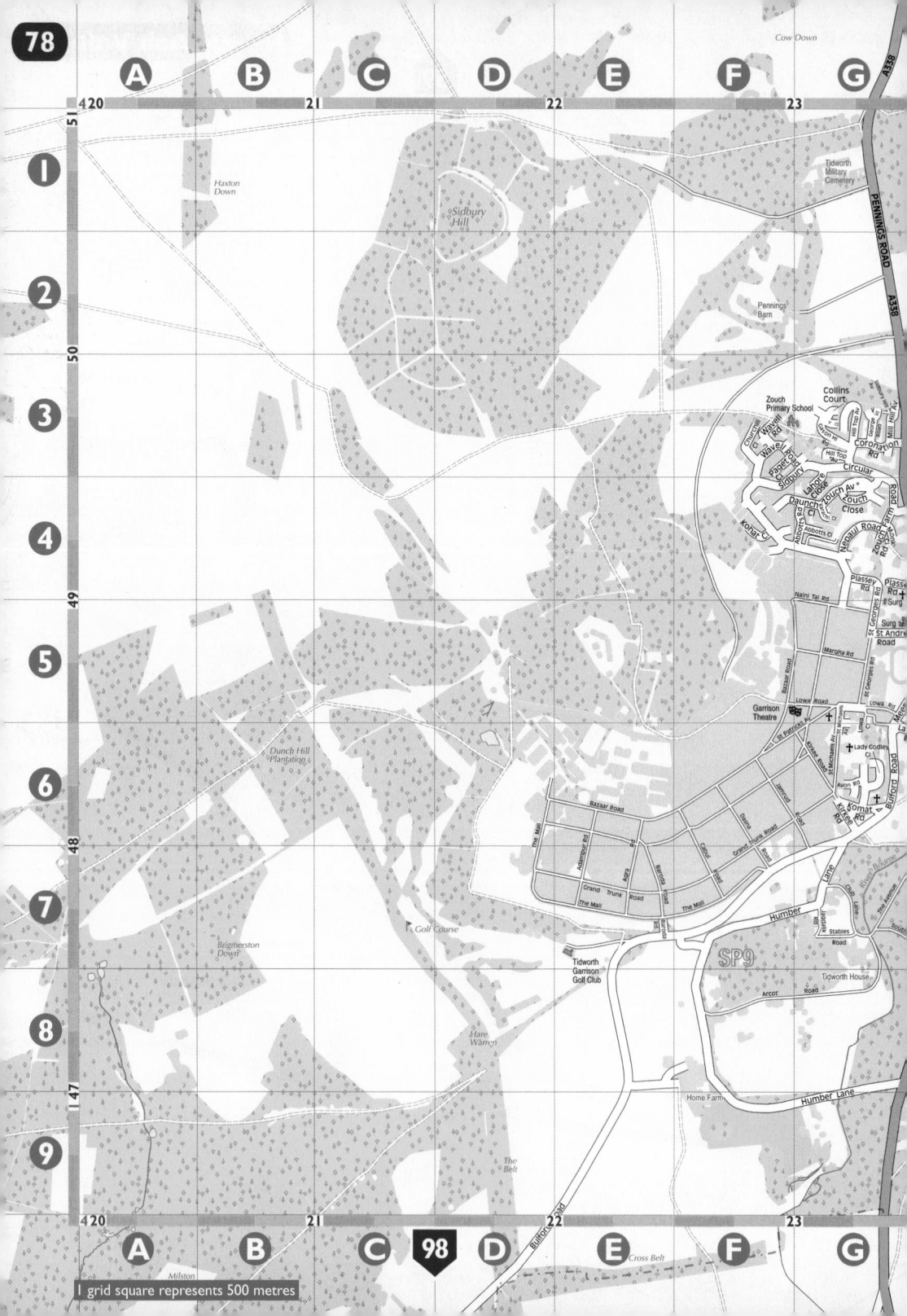

LUDGE

H **J** **K** **L** **M**

A342

Windmillhill
Down

24 25 26 27

Ludgershall
Castle and Cross

Deweys Lane

Byron Close

BUTT ST

CASTLE ST HIGH ST

Central

Surgery

Ludgershall Castle
Primary School

Perham

Shore

1

ANDOVER RD A342 TIDWORTH RD

TIDWORTH ROAD

Fleming Close

Eleanor Ct

Empress

Way

Clover Gdns

Primrose

Foxtail Gdns

Ludgershall
Sports Club

Roberts
Crescent

Camomile
Dr

Orchid
Drive

2

Somme Road

Aton Rd

Simond Rd

New Drove

New

Cornflower
Way

Castledown
School

50

A3026

3

Eiden Road

Somme Road

4

Manor Br
Ct

LUDGERSHALL ROAD

A3026

Chestnut Tree

Hawthorn

Beech Hill Rd

NORTH TIDWORTH

Perham
Down

Wouldham Ct

Uphor
Close

49

Manor Br

Wylye Rd

Ebble
Cl

Ash
Cl

Oak
Cl

Forest
Cl

Kestrel

Lambdown Terrace

Lambdown
Terrace

Kennmel

Somme Road

Fremantle Rd

4

Clarendon
J&I School

Bourne
Martin
Rd

Kennet
Road

Benin
Barrack
Rd

Fyfield
Way

Appleshaw
Way

Lamb
Down

Downsview
Way

5

t S

Ordnance Rd

Tidworth Leisure
Centre

Surgery

Surgery

Surgery

Station Road

80

Wiltshire County
Hampshire County

6

Ashdown Terrace

PARK ROAD

A338

Plantation
Rd

Furse Hill Road

Church Lane

Winton

Newdown
Copse

6

7

South Tidworth

A338

Kimpton
Down Farm

Down Road

8

Ashdown Copse

Kimpton
Wood

47

9

Wiltshire County
Hampshire County

Ox Drove

H **J** **K** **L** **M** **N** **P**

24 25 26 27

99

H   J   K   L   66   M   N
52   53   54   55   51

1

Foxdown

Polhampton Farm

2

ion Station
Works
Elm Rd
Beech Cl
Station Road
Road
Cl
Copse

Deane

PH

Quidhampton

50

3

+
Ashe
Source of
the River Test

ANDOVER ROAD

B3400

Cheesedown Farm

Turnpike
Cottages

49

4

LONDON ROAD B3400

The Green
Two Gate Mkt

TWO GATE LANE

Nightingale
Rise

Berrydown Court

Ashe
Park

Berrydown Lane

OVERTON

Berrydown
Farm

Waltham
Road

5

Pound Road

Burley
Wood

Burley Lane

88

Winchester St

Sapley
Farm House

6

48

Steventon

Waltham Lane

7

Brandown
Copse

Bassel's Farm

Waltham Lane

8

Lower
Whitehill
Cottages

47

9

Southley Farm

H   J   K   L   107   M   N   P
52   53   54   55

Pilgrim's Farm

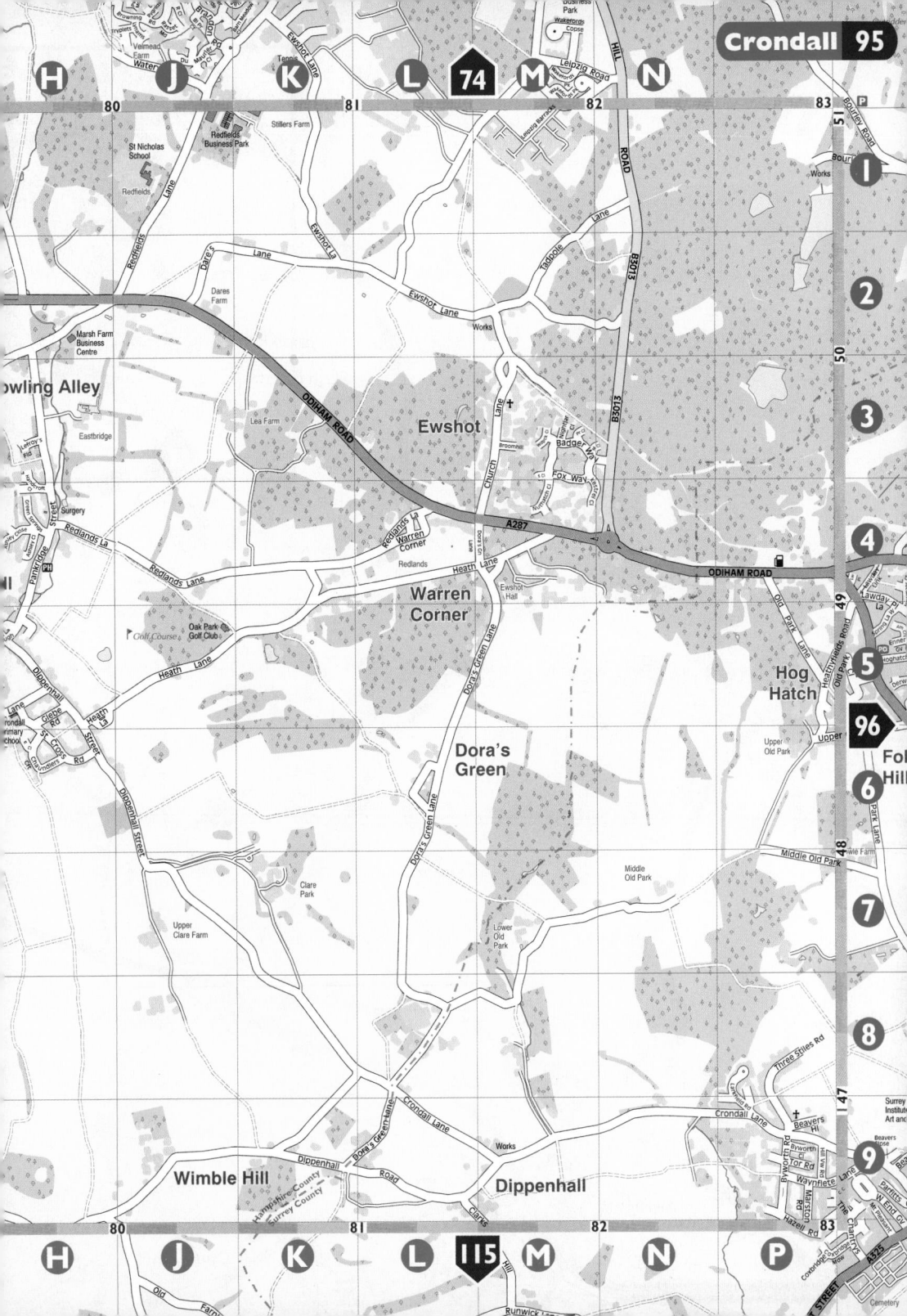

A B Kimpton† C 80 D E Fyfield F G

427 28 29 30

1

46

Snoddington Road

Kimpton CE
J&I School

Stanbury Road

Elm Cl

Lambourne
Way

Mullenspond

2

Thruxton Aerodrome &
Motor Racing Circuit

Thruxton

Stanbury Road

Beech Close

Von Dr

3

Thruxton
Industrial
Estate

45

Lovell Cl

A303

Bush Farm

East
Cholderton

Pithill Brook

Wiremead

4

Wiremead

Lane

Lains Farm

Hay Down Lane

Amport

Amport CE
J&I School

5

99

44

Furzedown

Amport House

Lane

Leggere's Hill

†

Parva Lane

Penna Lane

6

Quarley

Amport
Wood

Fox
Farm

Skew Road

7

Grateley Drove

43

Georgia Lane

Sarson
Wood

8

Quarley
Manor Farm

9

Grateley Drove

142

Grateley

Monxton Road

Lawrence Houses

Hawthorne

The
Deli

Gollard Farm

High

Georgia Farm

Chapel
Lane

Grateley
Primary

A B C 120 D E F G

427 28 29 30

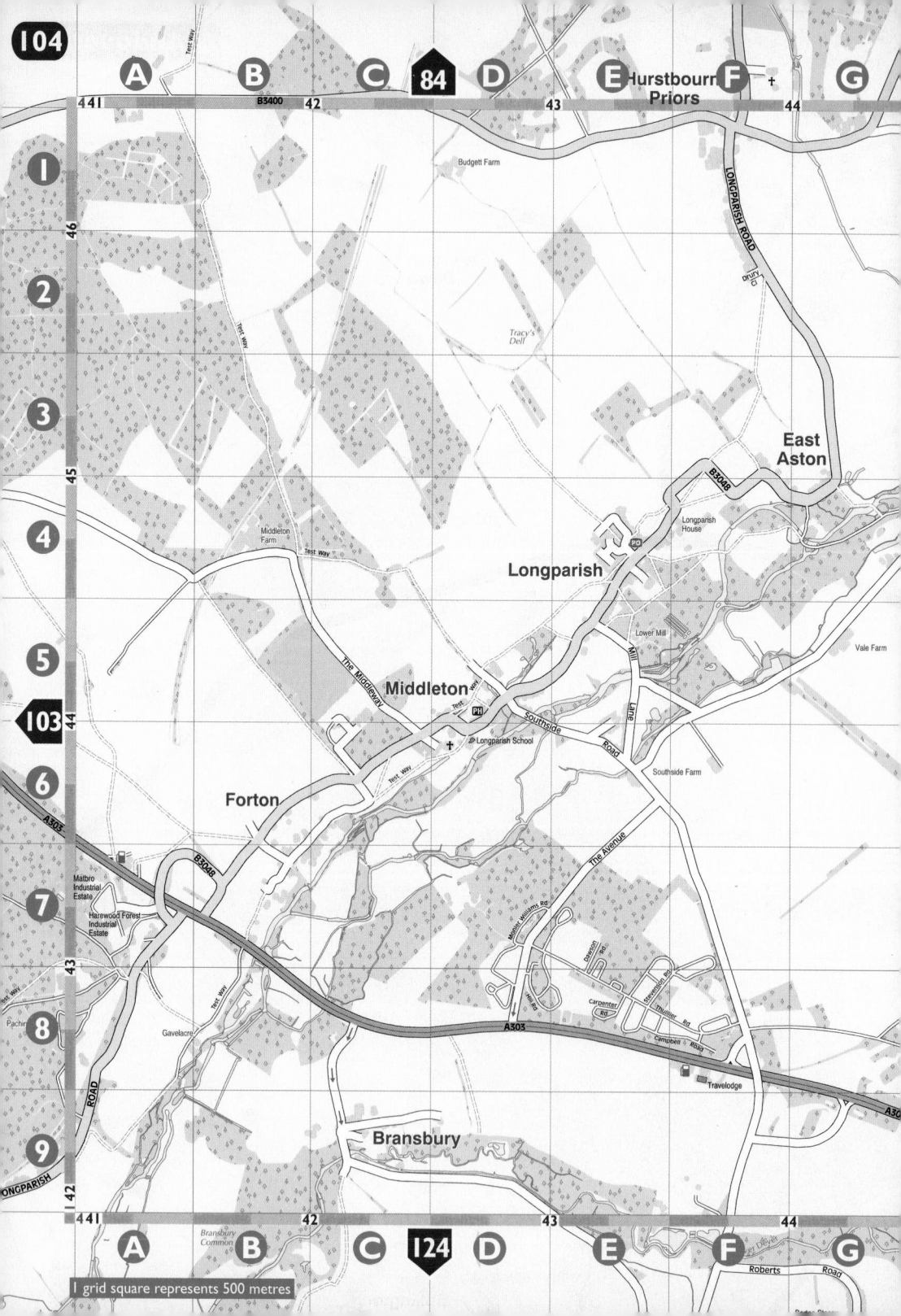

A B C 86 D E F G

86

448 49 50 51

New Barn
Cotts

Knowle
Hassock

Laverstoke
Grange Farm

White

1

46

Laverstoke Lane

Micheldever Road

New
Barn Farm

2

Buckkiln
Wood

Laverstoke
Wood

3

45

Roundwood Farm

4

Freefolk
Wood

5

105

105

44

6

Blind
End
Copse

7

43

Upper
Norton Farm

8

A303

9

A303

Upper
Cranbourne
Farm

42

448 49 50 51

A B C 126 D E F G

1 grid square represents 500 metres

H J K L **89** M N

59 60 61 62

I
46
2
3
45
4
Nutley Down
5
44 **110**
Ber
6

7
43
8
42
9

H J K L **129** M N P

59 60 61 62

Dummer Golf Club
Golf Course
Dummer
Farleigh Lane
Nutley Lane
Clump Farm
The Barns
Chapel
Down St
Glebe Close
Wayfarer's Walk
Inwood Copse
B3046
Gobley Hole
RG25
Nutley Wood
Nutley
Dummer Grange
Wayfarer's Walk
Dummer Grange Farm
Flockmoor Cottage
Breach Farm
PH
Axford
Damsel Lane
Fawkners
Preston House
PO
Garden
Preston Candover
CE Primary School
Preston Candover
Benbury Drive
Manor Farm

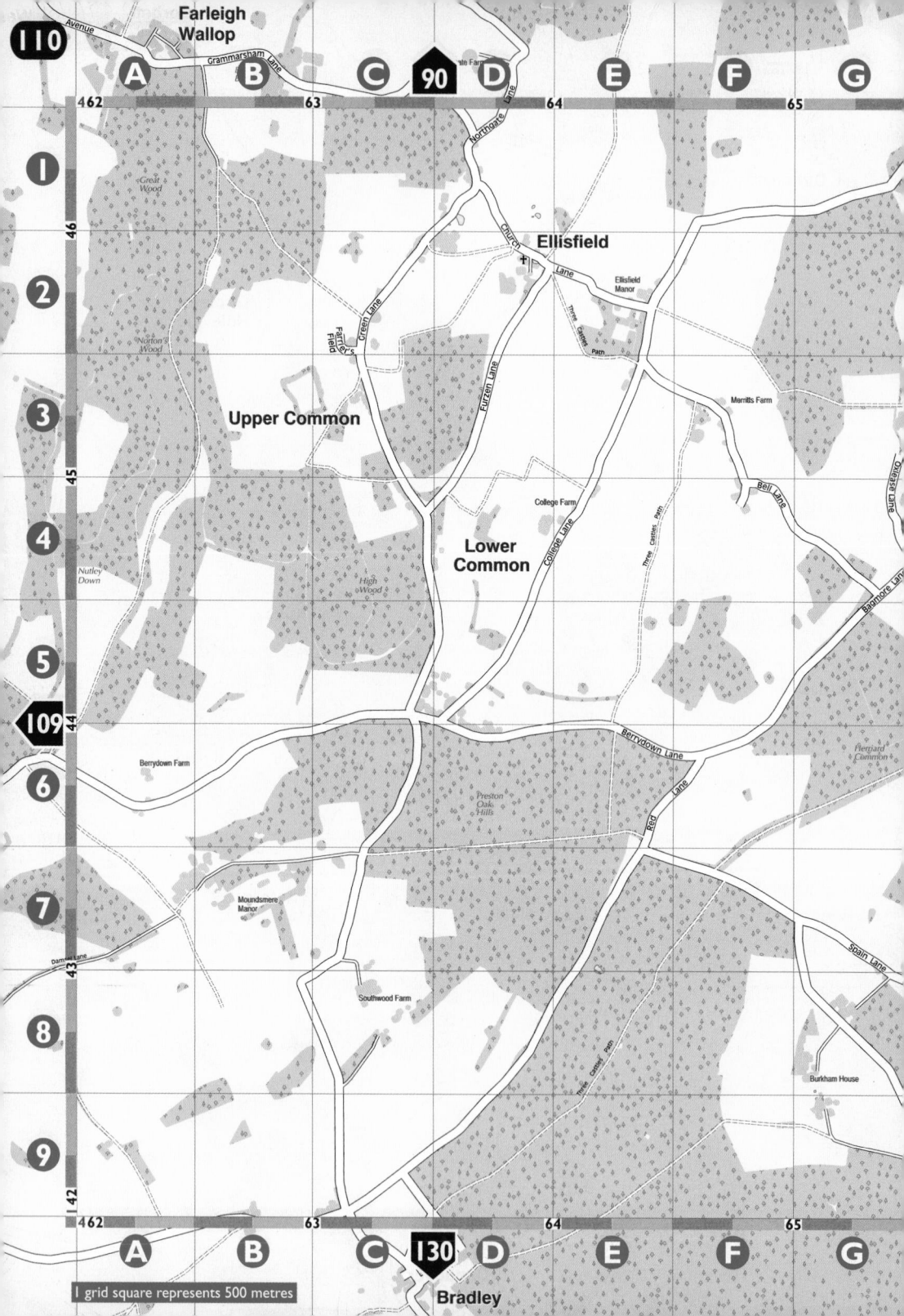

Hesters Copse

Lord Wandsworth College

Lord Wandsworth College

Lord Wandsworth College

Hyde Farm

93

H J K L M

73 74 75 76

PH

1

Well Lane

46

Lord Wandsworth College

New Farm

2

Sheephouse Copse

Vinney Copse

Froyle Lane

3

Crest Hill Farm

45

Sutton Common

Idighnam Copse

4

Well Lane

Lowe Froyl

5

Yarnhams

Hawkins Wood

44

114

Bambet Lane

6

Ham Wood

7

Old Lane

43

Spollycombe Copse

Upper Froyle

Treloar Trust

Treloar School

8

A31

River

Holybourne Down

PH

9

42

H J K L M N P

73 74 75 76

133

Bonhs Farm

Mill Court

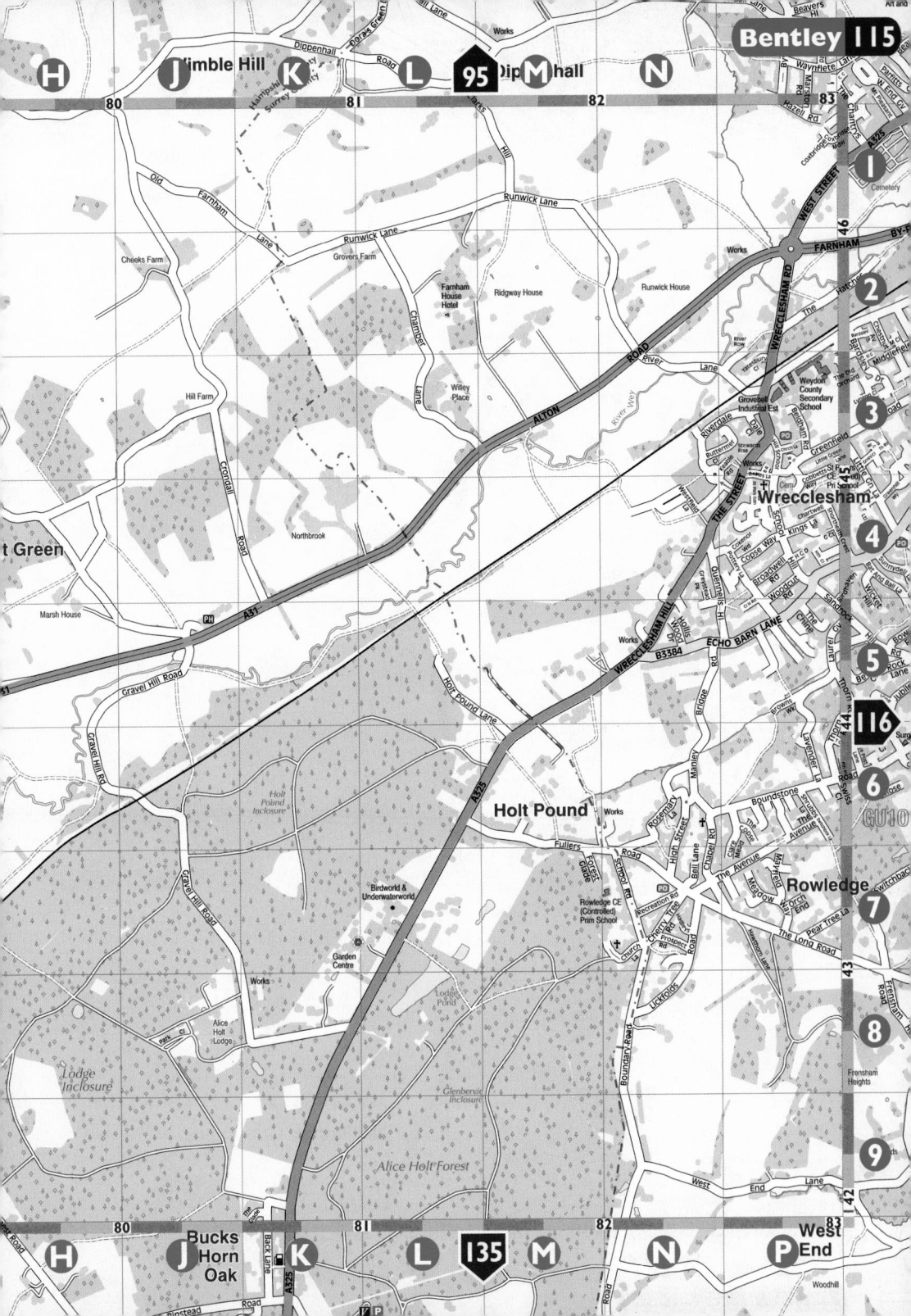

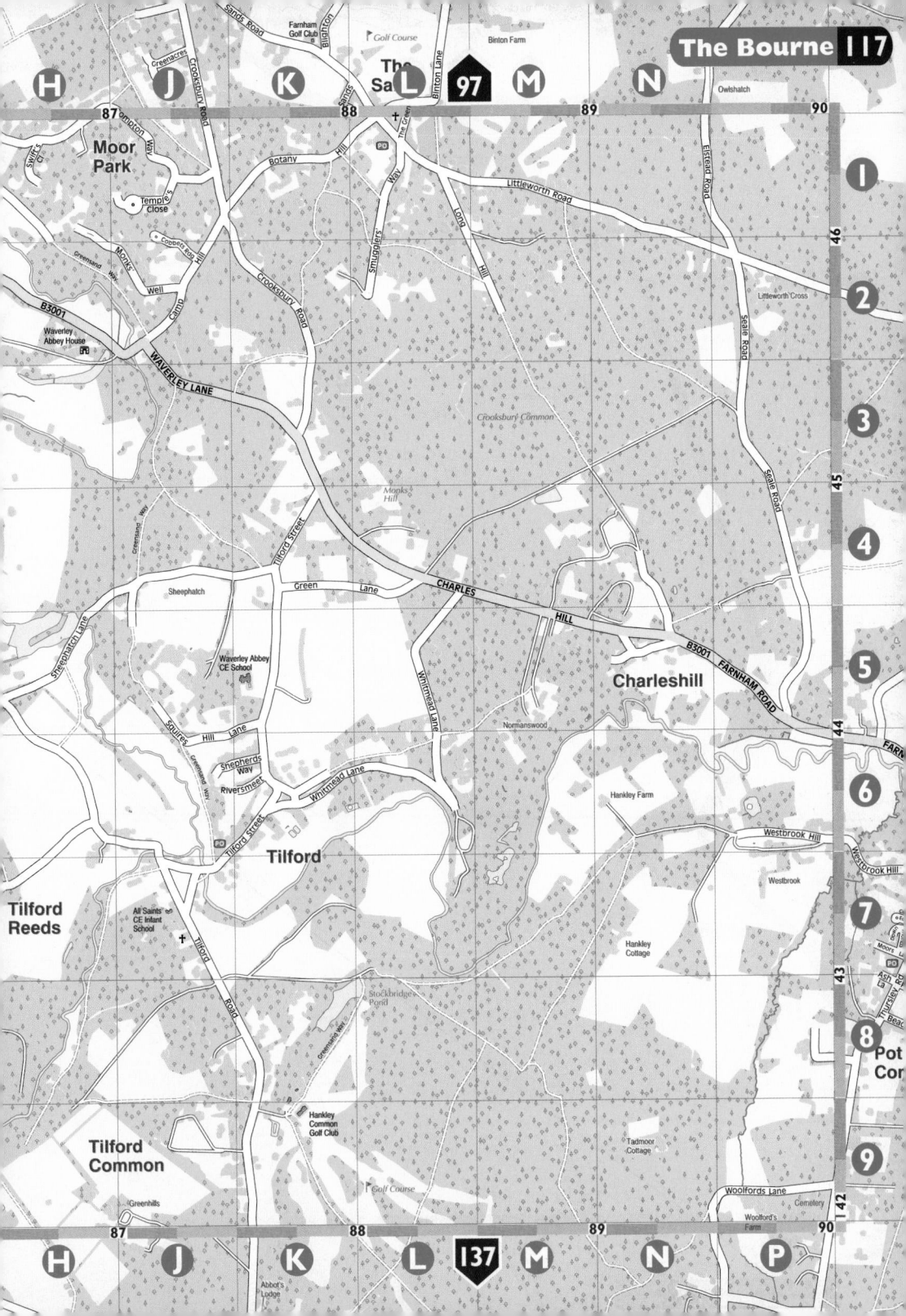

H J K L 99 M

24 25 26 27 42

Gra

Cholderton Lodge

Cholderton Road

Cholderton Road

1

Quarley Down Farm

Portway Farm

CHOLDERTON ROAD

Station Road

2

Grateley Business Park

Grateley Station

Station Ap

Campbell Cl

B3084

41

Streetway Road

Streetway Road

Hampshire County
Wiltshire County

Mount Hermon Road

Salisbury Road

3

Palestine

Zion Road

Palestine Road

Bournemouth Road

Orange Grove

Orange Grove

Olive Grove

40

4

Peach Grove

Peach Grove

Olive Grove

Mount Carmel Road

5

120

Castle Farm

6

Martin's Clump

39

7

Croft Fa

138

8

9

24 25 26 27

H J K L 138 M N P

Moxxton Farm

Farleigh School

Red ...

Prospect Farm

Stonehanger Copse

Down Farm

Dipden Bottom

Saxley Farm

122

Clatford Oakcuts

Kentsboro

Stockbridge Road

Stockbridge Road

A343

Road

Middle Wallop Airfield

Down Farm

Works

143

Danebury Hill

Danebury Ring

The Turret

Dane Down

140

122

A B C **102** D E F G

434 42 **35** **36** 37

Goodworth
Clatford

Clatford CE J&I School

The Crs

Barrow Hill

Red
Rice

1

Fullerton Road

Meadow Drive

Longstock Road

2

41

3

Flint Farm

Westover Farm

River Anton

4

40

Rowbury Farm

Fullerton Road

5

121

Longstock Road

Fullerton Manor

6

Fulle

Hazel Down

39

7

Longstock House

Charity Down Farm

8

Hazeldown Farm

38

9

434 **35** **36** 37

A B **141** C D E F G

Church Road

Church Road

Cemetery

Church Road

PH

PO

LECKFORD LANE

I grid square represents 500 metres

124

LONGPARISH

A **B** **C** **104** **D** **E** **F** **G**

Bransbury

441 42 42 43 44

Bransbury
Common

River Test

River Dever

Roberts Road

Barton Stacey
CE Primary
School

Roman Way

East Rd

Pheasant Cl

WEST ROAD

Bullingt

Works

Cravel Lane

King's Enter

King's

Greenacres

Ashfields

Barton Stacey

1

2

41

3

Newton Stacey

Manor Farm

4

40

5

B3420

123

6

Cocum Farm

39

Newton Down Farm

Moody's Down Farm

7

Drift Road

B3420

Middlebarn Farm

8

38

9

Harrows Lane

A30

Hill Farm

A272

441 42 43 44

A **B** **C** **143** **D** **E** **F** **G**

I grid square represents 500 metres

H J K L 105 M

45 46 47 48 42

Tidbury Farm

Cross Inn

A303

Upper
Bullington

1

Tidbury
Common

41

Colne Valley Way

Lower
Bullington

Colne

Barn Lane

2

Hill
Hill Barn

A34

BULLINGTON LANE

A30

Cranbourne
Grange

3

40

4

Egypt

Wonston Grange

Travelodge
Services

Travelodge

A30

Surgery

Wonston Lodge Lane

Hunton Lane

River Dever

5

126

BY PASS ROAD A30

Stockbridge Road

Sutton Scotney

PO

Wonston

6

Sutton
Manor

Barton

Drove

Winchester Hill

Christmas Hill

Holly Tree PH

39

A30

Wonston Lane

7

A34 WINCHESTER BY-PASS

8

38

Wonston Manor Farm

9

Sutton Down Farm

West Stoke Farm

A303

A   B   C   106   D   E   F   G

448   49   50   51
42

1

Upper
Cranbourne
Farm

2

41

Hunton
Down Farm

3

Hunton
Grange Farm

4

40

Hunton Down Lane

Norsebury
House

5

Hunton Lane

Hunton

ton Lane

Weston
Colley

Northbrook

Weston Down Road

Northbrook House

6

Stoke
Charity

PO

River Dever

River Dever

PO

Dever C

Church St

Mickl
Prim

Old Stoke Road

7

39

Borough Farm

8

138

9

448   49   50   51

A   B   C   145   D   E   F   G

1 grid square represents 500 metres

128

A   **B**   **C**   **108**   **D**   **E**   **F**   **G**

Woodmancott

55   56   57   58

42

1

2

41

3   Whiteway Farm

4   Candover Copse

40

Lone Farm

Lone Barn

Gunners Lane

5   Thorny Down Wood

Foxhill

Wayfarer's Walk

Grove Close

127

6   Candover House

Brown Candover

39

Copse Lane   Copse Lane   Bryce's Lane   Sorbush Lane

7   Burcot Farm

8

Stratton Lane

38

Totford Farm

9   Totford

Northington Down Farm

Northington

Swarraton

A   **B**   **C**   **147**   **D**   **E**   **F**   **G**

55   56   57   58

1 grid square represents 500 metres

Preston House

H J K L 109 M
59   60   61   62   42

I

Preston Candover CE Primary School

Preston Candover

Istenbury Drive

2

41

Preston Grange

3

Down Farm

Chilton Manor

Chilton Candover

4

B3046

40

B3046

The Avenue

5

130

Oxdrove Way

6

39

Oxdrove Way

Oxdrove Way

7

Wield Wood

Spiers Lane

Oxdrove Way

8

Armsworth Hill Farm

138

Godsfield Copse

Irene Castles Path

9

Armsworth Ho

59   60   61   62

H J K L 148 M N P

Hogga Lodge

Godsfield Farm

H   J   K   L   🏠   M   N

66   67   68   69   42

1
2
3
4
5
132
6
7
8
9

A339

Powells Farm

Wadgell's Copse

Bentworth Lodge

Drury Lane

Church Piece

Bentworth CE (Aided) Prim Sch
PO
Ashley Road
Church St
Village Street
Summerley
PH

Bentworth

Holt End Lane

Childer Hill Farm

Heathcroft Farm

Thedd Copse

Church Lane

Holt End

Bentworth Hall

Thedden Grange

Wivelrod Road

Lane

Jennie Green Lane

Wivelrod

Wellhouse

Medstead Grange

Wivelrod Road

King's Hill

Medstead Road

Bushy Leaze Wood

Jennie Green Lane

Rosewood Lane

Cem

The Abbey

Abbey Road

Old Park Farm

66   67   68   69

H   J   K   L   **150**   M   N   P

Hussell Lane

41

40

39

138

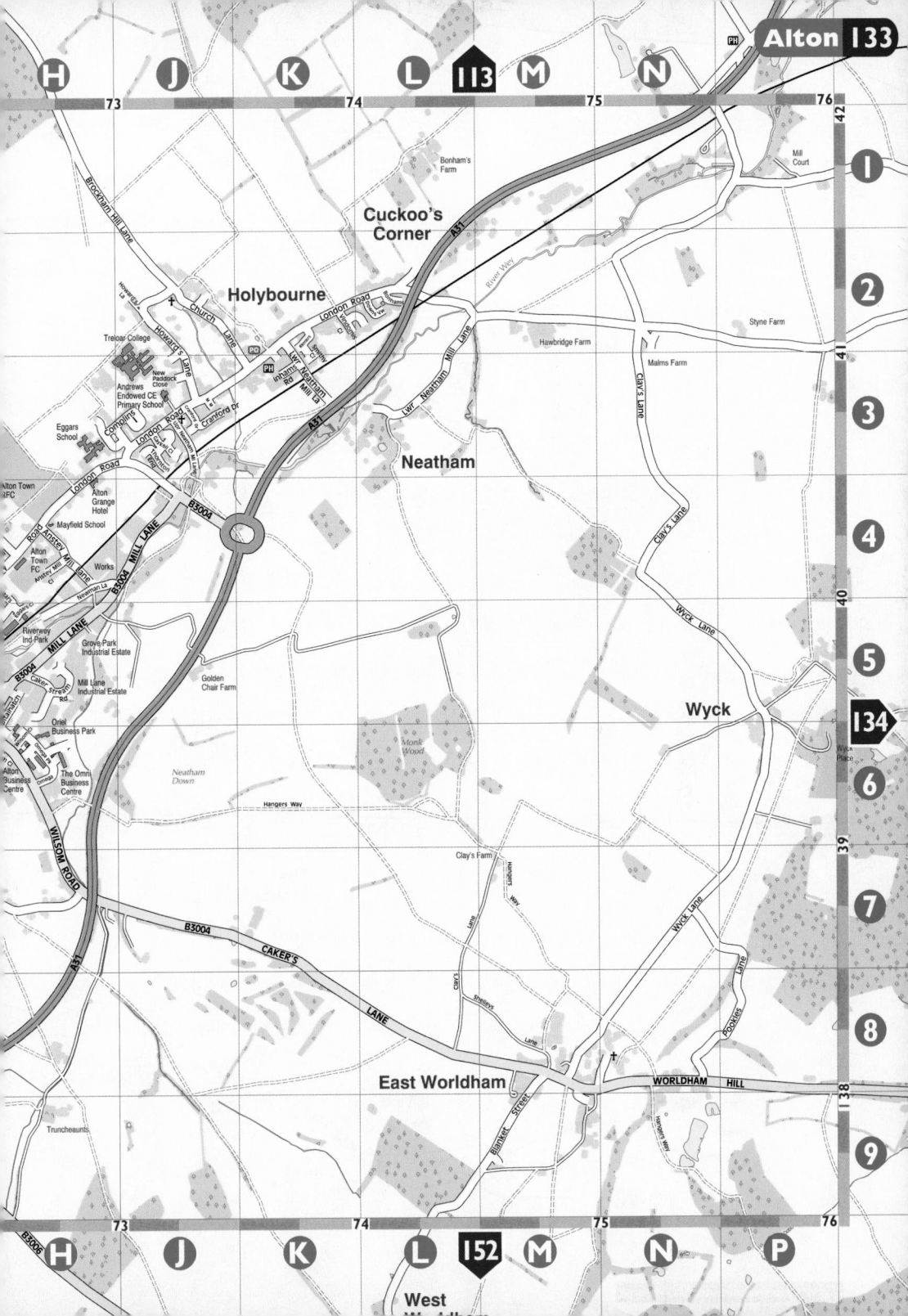

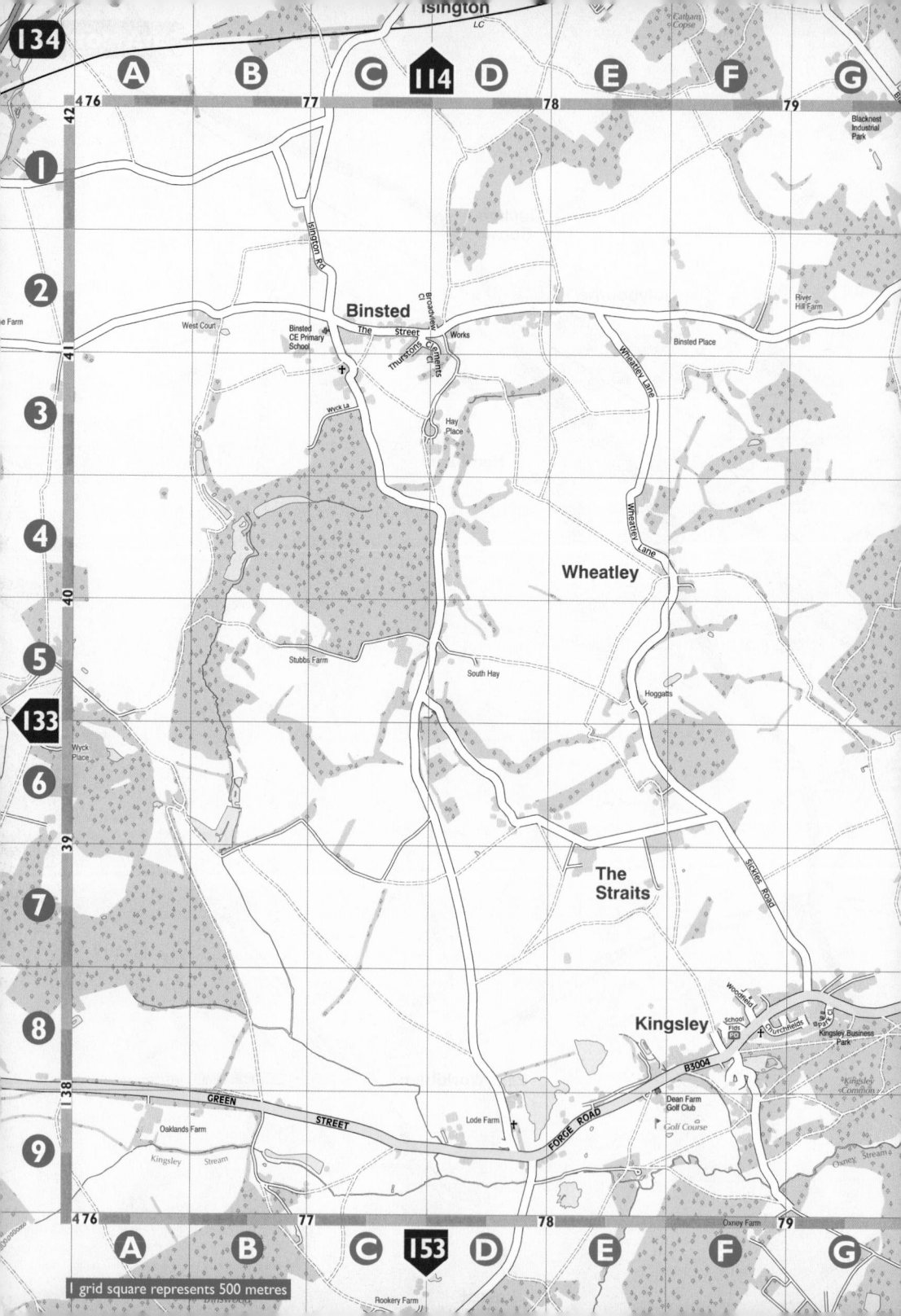

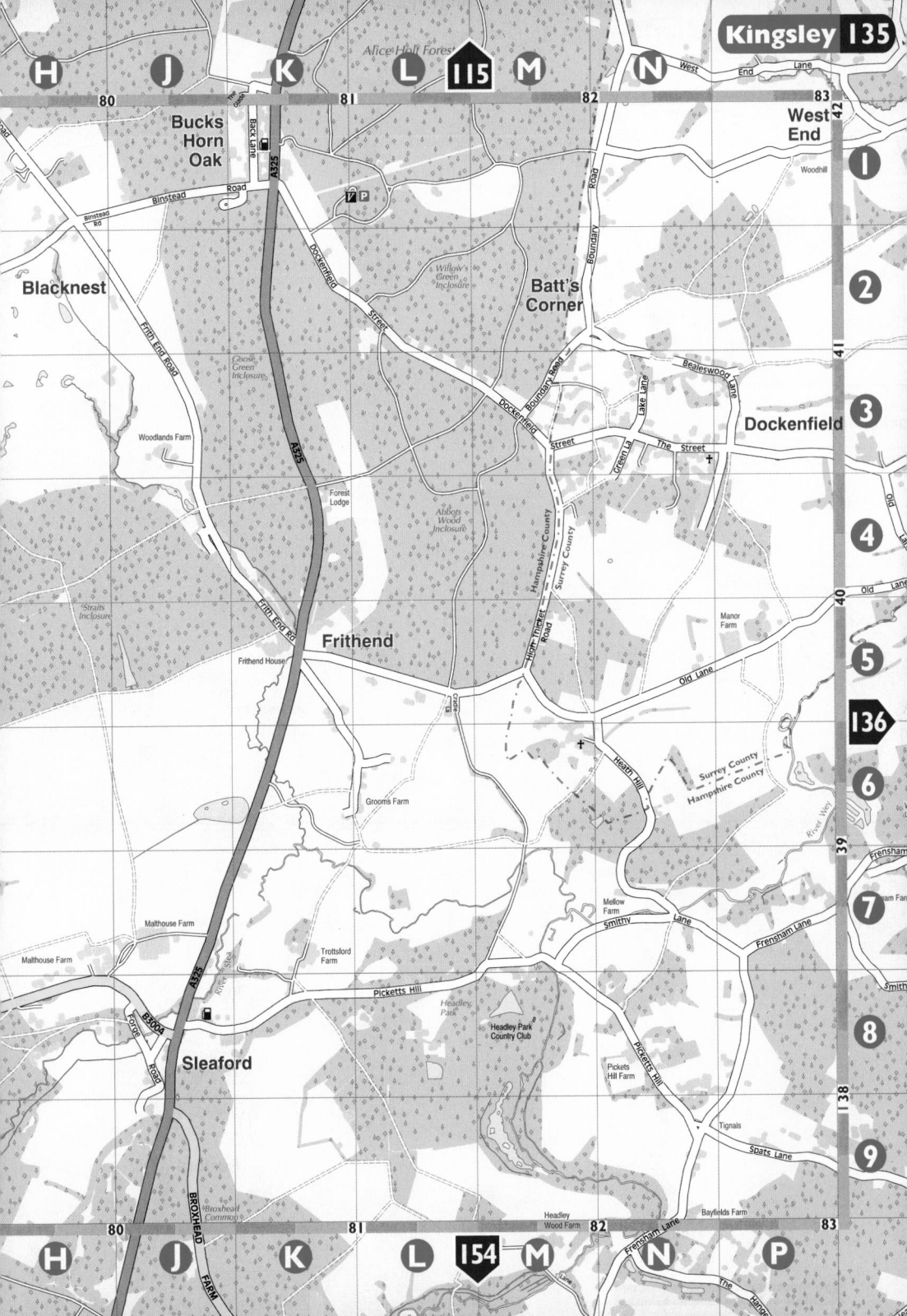

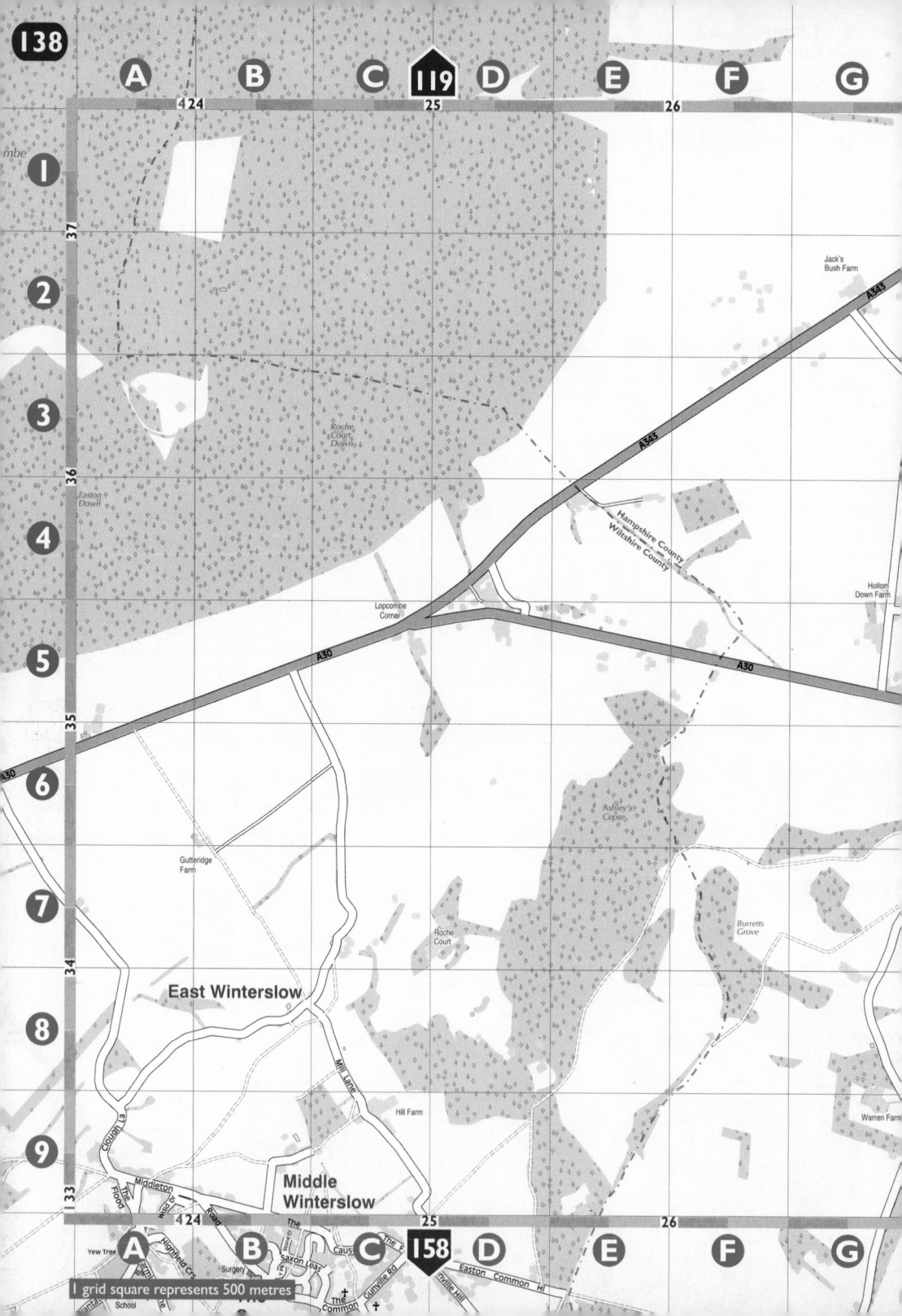

138

A B C 119 D E F G

424 25 26

mbe' 37

1

2

Jack's
Bush Farm

A343

3

Roche
Court
Down

A343

Easton
Down 36

4

Hampshire County
Wiltshire County

Hollom
Down Farm

Lopcombe
Corner

5

A30

A30

35

A30

6

Ashley's
Copse

Gutteridge
Farm

7

Burretts
Grove

Roche
Court

34

East Winterslow

8

Mill Lane

Warren Farm

Hill Farm

9

Middleton

33

Middle
Winterslow

424 25 26

Croucn Ln

The Flood

Yew Tree

A B C 158 D E F G

Surgery

Saxon Leaz

The Caus

Cunville Rd

Easton Common Hl

Ir'ula Hill

School

The Common

H J K L **122** M N

4   35   36   37   PO

Leckford Abbas

1

Church Road

Church Road

Church Road

Cemetery

PH

Longstock †

A3057

Test Way

Leckford Golf Club

2

Golf Course

Alners Towers

3

36

Works

A30

A3057

4

LONDON ROAD

Fairview Farm

A30

5

Stockbridge

HIGH STREET

A30

Old London Road

Stockbridge J&I School

WINTON HILL B3049

Cemetery

35 **142**

Roman Rd

Test Valley School

Town Hall

Wykeham Gallery

Newton

Ray

New St

Harold

Stockbridge Down

B3049

6

River Test

The Kelsons

Steepleton Home

Penny Lane

A3057

Somborne Park Road

7

Common Marsh (NT)

Test Way

34

North Park Farm

Homestead Farm

8

North Houghton

Marsh Court

North Park Wood

A3057

9

Houghton Lodge & Garden

33

4   35   36   37

H J K L **161** M N P

†

142 Leckford

123

141

162

A30

B3049

B3049

New Farm

Sandydown Farm

Heath House

Dumper's Oak

Stockbridge Down

Bushy Copse

Winter Down Copse

North Park Farm

Rookley Manor

Leckford Abbas

Course

Somborne Road

Whitehall Road

Little Somborne House

Little

1 grid square represents 500 metres

H   J   K   L   **124**   M   N

42   43   44

Martins Lane

A30

1

37

Brockley Warren

2

Chilbolton Down

Crawley Down

3

36

A272

Warren Wood

4

5

Hicks Lane

35   **144**

Cricket

Crawley Court

Close

Crawley

New Barn

6

+

PH

Copse

Cemetery

7

Beeches Farm

B3048

34

Folly Farm

Littleton Hi

8

STOCKBRIDGE ROAD B3049

Long Park

Folly Farm Touring
Caravan Park

Kirton Farm

9

133

H   J   K   L   **163**   M   N   P

42   43   44

Hill Farm

A272

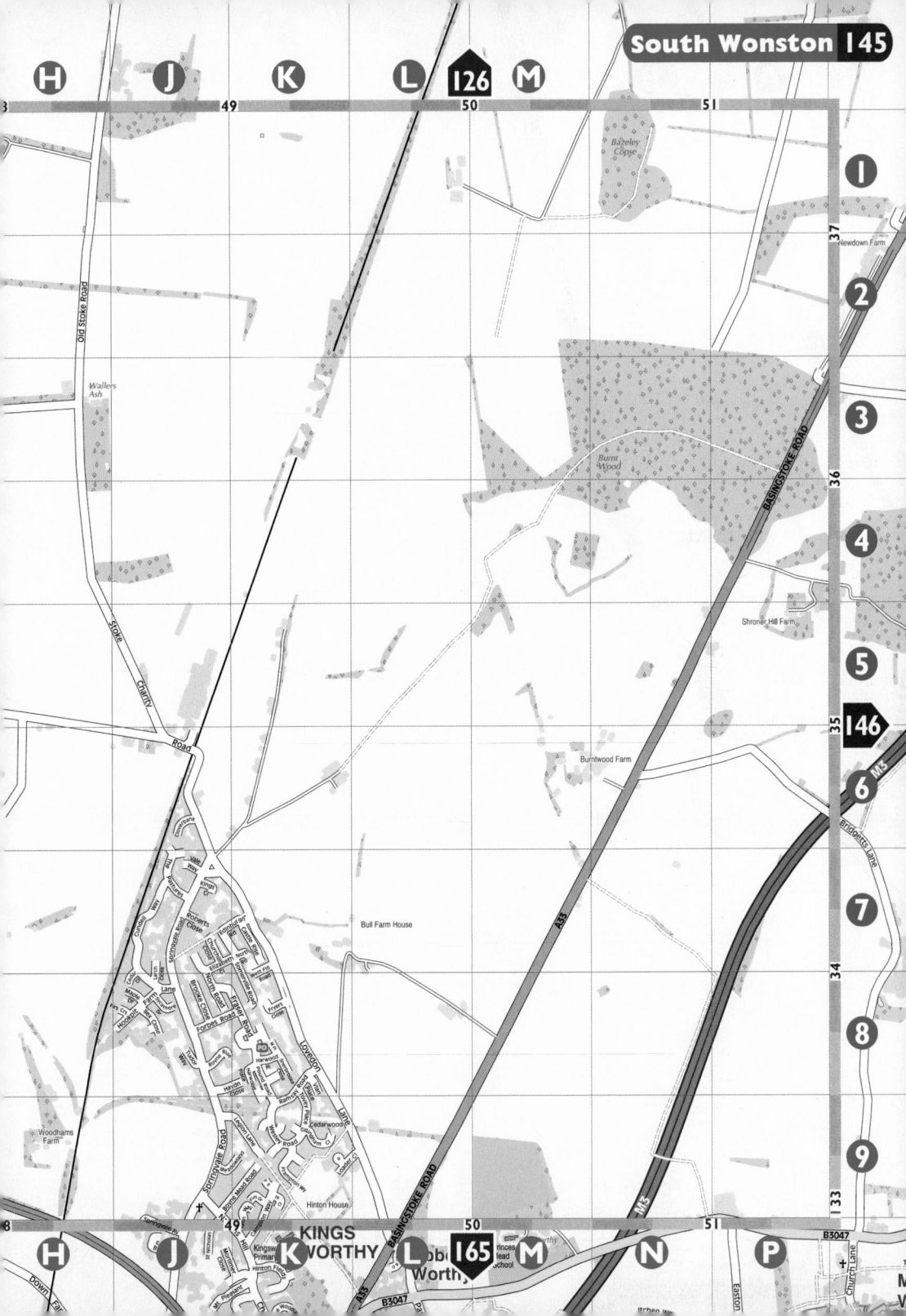

H J K L 128 M N

Northington

55 56 57 58

Northington Down Farm

Swarraton

B3046

Swarraton Farm

1

2

3

Abbotstone Down

4

The Grange Farm

The Grange

The Grange Lake

Warfarer's Walk

5

148

6

Northington Rd

Abbotstone

Itchen Stoke Down

Fobdown Farm

Three Castles Path

Old Alr orc 7

Green Cl

34

8

B3046

Outgrove Way

Warfarer's Walk

Folly Hill

Pinglestone Farm

9

133

55 56 57 58

Itchen

NEW ALRESFORD

Arle Industrial Estate
Arle Gdns

WEST ST

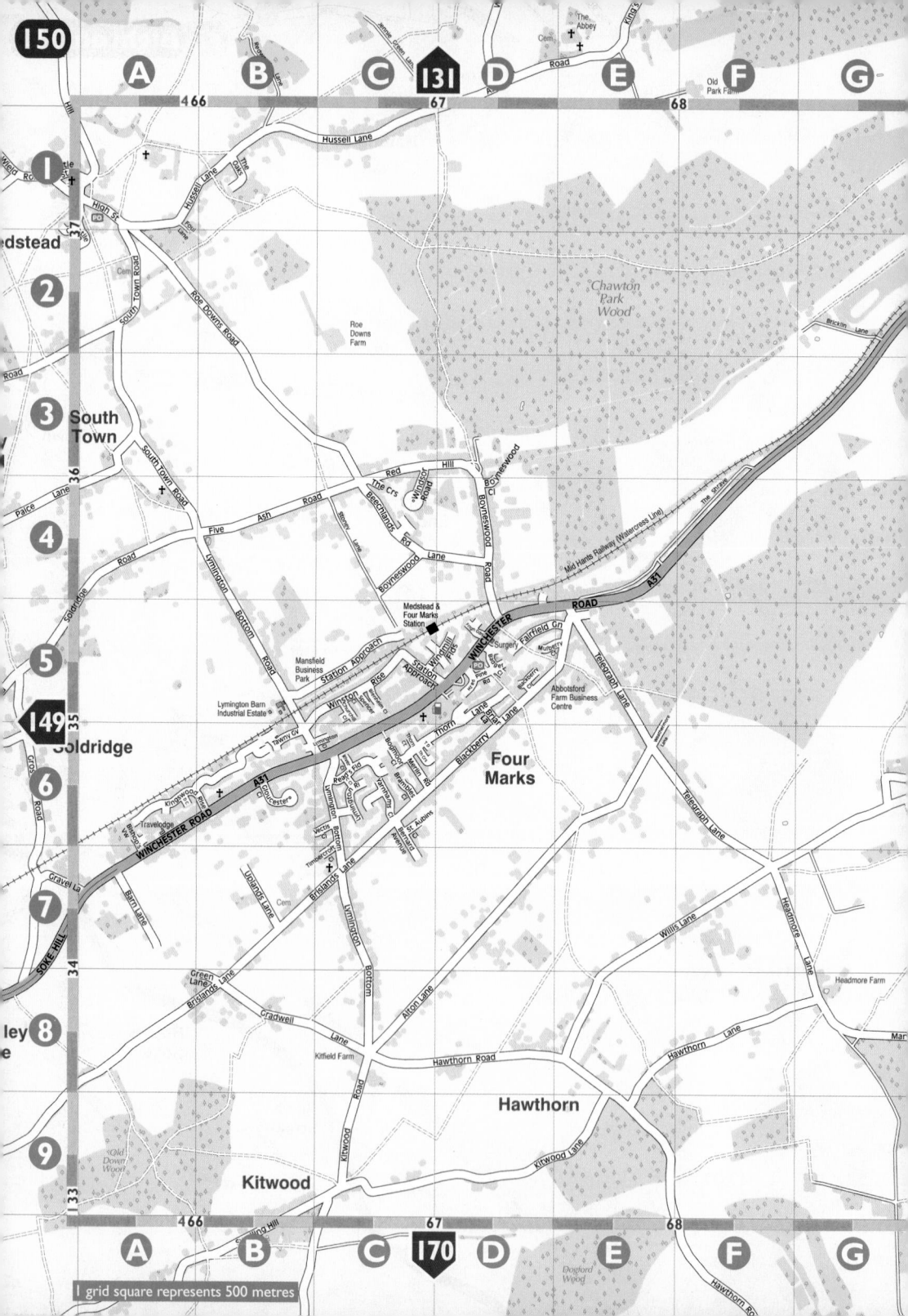

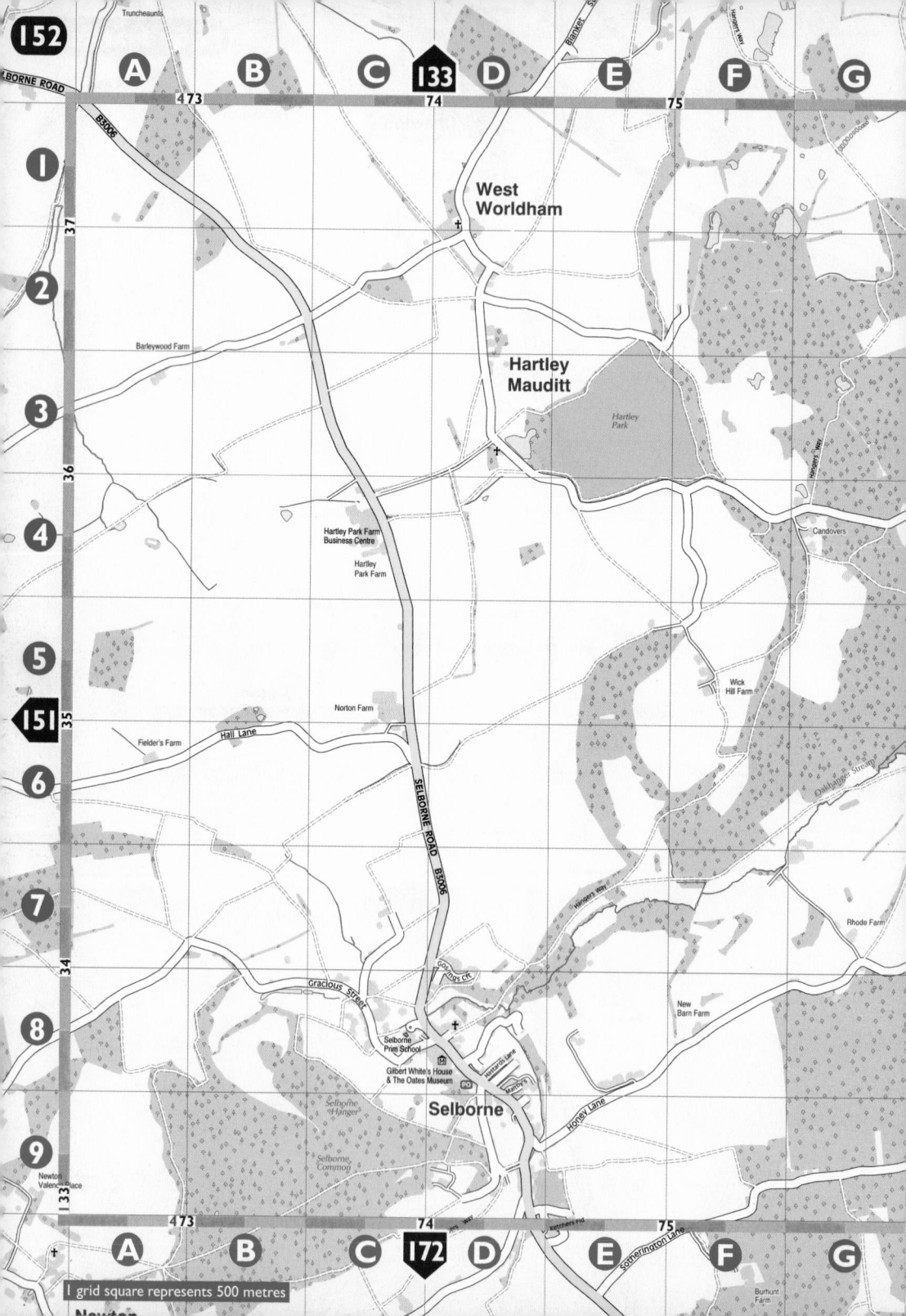

Middle Winterslow

138

The Common

Frenchmoor

1 grid square represents 500 metres

H   J   K   L   139   M

7   28   29   30   33

1
2
3
4
5
160
6
7
8
9

Broughton Primary

SAL
ROAD
whiteshoot
Greenwood
Queenwood Rise
Beeches
Cottage
Church Farm
ROMSEY ROAD
Clarendon Way
Monarch's Way
Buckholt Road
32
Clarendon Way
Monarch's Way
Buckholt Farm
31
Queenwood Farm
30
129

North Lane
Yew Tree Lane

Rectory Hill
Chalk Pit Lane
PO
West Tytherley Primary School
West Tytherley
North Lane
The Warren
Pug's Hole
Dean Road
Red Lane
The Coach Road
The Green
Pug's Hole
Bulls Drove

Stony Batter
Stride's Farm
The Coach Road
Manor Farm
Manor Rd
East Tytherley
Cedars Vw

Lockerley Hall
Lain Copse

H   J   K   L   178   M   N   P

27   28   29   30

Home Farm Business Centre

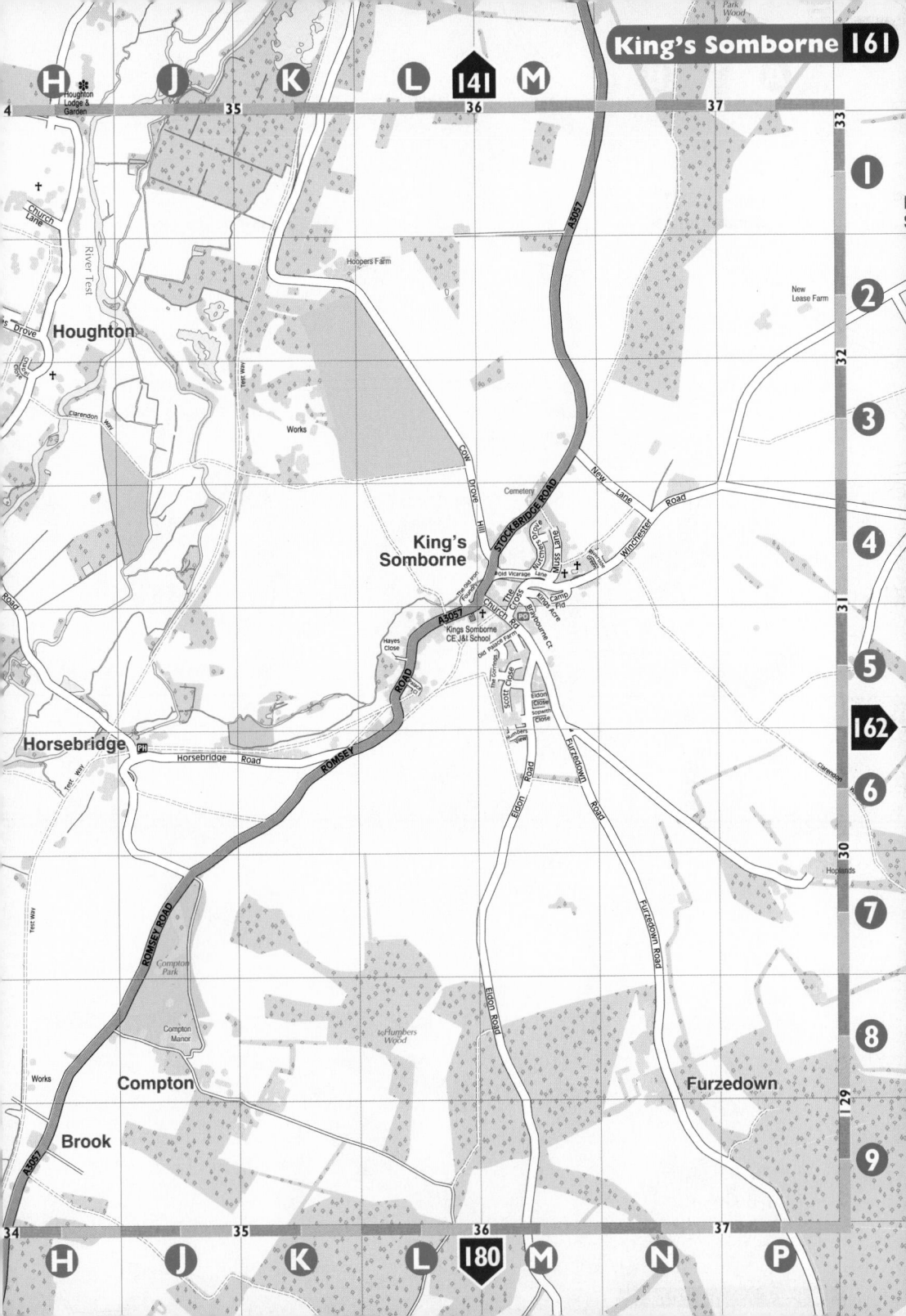

141

162

180

Houghton Lodge & Garden

Houghton

River Test

Church Lane

Clarendon Way

Hoopers Farm

Works

Cow Drove Hill

STOCKBRIDGE ROAD

Cemetery

New Lane

Winchester Road

King's Somborne

The Old Vicarage

Church Road

The Cross

Muss Lane

Eve Acre

Camp Fld

Eldon Road

Furzedown Road

A3057

Kings Somborne CE J&I School

Hayes Close

Scott Close

Eldon Close

Romsey Road

Horsebridge

PH

Horsebridge Road

Test Way

Romsey Road

Compton Park

Compton Manor

Works

Compton

Brook

A3057

Plumbers Wood

Eldon Road

Furzedown Road

Furzedown

New Lease Farm

Clarendon Av

Hoplands

H J K L M N P

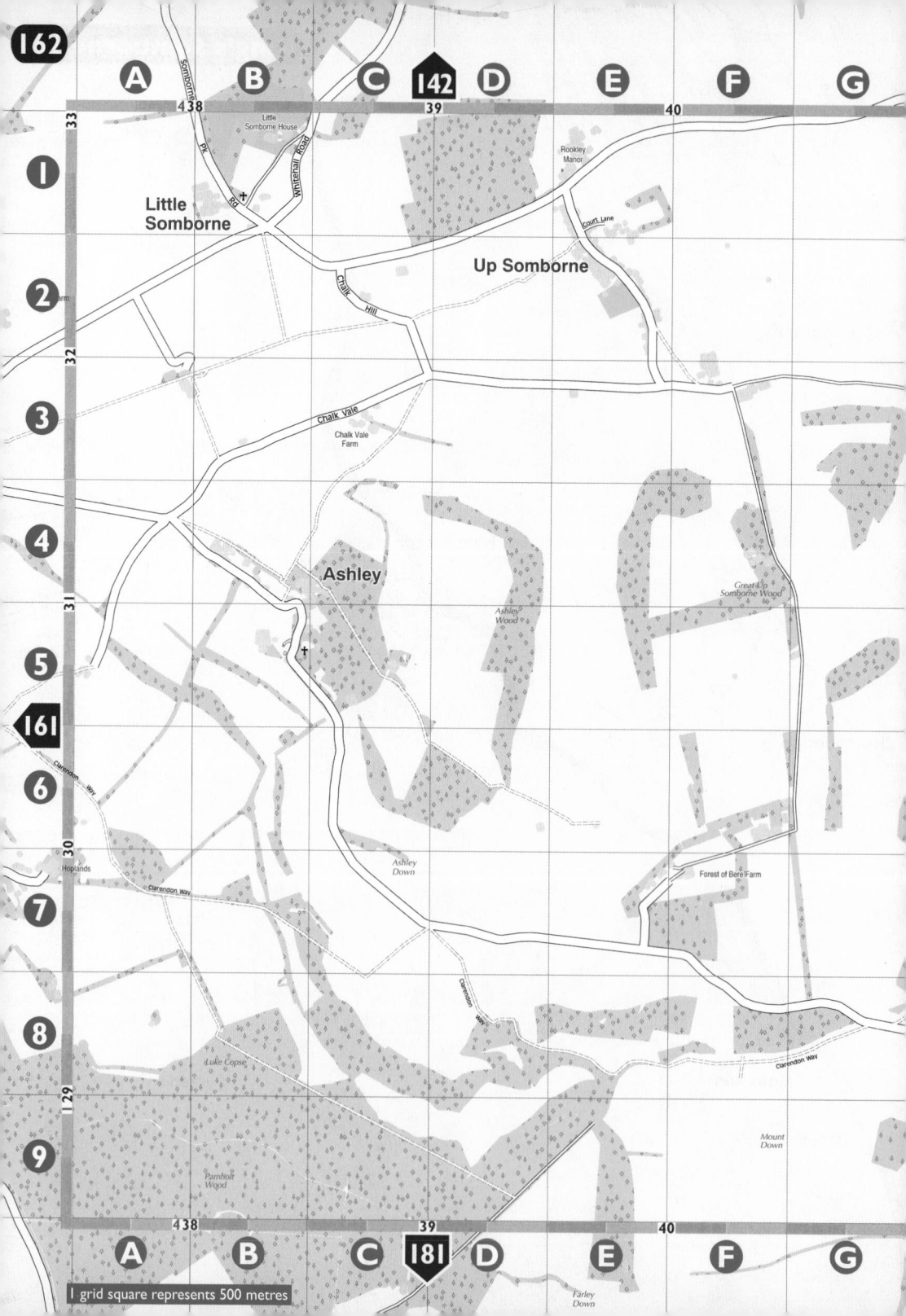

H   J   K   L   **151**   M   N

9   70   71   72   33

Place

A32

Lane

Newton Valence Place

1

Newton Valence

Plash Wood

Rotherfield Park

Shotters Lane

Shotters Farm

Hullam Lane

2

3

East Tisted

PO

Bridle

Appleton Ho

Old Place Farm

Heards Farm

32

4

Goleigh Wood

Shell Lane

31

5

Shell Lane

172

Colemore

6

Beckstedle Farm

Slade Farm

Church Farm

30

7

Field Farm

Five Ash Farm

8

Colemore Common

Hermitage Farm

Warren Farm

29

9

PH

Claypitt Lane

Claypit Farm

Barnet Side

Road

A32

39   70   71   72

H   J   K   L   **190**   M   N   P

Barnet Lane

more Lane

Alexander's Farm

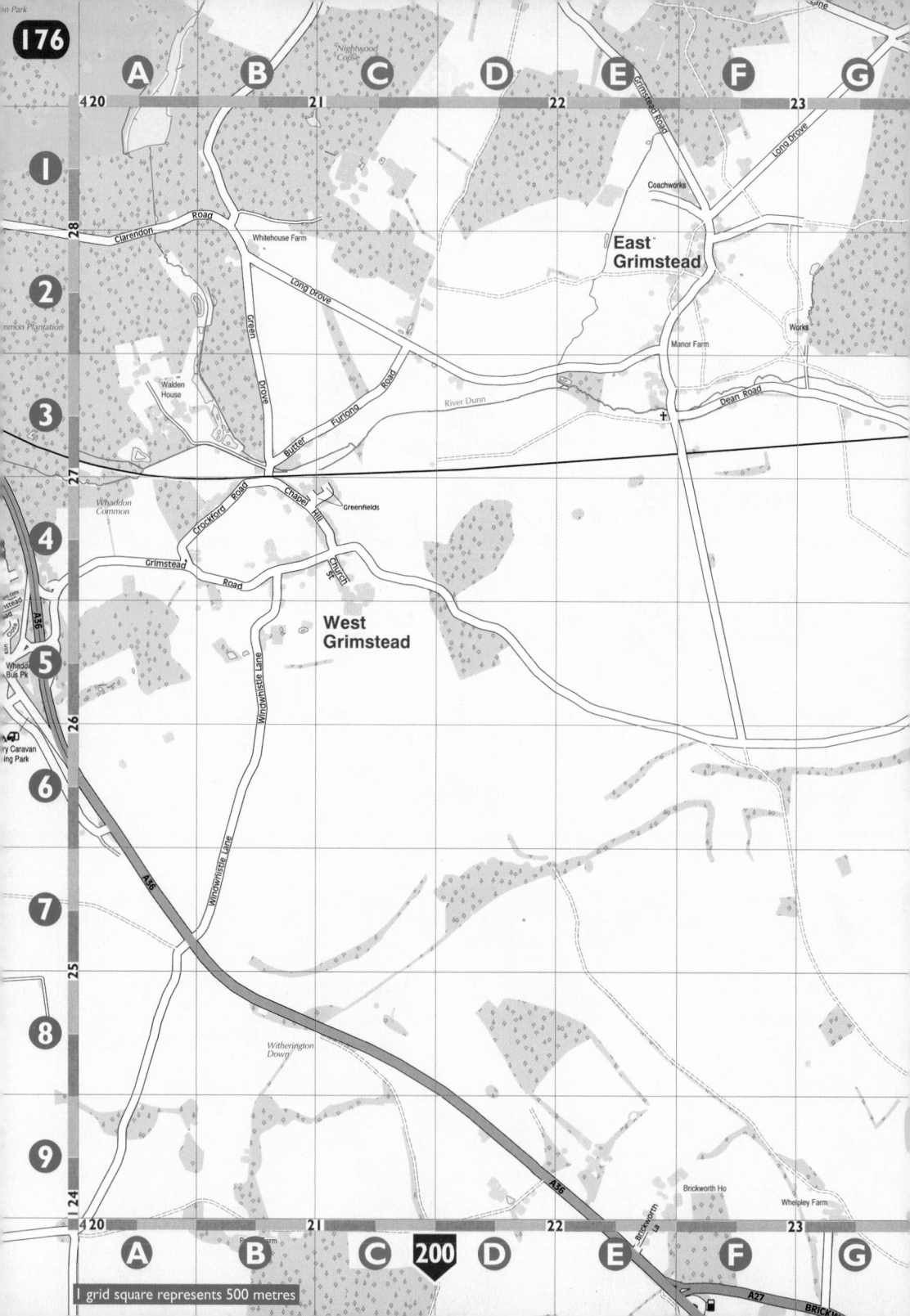

A B C D E F G

420 21 22 23

1

28

Clarendon Road
Whitehouse Farm

Common Plantation

Green Drove

Long Drove

Coachworks

East Grimstead

2

Walden House

Butter Furlong Road

Manor Farm

Works

Long Drove

3

27

River Dunn

Dean Road

Whaddon Common

Crockford Road

Chapel Hill

Greenfields

4

Grimstead Road

Church St

West Grimstead

A36

5

Whaddon Bus Pk

26

Caravan ing Park

Windwhistle Lane

6

A36

7

25

8

Witherington Down

9

24

A36

Brickworth Ho

Whelpley Farm

420 21 22 23

A B C **200** D E F G

Brickworth La

A27 BRICKU

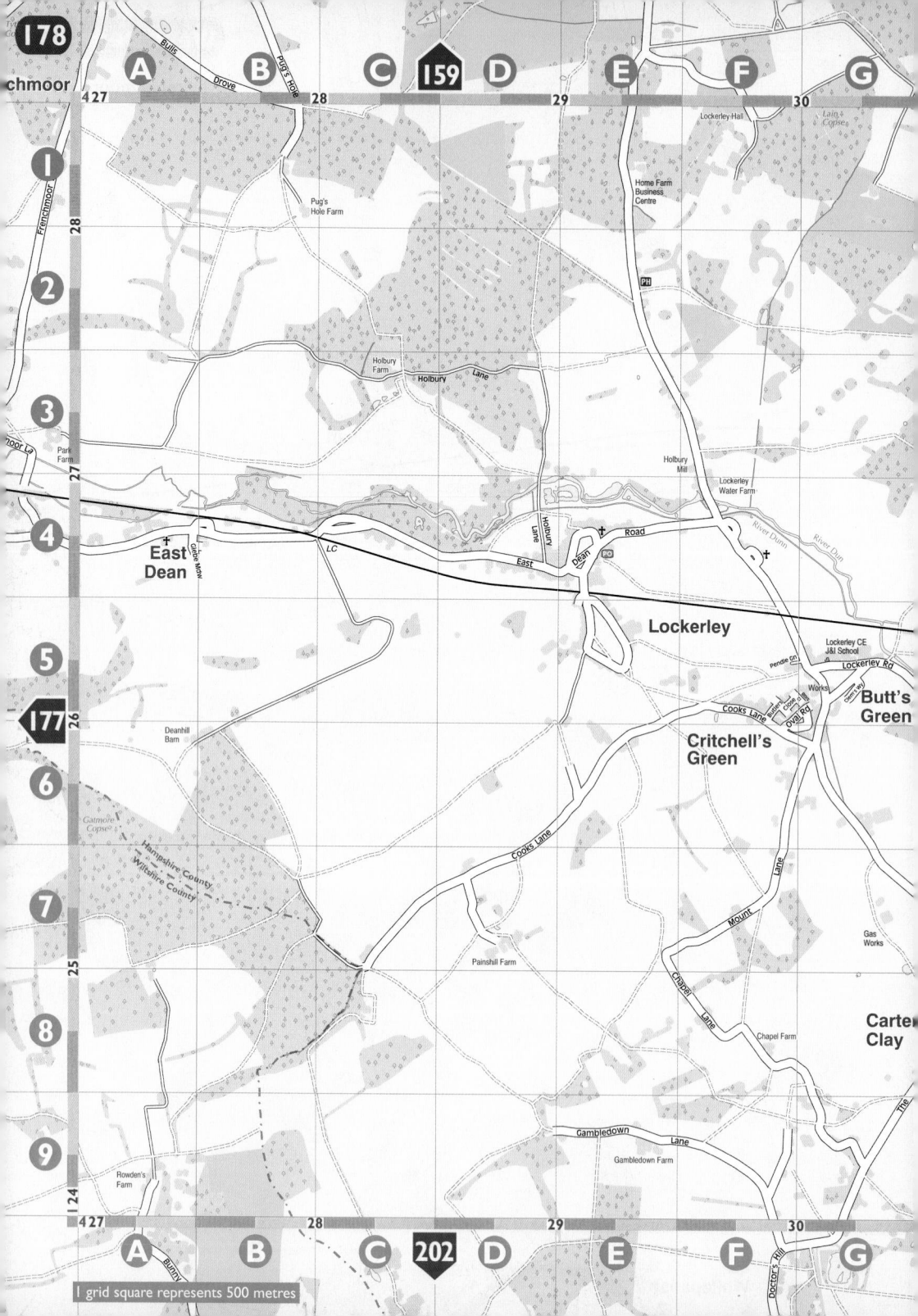

H J K L 162 M N

38 39 40 41

1
2
3
4
5
182
6
7
8
9

28
27
26
25
24

Farnholt Wood

Farley Down

Bailey's Down

Fishponds Fm

Farley Fm

Berrydown Farm

Furzedown Road

Farley Ho

Oakfield

Dores Lane

Farley Lane

Kings Somborne Road

Pitt Fm

Farley Lane

Gidge Copse

Merdon

Upper Slackstead

Monarch's Way

Fern Hill Lane

Dores Lane

Road

Church

Lower Slackstead

Dores Lane

Dores Lane

Woolley Green Fm

Monarch's Way

Dummers Rd

Monarch's Way

Claves Road

Gravel Rd

Pucknall

Common Hill Road

Braishfield Primary School

Braishfield Rd

Ampfield Wood

Monarch's Way

H J K L 205 M N P

38 39 40 41

The Sir Harold Hillier Gardens & Arboretum

Jermyns House Garden

Knapp Lane

Knapp

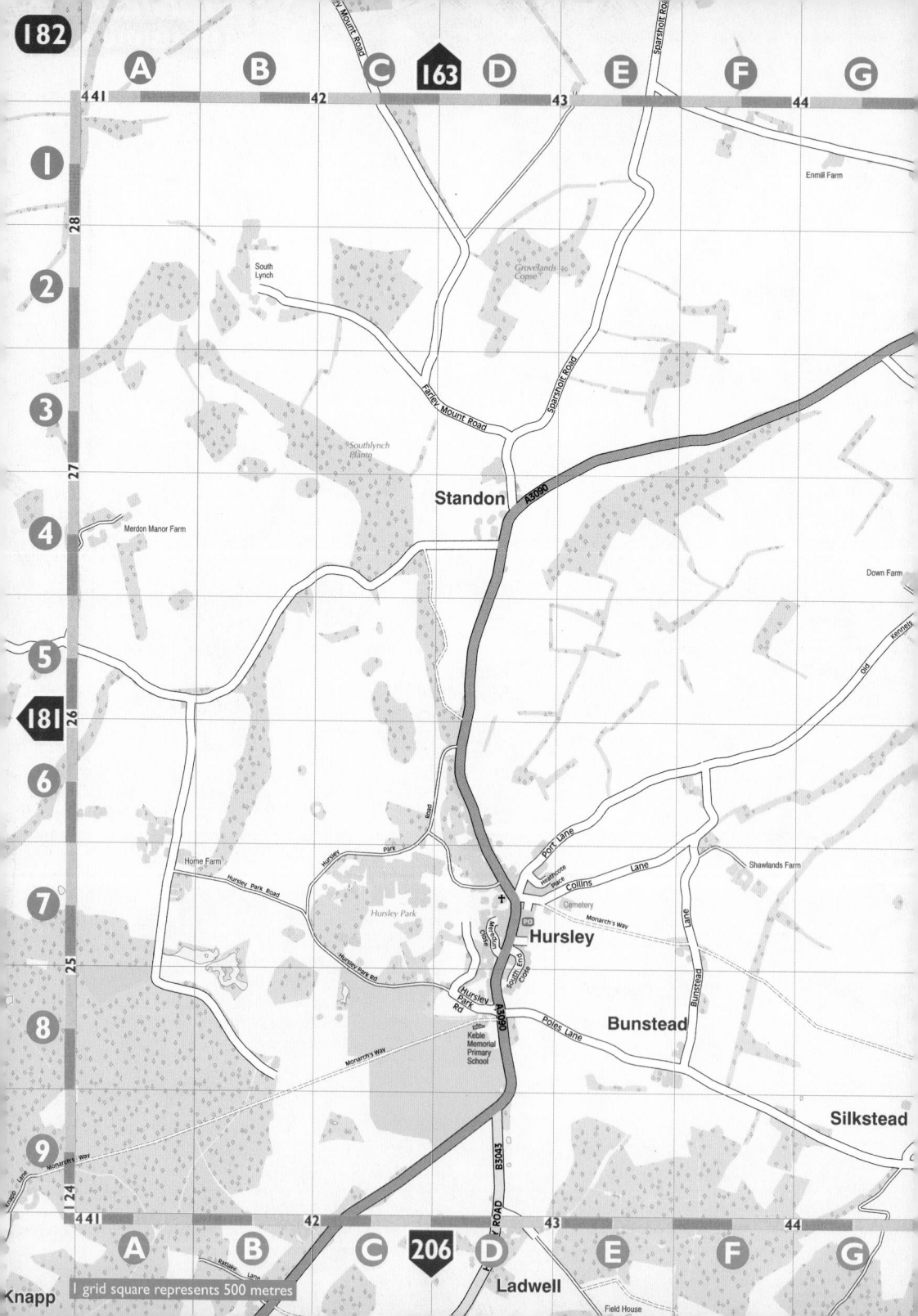

172

192

215

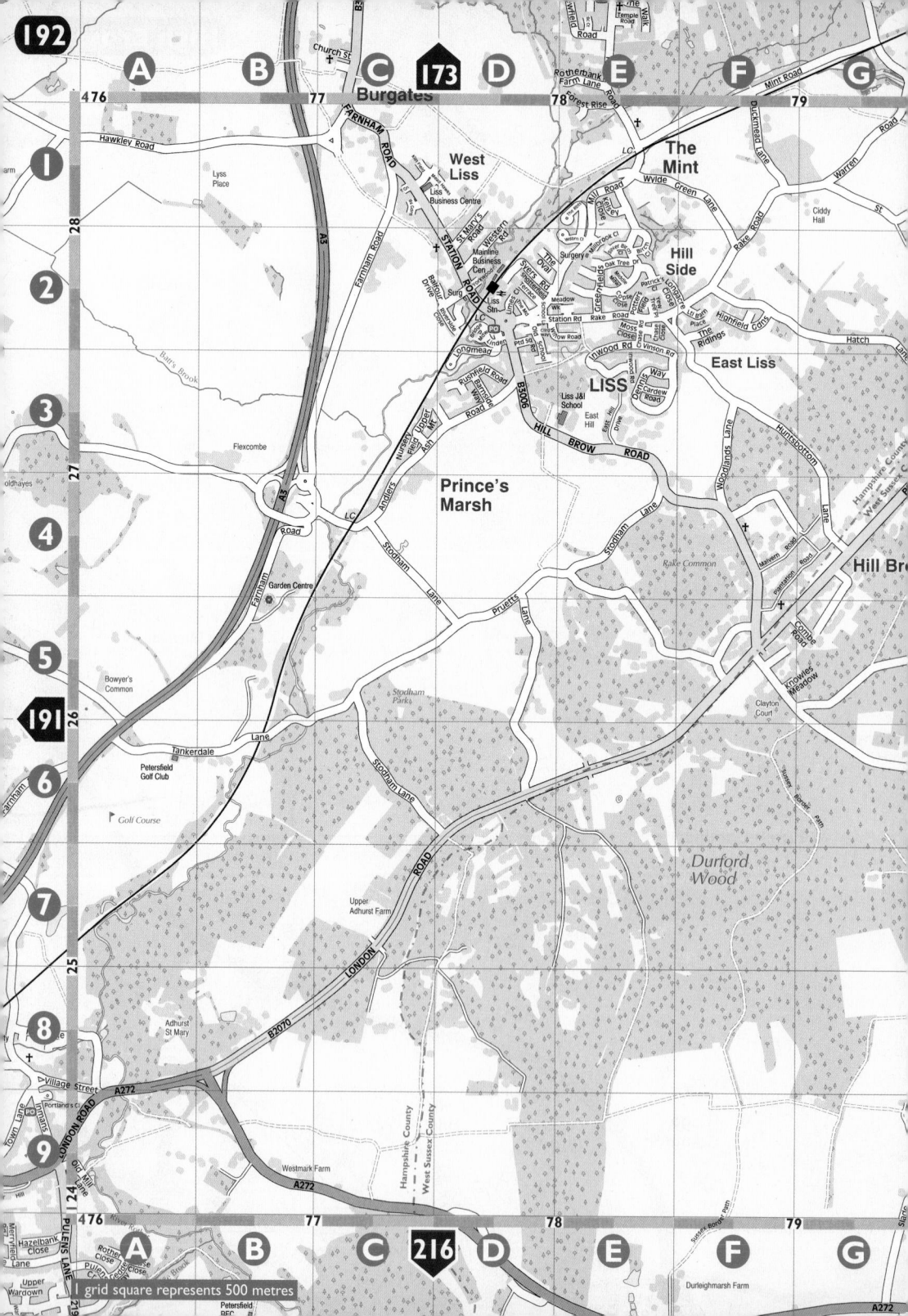

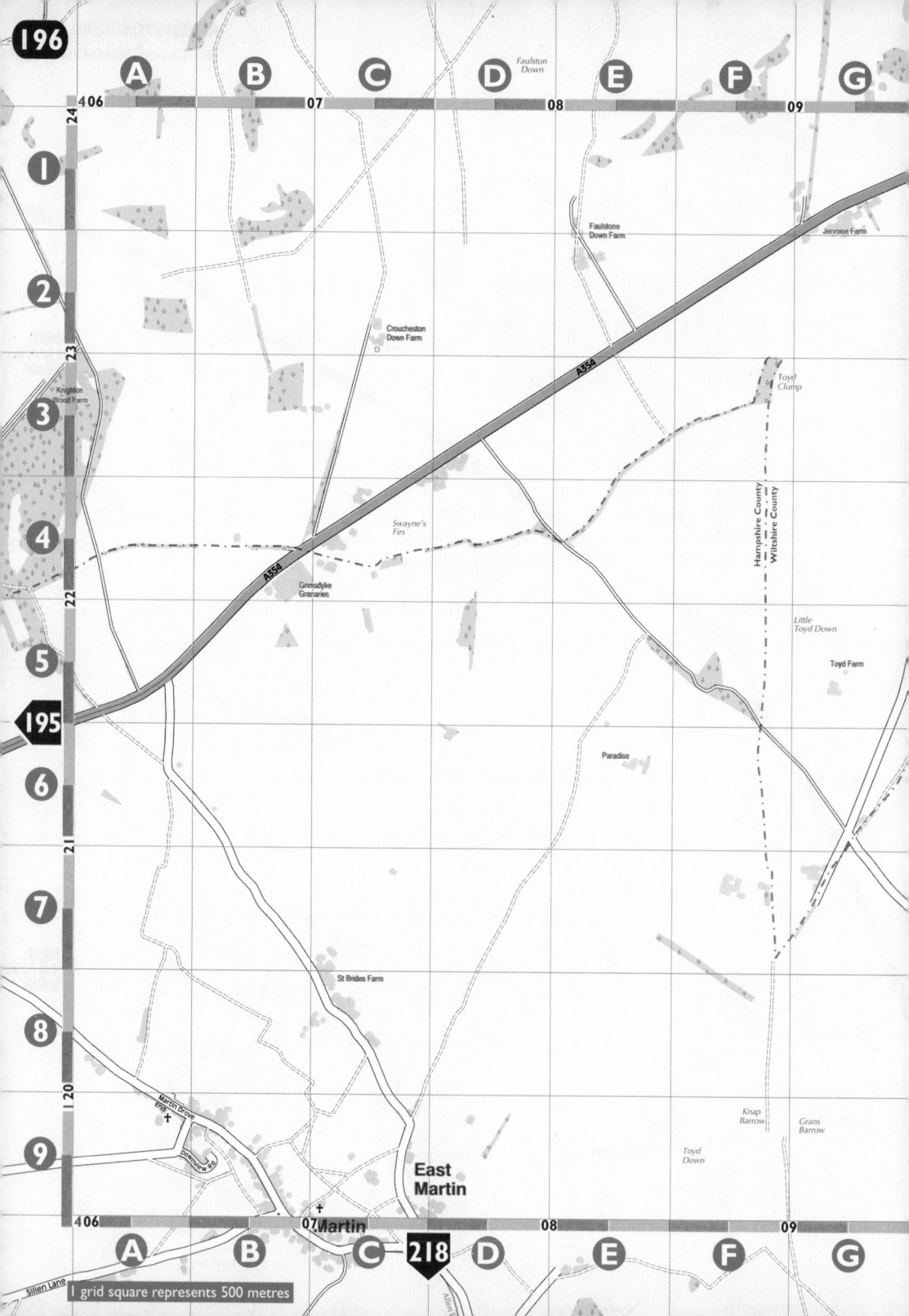

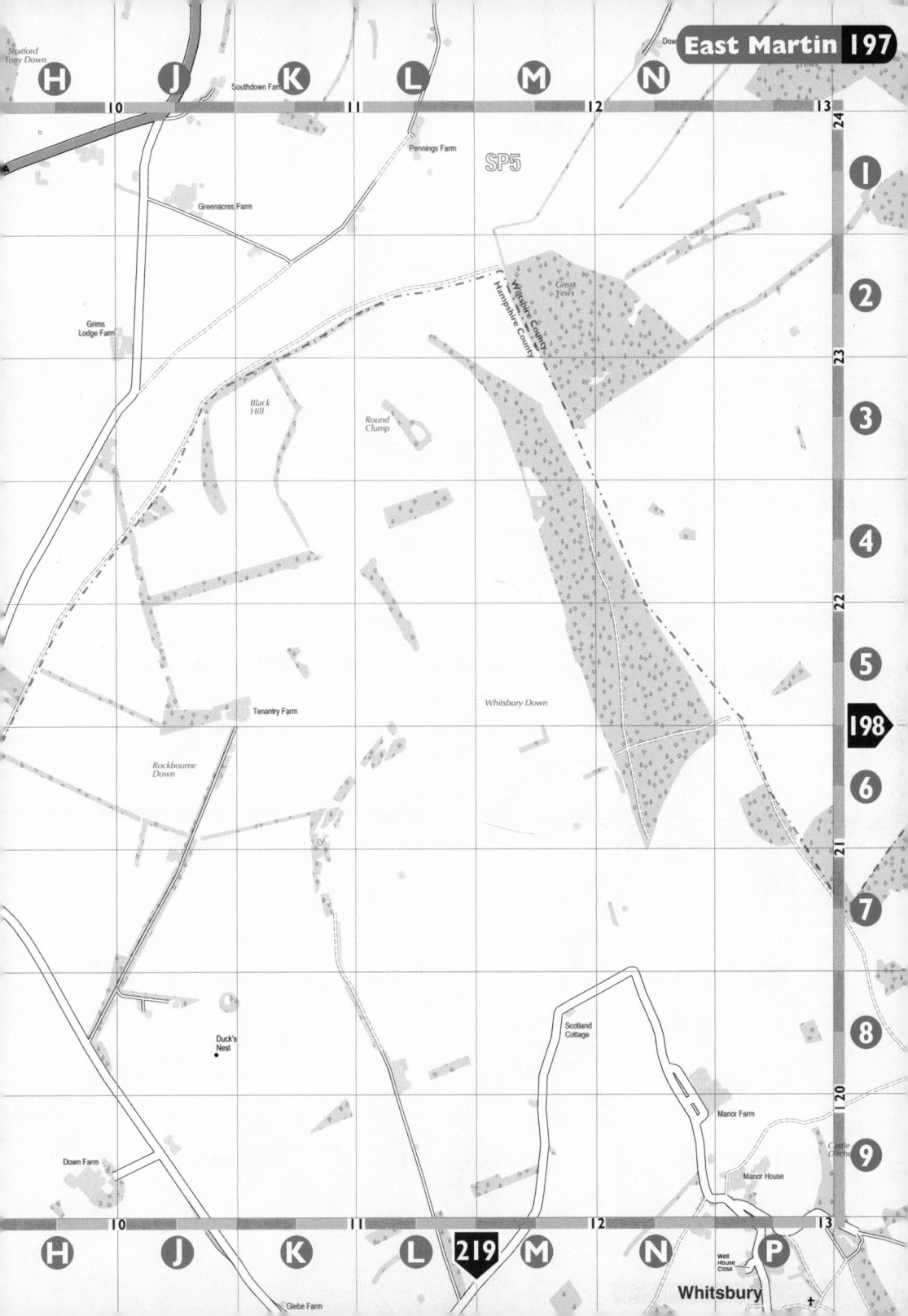

Stratford
Tony Down

H J K L M N

Southdown Farm

10 11 12 13

24

Pennings Farm

SP5

I

Greenacres Farm

2

Great
Yews

Grims
Lodge Farm

Wiltshire County
Hampshire County

23

Black
Hill

Round
Clump

3

4

22

5

Whitsbury Down

198

Tenantry Farm

6

Rockbourne
Down

21

7

Duck's
Nest

Scotland
Cottage

8

20

Manor Farm

Down Farm

Castle
Ditches

9

Manor House

10 11 12 13

H J K L 219 M N P

Well
House
Close

Whitsbury

198

A   B   C   D   E   F   G

Clearbury Down

4 13   14   15   16

24

Nunton Drove

1

Yews Farm

2

23

The
Giant's
Grave

3

New Court
Down Barn

The Giant's
Chair

4

New Court Down

22

5

Wick
Down

Wick Lane

197

Wic

Bosley's Farm

6

Wiltshire County
Hampshire County

North Charford Drove

21

7

Breamore
Down

South Charford Drove

8

North Charford
Drove

North Charford
Down Farm

20

Giant's Grave

9

Castle
Ditches

r House

Down Farm

Breamore

4 13   14   15   16

A   B   C   220   D   E   F   G

1 grid square represents 500 metres

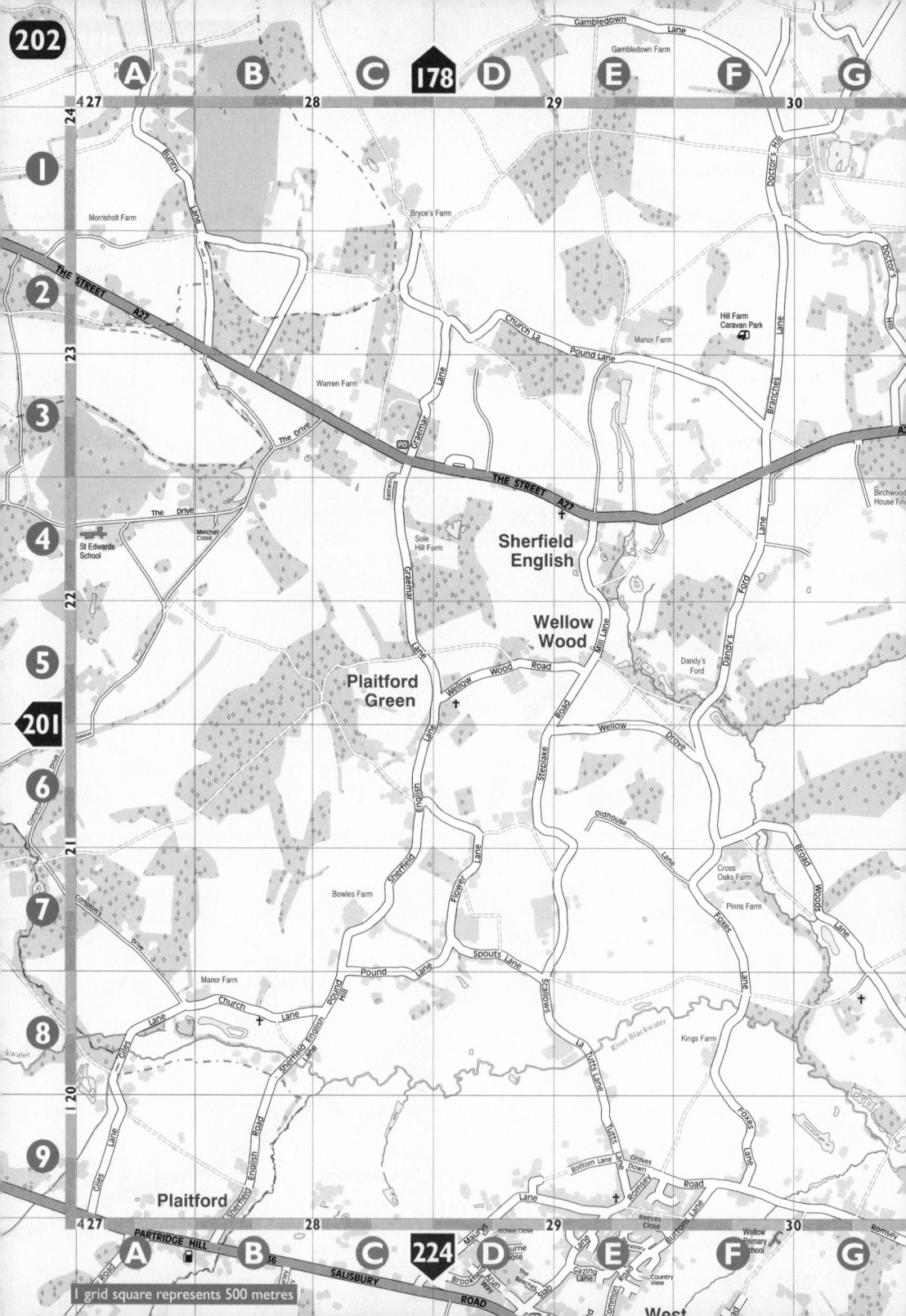

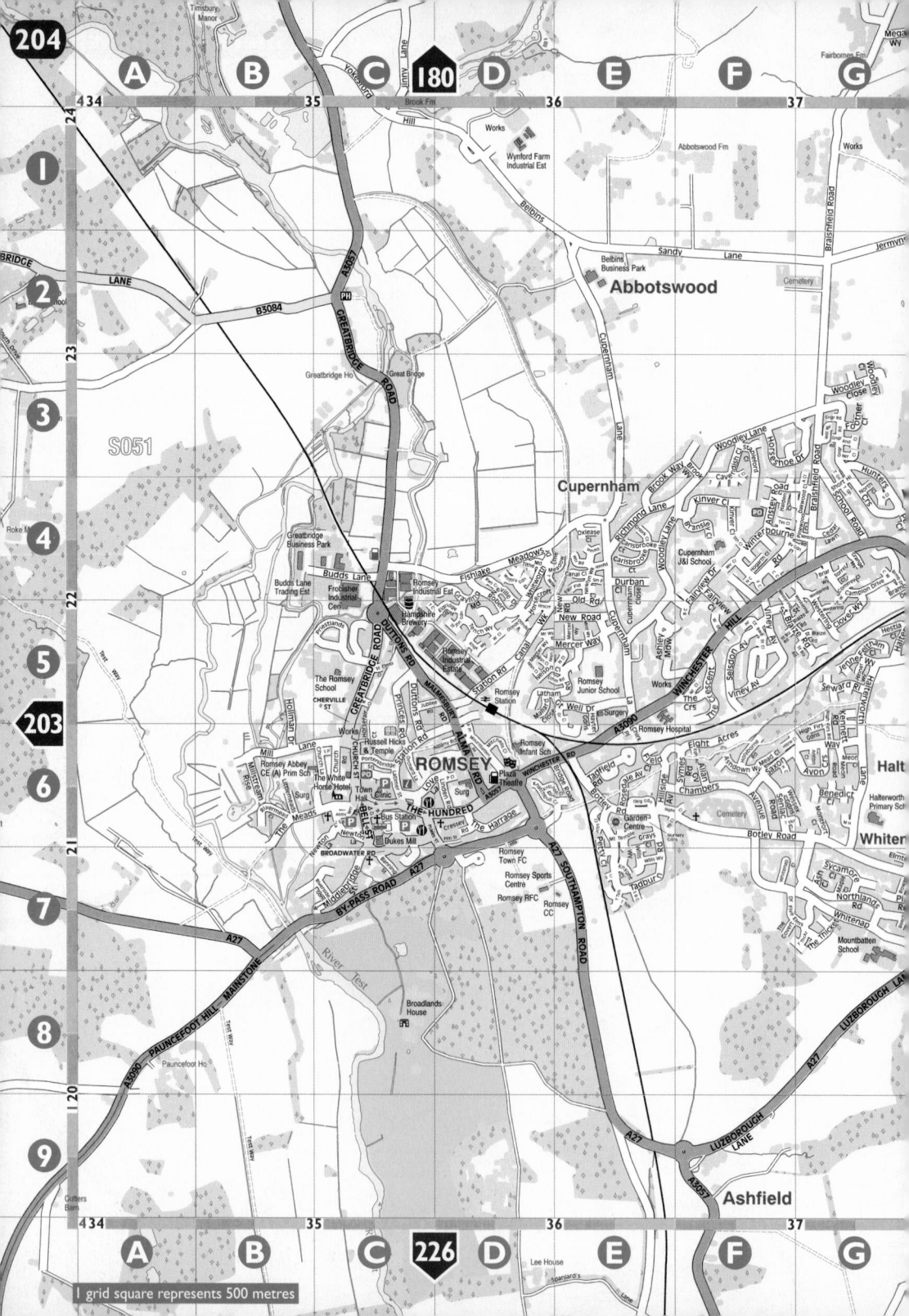

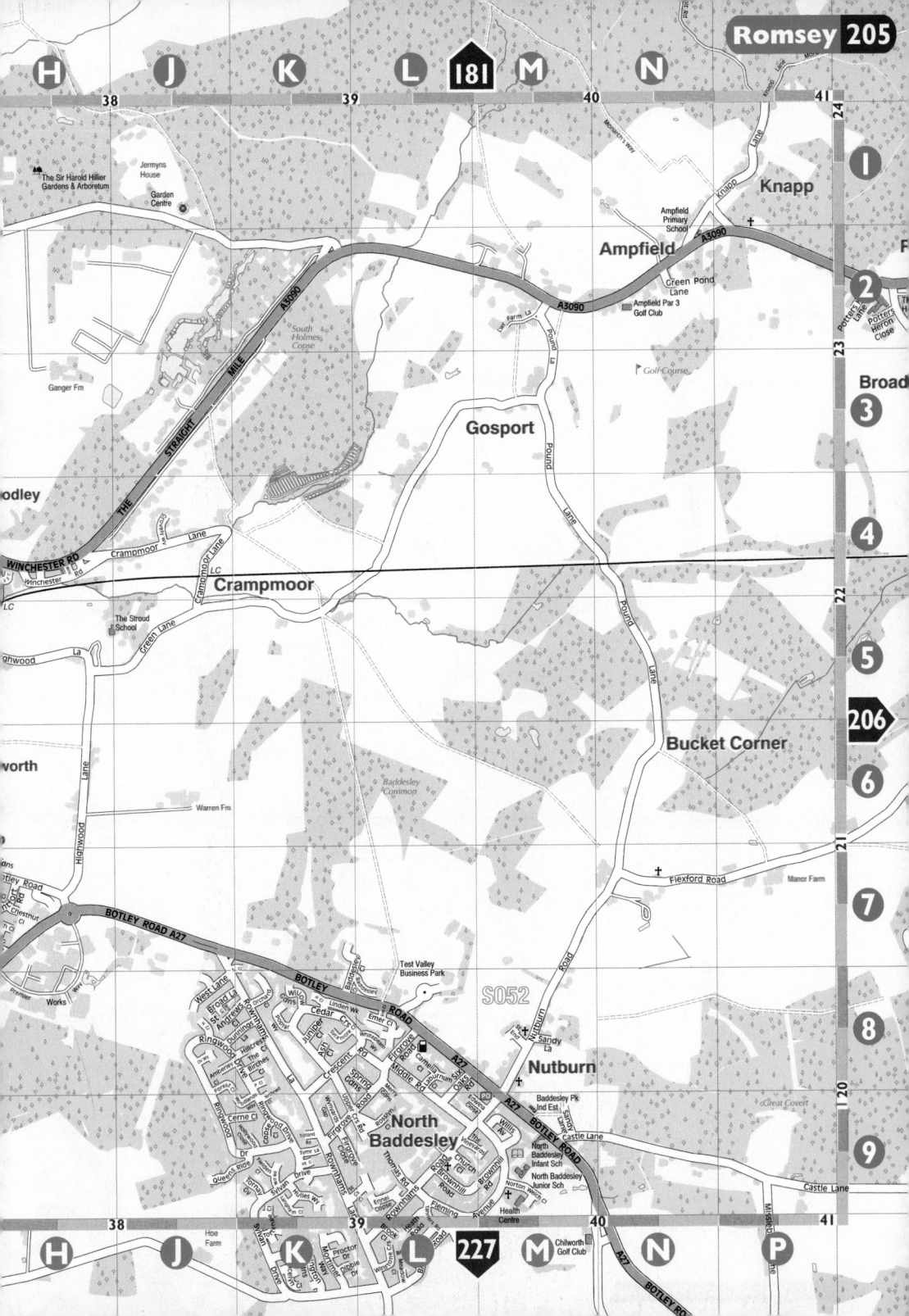

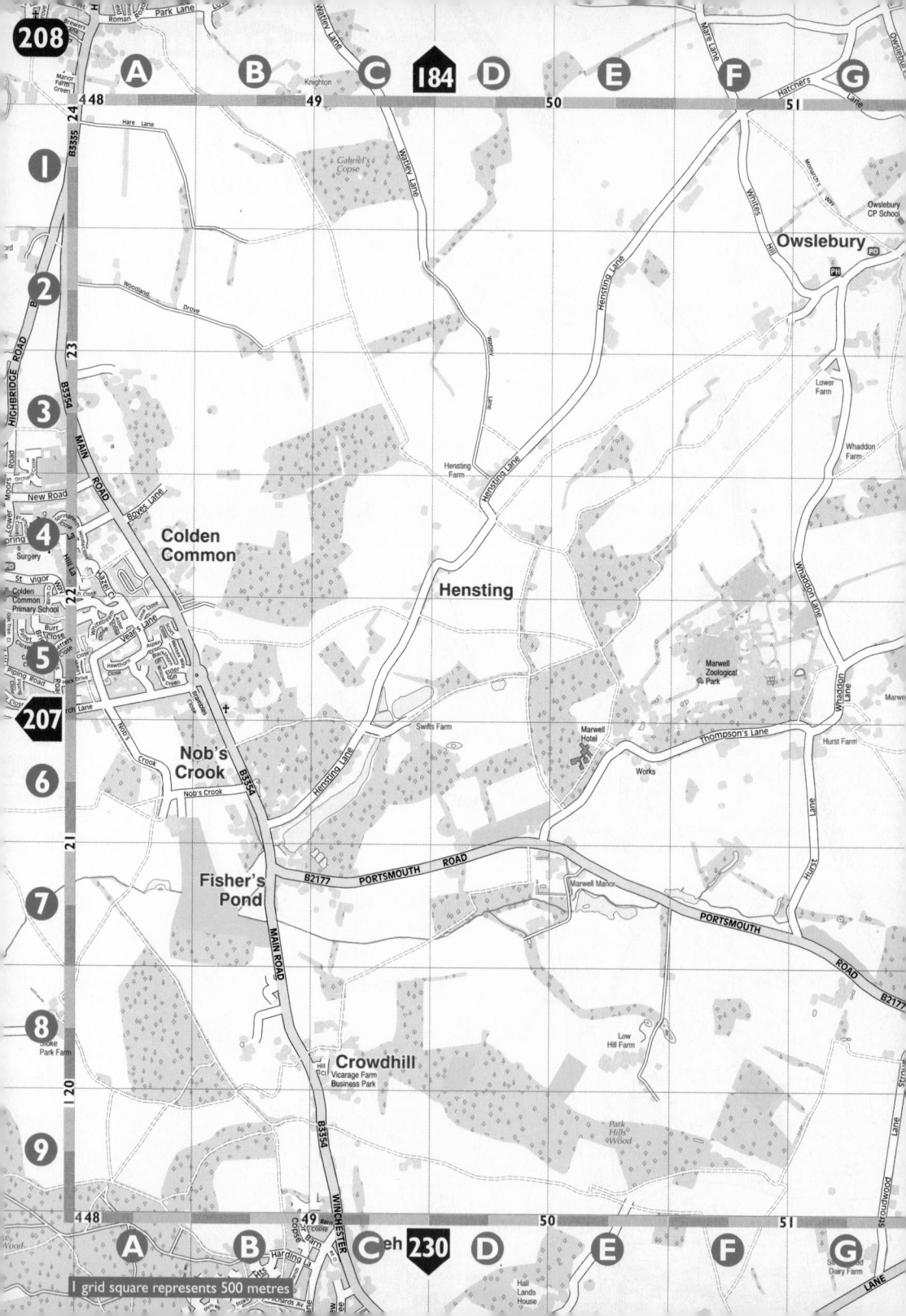

H J K L **189** M N

66 67 68 69

1

2

3

4

5

214

6

7

8

9

GU32

24

23

22

21

20

Westbury House

River Meon

Riplington

Drayton

Bereleigh House

Park Farm

Pidh

Hen Wood

Workhouse Lane
The Cross
Church Street
PH
PO
Chapel St
Chidd
Duncombe
Car Park
Washington
Milkhouse Meadow
Temple Lane
High Street

Coombe Road

East Meon

Lower House Farm

Oxenbourne

Duncombe Farm

l Farm

South Downs Way

South Downs Way

Coombe Cross

Coombe

Monarch's Way

South Downs Way

South Farm

Stonyl

233
▲
Salt Hill

H J K L **235** M N P

66 67 68 69

Chidden Down

South Downs Way

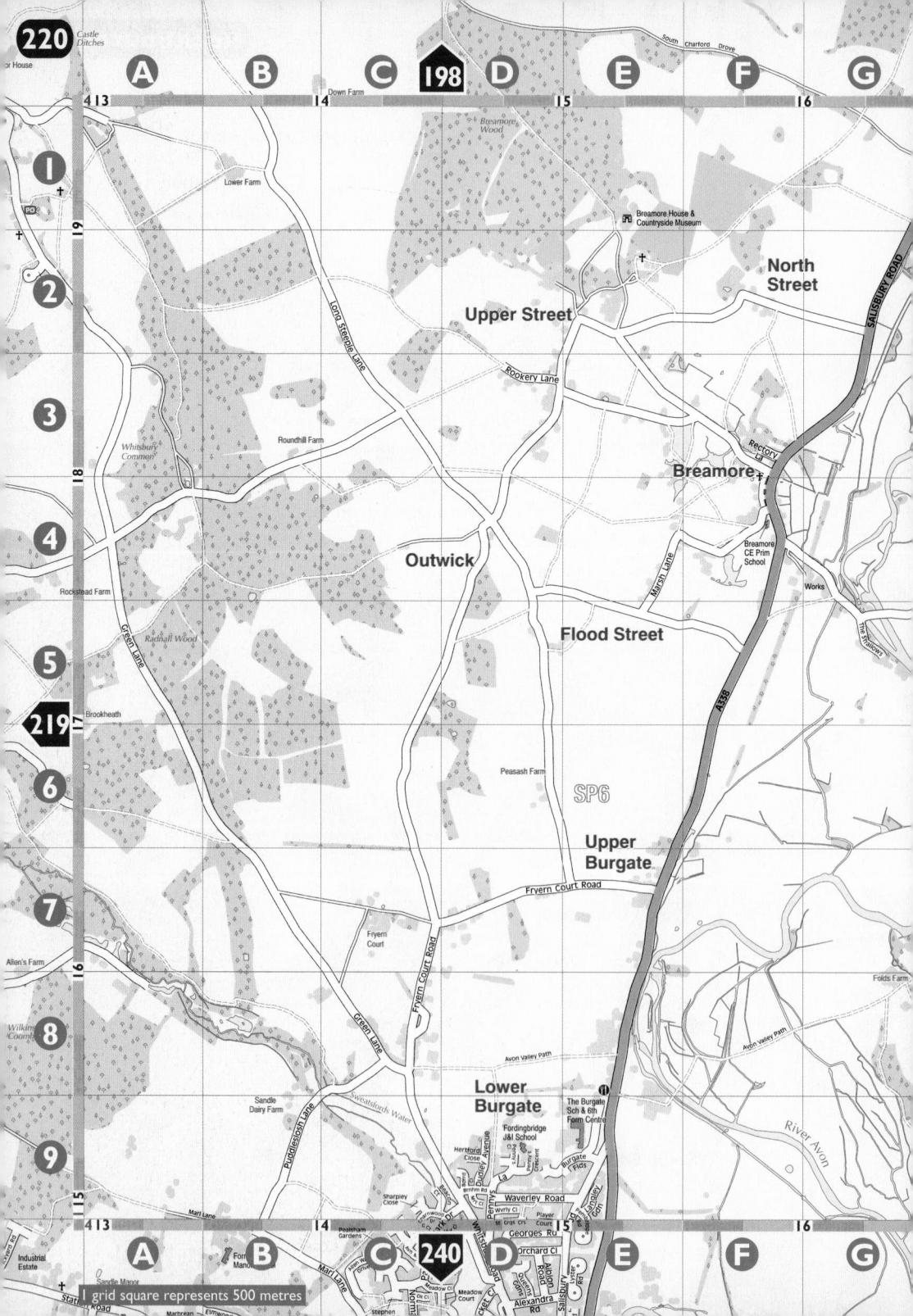

River Avon

N Charford Crossing

Wiltshire County
Hamp...

Searchfield Farm

199

North
Charford

North Charford
Manor House

Hatchet
Green

Hatchet

Carter's
Close

Whitsbro...

Tethering Drove

Tethering Drove

Hale Lane

Hale
Primary
School

Hale

South
Charford Farm

Moot Lane

Avon Valley Path

Queen Street

Hale Lane

Hale Road

Millersford
Plantation

Woodgreen

Cogdston

Lwr Densome Wd

Higherend Farm

Street

Love Lane

Grace Lane

Trimm's
Drove

Union Rd

Green
Drove

222

Brook Lane

Lane

Avon Valley Path

Drove

The Shallows

Godshill
Inclosure

Millersford
Bottom

B3078

Stone
Quarry
Bottom

New Forest

ROGER PENNY WAY

Brune's
Purlieu

Ditchend Brook

Purley
Lane

241

Works

Sandy Ball Ce...
Holiday Centre

The Pines

Godshill

Well
Lane

B3078

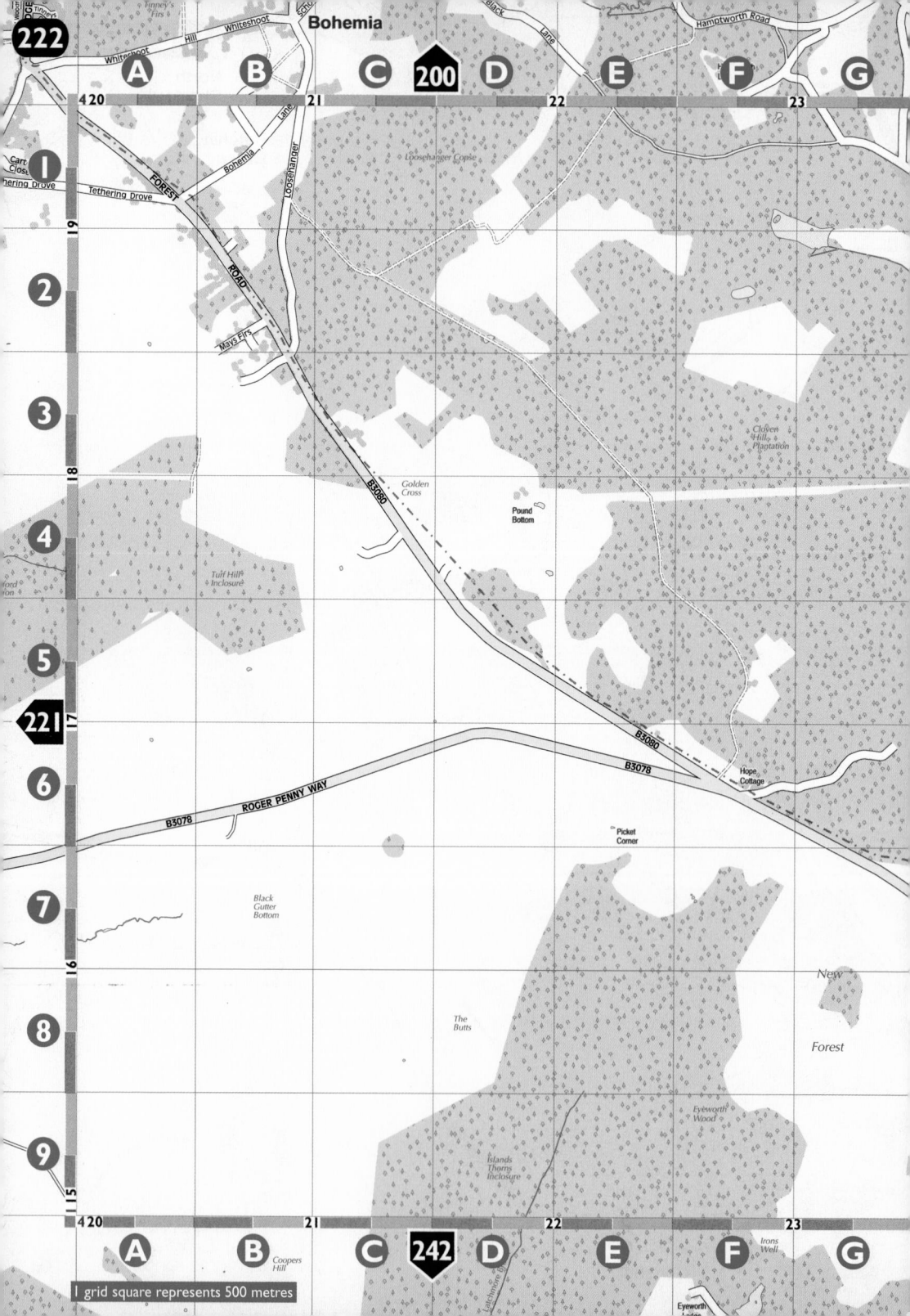

I grid square represents 500 metres

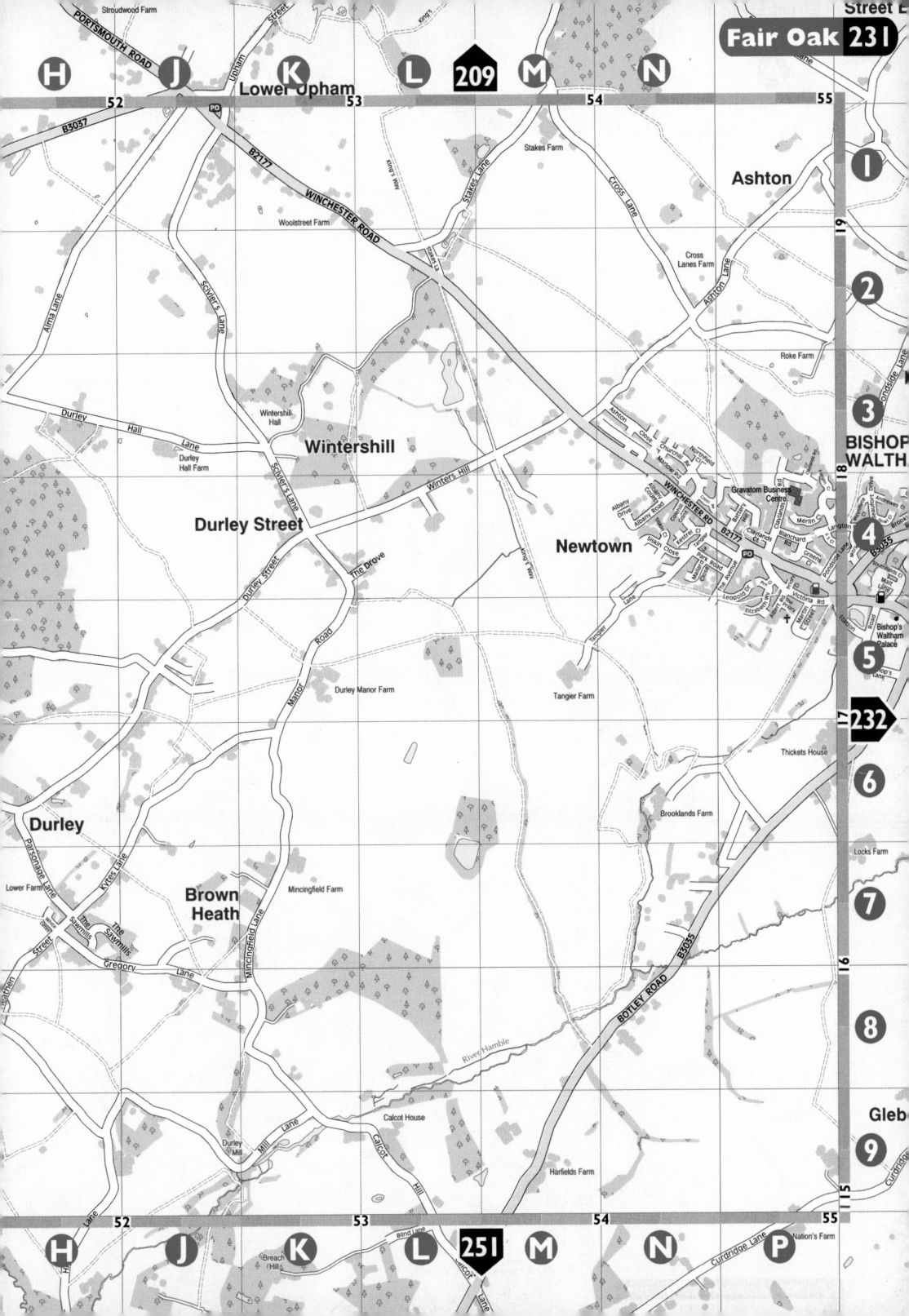

H J K L 211 M

59 60 61 WARNFORD 62

Meonstoke
CE School

New Road

1

Sheep Pond Lane

Sheep
Pond

Sheep Pond Lane

Shepherds Down

Hacketts Lane

Cem Crabbʼs La

19

Watton Lane

2

GARRISON HILL

Mill Lane

B2150 **Brockbridge**

Hacketts Lane Northend Lane

Waltham
Close
Union
La

Droxford

Surgery Townsendʼs The Lane

Station Road

18

PO

High St

Mill La.

3

Droxford
Junior
School

Wayfarerʼs Walk

4

Mayhill Lane

South Hill

A32

5

Oxford Lane

Swanmore Road

Middlington Ho

Midlington Hill Cutts

Soberton
Towers

117

234

6

Mayhill Farm

Swanmore Road

Midlington
Hill

MIDLINGTON ROAD

Arch

Long Road

Hill Place

Green Lane

River Meon

Cole Hill Chalk Hill

High St

Soberton

7

Kingʼs Way

West
St.

Wayfarerʼs Walk

16

Meon
Valley

Cole Hill

8

WICKHAM ROAD

Cott Street Lane Cott Street Lane

Cott Street Farm

High Street

Peststead

Lane

9

Cott Street

Cott Street

Dirty
Copse

A32

Hollywell House

St.Clairʼs Fm

Selworth Lane

Webbs Green
Fm

Ploughʼs Lane Rookʼs Hill Green Hill Hambledon Lane Taplands Roy's Lane Ainsworth Lane

59 60 Meon 61 62
Valley

H J K L 253 M N P

Chapel Road

233
▲
Salt Hill

213

I
J
K
L
M
N

66
67
68
69

1
19
2
3
18
4
5
236
17
6
7
16
8
9
15

Chidden Down

South Downs Way

Old Hambledonians CC

South Downs Way

Hyden Wood

Coombe Wood

Hyden Farm Lane

Chidden

Hermitage Farm

Monarch's Way

Hyden Farm

Monarch's Way

North Fm

Hyden Farm Lane

Chidden Holt

Stoneridge Fm

Old Mill Lane

Hinton Manor Lane

Broadhalfpenny Down

Dookennel Lane

Dookennel Lane

Lane

Dookennel Lane

Glidden Fm

Monarch's Way

Hinton Manor

H
J
K
L
M
N
P

66
67
68
69

255

A   B   C   214   D   E   F   G

469   70   71   72   A3

1

19

2

Hyden
Wood

3

18

Lowden's
Copse

4

235 17

5

6

Clanfield

7

16

8

9

115

469   70   71   72

A   B   C   256   D   E   F   G

South Downs Way

North   Lane

Hogs Lodge Lane

Newmans Fm

Byden Copse

Ditch
Acre Copse

Little   Hyden   Lane

North   Lane

Petersfield Lane

Oxenbourne
Down

Queen Elizabeth Country Park

War Dow

South Downs Way

Rangers   Way

Holt
Down
Plantat

Chalton
Down

Stourton   Way

Hambledon Road

Peak Rd

Tegg's Rd

Hinton Manor Lane

Downhouse   Road

Drift   Road

Hinton Manor Lane

Jamesgoan   Road

Dart   La

Brambie La
Clanfield
Junior School

church
Kingsbury court

Pond La

Nickelby Rd

Chalton La

Sword
mad

Chalton   Lane

Chalton   Lane   Chalton Lane

Sunderton

Farm Vw

Sandlewood Close

Copse Cl

St David's
Rd

Ridge
Cl

Kestrel

Maple
Crs

Beech Rd

White
Rd   Oak   Beam

Sycamore

Green

Hazelgrove

Blindon
Close

Fieldfare

Redwing

St James Cl

Puncton
Rd

Corhampton Av

Redhill

Green

Petersgate
Infant School

Surgery

Meon

Drift

Road

Hillcrest

Southdown Road

Grange Rd

White   Lane

Wode

Wessex
Rd

Viking Way

London Rd

London Rd

Butser Ancient
Farm

Horndean
Down

New
Barn Fm

Netherl

St
Andrew
Cl

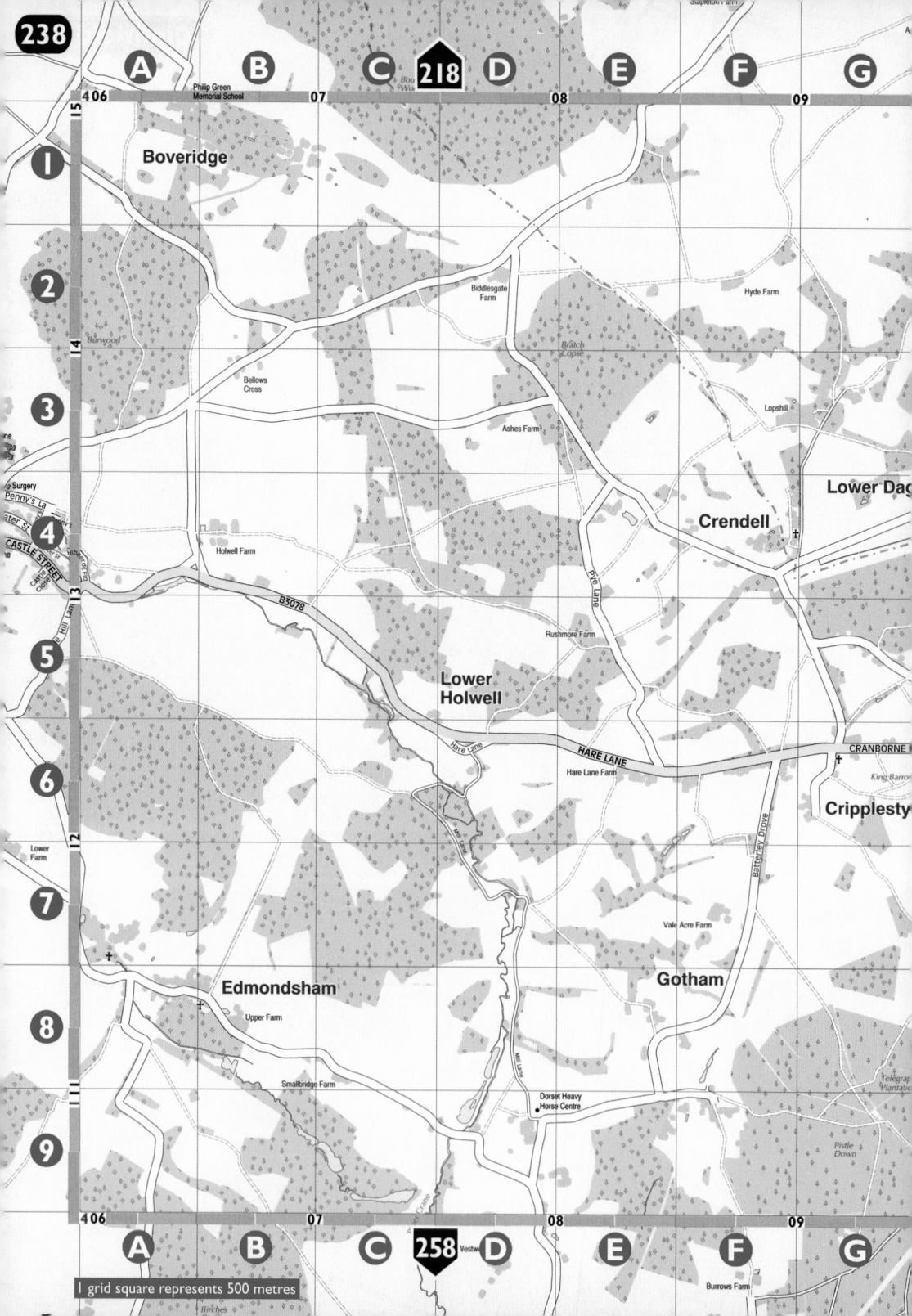

A B C **218** D E F G

15

1

Boveridge

Philip Green
Memorial School

2

Biddlesgate
Farm

Hyde Farm

14

Burwood

Bratch
Copse

Lopshill

3

Bellows
Cross

Ashes Farm

Lower Dag

ne

Surgery
Penny's La

Crendell

†

ater St

4

CASTLE STREET

Holwell Farm

Pye Lane

13

B3078

Rushmore Farm

III Hill Lane

ibson Ct Rd

Castle
Copse

5

Lower
Holwell

Hare Lane

HARE LANE

CRANBORNE

Hare Lane Farm

King Barro

6

12

Cripplesty

Lower
Farm

Mill Lane

Batterley Drove

7

Vale Acre Farm

Gotham

†

Edmondsham

Upper Farm

8

†

Telegrap
Plantatic

11

Smallbridge Farm

Pistle
Down

9

Dorset Heavy
Horse Centre

A B C **258** D E F G

Vestwe

Burrows Farm

Birches

1 grid square represents 500 metres

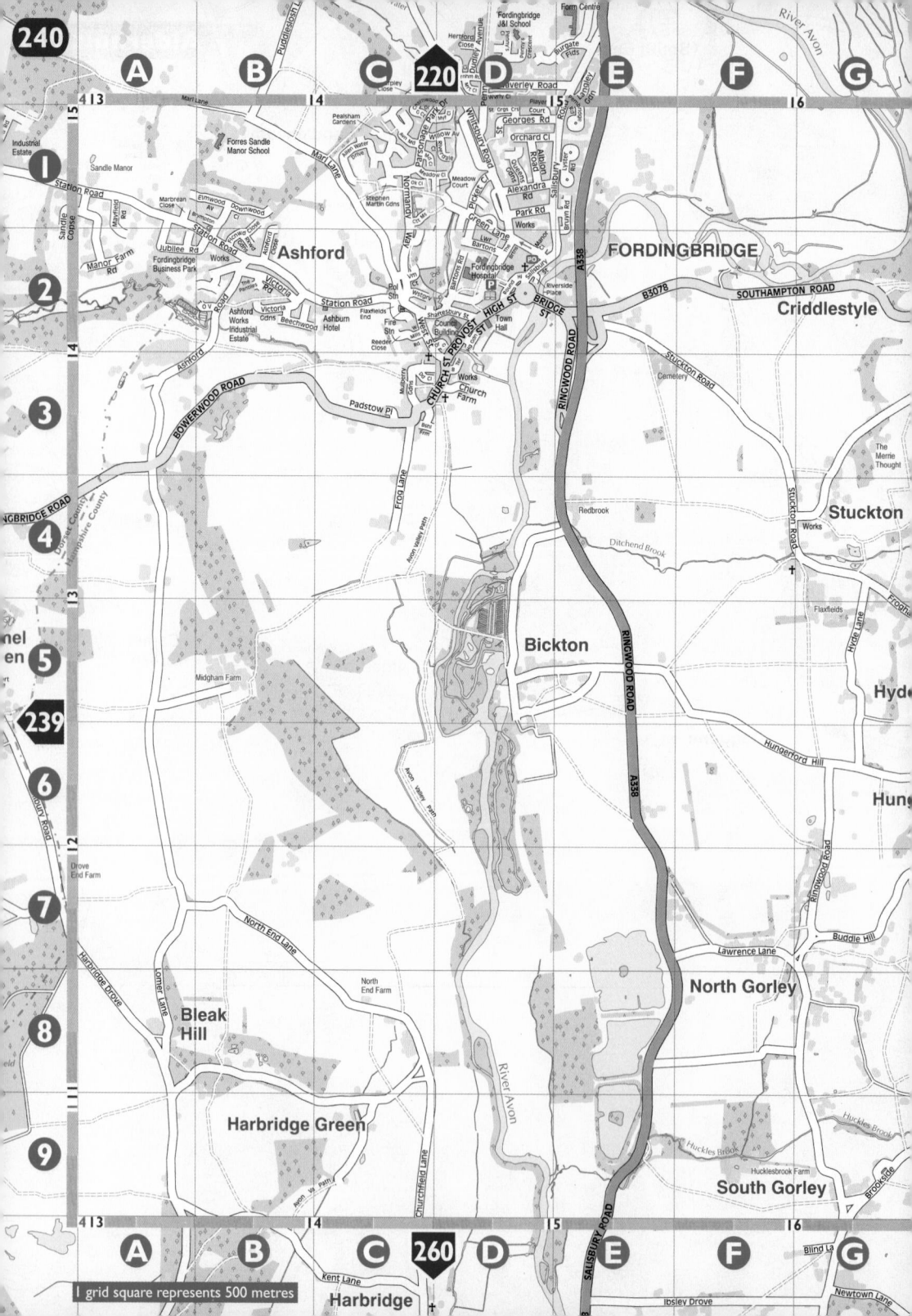

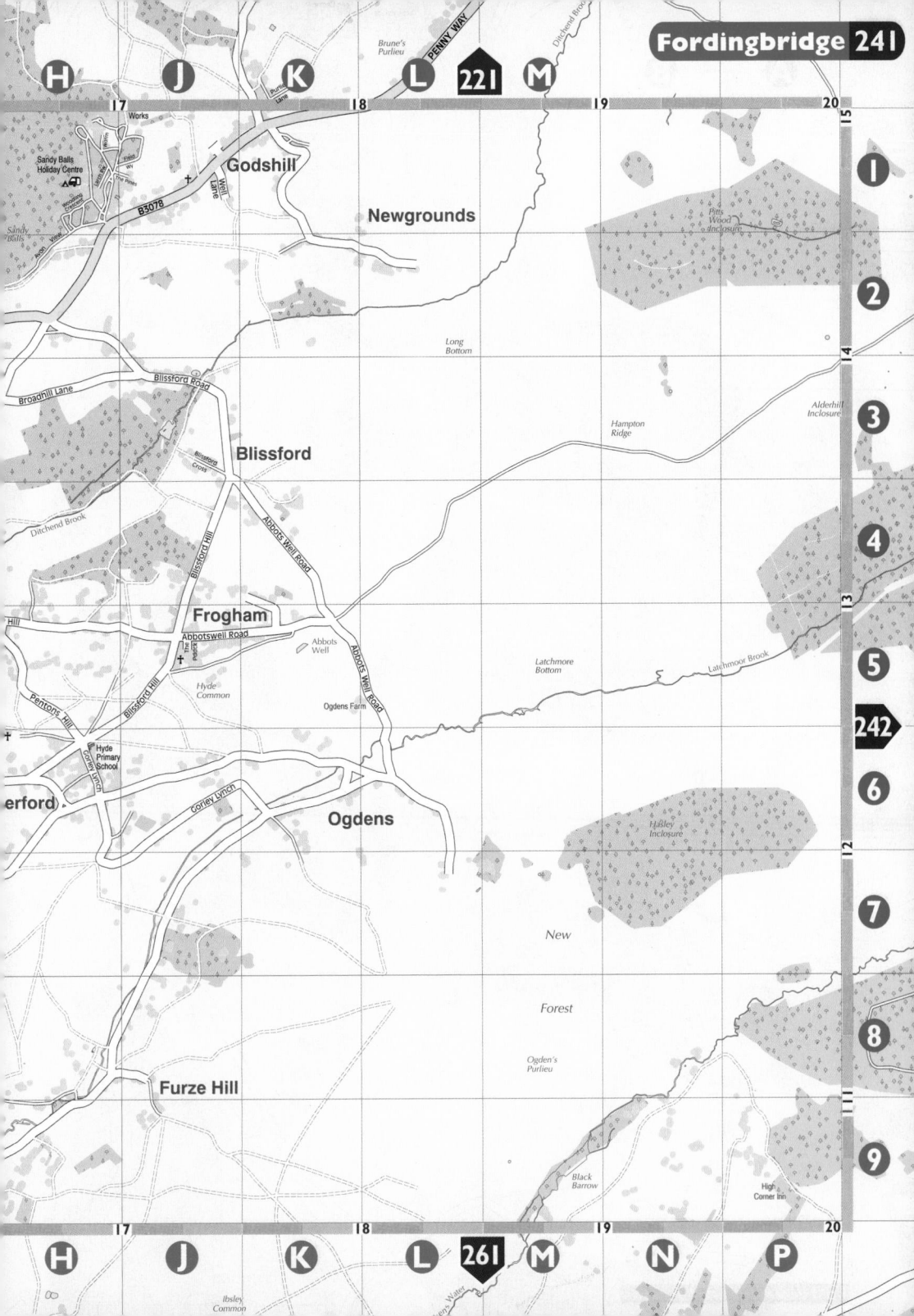

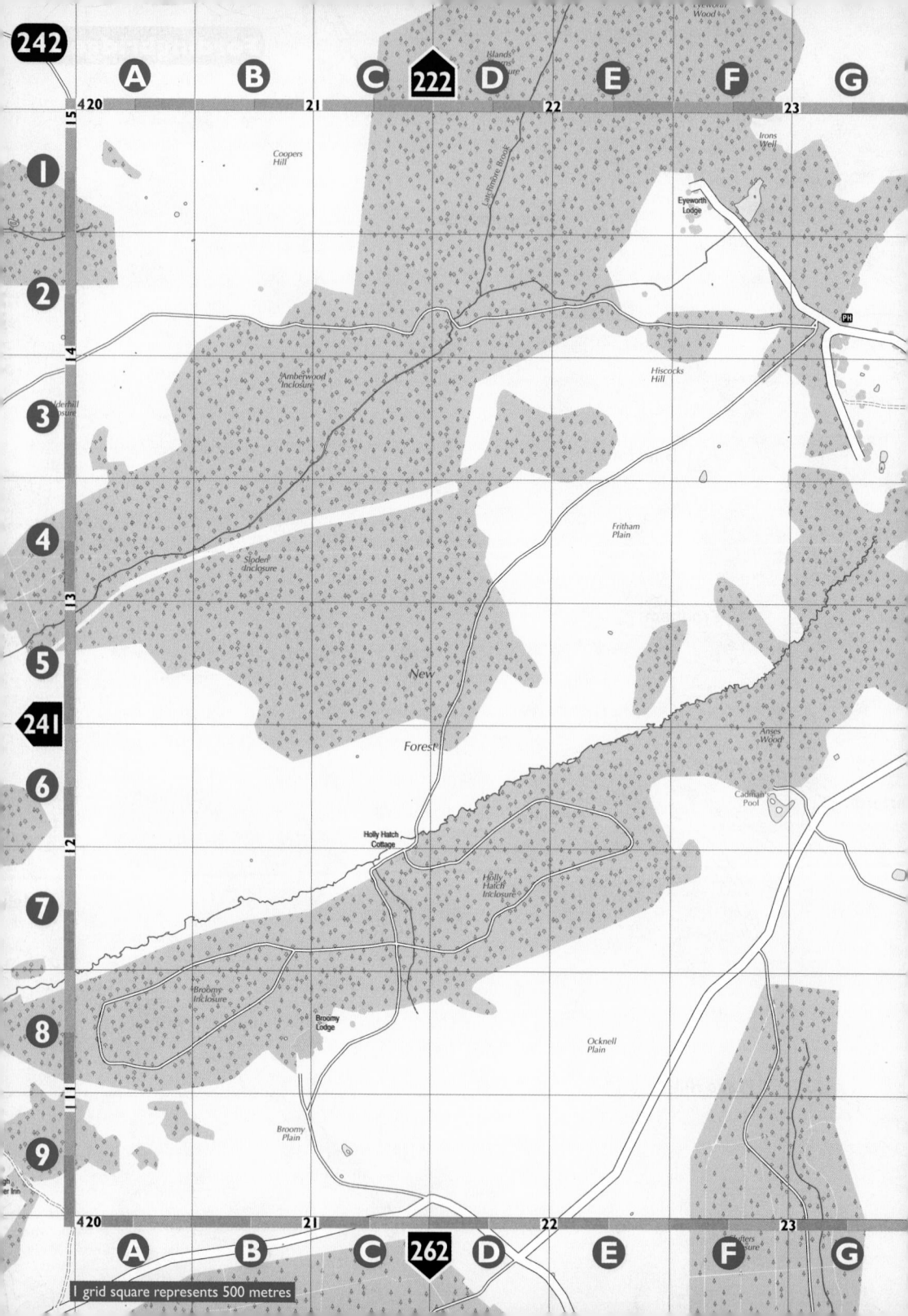

A   B   C   222   D   E   F   G

420   21   22   23

15

1   Coopers Hill

2

14

Irons Well

Eyeworth Lodge

PH

3   derhill closure

Amberwood Inclosure

Hiscocks Hill

4   Fritham Plain

13   Sloden Inclosure

5

New

6   Forest

Anses Wood

Cadman's Pool

12   Holly Hatch Cottage

7   Holly Hatch Inclosure

Broomy Inclosure

8   Broomy Lodge   Ocknell Plain

11

Broomy Plain

9

420   21   22   23

A   B   C   262   D   E   F   G

I grid square represents 500 metres

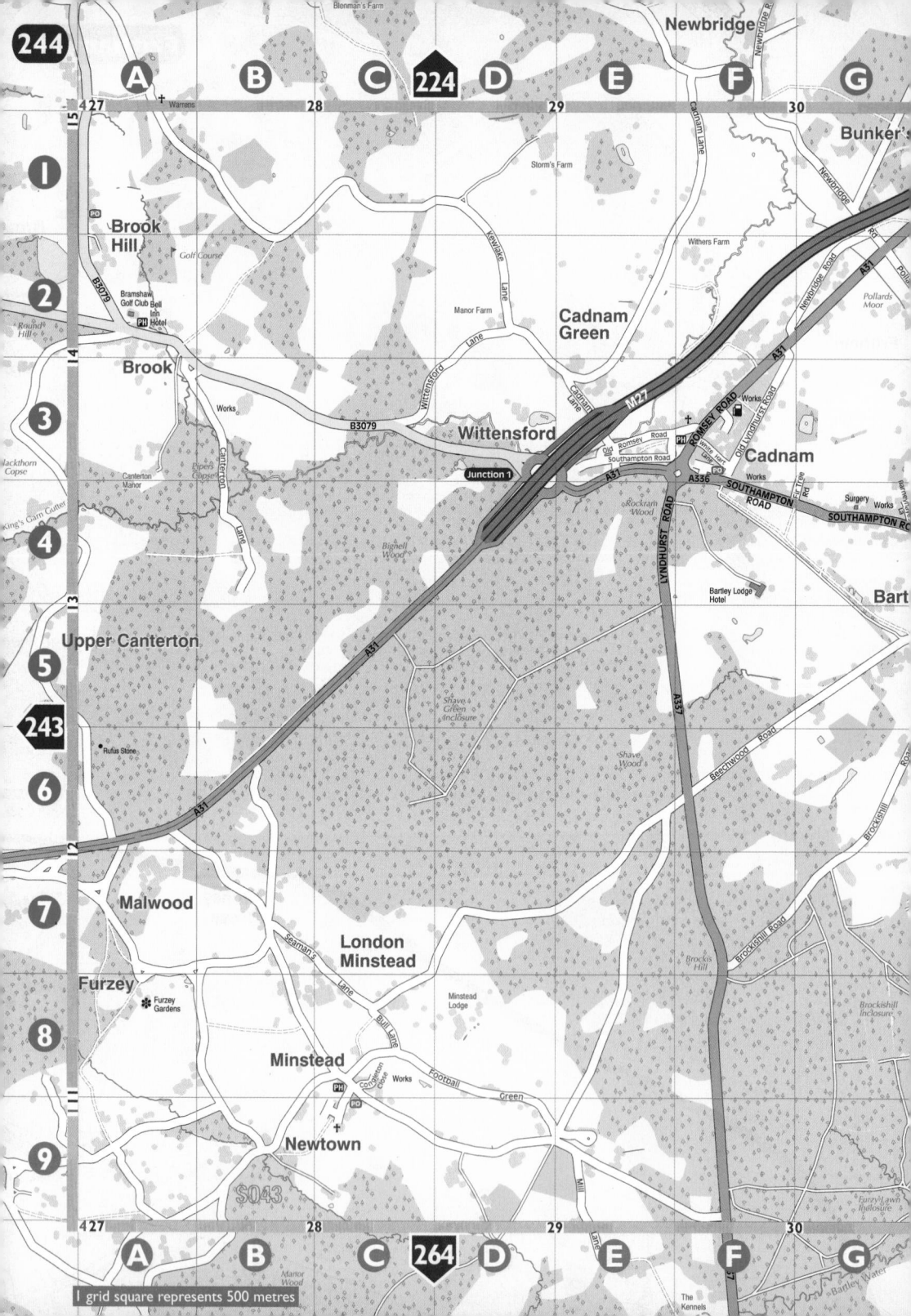

I grid square represents 500 metres

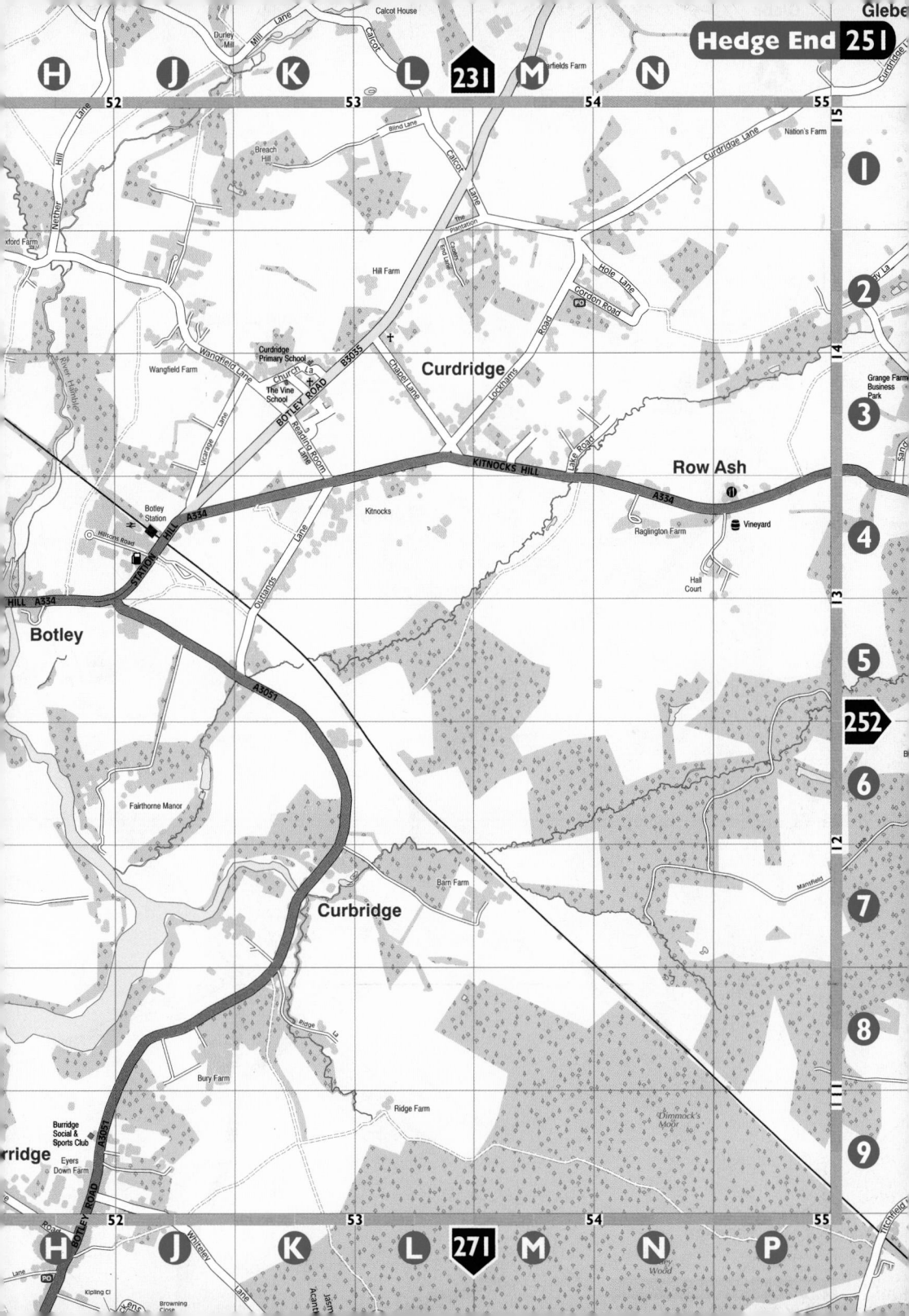

Glebe

H J K L M N

52 53 54 55

15

1

2

3

4

252

5

6

7

8

9

14

13

12

11

Calcot House

Durley Mill

Mill Lane

Calcot Lane

Berfields Farm

Nation's Farm

Curdridge Lane

Ly La

Blind Lane

Breach Hill

Hill Farm

Nether Hill

xford Farm

Hole Lane

The Plantation

End Lane

Gordon Road

Grange Farm Business Park

PO

River Hamble

Wangfield Lane

Wangfield Farm

Curdridge Primary School

Church La

The Vine School

Chapel Lane

Lockhams Road

Curdridge

Row Ash

BOTLEY ROAD

B3035

Reading Room

Vicarage Lane

Sandy

Lake Road

A334

Kitnocks

Raglington Farm

Vineyard

Botley Station

Hillsons Road

STATION HILL

A334

Outlands Lane

KITNOCKS HILL

Hall Court

HILL A334

Botley

A3051

Fairthorne Manor

Barn Farm

Mansfield Lane

Curbridge

rridge

Bury Farm

Ridge La

Ridge Farm

Dimmock's Moor

Burridge Social & Sports Club

Eyers Down Farm

A3051

BOTLEY ROAD

Road

PO

Kipling Cl

Browning Close

Whiteley Lane

Acacias

Jasm

ey Wood

Litchfield

H J K L M N P

52 53 54 55

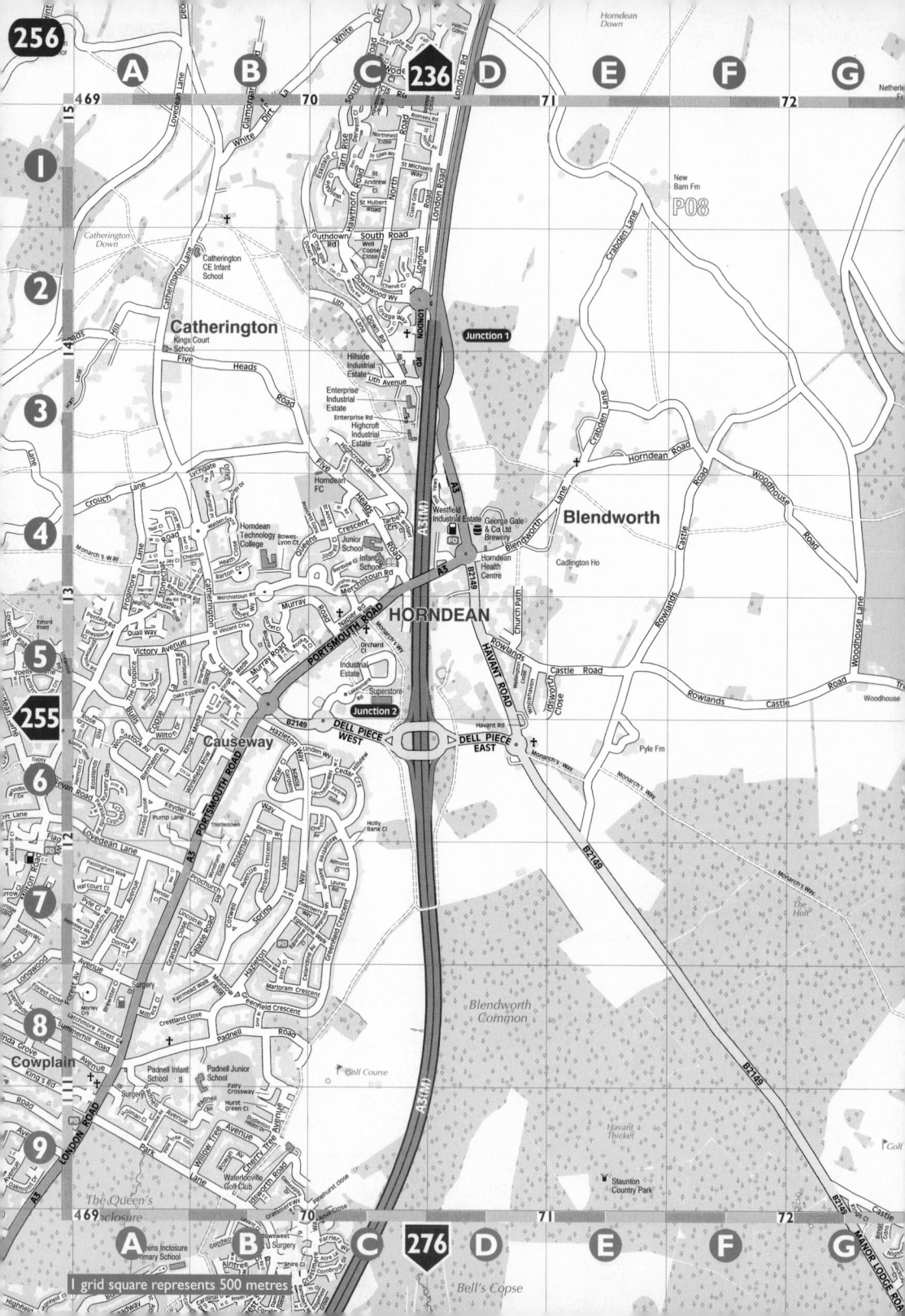

H J K L 241 M N

17 18 19 20

I
1

10

2

Linwood

3

60

4

Ibsley Common

Whitefield Plantn

Dockens Water

Toms Lane

Toms Lane

Toms Lane

Linwood Farm

Red Shoot Brewery

Black Barrow

High Corner Inn

Mockbeggar

Digden Bottom

Dockens Water

Appleslade Inclosure

Red Shoot Wood

5

80 262

6

Highwood

Rockford Common

Great Linford Inclosure

Linford Brook

Pinnick Wood

Handy Cross Plain

7

07

North Poulner

Highwood Lane

Wood Lane

Lin Brook

Cowpitts Lane

Works

Hangersley

St. Aubyns Lane

Linford

Little Linford Inclosure

Shobley

A31

8

9

06

The Mount

Linford Narrow Drake La

Poulner Road

disher

BH24

17 18 283 19 20

H ner J K L M N P

A31

BRUNER HILL

Picket Post

Picket

St.

Picket

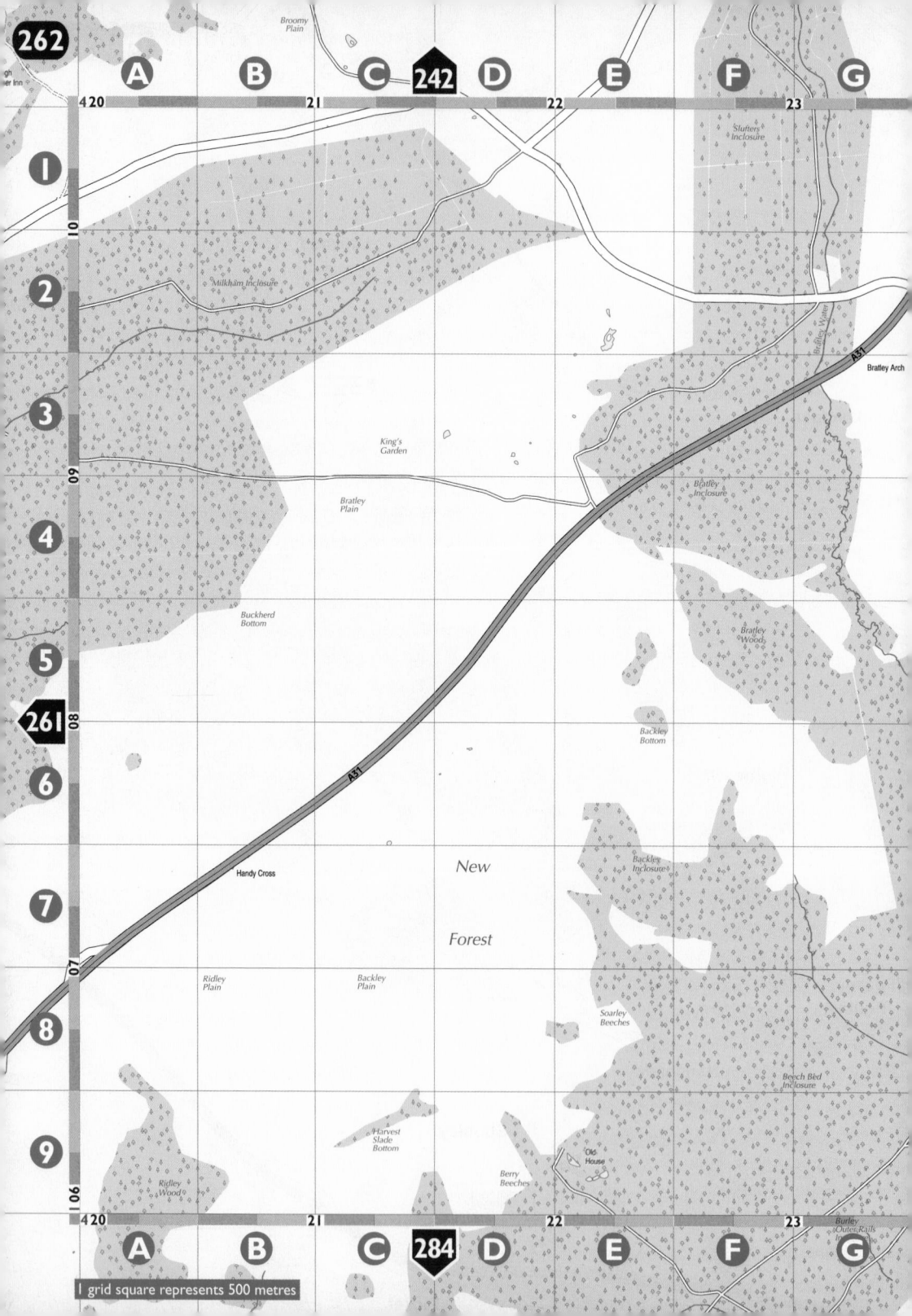

H   J   K   L ew 243   M   N

24   25   26   27

Forest

Fritham Cross

1

Acres Down House

10

2

Puckpits Inclosure

Highland Water

3

Wick Wood

Highland Water Inclosure

09

Acres Down

4

Bolderwood Farm

Holmhill Inclosure

Wood Crates

Highland   *Water*

5

Bolderwood Cottage

264

08

Bolderwood Grounds

Portuguese Fireplace   *Millyford*

6

Mark Ash Wood

Holidays Hill Inclosure

Barrow Moor

Wooson's Hill Inclosure

Nogh Oakley Inclosure

7

Church Moor

07

Warwick Slade

8

Bolderwood Arboretum Ornamental Drive

Winding Shoot

Bolderwood Arboretum Ornamental Drive

Knightwood Oak

A35

Anderwood Inclosure

Knightwood Inclosure

9

Eagle Oak

06

H   J   K   L 285   M   N   P

24   25   26   27

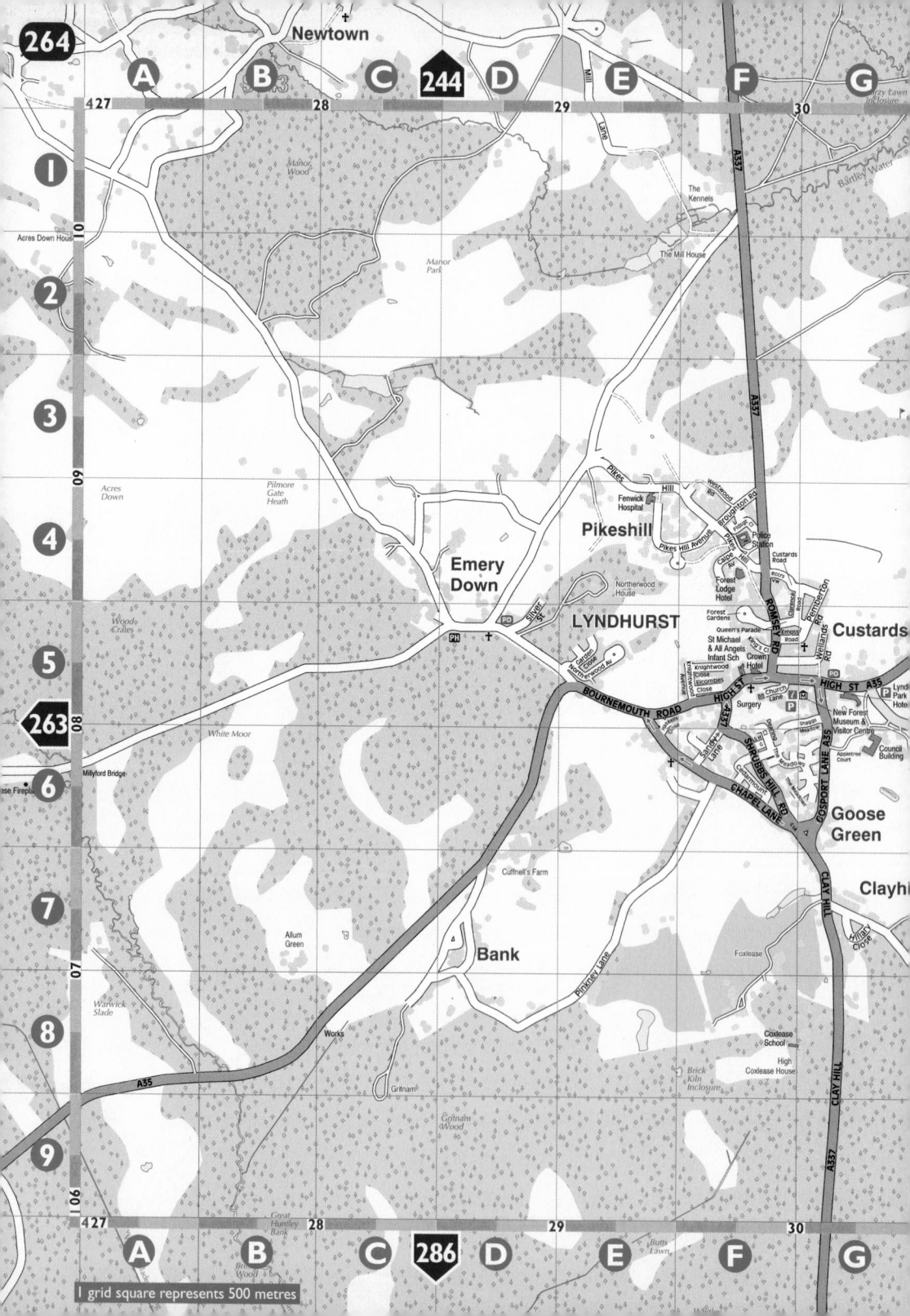

H J K L 245 M N

31 32 33 34

1

2

3

4

5

266

6

7

8

9

06

H J K L 287 M N P

31 32 33 34

Ironshill
Lodge

Buscketts
Lawn
Inclosure

Ironshill
Inclosure

Rushpole
Wood

Lodgehill
Cottage

A35

SOUTHAMPTON ROAD

Mallard
Wood

White
Moor

New Forest
Golf Club

Dunces Arch

Knightwood
Lodge

Ormonde House
Hotel

Cemetery

Beaulieu River

Ashurst
Wood

Ashurst Lodge

Ashurst Hospital

Works

LYNDHURST

Ashurst (New Forest)
Station

Church
Inclosure

BEAULIEU ROAD

B3056

Pondhead Inclosure

Le Poussin
at Parkhill
Hotel

Beechen Lane

Matley
Wood

Matley
Heath

Matley
Passage

Little
Holmhill
Inclosure

Denny
Inclosure

Park Hill

Denny
Wood

Princes St

Ocean Village

HYTHE

Langdown

Frostlane

Weston

Golsto

1 grid square represents 500 metres

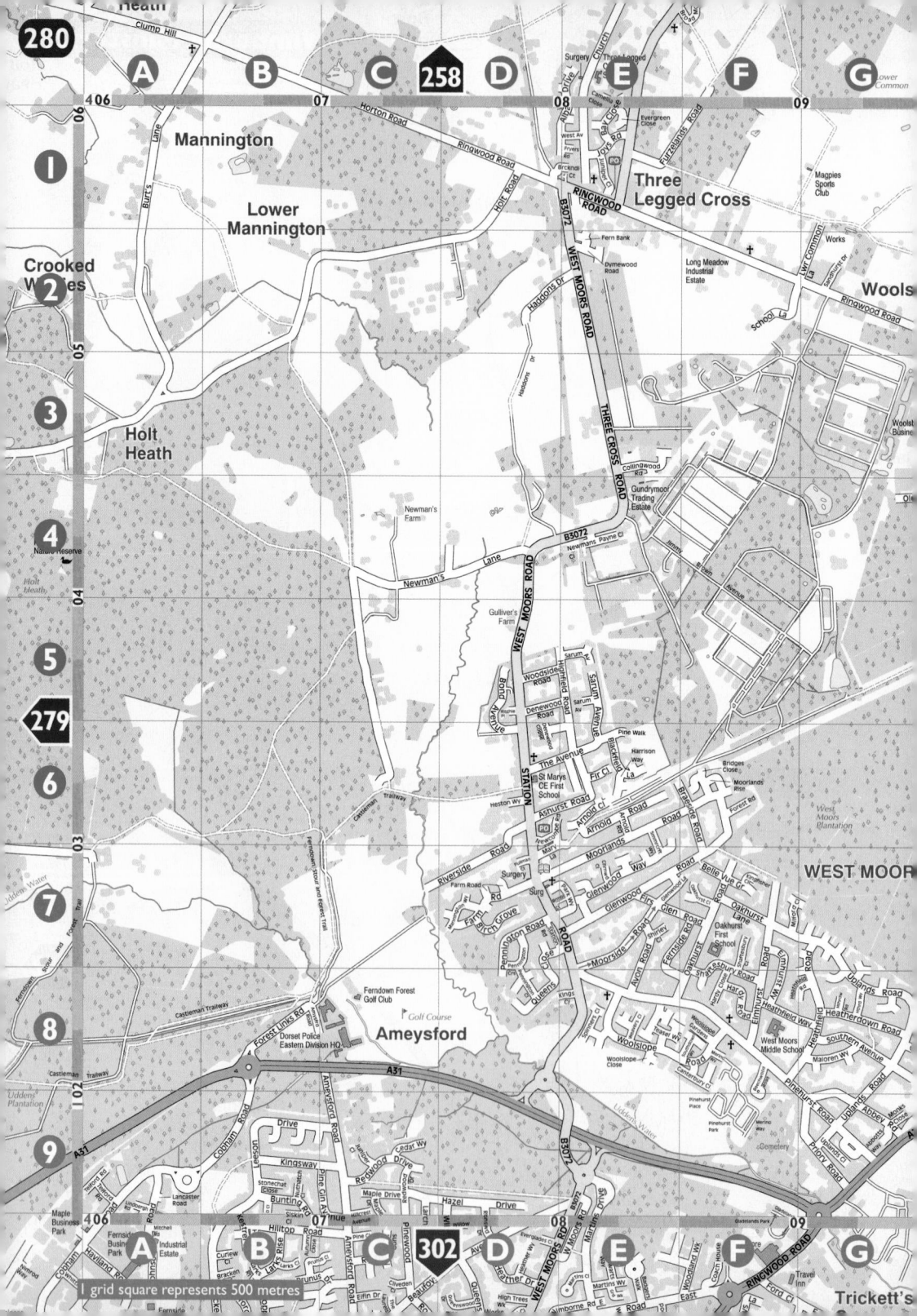

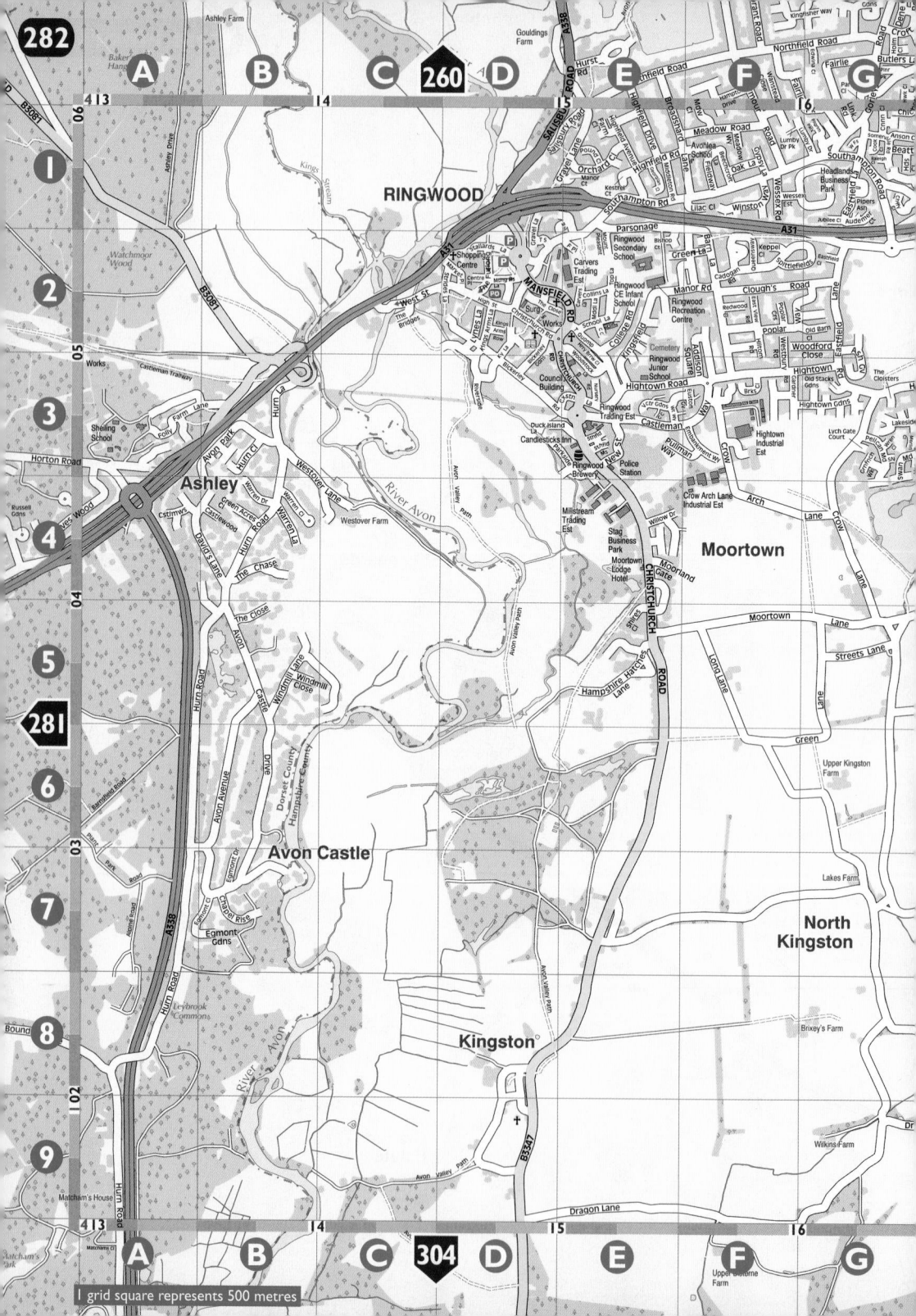

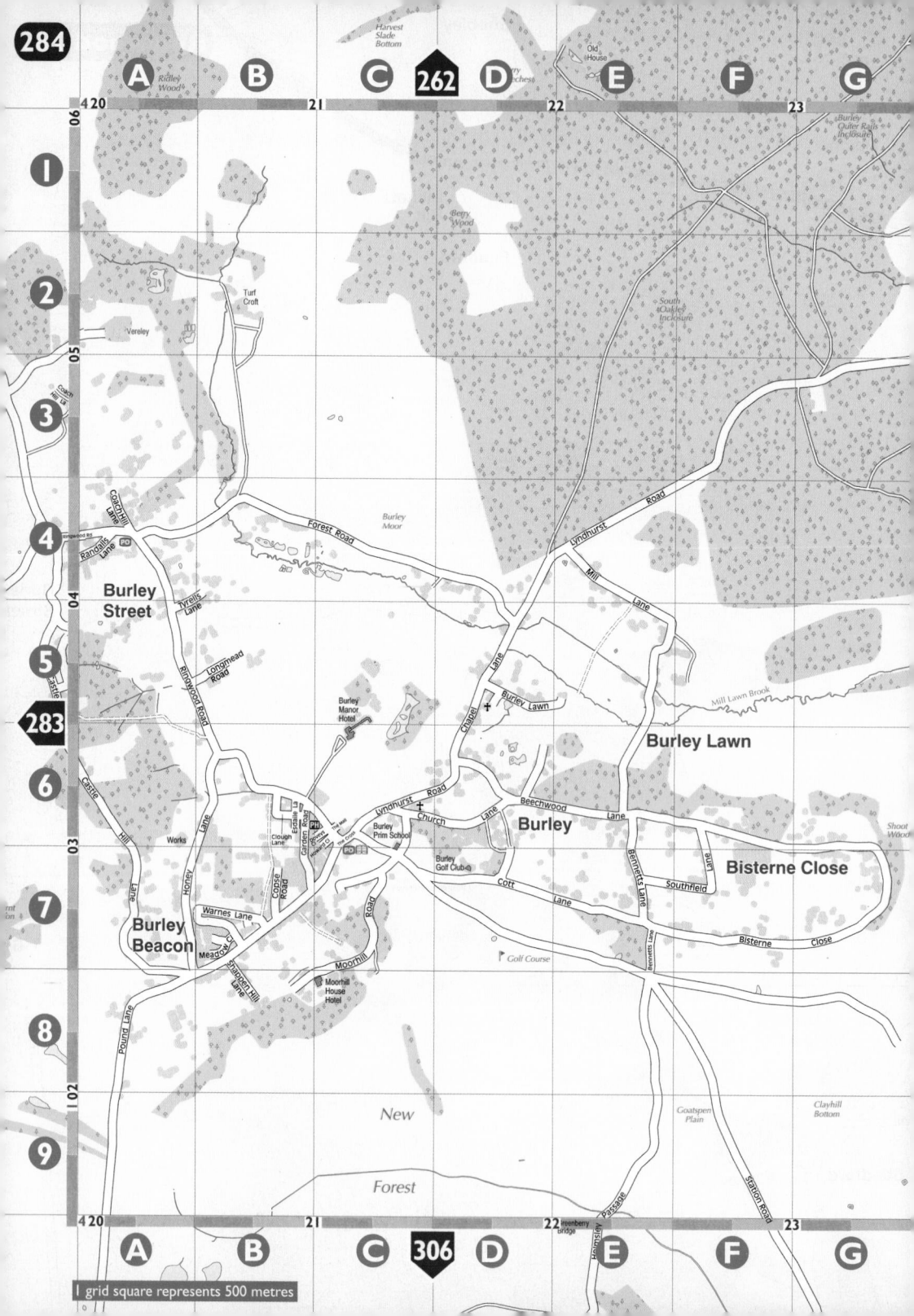

H J K L **263** M N

24 25 26 27 06

I

2

3

4

5

286

6

7

8

9

H J K L **307** M N P

24 25 26 27

Burley Lodge

Lyndhurst Road

Dames Slough Inclosure

Fletchers Thorns Inclosure

Vinney Ridge Inclosure

Pound Hill Inclosure

Rhinefield Ornamental Drive

Burley New Inclosure

Burley Old Inclosure

Rhinefield Sandy's Inclosure

Red Rise

A35

Rhinefield House Hotel

Aldridge Hill

Ober Water

Markway Inclosure

Crab Tree Earth

Duck Hole

A35

Wilverley Post

Naked Man

Wilverley Plain

Hincheslea Moor

Whit Moor

Burley Road

New For

Woosencroft Culvert

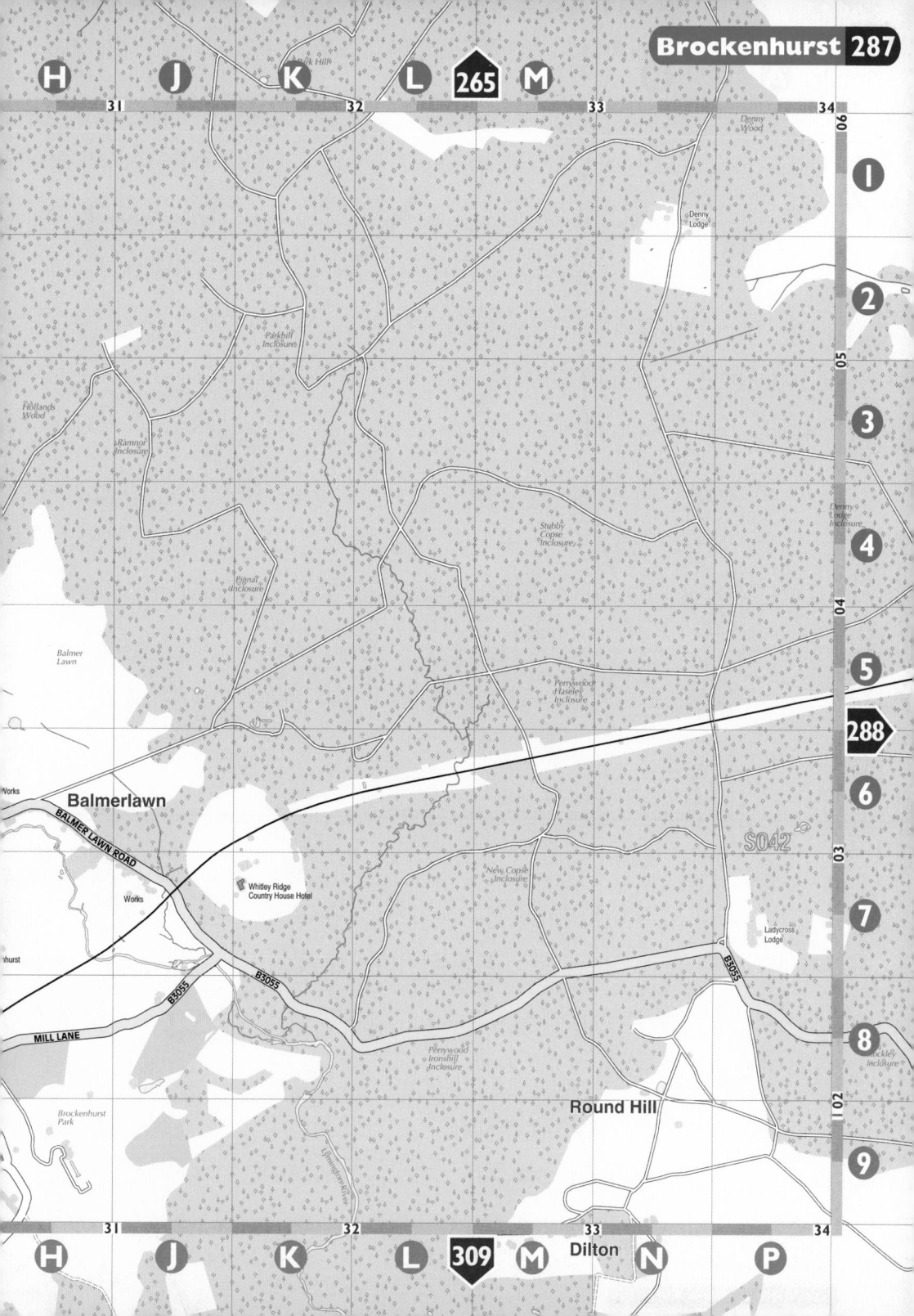

265
288
309

H **J** **K** **L** **M** **N** **P**

31 32 33 34

1 **2** **3** **4** **5** **6** **7** **8** **9**

06 05 04 03 02

Denny Wood

Denny Lodge

Parkhill Inclosure

Hollands Wood

Ramnor Inclosure

Denny Lodge Inclosure

Stubby Copse Inclosure

Dignal Inclosure

Balmer Lawn

Perrywood Haseley Inclosure

Balmerlawn

BALMER LAWN ROAD

Works

Works

S042

Whitley Ridge Country House Hotel

New Copse Inclosure

Ladycross Lodge

B3055

B3055

MILL LANE

B3055

Perrywood Ironshill Inclosure

Brockenhurst Park

Round Hill

Dilton

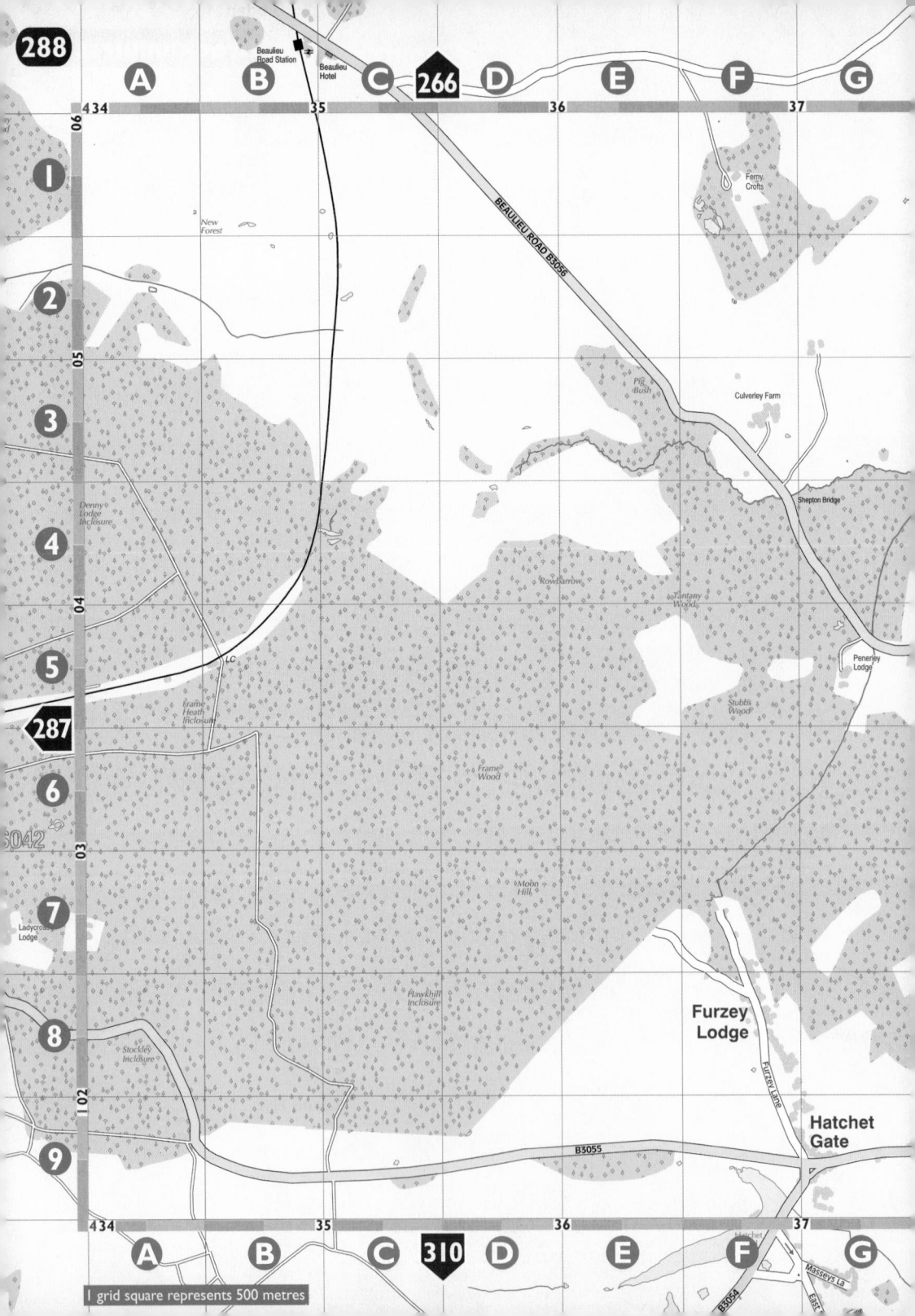

A B C D E F G

266

434   35   36   37

06

1

New
Forest

Ferny
Crofts

2

05

Pig
Bush

Culverley Farm

3

Denny
Lodge
Inclosure

Shepton Bridge

4

04

Rowbarrow

Tantany
Wood

5

LC

Peneley
Lodge

287

Frame
Heath
Inclosure

Stubbs
Wood

6

Frame
Wood

B3042

03

7

Ladycross
Lodge

Mobn
Hill

Furzey
Lodge

8

Stockley
Inclosure

Plawhill
Inclosure

Furzey Lane

02

Hatchet
Gate

9

B3055

434   35   36   37

A B C D E F G

310

Hatchet

Massey's La

B3054

1 grid square represents 500 metres

H J K L 269 M N

45 46 47 48

06

1
2
3
4
5
292
6
7
8
9

05
04
03
02

Cadland
Creek

J Av

H Avenue

Foreshore

Foreshore
North

North Trestle Road

Foreshore
Rd
South

Burnham
Road N

PL P.H.

Burnham
Road
South

Trestle
Road

Agel

South
Trestle
Road

Old

Agel
Road

Victor Rd

Palmer Rd

Oil Refinery

S045

Church
Rd

Marsh La

Marsh La

Fawley
Infant
School

Fawley
Business
Centre

Ashlett
Road

Copthorne Lane

Copthorne Lane

Ashlett

Ashlett Creek

ROAD

B3053

Ashdown
Road
Slades

Blackfield Rd

The
Pentagon

Hill

Fawley

FAWLEY BY-PASS

B3053

Stonehills

Northern Access
Road

Northern Access Rd

Fields Heath

Fields Farm

Badminston Farm

Badminston Lane

Badminston
Drove

Over

B3053

Calshot

Tom's Down

Mopley
Pond

Badminston
Common

Stanswood Road

Tristin
Close

Calshot
Lane

Castle
Lane

Hillhead

45 46 47 48

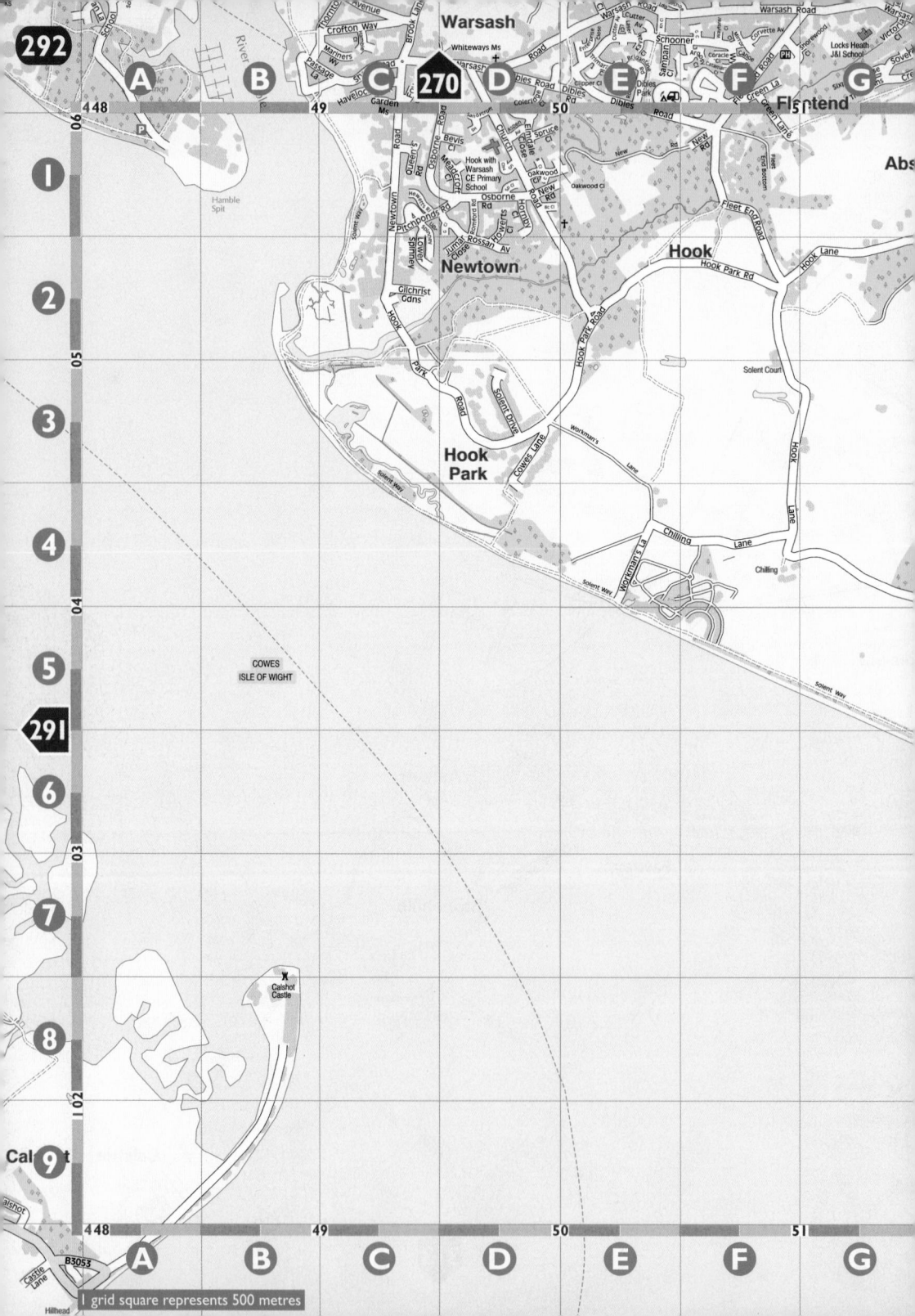

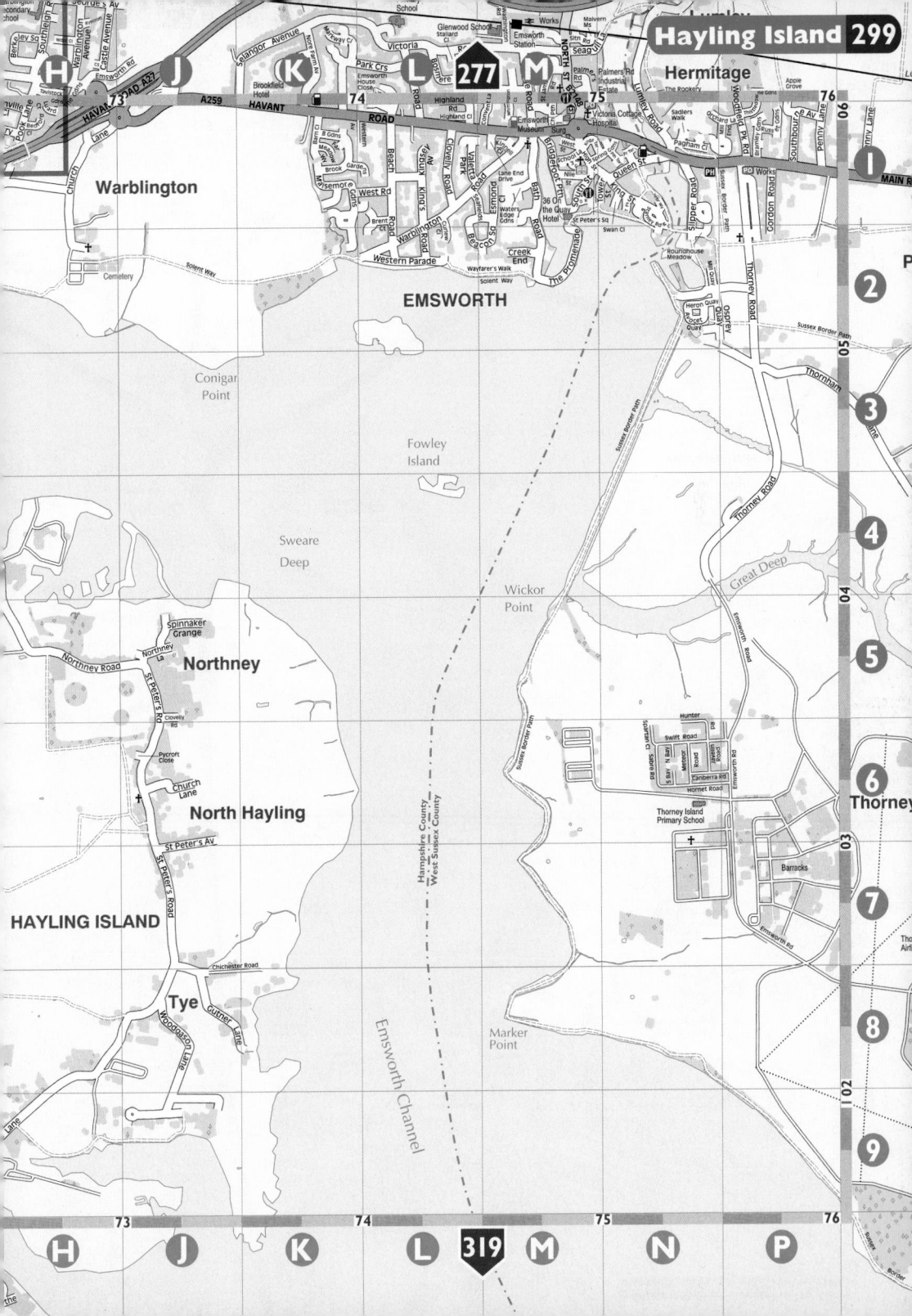

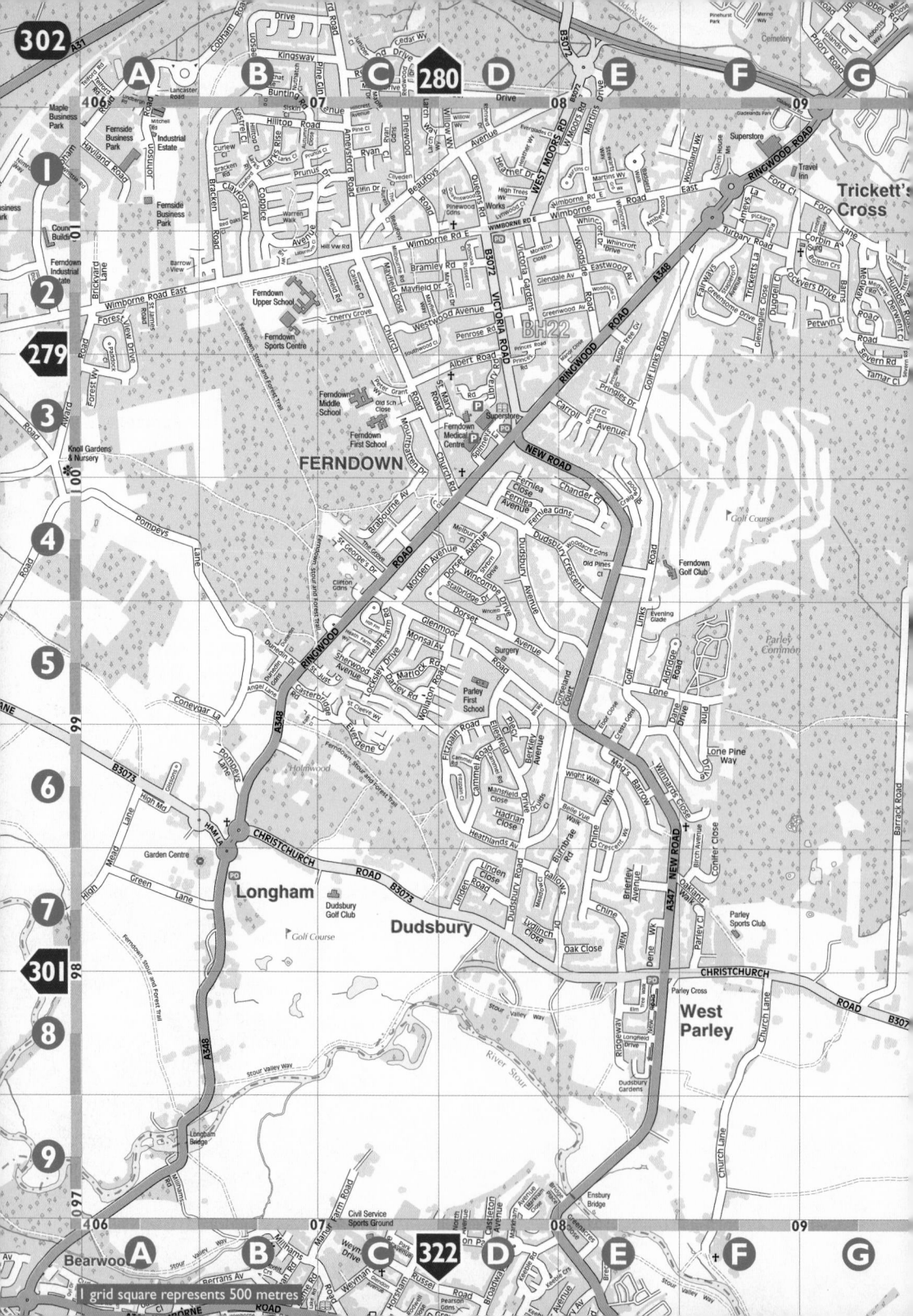

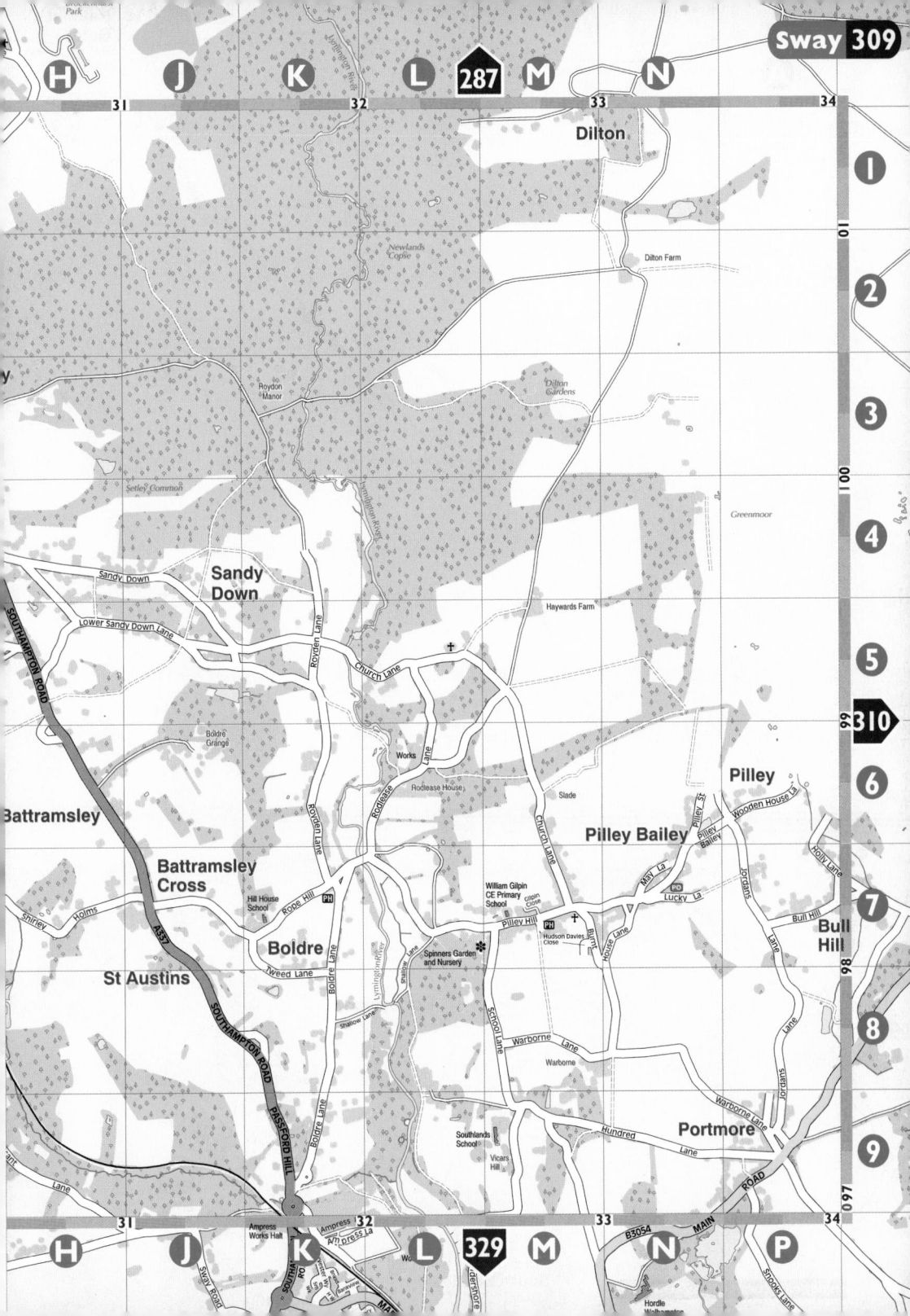

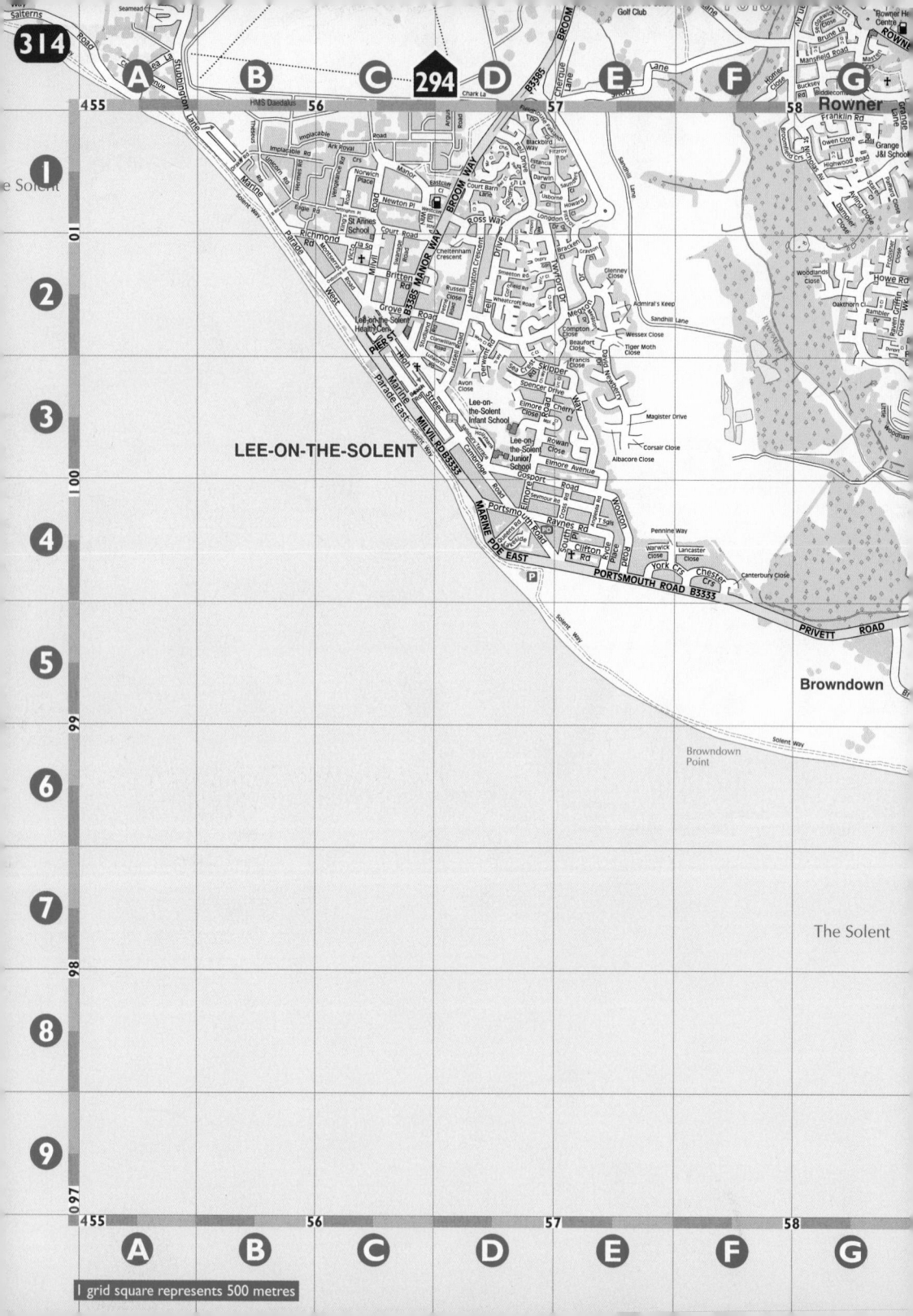

A   B   C   298   D   E   F   G

469   70   71   72

1

2

3

4

5

6

7

8

9

Langstone Channel

Sinah Lake

City of
Hamps

Hampshire County

University
of Portsmouth

Ferry Road

Golf Course

Sinah Common

Hayling
Golf Club

East Winner

Holiday Village

Warren Cl
Warren Close

Harbour
Road

Park Road

Catherine

St. Aubin's

St. Helen's Road

Sea Front

Hayling Billy Coastal Path

North Shore Road

Hayling Billy Business Cen
Station Theatre

Kurnss Wy

St. Thomas Av

St. Thomas Av

Richmond Dr

Station Road

Station
Road

St. Mary's
Road

Staunton Avenue

Bacon

Westmis

Sea Front

Sea Front

West Town

Westfield

SOUTH HAYLING

BEACH ROAD

Beach Rd

Victoria Av

Hollow
Lane

Hollow Lane

Woodlands
La

Brights La

Saltmarsh La

West

Dover
Court

Wardens

Atherley
Road

Charles

Gri Cl

Juces W

MANOR ROAD
A3023

A3023 MANOR ROAD

Southleigh Gv

MANOR ROAD
A3023

Hgerbrg

PO

P011

P011

Manor
House

Mill

A3023

Rest Wk Av
Pound
Lea

Kings Rd

The
Hayling School

Lulworth Cl

Katrina
Gdns

Works

Legion
Rd

Tournerbury

Mengham
Infant
School

Palmerston
Rd

Hayling Island
Health Centre

Cherrywood Gdns

Oakwood

Mengham Rd

Menol

Seismore

Grand Pde

Webb Cl

Manor

Church   Road

St. Mary's Road

St. Conrad's   Avenue

Elm

Ramsey Rd.

Alexandra Avenue

Chichester Avenue

Sea
Front

Westfield Avenue

Mengham   Lane

Fleet

Daw
Lane

HAVANT ROAD

Tree Rd

Cop

PD

Hayling Bay

1 grid square represents 500 metres

299

H J K L M

73 74 75 76

1
2
3
4
5
6
7
8
9

Mill Rithe

Holiday Centre

Mill Rythe J&I School

Eastwood Cl

Pilsey Sand

Stocker's Lake

Mengham Salterns

Mengham

Selsmore

Eastoke

Marine Road

Seaview Walk

Salterns Lane

Selsmore Avenue

Fishery Lane

Harold Road

Sea Front

Southwood

Bembridge Drive

Southwood Road

Wheatlands Avenue

Winsor Cl

Haven Road

Sandy Point

Eastoke Avenue

Bosmere Rd

Black Point

Bracklesham Rd

Eastoke Point

West Sussex County
Hampshire County

H J K L M N P

73 74 75 76

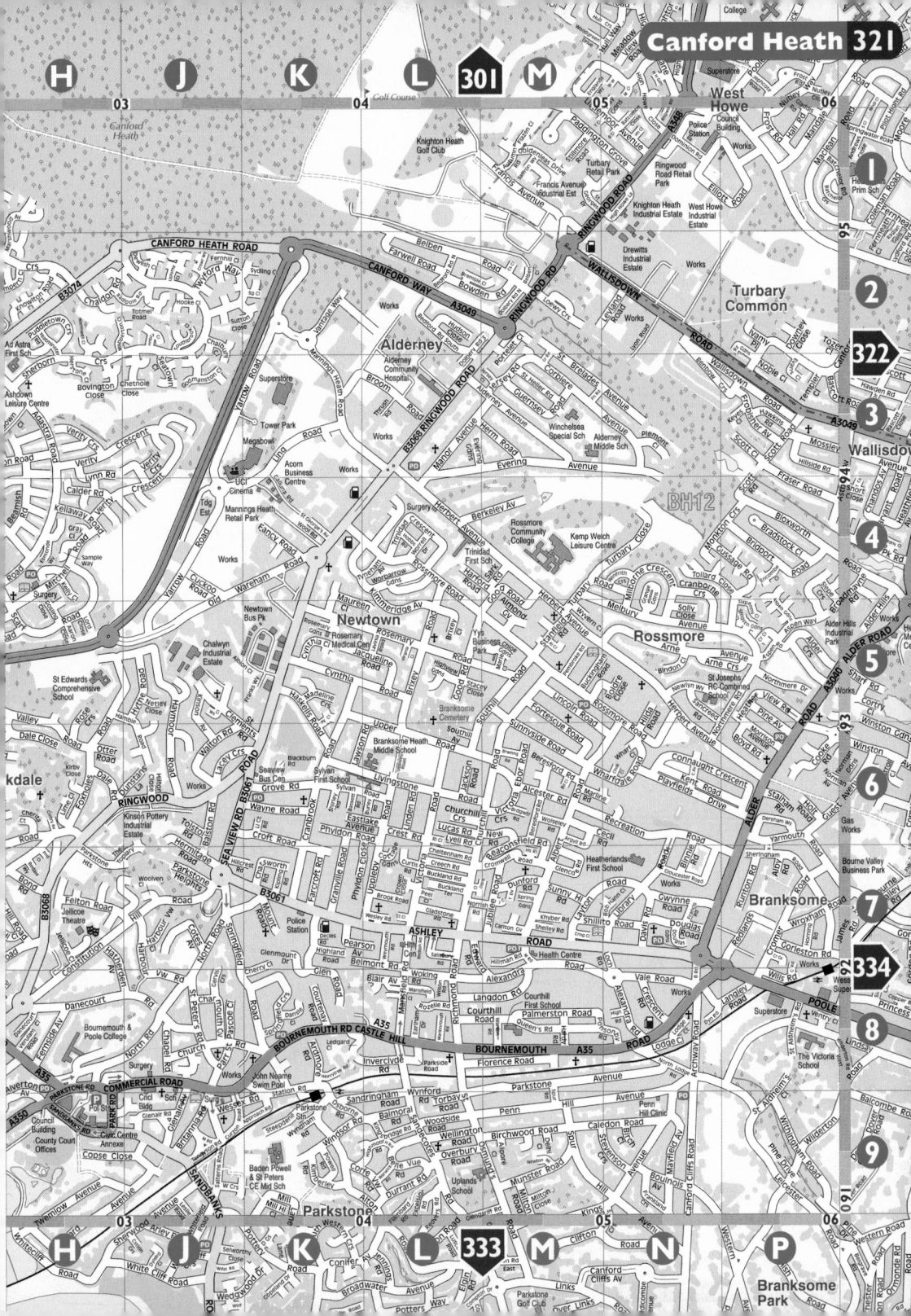

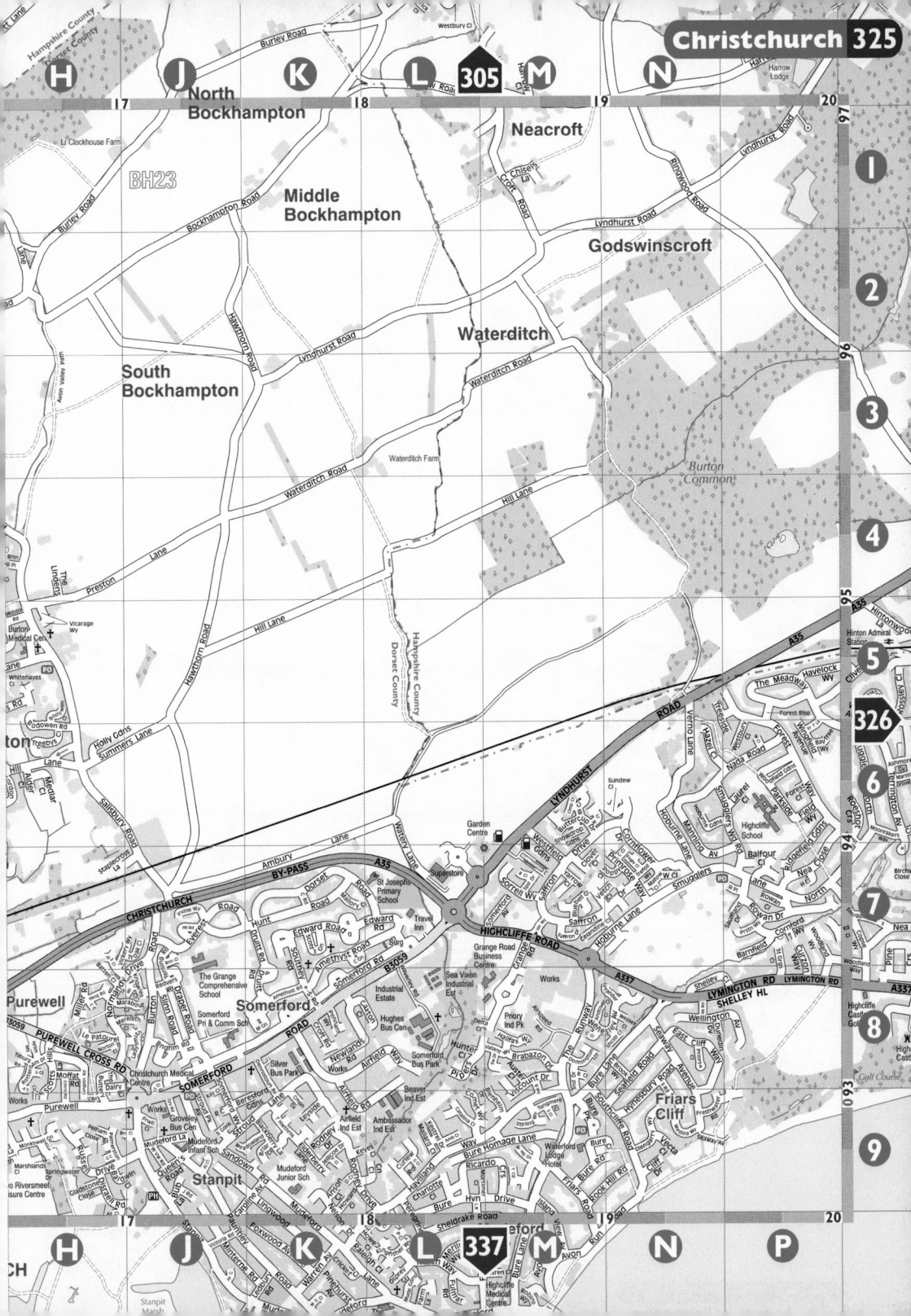

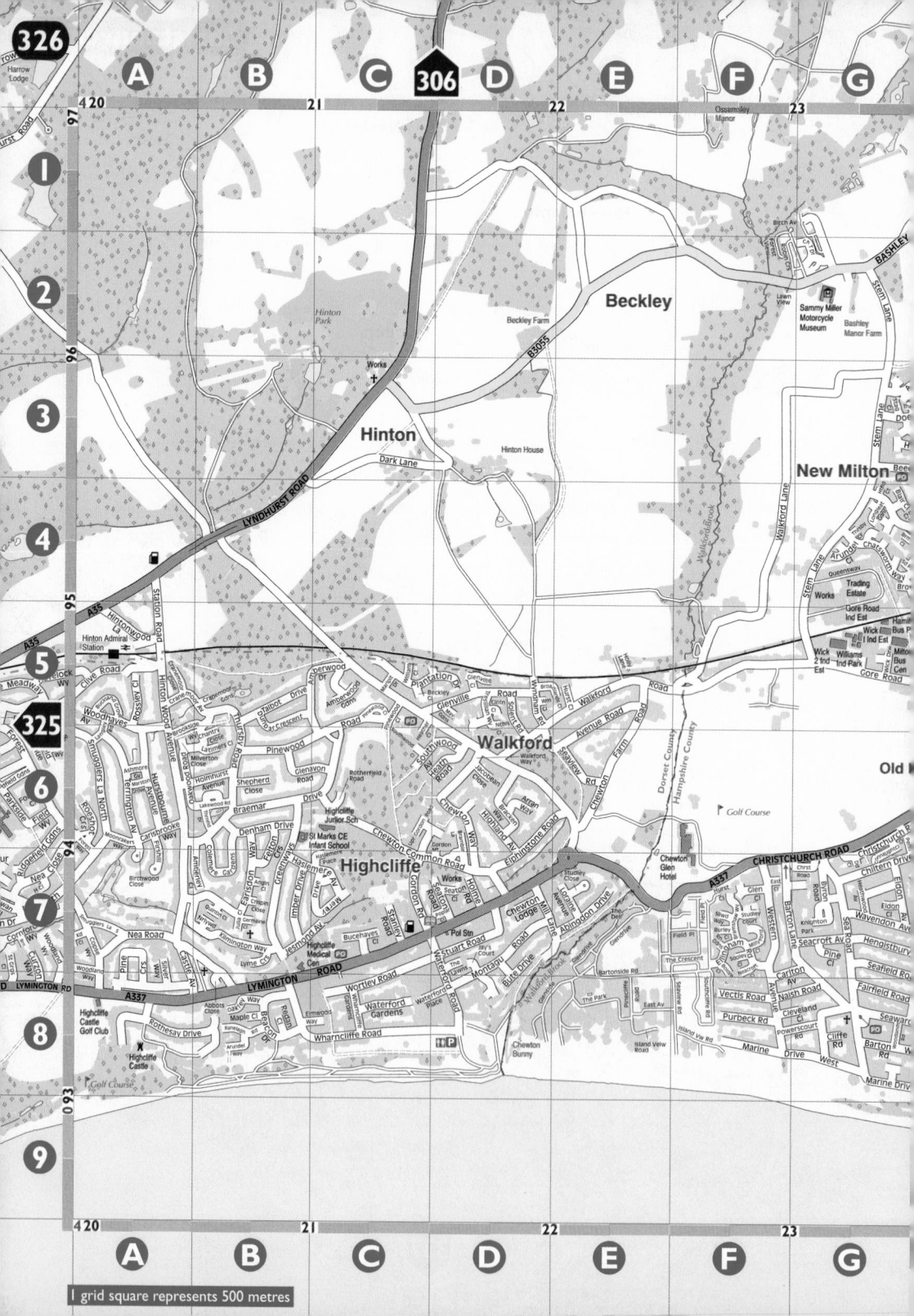

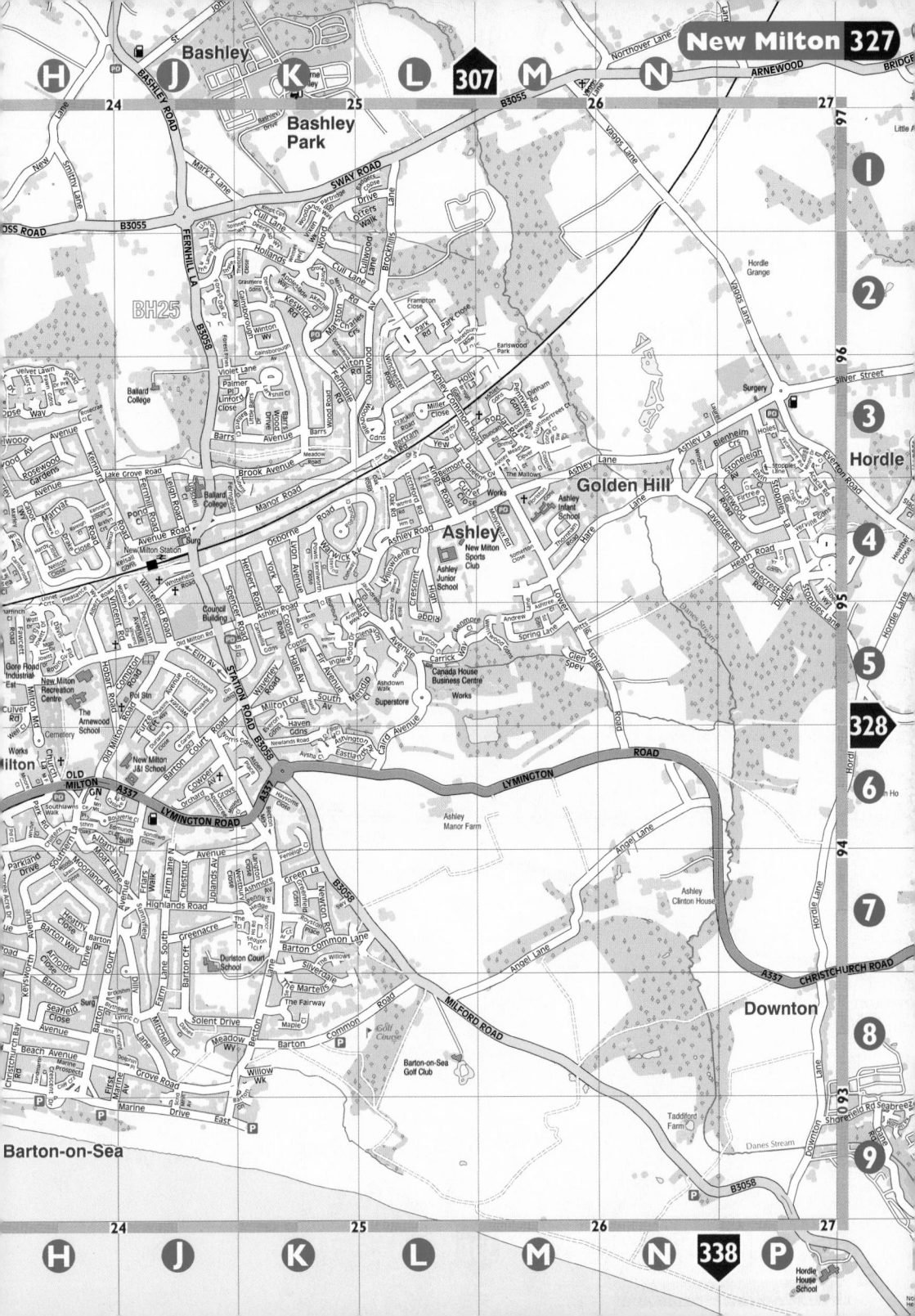

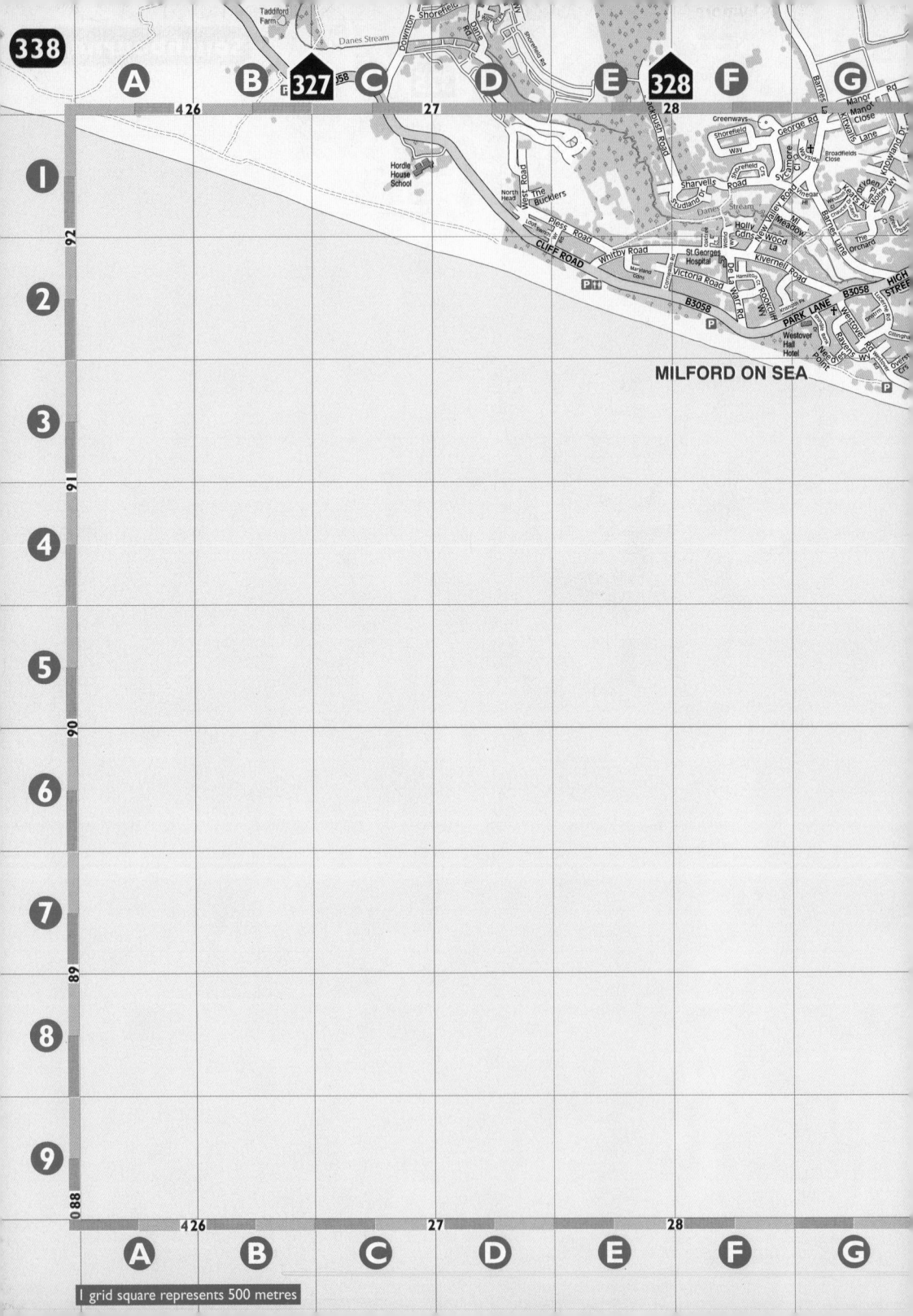

338

A B 327 C D E 328 F G

426   27   28

Taddiford Farm
Danes Stream
Downton
Shorefield

Hordle House School
North Head
The Bucklers
Pless Road
West Road
CLIFF ROAD
Whitby Road
Maryland Gdns
Victoria Road
B3058
St Georges Hospital

George Rd
Greenways Way
Shorefield
Sharvells Road
Studland
Danes Stream
Holly Gdns
Ash Wood
Kivernell Road
PARK LANE
Westover Hall Hotel
B3058
HIGH STREET
Manor Manor Close Lane
The Orchard
Broadfields Close

MILFORD ON SEA

1
2
3
4
5
6
7
8
9

92   91   90   89   0 88

426   27   28

A B C D E F G

I grid square represents 500 metres

Abbotstone ... 147 L6
Abbotswood ... 204 E2
Abbots Worthy ... 165 L1
Abbotts Ann ... 101 L7
Abshot ... 292 G1
Alderholt ... 239 M5
Aldermaston Soke ... 34 G3
Aldermoor ... 221 L9
Alderney ... 321 L2
Aldershot ... 3 C3
Allbrook ... 207 J7
Allington ... 118 B6
Alton ... 132 E6
Alverstoke ... 315 J6
Ameysford ... 280 C8
Ampfield ... 205 N2
Amport ... 100 F5
Anchorage Park ... 297 K5
Andover ... 4 E4
Andover Down ... 103 L2
Andwell ... 71 H7
Anmore ... 255 K7
Anna Valley ... 102 B5
Ann's Hill ... 315 K3
Ansteadbrook ... 157 P8
Anthill Common ... 254 F5
Applemore ... 267 L6
Appleshaw ... 81 H5
Arford ... 154 F2
Ash ... 76 F9
Ashe ... 87 L3
Ashfield ... 204 F9
Ashford ... 315 J6
Ashford Hill ... 33 H5
Ashington ... 300 C4
Ashlett ... 291 L6
Ashley ... 162 C4
Ashley ... 282 A4
Ashley ... 327 L4
Ashley Heath ... 281 N3
Ashmansworth ... 45 J6
Ashton ... 231 P1
Ashurst ... 246 A9
Ashurst Bridge ... 246 A6
Ash Vale ... 76 F6
Avington ... 166 D2
Avon ... 304 D6
Avon Castle ... 282 B7
Awbridge ... 203 L1
Axford ... 109 N7
Axmansford ... 33 M7
Baddesley Lea ... 97 J5
Baffins ... 317 K1
Bagmore ... 111 J4
Bailey Green ... 189 L3
Ball Hill ... 29 K3
Balmerlawn ... 287 H6
Bank ... 264 D7
Bar End ... 165 J9
Barford ... 136 E9
Barrow Hill ... 245 K1
Bartley ... 244 C4
Barton-on-Sea ... 327 H9
Barton Stacey ... 122 C3
Bashley ... 307 J9
Bashley Park ... 327 K1
Basingstoke ... 6 C4
Bassett ... 228 C7
Bassett Green ... 228 C7
Battramsley ... 308 G6
Battramsley Cross ... 309 J7
Batt's Corner ... 135 M2
Baughurst ... 33 M7
Baybridge ... 209 J2
Bear Cross ... 301 P7
Bearwood ... 301 P7
Beaulieu ... 289 J9
Beauworth ... 186 E6
Beckley ... 326 E2
Bedhampton ... 14 A5
Beech ... 132 A8
Beech Hill ... 37 H1
Bell Hill ... 191 L9
Bentley ... 114 D5
Bentworth ... 131 H4
Bickton ... 240 D5
Bidden ... 92 D4
Bighton ... 148 F7
Binley ... 63 J4
Binsted ... 134 C2
Birchy Hill ... 308 C7
Bishop's Hill ... 31 M3
Bishop's Sutton ... 168 E3
Bishopstoke ... 229 L1
Bishop's Waltham ... 232 A3
Bisterne ... 304 D2
Bisterne Close ... 284 F7
Bitterne ... 248 G4
Bitterne Park ... 248 F2
Black Dam ... 69 N9
Blackfield ... 290 F8
Blackhill ... 224 C5
Blackmoor ... 153 L9
Blacknest ... 135 H2
Blackwater ... 57 L1
Blackwater ... 323 P2
Blashford ... 260 E7
Bleak Hill ... 240 A8
Blendworth ... 256 C4
Blissford ... 241 J5
Boarhunt ... 273 M5
Bohemia ... 290 F4
Boldre ... 309 K7
Boorley Green ... 250 E1
Borden ... 193 P8
Bordon ... 154 B6
Boscombe ... 118 A7
Boscombe ... 355 L5
Bossington ... 144 A2
Botley ... 251 H5
Boundstone ... 116 B6
Bournemouth ... 9 F4
The Bourne ... 116 C4
Bourne Valley ... 322 B9
Boveridge ... 238 A1

Bowling Alley ... 94 G3
Bowling Green ... 328 E1
Boyatt Wood ... 207 H8
Bradley ... 130 D1
Braishfield ... 180 G7
Brambridge ... 207 M5
Bramdean ... 187 N1
Bramley ... 51 P1
Bramley Corner ... 51 L2
Bramley Green ... 52 C2
Bramshaw ... 223 P8
Bramshill ... 38 E7
Bramshott ... 175 K1
Branksome ... 321 P7
Branksome Park ... 321 P5
Bransbury ... 104 C9
Bransgore ... 305 M8
Breamore ... 220 E3
Bridgemary ... 294 F6
Brighton Hill ... 90 A3
Brimpton Common ... 33 M4
Broadgate ... 206 A3
Broad Layings ... 29 N5
Broadmere ... 89 P7
Broad Oak ... 72 F8
Broadoak ... 250 E4
Broadstone ... 300 D9
Brockbridge ... 233 P2
Brockhampton ... 14 C7
Brockenhurst ... 286 E8
Brockhurst ... 315 H2
Brock's Green ... 31 M6
Brook ... 161 H9
Brook ... 244 A5
Brooke's Green ... 225 P8
Brook Hill ... 244 A1
Broom Hill ... 279 K4
Broughton ... 160 B1
Brown Candover ... 128 F6
Browndown ... 219 K7
Brown Heath ... 231 J7
Browninghill Green ... 50 A2
Bucket Corner ... 205 N6
Buckland ... 329 J2
Bucklers Hard ... 311 N3
Bucks Horn Oak ... 135 J1
Buckskin ... 68 D8
Bull Hill ... 309 P7
Bunker's Hill ... 244 C1
Bunstead ... 182 E8
Burgates ... 173 K9
Burghclere ... 30 D7
Burghclere Common ... 30 F5
Burghfield ... 27 L2
Burghfield Common ... 27 J5
Burghfield Hill ... 27 L4
Buriton ... 215 L8
Burley ... 284 D6
Burley Beacon ... 284 A7
Burley Lawn ... 284 E6
Burley Street ... 284 A4
Burridge ... 250 G9
Burslendon ... 270 A2
Burton ... 324 G6
Bury's Bank ... 25 H8
Butlocks Heath ... 269 M3
Buttsash ... 290 D1
Butt's Green ... 178 G5
The Butts ... 132 E7
Cadnam ... 244 F3
Cadnam Green ... 244 E2
Calmore ... 246 A2
Calshot ... 291 P9
Camel Green ... 239 P6
Camelsdale ... 156 F8
Canada ... 243 D8
Canford Cliffs ... 333 M4
Canford Heath ... 320 G3
Canford Magna ... 301 J4
Carter's Clay ... 178 G8
Catherington ... 256 A2
Catisfield ... 271 N9
Causeway ... 215 L3
Causeway ... 256 B6
Chalton ... 237 H7
Chandler's Ford ... 206 F5
Chandlers Green ... 53 L3
Charleshill ... 117 N5
Charlton ... 82 C9
Charlton-All-Saints ... 199 K1
Charlwood ... 170 D4
Charminster ... 323 J6
Charter Alley ... 50 C5
Chawton ... 151 L1
Cheriton ... 187 H1
Chidden ... 235 H4
Chilbolton ... 123 L5
Chilbolton Down ... 143 H2
Chilcomb ... 184 F1
Chilton Candover ... 129 J2
Chilworth ... 227 P3
Chilworth Old Village ... 227 N2
Chineham ... 70 A1
Cholderton ... 98 E9
Christchurch ... 336 F1
Church Common ... 191 H6
Church Crookham ... 74 C7
Church End ... 52 D7
Church Oakley ... 88 C1
Churt ... 136 F8
Chute Cadley ... 60 C5
Chute Standen ... 60 A3
Clanfield ... 236 A6
Clanville ... 81 K4
Clapgate ... 278 E6
Clarken Green ... 88 B1
Clatford Oakcuts ... 121 N5
Clayhall ... 12 E7
Clayhill ... 264 C7
Cliddesden ... 90 B4
Cobley ... 194 G3
Cobley ... 195 H3
Coibury ... 246 B9
Cold Ash Hill ... 175 M2
Colden Common ... 208 A4

Cole Henley ... 64 E9
Colehill ... 279 H7
Colemore ... 171 L5
College Town ... 41 M5
Colt Hill ... 72 E9
The Common ... 158 B7
Compton ... 116 F1
Compton ... 161 H8
Compton ... 183 M1
Compton End ... 183 L5
Conford ... 154 C9
Coombe ... 213 H7
Copnor ... 297 J8
Copythorne ... 245 J8
Corhampton ... 211 M8
Corham ... 297 J1
Cottonworth ... 123 J5
Couch Green ... 146 B9
Court Corner ... 50 E2
Cove ... 57 M7
Cowesfield Green ... 201 L2
Cowplain ... 255 P8
Coxford ... 247 L1
Crab Orchard ... 258 E8
Crampmoor ... 205 J4
Cranbourne ... 219 K7
Crawley ... 143 L6
Creekmoor ... 320 C4
Crendell ... 238 F4
Cricket Hill ... 40 F9
Criddlestyle ... 240 F2
Cripplestyle ... 238 G6
Critchell's Green ... 201 L2
Critchmere ... 156 D6
Crockerhill ... 272 E3
Crondall ... 94 G4
Crookham ... 32 E1
Crookham Village ... 73 P6
Crosswater ... 136 E5
Crossways ... 219 K7
Crow ... 283 H5
Crowdhill ... 208 C8
Crowthorne ... 40 F1
Crux Easton ... 45 K8
Cuckoo's Corner ... 133 L1
Cufaude ... 51 P6
Cupernham ... 204 E4
Curbridge ... 251 K7
Curdridge ... 233 P6
Custards ... 264 C5
Daggons ... 239 J6
Damerham ... 219 K7
Daneshill ... 69 P4
Darby Green ... 41 H8
Deadwater ... 154 C5
Dean ... 163 P4
Dean ... 232 C1
Deane ... 87 N2
Deanland ... 194 A8
Deanlane End ... 257 K6
Deepcut ... 59 H7
The Dene ... 62 C4
Denmead ... 255 H6
Denvilles ... 277 J8
Dewlands Common ... 258 D5
Dibden ... 267 N9
Dibden Purlieu ... 267 N9
Dilton ... 309 M1
Dipley ... 54 D5
Dippenhall ... 94 F9
Dockenfield ... 135 P3
Dogmersfield ... 72 M6
Donnington ... 24 A1
Dora's Green ... 95 L6
Downton ... 199 M6
Downton ... 327 P8
Drayton ... 297 L1
Droxford ... 233 L3
Dry Hill ... 149 P3
Dudsbury ... 302 C7
Dummer ... 109 H1
Dunbridge ... 179 J5
Dundridge ... 232 F5
Dunley ... 64 B4
Durleighmarsh ... 216 E2
Durley ... 231 H6
Durley Street ... 231 J4
Durns Town ... 308 C6
Durrants ... 277 H2
Earlstone Common ... 30 E6
Eastleigh ... 229 K1
East Liss ... 192 F5
East Martin ... 196 C9
East Meon ... 213 M5
Eastney ... 317 L5
East Oakley ... 88 C1
Eastoke ... 319 J6
Easton ... 165 P2
East Parley ... 303 L8
Eastrop ... 71 J7
East Stratton ... 127 N5
East Tisted ... 171 K2
East Tytherley ... 159 N8
East Wellow ... 202 C8
East Winterslow ... 138 A8
East Woodhay ... 28 F7
East Worldham ... 151 P1
Ebblake ... 259 K6
Ecchinswell ... 47 L3
Edmondsham ... 238 B8
Egbury ... 63 N6

Egypt ... 125 M4
Eling ... 246 F6
Ellingham ... 260 C5
Ellisfield ... 110 D2
Elson ... 295 L9
Elsted ... 217 L9
Elvetham ... 55 N8
Elvetham Heath ... 56 B9
Emery Down ... 264 D4
Empshott ... 172 F4
Empshott Green ... 172 E4
Emsworth ... 299 L2
Enborne Row ... 30 A2
Enham Alamein ... 82 C4
Ensbury ... 322 E1
Ensbury Park ... 322 C5
Eversley ... 39 L5
Eversley Centre ... 39 N6
Eversley Cross ... 40 A6
Everton ... 328 E6
Ewshot ... 54 C6
Exbury ... 312 D5
Exton ... 211 N6
Faberstown ... 80 B2
Faccombe ... 44 C4
Fairmile ... 324 D6
Fair Oak ... 33 H7
Fair Oak ... 230 C2
Fair Oak Green ... 36 C8
Fareham ... 11 F4
Farleigh Wallop ... 90 A9
Farley Hill ... 38 C1
Farlington ... 297 M1
Farnborough ... 58 B8
Farnborough Green ... 58 D8
Farnborough Park ... 76 C1
Farnborough Street ... 58 B8
Farnham ... 57 M2
Fawley ... 291 K7
Ferndown ... 302 E3
Filmore Hill ... 189 J2
Finchampstead ... 39 N3
Finchdean ... 257 J5
Fisher's Pond ... 208 B7
Fleet ... 74 D3
Fleetend ... 270 F9
Fleetlands ... 294 C4
Flexford ... 206 B5
Flood Street ... 220 D5
Folly Hill ... 96 A6
Fordingbridge ... 240 E2
Forest Gate ... 254 F4
Forestside ... 257 P5
Forton ... 104 B6
Forton ... 315 M2
Fosbury ... 42 C4
Foulford ... 283 L2
Four Houses Corner ... 26 C7
Four Marks ... 150 D6
Foxdown ... 87 J1
Foxhills ... 246 B8
Fox Lane ... 57 N4
Foyers ... 245 J8
Fratton ... 316 G3
Freefolk ... 85 P5
Freemantle ... 247 N5
The Frenches ... 203 H5
Frenchmoor ... 158 C6
Frensham ... 136 B2
Friars Cliff ... 325 N9
Frimley ... 58 B4
Frimley Green ... 58 E6
Frimley Ridge ... 58 F2
Fritham ... 243 H2
Frithend ... 135 K5
Frogham ... 241 J5
Frogmore ... 41 J8
Frostlane ... 268 E8
Froxfield Green ... 190 C6
Fryern Hill ... 206 F7
Fulflood ... 164 E7
Fullerton ... 122 G6
Funtley ... 272 C5
Furzedown ... 161 N8
Furze Hill ... 241 J8
Furzey Corner ... 275 H1
Furzey Lodge ... 288 F8
Furzley ... 224 D7
Fyfield ... 80 E9
Fyning ... 216 E1

Habin ... 217 K3
Hale ... 96 D6
Hale ... 221 M5
Halecommon ... 193 J9
Halterworth ... 204 G6
Hambledon ... 254 D1
Hamble-le-Rice ... 269 P7
Hammer ... 156 B8
Hammer Bottom ... 156 A8
Hampreston ... 301 N3
Hampton Park ... 228 E9
Hamptworth ... 201 J9
Hamworthy ... 320 A9
Hangersley ... 261 J8
Hannington ... 48 E9
Harbridge ... 260 C1
Harbridge Green ... 240 B9
Hardley ... 290 E3
Hardway ... 315 M1
Harefield ... 249 L4
Harestock ... 164 D4
Hartfordbridge ... 55 L5
Hartley Mauditt ... 152 D3
Hartley Wespall ... 53 H4
Hartley Wintney ... 54 C6
Haslemere ... 157 J7
Hatch ... 70 D7
Hatch Bottom ... 249 M1
Hatchet Gate ... 288 C9
Hatchet Green ... 221 N1
Hatch Warren ... 89 L5
Hatherden ... 82 A2
Hatt Hill ... 179 K5
Hattingley ... 149 M1
Haughurst Hill ... 33 M5
Havant ... 15 C5
Hawkley ... 172 D8
Hawley ... 57 M2
Hawley Lane ... 57 M2
Hawthorn ... 150 D9
Hayling Island ... 299 H7
Hazeley ... 54 D2
Hazeley Bottom ... 54 C2
Hazeley Lea ... 64 G2
Headbourne Worthy ... 164 G2
Headley ... 32 B5
Headley ... 154 E3
Headley Down ... 155 J4
Hearn ... 155 J1
Heath End ... 29 H5
Heath End ... 96 A4
Heath End ... 96 D4
Heather Row ... 71 L6
Heatherside ... 59 H1
Heathfield ... 272 A9
Heath Green ... 149 K1
Heckfield ... 37 P8
Hedge End ... 250 B4
Hell Corner ... 28 C1
Henley ... 42 D2
Hensting ... 208 D4
Hermitage ... 277 N9
Herriard ... 111 H1
Hides Close ... 289 K5
Highbridge ... 207 M6
Highbury ... 297 H3
Highclere ... 29 N7
Highclere Street ... 45 L2
Highcliffe ... 326 C7
High Cross ... 190 F4
Higher Row ... 279 L1
Highfield ... 248 C1
Hightown ... 249 N7
Hightown ... 283 H2
Highwood ... 261 J6
Hilfield ... 320 C2
Hill Brow ... 192 G4
Hillbutts ... 278 B7
Hill Head ... 293 M8
Hill Park ... 272 B7
Hillpound ... 252 C8
Hillside ... 58 N1
Hill Street ... 192 E2
Hillstreet ... 225 P7
Hill Top ... 289 N5
Hillyfields ... 226 G8
Hilsea ... 297 H5
Hiltingbury ... 206 F3
Hindhead ... 156 E1
Hinton ... 326 C3
Hinton Ampner ... 187 J2
Hinton Parva ... 278 B1
Hocombe ... 206 D3
Hoe ... 252 D5
Hoe Gate ... 254 B4
Hog Hatch ... 95 P5
Holbury ... 290 E6
Holdenhurst ... 323 H4
Hollington ... 45 K1
Hollington Cross ... 45 L2
Hollywater ... 154 C7
Holt ... 72 C3
Holt ... 279 H2
Holt End ... 131 J6
Holt Heath ... 280 A3
Holt Pound ... 115 H3
Holybourne ... 133 J2
Hook ... 72 A3
Hook ... 292 E2
Hook Park ... 292 C5
Hordle ... 326 C5
Horndean ... 256 C5
Horsebridge ... 161 H6
Horton Common ... 258 C8
Horton Heath ... 230 C4
Horton Heath ... 258 A9
Houghton ... 161 N2
Hound ... 270 A5
Hound Green ... 54 B2
Hound Hill ... 278 A6
Houndmills ... 69 H5
Hounsdown ... 246 C2
Hungerford ... 240 G6
Hunton ... 126 A5
Hurn ... 303 P9

Hursley 182 D7
Hurstbourne Priors 84 E9
Hurstbourne Tarrant 62 B5
Hyde 23 F2
Hyde 240 G5
Hyde End 53 H2
Hythe 288 D6
Ibsley 260 E5
Ibthorpe 61 P4
Ibworth 67 L2
Iford 324 B8
Inhurst 33 M6
Inkpen Common 28 A1
Isington 114 A5
Itchen 248 C8
Itchen Abbas 166 D1
Itchen Stoke 167 J1
Jumpers Common 324 C7
Kempshott 89 L2
Kempshott Park 89 L2
Kent's Oak 179 L9
Keyhaven 339 K3
Kilmeston 187 H5
Kimbridge 179 L6
Kimpton 80 B9
Kingsclere 50 D6
Kingsclere Woodlands ... 32 D6
Kings Furlong 69 H8
Kingsley 134 E8
Kingsmead 252 G3
King's Somborne 161 L4
Kingston 282 D8
Kingston 317 H1
Kings Worthy 165 K1
Kinson 322 B2
Kitwood 150 B9
Knapp 205 P1
Knighton 301 M6
Knights Enham 82 E6
Knowle Village 272 C3
Ladwell 206 D1
Lambs Green 300 A3
Landford 201 N9
Landfordwood 201 M6
Lane End 136 D2
Lane End 170 E8
Lane End 186 A6
Langdown 268 D7
Langley 174 C9
Langley 312 F1
Langrish 214 C1
Langstone 298 E3
Lasham 111 M8
Latchmere Green 35 K9
Laverstoke 86 C6
Leagreen 328 A7
Leckford 123 H9
Lee 226 E4
Lee Ground 271 N5
Lee-on-the-Solent 314 B3
Leigh 301 H1
Leigh Park 276 D6
Lepe 313 J6
Liliput 333 L4
Linchmere 175 P4
Lindford 154 C4
Linford 261 L8
Linkenholt 43 N4
Linwood 261 M2
Liphook 175 H4
Liss 192 E3
Liss Forest 173 L8
Litchfield 64 D4
Little Ann 101 N6
Little Canford 301 L1
Littledown 43 J5
Littledown 323 N8
Little Hoddington 92 C6
Little Holbury 290 D4
Little London 50 G2
Little London 83 H5
Little Posbrook 293 L4
Little Sandhurst 41 H4
Little Shoddesden 80 C5
Little Somborne 162 A1
Littleton 164 C2
Locherley 178 E5
Locks Heath 270 C7
London Minstead 244 C7
Long Common 250 F2
Longfleet 320 E8
Longham 302 B7
Longparish 84 G9
Long Park 143 P8
Longstock 141 K1
Long Sutton 93 L8
Lord's Hill 227 L8
Lordswood 227 P8
Lovedean 255 N5
Lover 200 B8
Lower Bordean 190 A4
Lower Bourne 116 E4
Lower Brook 179 P2
Lower Buckland 329 L2
Lower Bullington 125 J9
Lower Burgate 220 D8
Lower Chute 60 A5
Lower Common 59 J5
Lower Common 110 D4
Lower Daggons 238 G4
Lower Farringdon 151 L5
Lower Froyle 114 A5
Lower Hamworthy 332 C2
Lower Holwell 238 D5
Lower Mannington 280 B1
Lower Pennington 329 J7
Lower Ratley 203 M7
Lower Slackstead 181 K7
Lower Swanwick 270 C2
Lower Turmer 260 A3
Lower Upham 209 N9
Lower Wield 130 D3
Lowford 270 A1
Lumley 277 N9
Lychpit 70 A5

Lyde Green 53 M6
Lymington 329 K3
Lymore 328 F9
Lynch 86 E3
Lynch Hill 85 M6
Lyndhurst 264 E5
Malwood 244 A7
Mannington 280 A1
Mapledurwell 70 F9
Marchwood 247 L9
Martin 218 C1
Martin Drove End 195 L2
Martyr Worthy 166 A1
Mattingley 54 A5
Maybush 247 J1
Mead End 307 N7
Medstead 149 P2
Mengham 319 H5
Meon 293 L6
Meonstoke 211 P9
Merley 300 G4
Merritown 303 L9
Merry Field Hill 278 G6
Merry Oak 248 G6
Meyrick Park 334 D1
Michelever 127 H6
Michelever Station ... 107 H8
Michelmersh 180 A5
Midanbury 249 H3
Middle Bockhampton . 325 K1
Middle Bourne 116 C3
Middleton 104 C5
Middle Wallop 120 E9
Middle Winterslow 138 B9
Milford on Sea 338 E3
Millbridge 116 D9
Millbrook 247 J4
Mill Green 52 C5
Mill Lane 94 E2
Milton 317 L4
Minstead 244 B8
The Mint 192 E1
Mockbeggar 261 H3
Monk Sherborne 50 E7
Monkwood 170 B5
Montgomery Lines 76 B8
Monxton 101 H5
Moorcourt 226 A5
Moordown 322 G6
Moorgreen 249 P9
Moor Park 117 H1
Moortown 282 F4
Morestead 184 F6
Morgan's Vale 199 N6
Mortimer 27 J9
Mortimer West End 35 L2
Mortisfont 179 L4
The Mount 29 N7
Mudeford 337 L1
Mullenspond 100 E2
Murrell Green 72 D1
Muscliff 323 H2
Mytchett 76 D1
Mytchett Place 76 G2
Nash's Green 111 L3
Nately Scures 71 K5
Neacroft 325 M1
Neatham 133 L3
Netherton 44 A5
Nether Wallop 139 P2
Netley 269 K4
Netley Hill 249 P7
Netley Marsh 245 N5
New Alresford 167 P1
Newbridge 224 E9
New Brighton 277 N7
Newbury 16 C2
New Cheriton 187 H2
Newfound 67 N9
Newgrounds 241 L1
New Milton 326 C3
Newnham 71 L4
Newton 201 H5
Newton Stacey 124 A4
Newton Tony 118 D4
Newton Valence 172 A1
New Town 269 J1
Newtown 30 G2
Newtown 132 D7
Newtown 175 J5
Newtown 203 H1
Newtown 231 M4
Newtown 244 B9
Newtown 253 N4
Newtown 292 D2
Newtown 321 K5
Nob's Crook 208 A6
No Man's Land 165 N7
Nomansland 223 M4
Norleywood 310 D3
Normandy 77 N8
Norman 21 H1
North Baddesley 205 L9
North Boarhunt 253 L9
North Bockhampton . 305 J9
Northbourne 322 D3
Northbrook 126 F5
Northbrook 232 A3
North Camp 76 A6
North Charford 199 N9
North End 68 C4
North End 167 P6
North End 219 J2
North End 297 H7
Northfields 184 A7
North Gorley 240 F8
North Hayling 299 J6
North Houghton 141 J8
Northington 128 D9
North Kingston 282 D7
Northney 299 J5
North Oakley 66 G5
North Poulner 261 H6
North Ripley 305 H4
North Stoneham 228 F5

North Street 149 M9
North Street 220 F2
North Tidworth 79 J4
North Town 97 L1
North Waltham 88 C9
North Warnborough 72 B8
North Weirs 286 C8
Nursling 226 G7
Nursted 216 A6
Nutburn 205 M8
Nutcombe 156 C3
Nutley 109 N5
Nyewood 217 J5
Oakdale 320 G6
Oakhanger 153 J4
Oakley 288 E2
Oakley 500 F4
Oakridge 6 E1
Oakshott 191 K2
Ocean Village 248 E9
Odiham 93 L1
Ogdens 241 K6
Old Alresford 147 P7
Old Basing 70 D5
Old Burghclere 46 D5
Old Milton 326 C6
Old Netley 269 K1
Old Portsmouth 18 C4
Old Shirley 247 L2
Oliver's Battery 183 J3
Ossemsley 306 G7
Otterbourne 207 K1
Otterwood 289 P9
Outwick 220 C4
Overton 87 H4
Over Wallop 120 C7
Ower 167 K3
Owslebury 208 F2
Oxenwood 42 A2
Padworth 26 A6
Padworth Common 26 A6
Palestine 119 N3
Pamber End 50 E4
Pamber Green 50 F1
Pamber Heath 34 E4
Pamphill 278 A8
Pardown 88 F5
Park Gate 271 H5
Parkstone 333 K1
Parley Green 323 J1
Passfield 154 G7
Paulsgrove 296 C1
Peartree Green 248 F7
Peel Common 294 D7
Pennington 329 J5
Penton Corner 101 N1
Penton Grafton 81 L8
Penton Mewsey 101 K9
Penwood 29 P6
Perham Down 79 L4
Petersfield 215 K2
Pheonix Green 54 F9
Picket Hill 283 L1
Picket Piece 102 F3
Pig Oak 278 C3
Pikeshill 264 E4
Pilford 279 J6
Pilley 309 P6
Pilley Bailey 309 M6
Pitch Place 137 N6
Pitt 183 J1
Plaitford 202 A9
Plaitford Green 202 C5
Plastow Green 32 D7
Pokesdown 335 N2
Pondtail 74 G4
Pooksgreen 247 H9
Poole 320 D9
Popham 108 C6
Popley 69 M5
Portchester 295 M1
Portmore 309 N9
Portsea 18 E2
Portsea Island 297 K9
Portsmouth 18 C1
Port Solent 296 B2
Portswood 248 D2
Potbridge 72 F4
Poulner 261 H1
Pound Green 49 N2
Pound Street 30 B7
Powntley Copse 112 D5
Preston Candover 129 L1
Priddy's Hard 315 N1
Prince's Marsh 192 C4
Privett 189 L4
Privett 315 J5
Pucknall 181 K8
Purbrook 275 M5
Purewell 337 H1
Pylehill 230 C1
Pyott's Hill 70 B3
Quarley 100 A6
Quidhampton 87 H2
Racedown 99 N4
Rafborough 75 M9
Ragged Appleshaw 81 J5
Rake 193 J2
Ramsdean 192 C4
Ramsdell 50 B6
Ratlake 206 G3
Redbridge 246 G5
Reddenham 80 F4
Red Hill 277 H1
Red Hill 322 F3
Redlynch 200 A6
Red Rice 122 A1
Ridge 226 A3
Ridge Common 191 J9
The Ridges 40 C2
Ringwood 282 C1
Ripley 304 G6

Riseley 37 P3
Rockbourne 219 L3
Rockford 260 C5
Rogate 217 J2
Romford 258 B5
Romsey 204 C6
Ropley 169 N3
Ropley Dean 169 L2
Ropley Soke 149 P8
Rossmore 321 N5
Rotherwick 53 M7
Rotten Green 56 A8
Round Hill 287 M9
Row Ash 251 N5
Rowland's Castle 257 K9
Rowledge 115 P7
Rowner 294 G9
Rownhams 227 K5
Runfold 97 J8
Rushcombe Bottom .. 300 A6
Rushington 246 D5
Rushmoor 137 J2
Rushmoor 254 C1
St Austins 309 H8
St Catherine's Hill .. 324 C4
St Cross 183 P1
St Denys 248 E3
St Giles's Hill 23 H5
St Leonards 281 L4
St Mary Bourne 84 C2
Salters Heath 50 G5
Sandbanks 333 L8
Sandford 283 H9
Sandhurst 41 J5
Sandleheath 219 H9
The Sands 97 J9
Sandy Cross 97 M7
Sandy Down 309 J4
Sarisbury 270 E5
Sarson 101 H4
Seale 97 P7
Selborne 152 D9
Selsmore 319 K6
Setley 308 G3
Shalden 132 A1
Shalden Green 112 A6
Shaw 24 N2
Shawford 183 P4
Shedfield 252 B4
Sheet 191 P6
Shepherd's Hill 157 H7
Sherborne St John 50 D9
Sherfield English 202 D4
Sherfield on Loddon .. 52 F5
Sherfield Park 52 B8
Shipton Bellinger 98 F3
Shirley 247 P3
Shirley 305 L6
Shirley Holms 308 G7
Shirley Warren 247 N1
Shirrell Heath 252 E2
Shobley 261 L9
Sholing 249 K7
Sholing Common 249 L8
Shootash 203 K4
Shorley 186 F5
Shorn Hill 225 N9
Shortfield Common ... 116 B8
Shortheath 116 B4
Shortheath 153 K2
Shottermill 184 E1
Silchester 35 J6
Silkstead 182 G9
Sladen Green 63 J3
Sleaford 135 J8
Sleepers' Hill 164 E9
Smannell 83 J5
Soake 255 K8
Soberton 233 N6
Soberton Heath 253 L2
Soldridge 149 N6
Somerford 325 J8
Sopley 304 F9
Southampton 248 C2
South Baddesley 330 C1
South Bockhampton . 325 H3
Southbourne 336 C3
South Down 183 M9
South End 219 J9
South Farnborough 76 C5
South Gorley 240 F9
South Ham 68 G9
South Harting 216 E9
South Hayling 318 G6
Southington 86 F4
Southsea 18 D6
Southsea 316 F2
South Tidworth 79 H7
South Town 149 P5
South View 6 E3
South Warnborough .. 92 C8
South Weirs 286 D9
Southwick 274 A4
South Wonston 144 D5
Southwood 75 J1
Spanish Green 52 G2
Sparsholt 163 M4
Spearywell 179 K3
Spreakley 116 B9
Springbourne 323 L9
Stamshaw 296 B6
Stanbridge 278 C2
Standford 154 D1
Standon 182 C4
Stanford End 37 K5
Stanley Green 320 D6
Stanmore 183 M1
Stanpit 325 J9
Stapehill 279 N9
Steep 191 L7
Steep Marsh 192 B1
Sterte 320 D9
Steventon 87 P1
Stockbridge 141 L5

Stockheath 14 D2
Stoke 62 F8
Stoke 298 G7
Stoke Charity 126 A6
Stoke Common 208 A7
Stonehills 291 L7
Stoner Hill 191 H6
Stoney Cross 243 N7
Stony Batter 159 K7
Stonyford 223 L8
Stony Heath 49 N4
Stonymarsh 179 N5
The Straits 134 E7
Stratfield Mortimer 36 C1
Stratfield Saye 36 C6
Stratfield Turgis 53 H1
Street End 210 A9
Stroud 214 C1
Strouden 323 K6
Stroud Green 17 G5
Stubbermere 277 N2
Stubbington 294 B6
Stuckton 240 G4
Sulhampstead 26 D1
Sulhampstead Abbots . 27 H3
Sulhampstead Bannister
   Upper End 26 F2
Sutton Scotney 125 M5
Swampton 84 G9
Swanmore 232 F7
Swanmore 252 D3
Swanwick 270 G3
Swarraton 147 L1
Sway 308 A7
Swaythling 228 G9
Sydmonton 47 J1
Tadley 34 D7
Talbot Heath 322 B8
Talbot Village 322 C7
Talbot Woods 322 D8
Tangley 60 D6
Tapnage 272 A1
Terwick Common 193 M9
Testwood 246 C2
Thatcham 25 M3
Thorney Hill 306 A4
Thornhill 249 N6
Thornhill Park 249 N4
Thorns Beach 331 M1
Three Ashes 35 L7
Three Legged Cross .. 280 E1
Throop 323 K5
Thruxton 100 D2
Tichborne 166 M6
Tigh 218 D2
Tilford 117 K7
Tilford Common 117 H9
Tilford Reeds 117 H9
Tilly Down 80 H4
Timsbury 180 A7
Tipner 296 A4
Tiptoe 307 M8
Titchfield 293 L1
Titchfield Common .. 271 K9
Titchfield Park 97 M5
Tongham 97 M5
Totford 227 J3
Totford 128 E9
Tot Hill 30 D5
Totton 246 E1
Townhill Park 249 H1
Towns End 49 K5
Trickett's Cross 302 C1
Trotten Marsh 193 N7
Trotts 5 J5
Tuckton 336 D1
Tufton 105 K9
Tullecombe 193 L9
Tunworth 89 L5
Turbary Common 321 P2
Turgis Green 53 H2
Turkey Island 252 B2
Turmer 260 B2
Twyford 184 A8
Tye 299 J6
Ufton Green 26 D3
Ufton Nervet 26 E3
Up Green 39 P8
Upham 209 M7
Up Nately 71 J9
Upper Bullington 125 J8
Upper Burgate 220 E6
Upper Canterton 243 P5
Upper Clatford 102 C6
Upper Common 110 B3
Upper Enham 82 F6
Upper Farringdon ... 151 N5
Upper Froyle 113 N8
Upper Hale 96 G3
Upper Pennington .. 328 G4
Upper Ratley 203 M1
Upper Shirley 247 P1
Upper Slackstead ... 181 L5
Upper Street 220 D2
Upper Swanmore 232 G4
Upper Wield 130 D2
Upper Wootton 67 P2
Up Somborne 162 D2
Upton 43 H4
Upton 227 H5
Upton 500 A8
Upton Grey 90 C2
Upwood 194 B7
Vernham Bank 42 G7
Vernham Dean 42 G7
Vernham Row 42 F7
Vernham Street 43 J5
Verwood 258 F4
Wadwick 63 N6
Walhampton 329 N3
Walkford 326 D8
Wallington 11 K4
Wallington 322 A6
Waltham Chase 252 B2
Walton Heath 273 N5
Warblington 299 H1
Warnborough Green .. 72 A7

Warnford	212 A1	West End	294 C1	West Stratton	127 L4	Wildern	250 C4	Woodgreen	221 H4
Warren Corner	95 L1	West End Green	36 C6	West Tisted	169 P8	Wildhern	82 C1	Woodhouse	82 G5
Warren Corner	190 C1	Westfield	318 E6	West Town	318 E5	Wildmoor	52 F8	Woodington	205 H7
Warsash	270 D9	West Fields	16 B5	West Tytherley	159 J7	Wilsom	132 G6	Woodlands	245 L8
Wash Common	30 C1	West Green	54 E8	West Wellow	224 E1	Wimble Hill	95 J9	Woodlands Common	258 A4
Wash Water	30 A3	West Grimstead	176 C5	West Woodhay	28 D3	Wimborne Minster	278 E9	Woodley	204 C4
Wasing	33 N1	West Ham	68 F7	West Worldham	152 D1	Wimpson	247 J2	Woodmancott	108 C9
Waterditch	325 L2	West Harting	216 E6	Weybourne	96 F5	Winchester	22 E6	Woodside	329 L6
Water End	71 J6	West Heath	50 B4	Weyhill	81 J9	Winchfield	73 H2	Woodyates	195 H6
Waterford	329 N5	West Heath	57 M8	Wheat Hold	33 H8	Winchfield Hurst	73 K4	Woolmer Hill	156 B6
Waterloo	320 C3	West Howe	301 N9	Wheatley	134 E4	Winklebury	51 M4	Woolsbridge	280 G2
Waterlooville	275 L2	West Hurn	323 M1	Wherwell	123 J3	Winkton	324 G2	Woolston	248 G9
Wecock	164 E5	West Leigh	276 G5	Whitchurch	85 L6	Winnall	23 J3	Woolton Hill	29 L7
Weeke	164 E5	West Liss	192 D1	Whitehall	72 E6	Winslade	91 H6	Wootton	307 J6
Well	94 A9	West Meon	212 D1	Whitehill	153 P6	Winsor	245 K2	Wootton St Lawrence	68 A5
Wellow Wood	202 D5	West Meon Woodlands	188 E4	Whitehouse Green	27 J1	Wintershill	251 K3	Worlds End	254 C6
Westbourne	277 P5	West Moors	280 C2	Whiteley	271 K2	Winton	273 F8	Worting	68 D7
Westbourne	334 B4	Weston	215 H5	Whitenap	204 C6	Winton	68 D7	Wrecclesham	115 P4
West Cliff	8 A6	Weston	268 C2	Whiteparish	201 J1	Wittensford	244 D3	Wyck	133 N5
West Common	312 C2	Weston Colley	126 E5	Whitsbury	219 N1	Wivelrod	131 L8	Wyke	77 L9
West Dean	197 M5	Weston Common	249 K7	Whitway	46 C1	Wolverton	49 J4	Wymering	296 G1
West Down	123 K7	Weston Corbett	91 P9	Wick	198 G6	Wolverton Common	49 K1	Yateley	40 E8
West End	135 P1	Weston Patrick	92 A9	Wick	294 E6	Wonston	125 P6	York Town	57 P1
West End	149 L4	West Parley	302 F8	Wickham	252 D7	Woodcot	63 N2		
West End	249 N2	West Southbourne	336 B1	Widley	275 L8	Woodfalls	199 N8		

USING THE STREET INDEX

Street names are listed alphabetically. Each street name is followed by its postal town or area locality, the Postcode District, the page number, and the reference to the square in which the name is found.

Standard index entries are shown as follows:

Aaron Cl *CFDH* BH17 ....**321** H5

Street names and selected addresses not shown on the map due to scale restrictions are shown in the index with an asterisk:

Abbeywood *ASHV* GU12 * **76** C8

GENERAL ABBREVIATIONS

ACC	ACCESS	CTYD	COURTYARD	HLS	HILLS	MWY	MOTORWAY	SCH	SCHOOL
ALY	ALLEY	CUTT	CUTTINGS	HO	HOUSE	N	NORTH	SE	SOUTH EAST
AP	APPROACH	CV	COVE	HOL	HOLLOW	NE	NORTH EAST	SER	SERVICE AREA
AR	ARCADE	CYN	CANYON	HOSP	HOSPITAL	NW	NORTH WEST	SH	SHORE
ASS	ASSOCIATION	DEPT	DEPARTMENT	HRB	HARBOUR	O/P	OVERPASS	SHOP	SHOPPING
AV	AVENUE	DL	DALE	HTH	HEATH	OFF	OFFICE	SKWY	SKYWAY
BCH	BEACH	DM	DAM	HTS	HEIGHTS	ORCH	ORCHARD	SMT	SUMMIT
BLDS	BUILDINGS	DR	DRIVE	HVN	HAVEN	OV	OVAL	SOC	SOCIETY
BND	BEND	DRO	DROVE	HWY	HIGHWAY	PAL	PALACE	SP	SPUR
BNK	BANK	DRY	DRIVEWAY	IMP	IMPERIAL	PAS	PASSAGE	SPR	SPRING
BR	BRIDGE	DWGS	DWELLINGS	IN	INLET	PAV	PAVILION	SQ	SQUARE
BRK	BROOK	E	EAST	IND EST	INDUSTRIAL ESTATE	PDE	PARADE	ST	STREET
BTM	BOTTOM	EMB	EMBANKMENT	INF	INFIRMARY	PH	PUBLIC HOUSE	STN	STATION
BUS	BUSINESS	EMBY	EMBASSY	INFO	INFORMATION	PK	PARK	STR	STREAM
BVD	BOULEVARD	ESP	ESPLANADE	INT	INTERCHANGE	PKWY	PARKWAY	STRD	STRAND
BY	BYPASS	EST	ESTATE	IS	ISLAND	PL	PLACE	SW	SOUTH WEST
CATH	CATHEDRAL	EX	EXCHANGE	JCT	JUNCTION	PLN	PLAIN	TDG	TRADING
CEM	CEMETERY	EXPY	EXPRESSWAY	JTY	JETTY	PLNS	PLAINS	TER	TERRACE
CEN	CENTRE	EXT	EXTENSION	KG	KING	PLZ	PLAZA	THWY	THROUGHWAY
CFT	CROFT	F/O	FLYOVER	KNL	KNOLL	POL	POLICE STATION	TNL	TUNNEL
CH	CHURCH	FC	FOOTBALL CLUB	L	LAKE	PR	PRINCE	TOLL	TOLLWAY
CHA	CHASE	FK	FORK	LA	LANE	PREC	PRECINCT	TPK	TURNPIKE
CHYD	CHURCHYARD	FLD	FIELD	LDG	LODGE	PREP	PREPARATORY	TR	TRACK
CIR	CIRCLE	FLDS	FIELDS	LGT	LIGHT	PRIM	PRIMARY	TRL	TRAIL
CIRC	CIRCUS	FLS	FALLS	LK	LOCK	PROM	PROMENADE	TWR	TOWER
CL	CLOSE	FLS	FLATS	LKS	LAKES	PRS	PRINCESS	U/P	UNDERPASS
CLFS	CLIFFS	FM	FARM	LNDG	LANDING	PRT	PORT	UNI	UNIVERSITY
CMP	CAMP	FT	FORT	LTL	LITTLE	PT	POINT	UPR	UPPER
CNR	CORNER	FWY	FREEWAY	LWR	LOWER	PTH	PATH	V	VALE
CO	COUNTY	FY	FERRY	MAG	MAGISTRATE	PZ	PIAZZA	VA	VALLEY
COLL	COLLEGE	GA	GATE	MAN	MANSIONS	QD	QUADRANT	VIAD	VIADUCT
COM	COMMON	GAL	GALLERY	MD	MEAD	QU	QUEEN	VIL	VILLA
COMM	COMMISSION	GDN	GARDEN	MDW	MEADOWS	QY	QUAY	VIS	VISTA
CON	CONVENT	GDNS	GARDENS	MEM	MEMORIAL	R	RIVER	VLG	VILLAGE
COT	COTTAGE	GLD	GLADE	MKT	MARKET	RBT	ROUNDABOUT	VLS	VILLAS
COTS	COTTAGES	GLN	GLEN	MKTS	MARKETS	RD	ROAD	VW	VIEW
CP	CAPE	GN	GREEN	ML	MALL	RDG	RIDGE	W	WEST
CPS	COPSE	GND	GROUND	ML	MILL	REP	REPUBLIC	WD	WOOD
CR	CREEK	GRA	GRANGE	MNR	MANOR	RES	RESERVOIR	WHF	WHARF
CREM	CREMATORIUM	GRG	GARAGE	MS	MEWS	RFC	RUGBY FOOTBALL	WK	WALK
CRS	CRESCENT	GT	GREAT	MSN	MISSION	CLUB		WKS	WALKS
CSWY	CAUSEWAY	GTWY	GATEWAY	MT	MOUNT	RI	RISE	WLS	WELLS
CT	COURT	GV	GROVE	MTN	MOUNTAIN	RP	RAMP	WY	WAY
CTRL	CENTRAL	HGR	HIGHER	MTS	MOUNTAINS	RW	ROW	YD	YARD
CTS	COURTS	HL	HILL	MUS	MUSEUM	S	SOUTH	YHA	YOUTH HOSTEL

POSTCODE TOWNS AND AREA ABBREVIATIONS

ALDT	Aldershot	CHFD	Chandler's Ford	HAV	Havant	NMIL/BTOS	New Milton/	SHAM	Southampton
ALTN	Alton	CHIN	Chineham	HEND	Hedge End		Barton on Sea	SHST	Sandhurst
AMSY	Amesbury	CHOB/PIR	Chobham/Pirbright	HISD	Hayling Island	NTHA	Thatcham north	SSEA	Southsea
AND	Andover	CWTH	Crowthorne	HLER	Hamble-le-Rice	NTID	North Tidworth	STHA	Thatcham south
ASHV	Ash Vale	DEAN	Deane/Oakley	HORN	Horndean	NWBY	Newbury	STOK	Stockbridge
BDST	Broadstone	ELGH	Eastleigh	HSEA	Hilsea	ODIM	Odiham	SWGE	Swanage
BH/HW/K	Brighton Hill/	EMRTH	Emsworth/Southbourne	HTWY	Hartley Wintney	OVTN	Overton/Rural Basingstoke	TADY	Tadley
	Hatch Warren/	ENEY	Eastney	HUNG	Hungerford/Lambourn	PEW/UP	Pewsey/Upavon	THLE	Theale/Rural Reading
	Kempshott	EPSF	Petersfield east	ITCH	Itchen	PLE	Poole	TOTT	Totton
BKME/WDN	Branksome/Wallisdown	EWKG	Wokingham east	KSCL	Kingsclere/Rural Newbury	PSEA	Portsea	TWDS	Talbot Woods
BLKW	Blackwater	FARN	Farnborough	LIPH	Liphook	PSF	Petersfield	UPTN	Upton
BMTH	Bournemouth	FAWY	Fawley/Hythe	LISS	Liss	PSTN	Parkstone	VWD	Verwood
BOR	Bordon	FBDG	Fordingbridge	LSOL/BMARY	Lee-on-the-Solent/	RAND	Rural Andover	WBNE	Westbourne
BOSC	Boscombe	FERN	Ferndown/West Moors		Bridgemary	RCCH	Rural Chichester	WCLF	West Cliff
BPWT	Bishop's Waltham	FHAM	Fareham	LTDN	Littledown	RDGW/BURGH	Reading west/	WEND	West End
BROC	Brockenhurst	FHAM/PORC	Fareham/Porchester	LYMN	Lymington		Burghfield	WHAM	Wickham
BSTK	Basingstoke	FHAM/STUB	Fareham/Stubbington	LYND	Lyndhurst	RFNM	Rural Farnham	WHCH	Whitchurch
BWD	Bearwood	FLEETN	Fleet north	MARL	Marlborough	RGUW	Rural Guildford west	WIMB	Wimborne Minster
CBLY	Camberley	FLEETS	Fleet south	MFD/CHID	Milford/Chiddingfold	RGWD	Ringwood	WINC	Winchester
CCLF	Canford Cliffs	FNM	Farnham	MIDH	Midhurst	ROMY	Romsey	WSHM	Southampton west
CFDH	Canford Heath	FRIM	Frimley	MOOR/WNTN	Moortown/Winton	ROWN	Rownhams	WVILLE	Waterlooville/Denmead
CHAM	Cosham	FUFL	Fulflood/Winchester west	NARL	New Alresford	RSAL	Rural Salisbury	YTLY	Yateley
CHAR	Charminster	GPORT	Gosport	NBAD	North Baddesley	RWIN	Rural Winchester		
CHCH/BSGR	Christchurch/	GSHT	Grayshott	NBNE	Northbourne	SBNE	Southbourne		
	Bransgore	HASM	Haslemere	NEND	North End	SD/PW	St Denys/Portswood		

1

1st St *FAWY* SO45 ....291 H5
2nd St *FAWY* SO45 ....291 H5
3rd St *FAWY* SO45 ....291 H5
4th St *FAWY* SO45 ....291 H5
5th St *FAWY* SO45 ....291 H5
6th St *FAWY* SO45 ....290 G5
7th St *FAWY* SO45 ....290 G4
8th St *FAWY* SO45 ....290 G5
9th St *FAWY* SO45 ....290 F5
10th St *FAWY* SO45 ....290 G5
11th St *FAWY* SO45 ....290 F4
12th St *FAWY* SO45 ....290 F4
13th St *FAWY* SO45 ....290 F5
14th St *FAWY* SO45 ....290 E4

A

Aaron Cl *CFDH* BH17 ....321 H5
Aaron Ct *TOTT* SO40 ....247 K9
A Av *FAWY* SO45 ....290 F4
Abbett La *CBLY* GU15 ....58 A2
Abbey Cl *FAWY* SO45 ....268 C2
 NWBY RG14 ....17 F7
Abbey Ct *CHIN* RG24 ....69 K3
Abbeydore Rd *CHAM* PO6 ....274 E9
Abbeyfield Dr *FHAM* PO15 ....272 A8
Abbeyfields Cl *HLER* SO31 ....269 M4
Abbey Gdns *WIMB* BH21 ....279 M9
Abbey Hi *HLER* SO31 ....269 H5
Abbey Hill Cl *WINC* SO23 ....165 H5
Abbey Hill Rd *WINC* SO23 ....164 G5
Abbey Pk *THLE* RG7 ....27 H4
Abbey Pas *WINC* SO23 ....23 F5
Abbey Rd *BDST* BH18 ....300 A8
 ELGH SO50 ....229 P2
Abbey Spring La *BROC* SO42 ....289 L5
Abbey St *FNM* GU9 ....116 C1
Abbey Water *ROMY* SO51 ....204 C6
Abbey Wy *FARN* GU14 ....58 B9
Abbeywood *ASHV* GU12 * 76 C8
Abbotsbury Rd *BDST* SO16 ....300 A8
 ELGH SO50 ....229 P2
Abbots Dr *FHAM* PO15 ....272 B8
Abbots Wy *FHAM* PO15 ....272 B8
 HLER SO31 ....269 M4
Abbotstone Av *HAV* PO9 ....276 C6
Abbots Wy *FHAM* PO15 * 272 B8
 HLER SO31 ....269 M4
Abbotswell Rd *FBDC* SP6 ....241 K4
Abbott Cl *KBH* RG22 ....89 N1
 MOOR/WNTN BH9 ....322 C7
Abbotts Ann Rd *FUFL* SO22 ......164 E4
 RAND SP11 ....101 J5
Abbotts Cl *NTID* SP9 ....78 C4
 RAND SP11 ....101 N6
Abbotts Dro *ROMY* SO51 ....224 E3
Abbotts Rd *RAND* SP11 ....101 N7
Abbotts Rd *ELGH* SO50 ....228 G3
 NTID SP9 ....78 C4
 WINC SO23 ....165 H5
Abbotts Wy *FERN* BH22 ....280 C9
 PTSW SO17 ....248 D2
Abbotswood Cl *TADY* RG26 ....34 C7
A'Becket Ct *PSEA* PO1 ....18 D5
Abercrombie Gdns
 ROWN SO16 ....227 L8
Aberdare Av *CHAM* PO6 ....275 K9
Aberdare Rd *NBNE* BH10 ....322 E4
Aberdeen Cl *FHAM* PO15 ....10 B2
Aberdeen Rd *PTSW* SO17 * 248 E2
Aberdeen Ter *GSHT* GU26 ....156 C2
Aberdour Cl *WEND* SO18 ....249 K3
Abex Rd *NWBY* RG14 ....17 K2
Abingdon Dr
 CHCH/BSGR BH23 ....326 E7
Abingdon Gdns *ROWN* SO16 ....228 A9
Abingdon Rd *CFDH* BH17 ....320 C4
 SHST GU47 ....41 K6
Abinger Rd *LTDN* BH7 ....323 N9
Abney Rd *NBNE* BH10 ....322 D4
Aborn Pde *THLE* RG7 * 27 J4
Above Bar St *SHAM* SO14 ....20 D2
Above Town *RAND* SP11 ....102 C6
Abraham Cl *HEND* SO30 ....250 D6
Abshot Cl *FHAM/STUB* PO14 ....271 H9
Abshot Rd *FHAM/STUB* PO14 ...271 H9
Acacia Av *SHST* GU47 ....41 L5
 VWD BH31 ....306 A1
Acacia Gdns *HORN* PO8 ....256 B6
Acacia Rd *ITCH* SO19 ....249 H6
 LYMN SO41 ....327 P3
Academy Pl *SHST* GU47 ....41 M7
Acanthas Rd *CHAM* PO6 * 274 A8
Accentors Cl *ALTN* GU34 ....132 E3
Acer Wy *HAV* PO9 ....277 H6
Acheulian Cl *FNM* GU9 ....116 C3
Achilles Cl *CHIN* RG24 ....52 A9
Ackender Rd *ALTN* GU34 ....132 E6
Ackrells Md *SHST* GU47 ....41 G7
Ackworth Rd *HSEA* PO3 ....297 J8
Acland Rd *MOOR/WNTN* BH9 ...323 H7
Acorn Cl *BSTK* RG21 ....69 J9
 CHAM PO6 ....297 N1
 CHCH/BSGR BH23 ....324 D7
 FUFL SO22 ....164 G5
 LSOL/BMARY PO13 ....295 H8

 NMIL/BTOS BH25 ....327 L3
 RGWD BH24 ....281 L6
 TOTT SO40 ....267 L1
Acorn Ct *HLER* SO31 ....269 P2
Acorn Dr *NTHA* RG18 ....25 N2
 ROWN SO16 ....227 J5
Acorn Gv *CHFD* SO53 ....206 B9
Acorn Keep *FNM* GU9 ....96 D3
Acorn Rd *BLKW* GU17 ....41 J9
The Acorns *HLER* SO31 ....269 P2
 RGWD BH24 ....281 H9
 WIMB BH21 ....301 J1
Acorn Wy *VWD* BH31 ....258 G4
Acre Cl *AND* SP10 ....5 F4
Acre La *HORN* PO8 ....276 C1
Acre Pth *AND* SP10 ....5 F4
Acres Rd *BWD* BH11 ....322 B5
Acton Rd *NBNE* BH10 ....322 B6
Adair Rd *ENEY* PO4 ....317 J6
Adam Cl *TADY* RG26 ....33 P5
Adams Rd *HLER* SO31 ....316 G2
Adampur Rd *NTID* SP9 ....78 E7
Adams Cl *HEND* SO30 ....230 B9
Adams Cft *CHOB/PIR* GU24 * 59 P6
Adams Dr *FLEETN* GU51 ....74 E4
Adamsfield Gdns *NBNE* BH10 ...322 C5
Adams Ms *LIPH* GU30 ....175 J5
Adamson Cl *CHFD* SO53 ....206 F5
Adams Park Rd *FNM* GU9 ....96 D7
Adams Rd *FAWY* SO45 ....268 C8
Adams Wy *ALTN* GU34 ....132 C5
Adams Wood Dr *TOTT* SO40 .....267 K1
Adastral Rd *CFDH* BH17 ....320 C5
Adderbury Av *EMRTH* PO10 ......277 M6
Addington Pl
 CHCH/BSGR BH23 ....325 H9
Addiscombe Rd
 CHCH/BSGR BH23 ....324 E8
 CWTH RG45 ....41 K2
Addison Gdns *BROC* SO42 ....286 F9
Addison Cl * 207 K8
 ELGH SO50 ....316 C5
 ENEY PO4 ....316 D5
 HLER SO31 ....270 F4
Addison Sq *HLER* BH24 ....282 F2
Addison Cl *FUFL* SO22 ....183 L1
Addis Sq *PTSW* SO17 * 248 D2
Adelaide Cl *CHCH/BSGR* BH23 .324 D7
Adelaide Pl *FHAM/PORC* PO16 ...11 J6
Adelaide Rd *AND* SP10 ....4 E4
 PTSW SO17 * 248 E3
Adela Verne Cl *ITCH* SO19 ....249 N8
Adeline Rd *BMTH* BH1 ....335 L2
Adey Cl *ITCH* SO19 ....249 K9
Adey's Cl *NWBY* RG14 ....17 G5
Adhurst Rd *HAV* PO9 ....276 G6
Adlam's La *FAWY* SO41 ....307 P5
Adlington Pl *FARN* GU14 ....76 D2
Admers Crs *LIPH* GU30 ....175 J6
The Admiral Pk *HSEA* PO3 ....297 K6
Admirals Cl *FAWY* SO45 ....291 K6
Admiral's Keep
 LSOL/BMARY PO13 ....314 C2
Admirals Rd *HLER* SO31 ....271 H6
Admirals Wk *GPORT* PO12 ....315 K5
 PSEA PO1 ....18 B1
 WCLF BH2 * 8 A6
Admirals Wy *AND* SP10 ....5 K3
Admiralty Cl *GPORT* PO12 ....315 M2
Admiralty Rd *PSEA* PO1 ....18 C2
Admiralty Wy *CBLY* GU15 ....57 N1
Adrian Cl *HTWY* RG27 ....55 J8
Adsdean Cl *HAV* PO9 ....276 E6
Adstone La *HSEA* PO3 ....297 L5
Adur Cl *GPORT* PO12 ....315 K1
 WEND SO18 ....249 K2
Adwood Ct *STHA* RG19 ....25 P4
Aerial Rd *CHAM* PO6 ....274 D8
Aerodrome Rd
 LSOL/BMARY PO13 ....295 H5
Aerospace Bvd *FARN* GU14 ....75 N5
Africa Dr *TOTT* SO40 ....267 K1
Agars La *LYMN* SO41 ....308 A9
Aggis Farm Rd *VWD* BH31 ....258 E4
Aghemund Cl *CHIN* RG24 ....69 P1
Agincourt Rd *NEND* PO2 ....316 F1
Agitor Rd *FAWY* SO45 ....291 L4
Agnew Rd *LSOL/BMARY* PO13 ...294 C6
Agra Rd *NTID* SP9 ....78 E7
Agravaine Cl *AND* SP10 ....82 E8
Agricola Wk *AND* SP10 ....82 K8
Aikman La *TOTT* SO40 ....246 F7
Ailsa La *ITCH* SO19 ....248 F7
Ainger Cl *ASHV* GU12 ....3 K1
Ainsdale Rd *CHAM* PO6 ....275 J9
Ainsley Gdns *ELGH* SO50 ....230 D5
Aintree Cl *ELGH* SO50 ....230 D5
 NWBY RG14 ....17 J6
Aintree Dr *WVILLE* PO7 ....276 B1
Aintree Rd *TOTT* SO40 ....246 A2
Aird Cl *KSCL* RG20 ....29 M6
Airetons Cl *BDST* BH18 ....320 E1
Airfield Rd *CHCH/BSGR* BH23 ...325 K8
Airfield Wy *CHCH/BSGR* BH23 ..325 K8
Airlie Cnr *FUFL* SO22 ....164 F9
Airlie Rd *FUFL* SO22 ....22 B7
Airport Service Rd *HSEA* PO3 ...297 K4
Airspeed Rd
 CHCH/BSGR BH23 ....325 M8
Aisne Rd *FRIM* GU16 ....59 K4
Ajax Cl *CHIN* RG24 ....52 A9
Akenfield Cl *NMIL/BTOS* BH25 ...327 K2
Alameda Rd *WVILLE* PO7 ....275 M6
Alameda Wy *WVILLE* PO7 ....275 M6
Alamein Rd *ALDT* GU11 ....3 C1
 RAND SP11 ....82 F4
Alanbrooke Cl *HTWY* RG27 ....55 H7
Alanbrooke Rd *ALDT* GU11 ....76 C6

Alandale Rd *ITCH* SO19 ....249 M7
Alan Drayton Wy *ELGH* SO50 ...229 N2
Alan Gv *FHAM* PO15 ....10 A4
Albacore Av *HLER* SO31 * 270 E9
Albacore Cl
 LSOL/BMARY PO13 ....314 E3
Albany Cl *FLEETN* GU51 ....74 E4
 NMIL/BTOS BH25 ....327 H6
Albany Ct *BPWT* SO32 ....231 M6
Albany Dr *BPWT* SO32 ....231 N4
 WIMB BH21 ....280 C1
Albany Gdns *PLE* BH15 ....332 B1
Albany Pk *FRIM* GU16 ....58 B4
Albany Rd *AND* SP10 ....102 C3
 BPWT SO32 ....231 N4
 FAWY SO45 ....290 E5
 FLEETN GU51 ....74 D4
 ROMY SO51 ....204 C6
 SSEA PO5 ....19 J7
 WSHM SO15 ....247 N5
Albatross Wk
 LSOL/BMARY PO13 ....294 F7
Albemarle Av *GPORT* PO12 ......315 M1
Albemarle Rd *TWDS* BH3 ....322 F8
Albert Cl *HLER* SO31 ....269 L5
Albert Gv *SSEA* PO5 ....19 K7
Albert Rd *FLEETN* GU51 ....74 C3
 GPORT PO12 ....12 E1
Albion Cl *BKME/WDN* BH12 ......321 J5
 FHAM/PORC PO16 ....295 M3
Albion Pl *SHAM* SO14 ....20 D5
Albion Rd *CHCH/BSGR* BH23 ....324 D6
 FBDC SP6 ....240 D1
 FRIM GU16 ....58 D1
Albion Wy *VWD* BH31 ....258 C5
Albretia Av *HORN* PO8 ....255 M8
Albury Pl *CHFD* SO53 * 206 D4
Albury Wy *STHA* RG19 ....31 L2
Alby Rd *BKME/WDN* BH12 ....321 P7
Alcantara Crs *SHAM* SO14 ....21 H7
Alcester Rd *BKME/WDN* BH12 ...321 M6
Alcot Cl *CWTH* RG45 ....41 J2
Alderbrook Cl *CWTH* RG45 ....40 F7
Alder Cl *ALTN* GU34 ....132 E4
 ASHV GU12 ....76 F5
 CHCH/BSGR BH23 ....325 H6
 FAWY SO45 ....291 H5
 NWBY RG14 ....17 K6
 ROMY SO51 ....208 A5
 RWIN SO21 ....208 A5
 TOTT SO40 ....247 K9
Alder Crs *BKME/WDN* BH12 .....321 P5
Alder Dr *FBDC* SP6 ....239 M6
Alderfield *PSF* GU32 ....215 L2
Alder Gld *THLE* RG7 ....27 H4
Alder Gv *YTLY* GU46 ....40 D5
Alder Hts *BKME/WDN* BH12 .....322 A9
Alder Hill Dr *TOTT* SO40 ....245 P3
Alder Hills *BKME/WDN* BH12 ....322 A8
Alderholt Rd *FBDC* SP6 ....239 N2
Alder La *LSOL/BMARY* PO13 .....315 H5
Alderley Rd *NBNE* BH10 ....322 D3
Aldermaston Rd *TADY* RG26 .....34 A9
 TADY RG26 ....34 E9
Aldermaston Road Rbt
 CHIN RG24 ....69 J4
Aldermaston Rd South
 BSTK RG21 ....6 A2
Aldermoor Av *ROWN* SO16 ......227 L8
Aldermoor Cl *ROWN* SO16 ....227 N8
Aldermoor Rd
 LSOL/BMARY PO13 ....315 H1
 ROWN SO16 ....227 M8
 WVILLE PO7 ....275 M1
Aldermoor Rd East
 WVILLE PO7 ....275 M5
Aldermey Av
 BKME/WDN BH12 ....321 L3
 KBH RG22 ....89 M4
Alderney Cl *ROWN* SO16 ....227 J8
Alder Rd *BKME/WDN* BH12 .....321 P6
 BOR GU35 ....155 J2
 ROWN SO16 ....227 K9
Alders Cl *BSTK* RG21 ....7 K6
Aldershot Rd *ASHV* GU12 ....74 D4
 FLEETN GU51 ....74 D4
 FLEETS GU52 ....74 D4
Alders Rd *FHAM/PORC* PO16 ....294 F2
The Alders *FNM* GU9 ....96 G5
 NTHA RG18 ....25 N3
Alderwood Cl *CHIN* RG24 ....70 A1
Alderwood Av *CHFD* SO53 ....206 C7
Alderwood Cl *HAV* PO9 ....276 A7
Alder Wood Dr *HTWY* RG27 ......72 A2
Aldis Gdns *PLE* BH15 ....332 A1
Aldrich Rd *PSEA* PO1 ....316 C2
Aldridge Cl *HORN* PO8 ....256 A7
Aldridge Rd *FERN* BH22 ....302 E5
 NBNE BH10 ....322 E3
Aldridge Wy *FERN* BH22 * 302 F5
Aldsworth Cl *CHAM* PO6 ....274 E9
Aldsworth Gdns *CHAM* PO6 .....297 L1
Aldwell St *SSEA* PO5 ....19 J4
Aldwick Cl *FARN* GU14 ....57 P7
Aldworth Crs *KBH* RG22 ....69 H8

Aldworth Gdns *CWTH* RG45 ......41 H1
Alec Rose La *PSEA* PO1 ....19 G3
Alecto Rd *GPORT* PO12 ....12 C5
Alencon Cl *GPORT* PO12 ....295 N9
Alencon Link *BSTK* RG21 ....6 E5
Alexander Cl
 CHCH/BSGR BH23 ....325 J9
 STOK SO20 ....160 G2
 TOTT SO40 ....246 B3
 WVILLE PO7 * 275 M5
Alexander Gv
 FHAM/PORC PO16 ....294 E1
Alexander Rd *OVTN* RG25 ....86 C4
 STHA RG19 ....25 J5
Alexandra Av *CBLY* GU15 ....41 P9
 HISD PO11 ....318 F6
Alexandra Cl *FAWY* SO45 ....268 C6
Alexandra Ct *BOR* GU35 ....154 A5
 FARN GU14 ....76 B3
Alexandra Pk *NEND* PO2 ....296 F6
Alexandra Rd *ALDT* GU11 * 2 B3
 ALTN GU34 ....132 F4
 AND SP10 ....4 B4
 ASHV GU12 ....97 M2
 BSTK RG21 ....6 B6
 CHFD SO53 ....206 C5
 FARN GU14 ....76 B2
 FAWY SO45 ....268 C6
 FBDC SP6 ....240 D1
 LYMN SO41 ....329 J2
 PSEA PO1 ....19 F2
 PSTN BH14 ....321 N8
 SBNE BH6 ....335 P1
 WSHM SO15 ....247 P5
Alexandra St *ALDT* GU11 * 2 D3
 ODIM RG29 * 72 B8
Alexandra Wy *WEND* SO18 ......250 C4
 WSHM SO15 ....247 N6
Alfonso Cl *ASHV* GU12 ....3 J6
Alford Rd *TWDS* BH3 ....322 D8
Alfred Cl *FLEETN* GU51 ....74 A1
 TOTT SO40 ....246 A4
Alfred Gdns *AND* SP10 ....82 D9
Alfred Rd *FHAM/STUB* PO14 ....294 B6
 FNM GU9 ....116 C1
 PSEA PO1 ....19 F2
 PSTN BH14 ....321 N8
 SBNE BH6 ....335 P1
 WSHM SO15 ....247 P5
Alfrey Cl *WEND* SO18 * 250 C4
Alfriston Gdns *ITCH* SO19 ....249 K8
Alfriston Rd *FRIM* GU16 ....59 H6
Algiers Rd *HSEA* PO3 ....297 K9
Alhambra Rd *ENEY* PO4 ....316 C7
Alice Rd *ALDT* GU11 ....3 H2
Alington Cl *PSTN* BH14 ....333 L4
Alington Rd *PSTN* BH14 ....333 L4
 TWDS BH3 ....322 D9
Alipore Cl *PSTN* BH14 ....321 M9
Alison Cl *FARN* GU14 ....75 N1
Alison Wy *ALDT* GU11 ....2 B3
 FUFL SO22 ....22 C3
Allan Gv *ROMY* SO51 ....204 F6
Allaway Av *CHAM* PO6 ....296 B1
Allbrook Cl *HAV* PO9 ....276 D6
Allbrook Hi *ELGH* SO50 ....207 K6
Allbrook Knoll *ELGH* SO50 ....207 J6
Allbrook Wy *ELGH* SO50 ....207 J5
Allcot Rd *HAV* PO9 ....297 H7
Aliden Av *ASHV* GU12 ....97 K4
Allden Gdns *ASHV* GU12 ....97 K4
Allee Dr *LIPH* GU30 ....175 J2
Allenby Cl *CFDH* BH17 ....320 D2
Allenby Ct *CFDH* BH17 ....320 D2
Allenby Gv
 FHAM/PORC PO16 ....295 N2
Allenby Rd *CBLY* GU15 ....41 P8
 CFDH BH17 ....320 D2
 GPORT PO12 ....315 J2
Allen Cl *ALTN* GU34 ....132 C4
 BSTK RG21 ....69 J9
Allen Ct *WIMB* BH21 ....278 E9
Allendale Av *EMRTH* PO10 ....277 L7
Allendale Cl *SHST* GU47 ....41 N6
Allen Rd *HEND* SO30 ....250 C4
 WIMB BH21 ....300 E1
Allens La *BPWT* SO32 ....211 N8
Allen's Rd *SSEA* PO5 ....316 C6
Allens Rd *FHAM/PORC* PO16 ...278 E9
Allen Water Dr *FBDC* SP6 ....240 C1
Allerton Cl *TOTT* SO40 ....245 P3
Alliance Cl *LSOL/BMARY* PO13 .295 H9
Allington La *ELGH* SO50 ....230 A5
Allington Rd *WSHM* SO15 ....247 H4
Alliston Wy *KBH* RG22 ....89 M7
 WHCH RG28 ....47 J3
Almara Dr *WVILLE* PO7 ....275 M5
Allnutt Av *BSTK* RG21 ....7 K6
Allotment Rd *HLER* SO31 ....270 E5
All Saints Crs *FARN* GU14 ....57 M4
All Saints Rd *LYMN* SO41 ....329 L5
 NTHA RG18 ....25 N3
Alma Gdns *FRIM* GU16 ....59 J5
Alma La *BPWT* SO32 ....231 H2
 FNM GU9 ....96 C4
Alma Rd *BOR* GU35 ....154 B5
 BOR GU35 ....154 A5
 MOOR/WNTN BH9 ....322 C8
 ROMY SO51 ....204 D6
 SHAM SO14 ....248 C3
Alma St *GPORT* PO12 ....315 L2
Almatade Rd *WEND* SO18 ....249 J4
Almer Rd *PLE* BH15 ....320 A9
Almond Av *NWBY* RG14 ....24 D2
Almond Cl *CHIN* RG24 ....70 B6
 CHAM PO6 ....297 P1
 FARN GU14 ....57 P6
 HORN PO8 ....256 C7

Almond Dr *NTHA* RG18 ....25 N3
Almond Gv *BKME/WDN* BH12 ...321 M5
Almond Rd *WSHM* SO15 ....247 N6
Almondsbury Rd *CHAM* PO6 .....274 B8
Almondside
 LSOL/BMARY PO13 ....295 J8
Almswood Rd *TADY* RG26 ....34 B4
The Aloes *FLEETN* GU51 ....74 B4
Alphage Rd
 LSOL/BMARY PO13 ....295 K8
Alpha Rd *FUFL* SO22 ....97 K2
Alphington Av *FRIM* GU16 ....58 E4
Alphington Gn *FRIM* GU16 ....58 E4
 WEND SO18 ....249 K3
Alpine Cl *KBH* RG22 ....89 P5
 BOR GU35 ....154 A7
 RGWD BH24 ....282 A7
 TOTT SO40 ....245 M8
Alresford Dro *RWIN* SO21 ....144 C3
Alresford Rd *HAV* PO9 ....42 B5
 NARL SO24 ....167 M3
 RWIN SO21 ....165 N8
 WINC SO23 ....23 J5
Alsford Rd *WVILLE* PO7 ....275 M5
Alston Ms *STHA* RG19 ....25 J5
Alswitha Ter *WINC* SO23 * 22 E2
Alten Rd *WVILLE* PO7 ....275 M5
Althorpe Dr *HSEA* PO3 ....297 L5
Altona Gdns *AND* SP10 ....82 D8
Alton Cl *ELGH* SO50 ....230 B2
Alton Ct *FHAM/PORC* PO16 .....295 M3
Alton La *ALTN* GU34 ....150 C8
Alton Ride *BLKW* GU17 ....41 K8
Alton Rd *FLEETN* GU51 ....74 F3
 NBNE BH10 ....322 B6
 ODIM RG29 ....93 H7
 PSTN BH14 ....321 K9
 RFNM GU10 ....115 M3
Alton Rd East *PSTN* BH14 ....333 M1
Alum Chine Rd *WBNE* BH4 ....334 B5
Alum Cl *FAWY* SO45 ....290 F6
Alumdale Rd *WBNE* BH4 ....334 B4
Alumhurst Rd *WBNE* BH4 ....334 B4
Alum Wy *FHAM/PORC* PO16 ....273 J9
 WEND SO18 ....249 K4
Alvara Rd *GPORT* PO12 ....12 B6
Alver Bridge Vw *GPORT* PO12 ..12 D5
Alvercliffe Dr *GPORT* PO12 ....12 D4
Alver Rd *GPORT* PO12 ....12 D4
 PSEA PO1 ....316 C2
Alverstoke Gdns *ALDT* GU11 .....2 A5
Alverstone Rd *ENEY* PO4 ....317 J4
Alverton Av *PLE* BH15 ....321 H9
Alveston Av
 FHAM/STUB PO14 ....294 A1
Alwin Pl *FNM* GU9 ....96 C4
Alyth Rd *TWDS* BH3 ....322 D9
Amaryllis Cl *BSTK* RG21 ....271 L6
Amazon Cl *BSTK* RG21 ....6 A7
Ambarrow Crs *SHST* GU47 ....40 E5
Ambarrow La *CWTH* RG45 ....40 E4
Ambassador Cl
 CHCH/BSGR BH23 ....325 L9
Amber Cl *BOR* GU35 ....154 B5
Amber Gdns *AND* SP10 ....102 B2
Amber Hl *CBLY* GU15 ....58 G1
Amberley Cl
 CHCH/BSGR BH23 ....326 A7
 HEND SO30 ....250 F5
 NBAD SO52 ....205 J8
 NWBY RG14 ....24 C3
Amberley Crt *TOTT* SO40 ....246 C5
Amberley Gra *ALDT* GU11 ....2 B6
Amberley Rd *GPORT* PO12 ....15 G3
 HORN PO8 ....236 D7
 NEND PO2 ....297 H6
Amberslade Wk *FAWY* SO45 ....268 E2
Amberwood Cl *TOTT* SO40 ....246 C5
Amberwood Dr
 CHCH/BSGR BH23 ....326 C5
Amberwood Gdns
 CHCH/BSGR BH23 ....326 C5
Ambledale *HLER* SO31 ....270 E6
Ambleside *FARN* GU14 ....57 M9
 FRIM GU16 ....76 F2
Ambleside Crs *FNM* GU9 ....96 A5
Ambleside Gdns *ITCH* SO19 ....249 J8
Ambleside Rd *LYMN* SO41 ....329 L5
Ambrose Rd *TADY* RG26 ....34 B4
Ambury La *CHCH/BSGR* BH23 ..325 K7
Amersham Cl *GPORT* PO12 ....315 J4
Amery Hl *ALTN* GU34 ....132 E5
Amery St *ALTN* GU34 ....132 E5
Amesbury Rd *AMSY* SP4 ....118 B3
 RAND SP11 ....100 C1
 SBNE BH6 ....324 A9
Amethyst Gv *WVILLE* PO7 ....275 J1
Amethyst Rd
 CHCH/BSGR BH23 ....325 K8
Amey Gdns *TOTT* SO40 ....245 P2
Ameysford Rd *FERN* BH22 ....302 E1
Amey La *FERN* BH22 ....302 F1
Amherst Rd *BOR* GU35 ....153 P2
Amoy St *WSHM* SO15 ....248 B3
Ampere Rd *NWBY* RG14 ....17 G1
Ampfield Cl *HAV* PO9 ....276 B6
Ampfield Rd *CHAR* BH8 ....323 K4
 TOTT SO40 ....70 B4
 FUFL SO22 ....164 D4
Amport Cl *HAV* PO9 ....276 D4
Ampress La *LYMN* SO41 ....329 K1
Ampthill Rd *WSHM* SO15 ....248 B2
Amsterdam Sq
 CHCH/BSGR BH23 ....325 H8
Amyas Ct *ENEY* PO4 ....317 L4
Ancasta Rd *SHAM* SO14 ....248 C4
Ancells Rd *FLEETN* GU51 ....57 K6
Anchorage Rd *HSEA* PO3 ....297 K6
The Anchorage *GPORT* PO12 ....13 F1
Anchor Cl *BWD* BH11 ....301 P8
 CHCH/BSGR BH23 ....337 L1

RGUW GU3 ....77 P8
Anchor Ga PSEA PO1 ....316 C2
Anchor La PSEA PO1 ....18 B1
Anchor Meadow FARN GU14 ....57 N9
Anchor Ms LYMN SO41 ....329 L3
Anchor Rd BWD BH11 ....301 P8
KSCL RG20 ....48 C3
Anchor Yd BSTK RG21 ....7 F7
KSCL RG20 ....48 C3
Andalusian Gdns HLER SO31 ....271 H2
Andeferas Rd AND SP10 ....82 D8
Anderby Rd ROWN SO16 ....247 H1
Andersen Cl HLER SO31 ....271 J2
Anderson Cl HAV PO9 ....15 H2
ROMY SO51 ....204 G3
Anderson's Rd SHAM SO14 ....21 H6
Anders Rd RWIN SO21 ....144 F4
Anderwood Dr LYMN SO41 ....308 B6
Andes Cl SHAM SO14 ....21 J7
Andes Rd ROWN SO16 ....226 F9
Andlers Ash Rd LISS GU33 ....192 C4
Andover Cl CHCH/BSGR BH23 ....325 M8
Andover Dro KSCL RG20 ....30 A2
Andover La RAND SP11 ....80 A4
Andover Rd BLKW GU17 ....41 K8
DEAN RG23 ....88 B2
ENEY PO4 ....317 H6
FUFL SO22 ....22 D1
KSCL RG20 ....30 B3
NWBY RG14 ....24 B8
OVTN RG25 ....87 N3
RAND SP11 ....79 P1
RAND SP11 ....80 D3
RAND SP11 ....81 H8
RAND SP11 ....101 L4
RWIN SO21 ....107 H8
WSHM SO15 ....247 P5
Andover Rd North FUFL SO22 ....144 D9
Andover Wy ALDT GU11 ....97 H4
Andrewartha Rd FARN GU14 ....76 D3
Andrew Bell St PSEA PO1 ....316 E2
Andrew Cl FAWY SO45 ....268 C9
PSEA PO1 ....317 H2
TOTT SO40 ....246 B4
Andrew Crs WVILLE PO7 ....275 M1
Andrewes Cl BPWT SO32 ....232 A4
Andrew La NMIL/BTOS BH25 ....327 M5
Andrew Pl FHAM/STUB PO14 ....293 P7
Andrews Cl BWD BH11 ....322 A4
FLEETS GU52 ....74 D6
Andrew's La NARL SO24 ....170 A2
ODIM RG29 ....93 M8
Andrews Rd FARN GU14 ....57 M8
Andromeda Rd ROWN SO16 ....227 J8
Andwell La HTWY RG27 ....71 H6
Anfield Cl ELGH SO50 ....230 C3
Angel Ct NWBY RG14 ....24 D3
Angel Crs ITCH SO19 ....249 J4
Angelica Gdns ELGH SO50 ....230 C5
Angelica Wy FHAM PO15 ....271 L2
Angeline Cl CHCH/BSGR BH23 ....326 B7
Angel La FERN BH22 ....302 B5
NMIL/BTOS BH25 ....327 M7
Angel Mdw ODIM RG29 ....72 D9
Angelo Cl WVILLE PO7 ....276 A2
Angelus Cl FHAM/STUB PO14 ....294 A7
Angerstein Rd NEND PO2 ....296 F8
Anglers Pl BSTK RG21 ....7 K6
Anglers Wy HLER SO31 ....270 D2
Anglesea Rd
LSOL/BMARY PO13 ....314 E4
PSEA PO1 ....19 F3
WSHM SO15 ....247 M2
Anglesea Ter SHAM SO14 ....21 H6
Anglesey Arms Rd
GPORT PO12 ....12 A7
Anglesey Av FARN GU14 ....57 N6
Anglesey Cl AND SP10 ....102 E5
CHIN RG24 ....69 M2
Anglesey Rd ASHV GU12 ....3 K4
GPORT PO12 ....12 A7
Anglesey Vw GPORT PO12 * 12 D4
Angora Wy FLEETN GU51 ....56 E9
Angus Cl FHAM PO15 ....10 A2
Anjou Cl BWD BH11 ....301 M8
Anjou Crs FHAM PO15 ....272 B8
Anker La FHAM/STUB PO14 ....294 A5
Ankerwyke
LSOL/BMARY PO13 ....294 F8
Anmore Cl HAV PO9 ....276 D6
Anmore Dr WVILLE PO7 ....255 M9
Anmore La WVILLE PO7 ....255 L7
Anmore Rd WVILLE PO7 ....255 J7
Anna La CHCH/BSGR BH23 ....304 E4
Annandale Dr RFNM GU10 ....116 D4
Anne Armstrong Cl ALDT GU11 ....76 C7
Anne Cl CHCH/BSGR BH23 ....324 E6
Anne Crs WVILLE PO7 ....275 N4
Annerley Rd BMTH BH1 ....9 K2
Annes Wy FLEETS GU52 ....74 E6
Annet Cl PLE BH15 ....332 A1
Annettes Cft FLEETS GU52 ....74 B8
Ann's Hill Rd GPORT PO12 ....12 A3
Ansell Rd FRIM GU16 ....58 D5
Anson Cl ALDT GU11 ....2 B1
CHCH/BSGR BH23 ....325 K9
LSOL/BMARY PO13 ....315 H3
RGWD BH24 ....282 C1
Anson Dr ITCH SO19 ....249 L7
Anson Gv FHAM/PORC PO16 ....273 P9
Anson Rd ELGH SO50 ....230 C5
ENEY PO4 ....317 H3
Anstey Cl BSTK RG21 ....90 C1
BWD BH11 ....322 A1
Anstey La ALTN GU34 ....132 F1
Anstey Mill Cl ALTN GU34 ....133 H4
Anstey Mill La ALTN GU34 ....133 H4
Anstey Pl THLE RG7 ....27 J4
Anstey Rd ALTN GU34 ....132 G5
BWD BH11 ....322 A2
ROMY SO51 ....204 F4
Antar Cl BSTK RG21 ....6 A7
Antell's Wy FBDG SP6 ....239 N5
Anthill Cl WVILLE PO7 ....254 E6
Anthony Gv GPORT PO12 ....295 K8
Anthony Pl GSHT GU26 * 156 E4
Anthony's Av PSTN BH14 ....333 L2
Antler Dr NMIL/BTOS BH25 ....326 G3
Anton Cl DEAN RG23 ....88 F2
ROMY SO51 ....204 G6
Anton La RAND SP11 ....82 F5
Anton Mill Rd AND SP10 ....4 C7
Anton Rd AND SP10 ....4 C7
Antrim Cl KBH RG22 ....68 E9
Anvil Cl HORN PO8 ....276 C1
TADY RG26 ....52 A2
Anvil Crs BDST BH18 ....300 A8
Anvil Wy TADY RG26 ....52 A2
Anzac Cl FHAM/STUB PO14 ....294 A5
Anzio Cl ALDT GU11 ....2 E2
Apex Dr FRIM GU16 ....58 C4
Apless La WVILLE PO7 ....254 B7
Apollo Cl BKME/WDN BH12 ....321 M5
Apollo Dr BOR GU35 ....154 B6
WVILLE PO7 ....275 P7
Apollo Pl WEND SO18 * 249 J4
Apollo Ri FARN GU14 ....57 L9
Apollo Rd CHFD SO53 ....207 H6
Appelford Cl STHA RG19 ....25 N5
Apple Cl BKME/WDN BH12 ....334 A2
Appledore Ms FARN GU14 ....57 P6
Appledown Cl NARL SO24 ....168 A3
Appledown La NARL SO24 ....168 B4
Applegarth Cl BSTK RG21 ....69 M9
Applegate Pl HORN PO8 * 256 C6
Apple Gv CHCH/BSGR BH23 ....324 C5
EMRTH PO10 ....277 P9
Applelands Cl RFNM GU10 ....116 A6
Appleshaw Cl FUFL SO22 ....164 E3
TADY RG26 ....34 C7
Appleshaw Gn HAV PO9 ....276 C6
Appleshaw Wy RAND SP11 ....79 M5
Appleslade Wy
NMIL/BTOS BH25 ....327 K2
Appleton Cl STOK SO20 ....120 C8
Appleton Rd FHAM PO15 ....272 B9
WEND SO18 ....248 G2
Appleton Vw ALTN GU34 ....171 L2
Apple Tree Cl NWBY RG14 ....24 B8
RSAL SP5 ....199 P6
Appletree Cl DEAN RG23 ....88 F3
NMIL/BTOS BH25 ....327 J6
SBNE BH6 ....336 A1
TOTT SO40 ....246 A3
Appletree Ct HEND SO30 ....250 G4
LYND SO43 ....264 G6
Apple Tree Gv AND SP10 ....102 B1
FERN BH22 ....302 E3
Apple Tree Rd FBDG SP6 ....239 M6
Appletree Rd RSAL SP5 ....199 P6
Apple Tree Wy SHST GU47 ....41 L5
Apple Wy CHIN RG24 ....70 C7
Applewood Gdns ITCH SO19 ....249 J8
Applewood Gv WVILLE PO7 ....275 L8
Applewood Pl TOTT SO40 ....246 A5
Approach Rd FNM GU9 ....116 C1
PSTN BH14 ....321 K9
The Approach HSEA PO3 * 297 J8
April Cl BWD BH11 ....322 A3
CBLY GU15 ....58 B3
WEND SO18 ....249 K4
April Gv HLER SO31 ....270 E7
April Sq PSEA PO1 ....19 J1
Apron Rd STHA RG19 ....31 M1
Apsley Cl AND SP10 ....102 D5
Apsley Crs CFDH BH17 ....320 E3
Apsley Pl CHFD SO53 ....206 D4
Apsley Rd ENEY PO4 ....317 J4
Aquila Wy HLER SO31 ....269 P8
Arabian Gdns FHAM PO15 ....271 J3
Aragon Rd YTLY GU46 * 56 D1
Aragon Wy MOOR/WNTN BH9 ....323 H2
The Arboretum OVTN RG25 ....92 B5
The Arcade ALDT GU11 * 2 E3
BMTH BH1 ....8 D4
LISS GU33 ....192 C1
Arcadia Av CHAR BH8 ....323 H8
Arcadia Cl DEAN RG23 ....89 L7
ROWN SO16 ....227 M9
Arcadia Rd CHCH/BSGR BH23 ....324 D6
Archdale Cl NBNE BH10 ....322 D5
Archers WSHM SO15 * 248 B4
Archers Cl TOTT SO40 ....246 A1
Archers Rd ELGH SO50 ....207 J9
WSHM SO15 ....248 A5
Archery Flds ODIM RG29 ....72 E9
Archery Gdns ITCH SO19 ....249 H9
Archery Gv ITCH SO19 ....248 G9
Archery La FHAM/PORC PO16 ....11 J4
WINC SO23 ....22 C5
Archery Ri ALTN GU34 ....132 E7
Archery Rd ITCH SO19 ....268 G1
Archway Rd CCLF BH13 ....321 N8
Arcot Rd NTID SP9 ....78 F8
Arden Cl WEND SO18 ....249 K2
Arden Rd MOOR/WNTN BH9 ....322 F4
Arden Wk NMIL/BTOS BH25 ....327 K5
Ardglen Rd WHCH RG28 ....85 K6
Ardingly Crs HEND SO30 ....250 D1
Ardington Ri WVILLE PO7 ....275 N7
Ardmore Rd PSTN BH14 ....321 K8
Ardrossan Av CBLY GU15 ....58 F1
Ardwell Cl CWTH RG45 ....40 F1
Arena La ALDT GU11 ....75 M8
Arenal Dr CWTH RG45 ....41 J3
Arford Common BOR GU35 ....154 G2
Arford Rd BOR GU35 ....154 G2
Argente Cl FLEETN GU51 ....56 E9
Argent Ter SHST GU47 * 41 M6
Argosy Cl HLER SO31 ....270 F9
Argus Rd LSOL/BMARY PO13 ....314 D1
Argyle Cl BOR GU35 ....154 A6
Argyle Crs FHAM PO15 ....10 B3
Argyle Rd CHCH/BSGR BH23 ....337 J1
NWBY RG14 ....16 D4
SHAM SO14 ....21 F2
Argyle St CHOB/PIR GU24 ....59 M7
Argyll Rd BKME/WDN BH12 ....321 M6
BOSC BH5 ....335 L2
Ariel Cl SBNE BH6 ....336 F2
Ariel Dr SBNE BH6 ....336 F2
Ariel Rd PSEA PO1 ....316 G3
Ark Dr FERN BH22 * 302 F5
Arkle Av STHA RG19 ....25 J4
Ark Royal Crs
LSOL/BMARY PO13 ....314 C1
Arkwright Cl KSCL RG20 ....29 N8
Arle Cl HORN PO8 ....236 C8
NARL SO24 ....167 P1
Arle Gdns NARL SO24 ....168 A1
Arley Rd PSTN BH14 ....333 J1
Arlington Ct NMIL/BTOS BH25 ....327 K7
Arlington Pl WINC SO23 ....22 E3
Arlington Ter ALDT GU11 ....2 C3
Arliss Rd ROWN SO16 ....247 L2
Arlott Ct WSHM SO15 ....248 A4
Arlott Dr BSTK RG21 ....7 F2
Armada Cl ROWN SO16 ....227 J5
Armada Dr FAWY SO45 ....268 B8
Arminers Cl GPORT PO12 ....315 M7
Armitage Av FAWY SO45 ....268 B9
Armitage Dr FRIM GU16 ....58 E4
Armory La PSEA PO1 ....18 D5
The Armoury TOTT SO40 * 247 L8
Armstrong Cl BROC SO42 ....286 E8
RWIN SO21 ....144 F4
WVILLE PO7 ....255 M9
Armstrong Ct ROWN SO16 ....227 K7
Armstrong La BROC SO42 ....286 E8
Armstrong Ml FARN GU14 ....57 L9
Armstrong Ri AND SP10 ....82 C8
Armstrong Rd BROC SO42 ....286 E8
CHIN RG24 ....69 P5
Armstrong Wy FARN GU14 ....75 J3
Armsworth La BPWT SO32 ....253 P1
Arnaud Cl NEND PO2 ....316 F1
Arne Av BKME/WDN BH12 ....321 N5
Arne Cl KBH RG22 ....89 P4
Arne Crs BKME/WDN BH12 ....321 N5
Arnewood Bridge Rd
LYMN SO41 ....307 P9
Arnewood Rd SBNE BH6 ....336 A1
Arnheim Cl ROWN SO16 ....227 N8
Arnheim Rd ROWN SO16 ....227 P8
Arnhem Cl ALDT GU11 ....3 G2
Arnhem Rd NWBY RG14 ....17 H2
Arnold Cl FERN BH22 ....280 E6
Arnold Rd ELGH SO50 ....229 J4
FERN BH22 ....280 E6
PTSW SO17 ....248 E1
Arnolds Cl NMIL/BTOS BH25 ....327 H7
Arnside Rd WVILLE PO7 ....275 N2
Arnwood Av FAWY SO45 ....290 B1
Aron Cl PSF GU32 ....215 L3
Arragon Ct WVILLE PO7 ....276 A2
Arran Cl CHAM PO6 ....275 H9
DEAN RG23 ....88 E1
Arran Wy CHCH/BSGR BH23 ....326 D6
Arreton HLER SO31 ....269 L4
Arrow Cl ELGH SO50 ....207 J9
ITCH SO19 ....268 F1
Arrow La HTWY RG27 ....54 G6
Arrow Rd FARN GU14 ....75 N2
Arrowsmith La WIMB BH21 ....300 G6
Arrowsmith Rd WIMB BH21 ....300 F7
Arters Lawn TOTT SO40 ....266 F4
Arthur Cl FNM GU9 ....116 B1
WCLF BH2 ....334 F1
Arthur La CHCH/BSGR BH23 ....324 E8
Arthur Rd CHCH/BSGR BH23 ....324 E8
ELGH SO50 ....207 J9
FNM GU9 ....116 C1
NWBY RG14 ....16 B4
WINC SO23 ....22 E1
WSHM SO15 ....247 P4
Arthurs Gdns HEND SO30 ....230 B9
Arthur St ALDT GU11 ....3 F4
NEND PO2 ....316 G1
Artillery Cl CHAM PO6 ....296 E1
Artillery Dr STHA RG19 ....25 P6
Artillery Rd ALDT GU11 * 3 F2
ALDT GU11 ....76 C5
Artillery Ter ENEY PO4 * 317 K4
Artists Wy AND SP10 ....4 C2
Arun Cl EPSF GU31 ....215 L3
Arun Ct BSTK RG21 ....7 J6
Arundel Cl FLEETN GU51 ....74 E4
LIPH GU30 ....154 E8
NARL SO24 ....168 A3
NMIL/BTOS BH25 ....326 G4
Arundel Dr FHAM/PORC PO16 ....10 E4
Arundel Gdns DEAN RG23 ....68 E5
Arundel Pl FNM GU9 * 96 B9
Arundel Rd CBLY GU15 ....59 H1
ELGH SO50 ....207 J7
GPORT PO12 ....315 K3
TOTT SO40 ....246 E3
Arundel St PSEA PO1 ....19 G2
Arundel Wy CHCH/BSGR BH23 ....326 B8
Arun Rd WEND SO18 ....249 K1
Arun Wy ROMY SO51 ....224 D1
Arwood Av TADY RG26 ....34 E6
Ascension Cl CHIN RG24 ....69 M3
Ascham Rd BMTH BH1 ....335 H1
Ascot Cl ALTN GU34 ....132 G7
FHAM/STUB PO14 ....271 J8
NWBY RG14 ....17 J7
Ascot Ct ALDT GU11 ....2 E4
Ascot Rd BDST BH18 ....300 C9
ELGH SO50 ....230 D5
HSEA PO3 ....317 J1
Ascott Wy NWBY RG14 ....24 G3
Ascupart St SHAM SO14 ....21 G4
Asford Gv ELGH SO50 ....207 M9
Ashbarn Crs FUFL SO22 ....183 M1
Ashbourne Cl ASHV GU12 ....77 H9
Ashbourne Rd BOSC BH5 ....335 P1
Ashbourne Wy STHA RG19 ....25 L4
Ashbridge Ri CHFD SO53 ....206 C4
Ashburn Garth RGWD BH24 ....283 H3
Ashburnham Cl ITCH SO19 ....248 F6
Ashburton Cl FAWY SO45 ....267 P7
NARL SO24 ....167 P2
Ashburton Gdns NBNE BH10 ....322 D6
Ashburton Rd GPORT PO12 ....315 K6
NARL SO24 ....167 P2
SSEA PO5 ....316 E6
Ashbury Dr FARN GU14 ....57 P4
Ashbury Rd BOR GU35 ....154 A6
Ashby Rd ITCH SO19 ....249 K8
TOTT SO40 ....246 B4
Ash Church Rd ASHV GU12 ....97 P1
Ash Cl ASHV GU12 ....76 G9
BLKW GU17 ....41 K9
FAWY SO45 ....290 C1
FBDG SP6 ....239 N6
FHAM/STUB PO14 ....10 A7
GPORT PO12 ....12 C3
HLER SO31 ....269 P2
HORN PO8 ....255 N8
ITCH SO19 ....249 L5
NBAD SO52 ....205 K8
NTID SP9 ....79 J4
ROMY SO51 ....204 G7
RWIN SO21 ....207 P5
Ash Copse HORN PO8 ....255 P6
Ashcroft La HORN PO8 ....257 K5
Ashdell Rd ALTN GU34 ....132 G6
Ashdene WSHM SO15 ....247 M3
Ashdene Cl WIMB BH21 ....278 F9
Ashdene Crs ASHV GU12 ....76 F9
Ashdene Rd ASHV GU12 ....76 F9
TOTT SO40 ....245 P9
Ashdown FAWY SO45 ....291 H6
LSOL/BMARY PO13 ....295 H8
Ashdown Av FARN GU14 ....76 D2
Ashdown Cl CFDH BH17 ....320 G3
CHFD SO53 ....206 E3
Ashdown Dr CHFD SO53 ....206 E3
Ashdown Rd CHFD SO53 ....206 E4
FAWY SO45 ....291 H7
Ashdown Ter NTID SP9 ....79 H6
Ashdown Wk
NMIL/BTOS BH25 ....327 L5
Ashdown Wy ROMY SO51 ....204 F6
Ashen Cl CHFD SO53 ....206 E5
Ashe Rd HAV PO9 ....277 H5
Ashfield CHIN RG24 ....70 A1
Ashfield Gn YTLY GU46 ....40 G9
Ashfield Rd AND SP10 ....102 B2
Ashfields RWIN SO21 ....124 F3
Ashford Cl CHAM PO6 ....274 G9
FBDG SP6 ....240 B2
Ashford Crs FAWY SO45 ....268 D7
Ashford Hill Rd STHA RG19 ....32 A4
Ashford Rd FBDG SP6 ....240 A3
SBNE BH6 ....324 B8
Ash Green La West ASHV GU12 ....97 M3
Ash Gv CHIN RG24 ....70 D6
KSCL RG20 ....48 C3
LIPH GU30 ....175 L4
LYMN SO41 ....328 D7
RGWD BH24 ....282 G2
TOTT SO40 ....246 A9
Ash Hill Rd ASHV GU12 ....76 G9
Ashington Cl HORN PO8 ....256 A8
Ashington Gdns WIMB BH21 ....300 B5
Ashington La WIMB BH21 ....300 C4
Ashington Pk
NMIL/BTOS BH25 ....327 K6
Ash La TADY RG26 ....33 P5
TADY RG26 ....35 L9
THLE RG7 ....27 J3
Ashlawn Gdns AND SP10 ....4 E7
Ashlea HTWY RG27 ....72 A2
Ashlea Cl ELGH SO50 ....230 D2
Ashleigh Cl FAWY SO45 ....290 C1
Ashleigh Ri NBNE BH10 ....322 D5
Ashlet Gdns NMIL/BTOS BH25 ....327 M3
Ashlett Cl FAWY SO45 ....291 L6
Ashlett Rd FAWY SO45 ....291 L6
Ashley Cl BMTH BH1 ....323 L9
FRIM GU16 ....58 F7
FUFL SO22 ....164 D4
HAV PO9 ....276 D6
HLER SO31 ....271 H3
HORN PO8 ....255 P6
RFNM GU10 ....95 H4
RGWD BH24 ....283 H3
Ashley Common Rd
NMIL/BTOS BH25 ....327 L3
Ashley Ct HLER SO31 ....250 A9
Ashley Crs ITCH SO19 ....249 L9
Ashleycross Cl FAWY SO45 ....290 F6
Ashley Dr BLKW GU17 ....57 K1
RGWD BH24 ....260 A6
Ashley Dr North RGWD BH24 ....281 M4
Ashley Dr South RGWD BH24 ....281 M4
Ashley Dr West RGWD BH24 ....281 M4
Ashley Dro MARL SN8 ....42 C1
Ashley Gdns BPWT SO32 ....232 C9
CHFD SO53 ....206 G8
DEAN RG23 ....88 F1
Ashley La LYMN SO41 ....329 L4
NMIL/BTOS BH25 ....327 M3
Ashley Mdw ROMY SO51 ....204 E5
Ashley Meads
NMIL/BTOS BH25 ....327 M3
Ashley Pk RGWD BH24 ....281 N3
Ashley Rd ALTN GU34 ....131 H4
BMTH BH1 ....323 L9
FARN GU14 ....58 C9
NMIL/BTOS BH25 ....327 L4
PSTN BH14 ....321 L7
Ashling Cl CHAR BH8 ....323 J7
WVILLE PO7 ....255 H7
Ashling Gdns WVILLE PO7 ....255 H7
Ashling La NEND PO2 ....296 F9
Ashling Park Rd WVILLE PO7 ....255 H7
Ash Lodge Cl ASHV GU12 ....97 N2
Ash Lodge Dr ASHV GU12 ....97 N2
Ashlyn Cl FHAM PO15 ....271 P9
Ashmead BOR GU35 ....154 A5
Ashmead Rd ROWN SO16 ....227 K9
Ashmeads Cl WIMB BH21 ....279 J8
Ashmeads Wy WIMB BH21 ....279 J8
Ashmoor La CHIN RG24 ....70 F6
Ashmore WIMB BH21 ....300 F1
Ashmore Av NMIL/BTOS BH25 ....327 K7
PLE BH15 ....332 B2
Ashmore Cl RSAL SP5 ....201 K1
Ashmore Crs PLE BH15 ....332 B2
Ashmore Gv
CHCH/BSGR BH23 ....326 A6
Ashmore La RSAL SP5 ....177 K9
Ashmore Rd FUFL SO22 ....164 D6
Ashridge FARN GU14 ....57 N6
Ashridge Av NBNE BH10 ....322 D2
Ashridge Cl WSHM SO15 ....248 B3
Ashridge Ct NWBY RG14 ....17 F4
Ashridge Gdns NBNE BH10 * 322 D2
Ash Rd ASHV GU12 ....3 K6
KSCL RG20 ....31 M3
TOTT SO40 ....245 P9
Ash St ASHV GU12 ....97 N2
Ashtead Cl FHAM/PORC PO16 ....295 L1
Ashton Cl BPWT SO32 ....231 N3
Ashton Cross ROMY SO51 ....224 G2
Ashton La BPWT SO32 ....231 N2
Ashton Pl CHFD SO53 * 206 D4
Ashton Rd MOOR/WNTN BH9 ....322 F5
NWBY RG14 ....17 G3
Ashton Wy FHAM/STUB PO14 ....294 B9
Ash Tree Cl DEAN RG23 ....88 E3
FARN GU14 ....75 K1
HASM GU27 ....157 L4
Ashtree Cl NMIL/BTOS BH25 ....327 M5
Ash Tree Rd AND SP10 ....102 A2
WEND SO18 ....248 G2
Ashurst Bridge Rd TOTT SO40 ....246 A5
Ashurst Cl FUFL SO22 ....164 E4
ITCH SO19 ....269 J1
TADY RG26 ....34 B6
TOTT SO40 ....245 P9
Ashurst Rd ASHV GU12 ....76 E8
CHAM PO6 ....296 G1
CHAR BH8 ....323 K4
FERN BH22 ....280 D6
Ashwood FHAM PO15 ....271 L5
HLER SO31 ....271 J8
Ashwood Cl HAV PO9 ....276 B7
HISD PO11 ....318 G5
Ashwood Dr BDST BH18 ....300 E9
NWBY RG14 ....24 G3
Ashwood Gdns ROWN SO16 ....228 A9
TOTT SO40 ....246 A5
Ashwood Wy DEAN RG23 ....68 G5
Ashworth Dr STHA RG19 ....25 M5
Aspen Av HLER SO31 ....292 D1
Aspen Cl BOR GU35 ....154 A7
HEND SO30 ....250 D4
RWIN SO21 ....208 A5
Aspen Dr VWD BH31 ....259 H4
Aspen Gdns BKME/WDN BH12 ....321 P5
HTWY RG27 ....72 A2
Aspen Gv ASHV GU12 ....97 L3
Aspengrove
LSOL/BMARY PO13 ....295 J8
Aspen Holt ROWN SO16 ....228 C7
Aspen Pl NMIL/BTOS BH25 ....327 K6
Aspen Rd BKME/WDN BH12 ....321 P5
Aspen Wk TOTT SO40 ....245 P3
Aspen Wy BKME/WDN BH12 ....321 P5
HORN PO8 ....256 A6
Aspin Wy BLKW GU17 ....41 J9
Asquith Cl CHCH/BSGR BH23 ....337 H1
Astbury Av BKME/WDN BH12 ....322 A7
Aster Ct AND SP10 * 102 B4
Aster Rd KBH RG22 ....89 L4
ROWN SO16 ....228 E8
Astley St SSEA PO5 ....19 G5
Aston Md CHCH/BSGR BH23 ....324 C3
Aston Rd ENEY PO4 ....317 H5
WVILLE PO7 ....275 N2
Astor Crs RAND SP11 ....79 N1
Astra Ct FAWY SO45 ....268 C5
Astral Gdns HLER SO31 ....269 P7
Astra Wk GPORT PO12 ....13 G3
Astrid Cl HISD PO11 ....319 J5
Asturias Wy SHAM SO14 ....21 J7
Asylum Rd WSHM SO15 ....20 E1
Atalanta Cl ENEY PO4 ....317 L3
Atbara Rd FLEETS GU52 ....74 D8
Atheling Rd FAWY SO45 ....268 C6
Athelstan Rd ITCH SO19 ....248 G4
SBNE BH6 ....336 C1
Athena Av WVILLE PO7 ....275 P7
Athena Cl ELGH SO50 ....230 A1
Atherfield Rd ROWN SO16 ....227 J9
Atherley Ct WSHM SO15 ....248 A3
Atherley Rd HISD PO11 ....318 E3
WSHM SO15 ....247 P5
Athlone Cl RAND SP11 ....82 F3
Atholl Ct AND SP10 ....82 E8
Atholl Rd BOR GU35 ....154 A7
Atkinson Cl GPORT PO12 ....12 B7
Atkins Pl FHAM PO15 ....272 A7
Atlantic Cl SHAM SO14 ....248 D9
Atlantic Park Vw WEND SO18 ....249 J1
Atlantis Av WVILLE PO7 ....275 P8
Atrebatti Rd SHST GU47 ....41 K5
Attenborough Cl FLEETN GU51 ....74 E1
Attfield Cl ASHV GU12 ....97 M2
Attlee Gdns FLEETS GU52 ....74 C8
Attwood Cl BSTK RG21 ....6 A7
FBDG SP6 ....239 M6
Attwoods Dro RWIN SO21 ....183 M6
Aubrey Cl HISD PO11 ....318 E4
LYMN SO41 ....339 J2
Auchinleck Wy ALDT GU11 ....2 A3
Auckland Cl NTID SP9 ....79 J5
Auckland Pl BROC SO42 ....286 F8
Auckland Rd
CHCH/BSGR BH23 ....325 N8
WSHM SO15 ....247 K4
Auckland Rd East SSEA PO5 ....316 E6
Auckland Rd West SSEA PO5 ....316 E6
Auclum Cl THLE RG7 ....27 K5
Auclum La THLE RG7 ....27 K5
Audemer Ct RGWD BH24 ....282 C1
Audley Cl NWBY RG14 ....24 G2
Audley Pl ELGH SO50 * 229 P2
Audret Cl FHAM/PORC PO16 ....295 M3
Augustine Rd CHAM PO6 ....275 L9
SHAM SO14 ....21 H1

Augustine Wy AND SP10 ....82 B8
Augustus Dr DEAN RG23 ....68 F5
Augustus Wk AND SP10 ....82 F8
Augustus Wy CHFD SO53 ....206 C6
Auckland Av BROC SO42 ....286 C8
Auklet Cl KBH RG22 ....89 K4
Auriol Dr CHAM PO6 ....298 A1
Aurora Dr DEAN RG23 ....89 L7
Austen Av FUFL SO22 ....183 L3
  NBNE BH10 * 522 D1
Austen Cl TOTT SO40 ....286 B5
  WINC SO23 ....165 H5
Austen Gdns HLER SO31 ....271 J2
  NWBY RG14 ....17 G7
Austen Gv KBH RG22 ....90 A1
Austen Rd FARN GU14 ....57 P7
Austerberry Wy
  LSOL/BMARY PO13 ....295 H9
Auster Cl CHCH/BSGR BH23 ....325 M8
Austin Av PSTN BH14 ....333 K1
Austin Cl BMTH BH1 ....335 K1
Austin Ct CHAM PO6 ....274 D9
Australia Cl PSEA PO1 ....102 C2
Aust Rd FHAM/STUB PO14 ....294 B1
Autumn Cl FERN BH22 ....302 B1
Autumn Rd BWD BH11 ....321 M1
  TOTT SO40 ....267 L1
Avalon PSTN BH14 ....333 L3
Avebury Av NBNE BH10 ....322 E1
Avebury Gdns CHFD SO53 ....206 C4
Aveley La FNM GU10 ....116 B3
Avenger Cl CHFD SO53 ....206 D8
Avens Cl ELGH SO50 ....230 C6
Avenue C SO45 ....290 C1
Avenue Cl AND SP10 ....102 C2
  LIPH GU35 ....175 J5
Avenue D FAWY SO45 ....290 C1
Avenue De Caen SSEA PO5 ....316 E6
Avenue E FAWY SO45 ....290 C1
Avenue La ALTN GU34 ....8 C4
Avenue Rd ALTN GU34 ....111 N6
  ALTN GU34 ....112 C7
  BROC SO42 ....286 F8
  CHCH/BSGR BH23 ....324 D8
  CHCH/BSGR BH23 ....326 E6
  FARN GU14 ....10 D6
  FHAM/STUB PO14 ....10 D6
  FLEETN GU51 ....74 C2
  FUFL SO22 ....22 B3
  GPORT PO12 ....12 E1
  GSHT GU26 ....156 C2
  HISD PO11 ....158 F5
  LYMN SO41 ....329 K5
  NMIL/BTOS BH25 ....327 J4
  SHAM SO14 ....248 C3
  WCLF BH2 ....8 B4
  WIMB BH21 ....300 F1
Avenue Sucy CBLY GU15 ....57 P1
The Avenue ALDT GU11 ....97 J4
  AND SP10 ....102 C2
  BPWT SO32 ....231 P4
  CBLY GU15 ....58 A1
  CCLF BH15 ....334 A6
  CWTH RG45 ....41 H1
  EPSF GU31 ....215 M2
  FERN BH22 ....280 D6
  FHAM PO15 ....10 B6
  FHAM PO15 ....293 P1
  FHAM/STUB PO14 ....10 D6
  FLEETN GU51 ....74 C2
  GPORT PO12 ....12 A6
  GSHT GU26 ....156 C2
  HASM GU27 ....156 E6
  LIPH GU30 ....175 H3
  NARL SO24 ....129 L6
  MOOR/WNTN BH9 ....322 F4
  NTID SP9 ....78 C7
  OVTN RG25 ....89 P8
  PTSW SO17 ....248 B1
  RAND SP11 ....82 C1
  RFNM GU10 ....115 N7
  RWIN SO21 ....104 E7
  RWIN SO21 ....184 A8
  THLE RG7 ....36 A1
Avery La GPORT PO12 ....315 L1
Aviary Ct CHIN RG24 ....69 P4
Aviation Pk West
  CHCH/BSGR BH23 ....303 K7
Avington Cl ELGH SO50 ....207 M8
Avington Ct ROWN SO16 ....228 B8
Avocet Crs SHST GU47 ....41 L6
Avocet Quay EMRTH PO10 ....299 N2
Avocet Wk
  LSOL/BMARY PO13 ....294 E7
Avocet Wy HORN PO8 ....256 A4
Avon Av RGWD BH24 ....282 B6
Avonborne Wy CHFD SO53 ....206 D5
Avon Buildings
  CHCH/BSGR BH23 ....324 F8
Avon Castle Dr RGWD BH24 ....282 B5
Avon Cswy CHCH/BSGR BH23 ....304 C8
Avoncliffe Rd SBNE BH6 ....336 C3
Avon Cl ASHV GU12 ....97 M2
  CHAR BH8 ....323 K9
  FARN GU14 ....57 M6
  LSOL/BMARY PO13 ....329 J4
  LYMN SO41 ....329 J4
  PSF GU31 ....215 L3
Avon Ct AND SP10 ....82 F9
Avon Crs ROMY SO51 ....204 C6
Avondale ASHV GU12 ....76 E5
Avondale Rd ALDT GU11 ....5 G6
  FLEETN GU51 ....74 D2
  PSEA PO1 ....317 H1
  WVILLE PO7 ....275 P2
Avon Gdns CHCH/BSGR BH23 ....305 M7
Avon Md CHFD SO53 ....206 F8
Avon Mdw FBDG SP6 ....240 C1
Avon Mead CHAR BH8 ....323 J9
Avon Pk RGWD BH24 ....282 B3
Avon Rd CHAR BH8 ....323 J9
  DEAN RG23 ....88 F2
  FERN BH22 ....280 E8
  FNM GU9 ....116 C1
  NTID SP9 ....78 C6
  WEND SO18 ....249 H2
Avon Rd East
  CHCH/BSGR BH23 ....324 E7
Avon Rd West
  CHCH/BSGR BH23 ....324 D7
Avon Run Cl
  CHCH/BSGR BH23 ....337 M1
Avon Run Rd
  CHCH/BSGR BH23 ....337 M1
Avon Valley Pth
  CHCH/BSGR BH23 ....304 E4
  CHCH/BSGR BH23 ....324 C1
  FBDG SP6 ....240 C4
  RGWD BH24 ....260 F7
  RGWD BH24 ....282 D5
Avon Vw FBDG SP6 ....241 H2
Avon View Rd
  CHCH/BSGR BH23 ....324 C4
Avon Wk FBSTK RG21 * 7 J6
Avon Wy HEND SO30 ....249 N1
Avonway WKBY RG14 ....24 C5
Avon Wy THLE RG7 ....26 A1
Avon Whf CHCH/BSGR BH23 * 324 C9
Avro Cl WSHM SO15 ....247 L4
Award Rd FLEETS GU52 ....74 D7
  WIMB BH21 ....279 K5
Awbridge Rd HAV PO9 ....276 C6
Axford Cl CHAR BH8 ....323 K4
Ayesgarth FLEETS GU52 ....74 E7
Ayjay Cl ALDT GU11 ....97 H4
Aylen Rd HSEA PO3 ....297 J7
Aylesbury Rd BMTH BH1 ....335 K2
  NEND PO2 ....297 H9
Aylesham Wy YTLY GU46 ....40 C8
Ayling Cl LSOL/BMARY PO13 ....314 C1
Ayling Ct FNM GU9 ....96 F4
Ayling Hl ALDT GU11 ....1 C6
Ayling La ALDT GU11 ....2 C6
Aylings Cl DEAN RG23 ....68 E8
Aylward's Dr ALTN GU34 ....151 K5
Aylward St PSEA PO1 ....18 D2
Aylwards Wy STOK SO20 ....139 N3
Aylwin Cl BSTK RG21 ....90 C1
Ayres La KSCL RG20 ....30 E6
Ayrshire Gdns FLEETN GU51 ....56 E3
Aysgarth Rd WVILLE PO7 ....275 N2
Aysha Cl NMIL/BTOS BH25 ....327 K6
Azalea Av BOR GU35 ....154 D3
Azalea Cl HAV PO9 ....276 G2
  RGWD BH24 ....281 N4
Azalea Ct AND SP10 * 102 B4
Azalea Dr HASM GU27 ....156 E5
Azalea Gdns FLEETS GU52 ....74 E7
Azura Cl WIMB BH21 ....281 H3

B

Babbs Md FNM GU9 ....116 A1
Babs Flds RFNM GU10 ....114 E5
Bach Cl KBH RG22 ....89 P4
Back Down La ADH RG24 ....283 H2
Back Dr CWTH RG45 * 41 J3
Back La LYMN SO41 ....308 C6
  OVTN RG25 ....111 M5
  RAND SP11 ....42 C7
  RAND SP11 ....81 J4
  RFNM GU10 ....135 K1
  ROMY SO51 ....179 K1
  THLE RG7 ....33 L3
  THLE RG7 ....35 K2
  WHAM PO17 ....274 A4
Back of the Walls SHAM SO14 ....20 E6
Back St WEND SO23 ....19 F3
Bacon Cl ITCH SO19 ....269 H1
  SHST GU47 ....41 L8
Bacon La HISD PO11 ....318 D5
  RFNM GU10 ....136 C5
Badajos Rd ALDT GU11 ....2 B1
Badbury Cl BDST BH18 ....320 E1
Badbury Vw WIMB BH21 ....278 F9
Baddesley Cl NBAD SO52 ....205 K3
Baddesley Rd CHFD SO53 ....206 C4
Baden Cl NMIL/BTOS BH25 ....327 K6
Baden Powell Rd LISS GU33 ....173 P5
Bader Cl HEND SO30 ....250 C3
Bader Rd CFDH BH17 ....320 C4
Bader Wy FHAM PO15 ....271 L5
Badger Brow WVILLE PO7 ....276 A4
Badger Cl ALTN GU34 ....150 D5
  ELGH SO50 ....229 P2
  ROMY SO51 ....272 D8
Badger Farm Rd FUFL SO22 ....22 B2
Badger's Bank CHIN RG24 ....70 A4
Badgers Cl FLEETS GU52 ....74 C4
  LYMN SO41 ....308 C6
  NMIL/BTOS BH25 ....281 M4
Badgers Cft THLE RG7 ....27 J9
Badgers Copse CBLY GU15 ....58 D2
  FHAM PO15 ....271 H5
  NMIL/BTOS BH25 ....327 L1
Badgers Gld THLE RG7 ....27 J5
Badgers Holt YTLY GU46 ....40 C9
Badgers Run HLER SO31 ....270 E4
Badgers Sett CWTH RG45 ....40 C1
The Badgers HLER SO31 ....269 L4
Badgers Wk FAWY SO45 ....268 B8
  FERN BH22 ....302 E1
Badgers Wy RFNM GU10 ....135 K5
  VWD BH31 ....258 F5
Badgewood Dr FHAM GU16... ....58 C3
Badminton Dro FAWY SO45 ....291 L9
Badminton La FAWY SO45 ....291 L8
Badshear La NARL SO24 ....168 B8
Badshot Lea Rd FNM GU9 ....96 G6
Badshot Pk FNM GU9 ....115 M1
Baffins Rd HSEA PO3 ....317 J2
Bagber Rd TOTT SO40 ....246 D4
Bagmore La OVTN RG25 ....110 C5
Bagnols Wy NWBY RG14 ....16 A4
Bagshaw Ms ITCH SO19 ....249 H8
Bagshot Ms ITCH SO19 * 249 H8
Bagwell La ODIM RG29 ....73 H5
Baigent Cl WINC SO23 ....23 J4
Bailey Cl FRIM GU16 ....58 C5
  FUFL SO22 ....164 E9
  HEND SO30 ....250 F5
  NMIL/BTOS BH25 ....327 M3
Bailey Crs PLE BH15 ....320 E5
Bailey Gn CHCH/BSGR BH23 ....325 G8
Bailey Gn WEND SO18 ....249 J1
Baileys Cl BLKW GU17 ....57 J1
Bailey's Rd SSEA PO5 ....19 J4
Baily Av NTHA RG18 ....25 L3
Bain Av CBLY GU15 ....58 A4
Baird Av KBH RG22 ....90 A1
Baird Wy CHCH/BSGR BH23 ....324 A2
Baiter Gdns PLE BH15 ....332 E2
Bakehouse Gdns FLEETS GU52 ....74 E7
Bakehouse Ms ALDT GU11 * 2 E2
Baker Rd BWD BH11 ....301 P8
Bakers Down Dr FUFL SO22 ....183 M2
Bakers Dro NMIL/BTOS BH25... ....258 E5
Bakers Fld LISS GU33 ....173 L5
Baker St NEND PO2 ....316 F1
Balaclava Rd WEND SO18 ....249 H1
Balcombe Rd CCLF BH13 ....334 A3
Balderton Cl NEND PO2 ....297 H5
Baldreys FNM GU9 ....116 A2
Baldwin Cl CHCH/BSGR BH23... ....325 H9
Balena Cl CFDH BH17 ....320 C4
Balfour Cl CHCH/BSGR BH23... ....325 P7
  LSOL/BMARY PO13 ....315 H2
Balfour Crs NWBY RG14 ....30 B1
Balfour Dr LISS GU33 ....173 L6
Balfour Rd ITCH SO19 ....249 K6
  MOOR/WNTN BH9 ....322 F6
  NEND PO2 ....296 G8
Balintore Ct SHST GU47 ....41 L7
Balksbury Hl RAND SP11 ....102 B5
Balksbury Rd RAND SP11 ....102 C5
Ballantyne Rd FARN GU14 ....57 P7
Ballard Cl KBH RG22 ....68 F9
  NMIL/BTOS BH25 ....327 K3
  PLE BH15 ....332 E2
Ballard La ROWN SO16 ....228 A1
Balliol Cl FHAM/STUB PO14 ....271 J9
Balliol Rd NEND PO2 ....316 G1
Balliol Wy SHST GU47 ....41 M5
Balloon Rd FARN GU14 ....76 A2
Ball & Wicket La FNM GU9 ....96 C4
Balmer Lawn Rd BROC SO42 ....287 H6
Balmoral Av CHAR BH8 ....323 L6
Balmoral Cl CFDH BH17 ....320 C4
  CHFD SO53 ....206 D5
  LSOL/BMARY PO13 ....295 H6
  ROWN SO16 ....227 N7
Balmoral Crs FNM GU9 ....96 F5
Balmoral Dr FRIM GU16 ....58 D5
  WVILLE PO7 ....275 L6
Balmoral Rd AND SP10 ....4 C4
  ASHV GU12 ....76 F8
  PLE BH15 ....10 B2
  PSTN BH14 ....321 L9
Balmoral Wk
  NMIL/BTOS BH25 ....327 H4
Balmoral Wy KBH RG22 ....89 H4
  PSF GU32 ....215 M1
  ROWN SO16 ....227 H6
Balsan Cl CHIN RG24 ....68 F4
Balston Rd PSTN BH14 ....321 J7
Balston Ter PLE BH15 ....332 D1
Baltic Rd HEND SO30 ....249 N2
Bamber La ALTN GU54 ....113 P6
Bampton Cl ROWN SO16 ....247 H3
Banbury Av ITCH SO19 ....249 L7
Banbury Cl FRIM GU16 ....58 E6
Banbury Rd CFDH BH17 ....320 E5
Band Hall Pl HTWY RG27 ....72 A3
Bangor Rd WSHM SO15 ....248 M5
Banister Gdns WSHM SO15 ....248 B4
Banister Ms WSHM SO15 * 248 B4
Banister Rd WSHM SO15 ....248 B4
Bankhill Dr LYMN SO41 ....329 K2
Bank Pde BKME/WDN BH12 * 322 A6
Bank Rd ALDT GU11 ....76 C7
Bankside FNM GU9 ....96 F4
Bank Side WEND SO18 ....249 K1
  LYMN SO41 ....329 K1
Bankside Rd
  MOOR/WNTN BH9 ....322 G4
Banks Rd CCLF BH13 ....333 K8
The Banks ROMY SO51 ....178 G9
Bank St BPWT SO32 ....232 B5
Bankview LYMN SO41 ....329 K1
Bannerman Rd PSF GU32 ....215 M1
Bannister Gdns HTWY RG27 ....39 P6
  YTLY GU46 ....40 D9
Bannister Rd FNM GU9 ....96 G5
Banstead Rd BDST BH18 ....300 C8
Bapaume Rd HSEA PO3 ....297 M5
Baptist Hl RAND SP11 ....84 B1
Barbara Cl FLEETS GU52 ....74 B6
Barberry Cl FLEETS GU52 ....74 C4
Barberry Dr TOTT SO40 ....245 P2
Barberry Wy BLKW GU17 ....57 N2
  VWD BH31 ....259 J5
Barbers Piles PLE BH15 ....332 D2
Barbican Cl CBLY GU15 ....59 J2
Barbour Cl ODIM RG29 ....93 J4
Barcelona Cl AND SP10 ....5 F2
Barclay Ms FAWY SO45 ....290 C1
Bardon Wy FHAM/STUB PO14... ....296 M1
Bardsley Dr FNM GU9 ....116 A2
Bardwell Cl KBH RG22 ....68 F8
The Baredown HTWY RG27 ....71 L5
Bar End Rd WINC SO23 ....184 B1
  WINC SO23 ....23 G7
Barfield Cl WINC SO23 ....23 K6
Barfield Rd NTHA RG18 ....25 K3
Barfields LYMN SO41 ....329 L3
Barfleur Cl FHAM PO15 ....272 B8
Barfleur Rd FHAM/STUB PO14... ....294 L6
Barford Cl CHFD SO53 ....206 D5
  FLEETN GU51 ....74 C5
Barford La RSAL SP5 ....199 L5
Bargates CHCH/BSGR BH23 ....324 F8
Bargate St SHAM SO14 ....20 D5
Barge Cl ALDT GU11 ....76 D7
Barge La FHAM/STUB PO14 ....294 A4
Barham Rd PSF GU32 ....215 M2
Barham Wy NEND PO2 ....296 F5
Baring Cl RWIN SO21 ....127 N5
  RWIN SO21 ....146 F9
Baring Rd SBNE BH6 ....336 E2
  WINC SO23 ....3 J3
Barker Mill Cl ROWN SO16 ....227 J6
Barkis Md SHST GU47 ....41 M4
Barlands Cl CHCH/BSGR BH23 ....324 C5
Barle Cl WEND SO18 ....249 K2
Barley Down Dr FUFL SO22 ....183 M2
Barley Mow Cl HTWY RG27 ....72 B4
Barley Mow Hl GU35 SO35 ....154 C2
Barley Vw OVTN RG25 ....108 D1
Barlow Cl FHAM/STUB PO14 ....293 P7
Barlows La AND SP10 ....102 D5
Barnard Cl TADY RG26 ....54 C7
Barnard Cl FRIM GU16 ....58 E5
Barnard Wy ALDT GU11 ....2 C1
Barnbrook Rd HLER SO31 ....270 E6
  ROWN SO16 ....299 K1
Barn Close La FLEETS GU52 ....45 J5
Barn Crs NWBY RG14 ....30 B1
Barncroft FNM GU10 ....116 C1
  RAND SP11 ....80 C6
Barncroft Wy HAV PO9 ....14 D2
Barnes Cl FARN GU14 ....58 C9
  HLER SO31 ....270 D6
  ITCH SO19 ....183 J1
  NBNE BH10 ....322 D4
  WINC SO23 ....183 N1
Barnes Crs NBNE BH10 ....322 D4
  WIMB BH21 ....300 C1
Barnes La HLER SO31 ....270 E6
  LYMN SO41 ....328 C7
Barnes Rd FRIM GU16 ....58 E5
  ITCH SO19 ....249 L5
  NBNE BH10 ....322 D4
  PSEA PO1 ....316 G2
Barnes Wallis Rd FHAM PO15 ....271 K6
Barnet Cl CHFD SO53 ....206 B5
Barnet Side La PSF GU32 ....190 D5
Barnetts Wood La NARL SO24 ....149 K8
Barney Evans Crs HORN PO8 ....255 M8
Barneyhayes La TOTT SO40 ....244 G3
Barnfield CHCH/BSGR BH23 ....325 P7
  YTLY GU46 ....40 G6
Barnfield Cl ALTN GU34 ....114 A6
  ITCH SO19 ....268 G1
Barnfield Ct
  FHAM/STUB PO14 ....294 C1
  ITCH SO19 ....269 H1
Barnfield Ri AND SP10 ....102 C4
Barnfield Rd EPSF GU31 ....216 A2
  ITCH SO19 ....268 G1
Barnfield Wy ITCH SO19 ....269 H1
Barn Fold HORN PO8 * 276 B1
Barn Green Cl WVILLE PO7 ....255 H7
Barn La ALTN GU34 ....150 A7
  DEAN RG23 ....68 C9
Barn Meadow Cl FLEETS GU52 ....74 C9
Barn Owl Wy THLE RG7 ....27 K4
Barn Piece CHFD SO53 ....206 B7
  BDST BH18 ....320 D1
Barnsfield Crs TOTT SO40 ....246 A4
Barnsfield Rd BWD BH24 ....181 N8
Barnside Wy LISS GU33 ....192 D5
Barnsley Cl FRIM GU16 ....76 C3
Barnsley Dro WIMB BH21 ....278 A3
Barns Rd FERN BH22 ....302 E9
The Barns CHFD SO53 * 109 H2
Barnwood Rd FHAM PO15 ....272 B9
Baroda Rd NTID SP9 ....78 E7
Barons Md ROWN SO16 ....227 J9
Barons Rd BWD BH11 ....301 M7
Barracane Dr CWTH RG45 ....41 J2
Barrack La RGWD BH24 ....283 H5
Barrack Rd ALDT GU11 ....2 D3
  CHCH/BSGR BH23 ....324 C7
  FERN BH22 ....302 C6
Barra Cl DEAN RG23 ....88 E1
Barrie Cl HLER SO31 ....271 J2
Barrie Rd FNM GU9 ....116 B1
  MOOR/WNTN BH9 ....322 F4
Barrington Cl ELGH SO50 ....207 H8
Barron Pl CHIN RG24 ....68 E4
Barrow Dr CHAR BH8 ....323 N4
Barrowgate Rd CHAR BH8 ....323 K3
Barrowgate Wy CHAR BH8 ....323 K4
Barrow Hl RAND SP11 ....122 C1
Barrow Hill Rd TOTT SO40 ....225 J8
Barrows La LYMN SO41 ....308 B9
  RSAL SP5 ....201 K7
Barrow Vw WIMB BH21 ....302 A2
Barrow Wy CHAR BH8 ....323 M5
Barrs Av NMIL/BTOS BH25 ....327 J3
Barrs Wood Dr
  NMIL/BTOS BH25 ....327 K3
Barrs Wood Rd
  NMIL/BTOS BH25 ....327 K3
Barry Gdns BDST BH18 ....300 B8
Barry Rd ITCH SO19 ....249 L6
Barrydene
  FHAM/STUB PO14 * 293 M1
Barry Wy KBH RG22 ....89 P4
Barters Cl ROWN SO16 ....247 K2
Barters La BDST BH18 ....300 B9
Bartholomew Cl HASM GU27 ....157 H5
  NWBY RG14 * 16 D4
  WINC SO23 ....22 E2
Bartholomew St NWBY RG14 ....16 D4
Bartlemy Cl NWBY RG14 ....16 A7
Bartlemy Rd NWBY RG14 ....16 A7
Bartlett Cl FHAM PO15 ....10 A2
  TADY RG26 ....52 C3
Bartlett Pl FRIM GU16 ....323 P7
Bartlett Rd LTDN BH7 ....10 A8
The Bartletts HLER SO31 ....270 A8
Bartley Av TOTT SO40 ....246 C5
Bartley Rd TOTT SO40 ....245 J8
Bartley Wy HTWY RG27 ....72 B4
Bartok Cl KBH RG22 ....90 A2
Barton Cha
  NMIL/BTOS BH25 * 327 H8
Barton Cl ALDT GU11 ....96 E2
  AND SP10 ....82 B8
  ROMY SO51 ....204 F5
Barton Common La
  NMIL/BTOS BH25 ....327 K7
Barton Common Rd
  NMIL/BTOS BH25 ....327 K8
Barton Court Av
  NMIL/BTOS BH25 ....327 J6
Barton Court Rd
  NMIL/BTOS BH25 ....327 J6
Barton Crs WEND SO18 ....249 H2
Barton Cft NMIL/BTOS BH25 * 327 J8
Barton Cross HORN PO8 ....256 B4
Barton Dr HEND SO30 ....250 D4
  HLER SO31 ....269 P7
  NMIL/BTOS BH25 ....327 H8
Barton Dro RWIN SO21 ....125 J5
Barton Gn NMIL/BTOS BH25 * 327 J9
Barton La NMIL/BTOS BH25 ....327 H8
Barton Pk ELGH SO50 ....229 L1
Bartons Ct ODIM RG29 ....72 C9
Barton's Dr YTLY GU46 ....56 E1
Bartonside Rd
  NMIL/BTOS BH25 ....326 E7
Bartons La CHIN RG24 ....70 B4
Bartons Rd FBDG SP6 ....240 D2
  HAV PO9 ....276 G5
The Bartons FBDG SP6 ....240 D2
Bartons Wy FARN GU14 ....57 K6
Barton Wy NMIL/BTOS BH25 ....327 H7
Barton Wood Rd
  NMIL/BTOS BH25 ....326 G8
Bartram Rd TOTT SO40 ....246 E5
Barwell Ct FHAM PO15 ....10 A6
Barwell Gv EMRTH PO10 ....177 L7
Bascott Cl BWD BH11 ....322 A6
Bascott Rd BWD BH11 ....321 P5
Bashley Common Rd
  NMIL/BTOS BH25 ....307 J8
Bashley Cross Rd
  NMIL/BTOS BH25 ....326 C2
Bashley Dr NMIL/BTOS BH25 ....327 K1
Bashley Rd NMIL/BTOS BH25... ....307 J9
Basingbourne Cl FLEETS GU52 ....74 D6
Basingbourne Rd FLEETS GU52... ....74 C7
Basing Dean ALTN GU34 ....149 N4
Basing Gdns KBH RG22 * 97 H4
Basingfield Cl CHIN RG24 ....70 C8
Basing Ms BPWT SO32 * 232 A5
Basing Rd CHIN RG24 ....69 P6
  HAV PO9 ....276 E5
Basingstoke Rd ALTN GU34 ....132 B5
  HTWY RG27 ....53 J3
  KSCL RG20 ....48 D3
  RWIN SO21 ....145 P4
  TADY RG26 ....50 B8
  WINC SO23 ....165 L1
Basing Vw BSTK RG21 ....7 H5
Basin Wy CHFD SO53 ....206 C9
Basingwell St BPWT SO32 ....232 A5
Basin St NEND PO2 ....316 F1
Bassenthwaite Gdns
  BOR GU35 ....154 A3
Bassett Av ROWN SO16 ....228 B7
  ROWN SO16 ....228 B8
Bassett Crs East ROWN SO16... ....228 B9
Bassett Crs West ROWN SO16... ....228 B9
Bassett Gdns ROWN SO16 ....228 A8
Bassett Grn Cl ROWN SO16 ....228 B7
Bassett Green Dr ROWN SO16... ....228 C7
Bassett Green
  ROWN SO16 ....228 C6
Bassett Heath Av
  ROWN SO16 ....228 B5
Bassett Meadow ROWN SO16... ....228 B9
Bassett Ms ROWN SO16 ....228 B6
Bassett Rd BKME/WDN BH12 ....321 K6
Bassett Rw ROWN SO16 ....228 B6
Bassett Wood Dr ROWN SO16... ....228 B6
Bassett Wood Rd
  ROWN SO16 ....228 B6
Bat & Ball La FNM GU9 ....116 A4
Batchelor Crs BWD BH11 ....321 P1
Batchelor Dr CHIN RG24 ....70 D7
Batchelor Gn HLER SO31 ....269 P2
Batchelor Rd BWD BH11 ....321 N1
Batcombe Cl BWD BH11 ....321 N1
Bath Cl ITCH SO19 ....249 K5
Bath Hill Rbt BMTH BH1 ....8 E5
Bathing La PSEA PO1 ....18 A5
Bath La FHAM/PORC PO16 ....11 K7
Bath La (Lower)
  FHAM/PORC PO16 ....11 K7
Bath Rd BMTH BH1 ....299 M1
  EMRTH PO10 ....317 H5
  ENEY PO4 ....288 K5
  ITCH SO19 ....339 M4
  NTHA RG18 ....25 J3
  NWBY RG14 ....24 A2
Bath Sq PSEA PO1 ....18 A5
Bath St SHAM SO14 ....248 C4
Bathurst Cl HISD PO11 ....318 E5

Batsford RAND SP11 .....84 B1
Batstone Wy FERN BH22 .....302 B2
Battalion Wy STHA RG19 .....25 P6
Battenburg Av NEND PO12 .....297 H7
Batten Cl CHCH/BSGR BH23 .....325 H7
Batten Rd RSAL SP5 .....199 J5
Battens Av OVTN RG25 .....87 H4
Battens Wy HAV PO9 .....276 F6
Batterley Dro WIMB BH21 .....258 F7
Battery Cl GPORT PO12 .....295 K9
Battery End NWBY RG14 .....24 A9
Battery HI BPWT SO32 .....231 P4
Battery Rw PSEA PO1 .....18 C7
Battle Cl HLER SO31 .....270 F6
  NWBY RG14 .....24 A3
Baughurst Rd TADY RG26 .....13 K3
  THLE RG7 .....26 C9
B Av HAV SO45 .....290 F4
Baverstock Rd
  BKME/WDN BH12 .....322 B7
Baverstocks ALTN GU34 .....132 C3
The Baxendales NWBY RG14 .....17 J6
Baxter Rd ITCH SO19 .....249 N7
Baybridge La RAND SP11 .....209 L3
Baybridge Rd HAV PO9 .....277 H5
Bay Cl ITCH SO19 .....249 J8
  WIMB BH21 .....280 E1
Bayfield Av FARN GU16 .....58 D3
Bayford Cl FARN GU14 .....57 P4
Bay Hog La PLE BH15 .....332 D1
Bayly Av FHAM/PORC PO16 .....295 P3
Baynard Cl BSTK RG21 .....7 G2
Bay Rd GPORT PO12 .....315 K5
  ITCH SO19 .....249 J8
Bays Ct TADY RG26 * 34 A5
Bays Rd LYMN SO41 .....329 J4
Baythorn Cl NEND PO2 .....316 F1
Bay Tree Gdns TOTT SO40 .....267 L1
Bay Trees ITCH SO19 .....249 N5
Bay Tree Wy
  CHCH/BSGR BH23 .....325 P6
Baywood Cl FARN GU14 .....57 K8
Bazaar Rd NTID SP9 .....78 F7
Beach Av NMIL/BTOS BH25 .....327 H8
Beach Dr CHAM PO6 .....296 B1
Beach Rd CCLF BH13 .....334 A6
  EMRTH PO10 .....299 L1
  HISD PO11 .....318 E6
  LSOL/BMARY PO13 .....314 C5
  SSEA PO5 .....316 F7
Beach's Crs TADY RG26 .....51 H2
Beach Wk AND SP10 * 102 B3
Beachway FHAM/PORC PO16 .....295 P5
Beacon Bottom HLER SO31 .....270 C4
Beacon Cl HLER SO31 .....270 C4
  LYMN SO41 .....328 D6
  RFNM GU10 .....116 A5
Beacon Ct FBDG SP6 .....220 C9
Beacon Dr CHCH/BSGR BH23 .....325 H7
Beacon Gdns BDST BH18 .....320 A1
  FLEETN GU51 * 74 B3
Beacon Hill La BPWT SO32 .....211 K6
Beacon Hill Rd FLEETS GU52 .....74 E8
  RFNM GU10 .....95 N2
Beacon Mt HLER SO31 .....270 C4
Beacon Rd FARN GU14 .....76 A4
  NEND SO30 .....249 M3
  WCLF BH2 .....8 C6
Beaconsfield Av CHAM PO6 .....297 J2
Beaconsfield Rd
  BKME/WDN BH12 .....321 M7
  BSTK RG21 .....69 L8
  CHCH/BSGR BH23 .....324 F8
  FHAM/PORC PO16 .....295 N3
  WVILLE PO7 .....275 N2
Beacon Sq EMRTH PO10 .....299 L2
  HLER SO31 .....270 C4
Beales Cl AND SP10 .....4 E4
Beales La RFNM GU10 .....115 P3
Bealeswood La RFNM GU10 .....135 N3
Bealing Cl ROWN SO16 .....228 D8
Beal's Pightle TADY RG26 .....50 C4
Beam Hollow FNM GU9 .....96 C4
Beamish Rd CFDH BH17 .....321 H4
Beancroft Rd STHA RG19 .....25 N5
Bear Cross Av BWD BH11 .....301 N7
Beard Ct RAND SP11 .....80 A1
Bear HI KSCL RG20 .....48 B4
Bear La FNM GU9 .....96 B8
  NWBY RG14 .....16 E2
Bearslane Cl TOTT SO40 .....246 B2
Bearwood Gdns FLEETN GU51 .....74 D5
  WSHM SO15 .....247 N4
Beatrice Rd ENEY PO4 .....316 C6
  WSHM SO15 .....247 N4
Beattie Ri HEND SO30 .....250 C1
Beattie Rd HLER SO31 .....271 H6
  RGWD BH24 .....282 C1
Beatty Ct AND SP10 .....5 J5
Beatty Dr GPORT PO12 .....315 K6
Beatty Rd MOOR/WNTN SO23 .....323 H6
Beauchamp Av
  LSOL/BMARY PO13 .....294 C7
Beauchamp Pl
  CHCH/BSGR BH23 .....324 E8
Beauchamps Gdns LTDN BH7 .....323 N7
Beauclerk Gn HTWY RG27 .....73 H3
Beaucroft La WIMB BH21 .....278 C8
Beaucroft Rd BPWT SO32 .....252 C9
  WIMB BH21 .....278 F8
Beaufighter Rd FARN GU14 .....75 J4
Beaufort Av FHAM/PORC PO16 .....12 C2
  LSOL/BMARY PO13 .....314 E2
Beaufort Dr BPWT SO32 .....232 A4
  WIMB BH21 .....278 E9
Beaufort Rd ASHV GU12 .....76 L6
  BOR GU35 .....154 A3
  FLEETS GU52 .....74 E5
  FNM GU9 .....96 C5
  HAV PO9 .....14 B4
  SBNE BH6 .....336 A1
  SSEA PO5 * 316 F7

WINC SO23 .....22 C7
Beaufoys Av FERN BH22 .....302 C1
Beaufoys Cl FERN BH22 .....302 C1
Beaulieu Av
  CHCH/BSGR BH23 .....324 C8
  FHAM/PORC PO16 .....295 L1
  HAV PO9 .....276 D4
Beaulieu Cl FUFL SO22 .....164 E3
  ROWN SO16 .....227 M7
  BSTK RG21 .....7 H6
Beaulieu Gdns BLKW GU17 .....41 K9
Beaulieu Pl
  LSOL/BMARY PO13 .....294 C7
Beaulieu Rd BROC SO42 .....288 D1
  BROC SO42 .....289 N5
  CHCH/BSGR BH23 .....324 C8
  ELGH SO50 .....207 J9
  FAWY SO45 .....268 B8
  LYND SO43 .....268 B8
  NEND PO2 .....296 C8
  TOTT SO40 .....267 H5
  WENH BH4 .....334 B5
Beaumaris Cl AND SP10 .....102 C4
Beaumaris Gdns FAWY SO45 .....268 B6
Beaumaris Pde FERN BH22 .....58 E5
Beaumont Dr AND SP10 * 102 A3
Beaumont Pl GPORT PO12 * 295 L9
  ROWN SO16 .....228 A9
Beaumont Ct GPORT PO12 .....12 E1
Beaumont Gv ALDT GU11 .....2 A3
Beaumont Ri FHAM PO15 .....272 B7
Beaumont Rd CCLF BH13 .....333 N4
  TOTT SO40 .....246 E4
Beaurepaire Cl TADY RG26 .....51 N2
Beauworth Av WEND SO18 .....249 L3
Beaver Dr ELGH SO50 .....230 A2
Beaver La YTLY GU46 .....40 F9
Beavers Cl ALTN GU34 .....132 E5
  FNM GU9 .....96 A9
  TADY RG26 .....34 A5
Beavers Hi FNM GU9 .....95 P9
Beavers Ms BOR GU35 .....154 B4
Beavers Rd FNM GU9 .....96 A9
Beccles Cl PLE BH15 .....332 D1
Becher Rd PSTN BH14 .....321 N8
Beck Cl HLER SO31 .....270 E7
Beckett Cl DEAN RG23 .....68 D7
Beckett Rd AND SP10 .....102 C2
Beckford La WHAM PO17 .....274 A1
Beck Gdns FNM GU9 .....96 A5
Beckham La PSF GU32 .....215 K1
Beckhampton Rd PLE BH15 .....320 A9
Beckley Copse
  CHCH/BSGR BH23 .....326 C5
Beck St SSEA PO1 .....18 E2
Becton La NMIL/BTOS BH25 .....327 K8
Becton Md NMIL/BTOS BH25 .....327 K6
Bedale Wy PLE BH15 .....321 H7
Beddington Ct CHIN RG24 .....70 B4
Bede Dr AND SP10 .....82 B8
Bedenham La
  LSOL/BMARY PO13 .....295 J6
Bedfield La WINC SO23 .....165 J2
Bedford Av FRIM GU16 .....58 E8
  ITCH SO19 .....248 C9
Bedford Cl BOR GU35 .....154 A7
  FBDG SP6 .....220 D9
  HAV PO9 .....15 K7
  HEND SO30 .....250 D5
  NWBY RG14 .....30 B1
Bedford Crs FRIM GU16 .....58 D7
  LTDN BH7 .....324 A8
Bedford La FARN GU16 .....58 E7
  WSHM SO15 .....20 D1
Bedford Rd PSF GU32 .....215 K2
Bedford Rd North
  BKME/WDN BH12 .....321 L2
Bedford Rd South
  BKME/WDN BH12 .....321 J2
  SSEA PO5 .....19 G4
Bedhampton HI CHAM PO6 .....276 A9
Bedhampton Hill Rd HAV PO9 .....276 B9
Bedhampton Rd HAV PO9 .....14 A4
  NEND PO2 .....297 H8
Bedser Sq AND SP10 .....82 E8
Bedwell Cl ROWN SO16 .....227 K7
Beecham Berry KBH RG22 .....89 P4
Beecham Rd PSEA PO1 .....316 C1
Beech Av CBLY GU15 .....58 C1
  RFNM GU10 .....116 C5
  SBNE BH6 .....336 A2
  STOK SO20 .....121 H5
  WEND SO18 .....248 G4
Beechbank Av CFDH BH17 .....320 A3
Beechbrook Av YTLY GU46 .....40 F9
Beech Cl ASHV GU12 .....97 L3
  CHFD SO53 .....206 F5
  FBDG SP6 .....239 N6
  FUFL SO22 .....185 K3
  HLER SO31 .....269 N8
  HORN PO8 .....255 P9
  LYMN SO41 .....328 E6
  OVTN RG25 .....87 H1
  RAND SP11 .....100 E2
  RAND SP11 .....101 N1
  RDGW/BURGH RG30 .....27 K3
  ROWN SO16 .....204 C7
  STOK SO20 .....121 H5
  TADY RG26 .....52 B5
  VWD BH31 .....258 E5
Beech Copse FUFL SO22 .....164 C6
  HEND SO30 * 249 M2
Beech Ct WIMB BH21 .....300 C1
Beech Crs FAWY SO45 .....290 D5
Beechcrest Vw HTWY RG27 .....72 A2
Beechcroft Cl AND SP10 .....4 C1
  CHFD SO53 .....206 F7
  FHAM PO15 .....272 A9
  LIPH GU30 .....174 E4
Beechcroft Cots
  STOK SO20 .....160 A1

Beechcroft La RGWD BH24 .....282 F1
Beechcroft Rd GPORT PO12 .....12 B5
Beechcroft Wy GPORT PO12 .....206 F7
Beechdale Cl TOTT SO40 .....246 A1
Beech Dr BLKW GU17 .....57 L1
Beechen La LYND SO43 .....265 H8
Beeches HI BPWT SO32 .....232 B2
The Beeches AND SP10 .....102 C2
  HAV PO9 .....76 E3
  ELGH SO50 .....230 D3
  KBH RG22 .....89 P5
  LTDN BH7 .....323 N7
  ROMY SO51 .....224 D1
Beechey Rd CHAR BH8 .....335 H1
Beechfield AMSY SP4 .....118 D3
Beechfield Ct WSHM SO15 .....247 L3
Beech Gdns HLER SO31 .....269 N8
Beech Gra RSAL SP5 .....223 M2
Beech Gv CHOB/PIR GU24 .....59 P6
  GPORT PO12 .....12 E4
  HISD PO11 .....319 H4
  RAND SP11 .....123 K3
  RWIN SO21 .....208 C1
Beech Hanger AMSY SP4 .....98 F9
Beech Hanger End
  GSHT GU26 .....156 A2
Beech HI BOR GU35 .....155 J4
Beech HI Rd BOR GU35 .....154 C2
  NTID SP9 .....79 J4
Beeching Cl ASHV GU12 .....76 G9
Beechlands Rd ALTN GU34 .....150 C4
Beech La GSHT GU26 .....156 A1
  RGWD BH24 .....281 L7
Beechleigh Pl RGWD BH24 * 282 E1
Beechmount Rd ROWN SO16 .....228 B7
Beechnut Dr BLKW GU17 .....41 J8
Beechnut Rd ASHV GU12 .....3 G4
Beech Ride FLEETS GU52 .....74 C5
  SHST GU47 .....41 J6
Beech Rd CHFD SO53 .....206 F5
  FARN GU14 .....58 A6
  FRIM GU16 .....58 E7
  HASM GU27 .....157 J6
  HISD PO11 .....250 D4
  HORN PO8 .....236 D7
  KSCL RG20 .....31 M4
  NARL SO24 .....168 A2
  TOTT SO40 .....245 P9
  WSHM SO15 .....247 M5
Beech Tree Cl DEAN RG23 .....68 E3
Beech Tree Dr FNM GU9 .....96 C6
Beech Tree Wk ROMY SO51 .....160 B4
Beech Wk AND SP10 .....102 B4
Beech Wy HORN PO8 .....256 B6
Beechwood CHIN RG24 * 69 P1
  FBDG SP6 .....240 B2
Beechwood Av BOSC BH5 .....335 M2
  NMIL/BTOS BH25 .....326 G3
  WVILLE PO7 .....275 N4
Beech Wood Cl BDST BH18 .....320 C7
Beechwood Cl CHFD SO53 .....206 C4
  FLEETN GU51 .....74 B6
  HLER SO31 .....292 D1
  WEND SO18 .....248 G3
Beechwood Crs CHFD SO53 .....206 B5
Beechwood Gdns CHFD SO53 .....335 N2
  WEND SO18 .....248 G3
Beechwood La RGWD BH24 .....284 D6
Beechwood Ri WEND SO18 .....248 F3
  FAWY SO45 .....290 E6
  FERN BH22 .....280 F8
  NEND PO2 .....296 C5
  TOTT SO40 .....246 D9
Beechwood Wy FAWY SO45 .....267 N8
Beechworth Rd HAV PO9 .....15 H5
Beehive Wk PSEA PO1 .....18 D5
Beethoven Rd KBH RG22 .....89 J7
Beeton's Av ASHV GU12 .....76 F8
Beggar's La WINC SO23 .....23 G4
Beggarwood La DEAN RG23 .....89 L7
Begonia Cl KBH RG22 .....89 L4
Begonia Rd ROWN SO16 .....228 G6
Behrendt Ct GPORT PO12 .....315 G6
Belaga Ct STOK SO20 .....120 C4
Belben Cl BKME/WDN BH12 .....321 M2
Belben Rd BKME/WDN BH12 .....321 L2
Belbins ROMY SO51 .....204 D1
Beldham Rd RFNM GU10 .....115 P9
Belfield Rd SBNE BH6 .....336 E2
Belfry Ms SHST GU47 .....40 C6
Belfry Cl HORN PO8 .....237 G8
Belfry Wk FHAM/STUB PO14 .....271 J8
Belgrave Ct BLKW GU17 .....57 L2
Belgrave Rd CCLF BH13 .....334 A4
  PTSW SO17 .....248 E1
Belgravia Rd NEND PO2 .....297 H8
Bellair Rd HAV PO9 .....15 H6
Belland Dr ALDT GU11 .....2 A4
Bell Cl FARN GU14 .....58 B7
Bell Crs WVILLE PO7 .....275 N4
Bell Davies Rd
  FHAM/STUB PO14 .....293 P8
Bellemoor Rd WSHM SO15 .....247 M3
Bellevue WHCH RG28 .....85 L6
Belle Vue Cl ASHV GU12 .....97 K1
  SBNE BH6 .....336 B2
Belle Vue Gv FERN BH22 .....336 D2
Belle Vue La EMRTH PO10 .....277 M8
Belle Vue Rd AND SP10 .....4 E7
  ASHV GU12 .....70 C6
  CHIN RG24 .....70 C6
  PSTN BH14 .....321 L9
  SBNE BH6 .....336 B3
Bellevue Ter SSEA PO5 .....18 E7
Belle Vue Wk FERN BH22 .....302 E6
Bellew Rd FRIM GU16 .....58 D7

Bellflower Cl
  CHCH/BSGR BH23 .....325 M7
Bellflower Wy CHFD SO53 .....206 B6
Bell HI PSF GU32 .....191 L9
Bell Holt NWBY RG14 .....30 B1
Bellingham Cl CBLY GU15 .....59 H1
Bell La BLKW GU17 .....41 K9
  OVTN RG25 .....110 F4
  RFNM GU10 .....115 N7
Bell Meadow Rd HTWY RG27 .....72 A3
Bell Rd AND SP10 .....5 J5
  CHIN RG24 .....69 P6
  CHAM PO6 .....296 F1
Bells La FHAM/STUB PO14 .....294 A7
Bell St RAND SP11 .....80 A1
  ROMY SO51 .....204 C6
  SHAM SO14 .....21 F6
  WHCH RG28 .....85 L6
Bell Vale La HASM GU27 .....183 G3
Belmont Av CHAR BH8 .....323 J5
Belmont Cl AND SP10 .....57 N6
  FARN GU14 .....268 C8
  FAWY SO45 .....294 B6
  FHAM/STUB PO14 .....256 C1
  HORN PO8 .....275 N4
  VWD BH31 .....258 C5
Belmont Gv HAV PO9 .....276 C8
Belmont Hts KBH RG22 .....89 N6
Belmont Ms CBLY GU15 .....58 B1
Belmont Pl SSEA PO5 .....19 H6
Belmont Rd AND SP10 .....4 E7
  CBLY GU15 .....58 B1
  CHFD SO53 .....206 G8
  NMIL/BTOS BH25 .....327 L3
  PSTN BH14 .....321 K7
  PTSW SO17 .....248 D1
Belmont St DEAN RG23 .....19 H6
Belmore Cl LYMN SO41 .....316 C1
Belmore La LYMN SO41 .....329 L4
  RWIN SO21 .....185 K9
Belney La LYMN SO41 .....329 K4
Belsize Rd FARN GU14 .....76 B3
Belstone Ms FARN GU14 .....76 B3
Belstone Rd TOTT SO40 .....246 C4
Belton Rd ITCH SO19 .....249 K8
Belvedere Cl DEAN RG23 .....68 F3
Belvedere Ct BLKW GU17 .....57 L2
Belvedere La NWBY RG14 .....16 E7
Belvedere Rd CHIN RG24 .....52 M9
Belvedere
  CHCH/BSGR BH23 .....324 E8
  FARN GU14 .....76 B2
  FAWY SO45 .....268 C8
  TWDS BH3 .....322 G9
Belvedere Ct PSF GU32 .....215 M1
Belvidere Rd SHAM SO14 .....21 J3
Belvidere Ter SHAM SO14 .....21 J3
Belvoir Cl FHAM/PORC PO16 .....11 C7
Bembridge HLER SO31 .....269 L4
Bembridge Cl ROWN SO16 .....228 E7
Bembridge Ct CWTH RG45 .....40 D2
Bembridge Crs ENEY PO4 .....316 C7
Bembridge Dr HISD PO11 .....319 J7
Bemister Rd
  MOOR/WNTN SO23 .....322 G7
Bemisters La GPORT PO12 .....13 J2
Benbow Cl HORN PO8 .....256 B6
Benbow Cr AND SP10 * 5 J5
Benbow Crs
  BKME/WDN BH12 .....321 N3
Benbow Pl PSEA PO1 .....18 C2
Benbridge Av BWD BH11 .....301 P8
Bendeng Cl FLEETN GU51 .....74 A1
Bendigo Rd CHCH/BSGR BH23 .....324 C7
Beneden Gn NARL SO24 .....168 A2
Benedict Cl ROMY SO51 .....204 C6
Benedict Wy
  FHAM/PORC PO16 .....274 A8
Beneficial St PSEA PO1 .....18 C3
Benellen Av WBNE BH4 .....334 C2
Benellen Gdns WBNE BH4 .....334 C2
Benellen Rd WBNE BH4 .....334 C2
Benenden Gn NARL SO24 .....168 A3
Benett Cl NWBY RG14 .....24 C2
Benett Gdns NWBY RG14 .....24 C2
Bengal Rd MOOR/WNTN SO23 .....322 E6
Benger's La FHAM/STUB PO14 .....179 K4
Benham Dr HSEA PO3 * 297 H5
Benham Gv
  FHAM/PORC PO16 .....295 P3
Benham HI NTHA RG18 .....25 J3
Benham La THLE RG7 .....38 A3
Benhams Farm Cl
  WEND SO18 .....249 J2
Benhams La LISS GU33 .....173 L5
Benhams Rd WEND SO18 .....249 J3
Benin Rd RAND SP11 .....79 M5
Benjamin Rd PLE BH15 .....332 A1
Benmoor Rd CFDH BH17 .....320 C4
Benmore Cl NMIL/BTOS BH25 .....327 L3
Benmore Gdns CHFD SO53 .....206 D5
Benmore Rd
  MOOR/WNTN SO23 .....322 G6
Bennet Cl ALTN GU34 .....132 E5
  BSTK RG21 .....7 J1
Bennett Rd CHAR BH8 .....323 J9
Bennetts La RGWD BH24 .....284 E7
Bennetts Rd ALDT GU11 .....3 J3
Bennion Rd NBNE BH10 .....322 C4
Benny Hill Cl ELGH SO50 .....229 H1
Benridge Cl CFDH BH17 .....320 C4
Benson Cl ASHV GU12 .....97 M2
Bentall Pl AND SP10 .....4 C6
Bentham Rd GPORT PO12 .....12 C5
Bentham Wy HLER SO31 .....270 D2
Bentley Cl HORN PO8 .....256 C5

WINC SO23 .....165 J1
Bentley Copse CBLY GU15 .....58 C1
Bentley Ct HAV PO9 .....277 H5
Bentley Crs FHAM/PORC PO16 .....19 D2
Bentley Rd MOOR/WNTN BH9 .....322 F4
Bentley Wy RSAL SP5 .....158 C2
Bentworth Cl HAV PO9 .....276 D6
Benwell Cl DDIM RG29 .....29 J3
Bepton Down EPSF GU31 .....215 N2
Berber Cl FHAM PO15 .....271 J3
Bercote Cl FUFL SO22 .....164 C2
Bere Cl CFDH BH17 .....320 F2
  CHFD SO53 .....206 C6
  FUFL SO22 .....164 E5
Bere Farm La WHAM PO17 .....273 K3
Bere HI WHCH RG28 .....85 L5
Bere Hill Crs AND SP10 .....5 G6
Berehurst ALTN GU34 .....132 F7
Bere Rd WVILLE PO7 .....255 J7
Beresford Cl AND SP10 .....102 E5
  BKME/WDN BH12 .....321 M6
  FRIM GU16 .....58 E7
  WVILLE PO7 .....275 N4
Beresford Gdns
  CHCH/BSGR BH23 .....325 J9
  CHFD SO53 .....206 G8
Beresford Ga AND SP10 * 103 J3
Beresford Rd
  BKME/WDN BH12 .....321 M6
  CHFD SO53 .....206 G8
  FHAM/STUB PO14 .....294 B6
  LYMN SO41 .....329 J3
  NEND PO2 .....296 C7
  SBNE BH6 .....335 P2
Bereweeke Av FUFL SO22 .....164 F4
Bereweeke Cl FUFL SO22 .....22 A1
Bereweeke Rd FUFL SO22 .....22 A1
Bereweeke Wy FUFL SO22 .....164 F5
Berewyk Cl KBH RG22 .....89 L4
Bergen Crs HEND SO30 .....250 C6
Berkeley Av
  BKME/WDN BH12 .....321 L4
Berkeley Cl FHAM/STUB PO14 .....293 P7
  FLEETN GU51 .....74 E3
  VWD BH31 .....258 E3
  WSHM SO15 .....248 A4
Berkeley Crs FRIM GU16 .....58 F5
Berkeley Gv BKME/WDN BH22 .....90 B3
Berkeley Gdns HEND SO30 .....250 C6
Berkeley Rd NWBY RG14 .....16 C5
  TWDS BH3 .....322 E8
Berkeley Sq HAV PO9 .....15 K5
Berkley Av FERN BH22 .....302 D6
Berkshire Circular Routes
  THLE RG7 .....27 K9
Berkshire Ct PSEA PO1 .....19 K3
Berkshire Corpse Rd
  ALDT GU11 .....75 M5
Bermuda Cl CHIN RG24 .....69 M3
Bernard Av ALTN GU34 .....150 C6
  CHAM PO6 .....297 J5
Bernards Ct CHCH/BSGR BH23 .....324 C7
Bernard St SHAM SO14 .....20 E6
Bernersh Ct SHST GU47 .....41 K5
Berney Rd ENEY PO4 .....317 L4
Bernina Cl WVILLE PO7 .....255 J5
Bernstein Rd KBH RG22 .....89 N3
Bernwood Gv FAWY SO45 .....312 G1
Berrans Av BWD BH11 .....322 B1
Berrybank SHST GU47 .....41 M8
Berry Cl HEND SO30 .....250 D5
  OVTN RG25 .....87 J4
Berrydown Rd HAV PO9 .....276 C3
Berryfield Rd LYMN SO41 .....328 A5
Berry HI NARL SO24 .....169 K2
Berrylands Cl LISS GU33 .....173 M8
Berry La FHAM/STUB PO14 .....293 N7
  RWIN SO21 .....185 K9
Berry Wy AND SP10 .....102 B4
Berrywood Gdns HEND SO30 .....250 B4
Berrywood La NARL SO24 .....130 D3
Bertie Rd ENEY PO4 .....317 K4
Bertram Rd NMIL/BTOS BH25 .....327 L3
Berwick Rd TWDS BH3 .....322 E8
Berwyn Cl KBH RG22 .....68 D9
Berwyn Wk FHAM/STUB PO14 .....10 B7
Beryl Av GPORT PO12 .....295 K9
Beryton Cl GPORT PO12 .....315 G2
Beryton Rd GPORT PO12 .....315 J2
Besomer Dro RSAL SP5 .....200 B9
Bessborough Rd CCLF BH13 .....333 N4
Bessemer Cl VWD BH31 .....259 J6
Bessemer Rd BSTK RG21 .....90 B1
Beswick Av NBNE BH10 .....322 D6
Beta Rd FARN GU14 .....57 N8
Bethel Cl FNM GU9 .....96 D5
Bethel La FNM GU9 .....96 D5
Bethia Cl CHAR BH8 .....323 K9
Bethia Rd CHAR BH8 .....323 K9
Betjeman Wk YTLY GU46 .....56 C1
Betsy Cl CHCH/BSGR BH23 .....305 M7
Betsy La CHCH/BSGR BH23 .....325 M7
Betteridge Dr ROWN SO16 .....227 H6
Bettesworth Rd PSEA PO1 .....316 C1
Bettiscombe Cl CFDH BH17 .....320 F2
Betula Cl WVILLE PO7 .....276 A4
Beulah Rd ROWN SO16 .....247 L2
Bevan Cl ITCH SO19 .....249 P8
Bevan Rd HORN PO8 .....255 P6
Beveren Cl FLEETN GU51 .....56 E9
Beverley Cl ASHV GU12 .....97 M2
  BSTK RG21 .....90 D2
  HLER SO31 .....271 J6
  NTHA RG18 18
Beverley Crs FARN GU14 .....76 N1
Beverley Gdns BPWT SO32 .....232 F7
  HLER SO31 .....269 N1
  NBNE BH10 .....322 D4
  ROMY SO51 .....204 F4
Beverley Hts WEND SO18 .....229 H9

Beverley Rd FAWY SO45 ....290 B1
  FHAM/STUB PO14 ....294 A8
Beverly Cl LSOL/BMARY PO13 ....295 H7
The Bevers THLE RG7 ....27 J9
Beverston Rd CHAM PO6 ....274 C9
Bevis Cl FAWY SO45 ....291 H7
  SO31 ....292 D1
  NEND PO2 ....296 F8
Bevis Rd GPORT PO12 ....12 D1
Bevois Gdns SHAM SO14 ....248 C4
Bevois HI PTSW SO17 ....248 D3
Bevois Valley Rd SHAM SO14 ....248 D4
Bexington Cl BWD BH11 ....321 N1
Bexmoor CHIN RG24 ....70 B6
Bexmoor Wy CHIN RG24 ....70 B6
Beyne Rd FUFL SO22 ....183 K3
Bible Flds OVTN RG25 ....108 G2
Bicester Cl WHCH RG28 ....85 L6
Bickerley Gdns RGWD BH24 ....282 D5
Bickerley Rd RGWD BH24 ....282 D5
Bicknell Rd FRIM GU16 ....58 D3
Bicton Rd BWD BH11 ....322 B4
Bidbury La HAV PO9 ....276 C9
Biddenfield La WHAM SO32 ....252 B7
Bidden Rd ODIM RG29 ....92 C6
  OVTN RG25 ....92 C6
Biddesden La RAND SP11 ....80 B1
Biddlecombe Cl
  LSOL/BMARY PO13 ....294 G9
Bideford Cl FARN GU14 ....57 P6
Biggin Wk FHAM/STUB PO14 ....294 C1
Bighton Dean La NARL SO24 ....148 G7
Bighton HI NARL SO24 ....169 K1
Bighton La NARL SO24 ....148 F7
Bighton Rd ALTN GU34 ....149 M3
Bilbao Ct AND SP10 ....5 J2
Bilberry Cl HLER SO31 ....270 F8
Bilberry Dr TOTT SO40 ....247 J9
Bilesden Rd CHOB/PIR GU 59 P1
Billett Av WVILLE PO7 ....275 P1
Billing Cl ENEY PO4 ....317 K5
Billington Gdns HEND SO30 ....250 D2
Billington Wy NTHA RG18 ....276 F6
Billy Lawn Av HAV PO9 ....276 F6
Bilton Rd CHIN RG24 ....69 P3
Bilton Wy HSEA PO3 ....297 L7
Bindon Cl BKME/WDN SO21 ....321 N5
Bindon Rd ROWN SO16 ....247 L1
Binfields Cl CHIN RG24 ....70 A3
Bingham Av PSTN BH14 ....333 N4
Bingham Dr LYMN SO41 ....329 L4
Bingham Rd
  CHCH/BSGR BH23 ....325 J8
  MOOR/WNTN BH9 ....322 C7
  VWD BH31 ....258 C6
Bingley Cl ALTN GU34 ....132 E5
  BSTK RG21 ....7 H2
Binley Bottom RAND SP11 ....62 G8
Binnacle Wy CHAM PO6 ....296 D1
Binness Wy CHAM PO6 ....297 N2
Binsey Rd BKME/WDN SO21 ....321 N7
Binsey Cl ROWN SO16 ....247 J3
Binstead Cl ROWN SO16 ....228 E7
Binstead Rd ALTN GU34 ....135 H1
Binsted Dr BLKW GU17 ....41 L9
Binsteed Rd NEND PO2 ....296 C9
Binton La RFNM GU10 ....97 L9
Birch Av CHCH/BSGR BH23 ....324 C4
  FERN BH22 ....302 F7
  FLEETN GU51 ....74 C3
  NMIL/BTOS BH25 ....326 F1
Birch Cl BOR GU35 ....154 B6
  HORN PO8 ....255 N8
  LISS GU33 ....192 E2
  PSTN BH14 ....321 N9
  RFNM GU10 ....116 A6
  RGWD BH24 ....281 K6
  ROWN SO16 ....247 J1
  RWIN SO21 ....207 P5
Birch Dr FAWY SO45 ....268 D8
Birchdale Cl HLER SO31 ....292 D1
Birchdale Rd WIMB BH21 ....278 F9
Birch Dr BLKW GU17 ....41 L7
  CHAR BH8 ....323 N5
  LSOL/BMARY PO13 ....294 G5
Birchen Cl HLER SO31 ....271 J4
The Birches CBLY GU15 ....51 J9
Birches Crest KBH RG22 ....89 P5
The Birches BLKW GU17 ....41 J9
  FARN GU14 ....57 L9
  WEND SO18 ....249 K3
Birchett Rd ALDT GU11 ....2 C4
  FARN GU14 ....57 M8
Birchfields CBLY GU15 ....58 B1
Birch Gv BOR GU35 ....154 A7
  ELGH SO50 ....207 H7
  FERN BH22 ....280 D7
  HTWY RG27 ....72 A2
  STOK SO20 ....123 M7
Birchland Cl THLE RG7 ....26 C9
Birchlands TOTT SO40 ....246 B6
Birch La THLE RG7 ....35 N1
Birchmore Cl
  LSOL/BMARY PO13 ....294 G7
Bircholt Rd LIPH SO30 ....174 L3
Birch Rd BOR GU35 ....155 J2
  HEND SO30 ....250 D4
  RGWD BH24 ....281 P5
  ROWN SO16 ....228 C4
  TADY RG26 ....33 P4
  THLE RG7 ....27 H4
Birch Tree Cl EMRTH PO10 ....277 M6
Birch Tree Dr EMRTH PO10 ....277 M6
Birchview Al YTLY GU46 ....56 D1
Birch Wk FERN BH22 * 302 F5
Birch Wy ASHV GU12 ....76 F5
Birchwood CHIN RG24 ....70 A1
Birch Wd ITCH SO19 ....249 N6
Birchwood Cl
  CHCH/BSGR BH23 ....326 A7
Birchwood Dr FBDG SP6 ....239 N6

Birchwood Gdns HEND SO30 ....250 C3
Birchwood Rd NWBY RG14 ....14 C8
  PSTN BH14 ....321 M9
Birchy HI LYMN SO41 ....308 C7
Bird Fld CHFD SO53 ....206 A7
Birdham Rd HISD PO11 ....319 L6
Birdhaven RFNM GU10 ....116 A5
Birdlip Cl HORN PO8 ....256 A5
Birdlip Rd CHAM PO6 ....274 D9
Bird's Hill Rd PLE BH15 ....320 G8
Birdwood Gv
  FHAM/PORC PO16 ....295 K1
Birinus Rd CBLY GU15 ....41 N8
Birinus Rd WINC SO23 ....23 F2
Birkbeck PI SHST GU47 ....41 M5
Birkdale Av CHAM PO6 ....275 L9
Birkdale Cl BDST BH18 ....300 C8
Birkdale Rd BDST BH18 ....300 C8
Birkenholme Cl BOR GU35 ....155 K4
Birmingham Ct
  LSOL/BMARY PO13 * 315 H3
Biscay Cl FHAM/STUB PO14 ....293 P6
Bishearne Gdns LISS GU33 ....192 C1
Bishop Cl BKME/WDN BH12 ....322 C8
Bishop Ct RCWD BH24 ....282 E2
Bishop Rd MOOR/WNTN BH9 ....322 C7
Bishops Cl FLEETS GU52 ....74 D5
  LTDN BH7 ....323 M9
  NTID SP9 ....79 H7
  SO40 ....246 C3
Bishops Crs ITCH SO19 ....249 H7
Bishopsfield Rd
  FHAM/STUB PO14 ....294 C2
Bishops Ga A BPWT SO32 ....252 F2
  BPWT SO32 ....252 F2
Bishop's Md FNM GU9 ....96 B9
Bishop Rd FNM GU9 ....96 B5
  ITCH SO19 ....248 G8
Bishopstoke La ELGH SO50 ....207 N7
Bishopstoke Mnr
  HAV PO9 ....229 M1
  HAV PO9 ....276 E5
Bishop St PSEA PO1 ....18 D2
Bishop Sumner Dr FNM GU9 ....96 C5
Bishop's Vw ALTN GU34 ....150 A6
Bishop's Wy AND SP10 ....4 A3
Bishopswood La TADY RG26 ....33 H5
Bishop's Wood Rd
  BPWT SO32 ....232 F9
Bishopswood Rd TADY RG26 ....34 A5
Bitterne Ct RGWD BH24 ....284 F7
Bittern Cl ALDT GU11 ....96 C4
  GPORT PO12 ....315 M1
  KBH RG22 ....89 K3
  SHST GU47 ....41 L6
Bitterne Cl HAV PO9 ....276 F4
Bitterne Crs ITCH SO19 ....249 P6
Bitterne Rd ITCH SO19 ....249 H5
Bitterne Rd East WEND SO18 ....249 K5
Bitterne Rd West WEND SO18 ....248 G4
Bitterne Village ITCH SO19 ....249 J5
Bitterne Wy ITCH SO19 ....248 G6
Bittern Rd ITCH SO19 ....249 H7
  LYMN SO41 ....329 K5
  VWD BH31 ....258 C5
Black Berry Cl HORN PO8 ....256 D8
Blackberry Cl ALTN GU34 ....150 D5
  THLE RG7 ....27 J5
Blackberry Dr ELGH SO50 ....230 B5
Blackberry La ALTN GU34 ....150 D6
  CHCH/BSGR BH23 ....325 K9
Blackberry Ter SHAM SO14 ....248 D4
  HORN PO8 ....255 P7
  KBH RG22 ....89 L6
  THLE RG7 * 27 K4
Blackbird Cl CFDH BH17 ....320 A4
Blackbird Rd ELGH SO50 ....228 F2
Blackbird Wy
  CHCH/BSGR BH23 ....305 N8
  LSOL/BMARY PO13 ....314 D1
Blackbrook House Dr
  FHAM PO15 ....10 B5
Blackbrook Park Av
  FHAM PO15 ....10 C5
Blackbrook Rd FHAM PO15 ....10 B5
Blackburn Ct
  LSOL/BMARY PO13 * 315 H3
Blackburn Rd
  BKME/WDN BH12 ....321 K6
Blackbushe Cl ROWN SO16 ....227 K7
Blackbushe Pk YTLY GU46 * 40 D9
Blackbushes Rd FLEETN GU51 ....56 B7
  HTWY RG27 ....55 P4
Blackcap Cl HAV PO9 ....276 C1
Blackcap PI SHST GU47 ....41 M6
Black Dam Rdbt CHIN RG24 ....69 P7
Black Dam Wy BSTK RG21 ....69 H8
Blackdown Cl FAWY SO45 ....267 P8
  KBH RG22 ....68 D9
Blackdown Crs HAV PO9 ....276 E6
Blackdown Wy FRIM GU16 ....59 H6
Blackdown Wy STHA RG19 ....25 M5
Blackfield La FARN BH22 ....280 B6
Blackfield Rd CHAR BH8 ....323 K4
  FAWY SO45 ....290 G8
Blackfriars Cl SSEA PO5 ....19 J4
Blackfriars Rd SSEA PO5 ....19 J3
Blackheath Rd FNM GU9 ....96 A4
Blackhill Rd ROMY SO51 ....224 F4
Black Horse La BPWT SO32 ....252 C2
Blackhouse La WHAM PO17 ....273 L2
Black La RSAL SP5 ....200 D9
Blackman Gdns ALDT GU11 ....2 C1
Black Moor Rd VWD BH31 ....259 J6
Blackmore La PSF GU32 ....190 E2
Blacknest Rd ALTN GU34 ....114 G8

Black Pond La RFNM GU10 ....116 C4
Blackstocks La HTWY RG27 ....71 J7
Blackstone Cl FARN GU14 ....57 L7
Black Swan Yd AND SP10 ....4 E4
Blackthorn Cl ITCH SO19 ....249 H6
  LYMN SO41 ....329 H5
  RWIN SO21 ....189 H2
Blackthorn Crs FARN GU14 ....57 N5
Blackthorn Dr GPORT PO12 ....295 L9
  HISD PO11 ....319 J5
  NTHA RG18 ....25 N2
Blackthorne Cl BOR GU35 ....154 B5
Blackthorn Gn HAV PO9 ....208 A5
Blackthorn Rd HISD PO11 ....319 J5
  ITCH SO19 ....249 H6
Blackthorn Wy DEAN RG23 ....248 F6
  VWD BH31 ....259 H5
Blackwater Cl ASHV GU12 ....97 N2
  BSTK RG21 ....7 H6
  CHAM PO6 ....296 F1
  DEAN RG23 ....88 F2
  FBDG SP6 ....239 L6
Blackwater Dr TOTT SO40 ....246 B2
  WIMB BH21 ....300 F6
Blackwater Gv FBDG SP6 ....239 L6
Blackwater Ms TOTT SO40 ....246 B2
Blackwater Pk ASHV GU12 ....97 L2
Blackwater Vw EWKG RG40 ....40 A4
Blackwell La ASHV GU12 ....97 N2
Bladon Cl HAV PO9 ....144 D6
Bladon Rd ROWN SO16 ....247 N1
Blagdon Cl STHA RG19 ....24 C8
Blair Av PSTN BH14 ....321 L8
Blair Cl NMIL/BTOS BH25 ....326 C4
Blaire Pk YTLY GU46 ....40 C7
Blair Rd BSTK RG21 ....69 K9
Blaise Cl FARN GU14 ....76 C1
Blake Cl CWTH RG45 ....41 K2
  ODIM RG29 ....93 J3
  ROWN SO16 ....226 C7
Blake Ct AND SP10 ....4 D1
Blakedene Rd PSTN BH14 ....333 L2
Blake Hill Av PSTN BH14 ....333 L2
Blake Hill Crs PSTN BH14 ....333 L2
Blakemere Crs CHAM PO6 ....274 E9
Blakeney Rd ROWN SO16 ....247 H1
Blake Rd CHAM PO6 ....275 M9
Blake's La TADY RG26 ....34 D5
Blakesley La HSEA PO3 ....297 L5
Blakes Ride YTLY GU46 ....40 C8
Blanchard Rd BPWT SO32 ....231 P4
Blandford Cl PLE BH15 ....332 B1
Blandford Rd CHCH/BSGR BH23 ....332 C2
Band's Ct THLE RG7 ....27 H5
Blanket St ALTN GU34 ....133 M9
Blankney Cl
  FHAM/STUB PO14 ....293 P7
Blann Cl ROWN SO16 ....226 C7
Blaven Wk FHAM/STUB PO14 ....10 B7
Bleaklow Cl ROWN SO16 ....247 K3
Blechynden Ter WSHM SO15 ....20 B3
Bledlow Cl NWBY RG14 ....30 C1
Blencowe Dr CHFD SO53 ....206 A8
Blendon Dr AND SP10 ....102 B1
Blendworth Crs HAV PO9 ....14 E1
Blendworth La HORN PO8 ....256 D4
  WEND SO18 ....248 G1
Blenheim Av PTSW SO17 ....248 C2
Blenheim Cl CHFD SO53 ....132 C6
  ALTN GU34 ....150 C5
  RFNM GU10 ....97 L4
  TOTT SO40 ....246 B5
Blenheim Crs FNM GU9 ....96 A5
  LYMN SO41 ....327 N3
Blenheim Dr
  CHCH/BSGR BH23 ....325 M8
Blenheim Gdns FAWY SO45 ....267 P8
  GPORT PO12 ....295 M9
  HAV PO9 ....277 H9
  PTSW SO17 ....248 D1
Blenheim Pk ALDT GU11 ....2 B5
Blenheim Rd ALDT GU11 ....2 B5
  CHIN RG24 ....70 D7
  ELGH SO50 ....229 J2
  HORN PO8 ....256 A6
  NWBY RG14 ....14 A5
Bliss Cl KBH RG22 ....90 A2
Blissford Cl HAV PO9 ....277 H4
Blissford Crs FBDG SP6 ....241 J3
Blissford HI FBDG SP6 ....241 J5
Blissford Rd FBDG SP6 ....241 J3
Bloomfield Av
  MOOR/WNTN BH9 ....322 F5
Bloomsbury Wk ITCH SO19 ....247 M5
Bloomsbury Wy BLKW GU17 ....57 K2
Blossom Cl AND SP10 ....102 A3
  HEND SO30 ....250 C7
Blossom Sq PSEA PO1 ....18 E1
Bloswood Dr WHCH RG28 ....85 K5
Bloswood La WHCH RG28 ....85 H3
Blount Rd PSEA PO1 ....18 D5
Bloxworth Rd
  BKME/WDN BH12 ....321 P4
Blue Ball Cnr WINC SO23 ....23 G4
Blue Ball HI WINC SO23 ....23 G4
Bluebell Cl AND SP10 ....102 A3
  CHCH/BSGR BH23 ....325 M7
  WVILLE PO7 ....275 P4
Bluebell Copse HLER SO31 ....270 F8
Bluebell Rd THLE RG7 ....27 H4

Bluebell La CFDH BH17 ....320 A3
Bluebell Rd BOR GU35 ....154 D3
  ROWN SO16 ....228 D8
Bluebell Wy HORN PO8 ....271 K2
  NTHA RG18 ....25 N2
Blueberry Gdns AND SP10 ....102 A3
Bluecoats NTHA RG18 ....25 M1
Bluehaven Wk HTWY RG27 ....71 N3
Blueprint Portfield Rd
  HSEA PO3 ....297 J2
Blue Prior Ct FLEETS GU52 ....74 B9
Bluestar Gdns HEND SO30 ....250 C1
Bluethroat Cl SHST GU47 ....41 M6
Bluff Cove ALDT GU11 ....3 J1
Blundell La HLER SO31 ....250 C9
Blunden Cl BSTK RG21 ....90 B2
Blunden Rd FARN GU14 ....57 N8
Blunt Rd DEAN RG23 ....88 E5
Blyth Av CHCH/BSGR BH23 ....305 L9
Blyth Cl CHCH/BSGR BH23 ....324 B3
Blyth Mws WSHM SO15 * 248 A1
Blythswood Ct
  NMIL/BTOS BH25 ....327 H8
Blythwood Dr FRIM GU16 ....58 C3
Boakes PI TOTT SO40 ....246 B2
Boames La KSCL RG20 ....29 N1
Boardwalk Wy TOTT SO40 ....247 L7
Boarhunt Cl PSEA PO1 ....19 J2
Boarhunt Rd WHAM PO17 ....273 J7
Boar's Br TADY RG26 ....51 H3
Bob Hann Cl
  BKME/WDN BH12 ....321 N7
Bockhampton Rd
  CHCH/BSGR BH23 ....325 J2
Bodin Gdns NWBY RG14 ....24 D7
Bodley Rd CCLF BH13 ....333 N4
Bodmin Cl KBH RG22 ....88 G2
  STHA RG19 ....25 M5
Bodmin Rd CHAM PO6 ....296 C1
  ELGH SO50 ....229 N1
Bodorgan Rd WCLF BH2 ....3 G2
Boirdre Cl HSEA PO3 ....297 K6
Boldens Rd GPORT PO12 ....315 M7
Bolderford Br BROC SO42 ....286 E4
Bolderwood Arboretum
  Ornamental Dr LYND SO43 ....263 J6
Bolderwood Cl ELGH SO50 ....229 P1
Boldre Cl BKME/WDN BH12 ....321 N5
  HAV PO9 ....276 C6
Boldre La LYMN SO41 ....309 K9
Boldrewood Rd ROWN SO16 ....228 E8
Boleyn Crs MOOR/WNTN BH9 ....323 J3
Bolhinton Av TOTT SO40 ....267 H1
Bolley Av BOR GU35 ....153 N5
Bolton Crs FERN BH22 ....302 G2
  KBH RG22 ....69 H9
Bolton Dr GPORT PO12 ....315 N1
Bolton Rd SBNE BH6 ....336 C3
The Boltons WVILLE PO7 ....275 N7
Bonchurch Cl ROWN SO16 ....228 E7
Bonchurch Rd ENEY PO4 ....317 J3
Bond Av FERN BH22 ....280 D5
Bond Cl CHIN RG24 ....69 A5
  LYMN SO41 ....308 B5
  TADY RG26 ....50 E5
Bondfields Crs HAV PO9 ....276 F4
Bond Rd PLE BH15 ....321 H7
  WEND SO18 ....248 G2
Bone La NWBY RG14 ....17 H2
Bone Rd PSTW RG14 ....277 H8
Bonfire Cnr PSEA PO1 ....18 C1
Bonham Rd TWDS BH5 ....322 F8
Bonhams Cl ALTN GU34 ....133 L2
Boniface Cl TOTT SO40 ....246 B5
Boniface Crs ROWN SO16 ....227 J9
Bonington Dr
  CHCH/BSGR BH23 ....325 J7
Bonners Fld RFNM GU10 ....114 C5
Boon Wy DEAN RG23 ....88 E1
Boothby Ct TOTT SO40 ....246 E5
Bordean La PSF GU32 ....190 C9
Borden Gates AND SP10 ....4 D6
Borden La LIPH GU30 ....193 P6
Border End HASM GU27 * 156 C7
Border La LIPH GU30 ....193 P6
Borderside YTLY GU46 ....40 B8
Bordon Rd TADY RG26 ....34 B6
Bordred Cross FBDG SP6 ....241 J3
Boreham Rd SBNE BH6 ....336 B1
Borelli Ms FNM GU9 ....4 E3
Borkum CI AND SP10 ....82 D8
Borley Rd CFDH BH17 ....320 C4
Borodin Cl KBH RG22 ....144 F4
Borough Court Rd HTWY RG27 ....54 D7
Borough HI PSF GU32 ....215 L2
Borough HI PSF GU32 ....215 L2
Borough Rd PSF GU32 ....215 K3
The Borough FNM GU9 ....96 G5
Bosanquet Cross FBDG SP6 ....241 J2
Bossington Cl ROWN SO16 ....227 J7

Boscombe Cliff Rd BOSC BH5 ....335 L3
Boscombe Grove Rd
  BMTH BH1 ....335 L1
Boscombe Overcliff Dr
  BOSC BH5 ....335 M3
Boscombe Spa Rd BOSC BH5 ....335 K2
Boscowen Cl AND SP10 ....5 P7
Bosham Rd NEND PO2 ....297 H9
Bosham Wk
  LSOL/BMARY PO13 ....294 F7
Bosley Cl CHCH/BSGR BH23 ....324 C5
Bosmere Gdns EMRTH PO10 ....277 L9
Bosmere Rd HISD PO11 ....319 L6
Bossington Cl ROWN SO16 ....163 N4
Boston Rd CHAM PO6 ....274 C9
Boston Rd CHCH/PORC PO16 ....207 J7
Bosville ELGH SO50 ....207 J7
Boswell Cl HEND SO30 ....250 F4
  ITCH SO19 ....249 L5
Bosworth Ms
  BKME/WDN BH9 ....322 G5
Botany Bay Rd ITCH SO19 ....249 K8
Botany HI RFNM GU10 ....117 K1
Botisdone Cl RAND SP11 ....42 G7
Botley Dr HAV PO9 ....276 D5
Botley Gdns ITCH SO19 ....249 K8
Botley Rd BPWT SO32 ....251 K3
  ELGH SO50 ....250 D4
  HEND SO30 ....249 P2
  HEND SO30 ....251 K5
  HLER SO31 ....249 L9
  ITCH SO19 ....249 L9
  NBAD SO52 ....205 K8
  ROMY SO51 ....200 E6
Bottle La HTWY RG27 ....53 L5
Bottom La ROMY SO51 ....202 E9
Boulevards ALDT GU11 * 2 E3
Boulnois Av PSTN BH14 ....321 N9
Boulter La WHAM SO17 ....274 C3
Boulters Rd ASHV GU12 ....2 C6
Boulton Rd PSEA PO1 ....19 J7
Boundary Acre HLER SO31 ....250 B7
Boundary Cl WSHM SO15 ....247 K5
Boundary Dr WIMB BH21 ....278 F8
Boundary La RGWD BH24 ....281 K8
Boundary Rd FARN GU14 ....75 K3
  CSHT GU26 ....269 P2
  HLER SO31 ....292 D7
  NWBY RG14 ....17 H3
  RFNM GU14 ....135 N2
Boundary Wk WHAM PO17 ....272 C3
Boundary Wy CHAM PO6 ....275 K5
  HAV PO9 ....14 E5
Bound La HISD PO11 ....318 G6
Boundstone Cl RFNM GU10 ....115 P6
Boundway LYMN SO41 ....307 M7
Bounty Rd BSTK RG21 ....69 K8
Bounty Rd BSTK RG21 ....69 K8
Bourley La RFNM GU10 ....95 P1
Bourley Rd FLEETS GU52 ....74 F8
Bourne Arch RTG18 ....25 L3
Bourne Av WCLF BH2 ....3 G5
  ROMY SO51 ....247 N2
Bourne Cl HORN PO8 ....256 B5
  ROMY SO51 ....224 D1
  RWIN SO21 ....207 K1
  WBNE BH4 ....334 D3
Bourne Dene RFNM GU10 ....116 A5
Bourne Fld CHIN RG24 ....51 H9
Bournefields RWIN SO21 ....116 D5
Bourne Firs RFNM GU10 ....116 D5
Bourne Grove Cl FNM GU9 ....116 E3
Bourne Grove Dr RFNM GU10 ....116 E3
Bourne Hts RFNM GU10 ....116 C2
Bourne La NTID SP9 ....198 A7
  RWIN SO21 ....207 K1
  TOTT SO40 ....245 K6
Bourne Meadow AND SP10 ....84 C2
Bournemouth Ar BMTH BH1 * 8 D4
Bournemouth International
  Centre Rbt WCLF BH2 ....8 B5
Bournemouth Rd CHFD SO53 ....206 E1
  CHFD SO53 ....206 E1
  LYND SO43 ....264 E5
  RAND SP11 ....119 N4
  ROWN SO16 ....228 E1
Bournemouth Rd Castle HI
  PSTN BH14 ....321 K8
Bournemouth Station Rbt
  BMTH BH1 ....9 H2
Bourne Rd CHAM PO6 ....296 D1
  NTID SP9 ....79 H5
  STHA RG19 ....25 L3
  TOTT SO40 ....245 P6
  WSHM SO15 ....247 P6
The Bourne FLEETS GU52 ....74 E7
Bourne Valley Rd
  BKME/WDN BH12 ....334 A1
Bourne Av AMSY SP4 ....118 A7
  NTID SP9 ....79 H4
  RAND SP11 ....84 D3
Bournewood Dr WBNE BH4 ....334 C2
Bourton Gdns CHIN RG24 ....70 D7
Bourton Cl NMIL/BTOS BH25 ....327 P7
Boveridge Gdns
  MOOR/WNTN BH9 ....323 H3
Bovington Cl CFDH BH17 ....320 A4
Bowater Cl TOTT SO40 ....246 A2
Bowater Wy TOTT SO40 ....246 A2
Bowcombe HLER SO31 ....269 L3
Bowcott HI BOR GU35 ....154 C3
Bowden La PTSW SO17 ....248 E1

Bowden Rd BKME/WDN BH12....321 L2
Bow Dr HTWY RG27....52 E5
Bowenhurst Gdns
FLEETS GU52....74 D8
Bowenhurst La FLEETN GU51....73 P9
RFNM GU10....94 F2
Bowenhurst Rd FLEETS GU52....74 D7
Bower Cl FAWY SO45....290 E6
ITCH SO19....269 H1
Bower Rd CHAR BH8....323 K7
RFNM GU10....116 A5
Bowers Cl HORN PO8....256 A7
Bowers Grove La ALTN GU34....149 M9
Bowers Hl RSAL SP5....200 A6
Bowers La RAND SP11....42 F6
Bowerwood Rd FBDG SP6....240 A3
Bowes Hl HAV PO9....257 J8
Bowes-lyon Ct HORN PO8....256 B4
Bowes Rd STHA RG19....25 N5
Bow Fld HTWY RG27....72 B3
Bow Gdns HTWY RG27....52 E5
Bow Gv HTWY RG27....52 E4
Bowland Ri CHFD SO53....206 C6
NMIL/BTOS BH25....327 L5
Bowland Wy FAWY SO45....312 G1
Bowler Av HSEA PO3....317 H2
Bowler Ct HSEA PO3....317 H2
Bowling Court Gn FRIM GU16....58 D6
Bowling Green Dr HTWY RG27....71 N3
Bowling Green La RSAL SP5....195 H8
Bowling Green Rd NTHA RG18....25 K2
Bowman Ct CWTH RG45....40 F2
ITCH SO19....249 K8
Bowman Rd CHIN RG24....52 A9
Bowmonts Rd TADY RG26....34 E6
Bow St ALTN GU34....132 E7
Bowyer Cl BSTK RG21 *....69 K8
Boxall's Gv ALDT GU11....2 D7
Boxall's La ALDT GU11....96 G4
FNM GU9....2 C7
Box Cl CFDH BH17....320 D5
Boxhalls La ALDT GU11....2 C7
Boxwood Cl WVILLE PO7....275 N4
Boyatt Crs ELGH SO50....207 J5
Boyatt La ELGH SO50....207 J6
Boyce Cl KBH RG22....89 N3
Boyd Cl FHAM/STUB PO14....293 P8
Boyd Rd BKME/WDN BH12....321 P6
LSOL/BMARY PO13....294 F6
Boyes La RWIN SO21....208 A4
Boyle Crs WVILLE PO7....275 M5
Boyne Mead Rd WINC SO23....145 J9
Boyne Ri WINC SO23....145 J8
Boyneswood Cl ALTN GU34....150 D4
Boyneswood La ALTN GU34....150 C4
Boyneswood Rd ALTN GU34....150 D4
Boynton Cl CHFD SO53....206 D5
Brabant Cl HLER SO31....271 H3
Brabazon Dr
CHCH/BSGR BH23....325 M8
Brabazon Rd FHAM PO15....271 K5
WIMB BH21....301 H4
Brabon Rd FARN GU14....57 N8
Brabourne Av FERN BH22....302 C4
Bracebridge CBLY GU15....41 P9
Bracher Cl AND SP10....4 E3
Bracken Bank CHIN RG24....70 A4
Brackenbury AND SP10....102 B1
Bracken Cl LSOL/BMARY PO13....314 E2
NBAD SO52....227 L1
RGWD BH24....281 K5
Bracken Crs ELGH SO50....229 P2
Brackendale Cl FRIM GU16....58 D2
Brackendale Ct WIMB BH21....280 E1
Brackendale Rd CBLY GU15....58 C1
CHAR BH8....323 J7
Brackendene ASHV GU12....77 H9
Bracken Gln PLE BH15....320 G8
Bracken Heath HORN PO8....276 B1
Brackenhill CCLF BH13....334 A5
Brackenhill Rd WIMB BH21....279 J7
Bracken La BOR GU35....153 M8
ROWN SO16....247 L2
YTLY GU46....40 B8
Bracken Pl ELGH SO50....228 C5
Bracken Rd EPSF GU31....216 A3
FERN BH22....302 B1
NBAD SO52....227 L1
SBNE BH6....336 A2
The Brackens FAWY SO45....267 P7
HLER SO31....271 H8
KBH RG22....89 N5
Brackens Wy LYMN SO41....329 M5
Bracken Wy
CHCH/BSGR BH23....326 D6
THLE RG7....27 J5
Brackenway Rd CHFD SO53....206 E5
Bracklesham Cl FARN GU14....57 P6
ITCH SO19....249 H8
Bracklesham Pl
NMIL/BTOS BH25....327 H8
Bracklesham Rd HISD PO11....319 N6
LSOL/BMARY PO13....295 H9
Brackley Av ELGH SO50....230 B2
HTWY RG27....54 G7
Brackley Cl CHCH/BSGR BH23....303 N8
Brackley Wy KBH RG22....89 N2
TOTT SO40....246 B3
Bracknell La HTWY RG27....55 H6
Bracknell Rd CWTH RG45....41 K1
Bradburne Rd WCLF BH2....8 B3
Bradbury Cl WHCH RG28....85 K6
Bradford Ct
LSOL/BMARY PO13 *....314 G2
Bradford Rd
MOOR/WNTN BH9....323 J3
SSEA PO5....19 K4
Brading Av ENEY PO4....317 J6
LSOL/BMARY PO13....294 G7
Brading Cl ROWN SO16....228 E7
Bradley Ct HAV PO9....277 H5
Bradley Gn ROWN SO16....227 M8
Bradley-Moore Sq NTHA RG18....25 P2
Bradley Peak FUFL SO22....164 D6
Bradley Rd FUFL SO22....164 D4
Bradly Rd FHAM PO15....272 A9
Bradman Sq AND SP10 *....82 F8
Bradpole Rd CHAR BH8....323 L6
Bradshaw Cl ELGH SO50....230 E2
Bradstock Cl
BKME/WDN BH12....321 P4
Bradwell Cl AND SP10....82 B8
Braehead FAWY SO45....268 B8
Braemar Av CHAM PO6....297 K2
SBNE BH6....336 E2
Braemar Cl FHAM PO15....10 B1
FRIM GU16....58 E5
LSOL/BMARY PO13....295 H7
SBNE BH6....336 E2
Braemar Dr CHCH/BSGR BH23....326 B6
DEAN RG23....88 E1
Braemar Rd
LSOL/BMARY PO13....295 H6
Braemore Cl STHA RG19....25 N6
Braeside Cl FUFL SO22....183 K2
HASM GU27....156 E5
Braeside Crs ITCH SO19....248 G6
Braeside Rd FERN BH22....280 E6
ITCH SO19....248 G6
RGWD BH24....281 L5
Brahms Rd KBH RG22....90 A3
Braidley Rd WCLF BH2....8 D2
Brailswood Rd PLE BH15....320 F8
Braintree Rd CHAM PO6....274 F9
Brairwood Gdns HISD PO11....318 F5
Braishfield Cl ROWN SO16....247 K2
Braishfield Gdns CHAR BH8....323 K5
Braishfield Rd HAV PO9....276 G6
ROMY SO51....204 G4
Brake Rd FARN GU14....75 M3
Bramber Rd GPORT PO12....315 L1
Bramble Bank FRIM GU16....58 F7
Bramble Cl ELGH SO50....207 K8
FAWY SO45....290 E6
FBDG SP6....240 B3
FHAM/STUB PO14....293 N8
HAV PO9....277 J7
Bramble Ct FERN BH22....280 D7
Bramble Dr ROMY SO51....204 G4
Bramblegate ELGH SO50 *....230 D3
Bramble Hl CHFD SO53....206 D7
NARL SO24....168 A2
Bramble La CHCH/BSGR BH23....326 D6
HLER SO31....270 E5
HORN PO8....236 B5
Bramble Ms WEND SO18....249 J3
Bramble Rd ENEY PO4....316 G4
EPSF GU31....216 A2
Brambles Cl ALTN GU34....150 C6
ASHV GU12....97 P2
RWIN SO21....208 A5
Brambles Rd
LSOL/BMARY PO13....314 B1
The Brambles NWBY RG14....24 B7
RFNM GU10 *....94 G5
Brambleton Av FNM GU9....116 B3
Bramble Wk LYMN SO41....329 J3
Bramble Wy CHIN RG24....70 D6
CHCH/BSGR BH23....305 M7
LSOL/BMARY PO13....294 E7
Bramblewood Pl FLEETN GU51....74 B3
Brambling Cl KBH RG22....89 K4
ROWN SO16....227 M6
Brambling Rd HAV PO9....277 H1
The Bramblings TOTT SO40....246 A4
Bramblys Cl BSTK RG21....6 D7
Bramblys Dr BSTK RG21....6 C7
Bramdean Cl TADY RG26....34 C7
Bramdean Dr HAV PO9....276 D5
Bramdean Rd WEND SO18....249 M4
Bramdown Hts KBH RG22....89 M5
Bramham Moor
FHAM/STUB PO14....293 P7
Bramley Cl ALTN GU34....132 G6
LYMN SO41....329 L5
WVILLE PO7....275 P2
Bramley Crs ITCH SO19....249 K9
Bramley Gdns EMRTH PO10....299 P1
GPORT PO12....315 L7
Bramley Green Rd TADY RG26....52 B3
Bramley Gv CWTH RG45....40 E1
Bramley La BLKW GU17....41 J9
TADY RG26....52 A1
Bramley Rd CBLY GU15....58 A3
FERN BH22....302 C2
HTWY RG27....52 E4
NBNE BH10....322 C2
TADY RG26....50 G4
THLE RG7....35 J5
The Bramleys RSAL SP5....201 K2
Bramley Wk BOR GU35....153 N6
Bramling Av YTLY GU46....40 C8
Brampton Gdns KBH RG22....89 M6
Brampton La HSEA PO3....297 L5
Brampton Rd PLE BH15....320 F6
Bramshaw Cl FUFL SO22....164 D4
Bramshaw Ct HAV PO9....277 H5
Bramshaw Gdns CHAR BH8....323 K4
Bramshaw Wy
NMIL/BTOS BH25....326 F7
Bramshot Dr FLEETN GU51....74 D2
Bramshot La FLEETN GU51....57 H8
Bramshott Ct LIPH GU30 *....155 H8
Bramshott Dr HTWY RG27....72 A3
Bramshott Rd ENEY PO4....317 H4
FARN GU14....75 H2
ITCH SO19....269 H2
Bramston Rd WSHM SO15....247 N3
Brancaster Av AND SP10....82 B8
Branches La ROMY SO51....202 F3
Branders Cl SBNE BH6....336 E2
Branders La SBNE BH6....336 E1
Brandon Cl ALTN GU34....132 D5
CBLY GU15....59 J1
Brandon Rd FLEETS GU52....74 B8
SSEA PO5....316 F6
Brandy Bottom BLKW GU17 *....56 F2
Brandy Mt NARL SO24....168 A1
Branewick Cl FHAM PO15....271 K7
Branksea Cl PLE BH15....332 A2
Branksome Av STOK SO20....123 L6
WSHM SO15....247 N2
Branksome Cl FUFL SO22....164 C9
NMIL/BTOS BH25....327 K5
STOK SO20....123 K6
Branksome Dene Rd
WBNE BH4....334 B4
Branksome Hill Rd SHST GU47....41 M7
WBNE BH4....334 B1
Branksome Towers CCLF BH13....334 B6
Branksome Wood Gdns
WCLF BH2....8 A1
Branksomewood Rd
FLEETN GU51....74 B3
Branksome Wood Rd
WBNE BH4....334 C1
Bransbury Cl ROWN SO16....227 N8
Bransbury Rd ENEY PO4....317 K5
Bransgore Av HAV PO9....276 C6
Bransgore Gdns
CHCH/BSGR BH23....305 M7
Bransley Cl ROMY SO51....204 F4
Branson Rd BOR GU35....154 B5
Branton Cl KBH RG22....68 F9
Branwell Cl CHCH/BSGR BH23....324 E6
Branwood Cl LYMN SO41....328 E6
Brasenose Cl
FHAM/STUB PO14....271 H9
Brasher Cl ELGH SO50....230 A2
Brassey Cl MOOR/WNTN BH9....322 G6
Brassey Rd FUFL SO22....22 C1
MOOR/WNTN BH9....322 F6
Brassey Ter
MOOR/WNTN BH9 *....322 F6
Brasted Ct ENEY PO4....317 K3
Braunfels Wk KSCL RG20....16 A4
Braybourne Ct STOK SO20....161 M5
Braye Cl SHST GU47....41 K5
Breachfield KSCL RG20....30 E7
Breach La HTWY RG27....52 F5
RAND SP11....60 A4
Breadels Fld DEAN RG23....89 L7
Breamore Cl ELGH SO50....207 J7
NMIL/BTOS BH25....326 G4
Breamore Rd RSAL SP5....199 H7
WEND SO18....249 M4
Brean Cl ROWN SO16....227 J9
Brecon Av CHAM PO6....275 K9
Brecon Cl CHFD SO53....228 D1
FARN GU14....57 L6
FAWY SO45....268 A7
FHAM/STUB PO14....10 A7
NBNE BH10....322 E1
NMIL/BTOS BH25....327 L5
Brecon Rd ITCH SO19....249 L6
Bredenbury Crs CHAM PO6....274 E9
Bredon Wk FHAM/STUB PO14....294 C1
Bredy Cl CFDH BH17....320 F3
Breech Cl HSEA PO3 *....297 H5
The Breech CBLY GU15....41 M7
Bremble Cl BKME/WDN BH12....321 L2
Bremen Gdns AND SP10....82 D9
Brenchley Cl
FHAM/PORC PO16....295 L2
Brendon Cl CHAR BH8 *....323 L5
FAWY SO45....267 P8
Brendon Gn ROWN SO16....247 K3
Brendon Rd FARN GU14....57 L6
FHAM/STUB PO14....294 B1
Brent Cl STHA RG19....25 N5
Brent Ct EMRTH PO10....299 L1
Brentwood Crs WEND SO18....249 J2
Bret Harte Rd FRIM GU16....58 D4
Breton Cl FHAM PO15....271 H3
Brewells La LISS GU33....174 B9
Brewer Cl HLER SO31....271 H6
KBH RG22....68 F9
Brewers Cl FARN GU14....57 P8
Brewers La
LSOL/BMARY PO13....294 G7
NARL SO24....170 C8
RWIN SO21....183 P9
Brewer St PSEA PO1....19 G1
Brewery Common THLE RG7....27 H9
Brewhouse La HTWY RG27....55 J6
Brewhouse Sq GPORT PO12....315 P3
Brewster Cl HORN PO8....256 A8
Briar Cl CHCH/BSGR BH23....325 K9
GPORT PO12....315 J5
HORN PO8....256 B6
PLE BH15....320 G7
Briardene Ct TOTT SO40....246 C4
Briarfield Gdns HORN PO8....256 B5
Briar La ALTN GU34....150 D5
Briarlea Rd THLE RG7....27 H9
Briars Cl FARN GU14....75 L1
The Briars ASHV GU12....97 P2
FLEETS GU52....74 D6
WVILLE PO7 *....275 L1
Briarswood ROWN SO16....247 M2
Briarswood Ri FAWY SO45....267 P8
Briar Wy ROMY SO51....204 G4
TADY RG26....34 D6
WIMB BH21....279 K9
Briar Wd LISS GU33....173 M8
Briarwood Cl
FHAM/PORC PO16....11 G7
Briarwood Rd TOTT SO40....246 A5
Brickfield La CHFD SO53....206 D8
LYMN SO41....329 M2
Brickfield Rd PTSW SO17....248 E1
Brickfields Cl CHIN RG24....70 A4
Brickiln La ALTN GU34....150 G2
Brick Kiln La ALTN GU34....132 C5
NARL SO24....170 A8
Brick La CHCH/BSGR BH23....306 A4
FLEETN GU51....74 D2
Brickmakers Rd RWIN SO21....207 P5
Bricksbury Hl FNM GU9....96 C4
Brickwoods ROMY SO51....204 F5
Brickworth La RSAL SP5....200 F4
Brickworth Rd RSAL SP5....200 G1
Brickyard La WIMB BH21....302 A2
Brickyard Rd BPWT SO32....232 D9
The Brickyard TOTT SO40....245 H3
Bricky Lake La ROMY SO51....225 J5
Bridefield Cl HORN PO8....255 M8
Bridefield Crs HORN PO8....255 M8
Bridge Ap PLE BH15....332 D2
Bridge Cl HLER SO31....270 B1
Bridge End CBLY GU15....58 A1
Bridgefield FNM GU9....96 D9
Bridgefoot Dr
FHAM/PORC PO16....11 K6
Bridgefoot Pth
EMRTH PO10....299 M1
Bridge Industries
FHAM/PORC PO16....11 K2
Bridge La RWIN SO21....183 N7
Bridgemary Av
LSOL/BMARY PO13....295 H6
Bridgemary Gv
LSOL/BMARY PO13....294 G4
Bridgemary Rd
LSOL/BMARY PO13....294 G4
Bridgemary Wy
LSOL/BMARY PO13 *....294 G4
Bridge Md BPWT SO32....211 P8
Bridgemead FRIM GU16....58 C5
Bridge Mdw LISS GU33....192 D2
Bridge Pl NBNE BH10....302 D9
Bridge Rd ALDT GU11....2 E6
CBLY GU15....58 A2
EMRTH PO10....277 M9
FARN GU14....57 N9
HASM GU27....157 H6
HLER SO31....270 B2
HLER SO31....270 F4
ITCH SO19....248 F8
LYMN SO41....329 M3
NARL SO24....167 N2
ODIM RG29....72 B8
ROMY SO51....204 D6
Bridgers Cl ROWN SO16....227 J7
Bridges Av CHAM PO6....274 B9
Bridges Cl ELGH SO50....229 H1
FERN BH22....280 F6
Bridgeside Cl PSEA PO1....19 K2
Bridge Sq FNM GU9....96 C9
The Bridges RGWD BH24 *....282 C2
THLE RG7....35 K1
Bridge St AND SP10....4 D5
CHCH/BSGR BH23....324 G9
FBDG SP6....240 D2
FHAM/STUB PO14....293 N1
NWBY RG14....16 E2
OVTN RG25....86 G3
WHAM PO17....252 E7
WHAM PO17....273 P4
WINC SO23....23 G5
Bridget Cl HORN PO8....256 C4
Bridge Ter SHAM SO14 *....21 H7
Bridgetts La RWIN SO21....146 A6
Bridge Wk YTLY GU46....40 E7
Bridgewater Rd
BKME/WDN BH12....321 M6
The Bridgeway ITCH SO19 *....248 G8
Bridgwater Ct WSHM SO15....247 P6
Bridle Cl ALTN GU34....171 L2
GSHT GU26....155 P5
Bridle Ct ALDT GU11....2 A3
Bridle Crs LTDN BH7....324 A7
Bridle Wy WIMB BH21....279 K8
Bridleways VWD BH31....258 E4
Bridlington Av WSHM SO15....247 P3
Bridport Rd BKME/WDN BH12....321 P4
VWD BH31....258 F4
Bridport St PSEA PO1....19 H2
Brierley Av FERN BH22....302 E7
Brierley Cl NBNE BH10....322 E2
Brierley Rd NBNE BH10....322 E3
Brigantine Rd HLER SO31....270 E9
Brighstone Cl ROWN SO16....228 E7
Brightlands Av SBNE BH6....336 D2
Brighton Av GPORT PO12....295 K9
Brighton Rd ALDT GU11....3 J7
LYMN SO41....308 A5
WSHM SO15....248 B4
Brighton Wy KBH RG22....89 P3
Bright Rd PLE BH15....320 F6
Brightside WVILLE PO7....275 M4
Brightside Rd ROWN SO16....247 K1
Brights La HISD PO11....318 F3
Brightstone La ALTN GU34....151 H6
Brightstone Rd CHAM PO6....296 G2
Brightwells Rd FNM GU9....96 C9
Brimley Hill Ct KSCL RG20....48 C3
Brimpton La THLE RG7....33 L3
Brimpton Rd THLE RG7....33 M4
Brindle Cl ALDT GU11....97 H4
ROWN SO16....228 C7
Brinksway FLEETN GU51....74 D4
Brinn's La BLKW GU17....41 K9
Brinsons Cl CHCH/BSGR BH23....324 G4
Brinton La FAWY SO45....268 C5
Brinton's Rd SHAM SO14....21 F2
Brinton's Ter SHAM SO14....21 F1
Brisbane Rd
CHCH/BSGR BH23....324 C6
Brislands La ALTN GU34....149 N9
Bristol Ct
LSOL/BMARY PO13 *....314 G2
Bristol Rd ENEY PO4....317 H6
Bristow Rd CBLY GU15....58 A2
Britain St PSEA PO1....18 D3
Britannia Cl BOR GU35....154 B5
Britannia Dr DEAN RG23....89 L7
Britannia Gdns HEND SO30....230 B9
Britannia Rd PSTN BH14....321 J9
SHAM SO14....21 H2
SSEA PO5....19 K5
Britannia Rd North SSEA PO5....19 K5
Britannia Wy
CHCH/BSGR BH23....325 M8
GPORT PO12....315 N1
Briton St SHAM SO14....20 D7
Britten Cl ASHV GU12....97 P1
Britten Rd KBH RG22....90 A3
LSOL/BMARY PO13....314 C2
Britten Wy WVILLE PO7....275 N6
Brixey Cl BKME/WDN BH12....321 L5
Brixey Rd BKME/WDN BH12....321 L5
Broadacres FLEETN GU51....74 A4
Broad Av CHAR BH8....323 K7
Broadbent Cl ROWN SO16....227 H6
Broad Chalke Down
FUFL SO22....183 L2
Broad Cft HAV PO9....257 J9
Broadcut FHAM/PORC PO16....11 K3
Broadfields Cl LYMN SO41....338 G1
Broad Gdns CHAM PO6....297 N1
Broad Gn SHAM SO14....21 F3
Broadhalfpenny La TADY RG26....34 D5
Broad Ha'Penny RFNM GU10....116 A5
Broadhill La FBDG SP6....241 H3
Broadhurst FARN GU14....57 K9
Broadhurst Av NBNE BH10....322 E3
Broadhurst Gv CHIN RG24....70 A5
Broadlands FARN GU14....76 D2
FRIM GU16....58 E5
Broadlands Av ELGH SO50....207 J8
SBNE BH6....336 D2
WVILLE PO7....275 N4
Broadlands Cl CHAR BH8....323 K4
CHCH/BSGR BH23....326 D5
Broadlands Rd BROC SO42....286 E8
PTSW SO17....228 D9
Broad La BPWT SO32....232 E7
LYMN SO41....329 M4
NBAD SO52....205 J8
WVILLE PO7....254 D5
Broadlaw Wk
FHAM/STUB PO14....294 C2
Broad Leaze HTWY RG27....71 P2
Broadley Cl FAWY SO45....290 E5
Broadly Cl LYMN SO41....329 H5
Broadmayne Rd
BKME/WDN BH12....321 P5
Broadmead FARN GU14....75 L1
Broadmeadow Cl TOTT SO40....246 C4
Broadmeadows La
WVILLE PO7....276 A3
Broadmead Rd ROWN SO16....227 H6
Broad Mead Rd WIMB BH21....258 E9
Broadmere Av HAV PO9....276 F5
Broadmere Rd DEAN RG23....89 L6
Broad Oak HEND SO30....250 E4
Broadoak TADY RG26....34 E6
Broadoak Cl FAWY SO45....290 E6
Broad Oak La ODIM RG29....72 F9
Broad Rd RAND SP11....101 H7
Broadsands Dr GPORT PO12....315 H5
Broadshard La RGWD BH24....260 E9
The Broads WIMB BH21....278 C8
Broadstone Wy BDST BH18....320 B3
BDST BH18....320 C1
Broad St NARL SO24....168 A1
PSEA PO1....18 B6
Broadview Cl ALTN GU34....134 C2
Broad View La FUFL SO22....183 J3
Broad Wk FRIM GU16....58 D3
Broadwater Av PSTN BH14....333 K1
Broadwater Rd ROMY SO51....204 C7
WEND SO18....229 H9
Broad Wy FARN GU14....75 P4
HLER SO31....269 N5
PSF GU32....190 D6
THLE RG7....37 J3
Broadway SBNE BH6....336 E2
STHA RG19....25 N4
WHCH RG28....85 M7
Broadway La CHAR BH8....323 J4
HORN PO8....255 M5
Broadway Pk EPSF GU31....215 M4
The Broadway AND SP10....4 C5
NBNE BH10....322 D1
PTSW SO17 *....248 D2
SHST GU47....41 J7
WINC SO23....23 F5
Broadwell Rd RFNM GU10....115 P4
Broad Woods La ROMY SO51....202 G6
Brocas Dr BSTK RG21....7 H2
Brocas Rd THLE RG7....27 H6
Brock Cl FRIM GU16....59 J5
Brockenhurst Av HAV PO9....276 D4
Brockenhurst Dr YTLY GU46....40 E9
Brockenhurst Rd ALDT GU11....3 F6
MOOR/WNTN BH9....323 H5
Brockham Hill La ALTN GU34....112 G7
Brockhampton La HAV PO9....14 E6
Brockhampton Rd HAV PO9....14 C7
Brockhills La
NMIL/BTOS BH25....327 L2
Brockhurst Ldg FNM GU9....116 B3
Brockhurst Rd GPORT PO12....315 K1
Brockishill Rd LYND SO43....244 F7
Brocklands HAV PO9....14 C5
YTLY GU46....56 C1
Brockley Rd NBNE BH10....322 D3
Brocks Cl FAWY SO45....267 P8
Brocks Pine RGWD BH24....281 M6
Brockwood Bottom
NARL SO24....188 A5
Brodrick Av GPORT PO12....12 B5
Brokenford Av TOTT SO40....246 E4
Brokenford La TOTT SO40....246 D4
Broken Wy KSCL RG20....30 G4
Brokle Cl FLEETS GU52....74 B8
Bromelia Cl TADY RG26....52 A1
Bromley Rd WEND SO18....249 H2
Brompton Rd ENEY PO4....317 H6
Bromyard Crs CHAM PO6....296 E1
Bronte Av CHCH/BSGR BH23....324 E6
Bronte Cl TOTT SO40....246 B5
Bronte Gdns FHAM PO15....271 J2
Bronte Ri NWBY RG14....24 E7
Bronte Wy ITCH SO19....248 G5
Bronze Cl DEAN RG23....89 L7
Brook Av FNM GU9....96 F4
HLER SO31....270 C7
NMIL/BTOS BH25....327 K3
Brook Cl FLEETN GU51....74 D4
HLER SO31....270 D7
NBAD SO52....227 L1
NBNE BH10....322 C3

SHST GU47........41 M5
Brookdale CI BDST BH18........300 C9
  WVILLE PO7........275 N2
Brook Dr VWD BH31........259 H6
Brooke CI WINC SO23........145 J8
Brookers Cnr CWTH RG45........41 K1
Brookers La
  LSOL/BMARY PO13........294 E6
Brook Farm Av FHAM PO15........10 C5
  HAV PO9........14 C9
Brookfield Gdns HLER SO31........270 F6
Brookfield PI PTSW SO17 *........248 D1
Brookfield Rd ASHV GU12........97 L1
  ELGH SO50........230 B2
  PSEA PO1........316 C2
Brookfields ROMY SO51........224 D1
Brook Gdns EMRTH PO10........299 K1
  FARN GU14........75 N2
Brook Gn TADY RG26........34 E6
Brook HI LYMN SO41........310 C9
Brookhouse Rd FARN GU14........75 N1
Brookland CI LYMN SO41........329 J4
Brooklands ALDT GU11........2 A4
Brooklands CI FNM SO09........96 D4
  RFNM GU10........114 F5
Brooklands Rd BPWT SO32........232 A4
  FNM GU9........96 C5
  HAV PO9........276 B8
Brooklands Wy FHAM PO15........96 L4
Brook La CHCH/BSGR BH23........305 L9
  FBDG SP6........221 J5
  HEND SO30........255 J4
  HLER SO31........270 C9
  WVILLE PO7........234 D6
Brookley CI RFNM GU10........97 H8
Brookley Rd BROC SO42........286 G8
Brookly Gdns FLEETN GU51........74 E3
Brooklyn CI RWIN SO21........20 D7
Brooklyn CI NMIL/BTOS BH25........327 H4
Brooklyn Dr WVILLE PO7........275 P2
Brooklyn CI BPWT SO32........252 C1
Brookmead Ct FNM GU9 *........96 A9
Brookmeadow FHAM PO15........10 C5
Brookmead Wy HAV PO9........298 F2
Brook Rd BKME/WDN BH12........321 L7
  CBLY GU15........58 A1
  ELGH SO50........230 C2
  LYMN SO41........329 M5
  NBNE BH10........322 C3
  WEND SO18........249 J4
  WIMB BH21........300 G2
Brook Rw FAWY SO45 *........268 D8
Brooksby CI BLKW GU17........41 J9
Brooks CI RGWD BH24........282 F3
  WHCH RG28........85 M7
Brookside FBDG SP6........240 D2
  FNM GU9........96 C5
  LSOL/BMARY PO13........294 F4
  SHST GU47........41 K7
  TOTT SO40........246 D6
Brookside CI
  CHCH/BSGR BH23........305 L7
  WVILLE PO7........255 H7
Brookside Pk FARN GU14 *........74 C9
  CHCH/BSGR BH23........305 L8
  HAV PO9........14 C7
Brookside Wk TADY RG26........34 D6
Brookside Wy
  CHCH/BSGR BH23........326 A6
  HEND SO30........229 N9
  WEND SO18........228 G8
Brooks Rd NTHA RG18........25 P3
The Brooks WINC SO23 *........25 F4
Brook St BPWT SO32........232 A5
The Brook NARL SO24........148 A8
Brookvale CI BSTK RG21........9 J6
Brookvale Rd PTSW SO17........248 C2
Brook Wy CHCH/BSGR BH23........325 N8
  ROMY SO51........204 F3
Brookway NWBY RG14........25 H4
  RAND SP11........102 A6
Brookwood Av SSEA PO5........229 H1
Brookwood Rd FARN GU14........247 H3
  ROWN SO16........247 H3
Broom Acres FLEETS GU52........74 C6
  SHST GU47........41 J6
Broom CI ENEY PO4........317 M4
  WVILLE PO7........276 A5
Broome CI YTLY GU46........40 D7
Broomfield Crs
  LSOL/BMARY PO13........314 F1
Broomfield Dr FBDG SP6........239 N6
Broomfield La LYMN SO41........329 L3
  RFNM GU10........95 N6
Broomfield Rd BOR GU35........153 N6
  RSAL SP5........223 M3
Broomhill FARN GU14........57 L8
Broomhill Rd FARN GU14........223 M2
Broom Hill Wy ELGH SO50........270 N6
Broomleaf Cnr FNM GU9........96 D9
Broomleaf Rd FNM GU9........96 D9
Broomrigg Rd FLEETN GU51........74 B2
Broom Rd BKME/WDN BH12........321 L3
  EPSF GU31........216 A5
Brooms Gv ITCH SO19........317 M4
Broom Sq ENEY PO4........317 M4
Broom Wy BLKW GU17........57 L1
  LSOL/BMARY PO13........314 D1
Broomwood Wy RFNM GU10........116 C4
Brougham La LYMN SO41........267 N6
Brougham PI FNM GU9........96 B4
Brougham Rd SSEA PO5........19 G5
Brougham St GPORT PO12 *........315 L2
Broughton Av NBNE BH10........322 E3
Broughton CI NBNE BH10........322 E4
  ROWN SO16........247 L2

Broughton Ct HSEA PO3........297 L5
Broughton Ms FRIM GU16........58 E4
Broughton Rd LYND SO43........264 F4
  STOK SO20........140 D6
Browndown Rd
  MOOR/WNTN BH9........323 H7
Brownhill CI CHFD SO53........206 E6
Brownhill Ct ROWN SO16........227 J9
Brownhill Rd CHFD SO53........206 E6
  NBAD SO52........205 M9
  NMIL/BTOS BH25........306 F5
Brownhill Wy ROWN SO16........226 C9
Browning Av BOSC BH5........335 M2
  ITCH SO19........249 M5
Browning CI CBLY GU15........59 H1
  CHIN RG24........69 M4
  ELGH SO50........229 H1
  HLER SO31........271 J1
  NTHA RG18........25 M3
  TOTT SO40........246 B4
Browning Dr FUFL SO22........164 E7
Browning Rd
  BKME/WDN BH12........321 M6
  FLEETS GU52........74 B9
Brownings CI LYMN SO41........328 C3
Brownlow Av ITCH SO19........249 J5
Brownlow CI PSEA PO1........316 F1
Brownlow Gdns ITCH SO19........249 J5
Browns CI TADY RG26........51 P1
Brownsea CI
  NMIL/BTOS BH25........326 C4
Brownsea Rd CCLF BH13........333 K8
Brownsea View Av
  PSTN BH14........333 K2
Brownsfield Rd NTHA RG18........20 D7
Browns La FBDG SP6........219 J7
  LYMN SO41........330 C2
Brownsover Rd FARN GU14........57 K9
Browns Wk RFNM GU10........115 P5
Brownwich La
  FHAM/STUB PO14........293 K4
The Brow WVILLE PO7........275 L8
Broxburn CI CHFD SO53........206 C4
Broxhead Farm Rd BOR GU35........135 J9
Broxhead Rd HAV PO9........276 C4
Bruan Rd NWBY RG14........24 C7
Brudenell Av CCLF BH13........333 M4
Brudenell Rd CCLF BH13........333 M4
Brue CI CHFD SO53........206 D6
Brummell Rd NWBY RG14........24 B2
Brune La LSOL/BMARY PO13........294 E8
Brunel CI HEND SO30........292 D2
  RWIN SO21........107 H8
  VWD BH31........259 J6
Brunel Rd BSTK RG21........69 H6
  NEND PO2........296 G6
  TOTT SO40........246 D6
  WSHM SO15........246 C4
Brunel Wy FHAM PO15........271 K5
Brune Wy FERN BH22........302 D5
Brunstead PI
  BKME/WDN BH12........334 B2
Brunstead Rd
  BKME/WDN BH12........334 A2
Brunswick CI ELGH SO50........230 B2
Brunswick Gdns HAV PO9........14 B4
  LYMN SO41........329 L3
  WSHM SO15........20 D1
Brunswick Rd ELGH SO50........230 B1
  FRIM GU16........59 J7
Brunswick Sq SHAM SO14........20 E7
Brunswick St SSEA PO5........19 G5
Bruntile CI FARN GU14........76 C3
Bruyn Rd FBDG SP6........240 E2
Bryanstone CI FLEETS GU52........74 D6
Bryanstone Rd TWDS BH3........322 E8
Bryanston Rd ITCH SO19........248 F7
Bryant Rd BKME/WDN BH12........322 A7
Bryce Gdns ALDT GU11........97 J4
Bryces La NARL SO24........128 E6
Bryce Rd RAND SP11........79 P5
Bryher Island CHAM PO6........296 D2
Brympton CI FBDG SP6........240 A1
Bryn Rd CHFD SO53........115 P3
Bryon Rd WIMB BH21........278 E8
Bryony CI BDST BH18........320 B1
  HLER SO31........270 F8
Bryony Gdns ELGH SO50........230 C6
Bryony Wy WVILLE PO7........276 A4
Bryson Rd FARN GU14........296 F1
Bubb La BPWT SO32........230 C8
Bub La CHCH/BSGR BH23........325 J9
Buccaneers CI
  CHCH/BSGR BH23........325 H9
Buccleuch Rd CCLF BH13........334 A4
Buchanan Av LTDN BH7........323 L9
Buchanan Rd ROWN SO16........227 K7
Buchan Av FHAM PO15........271 J2
Buchan Ct FAWY SO45........267 N8
Buckby La BSTK RG21........9 K2
  HSEA PO3........297 L5
Bucketts Farm CI BPWT SO32........232 F7
Buckfast CI CHIN RG24........70 B2
Buckholt Rd STOK SO20........159 P1
Buckhurst Rd FRIM GU16........58 E7
Buckhurst La ALTN GU34........132 D6
Buckingham Ct KBH RG22........89 L3
Buckingham Gn PSEA PO1........316 F1
Buckingham Pde KBH RG22........89 L3
Buckingham Rd
  BKME/WDN BH12........321 M5
  NWBY RG14........16 B5
  PSF GU32........215 K2
Buckingham St PSEA PO1........19 H1
Buckland Av KBH RG22........89 K5

Buckland CI ELGH SO50........207 J8
  FARN GU14........58 B6
  WVILLE PO7........58 B6
Buckland Dene LYMN SO41........329 K2
Buckland Gdns TOTT SO40........246 A1
Buckland Gv
  CHCH/BSGR BH23........326 A5
Buckland Pdn NEND PO2........316 F1
Buckland Rd
  BKME/WDN BH12........321 L7
Buckland St NEND PO2........316 D1
Buckland Ter
  BKME/WDN BH12........321 L7
Bucklers Ct HAV PO9........276 D3
Bucklers Rd GPORT PO12........295 N9
The Bucklers LYMN SO41........338 D4
Bucklers Wy CHAR BH8........323 K4
Buckmore Av PSF GU32........215 K1
Bucksey Rd
  LSOL/BMARY PO13........294 C9
Bucks Head HI BPWT SO32........211 N8
Buckskin La KBH RG22........89 J1
Buckstone CI LYMN SO41........329 M3
Buckthorn CI BDST BH18........320 B2
  TOTT SO40........245 N3
Budden's La WHAM PO17........253 J3
Buckland Pdn NEND PO2........252 E7
Buddle HI FBDG SP6........240 C7
Buddlesgate RWIN SO21........125 M6
Budd's CI BSTK RG21........6 C7
Budds La BOR GU35........153 P4
  ROMY SO51........204 C4
Bude CI CHAM PO6........204 B9
Buffbeards La HASM GU27........156 D6
Buffins Cnr ODIM RG29........93 J1
Buffins Rd ODIM RG29........93 J1
Bugkingham Wy FRIM GU16........58 E5
Bugle St SHAM SO14........20 D7
Bulbeck Rd HAV PO9........15 F6
Bulbery RAND SP11........101 N7
Buldowne Wk LYMN SO41........308 B3
Bulford Rd LYMN SO41........98 D1
Bullar Rd WEND SO18........248 G4
Bull Dro WINC SO23........184 B1
Buller Ct FARN GU14........76 E5
Buller Rd ALDT GU11........76 A8
Bullers Rd FNM GU9........96 F6
Bullfinch CI CFDH BH17........320 B3
  SHST GU47........41 M6
  TOTT SO40........246 A4
Bull HI LISS GU33........193 J2
  LYMN SO41........300 P7
Bullington La RWIN SO21........124 C2
Bull La BPWT SO32........232 B9
  LYND SO43........244 C8
  TADY RG26........34 A4
Bullrush CI FARN GU14........58 A7
Bulls Copse La HORN PO8........256 A5
Bulls Copse Rd TOTT SO40........246 A1
Bulls Down CI HTWY RG27........52 D4
Bulls Dro RSAL SP5........159 H9
Bulpits HI RAND SP11........43 H7
Bunces La THLE RG7........27 J5
Bunch La HASM GU27........156 F7
Bunch Wy HASM GU27........156 F7
Bungalow Rd FARN GU14........76 A2
Bunkers HI NWBY RG14........30 E9
  NBNE BH10........307 N6
Bunmian PI BSTK RG21........7 F4
Bunns La WVILLE PO7........254 A6
Bunny La ROMY SO51........180 D8
  RSAL SP5........202 A1
Bunstead La RWIN SO21........182 F8
Bunting Gdns HORN PO8........255 M9
Bunting Ms KBH RG22........89 L4
Buntingford Rd FERN BH22........280 E9
Buntings ALTN GU34........132 F3
Burbidge Gv FAWY SO45........317 J6
Burbridge CI CFDH BH17........320 C4
Burbush CI FAWY SO45........290 E6
Burchell Rd NWBY RG14........24 B2
Burcombe Rd NBNE BH10........322 C2
Burcote Dr HSEA PO3........297 K5
Burdale Dr HISD PO11........319 K5
Burdock CI CHCH/BSGR BH23........326 A6
  RAND SP11........142 F7
  THLE RG7........27 K5
Bure CI CHCH/BSGR BH23........325 M9
Bure Haven Dr
  CHCH/BSGR BH23........325 M9
Bure Homage Gdns
  CHCH/BSGR BH23........325 L9
Bure Homage La
  CHCH/BSGR BH23........325 L9
Bure La CHCH/BSGR BH23........337 M1
Bure Pk CHCH/BSGR BH23........325 M9
Bureland KSCL RG20........29 M9
Burford CI CHCH/BSGR BH23........324 D6
Burford La BROC SO42........286 C7
Burford Rd CBLY GU15........58 A1
Burgage Fld WHCH RG28........65 M5
Burgate CI HAV PO9........14 C1
Burgate Flds FBDG SP6........220 E9
Burgess CI BWD BH11........320 F9
Burgess Fld
  HISD PO11........319 K7
  ODIM RG29........93 J1
Burgess Gdns ROWN SO16........228 D1
Burgess La KSCL RG20........28 D1
Burgess Rd BSTK RG21........228 D1
  PTSW SO17........247 P1
  WSHM SO15........247 P1
Burghclere Rd HAV PO9........277 H4
  ITCH SO19........269 H2
Burgh La BPWT SO32........228 B4
Burghead CI SHST GU47........41 L7
Burgh Hill Rd LIPH GU30........154 C9
Burgoyne Rd ITCH SO19........249 N7
  SSEA PO5........316 F7
Burgundy CI HLER SO31........270 F8
Buriton CI FHAM/PORC PO16........279 P9
Buriton Rd FUFL SO22........164 E5
Buriton St PSEA PO1........19 J1

Burkal Dr AND SP10........82 E7
Burke Dr ITCH SO19........249 L5
Burleigh Rd FRIM GU16........58 C5
  NEND PO2........324 D9
  SBNE BH6........324 D9
Burley CI CHFD SO53........206 D9
  HAV PO9........277 H4
  NMIL/BTOS BH25........326 F7
  TOTT SO40........258 E5
  VWD BH31........258 E5
Burley Down CHFD SO53........206 D9
Burley La OVTN SO51........107 K1
Burley Lawn RGWD BH24........284 D5
Burley Rd BKME/WDN BH12........321 L6
  BROC SO42........308 A1
  CHCH/BSGR BH23........270 E7
  CHCH/BSGR BH23........324 C2
  FUFL SO22........164 E5
Burley Wy BLKW GU17........41 K9
Burlington Ar BMTH BH1 *........8 E3
Burlington Ct ALDT GU11........2 C5
  BLKW GU17........57 K2
Burlington Rd NEND PO2........296 G8
  WSHM SO15........248 A5
Burmah Rd North FAWY SO45........291 K4
Burmah Rd South FAWY SO45........291 K4
Burma Wy TOTT SO40........267 K2
Burmaby CI FHAM PO15........271 J3
Burnaby CI KBH RG22........69 M8
Burnaby Rd BMTH BH1........18 E3
  WBNE BH4........334 C5
Burnbake Rd VWD BH31........258 F5
Burnbank Gdns TOTT SO40........246 C4
Burnbrae Rd FERN BH22........302 D7
Burn CI VWD BH31........259 H6
Burne CI RWIN SO21........144 E6
Burne-Jones Dr SHST GU47........41 J5
Burnett Av FAWY SO45........324 C8
Burnett CI FAWY SO45........268 D8
  FUFL SO22........248 G2
  WEND SO18........248 G2
Burnett Rd CHCH/BSGR BH23........324 D8
  GPORT PO12........315 K2
Burnetts Flds ELGH SO50........230 C5
Burnetts Gdns ELGH SO50........230 D5
Burnetts La HEND SO30........230 D8
Burnett's Wy HAV PO9........14 C6
Burney Rd GPORT PO12........315 J5
Burngate Rd PLE BH15........331 M2
Burnham Beeches
  CHFD SO53........206 D7
Burnham Dr CHAR BH8........323 J8
Burnham Rd CHAM PO6........275 M9
  FBDG SP6........220 D9
  TADY RG26........34 A4
Burnham's Rd HEND SO30........230 D8
Burnhams Wk CPORT PO12........13 H1
Burnham Wd
  FHAM/PORC PO16........10 E1
Burnleigh Gdns
  NMIL/BTOS BH25........327 L3
Burnley CI TADY RG26........34 C7
Burnmoor Meadow
  EWKG RG40........39 P4
Burnsall CI FARN GU14........58 A7
Burns Av FLEETS GU52........74 E6
  ITCH SO19........249 M6
  SBNE BH6........324 D8
Burns CI CHCH/BSGR BH23........325 P7
  FLEETN GU51........74 D3
  LSOL/BMARY PO13........294 F4
  WVILLE PO7........276 A1
Burns Rd ROWN SO16........227 H5
Burns Rd ELGH SO50........229 H5
  ITCH SO19........249 M6
  SBNE BH6........324 D8
Burnside CHCH/BSGR BH23........325 P7
  FLEETN GU51........74 D3
  LSOL/BMARY PO13........294 F4
  WVILLE PO7........276 A1
Burnt Hill Rd RFNM GU10........116 A4
  WD My RFNM GU10........116 B5
Burnt House La
  CHCH/BSGR BH23........305 M7
  FHAM/STUB PO14........294 B6
  LYMN SO41........309 M7
Burrard Gv LYMN SO41........329 M5
Burri CI RWIN SO21........207 P5
Burrell Rd FRIM GU16........58 E6
Burrfields Rd HSEA PO3........297 K8
Burridge Rd HLER SO31........250 C9
Burrow CI RWIN SO21........163 M6
Burrows CI HAV PO9........15 J2
Burrows La VWD BH31........259 J6
The Burrows TADY RG26........34 B5
Burrwood Gdns ASHV GU12........76 F8
Bursledon Hts HLER SO31........270 D1
Bursledon PI WVILLE PO7........275 M5
Bursledon Rd HEND SO30........269 K5
  ITCH SO19........249 K5
  WVILLE PO7........275 M5
Bursledon Ter NTID SP9 *........98 C2
Burtley Rd SBNE BH6........336 C3
Burton CI CHCH/BSGR BH23........324 C6
  RGWD BH24........281 K4
Burtoncroft
  CHCH/BSGR BH23........324 C4
Burton Hall PI
  CHCH/BSGR BH23........324 C4
Burton Rd CCLF BH13........334 A3
  CHCH/BSGR BH23........325 J8
  NMIL/BTOS BH25........326 F7
Burton's Gdns CHIN RG24........70 C6
Burt's HI WIMB BH21........278 E8
Burt's La WIMB BH21........280 A1
Burwood Gv HISD PO11........318 G4
Bury Brickfield Pk
  TOTT SO40........246 C7
Bury CI GPORT PO12........12 D3
Bury Crs GPORT PO12........12 C3
Burydown Rd OVTN RG25........108 D1
Buryfields ODIM RG29........93 J1
Bury Hall La GPORT PO12........315 K5

Bury Hill CI RAND SP11........102 B6
Bury La TOTT SO40........246 F6
Bury Rd CCLF BH13........333 P2
  DEAN RG23........68 G6
  GPORT PO12........12 A3
  TOTT SO40........247 J9
Bury's Bank Rd STHA RG19........24 C8
Bushell Rd PLE BH15........320 E5
Bushells Farm FBDG SP6........240 C3
Bushey La ALTN GU34........132 E1
Bushey Rd CHAR BH8........323 J6
Bushmead Dr RGWD BH24........281 L4
Bushnells Dr KSCL RG20........48 B2
Bush St West SSEA PO5 *........19 G6
Bush St East SSEA PO5........19 G6
Bushy Md WVILLE PO7........275 L7
Bushywarren La OVTN RG25........111 H1
Busk Crs FARN GU14........75 N1
Busket La WINC SO23........23 F5
Busketts Wy TOTT SO40........245 N9
Butcher St PSEA PO1........18 C3
Bute CI KBH RG22........68 F8
Butler CI ROMY SO51........178 C5
Butlers La RWD BH24........260 C9
Butser Wk FHAM/STUB PO14........294 C1
Butson CI NWBY RG14........16 A2
Buttercup CI BOR GU35........153 N6
  FAWY SO45........268 C9
  ROWN SO16........250 A5
Buttercup Dr
  CHCH/BSGR BH23........325 M6
Buttercup PI NTHA RG18........25 N3
Butterfield CI RWD BH24........270 E7
Butterfield Wy HLER SO31........58 A1
Butterfield Rd ROWN SO16........228 A8
Butterfly Dr CHAM PO6........274 C8
Butter Furlong Rd RSAL SP5........176 B3
Butteridge Ri ROMY SO51........179 L8
Buttermer CI RFNM GU10........115 N5
Buttermere CI BOR GU35........154 A5
  FARN GU14........57 M9
  ROWN SO16........247 J1
Buttermere CI ASHV GU12 *........76 E8
Buttermere Dr CBLY GU15........59 J1
  89 L2
Buttermere Gdns NARL SO24........168 A3
The Buttery
  CHCH/BSGR BH23........325 H8
Button's La ALTN GU34........172 A5
  ROMY SO51........224 E1
Buttsash Av FAWY SO45........290 C1
Butts Ash Gdns FAWY SO45........290 D1
Butts Ash La FAWY SO45........290 B1
Butts Bridge HI FAWY SO45........268 C8
Buttsbridge Rd FAWY SO45........268 C8
Butts CI FUFL SO22........164 E6
  ITCH SO19........249 M7
Butt's Crs ITCH SO19........249 M7
Butts La BPWT SO32........232 B4
Butts Lawn BROC SO42........286 F7
Butts Md ALTN GU34........132 E7
Butts Paddock BROC SO42........286 F7
Butts Rd ALTN GU34........132 E8
  ITCH SO19........249 L7
Butt's Sq ITCH SO19........249 M7
The Butts BPWT SO32........211 M7
  THLE RG7........35 J6
  RAND SP11........79 N1
The Butts BSTK RG21........7 K1
Byerley CI EMRTH PO10........277 P5
Byerley Rd PSEA PO1........317 H2
Byes La THLE RG7........35 J7
Byeways FAWY SO45........268 B8
  KSCL RG20........29 N8
Byfields Rd KSCL RG20........40 B3
Byfleet Av CHIN RG24........70 C7
Byng Wk AND SP10........5 K3
By-Pass Rd ROMY SO51........204 C7
  RWIN SO21........125 K5
Byrd CI WVILLE PO7........275 N5
Byrd Gdns KBH RG22........89 L4
Byron Av FRIM GU16........58 G2
  FUFL SO22........164 E7
Byron CI BPWT SO32........232 C4
  CHIN RG24........69 M3
  FHAM/PORC PO16........10 E3
  NWBY RG14........24 C8
  RAND SP11........79 P1
  YTLY GU46........40 C9
Byron Dr CWTH RG45........41 J3
Byron Rd BOSC BH5........335 M2
  ELGH SO50........207 K9
  ITCH SO19........249 M7
  NEND PO2........297 H9
  NMIL/BTOS BH25........326 G7
Byways YTLY GU46........40 C9
Byworth CI FNM GU9........95 P9
Byworth Rd FNM GU9........95 P9

C

Cable St ELGH SO50........229 J2
  SHAM SO14........21 J2
Cabot Dr FAWY SO45........267 N7
Cabot La CFDH BH17........320 D4
Cabot Wy NMIL/BTOS BH25........327 H4
Cabul Rd WSHM SO15........57 F6
Cadet Wy FLEETS GU52........74 E8
Cadgwith PI CHAM PO6........296 D2
Cadhay CI NMIL/BTOS BH25........290 F2
Cadland Rd FAWY SO45........290 F2
Cadlands Park Est
  FAWY SO45........290 E3
Cadnam CI ALDT GU11........97 J5
  DEAN RG23........68 E3
Cadnam La RAND SP11........244 E3
Cadnam Rd ENEY PO4........317 K5
Cadnam Wy CHAR BH8........323 K4

Entry		
Cadogan Rd *ALDT* GU11	76	C5
RGWD BH24	282	F2
Cador Dr *FHAM/PORC* PO16	295	M3
Caerleon Av *ITCH* SO19	249	L5
Caerleon Dr *AND* SP10	82	E7
ITCH SO19	249	L5
Caer Peris Vw		
FHAM/PORC PO16	273	N8
Caesar Cl *SP* SO22	82	F8
Caesar Ct *ALDT* GU11	2	A3
Caesar's Wy *BDST* BH18	300	A3
WHCH RG28	85	K5
Cains Cl *FHAM/STUB* PO14	296	B6
Cairn Av *NMIL/BTOS* BH25	327	K4
Cairn Cl *FRIM* GU16	289	L4
Cairngorm Cl *KBH* RG22	68	E8
Cairngorm Pl *FARN* GU14	57	N6
Cairngorm Rd *STHA* RG19	25	N5
Cairns Cl *CHCH/BSGR* BH23	324	D7
Cairo Ter *NEND* PO2	316	F1
Caister Cl *FERN* BH22	302	C2
Caistor Cl *ROWN* SO16	227	L8
Caithness Cl *DEAN* RG23	88	E1
Caker's La *ALTN* GU34	133	K7
Caker Stream Rd *ALTN* GU34	133	H5
Calabrese *HLER* SO31	171	H5
Calard Dr *NTHA* RG18	17	J6
Calbourne *HLER* SO31	269	L3
Calcot Hi *BPWT* SO32	231	L9
Calcot La *BPWT* SO32	251	L1
Calcott Pk *YTLY* GU46	40	D8
Calder Cl *ROWN* SO16	247	J5
Calder Ct *AND* SP10	82	G9
Calder Rd *CFDH* BH17	321	H4
Caledonia Dr *FAWY* SO45	267	F7
Caledonian Cl		
CHCH/BSGR BH23	325	M8
Caledon Rd *PSTN* BH14	321	M9
Calender Cl *ALTN* GU34	132	F7
California Cl *TOTT* SO40	155	H6
Calkin Cl *CHCH/BSGR* BH23	324	E6
Calleva Cl *KBH* RG22	89	M4
Callowing Cl *RWIN* SO21	207	P5
Calluna Rd *BKME/WDN* BH12	321	K3
Calmore Cl *CHAR* BH8	323	K4
Calmore Crs *TOTT* SO40	245	P2
Calmore Dr *TOTT* SO40	246	A2
Calmore Gdns *TOTT* SO40	246	A4
Calmore Rd *TOTT* SO40	246	A1
Calpe Av *LYND* SO43	264	F4
Calshot Cl *FAWY* SO45	291	P9
Calshot Dr *CHFD* SO53	206	C9
Calshot Rd *FAWY* SO45	291	K6
HAV PO9	276	C3
Calshot Wy *FRIM* GU16	58	F6
LSOL/BMARY PO13	294	F8
Calthorpe Rd *FLEETN* GU51	74	B2
Calton Gdns *ALDT* GU11	97	J4
Calvecroft *LIPH* GU30	175	K5
Calvert Cl *ASHV* GU12	97	K2
Calvin Cl *CBLY* GU15	51	G4
Calvin Rd *MOOR/WNTN* BH9	322	F7
Camargue Cl *AND* SP10	271	H2
Camber Pl *PSEA* PO1	18	D6
Camberry Cl *BSTK* RG21	69	M9
Cambria Dr *FAWY* SO45	267	F7
Cambrian Cl *HLER* SO31	250	A9
Cambrian Rd *FARN* GU14	57	L6
Cambrian Ter *SSEA* PO5 *	19	J6
Cambrian Wk		
FHAM/STUB PO14	294	D2
Cambrian Wy *KBH* RG22	68	E9
Cambridge Gdns		
CHCH/BSGR BH23	324	D5
Cambridge Gn		
FHAM/STUB PO14	271	J8
Cambridge Rd *ALDT* GU11	2	B3
CWTH RG45	41	K2
GPORT PO12	315	J2
LSOL/BMARY PO13	314	D4
PSEA PO1	18	E5
SHAM SO14	5	G7
SHST GU47	41	M5
WCLF BH2	8	A3
Cambridge Rd East		
FARN GU14	76	C3
Cambridge Rd West		
FARN GU14	76	B3
Camcross Cl *CHAM* PO6 *	274	D9
Camden Cl *MOOR/WNTN* BH9 *	323	H6
Camden St *GPORT* PO12	315	L1
Camden Wk *FLEETN* GU51	74	F3
Camel Green Rd *FBDG* SP6	239	N5
Camelia Cl *HAV* PO9	277	H7
NBAD SO52	205	L8
Camelia Gdns *WEND* SO18	249	J1
Camelia Gv *ELCH* SO50	230	E2
Camellia Cl *WIMB* BH21	258	E9
Camellia Gdns		
NMIL/BTOS BH25	327	K5
Camelot Cl *AND* SP10	82	E9
Camelot Crs		
FHAM/PORC PO16	273	M9
Camelsdale Rd *HASM* GU27	156	E8
Camel Wy *FARN* GU14	75	P4
Cameron Cl		
LSOL/BMARY PO13	294	G6
Cameron Rd *ALDT* GU11	76	G6
CHCH/BSGR BH23	325	H8
Camfield Cl *BSTK* RG21	69	M9
Camford Ct *DEAN* RG23	89	L7
Camilla Cl *TOTT* SO40	245	P2
Camlea Cl *BSTK* RG21	69	M9
Camley Cl *ITCH* SO19	268	C1
Cammel Rd *FERN* BH22	302	D6
Cammomile Dr *RAND* SP11	79	H9
Campbell Cl *ALDT* GU11	97	H4
FLEETN GU51	74	B3
RAND SP11	119	N2
YTLY GU46	40	G8

Entry		
Campbell Pl *FRIM* GU16	58	E2
Campbell Rd *ALDT* GU11	2	D1
BMTH BH1	335	L1
CHCH/BSGR BH23	324	C4
ELGH SO50	229	K3
RWIN SO21	104	E8
SSEA PO5	19	K6
TADY RG26	52	C3
Campbell St *SHAM* SO14	21	J1
Campbell Wy *ELGH* SO50	230	C2
Camp Farm Rd *ALDT* GU11	76	C7
Camp Fld *STOK* SO20	161	M4
Camp Hi *RFNM* GU10	117	J2
Campion Cl *BLKW* GU17	57	N2
BOR GU35	154	D4
ELGH SO50	230	C5
HLER SO31	270	E9
LYMN SO41	329	L2
WVILLE PO7	276	A4
Campion Dr *ROMY* SO51	204	G4
Campion Gv		
CHCH/BSGR BH23	325	K9
Campion Rd *ITCH* SO19	249	M6
Campion Wy *HTWY* RG27	55	J6
LYMN SO41	329	L2
WINC SO23	165	K1
Camp Rd *BOR* GU35	154	A3
FARN GU14	58	F1
LSOL/BMARY PO13	295	H6
THLE RG7	26	E4
Campsie Cl *KBH* RG22	68	E8
Camrose Wy *BSTK* RG21	90	E1
Cams Bay Cl		
FHAM/PORC PO16	273	K9
Cams Hall Est		
FHAM/PORC PO16	295	H1
Cams Hi *FHAM/PORC* PO16	273	J9
WVILLE PO7	254	D2
Camus Cl *FLEETS* GU52	74	A7
Cam Wk *BSTK* RG21	7	J6
Camwood Cl *BSTK* RG21	69	M9
Canada Cl *BOR* GU35	154	A4
LIPH GU30	175	K4
Canal Cl *ALDT* GU11	76	F7
ODIM RG29	72	B8
Canal View Rd *NWBY* RG14	24	C4
Canal Wk *NWBY* RG14	16	E2
ROMY SO51	204	D5
SHAM SO14	20	E6
SSEA PO5	19	J5
Canberra Cl *GPORT* PO12	315	K4
HTWY RG27	40	B7
Canberra Rd		
CHCH/BSGR BH23	324	C6
EMRTH PO10	299	N6
ROWN SO16	226	F8
Canberra Wy *DEAN* RG23	89	L7
FARN GU14	75	N4
Candleford Ga *LIPH* GU30 *	175	J3
Candlemas Pl *PTSW* SO17 *	248	C3
Candover Cl *TADY* RG26	34	C7
Candy La *WEND* SO18	249	N4
Candys Cl *WIMB* BH21	300	A3
Candys La *WIMB* BH21	300	A3
Canes La *BOR* GU35	154	C5
Canford Av *BWD* BH11	321	P5
Canford Bottom *WIMB* BH21	279	L3
Canford Cliffs Av *PSTN* BH14	333	M1
Canford Cliffs Rd *CCLF* BH13	333	N1
Canford Cl *BPWT* SO32	252	C4
ROWN SO16	247	H1
Canford Crs *CCLF* BH13	333	N4
Canford Heath Rd		
CFDH BH17	320	C1
Canford Magna *WIMB* BH21	301	H3
Canford Rd *BWD* BH11	322	A6
PLE BH15	320	F8
Canford View Dr *WIMB* BH21	279	K8
Canford Wy		
BKME/WDN BH12	321	L2
Canhouse La *LISS* GU33...	193	K3
Canning Rd *ASHV* GU12	3	E3
Cannock Wk		
FHAM/STUB PO14	294	C2
Cannon Cl *BDST* BH18	320	E3
SHST GU47	41	N6
Cannon Hill Gdns *WIMB* BH21	279	K7
Cannon Hill Rd *WIMB* BH21	279	J7
Cannon St *SHAM* SO41	329	M5
WSHM SO15	247	N5
Canoe Cl *HLER* SO31	270	F9
Canon's Barn Cl		
FHAM/PORC PO16	273	N9
Canons Cl *NTID* SP9	79	H7
Canon's Ct *KSCL* RG20	48	B5
Canon St *WINC* SO23	22	C6
Cansfield End *NWBY* RG14	16	D1
Canterbury Av *ITCH* SO19	249	L5
Canterbury Cl *FERN* BH22	280	E8
KBH RG22	89	M3
LSOL/BMARY PO13	314	F4
Canterbury Dr *FAWY* SO45	267	N7
Canterbury Rd *ASHV* GU12	77	P8
ENEY PO4	317	H5
FARN GU14	76	C2
FHAM/STUB PO14	294	A4
Canterton La *LYND* SO43	244	B3
Canton St *WSHM* SO15	248	B5
Canute Dr *CHCH/BSGR* BH23	305	M7
Canute Rd *SHAM* SO14	9	H3
Capella Gdns *HAV* SO45	267	P7
Capel Ley *WVILLE* PO7	275	N6
Capers End La *BPWT* SO32	251	L2
Capesthorne		
CHCH/BSGR BH23	337	M1
Capper Ret *CBLY* GU15	41	P7
Capstone Cl *CHAR* BH8	323	K9
Capstone Rd *CHAR* BH8	323	J9
Captains Cl *GPORT* PO12	295	K9
Captains Pl *SHAM* SO14	21	G7

Entry		
Captain's Rw *LYMN* SO41	329	M3
PSEA PO1	18	C6
Carberry Dr		
FHAM/PORC PO16	295	M2
Carbery Av *SBNE* BH6	336	B2
Carbery Ct *HAV* PO9	276	D3
Carbery Gdns *SBNE* BH6	336	C1
Carbery Rw *SBNE* BH6 *	336	A2
Carbis Cl *CHAM* PO6	299	C8
Carbonel Cl *DEAN* RG23	68	D7
Cardew Rd *LISS* GU33	192	E5
Cardiff Rd *NEND* PO2	296	F7
Cardigan Rd		
BKME/WDN BH12	321	P8
MOOR/WNTN BH9	322	F7
Cardinal Dr *WVILLE* PO7	276	B1
Cardinal Ms *AND* SP10 *	4	B4
The Cardinals *RFNM* GU10	97	M4
Cardinal Wy *HLER* SO31	271	H8
Carey Rd *ITCH* SO19	249	L6
MOOR/WNTN BH9	322	E7
Carfax Av *RFNM* GU10	97	M3
Cargate Av *ALDT* GU11	2	D4
Cargate Gv *ALDT* GU11	2	C5
Cargate Hi *ALDT* GU11	2	C4
Cargate Ter *ALDT* GU11	2	C5
Carisbrooke *FRIM* GU16	58	E5
Carisbrooke Av		
FHAM/STUB PO14	293	N7
HAV PO9	15	K4
ROMY SO51	204	A3
Carisbrooke Ct		
NMIL/BTOS BH25	327	H4
ROMY SO51	204	E4
Carisbrooke Crs *CHFD* SO53	206	C8
Carisbrooke Dr *ITCH* SO19	249	H5
Carisbrooke Rd *ENEY* PO4	317	H4
LSOL/BMARY PO13	294	F6
Carisbrooke Wy		
CHCH/BSGR BH23	326	A6
Carless Cl *LSOL/BMARY* PO13	315	H1
Carlew Wy *RFNM* GU27	71	N6
Carlin Pl *CBLY* GU15	58	B1
Carlisle Cl *DEAN* RG23	68	F6
Carlisle Rd *RFNM* GU10	137	H2
ROWN SO16	247	M3
SSEA PO5	19	K3
Carlton Av *NMIL/BTOS* BH25	326	F4
Carlton Cl *CBLY* GU15	58	C2
Carlton Crs *FLEETS* GU52	74	E6
WSHM SO15	248	B5
Carlton Gv *PSTN* BH14	321	M7
Carlton Rd *BMTH* BH1	335	J2
BOR GU35	155	K4
FHAM/PORC PO16	273	P9
GPORT PO12	13	F2
WEND SO18	248	F3
WSHM SO15	248	B4
Carlton Wy *GPORT* PO12	13	F1
Carlyle Rd *GPORT* PO12	13	F2
SBNE BH6	336	B4
Carlyn Dr *CHFD* SO53	206	F6
Carlyon Cl *FARN* GU14	58	B9
FRIM GU16	58	E9
Carmans La *RWIN* SO21	183	M7
Carmarthen Av *CHAM* PO6	275	K9
Carmarthen Cl *FARN* GU14	57	N6
Carmichael Wy *KBH* RG22	89	N3
Carmine Ct		
LSOL/BMARY PO13 *	314	C2
Carmino Ter *LIPH* GU30 *	175	J3
Carnac Ct *FHAM/PORC* PO16 *	295	H1
Carnarvon Rd *BMTH* BH1	335	L2
GPORT PO12	12	A2
NEND PO2	297	H9
Carnation Rd *ROWN* SO16	228	E8
Carne Cl *CHFD* SO53	206	E5
Carnegie Cl *PSTN* BH14	321	M7
Carnegie Rd *NWBY* RG14	11	J4
Caroline Av *CHCH/BSGR* BH23	337	J1
Caroline Gdns *FHAM* PO15	272	A8
Caroline Pl *GPORT* PO12	315	M3
Caroline Rd *BWD* BH11	322	B4
Caroline Wy *FRIM* GU16	58	L4
Carpathia Cl *WEND* SO18	249	J1
Carpenter Cl *ENEY* PO4 *	317	J5
Carpenter Cl *SHAM* SO41	329	K2
Carpenters Rd *RWIN* SO21	104	E8
Carpenters La *HTWY* RG27	54	A6
Carpenters Ct *KBH* RG22	89	F1
Carpenter's Down *CHIN* RG24	69	L2
Carran Wk *FHAM/STUB* PO14	294	C2
Carraway *FHAM* PO15	271	K3
Carriage Cl *TWDS* BH3	334	C1
Carrbridge Rd *TWDS* BH3	322	D8
Carrick Cl *YTLY* GU46	40	F8
Carrick Wy *NMIL/BTOS* BH25	327	L5
Carrington Cl *LYMN* SO41	339	H2
Carrington Crs *TADY* RG26	34	C6
Carrington La *ASHV* GU12	78	B4
LYMN SO41	339	H1
Carroll Av *FERN* BH22	302	D3
Carroll Cl *BKME/WDN* BH12	322	A4
Carsthorn Wk *TOTT* SO40	246	B5
Carsworth Wy *CFDH* BH17	321	J2
Carter's Clay Rd *ROMY* SO51	179	H9
Carter's La *FBDG* SP6	221	P1
Carter's La *FLEETS* GU52	74	C5
Carter's Meadow *AND* SP10	82	E9
Carter Wk *FNM* GU9	96	D5
Carthage Cl *CHFD* SO53	207	H6
Carthagena *RWIN* SO21	125	M5
Carthona Dr *FLEETS* GU52	74	C5
Cartref Cl *VWD* BH31	258	F4
Cartwright Cl *NBNE* BH10	322	C3

Entry		
Cartwright Dr *FHAM* PO15	271	M8
Carvers La *RGWD* BH24	282	E2
Cary Cl *NWBY* RG14	24	A9
Carysfort Rd *BMTH* BH1	335	K2
Cascades Ap *PSEA* PO1	19	G1
Cashmoor Cl		
BKME/WDN BH12	321	P5
Cask St *BSTK* RG21	7	G2
Caslake Cl *NMIL/BTOS* BH25	327	H6
Caspar John Cl		
FHAM/STUB PO14	293	P8
Caspian Cl *HLER* SO31	271	H3
Cassel Av *WBNE* BH4	334	B5
Cassino Cl *ALDT* GU11	3	F2
Casterbridge La *RAND* SP11	81	K9
Casterbridge Rd *FERN* BH22	302	D5
Castle Cl *CBLY* GU15	58	E1
LYMN SO41	339	H3
Castle Ct *WSHM* SO15	247	L5
Castlecraig Ct *SHST* GU47 *	41	L7
Castledene Crs *PSTN* BH14	333	J1
Castle Farm La *WHAM* PO17	252	F3
Castle Fld *FNM* GU9	96	B8
Castle Gate Cl *CHAR* BH8	323	J6
Castle Gv *FHAM/PORC* PO16	295	P2
NWBY RG14	24	C2
Castle Hi *FNM* GU9	96	B8
Castle Hill La *RGWD* BH24	283	P5
Castle La *CHFD* SO53	206	E3
Castle La East *LTDN* BH7	323	P7
Castle La West		
MOOR/WNTN BH9	322	C3
MOOR/WNTN BH9	323	H4
Castlemain Av *SBNE* BH6	336	A1
Castlemans La *HISD* PO11	298	G3
Castleman Trailway		
CFDH BH17	320	A4
FERN BH22	280	C6
RGWD BH24	290	B4
WIMB BH21	281	K4
WIMB BH21	300	E5
Castle Point *CHAR* BH8 *	323	L5
Castle Ri *ODIM* RG29	72	B8
Castle Rd *ALDT* GU11	145	K7
BSTK RG21	69	L9
CBLY GU15	59	G5
HAV PO9	15	G5
HLER SO31	269	K4
MOOR/WNTN BH9	322	F6
SSEA PO5	19	F7
WEND SO18	248	B4
WHAM PO17	274	B4
Castle Rw *GPORT* PO12	13	J2
Castleshaw Cl *ROWN* SO16	247	H4
Castle Sq *SHAM* SO14	20	D6
Castle St *ALTN* GU34	149	P1
CHCH/BSGR BH23	324	F9
FHAM/PORC PO16	295	P2
FHAM/STUB PO14	293	M1
FLEETS GU52	74	C5
FNM GU9	96	B8
PLE BH15	332	E2
SHAM SO14	20	D6
Castleton Av *NBNE* BH10	322	D1
Castle Vw *GPORT* PO12	13	J2
Castle View Rd		
FHAM/PORC PO16	295	P3
Castleway *HAV* PO9	277	H9
Castle Wd *SHAM* SO14	20	D5
Castlewood *CHFD* SO53 *	206	E9
RGWD BH24	284	B4
Castle Woods *RSAL* SP5	199	P7
Caswall Ride *YTLY* GU46	40	F9
Caswell Cl *FARN* GU14	57	N7
Catalina Cl *CHCH/BSGR* BH23	326	A6
Catalina Dr *PLE* BH15	332	C2
Cateran Cl *ROWN* SO16	247	K3
Catesby Gdns *YTLY* GU46	40	B9
Cathay Gdns *FAWY* SO45	267	N7
Cathedral Vw *NWCI* SO23	23	G7
Catherine Cl *HEND* SO30	249	N1
Catherine Ct *RSAL* SP5	199	H6
Catherine Gdns *HEND* SO30	249	N1
Catherines Wk *RAND* SP11	101	M7
Catherington La *HORN* PO8	256	A2
Catherington Wy *HAV* PO9	256	A4
Catisfield La *FHAM* PO15	271	P9
Catisfield Rd *ENEY* PO4	317	K4
FHAM PO15	272	A9
Catkin Cl *CHIN* RG24	50	A1
Catmint Cl *CHFD* SO53	206	C4
Caton Cl *BKME/WDN* BH12	322	B7
Cattistock Rd *CHAR* BH8	323	L6
Cattle La *RAND* SP11	101	N6
Caunter Rd *NWBY* RG14	24	A3
Causeway Crs *TOTT* SO40	246	B5
Causeway Farm *HORN* PO8	256	B5
The Causeway *EPSF* GU31	143	M5
HTWY RG27	31	P7
RSAL SP5	273	J9
STOK SO20	139	N2
Causton Rd *CHAR* BH8	323	J9
Cavalier Cl *CHIN* RG24	70	D6
Cavalier Rd *CHIN* RG24	70	D6
Cavalier Wy *ALTN* GU34	132	D7
Cavalry Ct *ALDT* GU11	2	A3
Cavan Crs *CFDH* BH17	320	D3

Entry		
Cavanna Cl		
LSOL/BMARY PO13	294	F6
Cavan's Rd *ALDT* GU11	76	B6
Cavan Rd *CHIN* RG24	70	B4
Cavell Dr *CHAM* PO6	274	C9
Cavendish Cl *ROMY* SO51	204	F4
WVILLE PO7 *	275	P2
Cavendish Ct *ELGH* SO50 *	57	L2
NWBY RG14	11	L9
Cavendish Dr *WVILLE* PO7	275	P3
Cavendish Gv *WINC* SO23	165	J4
WSHM SO15	248	B3
Cavendish Ms *ALDT* GU11	2	D5
WSHM SO15	248	B5
Cavendish Pl *BMTH* BH1	334	G1
Cavendish Rd *ALDT* GU11	2	E4
FLEETS GU52	74	C8
SSEA PO5	19	J7
WCLF BH2	334	F1
C AV *FAWY* SO45	352	B4
Caversham Cl *HEND* SO30	249	M5
ITCH SO19	249	J7
PLE BH15	320	A9
Caves Farm Cl *SHST* GU47	41	H6
Cawdor Rd *TWDS* BH3	322	D8
Cawte Rd *WSHM* SO15	247	M5
Caxton Av *ITCH* SO19	249	K5
Caxton Cl *AND* SP10	102	A1
CHCH/BSGR BH23	325	K8
Cayman Cl *CHIN* RG24	69	M3
Cecil Av *CHAR* BH8	323	J7
SHAM SO14	247	N2
TOTT SO40	246	A9
Cecil Cl *WIMB* BH21	300	A7
Cecil Gv *SSEA* PO5	19	F7
Cecil Hi *CHAR* BH8	323	H7
Cecil Pl *SSEA* PO5	19	F7
Cecil Rd *BKME/WDN* BH12	321	M6
BOSC BH5	335	L2
ITCH SO19	249	H8
Cedar Av *BLKW* GU17	41	L9
GPORT PO12	295	L8
HEND SO30	250	C4
HLER SO31	269	P2
TADY RG26	52	B8
WINC SO23	165	J8
WVILLE PO7	275	N4
Cedar Cl *ASHV* GU12	97	L3
GPORT PO12	295	L8
HEND SO30	250	C4
HLER SO31	269	P2
TADY RG26	52	B8
WINC SO23	165	J8
WVILLE PO7	275	N4
Cedar Crs *HORN* PO8	256	C6
NBAD SO52	205	K8
Cedar Ct *DE FLEETN* GU51	74	F3
KSCL RG20	48	B5
LYMN SO41	328	D7
WIMB BH21	279	K9
Cedar Gdns *HAV* PO9	15	H3
SHAM SO14	248	C3
Cedar Gv *ASHV* GU12	317	K1
FHAM/STUB PO14	294	B4
Cedar Lawn *ROMY* SO51	204	G4
Cedar Lodge *HASM* GU27 *	157	K8
Cedarmount *LYND* SO43	264	F6
Cedar Mt *NWBY* RG14	24	C7
Cedar Rd *CHCH/BSGR* BH23	305	M7
FARN GU14	58	E2
FAWY SO45	290	C2
FHAM/STUB PO14	10	A7
Cedars Cl *SHST* GU47	40	G6
The Cedars *FHAM/PORC* PO16	10	C1
FLEETN GU51	54	B4
WIMB BH21	334	D2
Cedars Vw *RSAL* SP5	159	M8
Cedar Ter *HTWY* RG27 *	54	B7
Cedar Tree Cl *DEAN* RG23	88	E3
Cedar Vw *FLEETS* GU52	74	E6
Cedar Wk *AND* SP10	102	B4
FUFL SO32 *	306	E5
Cedar Wy *DEAN* RG23	68	G5
FERN BH22	280	C9
FHAM/STUB PO14	10	A7
Cedarways *FNM* GU9	116	B3
Cedarwood *CHIN* RG24 *	50	A1
WINC SO23	145	K9
Cedar Wood Cl *ELGH* SO50	230	E2
TOTT SO40	246	A3
Cedric Cl *FAWY* SO45	291	H9
Celandine Av *HLER* SO31	270	F8
HORN PO8	256	B8
Celandine Cl		
CHCH/BSGR BH23	325	M7
Celandine Ct *YTLY* GU46	40	B7
Celia Cl *WVILLE* PO7	276	B2
Cellars Farm Rd *SBNE* BH6	336	E3
Celtic Dr *AND* SP10	102	C4
Cement Ter *SHAM* SO14	20	C6
Cemetery Av *PLE* BH15	321	H6
Cemetery Hi *ODIM* RG29	93	L1
Cemetery La *OVTN* RG25	92	B6
WVILLE PO7	255	H6
Cemetery Rd *FLEETN* GU51	54	B5
WIMB BH21	278	D9
WSHM SO15	248	B5
Centaur St *NEND* PO2	296	F9
Centaury Gdns *ELGH* SO50	230	C5
Centenary Cl *LYMN* SO41	308	C6
Centenary Gdns *HAV* PO9	15	K4
Centenary Wy *BMTH* BH1	335	L1
Central Av *BKME/WDN* BH12	321	N6
Central Dr *FERN* BH22 *	281	H9
WCLF BH2	8	A4
Central Rd *BOR* GU35	154	A2
CHAM PO6	297	L2
FHAM/PORC PO16	295	M2
SHAM SO14	248	C9
Central Sq *WHAM* PO17	274	F1
Central Station Br *WSHM* SO15	20	A3
Central St *PSEA* PO1	19	J1

RAND SP11.............79 P1
Central Wy AND SP10.............103 J1
Centre Dr CHIN RG24.............70 A3
Centre La LYMN SO41.............328 E6
Centre Pl RGWD BH24.............282 D2
Centre Terrace Rd FARN GU14.............75 P4
Centurion Cl SHST GU47.............41 L6
Centurion Ga ENEY PO4.............317 M5
Centurion Wy HLER SO31.............270 G7
Century Cl OVTN RG25.............90 C4
Cerdic Ms HLER SO31.............270 A6
Cerne Dr MOOR/WNTN BH9.............323 H3
  NBAD SO52.............205 J9
  WEND SO18.............249 K2
Chadderton Gdns PSEA PO1.............18 E6
Chaddesley Gln CCLF BH13.............333 M5
Chaddesley Pines CCLF BH13.............333 L4
Chaddesley Wood Rd
  CCLF BH13.............333 N6
Chadwell Meadow HAV PO9.............14 B5
Chadwell Av ITCH SO19.............249 K7
Chadwick Rd ELGH SO50.............228 G2
Chafen Rd WEND SO18.............248 F3
Chaffers Cl ODIM RG29.............93 K9
Chaffey Cl RGWD BH24.............282 C1
Chaffinch Cl CFDH BH17.............320 B3
  KBH RG22.............68 F9
  NMIL/BTOS BH25.............327 H5
  TOTT SO40.............246 A3
Chaffinch Gn HORN PO8.............255 N7
Chaffinch Wy
  FHAM/PORC PO16.............295 K1
  LSOL/BMARY PO13.............314 D1
Chalbury Cl CFDH BH17.............321 J2
Chalcraft Cl LIPH GU30.............175 H3
Chalcrafts ALTN GU34.............132 C4
Chaldecott Gdns NBNE BH10.............322 C5
Chaldon Rd CFDH BH17.............321 H2
Chale Cl LSOL/BMARY PO13.............294 G7
Chalet Hl BOR GU35.............154 B5
Chalewood Rd FAWY SO45.............312 C1
Chalfont Av
  CHCH/BSGR BH23.............324 B4
Chalfont Dr FARN GU14.............76 B2
Chalford Rd NWBY RG14.............16 A3
Chalice Ct HEND SO30.............250 A5
Chalk Cl ALTN GU34.............150 C6
Chalkcroft La RAND SP11.............81 M7
Chalk Hl BPWT SO32.............233 N7
  STOK SO20.............102 C2
  WEND SO18.............249 L2
Chalk La WHAM PO17.............272 F3
Chalkpit La RAND SP11.............101 K5
Chalk Pit La RSAL SP5.............159 J6
Chalk Rd BOR GU35.............274 D8
Chalk Rdg HORN PO8.............236 D9
  WINC SO23.............
Chalkridge Rd CHAM PO6.............275 J9
Chalk's Cl RSAL SP5.............199 P6
Chalk V CHIN RG24.............70 D7
  STOK SO20.............162 C3
Chalky Copse HTWY RG27.............71 J7
Chalky Hl ALTN GU34.............149 K2
Chalky La HTWY RG27.............73 L9
Challenger Wy FAWY SO45.............267 P6
Challis Cl RAND SP11.............89 N1
Challis Ct RAND SP11.............80 A1
Champion Cl LYMN SO41.............339 H2
Champion Cl RGWD BH24.............52 C5
Champney Cl BOR GU35.............153 P7
Chancellors La BPWT SO32.............230 E9
Chancel Rd HLER SO31.............271 H7
Chandler Cl FHAM PO15.............272 B7
Chandler Rd BSTK RG21.............90 C1
Chandlers Cl HISD PO11.............319 J5
  LTDN BH7.............325 P7
Chandlers La YTLY GU46.............40 D7
Chandlers Rd ASHV GU12.............76 G8
Chandlers Wy HLER SO31.............271 H4
Chandos Av
  BKME/WDN BH12.............322 A7
Chandos Ri PSEA PO14.............19 H2
Chandos St SHAM SO14.............21 F6
Channels Farm Rd
  ROWN SO16.............228 F7
Channel Wy SHAM SO14.............21 H7
Chant Cl CHCH/BSGR BH23.............325 H8
  RAND SP11.............123 K3
Chantrell Wk FHAM PO15.............272 B7
Chantreys FLEETN GU51.............74 A4
Chantry Cl CHCH/BSGR BH23.............316 B6
  FNM GU9.............96 A9
  HTWY RG27.............71 P4
Chantry Ms KBH RG22.............89M4
Chantry Rd GPORT PO12.............315 L1
  HORN PO8.............256 B3
  SHAM SO14.............21 H6
The Chantry FNM GU9.............95 P9
The Chantry
  FHAM/STUB PO14.............271 J7
Chantry Wy AND SP10.............4 D4
Chapel Cl CHIN RG24.............70 C5

OVTN RG25.............109 H1
RAND SP11.............101 H4
ROMY SO51 *.............181 H8
STOK SO20.............161 H2
Chapel Ct NTHA RG18.............25 P3
Chapel Crs ITCH SO19.............249 J7
Chapel Dro ELGH SO50.............230 C5
  SO50.............250 B5
Chapel Gdns BOR GU35.............154 C3
Chapel Hl BSTK RG21.............6 D4
  RSAL SP5.............176 B4
Chapel La BPWT SO32.............251 L3
  BROC SO42.............310 C2
  CHCH/BSGR BH23.............303 J5
  FARN GU14.............207 K4
  FARN GU14.............57 N5
  FAWY SO45.............290 C9
  LYMN SO41.............308 D7
  LYND SO43.............264 F6
  PLE BH15.............332 E1
  RAND SP11.............62 F8
  RAND SP11.............79 N1
  RAND SP11.............82 F5
  RAND SP11.............120 B1
  RGWD BH24.............284 D6
  ROMY SO51.............178 E8
  ROMY SO51.............180 B6
  RSAL SP5.............200 A7
  RSAL SP5.............223 L5
  RWIN SO21.............165 P5
  STHA RG19.............33 J5
  STOK SO20.............140 A9
  TADY RG26.............49 J1
  THLE RG7.............54 C1
  THLE RG7.............37 P5
  TOTT SO40.............246 C6
  WIMB BH21.............278 D9
Chapel Md HTWY RG27.............39 P6
Chapel Pond Dr ODIM RG29.............72 B9
Chapel Ri RGWD BH24.............282 B7
Chapel River Cl AND SP10.............102 B3
Chapel Rd BPWT SO32.............232 F7
  BPWT SO32.............233 N1
  BPWT SO32.............233 N1
  HEND SO30.............249 N1
  HLER SO31.............270 E4
  PSTN RG29.............321 J8
  RFNM GU10.............115 N7
  SHAM SO14.............21 G5
Chapel Rw HTWY RG27.............
Chapelside FHAM/STUB PO14.............293 N1
Chapel Sq CBLY GU15.............45 H8
Chapel Sq CBLY GU15.............58 C7
  GPORT PO12.............295 M9
  NEND PO2 *.............296 C9
  NTHA RG18.............108 C1
  OVTN RG25.............108 C1
  PSF GU32.............213 M5
  PSF GU32.............215 M1
  SSEA PO5.............19 F6
Chaplains Av HORN PO8.............255 M8
Chaplains Cl HORN PO8.............255 M7
Chaplain's Hl CWTH RG45.............41 L2
Chaplins Ter NTID SP9 *.............9 H1
Chappell Cl LIPH GU30.............175 K3
Chapter Ter HTWY RG27.............
Charborough Rd BDST BH18.............320 D1
Charden Rd ELGH SO50.............230 A3
  LSOL/BMARY PO13.............295 H9
Charfield Cl FHAM/STUB PO14.............294 B1
  FUFL SO22.............183 N1
Charing Cl RGWD BH24.............282 E3
Charity Vw WHAM PO17.............272 C3
Chark La LSOL/BMARY PO13.............294 D9
Charlcot Cl WHCH RG28.............85 L8
Charlcot Farm WHCH RG28.............85 L8
Charldon Gn CHIN RG24.............70 B4
Charlecote Cl FARN GU14.............76 C5
Charlecote Dr CFDH BH17.............206 C5
Charledown Cl OVTN RG25.............86 G4
Charledown Rd OVTN RG25.............86 G4
Charles Av AGPORT PO12.............315 K5
Charles Cl HTWY RG27.............71 P5
  WINC SO23.............165 H5
  WVILLE PO7.............275M4
Charles Crs NMIL/BTOS BH25.............327 K2
Charles Dalton Ct AND SP10 *.............4 C5
Charles Dickens St PSEA PO1.............19 G5
Charles Gdns NBNE BH10.............322 C5
Charles Hl RFNM GU10.............117 L4
Charles Keightley Ct
  WIMB BH21.............300 F2
Charles Knott Gdns
  WSHM SO15.............248 B4
Charles Richards Cl BSTK RG21.............69 K9
Charles Rd CHCH/BSGR BH23.............325 K7
  PLE BH15.............331 H5
Charles's La RGWD BH24.............283 J6
Charles St KBH RG22.............68 G8
  NWBY RG14.............24 A9
  PSEA PO1.............215 L2
  SHAM SO14.............21 F6
Charleston Cl HISD PO11.............318 E4
Charleston Rd FAWY SO45.............290 B4
Charles Watts Wy HEND SO30.............249 N4
Charlesworth Gdns
  WVILLE PO7.............275M1
Charliejoy Gdns SHAM SO14.............21 J1
Charlie Soar Ct ELGH SO50.............228 E1
Charlock Cl NTHA RG18.............25 P2
Charlotte Cl AND SP10.............5 K3
  BKME/WDN BH12.............323 J7
  CHCH/BSGR BH23.............325 L9
  FNM GU9.............
Charlotte Dr GPORT PO12.............315 N1
Charlotte Pl SHAM SO14.............20 E1
Charlotte St PSEA PO1.............316 D2
  PSEA PO1 *.............19 G2
Charlton Cl LYMN SO41.............327 P4
  MOOR/WNTN BH9 *.............323 J3
Charlton Ct SHST GU47.............40 C5
Charlton La THLE RG7.............37 P1
Charlton Pl NWBY RG14.............24 D3

Charlton Rd AND SP10.............4 A2
  WSHM SO15.............247 P4
Charlwood La ALTN GU34.............170 D3
Charminster Av
  MOOR/WNTN BH9.............323 H6
Charminster Cl
  MOOR/WNTN BH9.............323 J5
  WVILLE PO7.............275 N2
Charminster Pl
  MOOR/WNTN BH9 *.............323 J5
Charminster Rd CHAR BH8.............323 H6
Charmouth Gv PSTN BH14.............321 J8
Charmouth Ter ROWN SO16 *.............247 L2
Charmus Rd TOTT SO40.............245 P1
Charmwood Crs HEND SO30.............249 L1
Charmwood Cl NWBY RG14.............24 C2
Charnock Cl LYMN SO41.............327 P4
Charnwood
  LSOL/BMARY PO13.............295 H7
Charnwood Av
  MOOR/WNTN BH9.............323 H4
Charnwood Cl AND SP10.............5 F7
  CHFD SO53.............206 E3
  FERN BH22.............280 E7
  KBH RG22.............89M2
  TOTT SO40.............246 B2
Charnwood Crs CHFD SO53.............206 E3
Charnwood Dr MOOR/WNTN BH9.............322 E5
Charnwood Gdns CHFD SO53.............206 E3
Charnwood Wy FAWY SO45.............312 F1
Charterhouse Wy HEND SO30.............250 B2
Charter Rd BWD BH11.............301 M7
  NWBY RG14.............24 C7
Charter Wk HASM GU27 *.............157 H7
Chart House Rd ASHV GU12.............116 F5
Chartwell FNM GU9.............115 P4
Chartwell Cl ELGH SO50.............207 K7
  FHAM/STUB PO14.............271 J9
Chartwell Dr WIMB BH21.............277 J7
Chartwell Gdns ALDT GU11.............76 B5
Chase Cl LISS GU33.............192 E2
Chase Farm Cl BPWT SO32.............232 C9
Chase Gv BPWT SO32.............232 C9
Chase La HASM GU27.............157 K9
Chase Pln GSHT GU26 *.............156 B4
Chase Rd BOR GU35.............154 C3
  LISS GU33.............192 E2
Chaseside LTDN BH7.............323 N7
The Chase FARN GU14.............58 C7
  FHAM/STUB PO14.............271 K8
  GPORT PO12.............315 K4
  RGWD BH24.............282 B4
  VWD BH31.............259 J4
Chasewater Av HORN PO8.............317 J1
Chatburn Av HORN PO8.............255 P8
Chatfield Av NEND PO2.............296 C8
Chatfield Cl FARN GU14.............76 B2
Chatfield Rd
  LSOL/BMARY PO13.............294 F5
Chatham Dr PSEA PO1.............18 E7
Chatham Gv FUFL SO22.............148 A1
Chatham Rd FUFL SO22.............148 A1
Chatsworth Av CHAR BH8.............297 J3
  HASM GU27.............157 H5
Chatsworth Cl FHAM PO15.............272 A9
Chatsworth Dr AND SP10.............102 B3
Chatsworth Gn KBH RG22.............89 N5
Chatsworth Gv FNM GU9.............96 B5
Chatsworth Rd CHAR BH8.............323 H9
  ELGH SO50.............207 K7
  FARN GU14.............76 D1
  ITCH SO19.............249 K6
  PSTN BH14.............321 K7
Chatsworth Wy
  NMIL/BTOS BH25.............326 C4
Chaucer Av AND SP10.............102 B1
  CHAM PO6.............274 A9
Chaucer Cl FERN BH22.............69M3
  FHAM/PORC PO16.............10 C4
  RWIN SO21.............144 F3
  WIMB BH21.............278 E8
  WVILLE PO7.............
Chaucer Crs FARN GU14.............24 E2
Chaucer Dr LYMN SO41.............338 C1
Chaucer Rd CCLF BH13.............333 N3
  CWTH RG45.............41 J2
  ITCH SO19.............14 U7
  ITCH SO19.............249M5
Chaucombe Pl
  NMIL/BTOS BH25.............327 H6
Chaundler Rd WINC SO23.............165 H5
Chaundlers Cft RFNM GU10.............136 A4
Chauntsingers Rd ALTN GU34.............132 T5
Chaveney Cl FAWY SO45.............268 B9
Chawton Cl FLEETN GU51.............73 P1
  FUFL SO22.............164 E5
  WEND SO18.............249M3
Chawton Park Rd ALTN GU34.............132 B9
Cheam Rd BDST BH18.............300 B9
Cheam Wy TOTT SO40.............245 P4
Cheap St NWBY RG14.............16 E2
Cheavley Cl AND SP10.............102 B1
Cheddar Cl ITCH SO19.............248 C8
Cheddington Rd
  MOOR/WNTN BH9.............322 G3
Chedington Cl CFDH BH17.............320 C2
Chedworth Crs CHAM PO6.............274 C9
Cheesecombe Farm La
  LISS GU33.............172 E9
Cheetah Rd FARN GU14.............76 A2
Chelmer Cl BSTK RG21.............7 J6
Chelmsford Rd NEND PO2.............297 H1
Chelsea Rd SSEA PO5.............19 K7
Cheltenham Crs
  LSOL/BMARY PO13.............314 D2
Cheltenham Gdns HEND SO30.............250 C9
Cheltenham Rd
  BKME/WDN BH12.............321 J7
  CHAM PO6.............296 E1
Chelveston Crs ROWN SO16.............227 K8
Chelwood Dr SHST GU47.............40 G5
Chene Rd WIMB BH21.............300 F1
Cheping Gdns HEND SO30.............250 G5

Chepstow Cl CHFD SO53.............206 D3
  TOTT SO40.............246 A3
Chepstow St WVILLE PO7.............276 B1
Chequer La THLE RG7.............37 K4
Chequers La HTWY RG27.............79 N8
Chequers Rd BSTK RG21.............7 F6
Cherberry Cl FLEETN GU51.............56 E9
Cherbourg Rd ELGH SO50.............229 H3
Cherford Rd BWD BH11.............322 B5
Cherita Ct PLE BH15.............331 J3
Cheriton Av LTDN BH7.............324 A7
  WEND SO18.............249 L4
Cheriton Cl FUFL SO22.............164 E6
  HAV PO9.............276 D5
  HORN PO8.............256 A4
  HORN PO8.............
Cheriton La NARL SO24.............168 D6
Cheriton Rd ELGH SO50.............229 H4
  FUFL SO22.............22 A2
  GPORT PO12.............315 K4
Cheriton Wy BLKW GU17.............41 L9
  WIMB BH21.............278 E8
Cherque La
  LSOL/BMARY PO13.............294 E9
Cherrett Cl BWD BH11.............301 P9
Cherries Dr MOOR/WNTN BH9.............322 E5
Cherrimans Orch HASM GU27.............156 C7
Cherry Cl HTWY RG27.............72 A2
  LSOL/BMARY PO13.............314 D3
  PSTN BH14.............321 K8
  RWIN SO21.............144 E4
Cherry Tree Cl FARN GU14 *.............57 K8
  LYMN SO41.............328 D7
  RGWD BH24.............281 K6
  SHST GU47.............41 L5
Cherry Tree Dr
  NMIL/BTOS BH25.............326 G2
Cherry Tree Rd AND SP10.............102 C1
  RFNM GU10.............116 B3
Cherry Wk WSHM SO15.............247 N3
Cherryway ALTN GU34.............132 E4
Cherrywood CHIN RG24.............69 P1
  HEND SO30.............250 B5
Cherrywood Gdns TOTT SO40.............246 A4
  HISD PO11.............319 L4
Cherrywood Rd FARN GU14.............57 P6
Chervil Cl CFDH BH17.............206 B7
  HORN PO8.............256 C2
Cherville St ROMY SO51.............204 C5
Chervil Wy THLE RG7.............27 K5
Cheshire Cl FHAM PO15.............272 A9
Cheshire Dr BSTK RG21.............69 K8
Chesil Av WINC SO23.............23 G6
Chesildene Av CHAR BH8.............323 K5
Chesildene Dr CHAR BH8.............323 K4
Chesil St WINC SO23.............23 G6
Chesil Ter WINC SO23.............23 G6
Cheslyn Rd HSEA PO3.............317 K2
Chessel Av BOSC BH5.............335M2
  ITCH SO19.............248 C4
Chessel Crs ITCH SO19.............248 C4
Chester Cl ASHV GU12.............97 P1
  NWBY RG14.............17 K7
Chester Crs
  LSOL/BMARY PO13.............294 D1
Chesterfield Cl CCLF BH13.............333 P5
Chesterfield Rd BSTK RG21.............69M3
  HSEA PO3.............317 J1
  NWBY RG14.............16 E5
Chester Pl BSTK RG21.............69 K8
  SSEA PO5.............316 F6
Chester Rd ASHV GU12.............76 G9
  CCLF BH13.............333 N4
  WEND SO18.............249 J2
  WINC SO23.............23 G5
Chesterton Gdns HORN PO8.............255 N8
Chesterton Pl FHAM PO15.............271 J2
Chesterton Rd NTHA RG18.............25M2
Chester Wy RFNM GU10.............95M1
Chestnut Av AND SP10.............102 D5
  ASHV GU12.............97 L4
  CHCH/BSGR BH23.............324 B7
  CHFD SO53.............228 E1
  FNM GU9.............317 H4
  FNM GU9.............96 E2
  FUFL SO22.............164 D2
  HASM GU27.............157 H6
  HAV PO9.............276 B7
  NMIL/BTOS BH25.............327 H6
  NTID SP9.............30 B1
  RGWD BH24.............259 P4
  RWIN SO21.............207 P4
  SBNE BH6.............336 A2
  TOTT SO40.............246 A8
Chestnut Bank CHIN RG24.............70 C5
Chestnut Cl ALTN GU34.............132 E6
  BLKW GU17 *.............41 M9
  CHFD SO53.............228 E2
  FLEETN GU51.............56 F9
  CSHT GU26.............156 A2
  LIPH GU30.............175 L4
  NWBY RG14.............16 D4
  RFNM GU10.............135 M8
  WBNE BH4.............334 C4
Chestnut Crs NWBY RG14.............24 D3
  STOK SO20.............121 H5

Chestnut Dr
  RDGW/BURGH RG30.............27 K3
Chestnut End BOR GU35.............154 C4
Chestnut Gv FLEETN GU51.............74 E2
  WIMB BH21.............279 N8
Chestnut Pl STOK SO20.............121 H5
  ELGH SO50.............228 B3
Chestnut Ri BPWT SO32.............233 L3
  ELGH SO50.............228 B3
Chestnut Rd BROC SO42.............286 G8
  FARN GU14.............57 P6
  BROC SO42.............247 L1
Chestnut Sq STOK SO20.............121 H5
The Chestnuts HLER SO31.............270 G8
Chestnut Wk GPORT PO12.............295 L9
Chestnut Wy
  CHCH/BSGR BH23.............324 G4
  FHAM/STUB PO14.............271 J3
Cheswell Gdns FLEETN GU51.............74 B6
Chetnole Cl CFDH BH17.............321 H3
Chettle Rd ITCH SO19.............249 N6
Chetwode Pl ALDT GU11.............97 J4
Chetwode Ter ALDT GU11.............96 E2
Chetwode Wy CFDH BH17.............320 D2
Chetwynd Dr ROWN SO16.............228 B8
Chetwynd Rd ENEY PO4.............316 C5
  ROWN SO16.............228 B8
Chevening Ct ENEY PO4 *.............317 K3
Cheviot Cl CBLY GU15.............59M1
  FARN GU14.............68 E9
  KBH RG22.............68 E9
  NWBY RG14.............30 B1
Cheviot Dr FAWY SO45.............267 P7
  FLEETN GU51.............56 E9
Cheviot Gn HLER SO31.............292 D1
Cheviot Rd ROWN SO16.............247 J4
  SHST GU47.............40 C5
Cheviot Wk FHAM/STUB PO14.............294 D2
Cheviot Wy VWD BH31.............258 F5
Chewter Cl ENEY PO4.............316 C7
Chewton Common Rd
  CHCH/BSGR BH23.............326 C6
Chewton Farm Rd
  CHCH/BSGR BH23.............326 E6
Chewton Ldg
  CHCH/BSGR BH23.............326 D7
Chewton Wy
  CHCH/BSGR BH23.............326 D7
Cheylesmore Dr FRIM GU16.............59 J3
Cheyne Gdns WBNE BH4.............334 C4
Cheyne Wy FARN GU14.............57 N6
  LSOL/BMARY PO13.............314 D3
Chichester Av HISD PO11.............318 F5
Chichester Cl AND SP10.............102 B2
  HEND SO30.............250 C2
  HLER SO31.............270 E7
  LSOL/BMARY PO13.............294 F7
  ROMY SO51.............225 H2
Chichester Pl KBH RG22.............90 A1
Chichester Rd ASHV GU12.............116 F9
  HSEA PO3.............297 J6
  NEND PO2.............296 C2
  RGWD BH24.............282 G1
  WEND SO18.............249 L3
Chichester Wk WIMB BH21.............300 G4
Chickenhall La ELGH SO50.............229 L2
Chickerell Cl
  MOOR/WNTN BH9.............323 N4
Chidden Cl PSF GU32.............213M4
Chidden Holt CFDH SO53.............206 C8
Chideock Cl BKME/WDN BH12.............321 N6
Chidham Cl HAV PO9.............14 E3
Chidham Dr HAV PO9.............14 D3
Chidham Rd CHAM PO6.............275 J9
Chidham Sq HAV PO9.............14 D4
Chidham Wk HAV PO9.............14 D4
Chigwell Rd CHAR BH8.............323 J6
Chilbolton Av FUFL SO22.............164 E7
Chilbolton Ct HAV PO9.............277 H4
Chilcomb Cl
  LSOL/BMARY PO13.............314 D2
Chilcombe Cl HAV PO9.............15 F1
Chilcombe Rd SBNE BH6 *.............335 P1
Chilcomb La WINC SO23.............184 B1
Chilcomb Rd WEND SO18.............249 L3
Chilcote Rd HSEA PO3.............317 J1
Chilcroft Rd HASM GU27.............156 E6
Childerstone Cl LIPH GU30.............175 K4
Childe Sq NEND PO2.............296 E2
Chilfrome Cl CFDH BH17.............320 E3
Chilgrove Rd CHAM PO6.............297 L1
Chilham Cl ELGH SO50.............207 J6
  FRIM GU16.............58 E5
Chillandham La RWIN SO21.............146 B3
Chilland La RWIN SO21.............166 B1
Chillenden Ct TOTT SO40.............246 A5
Chillerton HLER SO31.............248 C8
Chillingham Wy CBLY GU15.............58 B1
Chilling La HLER SO31.............292 E4
Chillington Gdns CHFD SO53.............206 B3
Chilmark Ct LISS GU33.............192 D2
Chilsdown Wy WVILLE PO7.............275 N5
Chiltern Av FARN GU14.............57 K9
Chiltern Cl FARN GU14.............57 K9
  FLEETS GU52.............74 E7
  HASM GU27.............156 G8
  NMIL/BTOS BH25.............327 H6
  NWBY RG14.............30 B1
  TOTT SO40.............245 P1
  WBNE BH4.............334 C4
Chiltern Dr NMIL/BTOS BH25.............326 G7
  VWD BH31.............258 F4
Chiltern Gn ROWN SO16.............247 J3
Chiltern Rd SHST GU47.............40 C5
Chiltley La LIPH GU30.............175 K4
Chiltley Mnr LIPH GU30.............175 L5
Chiltley La LIPH GU30.............175 L5
Chiltley Wy LIPH GU30.............175 L5
Chilton Farm Pk FARN GU14.............57 K9
Chilton Rdg KBH RG22.............89M6
Chilworth Cl ROWN SO16.............227 N4
Chilworth Dro ROWN SO16.............227 N4
Chilworth Gdns HORN PO8.............236 C3

Chilworth Gv *GPORT* PO12......315 L3
Chilworth Rd *ROWN* SO16......228 A3
Chine Av *ITCH* SO19......248 G5
Chine Cl *HLER* SO31......270 C6
Chine Crs *WCLF* BH2......8 A5
Chine Crescent Rd *WCLF* BH2......8 A5
Chineham Cl *FLEETN* GU51......73 P1
Chineham Farm Cots
......*CHIN* RG24......69 N5
Chineham La *CHIN* RG24......69 J2
Chineham Park Ct *CHIN* RG24......69 N4
The Chine *LSOL/BMARY* PO13......295 J8
......*RFNM* GU10......115 P5
Chine Wk *FERN* BH22......302 E7
Chingford Av *FARN* GU14......58 B8
Chinham Rd *TOTT* SO40......245 H5
Chinnock Cl *FLEETS* GU52......74 C5
Chippendale Cl *FHAM* RG26......53 P5
Chipstead Rd *CHAM* PO6......297 H1
Chirk Pl *ROMY* SO51......204 E6
Chisels La *CHCH/BSGR* BH23......325 M1
Chisholm Cl *ROWN* SO16......227 K7
Chiswell Rd *CFDH* BH17......320 B3
Chitty Rd *ENEY* PO4......317 J6
Chivers Cl *KBH* RG22......68 E9
......*SSEA* PO5......19 H6
Chloe Gdns *BKME/WDN* BH12...321 M5
Chobham Rd *FRIM* GU16......58 D5
Cholderton Rd *AMSY* SP4......118 C2
......*RAND* SP11......99 M7
Cholseley Dr *FLEETN* GU51......74 B1
Chopin Rd *KBH* RG22......89 P5
Chorley Cl *PLE* BH15......320 E6
Chrismas Av *ASHV* GU12......3 J5
Chrismas Pl *ASHV* GU12......3 J5
Christchurch Bay Rd
......*NMIL/BTOS* BH25......327 H8
Christchurch By-Pass
......*CHCH/BSGR* BH23......324 F8
Christchurch Cl *BLKW* GU17......41 K8
Christchurch Gdns *CHAM* PO6...275 K8
......*WINC* SO23......183 N1
Christchurch Rd *BMTH* BH1......9 J3
......*BMTH* BH1......335 L2
......*CHCH/BSGR* BH23......323 P1
......*FERN* BH22......302 B6
......*LYMN* SO41......327 P8
......*NMIL/BTOS* BH25......326 C7
......*RGWD* BH24......282 D2
......*WINC* SO23......22 C7
Christie Av *HLER* SO31......271 J2
Christie Hts *NWBY* RG14......24 E7
Christie Wk *YTLY* GU46......56 D1
Christine Cl *ASHV* GU12......97 M2
Christmas Hl *RWIN* SO21......125 L7
Christopher Ct *TADY* RG26......17 H4
Christopher Crs *PLE* BH15......320 E6
Christopher Wy *EMRTH* PO10...277 M8
Christy Ct *TADY* RG26......17 H5
Christy Est *ASHV* GU12 *......97 L1
Church Av *FARN* GU14......76 B2
Church Bank Rd *RWIN* SO21...127 M4
Church Cir *FARN* GU14......76 B3
Church Cl *AND* SP10......4 E4
......*ELGH* SO50......207 L9
......*HASM* GU27......157 L3
......*HLER* SO31......271 H7
......*HORN* PO8......236 B6
......*NBAD* SO52......205 L9
Church Ct *FLEETN* GU51......74 C1
Church End *WSHM* SO15......247 H7
Churcher Cl *GPORT* PO12......315 H5
Churcher Rd *EMRTH* PO10......277 P6
Church Farm *FBDC* SP6......240 D3
Church Farm Barns *THLE* RG7...36 C1
Church Farm Cl *FAWY* SO45...267 H7
......*OVTN* RG25......88 C9
Churchfield *VWD* BH31......258 E4
Churchfield Crs *PLE* BH15......320 G8
Churchfield La *RGWD* BH24......260 C1
Churchfield Rd *EPSF* SO21......215 P1
......*PLE* BH15......320 G9
Churchfields *BOR* GU35......134 F8
Church Flds *PLE* BH15......154 F3
Churchfields *FAWY* SO45......291 K6
Church Ga *STHA* PO19......74 B3
Church Gv *FLEETN* GU51......74 D3
Church Hatch *RSAL* SP5......199 L5
Church Hl *ALDT* GU11......2 D3
......*HEND* SO30......249 L2
......*LYMN* SO41......339 H1
......*RSAL* SP5......200 B8
......*STOK* SO20......35 J9
......*VWD* BH31......258 E4
Church Hill Ter *RFNM* GU10 *...95 H5
Churchill Av *ASHV* GU12......3 H4
......*BPWT* SO32......231 N3
......*ODIM* RG29......93 K3
Churchill Cl *ALTN* GU34......132 F7
......*ALTN* GU34......151 M5
......*FBDC* SP6......239 J6
......*FHAM/STUB* PO14......271 J9
......*HTWY* RG27......54 G6
......*NTID* SP9......78 F3
......*TADY* RG26......34 E7
......*WINC* SO23......145 J7
Churchill Ct *HORN* PO8 *......256 A5
Churchill Crs
......*BKME/WDN* BH12......321 L6
......*BOR* GU35......134 C4
......*FARN* GU14......76 B4
Churchill Dr *EMRTH* PO10......277 M6
Churchill Gdns
......*BKME/WDN* BH12......321 L7
Churchill Ms *GPORT* PO12 *...315 L2
Churchill Plaza *BSTK* RG21 *...7 F5
Churchill Rd
......*BKME/WDN* BH12......321 L7
......*BMTH* BH1......335 K1
......*WIMB* BH21......300 F2
Churchill Sq *ENEY* PO4......317 K6

Churchill Wy *AND* SP10......5 G1
......*BSTK* RG21......6 E5
Churchill Wy East *BSTK* RG21...7 H5
Churchill Wy West *AND* SP10...82 C9
......*AND* SP10......101 P2
......*BSTK* RG21......6 A6
......*KBH* RG22......68 C7
Church Lands *TADY* RG26......51 N2
Church La *ALTN* GU34......131 H7
......*ALTN* GU34......133 J2
......*ALTN* GU34......189 L3
......*ASHV* GU12......97 P1
......*BOR* GU35......154 E2
......*BPWT* SO32......230 F6
......*BPWT* SO32......232 C6
......*BPWT* SO32......251 K3
......*BROC* SO42......308 E4
......*BROC* SO42......311 H5
......*CHIN* RG24......70 C6
......*CHCH/BSGR* BH23......324 F9
......*DEAN* RG23......68 D8
......*ELGH* SO50......207 N5
......*EWKG* RG40......39 P7
......*FARN* GU14......76 A3
......*FAWY* SO45......291 J6
......*FBDC* SP6......219 K8
......*FERN* BH22......302 F9
......*FUFL* SO22......164 B1
......*GSHT* GU26......157 H6
......*HASM* GU27......157 H6
......*HAV* PO9......299 H1
......*HEND* SO30......250 B6
......*HEND* SO30......250 C6
......*HISD* PO11......299 J6
......*HLER* SO31......270 B2
......*HTWY* RG27......55 J9
......*HTWY* RG27......55 J9
......*KSCL* RG20......29 L6
......*KSCL* RG20......30 F7
......*LIPH* GU30......175 J1
......*LISS* GU33......172 C4
......*LYMN* SO41......308 B7
......*LYMN* SO41......309 K5
......*LYMN* SO41......329 L4
......*LYND* SO43......264 F5
......*NARL* SO24......168 E3
......*NARL* SO24......169 M3
......*NMIL/BTOS* BH25......327 H6
......*NTID* SP9......79 H7
......*NWBY* RG14......24 A3
......*OVTN* RG25......90 C4
......*OVTN* RG25......110 D1
......*PSF* GU32......188 D9
......*PTSW* SO17......248 D1
......*RAND* SP11......42 F5
......*RAND* SP11......79 N1
......*RAND* SP11......102 E9
......*RDGW/BURGH* RG30......101 M1
......*RFNM* GU10......95 M4
......*RFNM* GU10......114 E4
......*RFNM* GU10......115 N7
......*RFNM* GU10......115 P5
......*RGWD* BH24......284 C6
......*ROMY* SO51......179 M5
......*ROMY* SO51......202 B2
......*ROMY* SO51......203 L1
......*ROMY* SO51......204 C6
......*ROWN* SO16......226 D7
......*RWIN* SO21......165 N2
......*RWIN* SO21......166 A1
......*RWIN* SO21......184 A6
......*RWIN* SO21......207 P5
......*STHA* PO19......25 N4
......*STOK* SO20......139 P3
......*STOK* SO20......161 H1
......*TADY* RG26......48 G3
......*THLE* RG7......26 D5
......*THLE* RG7......35 M5
......*WINC* SO23......165 K1
......*WILLE* PO7......234 F9
Church Lane Cnr
......*LYMN* SO41......309 M7
Church La East *ALDT* GU11......2 C5
Church La West *ALDT* GU11......2 C5
Church Md *LYMN* SO41......329 L5
Church Mdw *NTID* SP9......98 C2
Church Ms *RAND* SP11 *......102 A5
Churchmoor Rd *WIMB* BH21...279 J9
Church Pth *ASHV* GU12......76 D7
......*EMRTH* PO10......299 M1
......*FHAM/PORC* PO16......11 J5
......*GPORT* PO12......12 A6
......*HORN* PO8......256 D5
......*HTWY* RG27......71 N4
Church Pth North *PSEA* PO1 *...19 H1
Church Rd *ALDT* GU11......3 H7
......*ALTN* GU34......151 M5
......*BPWT* SO32......230 D9
......*BPWT* SO32......252 B4
......*CBLY* GU15......41 N7
......*ELGH* SO50......207 M8
......*EMRTH* PO10......277 P7
......*FERN* BH22......302 C3
......*FHAM/PORC* PO16......296 A3
......*FLEETN* GU51......74 C4
......*FRIM* GU16......58 C5
......*GPORT* PO12......12 A6
......*HASM* GU27......157 H6
......*HISD* PO11......318 G4
......*HLER* SO31......311 M1
......*HLER* SO31......292 D1
......*ITCH* SO19......268 F1
......*LIPH* GU30......175 K1
......*NWBY* RG14......24 D2
......*OVTN* RG25......108 C1
......*OVTN* RG25......109 K5
......*PSEA* PO1......19 H3
......*PSF* GU32......191 L7
......*PSTN* BH14......321 J8
......*ROMY* SO51......180 B4
......*ROMY* SO51......204 G6

Church Rd East *CWTH* RG45......41 J1
......*FARN* GU14......76 C3
Church Rd West *CWTH* RG45......41 J2
......*FARN* GU14......76 B5
Church Sq *BSTK* RG21......6 E6
Church St *ALDT* GU11......2 C3
......*ALTN* GU34......131 J4
......*ALTN* GU34......151 M6
......*BPWT* SO32......209 M7
......*BSTK* RG21......6 E5
......*CHCH/BSGR* BH23......324 F9
......*DEAN* RG23......41 J2
......*DEAN* RG23......240 C3
......*FHAM/STUB* PO14......293 M1
......*KSCL* RG20......29 L7
......*LISS* GU33......173 J9
......*NARL* SO24......169 M3
......*ODIM* RG29......93 K1
......*PLE* BH15......332 D2
......*PSEA* PO1......316 E1
......*RAND* SP11......62 B5
......*RAND* SP11......125 L3
......*RFNM* GU10......95 M4
......*ROMY* SO51......204 C6
......*RSAL* SP5......176 C4
......*RWIN* SO21......126 G6
......*WCHR* RG28......85 L7
......*WIMB* BH21......278 D9
......*WSHM* SO15......247 G3
Church Street Rbt *PSEA* PO1...316 E1
Church Vw *ASHV* GU12......97 N1
......*EMRTH* PO10 *......277 P7
......*ENEY* PO4......317 J4
......*HTWY* RG27......55 H9
......*HTWY* RG27......72 A5
......*ODIM* RG29......93 M4
......*YTLY* GU46......40 F7
Church View *ITCH* SO19......249 J8
Church Vw *RSAL* SP5......200 C8
Churchward Gdns
......*HEND* SO30......250 C1
Clackton Rd *FARN* GU14......70 C5
Chute Ct *BOR* GU35......155 H1
Chute Cswy *RAND* SP11......60 A1
Chute Cl *TADY* RG26......52 A1
Cibbons Rd *CHIN* RG24......70 A1
Cinderford Cl *CHAM* PO6......274 D9
Cinnamon La *FAWY* SO45......291 J6
Circle Hill Rd *CWTH* RG45......41 K1
The Circle *MOOR/WNTN* BH9 *...322 C3
......*SSEA* PO5 *......316 F6
......*WHAM* PO17......252 D7
Circular Rd *PSEA* PO1......18 E1
The Circus *WVILLE* PO7......274 C8
Cirrus Gdns *HLER* SO31......269 P8
City Rd *WINC* SO23......22 D3
Civic Centre Rd *HAV* PO9......15 F5
......*SHAM* SO14......20 D3
Civic Wy *FHAM/PORC* PO16......11 J5
Clack La *FBDC* SP6......296 F1
Clacton Rd *CHAM* PO6......296 F1
Claire Gdns *HORN* PO8......256 C1
Clandon Ct *FARN* GU14......76 C1
Clandon Dr *ELGH* SO50......207 H7
Clanfield Cl *CHFD* SO53......206 F7
Clanfield Ride *BLKW* GU17......41 L9
Clanfield Rd *WEND* SO18......249 L4
Clanfield Wy *CHFD* SO53......206 F7
Clanwilliam Rd
......*LSOL/BMARY* PO13......314 C2
Clappers Farm Rd *THLE* RG7...35 P6
Clapps Gate Rd *TADY* RG26...34 F5
Clare Cl *FHAM/STUB* PO14......271 J9
Clare Gdns *EPSF* SO21......216 A2
......*FAWY* SO45......313 H1
Clare Lodge Cl
......*MOOR/WNTN* BH9......323 H5
Claremont Av
......*MOOR/WNTN* BH9......323 H5
Claremont Cl *ELGH* SO50......207 J7
Claremont Crs *NWBY* RG14......24 G3
......*WSHM* SO15......247 L4
Claremont Rd
......*MOOR/WNTN* BH9......323 H5
......*PSEA* PO1 *......316 C3
......*WSHM* SO15......247 L4
Clarence Cl *ASHV* GU12......3 J5
......*RAND* SP11......79 H7
Clarence Esp *SSEA* PO5......316 D6
Clarence Pde *SSEA* PO5......316 E6
Clarence Park Rd *LTDN* BH7...323 N9
Clarence Rd *FLEETN* GU51......74 C4
......*GPORT* PO12......13 H1
......*GPORT* PO12......315 K5
......*PSTN* BH14 *......321 J9
......*SSEA* PO5......316 F7
Clarence St *PSEA* PO1......316 E2
Clarence Whf *GPORT* PO12 *...13 H1
Clarendon Av *AND* SP10......102 C4
Clarendon Cl *BDST* BH18......300 C9
......*ROMY* SO51......204 F4
Clarendon Ct *BLKW* GU17......57 L2
Clarendon Crs
......*FHAM/STUB* PO14......271 H9
Clarendon Gdns *NWBY* RG14...24 D5
Clarendon Ms *SSEA* PO5 *......316 E6
Clarendon Pk *LYMN* SO41......329 K5
Clarendon Pl *PSEA* PO1......316 F2
Clarendon Rd *BDST* BH18......320 A1
......*CHCH/BSGR* BH23......324 E8
......*HAV* PO9......14 E6

Clingan Rd *SBNE* BH6......324 B9
Clinkley Rd *NARL* SO24......169 N8
Clinton Cl *CHCH/BSGR* BH23...326 D5
Clinton Rd *LYMN* SO41......329 L2
......*WVILLE* PO7......255 L8
Clipper Cl *HLER* SO31......270 E9
Clitheroe Rd *FARN* GU14......56 G4
Cliveden Cl *FERN* BH22......302 C1
Clive Gv *FHAM/PORC* PO16......295 N2
Clive Rd *ASHV* GU12......3 K5
......*CHCH/BSGR* BH23......326 A5
......*MOOR/WNTN* BH9......322 F6
......*PSEA* PO1......316 C2
Clock House Ct *HASM* GU27 *...157 H7
Clockhouse Rd *FARN* GU14......58 A9
Clock St *PSEA* PO1......18 C3
Clocktower Dr *ENEY* PO4......317 K6
The Cloisters *ALTN* GU34 *......132 F5
......*FHAM* PO15......272 A8
......*FRIM* GU16......58 C4
......*ROMY* SO51......204 B4
......*ROWN* SO16......204 C5
......*ROWN* SO16......228 C8
The Close Bellfield
......*FHAM/STUB* PO14......293 M2
The Close *BDST* BH18......320 A1
......*CHAM* PO6......297 J2
......*FAWY* SO45......290 F6
......*FHAM/PORC* PO16......295 N1
......*FNM* GU16......116 D1
......*FRIM* GU16......58 B5
......*HEND* SO30......250 A5
......*LYMN* SO41......308 A6
......*NMIL/BTOS* BH25......327 J7
......*NTHA* RG18......25 L3
......*PSF* GU32......214 B2
......*RAND* SP11......82 A1
......*RGWD* BH24......281 N5
......*RGWD* BH24......282 B5
......*RGWD* BH24......282 D2
......*RSAL* SP5......199 P6
......*RWIN* SO21......207 M4
......*SHST* GU47......41 M6
......*THLE* RG7......50 E7
......*WEND* SO18......249 M4
......*WINC* SO23......22 E6
Closewood Rd *WVILLE* PO7......275 J1
Closeworth Rd *FARN* GU14......76 D4
Clough La *RGWD* BH24......284 B6
......*RSAL* SP5......138 A9
Clough's Rd *RGWD* BH24......282 F2
Clouston Rd *FARN* GU14......57 N8
Clovelly Rd *EMRTH* PO10......299 L1
......*ENEY* PO4......317 J4
......*HISD* PO11......338 D9
......*SHAM* SO14......21 F1
Cloverbank *WINC* SO23......145 J6
Clover Cl *BOR* GU35......154 D3
......*CHCH/BSGR* BH23......325 M7
......*HLER* SO31......270 E8
......*LSOL/BMARY* PO13......314 B8
Clover Ct *NMIL/BTOS* BH25......327 M3
Clover Dr *CFDH* BH17......320 B3
Clover Fld *CHIN* RG24......70 A5
Clover Gdns *RAND* SP11......79 P1
Clover La *YTLY* GU46......40 B8
Cloverleaf Wy *CHIN* RG24......70 A6
......*HEND* SO30 *......250 A5
The Clovers *BKME/WDN* BH12...322 A7
Clover Wy *HEND* SO30......250 A5
......*ROMY* SO51......204 C5
Clowes Av *SBNE* BH6......336 F3
Club House La *BPWT* SO32......232 C9
Club House Rd *FRIM* GU16......58 D2
Club La *CWTH* RG45......41 L1
......*NTID* SP9......78 G7
Clump Hl *WIMB* BH21......258 A9
Clumps Rd *RFNM* GU10......116 A6
Clutebank Rd *NEND* PO2......296 F9
Clyde Ct *AND* SP10......82 G9
......*GPORT* PO12......315 K2
Clyde Rd *CFDH* BH17......320 D2
......*GPORT* PO12......315 K2
Clydesdale Dr *TOTT* SO40......245 F3
Clydesdale Rd *HLER* SO31......271 H3
Clydesdale Wy *TOTT* SO40......245 F3
Coach Hl *FHAM/STUB* PO14......293 M1
......*RAND* SP11......60 A8
Coach Hill Cl *CHFD* SO53......206 D6
Coach Hill La *RGWD* BH24......283 P5
Coach House Cl *FRIM* GU16......58 D2
Coach House Gdns
......*FLEETN* GU51......74 D1
Coach House Ms *ENEY* PO4......317 L4
......*FERN* BH22......302 F1
Coach House Pl *BMTH* BH1......334 C1
Coachmans Copse
......*WEND* SO18......249 J1
Coachman's Ct *NWBY* RG14......24 E2
Coachmans Halt
......*WVILLE* PO7 *......254 E1
Coach Rd *HLER* SO31......269 N8
Cuffe Ter *RSAL* SP5......159 J7
Coachways *AND* SP10......4 C7
Coal Park La *HLER* SO31......270 E1
Coalville Rd *ITCH* SO19......249 K7
Coastguard Cl *GPORT* PO12......315 K2
Coastguard Wy
......*CHCH/BSGR* BH23......337 J2
Coates Cl *RWIN* SO21......144 E6
Coates Rd *ITCH* SO19......249 M7
Coates Rd *ITCH* SO19......249 M7
Coates Wy *WVILLE* PO7......275 N5
Coat Gdns *FAWY* SO45......268 C2
Cobalt Ct
......*LSOL/BMARY* PO13......314 C2
Cobbetts Rdg *RFNM* GU10......117 J1
Cobbett Cl *FUFL* SO22......183 L1
Cobbett Gn *KBH* RG22......90 A1
Cobbett Rd *WEND* SO18......248 G4
Cobbett's La *BLKW* GU17......56 G1
......*YTLY* GU46......40 F7

Cobbetts Ms FNM GU9 * 96 B9
Cobbetts Wy FNM GU9 ....115 P4
Cobbetts Cnr LYMN SO41 ......308 G5
Cobblewood EMRTH PO10 ......277 M7
Cobbs La PLE BH15 ....320 C6
Cobb's Rd WIMB BH21 ....278 G8
Cobden Av HSEA PO3 ....297 J9
Cobden Crs WEND SO18 ....249 H3
Cobden Gdns WEND SO18 ......248 G2
Cobden La HASM GU27 ....157 J6
Cobden Ri WEND SO18 * 248 G2
Cobden St GPORT PO12 ....315 M3
Cobham Rd
 MOOR/WNTN BH9 ....322 G4
 WIMB BH21 ....279 P7
Cobham Wy WIMB BH21 ....300 G4
Coblands Av TOTT SO40 ......246 B4
Cobley Cl RSAL SP5 ....195 H6
Coburg St PSEA PO1 ....19 K2
 SHAM SO14 ....21 J1
Cochrane Cl
 LSOL/BMARY PO13 ....315 H2
Cochrane Cl STHA RG19 ....25 P4
Cock-a-Dobby SHST GU47 .....41 H6
Cockerell Cl FHAM PO16 ......11 G5
 WIMB BH21 ....301 H4
Cockleshell Gdns ENEY PO4...317 L5
Cockleshell Square
 GPORT PO12 ....13 C1
Cocklydown La TOTT SO40 ....246 C6
Cockshott La PSF GU32 ....160 G4
Cody Cl ASHV GU12 ....76 E7
Cody Rd FARN GU14 ....75 N1
Coe Cl ALDT GU11 ....2 D4
Cogdean Cl WIMB BH21 ....300 A5
Cogdeane Rd CFDH BH17 ......320 F2
Cogdean Wk WIMB BH21 ....300 A5
Cogdean Wy WIMB BH21 ......300 A5
Coghlan Cl FHAM/PORC PO16 ..11 G3
Cokenor Wd RFNM GU10 ......115 P4
Coker Cl FUFL SO22 ....22 B3
Colbeck FLEETS GU52 ....74 E8
Colborne Av WIMB BH21 ......299 J4
Colborne Cl LYMN SO41 ......329 L2
 PLE BH15 ....332 F2

PSEA PO1 ....18 C2
RGWD BH24 ....282 E2
SHST GU47 ....41 M7
WVILLE PO7 ....275 N8
College St EPSF GU31 ....215 M2
 PSEA PO1 ....18 C3
 SHAM SO14 ....21 F6
College Wk WINC SO23 ....23 F7
Collett Cl HEND SO30 ....250 B1
Colley Cl WINC SO23 ....165 H4
Collier Cl FARN GU14 ....57 L8
 PTSW SO17 ....248 E5
Collingbourne Av SBNE BH6 ..324 B9
Collingbourne Dr CHAM PO6 ..300 C7
Collington Crs CHAM PO6 ....274 D9
Collingwood Av WK AND SP10 ..5 K3
Collingwood Rd HSEA PO5 ...316 F6
 WIMB BH21 ....280 E5
Collingworth Cl FHAM SP10 .271 H4
Collingworth Ri FHAM PO15 .271 H5
Collins Cl AND SP10 ....82 C8
 CHFD SO53 ....206 B7
 NWBY RG14 ....24 F5
Collins Cl NTID SP9 ....78 C3
Collins Gdns ASHV GU12 .....97 P1
Collins La EPSF GU31 ....216 D6
 RGWD BH24 ....282 E2
 RWIN SO21 ....182 E7
Collins Rd ENEY PO4 ....317 J6
Collis Rd HSEA PO3 ....297 J9
Collwood Cl PLE BH15 ....320 E5
Collyers Cls LIPH GU30 .....175 M3
Collyers Rd BROC SO42 ......308 F1
Colne Av ROWN SO16 ....227 H9
Colne Valley Wy RWIN SO21 .125 P2
 WHCH RG28 ....86 B6
Colne Wy FARN GU14 ....57 N2
 BSTK RG21 ....7 L6
Colonnade Rd BOSC BH5 .....335 N1
The Colonnade ITCH SO19 * .248 F8
Colpoy St SSEA PO5 ....19 F5
Colson Cl WINC SO23 ....23 H3
Colson Rd WINC SO23 ....23 H5
Colt Cl ROWN SO16 ....227 K7
 PLE BH15 ....279 K8
Colton Copse CHFD SO53 ....206 B7
Coltsfoot Cl HEND SO30 .....250 B4
 THLE RG7 ....27 K4
Coltsfoot Dr HTWY RG27 .....72 B2
Colts Fmd Rd BOR GU35 .....154 D3
Coltsfoot Wk ROMY SO51 ....204 G4
Coltsmead CHAM PO6 ....296 B1
Columbian Wy WBNE BH10 ...287 J1
Columbia Rd NBNE BH10 ....322 D5
Columbia Trees La
 NBNE BH10 ....322 C6
Columbine Cl
 CHCH/BSGR BH23 ....325 M6
Columbine Rd KBH RG22 ......89 L5
Columbus Dr FARN GU14 .....75 K1
Columbus Wy AND SP10 ....5 H3
Colville Cl BOSC BH5 ....335 N1
Colville Dr BPWT SO32 ......232 B4
Colville Rd BOSC BH5 ....335 N1
Colvin Gdns CHAM PO6 ....287 J1
Colwell Cl ROWN SO16 ......247 H3
Colwell Rd CHAM PO6 ....297 H2
Colwyn Cl YTLY GU46 ....40 C8
Colyer Cl KBH RG22 ....89 N8
Combe La FARN GU14 ....57 P7
Combe Ri RFNM GU10 ....116 D5
Combe Rd LISS GU33 ....192 F5
Comber Rd MOOR/WNTN BH9...322 F4
Comet Cl ASHV GU12 ....76 E1
Comet Wy CHCH/BSGR BH23 ..325 L9
Comfrey Cl FARN GU14 ....57 K8
 HORN PO8 ....256 C2
 ROMY SO51 ....204 G4
Comines Wy HEND SO30 ......259 N5
Comley Hi HTWY RG27 ....277 J3
Comley Rd MOOR/WNTN BH9 .322 F5
Commercial Pl PSEA PO1 ....19 H1
Commercial Rd ASHV GU12 ....3 J6
 PLE BH15 ....321 H8
 PSEA PO1 ....19 G2
 TOTT SO40 ....226 B1
 WCLF BH2 ....8 C4
 SO18 ....20 D2
Commercial St WEND SO18 ..249 K4
Common Barn La
 LSOL/BMARY PO13 ....314 D1
Common Cl CHFD SO53 ....206 E5
Common Gdns CHFD SO53 ....206 E5
Common Ms ALTN SO24 ......149 N2
Common Hill Rd ROMY SO51 .185 H4
Common La
 FHAM/STUB PO14 ....293 K1
 WHAM PO17 ....274 A1
Common Rd CHFD SO53 ......206 E5
 RSAL SP5 ....201 K2
 STHA RG19 ....32 B6
Commonside EMRTH PO10 ....277 P5
Common St PSEA PO1 * 19 K1
The Common RSAL SP5 ......158 C1
Compass Cl
 LSOL/BMARY PO13 ....315 H2
Compass Fld HTWY RG27 .....72 A3
Compass Point HLER SO31 * .269 N8
Compass Rd CHAM PO6 ......296 D1
Complins ALTN SO24 ....133 H5
Compound Rd FARN PO14 ....333 M1
Compton Beeches
 RGWD BH24 ....281 N4
Compton Cl ELGH SO50 ......207 H7
 FLEETS GU52 ....74 E7
 FUFL SO22 ....183 K3
 HAV PO9 ....15 F2
Cook St SHAM SO14 ....21 F5
 HTWY RG27 ....72 A4

LSOL/BMARY PO13 ....314 E2
SHST GU47 ....41 K5
WBHI BH31 ....258 F4
Compton Crs NEND PO2 ......280 C8
Compton Dr PSTN BH14 ......333 L1
Compton Gdns FLEETS GU52 .74 E7
Compton Rd NEND PO2 ....297 H6
 NMIL/BTOS BH25 ....327 J5
 TOTT SO40 ....246 E3
Compton Sq AND SP10 ....82 G8
Compton St AWH SO21 ......183 K3
Compton Wy SHAM SO14 .....20 E2
Compton Wy FUFL SO22 ....183 K3
 RFNM GU10 ....96 C9
Conan Rd NEND PO2 ....296 C5
Concorde Wy FHAM PO15 ...271 L5
Conde Wy BOR GU35 ....154 B6
Condor Av FHAM/PORC PO16 .295 K2
Condor Cl ITCH SO19 ....248 F8
 WIMB BH21 ....281 H4
Conduit Rd FARN GU14 ......76 A2
Coney Gn WINC SO23 ....165 H5
Coneygar La LYMN SO41 ....329 M3
Conference Dr HLER SO31 ..271 H7
Conference Pl LYMN SO41 ..329 L5
Conford Ct HAV PO9 ....276 D4
Congleton Cl LYND SO43 ...244 C8
Conholt Hi RAND SP11 ......42 F8
Conholt La RAND SP11 ......60 C1
Conholt Rd AND SP10 ......102 E5
Conifer Av PSTN BH14 .....333 K1
Conifer Cl BOR GU35 ......153 P7
 CHCH/BSGR BH23 ....324 B4
 FAWY SO45 ....268 A7
 FERN BH22 ....282 F7
 FLEETS GU52 ....74 C2
 FUFL SO22 ....22 B2
 HORN PO8 ....256 A9
 RGWD BH24 ....281 K5
 TADY RG26 ....33 P4
Conifer Crest NWBY RG14 ...50 B2
Conifer Gv LSOL/BMARY PO13 .294 C5
Conifer Ms FHAM/PORC PO16 .275 P9
Conigar Rd EMRTH PO10 ....277 M7
Coniston Av BWD BH11 .....301 M8
 HSEA PO3 ....297 J8
Coniston Cl CBLY GU15 ......59 H2
 FARN GU14 ....75 M1
 STHA RG19 ....26 E6
 VWD BH31 ....258 F5
Coniston Ct ASHV GU12 * ...76 E8
Coniston Dr FNM GU9 ....96 C4
Coniston Gdns HEND SO30 ..250 C6
Coniston Gv NARL SO24 ....168 A3
Coniston Rd BOR GU35 .....153 P3
 ELGH SO50 ....229 H2
 KBH RG22 ....89 M3
 RGWD BH24 ....282 F3
 ROWN SO16 ....246 G3
Coniston Wk
 FHAM/STUB PO14 ....294 C2
Coniston Wy FLEETS GU52 ..74 B7
Connaught Barracks
 ALDT GU11 ....76 C6
Connaught Cl BOR GU35 ....154 A6
 CWTH RG45 ....40 C3
 NMIL/BTOS BH25 ....326 C7
 YTLY GU46 ....40 D8
Connaught Crs
 BKME/WDN BH12 ....321 N6
Connaught Rd ASHV GU12 ....3 J3
 BOSC BH5 ....335 P1
 FLEETN GU51 ....74 D4
 HAV PO9 ....15 J5
 NEND PO2 ....296 F7
 RGN RG14 ....17 C2
 RWIN SO21 ....144 D6
Connell Rd PLE BH15 ....320 E7
Connemara Crs HLER SO31 .271 H5
Connigar Cl
 LSOL/BMARY PO13 ....314 C1
Connop Wy FRIM GU16 ....58 E2
Conqueror Wy
 FHAM/STUB PO14 ....294 B7
Conrad Gdns FHAM PO15 ...271 J2
The Conservatory
 WINC SO23 * 23 C5
Consort Cl ELGH SO50 .....207 K8
Consort Ct FHAM/PORC PO16 *.11 J6
Consort Rd ELGH SO50 .....207 K8
Constable Ct BSTK RG21 ...69 N9
 FERN BH22 ....302 C4
 FHAM PO15 ....272 B6
 ITCH SO19 ....248 C5
Constable Gdns AND SP10 ...4 C2
Constable's Ga WINC SO23 .22 C5
Constantine Av CHFD SO53 .206 C7
Constantine Cl CHFD SO53 .206 C7
Constantine Sq AND SP10 ...82 G9
Constantine Wy KBH RG22 ..89 L1
Constant Rd FARN GU14 ....75 H2
Constitution Hill Rd
 PSTN BH14 ....321 H8
Convent La EMRTH PO10 ...299 M1
Conway Cl CHFD SO53 ......228 D1
 NMIL/BTOS BH25 ....327 K4
 NTHA RG18 ....25 J1
Conway Dr FARN GU14 ......75 N2
Conways Dr PSTN BH14 ....321 H6
Cook Cl RGWD BH24 ....282 C1
Cook's La RGWD BH24 ......280 D8
Cookham Cl SHST GU47 .....41 K5
Cook Rw WIMB BH21 ....300 D1
Cooks La ROMY SO51 ....178 D7
 ROMY SO51 ....203 N1
Cook St SHAM SO14 * 21 F5
Coolers Farm STOK SO20 ...160 B1

Coombe Av NBNE BH10 .....322 E5
Coombe Cl FERN BH22 ......282 E5
Coombe Ct STHA RG19 ......25 P4
Coombedale HLER SO31 ....271 H8
Coombe Dr FLEETS GU52 ...74 F3
Coombe Farm Av
 FHAM/PORC PO16 ....11 F7
Coombe Gdns NBNE BH10 ..322 D5
Coombehurst Dr BSTK RG21 .90 D1
Coombe La LYMN SO41 .....308 D7
 PSF GU32 ....212 G1
 ROMY SO51 ....203 M2
Coombe Rd GPORT PO12 ...315 M1
 HAV PO9 ....14 C2
 YTLY GU46 ....40 C7
Coombe Sq STHA RG19 .....25 P4
Coombs Ct HORN PO8 ......256 C2
The Cooperage ALTN GU34 .132 E6
Cooper Dean Dr CHAR BH8 .323 M6
Cooper Gv FHAM/PORC PO16 .295 P5
Cooper Rd HSEA PO3 ....317 K1
 TOTT SO40 ....246 A8
Cooper's Cl ROMY SO51 ...225 H2
 RWIN SO21 ....144 E6
Coopers Cl TADY RG26 .....52 A2
Coopers Crs NTHA RG18 ...25 M3
Cooper's Hl HTWY RG27 ....55 N2
Coopers Hill Dr
 CHOB/PIR GU24 ....59 P6
 KBH RG22 ....89 K3
Cooper's La ITCH SO19 ...248 F8
 STHA RG19 ....33 F1
 PSHT SO47 ....58 F3
Coopers Ter FNM GU9 * 96 C8
Copeland Dr PSTN BH14 ...333 K1
Copeland Rd ROWN SO16 ..247 H2
Copelands Cl CBLY GU15 ...59 J1
Copes La HTWY RG27 ....72 F4
Coplinger Cl TOTT SO40 ..246 A5
Copland Cl KBH RG22 ......89 N5
Copnor Cl ROMY SO51 .....29 K6
Copnor Rd NEND PO2 ......297 H5
Copper Beech Cl
 BKME/WDN BH12 ....334 A2
Copper Beech Dr CHAM PO6 .297 N1
Copper Beech Gdns
 NBNE BH10 ....322 D5
Copperfield Av SHST GU47 .41 M4
Copperfield Rd ROWN SO16 .228 C7
Copperfields TOTT SO40 ...245 P4
Coppers Cl FRIM GU16 .....58 A3
Copper St SSEA PO5 ....19 F6
Coppice Av FERN BH22 ....302 B1
 FUFL SO22 ....164 D6
 NMIL/BTOS BH25 ....327 M3
 NWBY RG14 ....17 C7
 RGWD BH24 ....281 M5
Coppice Cl FNM GU9 ....96 E5
 YTLY GU46 ....40 D9
Coppice Gdns CWTH RG45 ..40 C1
Coppice Hl BPWT SO32 ....232 A5
Coppice Ms BROC SO42 ....308 E2
Coppice Rd KSCL RG20 ....48 D5
 TOTT SO40 ....246 A1
The Coppice BROC SO42 ...286 D7
 CHCH/BSGR BH23 ....325 M9
 HORN PO8 ....256 A5
 LSOL/BMARY PO13 ....295 J9
Coppice Vw NBNE BH10 ....322 E4
Coppice Wy FHAM PO15 ...272 B7
Coppins Gv FHAM/PORC PO16 .295 N3
 NMIL/BTOS BH25 ....327 K5
Copse Cl EPSF GU31 ....216 H1
 LISS GU33 ....192 E2
 NBAD SO52 ....205 K9
 PLE BH15 ....321 H9
 RWIN SO21 ....207 L1
 STHA RG19 ....25 P5
 WVILLE PO7 ....275 N8
Copse Fn CHIN RG24 ....48 C4
Copse La HISD PO11 ....298 G9
 HLER SO31 ....269 P8
 LSOL/BMARY PO13 ....295 H8
 NARL SO24 ....128 C6
 RGWD BH24 ....280 E5
 ROWN SO16 ....247 H1
 WEND SO18 ....249 H1
The Copse CHFD SO53 .....206 B8
 DEAN RG23 ....89 H8
 FARN GU14 ....75 L1
 FHAM PO15 ....272 B6
 TADY RG26 ....34 B6
 TOTT SO40 ....245 K6
Copse Vw ITCH SO19 .....249 N6
Copse View CHIN RG24 ....70 A1
Copse Wy CHCH/BSGR BH23 .326 A7
 RFNM GU10 ....115 P4
Copsewood Av CHAR BH8 ...85 J4
Copsewood Rd FAWY SO45 .268 B7
 ITCH SO19 ....248 G1
 TOTT SO40 ....246 A8
Copythorne La FAWY SO45 .291 J4
Copythorne Cl CHAM PO6 ..297 M1
Copythorne Crs TOTT SO40 .245 J1
Coracle Cl HLER SO31 ....270 C6
Coral Cl FHAM/PORC PO16 .295 N3
Coral Cl BKME/WDN BH12 * .321 M9
Coralin Gv WVILLE PO7 ...276 B1
Coram Cl WINC SO23 .....165 H5
Coranation Rd WVILLE PO7 .275 M4
Corbar Rd CHCH/BSGR BH23 .324 C7
Corbett Rd WVILLE PO7 ...275 M4
Corbiere Av BKME/WDN BH12 .321 M5
Corbiere Cl ROWN SO16 ..227 J9

Corbin Av FERN BH22 .....302 G2
Corbin Rd LYMN SO41 ....329 H5
Corbould Rd FAWY SO45 ..295 K5
Corby Crs HSEA PO3 ......297 K5
Cordale Rd BSTK RG21 ....69 K9
Cordelia Cl FAWY SO45 ...267 P7
Cordery Gdns ASHV GU12 ..76 E4
Corfe Gdns FRIM GU16 ....58 E4
Corfe Halt Cl WIMB BH21 .300 A4
Corfe Lodge Rd PSTN BH14 .321 K9
Corfe Wk DEAN RG23 ......68 F6
Corfe Wy BDST BH18 .....320 A1
Corfield Cl EWKG RG40 ....40 B7
Corhampton Crs HAV PO9 .276 D6
Corhampton La BPWT SO32 .210 G7
Corhampton Rd SBNE BH6 .324 A9
Coriander Cl AND SP10 ...82 F7
Coriander Dr TOTT SO40 ..245 N4
Coriander Wy FHAM PO15 .271 K2
Corinna Gdns FAWY SO45 .267 P7
Corinthian Cl AND SP10 ..82 F7
 KBH RG22 ....89 N4
Corinthian Rd CHFD SO53 .206 G6
Cormorant Cl
 FHAM/PORC PO16 ....295 K1
 KBH RG22 ....89 K3
Cormorant Dr FAWY SO45 .268 D8
 PSHT SO47 ....41 L7
Cornaway La
 FHAM/PORC PO16 ....295 M2
Cornbrook Gv HORN PO8 ..256 C2
Cornbunting Cl SHST GU47 .41 L7
Cornelia Cl FARN GU14 * ..75 L1
Cornelia Crs
 BKME/WDN BH12 ....322 A9
Cornelius Dr WVILLE PO7 .276 B1
Cornel Rd ITCH SO19 .....249 H6
Corner Md WVILLE PO7 ...255 H7
Cornes Cl FUFL SO22 .....164 E7
Cornfield CHCH/BSGR BH23 .325 N6
Cornfield Cl CHFD SO53 ..206 B7
Cornfield Rd
 LSOL/BMARY PO13 ....314 D2
Cornfields AND SP10 .....102 F4
 YTLY GU46 ....40 D9
The Cornfields KBH RG22 .89 N4
Cornflower Cl HLER SO31 .270 E8
 RAND SP11 ....79 P2
Cornflower Dr
 CHCH/BSGR BH23 ....325 N6
Cornford Wy
 CHCH/BSGR BH23 ....325 P7
Cornforth Rd TOTT SO40 ..246 A2
Cornish Cl KBH RG22 ......68 F3
Cornish Gdns NBNE BH10 .322 D6
Corn Market ROMY SO51 ..204 C6
Compits La PSF GU32 .....219 J9
Cornwall Crs WEND SO18 .249 H1
Cornwall Rd AND SP10 ....82 F7
 BSTK RG21 ....7 H3
 HISD PO11 ....319 L7
 NTID SP9 ....78 C3
 RAND SP11 ....80 A1
 VWD BH31 ....258 F3
 YTLY GU46 ....40 E7
Cornwall Rd BOR GU35 ...154 A7
 CHFD SO53 ....206 E1
 PSEA PO1 ....316 G3
 WEND SO18 ....249 H1
Cornwell Cl
 LSOL/BMARY PO13 ....315 H1
 NEND PO2 ....296 D2
Coronado Rd GPORT PO12 .315 M2
Coronation Av
 MOOR/WNTN BH9 ....322 F5
Coronation Cl KSCL RG20 .60 B7
 ODIM RG29 ....72 E9
Coronation Pde HLER SO31 .269 N7
 ALDT GU11 ....97 H4
 BPWT SO32 ....232 F7
 BSTK RG21 ....7 H3
 HISD PO11 ....319 L7
 NTID SP9 ....78 C3
 RAND SP11 ....80 A1
 VWD BH31 ....258 F3
 YTLY GU46 ....40 E7
Corporation Rd BMTH BH1 ..9 J1
Correll Rd HSEA PO3 .....318 A1
Corringway FLEETS GU52 ..74 F6
Corsair Cl LSOL/BMARY PO13 .314 E3
Corsair Dr FAWY SO45 ...295 K5
Corscombe Cl CFDH BH17 .320 G2
Cortina Wy HEND SO30 ...250 C6
Cortry Cl BKME/WDN BH12 .322 A8
Corve La FHAM PO15 .....272 A6
Corunna Main AND SP10 ...5 F9
Corvette Av HLER SO31 ..270 F9
Cosford Cl ELGH SO50 ...230 A4
Cosham Park Av CHAM PO6 .297 H2
Cossack Cl AND SP10 .....23 F4
Cossack La WINC SO23 ...23 G4
Coster Cl NWBY RG14 ....24 A2
Cosworth Dr FAWY SO45 .268 B7
Cotes Av PSTN BH14 .....321 J7
Cotlands Rd BMTH BH1 .....9 J4
Cotsalls ELGH SO50 .....230 C3
Cotswold Cl FARN GU14 ..57 M6
 FAWY SO45 ....267 P3
 HAV PO9 ....276 E4
 KBH RG22 ....89 K5
 VWD BH31 ....258 F5
Cotswold Rd
 FHAM/STUB PO14 ....294 D2
Cotswold Wk
 FHAM/STUB PO14 * 255 H8
Cottage Gdns
 BKME/WDN BH12 ....321 L7
Cottage Gv ON HTWY RG27 .72 D1
 RAND SP11 ....122 C1
Cottage La LISS GU33 ...191 M2
 SSEA PO5 ....19 G5
Cottage Ms FBDC SP6 ....240 C1
 RGWD BH24 ....282 D2

Cottage Rd STOK SO20 .....120 C9
Cottagers La LYMN SO41 .....328 A4
Cottage Vw PSEA PO1 .....19 J2
Cottes Wy FHAM/PORC PO14 .....293 N8
Cottesway East
  FHAM/STUB PO14 .....293 P5
Cottington Cl KSCL RG20 .....48 D5
Cott La RGWD BH24 .....284 D7
Cottle Cl BSTK RG21 .....90 C1
Cotton Cl ALDT GU11 .....2 B1
  BDST BH18 .....300 B8
  ELGH SO50 .....229 N1
Cotton Dr EMRTH PO10 .....277 L7
Cott St BPWT SO32 .....233 H8
Cott Street La BPWT SO32 .....233 J8
Cotwell Av RGWD BH24 .....256 B7
Coulmere Rd GPORT PO12 .....315 G2
Coulsdon Rd HEND SO30 .....250 C5
Coultas Rd CHFD SO53 .....206 C8
Council Rd BSTK RG21 .....68 G3
Countess Cl WIMB BH21 .....300 C5
Countess Gdns LTDN BH7 .....323 M7
Country Vw
  FHAM/STUB PO14 .....293 P5
  ROMY SO51 .....224 E1
County Gdns
  FHAM/STUB PO14 .....294 A1
County Gates La WBNE BH4 .....334 B2
Course Park Crs
  FHAM/STUB PO14 .....271 K8
Court Barn La
  FHAM/STUB PO14 .....314 D1
Court Cl CHAM PO6 .....297 K2
  CHCH/BSGR BH23 .....325 J8
  LIPH GU30 .....175 J4
  LYMN SO41 .....329 K5
  TOTT SO40 .....246 B3
Court Dro OVTN RG25 .....65 N9
Courtenay Dr WIMB BH21 .....278 E8
Courtenay Pl LYMN SO41 .....329 L5
Courtenay Rd FNM GU9 .....96 E5
  PSTN BH14 .....321 K8
  WINC SO23 .....165 H5
Court Hl FBDG SP6 .....219 L7
Courthill Rd FERN BH22 .....321 J8
Court House Cl FAWY SO45 .....268 C6
Courtland Gdns ROWN SO16 .....228 D7
Courtlands Rd NWBY RG14 .....17 G6
Courtlands Ter HORN PO8 * 256 A7
Court La ALTN GU34 .....169 N1
  CHAM PO6 .....297 K2
  STOK SO20 .....162 E1
Court Ldg LYMN SO41 * 329 K5
Court Md CHAM PO6 .....297 K2
Courtmoor Av FLEETS GU52 .....74 C5
Courtmount Gv CHAM PO6 .....297 J1
Court Mt ALDT GU11 .....2 C4
  LSOL/BMARY PO13 .....314 C1
  MOOR/WNTN BH9 .....323 H6
  WINC SO23 .....165 K2
  WSHM SO15 .....4 C7
Court Royal Ms WSHM SO15 * 248 B3
Courts Hill Rd HASM GU27 .....156 G7
Courts Mount Rd HASM GU27 .....156 G7
The Courtyard EPSF GU31 .....215 M2
The Court Yd STHA RG19 * 20 F7
Cousins Gv ENEY PO4 .....317 J6
Covena Rd SBNE BH6 .....324 B9
Coventry Cl KBH RG22 .....89 M5
Coventry Ct
  LSOL/BMARY PO13 * 315 H2
Coventry Crs CFDH BH17 .....320 C2
Coventry Rd WSHM SO15 .....248 F3
Coverack Wy CHAM PO6 .....296 D2
Cove Rd FARN GU14 .....57 N9
  FLEETN GU51 .....74 F1
  NBNE BH10 .....322 C5
Covert Gv WVILLE PO7 .....276 A5
Coverts Cl FNM GU9 .....96 E7
The Covert FARN GU14 * 57 M5
  ROMY SO51 .....204 F7
Covey Cl FARN GU14 .....57 P5
Covey Wy NARL SO24 .....167 N3
Covington Rd EMRTH PO10 .....277 M5
Cowan Rd WVILLE PO7 .....275 M5
Coward Rd GPORT PO12 .....315 K6
Cowdown La HTWY RG27 .....53 F7
Cowdown La RAND SP11 .....102 F7
Cowdray Cl ELGH SO50 .....229 P6
  ROWN SO16 .....227 M8
Cowdray Pk ALTN GU34 .....132 F7
Cowdrey Hts CHIN RG24 .....69 P6
Cowdrey Sq AND SP10 .....82 F8
Cow Drove Hl STOK SO20 .....161 L3
Cowdrys Fld WIMB BH21 .....278 D8
Cowell Dr LTDN BH7 .....323 N7
Cowes La HLER SO31 .....298 D3
Cowfold La HTWY RG27 .....53 F7
Cowgrove Rd WIMB BH21 .....278 E2
Cow La CHAM PO6 .....296 E2
  EPSF GU31 .....216 E9
  FHAM/PORC PO16 .....296 A2
  RAND SP11 .....80 B8
Cowley Cl ROWN SO16 .....247 J1
Cowley Dr RWIN SO21 .....144 E6
Cowley Rd CFDH BH17 .....320 F4
  LYMN SO41 .....329 J3
Cowleys La BROC SO42 .....290 A9
Cowleys Rd CHCH/BSGR BH23 .....324 E1
Cowper Av NMIL/BTOS BH25 .....327 J6
Cowper Rd ITCH SO19 .....249 M5
  MOOR/WNTN BH9 .....322 F5
  PSEA PO1 * 316 C1
Cowpitts La RGWD BH24 .....284 H2
Cowslade NWBY RG14 .....24 A2
Cowslease Cl ROMY SO51 * 179 L9
Cowslease Cots
  ROMY SO51 .....179 L9
Cowslip Bank CHIN RG24 .....70 A4
Cowslip Cl BOR GU35 .....154 D4
  HLER SO31 .....270 D9
  LSOL/BMARY PO13 .....294 G7
Cowslip Crs NTHA RG18 .....25 N2

Cowslip Rd BDST BH18 .....320 A2
Cox Av MOOR/WNTN BH9 .....323 H4
Coxbridge FNM GU9 .....115 P1
Coxbridge Mdw FNM GU9 .....115 P1
Cox Cl MOOR/WNTN BH9 .....323 H5
Cox Dl FHAM/STUB PO14 .....271 J9
Coxes Meadow PSF GU32 .....191 L9
Coxeter Rd NWBY RG14 .....24 E3
Coxford Cl ROWN SO16 .....247 L1
Coxford Dro ROWN SO16 .....227 L9
Coxford Rd ROWN SO16 .....227 N9
Coxgreen SHST GU47 .....41 L8
Coxheath Rd FLEETS GU52 .....74 B6
Coxmoor Cl FARN GU14 .....58 D5
Cox Rw CHFD SO53 .....228 F1
Cox's Dr ITCH SO19 .....249 K9
Coxstone La RGWD BH24 .....282 E3
Coy Pond Rd
  BKME/WDN BH12 .....334 A1
Cozens Cl ITCH SO19 .....268 F1
Crabapple Cl TOTT SO40 .....246 A4
Crabbe Ct SSEA PO5 .....19 H5
Crabbs Wy TOTT SO40 .....245 P4
Crabbswood La LYMN SO41 .....307 N8
Crabden La HORN PO8 .....256 E3
Crableck La HLER SO31 .....270 C5
Crab Orchard Wy WIMB BH21 .....258 E8
Crabthorne Farm La
  FHAM/STUB PO14 .....293 P6
Crabton Close Rd BOSC BH5 .....335 M1
Crabtree ROWN SO16 .....247 K2
Crabtree Cl CHCH/BSGR BH23 .....324 G5
Crabtree La BOR GU35 .....154 F3
Crabtree La BOR GU35 .....154 F3
  RFNM GU10 .....136 G7
Crabtree Rd CBLY GU15 .....50 A3
Crabtree Wy FARN GU14 .....70 C8
Crabwood Cl ROWN SO16 .....247 K1
Crabwood Dr HAV PO9 .....276 D3
Crabwood Dr HEND SO30 .....249 N2
Crabwood Rd ROWN SO16 .....247 J1
Cracknore Hard TOTT SO40 .....248 B8
Cracknore Hard La TOTT SO40 .....267 M1
Cracknore Rd WSHM SO15 .....247 P5
Cradle La BOR GU35 .....135 L5
Craigmoor Av CHAR BH8 .....323 L6
Craigmoor Cl CHAR BH8 .....323 M6
Craigmoor Wy CHAR BH8 .....323 L5
Craigside Rd RGWD BH24 .....281 K5
Craigwell Rd WVILLE PO7 .....275 M6
Craigwood Dr FERN BH22 .....302 E4
Crake Pl SHST GU47 .....41 L6
Crampmoor La ROMY SO51 .....205 J3
Cramptons ALTN GU34 .....132 A7
Cranberry Cl TOTT SO40 .....267 K1
Cranborne Crs
  BKME/WDN BH12 .....321 N4
Cranborne Gdns CHFD SO53 .....206 D4
Cranborne Rd CHAM PO6 .....275 J9
  FBDG SP6 .....238 G6
  MOUY RG21 .....8 C5
  WIMB BH21 .....278 E6
Cranborne Wk
  FHAM/STUB PO14 .....294 C2
Cranbourne Cl WSHM SO15 .....247 P2
Cranbourne Ct BSTK RG21 .....90 B1
Cranbourne Dr RWIN SO21 .....207 K2
Cranbourne La BSTK RG21 .....90 B1
Cranbourne Rd GPORT PO12 .....12 E4
Cranbrook Ct FLEETN GU51 .....74 D1
Cranbrook Rd
  BKME/WDN BH12 .....321 K6
Cranbury Av SOTN SO14 .....248 D5
Cranbury Ct RSAL SP5 .....199 G7
  RWIN SO21 .....207 K2
Cranbury Ct ITCH SO19 .....249 H8
Cranbury Gdns HLER SO31 .....269 P1
Cranbury Pl SHAM SO14 .....248 C5
Cranbury Rd ELGH SO50 .....229 J3
  ITCH SO19 .....249 H8
Crane Cl LSOL/BMARY PO13 .....294 F7
  VWD BH31 .....258 E5
Crane Ct SHST GU47 .....41 L6
Crane Dr VWD BH31 .....258 E4
Cranemoor Av
  CHCH/BSGR BH23 .....326 A5
Cranemoor Cl
  CHCH/BSGR BH23 .....326 B5
Cranemoor Gdns
  CHCH/BSGR BH23 .....326 B5
Cranesfield CHIN RG24 .....51 H9
Cranes Cl FBL BH15 .....320 F9
Cranes Rd CHIN RG24 .....50 G9
Craneswater Av ENEY PO4 .....316 G6
Craneswater Ga ENEY PO4 .....316 G7
Craneswater Pk ENEY PO4 .....316 G7
Crane Wy WIMB BH21 .....278 A5
Cranfield Av WIMB BH21 .....278 F9
Cranford Av FLEETS GU52 .....74 B7
Cranford La ALTN GU34 .....133 J3
Cranford Gdns CHFD SO53 .....206 D5
Cranford Park Dr YTLY GU46 .....40 E8
Cranford Rd ALDT GU11 .....2 G5
Cranford Wy PTSW SO17 .....248 F1
Cranleigh Av PSEA PO1 .....316 G2
Cranleigh Cl SBNE BH6 .....336 C1
Cranleigh Ct FARN GU14 .....57 N9
Cranleigh Gdns SBNE BH6 .....336 C1
Cranleigh Rd
  FHAM/PORC PO16 .....295 L2
  HEND SO30 .....250 C5
  PSEA PO1 .....316 B9
  SBNE BH6 .....324 B9
Cranmer Dr WSHM SO15 .....226 C7
Cranmer Rd
  MOOR/WNTN BH9 .....322 F7
Cranmore HLER SO31 .....269 L5
Cranmore Av ALDT GU11 .....96 E2
Cranmore Gdns ALDT GU11 .....2 A3
Cranmore La ALDT GU11 .....96 E3
Cranmore Rd FHAM GU14 .....58 E9
Crantock Gv CHAR BH8 .....323 M5
Cranwell Cl BWD BH11 .....301 N9

CHCH/BSGR BH23 .....305 M7
Cranworth Rd FUFL SO22 .....22 C2
Crasswell St PSEA PO1 .....19 H1
Craven Cl FUFL SO22 .....116 C4
Craven Ct FHAM PO15 .....10 A2
Craven Dene NWBY RG14 .....24 E3
Craven Rd CHFD SO53 .....206 F7
  NWBY RG14 .....16 A3
Craven St SHAM SO14 .....21 F5
Craven Wk SHAM SO14 .....21 F5
Crawford Cl ROWN SO16 .....227 H7
Crawford Dr
  FHAM/PORC PO16 .....10 C1
Crawford Pl NWBY RG14 .....16 D1
Crawley Av HAV PO9 .....276 C4
Crawley Hl ROMY SO51 .....224 G3
Crawshaw Rd PSTN BH14 .....333 K1
Crawte Av FAWY SO45 .....290 F7
Crawts Rd OVTN RG25 .....86 C4
Craydown La STOK SO20 .....120 E7
Creasey Rd BWD BH11 .....322 A2
Credenhill Rd CHAM PO6 .....274 E9
Credon Cl FARN GU14 .....57 M8
Creech Rd BKME/WDN BH12 .....321 L1
Creech Vw WVILLE PO7 .....254 C7
Creedy Dr CHCH/BSGR BH23 .....325 J8
Creedy Gdns WEND SO18 .....229 J9
Creek Rd EMRTH PO10 .....299 M2
Creekmoor La CFDH BH17 .....320 C4
Creek Rd GPORT PO12 .....13 G2
  HISD PO11 .....319 K6
Creighton Rd WSHM SO15 .....247 N5
Cremorne Pl EPSF GU31 .....215 M1
Cremyll Cl FHAM/STUB PO14 .....294 A7
Crerar Cl FARN GU14 .....75 L1
Crescent Cl FUFL SO22 .....183 K2
Crescent Dr NMIL/BTOS BH25 .....327 H8
Crescent Gdns
  FHAM/PORC PO16 * 11 F6
Crescent La ASHV GU12 .....76 C7
Crescent Rd
  FHAM/PORC PO16 .....11 F6
  GPORT PO12 .....315 L7
  HLER SO31 .....269 L4
  NBAD SO52 .....205 K8
  PSTN BH14 .....321 N8
  VWD BH31 .....258 G4
  WCLF BH2 .....8 B3
  WIMB BH21 .....300 E1
The Crescent ALTN GU34 .....133 G2
  AND SO10 .....102 A2
  BPMT BH1 .....335 L2
  ELGH SO50 .....207 J9
  FARN GU14 .....76 B1
  FERN BH22 * 281 H9
  FLEETN GU51 .....73 P6
  FNM GU9 .....96 C8
  HLER SO31 .....269 L4
  ITCH SO19 .....249 J9
  NMIL/BTOS BH25 .....326 E7
  RAND SP11 .....104 A4
  RAND SP11 .....102 C9
  ROMY SO51 .....204 F5
  SHAM SO14 .....184 A8
  THLE RG7 .....27 J9
  TOTT SO40 .....245 L8
  TOTT SO40 .....246 A1
  WVILLE PO7 .....275 L6
  YTLY GU46 .....40 E7
Crescent Wk FERN BH22 .....302 E6
Cressey Rd ROMY SO51 .....204 D6
Cress Gdns AND SP10 .....4 A7
Cresswell Rd NWBY RG14 .....24 C5
Cressy Rd NEND PO2 .....316 F1
Cresta Gdns FERN BH22 .....302 E6
Crest Cl FHAM/PORC PO16 .....273 H9
Crestland Cl HORN PO8 .....256 A8
Crest Rd BKME/WDN BH12 .....321 L6
The Crest WVILLE PO7 .....275 L9
Crest Wv ITCH SO19 .....249 L7
Crete La FAWY SO45 .....268 B9
Crete Rd FAWY SO45 .....290 B1
Cribb Cl CFDH BH17 .....320 C5
Crichel Mount Rd PSTN BH14 .....333 L3
Crichel Rd MOOR/WNTN BH9 .....323 H2
Cricket Cl CHCH/BSGR BH23 .....337 K1
  RWIN SO21 .....143 L6
Cricket Dr WIMB BH21 .....256 A6
Cricketers Wy AND SP10 .....82 G8
Cricket Field Gv CWTH RG45 .....41 L2
Cricket Grn HTWY RG27 .....53 J7
Cricket Green La HTWY RG27 .....55 J7
Cricket Hl EWKG RG40 .....40 A4
Cricket Hill La BLKW GU17 .....56 E2
  YTLY GU46 .....40 F9
Cricket La RFNM GU10 .....116 D4
Cricket Lea BOR GU35 .....154 C5
Cricklade Pl AND SP10 .....4 A2
Cricklemede BPWT SO32 .....232 B5
Cricklewood Cl BPWT SO32 .....232 B5
Crigdon Cl ROWN SO16 .....247 J3
Crimea Rd ALDT GU11 .....3 G3
  MOOR/WNTN BH9 .....322 F1
Cringle Av SBNE BH6 .....336 E2
Crinoline Gdns ENEY PO4 .....317 J6
Cripley Rd FARN GU14 .....57 M8
Cripple Gate La BROC SO42 .....311 H5
Crispin Cl CHCH/BSGR BH23 .....326 B7
  ELGH SO50 .....206 E5
  HLER SO31 .....271 H6
Crispstead La WINC SO23 .....183 P1
Crisspyn Cl HORN PO8 .....256 B5
Critchmere Hl HASM GU27 .....156 C6
Critchmere La HASM GU27 .....156 D7
Critchmere V HASM GU27 .....156 C7
Criterion Ar BMTH BH1 * 8 C4
Crittall Ct LYMN SO41 .....308 C6
Crockford Br LYMN SO41 .....310 B6
Crockford Cl
  NMIL/BTOS BH25 .....327 K2
Crockford La CHIN RG24 .....69 N2
Crockford Rd EMRTH PO10 .....277 P6
  RSAL SP5 .....176 A4

HAV PO9 .....14 D4
  RAND SP11 .....183 M9
Crossways ASHV GU12 .....3 J5
  LYMN SO41 .....328 D6
  RFNM GU10 .....136 E8
Crossways Rd GSHT GU26 .....156 C2
The Crossways AND SP10 .....4 D5
  GPORT PO12 .....315 M2
The Crossway
  FHAM/PORC PO16 .....295 N1
Crossways Cl ITCH SO19 .....249 L6
Croucher's Cft FUFL SO22 .....164 C6
Crouch La HORN PO8 .....256 A4
Crow Arch La RGWD BH24 .....282 F5
Crowder Ter FUFL SO22 .....22 C5
Crowfield Dr STHA RG19 .....25 L4
Crow La RGWD BH24 .....282 G4
Crowle Cl BKME/WDN BH12 .....321 L7
Crown Cl BKME/WDN BH12 .....321 L7
  WVILLE PO7 .....275 L6
Crown Dr FNM GU9 .....96 C6
Crownfields ODIM RG29 .....93 K1
Crown Fields FLEETS GU51 .....74 E4
Crown La CHIN RG24 .....70 B6
Crown Md STHA RG19 * 25 M4
  WINC SO23 .....22 E3
Crown Pl SHST GU47 .....41 M5
  WINC SO23 .....22 E3
Crown Wk WINC SO23 * 22 E3
Crowsbury Cl EMRTH PO10 .....277 L7
Crows La ALTN GU34 .....151 M5
Crows Nest La BPWT SO32 .....250 F2
Crowsport HLER SO31 .....270 A7
Crowther Cl ITCH SO19 .....249 L7
Crowthorne Rd SHST GU47 .....41 J6
Croyde Cl FARN GU14 .....57 P7
Croydon Cl ROWN SO16 .....227 L8
Croye Cl AND SP10 .....4 A4
Cruikshank Lea SHST GU47 .....41 M8
Crummock Rd CHFD SO53 .....205 N2
Crundles EPSF GU31 .....215 N2
Crusader Ct GPORT PO12 .....315 N1
Crusader Gv CHFD SO53 .....206 B7
Cruse Cl LYMN SO41 .....308 B6
Crystal Wy WVILLE PO7 .....276 B2
Cucklington Gdns
  MOOR/WNTN BH9 .....323 H4
Cuckmere La ROWN SO16 .....247 H3
Cuckoo Bushes La CHFD SO53 .....206 C5
Cuckoo Hill Wy
  CHCH/BSGR BH23 .....305 N7
Cuckoo La FHAM/STUB PO14 .....293 N6
Cuckoo Rd BKME/WDN BH12 .....321 J4
Cudnell Av BWD BH11 .....301 P7
Cudworth Md HEND SO30 .....250 D2
Gufaude La TADY RG26 .....44 A2
Cuffelle Cl CHIN RG24 .....70 B1
Cuffnells Cl RGWD BH24 .....260 F2
The Cul-de-Sac
  NMIL/BTOS BH25 * 326 E7
Culford Av TOTT SO40 .....246 D5
Culford Cl CHAR BH8 .....323 M5
Cull Cl BKME/WDN BH12 .....322 C7
Cullen Cl YTLY GU46 .....40 D9
Cullens Ms ALDT GU11 * 2 D4
Culley Vw NARL SO24 .....168 A3
Culliford Crs CFDH BH17 .....320 G2
Cull La NMIL/BTOS BH25 .....327 K2
Culloden Cl FHAM PO15 .....319 J7
Culloden Rd
  FHAM/STUB PO14 .....294 D3
Cullwood La NMIL/BTOS BH25 .....327 L2
Culver HLER SO31 .....269 L3
Culver Cl ROWN SO16 .....247 H1
Culver Dr HISD PO11 .....319 J7
Culverhayes Pl WIMB BH21 .....278 D8
Culverhayes Rd WIMB BH21 .....278 D8
Culverlands Crs ASHV GU12 .....76 E3
Culverley Cl BROC SO42 .....286 F8
Culver Ms WINC SO23 * 22 E6
Culver Rd BSTK RG21 .....69 K9
  ENEY PO4 .....317 J6
  NMIL/BTOS BH25 .....327 H5
  SHST GU47 .....41 L5
  WINC SO23 .....22 D7
Culverwell Gdns WINC SO23 .....22 D6
Culvery Gdns WEND SO18 .....249 J1
Cumberland Av CHFD SO53 .....206 C8
  EMRTH PO10 .....277 P6
  KBH RG22 .....90 A2
Cumberland Pl WSHM SO15 .....20 C2
Cumberland Rd CBLY GU15 .....59 H1
  SSEA PO5 .....316 C3
Cumberland St PSEA PO1 * 30 C1
  SHAM SO14 .....21 G4
Cumberland Wy FAWY SO45 .....267 P2
Cumber Rd HLER SO31 .....270 E7
Cumbria Ct FARN GU14 .....76 D3
Cumbrian Wy ROWN SO16 .....247 J3
Cummins Cl AND SP10 .....4 A3
Cummins Gn HLER SO31 .....270 A1
Cumnor Rd BMTH BH1 .....9 F2
Cunard Av WSHM SO15 .....247 N3
Cunard Rd SHAM SO14 .....248 C9
Cundell Wy WINC SO23 .....145 J7
Cunningham Cl BWD BH11 .....322 A4
Cunningham Crs BWD BH11 .....322 A4
  CHCH/BSGR BH23 .....325 L9
Cunningham Dr HLER SO31 .....270 G6
  LSOL/BMARY PO13 .....295 H6

Cunningham Gdns
  HLER S031 ....269 N2
Cunningham Pl BWD BH11 ...322 A4
Cunningham Rd HORN P08....256 C4
  WVILLE P07................275 N5
Cunnington Rd FARN GU14 ....76 D3
Cupernham Cl ROMY S051....204 E5
Cupernham La ROMY S051 ...204 E4
Curdridge Cl HAV P09.......276 G5
Curdridge La BPWT S032....251 N1
Curlew Cl EMRTH P010 ....299 L1
  FERN BH22.................302 B1
  KBH R022 ....89 L2
  ROWN S016 ....227 M7
  STHA RG19 ....25 M4
Curlew Dr FAWY S045........268 D8
  FHAM/PORC P016..........295 K1
Curlew Gdns HORN P08 ....255 P7
Curlew Pth ENEY P04 * 317 K3
Curlew Rd CHAR BH8.........325 K5
  CHCH/BSGR BH23...........325 L9
Curlews ALTN GU34..........132 F3
Curlew Square ELGH S050....228 G2
The Curlews VWD BH31........258 C5
Curlieu Rd PLE BH15 ....320 C6
Curling La NWBY RG14 ....58 A6
Curly Bridge Gi FARN GU14...57 N5
Curnock Ct NWBY RG14 * 16 B5
Curtis Cl BOR GU35 ....154 F2
Curtis La BOR GU35 ....154 F2
Curtis Md NEND P02..........297 H5
Curtis Rd ALTN GU54........132 C7
  BKME/WDN BH12 ....321 L7
Curtiss Gdns GPORT P012....315 K4
The Curve HORN P08..........255 P5
  LSOL/BMARY P013.........294 F7
Curzon Br CHOB/PIR GU24....59 M8
Curzon Dr FLEETS GU52......74 C7
Curzon Howe Rd PSEA P01 ...18 D2
Curzon Pl LYMN S041........329 K5
  PSTN BH14 ....321 J9
Curzon Rd BMTH S041........323 K9
  WVILLE P07................275 N3
Curzon Wy CHCH/BSGR BH23..325 P7
Cusden Dr AND SP10 ....4 C1
Custards Rd LYND S043......264 F4
Cutbush La WEND S018.......229 J9
Cuthbert Rd ASHV GU12......76 F1
  PSEA P01...................317 H2
Cuthburga Rd WIMB BH21....278 C9
Cuthbury La WIMB BH21......278 C9
Cuthbury Gdns WIMB BH21...278 C9
Cutler Cl FHAM/PORC P016...295 K1
Cutlers La FHAM/STUB P014..294 A6
Cutters Pl WIMB BH21........279 J9
Cut Pound ALTN GU34.........132 C6
Cutter Av HLER S031.........270 E9
Cut Throat La BPWT S032....232 C6
  BPWT S032.................233 M3
Cutts Arch BPWT S032.......233 M5
Cutts Rd ALDT GU11 ....82 D8
Cygnet Cl STHA RG19.........25 L4
Cygnet Ct FHAM/PORC P016..295 K1
Cygnet Rd CHAM P06..........297 P2
Cygnus Gdns FAWY S045......267 K3
Cynthia Cl BKME/WDN BH12..321 K5
Cynthia Rd BKME/WDN BH12..321 K5
Cypress FARN GU14 ....57 N4
Cypress Av ITCH S019 ....249 H6
Cypress Crs HORN P08.......256 A6
Cypress Dr FLEETN GU51 .....74 F3
Cypress Gdns HEND S020....250 C4
  RAND SP11.................102 A3
Cypress Gv ASHV GU12........95 J5
Cypress Rd BOR GU35........153 M5
Cypress Wy GSHT GU26......156 C3
Cyprus Rd FHAM/STUB P014..271 J9
  FRIM GU16...................59 K6
  KBH R022...................89 N6
  NEND P02 ....296 C9
Cyril Rd CHAR BH8...........323 J9
Cyril Vokins Rd NWBY RG14..25 H5

D

Dacre Cl AND SP10............82 B8
Darracott Rd BSCR BH5.......335 N2
Daffodil Cl KBH R022.........89 L3
Daggons Rd FBDG SP6........239 J5
Dahlia Cl KBH R022..........89 L3
Dahlia Ct AND SP10 * 102 B4
Dahlia Rd ROWN S016........228 C8
Daintree Cl ITCH S019......249 M8
Dairy Cl CHCH/BSGR BH23...325 H8
  RSAL SP5...................199 P8
Dairy Gate Rd FARN GU14....76 A4
Dairymoor WHAM P017.......252 E7
Daisy La GPORT P012........12 B2
  HLER S031.................271 H7
Daisy Md WVILLE P07........276 A4
Daisy Rd ROWN S016.........228 E8
Dalby Crs NWBY RG14.........17 J7
Dale Cl FUFL S022...........164 B2
Dale PLE BH15 ....320 B3
  RFNM GU10.................115 P5
Dale Rd FAWY S045..........268 B7
  FHAM/STUB P014...........294 B6
  PLE BH15..................320 B3
  ROWN S016.................247 N1
Dales Cl WIMB BH21.........279 L8
Dales Dr WIMB BH21.........279 K9
Dales La CHCH/BSGR BH23...305 L9
Dales Wy TOTT S040.........245 P3
The Dale WVILLE P07........275 L8
Dale Valley Cl ROWN S016...247 N1
Dale Valley Gdns ROWN S016..247 N1

Dale Valley Rd PLE BH15....320 C5
  ROWN S016 ....227 N9
Dale Vw HASM GU27.........156 E6
Dalewood KBH R022...........89 L1
Dalewood Av BWD BH11......301 N8
Dalewood Rd FHAM P015....272 B9
Dalkeith Arcade BMTH BH1 ...8 E5
Dalkeith Rd CCLF BH13......334 A5
Dalkeith Steps BMTH BH1 *...8 E5
Dalley Ct SHST GU47 ....41 L7
Dalling Rd BKME/WDN BH12..334 A4
Dallington Cl
Dalmally Gdns WEND S018...248 G3
Dalmeny Rd SBNE BH6.......336 E3
Dalston Cl CBLY GU15.......59 J2
Damask Gdns WVILLE P07...276 B1
Damen Cl HEND S050 ....250 B6
Damerham Rd CHAR BH8....323 K4
Dampier Cl
  LSOL/BMARY P013..........314 G1
Damsel La OVTN RG25.......109 P7
Damsel Pth BSTK RG21........7 K6
Damson Crs ELGH S050......230 A3
Damson HI BPWT S032.......232 F4
Danbury Ct EMRTH P010.....277 N8
Dancers Meadow CHIN RG24..69 J1
Dances Cl AND SP10...........4 E2
Dances La WHCH RG28........85 L5
Dances Wy HISD P011.........249 L9
Dandelion Cl
  NMIL/BTOS BH25..........294 F6
Dando Rd WVILLE P07.......255 J7
Dandy's Ford La ROMY S051..202 F5
Danbury Cl HAV P09.........276 E4
Danebury Gdns CHFD S053...206 C9
Danebury Rd KBH R022......89 M5
Danebury Wy ROWN S016....227 N7
Dane Cl FAWY S045..........291 H8
Danecourt Cl PSTN BH14.....321 H8
Danecourt Rd PSTN BH14....321 H8
Danecrest Rd LYMN S041...327 P4
Dane Dr FERN BH22..........302 E5
Danegeld Cl AND SP10.......82 F7
Danehurst New Rd
  LYMN S041.................307 L8
Danehurst Pl AND SP10 ....102 A2
  HLER S031.................270 G8
Dane Rd LYMN S041.........328 A9
Danesbrook La WVILLE P07..276 A5
Danesbury Av SBNE BH6....336 D2
Danesbury Mdw
  NMIL/BTOS BH25..........327 L4
Danes Cl NMIL/BTOS BH25...327 J8
Daneshill Cl CHIN RG24......70 A4
Daneshill Dr CHIN RG24......70 B4
Danes Rd FHAM/PORC P016..273 M9
  ROMY S051.................203 K1
  WINC S023.................22 E1
The Danes BSTK RG21..........7 G6
Danestream Cl LYMN S041...338 C2
Daneswood Rd
  NMIL/BTOS BH25..........327 L4
Daniell's Cl LYMN S041......329 L4
Daniell's Wk LYMN S041....329 L5
Daniel Rd WHCH RG28.......85 M7
Dankworth Rd KBH R022....89 N5
Danley La HASM GU27.......175 P4
Dansie Cl PSTN BH14........321 K8
Danvers Cl STHA RG19........25 N5
Danvers Dr FLEETS GU52......74 B8
Daphne Dr FLEETS GU52.......74 B9
Dapple Pl TOTT S040........267 L1
Darby Green La BLKW GU17...41 J9
Darby Green Rd BLKW GU17..41 H9
Darby's Cl PLE BH15.........320 F6
Darby's Cnr CFDH BH17.....320 E2
Darby's La PLE BH15.........320 F5
Darby's La North CFDH BH17.320 F5
Darent Ct BSTK RG21..........7 J6
Dark La RFNM GU10...........95 J2
Dark La CHIN RG24...........69 H1
  CHCH/BSGR BH23..........326 C3
  FAWY S045.................291 K8
  NARL S024.................168 C5
  NARL S024.................187 H1
Darlee Ga HLER S031 * 269 P1
Daleydale Cl SHST GU47.....41 L4
Darley Rd FERN BH22.......302 C5
Darlington Gdns WSHM S015.247 P5
Darlington Rd BSTK RG21.....6 D2
  ENEY P04..................316 C5
Darset Av FLEETN GU51......74 D2
Dart Cl NTHA RG18...........25 L2
Dart Ct AND SP10............82 A9
Dartington Rd ELGH S050...207 M8
Dartmouth Rd HEEA P03....297 J7
Dartmouth Wk KBH R022....68 F9
Dartmouth Wy KBH R022....68 F9
Dart Rd FARN GU14...........57 L7
  WEND S018.................229 K9
Darvill Hts HAM GU9..........96 C9
Darvill Rd NARL S024........169 H8
Darvills La FNM GU9..........96 C9
Darwin Av CHCH/BSGR BH23.324 C6
Darwin Cl LSOL/BMARY P013.314 D1
Darwin Gv ALDT GU11..........3 J1
Darwin Rd ELGH S050........207 K9
  WSHM S015.................247 P4
Darwin Wy
  LSOL/BMARY P013.........315 H2
Dashwood Cl ALTN GU34....132 D7
Dasna Rd NTID SP9...........78 F6
Daulston Rd PSEA P01.......316 C1
Daunch Cl NTID SP9...........78 E6
Dauntless Rd THLE RG7.......27 K3
Dauntsey Dro RAND SP11....80 C9
Dauntsey La RAND SP11.....100 C1
Davenport Cl
  LSOL/BMARY P013.........314 G2
Davenport Ga AND SP10....102 A1
Daventry La HSEA P03.......297 L5
D Av FAWY S045.............290 F3

David Newberry Dr
  LSOL/BMARY P013.........314 F2
David's La RCWD BH24.......282 A4
Davidson Cl FAWY S045.....268 D6
Davis Cl LSOL/BMARY P013..294 C9
Davis Fld NMIL/BTOS BH25..327 H5
Davis Gdns SHST GU47......41 M7
Davis Rd PSTN BH14........321 N7
Davy Cl KBH R022............69 H7
Dawkins Wy
  NMIL/BTOS BH25..........327 J5
Daw La HISD P011...........298 F9
Daylesford Cl PSTN BH14...333 J1
Dayrell Cl TOTT S040.......245 P2
Day's Ct WIMB BH21.........300 F1
Dayshes Cl
  LSOL/BMARY P013.........294 B7
Deacon Cl ITCH S019........249 J6
Deacon Crs ITCH S019......249 J5
Deacon Gdns BWD BH11.....322 A2
Deacon Rd BWD BH11.......322 A2
  HLER S031.................271 H8
  ITCH S019.................249 J6
  RAND SP11.................80 B7
Deadbrook La ASHV GU12...76 D8
Deadman's La BSTK RG21......7 K6
  STHA RG19.................24 E9
Deadmoor La KSCL RG20.....30 D4
Deal Cl FHAM/STUB P014...294 A5
Deal Rd CHAM P06...........274 C9
Dean Cl FUFL S022..........164 D5
  PLE BH15..................320 A9
Dean Ct HEND S020 * 249 J1
Dean La CHAR P09 * 277 H5
Deane Down Dro FUFL S022..164 C5
The Deanery CHFD S053.....206 D5
Deanes Cl BSTK RG21...........1 J6
Deane's Park Rd
  FHAM/PORC P016..........273 H9
Deanfield Cl HLER S031.....269 P8
Dean La BPWT S032........210 C8
  HORN P08..................257 K6
  RSAL SP5...................194 A6
  RSAL SP5...................201 K1
  RWIN S021.................163 P4
Dean Park Crs BMTH BH1......8 E2
Dean Park Rd BMTH BH1.......8 E2
Dean Ri RAND SP11............62 C5
Dean Rd CHAM P06..........297 H2
  ELGH S050.................230 B3
  RSAL SP5...................176 F3
  RSAL SP5...................177 N1
  WEND S018.................249 J4
Deans Cl NTID SP9...........79 H7
Deans Court La WIMB BH21..338 C1
Deanscroft Rd NBNE BH10...322 E3
Deans Gdns PSF GU32.......190 C5
Deans Ga FHAM/STUB P014..294 A5
Dean Gv WIMB BH21.........278 F7
Deansleigh Rd LTDN BH7...323 P6
Dean's Rd BOSC BH5.........335 P1
The Deans BMTH BH1..........8 E1
Dean St SE PSEA P01........18 D3
Dean Swift Crs PSTN BH14..333 L3
Deanswood Rd TADY RG26....34 B6
The Dean NARL S024........167 P1
Dear Hay La PLE BH15......332 E1
Dearing Cl LYND S043.......264 F6
Dearlove Rd TOTT S040.....266 C2
De Courtenai Cl BWD BH11..301 N8
Decouttere Cl FLEETS GU52..74 B7
Dee Cl CHFD S053...........206 C8
Deedman Cl ASHV GU12......97 N1
Deepcut Bridge Rd FRIM GU16.59 J4
Deep Dene HASM GU27......156 C8
Deeping Cl ITCH S019.......269 H1
Deeping Ga WVILLE P07.....276 A3
Deep La BSTK RG21............6 A3
Deerfield Cl TADY RG26.......52 C3
Deerhurst Cl TOTT S040....246 A5
Deerhurst Crs CHAM P06...274 C9
Deerleap BOR GU35 * 155 K4
Deer Leap FHAM P015......272 B5
Deerleap La TOTT S040.....266 C2
Deerleap Wy FAWY S045....268 C7
Deer Park Cl
  NMIL/BTOS BH25..........327 K1
Deer Park Vw ODIM RG29...72 D9
Deeside ABEY P09 * 68 F9
De Grouchy La PTSW S017..248 C2
De Havilland Cl BWD BH11..301 H3
De Havilland Wy
  CHCH/BSGR BH23..........337 L1
Delamere Gdns NBNE BH10..322 E4
Delamere Rd ENEY P04.....316 G5
De La Warr Rd LYMN S041...338 F2
Delft Cl HLER S031..........270 F7
Delft Gdns WVILLE P07.....255 M9
Delft Ms CHCH/BSGR BH23..325 H8
Delhi Cl PSTN BH14.........321 M9
Delhi Rd NBNE BH10........322 E5
Delibes Rd KBH R022.........90 B3
De Lisle Cl NEND P02.......296 E7
De Lisle Rd TWDS BH3......322 F8
Delius Av ITCH S019........249 M8
Delius Cl KBH R022..........90 A2
Delius Wk KBH R022 * 275 N5
Dellands OVTN RG25..........86 C4
Dellands La OVTN RG25......86 C5

Dell Cl BDST BH18..........300 A9
  CHAM P06..................275 K8
  ELCH S050.................230 C3
  HASM GU27................156 F6
Dellcrest Pth CHAM P06....275 K9
Dellfield DEAN RG23.........67 N9
  PSF GU32..................190 D6
Dell Cv FRIM GU16...........58 E3
Dell Piece East HORN P08....256 D6
Dell Piece West HORN P08...256 C6
Dell Quay Cl
  LSOL/BMARY P013.........294 E7
Dell Rd AND SP10.............4 E6
  EWKG RG40.................40 B3
  WEND S018.................249 H1
  WINC S023.................23 J7
The Dell CHIN RG24..........70 D7
  FHAM/PORC P016..........273 H9
  FNM GU9...................90 D6
  HAV P09...................276 B8
  KSCL RG20.................48 C3
  NMIL/BTOS BH25..........326 E7
  RAND SP11.................43 H7
  YTLY GU46..................40 D9
Delme Dr FHAM/PORC P016..273 H8
Delphi Wy WVILLE P07......275 P8
Delph Rd WIMB BH21........300 F5
Delta Cl CHCH/BSGR BH23..325 L8
De-Lucy Av NARL S024......167 N2
Delville Cl FARN GU14.......75 L1
De Mauley Rd CCLF BH13...333 N5
De Montfort Rd NWBY RG14..24 A2
  RAND SP11.................80 B7
De Mowbray Wy LYMN S041.329 K5
Dempsey Cl ITCH S019......249 J7
Denbigh Cl ELGH S050......207 H8
  TOTT S040.................246 B6
Dene Cl AND SP10............4 E6
Dene Hollow CHAM P06.....297 M1
Dene La RFNM GU10.........116 D4
Dene La West RFNM GU10...116 D5
Dene Pth AND SP10............4 E6
Dene Rd CHAM P06..........297 M1
  FARN GU14.................75 M1
  TOTT S040.................246 A9
Deneside Copse LYMN S041.329 H6
Deneside Gdns LYMN S041..329 H5
Dene Wy NWBY RG14.........24 C2
Deneve Av CFDH BH17......320 E3
Dene Wk FERN BH22.........302 E7
Dene Wy AND SP10............4 E6
Denewood Copse FERN BH22.280 D6
Denewood Rd FERN BH22...280 D6
  WBNE BH4..................334 B4
Denewulf Cl BPWT S032.....232 A4
Denham Cl HLER S031.......320 G1
  FHAM/STUB P014..........293 P7
  WINC S023.................164 G5
Denham Dr CHCH/BSGR BH23.326 D6
  KBH R022..................89 M7
  YTLY GU46..................40 E9
Denham Gdns HLER S031....269 K5
Denhill Cl HISD P011.......318 E3
Denholm Cl RCWD BH24.....261 H9
Denison Rd CFDH BH17.....320 C5
Denman Cl FLEETN GU51.....74 F5
Denmark La PLE BH15.......320 E1
Denmark Rd
  MOOR/WNTN BH9...........322 F6
  NWBY RG14..................17 G2
Denmark Sq ASHV GU12......97 K1
Denmark St ASHV GU12.......97 K1
Denmead NMIL/BTOS BH25..327 M3
Denmead Rd SBNE BH6......324 B8
  TADY RG26..................34 C6
Dennett Cl
  NMIL/BTOS BH25..........327 J8
Denning Cl FLEETS GU52.....74 B5
Denning Md AND SP10........4 F6
Dennistoun Av
  CHCH/BSGR BH23..........325 K8
Dennis Wy LISS GU33.......192 E3
Denny Cl FAWY S045........291 K6
Denstone Rd ITCH S019....249 H7
Denton Wy FRIM GU16........59 J6
Denville Av FHAM/PORC P016.295 P6
Denville Cl CHAM P06.......297 P1
Denvilles Cl HAV P09........15 K3
Depedene Cl FAWY S045....290 E8
De Port Hts BPWT S032....211 N7
Deptford La ODIM RG29......72 B9
Derby Ct LSOL/BMARY P013.314 G2
Derby Flds ODIM RG29.......72 B6
Derby Rd BMTH BH1.........335 J2
  ELGH S050.................230 C2
  HASM GU27................156 G6
  NEND P02..................296 F8
  NWBY RG14.................13 K6
  SHAM S014.................21 G2
De Redvers Rd PSTN BH14..333 L1

Derwent Av ASHV GU12.......76 E8
Derwent Cl BOR GU35.......154 A3
  FARN GU14.................57 L9
  FERN BH22.................302 G2
  FHAM/STUB P014..........294 B5
  HAV P09....................96 A5
  HORN P08..................256 C1
  MOOR/WNTN BH9...........322 C5
  WEND S018.................249 K2
Derwent Ct AND SP10........82 C9
Derwent Dr TOTT S040......245 P3
Derwent Gdns NARL S024...168 A3
Derwent Rd BKME/WDN BH12.321 K2
  LSOL/BMARY P013.........294 B8
  ROWN S016.................247 J2
  STHA RG19.................25 K4
Derwentwater Rd
  WIMB BH21.................300 F3
Desborough Ct CHAM P06...274 C9
Desborough Rd ELGH S050..229 L3
Dettingen Crs FRIM GU16.....59 J5
Dettingen Rd FRIM GU16.....59 K5
Devenish Rd FUFL S022.....164 G4
Dever Cl AND SP10...........82 C9
Deverel Cl CHCH/BSGR BH23.324 E7
Deverill Pl WVILLE P07 * ..276 C1
Dever Wy DEAN RG23.........67 N9
The Devil's Hwy CWTH RG45..40 F1
Devils La LIPH GU30.........175 M4
Devine Gdns ELGH S050....229 M2
Devon Cl FLEETN GU51.......56 E9
  SHST GU47.................41 L7
Devon Dr CHFD S053........228 C1
Devon Rd ALDT GU11.........75 M5
  BOR GU35.................154 A5
  HSEA P03..................297 J6
  PLE BH15..................320 C7
Devonshire Av FAWY S045..317 J5
Devonshire Gdns FAWY S045.317 J1
  BSTK RG21.................69 K8
Devonshire Pl ALDT GU11...271 J5
Devonshire Rd WSHM S015..248 D4
Devonshire Sq ENEY P04...317 H4
Devonshire Wy
  FHAM/STUB P014..........294 A1
Dewar Cl FHAM P015........271 J5
Dewey's La NWBY RG14......79 P1
Dewlands Rd VWD BH31.....258 C4
Dewlands Wy VWD BH31....258 E4
Dew La ELGH S050...........229 H1
Dewlish Cl CFDH BH17......321 J2
Dewpond Wk CHAM P06......92 G8
Dexter Sq AND SP10 * 82 C8
Dexter Wy FLEETN GU51.....75 F3
Dial Cl CHCH/BSGR BH23...305 N6
Diamond Cl FBDG SP6.......221 H9
Diamond St SSEA PO5 * 19 F6
Diamond Wy FARN GU14....119 H4
Diana Cl EMRTH P010........277 L6
  GPORT P012................315 J4
  KBH R022..................89 H9
Diana Wy WIMB BH21........300 A9
Dibble Dr NBAD S052........227 K1
Dibden Cl CHAR BH8.........323 K4
Dibden Lodge Cl FAWY S045.268 E5
Dibles Pk HLER S031 * 270 E9
Dibles Rd HLER S031.......270 D9
Dibley Cl KBH R022..........68 F9
Dickens Cl NEND P02.......316 F1
Dickens Dell TOTT S040....245 P4
Dickens Dr HLER S031......271 J1
Dickens La CHIN RG24........91 H1
  OVTN RG25.................91 H1
Dickenson Wk NARL S024..168 A3
Dickens Rd SBNE BH6.......324 B8
Dickens Wk NWBY RG14.....24 C7
Dickens Wy YTLY GU46......40 D9
Dicker's La ALTN GU34......132 G5
Dickson Pl WHAM P017.....252 E7
Didcot Rd CFDH BH17.......320 F4
  WSHM S015.................247 N2
Dieppe Crs NEND P02.......296 C5
Dieppe Gdns GPORT P012...315 K4
Digby Rd NWBY RG14........24 B2
Diligence Cl HLER S031....270 A1
Dilly La HPWT P09............55 H9
  NMIL/BTOS BH25..........327 J8
Dimond Cl WEND S018......248 G1
Dimond HI WEND S018......248 G1
Dimond Rd WEND S018.....248 G1
Dines Cl RAND SP11..........62 A5
Dingle Rd BOSC BH5........335 P2
Dingle Wy NEND S031.......227 K8
Dingley Cl BSTK RG21.......316 F6
Dingley Wy FARN GU14......75 P4
Dinham Rd NMIL/BTOS BH25.327 M3
Dinorben Av FLEETS GU52...74 B5
Dinorben Beeches FLEETS GU52.74 B5
Dinorben Cl FLEETS GU52....74 C5
Dippenhall Rd RFNM GU10...10 A6
Dippenhall St RFNM GU10....95 J6
Diprose Rd WIMB BH21.......89 J6
Discovery Cl
  FHAM/STUB P014 * 294 A4
Disraeli Rd CHCH/BSGR BH23.325 H9
Ditcham Crs HAV P09........15 K3
Ditchbury LYMN S041.......329 K1
Dittany Gdns NTHA RG18....25 N2
Ditton Cl FHAM/STUB P014..294 B5
Divers Cl ALTN GU34........132 F3
Dixon La STOK S020.........102 F2
Dixons La STOK S020..........90 J3
Dockenfield Cl HAV P09 * ..276 C6
Dockenfield St RFNM GU10..135 K2
Dock La NEND S042..........289 N9
Dock Rd GPORT P012.........13 F3
Doctors Dro RAND SP11......62 A5
Doctor's La
Doctors La PSF GU32.........188 E9
Dodds La BPWT S032........232 F7
Dodgson Cl FBDG SP6.......221 J4

Dodwell La HLER SO31 .....250 B8
Doe Copse Wy
  NMIL/BTOS BH25 .....326 C3
Dogdean WIMB BH21 .....278 E6
Dogflug Wy FNM GU9 .....96 C8
Dogkennel La WVILLE PO7 .....235 H8
Dogwood Dell WVILLE PO7 .....275 P5
Dogwood Rd BDST BH18 .....320 A2
Doiley Bottom RAND SP11 .....62 C4
Dolbery Rd North
  BKME/WDN BH12 .....321 M2
Dolbery Rd South
  BKME/WDN BH12 .....321 L3
Dollis Dr FNM GU9 .....96 D8
Dollis Gn TADY RG26 .....52 A2
Dolman Rd GPORT PO12 .....13 F4
  NWBY RG14 .....24 D2
Dolomans La RAND SP11 .....62 A5
Dolphin Av NBNE BH10 .....322 E2
Dolphin Ct ELGH SO50 .....229 P2
Dolphin Ct CHIN RG24 .....156 D7
Dolphin Ct FHAM/STUB PO14 .....293 P5
Dolphin Crs GPORT PO12 .....12 D4
Dolphin HI RWIN SO21 .....184 A8
Dolphin PI NMIL/BTOS BH25 .....327 H8
Dolphin Wy GPORT PO12 .....13 H7
Dolton Rd RWIN SO16 .....227 K9
Doman Rd CBLY GU15 .....57 P1
Dome Aly WINC SO23 .....22 E6
Dominica CI CHIN RG24 .....69 M2
Dominion Rd BWD BH11 .....321 N1
Domitian Gdns CHIN RG24 .....64 B6
Domoney CI STHA RG19 .....25 P4
Domum Rd NEND PO2 .....297 H7
  WINC SO23 .....23 C7
Domvilles Ap NEND PO2 .....296 D8
Donaldson Rd CHAM PO6 .....297 H5
Doncaster Rd ELGH SO50 .....229 J4
Donigers Dell BPWT SO32 .....232 E6
Donlan Dr FARN GU14 .....75 K3
Donnelly Rd SBNE BH6 .....336 D1
Donnelly St GPORT PO12 .....315 L2
Donnington CI CBLY GU15 .....58 A1
Donnington Dr
  CHCH/BSGR BH23 .....325 M8
  CHFD SO53 .....228 C1
Donnington Gv PTSW SO17 .....248 D1
Donnington Pk NWBY RG14 .....24 C1
Donnington Sq NWBY RG14 .....24 C1
Donoughmore Rd BMTH BH1 .....335 J2
Dora's Green La RFNM GU10 .....95 K9
Dorcas CI WVILLE PO7 .....276 A1
Dorcas Ct CBLY GU15 .....58 A2
Dorchester Ct 68 E7
Dorchester Gdns PLE BH15 .....320 C7
Dorchester Rd HTWY PG27 .....P1 P3
  PLE BH15 .....320 C6
Dore Av FHAM/PORC PO16 .....295 M1
Doreen CI FARN GU14 .....57 L5
Dores La RAND SP11 .....181 K7
Dorian Gv NARL SO24 .....167 N5
Doric CI CHFD SO53 .....207 H6
Dorking Crs CHAM PO6 .....297 H2
Dorland Gdns TOTT SO40 .....246 B5
Dormer CI CWTH RG45 .....41 H1
  NWBY RG14 .....24 B9
Dormington Rd CHAM PO6 .....297 J4
Dormy CI HLER SO31 .....270 D7
Dormy Wy LSOL/BMARY PO13 .....294 F8
Dorneywood Wy NWBY RG14 .....24 C3
Dornie Rd CCLF BH13 .....333 M4
Dormmere La WVILLE PO7 .....276 A3
Dorothy Dymond St
  PSEA PO1 .....19 G3
Dorrel CI KBH RG22 .....89 M5
Dorrien Rd GPORT PO12 .....315 M1
Dorrita Av POB PO8 .....256 A7
Dorrita CI ENEY PO4 .....317 H6
The Dorrits TOTT SO40 .....245 N4
Dorset Av RFEN BH10 .....302 D5
Dorset CI HORN PO8 .....256 B5
Dorset Lake Av PSTN BH14 .....333 K3
Doric CI ASHV GU12 .....76 F7
  CHCH/BSGR BH23 .....325 K7
  CHFD SO53 .....228 C1
  WBNE BH4 .....334 C1
Dorset St PTSW SO17 .....248 C5
Dorset Wy PLE BH15 .....320 F5
Dorstone Rd CHAM PO6 .....274 E9
Doswell Wy BSTK RG21 .....7 G3
Douai CI FARN GU14 .....58 B9
Doublet CI STHA RG19 .....25 N6
Doughty Wy AND SP10 .....103 J1
Douglas Av CHCH/BSGR BH23 .....324 D9
Douglas Crs ITCH SO19 .....249M5
Douglas Gdns
  BKME/WDN BH12 .....321 N7
  HAV PO9 .....276 G6
Douglas Gv RFNM GU10 .....116 C5
Douglas Ms SBNE BH6 .....336 A1
Douglas Ride KSCL RG20 .....29 M6
Douglas Rd BKME/WDN BH12 .....321 N7
  HSEA PO3 .....317 H1
  RAND SP11 .....101 H3
  SBNE BH6 .....336 C5
Douglas Wy FAWY SO45 .....268 B6
Doulton Gdns PSTN BH14 .....333 K1
Dove CI AND SP10 .....82 F9
  HORN PO8 .....255 P7
  KBH RG22 .....88 C2
Dove Dr ELGH SO50 .....228 F2
Dovedale CI SHST SO47 .....41 L4
Dove Gdns HLER SO31 .....271 H5
Dover CI CCLF BH13 .....334 A3
  DEAN SO52 .....68 G6
  FHAM/STUB PO14 .....295 J6
  NARL SO24 .....168 A3
Dover CI HISD PO11 .....318 E3
Dovercourt Rd CHAM PO6 .....297 J3
Dover Rd CCLF BH13 .....334 A3
  HSEA PO3 .....317 J9
Dover St SHAM SO14 .....248 G4
Doves CI ALTN GU34 .....132 C5
Doveshill Crs NBNE BH10 .....322 D4

Doveshill Gdns NBNE BH10 .....322 D4
Doves La RSAL SP5 .....201 J2
Doveton Wy NWBY RG14 .....24 E3
Doveys CI RGWD BH24 .....284 B6
Dowden Gv ALTN GU34 .....132 F4
Dowds CI HEND SO30 .....250 B3
Dowland CI NBNE BH10 .....322 D3
Dowlands Rd NBNE BH10 .....322 C5
Dowley Ct
  FHAM/STUB PO14 * 293M1
Down End Rd CHAM PO6 .....275 L9
Down End Rd CHAM PO6 .....275 L9
Downend Rd
  FHAM/PORC PO16 .....273 L8
Down Farm La FUFL SO22 .....144 B8
Down Farm PI HORN PO8 * 256 C2
Down Ga NARL SO24 .....167 P3
Down La CHAM SO HORN PO8 .....255 P8
Downhouse Rd HORN PO8 .....236 A8
Downing St FNM GU9 .....4 C6
Downland CI HEND SO30 .....250 F4
  HLER SO31 .....270 C6
Downland PI CFDH BH17 * 320 C4
Downland Rd RSAL SP5 .....200 B7
Downlands CI RSAL SP5 .....199 K7
Downlands Rd FUFL SO22 .....183 K2
Downlands Wy RWIN SO21 .....144 E4
Down La OVTN RG25 .....70 C9
Downley Point HAV PO9 * 277 H6
Downley Rd HAV PO9 .....15 K1
Down Lodge CI FBDG SP6 .....255 P8
Down Rd HORN PO8 .....256 C2
  RAND SP11 .....79 P8
Downs CI FARN GU14 .....57M6
  WVILLE PO7 .....275 P7
Downscroft Gdns HEND SO30 .....250 B4
Downside LSOL/BMARY PO13 .....295 H7
Downside Av ITCH SO19 .....249 J5
Downside Rd FUFL SO22 .....164 C5
  WVILLE PO7 .....275 L7
Downsland Rd BSTK RG21 .....6 B7
Dryden Av CHAM PO6 .....274 A9
Down's Park Av TOTT SO40 .....246 E5
Down's Park Crs TOTT SO40 .....246 E5
Down's Park Rd TOTT SO40 .....246 E5
Down St RWIN SO21 .....144 E4
Down St OVTN RG25 .....109 H1
Downs Vw ALTN GU34 .....133 L2
Downsview Rd BOR GU35 .....155 K3
Downsview Wy RAND SP11 .....79M5
Downs Wy ALTN GU34 .....132 D7
The Downsway
  FHAM/PORC PO16 .....295 N1
Downton CI CHAR BH8 .....323 J4
Downton HI RSAL SP5 .....199 N6
Downton La LYMN SO41 .....327 P9
Downton Rd WEND SO18 .....249 H1
Downview Rd BDST BH18 * 196 A9
Downwood CI FAWY SO45 .....267 N4
Doyle Av NEND PO2 .....296 C5
Doyle CI NEND PO2 .....296 C5
Doyle CI ITCH SO19 .....269 H1
Doyne Rd PSTN BH14 .....321 N8
Dozel La BWD BH11 .....301 N8
Dradfield La BPWT SO32 .....253 N3
Dragon Est CHAM PO6 * 297 N2
Dragonfly Dr CHIN RG24 .....70 A4
Dragon La RGWD BH24 .....282 E9
Dragon St EPSF GU31 .....215M3
Dragoon CI ITCH SO19 .....249 L7
Dragoon Ct ALDT GU11 .....2 A3
Dragoon Wy
  CHCH/BSGR BH23 .....324 D8
Drake Av FRIM GU16 .....76 F3
Drake CI CHCH/BSGR BH23 .....325 K9
  HLER SO31 .....271 H5
  NMIL/BTOS BH25 .....327 M4
  RGWD BH24 .....260 G9
  TOTT SO40 .....247 K9
Drake Ct AND SP10 .....5 K3
Drake Rd ELGH SO50 .....207 N9
  LSOL/BMARY PO13 .....314 B1
  PLE BH15 .....319 M6
Drakes CI FAWY SO45 .....268 B8
Drakes Rd FERN BH22 * 302 F5
Draper CI STHA RG19 .....25 N5
Draper Rd BWD BH11 .....322 A3
Drapers Copse FAWY SO45 .....267 P6
Draycote Rd HORN PO8 .....256 D9
Draycott Rd NBNE BH10 .....322 A5
Draymans Wy ALTN GU34 .....132 F6
Drayton CI ITCH SO19 .....269 H2
Drayton La CHAM PO6 .....275 K9
Drayton PI TOTT SO40 .....246 B4
Drayton Rd NEND PO2 .....296 C8
Drayton St FUFL SO22 .....164 D9
Draytons Vw STHA RG19 .....24 F8
Dreadnought Rd
  FHAM/STUB PO14 .....294 C4
Dresden Dr HORN PO8 .....255M9
Dreswick Ct CHCH/BSGR BH23 .....324 B6
Drew CI BKME/WDN BH12 .....322 E8
Drifters Dr FRIM GU16 .....59 J4
Drift Rd BOR GU35 .....153 N8
  FHAM/PORC PO16 .....11 K3
The Drift HAV PO9 .....277 H1
Driftway Rd HTWY RG27 .....72 B3
Driftwood Gdns ENEY PO4 .....317 L4
  TOTT SO40 .....246 A1
Drill Shed Rd NEND PO2 .....296 D8
Drinkwater CI ELGH SO50 .....229 M1
The Drive BKME/WDN BH12 .....321M7
  DEAN SO52 .....88 F2
  FHAM/PORC PO16 .....10 E5
  FNM GU9 .....116 B3
  HEND SO30 .....229 L3
  LSOL/BMARY PO13 .....294 E7

NWBY RG14 .....16 B7
ROMY SO51 .....201 P4
ROMY SO51 .....224 Q2
TOTT SO40 .....246 D6
Drove CI RWIN SO21 .....183 P9
Drove HI STOK SO20 .....123 L6
Drove La NARL SO24 .....167 H1
Drove Rd ITCH SO19 .....249 K7
  STOK SO20 .....123 L6
  WHAM PO17 .....274 C6
Drovers End FLEETN GU51 .....56 F9
Drovers Wy FNM GU9 .....96 A5
The Drove AND SP10 .....102 B3
  BPWT SO32 .....231 K4
  BPWT SO32 .....232 F7
  ELGH SO50 .....230 D6
  FAWY SO45 .....290 G8
  HEND SO30 .....229 P9
  ROMY SO51 .....224 E1
  RWIN SO21 .....183 P9
  TOTT SO40 .....245 P2
  WEND SO18 .....249 J4
Droxford CI GPORT PO12 .....315 K4
Droxford Crs TADY RG26 .....34 B7
Droxford Rd BPWT SO32 .....233 L1
  LTDN BH7 .....323 P9
Druce Wy STHA RG19 .....25 N4
Druids CI HAV PO9 * 302 D6
Druitt Rd CHCH/BSGR BH23 .....325 K8
Drum Md PSF GU32 .....215 L2
Drummond CI ALTN GU34 .....150 A6
  FUFL SO22 .....183 N1
Drummond Rd BMTH BH1 .....335 K2
  FAWY SO45 .....268 C6
  HEND SO30 .....250 C2
  PSEA PO1 .....316 F2
Drummond Wy CHFD SO53 .....206 D5
Drury CI WHCH RG28 .....104 F9
Drury La ALTN GU34 .....131 J4
  THLE RG7 .....36 A2
Drury Rd WBNE BH4 .....334 B4
Dryden Av CHAM PO6 .....274 A9
Dryden CI CHIN RG24 .....69M4
  FHAM/PORC PO16 .....10 B6
  NTHA RG18 .....25M2
  RGWD BH24 .....281 L4
  WVILLE PO7 .....255M9
Dryden PI LYMN SO41 .....338 C1
Dryden Rd FARN GU14 .....57 N7
Drysdale Ms ENEY PO4 * 317 K6
Duchess CI ALTN GU34 .....132 E6
Duchess of Kent Barracks
  ALDT GU11 .....76 A9
Ducking Stool La
  CHCH/BSGR BH23 .....324 F9
Duck Island La RGWD BH24 .....282 D3
Ducklands BDST BH18 .....196 B7
Duck La STOK SO20 .....139 K2
Duckmead La LISS GU33 .....175 N9
Ducks La LISS GU33 .....175 M5
Duddon CI WEND SO18 .....249 K2
Duddon Wy BSTK RG21 * 7 K6
Dudleston Heath Dr
  HORN PO8 .....256 B9
Dudley Av FBDG SP6 .....220 D9
Dudley CI BOR GU35 .....153 P7
  DEAN SO52 .....68 E7
Dudley Gdns NBNE BH10 .....322 D2
Dudley Rd HSEA PO3 .....317 J1
  NBNE BH10 .....322 D2
Dudmoor Farm Rd
  CHCH/BSGR BH23 .....324 D4
Dudmoor La
  CHCH/BSGR BH23 .....324 D3
Dudsbury Av FERN BH22 .....302 D4
Dudsbury Crs FERN BH22 .....302 E8
Dudsbury Gdns FERN BH22 .....302 E8
Dudsbury Rd FERN BH22 .....302 D7
Dugald Drummond St
  PSEA PO1 .....19 G3
Dugdell CI FERN BH22 .....302 F2
Duisburg Wy SSEA PO5 .....18 E7
Duke CI AND SP10 .....5 K1
Duke Crs PSEA PO1 .....316 F1
Duke Rd HEND SO30 .....250 D6
Duke Ter HAV PO9 .....276 D6
Dulsie Rd TWDS BH3 .....322 C8
Dumas CI YTLY GU46 .....40 C9
Du Maurier CI FLEETS GU52 .....74 B9
Dumbarton CI NEND PO2 .....296 F9
Dumbleton CI ITCH SO19 .....249 P6
Dummer Ct HAV PO9 .....276 D4
Dummer Down La
  OVTN RG25 .....108 E3
Dummer La RAND SP11 .....60 A4
Dummers Wy WINC SO23 .....22 D6
Dummers Rd ROMY SO51 .....181 H7
Dumpers Dro ELGH SO50 .....230 D6
Dumpford La EPSF GU31 .....217 K5
Dump Rd FARN GU14 .....75M3
Dunbar CI ROWN SO16 .....227 K7
Dunbar Crs CHCH/BSGR BH23 .....326 B5
Dunbar Rd ENEY PO4 .....317 K4
Dunbridge La BPWT SO32 .....322 C3
Dundry Wy HEND SO30 .....250 D3
  NTID SP9 .....93 L2
Dunedin Dr FERN BH22 .....302 B5
Dunedin Gdns FERN BH22 .....302 B5
Dunedin Gv CHCH/BSGR BH23 .....325 N8
Dunford CI NMIL/BTOS BH25 .....326 G7
Dunford Rd BKME/WDN BH12 .....321M7
Dungells La YTLY GU46 .....40 D9
Dungells La YTLY GU46 .....40 D9
Dunhills La RAND SP11 .....82 G3
Dunhurst CI HAV PO9 .....15 H1
Dunkeld Rd GPORT PO12 .....315 L1
  TWDS BH3 .....322 D9
Dunkirk CI ROWN SO16 .....227 P8
Dunkirk Rd ROWN SO16 .....227 P8
Dunkirt La RAND SP11 .....101 L7
Dunley's HI ODIM RG29 .....44 B9
Dunlin CI CHCH/BSGR BH23 .....337 M1
  ENEY PO4 .....317 L5
Dunmow Rd FLEETN GU51 .....74 D2
Dunmow Rd AND SP10 .....4 E4
Dunn CI ENEY PO4 .....317 K5
Dunnings La NBAD SO52 .....205 J8
Dunnock CI FERN BH22 .....280 B9
  HAV PO9 .....277 H1
Dunsbury Wy HAV PO9 .....276 E5
Dunsell's La NARL SO24 .....169 N2
Dunsford Crs DEAN SO52 .....68 F5
Dunsmore CI SSEA PO5 .....19 G5
Dunsmore Gdns YTLY GU46 .....40 B9
Dunstable Wk
  FHAM/STUB PO14 .....294 B2
Dunstall Pk FARN GU14 .....57 P6
Dunstan Rd RFEN BH10 .....25 P3
Dunstan's Dro RAND SP11 .....61 P3
Dunstans La STHA RG19 .....321 H6
Dunster CI ROWN SO16 .....227 N7
Dunvegan Dr ROWN SO16 .....227 N7
Dunyeats Rd BDST BH18 .....300 F8
Dunyeats Rbt WIMB BH21 .....300 F8
Duouro CI TADY RG26 .....33 N6
Dupree Dr ENEY PO4 .....317 J3
Durban CI ROMY SO51 .....204 E4
Durban Rd PSEA PO1 .....317 H1
Durbidges STHA RG19 * 24 E8
Durdells Av BWD BH11 .....322 A2
Durdells Gdns BWD BH11 .....322 A2
Durford Ct HAV PO9 .....276 D4
Durford Rd EPSF GU31 .....216 A2
Durham Dr FRIM GU16 .....59 J4
Durham St GPORT PO12 .....315 L2
  PSEA PO1 .....19 H2
Durham Wy KBH RG22 .....89M3
Durland CI NMIL/BTOS BH25 .....327 J6
Durlands Rd HORN PO8 .....256 C5
Durley Av HORN PO8 .....255 P8
Durley Brook Rd BPWT SO32 .....230 F6
Durley Chine Rd WCLF BH2 .....8 A4
Durley Chine Rd South
  WCLF BH2 .....8 A5
Durley CI AND SP10 .....102 C3
Durley Crs TOTT SO40 .....246 B6
Durley Gdns WCLF BH2 .....8 A5
Durley Hall La BPWT SO32 .....231 H5
Durley Rd ELGH SO50 .....315 L2
  GPORT PO12 .....315 L2
Durley Rd North WCLF BH2 .....8 B5
Durley Rd South WCLF BH2 .....8 B5
Durley St BPWT SO32 .....231 K5
Durlston Crs
  CHCH/BSGR BH23 .....324 D3
Durlston Rd PSTN BH14 .....333 L1
Durnford CI STOK SO20 .....123 L5
Durnford Rd SHAM SO14 .....21 G1
Durngate Pl WINC SO23 .....23 G4
Durngate Ter WINC SO23 .....23 G4
Durnsford Av FLEETS GU52 .....74 D5
Durnstown LYMN SO41 .....308 G6
Durrant Rd PSTN BH14 .....321 L9
Durrants Gdns HAV PO9 .....277 H2
Durrant Wy LYMN SO41 .....308 B6
Dursley Crs CHAM PO6 .....296 E1
Durweston CI
  MOOR/WNTN BH9 .....323 H4
Dutton La ELGH SO50 .....229 K1
Duttons Rd ROMY SO51 .....223 N3
Dyehouse Rd MFD/CHID GU8 .....137 N5
Dyer Rd WSHM SO15 .....247 N4
Dymewood Rd WIMB BH21 .....280 E2
Dymoke St EMRTH PO10 .....277 P6
Dymott CI WSHM SO15 .....247 P6
Dyneley CI ROWN SO16 .....227 M1
Dyram CI ELGH SO50 .....207 H8
Dysart Av CHAM PO6 .....297 K2

Dyserth CI ITCH SO19 .....269 K1
Dyson Dr WINC SO23 .....165 H5
Dysons CI NWBY RG14 .....16 B2

E

Eadens La TOTT SO40 .....245 K4
Eagle Av HORN PO8 .....255M7
Eagle CI ALTN GU34 .....132 F3
  CHFD SO53 .....206 D9
  FHAM/PORC PO16 .....295 K1
  KBH RG22 .....89 K3
Eagle Rd BKME/WDN BH12 .....334 A2
  KSCL RG20 .....31M4
  LSOL/BMARY PO13 .....314 B1
Eagles Nest SHST SO47 .....41 H5
Eagle La LISS GU33 .....183 L2
Eardley Av AND SP10 .....102 B1
Earle Rd WBNE BH4 .....334 C5
Earlham Dr PSTN BH14 .....321 L9
Earl of Chester Dr FRIM GU16 .....59 J5
Earlsbourne FLEETS GU52 .....74 E8
Earls CI ELGH SO50 .....230 A2
Earlsdon St SSEA PO5 .....19 G4
Earlsdon Wy
  CHCH/BSGR BH23 .....326 B5
Earls Rd FHAM/PORC PO16 .....294 F2
  SHAM SO14 .....248 C3
Eariswood Dr FBDG SP6 .....239 M6
Eariswood Pk
  NMIL/BTOS BH25 .....327M2
Earnley Rd HISD PO11 .....319M6
Earthpits La RSAL SP5 .....195 K7
Eastacre FUFL SO22 .....164 C5
East Av FNM GU9 .....96 E8
  NMIL/BTOS BH25 .....326 E8
  TWDS BH3 .....322 C9
East Bank Rd BROC SO42 .....286 C9
East Bargate SHAM SO14 .....20 E5
East Beach BMTH BH1 * 8 E5
East Boldre Rd BROC SO42 .....310 C1
East Borough WIMB BH21 .....278 E9
Eastbourne Av GPORT PO12 .....295 L9
  WSHM SO15 .....247 P5
Eastbourne Rd GPORT PO12 .....295 L9
Eastbrook CI GPORT PO12 .....295 K9
  HLER SO31 .....270 C5
Eastbrooke Rd ALTN GU34 .....132 G5
Eastbrook Rw WIMB BH21 * 278 E9
East Cams CI
  FHAM/PORC PO16 .....273 K9
Eastchurch CI ROWN SO16 .....227 K9
Eastcliff CI LSOL/BMARY PO13 .....314 C1
East Cliffe WINC SO23 .....23 G6
East Cliff Wy
  CHCH/BSGR BH23 .....325 N8
East CI NMIL/BTOS BH25 .....326 F1
East Cosham Rd CHAM PO6 .....297 K1
Eastcot CI FAWY SO45 .....290 D6
Eastcote CI LTDN BH7 .....323 N7
East Ct CHAM PO6 .....297 K1
Eastcroft Rd GPORT PO12 .....315 L3
East Dean Rd ROMY SO51 .....178 D4
East Dr ELGH SO50 .....207M9
Eastern Av AND SP10 .....281 H9
  HSEA PO3 .....317 K2
Eastern La CWTH RG45 .....41 N2
Eastern Pde ENEY PO4 .....317 H7
  FHAM/PORC PO16 .....294 F2
Eastern Rd ASHV GU12 .....97 L1
  BOR GU35 .....154 A2
  ENEY PO4 .....317 K3
  HAV PO9 .....15 G4
  HEND SO30 .....249M2
  HSEA PO3 .....297 L5
  LYMN SO41 .....338 C2
  NEND PO2 .....296 D7
Eastern Ter ENEY PO4 * 317 J6
Eastern Villas Rd ENEY PO4 .....316 F7
Eastern Wy FHAM/PORC PO16 .....11 J6
  LYMN SO41 .....322 C2
Eastfield Av BSTK RG21 .....6 E4
Eastfield Rd AND SP10 .....5 K7
  FHAM/STUB PO14 .....294 D5
  RGWD BH24 .....282 G2
Eastfield La RGWD BH24 .....282 G2
Eastfield Rd AND SP10 .....5 K7
  CHAM PO6 .....274 D8
  ENEY PO4 .....317 J5
Eastgate St SHAM SO14 .....20 G5
  WINC SO23 .....23 G5
East Gn BLKW GU17 .....57 K1
East Harting St EPSF GU31 .....217 J9
East HI LYMN SO41 .....322 C2
East Hill CI FHAM/PORC PO16 .....273 H8
East Hill Dr LISS GU33 .....192 G3
East Hoe Rd WVILLE PO7 .....234 D9
East House Av
  FHAM/STUB PO14 .....294 B7
East Howe La NBNE BH10 .....322 C3
Eastlake Av BKME/WDN BH12 .....321 K6
Eastlake CI EPSF GU31 .....216 A2
Eastlands NMIL/BTOS BH25 .....327 K6
East La LYMN SO41 .....328 E6
Eastleigh Rd HAV PO9 .....15 J3
East Leigh Rd HAV PO9 .....277 J7
East Lodge Pk CHAM PO6 .....297 P1
Eastlyn Rd TADY RG26 .....34 F5
Eastman St EPSF GU31 .....215 L4
Eastmans Rd STOK SO20 .....123 L6
Eastmead FARN GU14 .....77 L4
Eastmeare Ct TOTT SO40 .....246 A5
Eastney Farm Rd ENEY PO4 .....317 L5
Eastney Rd ENEY PO4 .....317 K5
Eastney St ENEY PO4 .....317 J6
Eastney Wy ENEY PO4 .....317 J6
Eastoke Av HISD PO11 .....319 K7
Easton Common HI RSAL SP5 .....158 D1

Easton La RWIN SO21 ....165 L5
WINC SO23 ....23 J3
East Overcliff Dr BMTH BH1 .....9 G5
Eastover Ct HAV PO9 ....278 C4
East Park Ter SHAM SO14 ......20 E2
East Portway AND SO40 ....102 A2
East Quay Rd PLE BH15 ....332 E2
East Ring RFNM GU10 ....97 N4
East Rd FAWY SO45 ....290 F1
RWIN SO21 ....124 C2
WHAM PO17 ....274 C4
Eastrop La BSTK RG21 ....7 G6
Eastrop Rbt BSTK RG21 ....7 G5
Eastrop Wy BSTK RG21 ....7 G5
East Station Rd ASHV GU12 .....3 F4
East St AND SP10 ....4 E5
EMRTH PO10 ....277 P7
FHAM/PORC PO14...........11 K6
FHAM/STUB AND 293 M1
FNM GU9 ....96 C9
HAV PO9 ....15 G6
NARL SO24 ....168 A1
PLE BH15 ....332 E1
PSEA PO1 ....18 B5
SHAM SO14 ....20 E5
WIMB BH21 ....300 D1
WVILLE PO7 ....234 F9
East Surrey St PSEA PO1 ......19 H2
East View Rd RWD BH24 ....258 E7
Eastville Rd ELGH SO50 ....230 C3
East Wy CHAR BH8 ....325 H6
Eastways BPWT SO32 ....232 A5
Eastwood ROMY SO51 ....202 C4
Eastwood Av FERN BH22 ....302 E2
Eastwood CI HISD PO11 ....319 H4
Eastwood Ct ROMY SO51 *....204 C6
East Woodhay Rd FUFL SO22 ..164 E3
Eastwood Rd NEND PO2 ....296 C5
Eastworth Rd VWD BH31 ......258 E3
Eaton Rd CBLY GU15 ....4 E5
CCLF BH13 ....334 A4
E Av HAVY SO40 ....290 G4
Ebblake CI VWD BH31 ....259 J7
Ebble Cl NTID SP9 ....79 H4
Ebden Rd WINC SO23 ....23 H5
Ebenezer La HSEA PO3 ....317 K2
Ebor CI FERN BH22 ....302 E6
Ebor Rd BKME/WDN BH12 ...321 M6
Ecchinswell Rd KSCL RG20 ....48 A3
Eccles Rd PLE BH15 ....332 C1
Echo Barn La RFNM GU10 ....115 N5
Eccleston La HSEA PO3 ....297 L6
Eddeys CI BOR GU35 ....63 J7
Eddeys La BOR GU35 ....155 J3
Eddy Rd ASHV GU12 ....3 H4
Eddystone Rd TOTT SO40 .....226 B9
Edelvale Rd WEND SO18 ....249 K2
Edelweiss CI RAND SP11 ....79 P2
Edenbridge Rd ENEY PO4 .....317 K3
Edenbridge Wy HLER SO31...270 F4
Eden Gv WIMB BH21 ....300 F2
Eden Rd WEND SO18 ....249 K1
Eden St PSEA PO1 *...........19 H1
Eden Wk CHFD SO53 ....206 C8
Edgar CI AND SP10 ....82 F7
Edgar Crs FHAM/PORC PO16 ..295 P3
Edgar Rd WINC SO23 ....164 G9
Edgarton Rd CFDH BH17 ......320 F1
Edgbarrow Ct CWTH RG45 *...41 H3
Edgbarrowhill Star
CWTH RG45 ....41 H4
Edgbarrow Ri SHST GU47 ......41 H4
Edgcumbe Park Dr
CWTH RG45 ....41 H1
Edgecombe Crs
LSOL/BMARY PO13...........294 G9
Edgecombe La NWBY RG14 ...24 F2
Edgedale CI CWTH RG45 ....41 J2
Edgefield Gv HORN PO8 ....276 C1
Edgehill Rd MOOR/WNTN BH9...322 E7
WEND SO18 ....249 K1
Edgell Rd EMRTH PO10 ....277 P6
Edgemoor Rd FERN BH22 .....281 H8
FRIM GU16 ....59 H2
Edgerly Gdns CHAM PO6 .....297 H5
Edgeware Rd ENEY PO4 ......317 J3
Edifred Rd MOOR/WNTN BH9...322 G5
Edinburgh Rd PSEA PO1 ......145 J7
WINC SO23 ....145 J7
Edington CI BPWT SO32 ......231 P3
Edington Rd WINC SO23 ......165 H5
Edison Rd BSTK RG21 ....7 J6
Edith Haisman CI WSHM SO15...247 P4
Edmondsham Rd VWD BH31...258 E2
Edmund Rd ENEY PO4 ....316 C5
Edmunds CI HEND SO30 ......250 D6
NMIL/BTOS BH25 ....327 H6
Edney CI FLEETS GU52.........74 E6
Edneys La WVILLE PO7 ....255 J6
Edrich Sq AND SP10 *..........79 F9
Edric's Gn AMSY SP4 ....98 F9
Edward Av CBLY GU15 ....41 P9
Edward CI FHAM/PORC PO16...274 A9
Edward Gv FHAM/PORC PO16...274 A9
Edward Rd ALTN GU34 ....132 C4
BWD BH11 ....322 B4
CHCH/BSCR BH23 ....325 L7
FAWY SO45 ....268 C6
FNM GU9 ....96 F2
PSTN BH14 ....321 L7
WINC SO23 ....183 N2
WSHM SO15 ....247 N4
Edwards CI CHAM PO6 ....274 D9
WVILLE PO7 ....255 P9
Edward St ALDT GU11 ....2 C3
Edward Ter NARL SO24 *.....168 B2
Edwina CI ITCH SO19 ....249 H5
NBAD SO52 ....205 L9
Edwina Dr CFDH BH17 ....320 D2
Eeklo PI NWBY RG14 ....17 F6

Eelmoor Br ALDT GU11 ....75 K6
Eelmoor Plain Rd ALDT GU11...75 L8
Eelmoor Rd ALDT GU11 ....75 N2
Effingham Gdns ITCH SO19 ...299 L7
Efford Wy LYMN SO41 ....329 P5
Egan CI NEND PO2 ....297 H6
Egbert Rd WINC SO23 ....22 E1
Egbury Rd RAND SP11 ....84 C1
Egdon Cl FERN BH22 ....302 B6
Egdon Dr WIMB BH21 ....300 C5
Egerton Gdns CHAR BH8 * ...323 K9
Egerton Rd CHAR BH8 ....323 K9
SHST GU47 ....41 M8
Eggars CI ALTN GU34 ....132 C4
Eggars Fld RFNM GU10 ....114 F5
Eggar's HI ALDT GU11 ....2 D7
Eggleton CI FLEETS GU52 ....74 B7
Eglantine CI HORN PO8 ....256 B7
Eglantine Wk HORN PO8 ......256 B7
Eglinton Rd RFNM GU10 ......137 H3
Egmont CI RAND SP11 ....282 B7
Egmont Dr RWD BH24 ....282 B7
Egmont Gdns RGWD BH24 ...282 B7
Egret Gdns ALDT GU11 ....96 N6
Eight Acres ROMY SO51 ......204 F6
Elaine Gdns HORN PO8 ....255 P6
Eland CI WEND SO18 ....249 K2
Eland Rd ASHV GU12 ....3 K5
Elbe Wy AND SP10 ....82 D8
Elbow Cnr BSTK RG21 ....E6
Elcho Rd CHOB/PIR GU24 ....59 P5
Elcombes Cl LYND SO43 ......264 F5
Elden Rd NTID SP9 ....79 J2
Elderberry Bank CHIN RG24...70 A4
Elderberry CI ELGH SO50 .....230 A2
HORN PO8 ....236 D8
Elderberry La
CHCH/BSCR BH23 ....325 K9
Elderberry Rd BOR GU35 .....256 B7
Elderberry Wv HORN PO8 ....256 B7
Elder CI FUFL SO22 ....183 L2
HLER SO31 ....270 F8
TOTT SO40 ....226 B9
Elder Crs SP10 ....102 B4
Elderfield CI EMRTH PO10 ...277 N7
Elderfield Rd HAV PO9 ....276 D3
Elder Gn RWIN SO21 ....208 A5
Eldergrove FARN GU14 ....76 H2
Elder Rd HAV PO9 ....277 H7
Eldon Av NMIL/BTOS BH25...326 C7
Eldon CI NMIL/BTOS BH25...326 C7
STOK SO20 ....161 M5
Eldon Dr RFNM GU10 ....116 C5
Eldon PI WBNE BH4 * 334 B5
Eldon Rd MOOR/WNTN BH9...322 E6
ROMY SO51 ....180 F6
STOK SO20 ....161 M6
Eldon St SSEA PO5 ....19 G5
Eldridge Gdns ROMY SO51 ...204 D5
Eleanor CI LIPH GU30 ....154 E8
Eleanor Ct RAND SP11 ....79 N1
Eleanor Dr FERN BH22 ....301 M8
Eleanor Gdns
CHCH/BSCR BH23 ....324 C7
Eleanors Wd
FHAM/PORC PO16 * 275 M9
Electron Wy CHFD SO53 ......206 E7
Elettra Av FERN BH22 ....275 M1
Elfin Dr FERN BH22 ....302 C1
Elgar CI CHAM PO6 * 296 A1
GPORT PO12 ....315 K6
KBH RG22 ....90 A3
Elgar Rd ITCH SO19 ....249 L8
NBNE BH10 ....322 A1
Elgars Ct LYMN SO41* 329 M3
Elgar Wk WVILLE PO7 ....255 N5
Elgin CI FAWY SO45 ....268 C7
FHAM PO15 ....10 C3
Elgin Ct BLKW GU17 ....56 H7
CHAM PO6 ....297 H3
PSTN BH14 ....333 L1
WBNE BH4 ....334 D1
WSHM SO15 ....247 P6
Elgin Wy FRIM GU16 ....52 B8
Elijah CI PLE BH15 ....332 A1
Eling CI FUFL SO22 ....164 E4
Eling Ct HAV PO9 ....276 D4
Eling Hl TOTT SO40 ....246 E5
Eling La TOTT SO40 ....246 C5
Eliot CI NTHA RG18 ....25 M2
Eliot Dr HASM GU27 ....154 J7
Elise CI LTDN BH7 ....323 P7
Elizabethan Ri OVTN RG25 ...88 C3
Elizabeth Av
CHCH/BSCR BH23 ....324 D7
NWBY RG14 ....17 J4
Elizabeth CI
FHAM/STUB PO14 * 294 D2
Elizabeth Crs LYMN SO41 ...328 A5
Elizabeth Dr FLEETS GU52 ...74 D7
Elizabeth Gdns ENEY PO4 ...317 J3
WSHM SO15 ....268 C9
Elizabeth Rd
FHAM/STUB PO14 * 294 D2
KBH RG22 ....69 H8
PLE BH15 ....320 F9
WHAM PO17 ....252 D7
WIMB BH21 ....145 J7
WVILLE PO7 ....275 N5
Elizabeth Wy BPWT SO32....231 P5
ELGH SO50 ....207 K8
Eliza PI GPORT PO12 ....12 E1
Elkhams CI LYMN SO41 ......100 B8
Elkstone Rd CHAM PO6 ......274 D9
Ellachie Ms GPORT PO12 ....315 M7
Ellachie Rd GPORT PO12 ....315 M7
Elland CI ELGH SO50 ....230 C3
Eldene Ct TOTT SO40 ....246 C8
Ellen Dr FLEETN GU51 ....56 E9

Ellen Gdns CHFD SO53 ....206 C8
TADY RG26 ....51 P2
Elleray Ct ASHV GU12 ....76 F7
Ellerslie CI FHAM/STUB PO14...298 N8
Elley Gv LYMN SO41 ....329 L2
Elles CI FARN GU14 ....76 A1
Ellesfield Dr FERN BH22 .....302 D5
Ellesmere Orch EMRTH PO10...277 N6
Elles Rd FARN GU14 ....75 P2
Ellingham CI NARL SO24 ....168 A2
Ellingham Dr RGWD BH24 ...260 B5
Ellingham Dro RGWD BH24...260 C5
Ellingham Rd
NMIL/BTOS BH25 ....326 F7
Ellington CI RAND SP11 ......101 P3
Ellington Dr KBH RG22 ....89 N4
Elliot CI TOTT SO40 ....246 B5
Elliot Ri HEND SO30 ....250 C1
Elliott Rd BWD BH11 ....321 N1
Ellisfield Rd HAV PO9 ....276 E6
Ellison Wy RFNM GU10 ......97 M4
Ellwood Av ITCH SO19 ....249 N6
Ellwood CI ITCH SO19 ....249 N5
Elm Av CHCH/BSCR BH23 ...324 C6
LYMN SO41 ....329 J6
NMIL/BTOS BH25 ....327 J5
Elm Bank AND SP10 ....40 D7
Elm Bank Rd AND SP10 ......40 C7
Elm CI BOR GU35 ....154 B5
HISD PO11 ....318 C5
RAND SP11 ....80 B1
RAND SP11 ....100 D2
RWIN SO21 ....208 A5
STOK SO20 ....121 H5
Elm Crs BPWT SO32 ....209 L7
FAWY SO45 ....290 C2
FNM GU9 ....96 D4
Elmcroft CI FRIM GU16 ....58 E6
Elmdale CI HLER SO31 ....292 D1
Elmdale Gv HORN PO8 ....224 C5
Elm Dr RDGW/BURGH RG30 ...27 L2
Elmers Wy CHCH/BSCR BH23...305 M7
Elmes Dr WSHM SO15 ....247 M4
Elmesweslie Rd HORN PO8 ..256 A5
Elm Farm Gv KSCL RG20 *....48 C3
Elmfield CI RSAL SP5 ....199 P8
Elmfield West Block
WSHM SO15 * 247 P6
Elm Gdns HEND SO30 ....249 M1
WBNE BH4 ....334 C1
Elmgate Dr LTDN BH7 ....323 M8
Elm Gv ELGH SO50 ....229 H2
FNM GU9 ....96 C4
GPORT PO12 ....315 M3
HISD PO11 ....318 C5
KSCL RG20 ....48 C3
NTHA RG18 ....25 L2
SSEA PO5 ....19 H6
Elm Grove Rd FARN GU14 ....58 A9
Elmhurst Rd BWD BH11 .....322 A2
FERN BH22 ....280 F8
FHAM/PORC PO16 ....11 G2
GPORT PO12 ....12 C2
NTHA RG18 ....25 K2
Elmhurst Wy FERN BH22 ....280 F7
Elm La HAV PO9 ....15 F5
RFNM GU10 ....97 M4
Elmleigh Rd HAV PO9 ....15 G5
Elmore Av LSOL/BMARY PO13...314 C9
Elmore CI LSOL/BMARY PO13...314 D9
Elmore Dr RGWD BH24 ......281 L3
Elmore Rd LSOL/BMARY PO13...314 C9
Elm Park Rd HAV PO9 ....15 G4
Elm Rd ALDT GU11 ....3 H7
CHIN RG24 ....68 C2
FNM GU9 ....96 D4
FUFL SO22 ....22 B3
HAV PO9 ....15 J7
NARL SO24 ....168 A2
OVTN RG25 ....87 H1
Elms Av PSTN BH14 ....333 J2
STHA RG19 ....25 P4
Elms CI FBDG SP6 ....239 N1
PSTN BH14 ....333 J2
Elmside HTWY RG27 * 52 E4
Elmsleigh Gdns ROWN SO16...228 C8
Elmsleigh Rd FARN GU14 ....57 P9
Elmslie Gdns HLER SO31 ....269 P1
Elms Rd ALDT GU11 ....2 E4
FHAM/PORC PO16 ....294 F2
HTWY RG27 ....71 P3
Elmstead Rd CCLF BH13 ....333 P3
The Elms AND SP10 ....4 B5
BLKW GU17 * 57 L1
RFNM GU10 ....97 M4
SSEA PO5 * 19 F6
Elms Wy SBNE BH6 ....336 C2
Elm Ter LISS GU33 ....192 C1
SHAM SO14 ....21 H6
Elm Tree CI TOTT SO40 ......245 P9
Elmtree Gdns ROMY SO51 ...204 C7
Elmtree Rd CHAM PO6 ......297 N1
Elm Tree Wk FERN BH22 ....302 E8
Elm Vw ASHV GU12 ....76 C9
Elmwood Av FBDG SP6 ......240 B1
Elmwood Ct CHAM PO6 * ...274 M9
Elmwood CI ALTN GU34 ......132 D7
Elmwood Rd NEND PO2 .....296 C5
Elmwood Wy
CHCH/BSCR BH23 ....326 B8
Elphinstone Rd
CHCH/BSCR BH23 ....326 D7
SSEA PO5 ....19 K6
Elsfred Rd FHAM/STUB PO14...293 M8
Elsley CI FRIM GU16 ....59 H5
Elson La GPORT PO12 ....295 L9
Elson Rd GPORT PO12 ....295 L9

Elstead Gdns WVILLE PO7 ...275 L6
Elstead Rd RFNM GU10 ......97 N6
Elsted Rd MIDH GU29 ....217 M9
Elston PI ASHV GU12 ....3 J6
Elston Rd ASHV GU12 ....3 J6
Elswick Rd ITCH SO19 ....248 G6
Eltham CI LTDN BH7 ....323 P7
Elvetham CI FLEETS GU51 ...74 C1
Elvetham Crs FLEETS GU51...74 A1
Elvetham Dr FLEETS GU51...74 B1
Elvetham Heath Wy
FLEETN GU51 ....74 A1
Elvetham La HTWY RG27 .....55 L5
Elvetham PI FLEETS GU51...74 B1
Elvetham Rd FLEETS GU51...74 B1
Elvin CI LYMN SO41 ....329 L2
Elwell Gn HISD PO11 ....318 F5
Elwyn Rd BMTH BH1 ....335 J1
Ely CI LSOL/BMARY PO13 *...315 H3
Ely Rd ITCH SO19 ....248 G6
Emanuel St NEND PO2 ......316 F1
Embankment Wy
RGWD BH24 ....282 F3
Emberley CI FERN BH22 ....302 G2
Embleton Rd BOR GU35 ......155 J2
Embley CI TOTT SO40 ....246 B1
Embley La ROMY SO51 ......203 K7
Embsay Rd HLER SO31 ......270 D2
Emden Rd AND SP10 ....82 D8
Emerald CI ITCH SO19 ......249 J5
RGWD BH24 ....281 L3
WVILLE PO7 ....276 A3
Emer CI NBAD SO52 ....205 L8
Emmanuel CI
RGWD BH24 ....271 J8
Emmett Rd ROWN SO16 .....227 J7
Emmons CI HLER SO31 ....269 P9
Empress Av FARN GU14 ......58 A8
Empress Pk SHAM SO14 *...248 D4
Empress Rd LYND SO43 ......264 F5
SHAM SO14 ....248 D4
WINC SO23 ....268 D1
Empress Wy RAND SP11 .....79 P1
Empshott Rd ENEY PO4 ......317 H4
Empson Wk
LSOL/BMARY PO13...........314 D2
Emsbrook Dr EMRTH PO10...277 M8
Emsworth Common Rd
EMRTH PO10 ....277 K5
Emsworth House CI
EMRTH PO10 ....277 L9
Emsworth Rd EMRTH PO10...299 P5
HAV PO9 ....15 H6
LYMN SO41 ....329 L3
NEND PO2 ....296 D6
WSHM SO15 ....247 M3
Enborne CI
BKME/WDN BH12 ....321 P4
Enborne Ga NWBY RG14 .....24 A6
Enborne Gv NWBY RG14 .....16 B4
Enborne Pl NWBY RG14 ......16 B4
Enborne Rd NWBY RG14 .....16 A4
Enborne St KSCL RG20 ....29 P2
NWBY RG14 ....30 B1
Encombe CI
BKME/WDN BH12 ....321 P4
Endeavour CI GPORT PO12 ...13 G3
WSHM SO15 ....247 M3
Endeavour Wy FAWY SO45...268 B5
Enderwood Ct TOTT SO40 *...245 P3
Endfield CI CHCH/BSCR BH23...324 D1
Endfield Rd CHCH/BSCR BH23...324 D7
MOOR/WNTN BH9 ....322 G5
Endle St SHAM SO14 ....21 H6
Endofield CI
FHAM/STUB PO14 ....294 D3
Enfield Av PLE BH15 ....320 G6
Enfield Crs PLE BH15 ....320 G6
Enfield Gv ITCH SO19 ....248 G9
Enfield Rd ASHV GU12 ....76 B8
PLE BH15 ....320 G6
Englands Wy BWD BH11 ....301 M9
Englefield Rd WEND SO18 ...248 F4
English Av WSHM SO15 ......247 M4
English Wd CHIN RG24 ......68 F5
Enham Arch Rbt AND SP10 ....4 D1
Enham La AND SP10 ....82 C8
Enmill La FUFL SO22 ....183 H1
Ennel Copse NBAD SO52 ....205 L9
Ennerdale CI HORN PO8 .....256 C1
KBH RG22 ....89 M1
Ennerdale Gdns NARL SO24...168 A3
WEND SO18 ....249 K2
Ennerdale Gv FARN GU14 ....76 A5
Ennerdale Rd BOR GU35 .....154 A3
FHAM/STUB PO14 ....294 B5
ROWN SO16 ....247 J1
Ensbury Av NBNE BH10 .....322 D6
Ensbury Br FERN BH22 ......302 E9
Ensbury CI NBNE BH10 .....322 D6
Ensbury Park Rd
MOOR/WNTN BH9 ....322 E5
Ensign Wy FHAM/STUB PO14...293 J5
Ensign Wy HLER SO31 ......269 N8
Enterprise CI HLER SO31 ....270 E9
Enterprise Rd HORN PO8 ....256 C3
ROWN SO16 ....227 N3
Enterprise Wy
CHCH/BSCR BH23 ....303 K8
SHAM SO14 ....248 D9
Epping CI WEND SO18 ....249 K2
Epsom CI ELGH SO50 ....230 D5
Epsom Crs NWBY RG14 ......17 H6
Epsom Down ALTN GU34 ...112 F1
Epts Rd FARN GU14 ....75 H4
Epworth Rd NEND PO2 ....297 H8
Equine Wy NWBY RG14 ......24 E8
Erica CI HLER SO31 ....270 F7
HORN PO8 ....256 B8
Erica Wy HORN PO8 ....256 B7

Ericksen Rd BWD BH11 ......322 C4
Eric Rd FHAM/STUB PO14...294 A7
Erleigh Dene NWBY RG14 ...16 C6
Erles Rd LIPH GU30 ....175 K3
Ernest CI EMRTH PO10 ....277 M9
RFNM GU10 ....116 C6
Ernest Rd HAV PO9 ....276 C6
PSEA PO1 ....316 C1
Erpingham Rd
BKME/WDN BH12 ....334 A1
Erskine Ct TADY RG26 ....34 C5
Escombe Rd ELGH SO50 .....229 M1
Escur CI NEND PO2 ....297 H5
Esdaile La RGWD BH24 ......284 B6
Esher Ct KBH RG22 ....89 P2
Esher Gv WVILLE PO7 ....255 L9
Eskdale CI HORN PO8 ....256 C1
Eskdale Ct ASHV GU12 *......76 E8
Eskdale Wy CBLY GU15 ....59 H1
Esmond CI EMRTH PO10 .....299 M1
Esmonde CI
LSOL/BMARY PO13...........314 D2
Esmonde Wy CFDH BH17 ....321 H4
Esplanade CCLF BH13 ....333 P4
ENEY PO4 ....316 G7
PLE BH15 ....320 G8
Esplanade Gdns ENEY PO4 ...317 L6
The Esplanade GPORT PO12 ...13 C2
Essex Av CHCH/BSCR BH23...324 D5
Essex Pl NWBY RG14 *.......24 A2
Essex Rd BOR GU35 ....154 A4
BSTK RG21 7
Essex St NWBY RG14 ....24 A8
Esslemont Rd ENEY PO4 .....316 G5
Estancia CI
LSOL/BMARY PO13...........314 D1
Estella Rd NEND PO2 ....296 F7
Estridge CI HLER SO31 ......269 P1
Ethelbert Dr AND SP10 ....82 B8
Ethelbert Rd WIMB BH21 ...300 F1
Ethelburt Av ROWN SO16 ...228 E7
Ethelred Gdns TOTT SO40 ...246 A5
Ethel Rd PSEA PO1 ....316 G2
Eton CI KBH RG22 ....89 L5
Eton Gdns WBNE BH4 ......334 B2
Eton PI PSEA PO1 ....19 L5
Eton Rd SSEA PO5 ....316 G4
Ettrick Rd CCLF BH13 ....334 A5
Etwall RAND SP11 ....100 A6
Eucalyptus Av RGWD BH24...281 N7
Europa CI TADY RG26 ....52 A2
European Wy SHAM SO14 ...248 C9
Euryalus Rd
FHAM/STUB PO14 ....294 D5
Euskirchen Wy KBH RG22 ...68 A2
Euston Gv BWD BH24 ....282 F3
Euston Rd ENEY PO4 ....317 K3
Evans CI BWD BH11 ....321 P3
NEND PO2 ....296 D7
RGWD BH24 ....281 L3
STOK SO20 ....120 C7
Evans St SHAM SO14 ....21 J4
Evelegh Rd CHAM PO6 ......297 M1
Eveley CI BOR GU35 ....153 N8
Evelyn CI ALDT GU11 ....3 G7
Evelyn Crs BPWT SO32 ......232 C3
Evelyn Ms CHAR BH8 ....323 K5
Evelyn Rd MOOR/WNTN BH9...322 C6
Evelyn Woods Rd ALDT GU11...76 B5
Evening Gdns FERN BH22 ...302 E5
Evenlode Rd ROWN SO16 ...247 J2
Evenlode Wy SHST GU47 ....41 K6
Everdene Rd CHAM PO6 ....302 C6
Everdon La HSEA PO3 ....297 L6
Everest Rd CHCH/BSCR BH23...325 J7
Everglades Av HORN PO8 ...255 P8
Everglades CI FERN BH22 ...302 D5
Evergreen CI TOTT SO40 ....267 K1
WIMB BH21 ....280 E1
Evergreen Wy
WVILLE PO7 ....275 M5
Evergreen Rd FERN BH22 ...58 E5
Evergreens RGWD BH24 .....281 L4
TOTT SO40 ....246 E5
Evering Av BKME/WDN BH12...321 M3
BKME/WDN BH12 ....321 L3
Everlea CI LYMN SO41 ....328 D6
Everon Gdns
NMIL/BTOS BH25 ....327 K6
Eversfield CI AND SP10 ....4 A4
Evershot Rd CHAR BH8 ....323 L6
Eversley Crs HAV PO9 ....276 D6
Eversley Dr FLEETN GU51 ...73 P1
Eversley PI FUFL SO22 ....183 M1
Everton Rd LYMN SO41 ......327 P3
ROWN SO16 ....228 D7
Evesham Wk CHIN RG24 ....69 L3
SHST GU47 ....41 H8
Evingar Gdns WHCH RG28 ...85 L5
Evingar Rd WHCH RG28 ......85 L5
Ewart Rd PSEA PO1 ....316 C1
Ewell Wy TOTT SO40 ....227 J3
Ewer Common GPORT PO12 ...12 D6
Ewhurst CI HAV PO9 ....276 B2
Ewhurst Rd TADY RG26 ....49 P6
Ewins CI ASHV GU12 ....97 N1
Ewshot La FLEETS GU52 ....74 C9
Exbury CI ELGH SO50 ....206 A2
Exbury Dr BWD BH11 ....301 P8
Exbury Rd FAWY SO45 ....290 G9
HAV PO9 ....276 G5
Excellent Rd
FHAM/STUB PO14 ....294 D4
Excelsior Rd PSTN BH14 .....333 L1
Exchange Rd PSEA PO1 ......19 F3
Exeter CI ELGH SO50 ....207 H8

EMRTH PO10 ....277 M7
HLER SO31 ....270 F7
KBH RG22 ....89 M4
WEND SO18 ....249 J2

Exeter Cl
LSOL/BMARY PO13 *.....314 C2
Exeter Crs WCLF BH2 ....8 D5
Exeter Gdns YTLY GU46 ....40 C7
Exeter Park Rd WCLF BH2 ......8 D5
Exeter Rd ASHV GU12 ....76 F9
FERN PO4 ....317 H6
WCLF BH2 ....8 D5
WEND SO18 ....249 J3
Exford Av WEND SO18 ....249 L3
Exford Dr WEND SO18 ....249 L4
Exhibition Rd FARN GU14 ......75 P4
Exleigh Cl ITCH SO19 ....249 K5
Exmoor Cl KBH RG22 ....68 E9
Exmoor Rd SHAM SO14 ....21 F1
STHA RG19 ....25 M4
Exmouth Gdns ELGH SO50 ....230 C5
Exmouth Rd GPORT PO12 ......295 L9
SSEA PO5 ....316 F6
Express Wy NWBY RG14 ....25 H5

Exton Gdns
FHAM/PORC PO16 ....273 N9
Exton Rd HAV PO9 ....277 H5
SBNE BH6 ....324 B8
Eyebright Cl ELGH SO50 ....230 C6
Eyeworth Wk FAWY SO45 ......267 N6
Eynham Av ITCH SO19 ....249 L5
Eynham Cl ITCH SO19 ....249 K5
Eyre Cl TOTT SO40 ....246 B5

F

Faber Cl HAV PO9 ....276 C8
Fabian Cl BSTK RG21 ....6 C7
WVILLE PO7 ....276 A2
Factory Rd ELGH SO50 ....229 J2
Fairacre KSCL RG20 ....29 N6
Fairacre Ri FHAM/STUB PO14 ..293 F7
Fairacres RFNM GU14 ....115 P6
Fairbairn Wk CHFD SO53 ......206 B7
Fairbourne Cl HORN PO8 * ...355 N9
Fair Cl NWBY RG14 * 76 C1
WHCH RG28 ....85 L7
Fairclose WHCH RG28 ....85 K7
Fairclose Dr FUFL SO22 ....164 C2
Faircross Cl FAWY SO45 ....290 E6
Fairdown Cl WINC SO23 ....23 K5
Fairfax Cl FUFL SO22 ....183 K1
Fairfax Ct ITCH SO19 ....249 N5
Fairfax Ms FARN GU14 ....26 A7
ITCH SO19 ....249 N5
Fairfax Pl NWBY RG14 ....25 H2
Fairfax Rd FARN GU14 ....58 A6
Fair Fld ROMY SO51 ....49 L4
Fairfield CHCH/BSGR BH23....324 F8
WHCH RG28 ....85 L5
WVILLE PO7 ....255 H7
Fairfield Av FHAM/STUB PO14 ..294 C2
Fairfield Cl CHCH/BSGR BH23 ..324 F8
EMRTH PO10 ....277 M8
FAWY SO45 ....268 B6
LYMN SO41 ....329 L4
WIMB BH21 ....278 C9
Fairfield Dr FRIM GU16 ....58 D2
Fairfield Gn ALTN GU34 ....150 D5
Fairfield Pk THLE RG7 ....35 N1
Fairfield Rd FUFL SO22 ....22 B2
HAV PO9 ....277 H5
NMIL/BTOS BH25 ....326 G8
RWIN SO21 ....183 M9
Fairfield Sq CHAM PO6 ....296 C1
Fairfields RG BSTK RG21 ....69 L9
Fairfield Ter HAV PO9 * 15 G5
The Fairfield FNM GU9 ....96 C9
Fair Gn ITCH SO19 ....249 K6
The Fairground RAND SP11 .....81 K9
Fairholme Gdns FNM GU9 ....116 C1
Fairhome Cl GPORT PO12 ......315 L1
Fairies Dr FERN BH22 * 302 F5
Fair Isle Cl FHAM/STUB PO14 ..293 P6
Fairisle Rd NWBY SO16 ....227 J8
Fair La RWIN SO21 ....165 N7
Fairlawn Cl ROWN SO16 ....227 K6
Fairlawn Rd TADY RG26 ....34 E7

Fairlead Dr
LSOL/BMARY PO13 ....315 H2
Fairlead Rd EMRTH PO10 ......277 M7
LYMN SO41 ....329 L3
Fairlie RGWD BH24 ....260 C9
Fairlie Cl HEND SO30 ....230 B9
Fairlight La LYMN SO41 ....307 M7
Fairmead Cl SHST GU47 ....41 M7
Fairmead Ct CBLY GU15 ....58 B1
Fairmead Wk HORN PO8 ......256 A8
Fairmead Wy TOTT SO40 ......246 C6
Fairmile FLEETS GU52 ....74 D6
Fairmile Rd CHCH/BSGR BH23 ..324 E2
Fair Oak HAV PO9 ....15 F2
Fair Oak Dr HAV PO9 ....15 G1
Fair Oak La HAV PO9 ....15 H2
Fairoak Rd ELGH SO50 ....229 M2
Fairoak Wy TADY RG26 ....53 N5
Fairthorne Gdns GPORT PO12 ..12 B8
Fairthorne Ri CHIN RG24 ....20 D7
Fair Vw NARL SO24 ....167 P3
Fairview Cl FAWY SO45 ....268 C7
ROMY SO51 ....204 F4
Fairview Crs BDST BH18 ......300 C8
Fairview Dr BDST BH18 ....300 C8
ROMY SO51 ....204 F5
Fairview Gdns FNM GU9 ....96 C5
Fairview Meadow DEAN RG23 ..88 F3
Fairview Pde FAWY SO45 ......268 C8

Fairview Rd ASHV GU12 ....76 C9
BDST BH18 ....300 C8
BOR GU35 ....155 J3
RAND SP11 ....81 J9
Fairview Ter BOR GU35 * 155 H2

Fairwater Cl
LSOL/BMARY PO13 ....294 F8
Fairway Cl LIPH GU30 ....174 E4
Fairway Dr CHCH/BSGR BH23 ..324 D9
Fairway Gdns ROWN SO16 ....227 J7
Fairway Rd FAWY SO45 ....268 B6
PSTN BH14 ....333 L3
Fairways FERN BH22 ....302 F2
RAND SP11 ....81 H9
The Fairway BOR GU35 ....153 N7
FHAM PO15 ....75 J4
FHAM/PORC PO16 ....295 N1
FNM GU9 ....96 D4
FRIM GU16 ....58 F2
HAV PO9 ....257 J9
LSOL/BMARY PO13 ....294 G8
NMIL/BTOS BH25 ....327 K8
Fairwood Rd VWD BH31 ....256 B9
Fairy Crossway HORN PO8 ....258 B9
Faithfulls Dro STOK SO20 .....160 F3
Fakenham Wy SHST GU47 ......41 L5
Falaise Cl ALDT GU11 ....3 F2
ROWN SO16 ....227 N8
Falaise Rd STOK SO20 ....120 C5
Falcon Cl FHAM/PORC PO16 ..295 K1
GPORT PO12 ....315 N1
KBH RG22 ....89 K2
NTID SP9 ....79 H4
Falcon Coppice KSCL RG20 .....29 N6
Falcon Dr CHCH/BSGR BH23 ..337 M1
Falconer Cl FAWY SO45 ....290 D5
Falconer Dr PLE BH15 ....320 A8
Falcon Flds FAWY SO45 ....291 K6
TADY RG26 ....34 C4
Falcon House Gdns KSCL RG20 ..29 M6
Falcon Rd HORN PO8 ....256 C4
Falcon Sq ELGH SO50 ....228 C5
Falcon Vw FUFL SO22 ....183 C2
Falcon Wy BPWT SO32 ....250 F2
YTLY GU46 *...................40 C8
Falconwood Cl FBDG SP6 ......240 B2
Falkland Dr NWBY GU14 ....116 C7
Falkland Garth NWBY RG14 ....24 A8
Falkland Rd CHIN RG24 ....69 M3
CHFD SO53 ....228 E1
NEND PO2 ....296 F5
NWBY RG14 ....24 A9
WSHM SO15 ....247 L4

Falklands
LSOL/BMARY PO13 ....314 D1
Falklands Rd NEND PO2 * 296 C5
Falkner Rd FNM GU9 ....96 A9
Falkners Cl FLEETN GU51 ......56 F9
Fallowfield FLEETN GU51 ....56 F9
Fallow Fld FUFL SO22 ....183 L2
Fallowfield YTLY GU46 ....40 C7
Falmouth Cl CBLY GU15 ....58 F1
Falmouth Rd CHAM PO6 ....274 B9
Fancy Rd BKME/WDN BH12 ..321 K4
Fanshawe St SHAM SO14 ......21 F3
Fantails ALTN GU34 ....132 F3
Faraday Ct CHIN RG24 * 69 N4
Faraday Rd CHIN RG24 ....69 M3
FARN GU14 ....58 A3
NWBY RG14 ....58 B7
Farcroft Rd PSTN BH14 ....321 K7
Farcrosse Ct SHST GU47 ....41 M8
Fareham Dr YTLY GU46 ....40 C7

Fareham Hts
FHAM/PORC PO16 *..........273 H8
Fareham Park Rd
FHAM/PORC PO16 ....272 A6

Fareham Rd
LSOL/BMARY PO13 ....294 G4
WHAM PO17 ....252 E8
WHAM PO17 ....274 A5
Faringdon Cl SHST GU47 ....41 K5
Faringdon Rd WEND SO18 ....248 A9
Farleigh Cl HAV PO9 ....276 D5
Farleigh La OVTN RG25 ....109 L1
Farleigh Ri BSTK RG21 ....90 E1
Farleigh Rd OVTN RG25 ....90 D2
Farley Cl ELGH SO50 ....230 D3
FUFL SO22 ....183 K2
Farley Ct FARN GU14 * 76 C2
Farley La ROMY SO51 ....181 H5
Farley Mount Rd RWIN SO21 ..163 K9
Farley St STOK SO20 ....139 N2
Farlington Av CHAM PO6 ......275 L9
Farlington Rd NEND PO2 ......296 C8
Farm Cl RGWD BH24 ....282 E1
YTLY GU46 ....40 E9
Farm Ct FRIM GU16 ....58 E3

Farmdene Cl
CHCH/BSGR BH23 * 325 P7
Farm Dr FLEETN GU51 ....56 E9

Far Meadow Wy
EMRTH PO10 ....299 K1

Farm Edge Rd
FHAM/STUB PO14 ....294 A8
Farmers Wk LYMN SO41 ......328 D7
WIMB BH21 ....278 D8
Farmery Cl ELGH SO50 ....228 F8
Farm Gdns HSEA PO3 ....297 H5
Farm Ground Cl HTWY RG27 ..72 B5

Farm House Cl
FHAM/STUB PO14 ....294 A8
Farmhouse Wy HORN PO8 ....256 A6
Farm La CHCH/BSGR BH23 ...337 L1
RFNM GU10 ....95 H9
Farm Lane Cl WILLE PO7 .....275 M4

Farm La North
NMIL/BTOS BH25 ....327 J8

Farm La South
NMIL/BTOS BH25 ....327 J8
Farmlea Rd CHAM PO6 ....296 B1
Farm Rd ASHV GU12 ....76 C9
FERN BH22 ....280 D7
FHAM/STUB PO14 ....271 L8

FRIM GU16 ....58 D3
RAND SP11 ....101 N4
Farmside Gdns HSEA PO3 .....297 H5
Farm Vw EMRTH PO10 ....277 M7
YTLY GU46 ....40 E9
Farm View Av HORN PO8 ......256 B7
Farm View Dr CHIN RG24 ....70 B1
Farnborough Ga FARN GU14 * ..58 B8
Farnborough Rd ALDT GU11 ....2 B1
FARN GU14 ....58 B6
Farnborough St FARN GU14 ...58 C8
Farnham By-Pass FNM GU9 ..115 P2
Farnham La HASM GU27 ......156 F4
Farnham Park Cl FNM GU9 .....96 B5

Farnham Rd
BKME/WDN BH12 ....322 A8
BOR GU35 ....154 A2
FLEETN GU51 ....74 C3
LISS GU33 ....192 C2
ODIM RG29 ....70 F4
PSF GU32 ....191 P6
NMIL/BTOS BH25 ....322 A5
Farnleys Md LYMN SO41 ......329 L5
Faroe Cl CHIN RG24 ....69 N3
Faroes Cl FHAM/STUB PO14 * ..293 P6
Farrell Cl CBLY GU15 ....58 B2
Farriers Cl TADY RG26 ....52 A2
WIMB BH21 ....278 B8
Farriers Fld OVTN RG25 ....110 C2
Farriers Wk GPORT PO12 ....15 H1
Farrier Wy FHAM/PORC PO16 ..294 F3
Farringdon Rd HAV PO9 ....276 D6
Farringdon Wy TADY RG26 .....34 C7
Farringford Rd ITCH SO19 ....249 M5
Farrs Av AND SP11 ....5 F7
Farthing Ter PSEA PO1 * 18 D6
Farthing Flds BSTK RG21 ......154 F3
Farthings Ga WVILLE PO7 ....275 N7
Farwell Cl CHCH/BSGR BH23 ..324 C4
Farwell Rd BKME/WDN BH12 ..321 L2
Fastnet Cl ROWN SO16 ....227 J7
Fastnet Wy FHAM/STUB PO14 ..293 P6
Fathersfield BROC SO42 ....286 F8
Fathoms Reach HISD PO11 ....318 E4
F Av FAWY SO45 ....291 H3
Faversham Rd SHST GU47 .....41 L5
Fawcett Rd ENEY PO4 ....316 C5
NMIL/BTOS BH25 ....327 H5
Fawconer Rd KSCL RG20 ....48 C3
Fawley By-Pass FAWY SO45...291 K6
Fawley Cl HAV PO9 ....277 H5
Fawley Gn CHAR BH8 ....323 J5
Fawley La ALTN GU34 ....189 K2
RWIN SO21 ....184 F6

Fawley Rd FAWY SO45
FAWY SO45 ....290 D1
FAWY SO45 ....290 G6
NEND PO2 ....296 C4
WSHM SO15 ....247 K5
Fawn Gdns NMIL/BTOS BH25..327 H5
Fay Cl FHAM/STUB PO14 ......294 A7
Fayre Rd FHAM/PORC PO16 ..294 E2
Fayrewood Cha KBH RG22 .....89 M4
Fearon Rd NEND PO2 ....296 C7
Feathers La BSTK RG21 * 7 F2
Feildon Ct KSCL RG20 ....48 B4
Felbridge Cl FRIM GU16 ....58 E3
Feld Wy CHIN RG24 ....70 B5
Felix Rd GPORT PO12 ....315 M1
Fell Cl HLER SO31 ....270 G6
Fell Dr LSOL/BMARY PO13 ...314 D1
Fellows Rd FARN GU14 ....76 C3
Felmer Dr WINC SO23 ....145 K9
Feltham Cl ROMY SO51 ....204 G5
Felton Crs CHCH/BSGR BH23 ..326 B7
Felton Rd PSTN BH14 ....321 H7
Feltons Pl HSEA PO3 ....297 H4
Fen Av FHAM/PORC PO16 ....294 F2
Fencott Pl BSTK RG21 ....6 E3
Fenleigh Cl NMIL/BTOS BH25..327 K7
Fennel Cl CHIN RG24 ....52 B9
FARN GU14 ....57 J9
NWBY RG14 ....24 C2
Fennel Gdns LYMN SO41 .....329 J5
Fennel Cl WVILLE PO7 ....277 M1
Fenton Rd SBNE BH6 ....324 A9
Ferbies FLEETS GU52 ....74 D6
Ferguson Cl BSTK RG21 ....90 C1
Fermor Dr ALDT GU11 ....2 B1
Fern Bank WIMB BH21 ....280 E2

Fern Barrow
BKME/WDN BH12 ....322 B7
Fernbrae Cl RFNM GU10 ......116 B8
Fern Cl CHCH/BSGR BH23 ....324 C5
EPSF GU31 ....216 A2
FBDG SP6 ....150 B5
FRIM GU16 ....59 H2
Ferncote Rd BOR GU35 ....154 B5

Ferncroft Cl
FHAM/STUB PO14 ....294 A8
Ferncroft Gdns NBNE BH10 ...322 D2
Ferncroft Rd NBNE BH10 ......322 C2
Ferndale HEND SO30 ....250 D6
WVILLE PO7 ....275 P3
Ferndale Gdns HTWY RG27 ...71 P2

Ferndale Ms
FERN BH22 * 294 F5
Ferndale Rd AND SP10 ....102 C1
FLEETS GU52 ....74 C7
NMIL/BTOS BH25 ....327 K5
TOTT SO40 ....267 K1
Ferndene Wy WEND SO18 ....249 H3
Ferndown Cl ALDH RG23 ....89 L7
Ferndown Gdns FARN GU14 ...57 M5

Ferndown, Stour & Forest Trail
FERN BH22 ....302 A7
WIMB BH21 ....279 M5
Fern Heath FHAM PO15 ....272 A8
Ferney Cl ALTN GU34 ....151 L1
Ferney La ALTN GU34 ....130 B9
Fernglade NMIL/BTOS BH25 ..327 J4
Fernheath Cl BWD BH11 ......322 A5

Fernheath Rd BWD BH11 ......322 A4
Fernhill Cl CFDH BH17 ....321 J2
FARN GU14 ....57 M4
FNM GU9 ....96 B5
Fernhill Dr FNM GU9 ....96 B5
Fernhill La FARN GU14 ....57 M4
FNM GU9 ....96 B4
NMIL/BTOS BH25 ....327 J1
Fern Hill La ROMY SO51 ......181 H6
Fernhill Rd FARN GU14 ....57 M8
NMIL/BTOS BH25 ....327 J3
Fernhills Rd FAWY SO45 ......268 D9
Fernhill Wk FARN GU14 ....317 H4
Fernhurst Cl HISD PO11 ....318 E5
Fernhurst Rd ENEY PO4 ....317 H4
Fernlea FHAM/STUB PO14 ....293 P7
Fernlehurst CBLY GU15 ....58 E1
Fernlea BOR GU35 ....153 N7
Fernlea Av FERN BH22 ....302 D4
RGWD BH24 ....281 C5
Fernlea Cl CHAR BH8 ....302 D4
ROWN SO16 ....228 A9
Fernlea Wy FAWY SO45 ......267 P7
Fernleigh Ri FRIM GU16 ....59 H6
Fernleigh Rd FAWY SO45 .....268 B7
ITCH SO19 ....249 H9
Fernside Av PSTN BH14 ....321 H8
Fernside Rd FERN BH22 ....280 C7
MOOR/WNTN BH9 ....322 D7
PLE BH15 ....320 G8
Ferns Md FNM GU9 ....116 A1
Fern Wy FHAM PO15 ....96 C4
Fernway Cl WIMB BH21 ....271 K7
Fernwood Cl RGWD BH24 .....281 P4
Fernyhurst Av ROWN SO16 ...227 K6
Ferrell Fld HTWY RG27 ....71 N3
Ferrier Gv NWBY RG14 ....17 C7
Ferris Av CHAR BH8 ....323 J5
Ferris Cl CHAR BH8 ....323 K5
Ferris Pl CHAR BH8 ....323 K5
Ferrol Rd GPORT PO12 ....315 N2
Ferry Point LYMN SO41 * 329 K5
Ferry Rd ENEY PO4 ....317 M5
FAWY SO45 ....290 D1
HISD PO11 ....318 A4
PLE BH15 ....332 D2
SBNE BH6 ....336 D3
Ferry Wy CCLF BH13 ....333 K8
Festing Gv ENEY PO4 ....317 H6
Festing Rd ENEY PO4 ....317 H6
Festival Wy BSTK RG21 * 7 F6
Feversham Av CHAR BH8 .....323 L6
Fey Rd GPORT PO12 ....12 E1
Fibbards Rd BROC SO42 ......286 F8
Fiddlers Fld ALTN GU34 ......132 B1
Field Cl HLER SO31 ....270 G8
ROMY SO51 ....294 F4
ROWN SO16 ....204 E6
RWIN SO21 ....183 L8
THLE RG7 ....27 K5
Fielden Cl NBAD SO52 ....205 K9
ROMY SO51 ....204 F8
WINC SO23 ....145 K9
Fielders Ct ALTN GU34 ....132 F6
The Fielders HTWY RG27 ......39 P6
Fielders Wy ROMY SO51 .....225 H2
Fieldfare Av YTLY GU46 ....40 B8
Fieldfare Cl HORN PO8 ....256 C8
Fieldfare Ct SHST GU47 ....41 M5
Field Gate Dr KSCL RG20 ......48 B3

Fieldhouse Dr
LSOL/BMARY PO13 ....294 D9
Fielding Gdns CWTH RG45 .....41 J2
Fielding Rd SHST GU47 ....41 M8
Fields Cl FAWY SO45 ....290 G8
Field Stores Ap ALDT GU11 .....3 H1
Field Vw CHFD SO53 ....206 B7
Field Wk LYMN SO41 ....329 K2
Field Wy ASHV GU12 ....97 L1
CHCH/BSGR BH23 ....325 P6
FBDG SP6 ....241 J1
RFNM GU10 ....97 M4
RWIN SO21 ....183 L8
WIMB BH21 ....300 A5
WVILLE PO7 ....255 H7
Fieldway FLEETN GU51 ....74 A4
Fifehead Cl HASM GU27 ......157 H6
RGWD BH24 ....282 F1
Fifield La RFNM GU10 ....116 C8
Fifth Av CHAM PO6 ....296 C1
HAV PO9 ....277 H8
Fifth Rd NWBY RG14 ....16 A6
Fifth St PSEA PO1 ....317 H1
STHA RG19 ....25 M4
Filmer Cl LSOL/BMARY PO13 ..295 H9
Filmorehill La ALTN GU34 .....189 K8
Filton Cl TOTT SO40 ....246 A3
Filton Rd FLEETN GU51 ....329 K3
Fincham End Dr CWTH RG45 ..40 G2

Finchampstead Rd
EWKG RG40 ....39 P1
Finch Cl TADY RG26 ....34 D7
Finchdean Rd HAV PO9 ....257 J9
Finches Av ROWN SO16 ....276 D6
Finches Gn ALTN GU34 ....132 F5
The Finches PSTW SO17 ......248 D1
Finchfield Av BWD BH11 ......301 P7
Finchleigh Pl ODIM RG29 * 70 F4
Finchmead La PSF GU32 ......215 H1
Finch's Cl ALTN GU34 ....150 D7
Finch's La RWIN SO21 ....183 P8
Finch Wy THLE RG7 ....27 K4
Findhorn Cl HSST GU47 ....41 L5
The Findings FARN GU14 ....57 M5
Findon Rd GPORT PO12 ......295 M9

Fingle Dr AND SP10 ....102 C2

Finisterre St
FHAM GU14 ....293 P5
Finkley Rd RAND SP11 ....83 K6
Fintry H FARN GU14 ....57 M6
Finzi Cl ITCH SO19 ....249 L8
Fiona Cl WINC SO23 ....23 J5
Fir Acre Rd ASHV GU12 ....76 F6
Fir Av NMIL/BTOS BH25 ......327 K5
Firbank Rd MOOR/WNTN BH9..323 H7
Fir Cl FERN BH22 ....59 F4
FLEETN GU51 ....74 C4
Fir Copse Rd WVILLE PO7 ....275 M7
Fir Croft Dr CHFD SO53 ......206 F8
Fir Dr BLKW GU17 ....57 L2
Firecrest Cl ROWN SO16 ......227 M7
Firecrest Rd KBH RG22 ....89 K5
Fire Station Rd ALDT GU11 .....3 F1
Fire Thorn Cl FLEETS GU52 ....74 C8
Firfield Rd FNM GU9 ....116 A3
Firglen Dr YTLY GU46 ....40 E7
Firgrove Cl NBAD SO52 ....153 N7
Firgrove Cl FNM GU9 ....116 C1
Firgrove Crs HSEA PO3 ....297 H4
Firgrove Hl FNM GU9 ....116 C1
Firgrove La WHAM PO17 ......253 K9
Firgrove Pde FARN GU14 * 58 A9
Firgrove Rd BOR GU35 ....153 N7
FARN GU14 ....40 B8
HTWY RG27 ....40 B8
NBAD SO52 ....205 L8
WSHM SO15 ....247 N4
Firlands Ri CHAM PO6 ....296 C1
Firmain Rd BKME/WDN BH12 ..321 M3
Firmount Cl LYMN SO41 ......328 E6
Firmstone Rd WINC SO23 ......23 J4
Fir Rd TOTT SO40 ....245 P9
Firs Av WVILLE PO7 ....255 P9
Firs Cl FARN GU14 ....76 B2
Firs Dr HEND SO30 ....250 A6
Firs Av WINC SO23 ....145 H8
Fir's End THLE RG7 ....27 J5
Firs Glen Rd FERN BH22 ......280 E7
MOOR/WNTN BH9 ....322 D7
VWD BH31 ....258 F5
Firshill CHCH/BSGR BH23 .....326 A6
Firs La ODIM RG29 ....333 K3
First Av CHAM PO6 ....297 H1
CHAM PO6 ....297 N1
HAV PO9 ....15 K4
HEND SO30 ....250 A6
THLE RG7 ....54 D4
WSHM SO15 ....247 H4
The Firs AND SP10 ....102 C2
BMTH BH1 ....9 G2
LIPH GU30 ....175 J4
LSOL/BMARY PO13 ....295 H8
NTHA RG18 ....25 L3
WSHM SO15 ....228 B8

First Marine Av
NMIL/BTOS BH25 ....327 H8
First St FAWY SO45 ....290 C1
First St DEAN STHA RG19 ....31 M1
Firs Wy DEAN RG23 ....88 E5
WHCH RG28 ....85 L6
Firsway WHCH RG28 ....85 L6
Firth Cl THLE RG7 ....35 N2
Fir Tree Av HASM GU27 ....156 C7
Fir Tree Cl ELGH SO50 ....230 C5
RGWD BH24 ....281 K7
Fir Tree Cnr TADY RG26 ....33 P4
Firtree Crs HORN PO8 ....256 C6
Firtree Gdns HORN PO8 ......256 C6
Firtree Gv FAWY SO45 * 15 G6
Fir Tree Hl FBDG SP6 ....239 N5
Fir Tree La CHCH/BSGR BH23 ..325 P6
ELGH SO50 ....230 B5
NWBY RG14 ....25 H3
Fir Tree Rd HISD PO11 ....318 C5
TOTT SO40 ....244 C4
Firtree Wy FLEETN GU51 ....74 E4
ITCH SO19 ....249 K6
Fir Vale Rd BMTH BH1 ....8 E3
Firway GSHT GU26 ....155 M3
Fir Way Cl CHFD SO53 ....206 E5
Fisgard Rd GPORT PO12 ......315 M1
Fisher Cl AND SP10 ....5 K6
FHAM/STUB PO14 ....293 P6
Fisherman's Av ABNE BH6 ...335 P2
Fishermans Quay
LYMN SO41 * 329 M3
Fishermans Rd PLE BH15 .....332 E2
The Fishermans EMRTH PO10 ..319 L6
Fishermans Wk HISD PO11 ...319 J4
Fishermen's Cl ALDT GU11 ....76 D7
Fisher Rd LSOL/BMARY PO13 ..294 G6
Fishers Gv CHAM PO6 ....297 N2
Fishers Pl CHAM PO6 ....271 N8
Fisher's Rd TOTT SO40 ....245 P4
Fishery La HISD PO11 ....319 J6
Fishlake Mdw ROMY SO51 ...204 D4
Fiske Cl KBH RG22 ....68 F3
Fitzgerald Cl HLER SO31 .....271 J2

Fitzharris Av
MOOR/WNTN BH9 ....322 G8
Fitzherbert Rd CHAM PO6 ...297 M2
Fitzherbert Sp CHAM PO6 ...297 N2
Fitzpain Cl PSEA PO1 ....316 E2
Fitzpatrick Ct CHAM PO6 * ...274 F9
Fitzroy Cl ROWN SO16 ....228 B5
Fitzroy Rd FLEETN GU51 ......74 B5

Fitzwilliam Av
FHAM/STUB PO14 ....293 N7
Fitzwilliam Cl BWD BH11 .....301 N8
Fitzwygram Crs HAV PO9 .....15 F2

Five Acres Cl BOR GU35 ....154 C3
Five Ash Rd ALTN GU34 ....150 B4
Five Bells La STOK SO20 ....139 M3
Five Bridges Rd WINC SO23 ....183 N3
Five Elms Dr ROMY SO51 ....147 P6
Fivefields Cl WINC SO23 ....23 J6
Fivefields Rd WINC SO23 ....23 K6
Five Heads Rd HORN PO8 ......256 A3
Five Post La GPORT PO12 ....315M2
Flaghead Chine Rd
  CCLF BH13 ....333 N5
Flaghead Rd CCLF BH13 ....333 N4
Flag Staff Gdns
Flag Staff Rd GPORT PO12 .....315 P2
Flagstaff Sq STHA RG19 ....25 P5
Flag Wk HORN PO8 ....255 P6
Flambard Av
  FHAM/PORC BH23 ....324 D6
Flambard Rd PSTN BH14 ....333 L1
Flamborough Cl ROWN SO16....247 H1
Flamingo Ct
  FHAM/PORC PO16 ....295 K1
The Flashett RSAL SP5 ....158 C1
Flathouse Rd PSEA PO1 ....316 E1
The Flats BLKW GU17 ....57 J1
Flaxfield Ct BSTK RG21 ....6 D6
Flaxfield Rd BSTK RG21 ....6 C6
Flaxfields End FBDG SP6 ....240 C2
Flazen Cl BWD BH11 ....321 M1
Flecker Cl NTHA RG18 ....135M2
Fleet Cl LSOL/BMARY PO13 ....295 H8
Fleet End Bottom HLER SO31...292 F1
Fleetend Cl HAV PO9 ....276 E4
Fleet End Rd HLER SO31........292 F1
Fleet Hl EWKG RG40 ....39M4
Fleet Rd FARN GU14 ....57 K9
  FLEETN GU51 ....74 C3
  FLEETS GU51 ....75 H5
  HTWY RG27 ....55 J7
Fleet's Cnr CFDH BH17 ....320 D5
Fleets La PLE BH15 ....320 E6
Fleet Ter ELGH SO50 * 207 K4
Fleetwood Cl NWBY RG14 .....24 C2
Fleming Av NBAD SO52 ....205 L9
Fleming Cl FARN GU14 ....58 C7
Fleming Cl
  RAND SP11 ....79 J5
Fleming Ct NBAD SO52 * 205 M9
Fleming Pl ROMY SO51 ....204 D5
Fleming Rd FUFL SO22 ....164 D4
  NWBY RG14 ....17 C1
  ROWN SO16 ....228 F8
Flensburg Cl AND SP10 ....22 D8
Fletcher Cl BPWT SO32 ....69 J8
  FAWY SO45 ....267 P7
  NBNE BH10 * 322 D4
Fletcher Cl NBNE BH10 ....322 D4
Fletchers Fld LIPH GU30 ....175 J4
Fletchwood La TOTT SO40 ....245 P5
Fletchwood Rd TOTT SO40 ....245 M9
Fleur-de-Lys Pk LYMN SO41 * .309 M7
Fleuret Cl FARN GU14 ....290 C1
Flexford Cl CHFD SO53 ....206 C4
  KSCL RG20 ....29 H9
Flexford Gdns HAV PO9 ....115 K9
Flexford La AND SP10 ....328 C9
Flexford Rd NBAD SO52 ....206 B6
Flinders Cl AND SP10 ....103 K1
Flinders Ct ENEY PO4 ....317 K6
Flint Cl AND SP10 ....249 N7
Flint La RAND SP11 ....81 K5
Flint St SSEA PO5 ....19 F6
Floating Bridge Rd
  SHAM SO14 ....21 J7
The Flood RSAL SP5 ....138 A9
Floral Farm WIMB BH21 ....301 H5
Floral Wy AND SP10 ....6 B4
  NTHA RG18 ....25 N2
Floreat Gdns NWBY RG14 .....16 A5
Florence Cl ROMY SO51 ....225 H2
  YTLY GU46 ....40 D8
Florence Ct AND SP10 ....62 F8
Florence Portal Ut WHCH RG28..86 B6
Florence Rd BOSC BH5 ....335 L2
  FLEETS GU52 ....74 E6
  ITCH SO19 ....248 C9
  PSTN BH14 ....321 L8
  SHST GU47 ....49 M3
  SSEA PO5 ....316 F7
Florence Wy CHIN RG24 ....68 F4
Florentine Wy WVILLE PO7 ....276 A2
The Florins HLER SO31 ....270 C9
  WVILLE PO7 ....275 N7
Floriston Gdns
  NMIL/BTOS BH25 ....327 M4
Florrie Pl ALTN GU34 * 151 L5
Floud La PSF GU32 ....188 D9
Flowerdown Cl TOTT SO40 ....246 A3
Flower La MOOR/WNTN BH9 ..322 D7
Flowers Cl HLER SO31 ....269 N7
Flume Rd FAWY SO45 ....291 L5
Flushards LYMN SO41 ....329 M4
Focus Wy AND SP10 ....5 K1
Foden Rd ALDT GU11 ....2 E4
Foldsgate Cl LYND SO43 ......264 F4
Folkestone Rd PSEA PO1 ......317 J1
Folly Cl FLEETS GU52 ....74 D4
Folly Farm La RGWD BH24 ....282 A5
Folly Fld BPWT SO32 ....232 B5
Folly HI FNM GU9 ....96 A6
Folly La EPSF GU31 ....215M2
  TADY RG26 ....36 C9
  THLE RG7 ....27 J4
Folly La North FNM GU9 ....96 B4
Folly La South FNM GU9 ....96 A5
Folly Rbt AND SP10 ....4 C2
The Folly NWBY RG14 ....17 C6
Font Cl FHAM/STUB PO14 .....271 J7
Fontley Cl WSOL SO22 ....172 C7
Fontley Rd FHAM PO15 ....271 N7
Fontmell Rd BDST BH18 ....332 B2
Fontwell Cl ASHV GU12 ....3 K2
  TOTT SO40 ....246 A2
Fontwell Dr ALTN GU34 ....132 F7

Fontwell Gdns ELGH SO50 ....230 D5
Fontwell Ms HORN PO8 ....276 B1
Fontwell Rd NWBY RG14 ......17 H6
  SSEA PO5 ....316 F6
Foord Rd HEND SO30 ....250 B7
Football Gn LYND SO43 ....246 C7
Footner La ROMY SO51 ....204 C3
Footners La
  CHCH/BSGR BH23 ....324 G5
Forbes Cha SHST GU47 ....41 L7
Forbes Cl ROWN SO16 ....227 K6
Forbes Rd WINC SO23 ....145 J8
Forbury Rd SSEA PO5 ....206 F9
Ford Av CHFD SO53 ....206 F2
Ford Cl FERN BH22 ....302 F1
Fordingbridge Rd 317 K5
  FBDG SP6 ....239 P4
Fordington Rd FUFL SO22 ......22 A5
Ford La FERN BH22 ....302 G1
  ODIM RG29 ....58 D7
  RFNM GU10 ....116 B4
Ford Rd FARN GU14 ....58 D2
Ford Rd GPORT PO12 ....315 K2
Fore Br EPSF GU31 ....215M3
The Forehand THLE RG7 ....36 E2
Foreland Cl CHCH/BSGR BH23 ..324 B3
Foreland Ct HISD PO11 ....319 J6
Foreman Pk ASHV GU12 ....97 P1
Foreman Rd ASHV GU12 ....97 P2
Foreshore North FAWY SO45 ..291 K3
Foreshore South FAWY SO45 ..291 K3
Forest Av ROWN SO16 ....255 P8
Forest Centre BOR GU35 * 154 A5
Forest Cl BPWT SO32 ....232 C9
  CHCH/BSGR BH23 ....325 P6
  CHFD SO53 ....206 E5
  HORN PO8 ....255 P8
  NBAD SO52 ....205 J8
  TADY RG26 ....34 E8
  VWD BH31 ....259 K6
Forest Cnr LISS GU33 ....173 M8
Forest Court Hills
  RGWD BH24 ....283 H3
Forestdale GSHT GU26 ....156 C2
Forest Dean FLEETN GU51 ....56 F9
Forest Dr CHIN RG24 ....52 A9
  NTID SP9 ....79 J5
  RFNM GU10 ....116 C6
Forest Edge FAWY SO45 ....291 J6
Forest Edge Rd RGWD BH24 ..281 K4
Forest Edge Rd RGWD BH24 ..283 J4
Forest End FLEETS GU52 ......74 C6
Forest Gate Gdns LYMN SO41 .329 K6
Forest Gld FERN BH22 ....115M7
Forest Glade Cl BROC SO42 ...286 D8
Forest Hall BROC SO42 ....286 G8
Forest Hills CBLY GU15 ....58 A1
Forest Hills Dr WEND SO18 ...228 G9
Forest Hills Wy FAWY SO45 ...268 B8
Forestlake Av RGWD BH24 ....283 H5
Forest La BOR GU35 ....154 D2
  FAWY SO45 ....290 D3
  RAND SP11 ....103 K4
  RGWD BH24 ....283 K3
  TADY RG26 ....34 E8
  VWD BH31 ....258 E3
  WHAM PO17 ....272 G1
Forest Lane Cl LIPH GU30 .....175 H5
Forest Links Rd WIMB BH21 ...280 B8
Forest Md WVILLE PO7 ....255 H8
Forestmede FAWY SO45 ....290 C1
Forest Oak Dr
  NMIL/BTOS BH25 ....327 J2
Forest Park Rd BROC SO42 ....286 F7
Forest Pines
  NMIL/BTOS BH25 ....327 J2
Forest Ri CHCH/BSGR BH23 ...325 P5
  LISS GU33 ....173M9
Forest Rd BOR GU35 ....154 A7
  BPWT SO32 ....232 D9
  CFCL BH13 ....334 A4
  CHCH/BSGR BH23 ....306 A4
  CHFD SO53 ....206 F5
  CWTH RG45 ....41 K1
  FBDG SP6 ....289 F6
  FERN BH22 ....280 F6
  LISS GU33 ....173 K6
  RGWD BH24 ....284 D4
  RSAL SP5 ....223M4
  WVILLE PO7 ....254 C7
Forestside Av HAV PO9 ....275 N2
Forestside Gdns RGWD BH24 ..260 G9
The Forestside WIMB BH21 ....280 B8
Forest Vw BROC SO42 ....286 D8
  NMIL/BTOS BH25 ....326 F2
  SHAM SO14 ....20 D6
Forest View Cl
  MOOR/WNTN BH9 ....322 C5
Forest View Dr WIMB BH21 ...302 A2
Forest View Rd
  MOOR/WNTN BH9 ....322 C4
Forest Wy CHCH/BSGR BH23..325 P6
  LSOL/BMARY PO13 ....295 H7
  LYMN SO41 ....328 D6
  TOTT SO40 ....302 A3
Forfield Dr DEAN RG23 ....89 L6
Forge Cl FNM GU9 ....96 D8
  HLER SO31 ....270 A1
  TADY RG26 ....52 B3
Forge Fld AND SP10 ....4 E2
Forge La ALDT GU11 ....116 B4
Forge Rd BOR GU35 ....154 F8
  FAWY SO45 ....313 H1
Forneth Gdns FHAM PO15 ....295 P1
Forster Rd SHAM SO14 ....248 C4

Forsyth Gdns NBNE BH10 .....322 C6
Forsythia Cl HAV PO9 ....277 H6
  HEND SO30 ....250 B3
Forsythia Pl ITCH SO19 ....249 H6
Fort Cumberland Rd
  ENEY PO4 ....317 M5
Fortescue Rd
  BKME/WDN BH12 ....321 M5
  TWDS BH3 ....322 C9
Fort Fareham Rd
  FHAM/STUB PO14 ....294 D3
Fort Cl CHFD SO53 ....206 D8
  FARN GU14 ....57 L7
  FHAM/STUB PO14 ....293 P6
Forth Ct AND SP10 ....82 C9
Fort Hill Dr DEAN RG23 ....68 E6
Forties Cl FHAM/STUB PO14 * .293 P5
Forton Rd GPORT PO12 ....315 L2
  ITCH SO19 ....248 C8
Fortrose Cl SHST GU47 ....41 L7
Fortunes Wy CHAM PO6 ....275 P9
Forty Acre La EPSF GU31 ......215M2
Forum Cl DEAN RG23 ....68 E7
The Forum FHAM PO15 * 271 L4
Forward Dr LYMN SO41 ....329 J5
Fosseway CWTH RG45 ....40 C1
Foster Cl FHAM/STUB PO14 ...294 A5
Foster Rd GPORT PO12 ....12 C4
  PSEA PO1 ....316 F2
Foul La ALTN GU34 ....150 A1
Founders Wy
  LSOL/BMARY PO13 ....295 H7
Foundry Crs HLER SO31 ....270 A2
Foundry La FARN GU14 ....156 F7
  WSHM SO15 ....247 N5
Fountains Cl CHIN RG24 ....69 K3
Fountain Sq ENEY PO4 ....19 G2
Four Acre Rd HEND SO30 .....250 C5
Four Acre Coppice HTWY RG27..72 B3
Four Lanes Cl DEAN RG23 .....70 D1
Four Oaks KSCL RG20 ....29 N8
Four Posts HI WSHM SO15 ....20 A2
Fourshells Cl FAWY SO45 .....291 H7
Fouracre Av CHAM PO6 ....296 C1
  HAV PO9 ....15 K4
Fourth St PSEA PO1 ....317 H2
  STHA RG19 ....31 L1
Fourways RAND SP11 * 102 F7
Four Wells Rd WIMB BH21 ....279 J7
Fowey Cl CHFD SO53 ....206 B8
Fowey Ct GPORT PO12 * 295 N9
The Fowey FAWY SO45 ....290 C7
Fowler Av FARN GU14 ....75 P2
Fowler Rd ALDT GU11 ....76 B7
  HEND SO30 ....250 A3
Fowler's Wk NBAD SO52 ......227 P2
Foxbury Cl FAWY SO45 ....268 C8
Foxbury La
  FHAM/PORC PO16 ....295 M2
Foxbury La
  FHAM/PORC PO16 ....295 H5
Foxbury Rd RGWD BH24 ......303 C2
  THLE RG7 ....27 J4
Foxcombe Cl BPWT SO32 .....232 E6
Foxcote Gdns
  NMIL/BTOS BH25 * 327 H4
Foxcott Cl ITCH SO19 ....269 H2
Foxcott La AND SP10 ....82 B9
Foxcott La RAND SP11 ....81 P9
Foxcroft Gv FAWY SO45 ....276 F5
Foxcroft Dr FAWY SO45 ....290 D6
  WIMB BH21 ....279 K9
Foxdown OVTN RG25 ....86 C1
Fox Dr YTLY GU46 ....40 E7
Foxes Cl VWD BH31 ....258 F5
Foxes La ROMY SO51 ....202 F7
Fox Farm RAND SP11 ....100 F7
Fox Fld LYMN SO41 ....328 D6
Foxglade FAWY SO45 ....313 H4
Foxglove Cl
  CHCH/BSGR BH23 ....325 N7
  KBH RG22 ....89 L4
Foxglove Dr BOR GU35 ....154 B6
Foxglove Pl NMIL/BTOS BH25..327 M3
Foxgloves FHAM PO16 ....11 J1
The Foxgloves HEND SO30 ....250 D6
Foxhayes La FAWY SO45 ......313 H1
Fox Heath FARN GU14 ....75 K1
Foxhills TOTT SO40 ....246 A7
  VWD BH31 ....341 H4
Foxhills Cl TOTT SO40 ....246 A8
Foxhills La ASHV GU12 ....77 H9
Foxholes Rd PLE BH15 ....321 H6
  SBNE BH6 ....335 N9
Foxhunter Wy STHA RG19 ....25 J4
Foxhurst Rd ASHV GU12 ....76 F7
Foxlands FAWY SO45 ....313 H1
Fox La DEAN RG23 ....67 P9
  FUFL SO22 ....163 L5
  HTWY RG27 ....40 A6
  WIMB BH21 ....279 L2
Foxlea Gdns GPORT PO12 ....315M1
Foxley Cl BLKW GU17 ....41 K9
Foxley Dr HSEA PO3 ....297 K5
Fox Pond La LYMN SO41 ......329 J5
Fox Rd HASM GU27 ....156 D7
Fox's Furlong CHIN RG24 .....52 C9
Fox's La KSCL RG20 ....48 B4
Fox's Wk FAWY SO45 ....268 B9
Foxtail Dr FAWY SO45 ....268 B9
Foxtail Gdns RAND SP11 ......95 N3
Fox Wy RFNM GU10 ....95M3
Foxwood FLEETN GU51 ....74 F1

Foxwood Av CHCH/BSGR BH23..337 K1
Fox Yd FNM GU9 ....96 B9
Foxy Paddock FAWY SO45 .....313 H1
Foye La FLEETS GU52 ....74 D7
Foye Gdns HLER SO31 ....270 C9
Foyle Pk BSTK RG21 ....90 D1
Foyle Rd CHFD SO53 ....206 D7
Frampton Cl
  NMIL/BTOS BH25 ....327 L2
  RAND SP11 ....207 P4
Frampton Pl RGWD BH24 .....282 E2
Frampton Rd
  MOOR/WNTN BH9 ....322 G7
Frampton Wy TOTT SO40 .....246 D5
  WINC SO23 ....145 K9
Frances Rd BMTH BH1 ....9 J2
  BSTK RG21 ....9 E4
  WVILLE PO7 ....275M7
The Frances NTHA RG18 ......25 N3
Francis Av BWD BH11 ....321 M1
  ENEY PO4 ....317 H5
Francis Cl LSOL/BMARY PO13..314 E5
Francis Gdns WINC SO23 ......145 J5
Francis Pl FHAM/STUB PO14 ..294 B7
  HORN PO8 ....236 C9
Frankland Crs PSTN BH14 .....321 N9
Frankland Ter EMRTH PO10 ..299 N1
Franklin Av HTWY RG27 * 54 C6
Franklin Rd
  LSOL/BMARY PO13 ....314 C1
  MOOR/WNTN BH9 ....322 C4
  NMIL/BTOS BH25 ....327 L3
  RWIN SO21 ....184 A7
Frankum Av ITCH SO19 ....249 J7
Frankston Rd SBNE BH6 ....336 A2
Franks Wy PLE BH15 ....321 K5
Frankton Wy GPORT PO12 ....13 H1
Fraser Cl CHIN RG24 ....70 C6
Fraser Gdns FHAM PO15 ......10 A2
Fraser Md SHST GU47 ....41 M8
Fraser Rd BKME/WDN BH12 ..321 P3
  HAV PO9 ....14 C3
  LSOL/BMARY PO13 ....294 C5
  NEND PO2 ....296 D7
  SSEA PO5 ....19 J4
  WINC SO23 ....19 G1
Frater La GPORT PO12 ....295 L8
Fratfield Rd HAV PO9 ....277 H5
Fratton Rd PSEA PO1 ....316 G2
Fratton Wy ELGH SO50 ....230 C3
  ENEY PO4 ....317 H3
Frayslea FAWY SO45 ....268 C9
Freda Rd CHCH/BSGR BH23 ..524 D9
Freda Routh Gdns ELGH SO50..230 D2
Frederica Rd
  MOOR/WNTN BH9 ....322 E7
Frederick St ALDT GU11 ....2 D3
  SHAM SO14 ....248 D5
Freegrounds Av HEND SO30 ..250 C5
Freegrounds Cl HEND SO30 ..250 C5
Freegrounds Rd HEND SO30 ..250 C5
Freelands Dr FLEETS GU52 ...74 B7
Freemans Cl WIMB BH21 .....279 K8
Freemans La WIMB BH21 .....279 J9
Freemantle Cl BSTK RG21 ....7 M2
  ITCH SO19 ....249 H6
Freemantle Common Rd
  ITCH SO19 ....249 H6
Freemantle Rd GPORT PO12 ..315M1
Freestone Rd SSEA PO5 ....19 G6
Free St BPWT SO32 ....232 B4
Fremantle Rd RAND SP11 .....79 M4
Frenches La ROMY SO51 ......203 H4
French Gdns BLKW GU17 .....57 L1
Frenchies Vw WVILLE PO7 ....254 C7
Frenchmans Creek
  FLEETS GU52 ....74 B8
Frenchmans Rd NTID SP9 .....215 L1
Frenchmoor La RSAL SP5 .....177 P3
French Rd CFDH BH17 ....320 D3
  LISS GU33 ....174 A4
Frenchs Rd ITCH SO19 ....18 C6
Frendstaple Rd WVILLE PO7 ..276 A5
Frensham Av FLEETN GU51 ...74 F5
Frensham Cl HEND SO30 ......250 C5
  NBNE BH10 ....322 E4
Frensham Heights Rd
  RFNM GU10 ....116 A8
Frensham La BOR GU35 ....154 D2
Frensham Rd ENEY PO4 ....317 H4
  FNM GU9 ....116 C6
Frensham V FLEETN GU51 ....74 F5
Frere Av FLEETN GU51 ....74 B5
Frescade Crs BSTK RG21 ......6 K9
Freshfield Gdns WVILLE PO7 ..275 N2
Freshfield Rd WSHM SO15 ....247 M4
Freshfield Sq WSHM SO15 ....247 M4
Freshwater Rd CHAM PO6 ....296 C2
  CHCH/BSGR BH23 ....325 N9
Freshwood Dr YTLY GU46 .....56 D1
Friars Cft TOTT SO40 ....245 P1
Friars Fld FNM GU9 ....96 E8
Friarsgate WINC SO23 ....213 H8
Friars Pond Rd FHAM PO15 ..272 A9
Friars Rd CHCH/BSGR BH23 ..325M9
  ELGH SO50 ....229 H3
Friars Wk NMIL/BTOS BH25 ..327 J7
Friary Cl SSEA PO5 ....316 E6
Friend Av ASHV GU12 ....97 K2
Friesian Cl CHFD SO53 ....56 E9
Frimley Green Rd FRIM GU16..58 D6
Frimley Grove Gdns
  FRIM GU16 ....58 C5
Frimley Hall Dr CBLY GU15 ...58 C5
Frimley Rd ASHV GU12 ....76 F4
  CBLY GU15 ....41 P9
Fritham Cl TOTT SO40 ....246 A4

Fritham Gdns CHAR BH8 ......323 K4
Fritham Rd WEND SO18 ....249 L3
Frith End Rd ALTN GU34 ......135 J2
Frith Rd ALTN GU34 ....58 F4
Frith La WHAM PO17 ....252 E5
Frithmead Cl BSTK RG21 ......90 C1
Frobisher Av
  BKME/WDN BH12 ....321 P3
Frobisher Cl
  CHCH/BSGR BH23 ....325 K9
  LSOL/BMARY PO13 ....314 G2
  RGWD BH24 ....282 C1
Frobisher Gdns EMRTH PO10 ..299 M1
  ITCH SO19 ....249 L7
Frobisher Gv
  FHAM/PORC PO16 ....295 N2
Frobisher Rd SSEA PO5 ....19 K4
Frodsham Wy SHST GU47 .....41 M4
Froghall FAWY SO45 ....268 B9
Frogham HI FBDG SP6 ....240 C4
Frog La FBDG SP6 ....240 C4
  HTWY RG27 ....53 L6
  OVTN RG25 ....70 G7
Frogmore FHAM/STUB PO14 ..294 A1
Frogmore La HORN PO8 ....255 P9
  ROWN SO16 ....227 H9
Frogmore Pk Dr BLKW GU17 ..57 L1
Frogmore Rd BLKW GU17 .....57 M1
  ENEY PO4 ....317 H4
Frogs Hole KSCL RG20 ....48 B3
Frome Cl BSTK RG21 ....7 J5
  DEAN RG23 ....88 G2
  FARN GU14 ....57 L7
  TOTT SO40 ....247 L9
Frome Rd WEND SO18 ....229 J9
Fromond Cl LYMN SO41 ......329 L2
Fromond Rd FUFL SO22 ....164 D4
Fromont Dr STHA RG19 ....25 N4
Frosthole Cl FHAM PO15 .....10 A2
Frosthole Crs FHAM PO15 ....10 A2
Frost La FAWY SO45 ....268 E8
Frost Rd BWD BH11 ....321 M1
Froud Cl HTWY RG27 ....71 N4
Froxfield Cl FUFL SO22 ....164 E3
Froxfield Gdns
  FHAM/PORC PO16 ....273 N9
Froxfield Rd HAV PO9 ....277 H5
Froyle La ODIM RG29 ....92 G8
Fry Cl FAWY SO45 ....291 H7
Fry's Cl SSEA PO5 ....316 E6
Fryer Cl BWD BH11 ....322 B2
Fryern Ar CHFD SO53 * 206 C6
Fryern Cl CHFD SO53 ....206 C6
Fryers Cl WINC SO23 ....145 K8
Fryer's Copse WIMB BH21 ....279 L8
Fryers Rd WIMB BH21 ....279 L8
Fry's La BPWT SO32 ....211 P9
  LYMN SO41 ....328 D6
  YTLY GU46 ....40 F6
Fry Sq AND SP10 * 82 F9
Fugelmere Rd FLEETN GU51 ..74 F2
Fulbrook Wy ODIM RG29 ......93 K3
Fulflood Rd HAV PO9 ....276 E5
Fullers La KSCL RG20 ....29 J8
Fullers V BOR GU35 ....154 G3
Fullerton Cl HAV PO9 ....277 H5
Fullerton Rd LYMN SO41 ......329 J3
  RAND SP11 ....101 N8
  RAND SP11 ....101 N8
Fullerton Wy TADY RG26 .....34 D7
Fulmar Cl KBH RG22 ....89 K4
  ROWN SO16 ....227M7
Fulmar Dr FAWY SO45 ....268 C8
Fulmar Rd CHCH/BSGR BH23..337 L1
Fulmer Wk HORN PO8 ....255 N7
Fulwood Av BWD BH11 ....301 N8
Funtington Rd NEND PO2 .....297 H9
Furdies WVILLE PO7 ....272 C6
Furley Cl WINC SO23 ....23 H4
The Furlong RGWD BH24 .....282 D2
Furneaux Gdns
  FHAM/PORC PO16 ....11 G1
Furnell Rd PLE BH15 ....332 E7
Furness Rd SSEA PO5 ....316 F7
Furniss Wy HISD PO11 ....318 D4
Furse Cl CBLY GU15 ....58 A8
Furse Hill Rd NTID SP9 ....79 H6
Further Vell-Mead
  FLEETS GU52 ....74 B8
Furv Wy FHAM/STUB PO14 ...293 P6
Furzebrook Cl CFDH BH17 ....320 C2
Furze Cl ASHV GU12 ....76 F5
  ITCH SO19 ....249 J6
Furze Ct NMIL/BTOS BH25 ...327 J6
Furzedale Gdns FAWY SO45 ..268 D9
Furzedale Pk FAWY SO45 .....268 D9
Furzedown Crs HAV PO9 ......276 C5
Furzedown La RAND SP11 ....100 E5
Furzedown Ms FAWY SO45 ...268 D9
Furzedown Rd PTSW SO17 ...247 H2
  STOK SO20 ....161 N7
Furze Dr RAND SP11 ....79 M5
Furzehall Av
  FHAM/PORC PO16 ....11 J1
Furzehill WIMB BH21 ....278 F5
Furze Hill Crs CWTH RG45 ....41 K2
Furze Hill Dr PSTN BH14 ......333 L2
Furze Hill Rd BOR GU35 ....155 J3
Furzelands Rd WIMB BH21 ...280 E1
Furze La ENEY PO4 ....317M3
Furzeley Rd WVILLE PO7 .....255 N9
Furze Meadow EPSF GU31 ....217 J5
Furze Rd DTN RG25 ....110 D3
Furze Rd ITCH SO19 ....249 J6
  TADY RG26 ....52 B3
Furze Vale Rd BOR GU35 .....155 J4
Furze Wy HORN PO8 ....256 D7

Furzey Cl FAWY SO45 .....291 H8
Furzey La BROC SO42 .....288 F8
Furzley Ct HAV PO9 .....276 C4
Furzley La ROMY SO51 .....224 D7
Furzey Rd ROMY SO51 .....224 D7
Fushia Ct HAV PO9 .....277 J6
Fushsia Gdns ROWN SO16 .....247 P1
Fuzzy Dro KBH RG22 .....89 K3
Fyeford Cl ROWN SO16 .....227 K6
Fyfield Cl BLKW GU17 .....41 L9
　FHAM PO15 .....13 J9
Fyfield La RAND SP11 .....80 C9
Fyfield Rd RAND SP11 .....80 C9
　STHA RG19 .....25 N5
Fyfield Wy FUFL SO22 .....164 C2
　RAND SP11 .....79 M5
Fylingdales STHA RG19 .....25 M5
Fylingdales Cl KBH RG22 .....68 D9
Fyning St PSEA PO1 .....19 J1

G

Gable End FARN GU14 * 58 A9
Gables Cl ASHV GU12 .....76 F7
　FARN GU14 .....57 P9
Gables Ct WINC SO23 .....228 B7
Gables Rd FLEETS GU52 .....74 C8
Gabriel Dr CBLY GU15 .....58 C1
The Gabriels NWBY RG14 .....24 A9
Gaffney Cl ALDT GU11 .....76 C5
Gage Cl CHIN RG24 .....70 A5
　TOTT SO40 .....247 L9
Gaiger Av HTWY RG27 .....52 C8
Gainsborough Av
　NMIL/BTOS BH25 .....327 K2
Gainsborough Cl FARN GU14 .....76 C2
Gainsborough Ct AND SP10 .....4 B1
Gainsborough Ms
　FHAM/STUB PO14 .....293 M1
Gainsborough Rd BSTK RG21 .....90 E1
　LTDN BH7 .....323 M8
　RGWD BH24 .....281 L4
Gainsford Rd ITCH SO19 .....248 C6
Gain's Rd ENEY PO4 .....316 C6
Galahad Cl AND SP10 .....2 C4
Galaxie Rd HORN PO8 .....256 B7
Gale Barracks ALDT GU11 * 76 A8
Gale Moor Av GPORT PO12 .....315 H5
Galileo Pk AND SP10 * 102 A1
Gallaghers Md AND SP10 .....101 P2
Galleon Cl ROWN SO16 .....270 F9
Galleon Pl GPORT PO12 .....315 P2
The Galleries ALDT GU11 * 2 E2
Galley La STHA RG19 .....32 A5
The Gallops FHAM/STUB PO14...271 K8
The Gallop YTLY GU46 .....40 E7
Gallop Wy BKME/WDN BH12 .....322 C8
Galloway Cl FLEETS GU51 .....56 F9
　KBH RG22 .....68 E9
Gallows Dr FERN BH22 .....302 D7
Gallwey Rd ALDT GU11 .....76 B9
Gally Hill Rd FLEETS GU52 .....74 C8
Galsworthy Rd TOTT SO40 .....246 B4
Galton Av CHCH/BSGR BH23 .....324 D9
Galt Rd CHAM PO6 .....297 M1
Galway Rd YTLY GU46 * 56 D1
Gamble Cl ITCH SO19 .....249 H7
Gambledown La ROMY SO51 .....178 E9
Gamblins La BPWT SO32 .....204 C3
Gander Dr CHIN RG24 .....68 F4
Gangbridge La RAND SP11 .....62 C9
Ganger Rd NWBY RG14 .....204 C3
Gannet Cl FAWY SO45 .....268 D8
　KBH RG22 .....89 K5
　ROWN SO16 .....227 M7
The Gannetts
　FHAM/STUB PO14 .....293 P7
Gapemouth Rd FRIM GU16 .....59 K8
Garbett Rd WINC SO23 .....23 J4
Garbetts Wy RFNM GU10 .....97 L5
Garbitts La EPSF GU31 .....217 K2
Garden City HTWY RG27 .....338 F1
Garden Cl AND SP10 .....5 F5
　FARN GU14 .....75 M2
　HISD PO11 .....318 F5
　HTWY RG27 .....71 N3
　KSCL RG20 .....264 C5
　NMIL/BTOS BH25 .....327 J6
　OVTN RG25 .....109 M9
Garden Close La NWBY RG14 .....30 C2
Gardeners Gn NTID SP9 .....98 F3
Gardener's Hill Rd
　RFNM GU10 .....116 B6
Gardeners La ROMY SO51 .....205 M7
Gardenia Dr FHAM PO15 .....271 L7
Garden La RGWD BH24 .....281 L6
　SSEA PO5 .....19 C7
　WINC SO23 .....23 F4
Garden Ter SSEA PO5 .....316 F6
Gardiner Cl TOTT SO40 .....247 J8
Gardner Rd CHCH/BSGR BH23...324 C7
　FHAM/STUB PO14 .....293 M2
　RGWD BH24 .....282 F3
Garendon Ct FBDG SP6 .....240 C1
Garfield Av BMTH BH1 .....335 K1
Garfield Cl BPWT SO32 .....232 A4
Garfield Rd BMTH BH1 .....335 K1
　HLER SO31 .....269 J4
　ITCH SO19 .....248 C4
　NEND PO2 .....296 F9

Garford Crs NWBY RG14 .....24 A7
Garland Av EMRTH PO10 .....277 M7
Garland Rd PLE BH15 .....320 F8
Garlands Cl THLE RG7 .....27 J5
Garland Wy YTLY GU46 .....245 P3
Garnet Fld YTLY GU46 .....40 B9
Garnet Rd BOR GU35 .....154 B6
Garnett Cl FHAM/STUB PO14...294 A5
Garnier Pk WHAM PO17 .....252 E7
Garnier Rd WINC SO23 .....184 A1
Garnier St PSEA PO1 .....19 K2
Garnock Rd ITCH SO19 .....248 F9
Garratt Cl HEND SO30 .....250 C1
Garrett Cl ITCH SO19 .....269 J1
　KSCL RG20 .....48 B2
Garrick Gdns ITCH SO19 .....249 J9
Garrick Wy FRIM GU16 .....58 D7
Garrison Hl BPWT SO32 .....233 M2
Garrow Dr LYMN SO41 .....329 L2
Garsdale Cl BWD BH11 .....322 A1
Garston Cl PSF GU32 .....213 M5
Garston Mede STOK SO20 .....125 L5
Garston La FHAM/STUB PO14...293 M1
Garstons Rd
　FHAM/STUB PO14 .....293 M1
Gar St WINC SO23 .....22 D5
Garth Cl FNM GU9 .....116 A3
　RGWD BH24 .....281 K5
Garth Md MOOR/WNTN BH9 .....322 D6
　THLE RG7 .....35 P1
The Garth ALTN GU34 .....132 C5
　ASHV GU12 .....97 M2
　FARN GU14 .....58 C9
　FAWY SO45 .....268 A8
Garton Av ITCH SO19 .....248 F8
Gascoigne La NARL SO24 .....169 L2
Gashouse Hl HLER SO31 .....269 L5
Gaskell Cl ALTN GU34 .....133 J5
Gaskell Ms NWBY RG14 .....17 C7
Gason Hill Rd NTID SP9 .....78 G3
Gaston La ALTN GU34 .....151 M5
　ODIM RG29 .....92 F5
Gatcombe HLER SO31 .....269 L5
Gatcombe Av HSEA PO3 .....297 H7
Gatcombe Dr NEND PO2 .....297 H6
Gatcombe Gdns
　FHAM/STUB PO14 .....293 P1
　WEND SO18 .....249 J1
Gatehouse La EPSF GU31 .....195 P8
Gate House Rd
　FHAM/PORC PO16 .....295 L2
Gatekeeper Cl WINC SO23 .....25 K4
The Gates FLEETN GU51 .....56 F9
Gatwick Cl ROWN SO16 .....227 L8
Gaulter Cl HAV PO9 .....15 H2
Gauvain Cl ALTN GU34 .....132 C7
Gavan St ITCH SO19 .....249 M6
G Av FAWY SO45 .....291 H3
Gawaine Cl AND SP10 .....82 E7
Gaydon Rd BWD BH11 .....301 N9
Gaylyn Wy FHAM/STUB PO14...293 P1
Gaywood Dr NWBY RG14 .....24 C3
Gaza Av BROC SO42 .....310 C2
Gazing La ROMY SO51 .....224 E1
Geale's Crs ALTN GU34 .....132 C4
Geddes Wy EPSF GU31 .....216 A1
Gemini Cl ROWN SO16 .....227 K8
Geneva Av SBNE BH6 .....336 B1
Genoa Cl LYMN SO41 .....329 J6
Genoa Ct AND SP10 .....82 F8
Gento Cl HEND SO30 .....250 E5
Geoffrey Av WVILLE PO7 .....275 K8
Geoffrey Crs
　FHAM/PORC PO16 .....294 F5
George Byng Wy NEND PO2 .....296 F8
George Curl Wy ELGH SO50 .....229 H6
George Denyer Cl
　HASM GU27 .....157 H6
George Eyston Dr FUFL SO22...164 E9
George Gdns ALDT GU11 .....97 J4
Georgeham Rd SHST GU47 .....41 L4
George Rd FLEETN GU51 .....74 E5
　LYMN SO41 .....338 F1
George St BSTK RG21 .....6 B6
　CHOB/PIR GU24 .....59 M7
　ELGH SO50 .....229 J1
　GPORT PO12 .....315 N5
　KSCL RG20 .....48 C3
　PSEA PO1 .....316 C1
George W Rd NTID SP9 .....78 C5
George Yd NARL SO24 .....168 A1
The George Yd NARL SO24 .....168 A1
Georgia Cl AND SP10 .....102 B4
Georgia Gdns TADY RG26 .....34 F6
Georgian La RAND SP11 .....100 E7
Georgian Cl RGWD BH24 .....282 E1
Georgian Wy NBNE BH10 .....322 C7
Georgina Cl BKME/WDN BH12...322 C7
Gerald Rd TWDS BH3 .....322 G9
Gerald Sq ALTN GU34 .....132 C3
Gerard Crs ITCH SO19 .....249 M5
Germaine Cl
　CHCH/BSGR BH23 .....326 B7
German Rd TADY RG26 .....52 B5
Gershwin Rd KBH RG22 .....89 N3
Gervis Crs PSTN BH14 .....321 J8
Gervis Pl BMTH BH1 .....8 D4
Gervis Rd BMTH BH1 .....9 J4
Gibbons Cl SHST GU47 .....41 K7
Gibbs' La BOR GU35 .....153 M2
Gibbs Rd SHAM SO14 .....4 D5
Gibbs Wy YTLY GU46 .....56 C1
Gibraltar Cl FHAM PO15 .....272 B8
Gibraltar Rd ENEY PO4 .....317 M5
　FHAM/STUB PO14 .....294 D5
Gibson Cl FHAM PO15 .....271 L5
　LSOL/BMARY PO13 .....314 D2
Gibson Rd CFDH BH17 .....320 C5
Giddylake WIMB BH21 .....278 E8
Gid La ALTN GU34 .....113 P7
Giffard Dr FARN GU14 .....58 A4
Giffards Meadow FNM GU9 .....116 E1
Gifford Cl FHAM PO15 .....10 A2

Gilbard Cl CHIN RG24 .....70 B1
Gilbert Cl CHIN RG24 .....69 M3
　FBDG SP6 .....239 P5
　LSOL/BMARY PO13 .....295 H9
　LYMN SO41 .....329 K5
Gilbert Md HISD PO11 .....318 E4
Gilbert Rd CHAR BH8 .....323 K9
　FRIM GU16 .....58 B4
Gilbert's Gn NTID SP9 .....98 G3
Gilberts Mead Cl RAND SP11...101 P6
Gilbert Wy NARL SO24 .....169 L1
Gilbert Wy WVILLE PO7 .....275 N5
Gilbert White Wy ALTN GU34...132 F4
Gilbury Cl WEND SO18 .....228 G8
Gilchrist Gdns HLER SO31 .....292 C2
Giles Cl TADY RG26 .....34 D6
Giles La ROMY SO51 .....202 A8
Giles Rd TADY RG26 .....34 D6
Gilkicker Rd GPORT PO12 .....315 N7
Gillam Rd NBNE BH10 .....322 D3
Gillcrest FHAM PO15 .....271 J6
Gillett Rd BKME/WDN BH12...322 C8
Gillham's La HASM GU27 .....175 P3
Gillian Av ASHV GU12 .....3 J6
Gillian Cl ASHV GU12 .....3 K6
Gillies Dr CHIN RG24 .....68 F4
The Gillies FHAM/PORC PO16...11 F6
Gillingham Cl
　MOOR/WNTN BH9 .....323 J4
Gillingham Rd LYMN SO41 .....338 C2
Gillman Rd CHAM PO6 .....275 N9
Gilpin Cl ITCH SO19 .....249 M6
　LYMN SO41 .....309 M7
Gilpin Hl LYMN SO41 .....308 B6
Gins La BROC SO42 .....311 P7
Girton Cl FHAM/STUB PO14 .....271 J9
　SHST GU47 .....41 M5
Gisbourne Ct NTID SP9 .....79 J5
Gitsham Gdns WVILLE PO7 .....275 L7
Gladdis Rd BWD BH11 .....301 P9
Glade Cl CHIN RG24 .....70 A2
Gladeland Rd FERN BH22 .....280 F9
Gladelands Cl BDST BH18 .....300 A9
Gladelands Pk FERN BH22 .....302 F1
Gladelands Wy BDST BH18 .....300 A9
The Glades HLER SO31 .....270 G6
The Glade CHFD SO53 .....207 H4
　FAWY SO45 .....312 C1
　FHAM PO15 .....272 B6
　FNM GU9 .....96 D4
　HISD PO11 .....76 E2
　HISD PO11 .....319 J6
　NWBY RG14 .....24 C8
　RFNM GU10 .....115 K9
　WVILLE PO7 .....276 A2
Gladiator Wy FARN GU14 .....75 P4
Gladstone Cl
　CHCH/BSGR BH23 .....325 H9
Gladstone Gdns
　FHAM/PORC PO16 .....295 N2
Gladstone Rd
　BKME/WDN BH12 .....321 L7
　GPORT PO12 .....315 L1
　ITCH SO19 .....249 K7
　LTDN BH7 .....335 M1
Gladstone Rd East LTDN BH7...335 M1
Gladstone Rd West
　BMTH BH1 .....335 L1
Gladstone St WINC SO23 .....22 D3
Gladys Av HORN PO8 .....256 A7
　NEND PO2 .....296 F7
Glaisdale STHA RG19 .....25 M5
Glamis Av NBNE BH10 .....322 E2
Glamis Cl DEAN RG23 .....88 F1
　FRIM GU16 .....58 E6
　WVILLE PO7 .....276 A2
Glamorgan Rd HORN PO8 .....256 B1
Glasgow Rd ENEY PO4 .....317 K1
Glasgow Wy WEND SO18 .....249 J5
Glasspool WVILLE PO7 .....254 C6
Glastonbury Cl CHIN RG24 .....69 K4
Glaston Hill Rd HTWY RG27 .....39 L6
Glayshers Hl BOR GU35 .....155 H2
Glaziers La RGUW GU3 .....77 N9
Gleadowe Av
　CHCH/BSGR BH23 .....324 D9
Glebe Cl ALDT GU11 .....96 C4
　ALTN GU34 .....131 K3
　HISD PO11 .....318 E3
　RAND SP11 .....109 H1
　RGWD BH24 .....282 D1
　TADY RG26 .....34 C4
Glebe Cnr WHAM PO17 .....252 F8
Glebe Ct ELGH SO50 .....230 D2
　FLEETN GU51 .....74 C3
　HEND SO30 .....250 C3
　PTSW SO17 .....248 C1
Glebe Dr LSOL/BMARY PO13...314 B6
Glebefield Gdns CHAM PO6 .....296 C1
Glebe Flds ALTN GU34 .....131 K3
Glebefields LYMN SO41 .....338 C1
　NWBY RG14 .....24 E2
Glebeland Rd CBLY GU15 .....57 N1
Glebelands RAND SP11 .....102 E8
　STHA RG19 .....25 M4
Glebe La DEAN RG23 .....68 D8
　HTWY RG27 .....55 J8
　RFNM GU10 .....137 J4
　RSAL SP5 .....201 M9
Glebe Park Av CHAM PO6 .....276 A9
Glebe Rd BOR GU35 .....154 F3
　EPSF GU31 .....215 K8
　SHAM SO14 .....57 N8
　WVILLE PO7 .....275 P4
The Glebe BLKW GU17 .....41 J9
　FARN GU14 .....294 A8
Glenair Av PSTN BH14 .....321 J9
Glenair Rd PSTN BH14 .....321 J9

Glenavon NMIL/BTOS BH25 .....327 K5
Glenavon Gdns YTLY GU46 .....56 E1
Glenavon Rd
　CHCH/BSGR BH23 .....326 B6
Glenbrook Vk
　FHAM/STUB PO14 .....294 A1
Glencarron Wy ROWN SO16...228 A9
Glen Cl AND SP10 .....5 F3
　NMIL/BTOS BH25 .....326 F7
Glencoe Cl FRIM GU16 .....58 B3
Glencoe Rd BKME/WDN BH12...321 M7
　LTDN BH7 .....323 M8
　PSEA PO1 .....317 H1
Glencoyne Gdns ROWN SO16...227 K1
Glenda Cl HLER SO31 .....292 D1
Glendale BPWT SO32 .....232 F8
Glendale Cl CHCH/BSGR BH23...324 B4
　WIMB BH21 .....278 E9
Glendale Pk FLEETS GU51 .....73 P2
Glendale Rd SBNE BH6 .....336 E2
　TADY RG26 .....34 B5
Glendene Pk
　NMIL/BTOS BH25 * 326 G2
Glendon Av NBNE BH10 .....322 C1
Glendowan Rd CHFD SO53 .....206 B6
Glendrive NMIL/BTOS BH25...326 E7
Gleneagles Cl DEAN RG23 .....89 L6
　FERN BH22 .....302 F2
Gleneagles Dr FARN GU14 .....75 K1
　HORN PO9 .....256 B7
Glenelg FHAM PO15 .....10 C3
Glenesha Gdns FHAM PO15...272 B8
Glen Eyre Dr ROWN SO16 .....228 C8
Glen Eyre Rd ROWN SO16 .....228 B7
Glen Eyre Wy ROWN SO16 .....228 C8
Glenfernes Av TWDS BH3 .....322 D9
Glen Fern Rd BMTH BH1 .....9 F3
Glenfield Av WEND SO18 .....249 H4
Glenfield Cl RSAL SP5 .....158 C1
Glenfield Crs WEND SO18 .....249 H4
Glenfield Wy WEND SO18 .....249 H4
Glengariff Rd PSTN BH14 .....333 L1
Glengarry NMIL/BTOS BH25...327 L1
Glengarry Wy
　CHCH/BSGR BH23 .....325 N9
Glenhurst Cl BWD BH11 .....57 M1
Glen Innes SHST GU47 .....41 N5
Glenives Cl RGWD BH24 .....281 M5
Glenlea Cl GSHT GU26 .....156 D4
Glenlea Cl HEND SO30 .....249 M2
Glenlea Hollow GSHT GU26 .....156 M3
Glenleigh Av CHAM PO6 .....277 H8
Glenleigh Pk HAV PO9 .....277 H8
Glenmead Av FERN BH22 .....302 C5
Glenmere Adows Dr BWD BH11...322 B2
Glenmoor Cl NBNE BH10 .....322 D6
Glenmoor Rd FERN BH22 .....302 C5
　MOOR/WNTN BH9 .....322 D7
Glenmore Cl STHA RG19 * 25 N5
Glenmount Dr PSTN BH14 .....321 J3
Glenmount Rd FHAM GU16 .....76 F2
Glenney Cl LSOL/BMARY PO13...314 E2
Glenn Rd HEND SO30 .....249 M1
　HLER SO31 .....270 F3
Glen Rd BOSC BH5 .....335 L2
　FLEETN GU51 .....74 C4
　GSHT GU26 .....156 D4
　HLER SO31 .....270 F3
　ITCH SO19 .....268 F1
　PSTN BH14 .....321 K8
Glenroyd Gdns SBNE BH6 .....336 B2
Glenside FAWY SO45 .....268 B7
　HEND SO30 * 249 M2
　NMIL/BTOS BH25 .....326 D8
Glenside Av ITCH SO19 .....249 M7
The Glen CCLF BH13 .....333 N5
　FNM GU9 .....96 C5
　LSOL/BMARY PO13 .....295 J8
　TADY RG26 .....34 F5
Glenthorne Cl
　FHAM/STUB PO14 .....294 B8
Glenthorne Meadow
　PSF GU32 .....215 N7
Glenthorne Rd HSEA PO3 .....297 J8
Glenville Cl CHCH/BSGR BH23...326 D5
Glenville Gdns GSHT GU26 .....156 D4
　NBNE BH10 .....322 C5
Glenville Rd CHCH/BSGR BH23...326 D5
　NBNE BH10 .....322 C5
Glenwood Cl ELGH SO50 .....230 E2
Glenwood Ct ELGH SO50 .....230 E2
Glenwood Gdns HORN PO8 .....255 P9
Glenwood La FERN BH22 .....280 E7
Glenwood Rd FERN BH22 .....280 E7
　VWD BH31 .....258 F5
Glenwood Wy FERN BH22 .....280 E7
Glidden Cl PSEA PO1 .....19 J2
Glidden La WVILLE PO7 .....234 G8
Glissons FERN BH22 .....302 A6
Globe Farm La BLKW GU17 .....41 J9
Globe Yd AND SP10 .....4 D5
Glorney Md FNM GU9 .....96 G5
Gloster Ct FNM PO15 .....271 J5
Gloucester Cl ALTN GU34 .....150 B6
　PSF GU32 .....215 K2
Gloucester Dr KBH RG22 .....89 M4
Gloucester Rd ALDT GU11 .....97 J4
　BMTH BH7 .....335 H1
　LTDN BH7 .....335 M1
　NWBY RG14 .....16 B3
　PSEA PO1 .....316 C2
　WIMB BH21 .....300 G1
　WINC SO23 .....23 E7
　WVILLE PO7 .....275 M4

RFNM GU10 .....116 A6
Glynville Cl WIMB BH21 .....279 J7
Glynville Rd WIMB BH21 .....279 J7
Glyn Wy FHAM/STUB PO14 .....294 A7
Goatacre Rd ALTN GU34 .....149 M5
Goat La BSTK RG21 .....6 C4
Goch Wy AND SP10 .....82 D9
Goddards Cl HTWY RG27 .....52 E5
Goddards Firs DEAN RG23 .....88 C3
Goddards La CBLY GU15 .....58 A2
Goddards Md AND SP10 .....102 C3
Goddard Sq AND SP10 .....82 D9
Godfrey Cl SHST GU47 .....41 L7
Godfrey Pink Wy BPWT SO32...232 B5
Godmanston Cl CFDH BH17 .....321 J3
God's Blessing La WIMB BH21...278 C3
Godshill Cl CHAR BH8 .....323 K4
Godwin Cl EMRTH PO10 .....277 K1
　FUFL SO22 .....164 D4
Godwin Crs HORN PO8 .....236 C8
Godwit Cl GPORT PO12 .....295 M9
Godwit Rd ENEY PO4 .....317 L3
Gofton Av CHAM PO6 .....297 K2
Gogg's La RSAL SP5 .....200 B7
Goldcrest Cl
　FHAM/PORC PO16 .....295 J1
　HORN PO8 .....256 A4
　YTLY GU46 .....40 C8
Goldcrest Gdns ROWN SO16...227 L7
Goldcrest La TOTT SO40 .....246 A5
Golden Ct HEND SO30 .....249 P1
Golden Crs LYMN SO41 .....328 D6
Goldenfield Cl LIPH SO50 .....175 L4
Golden Flds LIPH GU30 .....175 L4
Golden Gv SHAM SO14 .....21 G3
Golden Hind Pk FAWY SO45...268 B8
Goldenleas Dr BWD BH11 .....321 M1
Golden Lion Rbt BSTK RG21 .....90 D2
Goldfinch Cl ALDT GU11 .....2 C7
　NMIL/BTOS BH25 .....327 H5
Goldfinch Rd KBH RG22 .....89 K5
Goldfinch La
　LSOL/BMARY PO13 .....314 D1
Goldfinch Rd CFDH BH17 .....320 A4
Goldfinch Rd RWIN SO21 .....144 F3
Gold Hl BOR GU35 * 134 G8
Goldhill RFNM GU10 .....116 C4
Gold La ALDT GU11 .....96 C3
Gold Mead Cl HLER SO31 .....329 L5
Goldney Rd CBLY GU15 .....58 C1
Goldring Cl HISD PO11 .....318 C5
Goldsmith Rd ELGH SO50 .....229 H5
Goldsmith Wy CWTH RG45 .....41 J2
Gold St SSEA PO5 .....19 F6
Goldwell Dr NWBY RG14 .....24 C3
Goldwire Dr CHFD SO53 .....206 B8
Golf Course Rd ROWN SO16...228 A6
Golf Dr CBLY GU15 .....69 J8
Golf La BOR GU35 .....153 N7
Golf Links Rd BDST BH18 .....300 D8
　HLER SO31 .....302 E3
Gomer La GPORT PO12 .....315 J4
Gondreville Gdns FLEETS GU52...74 B8
Gong Hl RFNM GU10 .....116 D7
Gong Hill Dr RFNM GU10 .....116 D6
Gooden Crs FARN GU14 .....75 N2
The Goodens NARL SO24 .....186 C1
Goodison Cl ELGH SO50 .....230 A3
Goodlands V HEND SO30 .....250 A5
Goodman Cl BSTK RG21 .....89 J8
Good Rd BKME/WDN BH12...321 M5
Goodsell Cl FHAM/STUB PO14...293 P7
Goodwin Cl ROWN SO16 .....247 N1
Goodwood Cl ALTN GU34 .....132 F7
　FHAM/STUB PO14 .....271 J8
　GPORT PO12 .....295 M9
　THLE RG7 .....276 B1
Goodwood Gdns TOTT SO40...246 A3
Goodwood Pl FARN GU14 .....76 D1
Goodwood Rd ELGH SO50 .....206 G9
　SSEA PO5 .....18 E5
Goodwood Wy NWBY RG14 .....17 K5
Goodwyns Cl NTID SP9 .....98 F3
Goodwyns Cl ALTN GU34 .....132 G3
Goodyers ALTN GU34 .....132 G6
Goose Gn HTWY RG27 .....71 N2
Goose Green Wy STHA RG19 .....25 P1
Goose La HTWY RG27 .....71 P2
Gordon Av CBLY GU15 .....58 A1
　FLEETS GU52 .....74 E6
　SHAM SO14 .....248 C3
　WINC SO23 .....23 K7
Gordon Cl BSTK RG21 .....6 C3
Gordon Crs CBLY GU15 .....58 B1
Gordon Mt CHCH/BSGR BH23...326 D5
Gordon Palmer Cl THLE RG7...36 C1
Gordon Rd ALDT GU11 .....2 E4
　BKME/WDN BH12 .....334 A1
　BMTH BH1 .....8 A3
　BPWT SO32 .....351 M2
　CBLY GU15 .....58 B1
　CHCH/BSGR BH23 .....326 C2
　CHFD SO53 .....206 F4
　ELGH SO50 .....41 L3
　EMRTH PO10 .....277 H7
　FARN GU14 .....76 C4
　FHAM/PORC PO16 .....10 E5
　GPORT PO12 .....12 B3
　LYMN SO41 .....329 J4
　NTHA RG18 .....25 K2
　NWBY RG14 .....16 B1
　PSEA PO1 .....18 E7
　WIMB BH21 .....300 G1
　WINC SO23 .....23 J7
　WVILLE PO7 .....275 M4
Gordon Rd South
　BKME/WDN BH12 .....334 A2
Gordon Ter ITCH SO19 .....249 J9
Gordon Wk YTLY GU46 .....56 D3
Gore End Rd KSCL RG20 .....29 J3

Gore Rd NMIL/BTOS BH25 ....326 G5
Gorey Rd BKME/WDN BH12 ...321 M5
Goring Av HORN PO8 ....236 D8
Goring Fld FUFL SO22 ....164 D6
Goring La THLE RG7 ....27 H6
Gorleston Rd
  BKME/WDN BH12 ....321 P7
Gorley Ct HAV PO9 ....276 C4
Gorley Lynch FBDG SP6 ....241 J6
Gorley Rd RGWD BH24 ....281 J6
Gorran Av LSOL/BMARY PO13 ...294 C8
The Gorrings STOK SO20 ....161 M5
Gorsecliff Rd BMTH BH10 ......322 D6
Gorse CI FNM GU9 ....116 A4
  HLER SO31 ....270 F8
  NMIL/BTOS BH25 ....327 K5
  RGWD BH24 ....281 K5
Gorsedown CI BOR GU35 ....153 N7
Gorsefield Rd
  NMIL/BTOS BH25 ....327 K2
Gorse Hill CI PLE BH15 ....320 C7
Gorse Hill Crs PLE BH15 ....320 C7
Gorse Knoll Dr VWD BH31 ......258 C3
Gorseland Ct FERN BH22 ....302 E5
Gorselands NBWY RG14 ....30 C1
  TADY RG26 ....34 C5
  YTLY GU46 ....64 D6
Gorselands CI ASHV GU12 ....76 F7
  BOR GU35 ....155 K4
Gorselands Rd WEND SO18 ....249 K2
Gorselands Wy
  LSOL/BMARY PO13 ....295 H9
Gorse La RFNM GU10 ....116 A4
Gorse Rd EPSF GU31 ....216 A2
  FRIM GU16 ....58 D3
Gorseway FLEETS GU52 ....74 D5
The Gorseway HISD PO11 ....318 D5
Gort CI ALDT GU11 ....76 D5
Gort Crs ITCH SO19 ....249 F7
Gort Rd BWD BH11 ....322 B4
  CFDH BH17 ....320 C3
Goscombs La NARL SO24 ....148 C9
Gosling CI CFDH BH17 ....321 H5
Goslings Cft ALTN GU34 ....152 D7
Gosnell CI FRIM GU16 ....59 J2
Gosport La LYND SO43 ....264 G6
Gosport Rd FHAM/PORC PO16 ...11 H7
  FHAM/STUB PO14 ....294 B7
  LSOL/BMARY PO13 ....314 D3
Gosport St LYMN SO41 ....329 M5
Gough Crs CFDH BH17 ....320 A2
Gough Rd FLEETN GU51 ....74 B2
Gough's Meadow SHST GU47 ....41 J7
Gould CI NBWY RG14 ....17 J2
  RAND SP11 ....79 N1
Government House Rd
  ALDT GU11 ....75 P5
Government Rd ALDT GU11 ......76 D8
Governor's Rd CBLY GU15 ....41 N8
Gover Rd ROWN SO16 ....246 C2
Gower CI BSTK RG21 ....6 E2
Gower Crs HTWY RG27 ....72 C7
Gower Pk SHST GU47 ....41 H6
Grace Bennett CI FARN GU14 * ...57 P6
Grace Dieu Gdns FARN SO31 * ...269 P1
Gracemere Crs KBH RG22 ....89 K4
Grace Sq AND SP10 ....82 C9
Gracious St ALTN GU34 ....152 C8
Graddidge Wy TOTT SO40 ....206 B4
Gradwell La ALTN GU34 ....150 B8
Graemar La ROMY SO51 ....202 C4
Grafton CI BOR GU35 ....154 B6
  CHCH/BSGR BH23 ....325 H9
  GPORT PO12 ....12 E7
  TWDS BH3 ....322 G8
Grafton Gdns LYMN SO41 ....329 J6
  ROWN SO16 ....227 N7
Grafton St NEND PO2 ....316 E1
Grafton Wy KBH RG22 ....68 G8
Graham Rd ENEY PO4 ....316 G5
  GPORT PO12 ....315 L2
  SHAM SO14 ....21 J1
Graham St SHAM SO14 ....21 J1
Grainger CI KBH RG22 ....90 A2
Grainger Gdns ITCH SO19 ....249 L8
Grammar School La
  WIMB BH21 ....300 D1
Grammarsham La OVTN RG25 ....90 B9
Grampian Rd SHST GU47 ....40 G4
Grampian Wy KBH RG22 ....68 E9
  CHCH BH23 ....256 A2
Granada PI AND SP10 ....256 F2
Granada Rd ENEY PO4 ....316 C7
  HEND SO30 ....250 A6
The Granary NBWY RG14 * 16 D2
Granby End THLE RG7 ....27 K4
Granby Rd BKME/WDN BH12 ....322 C3
Grand Av SBNE BH6 ....336 A2
Grand Pde FUFL SO22 ....164 D2
  HISD PO11 ....318 C6
  PLE BH15 * 332 D2
Grand Trunk Rd NTID SP9 ....78 E7
Grange WIMB BH21 ....278 E5
Grange CI GPORT PO12 ....315 K2
  HAV PO9 ....15 K4
  LYMN SO41 ....328 E7
Grange Ct HLER SO31 ....269 K4
  RFNM GU10 * 97 L5
Grange Crs GPORT PO12 ....315 K2
Grange Dr HEND SO30 ....250 D3
Grange Farm Rd ASHV GU12 .....76 F9
Grange Gdns
  BKME/WDN BH12 ....321 N5
Grange La HTWY RG27 ....54 G8
  LSOL/BMARY PO13 ....294 C9
Grange Ms ROMY SO51 ....204 C4
Grange Rd ASHV GU12 ....97 P2

BDST BH18 ....300 C9
CHCH/BSGR BH23 ....325 MB
FLEETS GU52 ....58 A6
FLEETS GU52 ....74 C7
HEND SO30 ....250 D4
HLER SO31 ....269 K4
LSOL/BMARY PO13 ....315 H4
NARL SO24 ....167 P2
NEND PO2 ....296 F8
PSF GU32 ....215 L3
RFNM GU10 ....97 L5
RFNM GU10 ....157 H1
RGWD BH24 ....281 K7
ROWN SO16 ....247 M2
SBNE BH6 ....336 B5
WINC SO23 ....185 N3
The Grange LYMN SO41 ....328 E7
  NWBY RG14 ....30 B1
Grangewood Gdns
  ELGH SO50 ....250 B2
Grantham Av HLER SO31 ....269 F2
Grantham Cl SHST GU47 ....41 M5
Grantham Rd BMTH BH1 ....335 L8
  ELGH SO50 ....229 J2
  ITCH SO19 ....249 H5
Grantley Ct FNM GU9 ....115 P4
Grantley Dr FLEETS GU52 ....74 C5
Grantley Rd BOSC BH5 ....335 M2
Grant Rd CHAM PO6 ....297 M1
  CWTH RG45 ....42 A3
Grant's Av BMTH BH1 ....323 K9
Grants Cl BMTH BH1 ....323 K9
Granville Cl HAV PO9 ....15 J6
Granville Pl WINC SO23 ....25 G7
Granville Rd BOSC BH5 ....335 N1
  PSTN BH14 ....321 K7
Granville St SHAM SO14 ....21 H5
Grasdean Cl WEND SO18 ....249 J2
Grasmere CI ELGH SO50 ....229 H2
Grasmere Ct BOR GU35 ....154 A3
  CHCH/BSGR BH23 ....324 B4
  WEND SO18 ....249 K2
Grasmere Gdns
  NMIL/BTOS BH25 ....327 K2
Grasmere Rd BOSC BH5 ....335 N2
  CCLF BH15 ....333 K8
  FARN GU14 ....75 M1
  FNM GU9 ....96 A5
Grasmere Wy
  FHAM/STUB PO14 ....294 B5
Graspan Rd RAND SP11 ....80 B2
Grassington Pl STHA RG19 ....25 N5
Grassmere Wy HORN PO8 ....256 B9
Grassymead FHAM PO15 ....271 J6
Grateley Cl ITCH SO19 ....269 H2
Grateley Crs HAV PO9 ....276 C6
Grateley Dro RAND SP11 ....99 P9
Grateley Rd AMSY SP4 ....86 F9
Gratton Cl RWIN SO21 ....125 M5
Gravel CI NARL SO24 ....128 G5
  RSAL SP5 ....99 J5
Gravel Hl BPWT SO32 ....232 F9
  CFDH BH17 ....320 E1
  WIMB BH21 ....300 F4
Gravel Hill Rd RFNM GU10 ....115 J5
Gravel La ALTN GU34 ....149 P7
  RGWD BH24 ....282 D2
  RWIN SO21 ....124 F3
Gravelly Cl KSCL RG20 ....29 H3
  TADY RG26 ....34 D8
Gravel Rd FARN GU14 ....76 C4
  FLEETS GU52 ....74 E6
  FNM GU9 ....96 B4
Graveney Sq AND SP10 ....82 F9
Gray CI CFDH BH17 ....321 H4
  HLER SO31 ....269 J4
Graycot CI NBNE BH10 ....322 C2
Grayland Cl HISD PO11 ....318 E5
Grayling Md ROMY SO51 ....204 D4
Graylings WSHM SO15 * 204 D4
Grays Av FAWY SO45 ....268 D7
Grays CI ELGH SO50 ....207 P5
  GPORT PO12 ....315 J5
  HASM GU27 ....157 K5
  ROMY SO51 ....204 D6
Grays Ct PSEA PO1 ....18 D5
Grayshot Dr BLKW GU17 ....41 K9
Grayshott Cl FUFL SO22 ....164 E5
Grayshott Laurels BOR GU35 ....154 D2
Grayshott Rd BOR GU35 ....155 K5
  ENEY PO4 ....317 H4
  GPORT PO12 ....315 K4
Grayson CI
  LSOL/BMARY PO13 ....314 C2
Grayswood Dr FRIM GU16 ....76 F3
Grayswood Ms HASM GU27 * ...157 L3
Grayswood Rd HASM GU27 ....157 J5
Gray's Yd PLE BH15 * 332 E2
Grazeley Rd THLE RG7 ....36 D1
Great Austins FNM GU9 ....116 D2
Great Binfields Crs CHIN RG24 ...70 A4
Great Binfields Rd CHIN RG24 ...70 A3
Great Br ROMY SO51 ....204 C3
Greatbridge Rd ROMY SO51 .....204 C2
Great Copse Dr HAV PO9 ....276 F5
Great Elms Cl FAWY SO45 ....290 D6
Greater Horseshoe Wy
  WHAM PO17 ....272 C2
Greatfield Cl FARN GU14 ....58 A5
Greatfield Rd FARN GU14 ....57 P5
Great Field Rd FUFL SO22 ....164 B7
Greatfield Wy HAV PO9 ....257 H9
Great Gays FHAM/STUB PO14 ...295 N8
Great Hanger EPSF GU31 ....215 P2
Great La WHCH RG28 ....85 L6
Great Md LYND SO43 * 80 F4
  WVILLE PO7 ....255 J8
Great Minster St WINC SO23 * ...22 E5
Great Oaks Cha CHIN RG24 ....69 P7
Great Sheldons Coppice
  HTWY RG27 ....71 N3
Great Southsea St SSEA PO5 .....19 G6
Great Well Dr ROMY SO51 ....204 D5
Greatwood Cl FAWY SO45 ....268 C8
Greaves Cl NBNE BH10 * 322 C4

Grebe Cl ALTN GU34 ....132 F3
  CFDH BH17 ....320 A4
  CHCH/BSGR BH23 ....325 L9
  EMRTH PO10 ....277 P6
  FHAM/PORC PO16 ....295 K1
  HORN PO8 ....255 N7
  KBH RG22 ....89 K4
  LYMN SO41 ....339 H2
Greenacre ALDT GU11 ....2 C5
Greenacre KSCL RG20 ....48 C3
  NMIL/BTOS BH25 ....327 J7
Greenacre Gdns WVILLE PO7 ...275 M6
Greenacres BOR GU35 ....154 C4
Green Acres Cl RGWD BH24 .....282 B4
Greenacres Dr RWIN SO21 ......207 L2
Greenaway La HLER SO31 ....270 E8
Green Banks Cl GPORT PO12 ....315 K1
Greenbanks La LYMN SO41 ......338 C1
Greenbanks Gdns
  FHAM/PORC PO16 ....273 H6
Greenberry Br RGWD BH24 ......306 E1
Greenbirch Cl KBH RG22 ....68 K4
Green Bottom WIMB BH21 ....279 J7
Greenbury Cl DEAN SO22 ....164 A7
Green Cl FAWY SO45 ....268 C6
  NARL SO24 ....148 A7
  PLE BH15 ....332 F2
  RSAL SP5 ....201 K1
  RWIN SO21 ....144 F4
  TOTT SO40 ....245 M7
Greenclose La WIMB BH21 ....300 F1
Green Crs LSOL/BMARY PO13 ...294 C8
Greencroft FARN GU14 ....58 A9
Green Cross La RFNM GU10 .....136 C8
Greendale Cl FHAM PO15 ....294 B6
The Greendale FHAM PO15 ......272 B6
Green Dro RAND SP11 ....92 F8
Greenfield CI LIPH GU30 ....175 K2
Greenfield Crs HORN PO8 ....256 C7
Greenfield Gdns
  NMIL/BTOS BH25 ....327 K7
Greenfield Ri HORN PO8 ....256 B8
Greenfield Rd FNM GU9 ....115 P3
  PLE BH15 ....320 C6
Greenfields EPSF GU31 ....217 J6
  LISS GU33 ....192 C3
  RAND SP11 ....101 N6
  RSAL SP5 ....176 C4
Greenfields CI ELGH SO50 ....217 J5
  TOTT SO40 ....246 C2
Greenfinch CI CFDH BH17 ....320 B3
  ELGH SO50 ....228 F3
Greenfinch Wk RGWD BH24 ....282 C3
Green Glades FLEETS GU52 ....74 C7
Greenham Cl STHA RG19 ....25 M5
Greenham Rd NWBY RG14 ....17 C5
Greenhanger RFNM GU10 ....136 F9
Greenhaven YTLY GU46 ....40 C9
Greenhaven Cl AND SP10 ....9 H5
Greenhayes BDST BH18 ....321 J2
Greenhays Ri WIMB BH21 ....278 E9
Greenhill Av FUFL SO22 ....22 A4
Greenhill Cl FUFL SO22 ....116 A5
  FUFL SO22 ....22 A4
  WIMB BH21 ....278 F8
Greenhill La ROWN SO16 ....227 J4
  WIMB BH21 ....278 F8
Greenhill Rd FNM GU9 ....116 D2
  FUFL SO22 ....164 E7
  WIMB BH21 ....278 F8
Greenhill Ter FUFL SO22 ....22 A4
Greenhill Wy FNM GU9 ....116 A4
Green Hollow Cl
  FHAM/PORC PO16 ....10 C1
Green Jacket Cl FUFL SO22 ......183 N1
Greenlands Rd CBLY GU15 ....58 A4
  KSCL RG20 ....48 C3
  NWBY RG14 ....17 C7
Green La ALTN GU34 ....150 A8
  ALTN GU34 ....170 D3
  BLKW GU17 ....57 J1
  BPWT SO32 ....232 C5
  FAWY SO45 ....291 H9
  FBDG SP6 ....220 A5
  FBDG SP6 ....240 D1
  FERN BH22 ....302 A7
  FNM GU9 ....116 A2
  GPORT PO12 ....295 N9
  GPORT PO12 ....12 A6
  HASM GU27 ....156 C9
  HISD PO11 ....318 E6
  HLER SO31 ....269 K4
  HLER SO31 ....270 A8
  HLER SO31 ....270 F9
  HLER SO31 ....270 C1
  HORN PO8 ....256 A2
  HSEA PO3 ....297 J6
  HTWY RG27 ....55 N4
  NARL SO24 ....168 F2
  NARL SO24 ....148 A2
  NBNE BH10 ....322 C4
  NMIL/BTOS BH25 ....327 K7
  NWBY RG14 ....16 A3
  OVTN RG25 ....110 C2
  PSF GU32 ....190 F1
  RAND SP11 ....101 J5
  RFNM GU10 ....110 A4
  RFNM GU10 ....183 N5
  RFNM GU10 ....136 F9
  RGWD BH24 ....281 N8
  ROMY SO51 ....228 D3
  ROWN SO16 ....247 J1

RSAL SP5 ....199 K5
SHST GU47 ....41 K6
STHA RG19 ....25 M4
TADY RG26 ....35 F2
THLE RG7 ....26 E5
THLE RG7 ....36 E6
TOTT SO40 ....226 A8
WVILLE PO7 ....234 D6
WVILLE PO7 ....254 D6
WVILLE PO7 ....254 G6
  ....40 C7
Green Leys FLEETS GU52 ....40 D7
Greenmead Av LYMN SO41 ....328 D6
Green Meadows La
  RAND SP11 ....102 E8
Green Park Cl WINC SO23 ....165 J5
Green Park Rd ROWN SO16 ......247 J4
Green Pond Cnr HAV PO9 ....15 K6
Green Pond Cl ROMY SO51 ......205 N2
Green Ride Cl HTWY RG27 ....54 C1
Green Rd FHAM/STUB PO14 .....294 A5
  GPORT PO12 ....12 A6
  GPORT PO12 ....315 M2
  PLE BH15 ....332 E1
  SSEA PO5 ....19 G6
  WINC SO23 ....165 J5
Greensand Wy FNM GU9 ....96 E9
  GSHT GU26 ....156 F3
  HASM GU27 ....157 H6
  RFNM GU10 ....117 K8
Green Sleeves Av HTWY RG27 ...54 E2
Greens Cl BPWT SO32 ....231 P4
  ELGH SO50 ....230 A3
Greenside CWTH RG45 ....40 G1
Greensleeves Av BDST BH18 ....300 D7
Greensleeves Av LISS GU33 .....199 P7
Greens Meade RSAL SP5 ....199 P7
Greensome Dr FERN BH22 ....302 D6
Green Springs RFNM GU10 ....95 H4
Green Stile ALTN GU34 ....149 P2
Green St BOR GU35 ....134 B9
The Green AND SP10 ....82 C9
  FNM GU9 ....96 C5
  FNM GU9 ....116 A2
  FRIM GU16 ....58 E7
  HLER SO31 ....270 E4
  HTWY RG27 ....55 K7
  LISS GU33 ....192 C5
  OVTN RG25 ....87 H5
  PSF GU32 ....190 F1
  RFNM GU10 ....117 L1
  ROMY SO51 ....204 C3
  RSAL SP5 ....201 K1
  RWIN SO21 ....124 G2
  STOK SO20 ....121 H5
  WBNE BH4 ....334 C1
  WHCH RG28 ....85 M6
Green Wk FHAM PO15 ....10 A1
Green Wy ASHV GU12 ....76 D9
  BSTK RG21 ....68 F8
Greenway HTWY RG27 ....52 E5
Greenway Cl LYMN SO41 ....329 J5
Greenway La EPSF GU31 ....215 J7
Greenway Rd GPORT PO12 ....315 M2
Greenways BPWT SO32 ....232 F7
  CHCH/BSGR BH23 ....326 B7
  FOLD SO53 ....206 F7
  FLEETS GU52 ....74 C7
  KSCL RG20 ....29 M5
  LYMN SO41 ....338 F1
  ROWN SO16 ....227 F8
  SHST GU47 ....41 J5
Greensways Av CHAM BH8 ......323 J4
Greenways Rd BROC SO42 ......266 D8
The Greenwich FAWY SO45 ......290 C7
Greenwich Wy AND SP10 ....82 E9
Greenwood Av CHAM PO6 ....296 F1
  FERN BH22 ....302 D2
  PSTN BH14 ....333 L3
  ROWN SO16 ....227 H6
Greenwood Cl
  FHAM/PORC PO16 ....272 E6
  ROMY SO51 ....204 E5
Greenwood Copse
  RGWD BH24 ....281 M5
Greenwood La CHIN RG24 ....52 A9
Greenwood La BPWT SO32 ......230 C4
Greenwood Rd
  CHOB/PIR GU24 ....59 N7
  MOOR/WNTN BH9 ....322 E6
Greenwoods
  NMIL/BTOS BH25 ....327 K6
  WHCH RG28 ....85 L5
Greenwood Wy RGWD BH24 ....281 M5
Greetham St SSEA PO5 ....19 H3
Gregory Cl BSTK RG21 ....7 H1
Gregory Gdns TOTT SO40 ....246 A2
Gregory St HTWY RG27 ....52 C1
Gregson Av
  LSOL/BMARY PO13 ....294 G6
Gregson Cl
  LSOL/BMARY PO13 ....294 G6
Greig Rd KBH RG22 ....90 A2
Grenadier Rd ASHV GU12 ....271 H8
Grenadier Rd ASHV GU12 ....75 K1
Grenadiers Wy FARN GU14 ....75 K1
Grendon Cl ROWN SO16 ....228 D7
Grenehurst Wy EPSF GU31 * 215 M2
Grenfell Rd MOOR/WNTN BH9 ...322 F4
Grenoble Cl HTWY RG27 ....52 B9
Grenville CI LIPH GU30 ....175 K5
  RGWD BH24 ....260 G9
Grenville Dr FLEETN GU51 ....74 B5
Grenville Gdns FAWY SO45 ....268 C9
  FRIM GU16 ....58 D7
Grenville Rd ENEY PO4 ....316 C4
  SSEA PO5 ....19 H1
Gresham Rd
  MOOR/WNTN BH9 ....322 C6
Gresham Wy FRIM GU16 ....58 D7
Gresley Gdns HEND SO30 ....250 C1
Gresley Rd BSTK RG21 ....7 H4

Grevillea Av FHAM PO15 ....271 L7
Greville Cl ALDT GU11 ....2 D2
Greville Rd ENEY PO4 ....277 L7
Greville Rd WSHM SO15 ....247 P4
Greyberry Copse Rd
  STHA RG19 ....24 C7
Greyfriars Rd FHAM PO15 ....272 A8
Greyhound Cl ASHV GU12 ....86 C4
  HEND SO30 ....230 B9
Greyshott Av
  FHAM/STUB PO14 ....294 A1
Greystead Pk RFNM GU10 ....115 N4
Greystoke Av BWD BH11 ....301 P7
Greystoke Ct CWTH RG45 ....41 H2
Greywell Av ROWN SO16 ....227 M6
Greywell Cl TADY RG26 ....34 B6
Greywell Rd CHIN RG24 ....70 E7
  HAV PO9 ....276 E5
Grieve Ct RFNM GU10 ....71 K8
Griffen Cl ELGH SO50 ....229 N2
Griffin Ct PTSW SO17 ....248 E1
Griffin Wk LSOL/BMARY PO13 ...314 G2
Griffin Wy North HTWY RG27 ......72 A1
Griffin Wy South HTWY RG27 .....72 A1
Griffiths Gdns BWD BH11 ....322 D2
Griffon CI FARN GU14 ....75 L1
  HLER SO31 ....270 A1
Grigg La BROC SO42 ....286 G8
Grimstead Rd RSAL SP5 ....176 A4
Grindle CI CHAM PO6 ....297 K5
Gritanwood Rd ENEY PO4 ....317 K5
Grosvenor Cl KBH RG22 ....89 M6
  PTSW SO17 ....248 E1
  RGWD BH24 ....281 K4
Grosvenor Ct BLKW GU17 ....57 L2
Grosvenor Dr WINC SO23 ....165 J5
Grosvenor Gdns BMTH BH1 .....335 L2
  HEND SO30 ....250 C8
  PTSW SO17 ....248 E1
Grosvenor House
  WSHM SO15 * 248 B5
Grosvenor Lawn
  NWBY RG14 * 16 A3
Grosvenor Ms LYMN SO41 * 329 L2
  PTSW SO17 * 248 E1
Grosvenor Rd ALDT GU11 ....2 D3
  ALTN GU34 ....149 P6
  CHFD SO53 ....206 E1
  PTSW SO17 * 248 E1
  WBNE BH4 ....334 C1
Grosvenor Sq WSHM SO15 ....20 D1
Grosvenor St SSEA PO5 ....19 H4
Grove Av FHAM/PORC PO16 .....295 N3
  GPORT PO12 * 12 B6
Groveburry HLER SO31 ....270 G8
Grove CI BSTK RG21 ....69 K1
Grove Cross Rd FRIM GU16 ....58 C4
Grove Farm Pk FRIM GU16 * 76 C1
Grovefields Av FRIM GU16 ....58 C4
Grove Gdns ITCH SO19 ....269 K1
Groveland Rd NBWY RG14 ....24 A2
Grovelands RFNM GU10 ....116 E3
Grovelands Rd FUFL SO22 ....164 C4
Grove La RSAL SP5 ....200 B6
Grovely Rd
  CHCH/BSGR BH23 ....325 J9
  WBNE BH4 ....334 B4
Grovely Av BOSC BH5 ....335 M2
Grovely Wy ROMY SO51 ....205 J4
Grove Pastures LYMN SO41 .....329 L4
Grove PI ITCH SO19 ....249 K9
  LYMN SO41 ....329 L4
Grove Rd ALTN GU34 ....132 F7
  ASHV GU12 ....76 F8
  BKME/WDN BH12 ....321 K6
  BMTH BH1 * 9 G4
  BSTK RG21 ....69 M9
  CHAM PO6 ....297 L2
  FHAM/PORC PO16 ....10 E6
  FLEETS GU52 ....74 E4
  GPORT PO12 ....315M2
  HAV PO9 ....15 G6
  LSOL/BMARY PO13 ....314 C2
  LYMN SO41 ....329 M4
  NMIL/BTOS BH25 ....327 J8
  NWBY RG14 ....24 A2
  SHAM SO14 ....21 H2
  WIMB BH21 ....300 A5
  WSHM SO15 ....247 N4
Grove Rd East
  CHCH/BSGR BH23 ....324 E7
Grove Rd North SSEA PO5 ....19 H6
Grove Rd South SSEA PO5 ....19 H7
Grove Rd West
  CHCH/BSGR BH23 ....324 C7
Grovers Cl SO51 ....144 D4
Grovers Down NWBY RG14 ......202 E9
Groves Lea THLE RG7 ....27 H9
The Grove ALDT GU11 ....2 C6
  CHCH/BSGR BH23 ....324 C6
  EMRTH PO10 ....277 P7
  FARN GU14 ....76 C3
  FERN BH22 ....302 C4
  FHAM/STUB PO14 ....295 P8
  FRIM GU16 ....58 C4
  HLER SO31 ....269M3
  HLER SO31 ....270 A1
  ITCH SO19 ....269 K1
  LIPH GU30 ....175 J3
  MOOR/WNTN BH9 ....322 F4
  NTHA RG18 ....5 H5
  RAND SP11 ....81 M7
  VWD BH31 ....258 C5
Grower Gdns BWD BH11 ....322 A3
Gubbins La NEND PO2 ....296 E9
Guardhouse Rd PSEA PO1 ....316 D1
Guardroom Rd NEND PO2 ....296 D8
Guernsey CI CHIN RG24 ....69 P6
  ROWN SO16 ....227 J9
Guernsey Dr FLEETN GU51 ....56 E9

Guernsey Rd
 BKME/WDN BH12 ......321 M3
Guessens La
 FHAM/STUB PO14 ......295 M1
Guest Av BKME/WDN BH12 ...321 P6
Guest Cl BKME/WDN BH12 ....322 A9
Guest Rd ELGH SO50 ......229 M1
Guildford Ct
 LSOL/BMARY PO13 * 315 H3
Guildford Dr CHFD SO53 ....228 D1
Guildford Rd ALDT GU11 ....97 K4
 ASHV GU12 ......77 J9
 FLEETN GU51 ......74 F3
 FNM GU9 ......96 D8
 FRIM GU16 ......96 D8
 PSEA PO1 ......316 G3
Guildford Rd East FARN GU14 ...76 B5
Guildford Rd West FARN GU14 ...76 B3
Guildford St SHAM SO14 * ...21 H2
Guildhall Sq PSEA PO1 ......19 C3
Guildhall Wk PSEA PO1 ......19 F4
Guillemard Rd SBNE BH6 ......336 C2
Guillemont Flds FARN GU14 ...57 L8
Guillemot Cl FAWY SO45 ....268 D7
Guillemot Gdns
 LSOL/BMARY PO13 ....294 F6
Guinea Ct CHIN RG24 ......52 B9
Gull Cl LSOL/BMARY PO13....296 F7
Gulley Rd FARN GU14 ......75 P4
Gulliver Cl PSTN BH14 ......333 L3
The Gulls TOTT SO40 ......247 K9
Gullycroft Md HEND SO30 ...250 B4
Gun HI ALDT GU11 ......3 F1
Gunner La RWIN SO21 ......128 E5
Gunners Ms BPWT SO32 ......232 B4
Gunners Pk BPWT SO32 ......232 C4
Gunners Rw ENEY PO4 ......317 K6
Gunners Wy GPORT PO12....295 K9
Gunns Farm LIPH GU30....175 K5
Gunwharf Rd HSEA PO3 ......297 J3
Gunville Crs
 MOOR/WNTN BH9 ....323 H4
Gunville HI RSAL SP5 ......158 D1
Gunville Rd RSAL SP5 ......158 C1
Gunwharf Quays PSEA PO1 ...18 C4
Gunwhard Rd PSEA PO1 ....18 B5
Gurdons ALTN GU34 ......132 D8
Gurnard Rd CHAM PO6 ......296 C2
Gurnays Md ROMY SO51....224 D1
Gurney Rd ENEY PO4 ......317 K4
 WIMB BH21 ......300 A7
Gussage Rd BKME/WDN BH12...321 N4
Gutner La HISD PO11 ......299 J8
Guttridge La TADY RG26 ......34 B6
Gwatkin Cl HAV PO9 ......276 C7
Gwyn Cl NWBY RG14 ......24 C7
Gwynne Rd BKME/WDN BH12...321 N7
Gypsy La HORN PO8 ......255 N6
 RGWD BH24 ......282 F1

H

Haarlem Ms
 CHCH/BSGR BH23 ....325 H8
Habershon Dr FRIM GU16 ......59 J3
Habin HI EPSF GU31 ......217 K1
Hack Dr RWIN SO21 ......207 P5
Hacketts La BPWT SO32 ......233 L2
Hackett Wy
 FHAM/STUB PO14 ......294 E3
Hackleys La RWIN SO51....295 P4
Hacks La RWIN SO21 ......143 L5
Hackupps La RWIN SO51....180 B5
Hackwood Cl AND SP10....102 B3
Hackwood Cots
 BSTK RG21 ......90 E1
Hackwood La OVTN RG25....90 D5
Hackwood Rd BSTK RG21...69 M9
Hackwood Road Rbt
 BSTK RG21 ......69 M9
Hackworths Gdns HEND SO30 ...250 C1
Hadden Rd CHAR BH8 ......323 K7
Haddon Cl FHAM PO15 ......10 B6
Haddon Dr ELGH SO50 ......207 J8
Haddon Dr WIMB BH21 ......280 D3
Hadleigh Gdns ELGH SO50 ....207 J8
Hadleigh Pl BSTK RG21 ......6 C6
Hadleigh Rd CHAM PO6 * ...296 F1
Hadley Fld FAWY SO45 ......290 D4
Hadleys RFNM GU10 ......115 N7
Hadow Rd BWD BH11 ......322 C4
Hadrian Cl FERN BH22....302 D6
Hadrian Rd AND SP10 ......82 F8
Hadrians FNM GU9 ......96 E7
Hadrians Wy DEAN RG23 ......88 B3
Hadrian Wy ROWN SO16....228 A5
 WIMB BH21 ......300 A5
Haflinger Dr HLER SO31 ......271 H2
Haglane Copse LYMN SO41...329 H5
Hagley Rd FLEETN GU51....74 B2
Hahnemann Rd WCLF BH2....8 B6
Haig Av PSTN BH14 ......333 N2
Haig La FLEETS GU52 ......74 E7
Haig Rd AND SP10 ......102 C2
 ASHV GU12 ......3 J4
 CBLY GU15 ......51 N8
 ELGH SO50 ......230 A3
 SAND GU47 ......168 A1
Haileybury Gdns HEND SO30...250 B2
Hailsham Cl SHST GU47 ......41 L5
Hailstone Rd BSTK RG21 ......69 L4
Hainault Dr VWD BH31 ......258 C4
Haining Gdns FRIM GU16 ......76 F1
Haking Rd CHCH/BSGR BH23...335 H8
Halcyon Dr RAND SP11 ......100 E2
Halden Cl ROMY SO51 ......204 F4
Hale Av NMIL/BTOS BH25....337 J3
Hale Cl NARL SO24 ......169 M2
Hale Gdns NMIL/BTOS BH25....327 K5

Hale House La RFNM GU10 ...136 G8
Hale La FBDG SP6 ......221 K3
Hales La FNM GU9 ......96 E6
Hale Reeds FNM GU9 ......96 D5
Hale Rd FBDG SP6 ......221 J3
 FNM GU9 ......96 D6
Hales Dr HEND SO30 ......250 A6
Hales Fld HASM GU27 ......157 H7
Hale St North PSEA PO1 ......316 F2
Hale St South PSEA PO1 ......316 F2
Hale Wy FRIM GU16 ......58 C4
Halewood Wy
 CHCH/BSGR BH23 ......324 D7
Half Moon HI HASM GU27....157 H7
Halfpenny La PSEA PO1 * ...18 D6
Halifax Cl AND SP10 ......4 A2
 FARN GU14 ......75 N1
Halifax Ct HEND SO30 * 249 L1
Halifax Pl NTHA RG18 ......25 M3
Halifax Wy CHCH/BSGR BH23...325 M8
 FARN GU14 ......75 N5
Halimote Rd ALDT GU11 ......2 E4
Hall Cl BPWT SO32 ......232 B4
Hall Dr FLEETS GU52 ......74 E6
Hallett Cl WEND SO18 ......249 J1
Hallett Cl WEND SO18 ......249 J1
Hallett Rd HAV PO9 ......277 H8
Halletts Cl FHAM/STUB PO14 ...294 A6
Hall Farm Crs YTLY GU46 ......40 D9
The Halliards
 FHAM/PORC PO16 ......294 F2
Halliday Cl BSTK RG21 ......90 C1
 GPORT PO12 ......12 D1
Halliday Crs ENEY PO4 ......317 L5
Hall Lands La ELGH SO50 ......230 D2
Hall La ALTN GU34 ......152 B6
 YTLY GU46 ......40 D9
Hallmark Cl SHST GU47 ......41 M6
Hall Rd ALTN GU34 ......132 C3
 BWD BH11 ......321 P1
 FARN GU14 ......76 A3
Halls Farm Cl FUFL SO22 ......164 F4
The Hall Wy FUFL SO22 ......164 C2
Halsey Cl GPORT PO12 ......315 K5
Halstead Rd CHAM PO6 ......296 F1
 WEND SO18 ......249 H1
Halstock Crs CFDH BH17 ......320 F2
Halter Pth PLE BH15 ......320 A9
Halter Ri WIMB BH21 ......279 L8
Halters End GSHT GU26 ......155 P5
The Halters NWBY RG14 ......24 E8
Halterworth Cl ROMY SO51...204 F6
Halterworth La ROMY SO51...204 G5
Halton Cl CHCH/BSGR BH23...305 M8
Halton Rd RAND SP11 ......79 M4
Haltons Cl TOTT SO40 ......246 B2
Halyard Cl LSOL/BMARY PO13...315 H1
Hambert Wy TOTT SO40 ......246 D6
Hamble Av BLKW GU17 ......41 L9
 HLER SO31 ......270 C9
Hamble Cl DEAN RG23....88 F2
 HLER SO31 ......270 C9
Hamble Dr TADY RG26 ......34 E6
Hamble House Gdns
 HLER SO31 ......270 A8
Hamble La HLER SO31 ......249 P9
 HLER SO31 ......269 N6
 WVILLE PO7 ......275 N5
Hamble Pk HLER SO31 * 270 F2
Hamble Rd GPORT PO12 ......315 K4
 PLE BH15 ......321 H5
Hamble Springs BPWT SO32...232 C5
Hambledon Cl CBLY GU15 ......58 G2
Hamblewood HEND SO30 ......250 C5
Hamble Wy HTWY RG27 ......52 C8
Hambledon Gdns SBNE BH6 ...324 A9
Hambledon La BPWT SO32 ...253 N1
Hambledon Pde
 WVILLE PO7 * 255 L9
Hambledon Rd HORN PO8 ......236 A7
 SBNE BH6 ......324 A9
 WVILLE PO7 ......254 F3
 WVILLE PO7 ......275 J2
Hambledon Wy HTWY RG27 ...52 C8

WIMB BH21 ......300 A8
Ham La FERN BH22 ......302 B6
 GPORT PO12 ......295 B8
 HORN PO8 ......255 P5
 TADY RG26 ......49 L1
 WIMB BH21 ......301 K1
Hamlash La RFNM GU10 ......116 C9
Hamlet Gdns RAND SP11 ......82 F5
Hamlet Wy GPORT PO12 ......295 H8
Hammer Hl HASM GU27 ......156 B9
Hammer La CSHT GU26 ......155 M1
 GSHT GU26 ......156 B5
Hammersley Rd ALDT GU11 ...76 A5
Hammerwood Copse
 HASM GU27 ......156 C8
Ham MI NWBY RG14 * 24 C4
Hammond Cl FHAM PO15 ......272 D8
 STHA RG19 ......25 P5
Hammond Meadow NWBY RG14 ...10 A3
Hammonds Cl TOTT SO40 ......246 D5
Hammond's Gn TOTT SO40 ......246 B3
Hammonds Heath THLE RG7 ...27 K9
Hammond's La NARL SO24 ...169 M3
 TOTT SO40 ......246 C3
Hammond Sq AND SP10 * 82 F9
Hammonds Wy TOTT SO40 ......246 D5
Hampden La ASHV GU12 ......97 J4
Hampshire Cl AND SP10 ......69 K8
Hampshire Ct FAWY SO45 ......290 D9
 BH22 ......280 F8
Hampshire Hatches La
 RGWD BH24 ......282 E5
Hampshire Rd BOR GU35 ......154 A4
Hampshire Ter PSEA PO1 ......19 F5
Hampton Cl FAWY SO45 ......290 C9
 FLEETS GU52 ......74 D8
 WVILLE PO7 ......256 A5
Hampton Dr RCWD BH24 ......260 F9
Hampton Gdns FAWY SO45 ......290 C9
Hampton Gv FAWY SO45 ......271 P9
Hampton HI BPWT SO32 ......232 F6
Hampton La FAWY SO45 ......290 C9
Hampton Rd FM GU9 ......96 A5
 NWBY RG14 ......16 D5
Hamptworth Rd RSAL SP5 ......200 D8
Hamtun Crs TOTT SO40 ......246 C2
Hamtun Gdns TOTT SO40 ......246 C2
Hamtun Rd ITCH SO19 ......249 L9
Hamtun St SHAM SO14 ......20 D6
Hanbidge Crs
 LSOL/BMARY PO13 ......295 H5
Hanbury Wy CBLY GU15 ......58 B2
Hancombe Rd SHST GU47 ......41 H4
Handcroft Cl RFNM GU10 ......95 K5
Handel Cl KBH RG22 ......89 P2
Handel Rd WSHM SO15 ......20 C1
Handel Ter WSHM SO15 ......20 B2
Handford La YTLY GU46 ......40 E9
Handford Pl WSHM SO15 ......20 D1
Handley Rd GPORT PO12 ......315 K2
Hangerfield Cl YTLY GU46 ......40 C9
Hanger Rd TADY RG26 ......34 A5
The Hangers BPWT SO32 ......210 E9
 BPWT SO32 ......232 B2
Hangers Wy ALTN GU34 ......132 C5
 LISS GU33 ......175 P1
 HORN PO8 ......236 C2
The Hanger BOR GU35 ......154 F1
Hanger Wy EPSF GU31 ......215 P2
Hanham Rd WIMB BH21 ......278 E9
Hankinson Rd
 MOOR/WNTN BH9 ......322 C7
Hanley Rd WSHM SO15 ......247 P3
Hanlon Cl BWD BH11 ......322 A3
Hanmore Rd CHIN RG24 ......69 P2
Hannah Gdns WVILLE PO7 ......275 P2
Hannah Wy LYMN SO41 ......328 F1
Hannam's Farm RFNM GU10 ...94 C5
Hannay Ri ITCH SO19 ......249 N9
Hannington Rd HAV PO9 ......276 D3
 LTDN BH7 ......324 D2
Hannings Wy THLE RG7 ......27 L4
Hann Rd ROWN SO16 ......227 J6
Hanns Wy ELGH SO50 ......229 J2
Hanover Buildings SHAM SO14 ...20 E5
Hanover Cl AND SP10 ......102 B4
 FRIM GU16 ......58 D4
 YTLY GU46 ......40 E7
Hanover Ct DR FLEETN GU51 ...56 F9
Hanover Ct PSEA PO1 ......18 D5
Hanover Gdns BSTK RG21 ......90 C1
 FARN GU14 ......M7
Hanover Gn CFDH BH17 ......321 H4
Hanoverian Wy FHAM PO15 ...271 J3
Hanover Md NWBY RG14 ......24 A9
Hanover St SHAM SO14 ......20 E5
Hanson Rd AND SP10 ......102 C1
Hanway Rd NEND PO2 ......296 F9
Ha'Penny Dell WVILLE PO7 * ...275 N7
Harbeck Rd CHAR BH8 ......323 J4
Harborough Rd WSHM SO15 ...248 B5
Harbour Cl FARN GU14 ......57 P5
 TOTT SO40 ......247 N9
Harbour Crs
 CHCH/BSGR BH23 ......337 J1
Harbour Hill Crs PLE BH15 ......320 C7
Harbour Hill Rd PLE BH15 ......320 G7
Harbour Pde WSHM SO15 ......20 E5
Harbour Rd GPORT PO12 ......13 H1
 HISD PO11 ......318 C4
 SBNE BH6 ......336 E3
Harbourside HAV PO9 ......298 F3
Harbour Vw
 FHAM/PORC PO16 ......295 N3
Harbour View Cl PSTN BH14 ...321 J7
Harbour View Rd PSTN BH14 ...321 J7
Harbour Wy EMRTH PO10 ......299 N1
 NEND PO2 ......296 F2
Harbridge Dro HAV PO9 ......276 D5

Harbridge Dro FBDG SP6 ......240 A7
Harbury Ct NWBY RG14 ......17 F4
Harcombe Ct CFDH BH17 ......320 G1
Harcourt Cl HORN PO8 ......256 A7
Harcourt Rd BOSC BH5 ......335 N1
 FHAM/STUB PO14 ......293 P2
 GPORT PO12 ......12 B1
 PSEA PO1 ......316 G3
 WEND SO18 ......248 F3
Harding La ELGH SO50 ......230 B1
Harding Rd GPORT PO12 ......315 J2
Hardings La HTWY RG27 ......55 J7
Hardley La FAWY SO45 ......290 D2
The Hard PSEA PO1 ......18 C2
Hardwick Cl ROWN SO16 ......247 K1
Hardwicke Wy HLER SO31 ......269 M8
Hardwick Rd CHFD SO53 ......206 F7
Hardy Av YTLY GU46 ......56 D1
Hardy Cl FERN BH22 ......280 F8
 HLER SO31 ......271 H6
 NMIL/BTOS BH25 ......327 H4
 NTHA RG18 ......25 M2
 WSHM SO15 ......247 M5
Hardy Crs WIMB BH21 ......300 F2
Hardy Dr FAWY SO45 ......290 D9
Hardyfair Cl RAND SP11 ......81 K9
Hardy Gn CWTH RG45 ......41 P2
Hardy La BSTK RG21 ......69 K8
Hardy Rd CHAM PO6 ......297 N2
 ELGH SO50 ......229 H3
 FERN BH22 ......280 F8
 PSTN BH14 ......321 M8
Hardys Fld KSCL RG20 ......30 D8
Harebell Cl FHAM/PORC PO16 ...11 J1
 HTWY RG27 ......55 J6
Harebell Dr NTHA RG18 ......25 P3
Harebell Gdns HTWY RG27 ......55 J6
Harefield Cl ROMY SO51 ......204 F5
Harefield Rd PTSW SO17 ......228 E9
Hare La FBDG SP6 ......239 H6
 NMIL/BTOS BH25 ......327 M4
 RWIN SO21 ......208 A1
 WIMB BH21 ......238 E5
Hares Gn LTDN BH7 ......323 N7
Hare's La HTWY RG27 ......55 K6
Harestock Cl FUFL SO22 ......164 E4
Harestock Rd FUFL SO22 ......164 E3
 HAV PO9 ......14 C2
Harewood Av LTDN BH7 ......323 N9
Harewood Cl ELGH SO50 ......207 J8
Harewood Crs LTDN BH7 ......323 N9
Harewood Gdns LTDN BH7 ......323 M8
Harewood Gn LYMN SO41 ......339 L2
Harewood Pl LTDN BH7 ......323 P9
Harfield Cl HTWY RG27 ......71 P3
Harford Cl LYMN SO41 ......329 H6
Harford Rd BKME/WDN BH12 ...321 L4
Harkness Dr WVILLE PO7 ......276 B2
Harkwood Dr PLE BH15 ......320 B8
Harland Crs WSHM SO15 ......247 P2
Harland Rd SBNE BH6 ......336 E3
Harlaxton Cl ELGH SO50 ......207 H8
Harlech Cl DEAN RG23 ......68 F7
Harlech Dr CHFD SO53 ......206 C9
Harlech Rd BLKW GU17 ......57 L1
Harlequin Gv FAREH PO15 ......10 B5
Harleston Rd CHAM PO6 ......274 F9
Harleston Vls WIMB BH21 ......300 F1
Harlington Wy FLEETN GU51 ...74 B4
Harlyn Rd ROWN SO16 ......247 H2
Harman Rd
 LSOL/BMARY PO13 ......294 D4
Harmsworth Rd TADY RG26 ......34 C6
Harness Cl WIMB BH21 ......279 K8
Harold Cl TOTT SO40 ......246 B5
Harold Gdns ALTN GU34 ......132 C6
Harold Jackson Ter BSTK RG21 ...69 M8
Harold Rd EMRTH PO10 ......277 P6
 ENEY PO4 ......316 G5
 FHAM/STUB PO14 ......319 H6
 WSHM SO15 ......247 N4
Harpdon Pde YTLY GU46 ......40 E7
Harpton Cl YTLY GU46 ......40 E7
Harpway La
 CHCH/BSGR BH23 ......324 G1
The Harrage ROMY SO51 ......204 D6
Harrier Cl HORN PO8 ......256 A5
 LSOL/BMARY PO13 ......314 D2
 ROWN SO16 ......227 H6
Harrier Dr WIMB BH21 ......280 B6
Harriers Cl CHCH/BSGR BH23 ...325 P7
Harrier Wy EPSF GU31 ......216 A3
 SSEA PO5 ......290 D3
Harrier Cl FHAM/STUB PO14 ...24 C2
Harris Av HEND SO30 ......250 C3
Harris HI KBH RG22 ......89 M4
Harris La HORN PO8 ......237 K7
Harrison Av BMTH BH1 ......323 K9
Harrison Cl CHCH/BSGR BH23 ...325 P6
Harrison Rd
 FHAM/PORC PO16 ......11 G3
 PTSW SO17 ......228 E9
Harrison's Cut SHAM SO14 ......20 E9
Harris Rd LSOL/BMARY PO13 ...294 G6
Harroway DEAN RG23 ......88 B2
Harroway La WHCH RG28 ......65 J1
Harrow Cl CHCH/BSGR BH23 ...305 M9
Harrow Down FUFL SO22 ......183 M2
Harrowgate La WVILLE PO7 ...255 H3
Harrow La PSF GU32 ......191 M8
Harrow Rd SSEA PO5 ......316 C4
Harrow Wy AND SP10 ......102 B1
 OVTN RG25 ......66 G9
 RAND SP11 ......81 N9
The Harrow Wy KBH RG22 ......90 A2
Harry Barrow Cl RGWD BH24 ...282 E2
Hart Cl FARN GU14 ......75 M5
 NMIL/BTOS BH25 ......327 H5
Hartford Bridge Flats
 HTWY RG27 ......55 M4
Hartford Ct HTWY RG27 ......55 H7
Hartford Rd HTWY RG27 ......55 H7

Hart HI FAWY SO45 ......268 E9
Harthill Dro RSAL SP5 ......200 A8
Harting Dr HORN PO8 ......236 D8
Harting Down EPSF GU31 ......215 P2
Harting Gdns
 FHAM/PORC PO16 ......273 N9
Harting Rd SBNE BH6 ......324 E8
Hartington Rd GPORT PO12 ...315 K2
 SHAM SO14 ......21 H2
Hartland Pl FARN GU14 ......57 P6
Hartland's Rd
 FHAM/PORC PO16 ......11 H6
Hart Plain Av HORN PO8 ......255 N9
Hartsbourne Dr LTDN BH7 ......323 P7
Harts Farm Wy HAV PO9 ......298 C1
Harts Hill Rd NTHA RG18 ......25 P3
Harthill Rd TADY RG26 ......34 A6
Harts La KSCL RG20 ......30 D8
 THLE RG7 ......26 D2
 WIMB BH21 ......279 J3
Hartsleaf Cl FLEETN GU51 ......74 C4
Harts Leap Cl SHST GU47 ......41 H5
Harts Leap Rd SHST GU47 ......41 H6
Harts Wy LYMN SO41 ......328 D6
Hartswood CHIN RG24 ......69 P2
The Hart FNM GU9 ......96 B9
Hartwell Rd HSEA PO3 ......297 K5
Hartwood Gdns HORN PO8 ......255 N9
Harvard Rd SHST GU47 ......41 N5
Harvest Cl FUFL SO22 ......183 M2
 YTLY GU46 ......56 C1
Harvest Crs FLEETN GU51 ......73 P9
Harvester Wy LYMN SO41 ......329 K1
Harvest Gn NWBY RG14 ......16 A6
Harvesting La PSF GU32 ......214 A7
Harvest Rd CHFD SO53 ......206 B7
 WVILLE PO7 ......254 G7
Harvest Wy CHIN RG24 ......70 A4
Harvey Crs FAWY SO45 ......290 G7
Harvey Gdns HLER SO31 ......270 F8
Harvey Gdns FAWY SO45 ......268 D7
Harvey Rd AND SP10 ......5 J3
Harvey Rd BOSC BH5 ......335 N1
 ELGH SO50 ......229 N1
 FARN GU14 ......300 C5
 WIMB BH21 ......300 C5
Harveys Fld OVTN RG25 ......86 G3
Harwell Rd CFDH BH17 ......320 F5
Harwich Rd CHAM PO6 ......274 F9
Harwood Cl
 LSOL/BMARY PO13 ......294 C5
 TOTT SO40 ......246 B3
Harwood Pl WINC SO23 ......145 K3
Harwood Rd KSCL RG20 ......29 N5
Harwood Rd
 LSOL/BMARY PO13 ......294 C6
Haselbury Rd TOTT SO40 ......246 D4
Haselfoot Gdns WEND SO18 ...249 N4
Haselworth Dr GPORT PO12 ...315 M7
Haskells Cl LYND SO43 ......264 E6
Haskells Rd BKME/WDN BH12 ...321 K5
Haslar Br GPORT PO12 ......13 J4
Haslar Crs WVILLE PO7 ......255 L9
Haslar La GPORT PO12 ......13 G6
Hasle Dr HASM GU27 ......156 G8
Haslemere Av
 CHCH/BSGR BH23 ......326 B7
Haslemere Cl FRIM GU16 ......59 H2
Haslemere Gdns HISD PO11 ...319 M6
Haslemere Pl
 CHCH/BSGR BH23 ......326 C7
Haslemere Rd ENEY PO4 ......317 H6
 LIPH GU30 ......175 L3
Hasler Rd CFDH BH17 ......320 E2
Haslop Rd WIMB BH21 ......279 M7
The Hassocks WVILLE PO7 ......276 A3
Hastards La ALTN GU34 ......152 D6
Hastie Dr NARL SO24 ......167 P3
Haste HI Top HASM GU27 ......157 J8
Hastings Av GPORT PO12 ......295 K9
Hastings Cl FRIM GU16 ......58 F6
 KBH RG22 ......68 E7
Hastings Rd CFDH BH17 ......320 D2
 CHAR BH8 ......323 M5
Hatchbury La RAND SP11 ......43 H7
Hatchet Cl FBDG SP6 ......221 P1
Hatchet La BROC SO42 ......310 E3
Hatchet La RWIN SO21 ......81 N2
Hatchers La CHIN RG24 ......70 C7
 LISS GU33 ......192 G2
 RDGW/BURGH RG30 ......27 M1
Hatch La CHIN RG24 ......70 C7
 LISS GU33 ......192 G2
Hatch Md HEND SO30 ......249 L1
Hatch Pond La CFDH BH17 ......320 E4
Hatch Pond Rd CFDH BH17 ......320 E4
Hatch Rw KBH RG22 ......89 N5
Hatchwarren Gdns KBH RG22 ...90 A4
Hatchwarren La KBH RG22 ......89 P6
Hatfield Ct NMIL/BTOS BH25 ...326 G4
Hatfield Gdns FARN GU14 ......76 D1
 LTDN BH7 ......323 P7
Hatfield Rd ENEY PO4 ......317 J3
Hathaway Cl ELGH SO50 ......230 K9

Hathaway Gdns CHIN RG24 ....69 M4
WVILLE PO7 ....276 B1
Hathaway Rd SBNE BH6 ....336 B2
Hatherden Av PSTN BH14 ....321 H7
Hatherden Ct AND SP10 * 4 E4
Hatherell Cl HEND SO30 ....249 M2
Hatherley Crs
FHAM/PORC PO16 ....295 M2
Hatherley Dr
FHAM/PORC PO16 ....295 M1
Hatherley Rd CHAM PO6 ....274 C9
FUFL SO22 ....22 B2
Hatherwood YTLY GU46 * 40 G9
Hatley Rd WEND SO18 ....249 K3
Hattem Pl AND SP10 ....82 D9
Hattingley Rd ALTN GU34 ....149 M1
Hatt La ROMY SO51 ....179 L4
Haughurst Hl STHA RG19 ....33 L6
Havant Farm Cl HAV PO9 ....15 G2
Havant Rd CHAM PO6 ....297 H1
HAV PO9 ....15 K7
HISD PO11 ....298 G9
HORN PO8 ....256 D6
NEND PO2 ....296 F8
Havant St PSEA PO1 ....18 C3
Havelock Rd
BKME/WDN BH12 ....334 A1
HLER SO31 ....270 C9
SSEA PO5 ....19 K5
WSHM SO15 ....20 C2
Havelock Wy
CHCH/BSGR BH23 ....325 P5
Haven Crs FHAM/STUB PO14 ....293 M8
Havendale HEND SO30 ....250 D6
Haven Gdns NMIL/BTOS BH25 ....327 K5
Haven Rd CCLF BH13 ....333 N5
HISD PO11 ....319 L7
Havenstone Wy WEND SO18 ....228 F8
The Haven ELGH SO50 ....207 K8
ENEY PO4 ....317 K3
GPORT PO12 ....12 C7
HEND SO30 * 250 B7
H Av FAWY SO45 ....291 H3
Haven Wy FNM GU9 ....96 D7
Haverstock Rd
MOOR/WNTN BH9 ....323 H5
Haviland Rd BMTH BH1 ....335 M1
WIMB BH21 ....302 A1
Haviland Rd East LTDN BH7 ....335 M1
Haviland Rd West BMTH BH1 ....335 L2
Havisham Rd NEND PO2 * 316 F1
Hawden Rd BWD BH11 ....322 A6
Haweswater Cl BOR GU35 ....154 A3
Haweswater Ct ASHV GU12 * 76 E8
Hawfinch Cl ROWN SO16 ....227 M6
Hawkchurch Gdns CFDH BH17 ....320 G2
Hawk Cl FHAM/STUB PO14 ....293 P7
KBH RG22 ....89 K3
WIMB BH21 ....279 J7
Hawke Cl AND SP10 ....5 K2
Hawker Cl WIMB BH21 ....301 H4
Hawker Rd ASHV GU12 ....76 E7
Hawkers Cl TOTT SO40 ....246 C2
Hawkes Cl HTWY RG27 ....55 H6
Hawke St PSEA PO1 ....18 C2
Hawkeswood Rd WEND SO18 ....248 E4
Hawkewood Av WVILLE PO7 ....255 M9
Hawkfield La BSTK RG21 ....69 K9
Hawkhill FAWY SO45 ....267 N6
Hawkhurst Cl ITCH SO19 ....269 J1
Hawkins Cl RGWD BH24 ....260 G9
Hawkins Gv FLEETN GU51 ....74 A6
Hawkins Rd
BKME/WDN BH12 ....321 P3
LSOL/BMARY PO13 ....295 H7
Hawkins Wy FLEETS GU52 ....74 F4
Hawkley Cl HAV PO9 ....276 E4
Hawkley Dr TADY RG26 ....34 D7
Hawkley Gn ITCH SO19 ....269 H2
Hawkley Rd LISS GU33 ....172 E8
Hawkshaw Cl LIPH GU30 ....175 L3
Hawkswood Av FRIM GU16 ....58 E3
Hawksworth Rd THLE RG7 ....27 K4
Hawkwell FHAM/PORC PO16 ....295 K1
FLEETS GU52 ....74 E8
Hawkwood Rd BOSC BH5 ....335 L2
Hawley Gn BLKW GU17 ....57 M2
Hawley Gv BLKW GU17 ....57 M3
Hawley La FARN GU14 ....58 A5
Hawley Rd BLKW GU17 ....57 N2
Haworth Cl CHCH/BSGR BH23 ....324 E6
Hawswater Cl ROWN SO16 ....247 K2
Hawthorn Cl ASHV GU12 ....97 L3
ELGH SO50 ....230 C2
FHAM/PORC PO16 ....273 M9
HEND SO30 ....250 D5
NARL SO24 ....168 A2
NMIL/BTOS BH25 ....327 L3
RWIN SO21 ....127 H7
RWIN SO21 ....208 A5
Hawthorn Ct EPSF GU31 ....216 A2
FARN GU14 ....76 B4
Hawthorn Crs CHAM PO6 ....297 J3
Hawthorn Dr CFDH BH17 ....320 B3
LYMN SO41 ....308 B6
Hawthorne Cl NTHA RG18 ....25 N2
RAND SP11 ....120 B1
Hawthorne Crs BLKW GU17 ....57 M1
Hawthorne Gv HISD PO11 ....318 G4
Hawthorne Rd TOTT SO40 ....246 B3
Hawthorn La ALTN GU34 ....150 E8
HLER SO31 ....270 E5
RFNM GU10 ....115 P7
Hawthorn Ri HTWY RG27 ....72 A2
Hawthorn Rd ALTN GU34 ....150 C8
CHCH/BSGR BH23 ....325 J5
FAWY SO45 ....268 B7
FRIM GU16 ....58 E3
HORN PO8 ....256 C2
MOOR/WNTN BH9 ....322 F7
NTID SP9 ....79 H4
NWBY RG14 ....24 D3
PTSW SO17 ....248 C1
WVILLE PO7 ....254 F7
Hawthorns ALTN GU34 ....132 E4
The Hawthorns BPWT SO32 * 231 N3
CHCH/BSGR BH23 ....325 K9
ELGH SO50 ....228 G3
TADY RG26 ....33 P6
TOTT SO40 ....267 L1
Hawthorn Wy DEAN RG23 ....68 F6
Hayburn Rd ROWN SO16 ....247 H1
Haydn Cl WINC SO23 ....145 J8
Haydn Rd KBH RG22 ....89 P3
Haydock Cl ALTN GU34 ....132 F7
TOTT SO40 ....246 A3
Haydock Ms WVILLE PO7 ....276 B1
Haydon Rd CCLF BH13 ....334 B5
Hay Down La RAND SP11 ....100 E5
Hayes Av LTDN BH7 ....323 L9
Hayes Cl FHAM PO15 ....272 B7
STOK SO20 ....161 L5
WIMB BH21 ....301 J1
Hayes La WIMB BH21 ....279 K9
Hayes Md FAWY SO45 ....290 D4
Hayeswood Rd WIMB BH21 ....279 J8
Hayle Rd WEND SO18 ....249 K1
Hayley Cl FAWY SO45 ....290 B1
Hayley La ODIM RG29 ....93 H6
Hayling Av HSEA PO3 ....317 K1
Hayling Billy Coastal Pth
HISD PO11 ....318 E1
Hayling Cl FHAM/STUB PO14 ....294 B1
GPORT PO12 ....295 N9
Haymoor Rd PLE BH15 ....321 J5
Haynes Av PLE BH15 ....320 F8
Haynes Wy FAWY SO45 ....268 A9
Haysoms Cl NMIL/BTOS BH25 ....327 K6
Haysoms Dr NWBY RG14 ....24 E8
Hay St PSEA PO1 ....18 E2
Hayter Gdns ROMY SO51 ....204 E5
Hayters Wy FBDG SP6 ....239 N5
Hayward Cl TOTT SO40 ....246 B4
Hayward Ct FAWY SO45 ....290 E5
Hayward Crs VWD BH31 ....258 E5
Haywarden Pl HTWY RG27 ....55 J6
Haywards Farm Cl VWD BH31 ....258 E5
The Haywards NTHA RG18 ....25 N3
Hayward Wy VWD BH31 ....258 D5
Haywood Dr FLEETS GU52 ....74 D5
Hazel Av FARN GU14 ....75 N2
Hazelbank Cl EPSF GU31 ....215 P1
LIPH GU30 ....175 L3
Hazel Cl AND SP10 ....102 B4
CHCH/BSGR BH23 ....325 N6
CHFD SO53 ....206 E3
DEAN RG23 ....88 F2
FBDG SP6 ....239 N6
RDGW/BURGH RG30 ....27 K2
RWIN SO21 ....208 A4
Hazelcombe OVTN RG25 ....87 H4
Hazel Coppice HTWY RG27 ....72 A2
Hazeldean Dr HAV PO9 ....277 H1
Hazeldene CHIN RG24 ....70 A2
Hazeldene Rd LIPH GU30 ....174 E3
Hazeldown Cl ROWN SO16 ....227 J7
Hazel Dr FERN BH22 ....280 D9
Hazeleigh Av ITCH SO19 ....248 G9
Hazeley Cl HTWY RG27 ....55 H6
Hazeley Rd RWIN SO21 ....184 A8
Hazel Farm Rd TOTT SO40 ....246 A4
Hazel Gn TADY RG26 ....33 N5
Hazel Gv FUFL SO22 ....183 M1
GSHT GU26 ....156 D4
HLER SO31 ....271 H8
NTHA RG18 ....25 N2
TOTT SO40 ....245 M8
Hazelgrove HORN PO8 ....236 C7
Hazelholt Dr HAV PO9 ....14 B2
Hazell Av NBNE BH10 ....322 B5
Hazell Rd FNM GU9 ....95 P9
Hazel Rd ALTN GU34 ....150 D5
FRIM GU16 ....76 F2
HORN PO8 ....236 C7
ITCH SO19 ....248 F8
LYMN SO41 ....328 G3
Hazelton Cl LTDN BH7 ....323 N7
Hazelwood CHIN RG24 * 51 P9
FHAM/STUB PO14 ....293 P4
Hazelwood Av HAV PO9 ....276 B7
NMIL/BTOS BH25 ....326 G3
Hazelwood Cl DEAN RG23 ....68 G5
Hazelwood Dr DEAN RG23 ....68 G5
VWD BH31 ....259 H6
Hazelwood Rd WEND SO18 ....249 J2
Hazely Cl HTWY RG27 ....55 H6
Hazlebury Rd CFDH BH17 ....320 G5
Hazlemere Dr RGWD BH24 ....281 L6
Hazleton Int HORN PO8 * 256 C5
Hazleton Wy HORN PO8 ....256 B6
Head Down EPSF GU31 ....215 P2
Headington Cl KBH RG22 ....89 P3
Headland Dr HLER SO31 ....270 G6
Headley Cl
LSOL/BMARY PO13 * 314 D2
NARL SO24 ....168 A3
Headley Flds BOR GU35 ....154 F4
Headley Hill Rd BOR GU35 ....154 G3
Headley La LIPH GU30 ....154 G3
Headley Rd BOR GU35 ....154 D3
GSHT GU26 ....155 N4
LIPH GU30 ....175 H1
Headmore La ALTN GU34 ....150 F7
Headon Vw PSF GU32 ....188 E9
Heads Farm Cl NBNE BH10 ....322 E2
Heads La HUNG RG17 ....28 B1
NBNE BH10 ....322 E2
Headswell Av NBNE BH10 ....322 E3
Headswell Crs NBNE BH10 ....322 E3
Headswell Gdns NBNE BH10 ....322 E3
Heanor Cl NBNE BH10 ....322 C5
Hearmon Cl YTLY GU46 ....40 E8
Hearne Gdns BPWT SO32 ....252 E2
Hearn V BOR GU35 ....155 H1
Hearsey Gdns BLKW GU17 ....41 K8
Heath Av PLE BH15 ....320 F6
Heath Cl ELGH SO50 ....230 D3
FNM GU9 ....96 C4
HORN PO8 ....256 B4
WIMB BH21 ....279 K7
Heathcote Cl ASHV GU12 * 76 F9
Heathcote Pl RWIN SO21 ....182 D7
Heathcote Rd ASHV GU12 ....76 G9
BMTH BH1 ....335 M2
BOR GU35 ....154 B5
CHFD SO53 ....206 F7
NEND PO2 ....297 H8
Heath End Farm TADY RG26 ....33 P5
Heath End Rd TADY RG26 ....33 P5
Heathen St BPWT SO32 ....231 H8
Heatherbank Rd WBNE BH4 ....334 C3
Heatherbrae Gdns
NBAD SO52 ....205 K9
Heather Cha ELGH SO50 ....230 A2
Heather Cl ALDT GU11 ....96 E2
ASHV GU12 ....76 G7
BOR GU35 ....153 N7
CHAR BH8 ....323 K3
CHCH/BSGR BH23 ....326 C6
FNM GU9 ....115 P4
LSOL/BMARY PO13 ....294 F7
LYMN SO41 ....328 A4
RGWD BH24 ....281 L6
TOTT SO40 ....246 C4
WIMB BH21 ....300 A7
WVILLE PO7 ....275 P4
Heather Ct WEND SO18 ....249 L4
Heatherdale Rd CBLY GU15 ....58 B1
Heatherdeane Rd PTSW SO17 ....248 C1
Heatherdene Av CWTH RG45 ....40 F2
Heatherdene Rd CHFD SO53 ....206 G4
Heatherdown Rd FERN BH22 ....280 G8
Heatherdown Wy FERN BH22 ....280 G8
Heather Dr AND SP10 ....4 B2
BOR GU35 ....154 C3
FERN BH22 ....302 D1
FLEETS GU52 ....74 C7
NTHA RG18 ....25 N2
TADY RG26 ....34 A4
Heatherfield EPSF GU31 ....215 K8
Heather Gdns FHAM PO15 ....272 B7
NWBY RG14 ....24 B8
Heather Gv HTWY RG27 ....55 H6
Heatherlands Ri
BKME/WDN BH12 ....321 M7
Heatherlands Rd ROWN SO16 ....228 B4
Heather La HTWY RG27 ....71 K7
Heatherlea Rd SBNE BH6 ....336 B2
Heather Md FRIM GU16 ....58 E3
Heather Rd EPSF GU31 ....216 A2
FAWY SO45 ....291 H7
NBNE BH10 ....322 D4
Heather Row La HTWY RG27 ....71 L7
Heatherstone Av FAWY SO45 ....290 B1
Heatherton Ms EMRTH PO10 ....277 M7
Heatherview Cl NBAD SO52 ....205 K8
Heather View Rd
BKME/WDN BH12 ....321 P5
Heatherway CWTH RG45 ....41 H1
Heather Wy FERN BH22 ....302 D1
GSHT GU26 ....156 E1
KBH RG22 ....89 L4
Heath Farm Cl FERN BH22 ....302 C5
Heath Farm Rd FERN BH22 ....302 C5
Heath Farm Wy FERN BH22 ....302 C5
Heathfield FAWY SO45 ....268 B8
Heathfield Av
BKME/WDN BH12 ....322 A7
FHAM/STUB PO14 ....272 B9
Heathfield Cl ITCH SO19 ....249 K8
Heathfield Ct FLEETN GU51 ....74 B5
Heathfield Rd CHFD SO53 ....206 E3
EPSF GU31 ....216 A2
FERN BH22 ....280 G8
ITCH SO19 ....249 K8
KBH RG22 ....89 P4
NEND PO2 ....296 F9
Heathfields TADY RG26 ....33 P5
Heathfield Wy FERN BH22 ....280 F8
Heath Gdns HLER SO31 ....269 M3
Heath Green La ALTN GU34 ....149 K1
Heath Hl RFNM GU10 ....135 N6
Heath Hill Rd North
CWTH RG45 ....41 J1
Heath Hill Rd South
CWTH RG45 ....41 J1
Heath House Cl HEND SO30 ....250 B7
Heath House Gdns
HEND SO30 ....250 B7
Heathhouse La HEND SO30 ....250 B7
Heathlands KSCL RG20 ....29 P6
Heathlands Av FERN BH22 ....302 D6
Heathlands Cl
CHCH/BSGR BH23 ....324 G4
CHFD SO53 ....206 E5
VWD BH31 ....258 G4
Heathlands Rd CHFD SO53 ....206 E5
Heathland St ALDT GU11 ....2 E3
Heath La BROC SO42 ....310 G1
FNM GU9 ....96 C4
NTHA RG18 ....25 M2
RFNM GU10 ....95 J5
Heath Lawns FHAM PO15 ....272 B9
Heathman St STOK SO20 ....139 P2
Heath Ride CWTH RG45 ....40 E2
Heath Rd CHCH/BSGR BH23 ....326 D6
EPSF GU31 ....215 N2
HASM GU27 ....156 C8
HLER SO31 ....270 F7
ITCH SO19 ....249 J6
LYMN SO41 ....327 P4
NBAD SO52 ....227 L1
RGWD BH24 ....281 K5
TADY RG26 ....34 F5
WHAM PO17 ....253 K3
Heath Rd East EPSF GU31 ....215 P3
Heath Rd North HLER SO31 ....270 F7
Heath Rd South HLER SO31 ....270 F7
Heath Rd West
CHCH/BSGR BH23 ....303 L2
EPSF GU31 ....215 N3
Heathrow Copse TADY RG26 ....33 N6
Heathside Wy HTWY RG27 ....55 H6
The Heath WVILLE PO7 ....255 J7
Heath V AND SP10 ....4 E6
Heathvale Bridge Rd
ASHV GU12 ....76 F6
Heathview HTWY RG27 ....72 B2
Heathwood Av
NMIL/BTOS BH25 ....326 G7
Heathwood Cl YTLY GU46 ....40 E7
Heathwood Rd
MOOR/WNTN BH9 ....322 E7
Heathy Cl NMIL/BTOS BH25 ....327 H7
Heathyfields Rd FNM GU9 ....95 P5
Heaton Rd GPORT PO12 ....315 L1
NBNE BH10 ....322 B5
Heavytree Rd PSTN BH14 ....321 K8
Hebden Cl STHA RG19 ....25 M6
Hebrides Cl FHAM/STUB PO14 ....293 P6
Heckfield Cl HAV PO9 ....277 H5
Heckford La PLE BH15 ....320 F8
Heckford Rd PLE BH15 ....320 F8
Hector Cl WVILLE PO7 ....275 N8
Hector Rd FHAM/STUB PO14 ....294 E4
Heddon Wk FARN GU14 ....57 P6
Hedera Rd HLER SO31 ....270 F7
Hedgecroft YTLY GU46 * 40 C8
Hedge End Rd AND SP10 ....5 G7
Hedgehog La HASM GU27 ....156 G8
Hedgerley NMIL/BTOS BH25 ....327 K7
Hedgerow Cl ROWN SO16 ....227 J6
Hedgerow Dr WEND SO18 ....249 K2
Hedgerow Gdns EMRTH PO10 ....277 M7
The Hedgerows CHIN RG24 ....70 B4
Hedges Cl NTID SP9 ....98 F3
The Hedges ELGH SO50 * 230 D6
Hedgeway NWBY RG14 ....24 F3
Hedley Cl FAWY SO45 ....291 H8
Hedley Gdns HEND SO30 ....230 B9
Heenan Cl FRIM GU16 ....58 D6
Heidelberg Rd ENEY PO4 ....317 H4
The Heights
FHAM/PORC PO16 ....273 H8
HEND SO30 ....250 A5
Hei-Lin Wy RAND SP11 ....79 N1
Heinz Burt Cl ELGH SO50 ....229 H1
Hele Cl BSTK RG21 ....90 C1
Helena Rd ENEY PO4 ....317 H6
Helen Ct FARN GU14 ....58 A9
Helford Ct AND SP10 ....82 G9
Helford Gdns WEND SO18 ....249 K1
Helksham Cl SHST GU47 ....41 L5
Hellyer Rd ENEY PO4 ....317 J5
Helm Cl LSOL/BMARY PO13 ....315 H2
Helsby Cl FHAM/STUB PO14 ....294 C1
Helsted Cl GPORT PO12 ....315 J4
Helston Dr EMRTH PO10 ....277 L7
Helston Rd CHAM PO6 ....274 B9
Helvellyn Rd ROWN SO16 ....247 K3
Helyar Rd CHAR BH8 ....323 M5
Hemdean Gdns HEND SO30 ....249 M2
Hemlock Rd HORN PO8 ....255 M7
Hemlock Wy CHFD SO53 ....206 B8
Hemming Cl TOTT SO40 ....246 C5
Hemmingway Gdns
FHAM PO15 ....271 J2
Hempland La ALTN GU34 ....189 L2
Hempsted Rd CHAM PO6 ....274 D9
Hemsley Wk HORN PO8 ....255 P7
Henbury Cl CFDH BH17 ....321 J2
Henderson Rd ENEY PO4 ....317 K5
Hendford Rd NBNE BH10 ....322 D5
Hendon Rd BOR GU35 ....154 B6
Hendren Sq AND SP10 ....82 F9
Hendy Cl SSEA PO5 ....19 J7
Henery St GPORT PO12 * 13 F2
Hengest Cl AND SP10 ....82 B8
Hengistbury Rd
NMIL/BTOS BH25 ....326 G7
SBNE BH6 ....336 D3
Hengist Pk SBNE BH6 * 336 F2
Hengist Rd BMTH BH1 ....335 K2
Henley Cl FARN GU14 ....57 M5
Henley Dr FRIM GU16 ....58 D6
Henley Gdns FHAM PO15 ....272 B6
LTDN BH7 ....323 N8
YTLY GU46 ....40 E9
Henley Ga CHOB/PIR GU24 ....77 P4
Henley Rd ENEY PO4 ....317 H5
Henning's Park Rd PLE BH15 ....320 F7
Henry Cl FAWY SO45 ....290 D3
Henry Rd ELGH SO50 ....207 M9
WSHM SO15 ....247 N4
The Henrys NTHA RG18 ....25 N3
Henry St WSHM SO15 * 248 B5
Henshaw Crs NWBY RG14 ....24 A7
Henstead Rd WSHM SO15 ....20 C1
Hensting La RWIN SO21 ....208 C6
Henty Rd ROWN SO16 ....247 L3
Henville Cl LSOL/BMARY PO13 ....295 H9
Henville Rd CHAR BH8 ....335 J1
Henwick Cl NTHA RG18 ....25 K1
Henwick La NTHA RG18 ....25 K3
Henwood Down EPSF GU31 ....215 N2
Hepplewhite Cl TADY RG26 ....33 P5
Hepplewhite Dr KBH RG22 ....89 L4
Hepworth Cl AND SP10 ....4 D1
ITCH SO19 ....249 L9
Hepworth Cft SHST GU47 ....41 M8
Herald Rd HEND SO30 ....250 B2
Herbert Av BKME/WDN BH12 ....321 L4
Herberton Rd SBNE BH6 ....336 A1
Herbert Rd ENEY PO4 ....316 G6
FLEETN GU51 ....74 B3
GPORT PO12 ....315 K3
NMIL/BTOS BH25 ....327 K4
RSAL SP5 ....199 P7
WBNE BH4 ....334 B4
Herbert St PSEA PO1 ....316 E1
Herbert Walker Av
WSHM SO15 ....20 C6
Herbs End FARN GU14 ....57 K8
Hercules St NEND PO2 ....296 F9
Hereford Cl ODIM RG29 ....93 J1
Hereford Ct
LSOL/BMARY PO13 * 314 G2
Hereford La FNM GU9 ....96 B5
Hereford Md FLEETN GU51 ....56 E9
Hereford Rd DEAN RG23 ....68 F7
SSEA PO5 ....19 J7
Hereward Cl ROMY SO51 ....204 F6
Herewood Cl NWBY RG14 ....24 C3
Heritage Gdns
FHAM/PORC PO16 ....295 L2
Heritage Pk DEAN RG23 ....89 M6
Heritage Vw DEAN RG23 ....89 M6
Heritage Wy GPORT PO12 ....295 N9
Hermes Cl FLEETN GU51 ....74 F3
Hermes Ct GPORT PO12 * 295 N9
Hermes Rd
LSOL/BMARY PO13 ....314 B1
Hermitage Cl ALTN GU34 ....132 E7
BPWT SO32 * 231 N4
FARN GU14 ....76 C3
FRIM GU16 ....58 E4
HAV PO9 ....276 E6
WIMB BH21 * 280 E1
Hermitage Rd PSTN BH14 ....321 J6
Hermits Cl THLE RG7 ....27 K4
Herm Rd BKME/WDN BH12 ....321 L3
Herne Rd CHAM PO6 ....296 G1
EPSF GU31 ....215 N2
Heron Cl ALTN GU34 ....132 F3
ENEY PO4 ....317 K3
FLEETS GU52 ....74 F7
FRIM GU16 ....58 E9
LYMN SO41 ....308 B6
Heron Court Rd
MOOR/WNTN BH9 ....322 G8
Herondale HASM GU27 ....156 D7
Heron Dr WIMB BH21 ....279 J7
Heron La ROMY SO51 ....180 B8
Heron Pk CHIN RG24 ....70 A3
Heron Quay EMRTH PO10 ....299 N2
Herons Cl FHAM/STUB PO14 ....294 A5
Heron Sq ELGH SO50 ....228 G3
Herons Ri AND SP10 ....102 F4
Heron Wy KBH RG22 ....89 L3
LSOL/BMARY PO13 ....294 E6
STHA RG19 ....25 L4
Heron Wood Rd ASHV GU12 ....97 K3
Herretts Gdns ASHV GU12 ....97 K2
Herrett St ASHV GU12 ....3 K6
Herriard PL DEAN RG23 ....89 L6
Herriard Wy TADY RG26 ....34 D7
Herrick Cl FRIM GU16 ....59 H2
ITCH SO19 ....249 M7
Herridge Cl TADY RG26 ....52 C3
Herriot Ct YTLY GU46 ....56 D1
Herriott Cl HORN PO8 ....256 A6
Herstone Cl CFDH BH17 ....321 H3
Hertford Cl FBDG SP6 ....220 D9
Hertford Pl PSEA PO1 ....316 F1
Hertsfield FHAM/STUB PO14 ....271 J6
Hesketh Cl RGWD BH24 ....281 N4
Hester Rd ENEY PO4 ....317 K4
Hesters Vw ODIM RG29 ....93 K9
Hestia Cl ROMY SO51 ....204 G5
Heston Cl CHCH/BSGR BH23 ....324 B3
Heston Wy FERN BH22 ....280 D6
Hewett Cl FHAM/STUB PO14 ....293 M2
Hewett Rd FHAM/STUB PO14 ....293 M2
NEND PO2 ....296 G7
Hewetts Ri HLER SO31 ....292 C1
Hewitt Cl GPORT PO12 ....315 L1
Hewitt Rd PLE BH15 ....320 A8
Hewitt's Rd WSHM SO15 ....247 P6
Hewshott Gv LIPH GU30 ....175 M2
Hewshott La LIPH GU30 ....175 L2
The Hexagon AND SP10 * 102 B4
Hexham Cl SHST GU47 ....41 L4
Heyes Dr ITCH SO19 ....249 L8
Heysham Rd BDST BH18 ....320 C1
WSHM SO15 ....247 M4
Heyshott Rd ENEY PO4 ....317 H4
Heytesbury Rd SBNE BH6 ....336 B1
Heyward Rd ENEY PO4 ....316 G4
Heywood Gn ITCH SO19 ....249 N6
Hibberd Wy NBNE BH10 ....322 D6
Hibiscus Crs AND SP10 ....102 A3
Hibiscus Gv BOR GU35 ....154 B6
Hickes Cl BWD BH11 ....301 P9
Hickory Dr FUFL SO22 ....164 D3
Hickory Gdns HEND SO30 ....229 M9
Hicks Cl TADY RG26 ....34 D6
Hicks La BLKW GU17 ....41 J9
Hides Cl WHCH RG28 ....85 L7
Highams Cl KSCL RG20 ....48 D3
Highbank Av WVILLE PO7 ....275 K7
Highbank Gdns FBDG SP6 ....240 D2
High Beeches FRIM GU16 ....58 G3
High Beech Gdns AND SP10 ....5 G6
Highbridge Rd ELGH SO50 ....207 M6
PSTN BH14 ....321 L9
Highbury Cl ELGH SO50 ....230 C3
NMIL/BTOS BH25 ....327 K4
Highbury Gv CHAM PO6 ....297 J3
HASM GU27 ....157 H5
Highbury Rd RAND SP11 ....102 B6
Highbury St PSEA PO1 ....18 D5
Highbury Wy CHAM PO6 ....297 H3
Highclere Av HAV PO9 ....276 D6
Highclere Rd ASHV GU12 ....3 K6
ROWN SO16 ....227 P9
Highclere Wy CHFD SO53 ....228 C1
Highcliff Av SHAM SO14 ....248 C3
Highcliffe Dr ELGH SO50 ....207 J6
Highcliffe Rd
CHCH/BSGR BH23 ....325 L7
GPORT PO12 ....315 K4
WINC SO23 ....23 G7
Highcroft La HORN PO8 ....256 C3
High Cross PSF GU32 ....190 E4
High Cross La PSF GU32 ....190 C5
Highcrown St PTSW SO17 ....248 C1
Highdown FLEETN GU51 ....74 D2
Highdowns KBH RG22 ....89 N5
High Dr KBH RG22 ....89 N1
LSOL/BMARY PO13 ....294 G8
Higher Blandford Rd
BDST BH18 ....300 C8
Highercombe Rd HASM GU27 ....157 K5
Higher Md CHIN RG24 ....70 A5
Higher Merley La WIMB BH21 ....300 A5

Highfield *LYMN* SO41 ....329 K4
RWIN SO21 ....184 A9
Highfield Av *ALDT* GU11 ....2 E7
FHAM/STUB PO14 ....294 D1
LYMN SO41 ....329 J4
NWBY RG14 ....16 E3
PTSW SO17 ....228 B9
RGWD BH24 ....282 E1
RWIN SO21 ....184 A9
WVILLE PO7 ....275 P1
Highfield Cha *BSTK* RG21 ....6 B6
Highfield Cl *ALDT* 3 F7
CHFD SO53 ....206 F7
FARN GU14 ....57 N9
FNM GU9 ....116 B3
LYMN SO41 ....308 B6
PTSW SO17 ....248 C1
WIMB BH21 ....300 A8
WVILLE PO7 ....275 P1
Highfield Crs *GSHT* GU26 ....156 D5
OVTN RG25 ....248 D1
RSAL SP5 ....158 A1
Highfield Dr *RGWD* BH24 ....260 E9
LISS GU33 ....192 F2
LYMN SO41 ....308 B6
Highfield La *LIPH* GU30 ....175 L5
MFD/CHID GU8 ....137 P8
RSAL SP5 ....199 P8
Highfield Pth *FARN* GU14 ....57 N9
Highfield Rd *CHFD* SO53 ....206 G7
FARN GU14 ....57 N9
FERN BH22 ....280 D5
GPORT PO12 ....315 K2
LYMN SO41 ....329 J3
MOOR/WNTN BH9 ....322 E5
NWBY RG14 ....16 D7
PSEA PO1 ....19 K2
PSF GU32 ....215 M1
PTSW SO17 ....248 B2
RGWD BH24 ....282 E1
WIMB BH21 ....300 A8
Highfields *OVTN* RG25 ....87 H4
Highfield Ter *FUFL* SO22 ....22 B5
High Firs Gdns *ROMY* SO51 ....204 C6
High Firs Rd *ITCH* SO19 ....249 K6
ROMY SO51 ....204 C5
Highgate La *FARN* GU14 ....58 B8
Highgate Rd *HSEA* PO3 ....297 J8
Highgrove *FARN* GU14 ....74 A4
Highgrove Cl *TOTT* SO40 ....246 B6
Highgrove Rd *HSEA* PO3 ....297 K9
High Howe Cl *BWD* BH11 ....301 N9
High Howe Gdns *BWD* BH11 ....301 N9
High Howe La *BWD* BH11 ....301 N8
Highland Av
CHCH/BSGR BH23 ....326 D6
Highland Dr *DEAN* RG23 ....88 E1
FLEETN GU51 ....74 E1
Highland Rd *ASHV* GU12 ....3 K3
ENEY PO4 ....277 L9
ENEY PO4 ....317 H5
PSTN BH14 ....321 K7
WIMB BH21 ....278 F9
Highlands Cl *FAWY* SO45 ....268 C8
FNM GU9 ....116 B3
NBAD SO52 ....205 J8
Highlands Gdns *NBNE* BH10 ....322 C5
Highlands Rd *AND* SP10 ....5 H5
CHAM PO6 ....297 M1
FHAM PO15 ....293 P1
FNM GU9 ....96 C4
KBH RG22 ....68 D9
NMIL/BTOS BH25 ....327 K7
Highland St *ENEY* PO4 ....317 J6
Highlands Wy *FAWY* SO45 ....268 B8
RSAL SP5 ....201 K1
Highland Ter *ENEY* PO4 ....317 H5
High Lawn Wy *HAV* PO9 ....276 E5
High Md *FERN* BH22 ....302 A6
FHAM PO15 ....10 A1
High Mead La *FERN* BH22 ....302 A7
High Meadow *ITCH* SO19 ....249 L5
Highmoor Rd *BWD* BH11 ....322 A2
PSTN BH14 ....321 L9
Highmoors *CHIN* RG24 ....69 P1
Highmount Cl *WINC* SO23 ....23 H6
Highnam Gdns *HLER* SO31 ....270 F6
High Oaks Cl *HLER* SO31 ....270 C7
High Oaks Gdns *BWD* BH11 ....301 N9
High Park Rd *BDST* BH18 ....300 A9
FNM GU9 ....96 B8
Highpath Wy *CHIN* RG24 ....68 F5
High Pitfold *GSHT* GU26 ....156 C4
Highridge *ALTN* GU34 ....132 D7
High Ridge Crs
NMIL/BTOS BH25 ....327 L5
High Rd *ELGH* SO50 ....228 F7
High St *ALDT* GU11 ....2 D2
ALTN GU34 ....132 F6
ALTN GU34 ....150 A1
AND SP10 ....4 E4
BOR GU35 ....154 A5
BOR GU35 ....154 F3
BPWT SO32 ....232 A5
BPWT SO32 ....233 M5
BPWT SO32 ....252 C4
BROC SO42 ....289 K9
CHAM PO6 ....297 H2
CHCH/BSGR BH23 ....324 F9
CWTH RG45 ....41 K2
ELGH SO50 ....229 J3
EMRTH PO10 ....299 M1
EPSF GU31 ....215 K8
EPSF GU31 ....215 M2
FARN GU14 ....76 B4
FAWY SO45 ....268 C5
FBDG SP6 ....219 J7
FBDG SP6 ....221 J5
FBDG SP6 ....240 D2

FHAM/PORC PO16 ....11 J4
FHAM/STUB PO14 ....293 M1
GPORT PO12 ....13 H2
HASM GU27 ....157 J6
HEND SO30 ....249 M2
HEND SO30 ....250 C4
HLER SO31 ....270 B3
HTWY RG27 ....55 J7
LSOL/BMARY PO13 ....314 C2
LYMN SO41 ....329 L4
LYMN SO41 ....338 C2
LYND SO43 ....264 F5
NTID SP9 ....98 C2
ODIM RG29 ....93 K1
OVTN RG25 ....86 C5
PLE BH15 ....332 D2
PSEA PO1 ....18 C6
PSF GU32 ....188 E9
PSF GU32 ....213 N4
RAND SP11 ....79 N1
RAND SP11 ....100 B9
RFNM GU10 ....115 N7
RGWD BH24 ....281 L3
RGWD BH24 ....282 D2
RWIN SO21 ....184 A9
SHAM SO14 ....20 E7
STOK SO20 ....139 P3
STOK SO20 ....140 A9
STOK SO20 ....141 K5
TOTT SO40 ....246 E4
WHAM PO17 ....274 B5
WIMB BH21 ....278 D9
WINC SO23 ....22 E4
WVILLE PO7 ....234 F9
High St North *PLE* BH15 ....320 F9
High Thicket Rd *RFNM* GU10 ....135 M5
Hightown Gdns *RGWD* BH24 ....282 F3
Hightown HI *RGWD* BH24 ....283 H5
Hightown Rd *RGWD* BH24 ....282 F5
High Trees *ELGH* SO50 ....230 E2
TOTT SO40 ....275 P2
Hightrees Av *CHAR* BH8 ....323 L6
High Trees Dr *FUFL* SO22 ....164 F5
High Trees Wk *FERN* BH22 ....302 D1
High Vw *FHAM/PORC* PO16 ....273 N3
PSF GU32 ....215 M1
Highview
CHCH/BSGR BH23 ....324 C4
High View Cl *FARN* GU14 ....57 P9
Highview Gdns
BKME/WDN BH12 ....321 L5
High View Rd *FARN* GU14 ....57 P9
High View Wy *WEND* SO18 ....249 H3
High Wk *FHAM* PO15 ....10 A1
Highway Cl *HAV* PO9 ....320 B1
Highway *CWTH* RG45 ....41 H1
Highways Rd *RWIN* SO21 ....183 L9
Highwood Cl *FBDG* SP6 ....239 K5
NWBY RG14 ....24 E1
YTLY GU46 ....56 D1
Highwood La *RGWD* BH24 ....260 C6
NWBY RG14 ....205 H5
Highwood Rdg *KBH* RG22 ....89 M5
Highwood Rd *BROC* SO42 ....286 F9
LSOL/BMARY PO13 ....314 C1
PSTN BH14 ....321 N8
Higworth La *HISD* PO11 ....318 F5
Hilary Av *CHAM* PO6 ....297 J2
Hilary Rd *CFDH* BH17 ....320 E5
Hilda Gdns *WVILLE* PO7 ....255 J8
Hilda Rd *BKME/WDN* BH12 ....321 N6
Hilden Wy *FUFL* SO22 ....164 B2
Hilder Gdns *FARN* GU14 ....76 C1
Hiley Rd *PLE* BH15 ....320 E6
Hilfield *BLKW* GU17 ....40 C3
Hilland Ri *IBOR* GU35 ....154 C4
Hillary Cl *FHAM/PORC* PO16 ....10 C3
FNM GU9 ....116 B3
LYND SO43 ....264 C7
Hillary Rd *BSTK* RG21 ....6 B2
CHCH/BSGR BH23 ....325 J7
FNM GU9 ....116 B3
Hillborough Cl *WVILLE* PO7 ....125 J3
Hill Barn La *RWIN* SO21 ....125 J3
Hillborough Crs *SSEA* PO5 ....19 J7
Hillbourne Rd *CFDH* BH17 ....320 C2
Hillbrook Ri *FHAM* 96 A5
Hillbrow Cl *FHAM* PO15 ....272 E7
Hill Brow Cl *HAV* PO9 ....277 N1
Hill Brow Rd *LISS* GU33 ....192 D3
Hillbrow Rd *SBNE* BH6 ....323 P9
Hillbury Av *FHAM* PO15 ....102 C4
Hillbury Pk *FBDG* SP6 ....239 P6
Hillbury Rd *FBDG* SP6 ....239 P6
Hill Cl *CHCH/BSGR* BH23 ....305 L9
ELGH SO50 ....208 C8
NWBY RG14 ....24 A3
Hill Ct *FARN* GU14 ....57 N4
Hillcrest *FLEETN* GU51 ....74 D1
FNM GU9 * 96 C5
Hillcrest Av *CHFD* SO53 ....206 F7
FERN BH22 ....302 C1
Hillcrest Cl *DEAN* RG23 ....68 E6
Hillcrest Dr *CHFD* SO53 ....206 F7
Hill Crest Dr *RFNM* GU10 ....115 P4
Hill Crest Gdns *BPWT* SO32 ....232 B3
Hill Crest Rd *BKME/WDN* BH12 ....321 J7
MOOR/WNTN BH9 ....322 C4
Hill Cft *FHAM* PO15 ....271 K7
Hillcroft *RSAL* SP5 * 199 P7
Hilldene Wy *HEND* SO30 ....249 N2
Hillditch *LYMN* SO41 ....329 K1
Hilldown Rd *PTSW* SO17 ....228 C9
Hilldowns Av *NEND* PO2 ....296 F7
Hill Dr *FHAM* PO15 ....272 B7
Hill Farm Cl *HASM* GU27 * 156 E8
Hill Farm Rd *NARL* SO24 ....170 C6
RWIN SO21 ....305 A5
Hillgrove Rd *WEND* SO18 ....229 H9
Hill Head Rd
FHAM/STUB PO14 ....293 N8
Hill House HI *LIPH* GU30 ....154 C9

Hillhouse La *STHA* RG19 ....32 D6
Hill Houses La *NARL* SO24 ....186 F1
Hillier Wy *WINC* SO23 ....165 H5
Hill La *CHCH/BSGR* BH23 ....305 L8
CHCH/BSGR BH23 ....325 K5
ROWN SO16 ....227 P9
RWIN SO21 ....207 P4
WSHM SO15 ....248 A2
Hillman Rd *PSTN* BH14 ....321 N7
Hillmead Gdns *HAV* PO9 ....276 B8
Hill Meadow *OVTN* RG25 ....86 C1
Hillmeadow *VWD* BH31 ....258 G6
Hill Park Rd *FHAM* PO15 ....272 B6
GPORT PO12 ....315 K2
Hill Ri *EPSF* GU31 ....270 B2
Hill Ri *BPWT* SO32 ....211 N8
RWIN SO21 ....184 A8
Hill Rd *DEAN* RG23 ....88 F3
FHAM/PORC PO16 ....273 P9
FNM GU9 ....96 A4
GSHT GU26 ....156 D7
HASM GU27 ....157 H7
NWBY RG14 ....24 B3
RGWD BH24 ....303 N2
SOUTH SO11 ....104 D8
Hillsborough Ct *FARN* GU14 ....57 M5
Hill School *RFNM* GU10 ....115 P5
Hillside *CBLY* GU15 ....41 N7
FUFL SO22 ....164 C2
RAND SP11 ....101 M6
TADY RG26 ....49 N1
THLE RG7 ....27 L4
WHCH RG28 ....86 A9
Hillside Av *ROMY* SO51 ....204 E6
WEND SO18 ....248 G2
WVILLE PO7 ....275 K8
Hillside Cl *ALTN* GU34 ....132 F4
BOR GU35 ....155 H2
CHFD SO53 ....206 F7
FLEETN GU51 ....73 P6
FUFL SO22 ....164 D5
RSAL SP5 ....177 M4
Hillside Ct *AND* SP10 ....4 A5
BKME/WDN BH12 ....321 P3
Hillside Dr *CHCH/BSGR* BH23 ....324 B3
Hillside La *FNM* GU9 ....96 C4
Hillside Rd *ALDT* GU11 ....2 C7
ASHV GU12 ....76 G9
BKME/WDN BH12 ....321 P3
HASM GU27 ....156 E8
LYMN SO41 ....329 J4
ODIM RG29 ....93 M2
RFNM GU10 ....116 B7
RWIN SO21 ....163 K3
RWIN SO21 ....183 P1
SHST GU47 ....41 M8
Hillside Vis *AND* SP10 ....82 C9
Hillsley Rd *CHAM* PO6 ....274 B8
Hillson Dr *FHAM* PO15 ....272 A7
Hillsons Rd *HEND* SO30 ....251 H4
Hillstead Ct *BSTK* RG21 ....69 L9
Hill St *PLE* BH15 ....332 E1
ROMY SO51 ....226 A6
Hilltop *FUFL* SO22 ....164 D2
Hilltop Av *YTLY* GU46 ....40 C9
Hillview *HORN* PO8 ....256 C6
Hill Vw *PSF* GU32 ....213 M4
Hill View Pk *ELGH* SO50 * 208 B8
Hill View Rd *FHAM* PO15 ....302 C2
FNM GU9 ....273 H9
FNM GU9 ....95 P9
KBH RG22 ....89 L6
ROMY SO51 ....180 A6
ROMY SO51 ....180 G8
Hillview Rd *FAWY* SO45 ....268 B7
NBNE BH10 ....322 D5
Hill Wk *FHAM* PO15 ....272 B7
Hill Wy *RGWD* BH24 ....281 L4
The Hillway *CHFD* SO53 ....206 F6
FHAM/PORC PO16 ....295 N1
Hilly Cl *RWIN* SO21 ....209 H1
Hillyfields *ROWN* SO16 ....227 P5
Hilsea Crs *NEND* PO2 ....296 C4
Hiltingbury Cl *CHFD* SO53 ....206 F4
Hiltingbury Rd *CHFD* SO53 ....206 D4
Hiltom Rd *RGWD* BH24 ....282 F2
Hilton Cl *PLE* BH15 ....321 J6
Hilton Rd *GPORT* PO12 ....13 F5
NMIL/BTOS BH25 ....327 K3
Hinaidi Wy *FARN* GU14 ....75 N4
Hinchliffe Cl *HISD* PO11 ....332 B1
Hinchliffe Rd *HISD* PO11 ....332 B1
Hindell Cl *FARN* GU14 ....57 P5
Hindhead Rd *HASM* GU27 ....156 D5
Hinkler Rd *ITCH* SO19 ....249 M6
Hinstock Cl *FARN* GU14 ....75 P1
Hinton Crs *ITCH* SO19 ....249 N6
Hinton Flds *WINC* SO23 ....165 L6
Hinton hl *NARL* SO24 ....187 K2
Hinton Manor La *HORN* PO8 ....255 N2
Hinton Rd *BMTH* BH1 ....8 E4
Hinton Wood Av
CHCH/BSGR BH23 ....326 A5
Hintonwood La
CHCH/BSGR BH23 ....326 A5
Hinwood Cl *STOK* SO20 ....140 A9
Ripley Rd *HAV* PO9 ....15 H1
Hirst Copse *RAND* SP11 ....84 C1
Hirst Rd *FAWY* SO45 ....268 D7
Hispano Av *FHAM* PO15 ....271 J3

Hitches La *FLEETN* GU51 ....73 P5
Hitherwood Cl *HORN* PO8 ....276 B1
Hives Wy *LYMN* SO41 ....329 K1
H Jones Crs *ALDT* GU11 ....3 J1
Hoadlands *EPSF* GU31 ....215 N1
Hoad's HI *WHAM* PO17 ....273 P2
Hobart Dr *FAWY* SO45 ....268 D7
Hobart Rd *NMIL/BTOS* BH25 ....327 H5
Hobb La *HEND* SO30 ....250 D5
Hobbs Ct *NARL* SO24 ....168 F5
Hobbs Pk *RGWD* BH24 ....281 M5
Hobbs Rd *BKME/WDN* BH12 ....321 L4
Hobbs Sq *AND* SP10 ....82 G9
Hobby Cl *HSEA* PO3 ....297 J5
Hobson Wy *FAWY* SO45 ....290 F6
Hoburne Gdns
CHCH/BSGR BH23 ....325 N6
Hoburne La *CHCH/BSGR* BH23 ....325 N6
Hockford La *THLE* RG7 ....33 K3
Hockham Ct *HAV* PO9 ....276 C3
Hockley La *CHAM* PO6 ....296 F1
Hockley Link *RWIN* SO21 ....183 N5
Hocombe Dr *CHFD* SO53 ....206 D3
Hocombe Park Cl *CHFD* SO53 ....206 D3
Hocombe Rd *CHFD* SO53 ....206 D3
Hocombe Wood Rd
CHFD SO53 ....206 C3
Hodder Cl *CHFD* SO53 ....206 D8
Hodges Cl *CFDH* BH17 ....320 C2
HAV PO9 ....15 H2
Hoeford Cl *FHAM/PORC* PO16 ....295 P2
Hoe La *ROMY* SO51 ....226 G2
Hoe Rd *BPWT* SO32 ....232 C5
Hoe St *WVILLE* PO7 ....254 B5
The Hoe *LSOL/BMARY* PO13 ....295 J8
Hogarth Cl *BSTK* RG21 ....6 P8
ITCH SO19 ....249 K9
ROMY SO51 ....204 F4
SHST GU47 ....41 M8
Hogarth Ct *AND* SP10 ....4 A1
Hogarth Wy *CHAR* BH8 ....323 M5
Hoggarth Cl *EPSF* GU31 ....191 M9
Hoghatch La *FNM* GU9 ....96 A5
Hogmoor Rd *BOR* GU35 ....153 N4
Hogs Lodge La *HORN* PO8 ....236 D2
Hogue Av *NBNE* BH10 ....322 D2
Hogwood La *HEND* SO30 ....229 N6
Holbeche Cl *YTLY* GU46 ....40 B9
Holbein Cl *BSTK* RG21 ....6 C4
Holborne Cl *NWBY* RG14 ....30 B1
Holbrook Cl *FNM* GU9 ....2 C7
Holbrook Rd
FHAM/PORC PO16 ....11 G7
PSEA PO1 ....19 K2
Holbrook Wy *ALDT* GU11 ....97 H4
Holbury Cl *CHAR* BH8 ....323 L4
Holbury Ct *HAV* PO9 ....277 H5
Holbury Dro *FAWY* SO45 ....290 D5
Holbury La *ROMY* SO51 ....178 D4
Holcot La *HSEA* PO3 ....297 L5
Holcroft Rd *ITCH* SO19 ....249 L6
Holdaway Cl *WINC* SO23 ....145 K9
Holdenhurst Av *LTDN* BH7 ....324 A8
Holdenhurst Cl *HORN* PO8 ....256 C2
Holdenhurst Rd *BMTH* BH1 ....9 H3
CHAR BH8 ....323 N4
Holden La *RWIN* SO21 ....185 D7
Holder Rd *ASHV* GU12 ....97 L2
Holding La *NARL* SO24 ....186 C8
Hole La *BPWT* SO32 ....251 N2
RFNM GU10 ....115 N7
WVILLE PO7 ....254 B3
Holes Bay Rd *PLE* BH15 ....320 D8
Holes Cl *LYMN* SO41 ....327 P5
Holkham Cl *ROWN* SO16 ....227 J9
Hollam Cl *FHAM/STUB* PO14 ....293 P1
Hollam Crs *FHAM/STUB* PO14 ....293 P1
Hollam Dr *FHAM* PO15 ....317 K4
Holland Cl *ALTN* GU34 ....150 A5
Holland Dr *AND* SP10 ....82 D8
Holland Gdns *FLEETN* GU51 ....74 D4
Holland Pk *HLER* SO31 ....270 F7
Holland Pl *LSOL/BMARY* PO13 ....295 H7
Holland Rd *ENEY* PO4 ....316 G4
ITCH SO19 ....248 F9
TOTT SO40 ....246 A4
The Hollands *STHA* RG19 ....25 P4
Hollands Wood Dr
NMIL/BTOS BH25 ....327 K2
Hollies Cl *HEND* SO30 ....300 B8
Hollies Cl *LYMN* SO41 ....308 B7
The Hollies *FARN* GU14 * 57 N4
NWBY RG14 ....30 C1
Hollingbourne Cl *WEND* SO18 ....230 B2
Hollington La *KSCL* RG20 ....29 P5
Hollington Dr *STHA* RG19 * 25 N8
Hollist La *EPSF* GU31 ....217 J9
Hollis Wood Dr *RFNM* GU10 ....115 N5
Hollow Av *BOR* GU35 ....154 F2
HISD PO11 ....318 F5
Hollowhut La *KSCL* RG20 ....48 B4
The Hollow *KSCL* RG20 ....48 B3
STOK SO20 ....160 B3
Holly Av *FRIM* GU16 ....58 G1
Hollybank *LSOL/BMARY* PO13 ....314 D3
Holly Bank Cl *HORN* PO8 ....256 C6
Hollybank Crs *FAWY* SO45 ....268 B6
Hollybank La *EMRTH* PO10 ....277 M6
Hollybank Rd *FAWY* SO45 ....268 B5
Hollybrook Cl *ROWN* SO16 ....247 M2
Hollybrook Gdns *HLER* SO31 ....154 E5
Hollybrook Rd *BOR* GU35 ....154 E5
Hollybrook Rd *ROWN* SO16 ....247 N1
Hollybush La *ALDT* GU11 * 3 J3
HTWY RG27 ....72 B2
TADY RG26 ....50 A3
THLE RG7 ....27 H5

Hollybush Ride *EWKG* RG40 ....40 D1
Holly Cl *ASHV* GU12 ....3 J3
BOR GU35 ....155 K5
FARN GU14 ....58 A7
FAWY SO45 ....290 G2
HLER SO31 ....270 E7
RGWD BH24 ....281 K5
TADY RG26 ....52 B3
Holly Ct *FHAM/PORC* PO16 ....272 C6
Holly Ct *CWTH* RG45 * 40 C1
Hollycroft *STHA* RG19 ....33 H5
Holly Dell *ROWN* SO16 ....228 A7
Holly Dr *CHIN* RG24 ....70 D6
WVILLE PO7 ....276 A4
Holly Gdns *CHCH/BSGR* BH23 ....325 H6
HEND SO30 ....250 C3
LYMN SO41 ....338 F1
Holly Green Ri *BWD* BH11 ....301 N9
Holly La *CHCH/BSGR* BH23 ....325 N6
VWD BH31 ....258 D5
Holly Hatch Rd *TOTT* SO40 ....246 C5
Holly Hedge Cl *FRIM* GU16 ....59 D5
Holly Hedge La *FRIM* GU16 ....58 D3
Holly HI *ROWN* SO16 ....228 B7
Holly Hill Cl *ROWN* SO16 ....228 A7
Holly HI *CHFD* SO53 * 206 G7
Hollyhock Cl *KBH* RG22 ....89 L5
Holly La *CHCH/BSGR* BH23 ....326 E5
LYMN SO41 ....309 P7
NMIL/BTOS BH25 ....327 L3
THLE RG7 ....35 J6
Holly Ldg *CHFD* SO53 * 228 E1
Holly Ms *ROWN* SO16 * 228 B8
Holly Oak Rd *ROWN* SO16 ....227 L9
Hollyridge *HASM* GU27 ....156 G7
Holly Rd *ASHV* GU12 ....3 J3
FARN GU14 ....57 N9
TOTT SO40 ....245 P9
Holly St *GPORT* PO12 ....13 F2
Hollytree Gdns *FRIM* GU16 ....58 C5
Holly Tree Pk *RWIN* SO21 ....125 L5
Hollytrees *FLEETN* GU51 ....74 B6
Hollywater Rd *BOR* GU35 * 102 B4
Holly Wk *BLKW* GU17 ....40 C3
Hollywell Dr *CHAM* PO6 ....296 D2
Hollywood Cl *NBAD* SO52 ....205 K9
Hollywood La *LYMN* SO41 ....329 K2
Holman Cl *HORN* PO8 ....256 A9
TADY RG26 ....49 H7
Holmbrook La *FARN* GU14 ....57 K3
Holm Cl *RGWD* BH24 ....260 C9
Holmdale Rd *GPORT* PO12 ....315 K3
Holmdene *THLE* RG7 ....27 K4
Holmefield Av
FHAM/STUB PO14 ....294 D5
Holme Rd *CHCH/BSGR* BH23 ....326 D7
Holmes Ct *HLER* SO31 ....269 K4
KBH RG22 ....89 N5
Holmes Ct *AND* SP10 ....102 C3
Holmesland Dr *HEND* SO30 ....250 F4
Holmesland La *HEND* SO30 ....250 F4
Holmfield Av *LTDN* BH7 ....271 J7
Holmgrove *FHAM/STUB* PO14 ....271 J7
Holm Hill La
CHCH/BSGR BH23 ....306 D9
Holmhurst Av
CHCH/BSGR BH23 ....326 B6
Holm Oak Cl *FUFL* SO22 ....164 B2
VWD BH31 ....258 E3
Holmsley Cl *LYMN* SO41 ....329 H5
WEND SO18 ....249 L4
Holmsley Ct *TOTT* SO40 * 245 P3
Holmsley Pas *RGWD* BH24 ....306 E1
Holmsley Rd
NMIL/BTOS BH25 ....306 F6
Holmwood Garth
RGWD BH24 ....283 H3
Holne Ct *ENEY* PO4 ....317 L5
Holne Rd *CFDH* BH17 ....320 F3
Holst Cl *KBH* RG22 ....89 M5
Holst Wy *WVILLE* PO7 ....275 P5
Holt Cl *FARN* GU14 ....58 B6
WHAM PO17 ....252 D7
Holt Cots *STHA* RG19 ....33 J6
Holt Ct *ITCH* SO19 ....249 L5
Holt Down *EPSF* GU31 ....215 P2
Holt End La *ALTN* GU34 ....130 C7
Holt Gdns *HAV* PO9 ....257 H8
RAND SP11 ....60 G4
Holt La *HTWY* RG27 ....72 B5
Holt Pound La *RFNM* GU10 ....115 L3
Holt Rd *BKME/WDN* BH12 ....321 P6
WIMB BH21 ....279 K1
WIMB BH21 ....280 D1
WSHM SO15 ....248 B4
Holt Wy *HTWY* RG27 ....72 B2
Holworth Cl *BWD* BH11 ....321 N1
Holy Barn Cl *KBH* RG22 ....89 L2
Holybourne Rd *HAV* PO9 ....15 F2
Holyrood Av *PTSW* SO17 ....248 D1
Holyrood Cl *WVILLE* PO7 ....276 A5
Holywell Cl *FARN* GU14 ....57 P6
Holywell Ct *STHA* RG19 ....25 M4
Home Cl *NARL* SO24 ....150 C7
NARL SO24 ....168 E2
Home Farm Cl *FARN* GU14 ....58 A5
Home Farm Gdns *AND* SP10 ....82 B8
Home Farm Rd *HTWY* RG27 ....55 M5
Home Farm Wy *VWD* BH31 ....258 E4
Homefield *ROMY* SO51 ....204 E4
Home Field Dr *ROWN* SO16 ....226 D7
Homefield Cl *CHAM* PO6 ....297 L2
EMRTH PO10 ....277 P6
Homefield Wy *HORN* PO8 ....236 B6
Home La *RWIN* SO21 ....163 M4
Homelea Cl *FARN* GU14 ....58 A5
Homeleigh Crs *ASHV* GU12 ....76 F4

Home Md OVTN RG25 ....108 D1
  WVILLE PO7 ....255 H8
Home Mead Cl NWBY RG14 ......24 B7
Home Park Rd YTLY GU46 ......40 D8
Homer Cl HORN PO8 ....255 N9
  LSOL/BMARY PO15 ......294 F9
Home Rd BWD BH11 ....322 B1
Home Pk FAWY SO45 * 312 G2
Home Rule Rd HLER SO31 ......270 G6
Homeside Rd MOOR/WNTN BH9 ......322 G6
Homestead Rd ALTN GU34 ...149 N3
Homesteads Rd KBH RG22 ......89 L3
Home Wy EPSF GU31 ......216 A2
Homewell HAV PO9 ......15 F6
Homewood Cl NMIL/BTOS BH25 ......327 L4
Hone HI SHST GU47 ......41 J7
Honeybottom Rd TADY RG26 ...54 C5
Honeybourne Crs SBNE BH6 ...336 E2
Honeycritch La PSF GU32 ......191 H5
Honey La ALTN GU34 ......152 E9
  FHAM PO15 ......272 B5
  RGWD BH24 ......284 A7
Honeysuckle DEAN RG23 ......89 J3
Honeysuckle Cl FUFL SO22 ...183 M2
  HLER SO31 ......270 C5
  KBH RG22 ......89 L3
  LSOL/BMARY PO13 * ...294 F6
  YTLY GU46 ......40 B8
Honeysuckle Ct WVILLE PO7 ...275 P5
Honeysuckle Gdns LYMN SO41 ......328 C6
Honeysuckle La BOR GU35 ...155 J3
  CFDH BH17 ......320 B3
Honeysuckle Rd ROWN SO16 ...228 E7
Honeysuckle Wy CHCH/BSGR BH23 ......325 M7
  CFDH SO53 ......206 C7
Honeywood Cl HSEA PO3 ......297 H5
  TOTT SO40 ......246 B2
Honister Gdns FLEETN GU51 ...74 F2
Hood Cl AND SP10 ......5 K3
  HLER SO31 ......271 H6
  NBNE BH10 ......322 B6
Hood Crs NBNE BH10 ......322 B6
Hood Rd WEND SO18 ......249 J3
Hook Cl CHFD SO53 ......206 C3
  NWBY RG14 ......24 F8
Hook Common HTWY RG27 ...71 N5
Hook Crs CHFD SO53 ......206 B3
Hook Cl CFDH BH17 ......321 J2
Hook La HLER SO31 ......292 G2
  NARL SO24 ......169 K3
  RFNM GU10 ......53 L8
  ROWN SO16 ......67 N4
Hook Park Est HLER SO31 * ...292 D3
Hook Park Rd HLER SO31 ...292 C4
Hookpit Farm La WINC SO23 ...145 J8
Hook Rd HTWY RG27 ......55 P8
  KSCL RG20 ......48 D5
  ODIM RG29 ......71 N8
  ROWY SO51 ......206 A2
Hook's Farm Wy HAV PO9 ...14 C2
Hook's La HAV PO9 ......14 C3
Hookside La FNM GU9 ......116 C1
Hook Water Rd CHFD SO53 ...206 B6
Hookwood La ROWY SO51 ...206 B5
Hooperstead OVTN RG25 ......90 C4
Hoopers Wy DEAN RG23 ......88 F2
Hope Fountain CBLY GU15 ...58 E1
Hope Grant's Rd ALDT GU11 ...75 P8
Hope La FNM GU9 ......116 C1
Hopeman Cl SHST GU47 ......41 L7
Hope Rd HEND SO30 ......249 N1
Hope St PSEA PO1 ......316 E2
Hopewood LISS GU33 ......173 L4
Hope Wy ALDT GU11 ......2 C1
Hopfield Cl WVILLE PO7 ......275 N4
Hopfield Ms WVILLE PO7 ...275 N4
Hopfield Rd HTWY RG27 ......55 H8
Hop Gdn FLEETS GU52 ......74 B6
Hop Garden Rd HTWY RG27 ...71 N3
Hop Gdns NWBY RG14 * 16 C1
Hopkins Cl CHAM PO6 ......296 A1
Hopkins Ct ENEY PO4 ......317 K6
Hopkinson Wy AND SP10 ...101 P1
Hopton Garth CHIN RG24 ......70 B3
Hopwood Cl NWBY RG14 ......24 C3
Horace Rd BOSC BH5 ......335 L2
Hordle La FHAM SO41 ......327 P7
Hordle Rd HAV PO9 ......276 C6
Horlock Rd BOSC SO42 ......286 C7
Hormer Cl SHST GU47 ......41 L5
Hornbeam Cl FARN GU14 ......
  HEND SO30 ......250 D5
  RWIN SO21 ......133 H4
  SHST GU47 ......41 L5
Hornbeam Gdns HEND SO30 ...249 M1
Hornbeam Pl HTWY RG27 ......72 A2
Hornbeam Rd CHFD SO53 ...206 A8
  HAV PO9 ......277 H7
Hornby Wy WIMB BH21 ......278 F9
Hornby Cl HLER SO31 ......292 D1
Hornchurch Rd ROWN SO16 ...227 K7
Horndean Prec HORN PO8 * ...256 D4
Horndean Rd EMRTH PO10 ...299 N6
  HORN PO8 ......256 E3
Horne Rd STHA RG19 ......25 P5
Hornet Cl FHAM PO15 ......272 B8
  GPORT PO12 ......13 F5
Hornet Rd EMRTH PO10 ......299 N6
  FHAM/STUB PO14 ......294 B3
Horning Rd BKME/WDN BH12 ...321 P7
Horn Rd FARN GU14 ......57 M8
Horns Dro ROWN SO16 ......227 J4
Horns HI BPWT SO32 ......253 M1
Horns Hill Cl ROWN SO16 ...227 H6
Horsa Cl SBNE BH6 ......336 C2
Horsa Ct SBNE BH6 ......336 C2
Horsa Rd SBNE BH6 ......336 C2
Horsea La NEND PO2 ......296 F5
Horsea Rd NEND PO2 ......296 G4

Horsebridge Rd HAV PO9 ......276 G6
  STOK SO20 ......160 D3
  STOK SO20 ......161 J6
Horsebridge Wy ROWN SO16 ...227 J7
Horsecroft ROMY SO51 ......204 D5
Horsefair Ct ROMY SO51 ......204 C6
Horse La ALTN GU34 ......149 N9
Horsepost La WVILLE PO7 ...255 K1
Horse Sands Cl ENEY PO4 ...317 N5
Horseshoe Bend GSHT GU26 ...155 P5
Horseshoe Cl FHAM/STUB PO14 ......271 K8
  WIMB BH21 ......279 K8
Horseshoe Crs BOR GU35 ...154 B5
  THLE RG7 ......27 J4
Horseshoe Rd ROMY SO51 ...204 F3
  TOTT SO40 ......245 N1
Horseshoe End NWBY RG14 ...24 E8
Horseshoe La ASHV GU12 ...76 F6
  RAND SP11 * 2 D2
Horseshoe Ldg HLER SO31 ...270 E9
Horsham Av NBNE BH10 ......322 C1
Horsham Rd SHST GU47 ......41 L5
Horton Cl MOOR/WNTN BH9 ...323 J4
Horton Rd LSOL/BMARY PO13 ...294 C5
  RGWD BH24 ......281 J5
  WIMB BH21 ......280 C1
Horton Wy ELGH SO50 ......229 P3
  VWD BH31 ......258 D5
Horwood Gdns BSTK RG21 ...90 B1
Hosker Rd BOSC BH5 ......335 P1
Hosketts La STOK SO20 ......139 M3
Hospital HI ALDT GU11 ......2 C2
Hospital La FHAM/PORC PO16 ...296 A3
Hospital Rd ALDT GU11 ......75 P9
  BPWT SO32 ......252 E2
Hostel Rd FARN GU14 ......1 A4
Hotspur Ct FAWY SO45 ......268 B5
Houchin St BPWT SO32 ......232 A5
Houghton Cl HAV PO9 * 277 H4
Houlton Rd PLE BH15 ......320 G8
Hound Cl HLER SO31 ......269 M5
Hound Green Cl HTWY RG27 ...54 A2
Houndmills Rd BSTK RG21 ...89 M5
Hound Rd HLER SO31 ......269 M4
Hound Road Gdns HLER SO31 ...269 M5
Hounds Wy WIMB BH21 ......279 K9
Houndwell Pl SHAM SO14 ...21 F5
Hounsdown Av TOTT SO40 ...246 D6
Hounsdown Cl TOTT SO40 ...246 D6
Hounslow Cl PLE BH15 ......332 A1
Hoursome Ct DEAN RG23 ......89 M7
House Cl RWIN SO21 ......208 A4
House Farm Rd GPORT PO12 ...315 J4
Houseman Rd FARN GU14 ...57 N7
Hoveton Gv CHFD SO53 ......206 D5
Howard Cl CHCH/BSGR BH23 ...325 K9
  CHFD SO53 ......206 F9
  ELGH SO50 ......230 C2
  FLEETN GU51 ......74 B6
  LSOL/BMARY PO13 ......314 E1
  RGWD BH24 ......284 B7
  WEND SO18 ......228 G8
Howard's Gv WSHM SO15 ...247 P5
Howard's La ALTN GU34 ......133 J2
Howards Md LYMN SO41 ......329 H5
Howe Cl CHCH/BSGR BH23 ...337 K1
  NMIL/BTOS BH25 ......327 H4
Howe La VWD BH31 ......258 F5
Howe Rd LSOL/BMARY PO13 ...314 G2
Howerts Cl HLER SO31 ......292 D2
Howes Gdns FLEETN GU51 ...74 B6
Howeth Cl NBNE BH10 ......322 D4
The Howe FARN GU14 ......75 J3
Howeth Rd NBNE BH10 ......322 C3
Howlett Cl LYMN SO41 ......329 J3
Howorth Cl NBNE BH10 * 322 C2
Howton Rd NBNE BH10 ......322 C2
Hoxley Rd NBNE BH10 ......322 D5
Hoylake Cl LSOL/BMARY PO13 ...294 G2
Hoyle Rd CHAM PO6 ......275 L9
Hoylecroft Cl FARN GU14 ...10 A1
Hubert Rd WINC SO23 ......185 N2
Huddington Gld HTWY RG27 ...40 B9
Hudson Cl BKME/WDN BH12 ...321 L2
  LIPH GU30 ......175 K4
  LSOL/BMARY PO13 ......314 G2
Hudson Ct TOTT SO40 ......246 A5
Hudson Davies Cl LYMN SO41 ...309 M7
Hudson Rd PSEA PO1 ......19 J5
Hudsons Meadow HTWY RG27 ...54 A2
Hugh's Cl FAWY SO45 ......290 G8
Hughs La OVTN RG25 ......107 L8
Hulbert Rd WVILLE PO7 ......275 P5
Hulbert Wy KBH RG22 ......89 N1
Hulfords La HTWY RG27 ......55 K4
Hullam La ALTN GU34 ......172 A2
Hull Crs BWD BH11 ......301 M9
Hulse La LYMN NBAD SO52 ...205 M9
Hull Rd BWD BH11 ......301 M9
Hull Wy BWD BH11 ......301 N9
Hulse Rd WSHM SO15 ......248 B3
Hulton Cl ITCH SO19 ......268 F1
Humber Cl FHAM/STUB PO14 ......295 P6
  NTHA RG18 ......25 L2
Humber Ct AND SP10 ......82 G9
Humber Gdns HLER SO31 ...270 A1
Humber La NTID SP9 ......78 F7
Humber Rd FERN BH22 ......302 G2
Humberstone Rd AND SP10 ...4 C7
Humber Vw STOK SO20 ......161 M6
Humber Wy SHST GU47 ......41 L6

The Hummicks BROC SO42 ...289 N9
Humming Bird Ct KBH RG22 ...89 K3
Hundred Acres Rd WHAM PO17 ......253 J8
Hundred La LYMN SO41 ......309 M9
The Hundred ROMY SO51 ......204 D5
Hungerfield Ct CHCH/BSGR BH23 ......305 L7
Hungerford HLER SO31 ......269 P3
Hungerford Cl SHST GU47 ...41 K6
Hungerford HI FBDG SP6 ...260 D2
Hungerford La RAND SP11 ...60 D2
  RAND SP11 ......60 D2
Hungerford Rd CHAR BH8 ...323 K4
Hunnels Cl FLEETS GU52 ......74 B9
Hunt Av HLER SO31 ......269 L4
Hunt Cl RWIN SO21 ......144 F4
Hunter Cl CHCH/BSGR BH23 ...325 L8
  FAWY SO45 ......290 D3
  LSOL/BMARY PO13 ......315 H1
  WIMB BH21 ......279 L8
Hunter Rd EMRTH PO10 ......299 N5
  ENEY PO4 ......317 H5
  GPORT PO12 ......75 N1
Hunters Cha BPWT SO32 ...232 G9
  LIPH GU30 ......175 J2
  VWD BH31 ......259 J5
Hunters Cl HLER SO31 * 250 B8
Hunters Crs ROMY SO51 ...204 C4
  TOTT SO40 ......245 P5
Hunter's HI THLE RG7 ......27 M9
  TOTT SO40 ......246 B8
Hunters Ldg FHAM PO15 ...293 P1
Hunters Ride WVILLE PO7 ...275 N3
Hunters Rd LISS GU33 ......174 A5
Hunters Wy ELGH SO50 ......230 A2
Huntfield Rd MOOR/WNTN BH9 ......323 H4
Huntingdon Cl FHAM/STUB PO14 ......271 J9
Huntingdon Dr WIMB BH21 ...300 G4
Huntingdon Gdns CHCH/BSGR BH23 ......324 D5
  ELGH SO50 ......230 D5
Huntingdon House Dr GSHT GU26 ......156 D1
Huntly Ga AND SP10 ......102 A2
Huntley Cl CHAM PO6 ......274 D9
Huntly Rd TWDS BH3 ......322 D9
Huntly Wy WEND SO18 ......249 H4
Hunton Down La RWIN SO21 ...126 A5
Hunton La RWIN SO21 ......125 P5
Hunton Rd HAV PO9 ......325 K7
  PLE BH15 ......320 G8
Huntsbottom La LISS GU33 ...192 F3
Hunts Cl HTWY RG27 ......72 B3
Hunts Common HTWY RG27 ...55 J6
Hunts Hill Rd RGUW GU3 ...77 M7
Huntsman's Ms FRIM GU16 ...58 E9
Huntsmead ALTN GU34 ......132 C6
Huntsmoor Rd TADY RG26 ...54 C4
Hunts Pond Rd HLER SO31 ...271 H6
Huntvale Rd MOOR/WNTN BH9 ......323 H4
The Hurdles CHCH/BSGR BH23 ......323 N2
  FHAM/STUB PO14 ......271 K8
Hurdle Wy RWIN SO21 ......183 L6
Hurland La BOR GU35 ......154 G4
Hurlands Cl FNM GU9 ......96 F7
Hurlands Pl FNM GU9 ......96 F7
Hurlingham Gdns ROWN SO16 ...228 C7
Hurn Br CHCH/BSGR BH23 ...282 B3
Hurn Cl RGWD BH24 ......282 B3
Hurn Ct HAV PO9 ......282 A9
Hurn La RGWD BH24 ......282 B3
Hurn Rd CHCH/BSGR BH23 ...282 A9
  RCWD BH24 ......282 A9
Hurn Wy CHCH/BSGR BH23 ...282 A9
Huron Cl LIPH GU30 ......175 L4
Hurricane Dr ROWN SO16 ...227 J6
Hurricane Wy FARN GU14 ...75 N5
Hursley Cl HLER SO31 ......324 A8
Hursley Dr FAWY SO45 ......312 C1
Hursley Park Rd RWIN SO21 ...182 D3
Hurst Av CHCH/BSGR BH23 ...323 N2
Hurst Cl ASHV GU12 ......3 H6
  WIMB BH21 * 206 D1
Hurst Court La CHCH/BSGR BH23 ......323 N2
Hurst HI PSTN BH14 ......333 L1
Hurst La ALTN GU34 ......190 B3
  RWIN SO21 ......208 C3
Hurst Lea LYMN SO41 * 329 K6
Hurstly La LYMN SO41 * 309 H5
Hurstmere Cl GSHT GU26 ...156 C2
Hurst Rd ALDT GU11 ......76 B9
  FARN GU14 ......58 A5
  NARL SO24 ......339 H5
  STHA RG19 ......33 L5
The Hurst HTWY RG27 ......73 L5
Hurstville Dr WVILLE PO7 ...275 P4
Hussar Cl CHCH/BSGR BH23 ...324 D8
Hussar Ct ALDT GU11 ......96 E1
  WVILLE PO7 * 275 P4
Hussell La ALTN GU34 ......150 A1
Hussey Cl WINC SO23 ......165 H5
Hussey's La ALTN GU34 ......114 A5

Hutton Cl NWBY RG14 ......24 E3
Hutton Rd ASHV GU12 ......76 F6
Hutton Sq AND SP10 ......82 G9
Hutwood Rd ROWN SO16 ...228 C4
Huxley Cl HLER SO31 ......271 H8
Huxley Rd FAWY SO45 ......267 N8
Hyacinth Cl CFDH BH17 ......320 B5
  KBH RG22 ......89 L3
Hyde Abbey Rd WINC SO23 ...22 E2
Hyde Church La WINC SO23 ...22 E2
Hyde Church Pth WINC SO23 ...22 E1
Hyde Cl LYMN SO41 ......308 B6
  TOTT SO40 ......246 B2
  WINC SO23 ......22 E2
  WSHM SO15 ......247 N2
Hyde End La STHA RG19 ......32 G1
Hyde Ga WINC SO23 ......22 E2
Hyde House Gdns CHCH/BSGR BH23 ......325 N9
Hyde La FBDG SP6 ......240 G5
  KSCL RG20 ......31 M8
  RFNM GU10 ......94 F4
  RFNM GU10 ......137 K8
Hyden Farm La HORN PO8 ...235 M6
Hyde Park Rd SSEA PO5 ......19 H4
Hyde Rd RBNE BH10 ......322 C2
Hydes Platt THLE RG7 ......35 H6
Hyde St SSEA PO5 * 19 G6
  WINC SO23 ......22 E3
The Hyde NMIL/BTOS BH25 ...326 C3
Hylton Rd TADY RG26 ......66 C1
Hylton Ct EPSF GU31 ......215 M2
Hynesbury Rd CHCH/BSGR BH23 ......325 N9
Hyson Crs RAND SP11 ......80 B1
Hyssop Cl FHAM PO15 ......271 K3
Hythe By-Pass FAWY SO45 ...267 M6
Hythe Cl TADY RG26 ......34 C7
Hythe Rd CHAM PO6 ......296 C1
  PLE BH15 ......321 J5
  TOTT SO40 ......267 K2

I

Ibbertson Cl CHAR BH8 ......323 M5
Ibbertson Rd CHAR BH8 ......323 M5
Ibbertson Wy CHAR BH8 ...323 M5
Ibbett Rd NBNE BH10 ......322 C5
Ibbotson Wy TOTT SO40 ...246 B6
Ibsen Cl HLER SO31 ......271 J2
Ibsley Cl CHAR BH8 ......323 J9
Ibsley Dro RGWD BH24 ...260 E1
Ibsley Gv HAV PO9 ......14 B2
Ibworth La TADY RG26 ......66 C1
Icarus Pl WVILLE PO7 ......275 P8
Icknield Wy AND SP10 ......82 F7
Iddesleigh Rd TWDS BH3 ...322 F9
Iden Ct NWBY RG14 ......24 A6
Idsworth Cl HORN PO8 ......256 E5
Idsworth Rd HORN PO8 ......256 E5
  HSEA PO3 ......297 J9
Iford Br CHCH/BSGR BH23 ...324 B7
Iford Cl HAV PO9 ......14 B2
Iford Gdns LTDN BH7 ......324 A8
Iford La SBNE BH6 ......324 C8
  WINC SO23 ......145 J8
  YTLY GU46 ......40 C8
Ilex Crs HLER SO31 ......271 H6
Ilex Wk HISD PO11 ......319 J5
Iley La LYMN SO41 ......329 J8
Ilford Cl SBNE BH6 ......324 A8
Ilkley Wy STHA RG19 ......25 M5
Illingworth Cl TADY RG26 ...52 C3
Imadene Crs BOR GU35 ...154 C4
Imber Cl ITCH SO19 ......249 J7
Imber Dr CHCH/BSGR BH23 ...305 J8
Imber Rd WINC SO23 ......23 J5
Imber Wy ITCH SO19 ......249 J7
Imbrecourt CCLF BH13 ......333 N4
Imjin Cl ALDT GU11 ......2 D1
Imperial Av WSHM SO15 ...247 M4
Imperial Rd WSHM SO15 ...247 M4
Imperial Wy WSHM SO15 ...248 D4
Implacable Rd LSOL/BMARY PO13 ......314 E1
Impstone Rd TADY RG26 ...34 C5
Imran Ct ASHV GU12 ......3 H6
Ingersley Ri HEND SO30 ...249 M2
Ingle Dell CBLY GU15 ......58 C1
Ingledene Cl GPORT PO12 ...14 B4
  HAV PO9 ......14 B4
Ingle Gln FAWY SO45 ......268 C9
Inglegreen La PLE BH15 ...320 A9
Ingleside HLER SO31 ......269 L8
Ingleside Cl FHAM/STUB PO14 ...293 P1
Ingleton Rd ROWN SO16 ...247 H2
Inglewood Av CBLY GU15 ...59 H1
Inglewood Dr KBH RG22 ...89 N5
  NMIL/BTOS BH25 ......327 K5
Inglis Rd SSEA PO5 ......316 G5
Ingoldfield La WHAM PO17 ...253 N4
Ingram Wk WIMB BH21 ......300 F1
Ings Cl ALTN GU34 ......132 F7
Ingworth Rd BKME/WDN BH12 ...334 A1
Inhams La WVILLE PO7 ......255 K1
Inhams Wy THLE RG7 ......35 H6
Inhurst Rd BWD BH11 ......
Inhurst Wy TADY RG26 ......34 A5
Inkerman Rd ITCH SO19 ......268 E2
Inkpen Gdns CHIN RG24 ...70 B4
Inmans La PSF GU32 ......190 E1
Innisfail Gdns ALDT GU11 ...2 A6
Insley Crs BDST BH18 ......300 A8
Institute Rd ASHV GU12 ......3 K6
Instow Gdns FARN GU14 ...57 P6

Interchange Pk HSEA PO3 * ...297 L6
International Wy ITCH SO19 ...268 G2
Inval HI HASM GU27 ......157 H5
Inveravon CHCH/BSGR BH23 ...337 K1
Inverclyde Rd PSTN BH14 ...321 L8
Invergordon Av CHAM PO6 ...297 K2
Inverkip Cl LSOL/BMARY PO13 * 314 C1
Inverleigh Rd SBNE BH6 ...336 B9
Inverness Av FHAM PO15 ...10 A2
Inverness Rd GPORT PO12 ...315 L3
  NEND PO2 ......316 C1
Inverness Wy SHST GU47 ...41 L7
Invincible Rd FARN GU14 ...75 P1
  FHAM/STUB PO14 ......293 H8
Inwood Rd LISS GU33 ......192 E3
Ionic Cl CHFD SO53 ......206 B8
Ipley Av FAWY SO45 ......290 C8
Ipley Wy FAWY SO45 ......268 C8
Ipoh Cl STOK SO20 ......120 G4
Ipswich Rd WBNE BH4 ......334 B2
Ireland Wy WVILLE PO7 ...275 N5
Iris Cl KBH RG22 ......89 J2
Iris Rd MOOR/WNTN BH9 ...322 F6
  ROWN SO16 ......228 D8
Ironbridge Crs HLER SO31 ...270 C4
Ironbridge La ENEY PO4 ...317 L4
Iron Mill Cl FHAM PO15 ...272 B7
Ironmill La FHAM PO15 ...271 P5
Irvine Cl CHAM PO6 ......296 A1
Irvine Dr FARN GU14 ......57 M5
Irvine Rd CHCH/BSGR BH23 ...325 J7
Irving Rd ROWN SO16 ......247 K2
  SBNE BH6 ......336 B1
Irwell Cl BSTK RG21 ......7 J6
  CHFD SO53 ......206 C8
Isaacs Cl BKME/WDN BH12 ...322 B8
Isambard Brunel Rd PSEA PO1 ...19 G3
Isington La ALTN GU34 ......114 C7
Isington Rd ALTN GU34 ......134 B1
Isis Cl ROWN SO16 ......247 J3
Isis Wy SHST GU47 ......41 M8
Island Cl HISD PO11 ......298 C6
Island Farm Rd THLE RG7 ...26 C6
Island View Av CHCH/BSGR BH23 ......325 M9
Island View Cl LYMN SO41 ...339 H3
Island View Rd NMIL/BTOS BH25 ......326 F8
Island View Ter NEND PO2 ...296 B8
Islay Gdns CHAM PO6 ......275 H9
Itchel La FARN GU14 ......94 F4
Itchen Av ELGH SO50 ......229 P2
The Itchen Br ITCH SO19 ...21 K7
Itchen Cl DEAN RG23 ......88 F2
  PSF GU32 ......215 L3
  ROMY SO51 ......224 D1
Itchen Ct AND SP10 ......82 G9
Itchenor Rd HISD PO11 ......319 M6
Itchen Rd HAV PO9 ......14 B2
Itchenside Cl WEND SO18 ...229 H8
Itchen St SSEA PO5 ......19 J4
Itchen Wy ELGH SO50 ......207 K7
  ITCH SO19 ......248 F8
  NARL SO24 ......167 N7
  RWIN SO21 ......166 F2
  WINC SO23 ......23 G7
Itchin Cl TOTT SO40 ......246 B5
Ithica Cl HISD PO11 ......318 C4
Ivamy Pl BWD BH11 ......321 P2
Ivanhoe Rd WSHM SO15 ...247 P2
Ivar Gdns CHIN RG24 ......70 A4
Ively Rd FARN GU14 ......75 K3
Ives Cl YTLY GU46 ......40 C7
Ivor Cl FAWY SO45 ......290 E5
Ivor Rd PLE BH15 ......332 C2
Ivy Cl FUFL SO22 ......183 L8
  RGWD BH24 ......281 K5
  TOTT SO40 ......246 C1
Ivy Ct WVILLE PO7 ......275 M6
Ivy Dene CHIN RG24 ......249 M7
Ivydene Gdns HORN PO8 ...256 A7
Ivy Down La DEAN RG23 ...87 P2
Ivyhouse Hi HTWY RG27 ...55 N5
Ivyhouse La PSF GU32 ......190 E5
Ivy La FNM GU9 ......96 B9
  HEND SO30 ......249 K1
  RGWD BH24 ......260 E7
Ivy Rd ASHV GU12 ......97 L1
  PTSW SO17 ......248 E3
  WIMB BH21 ......300 C5
Iwerne Cl MOOR/WNTN BH9 ...323 H5

J

Jacaranda Cl FHAM PO15 ...271 L7
Jacaranda Rd BOR GU35 ...154 A6
Jack Cl CHFD SO53 ......206 A7
Jack Cockerill Wy SSEA PO5 * ...316 F8
Jackdaw Cl HORN PO8 ......255 N7
  KBH RG22 ......89 K3
Jackdaw Ri ELGH SO50 ......228 F3
Jackie Wigg Gdns TOTT SO40 ...246 D4
Jacklyns Cl NARL SO24 ......167 P3
Jacklyns La NARL SO24 ......167 N3
Jackmans Cl ITCH SO19 ...248 F8
Jackman's Hi RWIN SO21 ...184 G1
Jackson Cl CHAM PO6 ......297 L3
Jackson Rd BKME/WDN BH12 ...321 L6
Jacobean Cl CHCH/BSGR BH23 ......326 D6
Jacob Rd CBLY GU15 ......41 P7
Jacobs Cl HORN PO8 ......236 C7
  ROMY SO51 ......204 E6
Jacob's Gutter La TOTT SO40 ...246 D6
Jacobs La PSF GU32 ......190 E5
Jacob's St PSEA PO1 ......19 H1
Jacobs Wk TOTT SO40 ......246 C7
Jacomb Pl LSOL/BMARY PO13 * 295 H7
Jacqueline Av WVILLE PO7 ...275 M6

Jacqueline Rd
BKME/WDN BH12 321 K5
Jade Ct LSOL/BMARY PO13 * 314 G2
Jagdalik Rd NTID SP9 78 G7
Jago Rd PSEA PO1 18 B1
Jaguar Rd FARN GU14 76 A2
Jamacia Pl GPORT PO12 12 E3
Jamaica Pl GPORT PO12 12 E3
Jamaica Rd GPORT PO12 315 P3
James Callaghan Dr
CHAM PO6 274 C8
James Cl BSTK RG21 7 G1
HISD PO11 318 E5
LSOL/BMARY PO13 294 G5
James Copse Rd HORN PO8 255 P6
James Grieve Av HLER SO31 270 G8
Jameson Rd MOOR/WNTN BH9 322 E6
James Rd ALDT GU11 76 C5
BKME/WDN BH12 334 A1
CBLY GU15 58 A3
HAV PO9 14 C3
LSOL/BMARY PO13 294 G5
James's La RDGW/BURGH RG30 27 M3
James St SHAM SO14 21 G4
James Wy CBLY GU15 58 A3
Jamrud Rd NTID SP9 78 F6
Janaway Gdns PTSW SO17 248 E3
Janes Cl FAWY SO45 290 G9
Jan Smuts Cl LISS GU33 174 A6
Janson Rd WSHM SO15 247 N4
Japonica Wy HAV PO9 277 J6
Jaques's La FLEET RG7 27 H1
Jardine Sq AND SP10 82 G9
Jarndyce Wk NEND PO2 * 316 E1
Jarvis Cl HTWY RG27 39 P6
Jarvis Flds HLER SO31 270 B2
Jasmine Ct AND SP10 * 102 B4
FHAM PO15 271 K1
LSOL/BMARY PO13 * 314 G2
LYMN SO41 329 K3
Jasmine Gv WVILLE PO7 276 A4
Jasmine Rd HEND SO30 250 B3
KBH RG22 89 M3
Jasmine Wk FHAM/STUB PO14 10 A7
Jasmine Wy BOR GU35 154 B6
HORN PO8 236 C7
Jasmond Rd CHAM PO6 297 H3
Jason Pl WVILLE PO7 275 N8
Jason Wy GPORT PO12 * 295 K9
Jaundrells Cl NMIL/BTOS BH25 327 L4
Java Dr FHAM PO15 271 J3
Java Rd SHAM SO14 268 D1
Javelin Rd EMRTH PO10 299 N6
J Av FAWY SO45 291 H3
Jay Cl FHAM/STUB PO14 293 P5
HORN PO8 256 A4
Jays Cl BSTK RG21 90 D2
KBH RG22 90 B3
Jay's Ct CHCH/BSGR BH23 326 D7
Jays Nest Cl BLKW GU17 57 L1
Jealous La LYMN SO41 308 G6
Jefferson Av CHAR BH8 323 K9
Jefferson Rd BSTK RG21 7 F1
Jeffries Cl ROWN SO16 227 J7
Jellicoe Av GPORT PO12 315 K6
Jellicoe Cl PSTN BH14 321 H7
Jellicoe Ct AND SP10 * 5 J3
Jellicoe Dr CHCH/BSGR BH23 325 K9
Jenkins Cl HEND SO30 250 G4
Jenkins Gv HSEA PO3 317 K1
Jenner Cl VWD BH31 258 E3
Jenner Wy ALTN GU34 132 G3
ROMY SO51 204 G5
Jennie Green La ALTN GU34 130 G7
Jennings Rd PSTN BH14 333 L1
TOTT SO40 246 E3
Jenny's Wk YTLY GU46 40 F8
Jenson Gdns AND SP10 102 C3
Jephcote Rd BWD BH11 301 P9
Jermyns La ROMY SO51 204 G2
Jerome Cnr CWTH RG45 41 K3
Jerome Ct ITCH SO19 249 M5
Jerram Cl GPORT PO12 315 K5
Jerrett's La ROWN SO16 227 H9
Jersey Brow Rd FARN GU14 75 P2
Jersey Cl BKME/WDN BH12 321 L3
CHIN RG24 69 M2
FHAM/STUB PO14 294 B8
FLEETN GU51 56 E9
ROWN SO16 227 J9
Jersey Rd BKME/WDN BH12 321 M3
NEND PO2 296 G9
Jervis Ct AND SP10 5 J2
Jervis Court La BPWT SO32 232 E4
Jervis Dr GPORT PO12 315 M2
Jervis Rd NEND PO2 296 E7
Jesmond Av CHCH/BSGR BH23 326 B7
Jesmond Dene NWBY RG14 24 C3
Jesmond Gv HLER SO31 270 G9
Jessamine Rd ROWN SO16 247 M1
Jesse Cl BLKW GU17 40 G9
Jessett Dr FLEETS GU52 74 B8
Jessica Av VWD BH31 258 D3
Jessica Cl WVILLE PO7 276 B1
Jessica Crs TOTT SO40 245 P2
Jessie Rd ENEY PO4 316 G4
GPORT PO12 12 B3
HAV PO9 14 A2
Jessie Ter SHAM SO14 21 F7
Jessop Cl FAWY SO45 268 B5
Jessopp Cl NBNE BH10 322 F3
Jessopp Rd WIMB BH21 279 K8
Jesty Rd NARL SO24 167 N3
Jetty Rd FAWY SO45 291 K4
Jewell Rd CHAR BH8 323 M6
Jewry St WINC SO23 22 E4
Jex Blake Cl ROWN SO16 227 M8
Jibbs Meadow TADY RG26 52 A2
Jimmy Brown Av WIMB BH21 280 E4
Jinny La ROMY SO51 180 C9
Joanna Cl RSAL SP5 199 H6
Jobson Cl WHCH RG28 85 L6
Jockey La ELGH SO50 207 N8
Jodrell Cl HORN PO8 256 C4
Joe Bigwood Cl ROWN SO16 227 H7
John Bunyan Cl FHAM PO15 271 J2
John Cl ALDT GU11 96 E3
John Darling Ml ELGH SO50 * 207 J9
John Eggars Sq ALTN GU34 132 G4
John Hunt Cl STHA RG19 25 P5
John King Shipyard
EMRTH PO10 * 299 N1
John Morgan Cl HTWY RG27 71 P2
Johnson Rd WIMB BH21 302 A1
Johnson St SHAM SO14 21 F4
Johnson Vw FHAM PO15 271 L4
Johnson Wy FLEETS GU52 74 C6
RAND SP11 79 N2
Johns Rd FHAM/PORC PO16 294 F2
ITCH SO19 248 F8
Johnstone Rd
CHCH/BSGR BH23 325 J9
Johnston Rd PLE BH15 320 F5
John St SHAM SO14 21 F7
Jolliffe Av PLE BH15 320 F8
Jolliffe Rd PLE BH15 320 F8
Jonas Nichols Sq SHAM SO14 21 G4
Jonathan Cl LYMN SO41 329 L2
Jonathan Hl KSCL RG20 30 G3
Jonathan Rd FHAM PO15 10 A5
Jones La FAWY SO45 268 B6
Jopps Cnr CHCH/BSGR BH23 324 G3
Jordans La LYMN SO41 308 C5
LYMN SO41 309 P7
THLE RG7 27 H5
Joseph St GPORT PO12 * 13 F2
Joshua Cl PLE BH15 332 A1
Josian Wk SHAM SO14 21 G3
Jouldings La HTWY RG27 38 G2
Joule Rd AND SP10 101 P1
BSTK RG21 6 B2
Jowitt Dr NMIL/BTOS BH25 327 H5
Joys La LYMN SO41 310 C8
STOK SO20 123 L5
WIMB BH21 279 N9
Joys Rd WIMB BH21 280 E1
Jubilee Av CHAM PO6 296 A1
Jubilee Cl ELGH SO50 229 H3
FARN GU14 57 K9
RGWD BH24 282 G1
TADY RG26 34 F5
WIMB BH21 300 A6
Jubilee Ct FHAM/STUB PO14 294 E2
LYMN SO41 308 B7
Jubilee Crs BKME/WDN BH12 321 M7
Jubilee Dr ASHV GU12 76 F6
Jubilee Gdns NBNE BH10 322 D5
WEND SO18 249 J4
Jubilee Hall Rd FARN GU14 58 B9
Jubilee La GSHT GU26 156 B2
RFNM GU10 116 A5
Jubilee Pth HAV PO9 14 A5
Jubilee Rd ALDT GU11 97 H4
BSTK RG21 69 L8
ENEY PO4 317 H5
EWKG RG40 40 A1
FBDG SP6 240 A2
FHAM/PORC PO16 295 P1
FRIM GU16 76 F2
GPORT PO12 315 M3
NWBY RG14 17 G4
PSTN BH14 321 M7
ROMY SO51 204 C5
WIMB BH21 300 A7
WVILLE PO7 275 N2
Jubilee Ter SSEA PO5 19 F6
Jukes Wk HEND SO30 249 P1
Julia Cl CHCH/BSGR BH23 326 B7
Julian Cl ROWN SO16 228 B6
Julian Rd ITCH SO19 249 K8
Julian Ter BOSC BH5 * 335 P1
Julie Av FHAM PO15 10 A5
Juliet Ct WVILLE PO7 * 276 A2
Julius Cl CHIN RG24 68 F4
CHFD SO53 206 G7
Julyan Av BKME/WDN BH12 322 A7
Jumar Cl HLER SO31 292 D2
Jumpers Av CHCH/BSGR BH23 324 C7
Jumpers Rd
CHCH/BSGR BH23 324 D7
Jumps Rd RFNM GU10 136 F6
Junction Rd AND SP10 4 A2
MOOR/WNTN BH9 322 F7
TOTT SO40 246 E4
Junction Ter NWBY RG14 17 J3
June Dr DEAN RG23 68 E7
Juniper Cl AND SP10 102 B3
BOR GU35 153 M6
CHIN RG24 70 B9
FERN BH22 280 C9
FUFL SO22 183 M1
LYMN SO41 329 H5
NBAD SO52 205 K8
WIMB BH21 280 E1
Juniper Rd FARN GU14 57 K8
HORN PO8 * 256 C2
WEND SO18 249 H4
Juniper Sq HAV PO9 15 G7
Jupiter Cl ROWN SO16 227 J8
Jupiter Wy WIMB BH21 300 A5
Jura Cl CHAM PO6 275 H9
Jurds Lake Wy ITCH SO19 268 F1
Jurd Wy HLER SO31 269 P1
Justin Cl FHAM/STUB PO14 10 A6
Justin Gdns NBNE BH10 322 E3
Justinian Cl CHFD SO53 207 H6
Jute Cl FHAM/PORC PO16 273 M9
Jutland Cl FHAM PO15 271 H3
Jutland Crs AND SP10 82 D7
Juventu Cl HAV PO9 15 H1

K

Kamptee Copse
NMIL/BTOS BH25 327 K1
Kanes Hl ITCH SO19 249 P5
Karachi Cl NTID SP9 78 G4
Karen Av CHAM PO6 297 L3
Kassassin St ENEY PO4 317 J6
Kassel Cl WVILLE PO7 276 B1
Katherine Chance Cl
CHCH/BSGR BH23 324 G4
Kathleen Cl BSTK RG21 90 C1
Kathleen Rd ITCH SO19 249 K8
Kathryn Cl TOTT SO40 245 P2
Katrina Gdns HISD PO11 318 G3
Katrine Crs CHFD SO53 206 C6
Katterns Cl CHCH/BSGR BH23 324 G5
Kayak Cl HLER SO31 270 E9
Kay Cl CHCH/BSGR BH23 325 J9
Kay Crs BOR GU35 155 J2
Kayleigh Cl TOTT SO40 246 B5
Keable Rd RFNM GU10 115 P3
Kealy Rd GPORT PO12 315 L2
Kearsney Av NEND PO2 296 G7
Keats Av CHAM PO6 274 A9
LYMN SO41 338 G1
Keats Cl CHIN RG24 69 M3
FUFL SO22 183 L2
HLER SO31 271 H1
HORN PO8 255 P7
RWIN SO21 144 E4
Keats Rd WEND SO18 249 L5
Keats Wy YTLY GU46 56 C1
Keble Cl CHFD SO53 206 E9
Keble Rd CHFD SO53 206 E9
Keble St FUFL SO22 164 D9
Keble Wy SHST GU47 41 M4
Keeble Cl NBNE BH10 322 D1
Keeble Crs NBNE BH10 322 D1
Keeble Rd NBNE BH10 322 D1
Keel Cl HSEA PO3 297 L6
LSOL/BMARY PO13 315 H1
Keepers Cl CHFD SO53 206 D7
Keeper's Hl RAND SP11 100 G5
Keepers La ROMY SO51 179 J4
WIMB BH21 279 N9
Keeps Md KSCL RG20 48 B2
The Keep FHAM/PORC PO16 295 P2
Kefford Cl HORN PO8 * 256 B5
Keighley Av BDST BH18 320 B2
Keighley Cl STHA RG19 25 M5
Keith Cl GPORT PO12 315 M2
Keith Lucas Rd FARN GU14 75 N2
Keith Rd TWDS BH3 322 C9
Kelburn Cl CHFD SO53 206 D6
Kellaway Rd CFDH BH17 321 H4
Kellett Rd WSHM SO15 247 P3
Kelly Cl CFDH BH17 321 H4
Kellynch Cl ALTN GU34 132 E5
Kelly Rd WVILLE PO7 275 N5
Kellys Wk AND SP10 102 C3
Kelmscott Gdns CHFD SO53 206 C4
Kelsall Gdns NMIL/BTOS BH25 327 J4
Kelsey Cl FHAM/STUB PO14 271 H9
LISS GU33 192 E1
Kelsey Gv YTLY GU46 40 F9
Kelvin Cl FAWY SO45 268 C7
Kelvin Gv FHAM/PORC PO16 295 P1
HLER SO31 269 L4
Kelvin Hl KBH RG22 90 A1
Kelvin Rd ELGH SO50 229 H2
NWBY RG14 24 E3
Kembers La OVTN RG25 70 F8
Kemmel Rd RAND SP11 79 L4
Kemmitt Wy AND SP10 102 C4
Kemnal Pk HASM GU27 157 J5
Kemp Rd MOOR/WNTN BH9 322 F7
Kempshott Gdns KBH RG22 89 L3
Kempshott Gv KBH RG22 68 D8
Kempshott La KBH RG22 89 L2
Kempton Cl ALTN GU34 132 F7
NWBY RG14 17 K6
Kempton Ct FARN GU14 75 N2
Kempton Pk WVILLE PO7 276 B1
Kemshott Ct HAV PO9 276 D4
Ken Berry Ct HAV PO9 277 H4
The Kench HISD PO11 * 318 A4
Kendal Av HSEA PO3 297 J8
ROWN SO16 247 J3
Kendal Cl CHFD SO53 206 G6
FARN GU14 * 57 M9
HORN PO8 256 A7
NTHA RG18 25 M3
Kendal Gdns KBH RG22 89 M2
Kendal Gv CBLY GU15 59 J1
Kendrick Rd NWBY RG14 30 C1
Kenilworth Cl
LSOL/BMARY PO13 314 D1
NMIL/BTOS BH25 327 K4
Kenilworth Crs FLEETN GU51 74 F2
Kenilworth Dr ELGH SO50 207 J7
Kenilworth Gdns HEND SO30 249 N2
Kenilworth Rd DEAN RG23 68 F6
FARN GU14 57 K8
FLEETN GU51 74 E3
SSEA PO5 * 316 F7
WSHM SO15 20 C1
Kenley Rd BOR GU35 155 J3
Kenmore Cl FLEETS GU52 74 E7
FRIM GU16 58 C5
TOTT SO40 246 B6
Kennard Ct NMIL/BTOS BH25 327 H4
Kennard Rd NMIL/BTOS BH25 327 H3
Kennart Rd CFDH BH17 320 C5
Kennedy Av FHAM PO15 10 A1
Kennedy Cl NWBY RG14 24 A9
WVILLE PO7 275 N6
Kennedy Crs GPORT PO12 315 J6
Kennedy Rd ROWN SO16 227 K9
Kennel La RFNM GU10 116 C8
Kennel Rd FUFL SO22 164 C3
Kennels La FARN GU14 75 K2
Kennet Cl ASHV GU12 97 N2
BSTK RG21 7 J6
FARN GU14 57 L7
GPORT PO12 315 M7
STHA RG19 25 P4
WEND SO18 229 K9
Kennet Ct AND SP10 * 82 G9
Kennet Pl THLE RG7 27 K4
Kennet Rd NTID SP9 79 J5
NWBY RG14 16 D3
PSF GU32 215 L3
Kennet Side NWBY RG14 17 J2
Kennett Pl NWBY RG14 * 24 E3
Kennett Rd ROMY SO51 204 G5
Kennet Wy DEAN RG23 88 F2
Kennington La TOTT SO40 245 H4
Kennington Rd CFDH BH17 320 F4
Ken Rd SBNE BH6 336 C2
Kensington Cl ELGH SO50 207 M8
Kensington Dr WCLF BH2 8 A1
Kensington Flds FAWY SO45 267 P8
Kensington Gdns
FHAM/STUB PO14 271 J8
Kensington Pk LYMN SO41 338 F2
Kensington Rd GPORT PO12 12 E4
NEND PO2 297 H7
Kenson Gdns ITCH SO19 249 J7
Kent Gv FHAM/PORC PO16 295 N3
Kentidge Rd WVILLE PO7 275 M5
Kentigern Dr CWTH RG45 41 M1
Kentish Rd WSHM SO15 247 N4
Kent La RGWD BH24 260 C1
Kenton Cl FRIM GU16 58 E3
Kent Rd BKME/WDN BH12 321 N6
BOR GU35 154 A6
CHFD SO53 228 E1
FLEETN GU51 74 E3
LSOL/BMARY PO13 294 F5
PTSW SO17 248 E2
SSEA PO5 19 G7
Kent St PSEA PO1 18 D3
SHAM SO14 21 J2
Kenwith Av FLEETN GU51 74 F3
Kenwood Rd
FHAM/PORC PO16 295 P4
Kenwyn Cl WEND SO18 249 K1
Kenya Rd FHAM/PORC PO16 295 M2
Kenyon Cl PLE BH15 320 G5
Kenyon Rd NEND PO2 297 H7
PLE BH15 320 G5
Kenyons Yd AND SP10 102 C2
Keogh Barracks FRIM GU16 76 F4
Keogh Cl FRIM GU16 76 G3
Keppel Cl RGWD BH24 282 F2
Kerchers Fld OVTN RG25 86 G4
Kerfield Wy HTWY RG27 72 A3
Kerley Rd WCLF BH2 * 8 C6
Kern Cl ROWN SO16 227 K9
Kerrfield FUFL SO22 164 E8
Kerrfield Ms FUFL SO22 164 E8
Kerry Cl CHFD SO53 206 E7
FLEETN GU51 56 E8
LYMN SO41 329 J4
Kersey Crs NWBY RG14 24 B2
Kersley Crs ODIM RG29 93 J3
Kersley Gdns ITCH SO19 249 J7
Kesteven Wy WEND SO18 249 J3
Kestrel Cl BPWT SO32 231 N4
BPWT SO32 250 F2
FERN BH22 302 B1
FHAM/STUB PO14 293 P5
FUFL SO22 183 M2
HORN PO8 236 C8
NTID SP9 79 J4
RFNM GU10 95 M4
ROWN SO16 227 M7
STHA RG19 25 L4
TOTT SO40 267 J1
Kestrel Ct RGWD BH24 282 E1
TADY RG26 * 51 J9
Kestrel Dr CHCH/BSGR BH23 325 L9
Kestrel Pl CHAM PO6 297 P2
Kestrel Rd ELGH SO50 228 G2
FARN GU14 76 A2
KBH RG22 89 L2
Kestrel Wy FBDG SP6 239 P6
THLE RG7 27 K3
Keswick Av HSEA PO3 297 J9
Keswick Cl CBLY GU15 59 H1
Keswick Rd BOSC BH5 335 M2
ITCH SO19 248 F8
NMIL/BTOS BH25 327 K2
Keswick Wy VWD BH31 258 E5
Ketchers Fld ALTN GU34 172 E1
Ketelbey Ri KBH RG22 90 B4
Kettering Ter NEND PO2 296 E9
Kevin Cl KSCL RG20 48 E3
Kevins Dr YTLY GU46 40 F7
Kevins Gv FLEETN GU51 74 E3
Kevlyn Crs HLER SO31 269 P1
Kewlake La ROMY SO51 244 D1
Kew La HLER SO31 270 A3
Kew Wk AND SP10 102 C3
Keydell Av HORN PO8 256 A6
Keydell Cl HORN PO8 256 A6
Keyes Cl BKME/WDN BH12 321 P3
CHCH/BSGR BH23 325 K9
LSOL/BMARY PO13 294 G5
Keyes Rd LSOL/BMARY PO13 294 G6
Keyhaven Cl
LSOL/BMARY PO13 294 E7
Keyhaven Dr HAV PO9 276 C5
Keyhaven Rd LYMN SO41 339 H2
Keynes Cl FLEETS GU52 74 E8
Keynsham Rd ITCH SO19 249 K5
Keynsham Wy SHST GU47 41 L4
Keysworth Av
NMIL/BTOS BH25 327 H8
The Key FLEETN GU51 74 A1
Khandala Gdns WVILLE PO7 275 P6
Khartoum Rd PTSW SO17 248 C1
Khyber Rd BKME/WDN BH12 321 M7
Kidmore La WVILLE PO7 255 H5
Kielder Cl CHFD SO53 206 C6
Kielder Gv LSOL/BMARY PO13 295 H7
Kiel Dr AND SP10 82 D8
Kildare Rd BOR GU35 154 A4
Kilford Ct HEND SO30 250 G5
Kilham La FUFL SO22 164 C9
Killarney Cl ITCH SO19 249 N8
Killinghurst La HASM GU27 157 P7
Kilmarnock Rd
MOOR/WNTN BH9 322 F6
Kilmartin Gdns FRIM GU16 58 E4
Kilmeston Rd NARL SO24 187 H2
Kilmington Wy
CHCH/BSGR BH23 326 B7
Kilmiston Cl PSEA PO1 316 G1
Kilmiston Dr
FHAM/PORC PO16 273 N9
Kilmore Dr CBLY GU15 58 G1
Kilmuir Cl SHST GU47 41 L7
Kiln Acre FHAM/PORC PO16 * 11 H2
Kiln Cl FAWY SO45 268 A7
Kiln Fld LISS GU33 192 C1
Kiln Flds HASM GU27 157 H5
Kiln Gdns HTWY RG27 55 H7
Kiln Hl BPWT SO32 253 M3
Kiln La EPSF GU31 215 K8
NARL SO24 148 A7
RFNM GU10 116 C4
ROMY SO51 180 F8
RSAL SP5 200 A6
RWIN SO21 207 K3
TADY RG26 50 D8
THLE RG7 36 B1
WVILLE PO7 253 P7
Kiln Rd CHIN RG24 69 H1
FHAM/PORC PO16 272 D6
HSEA PO3 297 J8
NWBY RG14 24 F3
Kilnside WVILLE PO7 255 H8
The Kilns ALTN GU34 * 133 H6
FNM GU9 * 96 D6
Kiln Wy ALDT GU11 97 H4
GSHT GU26 155 M3
VWD BH31 259 J6
Kilnyard Cl TOTT SO40 246 B2
Kilpatrick Cl NEND PO2 * 296 F9
Kilwich Wy FHAM/PORC PO16 295 M3
Kimbell Rd KBH RG22 90 B1
Kimber Cl CHIN RG24 70 A2
Kimberley FLEETS GU52 74 E8
Kimberley Cl AND SP10 82 B9
CHCH/BSGR BH23 324 D7
ELGH SO50 230 D2
Kimberley Rd ENEY PO4 317 J6
KBH RG22 69 H9
LISS GU33 173 P5
PSTN BH14 321 K9
SBNE BH6 324 A9
Kimber Rd BWD BH11 * 321 P1
Kimbers PSF GU32 215 L1
Kimbers Cl NWBY RG14 * 16 D2
Kimbers La FNM GU9 96 D8
TADY RG26 34 E9
Kimbolton Rd HSEA PO3 317 J2
Kimbridge Crs HAV PO9 276 G4
Kimbridge La ROMY SO51 179 M7
Kimmeridge Av
BKME/WDN BH12 321 L4
Kimpton Cl
LSOL/BMARY PO13 314 D2
Kimpton Ct HAV PO9 * 277 H4
Kimpton Dr FLEETN GU51 73 P1
Kineton Rd WSHM SO15 248 A2
King Alfred Pl WINC SO23 22 E2
King Alfred Ter WINC SO23 22 E2
King Arthur's Ct CHAM PO6 * 297 M1
King Arthur's Wy AND SP10 82 E8
King Charles St PSEA PO1 18 C5
King Cl RGWD BH24 281 M5
King Cup Av HLER SO31 270 F8
Kingcup Cl BDST BH18 320 A2
Kingdom Cl FHAM PO15 271 K5
King Edward Av
MOOR/WNTN BH9 322 F5
ROWN SO16 247 L3
King Edward's Crs NEND PO2 296 F7
Kingfisher Cl BOR GU35 154 B6
FARN GU14 57 K7
FERN BH22 280 F7
FLEETS GU52 74 D7
HAV PO9 277 H1
HISD PO11 319 J6
HLER SO31 270 A6
HORN PO8 255 N7
KBH RG22 89 K2
SBNE BH6 324 C9
WHCH RG28 * 85 L6
Kingfisher Copse HLER SO31 271 H7
Kingfisher Ct NWBY RG14 24 C5
Kingfisher Dr EMRTH PO10 277 P6
YTLY GU46 40 C8
Kingfisher Pk WIMB BH21 * 280 E3
Kingfisher Rd ELGH SO50 228 G2
Kingfishers
FHAM/PORC PO16 295 K1
NTID SP9 98 G3
The Kingfishers VWD BH31 258 G5
Kingfisher Wk ASHV GU12 76 E9
Kingfisher Wy
CHCH/BSGR BH23 337 L1
RGWD BH24 260 F9
ROMY SO51 204 D5
TOTT SO40 267 J1
King George Av EPSF GU31 215 M1
MOOR/WNTN BH9 322 F5
King George Cl FARN GU14 76 C2
King George Ms EPSF GU31 215 M1
King George Rd AND SP10 102 B2
FHAM/PORC PO16 295 N2
King George's Av
WSHM SO15 247 K5
King Henry I St PSEA PO1 19 F3
King John Av BWD BH11 301 M8
FHAM/PORC PO16 295 M2
King John Rd KSCL RG20 48 C3
King Johns Rd ODIM RG29 72 B8
Kingland Rd PLE BH15 320 F9
King La PSF GU32 190 F6
STOK SO20 120 B3
King Richard I Rd PSEA PO1 19 F4
King Richard Dr BWD BH11 301 M8
Kings Acre STOK SO20 161 M4
Kings Apartments CBLY GU15 58 B1
Kings Arms La RGWD BH24 282 D2
Kings Arms Rw RGWD BH24 282 D2
King's Av CHCH/BSGR BH23 324 D9
FUFL SO22 183 N1

HLER SO31 .....269 N7
PSTN BH14 .....333 M1
RFNM GU10 .....97 L3
Kingsbere Rd NBNE BH10....322 B5
Kingsbere Rd PLE BH15 .....320 C7
Kingsbridge Copse
　HTWY RG27 .....71 M4
Kingsbridge Rd NWBY RG14....16 A5
　PSTN BH14 .....321 L9
Kingsbury Ct HORN PO8 .....236 B6
Kingsbury Rd SHAM SO14 .....248 D4
Kingsbury's La RGWD BH24....282 D2
Kingsclear Pk CBLY GU15 .....58 C1
Kingsclere Av HAV PO9 .....276 D5
　ITCH SO19 .....269 H2
Kingsclere Cl ITCH SO19 .....269 H1
Kingsclere Rd BSTK RG21 .....6 B3
　DEAN RG23 .....68 B2
　OVTN RG25 .....86 C1
King's Cl CHFD SO53 .....206 F6
　FERN BH22 .....290 D8
　HAV PO9 .....256 C9
　LYND SO43 .....264 F5
　RWIN SO21 .....184 A7
　WINC SO23 .....145 J7
Kings Copse Av HEND SO30....200 D5
King's Copse Rd FAWY SO45....290 E9
　HEND SO30 .....200 C6
Kingscote Rd CHAM PO6 .....274 D8
　HORN PO8 .....255 M8
King's Ct RFNM GU10 .....97 L3
Kings Crs LYMN SO41 .....329 J3
　PSTN BH14 .....333 N1
Kingscroft FLEET GU51 .....74 D4
Kingscroft Ct HAV PO9 .....14 C6
King's Croft La HAV PO9 .....14 A5
Kingsdown Pl PSEA PO1 *....316 G3
Kingsdown Rd WVILLE PO7 .....255 L9
Kingsdown Wy WEND SO18....249 H1
King's Elms RWIN SO21 .....124 F2
Kingsey Av EMRTH PO10 .....299 L1
Kingsfernsden La PSF GU32....191 N9
Kings Fld HLER SO31 .....270 A1
Kingsfold Av WEND SO18....229 H9
Kings Furlong Dr BSTK RG21....69 J9
Kingsgate St WINC SO23 .....22 C7
Kings Head Ms EPSF GU31 *....193 M7
King's Hl ALTN GU34 .....131 M9
Kings Keep FLEETS GU52 .....74 D6
　SHST GU47 .....41 J5
Kingsland Cl CHAM PO6 .....274 E9
Kingsland Gra NWBY RG14....24 B7
Kingsland Rd ALTN GU34 .....132 G6
Kings La LYMN SO41 .....308 E8
　PSF GU32 .....190 C4
　RFNM GU10 .....115 P4
　RWIN SO21 .....165 N9
Kingsley Av CBLY GU15 .....58 B1
　SBNE BH6 .....336 E2
Kingsley Bungalows
　NARL SO24 * 167 N3
Kingsley Cl CWTH RG45 .....41 J3
　NWBY RG14 .....24 E2
　SBNE BH6 .....336 E2
Kingsley Gdns TOTT SO40....245 P4
Kingsley Pk WHCH RG28 .....85 L5
Kingsley Pl FUFL SO22 .....183 N1
Kingsley Rd ENEY PO4 .....317 K5
　FARN GU14 .....57 N7
　GPORT PO12 .....39 L6
　HTWY RG27 .....39 M6
　WSHM SO15 .....247 M4
Kingsley Sq FLEETN GU51 .....55 P9
Kingsmead ALTN GU34 .....132 F6
　FARN GU14 .....58 A9
　FLEETN GU51 .....58 D6
　RAND SP11 .....102 A6
　ROMY SO51 * 224 E1
　WHAM PO17 .....252 G4
Kingsmead Av
　FHAM/STUB PO14 .....294 B8
Kings Meadow AND SP10....8 E5
　OVTN RG25 .....86 B3
Kings Mede HORN PO8 .....256 B5
Kingsmill Cl GPORT PO12....315 K4
　CFDH BH17 .....320 G5
Kings Orch DEAN RG23 .....88 E7
Kingsmill Rd BSTK RG21 .....90 C1
　CFDH BH17 .....320 G5
Kings Pde PLE BH15 .....320 F8
Kings Peace GSHT GU26 *....156 B2
Kings Pightle CHIN RG24 .....70 A1
Kings Ride FAWY SO45 .....312 C1
King's Rd ALDT GU11 .....2 A4
　ALTN GU34 .....132 D7
　CHFD SO53 .....206 E7
　CWTH RG45 .....41 J2
　EMRTH PO10 .....299 L1
　FHAM/PORC PO16 .....11 G6
　FLEETN GU51 .....74 E3
　FUFL SO22 .....164 D9
　GPORT PO12 .....13 G1
　HASM GU27 .....156 F7
　HISD PO11 .....318 G3
　HORN PO8 .....255 P8
　KBH RG22 .....89 H9
　LSOL/BMARY PO13 .....314 C1
　LYMN SO41 .....329 K3
　NMIL/BTOS BH25 .....327 L3
　NWBY RG14 .....17 G3
　PSEA PO1 .....316 D4
　PSF GU32 .....215 K1
　RAND SP11 .....82 F4
　SSEA PO5 .....19 G6
　THLE RG7 .....35 H5
　TWDS BH3 .....322 G8
Kingsroad Rbt PSEA PO1 .....18 E6
Kings Rd West NWBY RG14....17 F3

King's Saltern Rd LYMN SO41 ....329 N5
Kings Somborne Rd
　ROMY SO51 .....181 H5
King's Ter EMRTH PO10 .....299 M1
　PSEA PO1 .....19 F6
Kingston Cl AND SO10 .....102 C4
Kingston Rd NEND PO2 .....296 F9
Kingston Gdns FHAM PO15....272 B6
Kingston La THLE RG7 .....26 E1
Kingston Pk LYMN SO41 .....329 J5
　ROMY SO51 .....224 E4
Kingston Rd GPORT PO12....315 K5
　NEND PO2 .....296 C9
　PLE BH15 .....320 F8
　WSHM SO15 .....247 P5
King St EMRTH PO10 .....277 P7
　EMRTH PO10 .....299 N1
　GPORT PO12 .....13 H1
　ODIM RG29 .....72 D9
　SHAM SO14 .....19 C5
　SSEA PO5 .....19 C5
　THLE RG7 .....27 J9
　WIMB BH21 .....300 D1
King's Wk CBLY GU15 .....41 N8
　WHCH RG28 .....85 L6
King's Warren BPWT SO32....209 L2
　BPWT SO32 .....231 L1
　BPWT SO32 .....233 L7
　BPWT SO32 .....234 B8
　FHAM/PORC PO16 .....295 K1
　NARL SO24 .....167 L5
　RWIN SO21 .....166 D1
　RWIN SO21 .....185 K2
　WHAM PO17 .....274 B1
　WINC SO23 .....165 K3
　WVILLE PO7 .....204 B3
Kingsway ALDT GU11 .....2 B5
　AND SP10 .....83 J9
　BLKW GU17 .....41 L9
　CHFD SO53 .....206 F7
　FERN BH22 .....280 B9
　HISD PO11 .....298 C6
　SHAM SO14 .....21 F3
Kingsway Cl
　CHCH/BSGR BH23 .....324 D6
Kingsway Gdns AND SP10....82 E8
　CHFD SO53 .....206 C5
The Kingsway
　FHAM/PORC PO16 .....295 N1
Kingswell Cl NBNE BH10....322 D5
Kingswell Gdns NBNE BH10....322 B5
Kingswell Gv NBNE BH10....322 B5
Kingswell Rd NBNE BH10....322 C5
Kingswell St PSEA PO1 * 19 G2
Kingswood Firs GSHT GU26....156 B3
Kingswood La GSHT GU26....156 B3
Kingswood Ri ALTN GU34....150 A6
Kings Worthy Rd FLEETN GU51....55 P9
Kingsworthy Rd HAV PO9....15 F1
Kings Yd AND SP10 * 83 J9
King William St PSEA PO1....18 D1
Kinnell Cl EMRTH PO10 .....299 M1
Kinross Crs CHAM PO6 .....297 K2
Kinross Rd TOTT SO40 .....246 D4
　TWDS BH3 .....322 E9
Kinsbourne Av NBNE BH10....322 D5
Kinsbourne Cl ITCH SO19....249 P5
Kinsbourne Ri ITCH SO19....249 P6
Kinsbourne Wy ITCH SO19....249 N6
Kinson Av PLE BH15 .....321 J6
Kinson Gv NBNE BH10 .....322 C1
Kinson Park Rd NBNE BH10....322 D1
Kintyre Cl CHAM PO6 .....297 M2
Kintyre Rd CHAM PO6 .....275 H9
Kinver Cl HLER SO31 .....271 H1
Kipling Cl FLEETN GU51 .....55 M9
Kipling Ct TOTT SO19 .....269 H1
Kipling Rd ELGH SO50 .....229 H1
　NEND PO2 .....296 C6
　PSTN BH14 .....321 K7
Kipling Wk KBH RG22 .....89 H9
Kirby Cl PLE BH15 .....321 H6
Kirby Rd NEND PO2 .....296 C7
Kirby Wy SBNE BH6 .....336 B2
Kirkee Rd NTID SP9 .....78 G6
Kirk Gdns TOTT SO40 .....246 D6
Kirkham Av CHCH/BSGR BH23....324 C4
Kirkham Cl SHST GU47 .....41 M4
Kirk Knoll BOR GU35 .....154 C3
Kirkstall Rd ENEY PO4 .....316 F7
Kirkstone Cl CBLY GU15 .....59 J1
Kirkway BDST BH18 .....300 D9
Kirkwood Crs THLE RG7 .....40 B1
Kirriemuir Gdns ASHV GU12....77 J9
Kirtley Cl CHAM PO6 .....297 L3
Kirton Rd CHAM PO6 .....297 L2
Kitchener Crs CFDH BH17....320 D2
Kitchener Rd ALDT GU11 .....76 C6
　LISS GU33 .....173 P5
　PTSW SO17 .....248 D8
Kitchers Cl LYMN SO41 .....308 B5
Kitcombe La ALTN GU34 .....151 K7
Kite Cl HORN PO8 .....255 N7
Kites Croft Cl
　FHAM/STUB PO14 .....271 J9
Kitnocks Hl BPWT SO32 .....251 L3
Kitscroft Rd NBNE BH10 .....322 C2
Kittiwake Cl
　LSOL/BMARY PO13 .....294 B7
　SBNE BH6 .....324 B9
Kitt's La NARL SO24 .....188 E4
Kitwalls La LYMN SO41 .....338 C1
Kitwood Gn HAV PO9 * 277 H5
Kitwood La ALTN GU34 .....150 D9
Kitwood Rd ALTN GU34 .....150 C9
Kivernell Rd LYMN SO41....338 F2
Kiwi Cl PLE BH15 .....320 C9
Knapp Cl CHCH/BSGR BH23....324 E7

Knapp La ROMY SO51 .....181 P9
　TADY RG26 .....34 E8
Knapp Mill Av
　CHCH/BSGR BH23 .....324 E7
Knapps Hard PSF GU32 .....188 D9
Knatchbull Cl ROMY SO51....204 D6
Knellers La TOTT SO40 .....245 J3
Knight Cl FLEETN GU51 .....55 P6
　WINC SO23 .....165 H5
Knightcrest Pk LYMN SO41 *....328 E6
Knight Gdns CHAM PO6 .....297 M2
Knighton Heath Cl BWD BH11....301 N9
Knighton Heath Rd
　BWD BH11 .....301 N9
Knighton La BWD BH11 .....301 M6
Knighton Pk
　NMIL/BTOS BH25 .....326 C9
Knighton Rd ITCH SO19 .....249 H8
Knights Bank Rd
　FHAM/STUB PO14 .....293 M8
Knightsbridge Dr STHA RG19....31 N3
Knightsbridge Rd RAND SP11....82 C4
Knights Cl HLER SO31 .....270 E9
Knights Lea KSCL RG20 .....29 J3
Knights Pk Rd BSTK RG21 .....6 A2
Knights Rd BWD BH11 .....301 M8
　FNM GU9 .....4 C5
Knightstone Gra FAWY SO45....268 C8
Knight St BSTK RG21 .....6 B7
Knights Wy ALTN GU34 .....132 D6
Knightswood Vw
　CHFD SO53 .....206 E7
Knightwood Av HAV PO9 .....276 C5
　LYND SO43 .....264 F5
Knightwood Cl
　CHCH/BSGR BH23 .....326 A7
　LYND SO43 .....264 F5
　TOTT SO40 .....245 P9
Knightwood Rd CHFD SO53....206 B9
　FAWY SO45 .....268 B9
Knobcrook Rd WIMB BH21....278 D8
Knockmundred La GSHT GU26....156 A5
Knockwood La STOK SO20....139 M1
Knole Gdns BMTH BH1 .....335 K2
Knole Rd BMTH BH1 .....335 K1
Knoll Cl FLEETN GU51 .....74 D1
Knoll Ct FLEETN GU51 .....74 D1
Knoll Gdns RGWD BH24 .....280 D5
Knoll Rd FLEETN GU51 .....74 D2
Knollys Rd ALDT GU11 .....75 N9
　THLE RG7 .....34 G5
The Knook SHST GU47 * 41 L7
Knottgrass Rd HLER SO31....270 E8
Knowland Dr LYMN SO41....338 C1
Knowle Av WHAM PO17 .....272 C3
Knowle Crs KSCL RG20 .....48 C3
Knowle Ga WHAM PO17 .....272 C3
Knowle Hl ELGH SO50 .....207 K6
Knowle La ELGH SO50 .....230 E4
Knowle Rd BROC SO42 .....288 E7
　WHAM PO17 .....272 D5
Knowles Av CWTH RG45 .....40 G2
Knowles Cl CHCH/BSGR BH23....325 J8
Knowles Meadow LISS GU33....192 F1
The Knowle BOR GU35 .....155 J2
The Knowlings WHCH RG28....85 M7
Knowlton Gdns
　MOOR/WNTN BH9 .....323 H3
Knowlton Rd CFDH BH17 .....321 H2
Knowsley Crs CHAM PO6 .....297 J2
Knowsley Rd CHAM PO6 .....297 J2
Knox Cl FLEETS GU52 .....74 B7
Knox Rd HAV PO9 .....14 C5
　NEND PO2 .....296 E8
Knox Ter ALTN GU34 * 132 C5
Knyght Cl ROMY SO51 .....204 E7
Knyveton Rd BMTH BH1 .....335 J2
Kohat Cl NTID SP9 .....78 F4
Kohat Ct ALDT GU11 .....3 G1
Kohima Cl ALDT GU11 * 3 G1
Komat Rd NTID SP9 .....78 F6
Kootenay Av WEND SO18....249 N4
Kooyong Cl WEND SO18....249 N4
Krooner Rd CBLY GU15 .....50 B3
Kynegils Rd FUFL SO22 .....164 G5
Kynon Cl GPORT PO12 .....295 N9
Kyrchil La WIMB BH21 .....278 G8
Kyrchil Wy WIMB BH21 .....279 H7
Kytes La BPWT SO32 .....231 H7

L

Labrador Dr PLE BH15 .....332 F2
Laburnum Av CHAM PO6 .....297 L2
Laburnum Cl ALDT GU11 .....2 D3
　FERN BH22 .....302 B2
　NBAD SO52 .....205 L8
　VWD BH31 .....259 J5
Laburnum Crs FAWY SO45....290 C2
Laburnum Dr LYMN SO41....338 C1
Laburnum Gv LYMN SO41....229 J1
　HISD PO11 .....319 H4
　NEND PO2 .....296 G8
　NWBY RG14 .....24 D3
Laburnum Pas ALDT GU11....2 D3
Laburnum Rd ALDT GU11....2 D4
　FHAM/PORC PO16 .....294 F3
　FNM GU9 .....96 E4
　HEND SO30 .....200 D5
　ROWN SO16 .....228 D8
　WVILLE PO7 .....275 H4
Laburnums HTWY RG27 .....41 J9
The Laburnums BLKW GU17....41 J9
Laburnum Wy DEAN RG23....68 G6
Lacey Crs PSTN BH14 .....321 J6
Lackford Av TOTT SO40 .....246 C5
Lacon Cl WEND SO18 .....248 G3
Lacy Cl WIMB BH21 .....278 E8
Lacy Dr WIMB BH21 .....278 E8
Ladram Rd GPORT PO12 .....315 J4

Ladwell Cl NWBY RG14 .....30 C1
Lady Betty's Dr FHAM PO15....271 L4
Ladybridge Rd WVILLE PO7....275 L6
Ladycross Rd FAWY SO45....268 C8
Lady Diana Ct RAND SP11....79 F1
Ladygate Dr GSHT GU26 .....155 P5
Lady Godley Cl NTID SP9 .....78 G6
Lady Jane Wk RAND SP11....79 F1
Ladysmith Cl
　CHCH/BSGR BH23 .....325 J8
Ladysmith Pl BOR GU35 .....153 P3
Ladywell La NARL SO24 .....148 A9
Ladywood ELGH SO50 .....207 H7
Lagado Cl PSTN BH14 .....333 L3
Lagland St PLE BH15 .....332 E1
Lagoon Rd PSTN BH14 .....333 K5
Lahore Cl NTID SP9 .....78 G6
Lahore Rd NTID SP9 .....78 G6
Laidlaw Cl BKME/WDN BH12....321 N3
Lainston Cl FUFL SO22 .....164 D5
Lake Cl CHFD SO53 .....206 G5
Lake Crs PLE BH15 .....320 A9
Lake End Wy CWTH RG45....41 H2
Lake Farm Cl HEND SO30....250 C3
Lake Grove Rd
　NMIL/BTOS BH25 .....327 H3
Lakeland Dr FRIM GU16 .....58 D4
Lakeland Gdns TOTT SO40....267 J1
Lakelands Dr WSHM SO15....247 N5
Lake Rd BPWT SO32 .....251 M3
　BWD BH11 .....322 B1
　CHFD SO53 .....206 G5
　FRIM GU16 .....58 F7
　ITCH SO19 .....5 K5
　PLE BH15 .....332 A1
　PSEA PO1 .....19 H1
　VWD BH31 .....258 D6
Laker Sq AND SP10 .....82 G9
Lakeside ELGH SO50 .....229 H4
　WHAM PO17 .....272 C5
Lakeside Av HSEA PO3 .....317 K2
　ROWN SO16 .....227 J7
Lakeside Cl AND SP10 .....82 D9
　ASHV GU12 .....77 J3
Lakeside Ct FLEETN GU51....74 E1
Lakeside Dr HTWY RG27 .....54 C1
Lakeside Gdns FARN GU14....57 L6
　WVILLE PO7 .....204 F1
Lakeside Rd ALDT GU11 .....2 E8
　ASHV GU12 .....76 E8
　CCLF BH13 .....334 A5
The Lake Side BLKW GU17....57 L1
Lakesmere Rd HORN PO8....256 C5
The Lakes BPWT SO32 .....232 C6
Lake Vw Dr HTWY RG27 .....55 J6
Lakeview Dr RGWD BH24....282 G3
Lakewood Cl CHFD SO53....206 F5
Lakewood Rd
　CHCH/BSGR BH23 .....326 B6
　CHFD SO53 .....206 F5
　TOTT SO40 .....246 A8
Lamb Cl AND SP10 .....5 G5
　NTHA RG18 .....25 M2
Lambdens Wk TADY RG26....34 C6
Lambdown Ap RAND SP11....79 L5
Lambdown Ter RAND SP11....79 L5
Lamberhurst Cl ITCH SO19....269 J2
Lambert Cl WVILLE PO7 .....275 N5
Lambert Crs BLKW GU17 .....57 K1
Lamborne Cl SHST GU47....155 H1
Lambourn Cl
　FHAM/STUB PO14 .....294 B1
Lambourne Cl FAWY SO45....268 B9
　FHAM/STUB PO14 .....294 B1
　RAND SP11 .....100 C2
　RWIN SO21 .....163 M4
Lambourne Dr HLER SO31....270 C7
Lambourne Rd WEND SO18....249 M1
Lambourn Sq CHFD SO53....206 C7
Lambourn Valley Wy
　NWBY RG14 .....16 B2
　NWBY RG14 .....24 D1
Lamb's Cl CFDH BH17 .....320 E3
Lambsgreen La WIMB BH21....300 B3
Lambs Rw CHIN RG24 .....24 D1
Lamden Wy THLE RG7 .....34 C1
Lamerton Cl BOR GU35 .....153 P4
Lamerton Rd BOR GU35 .....268 C8
Lamp Acres NWBY RG14 .....24 E2
Lanark Cl FRIM GU16 .....58 D3
Lancaster Cl AND SP10 .....116 C2
　ASHV GU12 .....77 J2
Lancaster Ct ALDT GU11 .....2 A5
　BDST BH18 .....300 B8
　CHCH/BSGR BH23 .....324 D8
　FHAM/PORC PO16 .....273 M9
　HLER SO31 .....270 A1
　LSOL/BMARY PO13 .....314 D4
　NTHA RG18 .....25 M3
Lancaster Dr BDST BH18 .....300 B8
　VWD BH31 .....258 E4
Lancaster Rd BSTK RG21 .....6 C3
　FERN BH22 .....290 B2
　ROWN SO16 .....228 C3
　WIMB BH21 .....280 A9
Lancaster Wy FARN GU14....58 B9
　WVILLE PO7 .....275 P4
Lancer Cl CHCH/BSGR BH23....324 D8
Lancer Ct ALDT GU11 .....2 A5
Lance's Hl ITCH SO19 .....249 H4

Landale Cl RAND SP11 .....82 F4
Lander Cl PLE BH15 .....332 F2
Landford Gdns CHAR BH8....323 K5
Landford Wy CHAR BH8....323 K5
Landguard Rd ENEY PO4....317 J5
　WSHM SO15 .....247 P5
Landon Cl GPORT PO12 .....12 A7
Landon Rd
　LSOL/BMARY PO13 .....295 H9
Landport St PSEA PO1 .....19 F5
　PSEA PO1 .....19 J1
Landport Ter PSEA PO1 .....19 F6
Landrake Cl BSTK RG21 .....69 N9
Landseer Cl BSTK RG21 .....69 N9
　SHST GU47 .....41 M8
Landseer Rd ITCH SO19 .....249 L8
　WBNE BH4 .....41 M8
Lands End La BOR GU35 .....154 B3
Lands End Rd HLER SO31....270 B3
Lane End Dr EMRTH PO10....299 M1
Lane End TADY RG26 .....52 A3
Lanehays Rd FAWY SO45....268 B7
Lanesbridge Cl TOTT SO40....245 K4
Lanes End FHAM/STUB PO14....294 A7
The Lanes NMIL/BTOS BH25....327 J2
Laneswood THLE RG7 .....35 M1
The Lane BMTH BH1 * 335 J1
　ENEY PO4 .....317 H6
　ENEY PO4 .....317 H6
　GPORT PO12 .....315 L7
　MFD/CHID GU8 .....137 P5
　TADY RG26 .....34 C6
Langbar Cl ITCH SO19 .....248 G5
Langbrook Cl HAV PO9 .....298 F1
Langdale Av CHAM PO6 .....297 K2
Langdale Cl FARN GU14 .....57 M9
　ROWN SO16 .....247 K5
Langdale Ct ASHV GU12 * 76 E7
Langdon Rd CBLY GU15 .....59 H1
Langdon Rd PSTN BH14 .....321 L8
Langdown Firs FAWY SO45 *....268 C7
Langdown Lawn FAWY SO45....268 C8
Langdown Lawn Cl
　FAWY SO45 .....268 C8
Langford La RSAL SP5 .....199 P5
　RSAL SP5 .....200 A2
Langford Rd NEND PO2 .....296 F8
Langham Cl NBAD SO52 .....205 K9
Langhorn Rd ROWN SO16....228 E8
Langley Cha RGWD BH24....281 N4
Langley Cl FLEETS GU52 .....74 C8
Langley Ct HAV PO9 .....1 E6
Langley Gdn FDBG SP6 .....220 E9
Langley Lodge Gdns
　FAWY SO45 .....312 C1
Langley Rd CHCH/BSGR BH23....326 A6
　NEND PO2 .....296 C9
　PSTN BH14 .....321 L9
　WSHM SO15 .....247 L5
Langrish Cl HAV PO9 .....276 C4
Langrish Rd ROWN SO16 .....227 M8
Langside Av
　BKME/WDN BH12 .....322 A7
Langstone Av HAV PO9 .....298 C4
Langstone Br HAV PO9 .....298 C4
Langstone High St HAV PO9....298 F3
Langstone Rd HAV PO9 .....298 F2
　HSEA PO3 .....317 J2
Langstone Wk
　FHAM/STUB PO14 .....294 A1
　LSOL/BMARY PO13 .....294 F7
Langton Cl FUFL SO22 .....22 A2
　NMIL/BTOS BH25 .....327 K7
Langton Dr BOR GU35 .....155 H1
Langton Farm Gdns
　PSEA PO1 .....316 C1
Langton Rd BPWT SO32 .....231 P4
　LTDN BH7 .....335 M1
Langtons NARL SO24 .....168 B2
Lanham La FUFL SO22 .....163 P8
Lankhills Rd WINC SO23 .....164 G5
Lansdown Av
　FHAM/PORC PO16 .....295 P3
Lansdowne Av AND SP10....102 C4
　WINC SO23 .....183 P1
　WVILLE PO7 .....275 K7
Lansdowne Cl ROMY SO51....204 C5
Lansdowne Gdns BMTH BH1....9 C1
Lansdowne Hl SHAM SO14....4 D4
Lansdowne Rd ALDT GU11....2 D4
　ALTN GU34 .....132 G4
　BMTH BH1 .....334 C1
　FRIM GU16 .....58 C8
　WSHM SO15 .....247 L4
The Lansdowne Rbt BMTH BH1....9 C5
Lansley Rd BSTK RG21 .....69 L4
Lantana Cl WVILLE PO7 .....275 P4
Lanyard Dr
　LSOL/BMARY PO13 .....315 H2
Lapin La KBH RG22 .....89 M6
Lapthorn Cl
　LSOL/BMARY PO13 .....294 F5
Lapwing Cl ENEY PO4 .....317 L3
　GPORT PO12 .....315 M1
　HORN PO8 .....256 A4
　KBH RG22 .....89 K4
　LSOL/BMARY PO13 .....314 C1
　LYMN SO41 .....327 P4
　NWBY RG14 .....24 A2
　RDGW/BURGH RG30 .....27 K3
　RGWD BH24 .....281 P5
Lapwing Gv
　FHAM/PORC PO16 .....295 K1
Lapwing Ri WHCH RG28 .....85 K5
Lapwing Rd WIMB BH21 .....279 J7

STOK SO20 ....121 H5
WINC SO23 ....145 J8
Larchdale CI HLER SO51 ....292 D1
Larch Dr AND SP10 ....102 A3
KSCL RG20 ....48 C3
Larches Gdns FHAM PO15 .....272 A9
Larchfield Rd FLEETS GU52 ....74 D5
Larchfield Wy HORN PO8 ....255 K6
Larch Rd BOR GU35 ....155 J2
ROWN SO16 ....227 L9
Larch Rw FBDG SP6 ....241 H1
Larch Wy FARN GU14 ....75 K1
FERN BH22 ....280 C9
HLER SO31 ....269 P2
Larchwood CHIN RG24 ....51 P9
Larchwood Av HAV PO9 ....276 B6
Larchwood Rd TOTT SO40 .....246 A5
Larcombe Rd PSF GU52 ....215 K4
Larg Dr FUFL SO22 ....164 D3
Lark CI AND SP10 ....82 F9
KBH RG22 ....89 K3
Larkfield CHIN RG24 ....70 A1
Larkfield Rd FHAM GU14 ....95 PB
Lark Hill Ri FUFL SO22 ....183 M2
Larkhill Rd HSEA PO3 ....297 H5
Larkin CI RAND SP11 * 80 A1
Lark Ri LIPH SO19 ....175 H2
Lark Rd FBDG SP6 ....325 L9
Larks Barrow Hl WHCH RG28 ...85 L1
Larks CI FERN BH22 ....302 B1
Larksfield Av
MOOR/WNTN BH9 ....323 H4
Larkshill Cl NMIL/BTOS BH25 ..327 K3
Larkspur Cha ITCH SO19 ....249 N6
Larkspur CI ALDT GU11 ....96 G4
BPWT SO32 ....232 E7
HLER SO31 ....270 E8
Larkspur Dr CHFD SO53 ....206 B6
TOTT SO40 ....267 J2
Larkspur Gdns FAWY SO45 ....290 D5
HEND SO30 ....250 C5
Larks Ri FERN BH22 ....302 B1
Larkswood CI SHST GU47 ....41 H5
Larkswood Dr CWTH RG45 ....41 L1
Larkwhistle Farm Rd
RWIN SO21 ....107 K9
Larmer CI FLEETN GU51 ....74 A5
Larwood Sq AND SP10 ....82 G8
Lascelles Rd LTDN BH7 ....323 P9
Laser CI HLER SO31 ....270 E9
Lasham Gn HAV PO9 * 277 H5
Lasham Rd FLEETN GU51 ....55 P9
Lasham Wk FHAM/STUB PO14...294 B2
Lashly Meadow WVILLE PO7 ...234 E9
Latch Farm Av
CHCH/BSGR BH23 ....324 E7
Latchmore Dr FAWY SO45 .....267 N6
Latchmore Forest Gv
HORN PO8 ....255 N8
Latchmore Gdns HORN PO8 ...255 N8
Latchmore La RFNM GU10 ......116 D5
Latelie CI HLER SO31 ....269 K5
Latham Av FRIM GU16 ....58 D5
Latham CI ELGH SO50 ....230 B2
Latham Ct WSHM SO15 ....247 M4
Latham Rd ELGH SO50 ....230 B2
ROMY SO51 ....204 D5
Latimer Ct HSEA PO3 * 297 K6
Latimer Rd MOOR/WNTN BH9 ..323 J7
Latimers CI CHCH/BSGR BH23 ..326 B6
Latimer St ROMY SO51 ....204 C6
SHAM SO14 ....21 F7
Laud CI NWBY RG14 ....24 C2
Lauder CI FRIM GU16 ....58 D3
Lauderdale FARN GU14 ....75 L2
Launcelot CI AND SP10 ....82 E8
Launcelyn CI NBAD SO52 ....227 K1
Launceston Dr ELGH SO50 ....207 H8
Laundry La CBLY GU15 ....41 M9
HTWY RG27 ....38 A9
LYMN SO41 ....339 H2
Laundry Rd ROWN SO16 ....247 M1
Laurel CI CBLY GU15 ....58 C1
CHCH/BSGR BH23 ....325 P6
DEAN RG23 ....88 F2
FARN GU14 ....75 K1
FAWY SO45 ....268 A7
GPORT PO12 ....315 N1
HLER SO31 ....271 H6
ITCH SO19 ....248 F8
LYMN SO41 ....327 N3
ODIM RG29 ....72 B9
RGWD BH24 ....281 L5
Laurel Dr BDST BH18 ....300 D9
BDST BH18 ....300 E9
HLER SO31 ....271 H6
Laurel Gv RFNM GU10 ....115 P5
Laurel La RGWD BH24 ....281 L6
Laurel Rd HLER SO31 ....271 H6
HORN PO8 ....256 C7
The Laurels AND SP10 ....102 C1
BROC SO42 * 286 F9
BSTK RG21 ....7 H3
FERN BH22 ....302 C1
FLEETN GU51 ....74 C5
FNM GU9 ....96 E7
NTHA RG18 * 25 M2
Laurence Ct RAND SP11 ....79 P1
Lauren Wy TOTT SO40 ....246 F7
Lauriston Dr CHFD SO53 ....206 D4
Laurus CI WVILLE PO7 ....276 A5
Lavant Dr HORN PO8 ....276 B1
Lavant Dr HAV PO9 ....276 B1
Lavant St PSF GU32 ....215 L2
Lavell's La THLE GU7 ....36 B6
Lavender CI ITCH SO19 ....249 H6
VWD BH31 ....259 J5
Lavender Ct AND SP10 * 102 C4
FHAM PO15 ....271 K1
Lavender Gdns BOR GU35 .....154 B4
Lavender La RFNM GU10 ....115 P6
Lavender Rd CHAR BH8 ....323 K3
KBH RG22 ....89 L4
LYMN SO41 ....327 N4

Laverock Lea
FHAM/PORC PO16 ....275 N9
Laverstoke CI ROWN SO16 .....227 J7
Laverstoke La OVTN RG25 .....106 C2
WHCH RG28 ....86 C6
Lavey's La FHAM PO15 ....271 P4
Lavington Gdns NBAD SO52 ...227 J1
Lavinia Rd BKME/WDN BH12 ...321-L5
GPORT PO12 ....12 B1
Lawday Link FNM GU9 ....96 A4
Lawday Pl FNM GU9 ....96 A4
Lawday Place La FNM GU9 ......96 A4
Lawford Crs YTLY GU46 ....40 E8
Lawford Ri
MOOR/WNTN BH9 * 322 C4
Lawford Rd
MOOR/WNTN BH9 ....322 C4
Lawford Wy TOTT SO40 ....246 C5
Lawn CI LSOL/BMARY PO13 ...295 H9
LYMN SO41 ....339 H2
Lawn Dr HLER SO31 ....270 C8
Lawn Rd ELGH SO50 ....207 K9
FUFL SO22 ....164 D2
LYMN SO41 ....329 H4
LYMN SO41 ....339 H2
PTSW SO17 ....248 D3
Lawns CI WIMB BH21 ....279 L8
Lawnside Rd WSHM SO15 .....247 L3
Lawnswood La FAWY SO45 .....279 K8
The Lawns CHCH/BSGR BH23 ...326 D7
FARN GU14 ....75 M1
Lawn St WINC SO23 ....23 F4
Lawnswood CI ELGH SO50 * ...230 D3
HORN PO8 ....255 P9
Lawn Vw NMIL/BTOS BH25 ....326 F2
Lawrence Av HORN PO8 ....255 N9
Lawrence CI AND SP10 ....82 D9
CHIN RG24 ....69 M3
Lawrence Ct CHAR BH8 ....323 J9
Lawrencedale Ct BSTK RG21 .....6 B7
Lawrence Dr PSTN BH14 ....333 N2
Lawrence Gdns CHIN RG24 .....69 M3
Lawrence Houses RAND SP11...100 B9
Lawrence La FBDG SP6 ....240 F7
Lawrence PI NWBY RG14 ....24 F2
Lawrence Rd ENEY PO4 ....316 C5
FHAM PO15 ....10 C4
FLEETS GU52 ....74 B7
RGWD BH24 ....260 G8
Lawrences La NTHA RG18 ....25 N1
Lawrence Wk
LSOL/BMARY PO13 *............315 H2
Lawrence Wy CBLY GU15 ....57 N1
Lawson CI HLER SO31 ....270 D2
Lawson Rd BKME/WDN BH12 ...321 K6
SSEA PO5 ....316 C4
Laws Ter ALDT GU11 ....3 H2
Laxton CI HLER SO31 ....271 H7
ITCH SO19 ....249 J9
Layard Dr WIMB BH21 ....300 F4
Lay Fld HTWY RG27 ....71 N3
Layton Rd BKME/WDN BH12 ...321 M7
LSOL/BMARY PO13 ....294 C6
Lea CI ASHV GU12 ....97 N2
BSTK RG21 ....7 K5
Leacock CI BPWT SO32 ....232 F6
Lea Ct FNM GU9 ....96 F4
Leaden Vere ODIM RG29 ....93 K7
Leafy La FHAM PO15 ....271 L4
Lealand Gv CHAM PO6 ....297 M1
Lealand Rd CHAM PO6 ....297 M2
Leamington Crs
LSOL/BMARY PO13 ....314 D2
Leamington Rd
MOOR/WNTN BH9 ....322 G8
Leander CI ELGH SO50 ....207 J8
Leander Dr GPORT PO12 ....315 N1
Lea-Oak Gdns FHAM PO15 ....272 B7
Leaphill Rd LTDN BH7 ....323 N9
Lea Rd CBLY GU15 ....58 A3
FAWY SO45 ....312 C1
Learoyd Rd CFDH BH17 ....320 F5
Lear Rd GPORT PO12 ....12 D1
Leaside Wy ROWN SO16 ....228 F7
Lea Springs FLEETN GU51 ....74 A5
The Lea FLEETN SO41 ....74 B5
VWD BH31 ....258 C5
Leatherhead Gdns
HORN PO8 ....250 D1
Lea Wy ASHV GU12 ....74 A5
BWD BH11 ....301 N7
Leaway FNM GU9 * 96 G6
The Leaway
FHAM/PORC PO16 ....295 P1
Leawood Rd FLEETN GU51 ......74 A5
Lea Wood Rd FLEETN GU51 ....74 A5
Lebanon Rd WSHM SO15 ....247 H4
Le Borowe FLEETS GU52 ....74 B8
Lechlade Gdns FHAM PO15 ....272 B6
LTDN BH7 ....323 N7
Leckford Cl
FHAM/PORC PO16 ....273 N9
WEND SO18 ....249 M3
Leckford La STOK SO20 ....141 M4
Leckford Rd HAV PO9 ....277 H4
Lecole Wk HEND SO30 * 250 C4
Ledbury Rd CHAM PO6 ....274 E9
CHFD SO53 ....206 A3
Lederle La LSOL/BMARY PO13 ..294 C4
Ledgard Cl PSTN BH14 ....321 K8
Ledwell Ct GPORT PO12 ....315 P2
Lee Church La ROMY SO51 ....226 D4
Lee Ct ALDT GU11 * 3 H6
Leedam Rd NBNE BH10 ....322 E2
Lee Dn ROMY SO51 ....226 E3
Lee Lands LYMN SO41 ....329 K6
Lee La FHAM GU14 ....226 E4
Leep La GPORT PO12 ....12 D7
Lee Rd ALDT GU11 ....96 E1
Lees CI CHCH/BSGR BH23 .....324 B5
Leesland Rd GPORT PO12 ....315 L3

Lees La GPORT PO12 ....315 M3
Lees La North GPORT PO12 ...315 M3
Leeson Dr FERN BH22 ....280 B9
Leeson Rd LTDN BH7 ....323 L8
Lefroy Av BSTK RG21 ....7 H2
Lefroy's Fld RFNM GU10 ....95 H5
Legge Ct FLEETS GU52 ....74 B7
Leger Cs ALDT GU11 ....96 E2
Legg La WIMB BH21 ....300 F1
Legion Cl PLE BH15 ....332 A1
Legion La WINC SO23 ....145 K9
Legion Rd HISD PO11 ....318 C4
PLE BH15 ....332 A1
Lehar Cl KBH RG22 ....89 P3
Leicester Ct
LSOL/BMARY PO13 * 315 H5
Leicester PI AND SP10 ....4 C5
Leicester Rd CCLF BH13 ....321 P9
WSHM SO15 ....247 P1
Leicester Wy WINC SO23 ....23 K1
Leigham Vale Rd SBNE BH6 ...336 B2
Leigh CI AND SP10 ....5 G6
Leigh Common WIMB BH21 ....278 G9
Leigh Fld THLE RG7 ....27 H9
Leigh Gdns AND SP10 ....5 G6
WIMB BH21 ....300 F1
Leigh La FNM GU9 ....116 E2
WIMB BH21 ....279 H9
Leigh Pk WINC SO23 ....329 J3
Leigh Rd AND SP10 ....5 G6
ELGH SO50 ....206 E9
FHAM/PORC PO16 ....10 E4
HAV PO9 ....15 C3
NMIL/BTOS BH25 ....327 J3
PTSW SO17 ....248 C2
Leighton Av WSHM SO15 ....247 M1
Leighton Rd ITCH SO19 ....248 GB
Leipzig Barracks FLEETS GU52 ..95 M1
Leipzig Rd FLEETS GU52 ....74 E9
Leith Av FHAM/PORC PO16 ....275 P9
Leith Dr ALDT GU11 ....2 C2
Le Marchant Rd FRIM GU16 ....58 E2
Lemon Gv BOR GU35 ....153 P7
Lemon Rd WSHM SO15 ....247 M4
Lena CI RAND SP11 ....79 N1
Lendorber Av CHAM PO6 ....297 J2
Lendore Rd FRIM GU16 ....58 C5
Lennel Gdns FLEETS GU52 ....74 E9
Lennon Wy KBH RG22 ....89 N4
Lennox CI CHFD SO53 ....206 C5
GPORT PO12 ....315 M7
ROWN SO16 ....227 K7
Lennox Rd KBH RG22 ....90 A1
Lennox Rd North SSEA PO5 ....316 F6
Lennox Rd South SSEA PO5 ...316 F6
Len Smart Ct BSTK RG21 ....7 H1
Lenten St ALTN GU34 ....132 E6
Lentham CI CFDH BH17 ....320 F2
Lent Hill Ct FUFL SO22 * 164 E9
Lentune Wy LYMN SO41 ....329 K5
Leofric Ct ENEY PO4 * 317 L5
Leominster Rd CHAM PO6 .....274 D9
Leonard CI FHAM PO15 ....58 C5
Leonard Rd GPORT PO12 ....13 F1
Leonardslee Crs NWBY RG14 ..24 G3
Leopold Av FARN GU14 ....58 A9
Leopold Dr BPWT SO32 ....231 P5
Leopold St ENEY PO4 ....316 G6
Le Patourel Cl
CHCH/BSGR BH23 ....325 H8
Lepe Rd FAWY SO45 ....313 H1
Leroux Cl WSHM SO15 ....20 C2
Lerryn Rd LSOL/BMARY PO13 ..295 H7
Leslie Rd MOOR/WNTN BH9 ...322 E7
PSTN BH14 ....321 J9
Leslie Southern Ct NWBY RG14 ..24 E3
Lesser Horseshoe Cl
WHAM PO17 ....272 C2
Lester Av HAV PO9 ....14 A4
Lester Rd GPORT PO12 ....315 K5
Lestock Wy FLEETN GU51 ....74 B7
Levell Ct RAND SP11 ....79 P1
Leven Av WBNE BH4 ....334 D1
Leven CI CHFD SO53 ....206 C5
KBH RG22 ....89 M4
Leventhorpe Ct GPORT PO12 ..12 E3
Levern Dr FNM GU9 ....96 C5
Leveson CI GPORT PO12 ....315 K5
Levet's La PLE BH15 ....332 D1
Leviathan Cl
FHAM/STUB PO14 ....294 B7
Levignen Ct FLEETS GU52 ......74 A7
Lewendon Rd NWBY RG14 .....24 B2
Lewens Ct WIMB BH21 ....300 E1
Lewes CI ELGH SO50 ....207 J7
Lewesdon Dr BDST BH18 ....300 B9
Lewes Rd FHAM PO15 ....208 A5
Lewins Wk HLER SO31 ....269 P1
Lewis CI BSTK RG21 ....7 H2
FAWY SO45 ....267 N8
Lewisham Wy SHST GU47 ....41 L5
Lewis Rd EMRTH PO10 ....277 N7
Lewis Silkin Wy ROWN SO16 ..227 L8
Lewry Cl HEND SO30 ....250 C4
Lexby Rd TOTT SO40 ....246 E5
Lexden Gdns HISD PO11 ....318 E4
Leybourne Av NBNE BH10 .....321 P2
WEND SO18 ....249 H3
Leybourne CI NBNE BH10 ......322 C2
Leydene Av CHAR BH8 ....323 M6
Leydene CI CHAR BH8 ....323 M6
Leydene Pk PSF GU32 * 235 N2
Leyland CI GPORT PO12 ....12 D5
Leyland Rd BKME/WDN BH12 ..321 N2
Ley Rd FARN GU14 ....75 P1
Leys Rd SBNE BH6 ....336 B1
Leyside CHCH/BSGR BH23 .....325 K9
CWTH RG45 ....41 H1
Leyton Rd SHAM SO14 ....21 J1
Leyton Wy AND SP10 ....102 C4
Liam CI HAV PO9 ....116 D1
The Liberties BPWT SO32 * 253 M1
Liberty CI WIMB BH21 ....281 H5

Liberty Rd BPWT SO32 ....253 L3
The Liberty WVILLE PO7 ....254 C8
Library Gdns HAV PO9 ....14 E2
Library La RWIN SO21 ....163 L3
Library Rd BKME/WDN BH12 ...321 N7
FARN GU14 ....76 A2
FERN BH22 ....302 D3
MOOR/WNTN BH9 ....322 E8
TOTT SO40 ....246 E4
Lichen Wy TOTT SO40 ....247 K9
Lichfield Ct
LSOL/BMARY PO13 * 315 H3
Lichfield Rd
FHAM/STUB PO14 ....271 J7
HSEA PO3 ....317 J2
Lickfolds Rd RFNM GU10 ....115 N8
Liddell Ct EWKG RG40 ....39 P3
Liddel Wy CHFD SO53 ....206 C8
Liddiards Wy WVILLE PO7 .....275 N7
Lidiard Gdns ENEY PO4 ....317 K6
Liederbach Dr VWD BH31 ......259 J6
Lightfoot Gv BSTK RG21 ....89 N6
Lightsfield DEAN RG23 ....88 F1
Lilac CI AND SP10 ....102 B3
BOR GU35 ....154 A6
HAV PO9 ....277 J7
RGWD BH24 ....282 F1
Lilac Rd ROWN SO16 ....228 G8
Lilac Wy DEAN RG23 ....68 G6
Lille Barracks ALDT GU11 ....76 C4
The Lillies ELGH SO50 ....230 D5
Lilliput Rd PSTN BH14 ....333 L3
Lillywhite Crs AND SP10 ....82 F7
Lily Av WVILLE PO7 ....275 K8
Lily CI KBH RG22 ....89 L4
Limberline Rd HSEA PO3 ....297 J5
Limberline Sp HSEA PO3 ....297 J4
Limbrey Hl OVTN RG25 ....92 B6
Lime Av ALTN GU34 ....132 E4
ITCH SO19 ....249 J6
Lime CI FAWY SO45 ....268 A6
ITCH SO19 ....249 J6
NWBY RG14 ....24 G3
PLE BH15 ....321 H6
RWIN SO21 ....163 M3
Limecroft YTLY GU46 ....40 D9
Lime Dr FLEETN GU51 ....58 C3
Lime Gdns BSTK RG21 ....69 P7
HEND SO30 ....229 M9
Lime Gv ALTN GU34 ....132 D4
CHAM PO6 ....274 D9
HISD PO11 ....318 C5
LYMN SO41 ....328 D7
Lime Kiln La FAWY SO45 ....290 D3
Limekiln La BPWT SO32 ....252 D1
PSF GU32 ....214 C6
Limekiln Lane Est
FAWY SO45 * 290 D4
Lime Rd NARL SO24 ....168 A2
Limes Av KSCL RG20 ....33 L3
Limes CI LIPH GU30 ....155 K9
LISS GU33 ....192 C2
Limes Rd FARN GU14 ....97 K8
The Limes LSOL/BMARY PO13 ..295 H8
TADY RG26 ....18 G2
TOTT SO40 ....267 L1
Lime St ALDT GU11 ....2 C3
KBH RG22 ....89 M4
RGWD BH24 ....260 G9
Limetree Av KSCL RG20 ....46 A5
Lime Tree CI FBDG SP6 ....239 M6
Limetree Wk WINC SO23 ....23 K4
Lime Tree Wy CHIN RG24 ....69 P1
Lime Wk AND SP10 * 102 B4
Limited Rd MOOR/WNTN BH9 ..322 F7
Linacre Rd ITCH SO19 ....249 M7
Lin Brook Dr RGWD BH24 ......260 G8
Linchmere Rd HASM GU27 ....156 C8
Lincoln Av BMTH BH1 ....323 K9
Lincoln Ct BDST BH23 ....324 D5
Lincoln CI ASHV GU12 ....76 E7
CBLY GU15 ....57 P4
FHAM/STUB PO14 ....271 J7
KBH RG22 ....89 M4
Lincoln Ct
LSOL/BMARY PO13 * 315 H5
NWBY RG14 ....16 C3
WSHM SO15 ....248 A1
Lincoln Gn ALTN GU34 ....132 E7
Lincoln Ri HORN PO8 ....256 A7
PSEA PO1 ....316 C3
Lincolns Ri ELGH SO50 ....207 K5
Linda Gv HORN PO8 ....255 P8
Linda Rd FAWY SO45 ....291 K6
Lindbergh Rd WIMB BH21 .....280 A9
Linden CI HEND SO30 ....271 L5
Lind CI WVILLE PO7 ....275 P9
Linden Av CHIN RG24 ....70 C7
ODIM RG29 ....72 E8
Linden CI BPWT SO32 ....232 C9
FERN BH22 ....302 D2
NWBY RG14 ....24 C3
RAND SP11 ....80 A1
Linden Dr LISS GU33 ....192 C2
Linden Gdns HEND SO30 ....250 D6
Linden Gv CHFD SO53 ....205 L4
GPORT PO12 ....12 C4
HISD PO11 ....318 D5
Lindens CI EMRTH PO10 ....277 M7
The Lindens
CHCH/BSGR BH23 ....325 H4
FNM GU9 ....116 D1
Linden Wk NBAD SO52 ....205 K3
Linden Wy HAV PO9 ....15 G1

HORN PO8 ....256 B6
LYMN SO41 ....329 J3
Lindford Cha BOR GU35 ....154 C5
Lindford Rd BOR GU35 ....154 B2
Lindford Wey BOR GU35 ....154 C5
Lindisfarne CI CHAM PO6 ......297 J2
Lindley Av ENEY PO4 ....317 J6
Lindley Gdns NARL SO24 ....168 A3
Lind Rd GPORT PO12 ....315 N7
Lindsay Rd CCLF BH13 ....334 A2
ITCH SO19 ....249 N5
Lindum Dene ALDT GU11 ....2 D5
Lindway HLER SO31 ....270 C5
Lineside CHCH/BSGR BH23 ....324 C7
The Lines KSCL RG20 ....48 C2
Linford CI NMIL/BTOS BH25 ...327 J3
Linford Ct HAV PO9 ....276 D3
Linford Crs ROWN SO16 ....227 P9
Linford Rd RGWD BH24 ....261 H9
Ling Cr BOR GU35 ....155 J2
Ling Dl ROWN SO16 ....228 B5
Lingdale Rd SBNE BH6 ....324 B9
Lingen CI AND SP10 ....82 D8
Lingfield CI ALTN GU34 ....132 F7
CHIN RG24 ....70 D7
Lingfield Gdns WEND SO18 ...229 H9
Lingfield Rd NWBY RG14 ....17 J2
Lingmala Gv FLEETS GU52 ......74 E7
Ling Rd BKME/WDN BH12 ......321 K3
Lingwood Av
CHCH/BSGR BH23 ....325 K9
Lingwood CI ROWN SO16 ......228 B5
Lingwood Wk ROWN SO16 .....228 B5
Linhorns La NMIL/BTOS BH25 ..327 J1
Linkenholt Wy HAV PO9 ....276 C5
Linklater Pth PSEA PO1 ....316 F1
Link Ri WIMB BH21 ....300 A1
Link Rd ALTN GU34 ....132 G3
CHAM PO6 ....274 D8
FARN GU14 ....75 L4
KSCL RG20 ....48 D3
NWBY RG14 ....16 E4
RGWD BH24 ....260 C9
ROWN SO16 ....227 K9
Links Dr CHCH/BSGR BH23 ...324 B6
Linkside Av CHAR BH8 ....323 L7
Links La HAV PO9 ....257 H8
HISD PO11 ....318 C5
Links Rd FUFL SO22 ....164 E6
PSTN BH14 ....333 M1
The Links BOR GU35
LSOL/BMARY PO13 ....294 G8
Links View Av PSTN BH14 ......333 N2
Links View Wy ROWN SO16 ...228 B6
Links Wy FARN GU14 ....75 K1
The Link AND SP10 ....102 A2
WVILLE PO7 ....276 A1
YTLY GU46 ....40 C9
Link Wy DEAN RG23 ....88 F2
NTHA RG18 ....25 L3
Linkway CBLY GU15 ....58 B1
CWTH RG45 ....40 G1
LISS GU33 ....192 C2
FLEETS GU52 ....74 C6
Linmead Dr BWD BH11 ....322 A1
Linnet CI EPSF GU31 ....216 A3
NTHA RG18 ....25 N7
Linnet Ct NMIL/BTOS BH25 ....327 H4
Linnet Rd CFDH BH17 ....320 A4
Linnet Sq ELGH SO50 ....228 F3
Linnets Rd NARL SO24 ....167 P3
The Linnets
FHAM/PORC PO16 ....295 K2
TOTT SO40 ....246 A3
Linnets Wy ALTN GU34 ....132 F4
Linnies La LYMN SO41 ....308 A9
Linsford La FRIM GU16 ....76 E1
Linstead Rd FARN GU14 ....57 M5
Linthorpe Rd PLE BH15 ....320 G8
Linton CI TADY RG26 ....34 D7
Linton Dr AND SP10 ....4 B1
Linwood CI FAWY SO45 ....268 C8
Linwood Rd
MOOR/WNTN BH9 ....323 H8
Lion CI OVTN RG25 ....86 C4
Lionheart CI BWD BH11 ....301 M8
Lionheart Wy HLER SO31 ....269 P1
Lion & Lamb Wy FNM GU9 ....96 B9
Lion & Lamb Yd FNM GU9 * 96 B9
Lion La GSHT GU26 ....156 E4
Lion Md HASM GU27 ....156 B4
Lion Rd FARN GU14 ....76 A2
Lions Fld BOR GU35 ....153 J4
Lions Ga FBDG SP6 * 240 D2
Lions Hill Wy RGWD BH24 .....281 J4
Lions La RGWD BH24 ....281 K5
Lion St PSEA PO1 ....18 E2
Lions Wd RGWD BH24 ....281 L5
Lion Ter PSEA PO1 ....18 E2
Lion Wy FLEETS GU52 ....74 E7
Liphook Rd BOR GU35 ....153 P8
BOR GU35 ....154 C3
HASM GU27 ....155 P5
Lipizzamer Flds HLER SO31 ...271 H2
Lippen La BPWT SO32 ....212 B2
Lipscombe CI NWBY RG14 ......16 A3
Lipscombe Ri ALTN GU34 ....132 F4
Lisbon Rd WSHM SO15 ....247 P5
Liskeard Dr FARN GU14 ....57 P2
Lisle CI FUFL SO22 ....183 J3
LYMN SO41 ....329 K4
NWBY RG14 ....24 C2
Lisle Ct FUFL SO22 ....164 F9
Lisle Court Rd LYMN SO41 .....329 P3
Lisle Wy EMRTH PO10 ....277 L7
Lismoyne CI FLEETN GU51 ......74 B4
Liss Rd ENEY PO4 ....317 H4
Lister Rd KBH RG22 ....90 B2
Litchfield CI AND SP10 ....82 B8
Litchfield Crs WEND SO18 .....249 H2
Litchfield Rd FUFL SO22 ....164 E5
WEND SO18 ....249 H2

Litchford Rd
NMIL/BTOS BH25 327 L3
Lith Av HORN PO8 256 C3
Lith La HORN PO8 256 C2
The Litter KSCL RG20 48 C3
Little Abshot Rd
FHAM/STUB PO14 293 H1
Little Aldershot La STHA RG19 33 M4
Little Anglesey Rd
GPORT PO12 12 A6
Little Arthur St NEND PO2 * 316 G1
Little Ashton La BPWT SO32 232 B1
Little Austins Rd FNM GU9 116 D2
Little Barn Pl LISS GU33 192 F2
Little Barrs Dr
NMIL/BTOS BH25 327 K3
Little Basing CHIN RG24 70 A5
Little Binfield CHIN RG24 70 B3
Little Bull La BPWT SO32 252 B1
Little Copse AND SP10 102 C4
FLEETS GU52 74 C5
YTLY GU46 40 D7
Little Copse Cha CHIN RG24 69 P2
Little Cnr WVILLE PO7 255 H8
Littlecroft Av
MOOR/WNTN BH9 323 H4
Little Croft Rd
BKME/WDN BH12 321 K6
Little Dean La OVTN RG25 92 E6
Little Dene Copse LYMN SO41 329 H5
Little Dewlands VWD BH31 258 D4
Littledown Av LTDN BH7 323 L8
Littledown Dr LTDN BH7 323 L8
Little Dro FBDG SP6 221 J5
Little Drove Rd STOK SO20 123 L6
Little Fallow CHIN RG24 70 A4
Littlefield Cl ASHV GU12 97 N2
Littlefield Crs CHFD SO53 206 A7
Littlefield Gdns ASHV GU12 97 N2
Littlefield Rd ALTN GU34 132 G5
Little Forest Rd WBNE BH4 334 D1
Little Fox Dr FHAM PO15 271 H5
Little Gays FHAM/STUB PO14 293 M7
Little George St PSEA PO1 316 G1
Little Gn GPORT PO12 12 A6
Littlegreen Av HAV PO9 15 J1
Little Green La FNM GU9 115 P3
Little Green Orch
GPORT PO12 * 12 A5
Little Hambrook St SSEA PO5 * 19 F6
Little Hayes La RWIN SO21 146 E9
Little Hoddington Cl
OVTN RG25 92 C6
Little Hyden La HORN PO8 236 B5
Little Knowle Hl KSCL RG20 48 E1
STHA RG19 32 G8
Little Lance's Hl ITCH SO19 249 H4
Little La GPORT PO12 12 A6
Little London Rd THLE RG7 35 H8
Little Lonnen WIMB BH21 279 H6
Little Md WVILLE PO7 255 J8
Littlemead Cl CFDH BH17 320 C5
Littlemeads ROMY SO51 204 B6
Littlemill La FBDG SP6 219 J7
Little Minster St WINC SO23 22 E5
Little Moor SHST GU47 41 K5
Littlemoor Av BWD BH11 301 M9
Little Oak Rd ROWN SO16 228 B8
Littlepark Av HAV PO9 276 B7
Little Park Cl HEND SO30 250 B5
Little Park Farm Rd
FHAM PO15 271 J5
Little Quob La HEND SO30 249 N1
Little Shore La BPWT SO32 232 A5
Little Southsea St SSEA PO5 19 F6
Little Thurbans Cl FNM GU9 116 A4
Littleton Gv HAV PO9 276 F6
Littleton La RWIN SO21 163 N5
Little Vigo YTLY GU46 56 C1
Little Wellington St ALDT GU11 2 E3
Little Woodfalls Dr RSAL SP5 199 P9
Littlewood Gdns HEND SO30 249 M2
HLER SO31 270 E7
Little Woodham La
LSOL/BMARY PO13 314 G3
Littleworth Rd RFNM GU10 117 M1
Litton Gdns DEAN RG23 88 F2
Liverpool Ct
LSOL/BMARY PO13 * 315 H3
Liverpool Rd
FHAM/STUB PO14 294 D3
PSEA PO1 316 G3
Liverpool St SHAM SO14 248 C4
Livery Rd RSAL SP5 158 A9
Livesay Gdns HSEA PO3 317 H2
Livia Cl AND SP10 82 F7
Livingstone Rd AND SP10 103 J1
BKME/WDN BH12 321 L6
BOSC BH5 335 P2
CHCH/BSGR BH23 325 H9
NWBY RG14 17 G3
SHAM SO14 248 C3
SSEA PO5 19 K6
WIMB BH21 300 G1
Llangar Gv CWTH RG45 41 H1
Lloyd Av TOTT SO40 267 J1
Lloyd's La TADY RG26 49 M8
Loader Cl WINC SO23 145 K9
Loaders Cl MOOR/WNTN BH9 322 G7
Loane Rd ITCH SO19 249 H8
Lobelia Rd ROWN SO16 228 E8
Locarno Rd HSEA PO3 297 H7
Loch Rd PSTN BH14 321 N7
Lock Approach CHAM PO6 296 C2
Locke Cl RAND SP11 119 N2
Lockerley Cl LYMN SO41 329 L5
Lockerley Crs ROWN SO16 247 K1
Lockerley Rd HAV PO9 15 H1
ROMY SO51 178 G5
ROMY SO51 179 K9
Locke Rd HEND SO30 250 C3
LIPH GU30 175 L3
Locke's Dro RAND SP11 61 K4
Lockhams Rd BPWT SO32 251 M3
Lockram La THLE RG7 27 L6
Lock Rd ALDT GU11 76 C7
Locksbridge La TADY RG26 51 N3
Locksheath Cl HAV PO9 276 D4
Locksheath Park Rd
HLER SO31 271 H9
Lock's La RWIN SO21 163 N4
Locksley Dr FERN BH22 302 C5
Locksley Rd ELGH SO50 228 G3
Locksmead BSTK RG21 7 K5
Lock Sq AND SP10 82 G9
Locks Rd HLER SO31 270 G6
Locksway Rd ENEY PO4 317 L4
Lockswood Keep
HLER SO31 * 270 G6
Lockswood Rd HLER SO31 270 F7
Lock Vw CHAM PO6 296 C2
Lockwood Cl FARN GU14 57 M5
Lockyers Dr FERN BH22 302 F2
Lockyers Rd WIMB BH21 300 A5
Loddon Ct BSTK RG21 90 D1
Loddon Dr BSTK RG21 7 J6
Loddon Rd FARN GU14 57 L7
Loddon Wy ASHV GU12 97 N2
Lode Hl RSAL SP5 199 M6
Loders Cl CFDH BH17 320 E1
Lodge Av CHAM PO6 297 J1
Lodge Cl AND SP10 102 C2
PSTN BH14 321 N8
Lodge Ct PSTN BH14 321 N8
Lodge Dr FAWY SO45 268 B9
RAND SP11 81 K9
Lodge Dro RSAL SP5 199 N9
Lodge Gdns GPORT PO12 12 A4
Lodge Gv YTLY GU46 40 G8
Lodge Hill Cl RFNM GU10 116 D4
Lodge Hill Rd RFNM GU10 116 D4
Lodge La BROC SO42 311 J2
RAND SP11 60 A9
Lodge Rd CHCH/BSGR BH23 324 C7
HAV PO9 276 B9
HLER SO31 271 H7
LYMN SO41 329 H4
SHAM SO14 248 C4
WIMB BH21 279 H1
The Lodge WSHM SO15 * 248 B4
Lodge V ROMY SO51 225 H2
Lodsworth FARN GU14 75 L1
Lodsworth Cl HORN PO8 236 D8
Loewy Crs BKME/WDN BH12 321 M2
Lofting Cl ELGH SO50 229 N2
Logan Cl ROWN SO16 227 K7
Loggon Rd BSTK RG21 90 C2
Loman Rd FRIM GU16 76 F1
Lomax Cl HEND SO30 250 C2
Lombard Av SBNE BH6 336 B1
Lombard St PSEA PO1 18 C5
Lombardy Cl
LSOL/BMARY PO13 295 J7
VWD BH31 259 H5
Lombardy Ri WVILLE PO7 275 P5
Lomer La RGWD BH24 240 A7
Lomond Cl DEAN RG23 88 E2
NEND PO2 296 F9
Londesborough Rd
ENEY PO4 316 G5
Londlandes FLEETS GU52 74 B8
London Av NEND PO2 296 F7
London La CHCH/BSGR BH23 304 E6
London Ml NEND PO2 * 296 F8
London Rd ALTN GU34 133 J3
AND SP10 5 G4
BLKW GU17 57 M1
BSTK RG21 7 G7
CBLY GU15 41 N9
CHIN RG24 70 C8
CHAM PO6 297 H1
EPSF GU31 191 P9
HORN PO8 236 D9
HORN PO8 255 P9
HTWY RG27 55 H8
HTWY RG27 71 H5
LIPH GU30 175 K3
NEND PO2 296 F9
NWBY RG14 17 J1
ODIM RG29 72 E8
OVTN RG25 86 F4
RAND SP11 103 N1
STHA RG19 25 P4
STOK SO20 141 M4
WHCH RG28 85 N6
WINC SO23 165 J3
WSHM SO15 20 D1
WVILLE PO7 275 K8
London St AND SP10 4 E5
BSTK RG21 7 F7
WHCH RG28 85 L6
Lone Barn La BPWT SO32 211 J6
Lone Pine Dr FERN BH22 302 E5
Lone Pine Wy FERN BH22 302 F6
Lone Va WVILLE PO7 275 L7
Longacre ASHV GU12 97 N1
NWBY RG14 24 A7
Longacre Cl LISS GU33 192 E2
Long Acre Ct PSEA PO1 316 G1
Longacre Ri CHIN RG24 69 P2
Longacres FHAM/STUB PO14 271 J6
Longbarrow Cl CHAR BH8 * 323 M6
Long Barrow Cl RWIN SO21 144 F3
Long Beech Dr FARN GU14 75 K1
TOTT SO40 246 B5
Long Br FNM GU9 96 C9
Longbridge Cl HTWY RG27 52 F4
TOTT SO40 246 B1
Longbridge Rd TADY RG26 52 A2
Long Cl RSAL SP5 199 J5
Longclose Rd HEND SO30 250 D4
Long Cl West RSAL SP5 199 J5
Long Copse FAWY SO45 290 G6
Long Copse Cha CHIN RG24 69 P2
Long Copse La EMRTH PO10 277 M6
Longcroft RFNM GU10 114 E5
Longcroft Cl BSTK RG21 6 C7
Longcroft Rd KSCL RG20 48 B2
STHA RG19 25 P5
Long Cross Hl BOR GU35 154 F3
Long Cross La KBH RG22 89 L5
Long Curtain Rd PSEA PO1 18 D7
Longdean Cl CHAM PO6 274 C9
Longdene Rd HASM GU27 156 G7
Longdon Dr
LSOL/BMARY PO13 314 D1
Long Down EPSF GU31 215 P1
Longdown FLEETS GU52 74 C6
Longdown Cl RFNM GU10 116 C4
Longdown Rd RFNM GU10 116 B5
SHST GU47 41 H5
Long Dr HEND SO30 249 N1
LSOL/BMARY PO13 294 G8
Long Dro RSAL SP5 176 B2
Longespee Rd WIMB BH21 300 F5
Longfellow Pde CHIN RG24 * 69 M4
Longfield DEAN RG23 67 M9
Longfield Av FHAM/STUB PO14 294 C2
Longfield Cl ENEY PO4 317 L3
FARN GU14 57 P5
OVTN RG25 108 C1
Longfield Dr BWD BH11 322 A1
FERN BH22 302 E8
Longfield Rd ASHV GU12 97 N1
EMRTH PO10 277 L7
LYMN SO41 328 B5
WINC SO23 165 L7
Longfleet Dr WIMB BH21 301 J6
Longfleet Rd PLE BH15 320 G8
Longford Cl CBLY GU15 58 C1
Long Garden Pl FNM GU9 * 96 B8
Long Garden Wk FNM GU9 96 B9
Long Garden Wk East
FNM GU9 96 B8
Long Garden Wk West
FNM GU9 96 B8
Long Garden Wy FNM GU9 96 B9
Long Gv TADY RG26 33 N4
Longham Br NBNE BH10 302 A9
Long Hl RFNM GU10 117 L1
Longhope Dr RFNM GU10 116 A4
Longhouse Gn WINC SO23 23 K4
Long La CHIN RG24 70 B2
FAWY SO45 290 E4
HLER SO31 270 A2
ODIM RG29 93 M3
RGWD BH24 282 F5
TOTT SO40 267 H1
WIMB BH21 278 G6
Long Lane Cl FAWY SO45 290 F6
Longleat Gdns
NMIL/BTOS BH25 326 G4
ROWN SO16 227 M7
Longleat Sq FARN GU14 76 D1
Long Leaze RAND SP11 62 F8
Longley Rd FNM GU9 116 D1
Longmead FLEETS GU52 74 D6
KSCL RG20 29 N5
LISS GU33 192 D3
Longmead Av ELGH SO50 207 M9
Longmead Gdns HAV PO9 298 F2
Longmeadow FRIM GU16 58 E2
Longmeadow Gdns
FAWY SO45 268 C6
Longmeadow La CFDH BH17 320 A4
Longmead Rd RGWD BH24 284 B5
WEND SO18 249 H1
Long Mickle SHST GU47 41 H5
Longmoor Dr LIPH GU30 174 E3
Longmoor La THLE RG7 27 J8
Longmoor Rd BSTK RG21 69 K8
LIPH GU30 174 D3
LISS GU33 173 M5
Longmore Av ITCH SO19 248 F9
Longmore Crs ITCH SO19 248 F9
Longmynd Dr
FHAM/STUB PO14 294 B1
Longparish Rd RAND SP11 123 L2
WHCH RG28 104 F1
Long Priors PSF GU32 188 D9
Longridge Rd HEND SO30 250 C5
Long Rd BPWT SO32 233 N6
NBNE BH10 322 C3
PSF GU32 191 N9
The Long Rd RFNM GU10 115 P7
Longroden La OVTN RG25 91 K4
Longs Ct WHCH RG28 85 L6
Longshore Wy ENEY PO4 317 M4
Longs La FHAM/STUB PO14 294 A6
Longstaff Gdns
FHAM/PORC PO16 10 D2
Long Steeple La FBDG SP6 220 C2
Longstock Cl AND SP10 102 C3
CHIN RG24 52 C9
ITCH SO19 269 J2
Longstock Crs TOTT SO40 246 B4
Longstock Rd HAV PO9 277 H4
RAND SP11 122 D5
Longs Wk PSEA PO1 316 F1
Long Wk RWIN SO21 165 M3
Long Water Dr GPORT PO12 315 N7
Longwater La EWKG RG40 39 P4
Longwater Rd HTWY RG27 40 A6
Longwood Av HORN PO8 255 P8
Longwood Copse La
DEAN RG23 89 K7
Longwood Dean La
RWIN SO21 186 A8
Longwood Rd RWIN SO21 209 J1
Lonnen Rd WIMB BH21 279 J6
Lonnen Wood Cl WIMB BH21 279 J6
Lonsdale Av CHAM PO6 297 J2
FHAM/PORC PO16 295 P3
Lonsdale Rd TWDS BH3 322 F8
Loosehanger RSAL SP5 222 B1
Loperwood TOTT SO40 245 M1
Loperwood La TOTT SO40 225 N8
Loraine Av CHCH/BSGR BH23 326 E7
Lord Cl CFDH BH17 321 H5
Lordington Cl CHAM PO6 297 K1
Lord Mountbatten Cl
WEND SO18 228 G8
Lordsfield Gdns OVTN RG25 86 F3
Lord's Hill Centre East
ROWN SO16 227 K7
Lord's Hill Centre West
ROWN SO16 227 K8
Lord's Hill Wy ROWN SO16 227 K8
Lordswood ELGH SO50 207 N6
THLE RG7 35 H6
Lordswood Cl ROWN SO16 227 P9
Lordswood Gdns ROWN SO16 227 P8
Lordswood Rd ROWN SO16 227 N8
Loreille Cl ROWN SO16 227 J5
Lorne Park Rd BMTH BH1 9 F3
Lorne Pl WEND SO18 * 249 J4
Lorne Rd SSEA PO5 316 G5
Lothian Rd CHOB/PIR GU24 59 M7
Loughwood Cl ELGH SO50 207 J7
Louisburg Rd BOR GU35 154 A2
Louise Margaret Rd ALDT GU11 3 G1
Loundyes Cl NTHA RG18 25 L3
Lovage Gdns TOTT SO40 246 A4
Lovage Rd FHAM PO15 271 K3
Lovage Wy HORN PO8 256 C2
Lovatt Gv FHAM PO15 272 B7
Lovedean La HORN PO8 255 N3
HORN PO8 256 A1
Lovedon La WINC SO23 145 K8
Lovegroves CHIN RG24 70 B1
Love La AND SP10 4 E6
BPWT SO32 210 F2
EPSF GU31 215 N1
FBDG SP6 221 J4
KSCL RG20 48 C3
NWBY RG14 24 C1
ODIM RG29 93 K3
PSF GU32 212 E1
ROMY SO51 204 C6
RWIN SO21 184 B9
Lovell Cl RAND SP11 100 D3
RWIN SO21 144 F4
Lovells Wk NARL SO24 167 P2
Loveridge Cl AND SP10 82 F7
BSTK RG21 90 C1
Lovers La RFNM GU10 136 C2
Love's Cl THLE RG7 27 H4
Loves Wd THLE RG7 35 N1
Lovett Rd HSEA PO3 297 H6
Lovington La RWIN SO21 167 H3
Lowa Cl NTID SP9 78 G6
Lowa Rd NTID SP9 78 G5
Lowcay Rd SSEA PO5 316 F6
Lowden Cl FUFL SO22 183 M2
Lowe Cl ALDT GU11 2 B1
Lower Ashley Rd
NMIL/BTOS BH25 327 M4
Lower Banister St WSHM SO15 20 D1
Lower Bartons FBDG SP6 240 D2
Lower Baybridge La
RWIN SO21 209 H4
Lower Bellfield
FHAM/STUB PO14 293 M2
Lower Bere Wd WVILLE PO7 275 P3
Lower Blandford Rd
BDST BH18 300 C9
Lower Broadmoor Rd
CWTH RG45 41 L2
Lower Brook St BSTK RG21 6 A6
WINC SO23 23 F4
Lower Brownhill Rd
ROWN SO16 246 G1
Lower Buckland Rd
LYMN SO41 329 K2
Lower Canal Wk SHAM SO14 20 E7
Lower Canes YTLY GU46 40 B8
Lower Chase Rd BPWT SO32 232 E7
Lower Chestnut Dr BSTK RG21 69 J9
Lower Church La FNM GU9 96 B9
Lower Church Pth PSEA PO1 19 H2
Lower Church Rd
FHAM/STUB PO14 271 J7
SHST GU47 40 F5
Lower Common HTWY RG27 39 H5
Lower Common La
WIMB BH21 280 G2
Lower Common Rd
ROMY SO51 224 E2
Lower Crabbick La
WVILLE PO7 254 D7
Lower Densome Wd
FBDG SP6 221 J4
Lower Derby Rd NEND PO2 296 E8
Lower Drayton La CHAM PO6 297 L2
Lower Duncan Rd HLER SO31 271 H5
Lower Evingar Rd WHCH RG28 85 L6
Lower Farlington Rd
CHAM PO6 297 N1
Lower Farm Ct STHA RG19 25 J6
Lower Farm La ROMY SO51 205 M2
Lower Farnham Rd ALDT GU11 97 J4
Lower Forbury Rd SSEA PO5 * 19 J6
Lower Golf Links Rd
BDST BH18 300 D8
Lower Gv FBDG SP6 219 P2
Lower Grove Rd HAV PO9 15 H7
Lower Hanger HASM GU27 156 B7
Lower Heyshott EPSF GU31 215 N1
Lower Lamborough La
NARL SO24 187 H1
Lower La BPWT SO32 232 B4
Lower Md EPSF GU31 215 P2
LISS GU33 192 D2
STOK SO20 121 H5
Lower Mead End Rd
LYMN SO41 307 P8
Lower Moor YTLY GU46 40 E9
Lower Moors Rd RWIN SO21 207 P4
Lower Mortimer Rd
ITCH SO19 248 F8
Lower Mount St
FLEETN GU51 73 P1
Lower Mullin's La FAWY SO45 268 B6
Lower Neatham Mill La
ALTN GU34 133 L3
Lower Nelson St ALDT GU11 2 D2
Lower Newport Rd ASHV GU12 97 K2
Lower New Rd HEND SO30 249 M2
Lower Northam Rd
HEND SO30 250 C5
Lower Paice La ALTN GU34 149 M4
Lower Pennington La
LYMN SO41 329 K6
Lower Pool Rd HTWY RG27 54 G1
Lower Preshaw La
BPWT SO32 210 D5
Lower Quay Cl
FHAM/PORC PO16 294 F1
Lower Quay Rd
FHAM/PORC PO16 294 F1
Lower Rd HASM GU27 157 L3
HAV PO9 276 C9
RSAL SP5 199 K1
RWIN SO21 144 D4
Lower St Helens Rd
HEND SO30 250 C6
Lower Sandhurst Rd
EWKG RG40 40 B4
Lower Sandy Down La
LYMN SO41 309 H5
Lower South Vw FNM GU9 96 C8
Lower Spinney HLER SO31 292 C2
Lower St HASM GU27 156 G7
ROMY SO51 180 F7
Lower Swanwick Rd
HLER SO31 270 D2
Lower Terrace Rd FARN GU14 75 P4
Lower Turk St ALTN GU34 132 F6
Lower Vicarage Rd ITCH SO19 248 F8
Lower Wardown EPSF GU31 215 P1
Lower Wy STHA RG19 25 K4
Lower Weybourne La
FNM GU9 96 F5
Lower William St SHAM SO14 248 F5
Lower Woodside LYMN SO41 329 L7
Lower York St SHAM SO14 21 K1
Lowestoft Rd CHAM PO6 274 F9
Loweswater Gdns BOR GU35 154 A3
Lowford Hl HLER SO31 269 P1
Lowicks Rd RFNM GU10 137 H3
Lowland Rd WVILLE PO7 254 G7
Lowlands Rd BLKW GU17 57 K1
KBH RG22 68 D9
Low La FNM GU9 97 H5
Lowndes Buildings
FNM GU9 * 96 B8
Lowry Cl SHST GU47 41 L8
Lowry Ct AND SP10 4 B1
Lowry Gdns ITCH SO19 249 L9
Lowther Gdns CHAR BH8 335 J1
Lowther Rd CHAR BH8 322 G9
Loxwood Av FLEETN GU51 74 B5
Loxwood Rd HORN PO8 255 P5
Loyalty La CHIN RG24 70 C6
Luard Ct HAV PO9 15 K6
Lubeck Dr AND SP10 82 D8
Lucas Cl ROWN SO16 227 K7
YTLY GU46 40 E9
Lucas Fld HASM GU27 156 D7
Lucas Rd BKME/WDN BH12 321 L6
Luccombe Pl WSHM SO15 247 P1
Luccombe Rd WSHM SO15 247 P1
Lucerne Av SBNE BH6 336 B1
WVILLE PO7 275 L1
Lucerne Gdns HEND SO30 250 B5
Lucerne Rd LYMN SO41 338 G2
Luckham Cl
MOOR/WNTN BH9 323 H5
Luckham Pl
MOOR/WNTN BH9 323 H5
Luckham Rd
MOOR/WNTN BH9 323 H5
Luckham Rd East
MOOR/WNTN BH9 323 H5
Lucknow St PSEA PO1 316 G3
Lucky La LYMN SO41 309 N7
Ludcombe WVILLE PO7 255 H6
Ludgershall Rd NTID SP9 79 H4
Ludlow Cl DEAN RG23 68 G7
FRIM GU16 58 F6
NWBY RG14 25 H3
Ludlow Gdns DEAN RG23 68 G7
Ludlow Rd CHAM PO6 274 E9
ITCH SO19 248 G7
Ludshott Gv BOR GU35 155 J3
Ludwell's La BPWT SO32 232 D8
Lugano Cl WVILLE PO7 275 M1
Luke Rd ALDT GU11 96 E3
Luke Rd East ALDT GU11 2 A6
Lukin Dr ROWN SO16 226 G7
Lulworth Av PLE BH15 332 A2
Lulworth Cl CHFD SO53 228 D1
FARN GU14 57 P6
HISD PO11 318 G3
PLE BH15 332 A1
ROWN SO16 247 J1
Lulworth Crs PLE BH15 332 A2
Lulworth Gn ROWN SO16 247 J1
Lulworth Rd
LSOL/BMARY PO13 314 C2
Lumby Dr RGWD BH24 282 F1
Lumby Drive Pk RGWD BH24 282 F1
Lumley Rd EMRTH PO10 277 N9
Lumsden Av WSHM SO15 247 N4
Lumsden Rd ENEY PO4 317 M5
Lundy Cl CHIN RG24 69 N3
ROWN SO16 227 J7
Lune Cl BSTK RG21 7 J6
Lune Ct AND SP10 82 G9
Lunedale Rd FAWY SO45 290 A1
Lupin Cl KBH RG22 89 L3
Lupin Gdns FUFL SO22 164 C5
Lupin Rd ROWN SO16 228 E7
Luscombe Rd PSTN BH14 333 L1
Luther Rd MOOR/WNTN BH9 322 F7
Lutman St EMRTH PO10 277 L6
Luton Rd ITCH SO19 249 K7
Lutyens Cl CHIN RG24 70 A4
Luxton Cl HEND SO30 250 F3
Luzborough La ROMY SO51 204 G8
Lyall Pl FNM GU9 96 B4
Lyburn Cl ROWN SO16 227 N8
Lyburn Rd RSAL SP5 223 J2
Lych Gate Cl SHST GU47 40 G6
Lych Gate Ct RGWD BH24 282 G3

Lychgate Dr HORN PO8 .....256 B4
Lychgate Gn
  FHAM/STUB PO14 .....294 A4
Lyde Cl DEAN RG23 .....88 F2
Lydford Cl FARN GU14 * 57 P6
  FRIM GU16 .....58 H6
Lydford Gdns BWD BH11 .....322 A5
Lydford Rd BWD BH11 .....322 A5
Lydgate LYMN SO41 .....338 D1
  TOTT SO40 .....246 B4
Lydgate Cl ITCH SO19 .....249 M7
Lydgate Gn ITCH SO19 .....249 M7
Lydgate Rd ITCH SO19 .....249 M7
Lydiard Cl ELGH SO50 .....207 J8
Lydlinch Cl FERN BH22 .....302 D7
Lydlynch Rd FUFL SO40 .....246 E5
Lydney Cl CHAM PO6 .....296 E1
Lydney Rd HLER SO31 .....270 F8
Lydwell Cl BWD BH11 .....301 P8
Lye Copse Av FARN GU14 .....58 A5
Lyell Rd BKME/WDN BH12 .....321 L6
Lyeway La NARL SO24 .....169 N3
Lyeway Rd ALTN GU34 .....170 B2
Lyford Rd BSTK RG21 .....7 F3
Lymbourn Rd HAV PO9 .....15 H6
Lyme Cl ELGH SO50 .....207 H8
Lyme Cl CHCH/BSGR BH23 .....326 B7
Lymefields LYMN SO41 .....226 C6
Lymer La ROWN SO16 .....226 C6
Lymer Vls ROWN SO16 .....226 C6
Lymington Av YTLY GU46 .....40 D9
Lymington Bottom
  ALTN GU34 .....150 C7
Lymington Bottom Rd
  ALTN GU34 .....150 B6
  KBH RG22 .....89 M5
Lymington Cl ALTN GU34 .....150 C6
Lymington Rd BROC SO42 .....308 G2
  CHCH/BSGR BH23 .....325 P8
  LYMN SO41 .....328 E9
  LYMN SO41 .....330 E2
  NMIL/BTOS BH25 .....327 H6
Lymington Road Shelley Hl
  CHCH/BSGR BH23 .....325 N8
Lymore La LYMN SO41 .....328 F8
Lymore Va LYMN SO41 .....328 F9
Lynams FLEETS GU52 .....74 B9
Lynchborough Rd LIPH GU30 .....154 E8
Lynch Cl FUFL SO22 .....164 F5
Lynchford La FARN GU14 .....76 D3
Lynchford Rd ALDT GU11 .....76 C4
Lynch Hl WHCH RG28 .....85 L6
Lynch Hill Pk WHCH RG28 .....85 M6
Lynch La PSF GU32 .....212 E1
Lynch Rd FNM GU9 .....96 D9
The Lynch OVTN RG25 .....86 E3
  WHCH RG28 .....85 L6
Lyn Ct BSTK RG21 .....7 J5
Lyndale Cl LYMN SO41 .....339 H1
Lyndale Dr FLEETN GU51 .....74 G3
Lyndale Rd HLER SO31 .....271 H6
Lynden Cl FHAM/STUB PO14 .....296 C1
Lynden Ga ITCH SO19 .....249 J8
Lyndford Ter FLEETS GU52 .....74 C5
Lyndhurst Av BLKW GU17 .....41 K8
  FNM GU9 .....97 J5
Lyndhurst Cl FUFL SO22 .....164 E3
  HISD PO11 .....318 C6
Lyndhurst Dr KBH RG22 .....89 K5
Lyndhurst Rd BROC SO42 .....286 C7
  CHCH/BSGR BH23 .....325 K3
  CHCH/BSGR BH23 .....325 M6
  FLEETS GU51 .....55 P9
  GPORT PO12 .....12 A1
  NEND PO2 .....297 H7
  RGWD BH24 .....284 D6
  RGWD BH24 .....285 J2
  RSAL SP5 .....223 L1
  TOTT SO40 .....244 E4
  TOTT SO40 .....265 P1
Lyndock Cl ITCH SO19 * 248 C9
Lyndock Pl ITCH SO19 .....248 C9
Lyndsey Cl FARN GU14 .....57 J9
Lyndum Cl EPSF GU31 .....215 M2
Lyndum Pl BOR GU35 * 154 C7
Lyneham Rd CWTH RG45 .....41 J1
Lyne Pl HORN PO8 .....256 B5
Lynes La RGWD BH24 .....282 D2
Lynford Av FUFL SO22 .....164 F1
Lynford Wy FUFL SO22 .....164 F5
Lynn Rd CFDH BH17 .....321 H4
  NEND PO2 .....297 H9
Lynn Wy FARN GU14 .....57 N6
  WINC SO23 .....165 K1
Lynric Cl NMIL/BTOS BH25 .....327 H8
Lynton Cl TOTT SO40 .....116 A3
Lynton Ct TOTT SO40 .....246 C5
Lynton Crs CHCH/BSGR BH23 .....324 B4
Lynton Gdns
  FHAM/PORC PO16 .....10 C1
Lynton Gv HSEA PO3 .....297 P4
Lynton Meadow STOK SO20 .....123 L4
Lynton Rd BOR GU35 .....154 A5
  HEND SO30 .....250 C4
  PSF GU32 .....215 L1
Lynwood Av WILLE PO7 .....255 M8
Lynwood Cl BOR GU35 .....154 D3
  FERN BH22 .....302 D1
Lynwood Dr AND SP10 .....102 C2
  FRIM GU16 .....76 F1
Lynwood Gdns HTWY RG27 .....71 P3
Lynx Cl CLAY SO21 .....200 D6
Lyon Av NMIL/BTOS BH25 .....327 K4
Lyon Rd BKME/WDN BH12 .....321 N2
Lyon St SHAM SO14 .....248 C5
Lyon Wy FRIM GU16 .....76 F1
Lysander Ct CHCH/BSGR BH23 .....325 M8
Lysander Wy FARN GU14 .....76 A3
  WILLE PO7 .....276 A2
Lysons Av ASHV GU12 .....76 E4
Lysons Rd ALDT GU11 .....2 E4
Lyss Ct LISS GU33 .....192 D2
Lysses Ct FHAM/PORC PO16 .....11 K5

Lysses Pth FHAM/PORC PO16 .....11 K5
Lyster Rd FBDG SP6 .....240 E1
Lystra Rd MOOR/WNTN BH9 .....322 G4
Lytchett Dr BDST BH18 .....320 C1
Lyteltane Rd LYMN SO41 .....329 K5
Lytham Rd BDST BH18 .....320 C1
  WEND SO18 .....249 J3
Lytte La PSF GU32 .....190 C9
Lytton Rd BMTH BH1 .....335 J1
  BSTK RG21 .....7 H5
  FAWY SO45 .....268 D8

M

Mabbs La HTWY RG27 .....55 H9
Mabey Av NBNE BH10 .....322 D5
Mabey Cl GPORT PO12 .....12 E7
Mablethorpe Rd CHAM PO6 .....274 C9
Macadam Wy AND SP10 .....77 H1
Macandrew Rd CCLF BH13 .....333 N4
Macarthur Crs WEND SO18 .....249 J3
Macaulay Av CHAM PO6 .....274 B9
Macaulay Rd BDST BH18 .....300 C9
Maccullum Rd AND SP11 .....82 F3
Macdonald Rd FNM GU9 .....96 B4
Maclaren Rd
  MOOR/WNTN BH9 .....322 F4
Maclean Rd BWD BH11 .....321 P1
Macnaghten Rd WEND SO18 .....248 F4
Macrae Rd YTLY GU46 .....40 D6
Madden Cl GPORT PO12 .....315 K5
Maddison St SHAM SO14 .....21 K5
Maddocks Hl NARL SO24 .....169 L3
Maddoxford Wy BPWT SO32 .....250 F2
Madeira Cl CHIN RG24 .....69 N3
Madeira Pl NWBY RG14 .....16 E4
Madeira Rd BMTH BH1 .....311 K3
  NEND PO2 .....296 C6
  PSTN BH14 .....321 M7
Madeley Rd FLEETS GU52 .....74 E6
Madeline Ct
  BKME/WDN BH12 .....321 K5
Madeline Rd EPSF GU31 .....215 M1
Madison Av BMTH BH1 .....323 K9
Madison Cl
  LSOL/BMARY PO13 .....295 J9
Madison Ct FHAM/PORC PO16 .....11 K6
Madox Brown End SHST GU47 .....41 M8
Madrid Rd AND SP10 .....5 H2
Mafeking Rd ENEY PO4 .....317 H5
Magazine La TOTT SO40 .....247 L8
Magdala Rd FARN GU14 .....75 L4
  HISD PO11 .....318 E5
Magdalene Rd SHST GU47 .....41 N4
Magdalene Wy
  FHAM/STUB PO14 .....271 J9
Magdalen Hl WINC SO23 .....23 G5
Magdalen La
  CHCH/BSGR BH23 .....324 E9
Magdalen Ms WINC SO23 * 23 G5
Magdalen Rd NEND PO2 .....296 C6
Magdalen Rw PSF GU32 .....215 L2
Magellan Cl AND SP10 .....103 J1
Magennis Cl
  LSOL/BMARY PO13 .....315 H1
Magenta Ct
  LSOL/BMARY PO13 * 314 G2
Magister Dr
  LSOL/BMARY PO13 .....314 E3
Magna Cl BWD BH11 .....301 P7
Magna Gdns BWD BH11 .....301 P7
Magna Rd WIMB BH21 .....301 K5
Magnolia Cl AND SP10 .....102 C3
  FAWY SO45 .....267 N6
  FHAM/STUB PO14 .....10 A7
  SBNE BH6 .....336 E1
  SHST GU47 .....41 L5
  VWD BH31 .....259 J6
Magnolia Ct CHAM PO6 .....274 E9
Magnolia Gv ELGH SO50 .....230 E2
Magnolia Rd ITCH SO19 .....249 H6
Magnolia Wy FLEETS GU52 .....74 D5
  HORN PO8 .....256 C7
Magnus Dr KBH RG22 .....89 M4
Magpie Cl BOR GU35 .....154 B6
  CHAR BH8 .....323 J4
  FHAM/PORC PO16 .....295 J1
  KBH RG22 .....89 K3
  RFNM GU10 .....95 M3
Magpie Dr TOTT SO40 .....246 A4
Magpie Gdns ITCH SO19 .....249 K7
Magpie Gv NMIL/BTOS BH25 .....327 H5
Magpie La ELGH SO50 .....228 G2
Magpie Rd HORN PO8 .....257 J6
Magpie Wk HORN PO8 .....255 M7
Mag's Barrow FERN BH22 .....302 E6
Maguire Dr FRIM GU16 .....99 H2
Mahler Cl KBH RG22 .....90 B3
Maida Rd ALDT GU11 .....76 A8
Maiden La LYMN SO41 .....329 M6
Maidenthorn La OVTN RG25 .....108 D1
Maidford Gv HSEA PO3 * 297 J1
Maidment Cl BWD BH11 .....301 N9
Maidstone Crs CHAM PO6 .....274 D9
Main Dr FAWY SO45 .....312 C2
  WHAM PO17 .....274 C4
Main Gate Rd FARN GU14 .....76 A2
Main Rd ELGH SO50 .....208 B7
  FAWY SO45 .....267 L3
  FAWY SO45 .....267 P5
  FAWY SO45 .....290 E3
  FUFL SO22 .....164 B1
  LSOL/BMARY PO13 .....295 H5
  LYMN SO41 .....310 F7
  LYMN SO41 .....329 N1
  PSEA PO1 .....18 C2
  RWIN SO21 .....207 K3
  RWIN SO21 .....207 P3
  RWIN SO21 .....208 B6
  RWIN SO21 .....209 H1
  TADY RG26 .....34 E8
  TOTT SO40 .....246 C7
  TOTT SO40 .....267 K1
Mainsail Dr FHAM/PORC PO16 .....294 F1
Mainstone Rd ROMY SO51 .....204 B8
Mainstone Cl FRIM GU16 .....59 H6
Mainstream Ct ELGH SO50 .....229 M1
Main St STHA RG19 .....31 M2
Maisemore Gdns
  EMRTH PO10 .....299 K1
Maison Belle Vue ITCH SO19 * 269 H1
Maitland Rd FARN GU14 .....76 A4
Maitlands Cl RFNM GU10 .....97 L5
Maitland St PSEA PO1 .....316 F1
Majendie Cl NWBY RG14 .....24 A5
Majestic Rd KBH RG22 .....89 L6
  ROWN SO16 .....226 F8
Majorca Av AND SP10 .....5 C1
Malan Cl CFDH BH17 .....320 C4
Malcolm Cl CHFD SO53 .....206 G4
  HLER SO31 .....271 K1
Malcolm Rd CHFD SO53 .....206 G4
Malcomb Cl SBNE BH6 .....336 E5
Malcroft Ms TOTT SO40 .....267 L1
Maldive Rd CHIN RG24 .....69 N3
Maldon Cl ELGH SO50 .....229 M1
Maldon Rd CHAM PO6 * 296 E1
Malham Gdns KBH RG22 .....89 M6
Malham Rd STHA RG19 .....29 N6
Mallbres Rd CHFD SO53 .....207 H5
Malin Cl FHAM/STUB PO14 .....295 P6
  HLER SO31 .....271 K1
Malins Rd NEND PO2 .....316 F1
Mallard Cl AND SP10 .....82 F9
  ASHV GU12 .....97 M1
  CHAR BH8 .....323 J6
  CHCH/BSGR BH23 .....325 L9
  HASM GU27 .....156 D7
  KBH RG22 .....89 K4
  NARL SO24 .....168 A1
  NEND PO2 .....204 D5
Mallard Ct NWBY RG14 .....16 C2
Mallard Gdns HEND SO30 .....250 C1
  LSOL/BMARY PO13 * 294 F7
Mallard Rd CHAR BH8 .....323 K6
  HAV PO9 .....15 H9
  PLE PO4 .....317 K3
  WIMB BH21 .....279 J7
Mallards Al ALTN GU34 .....132 F4
Mallards Rd HLER SO31 .....271 J6
The Mallards
  FHAM/PORC PO16 .....11 F1
  FRIM GU16 .....58 E3
  HAV PO9 .....298 F2
Mallett Cl HEND SO30 .....250 E1
Mallory Cl CHCH/BSGR BH23 .....325 K7
Mallory Crs FHAM/PORC PO16 .....10 E2
Mallow Cl BDST BH18 .....320 A1
  BOR GU35 .....154 A6
  CHAM PO6 .....297 H1
  CHCH/BSGR BH23 .....325 N7
  WILLE PO7 .....275 P4
Mallow Gdns NTHA RG18 .....25 N2
Mallow Rd HEND SO30 .....250 A5
The Mallows
  NMIL/BTOS BH25 .....327 M3
The Mall CHFD SO53 * 206 G6
  NEND PO2 * 296 F8
  NTID SP9 .....78 E7
  RGWD BH24 .....284 C6
Malmesbury Cl ELGH SO50 .....230 C2
Malmesbury Ct CHAR BH8 .....323 J3
Malmesbury Fld KBH RG22 .....89 P3
Malmesbury Flds HEND SO30 .....249 P5
Malmesbury Gdns FUFL SO22 .....164 E5
Malmesbury Park Pl
  CHAR BH8 .....335 J1
Malmesbury Park Rd
  CHAR BH8 .....323 J9
Malmesbury Pl WSHM SO15 .....247 P4
Malmesbury Rd RGWD BH24 .....281 L6
  ROMY SO51 .....204 C5
  RWIN SO21 .....165 N2
Malmsbury Cl
  CHCH/BSGR BH23 .....336 F1
Malmsbury Rd BOR GU35 .....154 A6
Maloren Wy FERN BH22 .....280 C8
Malory Cl ITCH SO19 .....249 M7
Malpass Rd RWIN SO21 .....144 D6
Malshanger La DEAN RG23 .....67 M9
Malta Cl CHIN RG24 .....69 H6
Malta Rd FRIM GU16 .....59 J5
  NEND PO2 .....296 C9
Maltby's ALTN GU34 .....152 D8
Malthouse Cl FLEETS GU52 .....74 B7
Malthouse La ALTN GU34 .....152 A6
  ROMY SO51 .....165 N2
Malthouse Gdns TOTT SO40 .....267 K1
Malthouse La
  FHAM/PORC PO16 .....11 G5
  LIPH GU30 .....175 L3
  NWBY RG14 .....16 D3
  TADY RG26 .....52 A3
Malt La BPWT SO32 .....232 A4
Malus Cl FHAM/STUB PO14 .....294 D2
Malvern Av FHAM/STUB PO14 .....294 C2
Malvern Cl BPWT SO32 .....232 B5
  KBH RG22 .....68 D9
  MOOR/WNTN BH9 .....322 G2
Malvern Dr FAWY SO45 .....267 P7
Malvern Gdns HEND SO30 .....250 D1
Malvern Ms EMRTH PO10 .....277 M9
Malvern Rd BLKW GU17 .....56 C4
  FARN GU14 .....315 K3
  GPORT PO12 .....315 K3
  LISS GU33 .....192 F4
  MOOR/WNTN BH9 .....322 G5
  ROWN SO16 .....226 G6
Malvern Ter ROWN SO16 * 247 P1
Malwood Av ROWN SO16 .....227 P9
Malwood Cl HAV PO9 .....276 C4
Malwood Gdns TOTT SO40 .....246 A3
Malwood Rd FAWY SO45 .....268 B6
Malwood Rd West
  FAWY SO45 .....268 B6
Manaton Wy HEND SO30 .....250 B2
Manchester Ct
  LSOL/BMARY PO13 * 315 H5
Manchester Rd HLER SO31 .....269 J5
  SWAY SO41 .....308 B5
  PSEA PO1 .....316 C3
Mancroft Av
  FHAM/STUB PO14 .....294 A8
Mandale Cl BWD BH11 .....322 A4
Mandale Rd BWD BH11 .....321 P1
Mandarin Ct NWBY RG14 * 17 J3
Mandarin Wy
  LSOL/BMARY PO13 .....314 G2
Mandela Wy WSHM SO15 .....21 A2
Manderley LYMN SO41 .....339 H5
Mandora Rd ALDT GU11 .....76 A8
Manfield Rd ASHV GU12 .....97 N1
Manley Bridge Rd
  RFNM GU10 .....115 N6
Manley James Cl ODIM RG29 * 72 D9
Manley Rd HLER SO31 .....269 P1
Mann Cl WHCH RG28 .....85 M7
Manners Rd ENEY PO4 .....316 C4
Manning Av
  CHCH/BSGR BH23 .....325 J4
Manningford Cl WINC SO23 .....165 H4
Mannings Heath Rd
  BKME/WDN BH12 .....321 K2
Mannington Pl WCLF BH2 .....8 B4
Mannington Wy FERN BH22 .....280 D7
Manns Cl WEND SO18 .....249 L1
Mannyngham Wy
  ROMY SO51 .....180 B7
Manor Av BKME/WDN BH12 .....321 L3
Manor Bridge Ct NTID SP9 .....79 H4
Manor Cl ALTN GU34 .....132 C5
  FBDG SP6 .....238 E2
  FERN BH22 .....302 E3
  HASM GU27 .....156 D7
  HAV PO9 .....15 G5
  HLER SO31 .....269 P1
  KBH RG22 .....89 J5
  LYMN SO41 .....338 C1
  NTID SP9 .....78 F3
  RAND SP11 .....101 N7
  RFNM GU10 .....97 M4
  TOTT SO40 .....246 C6
  WHAM PO17 .....252 E9
  WINC SO23 .....25 F8
Manor Copse AND SP10 .....82 F6
Manor Ct FLEETS GU52 .....74 D8
  RGWD BH24 .....282 E1
  VWD BH31 .....258 F4
Manor Crs CHAM PO6 .....296 E1
  HLER SO31 .....269 P1
Manor Farm Cl ASHV GU12 * 97 M3
  NMIL/BTOS BH25 .....327 H6
Manor Farm Gn RWIN SO21 .....183 P9
Manor Farm Gv ELGH SO50 .....229 N2
Manor Farm La ROMY SO51 .....180 B5
Manor Farm Rd FBDG SP6 .....240 A2
  NBNE BH10 .....322 C1
  WEND SO18 .....248 F2
Manor Flds LIPH GU30 .....175 L3
Manor Gdns RFNM GU10 .....282 E1
  VWD BH31 .....258 F4
Manor House Av WSHM SO15 .....247 P4
Manor La CHIN RG24 .....70 C6
  NTHA RG18 .....25 H3
  VWD BH31 .....258 F4
Manor Lodge Rd HAV PO9 .....276 C1
Manor Ms CHAM PO6 .....297 H1
Manor Park Av HSEA PO3 .....297 J9
Manor Park Dr YTLY GU46 .....40 F9
Manor Park East ASHV GU12 * 3 H9
Manor Pl NWBY RG14 .....24 A2
Manor Rd RAND SP11 .....102 C6
  ALTN GU34 .....132 C7
  AND SP10 .....4 G2
  ASHV GU12 .....97 P4
  BMTH BH1 .....9 K4
  CHCH/BSGR BH23 .....324 E9
  CHIN RG24 .....49 H4
  CHCH/BSGR BH23 .....324 E9
  ELGH SO50 .....229 N2
  FARN GU14 .....76 C1
  FAWY SO45 .....290 E5
  FNM GU9 .....96 F7
  HISD PO11 .....318 E6
  LYMN SO41 .....341 J5
  NMIL/BTOS BH25 .....327 K4
  PSEA PO1 .....316 D1
  RGWD BH24 .....282 E2
  RSAL SP5 .....159 M6
  RWIN SO21 .....183 P9
  TOTT SO40 .....265 P1
  VWD BH31 .....258 F4
Manor Rd North ITCH SO19 .....248 F7
Manor Rd South ITCH SO19 .....248 F8
Manorside Cl RFNM GU10 .....97 M3
Manor Wk ASHV GU12 .....3 H3
  VWD BH31 .....258 F4
Mansbridge Rd ELGH SO50 .....229 J3
  WEND SO18 .....229 H8
Manse La TADY RG26 .....34 E8
Mansel Cl BKME/WDN BH12 .....322 C8
Mansel Ct ROWN SO16 .....247 J1
Mansell Cl FAWY SO45 .....290 A1
Mansell Dr NWBY RG14 .....30 B1
Mansel Rd East ROWN SO16 .....247 J2
Mansel Rd West ROWN SO16 .....247 H1
Mansfield Ct BARTON * 302 D6
  PSTN BH14 .....321 L8
Mansfield La WHAM PO17 .....251 P7
Mansfield Rd KBH RG22 .....90 A1
  LSOL/BMARY PO13 .....294 C9
  MOOR/WNTN BH9 .....322 E6
  PSTN BH14 .....321 L8
  RGWD BH24 .....282 D2
Man's Hl THLE RG7 .....27 L4
Mansion Dr HTWY RG27 .....54 C1
Mansion House St
  NWBY RG14 * 16 D2
Mansion Rd ENEY PO4 .....316 C7
  WSHM SO15 .....247 P5
Mansvid Av CHAM PO6 .....297 K2
Mantle Cl LSOL/BMARY PO13 .....315 H1
Mantle Sq NEND PO2 .....296 D7
Manton Rd PLE BH15 .....320 A9
Maple Cl ALDT GU11 .....3 J2
  ASHV GU12 .....76 E5
  BLKW GU17 .....41 K9
  CHCH/BSGR BH23 .....326 B8
  EMRTH PO10 .....277 M8
  FHAM PO15 .....272 A9
  LSOL/BMARY PO13 .....294 C9
  NARL SO24 .....167 P5
  NMIL/BTOS BH25 .....327 K8
  ROMY SO51 .....204 C7
  SHST GU47 .....40 G5
  STOK SO20 .....121 H5
Maple Crs BSTK RG21 .....6 E1
  HORN PO8 .....256 C6
  NWBY RG14 .....24 D3
  RAND SP11 .....80 B1
Maple Dr FERN BH22 .....280 C9
  WINC SO23 .....145 J8
  WILLE PO7 .....255 J8
Maple Gdns TOTT SO40 .....246 A5
  YTLY GU46 .....40 E9
Maple Gv TADY RG26 .....34 D6
Maplehurst Cha KBH RG22 .....89 M6
Maple Leaf Cl FARN GU14 .....75 N1
Maple Lear Dr BOR GU35 .....154 A4
Maple Ldg HASM GU27 * 157 K9
Maple Rd FAWY SO45 .....290 D1
  MOOR/WNTN BH9 .....322 F7
  PLE PO4 .....320 F9
  SSEA PO5 .....316 F6
Maple Sc ELGH SO50 .....228 G5
The Maples CHFD SO53 .....206 E5
Maple Ter NTID SP9 * 79 J4
Mapleton Rd HEND SO30 .....250 D5
Mapletree Av HORN PO8 .....256 C6
Maple Wk AND SP10 .....102 D4
  ASHV GU12 .....3 J3
Maple Wd HAV PO9 .....276 B9
Maplewood Cl TOTT SO40 .....246 A5
Maplin Rd ROWN SO16 .....246 H1
Mapperton Cl FBDG BH17 .....321 J2
Marabout Cl
  CHCH/BSGR BH23 .....325 H8
Maralyn Av WILLE PO7 .....275 N4
Marathon Pl ELGH SO50 .....230 B2
Marazan Rd HSEA PO3 .....297 K7
Marbrean Cl FBDG SP6 .....240 A1
Marchant Cl STHA RG19 .....29 N6
Marchant Rd AND SP10 .....102 C5
March Cl AND SP10 .....5 F2
Marchwood By-Pass
  TOTT SO40 .....246 E6
Marchwood Rd HAV PO9 .....276 A4
  NBNE BH10 .....322 C4
  TOTT SO40 .....246 G7
  WSHM SO15 .....248 C1
Marchwood Ter TOTT SO40 * 247 K9
Marconi Rd NWBY RG14 .....24 E3
Marcus Cl ELGH SO50 .....230 B2
Mardale CBLY GU15 .....59 H1
Mardale Rd ROWN SO16 .....247 H3
Marden Wy EPSF GU31 .....215 N2
Mardon Cl ELGH SO50 .....228 C7
Mare La RWIN SO21 .....184 E3
Mareth Cl ALDT GU11 .....3 G2
Margam Av ITCH SO19 .....249 N8
Margaret La BWD BH11 .....258 E5
Margaret Cl WILLE PO7 .....275 M1
Margaret Rd BWD BH11 .....68 G8
Margarita Rd FHAM PO15 .....10 A4
Margate Rd SSEA PO5 .....19 J5
Marguerite La TADY RG26 .....52 A2
Marianne Rd WSHM SO15 .....247 K5
Marianne Rd
  BKME/WDN BH12 .....322 C7
  BKME/WDN BH12 .....279 J7
Marie Av RSAL SP5 .....199 H6
Marie Ct BKME/WDN BH12 .....321 M5
Marie Rd ITCH SO19 .....249 L8
Marigold Cl FHAM PO15 .....10 A4
  KBH RG22 .....89 L3
Marina Ct EMRTH PO10 .....299 H7
Marina Dr HAV PO9 * 270 A8
  PSTN BH14 .....333 K2
Marina Gv FHAM/PORC PO16 .....295 N3
  HSEA PO3 .....317 K2
Marina Keep CHAM PO6 .....296 C2
The Marina BOSC BH5 .....335 L3
Marine Ct ENEY PO4 .....317 J6
  NMIL/BTOS BH25 .....326 G8
Marine Dr East
  NMIL/BTOS BH25 .....327 J9
Marine Dr West
  NMIL/BTOS BH25 .....326 F8

Marine Pde SHAM S014 ......21 H5
Marine Pde East
LSOL/BMARY P013 ......314 D4
Marine Pde West
LSOL/BMARY P013 ......314 B1
Marine Prospect
NMIL/BTOS BH25 ......327 H8
Marine Rd SBNE BH6 ......336 B3
Mariner's CI HLER S031 ......270 A6
TADY RG26 ......34 E8
Mariners Dr RGUW GU3 ......77 N9
Mariners Ms FAWY S045 ......268 C6
Mariners Wk ENEY P04 ......317 K3
Mariners Wy GPORT P012 ......13 G4
HLER S031 ......270 C9
Maritime Wk HISD P011 ......319 K5
Marion Rd ENEY P04 ......316 G6
Maritime Av TOTT S040 ......247 K8
Maritime Wy SHAM S014 ......248 C9
Marjoram CI FARN GU14 ......57 J7
Marjoram Crs HORN P08 ......256 B8
Marjoram Wy FHAM P015 ......271 K3
Markall CI NARL S024 ......187 H1
Mark CI FHAM P03 ......297 H5
WSHM S015 ......247 L4
Marken CI HLER S031 ......270 E7
Market CI PLE BH15 ......332 E1
Market La WINC S023 ......22 E5
Market Pde HAV P09 ......15 F5
Market PI BSTK RG21 ......7 F7
NWBY RG14 ......16 E2
RGWD BH24 ......282 D2
SHAM S014 ......20 C7
Market Sq ALTN GU34 ......132 F6
Market St ALTN GU34 ......132 F6
ELGH S050 ......229 K3
NWBY RG14 ......16 E3
PLE BH15 ......332 D2
WINC S023 ......22 E5
Marketway PSEA P01 ......316 E2
Market Wy WIMB BH21 ......300 F1
Markham Cl NBNE BH10 ......322 D1
Markham CI NBNE BH10 ......302 D9
Markham Rd
MOOR/WNTN BH9 ......322 G7
Mark's La NMIL/BTOS BH25 ......327 J1
Markson Rd RWIN SO21 ......144 D4
Mark's Rd FHAM/STUB P014 ......294 C7
MOOR/WNTN BH9 ......322 F4
Marks Tey Rd
FHAM/STUB P014 ......294 A4
Markway CI EMRTH P010 ......317 J5
Marlborough CI FLEETN GU51 ......74 C4
WVILLE P07 ......275 M5
Marlborough Ct FAWY S045 ......268 A8
Marlborough Gdns DEAN RG23 ......88 F1
HEND SO30 ......230 C9
Marlborough Gv
FHAM/PORC P016 ......295 N2
Marlborough Pk HAV P09 ......277 N1
Marlborough PI LYMN S041 ......329 K2
WBNE BH4 ......278 F9
Marlborough Rd CHFD SO53 ......206 C4
GPORT P012 ......315 K2
PSTN BH14 ......321 L8
WBNE BH4 ......334 C3
WSHM S015 ......247 M5
Marlborough Rw PSEA P01 ......18 D1
Marlborough St AND SP10 ......4 D3
Marlborough Vw FARN GU14 ......57 K8
Marldell CI HAV P09 ......276 C5
Marles CI LSOL/BMARY P013 ......315 H1
Marley Av NMIL/BTOS BH25 ......326 C3
Marley CI NMIL/BTOS BH25 ......327 H4
Marley Combe Rd
HASM GU27 ......156 E8
Marley La HASM GU27 ......156 D8
Marley Mt LYMN S041 ......307 N7
Marlhill CI WEND SO18 ......249 H1
Marlin CI LSOL/BMARY P013 ......315 H1
Marline Rd BKME/WDN BH12 ......321 M6
Marl La FBDG SP6 ......320 A9
Marlott Rd PLE BH15 ......320 E7
Marlow CI FHAM P015 ......272 C6
Marlow Dr CHCH/BSGR BH23 ......324 C4
Marlowe Ct WVILLE P07 ......275 M1
The Marlowes NWBY RG14 ......24 C7
Marlow Rd BPWT SO32 ......231 N3
Marlpit Dr CHCH/BSGR BH23 ......326 C5
Marlpit La NMIL/BTOS BH25 ......307 J8
Marl's La TADY RG26 ......51 L9
Mars Rd HEND SO30 ......250 C5
Marmion Av SSEA P05 ......316 F6
Marmion Gn CHCH/BSGR BH23 ......325 K8
Marmion Rd SSEA P05 ......316 E6
Marne Rd WEND SO18 ......249 J4
Marnhull Rd PLE BH15 ......320 F8
Marple CI BWD BH11 ......321 N1
Marples Wy HAV P09 ......14 C6
Marquis Wy BWD BH11 ......301 M8
Marram CI LYMN S041 ......329 L1
Marrels Wd WVILLE P07 ......275 L6
Marrowbrook CI FARN GU14 ......75 P1
Marrowbrook La FARN GU14 ......75 N2
Marryat Rd NMIL/BTOS BH25 ......327 H4
Marsden Ct WHCH RG28 ......86 C5
Marsden Rd CHAM P06 ......296 D1
Marshal CI ALTN GU34 ......132 E7
Marshall Rd FARN GU14 ......57 N6
FRIM GU16 ......59 J3
Marshall Gdns BSTK RG21 ......7 G5
Marshall Rd HISD P011 ......319 J6
SHST GU47 ......41 L7
Marshall Sq AND SP10 ......82 G9
Marshall Wy HEND SO30 ......249 P2
Marshal Rd CFDH BH17 ......320 D3
Marsh CI BOR GU35 ......154 C5
Marshcourt CHIN RG24 ......70 A4
Marshfield WIMB BH21 ......279 H7

Marshfield CI TOTT S040 ......267 H1
Marsh Gdns HEND SO30 ......230 C9
Marshlands CI
CHCH/BSGR BH23 ......325 H9
Marshlands Rd CHAM P06 ......297 M2
Marshlands Sp CHAM P06 ......297 N2
Marsh La CHCH/BSGR BH23 ......324 D5
FAWY S045 ......291 K6
FBDG SP6 ......220 E4
HTWY RG27 ......39 P9
LYMN S041 ......329 L1
NWBY RG14 ......16 E1
SHAM S014 ......21 F6
Marsh Rd NTHA RG18 ......25 P3
The Marsh FAWY S045 ......268 C5
Marshwood Av CFDH BH17 ......321 H2
WVILLE P07 ......276 A3
Marston CI NMIL/BTOS BH25 ......327 K2
Marston Dr FARN GU14 ......58 A6
NWBY RG14 ......16 F2
Marston Gn RWIN SO21 ......22 E3
Marston Gv CHCH/BSGR BH23 ......326 A6
Marston La FAWY S045 ......297 K5
Marston Rd FNM GU9 ......95 P9
ITCH S019 ......249 M6
NMIL/BTOS BH25 ......327 K2
PLE BH15 ......332 D1
Marsum CI AND SP10 ......82 D7
Martello CI GPORT P012 ......315 H5
Martello Pk CCLF BH13 ......333 P4
Martello Rd CCLF BH13 ......333 N7
The Martells NMIL/BTOS BH25 ......327 K8
Martin Av FHAM/STUB P014 ......294 B7
WVILLE P07 ......255 J7
Martin CI BPWT SO32 ......232 F8
BSTK RG21 ......7 H1
CFDH BH17 ......320 B5
LSOL/BMARY P013 ......314 D1
NTID SP9 ......79 J5
Martindale Av CBLY GU15 ......59 H2
WIMB BH21 ......279 K9
Martin Drove End FBDG SP6 ......195 N3
Martingale CI ALDT GU11 ......2 A3
Martin Rd FHAM/STUB P014 ......294 B7
HAV P09 ......276 C6
HSEA P03 ......297 J9
Martins CI ALTN GU34 ......132 G4
BLKW GU17 ......57 L1
FERN BH22 ......302 E1
Martins Dr FERN BH22 ......302 E1
Martins Flds RWIN SO21 ......183 L5
Martins Hill CI
CHCH/BSGR BH23 ......324 C6
Martins Hill La
CHCH/BSGR BH23 ......324 C6
Martins La STOK SO20 ......123 N6
Martins Pk FARN GU14 ......57 L6
Martin's Rd RSAL SP5 ......201 N7
Martin's Rd BROC SO42 ......286 C7
The Martins ELGH SO50 ......230 D3
Martin St BPWT SO32 ......231 P5
Martins Wy FERN BH22 ......302 E1
Martins Wd CHIN RG24 ......70 A1
Martin Wy AND SP10 ......82 F8
FRIM GU16 ......58 D4
Martley Gdns HEND SO30 ......250 D1
Marvic CI HAV P09 ......276 E4
Marvin Wy HEND SO30 ......250 E4
WEND SO18 ......249 L5
Marwell CI LTDN BH7 ......323 N8
Marwell Rd FLEETN GU51 ......55 P9
Marybridge CI TOTT S040 ......246 C5
Maryland CI SHAM S014 ......21 G5
Maryland CI WEND SO18 ......229 H9
Maryland Gdns LYMN S041 ......338 E2
Mary La ALTN GU34 ......150 G8
FERN BH22 ......280 D7
OVTN RG25 ......88 C9
Mary Rose CI FHAM P015 ......10 A1
The Mary Rose St PSEA P01 * 19 G3
Masefield CI FHAM P015 ......271 H8
Masefield CI ELGH SO50 ......206 D4
Masefield Crs HORN P08 ......255 P6
Masefield Gn ITCH S019 ......249 M5
Masefield Rd NTHA RG18 ......25 M3
Maskell Wy FARN GU14 ......75 K1
Maslen Mws DEAN RG23 ......89 M7
Mason Ct YTLY GU46 * 40 F9
Mason PI SHST GU47 ......40 G6
Mason Rd FARN GU14 ......57 M7
Masons Yd WINC S023 * 22 D5
Masons Wy ALDT GU11 ......97 H4
Masseys La BROC SO42 ......310 C1
Masten Crs
LSOL/BMARY P013 ......294 C9
Matapan Rd NEND P02 ......296 F5
Matchams CI RGWD BH24 ......304 A1
Matchams La RGWD BH24 ......303 P3
Matchlock Ms NWBY RG14 * 24 F2
Matheson Rd ROWN SO16 ......227 K6
Matthews Ter ALDT GU11 * 3 H2
Mathias Wk KBH RG22 ......89 P5
Matilda Dr KBH RG22 ......89 M4
Matilda PI WINC S023 * 23 F3
Matley Gdns TOTT S040 ......245 P4
Matlock Rd FERN BH22 ......302 C5
Matthew Rd FNM GU9 ......96 E3
Matthews CI HAV P09 ......276 C7
STHA RG19 ......25 L4
Matthews La BROC SO42 ......310 C2
Matthews Wy DEAN RG23 ......88 G2
Mattock Wy CHIN RG24 ......70 A1
Maturin CI LYMN S041 ......329 K4
The Maultway CBLY GU15 ......59 J1
Maundville Crs
CHCH/BSGR BH23 ......324 C7
Maundville Rd
CHCH/BSGR BH23 ......324 C7
Maunsell Wy HEND SO30 ......230 C9
Maureen Ct BKME/WDN BH12 ......321 K4
Maurepas Wy WVILLE P07 ......275 M3
Mauretania Rd ROWN SO16 ......226 F8
Maurice Rd ENEY P04 ......317 L4
Maurys La ROMY SO51 ......224 D1
Mavins Rd FNM GU9 ......116 D2

Mavis Crs HAV P09 ......15 F4
Mavis Rd MOOR/WNTN BH9 ......323 H6
Maw Ct KBH RG22 ......90 B3
Maxine CI SHST GU47 ......41 J5
Maxstoke CI SSEA P05 ......19 J5
Maxwell Rd CCLF BH13 ......333 P4
ENEY P04 ......317 J3
ITCH S019 ......249 J8
MOOR/WNTN BH9 ......322 C8
May Av LYMN S041 ......329 K2
Maybray King Wy ITCH S019 ......249 J4
Maybrick CI SHST GU47 ......40 C5
Maybrook CHIN RG24 ......52 A9
Maybury CI FRIM GU16 ......58 C5
Maybush CI FRIM GU16 ......58 C5
Maybush Rd ROWN SO16 ......247 J1
May CI BOR GU35 ......154 F4
CHIN RG24 ......70 D6
FAWY S045 ......290 F6
SHST GU47 ......41 L6
May Copse FAWY S045 ......290 F6
May Crs ASHV GU12 ......97 L2
FAWY S045 ......290 F6
Maydman Sq HSEA P03 ......317 J2
Mayfair CI NEND SO30 ......250 C4
Mayfair Dr NWBY RG14 ......16 A5
Mayfair Gdns BWD BH11 ......322 A3
WSHM S015 ......248 B4
Mayfield RFNM GU10 ......115 P7
Mayfield Av PSTN BH14 ......321 N9
TOTT S040 ......246 C3
Mayfield CI FERN BH22 ......302 C2
FHAM/STUB P014 ......294 B6
HAV P09 ......97 H5
LYMN S041 ......329 J4
NTID SP9 ......98 F3
Mayfield Ct HTWY RG27 ......39 N6
Mayfield Dr FERN BH22 ......302 D2
Mayfield Rdg KBH RG22 ......89 M6
Mayfield Rd CBLY GU15 * 58 A4
FARN GU14 ......57 N6
FBDG SP6 ......240 A1
GPORT P012 ......12 D4
MOOR/WNTN BH9 ......322 C5
NEND P02 ......296 C7
PTSW S017 ......228 D9
Mayfield Wy FERN BH22 ......302 C2
Mayflower CI CHIN RG24 ......69 P2
CHFD S053 ......206 D8
FHAM/STUB P014 ......294 A8
LYMN S041 ......329 N4
Mayflower Dr YTLY GU46 ......40 B7
Mayflower Rd BOR GU35 ......153 P8
WSHM S015 ......20 C7
Mayflower Rbt WSHM S015 ......20 C7
The Mayflowers ROWN SO16 ......228 C9
Mayfly CI FBDG SP6 ......240 D1
Mayford Rd
BKME/WDN BH12 ......322 B9
May Gdns BWD BH11 ......321 N1
CHCH/BSGR BH23 ......326 D5
Mayhall Rd HSEA P03 ......297 J8
Mayhill La BPWT SO32 ......233 H5
Maylands Av FAWY P04 ......317 J4
Maylands Rd HAV P09 ......276 B8
May La LYMN S041 ......309 N7
Mayles CI WHAM P017 ......252 E8
Mayles Cnr WHAM P017 ......272 B2
Mayles La WHAM P017 ......272 B2
Mayles Rd ENEY P04 ......317 K4
Maylings Farm Rd
FHAM/PORC P016 ......10 D2
Maynard CI
LSOL/BMARY P013 ......294 C5
NTHA RG18 ......25 M2
Maynard PI HORN P08 ......256 B4
Maynard Rd TOTT S040 ......246 D4
Maynards Wd CHIN RG24 ......69 P2
Mayo CI PSEA P01 ......316 F1
Mayors La NWBY RG14 ......16 E3
May PI BSTK RG21 ......7 F7
Mayridge FHAM/STUB P014 ......271 J7
May Rd WSHM S015 ......248 B5
Mays Firs FBDG SP6 ......222 B2
May's La FHAM/STUB P014 ......294 D5
May Tree CI FUFL SO22 ......183 L2
Maytree CI HLER S031 ......270 C7
Maytree Gdns HORN P08 ......255 N8
May Tree Rd AND SP10 ......102 B1
Maytree Rd CHFD S053 ......206 F7
FHAM/PORC P016 ......10 E6
HORN P08 ......256 A4
Mayvale CI TOTT S040 ......267 K1
McCartney Wk KBH RG22 ......89 N4
McFauld Wy WHCH RG28 ......85 E7
McGrigor Barracks ALDT GU11 ......76 A9
McIntyre Rd
CHCH/BSGR BH23 ......303 J1
McKay CI ALDT GU11 ......3 J4
McKinley Rd WBNE BH4 ......334 C4
McNaughton CI FARN GU14 ......75 K1
McWilliam CI
BKME/WDN BH12 ......322 C7
McWilliam Rd
MOOR/WNTN BH9 ......322 C5
Meacher CI TOTT S040 ......246 C3
Meadbrook Gdns CHFD S053 ......206 C7
Mead CI FBDG SP6 ......240 C1
AND SP10 ......4 A6
CFDH BH17 ......320 C5
ROMY S051 ......204 F6
Mead Crs BKME/WDN BH12 ......321 J7
Meadcroft CI HLER S031 ......292 D1
Meadend CI HAV P09 ......277 H5
Mead End Rd LYMN S041 ......307 P7
WVILLE P07 ......255 J8
Meade Rd RAND SP11 ......80 A1
Mead Gdns HTWY RG27 ......54 G6
Meadham La OVTN RG25 ......86 B3
Mead Hatchgate HTWY RG27 ......71 P2
Mead Hawks LISS GU33 ......192 C1
Mead Hedges AND SP10 ......4 B6
Mead La FARN GU14 ......116 B1
Meadow Av HLER S031 ......270 C6
Meadow Bank FNM GU9 ......116 B1
Meadowbank RWIN SO21 ......163 K2

Meadowbank Rd FHAM P015 ......272 B9
Meadow CI ASHV GU12 ......76 E3
BLKW GU17 ......57 L1
BPWT SO32 ......232 B8
CHCH/BSGR BH23 ......304 F9
CHCH/BSGR BH23 ......305 L9
FBDG SP6 ......240 C1
FERN BH22 ......302 D7
HEND SO30 ......249 J8
HISD P011 ......298 F6
LIPH GU30 ......175 K3
NARL S024 ......168 A2
NBAD S052 ......227 L1
RGWD BH24 ......260 F9
RGWD BH24 ......284 B7
STHA RG19 ......26 B4
TOTT S040 ......246 D6
RSAL SP5 ......201 L1
Meadow Ct FBDG SP6 ......240 D1
MOOR/WNTN BH9 ......322 G4
Meadowcroft CI RWIN SO21 ......207 L2
Meadow Dr RAND SP11 ......122 D1
Meadow Edge WVILLE P07 ......275 K8
Meadow Gdns BPWT SO32 ......232 C1
Meadow Gate Av FARN GU14 ......75 N2
Meadow Gv VWD BH31 ......258 D7
Meadowhead Rd ROWN SO16 ......228 F9
Meadowland CHIN RG24 ......69 P1
CHCH/BSGR BH23 ......325 J9
WINC S023 ......145 J9
Meadowlands HAV P09 ......15 J6
LYMN S041 ......329 J3
Meadow La CHCH/BSGR BH23 ......305 J5
HLER S031 ......270 A8
HTWY RG27 ......55 H7
Meadowmead Av
WSHM S015 ......247 L4
Meadow Pound WHCH RG28 ......85 M6
Meadowridge KBH RG22 ......89 N6
Meadow Ri BDST BH18 ......300 B8
HORN P08 ......256 B8
OVTN RG25 ......108 D1
Meadow Rd BSTK RG21 ......90 C2
FARN GU14 ......58 A6
LYMN S041 ......315 L1
NMIL/BTOS BH25 ......327 K8
NWBY RG14 ......16 D7
RGWD BH24 ......282 F1
Meadowside CI WEND SO18 ......228 G8
The Meadows
FHAM/PORC P016 ......11 K1
HTWY RG27 ......52 E4
LYND SO43 ......264 F6
RFNM GU10 ......136 F8
Meadow St SSEA P05 * 19 F6
Meadowsweet CI WVILLE P07 ......276 B1
Meadowsweet CI NTHA RG18 ......25 P3
Meadowsweet Wy
CHAM P06 ......274 F9
ELCH SO50 ......230 C6
Meadow Ter
FHAM/PORC P016 * 11 F5
The Meadow ROMY SO51 ......204 G4
WVILLE P07 ......255 H7
Meadow V HASM GU27 ......156 F7
Meadow Vw BOR GU35 ......154 B5
FLEETS GU52 ......74 B7
RAND SP11 * 81 H9
WHCH RG28 ......85 M6
Meadow View Rd BWD BH11 ......321 N1
LSOL/BMARY P013 ......294 F4
Meadow Wy AND SP10 ......102 B2
ASHV GU12 ......97 J5
BLKW GU17 ......41 K9
FAWY S045 ......291 L6
FUFL SO22 ......183 L2
LIPH GU30 ......175 K2
NMIL/BTOS BH25 ......327 J8
RFNM GU10 ......113 P6
RGWD BH24 ......282 F1
VWD BH31 ......259 H6
Mead Park Sq STOK SO20 ......121 H5
Mead Rd AND SP10 ......4 A6
CHFD S053 ......206 E7
GSHT GU26 ......156 D4
LYMN S041 ......329 H5
WINC S023 ......183 N2
The Meads CHFD S053 ......206 C8
HASM GU27 ......156 E7
ROMY SO51 ......204 B6
The Mead CHIN RG24 ......70 C6
FARN GU14 * 76 A1
FAWY S045 ......268 A7
LIPH GU30 ......175 J2
LISS GU33 ......192 D2
LSOL/BMARY P013 ......294 F6
Meadway FRIM GU16 ......58 E3
HASM GU27 ......156 E7
WVILLE P07 ......276 A1
Meaker CI CHIN RG24 ......70 C6

Medway Av DEAN RG23 ......88 F1
Medway CI NTHA RG18 ......25 L2
FARN GU14 ......7 K6
Medway Dr CHFD S053 ......206 C5
FARN GU14 ......57 M6
Medway Rd FERN BH22 ......302 G2
Meerut Rd BROC S042 ......286 C7
Meeting House La
RGWD BH24 ......282 D2
Megana Wy ROMY SO51 ......180 G9
Megan Rd HEND SO30 ......299 M1
Meggeson Av WEND SO18 ......249 J1
Megson Dr
LSOL/BMARY P013 ......314 E2
Meitner CI TADY RG26 ......52 A1
Melbourne Rd CHAR BH8 ......323 J9
CHCH/BSGR BH23 ......324 C6
HEND SO30 ......230 C9
Melbourne St SHAM S014 ......21 H5
Melbury Av BKME/WDN BH12 ......321 N5
Melbury CI FHAM P015 ......302 D4
LYMN S041 ......329 K4
Melchet CI ROMY SO51 ......202 B4
Melchet Rd WEND SO18 ......249 L3
Melford Gdns KBH RG22 ......90 C1
Melick CI TOTT S040 ......247 K9
Meliot Ri AND SP10 ......82 E7
Mellersh CI FLEETS GU52 ......74 B8
Mellor CI CHAM P06 ......297 N1
Mellstock Rd PLE BH15 ......320 E7
Melrose Av FARN GU14 ......57 K8
Melrose CI BOR GU35 ......154 A6
ENEY P04 ......317 K4
Melrose Ct NMIL/BTOS BH25 * 327 L4
TOTT S040 ......246 A2
Melrose Gdns GPORT P012 ......315 K1
Melrose Rd WSHM S015 ......247 P1
Melrose Wk CHIN RG24 ......69 K4
Melverley Gdns WIMB BH21 ......278 F9
Melville CI ROWN SO16 ......227 N7
Melville Rd ENEY P04 ......317 L6
ITCH S019 ......315 L1
MOOR/WNTN BH9 ......322 E7
Melville Ter FNM GU9 * 96 E9
Membury CI FRIM GU16 ......58 F6
Memorial Rd HTWY RG27 ......71 P4
Mendip CI KBH RG22 ......89 K6
NMIL/BTOS BH25 ......327 K5
VWD BH31 ......258 F5
Mendip Gdns FAWY S045 ......267 P8
Mendip Rd FARN GU14 ......57 M6
ROWN SO16 ......228 A4
VWD BH31 ......258 F4
Mendips Rd
FHAM/STUB P014 ......294 B1
Mengham Av HISD P011 ......318 G6
Mengham La HISD P011 ......318 G5
Mengham Rd HISD P011 ......318 G6
Menin Wy FNM GU9 ......116 D1
Menslands La WVILLE P07 ......254 B3
Mentone Rd PSTN BH14 ......321 J9
Menzies CI ROWN SO16 ......227 K7
Meon CI FARN GU14 ......57 L7
HORN P08 ......256 C8
LSOL/BMARY P013 ......294 F7
PSF GU32 ......215 L1
ROMY SO51 ......204 G6
TADY RG26 ......34 B5
Meon Ct WEND SO18 ......249 M3
Meon Crs CHFD S053 ......206 F7
Meon Rd DEAN RG23 ......317 K4
ENEY P04 ......317 K4
LTDN BH7 ......323 P8
ROMY SO51 ......204 G6
Meon Wk BSTK RG21 * 7 H6
Meonwara Crs PSF GU32 ......188 F9
Mercer CI KBH RG22 ......90 B4
Mercer Wy RGWD BH24 * 254 E5
Merchants PI WINC SO23 ......23 F4
Merchants Wk SHAM S014 ......20 C7
Merchistoun Rd HORN P08 ......256 C4
Mercia Av AND SP10 ......82 B6
Mercury Gdns BOR GU35 ......154 B5
ROWN SO16 ......227 K8
Mercury Gdns HLER S031 ......270 A6
Mercury PI WVILLE P07 ......275 N8
Merdon Av CFDH BH17 ......205 N8
Merdon CI CHFD S053 ......206 D7
Mere Cft FHAM P015 ......271 K7
Meredith CI CHCH/BSGR BH23 ......325 H8
Meredith Gdns TOTT S040 ......246 B5
Meredith Rd NEND P02 ......296 G6
Meredun Ct RWIN SO21 ......182 D7
Merepond La ALTN GU34 ......189 N3
Merganser CI GPORT P012 ......315 H1
Meriden CI CCLF BH13 ......333 P4
Meriden Rd SSEA P05 ......19 F4
Meridian Pk AND SP10 ......82 G9
The Meridians
CHCH/BSGR BH23 ......336 D1
Merino Wy FERN BH22 ......280 F9
Merivale FLEETN GU51 ......74 A4
Merlewood Dr CHCH/BSGR BH23 ......326 C7
Merley Gdns WIMB BH21 ......300 F4
Merley La WIMB BH21 ......300 F5
Merley Park Rd WIMB BH21 ......300 F2
Merley Ways WIMB BH21 ......300 F3
Merlin CI AND SP10 ......82 E8
BPWT SO32 ......232 B8
HORN P08 ......255 N7
RGWD BH24 ......282 G5
Merlin Dr HSEA P03 ......297 J5
Merlin Gdns
FHAM/PORC P016 ......273 M9
HEND SO30 ......249 K9
Merlin Md KBH RG22 ......89 K5
Merlin Rd ALTN GU34 ......150 C6
FARN GU14 ......76 A2

Merlins Cl FNM GU9 ....116 C1
Merlin Wy CHCH/BSGR BH23 ...337 L1
CHFD SO53 ....206 B6
FARN GU14 ....75 L1
Mermaid Rd
FHAM/STUB PO14 ....294 D4
Mermaid Wy SHAM SO14 ....248 D9
Merriatt Cl BSTK RG21 ....90 D1
Merrick Wy CHFD SO53 ....206 B5
Merridale Rd ITCH SO19 ....248 C8
Merrifield Av BDST BH18 ....300 E7
Merrifield Dr BDST BH18 ....300 D7
Merrileas Cl CHFD SO53 ....206 E6
Merriemeade Cl FAWY SO45 ...268 A9
Merrifield WIMB BH21 ....278 C7
Merrileas Gdns KBH RG22 ....89 L3
Merritown La
CHCH/BSGR BH23 ....303 K9
Merrivale Av SBNE BH6 ....296 E7
Merrivale Rd FAWY SO45 ....268 A7
Merrivale Rd NEND PO2 ....296 E3
Merron Cl YTLY GU46 ....40 D9
Merrow Av BKME/WDN BH12 ...322 B9
Merrydown La CHIN RG24 ....69 P1
Merryfield CHIN RG24 ....69 P1
FHAM/STUB PO14 ....294 E7
Merryfield Cl
CHCH/BSGR BH23 ....305 L8
VWD BH31 ....258 F4
Merryfield La NBNE BH10 ....322 C3
Merryfield Rd EPSF GU31 ....215 P1
Merry Gdns NBAD SO52 ....205 J8
Merryoak Rd ITCH SO19 ....249 H6
Merryoak Pk CBLY GU15 ....58 E1
Mersea Gdns ITCH SO19 ....249 J7
Mersey Cl AND SP10 ....82 G9
Mersey Wy NTHA RG18 ....25 L2
Mersham Gdns WEND SO18 ...249 J4
Merstone Rd
LSOL/BMARY PO13 ....294 C7
Merthyr Av CHAM PO6 ....275 K9
Merton Av FHAM/PORC PO16 ...295 P3
Merton Cl FBDG SP6 ....220 D9
SHST GU47 ....41 N4
Merton Crs FHAM/PORC PO16 ...295 P3
Merton Rd BSTK RG21 ....6 B3
PTSW SO17 ....248 D1
SSEA PO5 ....19 H7
Meryl Rd ENEY PO4 ....317 L4
Meryon Rd NARL SO24 ....167 P3
Mesh Pond RSAL SP5 ....199 H5
Mesh Rd HORN PO8 ....180 A4
Metcalfe Av
FHAM/STUB PO14 ....294 B6
Meteor Rd FHAM/PORC PO10 ...299 N6
Meteor Wy FARN GU14 ....75 P3
Methuen Cl CHAR BH8 ....335 J1
Methuen Rd CFDH BH17 ....320 D2
CHAR BH8 ....335 H1
ENEY PO4 ....317 J5
LISS GU33 ....173 P4
Methuen St SHAM SO14 ....248 C4
Metuchen Wy HEND SO30 ...250 C7
Meudon Av FARN GU14 ....76 A1
Mewsey Ct HAV PO9 ....276 D5
The Mews AND SP10 ....5 F7
CHFD SO53 ....228 E1
EPSF GU31 ....215 N1
FAWY SO45 ....313 H1
ROWN SO16 ....227 K6
TADY RG26 ....52 C3
Mey Cl WILLE PO7 ....275 P3
Meynell Cl ELGH SO50 ....229 H1
Meyrick Cl CHCH/BSGR BH23 ...305 L9
Meyrick Dr NWBY RG14 ....30 B1
Meyrick Park Crs TWDS BH3 ...322 F9
Meyrick Rd BMTH BH1 ....9 H4
HAV PO9 ....14 C5
NEND PO2 ....296 E2
Michael Crook Cl HAV PO9 ...14 A2
Michaelmas Cl YTLY GU46 ....56 E1
Michaelmas Dro RAND SP11 ...101 H1
Michaels Wy ELGH SO50 ....229 L5
FAWY SO45 ....268 B6
Micheldever Cl WHCH RG28 ...85 M8
Micheldever Gdns WHCH RG28 ...85 M8
Micheldever Rd AND SP10 ....5 F1
WHCH RG28 ....85 M7
Michelgrove Rd BOSC BH5 ....335 L3
Michelmersh Cl ROWN SO16 ...227 J7
Michelmersh Gn CHAR BH8 ...323 K5
Michigan Wy TOTT SO40 ....245 P3
Mickle Hi SHST GU47 ....41 H5
Midanbury Broadway
WEND SO18 ....249 H2
Midanbury Crs WEND SO18 ...249 H2
Midanbury La WEND SO18 ...248 G3
Midanbury Rd WEND SO18 ...249 H3
Midas Cl WVILLE PO7 ....275 P7
Middle Av FNM GU9 ....116 D2
Middle Bourne La
RFNM GU10 ....116 B4
Middlebridge St ROMY SO51 ...204 C7
Middlebrook BPWT SO32 ....233 J3
Middle Brook St WINC SO23 ...23 F5
Middle Church La FNM GU9 * ...96 B9
Middle Cl NWBY RG14 ....24 A8
Middle Common Rd
LYMN SO41 ....328 G4
Middlecroft La GPORT PO12 ...315 K2
Middlefield FNM GU9 ....116 A3
Middlefield Cl FNM GU9 ....116 A3
Middle Hi ALDT GU11 ....2 C2
Middlehill Dr WIMB BH21 ....279 K8
Middlehill Rd WIMB BH21 ....279 J7
Middle La RGWD BH24 ....282 E2
Middle Md FHAM/STUB PO14 ...293 P1

HTWY RG27 ....71 P3
Middle Meadow LISS GU33 ...192 E2
Middlemoor Rd FRIM GU16 ...58 D5
Middle Old Pk FNM GU9 ....95 P7
Middle Park Wy HAV PO9 ....276 D4
Middle Rd FUFL SO22 ....22 B3
HLER SO31 ....271 H5
ITCH SO19 ....249 J8
LYMN SO41 ....307 M8
LYMN SO41 ....329 K4
NBAD SO52 ....205 L8
NBNE BH10 ....322 C2
PLE BH15 ....320 G6
Middlesex Rd ENEY PO4 ....317 J5
Middle St CCLF BH15 ....113 M4
SHAM SO14 ....248 C4
SSEA PO5 ....19 G4
Middleton Cl
FHAM/STUB PO14 ....294 C2
WEND SO18 ....249 J1
Middleton Ct NWBY RG14 ....25 H2
Middleton Gdns BSTK RG21 ...7 F2
FARN GU14 ....57 M7
Middleton Ms
NMIL/BTOS BH25 ....327 H6
Middleton Park Farm
RAND SP11 * 104 B4
Middleton Ri HORN PO8 * 236 D8
Middleton Rd NBNE BH10 ....322 E5
RGWD BH24 ....282 E1
RSAL SP5 ....138 A9
The Middleway RAND SP11 ...103 M2
Midfield Cl FHAM/STUB PO14 ...294 D2
Midhurst Rd HASM GU27 ....156 G8
LIPH GU30 ....175 K4
Midland Rd MOOR/WNTN BH9 ...322 F6
Midlands Est HEND SO30 ....249 L2
Midlane Cl BSTK RG21 ....90 C1
Midlington Hi BPWT SO32 ....233 L5
Midlington Rd BPWT SO32 ....233 M5
Midway FAWY SO45 ....268 B7
Midway Rd NEND PO2 ....296 G4
Midwood Av CHAR BH8 ....323 M6
Mike Hawthorn Dr FNM GU9 ...96 C8
Milbeck Cl HORN PO8 ....256 A8
Milborne Crs
BKME/WDN BH12 ....321 N5
Milbourne Rd FERN BH22 ....302 C2
Milburn Cl WBNE BH4 ....334 C2
Milburn Rd WBNE BH4 ....334 D2
The Milburns ROMY SO51 ....180 B7
Milbury Crs ITCH SO19 ....249 J5
Milden Cl FHAM SO15 ....58 F7
Milden Gdns FRIM GU16 ....58 F7
Mildmay Ct ODIM RG29 ....93 L1
Mildmay St FUFL SO22 ....183 M1
Milebush Rd ENEY PO4 ....317 L5
Mile End Rd PSEA PO1 ....316 E1
Miles Rd ASHV GU12 ....76 G9
Miles's La RSAL SP5 ....177 L7
Milestone Rd PLE BH15 ....320 F6
Milford La FERN BH22 ....280 F7
HAV PO9 ....14 B9
Milford Ct LYMN SO41 ....339 H2
Milford Crs LYMN SO41 ....339 H2
Milford Dr BWD BH11 ....301 P8
Milford Gdns CHFD SO53 ....206 C7
Milford Rd LYMN SO41 ....328 F6
NMIL/BTOS BH25 ....339 L1
PSEA PO1 ....19 J2
Military Rd FHAM/PORC PO16 ...273 J8
GPORT PO12 ....315 J1
HSEA PO3 ....297 H4
PSEA PO1 ....316 D2
Milkingpen La CHIN RG24 ....69 K6
Milkwood Ct TOTT SO40 ....245 P4
Millais Rd ITCH SO19 ....248 G8
Milland La LIPH GU30 ....175 H9
Milland Rd WINC SO23 ....165 J9
Millbank St SHAM SO14 ....21 K2
Millbridge Gdns ITCH SO19 ...249 K7
Millbridge Rd YTLY GU46 ....40 G7
Millbrook CHFD SO53 ....206 D8
LISS GU33 ....192 E2
Millbrook Dr HAV PO9 ....276 G4
Millbrook Point Rd
WSHM SO15 ....247 L5
Millbrook Rd East
WSHM SO15 ....247 N6
Millbrook Rd West
WSHM SO15 ....247 K5
Mill Chase Rd BOR GU35 ....154 B5
Mill Cl HASM GU27 ....156 D7
HISD PO11 ....298 F7
ROWN SO16 ....227 H7
WVILLE PO7 ....255 K7
Mill Copse Rd HASM GU27 ...156 C9
Mill Cnr FLEETN GU51 ....74 B6
Mill Ct FBDG SP6 * 240 C2
Mill End GPORT PO12 ....299 P1
FBDG SP6 ....219 K8
Millennium Ct BSTK RG21 ....6 A6
Millenium Cl NMIL/BTOS BH25 ...327 L3
Miller Dr FHAM/PORC PO16 ...10 D2
Miller Rd CHCH/BSGR BH23 ...325 H8
Millers La FUFL SO22 ....183 H5
Miller's Pond Gdns ITCH SO19 ...249 H8
Millers Rd TADY RG26 ....34 C6
Millers Yd RWIN SO21 * 125 L5
Millfield CFDH BH17 ....320 C5
Millgreen La STHA RG19 ....32 F4
Millhams Rd BWD BH11 ....302 A9
NBNE BH10 ....322 B1
Millhams St CHCH/BSGR BH23 ...324 F9
Millhams St North
CHCH/BSGR BH23 ....324 F9
Mill Hi HEND SO30 ....250 G4
NARL SO24 ....148 A9
Mill Hill Av NTID SP9 ....78 G3
Mill Hill Cl PSTN BH14 ....321 K9
Milliken Cl FAWY SO45 ....291 H7
Millins Cl SHST GU47 ....41 L5
Mill La ALTN GU34 ....133 J4

BOR GU35 ....154 E3
TADY RG26 ....34 C8
BPWT SO32 ....231 K9
BPWT SO32 ....233 M3
BROC SO42 ....287 H8
BROC SO42 ....287 P7
CHCH/BSGR BH23 ....323 P1
CHCH/BSGR BH23 ....326 D7
EMRTH PO10 ....277 P8
EPSF GU31 ....217 P5
FHAM PO15 ....271 N9
GPORT PO12 ....315 M2
HAV PO9 ....14 A6
HTWY RG27 ....53 K7
KSCL RG20 ....47 M1
LISS GU33 ....172 E5
LYMN SO41 ....308 E9
LYMN SO41 ....329 M3
LYMN SO41 ....330 D3
LYND SO43 ....244 E9
NWBY RG14 ....17 F2
ODIM RG29 ....72 B7
PSF GU32 ....191 L6
PSTN BH14 ....321 K9
RFNM GU10 ....114 C5
RGWD BH24 ....282 D4
ROMY SO51 ....204 C6
ROMY SO51 ....202 E5
ROMY SO51 ....204 B6
ROWN SO16 ....226 C8
RSAL SP5 ....138 C8
THLE RG7 ....36 D9
WHAM PO17 ....252 E6
WIMB BH21 ....238 D6
WIMB BH21 ....278 D9
WIMB BH21 ....278 D9
WVILLE PO7 ....255 J9
YTLY GU46 ....40 F7
Mill Meadow LYMN SO41 ....338 F1
Millmere YTLY GU46 ....40 E7
Mill Pond Rd GPORT PO12 ...315 M2
The Mill Pond FAWY SO45 ...290 D3
Mill Quay EMRTH PO10 ....299 N2
Mill Reef Cl STHA RG19 ....25 J4
Mill Ri HORN PO8 * 179 K6
CHIN RG24 ....68 F4
CHCH/BSGR BH23 ....324 E7
EMRTH PO10 ....277 P6
FHAM/PORC PO16 ....294 E1
GPORT PO12 ....315 J2
LISS GU33 ....192 E1
TOTT SO40 ....246 E4
WSHM SO15 ....247 L4
WVILLE PO7 ....255 J7
WVILLE PO7 ....275 M4
Mill Rd (North) CHAR BH8 ...323 K4
Mill Rd (South) CHAR BH8 ...323 J5
Mill Rythe La HISD PO11 ....318 C1
Mills Rd NEND PO2 ....296 F9
Mill Stream HAV PO9 ....96 E5
Millstream Cl AND SP10 ....102 E4
CFDH BH17 ....320 C5
WSHM SO15 ....247 L4
Millstream Ri ROMY SO51 ...204 B6
The Millstream HASM GU27 ...156 D8
Mill St FHAM/STUB PO14 ....293 N1
Millvina Cl TOTT SO40 ....245 M7
Mill Wy TOTT SO40 ....246 C6
Millway Cl AND SP10 ....102 C3
Millway Rd AND SP10 ....102 C3
Millyford Br LYND SO43 ....264 A6
Millyford Cl NMIL/BTOS BH25 ...326 F7
Milne Cl FAWY SO45 ....267 N8
Milner Ct WSHM SO15 ....247 N3
Milner Cl CHIN RG24 ....69 K5
Milner Pl FUFL SO22 ....164 F9
Milner Rd WBNE BH4 ....334 C4
Milnthorpe La FUFL SO22 ....22 A6
The Milsons STOK SO20 ....141 L6
Milton Av AND SP10 ....102 B1
Milton Cl CHIN RG24 ....69 J6
PSTN BH14 ....321 M9
Milton Gn NMIL/BTOS BH25 ...327 H6
NMIL/BTOS BH25 ....327 K5
Milton Md NMIL/BTOS BH25 ...327 H5
Milton Pde WVILLE PO7 ....255 N6
Milton Park Av ENEY PO4 ....317 J4
Milton Rd BMTH BH1 ....334 C1
ELGH SO50 ....207 K8
ENEY PO4 ....317 H5
PSTN BH14 ....321 M9
WIMB BH21 ....278 B8
WVILLE PO7 ....255 M1
WVILLE PO7 ....248 A5
Milverton Cl
CHCH/BSGR BH23 ....326 A6
Milverton Rd FUFL SO22 ....22 A3
TOTT SO40 ....246 E5
Milvil Rd LSOL/BMARY PO13 ...314 C3
Mimosa Av AND SP10 ....300 C5
Mimosa Cl BOR GU35 ....154 D3
FHAM PO15 ....271 L6
Mimosa Ct AND SP10 * 102 B3
Mimosa Dr ELGH SO50 ....230 C2
Minchens La TADY RG26 ....35 J3
Mincingfield La BPWT SO32 ...231 K8
Minden Cl AND SP10 ....82 D8
CHIN RG24 ....69 P5
The Mindens NTID SP9 * 98 C3
Minden Wy FUFL SO22 ....185 L1
Minehurst Rd FRIM GU16 ....58 D9
Minerva Cl WVILLE PO7 ....275 N8
Minerva Crs PSEA PO1 * 18 C5
Minerva Rd FARN GU14 ....76 A3
Ministry Rd STHA RG19 ....31 M1
Miniey Cl FARN GU14 ....57 M9
Minley Ct FARN GU14 ....57 M9
Minley Gv FLEETN GU51 ....74 E1
Minley Rd FARN GU14 ....56 F4
FLEETN GU51 ....56 E9
Minnitt Rd GPORT PO12 ....13 J2
Minorca Av FRIM GU16 ....59 K3
Minorca Rd FRIM GU16 ....59 K4
Minstead Av WEND SO18 ....249 L3

Minstead Cl FUFL SO22 ....164 E3
TADY RG26 ....34 C8
Minstead Dr YTLY GU46 ....40 C9
Minstead Rd ENEY PO4 ....317 K5
NBNE BH10 ....322 C4
Minster Cl FHAM PO15 ....272 A9
Minster Ct CBLY GU15 * 57 N1
Minster Gdns WINC SO23 ....22 E5
Minster Pk WIMB BH21 * 280 L5
Minster Vw WIMB BH21 ....278 E9
Mintern Cl ELGH SO50 ....207 M8
Minterne Rd
CHCH/BSGR BH23 ....337 J1
MOOR/WNTN BH9 ....322 G5
PSTN BH14 ....333 L4
Minters Lepe WVILLE PO7 ...275 N7
Mint Rd LISS GU33 ....173 N9
Mirabella Cl ITCH SO19 ....248 F9
Mirror Cl HLER SO31 ....270 F9
Mislingford Rd BPWT SO32 ...232 G9
Missenden Acres HEND SO30 ...250 J5
Mission Rd BDST BH18 ....320 C2
Missiebrook La NBAD SO52 ...205 P9
Mistletoe Rd YTLY GU46 ....56 E1
Mitchell Av HTWY RG27 ....55 H8
Mitchell Cl AND SP10 ....101 P1
FHAM PO15 ....271 K5
ITCH SO19 ....248 F8
NMIL/BTOS BH25 ....327 J8
Mitchell Dr ELGH SO50 ....230 C1
Mitchell Gdns KBH RG22 ....89 N4
Mitchell Rd CFDH BH17 ....321 H4
ELGH SO50 ....230 C1
HAV PO9 ....276 B7
WIMB BH21 ....302 A1
Mitchells Cl ROMY SO51 ....204 D6
RSAL SP5 ....199 P7
Mitchell Wy ELGH SO50 ....229 J5
HSEA PO3 ....297 K6
Mitford Rd NARL SO24 ....167 N2
Mitre Copse ELGH SO50 ....229 P2
Moat Cl FAWY SO45 ....290 D6
TADY RG26 ....51 P1
Moat Dr GPORT PO12 ....315 H5
Moat Hi WEND SO18 ....229 H9
Moat La NMIL/BTOS BH25 ....339 K6
Mockbeggar La RGWD BH24 ...260 E3
Moffat Rd CHCH/BSGR BH23 ...325 N8
Moffatts Cl SHST GU47 ....41 L5
Moggs Md ENEY PO4 ....215 N2
Moira Cl FARN GU14 ....57 J7
Mole Hi WVILLE PO7 ....275 P5
Molesworth Rd GPORT PO12 ...12 L4
Mollison Ri FHAM PO15 ....271 K4
Molyneux Rd
NMIL/BTOS BH25 ....327 M4
MOOR/WNTN BH9 ....273 M6
Monachus La HTWY RG27 ....55 J6
Monarch Cl HLER SO31 ....271 H8
KBH RG22 ....89 L7
WVILLE PO7 ....276 A3
Monarch's Wy BPWT SO32 ...209 J6
BPWT SO32 ....212 D8
HAV PO9 ....277 M1
HORN PO8 ....256 D6
ROMY SO51 ....179 M6
ROMY SO51 ....205 N1
STOK SO20 ....159 K2
WVILLE PO7 ....275 L5
Monarch Wy FUFL SO22 ....164 D9
HEND SO30 ....249 N1
Monastery Rd WEND SO18 ...248 G4
Monckton Rd GPORT PO12 ...315 M7
HSEA PO3 ....297 L1
Mon Crs WEND SO18 ....249 L4
Moneyer Rd AND SP10 ....82 E8
Moneyfield Av HSEA PO3 * ...297 J9
Moneyfield La HSEA PO3 * ...297 J9
Moneyfly Rd VWD BH31 ....259 H5
Mongers Piece CHIN RG24 ...52 D2
Monier Williams Rd
RWIN SO21 ....104 D7
Moniton Est KBH RG22 * 89 E8
Monks Brook Cl ELGH SO50 ...228 G3
Monks Cl FARN GU14 ....58 B9
FERN BH22 ....280 C9
NTID SP9 ....78 D2
Monkshanger FNM GU9 ....96 E9
Monk Sherborne Rd
TADY RG26 ....50 A6
Monk's Hi EMRTH PO10 ....277 N4
Monkswell Gn
CHCH/BSGR BH23 ....325 M6
Monks La NWBY RG14 ....24 C8
Monks Orch PSF GU32 ....191 M9
Monks Pl TOTT SO40 ....246 B5
Monks Ri FLEETN GU51 ....74 A3
Monks Rd ELGH SO50 ....229 K4
WINC SO23 ....23 G2
Monks Wk FAWY SO45 ....290 A1
RFNM GU10 ....116 F3
Monks Wy ELGH SO50 ....229 H3
FHAM/STUB PO14 ....293 P9
WIMB BH21 ....301 L8
Monks' Well RFNM GU10 ....117 J2
Monkswell Gn
CHCH/BSGR BH23 ....325 H9
Monks Wd PSF GU32 ....191 M9
Monks Wood Cl ELGH SO50 ...228 D6
Monkswood Ct NWBY RG14 ...24 A8
Monks Wood Crs TADY RG26 ...34 C7
Monkton Cl FERN BH22 ....302 D2
Monkton Crs
BKME/WDN BH12 ....321 N4
Monktons La THLE RG7 ....36 B1
Monkwood Cl HAV PO9 ....96 F3
Monkworthy Dr RGWD BH24 ...281 M4
Monmouth Cl CHFD SO53 ....206 C7
VWD BH31 ....259 H6
Monmouth Dr VWD BH31 ....259 H6

Monmouth Rd NEND PO2 ....296 F7
Monmouth Sq FUFL SO22 * ...164 C9
Monnow Gdns WEND SO18 ...249 K2
Monroe Cl GPORT PO12 ....315 J5
Monsal Av FERN BH22 ....302 C5
Mons Barracks ALDT GU11 ...76 B7
Mons Cl ALDT GU11 ....76 D5
Mons Ct WINC SO23 ....22 E5
Montacute Cl AND SP10 ....58 C9
Montacute Wy WIMB BH21 ...300 C5
Montagu Cl GPORT PO12 ....295 N9
Montague Av ITCH SO19 ....249 M8
Montague Cl ITCH SO19 ....249 M8
Montague Gdns EPSF GU31 ...216 A2
Montague Rd BOSC BH5 ....335 P2
NEND PO2 ....296 E3
Montague Ter NWBY RG14 ...16 E7
Montagu Rd
CHCH/BSGR BH23 ....326 D8
Monteagle La LYMN SO41 ....327 P3
Monterey Dr HAV PO9 ....276 C6
HLER SO31 ....270 G8
Montfort Cl ROMY SO51 ....204 C6
Montfort Hts ROMY SO51 ....204 C6
Montfort Rd ROMY SO51 ....204 C2
Montgomerie Rd SSEA PO5 ...19 J4
Montgomery Av BWD BH11 ...322 B4
TOTT SO40 ....246 B3
Montgomery Cl FUFL SO22 ...183 L1
FARN GU14 ....41 J6
Montgomery Rd FARN GU14 ...75 N1
HAV PO9 ....276 A5
LSOL/BMARY PO13 ....294 C5
NWBY RG14 ....16 A7
RAND SP11 ....25 J3
WEND SO18 ....249 J3
Montgomery Wk WVILLE PO7 ...275 L5
Montgomery Wy CHFD SO53 ...220 D1
Montpelier Cl HLER SO31 ....271 J7
Montrose Av
FHAM/PORC PO16 ....274 A7
Montrose Cl BOR GU35 ....154 A7
FLEETN GU51 ....74 E4
FRIM GU16 ....58 D5
HEND SO30 ....250 E5
VWD BH31 ....258 F4
Montrose Rd NBNE BH10 ....322 D5
Monument Cha BOR GU35 ...154 E7
Monument Cl NWBY RG14 ...24 A8
Monument La LYMN SO41 ....329 N3
WHAM PO17 ....273 M6
Monxton Rd RAND SP11 ....101 M3
RAND SP11 * 101 M3
Moody Rd FHAM/STUB PO14 ...293 P8
Moody's Hi RSAL SP5 ....177 L4
Moon Cl SHST GU47 ....267 J1
Moonhills La BROC SO42 ....289 M7
Moonrakers Wy
CHCH/BSGR BH23 ....326 A6
Moonscross Av TOTT SO40 ...246 D7
Moons Hi RFNM GU10 ....116 B8
Moor Cl BOR GU35 ....153 N5
SHST GU47 ....41 M5
Moor Court La RWIN SO21 ...163 L4
Moorcroft Av
CHCH/BSGR BH23 ....324 C5
Moorcroft Cl RWIN SO21 ....125 M6
Moordown Cl
MOOR/WNTN BH9 ....322 G4
Moore Av BWD BH11 ....322 A4
Moore Cl AND SP10 ....5 D1
FLEETS GU52 ....74 D1
NMIL/BTOS BH25 ....327 H6
RFNM GU10 ....97 M3
Moore Crs HLER SO31 ....269 K4
Moore Gdns GPORT PO12 ....315 J4
Moore Rd CHOB/PIR GU24 ...59 N7
FLEETS GU52 ....74 D7
Moorfield HASM GU27 ....156 E8
Moorfield Gv
MOOR/WNTN BH9 ....322 F5
Moorfoot Gdns CHFD SO53 ...333 P3
Moorfoot Gdns KBH RG22 ....89 G8
Moorgreen Pk HEND SO30 * ...249 P1
HEND SO30 ....249 N1
Moorhams Av KBH RG22 ....89 L5
Moorhill Gdns WEND SO18 ...249 N4
Moorhill Rd HEND SO30 ....249 N1
Moorings Cl PLE BH15 ....332 B2
The Moorings BSTK RG21 ....7 K5
FHAM/PORC PO16 ....294 F2
Moorings Wy ENEY PO4 ....317 L2
Moorland Av
NMIL/BTOS BH25 ....327 H7
Moorland Cl HASM GU27 ....156 E8
HLER SO31 ....270 C6
Moorland Ga RGWD BH24 ....282 E4
Moorland Rd BMTH BH1 ....335 K2
PSEA PO1 ....316 D2
Moorlands Cl BROC SO42 ....288 D8
FLEETN GU51 ....74 E4
GSHT GU26 ....156 D1
Moorlands Crs WEND SO18 ...249 J3
Moorlands Ri FERN BH22 ....280 F6
Moorlands Rd BPWT SO32 ...232 G6
CBLY GU15 ....50 F7
FERN BH22 ....280 C7
VWD BH31 ....258 F3
Moor La RSAL SP5 ....200 C4
Moor Pk HORN PO8 ....256 B9
Moor Park La FNM GU9 ....96 E8
Moor Park Vw FNM GU9 ....96 F8
Moor Rd BDST BH18 ....300 D8
FARN GU14 ....58 B7
FRIM GU16 ....58 E5
HASM GU27 ....156 B8
LISS GU33 ....173 N6
Moors Cl CHCH/BSGR BH23 ...303 P9

RWIN SO21 ....207 P4
Moorside FERN BH22 * 281 H9
Moorside CI BWD BH11 ......322 B4
FARN GU14 ....57 P4
Moorside Rd BWD BH11 .....322 A4
FERN BH22 ....280 E7
WINC SO23 ....165 K5
The Moors RFNM GU10 ....97 M4
STHA RG19 ....25 N5
Moorton Av CHAM PO6.....275 L9
Moortown Dr WIMB BH21 .....145 K5
Moortown La RGWD BH24.....282 F5
Moorvale Rd
MOOR/WNTN BH9 ....322 C5
Moor Vw CHIN RG24 ....70 B5
Moor View Rd PLE BH15 ....322 C6
Moot CI AND SP10 ....82 F7
RSAL SP5 ....199 L7
Moot Gdns RSAL SP5 ......199 K3
Moot La FBDG SP6 ....221 K2
RSAL SP5 ....199 K7
Mopley FAWY SO45 ....313 H1
Mopley CI FAWY SO45 ......313 H1
Morant Rd RGWD BH24 ......260 F9
Moraunt CI GPORT PO12 .....295 M9
Moraunt Dr
FHAM/PORC PO16.......295 M3
Moray Av SHST GU47 ....41 J3
Mordaunt Dr CWTH RG45 .....41 J3
Mordaunt Rd SHAM SO14....248 C4
Morden Av FERN BH22 ....302 C4
Morden Rd MOOR/WNTN BH9 .322 F6
Moreland CI ALTN GU34 .....132 F7
Morelands Rd WVILLE PO7 ...275 N6
Morestead Rd RWIN SO21 ....184 C1
Moreton CI FLEETS GU52 .....74 C8
RFNM GU10 ....136 E8
Moreton Rd
MOOR/WNTN BH9 ....323 H5
Morgan Le Fay Dr CHFD SO53..206 B6
Morgan Rd ENEY PO4 ....317 L4
HEND SO30 ....250 C6
Morgans Dr FHAM/STUB PO14..294 A4
Morgan's La RSAL SP5 ......195 J8
Morgans Rise Rd RSAL SP5 ...199 P6
Morgans Vale Rd RSAL SP5 ...199 P7
Morgaston Rd TADY RG26.....91 J6
Morland Rd ALDT GU11 ....97 J4
WSHM SO15 ....247 N2
Morland's Rd ALDT GU11 .....76 C7
Morley CI BOSC BH5 ....335 N1
CHCH/BSGR BH23 .....324 C4
ITCH SO19 ....249 H5
YTLY GU46 ....40 C9
Morley College WINC SO23 *...22 E5
Morley Crs HORN PO8 ....256 A8
Morley Dr BPWT SO32 ....232 A4
Morley Rd BOSC BH5 ......335 N1
BSTK RG21 ....0 C2
ENEY PO4 ....317 J6
FNM GU9 ....116 C1
Morningside Av
FHAM/PORC PO16.......273 P9
Mornington CI AND SP10 ....102 E5
TADY RG26 ....33 N5
Mornish Rd CCLF BH13 .....333 P1
Morpeth Av CWTH RG45 .....246 D3
Morris CI FAWY SO45 ....267 P6
LSOL/BMARY PO13 .....294 C5
Morrison Av
BKME/WDN BH12 ....321 P6
Morris Ri CHIN RG24 ....69 P2
Morris Rd CFDH BH17 .....320 F4
FARN GU14 ....76 C4
WSHM SO15 ....247 N2
Morris St HTWY RG27 ....71 M4
Morse Rd KBH RG22 ....69 H8
Morshead Crs
FHAM/PORC PO16.......10 D2
Mortimer CI
CHCH/BSGR BH23 .....325 L9
HLER SO31 ....269 K4
HTWY RG27 ....54 C9
TOTT SO40 ....246 B2
WINC SO23 ....165 J1
Mortimer La BSTK RG21 .....26 D7
Mortimer Rd CHAM PO6 .....274 E9
CHAR BH8 ....323 H6
HEND SO30 ....250 C5
ITCH SO19 ....248 G7
Mortimers Dr ELGH SO50 ....230 D2
Mortimers La ELGH SO50 ....230 D2
Mortimer Wy NBAD SO52 ....227 K1
Mortimore Rd GPORT PO12 ..315 K2
Morton CI FRIM GU16 ....58 E6
Morval CI FARN GU14 ....57 L8
Mosaic CI ITCH SO19 ....249 P7
Moselle CI FARN GU14 ....57 L8
Moss CI LISS GU33 ....192 E2
Mosscrop CI BSTK RG21 *....69 K8
Moss Dr TOTT SO40 ....247 K9
Mossleigh Av ROWN SO16 ...227 K7
Mossley Av BKME/WDN BH12 .321 P5
Moss Rd WINC SO23 ....23 H4
Motcombe Rd CCLF BH13....334 A5
Mothes House TADY RG26....34 D7
Motisfont CI WSHM SO15 ....247 L5
Mottisfont Rd ELGH SO50....207 J9
Moulsham Copse La
YTLY GU46 ....40 C7
Moulsham La YTLY GU46 .....40 C7
Moulshay La HTWY RG27 .....52 D8
Mound CI GPORT PO12 ....12 A4
Mountain Ash CI WEND SO18 .249 L4
Mountbatten Av ROMY SO51 .204 D6
Mountbatten CI
CHCH/BSGR BH23 .....337 L1
LSOL/BMARY PO13 ....294 C5
NWBY RG14 ....34 F2

Mountbatten Ct AND SP10 ......5 J3
FUFL SO22 ....164 F4
Mountbatten Dr FERN BH22 ...302 C3
WVILLE PO7 ....275 L4
Mountbatten PI WINC SO23...145 K8
Mountbatten Ri CCLF SO47 ...40 C5
Mountbatten Rd CCLF BH13 .334 B5
CHAR BH8 ....323 M5
ELGH SO50 ....207 J8
TOTT SO40 ....246 B3
Mountbatten Sq ENEY PO4 ..317 K6
Mountbatten Wy
WSHM SO15 ....247 P6
Mount Carmel Rd RAND SP11 .119 M4
Mount CI FUFL SO22 ....164 F4
KSCL RG20 ....29 N8
NMIL/BTOS BH25 .....327 J6
NWBY RG14 ....16 E6
Mount Dr CHFD SO53 ....206 C9
FHAM PO15 ....293 P1
Mounters La ALTN GU34 .....132 D8
Mountfield FAWY SO45 ......268 A6
Mount Grace Dr PSTN SO41 .333 L4
Mount Hermon Rd
RAND SP11 ....119 N3
Mount House CI FAWY SO45 ..268 C5
Mountjoy CI WIMB BH21 .....301 H3
Mount La ROMY SO51 ....178 F7
Mount Pleasant FNM GU9 ....96 A9
HTWY RG27 ....55 J7
RGWD BH24 ....282 E1
ROMY SO51 * 204 C7
SHST GU47 ....41 H5
TADY RG26 ....34 D6
WINC SO23 ....165 J1
Mount Pleasant Dr CHAR BH8..323 M6
CHCH/BSGR BH23 ....305 N7
Mount Pleasant La
LYMN SO41 ....308 C8
Mount Pleasant Rd
ALTN GU34 ....132 F7
ASHV GU12 ....3 H3
BOR GU35 ....154 C3
GPORT PO12 ....12 C6
PLE BH15 ....332 F1
SHAM SO14 ....248 D4
Mount Rd BWD BH11 ....322 A3
KSCL RG20 ....29 N7
NTHA RG18 ....25 N3
PSTN SO41 ....321 K7
Mountsom's La ALTN GU34...151 N4
Mounts Wy FLEETS GU51 .....73 P1
Mount Temple ROMY SO51 ..204 E6
The Mount BOR GU35 ....155 H2
FLEETN GU51 ....74 D2
HASM GU27 ....187 L5
LSOL/BMARY PO13 .....295 J8
NWBY RG14 * 16 E7
RGWD BH24 ....283 H1
ROWN SO16 ....228 D8
ROWN SO16 ....247 L2
Mount Vw ALDT GU11 ....2 D5
Mountview Av
FHAM/PORC PO16.......274 A9
Mourne CI KBH RG22 ....68 E8
Mousehole La FAWY SO45 ...268 C7
WEND SO18 ....249 K7
Mousehole Rd CHAM PO6 ...274 B9
Mowbray Rd ITCH SO19 .....249 K7
Moxhams FBDG SP6 * 240 D2
Mozart CI KBH RG22 ....90 A3
Mucclesfield CI HAV PO9 ....276 C6
Muddyford Rd RSAL SP5 .....199 P4
Mudeford CHCH/BSGR BH23 .337 K1
Mudeford Green CI
CHCH/BSGR BH23 .....337 K1
Mudeford La
CHCH/BSGR BH23 .....325 K9
Mude Gdns CHCH/BSGR BH23 .337 J1
Mud La HTWY RG27 ....39 J5
Mulberry Av CHAM PO6 .....297 J2
FHAM/STUB PO14 ......294 A8
Mulberry CI ASHV GU12 ......76 E5
CWTH RG45 ....41 K2
GPORT PO12 ....12 C3
SHST GU47 ....41 L6
Mulberry Cnr CHFD SO53 *..206 C9
Mulberry Gdns FBDG SP6 ...240 C3
Mulberry Gdns FHAM PO16 ..297 J2
Mulberry La CHAM PO6 ......297 J2
Mulberry Rd TOTT SO40 ....246 C7
Mulberry Wk WSHM SO15 ...247 N3
Mulberry Wy CHIN RG24 .....70 A1
Mulfords Hl TADY RG26 ......34 D8
Mulgrave Rd FRIM GU16 .....58 E5
Mull CI DEAN RG23 ....69 H8
Mullen CI ITCH SO19 ....248 G7
Mullins CI BKME/WDN BH12..322 C7
BSTK RG21 ....69 L4
Mullion CI CHAM PO6 ......296 D2
Mumby Rd GPORT PO12 ......13 H1
Mundays Rw HORN PO8 .....256 C5
Mundays Rd CHCH/BSGR BH23..325 N7
Munnings CI BSTK RG21 .....69 N9
Munnings Ct AND SP10 ....41 A1
Munnings Dr SHST GU47 ....41 L8
Munns Crs WSHM SO15 ....247 N4
Munster Rd NEND PO2 ......296 F3
PSTN BH14 ....321 M9
Murefield Rd PSEA PO1 .....19 N2
Muriel Rd WVILLE PO7 ......275 N4
Murley Rd MOOR/WNTN BH9 .322 C7
Murray CI AND SP10 ....100 D5
FHAM PO15 ....10 B4
ITCH SO19 ....249 N5
Murray Rd FARN GU14 ....75 N1
Murray's La PSEA PO1 ......316 B2
Murray's Rd ALDT GU11 ....76 F9
Murrell Rd ASHV GU12 ....76 F9
Murrells La CBLY GU15 ....58 A2
Muscliffe CI HAV PO9 ......277 H5
Muscliffe La
MOOR/WNTN BH9 ....322 G3

Muscliffe Pk
MOOR/WNTN BH9 ....323 J3
Muscliffe Rd
MOOR/WNTN BH9 ....322 F7
Muscott CI NTID SP9 ....98 F5
Museum HI HASM GU27 .....157 J7
Museum Rd PSEA PO1 ....18 E5
Musgrave CI KBH RG22 ......89 P3
Musgrove Gdns ALTN GU34...132 E5
Musket Copse CHIN RG24.....70 B6
Mussett CI TOTT SO40 ......246 C4
Muss La STOK SO20 ....161 M4
Mustang Av FHAM PO15.....271 H3
Myers CI BPWT SO32 ....232 F7
Myers Wy FRIM GU16 ....59 J3
Mylen CI BSTK RG21 ....7 G1
Mylen Rd AND SP10 ....102 C1
My Lords La HISD PO11 ......35 H3
Myrtle CI LSOL/BMARY PO13 .294 F6
LYMN SO41 ....327 P3
THLE RG7 ....27 L4
Myrtle Dr BLKW GU17 ....57 L1
Myrtle Gv HSEA PO3 ....317 K2
Myrtle Rd CHAR BH8 ....323 J9
ROWN SO16 ....227 M8
Mytchett Farm Pk
FRIM GU16 * 76 E2
Mytchett Heath FRIM GU16...76 F1
Mytchett Lake Rd FRIM GU16..76 F1
Mytchett Place Rd FRIM GU16 .76 F1
Mytchett Rd FRIM GU16 .....58 E9
Myvern CI FAWY SO45 ......290 F6

N

Nada Rd CHCH/BSGR BH23...325 P6
Nadder Rd NTID SP9 ....79 H5
Nailsworth Rd CHAM PO6 ....274 D9
Naini Tal Rd NTID SP9 ....78 G4
Nairn CI FRIM GU16 ....58 D3
Nairn Rd CCLF BH13 ....333 N4
TWDS BH3 ....322 E9
Naish CI HAV PO9 ....276 C3
Naish Est NMIL/BTOS BH25 *.326 F7
Naish Rd NMIL/BTOS BH25 ..326 F7
Namu Rd MOOR/WNTN BH9 .322 E6
Nansen Av PLE BH15 ....320 F7
Napier CI ALDT GU11 ....76 D5
CWTH RG45 ....41 K2
NTID SP9 ....79 J5
Napier Crs FHAM PO15 .....272 A9
Napier Rd CWTH RG45 ......41 K2
HORN PO8 ....256 D1
ITCH SO19 ....249 N6
SSEA PO5 ....316 F6
Napier Wk AND SP10 ....5 J2
Napoleon Av FARN GU14 .....58 A7
Napoleon Dr DEAN RG23 .....68 F5
Narrow La RGWD BH24 .....261 H9
Narvik Rd NWBY RG14 ....8 C6
Naseby Ri NWBY RG14 ....8 C6
Naseby Rd MOOR/WNTN BH9 .322 C6
Nash CI BSTK RG21 ....7 G2
FAWY SO45 ....267 P9
Nashe CI FHAM PO15 ....272 B7
Nashe Wy FHAM PO15 ......272 A8
Nash Mdw ODIM RG29 ....92 C7
Nash Rd FAWY SO45 ....267 P9
Nasmith CI
LSOL/BMARY PO13 .....315 H4
Nately Rd OVTN RG25 ....71 J3
Nations HI WINC SO23 ......145 J9
Navarino Ct LYMN SO41 *....329 M4
Navigator's Wy HEND SO30..250 C3
Navy Rd PSEA PO1 ....316 C2
Naylor Dr CHCH/BSGR BH23..325 P7
Neacroft CI NMIL/BTOS BH25 .326 F2
Nea Dr RGWD BH24 ....259 N5
Nea Rd CHCH/BSGR BH23 ..326 A7
Neath Rd BSTK RG21 ....7 J5
Needles Point LYMN SO41...338 C2
Neelands Gv CHAM PO6 ....296 A1
Neilson CI CHFD SO53 ......206 B6
Neilson Av WSHM SO15 ....247 N4
NEND PO2 ....3 J4
Nelson CI ASHV GU12 ....3 J4
FAWY SO45 ....290 E6
FHAM PO16 ....96 D3
NMIL/BTOS BH25.....327 H4
ROMY SO51 ....204 E5
STOK SO20 ....141 L5
Nelson CI FHAM/STUB PO14..294 B8
Nelson Crs HORN PO8 * 256 C1
Nelson Dr CHCH/BSGR BH23 .325 K9
Nelson Ga WSHM SO15 .....141 L5
Nelson La WHAM SO17 .....273 N7
Nelson PI LYMN SO41 ......329 M4
Nelson Rd BKME/WDN BH12..334 B2
ELGH SO50 ....207 J8
FNM GU9 ....96 C3
GPORT PO12 ....12 D3
PSEA PO1 ....316 D1
SSEA PO5 ....316 F7
WINC SO23 ....23 J6
Nelsons Gdns HEND SO30 ..230 C9
Nelson St ALDT GU11 ....2 D2
Nelson Wk AND SP10 ....5 J2
Nene CI AND SP10 * 82 G9
Nene Ct FARN GU14 ....75 H9
Nepaun CI GPORT PO12 ....315 M7
Neptune Rd BOR GU35 .....154 B6
FHAM PO15 ....294 D4
Neptune Wy SHAM SO14 ...248 D9

Nerissa CI WVILLE PO7 ......276 D2
Nerquis CI ROMY SO51 .....204 F5
Nesbitt CI LSOL/BMARY PO13..294 F6
Nessus St ENEY PO4 ....296 F9
Nestor CI AND SP10 ....4 A1
Netherfield CI ALTN GU34....132 E5
HAV PO9 ....15 J7
Netherhall Gdns WBNE BH4..334 C3
Nether Hill La BPWT SO32 ..251 H1
Netherhouse Moor
FLEETN GU51 ....74 B6
Netherton Rd GPORT PO12..315 K1
Nether Vell-Mead FLEETS GU52..74 B8
Netherwood PI WIMB BH21..278 C9
Netley Cliff HLER SO31 * 269 K5
Netley CI CHFD SO53 ....228 D1
PLE BH15 ....321 J5
Netley Firs Rd ITCH SO19 ...249 P7
Netley Hill Est ITCH SO19 *..249 P7
Netley Lodge CI HLER SO31 .269 L5
Netley Rd FHAM/STUB PO14 .271 J9
SSEA PO5 ....316 E6
Netley St FARN GU14 ....76 B4
Nettlebeds La NARL SO24....148 E6
Nettlestone HLER SO31 .....269 L3
Nettlestone Rd ENEY PO4 ...317 K6
Nettleton CI CFDH BH17 ....320 C5
Neuvic Wy WHCH RG28 ....85 M7
Nevada CI FARN GU14 ......321 J5
Neva Rd WEND SO18 ....249 H5
Neville Av FHAM/PORC PO16 .295 P5
Neville CI AND SP10 ....102 F4
BSTK RG21 ....90 D1
Neville Dr ROMY SO51 ......204 D4
Neville Duke Rd FARN GU14 ..57 N5
Neville Gdns EMRTH PO10 ..277 L7
Neville HSEA PO3 ....317 J1
Neville Shute Rd FARN GU14 .57 N5
Newall Rd RAND SP11 ......101 N5
Newball CI BWD BH11 *......56 F4
New Barn CI FLEETN GU51 ...74 A5
New Barn La ALTN GU34.....132 F7
RAND SP11 ....123 K1
Newbarn Rd EPSF GU31 ....237 J1
HAV PO9 ....276 C7
Newbold Rd NWBY RG14 .....24 A2
Newbolt CI HORN PO8 ......255 N8
NTHA RG18 ....25 M2
Newbolt Rd CHAM PO6 .....274 B9
New Borough Rd WIMB BH21.300 C2
New Br CHCH/BSGR BH23 ..323 N4
Newbridge HLER SO31 ......269 L4
New Bridge La BSTK RG21 ....7 K5
Newbridge Rd TOTT SO40 ..224 F9
New Brighton Rd
EMRTH PO10 ....277 M8
Newbroke Rd
LSOL/BMARY PO13 .....295 J8
Newbury CI ELGH SO50 .....230 B2
Newbury Dr NBNE BH10 ....322 D6
Newbury PI HLER SO31 .....270 F8
Newbury Rd AND SP10 ....82 F9
KSCL RG20 ....29 N7
WHCH RG28 ....85 L6
WSHM SO15 ....247 N2
Newbury St AND SP10 ....4 E4
BSTK RG21 ....85 L6
Newchurch Rd TADY RG26 ...34 B5
New Cliffe Gdns HEND SO30 .250 B6
Newcomb CI AND SP10 .....100 D5
Newcombe Rd FERN BH22 ..280 D6
SBNE BH6 ....324 C9
WSHM SO15 ....248 A5
Newcomen Rd NEND PO2 ...296 E7
Newcome PI ASHV GU12 .....92 F4
Newcome Rd FNM GU9 ......96 E4
PSEA PO1 ....316 C2
New Cottages Lane End
RWIN SO21 * 186 A6
New Crs RAND SP11 ....79 N2
Newcroft Gdns
CHCH/BSGR BH23 .....324 E7
New Cut HISD PO11 ....298 F6
New Dawn CI FARN GU14 ....75 L1
New Down La WVILLE PO7 ..275 J8
New Dro RAND SP11 ....79 N2
Newenham Rd LYMN SO41 ..329 L5
New Farm Rd NARL SO24....167 N2
Newfield Av FARN GU14 .....57 M7
Newfield Rd ASHV GU12 .....76 F6
LISS GU33 ....173 M9
New Forest Dr BROC SO42 ..286 D8
New Harbour Rd PLE BH15 .332 F2
New Harbour Rd South
PLE BH15 ....332 D3
New House La AND SP11 .....80 G4
New Inn La BROC SO42 ......310 C3
New Inn Rd TOTT SO40 .....245 H5
New La ANGL GU14 * 329 L5
FARN GU14 ....58 C7
NMIL/BTOS BH25.....327 K7
New Lane CI PLE BH15 * 19 H7
LIPH GU30 ....175 K4
NWBY RG14 ....16 E6
New La HAV PO9 ....15 H4

LYMN SO41 ....339 J3
NMIL/BTOS BH25 ....327 H1
STOK SO20 ....161 M5
Newlease Rd WVILLE PO7 ...275 P5
Newlyn Wk ROMY SO51 .....204 F5
Newlyn Wy BKME/WDN BH12 .321 N5
CHAM PO6 ....296 C2
Newman La ALTN GU34 .....133 H4
Newmans CI FERN BH22 ....280 E4
Newmans Copse Rd
TOTT SO40 ....246 E7
Newmans Ct FNM GU9 ......96 A5
Newman Rd MHOP17 ....252 C3
Newman's La FERN BH22 ...280 C4
Newman St ROWN SO16....247 M5
Newmarket CI ELGH SO50 ..230 D5
Newmer Ct HAV PO9 ....277 H7
New Merrifield WIMB BH21 ..278 C7
New Mill La HTWY RG27 .....39 H4
New Mill Rd HTWY RG27 .....39 H4
Newmorton Rd
MOOR/WNTN BH9 ....322 G3
Newney CI NEND PO2 ....297 H5
Newnham Ct HAV PO9 * 277 H5
Newnham La CHIN RG24 .....70 E4
HTWY RG27 ....71 K3
Newnham Pk HTWY RG27 ...71 M4
Newnham Rd HTWY RG27 ...71 L4
New Odiham Rd ALTN GU34..133 J5
New Orch PLE BH15 ....332 D1
New Paddock CI ALTN GU34 .133 J3
New Pde NBNE BH10 * 322 E2
New Park Rd SBNE BH6 ....336 A2
Newport CI CHFD SO53 .....206 C9
NWBY RG14 ....24 E3
Newport La ROMY SO51 ....180 F8
Newport Rd ASHV GU12 ......3 J5
GPORT PO12 ....315 K3
NWBY RG14 ....24 E3
New Quay Rd PLE BH15 ....332 C2
New Rd BKME/WDN BH12....321 N6
BLKW GU17 ....153 P7
BPWT SO32 ....232 D8
BPWT SO32 ....232 D8
BSTK RG21 ....7 F7
CWTH RG45 ....41 K1
ELGH SO50 ....230 D2
EMRTH PO10 ....277 P7
FAWY SO45 ....290 C8
FBDG SP6 ....219 L3
FERN BH22 ....302 D3
FHAM/PORC PO16.......302 E8
FHAM/PORC PO16.......11 F5
FLEETS GU52 ....74 E6
FUFL SO22 ....164 B1
HASM GU27 ....156 E8
HAV PO9 ....14 C4
HLER SO31 ....269 K4
HLER SO31 ....270 F2
HLER SO31 ....271 J8
HORN PO8 ....256 F5
HORN PO8 ....255 N5
HTWY RG27 ....71 P3
LYMN SO41 ....339 K2
NBNE BH10 ....322 E2
NEND PO2 ....316 C1
NTHA RG18 ....17 G5
ODIM RG29 ....72 B8
RFNM GU10 ....97 M5
RGWD BH24 ....260 A7
ROMY SO51 ....204 E5
RSAL SP5 ....223 N3
RWIN SO21 ....107 H8
RWIN SO21 ....207 N4
SHAM SO14 ....20 E3
SHST GU47 ....41 H6
STOK SO20 ....120 C9
STOK SO20 ....34 B7
TADY RG26 ....50 F2
THLE RG7 ....27 M7
TOTT SO40 ....246 A4
WEND SO18 ....258 A3
New Rd East NEND PO2 ....297 H9
Newstead Rd SBNE BH6....336 B2
New St AND SP10 ....4 E1
BSTK RG21 ....7 E7
LYMN SO41 ....329 L3
PLE BH15 ....332 D1
RGWD BH24 ....282 E3
STOK SO20 ....141 L6
THLE RG7 ....36 F6
Newton CI FHAM/STUB PO14..294 A5
RSAL SP5 ....201 J2
Newton La ALTN GU34 ......151 M8
ROMY SO51 ....204 C6
RSAL SP5 ....200 F5
Newton Morrell PSTN BH14..321 N9
Newton PI LSOL/BMARY PO13..314 C1
Newton Rd CCLF BH13 .....333 N3
FARN GU14 ....58 C7
NMIL/BTOS BH25.....327 K7
RWIN SO21 ....184 A7
WEND SO18 ....248 C2
Newton VIs RFNM GU10 * 80 E2
Newton Wy RFNM GU10 ......97 L4
New Town
FHAM/PORC PO16.......295 P1
Newtown TADY RG26 ....34 B6
Newtown CI AND SP10 ......102 C5
Newtown La HISD PO11 .....318 E4
RGWD BH24 ....260 B8
Newtown Rd ELGH SO50 ....207 J9
HLER SO31 ....292 C1
ITCH SO19 ....249 J2
LIPH GU30 ....175 K4
NWBY RG14 ....16 E6
ROMY SO51 ....203 H2

SHST GU47 41 J6
VWD BH31 258 G4
New Valley Rd LYMN SO41 338 F2
New Vis KSCL RG20 * 29 J3
Nexus Pk ASHV GU12 76 E4
Nicholas Cl CHCH/BSGR BH23 326 D5
Nicholas Crs FHAM PO15 10 C4
Nicholas Gdns NBNE BH10 322 C5
Nicholas Rd FAWY SO45 312 G1
Nicholl Pl LSOL/BMARY PO13 294 G7
Nichol Rd CHFD SO53 206 F4
Nicholson Cl CFDH BH17 320 G4
Nicholson Wk ROWN SO16 227 H6
Nicholson Wy HAV PO9 14 E2
Nichols Rd SHAM SO14 21 G2
Nickel Cl WINC SO23 23 H3
Nickel St SSEA PO5 19 F7
Nickleby Gdns TOTT SO40 245 P4
Nickleby Rd HORN PO8 236 B6
Nickson Cl CHFD SO53 206 D5
Nideggan Cl STHA RG19 25 N4
Nightingale Av ELGH SO50 228 F2
Nightingale Cl FARN GU14 57 K7
FUFL SO22 164 C9
GPORT PO12 315 K2
HAV PO9 276 G1
ROMY SO51 204 E6
VWD BH31 258 G5
Nightingale Ct EMRTH PO10 277 P6
Nightingale Crs BPWT SO32 252 D3
Nightingale Dr FRIM GU16 76 F1
TOTT SO40 246 A3
Nightingale Gdns CHIN RG24 68 F4
HTWY RG27 71 P3
SHST GU47 41 J6
Nightingale Gv WSHM SO15 247 N4
Nightingale La THLE RG7 27 M9
Nightingale Pk HAV PO9 15 K6
Nightingale Ri OVTN RG25 87 H4
Nightingale Rd ASHV GU12 77 H9
BOR GU35 154 B6
HLER SO31 269 P2
PSF GU32 215 K3
SSEA PO5 316 D6
The Nightingales NWBY RG14 17 G7
Nightingale Wk HLER SO31 269 L6
Nightjar Cl CFDH BH17 320 A4
HORN PO8 256 A5
RFNM GU10 95 M3
Nile Rd PTSW SO17 248 C1
Nile St EMRTH PO10 299 M1
Nimrod Dr LSOL/BMARY PO13 315 H2
Nimrod Wy WIMB BH21 279 P8
Nine Elms La WHAM PO17 273 J6
Ninian Cl ELGH SO50 230 C3
Ninian Park Rd HSEA PO3 297 J7
Niton Cl LSOL/BMARY PO13 294 G7
Noads Cl FAWY SO45 268 B8
Noads Wy FAWY SO45 268 B8
Nobbs La PSEA PO1 18 D5
Nobes Av LSOL/BMARY PO13 294 G6
Nobes Cl LSOL/BMARY PO13 295 H7
Noble Cl BWD BH11 321 P3
Noble Rd HEND SO30 250 D5
Nob's Crook RWIN SO21 208 A6
Noctule Ct WHAM PO17 272 B2
Noel Cl BROC SO42 286 G8
Noel Rd NBNE BH10 322 B6
Nogarth Cl ROMY SO51 204 F4
Nomad Cl WEND SO18 249 K2
The Nook ELGH SO50 207 K8
LSOL/BMARY PO13 295 J8
Noon Gdns VWD BH31 259 H4
Noon Hill Dr VWD BH31 259 H4
Noon Hill Rd VWD BH31 259 H4
Norbury Cl CHFD SO53 206 D6
Norbury Gdns HLER SO31 269 N8
Norcliffe Cl BWD BH11 322 B4
Norcliffe Rd PTSW SO17 248 C3
Norden Cl BSTK RG21 7 F3
Nordik Gdns HEND SO30 250 C6
Nore Crs EMRTH PO10 277 K9
Nore Farm Av EMRTH PO10 277 K9
Noreuil Rd PSF GU32 215 K2
Norfolk Av CHCH/BSGR BH23 324 D6
Norfolk Rd GPORT PO12 315 K1
WSHM SO15 247 P3
Norfolk St SSEA PO5 19 G6
Norgett Wy
FHAM/PORC PO16 295 M3
Norham Av ROWN SO16 247 N1
Norham Cl ROWN SO16 247 N1
Norland Rd ENEY PO4 * 316 G5
Norlands NTHA RG18 25 M2
Norlands Dr RWIN SO21 207 L1
Norley Cl HAV PO9 276 E5
Norleywood
CHCH/BSGR BH23 326 B7
Norleywood Rd LYMN SO41 310 B7
Norman Av BKME/WDN BH12 321 P6
Norman Cl BOR GU35 154 B5
FHAM/PORC PO16 295 P3
Norman Court La RAND SP11 102 D6
Normandy Cl FRIM GU16 59 K5
LYMN SO41 308 A6
ROWN SO16 227 H6
Normandy Common La
RGUW GU3 77 N8
Normandy Dr
CHCH/BSGR BH23 325 H8
Normandy Gdns GPORT PO12 315 K4
Normandy La LYMN SO41 329 M5
Normandy Rd NEND PO2 296 F5
Normandy St ALTN GU34 132 G5
Normandy Wy FBDG SP6 240 C1
TOTT SO40 247 K8
Norman Gdns
BKME/WDN BH12 322 A9
HEND SO30 250 A6
Normanhurst Av CHAR BH8 323 K6
Norman Rd ENEY PO4 316 G5
FAWY SO45 291 H9
GPORT PO12 315 L3
HISD PO11 319 H6
WINC SO23 164 G9
WSHM SO15 247 P6
Normanton Cl
CHCH/BSGR BH23 324 D6
Normanton Rd BSTK RG21 69 L4
Norman Wy HAV PO9 276 C8
Normay Ri NWBY RG14 30 B1
Normoor Rd THLE RG7 27 H6
Norn Hl BSTK RG21 7 H3
Norn Hill Cl BSTK RG21 7 H3
Norris Br FARN GU14 75 H4
Norris Cl BOR GU35 153 N7
RGWD BH24 281 L5
ROMY SO51 204 G3
Norris Gdns HAV PO9 15 J7
NMIL/BTOS BH25 327 J6
RWIN SO21 144 E4
Norris Hl WEND SO18 248 G2
Norris Hill Rd FLEETS GU52 74 G5
Norrish Rd BKME/WDN BH12 321 L7
Norset Rd FHAM PO15 272 A8
Northam Br WEND SO18 248 E5
Northam Ms PSEA PO1 * 19 J2
Northampton La FAWY SO45 290 G9
Northam Rd SHAM SO14 21 H2
Northam St PSEA PO1 19 K2
Northanger Cl ALTN GU34 132 E5
Northarbour Rd CHAM PO6 296 F2
North Av FNM GU9 96 D4
NBNE BH10 322 D1
NEND PO2 296 G4
North Battery Rd NEND PO2 296 D7
North Bay EMRTH PO10 299 N6
Northbourne Av NBNE BH10 322 D3
Northbourne Cl FAWY SO45 268 C9
Northbourne Gdns NBNE BH10 322 E2
Northbourne Pl NBNE BH10 322 D2
Northbrook Av WINC SO23 23 H5
Northbrook Cl PSEA PO1 316 F1
WINC SO23 23 J5
Northbrook Rd ALDT GU11 3 F6
BDST BH18 320 C2
SHAM SO14 21 G2
Northbrook St NWBY RG14 16 E1
North Charford Crossing
FBDG SP6 199 H9
North Charford Dro
FBDG SP6 198 B6
North Cl ASHV GU12 97 L2
FARN GU14 57 P5
GPORT PO12 315 K4
HAV PO9 15 H7
LYMN SO41 329 M3
ROMY SO51 204 G4
North Common La
LYMN SO41 308 F9
RSAL SP5 201 K7
Northcote Av NEND PO2 297 H9
Northcote Rd ASHV GU12 76 F5
BMTH BH1 9 J1
ENEY PO4 316 G5
FARN GU14 57 M7
PTSW SO17 248 E1
North Crs HISD PO11 319 H5
Northcroft La NWBY RG14 16 C1
Northcroft Rd GPORT PO12 315 K2
Northcroft Ter NWBY RG14 16 D2
North Cross St GPORT PO12 13 H2
Northdene Rd CHFD SO53 206 E8
North Downs Wy RFNM GU10 96 G9
North Dr CHOB/PIR GU24 59 P7
FERN BH22 * 281 H9
FUFL SO22 164 C2
NMIL/BTOS BH25 306 G7
North East Cl ITCH SO19 249 K6
North East Rd ITCH SO19 249 J7
North End Av NEND PO2 296 F7
North End Cl CHFD SO53 206 E9
North End Gv NEND PO2 296 F7
Northend La BPWT SO32 233 L2
North End La FBDG SP6 240 B7
NARL SO24 168 A8
Northern Access Rd
FAWY SO45 291 M7
Northern Anchorage
ITCH SO19 248 F8
Northern Av AND SP10 4 D2
NWBY RG14 24 D1
Northern Pde NEND PO2 296 F6
Northern Rd CHAM PO6 297 H1
Northerwood Av LYND SO43 264 E5
Northerwood Cl NBAD SO52 205 K9
Northey Rd SBNE BH6 324 C9
North Farm Rd FARN GU14 57 M5
North Fld OVTN RG25 86 G2
Northfield Av
FHAM/STUB PO14 294 D2
Northfield Cl ASHV GU12 97 K2
BPWT SO32 231 N3
FLEETS GU52 * 74 E6
HORN PO8 256 C1
Northfield La ALTN GU34 132 G9
Northfield Pk
FHAM/PORC PO16 * 273 M9
Northfield Rd FLEETS GU52 74 E6
HTWY RG27 52 E4
LYMN SO41 339 H1
NTHA RG18 25 L3
RGWD BH24 260 E9
WEND SO18 229 H9
Northfields Farm La
WHAM PO17 252 E6
North Front SHAM SO14 20 E3
North Fryerne YTLY GU46 40 E6
Northgate Av NEND PO2 317 H1
Northgate La OVTN RG25 110 D1
North Gate Rd FARN GU14 76 A2
Northgate Wy KBH RG22 89 L5
North Greenlands LYMN SO41 329 J5
North Head LYMN SO41 338 D1
North Hl CHAM PO6 274 D8
FHAM/PORC PO16 11 G1
North Hill Cl FUFL SO22 164 C5
Northington Rd NARL SO24 147 H2
RWIN SO21 146 G7
Northlands Cl TOTT SO40 246 B3
Northlands Dr WINC SO23 165 H5
Northlands Gdns WSHM SO15 248 A4
Northlands Rd ELGH SO50 229 J1
ROMY SO51 204 G7
TOTT SO40 246 B3
WSHM SO15 248 A4
North La ALDT GU11 3 K1
BROC SO42 289 J4
EPSF GU31 215 L8
EPSF GU31 216 F9
HORN PO8 236 B3
HORN PO8 236 B6
RSAL SP5 159 H5
RSAL SP5 223 L5
Northleigh Cnr WEND SO18 * 228 G7
Northleigh La WIMB BH21 278 G8
North Ldg FBDG SP6 * 239 M3
North Lodge Rd PSTN BH14 321 N8
Northmead FARN GU14 58 A9
Northmead Dr CFDH BH17 320 B4
Northmere Dr
BKME/WDN BH12 321 P5
Northmere Rd
BKME/WDN BH12 321 N6
North Millers Dl CHFD SO53 206 C4
Northmore Cl HLER SO31 271 H5
Northmore Rd HLER SO31 271 H5
Northney La HISD PO11 299 J5
Northney Rd HISD PO11 298 G4
Northolt Gdns ROWN SO16 227 L8
Northover La LYMN SO41 307 N9
Northover Rd HSEA PO3 297 K9
LYMN SO41 328 G3
North Pde BOR GU35 153 P2
North Poulner Rd
RGWD BH24 260 F8
North Rd ALDT GU11 76 C5
ASHV GU12 76 E8
BROC SO42 286 G8
FAWY SO45 267 P8
HORN PO8 256 C1
LTDN BH7 335 L1
PLE BH15 332 C1
PSF GU32 215 M1
PSTN BH14 321 J8
PTSW SO17 248 E3
WINC SO23 145 K7
WVILLE PO7 274 C8
North Rd East WHAM PO17 274 C4
North Rd West WHAM PO17 274 B4
North Shore Rd HISD PO11 318 D4
North Side RFNM GU10 97 N4
Northside La NARL SO24 148 G9
North Sq WHAM PO17 272 C3
North St EMRTH PO10 277 M9
HAV PO9 14 B4
HAV PO9 15 G5
KSCL RG20 48 C3
LYMN SO41 329 J5
NARL SO24 168 E2
PLE BH15 332 E1
PSEA PO1 18 D2
North Street Ar HAV PO9 15 G4
North Stroud La PSF GU32 214 E3
North Town RWIN SO21 184 A7
North Trestle Rd FAWY SO45 291 K3
Northumberland Rd
BOR GU35 154 A7
SHAM SO14 21 H2
North Vw FUFL SO22 22 B3
North View Rd TADY RG26 34 E7
North Wallington
FHAM/PORC PO16 11 K3
North Walls WINC SO23 23 G4
North Warnborough St
ODIM RG29 72 A9
North Wy AND SP10 83 J9
HAV PO9 14 E3
Northway FHAM PO15 271 L7
NTHA RG18 25 M2
NWBY RG14 17 G4
Northways FHAM/STUB PO14 294 B7
North Weirs BROC SO42 286 D8
Northwick HTWY RG27 39 P7
Northwood Cl ROWN SO16 228 C6
Northwood Dr NWBY RG14 24 F3
Northwood La HISD PO11 298 G8
Northwood Rd NEND PO2 296 G5
Northwood Sq
FHAM/PORC PO16 11 G4
Nortoft Rd CHAR BH8 323 H9
Norton Cl CHCH/BSGR BH23 325 H8
ITCH SO19 248 G8
WHAM PO17 274 B4
WVILLE PO7 275 M3
Norton Dr FHAM/PORC PO16 10 E2
Norton Ride CHIN RG24 70 A5
Norton Rd CBLY GU15 59 H1
MOOR/WNTN BH9 322 E6
THLE RG7 37 P4
WHAM PO17 274 B4
Norton Wy PLE BH15 332 C2
Norton Welch Cl NBAD SO52 205 M9
Norway Rd HSEA PO3 297 J5
Norwich Av CBLY GU15 58 D2
WCLF BH2 8 A3
Norwich Av West WBNE BH4 334 D3
Norwich Cl HLER SO31 270 E6
KBH RG22 89 M4
Norwich Pl
LSOL/BMARY PO13 314 C1
Norwich Rd CHAM PO6 274 F9
WCLF BH2 8 B4
WEND SO18 249 H1
Norwood Pl BOSC BH5 335 P1
Nottingham Pl
LSOL/BMARY PO13 314 C1
Nouale La RGWD BH24 283 H2
Novello Cl KBH RG22 89 P4
Novello Gdns WVILLE PO7 275 N5
Noyce Dr ELGH SO50 230 D3
Noyce Gdns CHAR BH8 323 P5
Nuffield Dr SHST GU47 41 N5
Nuffield Rd CFDH BH17 320 F5
Nugee Ct CWTH RG45 41 J1
Nugent Rd SBNE BH6 336 D2
Nunns Pk RSAL SP5 201 K1
Nuns Rd WINC SO23 23 F1
Nuns Wk WINC SO23 23 F1
Nunton Dro RSAL SP5 198 B1
Nursery Cl CHIN RG24 70 B1
EMRTH PO10 277 M7
FLEETN GU51 74 G4
FRIM GU16 58 E6
HTWY RG27 71 P2
LSOL/BMARY PO13 294 F6
Nursery Fld LISS GU33 192 C3
Nursery Gdns CHFD SO53 228 E1
FUFL SO22 164 E7
HORN PO8 256 A6
ITCH SO19 249 K5
ROMY SO51 204 E6
Nursery Gv HEND SO30 250 C6
Nursery La FHAM/STUB PO14 294 A8
Nursery Rd ALTN GU34 132 G5
HAV PO9 276 C8
MOOR/WNTN BH9 322 G4
NARL SO24 168 A2
RGWD BH24 282 E3
WEND SO18 248 F2
Nursery Ter ODIM RG29 * 72 B8
Nursling Crs HAV PO9 276 G5
Nursling Gn CHAR BH8 323 K5
Nursling St ROWN SO16 226 G7
Nutash FHAM PO15 271 J6
Nutbane Cl AND SP10 102 B3
Nutbane La RAND SP11 81 M4
Nutbean La THLE RG7 38 C1
Nutbeem Rd ELGH SO50 229 J2
Nutbourne FNM GU9 96 E4
Nutbourne Rd CHAM PO6 297 M2
HISD PO11 319 L7
Nutburn Rd NBAD SO52 205 M9
Nutchers Dro STOK SO20 161 M4
Nutcombe La GSHT GU26 156 D4
Nutfield Ct ROWN SO16 227 J9
Nutfield Pl PSEA PO1 316 F2
Nutfield Rd ROWN SO16 227 H6
Nuthatch Cl CFDH BH17 320 B5
FERN BH22 280 B9
HAV PO9 277 H1
KBH RG22 89 K4
RFNM GU10 95 M4
Nutley Cl BOR GU35 154 A6
BWD BH11 301 P9
YTLY GU46 40 E9
Nutley La OVTN RG25 109 K1
Nutley Rd HAV PO9 276 D5
Nutley Wy BWD BH11 321 P1
Nutmeg Ct FARN GU14 57 K8
Nutsey Av TOTT SO40 246 B1
Nutsey La TOTT SO40 246 C1
Nutshalling Av ROWN SO16 227 J7
Nutshalling Cl TOTT SO40 246 A1
Nutshell La FNM GU9 96 C5
Nutwick Rd HAV PO9 277 H7
Nutwood Wy TOTT SO40 246 C1
Nyewood Av
FHAM/PORC PO16 273 P9
Nyria Wy GPORT PO12 13 G3

O

Oakapple Gdns CHAM PO6 297 N1
Oak Av CHCH/BSGR BH23 324 B7
SHST GU47 41 L5
Oak Bank AND SP10 4 D7
Oakbank Rd ELGH SO50 229 L1
ITCH SO19 248 F8
Oak Cl BPWT SO32 209 M8
BSTK RG21 7 K6
DEAN RG23 88 F2
FAWY SO45 268 A9
FERN BH22 302 E7
HORN PO8 255 N9
KSCL RG20 48 D3
LYND SO43 * 264 F6
NTID SP9 79 J4
OVTN RG25 86 G4
STOK SO20 121 H5
TADY RG26 33 N6
WSHM SO15 246 G4
Oak Coppice Cl ELGH SO50 230 A2
Oak Ct FNM GU9 116 B1
LYMN SO41 * 329 J5
Oakcroft La
FHAM/STUB PO14 294 A4
Oakdale Rd PLE BH15 320 G6
Oakdene ALTN GU34 132 E4
LSOL/BMARY PO13 295 H8
THLE RG7 27 J4
TOTT SO40 245 P4
Oakdene Cl WIMB BH21 278 F9
Oakdown Rd
FHAM/STUB PO14 294 B6
Oak Dr ELGH SO50 230 C2
NWBY RG14 16 C4
THLE RG7 27 H5
Oakenbrow FAWY SO45 267 P8
LYMN SO41 308 A5
Oaken Copse FLEETS GU52 74 E8
Oaken Copse Crs FARN GU14 58 A6
Oaken Gv NWBY RG14 24 A7
The Oakes FHAM/STUB PO14 293 P5
Oak Farm Cl BLKW GU17 41 K9
Oakfield Ct HAV PO9 * 277 H5
Oakfield Pl FARN GU14 57 K9
Oakfield Rd BLKW GU17 57 M1
PLE BH15 320 E6
TADY RG26 34 F5
TOTT SO40 245 H4
TOTT SO40 246 D4
Oakfields ELGH SO50 207 J6
Oakfields Cl KSCL RG20 47 L1
Oak Gdns LYMN SO41 328 D7
Oak Gn ALTN GU34 * 150 D5
Oak Green Wy WEND SO18 249 J3
Oak Grove Crs CBLY GU15 41 N8
Oakgrove Rd ELGH SO50 229 N2
Oak Hanger Cl HTWY RG27 72 A3
Oakhanger Rd BOR GU35 153 M3
Oakhill HLER SO31 270 B1
Oak Hl NARL SO24 168 A3
Oakhill Cl CHFD SO53 206 G8
HLER SO31 270 B1
Oakhill Ct CHFD SO53 206 G8
Oakhill Rd BOR GU35 155 J3
Oakhurst GSHT GU26 156 C2
Oakhurst Cl FERN BH22 280 F7
HLER SO31 269 L4
Oakhurst Dr WVILLE PO7 276 A2
Oakhurst Gdns CHAM PO6 275 K8
Oakhurst La FERN BH22 280 F7
Oakhurst Rd FERN BH22 280 F8
PTSW SO17 228 C9
Oakhurst Wy HLER SO31 269 L4
Oakland Av FNM GU9 96 E4
Oakland Dr TOTT SO40 267 K1
Oakland Rd WHCH RG28 85 L6
Oaklands HASM GU27 157 H6
HTWY RG27 55 H8
LYMN SO41 329 M5
RWIN SO21 144 E4
YTLY GU46 40 E8
Oaklands Av TOTT SO40 246 D4
Oaklands Cl FBDG SP6 240 C1
FUFL SO22 164 C9
VWD BH31 258 E4
Oaklands Gdns
FHAM/STUB PO14 271 J9
Oaklands Gv HORN PO8 255 N8
Oaklands Rd HAV PO9 15 J5
PSF GU32 215 L1
The Oaklands CHFD SO53 228 D1
Oaklands Wy DEAN RG23 68 F6
FAWY SO45 267 N8
FHAM/STUB PO14 271 J9
ROWN SO16 228 B8
Oakland Wk FERN BH22 302 E7
Oak La RGWD BH24 282 F1
Oaklea ASHV GU12 76 F7
Oaklea Dr HTWY RG27 39 H4
Oaklea Gdns TADY RG26 52 C3
Oakleigh Crs TOTT SO40 246 C5
Oakleigh Dr RSAL SP5 223 M3
Oakleigh Gdns ROMY SO51 204 E6
Oakleigh Wy
CHCH/BSGR BH23 326 B8
Oakley Cl FAWY SO45 290 E5
Oakley Dr FLEETN GU51 74 D4
Oakley Hl WIMB BH21 300 F2
Oakley La DEAN RG23 88 F1
WIMB BH21 301 H3
Oakley Rd BOR GU35 154 A3
CBLY GU15 58 A1
HAV PO9 276 D5
NWBY RG14 24 G3
ROMY SO51 179 L4
ROWN SO16 247 K3
TADY RG26 66 E1
WIMB BH21 300 F3
Oakley Straight WIMB BH21 300 G4
Oak Ldg HASM GU27 * 157 K9
Oakmead TADY RG26 51 P1
Oakmead Gdns BWD BH11 301 N9
Oakmeadow Cl EMRTH PO10 277 N7
Oakmead Rd CFDH BH17 320 B5
Oakmont Dr WVILLE PO7 255 P9
Oakmount Av CHFD SO53 206 F9
PTSW SO17 248 C2
TOTT SO40 246 D3
Oakmount Rd CHFD SO53 206 F9
Oak Park Dr HAV PO9 15 H2
Oakridge Centre BSTK RG21 7 G1
Oak Ridge Cl NWBY RG14 24 B7
Oakridge Rd BSTK RG21 6 B1
WSHM SO15 247 H3
Oak Rd BPWT SO32 232 B4
CHAR BH8 323 J9
FARN GU14 76 B1
FAWY SO45 268 A9
FBDG SP6 239 M6
FHAM PO15 272 B8
HLER SO31 269 N2
HORN PO8 236 C7
ITCH SO19 248 F9
NMIL/BTOS BH25 327 L4
Oaks Coppice HORN PO8 256 A5
Oaks Dr RGWD BH24 281 K6
Oakshott Dr HAV PO9 276 G5
Oaks Md VWD BH31 * 258 F4
The Oaks ALTN GU34 150 B1
AND SP10 * 102 C2
FLEETN GU51 74 A3
HLER SO31 269 P2
ITCH SO19 249 H6
TADY RG26 34 B6
VWD BH31 258 E3
YTLY GU46 40 E9
Oak St GPORT PO12 13 F2
Oakthorn Cl
LSOL/BMARY PO13 314 G2
Oak Tree Cl ASHV GU12 76 E3
ASHV GU12 97 K3
BOR GU35 154 G4
RWIN SO21 207 P5
TADY RG26 34 C5
Oaktree Ct LYMN SO41 338 F2
Oak Tree Dr EMRTH PO10 277 L6
HTWY RG27 72 A2
LISS GU33 192 E2
Oak Tree Gdns HEND SO30 250 B5
Oak Tree La HASM GU27 156 C7
Oak Tree Rd BOR GU35 153 P7
STHA RG19 25 P5
WEND SO18 248 F2
Oaktrees ASHV GU12 97 M2
FNM GU9 96 B5
Oak Tree Ter AND SP10 * 4 E4
Oak Tree Vw FNM GU9 96 D5
Oak Tree Wy ELGH SO50 207 J8
Oaktree Wy SHST GU47 41 H5

Oak V HEND SO30 ....229 K9
Oakway ASHV GU12....97 K3
  RFNM GU10 ....114 E6
Oakway Dr FRIM GU16....58 D4
Oakwood CHIN RG24....70 A1
  FLEETS GU51....74 D8
Oakwood Av HAV PO9....276 B7
  NMIL/BTOS BH25....327 L3
  RWIN SO51....207 L2
Oakwood Cl CHFD SO53....206 A4
  HLER SO31....292 E1
  MOOR/WNTN BH9....323 H5
  ROMY SO51....204 C4
  RWIN SO51....207 L1
Oakwood Ct HEND SO30....249 N1
Oakwood Dr ALTN GU34 *....132 E6
  ROWN SO16....227 N7
Oakwood Rd
  CHCH/BSGR BH23....326 B6
  CHFD SO53....206 F5
  HISD PO11....318 F5
  MOOR/WNTN BH9....322 C5
Oakwood Wy HLER SO31....270 A7
Oasthouse Dr FLEETN GU51....56 F9
Oast House La FNM SO30....96 D6
Oast La ALDT GU11....97 M7
Oates Rd MOOR/WNTN BH9....322 E2
Oatfield Gdns TOTT SO40....246 A2
Oatlands ROMY SO51....204 D5
Oatlands Cl BPWT SO32....250 F2
Oatlands Rd BPWT SO32....250 F2
Oatsheaf Pde FLEETS GU51 *....74 C4
Oban Cl DEAN RG23....88 E1
Oban Rd TWDS BH3....322 E8
O'Bee Gdns TADY RG26....34 A5
Obelisk Rd ITCH SO19....248 F9
Oberfield Rd BROC SO42....286 D7
Oberon Cl WVILLE PO7....276 A2
Ober Rd BROC SO42....286 E7
Oberursel Wy ALDT GU11....2 C2
Occupation La
  FHAM/STUB PO14....293 L2
Ocean Cl FHAM PO15....272 B8
Oceania Crs DEAN RG23....89 K7
Ocean Pk HSEA PO3 *....297 K8
Ocean Rd FHAM/STUB PO14....
  SHAM SO14....268 C1
Ocean Wy SHAM SO14....248 D9
Ochil Cl KBH RG22....68 E9
Ockendon Cl ELCH SO50....19 G5
Ocknell Gv FAWY SO45....267 N7
O'Connell Rd ELCH SO50....228 G2
O'Connor Rd ALDT GU11....76 C5
Octavia Gdns CHFD SO53....207 H6
Octavia Cl FUFL SO22....164 E9
Octavia Rd WEND SO18....228 G8
Octavius Ct WVILLE PO7....276 B1
Oddfellows Rd NWBY RG14....16 D5
Odell Cl FHAM/PORC PO16....10 C1
Odette Gdns TADY RG26....34 C5
Odiham Cl ROWN SO16....227 K8
Odiham Rd HTWY RG27....38 A5
  HTWY RG27....72 F5
  RFNM GU10....95 K3
  THLE RG7....37 P3
Officers Rw TADY RG26....52 C3
Oglander Rd WINC SO23....165 H5
Ogle Rd SHAM SO14....20 D4
O'Gorman Av FARN GU14....76 A2
Okeford Rd BDST BH18....320 D2
Okement Cl WVILLE PO7....249 N1
Okingham Cl SHST GU47....41 L5
Olaf Cl AND SP10....82 F7
Olave Cl LSOL/BMARY PO13 *....314 C2
Old Acre Rd ALTN GU34....120 C7
Old Agwi Rd FAWY SO45....291 L4
Old Barn Cl CHCH/BSGR BH23....324 B5
  OVTN RG25....108 C1
  RGWD BH24....282 G2
Oldbarn Cl TOTT SO40....246 A1
Old Barn Crs WVILLE PO7....254 E1
Old Barn Farm Rd
  WIMB BH21....280 C4
Old Barn La RFNM GU10....137 H7
Old Barn Rd
  CHCH/BSGR BH23....324 B5
Old Basing MI BSTK RG21....7 F5
Old Bath Rd NWBY RG14....24 B3
Old Beggarwood La
  DEAN RG23....89 L6
Oldberg Gdns KBH RG22....90 B3
Old Bisley Rd FLEETS GU51....58 F3
Old Brickfield Rd ALDT GU11....97 H4
Old Brickyard Rd FBDG SP6....239 P1
Old Bridge House Rd
  HLER SO31....270 B2
Old Bridge Rd ENEY PO4....316 D6
  LTDN BH7....324 B7
Oldbury Cl FRIM GU16....58 E5
Oldbury Ct ROWN SO16....247 H1
Oldbury Wy
  FHAM/STUB PO14....294 A1
Old Canal ENEY PO4 *....317 K4
Old Canal Pl BSTK RG21....7 K5
Old Chapel La ASHV GU12....97 N1
Old Christchurch Rd
  BMTH BH1....8 E3
  LYMN SO41....328 D6
Old Church La FNM GU9....116 D3
Old Coach Rd NTID SP9....99 K2
Old Coastguard Rd
  CCLF BH13....333 K7
Old Commercial Rd
  NEND PO2....316 E1
Old Common HLER SO31....270 C6
Old Common Gdns
  HLER SO31....270 C7
Old Common Rd BSTK RG21....69 H8
Old Common Wy RAND SP11....79 P1
Old Compton La FNM GU9....116 E1
Old Copse Rd HAV PO9....276 F5
Oldcorne Hollow HTWY RG27....40 B9
Old Cove Rd FLEETN GU51....74 E1

Old Cracknore Cl TOTT SO40....247 K9
Old Cricket Ms WSHM SO15....248 B3
Old Down RWIN SO21....185 H7
Old Down Cl ALTN RG22....89 L2
Old Down Rd AND SP10....4 A1
Olde Farm Dr BLKW GU17....41 J9
Oldenburg HLER SO31....271 H2
Old English Dr AND SP10....82 D7
Old Farm Cl RCWD BH24....260 G8
Old Farm Dr WEND SO18....249 H1
Old Farm La EMRTH PO10....277 P7
  FHAM/STUB PO14....294 A8
Old Farm Pl ASHV GU12....76 E8
Old Farm Rd PLE BH15....320 C6
Old Farm Wk LYMN SO41....329 K4
Old Farm Wy CHAM PO6....297 N2
Old Farnham La FNM GU9....116 C2
Oldfield Vw HTWY RG27....55 H8
The Old Flour MI
  EMRTH PO10 *....299 N1
Old Forge End SHST GU47....41 J7
Old Forge Gdns STOK SO20 *....140 A9
Old Forge Rd WIMB BH21....279 P8
Old Foundry Mews HTWY RG27....11 J5
Old Frensham Rd RFNM GU10....116 D4
Old Garden Cl
  FHAM/STUB PO14....271 J8
Old Gdns FUFL SO22....164 G5
Oldgate Gdns NEND PO2 *....297 H5
Old Gosport Rd
  FHAM/PORC PO16....294 F1
Old Guildford Rd FRIM GU16....58 G8
Old Ham La WIMB BH21....301 M1
Old Haslemere Rd
  HASM GU27....157 H9
Old Heath Wy FNM GU9 *....96 C4
Old Hillside Rd FUFL SO22....164 D6
The Old HI RAND SP11....123 K3
Oldhouse La RFNM GU10....202 E6
The Old Iron Foundry
  STOK SO20....161 L4
Old Ivy La WEND SO18....249 K1
Old Kempshott La KBH RG22....68 D9
Old Kennels Cl FUFL SO22....183 J3
Old Kennels La RWIN SO21....182 G5
Old Kiln Cl RFNM GU10....136 F7
Old Kiln La RFNM GU10....136 F7
Old La ALDT GU11....96 C4
  ASHV GU12....76 D9
  RFNM GU10....135 N5
  STHA RG19....33 H5
Old Litten La PSF GU32....191 J3
Old London Rd STOK SO20....141 M5
Old Lyndhurst Rd TOTT SO40....244 F3
Old Magazine Cl TOTT SO40....247 K9
Old Manor Cl WIMB BH21....300 C1
Old Manor Farm HAV PO9 *....276 B9
Old Manor Wy CHAM PO6....297 K2
Old Market Sq BSTK RG21....7 F7
Old Micheldever Rd
  RAND SP11....103 L5
Old Mill La EPSF GU31....191 P9
  HORN PO8....255 K3
Old Mill PI HASM GU27....156 E6
Old Mill Wy ROWN SO16....247 L2
Old Milton Cn
  NMIL/BTOS BH25....327 H6
Old Milton Rd
  NMIL/BTOS BH25....327 J5
Old Mulberry Cl NBNE BH10....322 A6
Old Newtown Rd NWBY RG14....16 B6
Old Odiham Rd ALTN GU34....112 D7
Old Orch PLE BH15....332 E2
Old Orchards LYMN SO41....329 N5
  ODIM RG29....92 F7
The Old Orch FNM GU9....115 P3
Old Palace Farm STOK SO20....161 M5
Old Park Cl FNM GU9....96 A5
Old Park La FNM GU9....95 P4
Old Park Rd NARL SO24....169 H4
Old Parsonage Ct RWIN SO21....207 L2
Old Pasture Rd FRIM GU16....58 E2
Old Pharmacy Ct CWTH RG45 *....41 K2
Old Pines Cl FERN BH22....302 E4
Old Pond Cl FRIM GU16....58 A4
Old Portsmouth Rd CBLY GU15....58 F1
Old Potbridge Rd HTWY RG27....72 F5
Old Priory Cl HLER SO31....270 A8
Old Priory Rd SBNE BH6....336 D2
Old Pumphouse Cl
  FLEETN GU51....74 E2
The Old Quarry HASM GU27....156 E9
Old Reading Rd BSTK RG21....7 G5
Old Rectory Cl EMRTH PO10....277 P7
Old Rectory Dr ASHV GU12....97 P1
Old Rectory Gdns FARN GU14....58 C9
  WINC SO23....165 L1
Old Rectory La RWIN SO21....184 A7
Old Rectory Rd CHAM PO6....297 N1
Old Redbridge Rd
  WSHM SO15....246 C3
Old Reservoir Rd CHAM PO6....297 M2
Old River WVILLE PO7....255 H8
Old Rd GPORT PO12....12 E4
  ROMY SO51....204 E5
  WIMB BH21....300 D1
Old Rd Chale CHAM PO6....297 H5
Old Romsey Rd TOTT SO40....244 E5
The Old Rope Wk PLE BH15 *....332 B2
Old St John's Ms
  MOOR/WNTN BH9....322 F4
Old Salisbury La RWIN SO21....203 L4
Old Salisbury Rd RAND SP11....101 P7
  ROMY SO51....225 L5
Old Sawmill La VWD BH31....258 E4
Old School Cl ASHV GU12....76 F9
  FAWY SO45....290 D3
  FERN BH22....302 C5
  FLEETN GU51 *....
  HLER SO31....269 L3
  HTWY RG27....55 J7
Old School Dr HISD PO11....319 H6
Old School Gdns HEND SO30....249 N1
Old School La YTLY GU46....40 D8

Old School Pl STOK SO20 *....140 A9
Old School Rd HTWY RG27....71 M4
  LISS GU33....192 D2
Old Shamblehurst La
  HEND SO30....250 C1
Old Stacks Gdns RGWD BH24....282 C3
Old Star PSEA PO1....18 C2
Old Station Ap WINC SO23....23 H5
Old Station Rd RWIN SO21....146 D9
Old Station Wy BOR GU35....153 M3
Old Stockbridge Rd
  RAND SP11....120 B3
Old Stoke Rd RWIN SO21....145 H2
Old St FHAM/STUB PO14....295 N7
Old Timbers HISD PO11....318 F5
Old Town Ms FNM GU9 *....96 A9
Old Turnpike FHAM/PORC PO16....11 H5
Old Vicarage Cl NBNE BH10....322 E1
Old Vicarage La STOK SO20....161 M4
The Old Vineries FBDG SP6....240 B2
Old Vyne La TADY RG26....50 A4
Old Wareham Rd
  BKME/WDN BH12....321 J5
Old Well Cl ITCH SO19....249 L8
Old Welmore YTLY GU46....40 F9
Old Winchester Hill La
  BPWT SO32....212 B2
Old Winton Garages AND SP10....4 E7
Old Winton Rd AND SP10....4 E6
Old Wodwood Chine FARN GU14....75 J1
Old Worting Rd KBH RG22....68 F8
Old Wymering La CHAM PO6....296 C1
Oleander Cl HLER SO31....270 C5
Oleander Dr TOTT SO40....246 B1
Olive Crs FHAM/PORC PO16....295 P3
Olive Gv RAND SP11....119 N4
Olive Rd ROWN SO16....227 L8
Oliver Ri ALTN GU34....132 F5
Oliver Rd ENEY PO4....317 H5
  LYMN SO41....329 J4
  WEND SO18....228 F9
Oliver's Battery Crs
  FUFL SO22....183 K2
Oliver's Battery Gdns
  FUFL SO22....183 K1
Oliver's Battery Rd North
  FUFL SO22....183 K1
Oliver's Battery Rd South
  FUFL SO22....183 K3
Olivers Cl TADY RG26....52 B3
  TOTT SO40....245 P4
Olivers Rd WIMB BH21....279 J8
Oliver's Wk CHIN RG24....70 A5
Olivers Wy WIMB BH21....279 J8
Olivia Cl WVILLE PO7....276 A1
Olympic Wy ELGH SO50....230 B1
Omdurman Rd PTSW SO17....248 C1
Omega ALTN GU34....133 H6
Omega Pk ALTN GU34....133 H6
Omega St SSEA PO5....19 J5
Omer's Ri THLE RG7....37 J4
Onibury Cl WEND SO18....249 J2
Onibury Rd WEND SO18....249 J2
Onslow Cl CHIN RG24....69 P3
Onslow Gdns WIMB BH21....280 B4
Onslow Rd SHAM SO14....248 C5
  SSEA PO5....316 F7
Ontario Wy LIPH GU30....175 K4
Openfields BOR GU35....154 F2
Ophir Gdns CHAR BH8....335 H1
Ophir Rd CHAR BH8....335 H1
  NEND PO2....296 F7
Oracle Dr WVILLE PO7....275 N7
Orange Gv LSOL/BMARY PO13....295 H8
  RAND SP11....119 N4
Orange La STOK SO20....161 M1
Orange Rw EMRTH PO10....299 P1
Oratory Gdns CCLF BH13....333 J5
Orchard Av ELGH SO50....229 P3
  PSTN BH14....333 H1
Orchard Cl ASHV GU12....76 F7
  CHCH/BSGR BH23....324 D9
  EPSF GU31....217 J9
  FARN GU14....57 N4
  FAWY SO45....291 K6
  FBDG SP6....302 E3
  FERN BH22....302 E3
  FNM GU9....96 C5
  GPORT PO12....295 L8
  HISD PO11....318 F6
  HORN PO8....256 C5
  NARL SO24....168 A3
  NBAD SO52....205 K8
  NWBY RG14....24 F2
  RGWD BH24....282 E1
  RWIN SO21....144 D4
  RWIN SO21....207 P4
  TOTT SO40....245 P4
Orchard Ct HEND SO30....250 E4
  VWD BH31....258 C5
Orchard Dro ELGH SO50 *....230 B2
Orchard End RFNM GU10....115 P7
Orchardene NWBY RG14....24 E3
Orchard Gdns ALDT GU11....3 J7
  FBDG SP6....240 D2
Orchard Ga SHST GU47....41 J6
Orchard Gv
  FHAM/PORC PO16....295 L2
  HORN PO8....255 P8
  NMIL/BTOS BH25....327 J6
Orchard La ALTN GU34....132 G5
  EMRTH PO10....299 N1
  ROMY SO51....204 C6
  SHAM SO14....5 K6
Orchardlea BPWT SO32....232 F9
Orchard Mt RGWD BH24....282 E1
Orchard PI SHAM SO14....21 F7
Orchard Rd AND SP10....102 C1
  ELGH SO50....230 C2
  ENEY PO4....316 G4
  FARN GU14....57 P9
  FNM GU9....96 C5
  GPORT PO12....315 P2
  HAV PO9....15 G7

  HISD PO11....318 G6
  HLER SO31....270 F8
  KBH RG22....68 F8
  RSAL SP5....199 P6
  SBNE BH6....336 D4
  WEND SO18....144 D4
  THLE RG7....36 A1
Orchard St WCLF BH2....8 C4
Orchards Wy HEND SO30....249 M2
  PTSW SO17....248 C1
Orchard Ter ALTN GU34....132 G5
The Orchard BWD BH11....301 M7
  CHAM PO6....297 H2
  CHCH/BSGR BH23....305 N8
  HASM GU27....156 E8
  HTWY RG27....71 P2
  LYMN SO41....338 G2
  ODIM RG29....86 G5
  ROWN SO16....227 L6
  STHA RG19....25 J4
  TADY RG26....34 E6
  TOTT SO40....245 K6
  WVILLE PO7....255 H7
Orchard Wk FUFL SO22....183 H1
Orchard Wy ALDT GU11....3 J7
  CBLY GU15....58 A3
  FAWY SO45....268 A8
Orcheston Rd CHAR BH8....323 J9
Orchid Cl AND SP10 *....102 B4
Orchid Dr RAND SP11....79 P2
Orchid Wy CHCH/BSGR BH23....324 C8
Ordnance Cl HSEA PO3 *....297 J4
Ordnance Rd ALDT GU11....3 C2
  GPORT PO12....13 G2
  NTID SP9....79 H5
  WSHM SO15....248 C5
Ordnance Rw PSEA PO1....18 E1
Oregon Cl ITCH SO19....249 J7
Orford Cl CHCH/BSGR BH23....324 B3
Oriana Wy ROWN SO16....226 F8
Oriel Dr FHAM/STUB PO14....271 J9
Oriel HI CBLY GU15....58 A7
Oriel Rd NEND PO2....296 F7
Orient Dr FUFL SO22....164 D4
Orion Av GPORT PO12....315 N1
Orion Cl FHAM/STUB PO14....294 B7
  ROWN SO16....227 K8
Orkney Cl CHIN RG24....69 N3
  ROWN SO16....227 J8
Orkney Rd CHAM PO6....275 H9
Ormesby Dr CHFD SO53....206 D5
Ormond Cl ELGH SO50....230 B1
Ormonde Rd CCLF BH13....334 A4
Ormsby Rd SSEA PO5....19 H7
Orpen Rd ITCH SO19....249 M7
Orpine Cl FHAM PO15....272 B7
Orsmond Cl WVILLE PO7....275 N4
Orwell Cl FARN GU14....57 M6
  ROWN SO16....247 J2
Orwell Crs FHAM/STUB PO14....271 J8
Orwell Rd PSF GU32....215 L3
Osborn Crs
  LSOL/BMARY PO13....294 F5
Osborne Cl ALTN GU34....132 D6
  BSTK RG21....6 C2
  WVILLE PO7....256 F3
Osborne Dr CHFD SO53....206 G8
  FLEETS GU51....74 E5
Osborne Gdns ELGH SO50....230 E2
Osborne PI WHAM PO17....272 C3
Osborne Rd AND SP10....4 B5
  FARN GU14....77 J5
  GPORT PO12....315 P9
  HLER SO31....292 D1
  LSOL/BMARY PO13....314 C2
  MOOR/WNTN BH9....322 K5
  NMIL/BTOS BH25....327 K4
  PSF GU32....215 M1
  SSEA PO5....316 E6
  TOTT SO40....246 E4
  WIMB BH21....300 F1
Osborne Rd North
  PTSW SO17....248 C3
Osborne Rd South
  PTSW SO17....248 C3
Osborne View Rd
  FHAM/STUB PO14....295 M8
Osborn Rd FHAM/PORC PO16....11 G6
Osborn Rd South
  FHAM/PORC PO16....11 G5
Osborn Sq FHAM/PORC PO16....11 G5
Osborn Sq HTWY RG27....72 A4
Osier Cl NEND PO2....296 E7
Oslands Dr HLER SO31....270 D5
Osmund Cl KBH RG22....52 K2
Osprey Cl CHCH/BSGR BH23....337 L1
  ROWN SO16....227 M7
  TOTT SO40....267 J7
Osprey Dr HISD PO11....319 H5
Osprey Gdns LSOL/BMARY PO13....96 C4
Osprey Quay EMRTH PO10....299 P2
Osprey Rd DEAN RG23....88 G5
Ossemsley South Dr
  NMIL/BTOS BH25....306 G8
Osterley Cl HEND SO30....250 C4
Osterley Rd ITCH SO19....248 E8
Oswald Cl MOOR/WNTN BH9....322 E5
Oswald Rd MOOR/WNTN BH9....322 E5
Othello Dr WVILLE PO7....276 A2
Ottawa Dr LIPH GU30....175 K4
Otterbourne Crs HAV PO9....276 D5
Otterbourne HI CHFD SO53....207 J4
Otterbourne Rd RWIN SO21....207 L1
Otter Cl ELGH SO50....230 A2
  VWD BH31....258 G5
Otter Dr PLE BH15....321 H6
Otters Wk NMIL/BTOS BH25....327 L1
Ouse Cl CHFD SO53....206 D5
Ouse Ct AND SP10....82 G9
Outer Cir ROWN SO16....227 L8
Outlands La HEND SO30....251 K5

Outram Rd SSEA PO5....19 K6
Oval Gdns GPORT PO12....315 K5
Oval Rd ROMY SO51....178 F6
The Oval AND SP10 *....82 G8
  LISS GU33....192 D2
  STHA RG19....25 H8
Overbecks NWBY RG14....24 G5
Overbridge Sq NWBY RG14....25 H4
Overbrook FAWY SO45....268 B8
Overbury Av NBAD SO52....205 J8
Overbury Rd PSTN BH14....321 C9
Overcliff Ri ROWN SO16....228 A8
Overcombe Cl CFDH BH17....320 C2
Overdale Pl BOR GU35 *....154 A7
Overdale Ri FRIM GU16....58 D2
Overdale Wk BOR GU35....154 A7
Overlands Crs LYMN SO41....333 H4
Overt Links Dr PSTN BH14....333 M1
Overton Cl ALDT GU11....97 J5
Overton Crs HAV PO9....276 D5
Overton Rd RWIN SO21....107 H8
Oviat Cl TOTT SO40....245 P4
Ovington Av LTDN BH7....324 A8
Ovington Rd RWIN SO21....324 P4
Owen Cl LSOL/BMARY PO13....314 C1
Owen Rd ELGH SO50....229 H2
  NWBY RG14....24 E1
Owen's Rd FUFL SO22....22 C1
Owen St ENEY PO4....317 J6
Owlsmoor Rd SHST GU47....40 G5
Owls Rd BOSC BH5....335 L5
  VWD BH31....258 G5
Owslebury Bottom
  RWIN SO21....184 D9
Owslebury Gv HAV PO9....276 F5
Oxburgh Cl ELGH SO50....207 H8
Ox Dro RAND SP11....79 P9
  RAND SP11....83 L9
  RSAL SP5....194 C2
  RWIN SO21....144 G4
Ox Drove Ri RAND SP11....83 M8
Oxdrove Wy NARL SO24....129 K7
  NARL SO24....148 E4
  OVTN RG25....129 P3
  RWIN SO21....146 B4
Oxenden Ct RFNM GU10....97 L3
Oxenden Rd RFNM GU10....97 L5
Oxford Av SBNE BH6....336 A1
  SHAM SO14....21 F2
Oxford Cl FHAM/PORC PO16....10 C3
Oxford La BPWT SO32....233 K5
  BWD BH11....322 B1
Oxford Rd SHAM SO14 *....21 F7
Oxford St NWBY RG14....24 C3
  SHAM SO14....21 F7
Oxford Ter LYMN SO41 *....308 G6
Oxlease Cl ROMY SO51....204 E4
Oxlease La OVTN RG25....110 G5
Oxleys Cl FHAM/STUB PO14....271 J8
Oxted Ct ENEY PO4....317 K3
Oyster Cl KBH RG22....89 L4
Oyster Est CHAM PO6 *....297 M3
Oyster Ms PSEA PO1....18 C6
Oyster Quay CHAM PO6....296 D3
Oyster St PSEA PO1....18 C6
Ozier Rd WEND SO18....249 J1

P

Pacific Cl SHAM SO14....248 E9
Packenham Rd BSTK RG21....69 J9
Pack La DEAN RG23....67 N9
  KBH RG22....89 M1
Packridge La ROMY SO51....227 K3
Packway FNM GU9....116 C3
Padbury Cl NTID SP9....297 H5
Paddington Gv BWD BH11....321 M1
Paddington Rd NEND PO2....297 H8
Paddock Cl BKME/WDN BH12....321 K6
  RGWD BH24....144 F4
  RWIN SO21....144 F4
  WIMB BH21....302 A2
Paddock Ct HTWY RG27....68 G9
Paddock End WVILLE PO7....255 H8
Paddockfields CHIN RG24....70 C5
Paddock Gdns LYMN SO41....329 K2
Paddock Gv VWD BH31....258 G5
Paddock Rd KBH RG22....68 G9
  NWBY RG14....24 C1
The Paddocks FAWY SO45....291 K6
The Paddock BOR GU35....154 F3
  BROC SO42....286 F8
  FBDG SP6....207 K7
  FHAM/STUB PO14....294 A5
  GPORT PO12....12 A4
  GSHT GU26....155 P4
  HASM GU27....156 E8
  HTWY RG27....72 B2
  KSCL RG20....48 B3
  NWBY RG14....16 F6
  RFNM GU10 *....115 P7
  RWIN SO21....281 H9
  TOTT SO40....246 A1
  WINC SO23....165 K1
Paddock Wy HASM GU27....157 M3
  LIPH GU30....175 J2
  NARL SO24....129 P7
  PSF GU32....215 K3
Padfield Cl SBNE BH6....324 C9
Padget Rd RGWD BH24....260 G9
Padnall Av HORN PO8....256 B9
Padnell Rd HORN PO8....256 B9

Padstow Pl *FBDG* SP6............240 C3
Padwell Rd *SHAM* SO14.........248 C4
Padwick Av *FHAM* PO6..........297 J1
Padwick Cl *BSTK* RG21..........69 K8
Padworth La *THLE* RG7..........26 A4
Padworth Rd *THLE* RG7..........26 C7
Paffard Cl
  LSOL/BMARY PO13..........314 G1
Page Cl *FAWY* SO45..........290 F7
Pages La *BROC* SO42..........310 C2
Paget Cl *NTID* SP9..........78 F3
  WIMB BH21..........279 J7
Paget Rd *BWD* BH11..........322 A3
  GPORT PO12..........12 A7
Paget St *SHAM* SO14..........21 H6
Pagham Cl *EMRTH* PO10..........299 N1
Pagham Gdns *HISD* PO11..........319 M6
Paice La *ALTN* GU34..........149 P4
Paices Hl *THLE* RG7..........34 B2
Paignton Av *HSEA* PO3..........297 J9
Paignton Rd *ROWN* SO16..........247 K3
Paimpol Pl *ROMY* SO51 *..........204 C7
Pain's Rd *SSEA* PO5..........19 J5
Painswick Cl *CHAM* PO6..........296 E1
  HLER SO31..........270 F4
Painter Cl *HSEA* PO3..........297 K6
Painters Pightle *HTWY* RG27..........71 N3
Paisley Rd *SBNE* BH6..........336 A1
Pakenham Cl *ALDT* GU11..........2 D1
Palace Cl *STOK* SO20..........161 L5
Palace Ga *ODIM* RG29..........72 C9
Palace La *BROC* SO42..........289 L8
Palace Ms *BPWT* SO32..........232 A5
Pale La *HTWY* RG27..........73 M2
Palestine Rd *RAND* SP11..........119 M3
Palfrey Rd *NBNE* BH10..........322 D3
Palk Rd *HAV* PO9..........14 C5
Pallant Gdns
  FHAM/PORC PO16..........273 H8
The Pallant *HAV* PO9..........15 G5
Pallet Cl *RWIN* SO21..........207 P5
Pallot Cl *HLER* SO31..........269 P2
Palmer Dr *AND* SP10..........5 J4
Palmer Rd *NMIL/BTOS* BH25 *..........327 J3
Palmers Cl *ELCH* SO50..........230 D2
Palmers La *THLE* RG7..........27 J5
Palmer's Rd *EMRTH* PO10..........277 M7
Palmerston Av
  CHCH/BSGR BH23..........325 H9
  FHAM/PORC PO16..........11 H5
Palmerston Dr
  FARN GU14..........294 E2
Palmerstone Ms *BMTH* BH1..........335 J2
Palmerston Rd *BMTH* BH1..........335 L2
  HISD PO11..........318 G4
  PSTN BH14..........321 M8
  SHAM SO14..........20 E3
  SSEA PO5..........316 E6
Palmerston St *ROMY* SO51..........204 D6
Palmerston Wy *GPORT* PO12..........315 J6
Palmers Yd *KSCL* RG20..........31 M8
Palm Hall Cl *WINC* SO23..........23 J5
Palm Rd *ROWN* SO16..........227 L8
Pamber Heath Rd *TADY* RG26..........34 E6
Pamber Rd *THLE* RG7..........35 H4
Pamela Av *CHAM* PO6..........296 B1
Pamplyn Cl *RWIN* SO21..........329 J3
Pangbourne Av *CHAM* PO6..........297 K2
Pangbourne Cl *PSTN* SO14..........249 J7
Pankridge St *FARN* GU10..........95 H4
Pannall Rd *GPORT* PO12..........315 L1
Pannells *RFNM* GU10..........116 D5
Panorama Rd *CCLF* BH13..........333 K8
Pans Cnr *FERN* BH22 *..........302 F5
Pan's Gdns *CBLY* GU15..........58 F3
Pan St *PSEA* PO1 *..........19 H1
Pansy Rd *ROWN* SO16..........228 C8
Pantheon Rd *CHFD* SO53..........207 H6
Pantile Dr *HTWY* RG27..........72 B3
Pantiles *BOR* GU35 *..........155 J3
The Pantiles *FBDG* SP6..........240 B2
Pantings La *KSCL* RG20..........29 N8
Panton Cl *EMRTH* PO10 *..........277 L7
Panwell Rd *WEND* SO18..........249 J4
Papermakers *OVTN* RG25..........87 H4
Paper Mill La *ALTN* GU34..........132 C5
The Parade *ASHV* GU12 *..........76 F8
  BSTK RG21 *..........7 H4
  FRIM GU16 *..........
  LSOL/BMARY PO13 *..........294 F6
  NMIL/BTOS BH25..........327 M4
  PSEA PO1..........18 C1
  TADY RG26 *..........34 C5
Paradise La *BPWT* SO32..........232 C6
  EMRTH PO10..........277 H6
  FHAM/PORC PO16..........273 J9
  TOTT SO40..........245 K5
Paradise St *PLE* BH15..........332 D2
  PSEA PO1..........19 H2
Parchment St *WINC* SO23..........23 F5
The Parchment *HAV* PO9..........15 F6
Pardoe Cl *HEND* SO30..........250 C6
Pardown *DEAN* RG23..........88 A2
Parfitts Cl *FNM* GU9..........96 A9
Parham Dr *ELCH* SO50..........207 H9
Parham Rd *GPORT* PO12..........315 N2
  NBNE BH10..........322 C5
Parish Cl *ASHV* GU12..........97 P2
  FNM GU9..........96 A5
Parish Rd *FARN* GU14..........76 A4
  PLE BH15..........320 C9
Park Av *WHAM* PO17..........272 C5
Park Av *CBLY* GU15..........58 B1
  CHIN RG24..........70 C7
  LYMN SO41..........329 K3
  NBNE BH10..........322 C1
  NTHA RG18..........23 F3
  WVILLE PO7..........255 H6
Park Cl *BOR* GU35..........134 G8
  BROC SO42..........286 D7
  CHCH/BSGR BH23..........324 G4

DEAN RG23..........88 E1
FAWY SO45..........268 D6
GPORT PO12..........315 K2
Park Cnr *HTWY* RG27..........157 L4
  LYMN SO41..........339 H1
  NMIL/BTOS BH25..........327 L2
  RFNM GU10..........115 J8
  TOTT SO40..........267 H1
  WINC SO23..........165 H5
Park Close Rd *ALTN* GU34..........132 C4
Park Corner Rd *HTWY* RG27..........55 J6
Park Ct *EMRTH* PO10..........277 K9
Park Dr *WBD* BH31..........258 E3
Park Dro *STOK* SO20..........120 E5
Park End *NWBY* RG14..........24 D3
Parker Cl *GPORT* PO12..........295 L8
Parker Gdns *WVILLE* PO7..........275 LB
Parker Rd *MOOR/WNTN* BH9..........322 F8
Parkers Cl *RCWD* BH24..........260 C9
Park Farm Av *FHAM* PO15..........272 A6
Park Farm Cl *FHAM* PO15..........272 B7
Park Farm Rd *WVILLE* PO7..........275 M6
Parkfields *YTLY* GU46..........40 E9
Park Gdns *BSTK* RG21..........59 M8
Park Gln *FHAM* PO15..........271 J6
Park Gv *CHAM* PO6..........297 H2
Park Hl *FLEETS* GU52..........74 C8
Park Hill Cl *FAWY* SO45..........290 E6
Parkhill Cl *BLKW* GU17..........57 L1
Parkhill Rd *BLKW* GU17 *..........57 L1
Park Homer Dr *WIMB* BH21..........279 H8
Park Homer Rd *WIMB* BH21..........279 H7
Park House Farm Wy
  HAV PO9..........276 C5
Parkhurst Flds *RFNM* GU10..........136 F8
Park Lake Rd *PLE* BH15..........332 C1
Parkland Cl *WBD* BH31..........259 K6
Parkland Dr *NMIL/BTOS* BH25..........327 H7
Parkland Gv *FNM* GU9..........2 B7
Parklands Av *HORN* PO8..........256 A9
Parklands Cl *CHFD* SO53..........206 E6
  GPORT PO12..........315 M2
Park La *ALTN* GU34..........114 A6
  BPWT SO32..........232 G3
  BPWT SO32..........233 M3
  BROC SO42..........287 M8
  CHAM PO6..........297 J2
  ELCH SO50..........207 K5
  EMRTH PO10..........277 P2
  EWKG RG40..........39 K3
  FDBG SP6..........239 M5
  FHAM/PORC PO16..........11 F3
  FHAM/STUB PO14..........294 A6
  HAV PO9..........14 A3
  HAV PO9..........276 C2
  HORN PO8..........256 A9
  LYMN SO41..........311 M9
  LYMN SO41..........338 G2
  NARL SO24..........169 L4
  NBNE BH10..........322 F3
  NTHA RG18..........25 N2
  NWBY RG14..........24 B8
  RAND SP11..........100 A6
  RSAL SP5..........158 B7
  RWIN SO21..........165 L1
  RWIN SO21..........184 A9
  THLE RG7..........36 B4
  THLE RG7..........36 G4
  TOTT SO40..........244 B5
  WIMB BH21..........300 E1
Park Pde *HAV* PO9..........276 E6
Park Pl *FLEETS* GU52..........74 C7
Park Prewett *CHIN* RG24 *..........69 H5
Park Rd *ALDT* GU11..........3 G1
  BMTH BH1..........335 H4
  BPWT SO32..........231 N4
  CBLY GU15..........58 B2
  CHFD SO53..........206 E5
  FARN GU14..........76 D3
  FBDG SP6..........240 D1
  FNM GU9..........96 C5
  FUFL SO22..........164 G5
  GPORT PO12..........12 D6
  HASM GU27..........157 H7
  HISD PO11..........318 C4
  LYMN SO41..........329 K3
  LYMN SO41..........339 H2
  NMIL/BTOS BH25..........327 L2
  NTID SP9..........79 H5
  PLE BH15..........321 H9
  PSEA PO1..........18 C4
  PSF GU32..........215 M2
  SHST GU47..........41 K7
  WSHM SO15..........247 N5
  WVILLE PO7..........255 H6
  WVILLE PO7..........275 L6
Park Rd North *HAV* PO9..........14 E4
Park Rd South *HAV* PO9..........15 F6
Park Rw *FNM* GU9..........96 B9
Parkside *CHCH/BSGR* BH23..........325 P6
  FNM GU9..........96 C5
  HAV PO9..........276 C8
  RCWD BH24..........282 D3
  TOTT SO40..........244 B6
Parkside Av *ROWN* SO16..........247 H5
Parkside Gdns *FUFL* SO22..........164 D5
  NBNE BH10..........322 E5
Parkside La *NARL* SO24..........169 K5
Parkside Rd *BSTK* RG21..........69 M9
  NTHA RG18..........25 N1
Parkstone Av *ENEY* PO4..........316 G7
  PSTN BH14..........321 M8
Parkstone Hts *PSTN* BH14..........321 J7
Parkstone Rd *NARL* SO24..........169 N5
  PLE BH15..........332 B2
Park St *BOR* GU35 *..........154 A5
  GPORT PO12..........12 D3
  NWBY RG14..........24 D3
  ROWN SO16..........247 M3

SSEA PO5..........19 F5
Park Ter *NWBY* RG14..........24 D3
Park Terraces *GPORT* PO12 *..........13 F2
The Park *BPWT* SO32..........233 L5
  NMIL/BTOS BH25..........326 EB
Park Vw *ELGH* SO50 *..........207 K4
  HEND SO30..........250 B4
  HEND SO30..........250 C4
Parkview Cl *AND* SP10..........82 C9
Parkville Rd *ROWN* SO16..........228 F8
Park Vw *FHAM* PO15..........25 J6
  SHAM SO14..........20 E3
Parkwater Rd *RSAL* SP5..........201 L4
Park Wy *FARN* GU14..........280 E7
  HAV PO9..........14 E5
Parkway *CBLY* GU15..........58 B2
  CWTH RG45..........41 H1
  FHAM PO15..........271 M3
Parkway Dr *CHAR* BH8..........323 L7
Parkway Gdns *CHFD* SO53..........206 E6
The Parkway
  LSOL/BMARY PO13..........294 F7
  WIMB BH21..........228 C7
Parkwood Cl *CHIN* RG24..........52 A9
Parkwood Rd *BOSC* BH5..........335 N2
  WIMB BH21..........300 E1
Parley Cl *FERN* BH22..........302 F7
Parley Cross *FERN* BH22..........302 E8
Parley La *CHCH/BSGR* BH23..........303 H8
Parley Rd *MOOR/WNTN* BH9..........322 G5
Parliamentary Rd
  CHOB/PIR GU24..........59 M7
Parliament Pl *FUFL* SO22..........183 J2
Parmiter Dr *WIMB* BH21..........300 C1
Parmiter Rd *WIMB* BH21..........300 D1
Parmiter Wy *WIMB* BH21..........300 C1
Parnell Ct *AND* SP10..........102 A1
Parnell La *ROMY* SO51..........180 E4
Parnell Rd *ELCH* SO50..........229 H2
Parr St *PSTN* BH14..........321 J8
Parry Cl *CHAM* PO6..........296 A1
Parry Rd *ITCH* SO19..........249 M7
Parsonage Barn La
  RGWD BH24..........282 E1
Parsonage Cl *ALTN* GU34..........151 M5
  EPSF GU31..........197 N9
Parsonage Est *EPSF* GU31..........217 J1
Parsonage La *BPWT* SO32..........231 H6
Parsonage Park Dr *FBDG* SP6..........240 C1
Parsonage Rd *BMTH* BH1..........9 F4
  SHAM SO14..........21 H1
Parsonage Wy *FRIM* GU16..........58 D4
Parsons Cl *FLEETS* GU52..........74 C7
  HASM GU27..........157 H5
  NWBY RG14..........16 A3
Parsons Fld *SHST* GU47..........41 H6
Parsons On *HASM* GU27..........157 H5
Part La *THLE* RG7..........37 J9
Partridge Av *FHAM* PO15 *..........40 C8
Partridge Cl
  CHCH/BSGR BH23..........337 L1
  FHAM/PORC PO16 *..........295 J1
  KBH RG22..........88 K4
  RFNM GU10..........95 M3
Partridge Down *FUFL* SO22..........183 K3
Partridge Dr *PSTN* BH14..........333 K2
Partridge Gdns *HORN* PO8..........256 A7
Partridge Gn *ALTN* GU34..........132 F4
  NMIL/BTOS BH25..........327 K1
Partridge HI *RSAL* SP5..........224 A1
Partridge Rd *BROC* SO42..........286 F9
  FAWY SO45..........268 B9
Partrige Wk *PSTN* BH14..........333 L2
Partry Cl *CHFD* SO53..........206 D5
Pascoe Cl *PSTN* BH14..........321 J8
Passage La *HLER* SO31..........270 B9
Passfield Av *ELCH* SO50..........228 G2
Passfield Cl *ELCH* SO50..........228 G2
Passfield Rd *LIPH* GU30..........154 FB
Passfield Wk *HAV* PO9 *..........277 H5
Passford HI *LYMN* SO41..........309 K9
Passingham Wk *HORN* PO8..........256 A7
The Pastures
  FHAM/STUB PO14..........271 J6
  NARL SO24..........167 P9
  WINC SO23..........165 J7
  WVILLE PO7..........254 CB
Pat Bear Cl *WSHM* SO15..........246 C3
Patchway Dr
  FHAM/STUB PO14..........294 A1
Paternoster Rw *WINC* SO23..........23 F5
Paterson Cl *FRIM* GU16..........58 B2
Paterson Rd AD *LISS* SO33..........173 P5
Pathfields Cl *HASM* GU27..........157 J6
The Pathfinders *FARN* GU14..........75 K1
Patricia Cl *HEND* SO30..........249 M1
Patricia Dr *HEND* SO30..........249 M1
Patrick's Cl *LISS* GU33..........192 E2
Patten Av *YTLY* GU46..........40 D9
Pattinson Crs *RAND* SP11..........101 N3
Paul Cl *ALDT* GU11..........2 A6
Paulet Cl *WEND* SO18..........249 J2
Paulet Lacave Av *ROWN* SO16..........227 H6
Paulet Pl *CHIN* RG24..........70 C6
  FUFL SO22..........183 H1
Pauletts La *TOTT* SO40..........225 P9
Paul's Fld *HTWY* RG27..........39 P6
Paulsgrove Rd *NEND* PO2..........297 H9
Paulus La *LYMN* SO41..........338 D3
Paulson Cl *CHFD* SO53..........206 E5
Pauncefoot HI *ROMY* SO51..........204 AB
Pauncefote Rd *BOSC* BH5..........335 N1
Pauntley Rd
  CHCH/BSGR BH23..........337 J1
Pavan Gdns *NBNE* BH10..........322 C4
Pavilion Cl *ELGH* SO50..........230 C9
Pavilion Rd *ALDT* GU11..........75 K6
  ALDT GU11..........96 E2
  HEND SO30..........250 D3
The Pavilions End *CBLY* GU15..........58 C2

Pavilions Wy *GPORT* PO12..........13 G1
Pawley Cl *RFNM* GU10..........97 M4
Pawmers Md *FLEETS* GU52..........74 B9
The Park *BPWT* SO32..........233 L5
Paxton Cl *HEND* SO30..........250 D6
  KBH RG22..........88 D5
Paxton Rd *FHAM/STUB* PO14..........10 D6
Payne Cl *WIMB* BH21..........280 E4
Paynes Rd *WSHM* SO15..........32 B6
  STOK SO20..........120 E5
Paynesdown Rd *STHA* RG19..........13 J9
Paynes Hay Rd *ROMY* SO51..........180 F6
Paynes La *STOK* SO20..........140 A4
Payne's Meadow *CHIN* RG24..........70 B4
Payne's Rd *WSHM* SO15..........247 N5
Peabody Rd *FARN* GU14..........76 C3
Peace Cl *CHCH/BSGR* BH23..........305 LB
Peach Cl *RAND* SP11..........119 N4
Peach Rd *ROWN* SO16..........227 L8
Peach Tree Cl *FARN* GU14..........57 P6
Peacock La *CHIN* RG24..........52 A9
Peacock Pl *WINC* SO23..........23 K4
Peak Cl *ROWN* SO16..........247 K5
Peak Dr *FHAM/STUB* PO14..........294 B1
Peake New Rd *BPWT* SO32..........212 B5
Peakfield *RFNM* GU10..........136 C2
  WVILLE PO7..........
Peak La *BPWT* SO32..........209 N8
  FHAM/STUB PO14..........294 B2
Peak Rd *HORN* PO8..........236 A7
Peak Wy *FARN* GU14..........59 N9
The Peak *HAV* PO9..........257 J9
Pealsham Gdns *FBDG* SP6..........240 C1
Pearce Av *PSTN* BH14..........333 J2
Pearce Ct *GPORT* PO12..........13 F1
Pearces Pl *KSCL* RG20 *..........48 C3
Pear Cl *BKME/WDN* BH12..........334 B2
Pearl Gdns *NBNE* BH10..........322 C5
Pearl Rd *NBNE* BH10..........322 C5
Pearman Dr *AND* SP10..........5 J4
Pearson Av *CHAM* PO6 *..........321 K7
Pearson Gdns *RAND* SP11..........322 D1
Peartree Av *ITCH* SO19..........248 G7
Pear Tree Cl *BOR* GU35..........154 C4
Pear Tree Cl *BOR* GU35..........154 C4
Peartree Cl *FHAM/STUB* PO14..........294 B6
  ITCH SO19..........248 F7
Peartree Ct *LYMN* SO41..........329 L5
Pear Tree Dr *RSAL* SP5..........233 M4
Pear Tree La *NWBY* RG14..........26 B2
  RFNM GU10..........115 P7
Pear Tree Rd *BOR* GU35..........154 C3
Pear Tree Rd *FAWY* SO45..........268 A3
  ITCH SO19..........248 F7
Peat Moor Cl *FLEETN* GU51..........74 B2
Peatmoor Cl *FLEETN* GU51..........74 B2
Peatmore Dr *CHOB/PIR* GU24..........59 P7
Pebble Cl *HISD* PO11..........319 H6
Pebble Ct *TOTT* SO40..........247 K9
Pebmarsh Rd *CHAM* PO6..........296 F1
Peckham Av
  NMIL/BTOS BH25..........327 J5
Peckham Cl *HLER* SO31..........271 J8
Peckmoor Dr *STHA* RG19..........24 F8
Pedam Cl *ENEY* PO4..........317 J5
Peddlars Gv *YTLY* GU46..........40 E8
Peel Av *FRIM* GU16..........58 F6
Peel Cl *BKME/WDN* BH12..........333 N1
  ROMY SO51..........204 G4
Peel Gdns *KSCL* RG20..........48 D3
Peel Pl *SSEA* PO5..........19 G5
Peel Rd *GPORT* PO12..........13 F1
Peel St *SHAM* SO14..........21 J2
Peewit Wk *HLER* SO31..........250 A8
Peewit Hill Cl *HLER* SO31..........250 A8
Pegasus Av *ASHV* GU12..........76 D9
Pegasus Cl *ASHV* GU12..........
  HLER SO31..........328 A5
Pegasus Ct *HASM* GU27..........196 F9
  HLER SO31..........269 P8
  ROWN SO16..........227 KB
  STHA RG19..........25 K3
Pegasus Cl *WHCH* RG28 *..........85 L5
Pegasus Rd *FARN* GU14..........57 N6
  FARN GU14..........76 A2
Peggotty Pl *SHST* GU47..........41 H6
Pelham Cl *BOR* GU35..........154 A7
  CHIN RG24..........70 C7
Pelham Cl *RFNM* GU10..........116 A6
Pelham Rd *GPORT* PO12..........12 C1
  SSEA PO5..........19 H7
Pelhams Pk *NBNE* BH10 *..........322 C1
Pelham Ter *EMRTH* PO10..........299 N1
Pelican Cl *FHAM* PO15..........272 BB
Pelican Ct *AND* SP10..........4 E2
Pelican La *NWBY* RG14..........24 C3
Pelican Md *RCWD* BH24..........283 G3
Pelican Rd *FHAM/STUB* PO14..........294 D4
  TADY RG26..........34 F4
Pelton Rd *BSTK* RG21..........6 B4
Pembers Cl *ELCH* SO50..........230 D2
Pemberton Rd *LYND* SO43..........256 H5
Pembrey Cl *ROWN* SO16..........227 K7
Pembridge Rd *FBDG* SP6..........240 D1
Pembroke Cl *ELGH* SO50..........207 H8
  PSEA PO1..........18 D6
  ROMY SO51..........204 D6
  THLE RG7..........37 J9
  TOTT SO40..........246 E3
Pembroke Crs
  FHAM/STUB PO14..........293 N7
Pembroke Rd
  BKME/WDN BH12..........321 M5
  DEAN RG23..........87 P5
  FUFL SO22..........164 D2
  ITCH SO19..........17 K9
  NWBY RG14..........16 D1
  PSEA PO1..........18 E7

WBNE BH4..........334 B4
Pembury Pl *ASHV* GU12..........3 H5
Pembury Rd
  FHAM/STUB PO14..........294 B5
  HAV PO9..........15 J7
Pemerton Rd *BSTK* RG21..........7 H2
  FUFL SO22..........164 E4
Penarth Av *CHAM* PO6..........297 K1
Penarth Ms *WINC* SO23 *..........22 C5
Pen Cl *AND* SP10..........5 J4
Pendennis Cl *DEAN* RG23..........68 E6
Pendennis Rd *CHAM* PO6..........296 B1
Pendle Cl *ROWN* SO16..........247 K3
Pendle Gn *ROMY* SO51..........178 F5
Pendleton Gdns *FAWY* SO45..........290 C8
Pendragon Wy *CBLY* GU15..........59 J1
Pendula Wy *ELCH* SO50..........207 N8
Penelope Gdns *HLER* SO31..........249 P9
Penfold Cft *FNM* GU9..........96 F7
Penfords Paddock
  BPWT SO32..........232 B5
Pengilly Rd *FNM* GU9..........96 B9
Penhale Gdns
  FHAM/STUB PO14..........271 J9
Penhale Rd *PSEA* PO1..........316 G3
Penhale Wy *TOTT* SO40..........246 C6
Penhurst Rd *HAV* PO9..........276 BB
Peninsula Rd *FUFL* SO22..........164 D2
Peninsula Sq *WINC* SO23..........22 C5
Penistone Cl *ITCH* SO19..........269 K1
Penjar Av *WVILLE* PO7..........275 L6
Penk Rdg *CHAM* PO6..........297 P1
Pennant Hills *HAV* PO9..........276 BB
Pennant Plc
  FHAM/PORC PO16 *..........11 J1
Pennant Wy
  CHCH/BSGR BH23..........325 K8
Pennard Wy *CHFD* SO53..........206 C9
Penn Cl *NMIL/BTOS* BH25..........327 K1
Pennefathers Rd *ALDT* GU11..........75 N9
Pennerly Ct *HAV* PO9..........276 D3
Penner Rd *HAV* PO9..........298 E2
Penn Hill Av *PSTN* BH14..........321 M9
Pennine Gdns *FAWY* SO45..........267 P8
Pennine Rd *ROWN* SO16..........247 K4
Pennine Wk
  FHAM/STUB PO14..........294 C2
Pennine Wy *CHFD* SO53..........206 F9
  FARN GU14..........57 M6
  KBH RG22..........68 E9
  LSOL/BMARY PO13..........314 E4
  VWD BH31..........258 F5
Pennings Rd *NTID* SP9..........78 C1
Pennington Cl *ELGH* SO50..........207 P5
  FERN BH22..........280 DB
  LYMN SO41..........329 J5
Pennington Crs *FERN* BH22..........280 D7
Pennington Ov *LYMN* SO41..........329 H5
Pennington Rd *FERN* BH22..........280 DB
Pennington Wy *FHAM* PO15..........272 B7
Penn Rd *NWBY* RG14..........24 A2
Penns Pl *EPSF* GU31..........216 B2
Penns Rd *PSF* GU32..........215 L1
Penns Yd *FNM* GU9..........96 B9
Pennycress *HLER* SO31..........270 E6
Penny Hedge
  NMIL/BTOS BH25..........327 K7
Penny Pl *WVILLE* PO7..........299 P1
Penny St *PSEA* PO1..........141 M7
Penny's Cl *FBDG* SP6..........220 D9
Penny's Crs *FBDG* SP6..........220 D9
Penny's Hatch *KSCL* RG20..........48 D3
Pennys La *FBDG* SP6..........240 C5
Pennys Wk *FNM* GU9 *..........18 C7
Pennywell Gdns
  NMIL/BTOS BH25..........327 M3
Penrhyn Av *CHAM* PO6..........297 K1
Penrhyn Cl *ALDT* GU11..........3 F5
Penrith Cl *VWD* BH31..........258 E5
Penrith Rd *BOSC* BH5..........335 N4
Penrose Cl *NEND* PO2..........296 F7
  NWBY RG14..........24 C2
Penrose Rd *FERN* BH22..........302 D7
Penror Cl *BOR* GU35..........155 K3
Penshurst Ri *FRIM* GU16..........58 E5
Penshurst Wy *ELGH* SO50..........207 J7
Pentere Rd *HORN* PO8..........256 A5
Pentere Av *WSHM* SO15..........247 P1
Pentire Wy *WSHM* SO15..........247 P1
Pentland Cl *FAWY* SO45..........267 P8
  KBH RG22..........68 E9
Pentland Ri
  FHAM/PORC PO16..........273 P9
Penton Cl *HAV* PO9..........277 H4
Penton La *RAND* SP11..........81 M5
Penton Pl *WINC* SO23 *..........23 H7
Penton Rd *RWIN* SO21..........184 A1
Pentons Hl *FBDG* SP6..........241 H5
Pentridge Wy *TOTT* SO40..........246 B6
Penwith Dr *HASM* GU27..........156 C9
Penwood Cl *HAV* PO9 *..........277 H5
Penwood Hts *KSCL* RG20..........29 P6
Penwood Rd *KSCL* RG20..........30 B3
Peperham Rd *HASM* GU27..........157 H5
Peper Harow *Horn* PO8..........256 B5
Peppard Cl *WEND* SO18..........249 J4
Peppercorn Wy *HEND* SO30..........230 B9
Pepys Av *ITCH* SO19..........249 M6
Pepys Cl *ENEY* PO4..........317 H5
  GPORT PO12..........315 M7
Percival Rd *CHFD* SO53..........206 B9
Percival Rd *NEND* PO2..........297 H9
Percy Chandler St *PSEA* PO1..........19 H3
Percy Cl *FAWY* SO45..........268 B5
Percy Rd *BOSC* BH5..........335 L3
  ENEY PO4..........316 G4
  GPORT PO12..........12 E7

ROWN SO16 ...247 L3
Peregrine Cl TOTT SO40 ...246 A5
Peregrine Rd
　CHCH/BSGR BH23 ...325 L9
The Peregrines
　FHAM/PORC PO16 ...295 K1
Pergin Crs CFDH BH17 ...320 D5
Pergin Wy CFDH BH17 ...320 D5
Perham Crs RAND SP11 ...80 A1
Peris Cl NARL SO24 ...167 N3
Periwinkle Cl BOR GU35 ...154 D3
Pern Dr HEND SO30 ...250 C4
Peronne Cl HSEA PO3 ...297 H4
Peronne Rd HSEA PO3 ...297 H4
Perowne St ALDT GU11 ...2 C3
Perran Rd ROWN SO16 ...247 H2
Perring Av FARN GU14 ...57 M5
Perring Rd FARN GU14 ...75 P3
Perry Dr FLEETN GU51 ...74 A3
Perryfield Gdns LTDN BH7 ...323 P7
Perry Gdns PLE BH15 ...332 E2
Perryhill Dr SHST GU47 ...40 G5
Perry Wy BOR GU35 ...154 G4
　FNM GU9 ...96 B4
Perrywood Cl FAWY SO45 ...290 E6
Perrywood Gdns TOTT SO40 ...245 P4
Perseus Pl WVILLE PO7 ...275 P7
Perseus Ter PSEA PO1 * ...18 C5
Pershore Cl HLER SO31 ...270 C7
Pershore Rd CHFD SO24 ...69 L3
Persian Dr HLER SO31 ...271 H5
Persley Rd NBNE BH10 ...322 D5
Perth Cl CHCH/BSGR BH23 ...324 C6
Perth Rd ENEY PO4 ...317 K4
　LSOL/BMARY PO13 ...295 H6
　RAND SP11 ...79M4
Pervin Rd CHAM PO6 ...297 H2
Peststead La BPWT SO32 ...233 N8
Peter Ashley Rd CHAM PO6 ...275 N1
Peterborough Ct
　LSOL/BMARY PO13 * ...315 H3
Peterborough Rd CHAM PO6 ...274 C9
Peter Grant Wy FERN BH22 ...302 C3
Peterhouse Cl SHST GU47 ...41 N4
Peters Cl HLER SO31 ...270 F7
Peterscroft Av TOTT SO40 ...265 N1
Petersfield DEAN RG23 ...88 A1
Petersfield Cl CHIN RG24 ...52 B9
Petersfield La HORN PO8 ...256 C6
Petersfield Rd IH LTDN BH7 ...323 P8
Petersfield Rd BOR GU35 ...153 P7
　EPSF GU31 ...215 K8
　HAV PO9 ...15 G2
　LISS GU33 ...173 K6
　LTDN BH7 ...323 N9
　NARL SO24 ...169 J3
　NARL SO24 ...167 H2
　RWIN SO21 ...165 P9
　WINC SO23 ...23 J6
Petersham Cl MOOR/WNTN BH9 ...322 C4
Petersham Rd FRIM GU16 ...275M1
Petersham Rd FERN BH22 * ...302 F5
　HLER SO31 ...270 F7
Petit Rd MOOR/WNTN BH9 ...322 E4
Petrel Cft KBH RG22 ...89 L3
Petrel Wk LSOL/BMARY PO13 ...296 F7
Petrie Rd LSOL/BMARY PO13 ...314 D2
Petticoat La RSAL SP5 ...200 A6
Pettinger Gdns PTSW SO17 ...248 F3
Pettry Cl ROMY SO51 ...158 E1
Pettycot Crs
　LSOL/BMARY PO13 ...294 F6
Petty's Brook Rd CHIN RG24 ...52 A9
Petunia Cl KBH RG22 ...88 C8
Petworth Cl FRIM GU16 ...58 E5
　KBH RG22 ...88 C8
Petworth Gdns ELGH SO50 ...207 J8
　ROWN SO16 ...227 N7
Petworth Rd HASM GU27 ...157 J8
　HSEA PO3 ...317 K2
Petwyn Cl FERN BH22 ...302 C2
Pevensey Cl ROWN SO16 ...247 H2
Pevensey Wy FRIM GU16 ...58 F5
Peveral Wk KBH RG22 ...68 C9
Peverells Rd CHFD SO53 ...206 G7
Peverells Wood Av
　CHFD SO53 ...206 G6
Peveril Wood Cl
　CHFD SO53 ...207 H6
Peveril Cl RGWD BH24 ...281M3
Peveril Rd ITCH SO19 ...248 C7
Pewsey Pl WSHM SO15 ...247 P7
Phealden's Rd TADY RG26 ...51 P2
Pheasant Cl KBH RG22 ...89 K3
　NTID SP9 ...119 H5
　RWIN SO21 ...124 F2
Pheasant Copse FLEETN GU51 ...74 A3
Pheby Rd KBH RG22 ...89 P1
Phelipps Rd WIMB BH21 ...300 A7
Phoenix Wy
　LSOL/BMARY PO13 ...294 G8
Philip Rd WVILLE PO7 ...275 P5
Philips Crs BOR GU35 ...154 G3
Phillimore Rd ROWN SO16 ...228 F7
Phillips Cl BOR GU35 ...154 G3
　RFNM GU10 ...97 L3
　ROWN SO16 ...227 J6
Philpott Dr TOTT SO40 ...267 K1
Phoenix Cl HLER SO31 ...270 A1
　KSCL RG20 ...8 B2
Phoenix Park Ter BSTK RG21... 6 E4
Phoenix Sq NEND PO2 ...296 G5
Phoenix Ter HTWY RG27 ...54 C9
Phyldon Cl BKME/WDN BH12 ...321 K7
Phyldon Rd BKME/WDN BH12... 321 K6
Pickard Rd FERN BH22 ...302 F1
Pickaxe La ODIM RG29 ...112 F2
Pickering Cl BDST BH18 ...310 G4
Picket Cl FBDG SO45 ...240 D1
Picketts Hl BOR GU35 ...155 J2
Picket Twenty RAND SP11 ...103 J2
Pickford Rd
　MOOR/WNTN BH9 ...322 E6
Pickford St ALDT GU11 ...3 F3

Pickwick Cl TOTT SO40 ...245 P4
Pickwick Gdns CBLY GU15 ...58 G1
Picton Rd AND SP10 ...102 D5
Pier Ap BMTH BH1 * ...8 E6
Pier Head Rd NEND PO2 ...296 D9
Pierrefondes Av FARN GU14 ...57 P8
Pier St LSOL/BMARY PO13 ...314 C2
Pigeon Cl TADY RG26 ...52 B3
Pigeonhouse Fld RWIN SO21 ...125 L5
Pigeon House La WVILLE PO7 ...254 F7
Pigeonhouse Yd RWIN SO21 ...125 L5
Pigeons Farm Rd STHA RG19 ...24 C8
Pike Cl ALDT GU11 ...3 J2
Pikes Hl LYND SO43 ...264 F4
Pikes Hill Av LYND SO43 ...264 E4
Pike St NWBY RG14 ...24 C5
Pilands Wood Rd HLER SO31 ...269 P2
Pilchards Av ELGH SO50 ...230 B1
Pilcot Rd HTWY RG27 ...73 N6
Pilford Heath Rd WIMB BH21 ...279 J7
Pilford La WIMB BH21 ...279 K4
Pilgrim Cl NMIL/BTOS BH25 ...327 L3
Pilgrim Pk RGWD SO22 ...282 C1
Pilgrim Pl WEND SO18 ...228 G8
Pilgrims Cl CHFD SO53 ...206 B5
　FNM GU9 ...116 A2
Pilgrims Ga FUFL SO22 ...22 A2
Pilgrims Pk RGWD BH24 * ...282 C1
Pilgrims Wy AND SP10 ...5 C1
　BOR GU35 ...154 F5
　CHFD SO53 ...320 C5
　FNM GU9 ...116 A2
　FHAM/STUB PO14 ...295 P8
Pilley Bailey LYMN SO41 ...309 N6
Pilley Hl LYMN SO41 ...309M7
Pilley St LYMN SO41 ...309 N6
Pill Hl RSAL SP5 ...201 J1
Pilning Cl FHAM/STUB PO14 ...294 A1
Pilot Hight Rd BWD BH11 ...322 A4
Pilsdon Dr CFDH BH17 ...320 C2
Pimpern Cl CFDH BH17 ...320 C2
Pimpernel Cl LISS GU33 ...173 K5
Pimpernel Wy CHIN RG24 ...70 A5
Pinchcut THLE RG7 ...27 J4
Pinchington La NWBY RG14 ...24 E8
Pindar Pl NWBY RG14 ...25 H2
Pine Av BKME/WDN BH12 ...321 P5
　CBLY GU15 ...41M7
　FAWY SO45 ...268 B8
　FERN BH22 ...302 C1
　FUFL SO22 ...183 K3
　NBAD SO52 ...205 K8
　NMIL/BTOS BH25 ...326 G7
　SSEA PO5 ...223M2
　RWIN SO21 ...144 F4
　STOK SO20 ...121 H5
　TOTT SO40 ...246 A8
Pine Cft FRIM GU16 * ...76 F1
Pine Crs CHCH/BSGR BH23 ...326 A8
　CCLF BH13 ...305 E5
　RGWD BH24 ...281M5
　THLE RG7 ...27 H9
　WEND SO18 ...249M4
Pine Dr East WEND SO18 ...249 N4
Pine End FERN BH22 * ...302 F5
Pinefield Rd WEND SO18 ...249 H1
Pinefields Cl CWTH RG45 ...41 J1
Pine Glen Av FERN BH22 ...280 B9
Pine Gv FLEETS GU52 ...74 E7
　FNM GU9 ...116 E4
　RFNM GU10 ...116 E4
Pinegrove Rd ITCH SO19 ...249 H8
Pinehill Rd BOR GU35 ...154 B6
　CWTH RG45 ...41 J2
Pineholt Cl RGWD BH24 ...281 N4
Pinehurst TADY RG26 ...34 C7
Pinehurst Av
　CHCH/BSGR BH23 ...337 K1
　FARN GU14 ...76 A2
Pinehurst Cl HORN PO8 ...256 C9
Pinehurst Pk FERN BH22 ...280 F9
Pinehurst Pl FERN BH22 ...280 F9
Pinehurst Rd FARN GU14 ...75 P2
　FERN BH22 ...280 F8
　ROWN SO16 ...228 B6
Pinelands Rd ROWN SO16 ...228 B4
Pine Manor Rd RGWD BH24 ...281 H9
Pine Mount Rd CBLY GU15 ...58 C1
Pine Rdg NWBY RG14 ...24 F2
Pine Ridge Dr RFNM GU10 ...116 B5
Pine Ridge Rd THLE RG7 ...27 J5
Pine Rd ALTN GU34 ...150 D5
　BPWT SO32 ...232 B4
　FBDC SO45 ...238 C5
　FBDG SP6 ...239M6
　MOOR/WNTN BH9 ...322 B1
　ROMY SO51 ...204 G7
　WIMB BH21 ...300 A7
Pinesprings Dr BDST BH18 ...310 A2
Pines Rd FLEETN GU51 ...74 C2
　LIPH GU30 ...174 F3
The Pines AND SP10 ...4 A3
　FBDC SP6 ...241 H1
　FHAM/PORC PO16 ...273 L9
Pinetops Cl LYMN SO41 ...328 G4
Pine Tree Cl WIMB BH21 ...278 F9
Pine Tree Gdns HORN PO8 ...256 A9
Pine Tree Gln WBNE BH4 ...118 F2
Pinetree Houses NTID SP9 * ...79 J4
Pine Trees Cl
　FHAM/STUB PO14 ...294 B1
Pinetree Wk CFDH BH17 ...320 D4
Pine Vale Crs NBNE BH10 ...322 D5
Pine Vw BOR GU35 ...155 J2

Pine View Cl FNM GU9 ...96 C6
　HASM GU27 ...157 H5
Pineview Cl HLER SO31 ...270 A1
　RSAL SP5 ...199 P9
Pine Vw AND SP10 ...102 B4
Pine Wk AND SP10 ...280 E6
　HLER SO31 ...270 C5
　LISS GU33 ...173M9
　ROWN SO16 ...228 B5
Pine Wy ROWN SO16 ...228 B5
Pinewood CHIN RG24 * ...69 P1
　LSOL/BMARY PO13 ...295 J8
Pinewood Av HAV PO9 ...276 B7
　NBNE BH10 ...322 D2
Pinewood Cl
　CHCH/BSGR BH23 ...326 C6
　FHAM/STUB PO14 ...294 B5
　NBNE BH10 ...322 D2
　ROMY SO51 ...204 G4
　SHST GU47 ...40 G6
　TADY RG26 ...33 N5
Pinewood Crs FARN GU14 ...57 K8
　FAWY SO45 ...268 D8
Pinewood Dr FARN GU14 ...57 K8
　KSCL RG20 ...30 F4
Pinewood Gdns FERN BH22 ...302 D1
Pinewood Hl FLEETN GU51 ...74 D2
Pinewood Pk FARN GU14 ...57 J8
　ITCH SO19 ...249 P6
Pinewood Rd ASHV GU12 ...77 J9
　CCLF BH13 ...334 B5
　CHCH/BSGR BH23 ...326 B6
　FERN BH22 ...302 C1
　LYMN SO41 ...327 P4
Pinkerton Rd KBH RG22 ...89 N1
Pinkney La LYND SO43 ...264 E8
Pink Rd NEND PO2 ...296 C9
Pinks Hl FHAM/PORC PO16 ...273 H8
Pinks La TADY RG26 ...33 P5
Pinnell Cl KBH RG22 ...89 L5
Pinsley Dr WHAM PO17 ...274 C4
Pintail Cl KBH RG22 ...89 K4
Pinto Cl FHAM PO15 ...271 H3
Pipers Ash TADY RG26 ...282 C1
Pipers Cl TOTT SO40 ...246 B5
Pipers Cft FLEETS GU52 ...74 E8
Pipers Dr CHCH/BSGR BH23 ...325 L8
Pipers Md HORN PO8 ...236 A7
Pipers Patch FARN GU14 ...58 A9
Piping Cl RWIN SO21 ...207 P5
Piping Rd RWIN SO21 ...207 P5
Pipistrelle Wk WHAM PO17 ...272 C2
Pipit Cl GPORT PO12 ...315M1
　STHA RG19 ...25 L4
Pippin Cl CHCH/BSGR BH23 ...324 C5
　LYMN SO41 ...329 L5
Pipsons Cl YTLY GU46 ...40 E8
Pirbright Rd FARN GU14 ...77 J4
　RGUW GU3 ...77 L8
Pirelli St SHAM SO14 ...20 C4
Pirrie Cl WSHM SO15 ...247 P2
Pitcairn Cl CHIN RG24 ...69M2
Pitcairn Ms ENEY PO4 * ...317 K6
Pitchponds Rd HLER SO31 ...292 C1
Pitcot La RWIN SO21 ...209 H2
Pitcroft La EPSF GU31 ...215M8
Pitcroft Rd NEND PO2 ...296 F8
Pitfield La THLE RG7 ...36 B2
Pitfold Av HASM GU27 ...156 C7
Pitfold Cl HASM GU27 ...156 D7
Pither Rd ODIM RG29 ...93 J5
Pithouse La CHCH/BSGR BH23 ...304 B8
Pitman Cl KBH RG22 ...89M1
Pitmore Cl ELGH SO50 ...207 K5
Pitmore La LYMN SO41 ...308 D6
Pitmore Rd ELGH SO50 ...207 K5
Pitreavie Rd CHAM PO6 ...297 N1
Pittard Rd BSTK RG21 ...69 J9
Pitter Cl FUFL SO22 ...164 C2
Pitthall TADY RG26 * ...49 L8
Pitt Hill La WVILLE PO7 ...254 C2
Pitt La RFNM GU10 ...136 A3
Pittmore Rd
　CHCH/BSGR BH23 ...324 C5
Pitt Rd WSHM SO15 ...247 N5
Pitts Deep La LYMN SO41 ...330 C2
Pitts La AND SP10 ...4 C7
Pitts Pl NMIL/BTOS BH25 ...327M5
Pitt Wk AMSY SP4 ...118 F2
Pitwines Cl PLE BH15 ...332 F1
Pitymoor La WHAM PO17 ...274 D6
Place Crs WVILLE PO7 ...275 P5
Place House Cl FHAM PO15 ...272 A9
Place La RWIN SO21 ...180M6
Plaitford Gv HAV PO9 ...276 C6
Plantagenet Crs BWD BH11 ...301M4
Plantation Dr
　CHCH/BSGR BH23 ...325 N8
　TOTT SO40 ...267 J1
Plantation Rd AND SP10 ...102 E5
　CFDH BH17 ...320 E3
　CHCH/BSGR BH23 ...305 P4
　LISS GU33 ...192 F4
　NTID SP9 ...79 H6
　ROMY SO51 ...224 D4
　TADY RG26 ...34 C3
The Plantation BPWT SO32 ...251 L1
Plantation Wy BOR GU35 ...153M8
Plant Park Rd RGWD BH24 ...282 A6
Plants Cl ROMY SO51 ...225 H3
Plassey Crs BWD BH11 ...322 B2
Plassey Rd NTID SP9 ...78 C6
Platoff Rd LYMN SO41 ...329 L7
Player Cl FBDG SP6 ...220 D9
Players Crs TOTT SO40 ...246 C6
Playfair Rd SSEA PO5 ...19 J5
Playfields Dr
　BKME/WDN BH12 ...321 N6
Pleasance Wy
　NMIL/BTOS BH25 ...327 H4

Pleasant Hl TADY RG26 ...34 C6
Pleasant Rd ENEY PO4 ...317 K4
Plecy Cl FERN BH22 ...302 D5
Plemont Cl BKME/WDN BH12 ...321 N3
Pless Rd LYMN SO41 ...338 D1
Plough Gdns STOK SO20 ...160 A1
Plough La BPWT SO32 ...253 N1
　HTWY RG27 ...54 E2
Plough Rd YTLY GU46 ...40 F7
Plough Wy FUFL SO22 ...183M2
Plover Cl AND SP10 ...82 F9
　FHAM/STUB PO14 ...295 P7
　KBH RG22 ...89M7
　ROWN SO16 ...228M7
Plover Dr LYMN SO41 ...339 J2
Plover Reach ENEY PO4 * ...317 K3
Plover Rd TOTT SO40 ...246 A4
Plovers Down FUFL SO22 ...183 K5
Plovers Rd HORN PO8 ...236 A6
Plovers Wy ALTN GU34 ...132 C4
Plowman Ct WVILLE PO7 ...276 D1
P.L.P.H. Rd FAWY SO45 ...291 K4
Plumer Rd CFDH BH17 ...320 C5
　LISS GU33 ...173M9
Plumpton Gdns HSEA PO3 ...297 K6
Plumpton Gv WVILLE PO7 ...276 B1
Plumpton Rd HAV PO9 ...192 A6
Plumpton Wy ALTN GU34 ...132 F7
Pluto Rd ELGH SO50 ...230 D1
Plymouth Dr
　FHAM/STUB PO14 ...295 P7
Plymouth St SSEA PO5 ...19 H4
Poachers Fld ODIM RG29 ...92 G8
Pococks La LISS GU33 ...172 E8
Poets Wy FUFL SO22 ...164 E7
Poinsettia Cl FHAM PO15 ...271 L7
Pointout Cl ROWN SO16 ...228 A9
Pointout Rd ROWN SO16 ...228 A9
Poland La ODIM RG29 ...72 C6
Polden Cl FARN GU14 ...57M6
Polesden Cl CHFD SO53 ...206 D5
Poles La LYMN SO41 ...329 L6
　RWIN SO21 ...144 C6
Police Station La BPWT SO32 ...233M5
Policerin Wy FLEETS GU52 ...74 E8
Pollard Gv CBLY GU15 ...59 H1
Pollards Moor Rd TOTT SO40 ...244 G2
Polmear Cl FLEETS GU52 ...74 E8
The Polygon WSHM SO15 ...20 C2
Pomona Cl FERN BH22 ...302 D2
Pompeys La FERN BH22 ...302 A4
Pond Cl NMIL/BTOS BH25 ...327 J4
　NWBY RG14 ...86 C5
　OVTN RG25 ...86 D5
　TOTT SO40 ...247 K9
Pond Cft YTLY GU46 ...40 F7
Pond Head WIMB BH21 ...279 J1
Pondhead Cl FAWY SO45 ...290 E6
Pond La HORN PO8 ...236 B6
　RFNM GU10 ...136 C5
Pond Piece WVILLE PO7 ...255 H6
Pond Rd BOR GU35 ...155 H4
　FARN GU14 ...57 J4
　HLER SO31 ...270 F4
　TADY RG26 ...52 B3
Pondside La BPWT SO32 ...231 P4
Pondtail Cl FLEETS GU52 ...74 F4
Pondtail Gdns FLEETN GU51 ...74 F4
Pondtail Rd FLEETN GU51 ...74 E4
Pondview Cl FLEETN GU51 ...74 F4
Ponsonby Rd PSTN BH14 ...321M8
Pook La HAV PO9 ...277 K6
　WHAM PO17 ...272 F6
Pookles La ALTN GU34 ...133 P8
Pooksgreen TOTT SO40 ...247 H9
Poole Br PLE BH15 ...332 D2
Poole Hl WCLF BH2 ...8 B4
Poole La BWD BH11 ...301 P9
Poole Rd CCLF BH13 ...321 P8
　ITCH SO19 ...320 A5
　UPTN BH16 ...320 A5
　WBNE BH4 ...334 B2
　WCLF BH2 ...8 A4
Pool Rd ALDT GU11 ...97 J4
　HTWY RG27 ...55 H6
Popes Farm Rd CHIN RG24 ...70 F4
Popes Hl KSCL RG20 ...48 B5
Popes La BPWT SO32 ...209 J9
　TOTT SO40 ...246 D4
Popes Md NMIL/BTOS BH25 ...327 H6
Popham La OVTN RG25 ...108 C2
Poplar Cl CHCH/BSGR BH23 ...305 N8
　FRIM GU16 ...76 E1
　HTWY RG27 ...54 E2
　WIMB BH21 ...278 F9
Poplar Crs RGWD BH24 ...282 C2
Poplar Dr FHAM/STUB PO14 ...294 C1
Poplar Gv HISD PO11 ...318 G4
Poplar La CHCH/BSGR BH23 ...325 N8
Poplar Pl NWBY RG14 ...24 D2
Poplar Rd ITCH SO19 ...249 H5
　NMIL/BTOS BH25 ...326 E3
The Poplars BPWT SO32 ...232 C9
Poplar Wk CHIN RG24 ...96 D4
Poppy Cl Wy HEND SO30 ...250 E3
　NBAD SO52 ...205 K8
　RGWD BH24 ...282 F2
Popley Wy CHIN RG24 ...69 L3
Poppy Cl CHCH/BSGR BH23 ...325M7
　HLER SO31 ...270 F8
　RAND SP11 ...102 A3
Poppy Flds CHIN RG24 ...70 B4
Poppyfields CHFD SO53 ...206 B5
Poppy Wy ROWN SO16 ...228 E3
Porchester Cl HSEA PO3 ...297 L4
Porchester Rd ITCH SO19 ...248 G8
　NWBY RG14 ...24 B4
Porlock Cl STHA RG19 * ...25 N5
Porlock Rd ROWN SO16 ...246 G2

Portacre Ri BSTK RG21 ...69 J9
Portal Cl RAND SP11 ...101 P3
Portal Rd ELGH SO50 ...229M1
　ITCH SO19 ...249 K7
　LSOL/BMARY PO13 ...294 G6
　TOTT SO40 ...247 N4
　WINC SO23 ...25 H7
Portarlington Cl WBNE BH4 ...334 D4
Portarlington Rd WBNE BH4 ...334 C3
Portchester Ct CHAR BH8 * ...335 H1
Portchester Hts
　CHAM PO6 ...273 P9
Portchester La WHAM PO17 ...273 N4
Portchester Ri ELGH SO50 ...207 J6
Portchester Rd BMTH BH8 ...335 H1
　FHAM/PORC PO16 ...295 L1
Portchester Rd CHAR BH8 ...322 C9
Portelet Cl BKME/WDN BH12 ...321M3
Portelet Pl HEND SO30 ...250 C6
Porteous Crs CHFD SO53 ...207 H7
Porter Cl ODIM RG29 ...93 J5
Porter End NWBY RG14 ...24 D7
Porter Rd CFDH BH17 ...320 D5
　KBH RG22 ...90 B2
Porterbridge St ROMY SO51 ...204 C6
Porters Cl AND SP10 ...102 B1
　OVTN RG25 ...109 H1
Porter's La SHAM SO14 ...20 D7
　SHAM SO14 ...279 L8
Portesham Gdns
　MOOR/WNTN BH9 ...323 H5
Portesham Wy CFDH BH17 ...320 C1
Portfield Cl CHCH/BSGR BH23 ...324 E7
Portfield Rd
　CHCH/BSGR BH23 ...324 E8
Port Hamble HLER SO31 * ...270 A7
Portiswood Cl TADY RG26 ...34 E6
Portland Dr FLEETS GU52 ...74 C8
　GPORT PO12 ...315 H5
Portland Gv AND SP10 ...4 D4
Portland Rd
　MOOR/WNTN BH9 ...322 G7
　SSEA PO5 ...316 E6
　WVILLE PO7 ...275 N3
Portland's Cl PSF GU32 ...191 P9
Portland Sq LISS GU33 ...192 D2
Portland St FHAM/PORC PO16 ...11 H6
　PSEA PO1 ...18 E3
　SHAM SO14 ...20 D4
Portland Ter FNM GU9 * ...96 D7
　SSEA PO5 * ...316 E6
Port La RWIN SO21 ...182 D7
Portman Crs SBNE BH6 ...335 M1
Portman Rd LTDN BH7 ...335M1
Portman Ter SBNE BH6 * ...335 P2
Portmore Cl BDST BH18 ...300 D7
Portobello Gv
　FHAM/PORC PO16 ...273 P9
Port Royal St SSEA PO5 * ...19 L3
Portsdown Av CHAM PO6 ...297 L1
Portsdown Hill Rd CHAM PO6 ...275 H9
　FHAM/PORC PO16 ...273 L8
Portsdown Rd BPWT SO32 ...209 H9
　CHAM PO6 ...297 P5
　ELGH SO50 ...208 C7
　FRIM GU16 ...58 D2
　GSHT GU26 ...156 B4
　HORN PO8 ...256 C5
　ITCH SO19 ...248 G9
　LIPH GU30 ...155 P9
　LIPH GU30 ...175 J6
　LSOL/BMARY PO13 ...314 E4
Portsmouth Wk KBH RG22 ...89 P1
Portsmouth Wy KBH RG22 ...89 P1
Portsview Av
　FHAM/PORC PO16 ...295 P1
Portsview Gdns
　FHAM/PORC PO16 ...273 P9
Portswood Av PTSW SO17 ...248 D3
Portswood Dr
　MOOR/WNTN BH9 ...322 G3
Portswood Pk PTSW SO17 ...248 D3
Portswood Rd HAV PO9 ...276 D4
　NEND PO2 ...296 G4
　PTSW SO17 ...248 D3
Portview Rd WEND SO18 ...249 K4
Port Wy CHAM PO6 ...296 C1
Portway TADY RG26 ...33 N5
　THLE RG7 ...37 P4
Portway Cl AND SP10 ...102 B2
　WEND SO18 ...249 K4
Posbrook Dr Pl DEAN RG23 ...68 E7
Posbrook La ENEY PO4 ...317 J4
Posbrook La
　FHAM/STUB PO14 ...293 L4
Postern Cl FHAM/PORC PO16 ...295 P1
Post Horn La HTWY RG27 ...53M8
Posting House Ms NWBY RG14 ...24 D5
Post Office La TOTT SO40 ...109 H1
　RDGW/BURGH RG30 ...27 L2
　RGWD BH24 ...281 N4
Post Office Rd BMTH BH1 * ...8 D4
　CHCH/BSGR BH23 ...275 L5
Pottbridge Rd ODIM RG29 ...72 E4
Pot La CHIN RG24 * ...71 H8
Potley Hill Rd YTLY GU46 ...40 G9
Potteries La FRIM GU16 ...76 E1
The Potteries FARN GU14 ...57 L7
　FHAM/PORC PO16 ...11 H2
Potterne Wy WIMB BH21 ...299 N8
Potterne Wood Cl VWD BH31 ...259 J6
Potters Cl LISS GU33 ...192 E2
Potters Ga FNM GU9 ...96 A9
Potters Heron Cl ROMY SO51 ...206 A2
Potters Heron La ROMY SO51 ...206 A2
Potters La HTWY RG27 ...55 J8
Potters Wy PSTN BH14 ...333 L1
Pottery Dro STOK SO20 ...120 A7

Pottery La RFNM GU10 .....115 P4
Pottery Rd PSTN BH14 .....333 J1
Poulner Cl ITCH SO19 .....269 J1
Poulner Ct HAV PO9 .....276 C4
Poulner Hl RGWD BH24 .....283 H1
Poulner Pk RGWD BH24 .....260 C9
Poultons Cl OVTN RG25 .....86 C4
Poultons Rd OVTN RG25 .....86 C4
Pound Bar GU35 .....154 C3
 LSOL/BMARY PO13 .....295 H9
 NARL SO24 .....130 B7
 PLE BH15 .....321 H7
 RGWD BH24 .....282 E1
 TADY RG26 .....51 P2
Pound Cots
 BPWT SO32 .....211 N8
Pound Ga ALTN GU34 .....132 C4
Pound Gate Dr
 FHAM/STUB PO14 .....271 J9
Pound Hl NARL SO24 .....167 P1
 ROMY SO51 .....202 C8
Pound La BPWT SO32 .....211 P8
 FBDG SP6 .....219 H7
 KSCL RG20 .....30 D8
 NWBY RG14 .....24 A3
 PLE BH15 .....320 C7
 RGWD BH24 .....284 A8
 ROMY SO51 .....202 C8
 ROMY SO51 .....205 M3
 STHA RG19 .....25 K4
 TOTT SO40 .....137 J8
 TOTT SO40 .....246 D9
Pound Lea HISD SP11
Pound Meadow HTWY RG27 .....52 F5
Pound Rd ASHV GU12 .....3 C4
 CHAM PO6 .....274 D8
 HLER SO31 .....260 D1
 LYMN SO41 .....329 H4
 OVTN RG25 .....87 H4
 STOK SO20 .....120 C7
 WINC SO23 .....145 K8
Pound St NWBY RG14 .....16 C4
 WEND SO18 .....249 J4
Pound Tree Rd SHAM SO14 .....20 E4
Poveys Md KSCL RG20 .....30 D8
Powell Crs PSTN BH14 .....321 K9
Powell Rd PSEA PO1 .....316 C2
Power Rd PSEA PO1 .....316 C2
Powerscourt Rd NEND PO2 .....296 C9
 NMIL/BTOS BH25 .....327 K4
Powis Cl NMIL/BTOS BH25 .....327 K4
Poyle Rd RFNM GU10
Poyner Cl FHAM/PORC PO16 .....11 C4
Poynings Crs BSTK RG21 .....90 E1
Poynings Pl PSEA PO1 .....18 D6
Poynters Cl AND SP10 .....82 D9
Poyntz Rd OVTN RG25 .....86 C3
Prancing Horse La STHA RG19 .....25 P4
The Precinct GPORT PO12 * 13 L2
 HISD PO11 * 318 C5
 WVILLE PO7 .....275 N3
Precosa Rd HEND SO30 .....250 B6
Prelate Wy FHAM/STUB PO14 .....271 J8
Premier Pde WEND SO18 * 229 J1
Premier Rd ROMY SO51 .....205 H8
Prentice Cl FARN GU14 .....58 A5
Prescelly Cl KBH RG22 .....68 E8
Preshaw Cl ROWN SO16 .....227 N8
Preston La CHCH/BSGR BH23 .....325 H4
Preston Pl NEND PO2 .....297 H8
 PLE BH15 .....320 E6
Preston Wy CHCH/BSGR BH23 .....325 P7
Prestwick La HASM GU27 .....157 M3
Prestwood Cl
 NMIL/BTOS BH25 .....327 H6
Pretoria Cl LISS GU33 .....173 P5
Pretoria Rd ENEY PO4 .....317 H5
 HEND SO30 .....250 B6
 RAND SP11 .....80 E2
Pricketts Hl BPWT SO32 .....252 D4
Prideaux-Brune Av
 LSOL/BMARY PO13 .....294 C5
Priest Croft Dr FAWY SO45 .....255 J7
Priest Down DEAN RG23 .....89 M6
Priestfields FHAM/STUB PO14 .....271 J8
Priestlands ROMY SO51 .....204 C5
Priestlands La TOTT SO40 .....245 N5
Priestlands La LYMN SO41 .....329 J4
Priest La CHCH/BSGR BH23 .....304 F9
 CHOB/PIR GU24 .....59 P7
Priestley Cl TOTT SO40 .....246 B4
Priestley Rd CHIN RG24 .....69 H3
 NBNE BH10 .....322 B6
Priestwood Cl WEND SO18 .....249 M4
Primate Rd FHAM/STUB PO14 .....271 K8
Prime One AND SP10 * 103 J1
Primrose Cl CHFD SO53 .....206 B9
 HEND SO30 .....250 C6
 LSOL/BMARY PO13 .....294 C4
Primrose Dr HTWY RG27 .....55 N6
Primrose Gdns CFDH BH17 .....320 B3
 FARN GU14 .....89 M6
 KBH RG22 .....89 H8
Primrose La LISS GU33 .....193 J2
 RSAL SP5 .....199 N7
Primrose Rd RAND SP11 .....79 P1
 ROWN SO16 .....228 C8
Primrose Wy
 CHCH/BSGR BH23 .....325 N7
 HLER SO31 .....270 F8
 ROMY SO51 .....204 C5
 SHST GU47 .....41 J5
 WIMB BH21 .....300 A6
Primula La BOR GU35 .....154 D8
Prince Albert Gdns AND SP10 .....4 B5
Prince Albert Rd ENEY PO4 .....317 H1
Prince Alfred St GPORT PO12 .....12 C4
Prince Charles Crs FARN GU14 .....58 A5
Prince Cl AND SP10 .....83 H9
Prince Dr SHST GU47 .....41 H5
Prince George's St HAV PO9 .....15 C5
Prince George St PSEA PO1 .....18 D2

NEND PO2 .....316 E1
RFNM GU10 .....115 N7
Protea Gdns
 FHAM/STUB PO14 .....293 M1
Provene Cl BPWT SO32 .....232 C8
Providence Hl HLER SO31 .....250 A9
Providence Pl ROWN SO16 .....228 B7
Provident Wy BSTK RG21 .....6 A1
Provost St FBDG SP6 .....240 D3
Pruetts La LISS GU33 .....192 D5
Prunus Cl FERN BH22 .....302 B1
Prunus Dr FERN BH22 .....302 B1
Puckridge Gate Rd ALDT GU11 .....75 L6
Puckridge Hill Rd ALDT GU11 .....75 M7
Puckshott Wy HASM GU27 .....157 J5
Pudbrooke Gdns HEND SO30 .....250 B3
Pudding La WINC SO23 .....165 J3
Puddledish La FBDG SP6 .....220 B9
Puddletown Cr CFDH BH17 .....321 H2
Puffers Wy NWBY RG14 .....16 A4
Puffin Cl KBH RG22 .....89 K5
 ROWN SO16 .....227 M7
Puffin Crs FHAM/STUB PO14 .....293 P5
Puffin Gdns
 LSOL/BMARY PO13 .....294 E8
Puffin Wk HORN PO8 .....255 M7
Pug's Hole RSAL SP5 .....159 H8
Pulens Crs EPSF GU31 .....216 A1
Pulens La EPSF GU31 .....215 P1
Pullman Ct FERN BH22 .....280 D7
Pullman Wy RGWD BH24 .....282 B8
Pump La HORN PO8 .....256 A6
 LSOL/BMARY PO13 .....294 G8
Punshott La NARL SO24 .....188 C3
Purbeck Av PLE BH15 .....332 A2
Purbeck Dr FHAM/STUB PO14 .....294 B1
 VWD BH31 .....258 F5
Purbeck Rd NMIL/BTOS BH25 .....326 F8
 WCLF BH2 .....8 B4
Purbrook Gdns WVILLE PO7 .....275 L5
Purbrook Heath Rd
 WVILLE PO7 .....275 H5
Purbrook Rd PSEA PO1 .....316 C3
 TADY RG26 .....51 K4
Purbrook Wy HAV PO9 .....276 B6
 WVILLE PO7 .....275 P6
Purcell Cl KBH RG22 .....90 B2
 WVILLE PO7 .....275 N5
Purchase Rd
 BKME/WDN BH12 .....322 C8
Purewell CHCH/BSGR BH23 .....325 H9
Purewell Cl
 CHCH/BSGR BH23 .....325 J9
Purewell Cross Rd
 CHCH/BSGR BH23 .....325 J9
Purkess Cl CHFD SO53 .....206 F6
Purkiss Cl TOTT SO40 .....245 J6
Purley Wy FRIM GU16 .....58 D5
 ROMY SO51 .....224 D1
Purlieu La FBDG SP6 .....221 K9
Purmerend Cl FARN GU14 .....57 K8
The Purrocks PSF GU32 .....191 M9
Purslane Gdns FHAM PO15 .....271 M7
Pursuit Cl WVILLE PO7 .....275 N3
Pussex La CHCH/BSGR BH23 .....305 N8
Putmans Cl EPSF GU31 .....216 D1
Puttenham Rd CHIN RG24 .....27 G8
 RFNM GU10 .....97 P7
Puttock Cl HASM GU27 .....156 C8
Pycroft Cl HISD PO11 .....299 J6
 ITCH SO19 .....249 H6
Pye La WIMB BH21 .....238 E4
 WIMB BH21 .....300 D1
Pyestock Crs FARN GU14 .....57 J9
Pye St PSEA PO1 .....316 E2
Pyland's La HLER SO31 .....250 B8
Pyle Cl HORN PO8 .....256 A7
Pyle Hl NWBY RG14 .....17 H6
Pylewell Rd FAWY SO45 .....268 C5
Pyotts Copse CHIN RG24 .....70 B3
Pyotts Ct CHIN RG24 .....70 B3
Pyotts Hl CHIN RG24 .....70 B3
Pyrford Cl GPORT PO12 .....315 J5
 WVILLE PO7 .....255 M9
Pyrford Ms LYMN SO41 .....329 L5
Pytchley Cl FHAM/STUB PO14 .....293 N7

Q

The Quadrangle ELGH SO50 .....207 J9
 FARN GU14 * 58 B5
The Quadrant ASHV GU12 .....76 F8
Quail Wy HORN PO8 .....256 A5
Quantock Cl KBH RG22 .....89 K3
Quantock Rd ROWN SO16 .....227 P8
The Quantocks FAWY SO45 .....267 P8
 STHA RG19 .....25 N5
Quarely Rd HAV PO9 .....276 A4
Quarrington Cl STHA RG19 .....25 P5
Quarry La YTLY GU46 .....40 F9
Quarry Rd WIMB BH21 .....279 J7
 WINC SO23 .....3 G2
Quarterdeck Av NEND PO2 .....296 D8
Quarterjack Rd FARN GU14 .....76 B2
Quartremaine Rd HSEA PO3 .....297 M3
Quavey Rd RSAL SP5 .....200 A7
Quay Hvn HLER SO31 .....270 D4
Quay La GPORT PO12 .....13 J7
Quayle Dr BWD BH11 .....301 P7
Quay Point CHAM PO6 .....296 F4
Quay Rd CHCH/BSGR BH23 .....324 E1
Quayside HISD PO11 .....299 J6
Quayside Rd WEND SO18 .....248 F4
Quayside Wk TOTT SO40 .....246 K7
Quay St FHAM/PORC PO16 .....11 J7
 LYMN SO41 .....329 M5
The Quay PLE BH15 .....332 E2
Quebec Cl LIPH GU30 .....175 K4

Quebec Gdns BLKW GU17 .....57 L1
Queen Anne Dr WIMB BH21 .....300 E6
Queen Anne's Dr HAV PO9 .....276 C8
Queen Anne's Ga FNM GU9 .....96 B4
Queen Elizabeth Av
 LYMN SO41 .....329 K3
Queen Elizabeth Ct ASHV GU12 .....97 N1
Queen Elizabeth Dr ALDT GU11 .....2 C3
Queen Katherine Rd
 LYMN SO41 .....329 M4
Queen Mary Av BSTK RG21 .....7 F5
 CBLY GU15 .....41 P9
 MOOR/WNTN BH9 .....322 F5
Queen Mary Cl FLEETN GU51 .....74 C2
Queen Mary Rd
 FHAM/PORC PO16 .....295 P2
Queen Rd FHAM/STUB PO14 .....294 D5
Queen's Av ALDT GU11 .....76 A1
 AND SP10 .....64 A2
 CHCH/BSGR BH23 .....336 F1
Queensbury Pl BLKW GU17 .....57 K2
Queen's Cl FARN GU14 .....76 A4
 FERN BH22 .....280 D8
 LSOL/BMARY PO13 * 314 C2
 RAND SP11 .....63 H1
Queens Crs FHAM/STUB PO14 .....294 B6
 HORN PO8 .....256 B4
Queensfield OVTN RG25 .....109 H1
Queens Gdns FBDG SP6 .....240 D1
Queen's Gate Rd FARN GU14 .....76 A5
Queens Gv NMIL/BTOS BH25 .....327 L3
 SSEA PO5 .....316 E6
 WVILLE PO7 .....275 M5
Queensland Rd BOSC BH5 .....335 N1
Queens La FNM GU9 .....96 C5
Queensmead
 CHCH/BSGR BH23 .....324 E6
 FARN GU14 .....76 A1
Queens Md FUFL SO22 .....164 F5
Queens Pde WINC SO23 * 264 F5
 WVILLE PO7 .....275 N5
Queen's Park Av CHAR BH8 .....323 J7
Queen's Park Gdns CHAR BH8 .....323 J8
Queen's Park Rd CHAR BH8 .....323 K8
Queen's Park South Dr
 CHAR BH8 .....323 J8
Queen's Park West Dr
 CHAR BH8 .....323 J8
Queen's Pl SSEA PO5 .....19 H7
Queens Ride NBAD SO52 .....205 J9
Queens Rd ALDT GU11 .....2 C3
 ALTN GU34 .....132 E6
 BSTK RG21 .....58 A1
 CBLY GU15 .....58 A1
 CHCH/BSGR BH23 .....325 J9
 CHFD SO53 .....206 F4
 FARN GU14 .....76 C4
 FERN BH22 .....302 D1
 FHAM/PORC PO16 .....11 C4
 FLEETS GU52 .....74 D5
 FNM GU9 .....96 C5
 FUFL SO22 .....164 E8
 GPORT PO12 .....12 E1
 KSCL RG20 .....30 D8
 LIPH GU30 .....174 D4
 LSOL/BMARY PO13 .....314 D4
 LYND SO43 .....264 C5
 NEND PO2 .....296 C9
 NWBY RG14 .....16 A4
 ODIM RG29 .....72 B9
 PSEA PO1 .....316 B2
 PSF GU32 .....215 K1
 PSTN BH14 .....321 M8
 WBNE BH4 .....334 D3
 WHCH RG28 .....85 M8
 WSHM SO15 .....247 N1
 WVILLE PO7 .....275 N1
Queen's Ter ASHV GU12 .....97 N1
Queen's Ter SHAM SO15 .....21 F7
Queenstown Rd WSHM SO15 .....247 N5
Queen St ASHV GU12 .....97 K1
 EMRTH PO10 .....299 N1
 FBDG SP6 .....221 M5
 PSEA PO1 .....18 E3
 RWIN SO21 .....183 P9
Queen's Vw HLER SO31 .....269 K4
Queen's Wy SHAM SO14 .....20 E7
 SSEA PO5 .....19 H7
The Queensway
 FHAM/PORC PO16 .....295 M1
Queenswood Av CHAR BH8 .....323 L6
Queenswood Dr FERN BH22 .....302 D1
Queenwood Ri STOK SO20 .....160 A1
Queenwood Rd STOK SO20 .....160 A1
Quennells Hl RFNM GU10 .....115 N4
Querida Cl HLER SO31 .....270 D2
Quilter Cl ITCH SO19 .....249 M7
Quilter Rd KBH RG22 .....89 K5
Quince La WIMB BH21 .....278 F8
Quince Tree Wy HTWY RG27 .....72 A3
Quinton Cl CHCH/BSGR BH23 .....326 B7
Quintin Cl SSEA PO5 .....19 J4
Quintrell Av
 FHAM/PORC PO16 .....295 L1
Quob Farm Cl HEND SO30 .....229 N1
Quob La HEND SO30 .....229 N9
The Quomp RGWD BH24 .....282 E2

R

Racecourse Vw LYND SO43 .....264 F4
Rachel Cl ELGH SO50 .....230 B2
Rack Cl AND SP10 .....4 E4
Rackclose Rd ALTN GU54 .....132 E6

Rackfield HASM GU27 .....156 C6
Rackstraw Rd SHST GU47 .....41 L5
Racton Av CHAM PO6 .....297 K2
Racton Rd EMRTH PO10 .....277 M7
Radar Rd FARN GU14 .....75 L3
Radcliffe Cl FRIM GU16 .....58 E6
Radcliffe Rd SHAM SO14 .....21 H1
Radclyffe Rd
 FHAM/PORC PO16 .....11 K3
Radford Cl FNM GU9 .....96 E6
Radford Gdns BSTK RG21 .....90 B1
Radipole Rd CFDH BH17 .....321 H2
Radleigh Gdns TOTT SO40 .....245 P3
Radley Cl HEND SO30 .....250 C2
Radnor St SSEA PO5 .....19 H4
Radstock Rd ITCH SO19 .....248 G8
Radway Crs WSHM SO15 .....247 P5
Radway Rd WSHM SO15 .....247 P5
Raeburn Cl NARL SO24 .....187 H1
Raeburn Dr HEND SO30 .....250 B4
Raeburn Wy SHST GU47 .....41 L8
Rae Rd FARN GU14 .....76 A3
RAF Gate Rd FARN GU14 .....76 A3
Ragdale THLE RG7 .....27 J4
Raglan Cl ASHV GU12 .....97 P3
 CHFD SO53 .....206 C9
 FRIM GU16 .....58 E5
Raglan Gdns BWD BH11 .....322 A5
Ragmore La PSF GU32 .....190 E1
Rails La HISD PO11 .....319 H6
Railway Rd LISS GU33 .....193 J5
 NWBY RG14 .....17 G3
Railway Triangle CHAM PO6 * 297 K3
Railway Vw PSEA PO1 .....19 J2
Rainbow Cl CHIN RG24 .....70 D7
Rainham Cl KBH RG22 .....89 K4
Rakemakers ALTN GU34 .....133 L6
Rake Rd LIPH GU30 .....193 P4
 LISS GU33 .....192 F2
Raleigh Cl CHCH/BSGR BH23 .....337 K1
 NMIL/BTOS BH25 .....327 H4
 RGWD BH24 .....282 C1
Raleigh Wy CBLY GU15 .....58 B2
Raley Rd HLER SO31 .....270 C8
Ralph Rd WIMB BH21 .....300 A6
Ram Aly STHA RG19 .....32 F6
Ramalley La CHFD SO53 .....206 D6
Rambler Dr
 LSOL/BMARY PO13 .....314 C2
Ramblers Md RAND SP11 .....81 M8
Ramblers Wy HORN PO8 .....276 B1
Ramillies Cl ALDT GU11 .....76 D5
Ramley Rd LYMN SO41 .....328 C3
Rampart Rd HSEA PO3 .....297 H4
Rampart Rd WEND SO18 .....248 E7
Rampart Rw GPORT PO12 .....13 J4
Rampton La WHCH RG28 .....85 M7
Ramptons La THLE RG7 .....26 D9
Rampton's Meadow
 TADY RG26 .....34 E7
Ramsay Pl LSOL/BMARY PO13 .....294 C7
Ramsay Rd WINC SO23 .....145 K9
Ramsdale Av HAV PO9 .....276 C5
Ramsdean Rd PSF GU32 .....214 D4
Ramsdell Cl TADY RG26 .....34 C7
Ramsdell Rd FLEETN GU51
 TADY RG26 .....49 H4
 TADY RG26 .....50 E4
Ramsey Rd HISD PO11 .....318 C5
Ramshill EPSF GU31 .....215 N1
Ramsholt Cl OVTN RG25 .....108 C1
Rances Wy FUFL SO22 .....164 F5
Randall Cl TOTT SO40 .....246 A1
Randall Rd CHFD SO53 .....206 F5
Randalls La RGWD BH24 .....284 A4
Randolph Dr FARN GU14 .....75 K1
Randolph Rd BMTH BH1 .....335 L2
 NEND PO2 .....296 C9
 PSTN BH14 .....321 L7
Randolph St WSHM SO15 .....247 N4
Ranelagh Gdns WSHM SO15 .....248 A4
Ranelagh Rd
 CHCH/BSGR BH23 .....326 B8
 HAV PO9 .....296 E8
 NEND PO2 .....296 E8
 WINC SO23 .....164 F9
Ranfurly Gdns FAWY SO45 .....268 A8
Range Gdns ITCH SO19 .....249 K8
Range Gn NEND PO2 .....296 E6
Range Ride CBLY GU15 .....41 P7
Range Rd FARN GU14 .....75 L2
Range Vw SHST GU47 .....41 M6
Rankine Cl FNM GU9 .....96 C5
Rankine Rd CHIN RG24 .....70 B4
Rannoch Cl FHAM PO15 .....10 A2
Ransome Ct
 FHAM/STUB PO14 .....293 M2
Ranvilles La
 FHAM/STUB PO14 .....293 P2
Rapallo Cl FARN GU14 .....58 B9
Raphael Cl BSTK RG21 .....69 N9
Rapson Cl CHAM PO6 .....297 J2
Rareridge La BPWT SO32 .....232 C4
Rashleigh Ct FLEETS GU52 .....74 E8
Rasset Md FLEETS GU52 .....74 B9
Ratcliffe Rd FARN GU14 .....57 N5
 FAWY SO45 .....268 B9
Ratlake La ROMY SO51 .....206 B1
Rattigan Gdns HLER SO31 .....271 J2
Ravel Cl KBH RG22 .....90 A2
Ravelin Cl RFNM GU10 .....95 H6
Raven Cl LSOL/BMARY PO13 .....314 C2
 NTID SP9 .....79 H5
 YTLY GU46 .....40 D9
Raven Rd HTWY RG27 .....71 P3
 SHAM SO14 .....21 C1
Ravens Cl FHAM/STUB PO14 .....294 B6
Ravenscourt Rd LYMN SO41 .....329 K4
 BMTH BH6 .....336 A1
Ravenscroft HTWY RG27 .....72 A2
Ravens Cft HTWY RG27 * 72 A2

Ravenscroft Cl ASHV GU12 .....77 H9
 HLER SO30 .....269 P1
Ravenscroft Wy BPWT SO32 .....250 F2
Ravensdale Cl
 BKME/WDN BH12 .....321 L6
Raven Sq ALTN GU34 .....132 F5
 ELGH SO50 .....149 J2
Ravens Wy LYMN SO41 .....338 C2
Ravenswood
 FHAM/STUB PO14 * 271 J7
Ravenswood Av CWTH RG45 .....40 F1
Ravensworth Rd THLE RG7 .....26 C9
Ravine Rd BOSC BH5 .....335 P2
 CCLF BH13 .....333 P3
Rawlings Ct RAND SP11 .....79 P1
Rawlings Rd HTWY RG27 .....72 A4
Rawlinson Rd ALDT GU11 .....76 B6
 CBLY GU15 .....41 N8
Raygnoldes FLEETS GU52 .....74 B9
Rayleigh Rd BSTK RG21 .....6 D6
Raymond Cl FAWY SO45 .....290 F6
 HEND SO30 .....229 P9
 VWD BH31 .....305 J2
Raymond Rd CHAM PO6 .....274 A9
 WSHM SO15 .....247 P4
Rayners Gdns ROWN SO16 .....228 F8
Raynes Rd LSOL/BMARY PO13 ..314 D4
Reading Dr North HTWY RG27 .....58 G9
Reading Rd BLKW GU17 .....41 H9
 BLKW GU17 .....57 J1
 CHIN RG24 .....69 N4
 CHIN RG24 .....70 B1
 EWKG RG40 .....39 J2
 FARN GU14 .....76 B3
 HTWY RG27 .....39 N6
 HTWY RG27 .....52 E5
 HTWY RG27 .....54 J5
 HTWY RG27 .....71 P2
 RDGW/BURGH RG30 .....27 L3
 THLE RG7 .....34 G1
 THLE RG7 .....40 B7
Reading Rd North
 FLEETN GU51 .....74 B3
Reading Road Rbt
 CHIN RG24 .....69 N4
Reading Rd South
 FLEETN GU51 .....74 C4
Reading Room La
 BPWT SO32 .....251 K3
Readon Cl EPSF GU31 .....215 N1
Read's Fld ALTN GU34 .....150 C6
Rebbeck Rd LTDN BH7 .....335 N1
Rebecca Cl FLEETS GU52 .....74 B9
The Recess ELGH SO50 .....207 K8
Record Rd EMRTH PO10 .....277 L9
Recreation Cl FARN GU14 .....57 N4
Recreation Rd AND SP10 .....4 D3
 BKME/WDN BH12 .....321 N6
 ODIM RG29 .....93 J1
 RAND SP11 .....79 P1
 RFNM GU10 .....115 N7
 THLE RG7 .....27 J5
Rectory Av CHAM PO6 .....275 P9
Rectory Cl FHAM/STUB PO14 .....294 A6
 GPORT PO12 .....12 B6
 NWBY RG14 .....16 C5
 SHST GU47 .....40 C6
 TADY RG26 .....34 D8
Rectory Ct HEND SO30 .....250 F4
Rectory Hl RSAL SP5 .....159 H6
 RSAL SP5 .....177 M3
Rectory La BPWT SO32 .....211 N8
 FBDG SP6 .....220 F3
 LIPH GU30 .....155 L9
 RFNM GU10 .....114 F6
 RWIN SO21 .....146 F8
 STOK SO20 .....160 A1
 TADY RG26 .....48 F6
Rectory Pl RAND SP11 .....81 K9
Rectory Rd DEAN RG23 .....58 B9
 FARN GU14 .....58 B9
 HAV PO9 .....15 F7
 HTWY RG27 .....71 P4
 PLE BH15 .....320 E6
 THLE RG7 .....26 B8
Reculver Wy AND SP10 .....82 B8
Redan Cl CHCH/BSGR BH23 .....326 E8
Redan Gdns ASHV GU12 .....3 G3
Redan Hill Est ASHV GU12 * 3 J3
Redan Rd ASHV GU12 .....3 H3
The Redan GPORT PO12 .....315 N7
Red Barn Av
 FHAM/PORC PO16 .....273 N9
Red Barn La FHAM PO15 .....272 C4
Redbreast Rd
 MOOR/WNTN BH9 .....322 C4
Redbreast Rd North
 MOOR/WNTN BH9 .....322 C4
Redbridge Cswy WSHM SO15 ..246 F3
Redbridge Dr AND SP10 .....4 A7
Redbridge Gv HAV PO9 .....14 B1
Redbridge Hl ROWN SO16 .....247 K2
Redbridge La CHIN RG24 .....69 P7
 ROWN SO16 .....246 G1
Redbridge Rd WSHM SO15 ..247 H3
Redbrook Ter FBDG SP6 * 220 C4
Redcar Av HSEA PO3 .....297 J8
Redcliffe Cl CHCH/BSGR BH23 .324 C6
Redcotts La WIMB BH21 .....249 K4
Redcotts Rd WIMB BH21 .....249 K4
Redcroft La HLER SO31 .....270 A1
Redenham Dro RAND SP11 .....80 G3
Redfield Ct NWBY RG14 .....16 C5
Redfields La FLEETS GU52 .....95 J2
The Redfords TOTT SO40 .....246 F2
Redheame Flds RFNM GU10 ..136 E7
Red Hl ALTN GU34 .....150 C5
 HTWY RG27 .....54 D4
 KSCL RG20 .....45 K7
 RAND SP11 .....79 N1

ROWN SO16 .....228 A8
Redhill Ct NBNE BH10 * 322 C5
Redhill Crs MOOR/WNTN BH9 .322 F4
Red Hill Crs ROWN SO16 .....228 A8
Redhill Dr NBNE BH10 .....322 E5
Redhill Rd HAV PO9 .....277 H1
Red Hill Wy ROWN SO16 .....228 A9
Redhoave Rd CFDH BH17 .....320 C3
Red House Ct EPSF GU31 .....217 K1
Redhouse Park Gdns
 GPORT PO12 .....315 J2
Redlands BKME/WDN BH12 ..321 P7
Redlands Dr ITCH SO19 .....249 H5
Redlands Gv ENEY PO4 .....317 L4
Redlands La EMRTH PO10 .....277 M6
 FHAM/STUB PO14 .....10 C6
 RFNM GU10 .....95 J4
Red La BOR GU35 .....155 J1
 OVTN RG25 .....110 E6
 RSAL SP5 .....159 H8
 THLE RG7 .....34 E1
Red Leaves BPWT SO32 .....252 C1
Red Lion La BSTK RG21 .....7 F7
 FNM GU9 .....116 B1
 OVTN RG25 .....86 C3
Red Ldg CHFD SO53 .....228 D1
Redlynch Cl HAV PO9 * 277 H6
Redmans Vw VWD BH31 .....258 D4
Redmayne CBLY GU15 .....59 H1
Redmoor Cl ITCH SO19 .....248 G5
Red Oaks RFNM GU10 * 115 N7
Red Oaks Dr FERN BH22 .....302 B1
Red Oaks Dr FHAM PO15 .....271 J5
Redon Wy AND SP10 .....4 A1
Red Post La RAND SP11 .....101 L2
Red Rice Rd RAND SP11 .....102 A9
Redrise Cl FAWY SO45 .....290 D6
Redshank La CFDH BH17 .....320 B3
Redshank Rd STHA RG19 .....25 K4
Redshank Rd HORN PO8 .....256 A4
Redvers Buller Rd ALDT GU11 ..76 B5
Redvers Rd CHCH/BSGR BH23 ..325 J8
Redward Rd ROWN SO16 .....227 K7
Redwing Ct ENEY PO4 .....317 L3
Redwing Gdns TOTT SO40 .....246 A3
Redwing Rd HORN PO8 .....236 C8
 KBH RG22 .....89 K4
Redwood Cl FAWY SO45 .....267 P7
 HEND SO30 .....250 F5
 LYMN SO41 .....329 J2
 RGWD BH24 .....282 F2
Redwood Dr CBLY GU15 .....59 J1
 FERN BH22 .....280 C9
 FHAM/PORC PO16 .....295 M1
Redwood Gdns TOTT SO40 ....246 A4
Redwood Gv HAV PO9 .....276 G6
Redwood La ALTN GU34 .....131 J9
Redwood Wy ROWN SO16 .....228 C6
Reed Cl ALDT GU11 .....76 C6
Reed Dr TOTT SO40 .....247 K9
Reeder Cl FBDG SP6 .....240 C2
Reedmace Cl WVILLE PO7 * 276 A4
Reeds La LISS GU33 .....174 B9
Reed's Pl GPORT PO12 .....315 L3
Reed's Pl GPORT PO12 .....315M1
The Reeds Rd RFNM GU10 ....116 D9
Reed Wk NWBY RG14 .....16 C1
Rees Rd RWIN SO21 .....144 D6
Reeves Cl BSTK RG21 .....224 E1
Reeves La ASHV GU12 .....3 H4
Reeves Wy HLER SO31 .....269 P2
Regal Cl CHAM PO6 .....297 H1
Regency Crs
 CHCH/BSGR BH23 .....324 D7
Regency Gdns WVILLE PO7 ...275M4
Regency Pl FHAM PO15 .....10 A1
Regent Ct BSTK RG21 .....6 C3
Regent Dr LTDN BH7 .....323 M7
Regent Pl SSEA PO5 .....19 F7
Regent Pl CHFD SO53 .....206 F7
Regents Ct HAV PO9 .....298 F1
 NWBY RG14 .....16 D1
Regents Ga HLER SO31 .....270 E5
Regent's Gv WSHM SO15 * ...247 M5
Regent's Park Gdns
 WSHM SO15 .....247 M4
Regent's Park Rd
 WSHM SO15 .....247 L4
Regents Pl SHST GU47 .....41 M6
Regent St FLEETN GU51 .....74 D4
 PSEA PO1 .....316 E1
 SHAM SO14 .....20 D4
Regent Wy CHCH/BSGR BH23 .324 F9
Regiment Cl FARN GU14 * 75 K1
Reginald Rd ENEY PO4 .....317 L2
Regnum Dr NWBY RG14 .....24 E2
Reid St CHCH/BSGR BH23 .....324 E8
Reith Wy AND SP10 .....101 P1
Relay Rd WVILLE PO7 .....275M2
Reliant Cl CHFD SO53 .....206 D8
Rembrandt Cl BSTK RG21 .....69 N9
Remembrance Gdns
 CHIN RG24 .....69 P2
Remembrance Rd
 NWBY RG14 .....16 A4
Renaissance Rd WIMB BH21 ..300 F4
Renault Dr BDST BH18 .....320 C3
Renda Rd HAV PO9 .....290 E5
Renny Rd PSEA PO1 .....317 H5
Renouf Cl LYMN SO41 .....329 J4
Renoun Cl CHFD SO53 .....206 D8
Renown Gdns HORN PO8 .....255 P6
Renown Wy CHIN RG24 .....52 A9
Repton Cl GPORT PO12 .....315 J4
Repton Gdns HEND SO30 .....250 D1
Reservoir La HEND SO30 .....250 A5
 PSF GU32 .....191 M9
Reservoir Rd FARN GU14 .....75 J4
Rest-a-wyle Av HISD PO11 ...318 C3
Restormel Cl DEAN RG23 .....68 E6

Retreat Rd WIMB BH21 .....300 F1
The Retreat ELGH SO50 .....19 H7
 SSEA PO5 .....19 H7
 TOTT SO40 .....246 E6
Reuben's Crs TADY RG26 .....34 A1
Revelstoke Av FARN GU14 .....58 A7
Revenge Cl ENEY PO4 .....317 L2
Rewlands Dr FUFL SO22 .....164 D3
Reynards Cl TADY RG26 .....34 A1
Reynolds Cl BSTK RG21 .....69 N8
Reynolds Ct AND SP10 .....4 B1
Reynolds Dl TOTT SO40 .....246 B6
Reynolds Gn SHST GU47 .....41 L8
Reynolds Rd ELGH SO50 .....250 D3
 WSHM SO15 .....247 N3
Reyntiens Vw ODIM RG29 .....93 L1
Rhine Banks FARN GU14 .....57 L8
Rhinefield Cl BROC SO42 .....286 E7
Rhinefield Dr BROC SO42 .....286 E7
 ELGH SO50 .....229 P2
 HAV PO9 * 277 C6
Rhinefield Ornamental Dr
 BROC SO42 .....285 P4
Rhinefield Rd BROC SO42 ....286 D7
 NMIL/BTOS BH25 .....306 G6
Rhiners Cl LYMN SO41 .....308 B5
Rhodes Sq AND SP10 .....82 G8
Rhododendron Rd FRIM GU16 .58 G5
Rhyme Hall Ms FAWY SO45 ...291 K6
Ribble Cl BDST BH18 .....320 C2
 ROWN SO16 .....206 F8
Ribble Ct AND SP10 * 82 G9
 ROWN SO16 .....247 J2
Ribble Pl FARN GU14 .....57 M7
Ribble Wy BSTK RG21 .....7 J6
Ricardo Crs CHCH/BSGR BH23 .325 L9
Richard Cl FAWY SO45 .....74 B5
Richard Cv GPORT PO12 .....295 L8
Richards Cl ASHV GU12 * 3 H7
 HLER SO31 .....271 H7
Richborough Dr AND SP10 .....82 A8
Richlans Rd HEND SO30 .....250 C5
Richmond Av STHA RG19 .....25 K4
Richmond Cl BOR GU35 .....154 A7
 CHFD SO53 .....206 D4
 FARN GU14 .....75 L1
 FLEETS GU52 .....74 C6
 FRIM GU16 .....58 E4
 HISD PO11 .....318 E4
 TOTT SO40 .....245 P2
Richmond Dr HISD PO11 .....318 D4
Richmond Hill BMTH BH1 .....8 E3
Richmond Hill Dr WCLF BH2 ....8 D3
Richmond Hill Rbt WCLF BH2 ...8 D2
Richmond La ROMY SO51 .....204 E4
Richmond Pk RWIN SO21 ....207M1
Richmond Park Av CHAR BH8 .323 J8
Richmond Park Cl
 CHAR BH8 * 323 K9
Richmond Park Crs
 CHAR BH8 .....323 J8
Richmond Park Rd CHAR BH8 .323 H9
Richmond Pl PSEA PO1 .....18 E3
Richmond Rd
 FHAM/PORC PO16 .....273 N9
 GPORT PO12 .....12 A3
 LSOL/BMARY PO13 .....314 B2
 PSTN BH14 .....321 L8
 SHST GU47 * 41 M7
 SSEA PO5 .....316 F6
 WIMB BH21 .....300 F1
 WSHM SO15 .....247 N5
Richmond St SHAM SO14 .....21 F6
Richmond Ter SSEA PO5 * 316 E6
Richmond Wood Rd
 CHAR BH8 .....323 J8
Richville Rd ROWN SO16 .....247 L3
Ridding Cl WSHM SO15 .....247 N2
Riddings La STHA RG19 .....32 F4
Riders La HAV PO9 .....276 E6
Rideway Cl CBLY GU15 .....58 A1
Ridge Cl HORN PO8 .....236 C8
 KBH RG22 .....89 N6
Ridge Common La PSF GU32 ..191 J8
Ridgefield Gdns
 CHCH/BSGR BH23 .....325 P7
Ridge La HEND SO30 .....251 K8
 HTWY RG27 .....71 M2
 ROMY SO51 .....225 P3
Ridgemount Av ROWN SO16 ..228 B7
Ridgemount Gdns PLE BH15 ..320 A9
Ridges Cl RAND SP11 .....83 H5
The Ridge RSAL SP5 .....199 P9
Ridge Top La PSF GU32 .....190 D8
Ridgeway BDST BH18 .....300 D9
 FERN BH22 .....302 E8
 FUFL SO22 .....183 L1
Ridgeway Cl CHAM PO6 .....274 B9
 CHFD SO53 .....206 D4
 ELGH SO50 .....230 C1
Ridgeway La LYMN SO41 .....329 K5
The Ridgeway AND SP10 .....5 K4
 FHAM/PORC PO16 .....273 J9
Ridgeway Cl FAWY SO45 .....267 N7
Ridgewood Dr FRIM GU16 .....59 J2
Ridgway Hl FNM GU9 .....116 C2
Ridgway Hill Rd FNM GU9 ....116 C2
Ridgway Pde FNM GU9 * 116 C2
Ridgway Rd FNM GU9 .....116 C2
The Ridings BPWT SO32 .....232 C8
 ELGH SO50 .....230 A2
 FNM GU9 .....116 D7
 LISS GU33 .....192 F2
 NEND PO2 .....297 H6
Ridley Cl FAWY SO45 .....290 E5
 FLEETS GU52 .....74 C5
Ridley Rd MOOR/WNTN BH9 ...322 F7
Ridleys Piece ODIM RG29 * 92 E9
Ridout Cl NBNE BH10 .....322 B6
Rifle Wy FARN GU14 .....75 K1
Rigby Rd SHAM SO14 .....248 D3

Riggs Gdns BWD BH11 .....321 P2
Rigler Rd PLE BH15 .....332 C2
Riley La CHIN RG24 .....70 C5
Riley Rd RWIN SO21 .....124 F1
Rimbault Cl ALDT GU11 .....76 C5
Rimbury Wy
 CHCH/BSGR BH23 .....324 E7
Rimes's Crs TADY RG26 .....34 A1
Rimmington Rd HORN PO8 ...255 N8
Ringbury LYMN SO41 .....329 K1
Ringlet Wy WINC SO23 .....23 K4
Ringsgreen La PSF GU32 .....176 D5
Ringshall Gdns TADY RG26 ....51 P2
The Ring ROWN SO16 .....228 A5
Ringway East CHIN RG24 .....7 K1
Ringway North CHIN RG24 .....69 H5
Ringway South BSTK RG21 ....69M9
Ringway West KBH RG22 .....69 H9
Ringwood Dr NBNE BH10 .....322 A4
Ringwood Rd BLKW GU17 .....41 K8
 BWD BH11 .....322 F3
 CHCH/BSGR BH23 .....304 E8
 ENEY PO4 .....317 K5
 FARN GU14 .....58 B6
 FBDG SP6 .....239 N7
 FBDG SP6 .....282 B8
 FERN BH22 .....302 B8
 PSTN BH14 .....321 K6
 RGWD BH24 .....243 N9
 TOTT SO40 .....245 N4
 VWD BH31 .....258 F3
 WIMB BH21 .....280 E1
Ripley Gv HSEA PO3 .....297 L6
Ripon Cl CBLY GU15 .....59 J2
Ripon Ct LSOL/BMARY PO13 ...315 H3
Ripon Gdns WVILLE PO7 .....276 A4
Ripon Rd BLKW GU17 .....56 G4
 MOOR/WNTN BH9 .....322 C7
Ripplesmore Cl SHST GU47 ....41 J6
Ripplewood TOTT SO40 .....267 L1
Ripstone Gdns PTSW SO17 ...228 D9
The Rise BROC SO42 .....286 F8
 CWTH RG45 .....40 G1
 EWKG RG40 .....39 K4
 THLE RG7 * 36 B1
 WVILLE PO7 .....275MB
Ritchie Ct ITCH SO19 .....249 K7
Ritchie Rd FERN BH22 .....280 D5
Ritchie Rd BWD BH11 .....322 E5
Rival Moor Rd EPSF GU31 ....215 P3
River Cl ALTN GU34 .....150 C6
 WIMB BH21 .....115 N3
Riverdale RFNM GU10 .....115 N3
River Gdns LYMN SO41 .....339 H2
River Gn HLER SO31 .....287 N8
Riverhead NARL SO24 .....168 F3
Riverhead Cl ENEY PO4 .....317 K3
River La FHAM SO31 .....272 A4
 FNM GU9 .....116 D1
Riverlea Rd CHCH/BSGR BH23 .324 E9
Rivermead CI ROWN SO16 ....227 N7
Rivermead Gdns
 CHCH/BSGR BH23 .....324 C5
Rivermead Rd CBLY GU15 ....58 G3
Rivermede BOR GU35 .....154 B4
River Pde AND SP10 .....82 G9
River Pk HTWY RG27 .....17 H1
River Rd YTLY GU46 .....40 C7
River Rnw FNM GU9 .....115 P2
Rivers Cl FARN GU14 .....76 D3
Riversdale Cl ITCH SO19 .....268 G2
Riverside CI LYMN SO41 .....339 H1
Riverside ELGH SO50 .....229M1
 RGWD BH24 .....282 D3
 WHCH RG28 * 85 L6
Riverside Av
 FHAM/PORC PO16 .....273 H7
 LTDN BH7 .....324 A6
Riverside Cl CHAM PO6 .....70 C5
 FARN GU14 .....76 B6
 LISS GU33 .....192 C2
 OVTN RG25 .....86 F2
 TOTT SO40 .....245 J5
Riverside Gdns ROMY SO51 ...204 C7
Riverside La SBNE BH6 .....336 D1
Riverside La SBNE BH6 .....336 D3
Riverside Ms WHAM PO17 ....272 B3
Riverside Pl FBDG SP6 .....240 D1
Riverside Rd FERN BH22 .....302 B9
 SBNE BH6 .....336 D1
Riverside Wy CBLY GU15 .....59 H3
Riversmeet Athran GU12 ....117 J6
Rivers Reach LYMN SO41 * ...329M4
River's St SSEA PO5 .....19 G6
Riverview LTDN BH7 .....324 A6
River View Cl STOK SO20 ....123 K5
River View Rd WEND SO18 ...248 F1
River Wk NWBY RG14 .....16 D1
 WEND SO18 .....228 G9
River Wy AND SP10 .....5 K2
 CHCH/BSGR BH23 .....324 B5
RL Stevenson Av WBNE BH4 .334 G3
Roads HI HORN PO8 .....255 P2
Road Vw NEND PO2 .....296 G3
Robert Cecil Av WEND SO18 ..228 G4
Robert Mays Rd ODIM RG29 ..93 M7
Roberts Cl LPHA GU34 * 3 K4
Roberts La CFDH BH17 .....41 P8
Roberts Gv FHAM/PORC PO16 ..295 P5
Robertson Rd NARL SO24 ....167M2
Robertson Wy ALTN GU34 * 97M2
Roberts Rd ASHV GU12 .....3 H4
 CBLY GU15 .....41 P8
 FAWY SO45 .....267 N8
 ROWN SO16 .....228 A3

Romans Fld THLE RG7 ....35 J6
Romans Ga THLE RG7 ....34 G5
Romans' Rd WINC SO23 ....22 D7
Roman Wy AND SP10 ....82 F8
  DEAN SO21 ....68 D7
  FAWY SO45 ....267 P9
  FNM GU9 ....96 E7
  HAV PO9 ....276 C8
  NTHA RG18 ....35 K3
  RWIN SO21 ....124 G2
The Romany FARN GU14 ....75 H3
Romayne Cl FARN GU14 ....57 P8
Romford Rd HLER SO31 ....292 D1
Romill Cl WEND SO18 ....229 K6
Romney Cl NBNE BH10 * 322 E4
Romney Rd FARN GU14 ....51 N3
  NBNE BH10 ....322 E3
Romsey Av
  FHAM/PORC PO16 ....295 L1
  HSEA PO3 ....317 K2
Romsey Cl ALDT GU11 ....97 J5
  BLKW GU17 ....41 K8
  CHIN RG24 ....69 K3
  ELGH SO50 ....229 J1
Romsey Rd ELGH SO50 ....229 J1
  FHAM/STUB PO14 ....22 A5
  HORN PO8 ....22 A5
  LYND SO43 ....264 F4
  RAND SP11 ....122 C1
  ROMY SO51 ....202 E9
  ROMY SO51 ....225 M6
  ROWN SO16 ....227 H7
  RSAL SP5 ....201 K1
  STOK SO20 ....139 L1
  STOK SO20 ....160 A2
  STOK SO20 ....161 K6
  TOTT SO40 ....225 K8
  TOTT SO40 ....244 D7
Romyns Ct FHAM/STUB PO14 ......10 C6
Ronckliff Wy RAND SP11 ....338 F2
Rookery Av FHAM PO15 ....295 K1
Rookery Gra HLER SO31 ....271 K5
Rookery La FBDG SP6 ....220 D3
  STOK SO20 ....160 B1
The Rookery EMRTH PO10 ....277 N9
  WHCH RG28 ....85 L6
Rookes Cl HORN PO8 ....256 B5
Rookes La LYMN SO41 ....329 K5
Rook Hill Rd
  CHCH/BSGR BH23 ....325 M9
Rook La HAV PO9 ....126 C6
Rookley HLER SO31 ....269 L5
Rooksbridge FAWY SO45 ....267 N7
Rooksbury Cft HAV PO9 ....276 C5
Rooksbury Rd AND SP10 ....102 C4
Rooksdown La CHIN RG24 ....68 F4
Rooks Down Rd FUFL SO22 ....183 J4
Rooksfield KSCL RG20 ....31 M4
Rooksnest La HUNG RG17 ....28 B1
Rooksway Gv
  FHAM/PORC PO16 ....295 K1
Rookwood Cl ALTN GU34 ....132 F4
Rookwood Cl HTWY RG27 ....72 A3
Rookwood Vw SHST GU47 ....41 M5
Rookwood Cl ALTN GU34 ....149 M5
Rookwood Vw WVILLE PO7 ....255 H6
Roosevelt Crs BWD BH11 ....322 D1
Rope Hl LYMN SO41 ....309 K7
Rope Wk STHA RG19 ....25 M4
The Rope Wk
  FHAM/PORC PO16 * 294 F1
Ropley Cl ITCH SO19 ....269 J2
  TADY RG26 ....84 F7
Ropley Rd ALTN GU34 ....170 C2
  HAV PO9 ....287 H5
  LTDN BH7 ....324 A8
Rorkes Drift FRIM GU16 ....58 D1
Rosamund Av WIMB BH21 ....300 G4
Rosary Gdns YTLY GU46 * 40 E8
Roscrea Cl SBNE BH6 ....346 D1
Roscrea Dr SBNE BH6 ....336 F2
Rosebank Cl ROWN SO16 * 227 J7
  TADY RG26 ....34 C6
Rosebank Ldg ROWN SO16 * 227 J7
Rosebay Cl ELGH SO50 ....230 C6
Rosebay Ct WVILLE PO7 ....275 P5
Rosebay Gdns HTWY RG27 ....72 B2
Roseberry Av CHAM PO6 ....297 J2
Rosebery Av VWD BH31 ....259 J5
Rosebery Cl BOSC BH5 ....335 N1
Rosebery Rd BOSC BH5 ....335 N1
  NARL SO24 ....189 P4
Rosebud Av
  MOOR/WNTN BH9 ....322 G5
Rosebury Av FAWY SO45 ....268 C9
Rose Cl FAWY SO45 ....268 C8
  HEND SO30 ....250 C3
  KBH RG22 ....89 M3
Rosecrae Cl NMIL/BTOS BH25 ....327 H3
Rose Crs PLE BH15 ....321 H6
Rosedale ASHV GU12 ....3 H3
Rosedale Av ROMY SO51 ....226 C6
Rosedale Cl CHCH/BSGR BH23 ...325 J9
  FHAM/STUB PO14 ....293 M1
Rosedale Gdns STHA RG19 ....25 M5
Rosedene Gdns FLEETN GU51 * 41 L7
Rosedene La SHST GU47 ....41 L7
The Rose Est HTWY RG27 * 72 A4
Rose Gdns FARN GU14 ....75 L1
  MOOR/WNTN BH9 ....322 G5
Rose Hl HORN PO8 ....256 A5
Rosehill CHCH/BSGR BH23 * 305 M7
Rosehill Dr CHCH/BSGR BH23 ....305 M7
Roseship Vw CHIN RG24 ....69 K5
Rose Hodson Pl DEAN RG23 ....68 F5
Roselands HEND SO30 ....249 M3
  HORN PO8 ....256 A6

Roselands Cl ELGH SO50 ....230 B1
Roselands Gdns PTSW SO17 ....248 C1
Roseleigh Dr TOTT SO40 ....246 C5
Rosemary Av WILLE GU12 ....76 F4
Rosemary Ct FARN GU14 ....57 L8
Rosemary Dr TADY RG26 ....34 C8
Rosemary Gdns
  BKME/WDN BH12 ....321 K5
  BLKW GU17 ....41 K9
  FHAM PO15 ....271 K2
  HEND SO30 ....250 C6
Rosemary La BLKW GU17 ....41 K9
  PSEA PO1 ....18 C3
  RFNM GU10 ....115 N6
Rosemary Price Ct
  HEND SO30 * 250 C3
Rosemary Rd
  BKME/WDN BH12 ....321 L5
Rosemary Wy HORN PO8 ....256 B7
Rosemoor Gdns NWBY RG14 ....24 F3
Rosemoor Gv CHFD SO53 ....206 D4
Rosendale Rd CHFD SO53 ....206 F9
Roseneath La SHAM SO14 ....248 C5
  TOTT SO40 ....246 E5
The Rosery GPORT PO12 ....315 M7
Rosetta Rd ENEY PO4 ....317 K4
Rose Wk FLEETN GU51 ....74 C2
Rosewall Rd ROWN SO16 ....227 K9
Rosewarne Ct WINC SO23 * 22 D2
Rosewood CHIN RG24 * 69 P1
  LSOL/BMARY PO13 ....295 J8
Rosewood Gdns HORN PO8 ....236 C7
  NMIL/BTOS BH25 ....327 H3
  TOTT SO40 ....267 L1
Rosewood Ter NTID SP9 * 79 J4
Rosina Cl WVILLE PO7 ....276 B2
Roslin Rd TWDS BH3 ....322 E8
Roslin Rd South TWDS BH3 ....322 D8
Rosoman Rd ITCH SO19 ....249 H7
Rossan Av HLER SO31 ....292 D2
Ross Cl BSTK RG21 ....90 C1
Ross Gdns BWD BH11 ....301 L8
  ROWN SO16 ....247 L1
Rossington Av WEND SO18 ....249 H4
Rossington Wy WEND SO18 ....249 H4
Rossini Cl KBH RG22 ....90 A3
Rossiters Quay
  CHCH/BSGR BH23 * 324 C9
Rossley Cl CHCH/BSGR BH23 ......326 A5
Rosslyn Cl NBAD SO52 ....205 L9
Rossmore Gdns ALDT GU11 ....2 A5
Rossmore Rd
  BKME/WDN BH12 ....321 L4
Ross Rd RGWD BH24 ....260 C9
Ross Wy LSOL/BMARY PO13 ....314 D1
Rostron Cl WEND SO18 ....229 J9
Rosyth Rd WEND SO18 ....249 H4
Rotary Cl WIMB BH21 ....279 H7
Rotary Ct HLER SO31 ....269 K4
Rothay Ct BSTK RG21 ....7 J6
Rothbury Cl ITCH SO19 * 249 J7
  TOTT SO40 ....246 B2
Rothbury Pk
  NMIL/BTOS BH25 ....327 K5
Rotherbank Farm La
  LISS GU33 ....173 L9
Rother Cl EPSF GU31 ....216 A1
  SHST GU47 ....41 K6
  WEND SO18 ....249 K2
Rothercombe La PSF GU32 ....214 C1
Rother Di ITCH SO19 ....249 N8
Rotherfield Rd BOSC BH5 ....335 P3
  CHCH/BSGR BH23 ....326 C6
Rother Rd FARN GU14 ....57 M7
Rotherwick Cl HAV PO9 ....277 H5
Rotherwick La HTWY RG27 ....53 K5
Rotherwick Rd TADY RG26 ....34 C7
Rothesay Dr
  CHCH/BSGR BH23 ....326 A8
Rothesay Rd GPORT PO12 ....315 L1
  TWDS BH3 ....322 C9
Rothsbury Dr CHFD SO53 ....206 D7
Rothschild Cl ITCH SO19 ....269 L1
Rothville Pl CHFD SO53 ....206 D3
Rothwell Cl CHAM PO6 ....274 C9
Rotten Green Rd FLEETN GU51 .....56 B7
Rotten Hl OVTN RG25 ....86 E5
Rotterdam Dr
  CHCH/BSGR BH23 ....325 H8
Rotunda Est ALDT GU11 ....3 G5
Roughdown La FAWY SO45 ....290 E8
Roumelia La BMTH BH1 ....335 L2
The Roundabouts LISS GU33 ....192 E1
Roundaway La RAND SP11 ....81 L1
Round Cl YTLY GU46 ....40 C9
Round End NWBY RG14 ....30 C1
Roundhaye Rd BWD BH11 ....301 P8
Roundhill Cl WEND SO18 ....249 J2
Roundhouse Dr TOTT SO40 ....245 P5
Roundhouse Meadow
  EMRTH PO10 ....299 N2
Roundnuts Ri WINC SO23 ....23 K4
Roundmead Rd BSTK RG21 ....6 C7
Roundway WVILLE PO7 ....275 P2
Roundways BWD BH11 * 321 P1
Rounton Rd FLEETN GU51 ....74 B2
Routs Wy ROWN SO16 ....227 J5
Rowallan Av
  LSOL/BMARY PO13 ....294 F8
Rowan Av HORN PO8 ....256 B9
Rowan Cha RFNM GU10 ....16 B3
Rowan Cl BPWT SO32 ....232 F6
  CHCH/BSGR BH23 ....325 P7
  FLEETN GU51 ....74 F3
  HLER SO31 ....269 P2
  LSOL/BMARY PO13 ....314 D3
  RGWD BH24 ....201 K5
  ROMY SO51 ....204 C7
  ROWN SO16 ....227 K9

RWIN SO21 ....144 F4
TOTT SO40 ....246 B5
Rowan Ct ENEY PO4 ....317 H4
  NTID SP9 * 79 H4
Rowan Dr FLEETS GU52 ....74 C7
Rowan Dr CFDH BH17 ....320 A3
  CHCH/BSGR BH23 ....325 P7
  RWY RG14 ....24 D2
  VWD BH31 ....259 H6
Rowan Gdns HEND SO30 ....250 D5
Rowan Rd HAV PO9 ....277 H7
  TADY RG26 ....34 D3
Rowans Cl FARN GU14 ....57 M4
Rowanside Cl BOR GU35 ....155 K4
Rowans Pk LYMN SO41 ....329 K4
The Rowans GSHT GU26 ....156 C5
  TOTT SO40 ....267 K1
Rowan Wy FHAM/STUB PO14 ......294 A1
  RDGW/BURGH RG30 ....27 K3
Rowbarrow Cl CFDH BH17 ....320 C2
Rowborough Rd WEND SO18 ....249 H3
Rowbury Rd HAV PO9 ....276 D4
Rowcroft Cl ASHV GU12 ....76 F6
Rowdell Cots NARL SO24 ....169 K2
Rowden Cl ROWN SO16 ....224 E2
Rowe Ashe Wy HLER SO31 ....270 F7
Rowena Rd SBNE BH6 ....336 D1
Rowes La LYMN SO41 ....310 F9
Rowhay La BPWT SO32 ....209 J8
Rowhill Av ALDT GU11 ....2 B6
Rowhill Crs ALDT GU11 ....2 B7
Rowhill Dr FAWY SO45 ....267 N7
Rowhills FNM GU9 ....96 D3
Rowhills Rd FNM GU9 ....2 B7
Rowin Cl HISD PO11 ....319 K6
Rowland Av PLE BH15 ....320 C7
Rowland Rd CHAM PO6 ....274 A4
  FHAM PO15 ....10 C4
Rowlands Av HAV PO9 ....275 N1
Rowlands Castle Rd
  HORN PO8 ....256 F5
Rowlands Cl CHFD SO53 ....206 C9
  THLE RG7 ....35 L5
Rowlands Hl WIMB BH21 ....278 E9
Rowlands Wk WEND SO18 ....249 J1
Rowlett Rd LYMN SO41 ....329 L4
Rowley Cl BLKW GU17 * 41 L9
Rowley Dr HEND SO30 ....250 D5
Rowlings Rd FUFL SO22 ....164 E4
Rowner Cl LSOL/BMARY PO13 .....294 G8
Rowner La
  LSOL/BMARY PO13 ....294 G9
Rowner Rd
  LSOL/BMARY PO13 ....294 F8
Rownhams Cl ROWN SO16 ....227 J6
Rownhams La NBAD SO52 ....205 K8
  ROWN SO16 ....227 K5
Rownhams Pk ROWN SO16 * 227 J4
Rownhams Rd CHAR BH8 ....323 J4
  HAV PO9 ....276 D5
  NBAD SO52 ....205 L6
  ROWN SO16 ....247 K1
Rownhams Rd North
  ROWN SO16 ....227 K7
Rownhams Wy ROWN SO16 ....227 J6
Rowse Cl ROMY SO51 ....204 A6
Row RSAL SP5 ....200 A6
Row Wood La
  LSOL/BMARY PO13 ....294 F8
Roxbee Cox Rd FARN GU14 ....75 H3
Roxburgh Cl CBLY GU15 ....59 H1
Roxburghe Cl BOR GU35 ....154 A6
Royal Albert Wk ENEY PO4 * 316 C6
Royal Clarence Yd
  GPORT PO12 ....315 P2
Royal Cl DEAN RG23 ....89 L6
Royal Crescent Rd SHAM SO14 .....21 H6
The Royal Crs NTID SP9 ....79 J4
Royale Cl ALDT GU11 * 3 J7
Royal Gdns HAV PO9 ....276 C1
Royal Oak Cl YTLY GU46 ....40 F8
Royal Oak Rd NBNE BH10 ....322 C2
Royal Sovereign Av
  CHCH/BSGR BH23 ....324 D4
Royal Wy WVILLE PO7 ....276 A5
Royce Cl AND SP10 ....101 P1
Royden La LYMN SO41 ....309 K5
Roydon Cl FUFL SO22 ....183 M1
Royster Cl CHFD SO53 ....320 E3
Royston Av ELGH SO50 ....230 B7
Royston Cl PTSW SO17 ....248 D1
Royston Dr WIMB BH21 ....278 F9
Royston Pl NMIL/BTOS BH25 ....327 K7
Rozelle Cl FUFL SO22 ....164 B2
Rozelle Rd PSTN BH14 ....321 L8
Rubens Cl BSTK RG21 ....90 F1
  NMIL/BTOS BH25 * 327 J3
Ruby Rd ITCH SO19 ....249 J5
Rudd Hall Ri CBLY GU15 ....58 C2
Rudd La ROMY SO51 ....180 C7
Rudgwick Cl
  FHAM/PORC PO16 ....295 M1
Rudland Ct STHA RG19 ....25 N5
Rudmore Sq NEND PO2 ....296 F9
Ruffield Cl FUFL SO22 ....164 D5
  FLEETS GU52 ....74 D6
Rufford Gdns SBNE BH6 ....336 C1
Rufus Ct CHFD SO53 ....206 C5
  ROWN SO16 * 227 H6
Rufus Gdns TOTT SO40 ....246 A4
Rugby Cl SHST GU47 ....41 M5
Rugby Rd CFDH BH17 ....320 C3
  ENEY PO4 ....317 H3
Rumbridge Gdns TOTT SO40 ....246 E4
Rumbridge St TOTT SO40 ....246 D5
Rune Dr AND SP10 ....82 A7
Runnymede FHAM PO15 ....272 B6
  HEND SO30 ....250 G1
Runnymede Av BWD BH11 ....301 M7
Runnymede Ct HEND SO30 ....249 L2
Runton Rd
  BKME/WDN BH12 * 321 P7

The Runway
  CHCH/BSGR BH23 ....325 M8
Runwick La RFNM GU10 ....115 M1
Rupert Rd NWBY RG14 ....24 A4
Ruscombe Wy WIMB BH21 ....300 A3
Rushden Wy FNM GU9 ....96 D4
Rushes Farm PSF GU32 ....215 L1
Rushes Rd PSF GU32 ....215 L5
The Rushes BSTK RG21 ....7 K6
  TOTT SO40 ....247 K9
Rushfield Rd LISS GU33 ....192 D3
Rushford Warren
  CHCH/BSGR BH23 ....337 K2
Rushington Av TOTT SO40 ....246 D5
Rushington La TOTT SO40 ....246 C6
Rushmere La WILLE PO7 ....254 F4
Rushmere Rd SBNE BH6 ....324 A8
Rushmoor Cl FLEETS GU52 ....74 D5
Rushmoor Rd ALDT GU11 ....75 M9
Rushton Crs TWDS BH5 ....322 F9
Ruskin Av MOOR/WNTN BH9 ....323 H4
Ruskin Cl BSTK RG21 ....69 N9
Ruskin Ct CWTH RG45 ....40 G2
Ruskin Rd ELGH SO50 ....207 J9
  ENEY PO4 ....317 J4
Ruskin Wy HORN PO8 ....255 P7
Rusland Cl CHFD SO53 ....206 D6
Russell Cl LSOL/BMARY PO13 .....314 D2
Russell Cotes Rd BMTH BH1 ....9 F5
Russell Ct BLKW GU17 ....41 L9
Russell Dr CHCH/BSGR BH23 .....326 C6
  ROMY SO51 ....179 K6
Russell Gdns RGWD BH24 ....203 J9
Russell Pl FHAM/PORC PO16 ....11 F5
  PTSW SO17 ....248 D2
Russell Rd BSTK RG21 ....69 L9
  HAV PO9 ....277 K1
  LSOL/BMARY PO13 ....314 D3
  NWBY RG14 ....16 B3
  WINC SO23 ....165 H5
Russell St GPORT PO12 ....315 L2
  SHAM SO14 ....21 F6
Russell St NBNE BH10 ....322 C1
Russet Cl NBNE BH10 ....322 C1
Russet Cl DEAN RG23 ....88 C2
  LYMN SO41 ....329 M4
  NARL SO24 ....167 P3
  RFNM GU10 ....97 L4
Russet Gdns CBLY GU15 ....58 C2
  EMRTH PO10 ....299 P1
Russet Gld FNM GU9 ....96 D3
  THLE RG7 ....35 J5
Russett Cl BPWT SO32 ....232 F8
Russett Rd ALTN GU34 ....132 G6
Russetts Dr FLEETN GU51 ....74 C4
Rustan Cl ELGH SO50 ....230 D2
  HEND SO30 ....250 B5
Rustic Gln FLEETS GU52 ....74 K8
Ruth Cl FARN GU14 ....57 K8
Rutherford Rd CHIN RG24 ....69 N4
Rutland Cl ALDT GU11 ....54 D1
Rutland Gdns HLER SO31 * 270 A1
Rutland Rd CHCH/BSGR BH23 .....324 D6
  MOOR/WNTN BH9 ....323 H7
Rutland Wy WEND SO18 ....249 J2
Ruxley Cl HAV PO9 ....290 E5
Ryall Dr CFDH BH17 ....320 F5
Ryan Cl FERN BH22 ....302 C1
Ryan Gdns FERN BH22 ....302 C1
Ryan Mt SHST GU47 ....41 H6
Rycroft Meadow DEAN RG23 ....89 L7
Rydal Cl BOR GU35 ....154 A3
  CHAM PO6 ....276 D3
  CHCH/BSGR BH23 ....324 B3
  FARN GU14 ....75 L1
  FERN BH22 ....302 A5
Rydal Dr FLEETS GU52 ....74 B7
  STHA RG19 ....25 K3
Rydal Rd GPORT PO12 ....295 L3
Ryde Pl LSOL/BMARY PO13 ....314 E4
Ryde Ter SHAM SO14 ....21 H6
Ryebeck Rd FLEETS GU52 ....74 D7
Rye Cl CHFD SO53 ....206 B5
  FARN GU14 ....57 M7
  FLEETN GU51 ....56 F8
Ryecroft FHAM/STUB PO14 ....271 J8
Ryecroft La HAV PO9 ....290 C6
Ryecroft Rd FNM GU9 ....277 H9
Rye Dl TOTT SO40 ....246 A8
Ryedown La ROMY SO51 ....203 J9
Ryefield Cl EPSF GU31 ....216 A2
Ryeland Cl FLEETN GU51 * 56 F8
Ryelaws Dr HAV PO9 ....276 K9
Rye Paddock La FAWY SO45 ....291 K5
Rylandes Cl ROWN SO16 ....227 K9
Rye Rd FNM GU9 ....116 B2
Ryon Cl AND SP10 ....82 E7
Ryves Av YTLY GU46 ....40 B9

Sages La ALTN GU34 ....189 L1
Sailor's La BPWT SO32 ....210 G6
  MFD/CHID GU8 ....137 M7
Sainfoin La DEAN RG23 ....88 F3
Sainsbury Cl AND SP10 ....4 A7
St Agatha's Rd HLER SO31 ....270 A6
St Alban's Av CHAR BH8 ....323 J8
St Albans Ct
  LSOL/BMARY PO13 * 315 H3
St Alban's Crs CHAR BH8 ....323 H8
St Alban's Rd CHAR BH8 ....323 H8
  ENEY PO4 ....317 H5
  HAV PO9 ....276 C6
  SHAM SO14 ....21 H2
St Aldhelm's Cl CCLF BH13 ....321 C9
St Aldhelm's Rd CCLF BH13 ....321 P8
St Alphege Gdns AND SP10 ....82 D9
St Andrew Cl HORN PO8 ....256 C1
St Andrews Cl NBAD SO52 ....205 J8
  ROMY SO51 ....179 N9
St Andrews Rd ELGH SO50 ....230 C6
  BDST BH18 ....300 C8
  BOR GU35 ....153 N6
  CHAM PO6 ....297 P1
  FUFL SO22 ....12 D3
  HISD PO11 ....319 H6
  KBH RG22 ....68 G9
  NTID SP9 ....78 C5
  SHAM SO14 ....20 E2
  SSEA PO5 ....19 J6
St Andrew's Wy FRIM GU16 ....158 D3
St Anne's Av SBNE BH6 ....336 C1
St Annes Ct FUFL SO22 ....183 L1
  RAND SP11 ....122 D1
St Anne's Gdns ITCH SO19 ....248 C9
  LYMN SO41 ....329 K4
St Anne's Gv
  FHAM/STUB PO14 ....294 D2
St Annes La BPWT SO32 ....252 B4
St Ann's Cl ITCH SO19 ....248 C9
St Ann's Cl AND SP10 ....4 C1
St Ann's Crs GPORT PO12 ....315 L2
St Ann's Rd HAV PO9 ....276 C4
St Anthony's Rd WCLF BH2 ....334 B5
St Aubin's Av ITCH SO19 ....249 J6
St Aubins Cl ALTN GU34 ....150 C6
St Aubin's Pk HISD PO11 ....318 D5
St Aubyns Ct PLE BH15 * 332 D1
St Aubyns La RGWD BH24 ....261 J9
St Augustine Gdns
  PTSW SO17 ....248 D2
St Augustine Rd ENEY PO4 ....317 H5
St Augustine's Av ASHV GU12 ....97 K2
St Augustin's Rd WCLF BH2 ....334 F1
St Austell Cl ELGH SO50 ....229 N1
St Barbara's Cl PADY RG26 ....52 C5
St Barbara's Wy NEND PO2 ....297 H5
St Barbe Cl ROMY SO51 ....204 E7
St Bartholomew Gdns
  SSEA PO5 ....19 K6
St Benedict's Cl ALDT GU11 ....2 D8
St Birinus Gdns AND SP10 ....82 D9
St Birstan Gdns AND SP10 ....82 D9
St Blaize Rd ROMY SO51 ....204 G5
St Bonnet Dr BPWT SO32 ....232 A4
St Brelades Av
  BKME/WDN BH12 ....321 M3
St Catherines HMCH BH21 * 300 E1
St Catherine's HI THLE RG7 ....35 M1
St Catherine's Rd ELGH SO50 .....207 J8
  FRIM GU16 ....58 F4
  HISD PO11 ....318 C5
  SBNE BH6 ....336 C3
  WEND SO18 ....248 G2
  ....23 H7
St Catherines's Wy
  CHCH/BSGR BH23 ....324 B4
St Catherine St SSEA PO5 ....316 F7
St Catherines Wy
  FHAM/PORC PO16 ....273 J9
  HEND SO30 * 250 A5
St Chad's Av NEND PO2 ....296 C7
St Christopher Av
  FHAM/PORC PO16 ....11 K2
St Christophers Cl ASHV GU12 ....3 K2
  HASM GU27 * 156 F7
  KBH RG22 ....68 F9
  NBAD SO52 ....205 K9
St Christophers Pl FARN GU14 .....75 N1
St Christopher's Rd
  FARN GU14 ....75 P1
  HASM GU27 ....156 F7
  HAV PO9 ....276 C7
St Clair Rd CCLF BH13 ....333 N5
St Clares Av HAV PO9 ....276 D3
St Cleeve Wy FERN BH22 ....302 C5
St Clements Cl ROMY SO51 ....204 D5
St Clements Gdns BMTH BH1 ....335 K1
St Clement's Rd BMTH BH1 ....335 K1
  PLE BH15 ....321 K5
St Clement St WINC SO23 ....22 D5
St Colman's Av CHAM PO6 ....297 J1
St Cross Rd FNM GU9 ....96 D4
  FRIM GU16 ....58 F6
  RFNM GU10 ....95 H6
  WINC SO23 ....183 N3
St Cuthberts Cl HLER SO31 ....271 H6
St Cuthberts La HLER SO31 ....271 H6
St David's Cl FARN GU14 ....57 N8
  FNM GU9 ....96 E4
  ODIM RG29 ....93 J1
  TOTT SO40 ....246 A2
St Davids Ct
  LSOL/BMARY PO13 * 314 C2
St Davids Rd HLER SO31 ....270 F7
  HORN PO8 ....236 C7
  KBH RG22 ....69 H9
  NWBY RG14 ....16 D3
  SSEA PO5 ....19 K5
St Denys' Rd PTSW SO17 ....248 E2
St Donats Pl FARN GU14 ....17 F4
St Edmondsbury Ct
  LSOL/BMARY PO13 * 315 H3

St Edmund Cl
FHAM/STUB PO14 271 H9
St Edmund's Rd ROWN SO16 247 M3
St Edward's Rd GPORT PO12 12 D3
HLER SO31 269 K3
SSEA PO5 19 G7
St Elizabeth's Av WEND SO18 249 K4
St Evox Cl ROWN SO16 227 K7
St Faith's Cl GPORT PO12 12 A1
St Faiths Rd PSEA PO1 19 H1
WINC SO23 183 P1
St Francis Av WEND SO18 249 K3
St Francis Cl FAWY SO45 312 G1
St Francis Ct NEND PO2 * 296 G5
St Francis Pl HAV PO9 14 D1
St Francis Rd FAWY SO45 312 G1
GPORT PO12 315 N7
St Gabriels Lea CHIN RG24 70 B1
St Gabriel's Rd WEND SO18 249 K4
St George Cl HLER SO31 269 P1
St Georges PLE BH15 * 332 D2
St George's Av
BKME/WDN BH12 321 K4
CHAR BH8 323 J7
HAV PO9 277 H9
NWBY RG14 16 C4
St George's Cl CHAR BH8 323 J7
CHCH/BSGR BH23 325 P7
FNM GU9 * 97 H5
St Georges Ct
FHAM/PORC PO16 294 F1
St Georges Crs FBDG SP6 240 D1
St Georges Dr BWD BH11 321 M1
CHCH/BSGR BH23 305 N8
FERN BH22 302 C4
St Georges Ms FNM GU9 * 96 B8
St George's Rd ASHV GU12 3 F5
CHAM PO6 297 H1
ENEY PO4 317 J6
FBDG SP6 240 D1
FNM GU9 116 D1
HISD PO11 318 D5
HLER SO31 270 F7
NTID SP9 78 G5
PSEA PO1 18 D4
RFNM GU10 97 H7
St George's Rd East ASHV GU12 3 G4
St Georges Sq PSEA PO1 * 18 D3
St Georges St SHAM SO14 21 F5
WINC SO23 22 E4
St George's Wk GPORT PO12 13 G1
WVILLE PO7 275 N3
St George's Wy PSEA PO1 18 D3
St Georges Yd FNM GU9 * 96 B9
St Giles Cl WINC SO23 23 H6
St Giles Hl WINC SO23 23 H5
St Giles Wy HORN PO8 256 C1
St Helena Gdns WEND SO18 229 H9
St Helena Wy
FHAM/PORC PO16 295 N1
St Helen's Cl ENEY PO4 317 H6
St Helens Crs SHST GU47 41 J6
St Helens Pde ENEY PO4 316 G7
St Helens Rd GPORT PO12 315 J5
HISD PO11 318 D5
St Helier Rd BKME/WDN BH12 321 M3
St Hellen's Rd CHAM PO6 297 M1
St Hermans Rd HISD PO11 319 J6
St Hilda Av HORN PO8 256 C1
St Hubert Rd AND SP10 102 C3
HORN PO8 256 C1
St Ives End La RGWD BH24 281 N4
St Ives Gdns WCLF BH2 334 F1
St Ives Pk RGWD BH24 281 N4
St Ives Wd RGWD BH24 281 P4
St James' Av FNM GU9 96 D7
St James Cl HORN PO8 236 C8
PLE BH15 332 D2
TADY RG26 52 C4
St James' La FUFL SO22 22 B5
St James Pk CHFD SO53 * 206 C5
St James' Rd EMRTH PO10 277 M9
FLEETN GU51 74 C4
HEND SO30 249 M1
LYMN SO41 308 C6
WIMB BH21 302 A2
St James's Cl WSHM SO15 247 N2
St James's Park Rd
ROWN SO16 247 N1
St James's Rd SSEA PO5 19 G5
WSHM SO15 247 N2
St James's Sq BOSC BH5 335 N1
St James's St PSEA PO1 18 E2
St James St RAND SP11 79 N1
St James' Ter FNM GU9 96 C8
FUFL SO22 22 C5
St James' Vls WINC SO23 22 C6
St James Wy
FHAM/PORC PO16 295 P1
St John Cl TADY RG26 52 B3
St John's Av WVILLE PO7 275 N7
St John's Cl GPORT PO12 315 M3
HISD PO11 318 E5
HTWY RG27 72 A3
ROWN SO16 227 J5
WIMB BH21 300 F1
St Johns Ct FARN GU14 * 57 L8
TOTT SO40 267 K1
St Johns Dr TOTT SO40 267 J1
St John's Gdns
MOOR/WNTN BH9 322 F6
ROMY SO51 204 D5
St Johns Glebe ROWN SO16 227 K6
St Johns Gv FNM GU9 116 B3
St John's Hl WIMB BH21 278 F9
St Johns North WINC SO23 23 G5
St John's Piece DEAN RG23 88 F3
St John's Rd AND SP10 4 E3
BOSC BH5 335 L3
CHAM PO6 297 J1
CHCH/BSGR BH23 324 E9
DEAN RG23 88 F1
ELGH SO50 207 K9
FARN GU14 57 M9
FNM GU9 116 B2
HAV PO9 276 C6
HEND SO30 250 A7
HLER SO31 271 H8
HTWY RG27 55 J8
NMIL/BTOS BH25 307 J9
NWBY RG14 16 E5
PLE BH15 320 F8
SHST GU47 41 J7
STHA RG19 25 M4
THLE RG7 35 P1
WINC SO23 23 H4
St Johns South WINC SO23 23 G5
St Johns Sq GPORT PO12 315 M3
St John's St FAWY SO45 268 C6
WINC SO23 23 G5
St Joseph's Crs CHIN RG24 70 A2
St Josephs Ms SSEA PO5 * 19 H6
St Joseph's Rd ALDT GU11 2 E5
ASHV GU12 3 F5
St Just Cl AMSY SP4 118 D4
FERN BH22 302 B5
St Lawrence Rd ALTN GU34 132 F5
ELGH SO50 207 J9
SHAM SO14 21 G7
St Ledger's Pl CHAR BH8 * 323 K9
St Ledger's Rd CHAR BH8 323 K8
St Leger Ct NWBY RG14 * 24 B3
St Leonards RAND SP11 100 B9
St Leonard's Av CHIN RG24 70 B1
HISD PO11 318 G5
St Leonards Cl FHAM PO15 271 L7
St Leonard's Rd CHAR BH8 323 H9
LYMN SO41 310 F9
WINC SO23 23 J7
St Leonards Wy RGWD BH24 281 K4
St Lukes Cl HEND SO30 250 C2
KBH RG22 89 N1
St Luke's Rd GPORT PO12 315 L2
TWDS BH3 322 F8
St Margaret's Av
CHCH/BSGR BH23 324 E9
St Margaret's Cl WEND SO18 249 K4
WIMB BH21 278 C9
St Margaret's Hl WIMB BH21 278 C8
St Margarets La
FHAM/STUB PO14 271 L9
St Margarets Rd ELGH SO50 207 L9
HISD PO11 318 G5
NBNE BH10 322 B5
PLE BH15 320 E8
St Marks Cl CHFD SO53 * 207 H4
FARN GU14 76 B3
GPORT PO12 315 L7
STHA RG19 25 M4
TADY RG26 52 B3
St Marks Pl FNM GU9 * 96 B4
St Mark's Rd BWD BH11 322 B4
GPORT PO12 315 L7
LYMN SO41 329 H4
NEND PO2 296 F8
St Martin's Cl ROWN SO16 227 J9
WINC SO23 23 H4
St Mary Gv LYMN SO41 328 A5
St Marys ROMY SO51 * 204 C7
St Mary's Av GPORT PO12 12 B6
TADY RG26 52 C3
St Marys Cl ALTN GU34 132 F7
CHCH/BSGR BH23 305 M8
RSAL SP5 200 B8
SHST GU47 41 K6
WINC SO23 165 K2
St Mary's Ct BSTK RG21 7 G6
TADY RG26 52 C3
St Mary's Meadow
RAND SP11 101 N6
St Marys Pl FNM GU9 * 96 C8
NWBY RG14 24 D3
SHAM SO14 21 F5
St Mary's Rd ASHV GU12 76 F7
BMTH BH1 323 K9
ELGH SO50 207 M9
FERN BH22 302 C3
FHAM/STUB PO14 294 A5
HISD PO11 318 G4
HLER SO31 269 L4
HTWY RG27 55 H8
KSCL RG20 48 C3
LISS GU33 192 D2
NWBY RG14 24 D3
PLE BH15 320 G8
PSEA PO1 316 G2
SHAM SO14 21 F2
THLE RG7 27 J9
St Mary's Ter RWIN SO21 184 A8
St Mary St FUFL SO22 183 M1
SHAM SO14 21 G5
St Mary's Wy THLE RG7 27 L4
St Matthews Cl SHAM SO14 21 F2
St Matthews Ct GPORT PO12 13 H1
St Matthew's Rd CHAM PO6 297 J1
FUFL SO22 164 E5
St Merrin's Cl NBNE BH10 322 C3
St Michaels Av NTID SP9 78 G6
St Michaels Cl FAWY SO45 290 G8
FLEETN GU51 74 F4
OVTN RG25 108 C1
PLE BH15 320 A9
VWD BH31 258 F5
St Michaels Ct CHAM PO6 274 D9
St Michael's Gdns WINC SO23 22 D6
St Michael's Gv
FHAM/STUB PO14 294 D2
St Michaels La THLE RG7 26 F2
St Michael's Rd ASHV GU12 3 F5
FARN GU14 58 A7
HAV PO9 276 C7
HLER SO31 270 F8
KBH RG22 68 F9
NWBY RG14 16 C4
PSEA PO1 19 F4
SHST GU47 40 G6
TOTT SO40 246 D2
VWD BH31 258 F6
WCLF BH2 8 B4
WINC SO23 22 D7
St Michaels Sq SHAM SO14 20 D6
St Michael's St SHAM SO14 20 D6
St Michaels Wy HORN PO8 256 C1
St Monica Rd ITCH SO19 249 J8
St Neot's Rd HTWY RG27 39 J7
St Nicholas WINC SO23 165 J1
St Nicholas Av
LSOL/BMARY PO13 314 G1
St Nicholas Cl FLEETN GU51 74 C3
RAND SP11 80 B1
St Nicholas Ct KBH RG22 68 G8
St Nicholas' Rd NWBY RG14 16 D3
St Nicholas St PSEA PO1 18 D6
St Omer Barracks ALDT GU11 76 C7
St Osmund's Rd PSTN BH14 321 L9
St Patricks Av NTID SP9 78 F6
St Patrick's La LISS GU33 192 G1
St Patrick's Rd KBH RG22 69 H9
St Pauls Cl RFNM GU10 97 M4
St Paul's Hl FUFL SO22 22 C3
St Paul's La BMTH BH1 9 H2
St Paul's Pl BMTH BH1 9 H2
St Pauls Rd BMTH BH1 9 H1
HLER SO31 270 E4
KBH RG22 69 H9
SSEA PO5 19 F4
St Pauls Rbt BMTH BH1 9 G1
St Paul's Sq SSEA PO5 * 19 F5
St Peter's Av HISD PO11 299 J7
St Peters Cl NTID SP9 98 G3
RAND SP11 102 F8
St Peter's Gdns RFNM GU10 115 P4
YTLY GU46 40 E8
St Peters Gv SSEA PO5 19 J6
St Peters Md ASHV GU12 97 P1
St Peters Pk FNM GU9 96 E3
St Peter's Rd BMTH BH1 8 E3
HISD PO11 299 J7
KBH RG22 68 F9
PSF GU32 215 M2
PSTN BH14 321 J8
St Peters Rbt BMTH BH1 9 F4
St Peter's Sq EMRTH PO10 299 M1
St Peter's St BPWT SO32 232 A4
St Peter St WINC SO23 22 E4
St Peter's Wy FRIM GU16 58 E6
St Philip's Wy WEND SO18 249 K4
St Pirans Av HSEA PO3 317 J1
St Richards Gdns
WVILLE PO7 * 275 L5
St Richards Rd NWBY RG14 24 E2
St Ronan's Av ENEY PO4 316 G6
St Ronan's Rd ENEY PO4 316 G6
St Sebastian Crs
FHAM/PORC PO16 11 H1
St Simon Cl HLER SO31 271 H7
St Simon's Rd SSEA PO5 316 F6
St Stephens Cl HASM GU27 157 H6
St Stephens La VWD BH31 258 G4
St Stephen's Rd FUFL SO22 164 E5
NEND PO2 296 G9
WCLF BH2 8 B2
St Stephen's Wy WCLF BH2 8 D3
St Swithin Wy AND SP10 82 D9
St Swithun Cl BPWT SO32 231 P4
St Swithun's Cl ROMY SO51 205 H4
St Swithun's Rd BMTH BH1 9 J1
NEND PO2 297 H7
St Swithun's Rd South
BMTH BH1 9 J2
St Swithuns Ter WINC SO23 * 22 E6
St Swithun St WINC SO23 22 D6
St Theresas Cl HAV PO9 14 A2
St Thomas Av HISD PO11 318 D5
St Thomas Cl AND SP10 82 C8
BSTK RG21 6 D2
FHAM/PORC PO16 11 J2
St Thomas Pk LYMN SO41 329 K3
St Thomas's Cl NBNE BH10 322 D5
St Thomas's Ct PSEA PO1 18 D5
St Thomas's Rd GPORT PO12 295 M9
St Thomas's St LYMN SO41 329 K4
PSEA PO1 18 C6
St Thomas St WINC SO23 22 D6
St Tristan Cl HLER SO31 271 H7
St Ursula Gv SSEA PO5 19 J6
St Valerie Rd GPORT PO12 12 D5
WCLF BH2 334 F1
St Vigor Wy RWIN SO21 207 P4
St Vincent Crs HORN PO8 256 B5
St Vincent Rd GPORT PO12 315 M2
SSEA PO5 316 F6
St Vincent St SSEA PO5 * 19 F4
St Winifred's Rd ROWN SO16 247 N1
WCLF BH2 334 F1
Salamanca CWTH RG45 40 F1
Salcombe Av HSEA PO3 297 J8
Salcombe Cl CHFD SO53 206 D9
Salcombe Crs TOTT SO40 246 C5
Salcombe Rd NWBY RG14 16 A5
TOTT SO40 246 C5
WSHM SO15 247 N4
Salcot Rd WINC SO23 165 H5
Salem St WSHM SO15 247 N2
Salerno Cl ALDT GU11 2 E2
Salerno Dr GPORT PO12 315 K4
Salerno Rd NEND PO2 296 F5
ROWN SO16 227 N8
Salesian Vw FARN GU14 76 D4
Salet Wy WVILLE PO7 276 B1
Salisbury Cl ALTN GU34 132 G7
ELGH SO50 207 K9
ODIM RG29 93 J1
Salisbury Gdns KBH RG22 68 F8
Salisbury Gv FRIM GU16 76 F1
Salisbury La STOK SO20 120 G9
Salisbury Rd ASHV GU12 97 N1
BLKW GU17 41 K9
BMTH BH1 335 L2
CHAM PO6 297 J2
CHCH/BSGR BH23 324 F1
ENEY PO4 317 H6
FARN GU14 58 B9
FBDG SP6 220 G2
FBDG SP6 240 E1
NARL SO24 167 P2
NTID SP9 98 G5
PSTN BH14 321 L7
PTSW SO17 228 C9
RAND SP11 101 N9
RAND SP11 102 A5
RAND SP11 119 N3
RAND SP11 121 K3
RGWD BH24 260 E1
RGWD BH24 282 D1
ROMY SO51 203 H3
ROMY SO51 224 C1
ROMY SO51 225 J4
RSAL SP5 199 J4
STOK SO20 139 N6
TOTT SO40 246 C1
Salisbury Road Ar
TOTT SO40 * 246 D4
Salisbury St FBDG SP6 240 D2
WSHM SO15 20 D1
Salisbury Ter FRIM GU16 76 F1
LSOL/BMARY PO13 314 D3
Salmon Dr ELGH SO50 229 P2
Salmond Rd RAND SP11 101 P2
Salmons Rd ODIM RG29 93 J1
Salterns Av ENEY PO4 317 K3
Salterns Cl HISD PO11 319 J5
Salterns Est
FHAM/PORC PO16 294 F2
Salterns La FAWY SO45 291 K5
FHAM/PORC PO16 294 F2
HISD PO11 319 H5
HLER SO31 270 A4
Salterns Rd FHAM/STUB PO14 293 P9
PSTN BH14 321 J9
Salterns Wy PSTN BH14 333 K3
Salter Rd CCLF BH13 333 K8
Salters Acres FUFL SO22 164 D5
Salters Heath Rd TADY RG26 50 E7
Salters La FUFL SO22 164 C5
Saltgrass La LYMN SO41 339 K3
The Saltings CHAM PO6 297 N2
HAV PO9 298 F3
Salt La BPWT SO32 210 C2
Saltmarsh La HISD PO11 318 E3
Saltmarsh Rd SHAM SO14 21 H7
Saltmead PTSW SO17 248 F2
Salt Meat La GPORT PO12 315 P2
Saltram Rd FARN GU14 76 D2
Salvia Cl WVILLE PO7 276 A4
Salwey Rd HEND SO30 250 D6
Samarkand Cl CBLY GU15 58 G1
Samber Cl LYMN SO41 329 J3
Sampan Cl HLER SO31 270 E9
Samples Wy CFDH BH17 321 H4
Sampson Rd
FHAM/STUB PO14 294 D3
PSEA PO1 18 B1
Samson Cl LSOL/BMARY PO13 315 H1
Samuel Rd PSEA PO1 317 H2
Sam Whites Hl RAND SP11 102 C6
San Carlos Ap ALDT GU11 3 J2
Sancreed Rd
BKME/WDN BH12 321 N5
Sanctuary Pl HTWY RG27 55 J6
Sandbanks Dr KBH RG22 89 M4
Sandbanks Rd PLE BH15 321 H9
Sandbourne Rd CCLF BH13 334 B5
PLE BH15 320 F8
Sandcroft Cl GPORT PO12 315 J5
Sandecotes Rd PSTN BH14 321 L9
Sanderling Rd ENEY PO4 317 L3
Sanderlings RGWD BH24 282 G3
The Sanderlings HISD PO11 318 G6
Sandford Av GPORT PO12 315 H4
Sandford Cl KSCL RG20 48 E3
MOOR/WNTN BH9 323 J4
Sandford Ct ALDT GU11 2 A4
Sandford Rd ALDT GU11 2 C3
FNM GU9 96 B4
TADY RG26 34 B6
Sandford Wy BDST BH18 320 B1
Sand Hl FARN GU14 58 A6
Sandhill La
LSOL/BMARY PO13 314 E1
Sandhills Cl CFDH BH17 320 F2
Sandhurst Dr WIMB BH21 280 G2
Sandhurst La BLKW GU17 41 J8
Sandhurst Rd CWTH RG45 41 J3
WSHM SO15 20 B1
YTLY GU46 40 F8
San Diego Rd GPORT PO12 315 M2
Sandisplatt
FHAM/STUB PO14 294 A1
Sandle Copse FBDG SP6 239 P2
Sandleford Pde NWBY RG14 * 24 D8
Sandleford Ri NWBY RG14 24 D8
Sandleford Rd HAV PO9 276 D3
Sandleheath Rd FBDG SP6 239 M3
Sandlewood Cl HORN PO8 236 C9
Sandmartin Cl
NMIL/BTOS BH25 327 H8
Sandown Cl ALTN GU34 132 G7
BLKW GU17 41 L9
GPORT PO12 315 J5
Sandown Crs ALDT GU11 97 H4
Sandown Dr FRIM GU16 58 C3
Sandown Rd CHAM PO6 296 G2
CHCH/BSGR BH23 325 J9
WSHM SO15 247 M2
Sandown Wy NWBY RG14 17 J6
Sandpiper Cl CFDH BH17 320 B3
HORN PO8 256 A4
TOTT SO40 267 J1
Sandpiper Rd ROWN SO16 227 L7
Sandpiper Wy KBH RG22 89 K4
Sandpit Hl KSCL RG20 30 B3
Sandpit La LYMN SO41 331 J3
THLE RG7 38 E1
Sandport Gv
FHAM/PORC PO16 295 M2
Sandringham Cl ALTN GU34 132 D6
CHFD SO53 206 B9
MOOR/WNTN BH9 323 H3
Sandringham Gdns
MOOR/WNTN BH9 323 H3
Sandringham La PSEA PO1 * 316 G3
Sandringham Rd
FHAM/STUB PO14 293 P1
PSEA PO1 316 G3
PSF GU32 215 M1
PSTN BH14 321 K9
WEND SO18 248 G2
Sandringham Wy FRIM GU16 58 E5
Sandrock HASM GU27 157 H7
Sandrock Hill Rd RFNM GU10 115 P4
Sandsbury La PSF GU32 191 H9
Sands Cl RFNM GU10 97 K9
Sands Rd RFNM GU10 97 J9
The Sands BOR GU35 153 M6
Sandy Brow WVILLE PO7 275 M6
Sandy Cl EPSF GU31 216 A2
WIMB BH21 279 J6
Sandycroft HLER SO31 292 D1
Sandy Down LYMN SO41 309 H4
Sandy Field Crs HORN PO8 255 N8
Sandy Hill Rd FNM GU9 96 A4
Sandyhurst Cl CFDH BH17 320 E3
Sandy La BPWT SO32 252 A2
CHCH/BSGR BH23 324 C5
ELGH SO50 230 B2
FARN GU14 57 K7
FHAM/STUB PO14 293 M1
FLEETS GU52 74 D8
HASM GU27 156 B6
HASM GU27 157 K4
HTWY RG27 55 J8
LISS GU33 193 J3
LYND SO43 264 F6
NBAD SO52 205 M9
RFNM GU10 116 C9
RFNM GU10 136 G3
RGWD BH24 281 M5
ROMY SO51 204 E2
RSAL SP5 200 A6
SBNE BH6 335 P1
SHST GU47 40 G5
TADY RG26 34 E6
VWD BH31 258 G4
WIMB BH21 258 E8
WIMB BH21 279 J6
Sandy Mead Rd CHAR BH8 323 M6
Sandy Plot CHCH/BSGR BH23 324 G6
Sandy Point Rd HISD PO11 319 L7
Sandys Cl KBH RG22 69 H9
Sandys Rd KBH RG22 69 H8
Sandy Wy NBNE BH10 322 E4
Sankey La FLEETN GU51 56 G9
Sanross Cl FHAM/STUB PO14 293 N8
Santina Cl FNM GU9 96 D3
Saor Ms AND SP10 4 B3
Sapley La OVTN RG25 86 G4
The Saplings FAWY SO45 290 D4
Sapphire Cl GPORT PO12 315 M1
WVILLE PO7 * 276 A3
Sapphire Rdg WVILLE PO7 276 A3
Saracen Cl LYMN SO41 329 J6
Saracens Rd CHFD SO53 207 H6
Sarah Cl LTDN BH7 323 P7
Sarah Sands Cl
CHCH/BSGR BH23 325 H7
Sarah Wy FARN GU14 58 A9
Sargood Cl STHA RG19 25 P5
Sarisbury Cl TADY RG26 34 B6
Sark Rd BKME/WDN BH12 321 M4
Sarnia Ct ROWN SO16 227 J9
Sarson Cl RAND SP11 101 H4
Sarson La RAND SP11 101 H3
Sarum Av FERN BH22 280 E5
Sarum Cl FUFL SO22 164 D8
NTID SP9 98 F3
STOK SO20 120 D9
Sarum Hl BSTK RG21 6 D7
Sarum Rd CHFD SO53 206 G7
FUFL SO22 163 N8
FUFL SO22 164 E8
TADY RG26 34 B5
Sarum St PLE BH15 332 D2
Sarum Vw FUFL SO22 164 C9
Sarum Wk LYMN SO41 329 K1
Satchell La HLER SO31 270 A7
Saturn Cl ROWN SO16 227 K8
Saulfland Dr
CHCH/BSGR BH23 325 P7
Saulfland Pl
CHCH/BSGR BH23 325 P7
Saunders Cl
LSOL/BMARY PO13 314 E1
Saunders Gdn TADY RG26 34 C6
Saunders La ROMY SO51 179 L9
Saunders Ms ENEY PO4 317 K6
Saunton Gdns FARN GU14 57 P7
Savernake Cl
LSOL/BMARY PO13 295 H7
ROMY SO51 204 F4
Savile Crs BOR GU35 154 B5
Saville Cl ELGH SO50 207 M8
GPORT PO12 315 K5
Saville Gdns
FHAM/PORC PO16 10 D1
Savoy Cl AND SP10 4 E5
Savoy Gv BLKW GU17 57 L2
The Sawmills BPWT SO32 231 H7
Sawyer Cl FUFL SO22 164 D6
Sawyers Ley THLE RG7 27 M7
Saxby Cl THLE RG7 27 K4
Saxholm Cl ROWN SO16 228 B6
Saxholm Dl ROWN SO16 228 B6
Saxholm Wy ROWN SO16 228 B6
Saxley Ct HAV PO9 276 C4
Saxonbury Rd SBNE BH6 324 C9
Saxon Cl FHAM/PORC PO16 273 M9
HLER SO31 270 E9
HORN PO8 236 C8
Saxon Ct AND SP10 82 E8
STHA RG19 25 K4
Saxon Cft FNM GU9 116 C1
Saxonford Rd
CHCH/BSGR BH23 325 N8

Saxon Gdns *HEND* SO30 ....250 A6
Saxonhurst *RSAL* SP5 ....199 L6
Saxonhurst Cl *NBNE* BH10 ....322 E2
Saxonhurst Gdns *NBNE* BH10 .....322 D3
Saxonhurst Rd *NBNE* BH10 ....322 D3
Saxon King Gdns *SBNE* BH6........336 E7
Saxon Leas *RSAL* SP5 ....158 B1
Saxon Pl *LYMN* SO41 ....329 K1
Saxon Rd *FAWY* SO45 ....291 K6
 WINC SO23 ....22 E2
 WSHM SO15 ....247 P6
Saxon Wk *CHFD* SO53 ....206 G8
Saxon Wy *AND* SP10 ....82 D8
 CHIN RG24 ....70 A5
 FBDG SP6 ....239 N6
 ROMY SO51 ....204 F6
Saxony Wy *YTLY* GU46 * 56 D1
Sayers Cl *FRIM* GU16 ....58 D6
 NWBY RG14 ....24 C2
Sayers Rd *ELGH* SO50 ....229 M2
SBAC Tr *ALDT* GU11 ....75 M6
Scafell Av *FHAM/STUB* PO14 ......294 B1
Scallows La *RSAL* SO51 ....202 D8
Scantabout Av *CHFD* SO53...........206 G6
Scarf Rd *CFDH* BH17 ....321 H5
Scarlet Rd *KBH* RG22 ....90 B5
Scarlet Oaks *CBLY* GU15 ....58 D2
Scarlett's Rd *ALDT* GU11 ....75 P9
Scholars' Wk *CHAM* PO6 ....297 L2
School Cl *CHFD* SO53 ....206 D8
 LYMN SO41 ....329 J5
 RAND SP11 ....43 H8
 VWD BH31 ....258 C5
School Flds *BOR* GU35 ....134 F8
School HI *BPWT* SO32 ....233 N6
 CWTH RG45 ....41 L2
 RFNM GU10 ....97 P7
 SHST GU47 ....115 P4
 SHST GU47 ....41 H5
School La *BWD* BH11 ....322 B2
 CHCH/BSGR BH23 ....306 A4
 CHFD SO53 ....206 D8
 EMRTH PO10 ....277 P5
 EMRTH PO10 ....299 M1
 HLER SO31 ....183 J2
 LISS GU33 ....192 D2
 LYMN SO41 ....309 M8
 LYMN SO41 ....328 E9
 LYMN SO41 ....329 L3
 NARL SO24 ....168 E2
 NARL SO24 ....169 H3
 PLE BH15 ....320 E7
 PSF GU32 ....191 N8
 RFNM GU10 ....114 F5
 RFNM GU10 ....116 D4
 RGUW GU3 ....77 L8
 RWIN SO21 ....281 N4
 RWIN SO21 ....282 E2
 RWIN SO21 ....146 E9
 STOK SO20 ....120 F9
 STOK SO20 ....139 P9
 THLE RG7 ....27 H5
 THLE RG7 ....35 J5
 THLE RG7 ....58 B5
 WIMB BH21 ....278 D9
 WIMB BH21 ....280 F2
 WINC SO23 ....165 J2
 WVILLE PO7 ....254 F6
 YTLY GU46 ....40 C8
School Rd *BOR* GU35 ....154 A4
 BPWT SO32 ....253 K1
 CHCH/BSGR BH23 ....306 A4
 FAWY SO45 ....268 C6
 FAWY SO45 ....291 K6
 GPORT PO12 ....295 K8
 GSHT GU26 ....156 A2
 HASM GU27 ....156 E8
 HAV PO9 ....14 E6
 HLER SO31 ....270 A2
 RDGW/BURGH RG30 ....27 L1
 RFNM GU10 ....115 N7
 ROMY SO51 ....204 G4
 ROMY SO51 ....224 F2
 RSAL SP5 ....200 C8
 RSAL SP5 ....183 P8
 THLE RG7 ....26 B6
 THLE RG7 ....38 B2
 TOTT SO40 ....246 E5
 WHAM PO17 ....179 J4
Schooner Wy *HLER* SO31 ....270 E9
 HSEA PO3 ....317 L2
Schroeder Cl *BSTK* RG21 ....90 C1
Schubert Rd *KBH* RG22 ....90 A5
The Scimitars
 FHAM/STUB PO14 ....293 P6
Scivier's La *BPWT* SO32 ....231 J2
Scotland Cl *ASHV* GU12 ....76 F7
Scotland *ELGH* SO50 ....228 C2
Scotland Farm Rd *ASHV* GU12 ......76 F7
Scotland HI *SHST* GU47 ....41 H6
Scotland La *HASM* GU27 ....156 A7
 RSAL SP5 ....201 J6
Scotlands Cl *HASM* GU27 ....156 C8
Scotlands Dr *HASM* GU27 ....156 C8
Scotney Ct *HAV* PO9 ....277 H4
Scotney Rd *BSTK* RG21 ....6 E1
Scots Ct *HTWY* RG27 ....72 B2
Scott Cl *AND* SP10 ....103 J1
 BKME/WDN BH12 ....321 P3
 FHAM/STUB PO14 ....294 A5
 RWIN SO21 ....208 A5
 STOK SO20 ....161 M5
Scotter Rd *ELGH* SO50 ....229 M1
 LTDN BH7 ....335 P1
Scott-paine Cl *FAWY* SO45 ....268 D6
Scott Rd *BKME/WDN* BH12 ....321 P4
 ELGH SO50 ....229 H2
 HSEA PO3 ....297 H4
 ITCH SO19 ....269 H1
 PSEA PO1 ....18 B1
Scott's Ct *FARN* GU14 ....58 A6
Scott's Gn *CHCH/BSGR* BH23 ....325 K7
Scotts Hills La
 CHCH/BSGR BH23 ....325 H9
Scratchface La *HAV* PO9 ....276 C8
 WVILLE PO7 ....275 P6
Scrubbs La *NARL* SO24 ....168 D4
Scullards La *SHAM* SO14 ....20 D4
Scures Rd *HTWY* RG27 ....71 N3
Seabird Wy
 FHAM/PORC PO16 ....294 F2
Seabourne Rd *BOSC* BH5 ....335 P1
Seabourne Rd *BOSC* BH5 ....335 N1
Sea Breeze Gdns *ENEY* PO4 ....317 L5
Seabreeze Wy *LYMN* SO41 ....328 A9
Seacombe Gn *ROWN* SO16 ....247 H2
Seacombe Rd *CCLF* BH13 ....333 K8
Sea Crest Rd
 LSOL/BMARY PO13 ....314 D3
Seacroft Av *NMIL/BTOS* BH25 ....326 C2
Seafield Cl *NMIL/BTOS* BH25 ......327 H8
Seafield Dr *SBNE* BH6 ....324 C9
Seafield Park Rd
 FHAM/STUB PO14 ....293 P8
Seafield Rd *CHCH/BSGR* BH23 ...325 N9
 FHAM/PORC PO16 ....295 M2
 HSEA PO3 ....297 J8
 NMIL/BTOS BH25 ....326 C7
 ROWN SO16 ....247 H1
 SBNE BH6 ....336 C3
Seafields *EMRTH* PO10 ....299 L1
Seafire Wy *FARN* GU14 ....75 M5
Seaford Cl *HLER* SO31 ....269 P1
Sea Front *HISD* PO11 ....318 F6
Seagarth La *ROWN* SO16 ....227 P9
Seagers Ct *PSEA* PO1 ....18 B6
Seagrim Rd *CHAM* PO6 ....323 A4
Sea Grove Av *HISD* PO11 ....318 C6
Seagrove Rd *HISD* PO11 ....318 C6
Seagull Cl *ENEY* PO4 * 317 L2
 KBH RG22 ....89 K3
Seagull La *EMRTH* PO10 ....277 M9
Seagull Rd *CHAR* BH8 ....323 J6
The Seagulls
 LSOL/BMARY PO13 ....314 E4
Seahorse Wk *GPORT* PO12 ....315 H7
Sea Kings *FHAM/STUB* PO14 .....293 P7
Sea La *LSOL/BMARY* PO13 ....294 A9
Sealark Rd *GPORT* PO12 ....315 N1
Seale La *RFNM* GU10 ....97 K7
Seale Rd *MFD/CHID* GU8 ....117 P2
Seaman's La *LYND* SO43 ....244 B7
Seamead *FHAM/STUB* PO14 ......294 A7
Sea Mill Gdns *PSEA* PO1 ....18 D3
Seamoor La *WBNE* BH4 ....334 B5
Seamoor Rd *CCLF* BH13 ....334 B3
Searing Wy *TADY* RG26 ....34 B5
Searle Rd *FNM* GU9 ....116 C2
Searles Cl *NARL* SO24 ....168 A2
Searles HI *RWIN* SO21 ....184 A8
Searl's La *HTWY* RG27 ....54 A9
Sea Rd *BOSC* BH5 ....335 L3
 ITCH SO19 ....248 F7
 LYMN SO41 ....339 H2
 NMIL/BTOS BH25 ....326 C5
 SBNE BH6 ....336 D5
Seaton Av *HAV* PO9 ....297 J9
Seaton Cl *CHCH/BSGR* BH23 .....326 D7
 FHAM/STUB PO14 ....294 A7
 LYMN SO41 ....329 L2
 WEND SO18 ....248 E1
Seaton Rd *CHCH/BSGR* BH23 ....326 D7
Seatown Ct *CFDH* BH17 ....321 J3
Sea Vw *LYMN* SO41 * 308 B8
Seaview Av
 FHAM/PORC PO16 ....274 A9
Seaview Est *HLER* SO31 ....269 K5
Sea View Rd
 BKME/WDN BH12 ....321 J7
 CHAM PO6 ....297 L1
 HISD PO11 ....319 K5
Seaward Av *NMIL/BTOS* BH25 ....326 G8
 SBNE BH6 ....335 P2
Seaward Rd *FAWY* SO45 ....268 D7
 ITCH SO19 ....248 G7
Seaway *NMIL/BTOS* BH25 ....327 K7
Seaway Av *CHCH/BSGR* BH23 ....325 N9
Seaway Crs *ENEY* PO4 ....317 L4
Seaway Gdns *ENEY* PO4..............295 N3
Seawinds *LYMN* SO41 ....309 M1
Sebastian Gv *WVILLE* PO7 ....276 A2
Sebastopol Rd *ALDT* GU11 ....3 F5
Second Av *CHAM* PO6 ....296 C1
 CHAM PO6 ....297 N2
 HAV PO9 ....14 A3
 THLE RG7 ....34 C4
 WSHM SO15 ....247 H4
Second Marine Av
 NMIL/BTOS BH25 ....327 J9
Second St *FAWY* SO45 ....290 C1
 STHA RG19 ....31 M2
Second St East *STHA* RG19 ....31 M1
Sedbergh Rd *ROWN* SO16 ....247 H2
Seddon Cl *NMIL/BTOS* BH25 ......327 K7
Sedgefield Cl *CHAM* PO6 ....296 B1
 TOTT SO40 ....246 A3
Sedgefield Rd *NWBY* RG14 ....17 J7
Sedgeley Gv *GPORT* PO12 ....295 L9
Sedgemead *HLER* SO31 ....269 K5
Sedgemoor *FARN* GU14 ....58 A6
Sedgewick Cl
 LSOL/BMARY PO13 ....294 C9
Sedgewick Rd *ELGH* SO50 ....229 M1
 ITCH SO19 ....249 L6
Sedgley Cl *SSEA* PO5 ....19 J5
Sedgley Rd *MOOR/WNTN* BH9 ...322 E7
Seebys Oak *SHST* GU47 ....41 L8
Seeviours Ct *WHCH* RG28 ....85 L6
Segars La *RWIN* SO21 ....183 P9
Segensworth Rd *FHAM* PO15 ......271 K6
Sek Kong Cl *STOK* SO20 ....120 G5
Selangor Av *EMRTH* PO10 ....277 K9
Selborne Av *ALDT* GU11 ....97 J4
 HAV PO9 ....276 D5
 WEND SO18 ....249 L3
Selborne Cl *BLKW* GU17 ....41 K8
Selborne Gdns *FNM* GU9 ....116 A3
 GPORT PO12 ....12 A2
Selborne Pl *FUFL* SO22 ....183 M1
Selborne Rd *ALTN* GU34 ....132 E8
 LISS GU33 ....173 H5
Selborne Wk *WEND* SO18 ....249 L5
Selborne Wy *BOR* GU35 ....153 M6
Selbourne Dr *ELGH* SO50 ....207 J9
Selbourne Rd *HAV* PO9 ....14 E6
 TOTT SO40 ....246 B3
Selbourne Ter *PSEA* PO1 ....316 C5
Selby Cl *BDST* BH18 ....320 C1
Selby Wk *CHIN* RG24 ....69 L4
Seldon Cl *FUFL* SO22 ....183 K2
Seldown PLE BH15 ....320 F9
Seldown Br *PLE* BH15 ....332 F1
Seldown La *PLE* BH15 ....320 F9
Seldown Rd *PLE* BH15 ....320 F9
Selfridge Av *SBNE* BH6 ....336 F3
Selfridge Cl *SBNE* BH6 ....336 F5
Selhurst Wy *ELGH* SO50 ....230 C3
Seliot Cl *PLE* BH15 ....320 F7
Selkirk Cl *WIMB* BH21 ....300 C4
Selkworthy Cl *PSTN* BH14 ....333 J1
Sellwood Wy
 NMIL/BTOS BH25 ....326 F7
Selman Cl *FAWY* SO45 ....268 D6
Selsdon Av *ROMY* SO51 ....204 F5
Selsey Av *ENEY* PO4 ....317 J4
 GPORT PO12 ....295 K9
Seisey Cl *HISD* PO11 ....319 M6
 ROWN SO16 ....247 J1
Selsmore Av *HISD* PO11 ....319 J6
Selsmore Rd *HISD* PO11 ....318 G5
Selwood Pk *NBNE* BH10 * 302 C9
Selworthy Cl *LB* BPWT SO22 ....233 M9
Selworthy Cl *PSTN* BH14 ....335 J1
Selwyn Cl *WEND* SO18 ....40 C3
Selwyn Gdns *ELGH* SO50 ....207 J8
Sengana Cl *HEND* SO30 ....250 D5
Senlac Rd *ROMY* SO51 ....204 F6
Sennen Pl *CHAM* PO6 ....296 C2
Sentinel Cl *WVILLE* PO7 ....276 B1
Sepen Meade *FLEETS* GU52 ....74 B8
Seps 4 Rd *FAWY* SO45 ....291 K5
September La *WVILLE* PO7 ....276 B1
Seremban Cl *STOK* SO20 ....120 C4
Serle Cl *TOTT* SO40 ....246 B5
Serle Gdns *TOTT* SO40 ....246 B5
Sermon Rd *FUFL* SO22 ....164 C6
Serpentine Rd
 FHAM/PORC PO16 ....11 G2
 PLE BH15 ....320 E9
 SSEA PO5 ....316 E6
 WVILLE PO7 ....275 L7
Setley Gdns *CHAR* BH8 ....323 L4
Seton Dr *HTWY* RG27 ....71 N4
Setters Cl *RWIN* SO21 ....207 P5
Set Thorns Rd *LYMN* SO41 ....308 C6
Settle Cl *ROWN* SO16 ....247 H1
Settlers Cl *PSEA* PO1 ....19 J1
The Sett *YTLY* GU46 ....40 C9
Sevenoaks Dr *LTDN* BH7 ....323 N7
Sevenoaks Rd *CHAM* PO6 ....296 C1
Seventh St *STHA* RG19 ....31 L1
The Severals *CHIN* RG24 ....69 K1
Severn Cl *CHAM* PO6 ....274 D9
 FHAM/PORC PO16 ....295 L1
 NTHA RG18 ....25 L2
 SHST GU47 ....41 K6
Severn Ct *AND* SP10 ....82 C9
Severn Gdns *DEAN* RG23 ....88 F2
Severn Rd *FARN* GU14 ....57 M7
 FERN BH22 ....302 C3
 ROWN SO16 ....247 J3
Severn Wy *BSTK* RG21 ....7 K6
 HEND SO30 ....249 M1
Seville Crs *AND* SP10 ....82 C9
Seward Ri *ROMY* SO51 ....204 G5
Seymour Cl *CHFD* SO53 ....206 G8
 NEND PO2 ....316 F1
 TOTT SO40 ....246 A2
Seymour La *NBAD* SO52 ....205 K9
Seymour Rd *BOR* GU35 ....155 K4
 KBH RG22 ....89 H1
 LSOL/BMARY PO13 ....314 D4
 RGWD BH24 ....260 F9
 ROWN SO16 ....227 N9
Shackleton Cl *ASHV* GU12 ....76 B1
Shackleton Rd
 LSOL/BMARY PO13 ....295 H9
Shackleton Sq *AND* SP10 * 82 G8
Shadwell Rd *NEND* PO2 ....296 C2
Shady Nook *FNM* GU9 ....96 B5
Shaftesbury Av *CHFD* SO53 ....206 E9
 ENEY PO4 ....248 D2
 WVILLE PO7 ....275 M6
Shaftesbury Cl *FERN* BH22 ....280 F7
Shaftesbury Mt *BLKW* GU17 ....57 K2
Shaftesbury Rd *CHAR* BH8 ....323 J9
 FERN BH22 ....280 F8
 GPORT PO12 ....13 G3
 PSEA PO1 ....316 E6
Shaftesbury St *FBDG* SP6 ....240 C2
Shaftsbury La *LYND* SO43 ....264 G5
Shaggs Meadow *LYND* SO43 ......264 G5
Shakespeare Av *SHAM* SO14 ....90 A1
Shakespeare Dr *TOTT* SO40 ....246 B1
Shakespeare Gdns *FARN* GU14 .....57 L8
 HORN PO8 ....255 N8
Shakespeare Rd *CHIN* RG24 ....69 M4
 ELGH SO50 ....207 J9
 NTHA RG18 ....25 M3
 PSEA PO1 ....316 G2
 SBNE BH6 ....324 B8
 WIMB BH21 ....278 E8
Shalbourne Rd *GPORT* PO12 ....315 L1
Shalcombe *HLER* SO31 ....269 L3
Shalden Rd *ASHV* GU12 ....3 K6
Shaldon Cl *ROWN* SO16 ....227 N8
Shaldon Rd *HAV* PO9 ....277 H4
Shaldon Wy *FLEETS* GU51 ....74 A4
Shales Rd *WEND* SO18 ....249 K4
Shallow La *LYMN* SO41 ....309 K8
The Shallows *FBDG* SP6 ....220 C5
Shamblehurst La *HEND* SO30 .....250 C2
Shamblehurst La
 North *BPWT* SO32 ....230 D9
Shamblehurst La South
 HEND SO30 ....250 C3
Shamrock Cl *FRIM* GU16 ....58 C5
 GPORT PO12 ....13 J3
Shamrock Quay *SHAM* SO14 * 248 F5
Shamrock Rd *ITCH* SO19 ....248 A3
Shamrock Wy *FAWY* SO45 ....268 C5
Shanklin Ct *ASHV* GU12 ....3 J5
Shanklin Crs *WSHM* SO15 ....247 P2
Shanklin Rd *ENEY* PO4 ....316 C4
 WSHM SO15 ....247 P1
Shannon Cl *FHAM* PO15 ....272 B8
Shannon Ct *AND* SP10 ....82 C9
Shannon Rd
 FHAM/STUB PO14 ....293 P6
Shannon Wy *CHFD* SO53 ....206 D7
Shapland Av *BWD* BH11 ....301 N8
Shappen Hill La *RGWD* BH24 ....256 B7
Shapton Cl *FAWY* SO45 ....290 C6
Shapwick Rd *PLE* BH15 ....332 C2
Shard Cl *VWD* BH31 ....258 C4
Sharf Rd *BKME/WDN* BH12 ....322 A8
Sharlands Cl *BDST* BH18 ....320 D2
Sharon Rd *HEND* SO30 ....249 L1
Sharon Wy *CHFD* SO53 ....205 N3
Sharpness Cl
 FHAM/STUB PO14 ....294 A1
Sharps Cl *HSEA* PO3 ....297 K6
Sharps Rd *HAV* PO9 ....277 H5
Sharvells Rd *LYMN* SO41 ....338 F1
Slavard La *BPWT* SO22 ....211 P8
Shaves La *NMIL/BTOS* BH25 ....327 J2
Shaw Br *NWBY* RG14 * 24 E2
Shaw Cl *AND* SP10 ....102 A2
 TOTT SO40 ....246 B4
 WEND SO18 ....249 J1
Shaw Farm Rd *NWBY* RG14 ....24 E2
Shawfield La *ASHV* GU12 ....97 M1
Shawfield Rd *ASHV* GU12 ....97 M2
 HAV PO9 ....15 J7
Shawford Cl *ROWN* SO16 ....228 A3
Shawford Gv *HAV* PO9 ....275 J3
Shawford Rd *CHAR* BH8 ....183 P8
 RWIN SO21 ....183 P8
Shaw HI *NWBY* RG14 ....24 E2
Shaw La *TADY* RG26 ....34 A8
Shaw Pk *CWTH* RG45 ....41 J5
Shaw Pightle *HTWY* RG27 ....71 N3
Shaw Rd *NWBY* RG14 ....24 E3
 RGWD BH24 ....260 G8
Shaws Wk *AND* SP10 * 4 D5
Sheardley La *BPWT* SO32 ....234 B4
Shearer Rd *PSEA* PO1 ....316 C1
Shears Brook Cl
 CHCH/BSGR BH23 ....305 M7
Shears Rd *ELGH* SO50 ....229 N1
Shearwater Av
 LSOL/BMARY PO13 ....294 F7
Shearwater Dr *CHAM* PO6 ....297 J2
Sheepcroft La *WIMB* BH21 ....279 K2
Sheep Dro *STOK* SO20 ....139 L4
Sheep Fair *AND* SP10 ....5 G4
Sheep Fair Rd *AND* SP10 ....5 G4
Sheephatch La *RFNM* GU10 ....117 H5
Sheephouse La *RFNM* GU10 ....116 C2
Sheep Pond La *BPWT* SO32 ....233 J1
Sheep St *PSF* GU32 ....215 M2
Sheepwash La *KSCL* RG20 ....50 A7
Sheffield Cl *ELGH* SO50 ....207 M8
 FARN GU14 ....57 N9
Sheffield Ct
 LSOL/BMARY PO13 ....314 C2
Sheffield Rd *PSEA* PO1 ....316 G3
Shelbourne Cl *CHAR* BH8 ....323 J9
Shelbourne Rd *CHAR* BH8 ....323 J9
Sheldon's La *HTWY* RG27 ....71 N3
Sheldon's Rd *HTWY* RG27 ....71 N3
Sheldrake Gdns *LYMN* SO41 ....328 B5
Sheldrake Rd
 CHCH/BSGR BH23 ....337 L1
Shelford Rd *ENEY* PO4 ....317 K4
Shellcroft *HLER* SO31 ....292 D1
Shelley Av *CHAM* PO6 ....274 A9
Shelley Cl *BMTH* BH1 ....335 L1
 CHIN RG24 ....69 M4
 CHCH/BSGR BH23 ....325 N8
 FLEETS GU51 ....74 C7
 FUFL SO22 ....164 C7
 RGWD BH24 ....260 F9
 WIMB BH21 ....166 D1
Shelley Gdns *BMTH* BH1 ....335 L1
 HORN PO8 ....255 N8
Shelley La *ROMY* SO51 ....225 L3
Shelley Rd *WTLY* GU46 ....40 C9
 ELGH SO50 ....229 H5
Shelley Rd East *BMTH* BH1 ....335 L1
Shelleys La *ALTN* GU34 ....133 L8
Shelley Wk *BLKW* GU17 ....57 K2
Shell La *ALTN* GU34 ....171 K5
Shelly Ri *FARN* GU14 ....57 N7
Shelton Rd *SBNE* BH6 ....324 A9
Shenley Cl *FHAM* PO15 ....272 A8
Shenstone Ct
 NMIL/BTOS BH25 * 327 J6
Shepards Cl
 FHAM/STUB PO14 ....294 A1
Shepherd Cl
 CHCH/BSGR BH23 ....326 B6
Shepherd & Flock Roundabout
 RFNM GU10 ....96 E8
Shepherds Cl *FUFL* SO22 ....183 K5
 TOTT SO40 ....245 H5
Shepherds Down *NARL* SO24 .....245 P2
Shepherds Hey Rd *TOTT* SO40 ....245 P2
Shepherd's HI *HASM* GU27 ....157 H7
 RGWD BH24 ....260 A4
Shepherds La *RGWD* BH24 ....259 N4
 RWIN SO21 ....183 H8
Shepherds Purse Cl
 HLER SO31 ....270 E8
Shepherds Ri *RAND* SP11 ....43 H8
Shepherds Rd *TOTT* SO40 ....245 H5
 WINC SO23 ....23 K4
Shepherds Rw *AND* SP10 ....5 G5
Shepherds Spring La *AND* SP10 .....4 D3
Shepherds Wk *FARN* GU14 ....57 M6
 LIPH GU30 ....175 L4
 LTDN BH7 ....323 N8
 LYMN SO41 ....328 C6
 RFNM GU10 ....117 J6
 ROWN SO16 ....226 C7
Sheppard Cl *HORN* PO8 ....256 A5
 WHCH RG28 ....85 L7
Sheppard Rd *BSTK* RG21 ....90 C1
Sheppards Fld *WIMB* BH21 ....278 D8
Sheppard Sq *AND* SP10 * 82 G8
Shepton Br *BROC* SO42 ....288 F4
Sheraton Av *KBH* RG22 ....89 M4
Sheraton Cl *BLKW* GU17 ....57 M1
Sherborn Crs *CFDH* BH17 ....321 H5
Sherborne Ct *ELGH* SO50 ....207 H7
Sherborne Dr *FERN* BH22 ....302 D4
Sherborne Rd *BSTK* RG21 ....6 C2
 CHIN RG24 ....69 J2
 FARN GU14 ....76 C4
 PTSW SO17 ....248 D1
Sherborne Wy *HEND* SO30 ....250 C5
Sherbrooke Cl *WINC* SO23 ....145 K8
Sherfield Av *HAV* PO9 ....276 G5
Sherfield Cl *CHAR* BH8 ....323 K5
Sherfield English La
 ROMY SO51 ....202 C7
Sherfield English Rd
 RSAL SP5 ....224 B1
Sherfield Rd *TADY* RG26 ....52 A2
Sheridan Cl *ALDT* GU11 ....2 E6
 FUFL SO22 ....183 L1
 ITCH SO19 ....249 L6
Sheridan Gdns *HLER* SO31 ....271 J2
Sheridan Rd
 FHAM/PORC PO16 ....33 P5
Sheringham Rd
 BKME/WDN BH12 ....321 P7
 CHAM PO6 * 274 F9
Sherington Cl *FARN* GU14 ....58 A7
Sherley Gn *HLER* SO31 ....269 P1
Sherlock Lea *HTWY* RG27 ....59 P7
Shermin's Bank
 CHCH/BSGR BH23 ....337 J1
Sherrardmead *NWBY* RG14 ....24 E2
Sherrin Cl *PLE* BH15 ....320 F7
Sherrington Av *CHFD* SO53 ....291 K6
Sherrington Wy *KBH* RG22 ....89 L4
Sherwin Crs *FARN* GU14 ....58 A5
Sherwin Wk *GPORT* PO12 ....12 A5
Sherwood Av *FERN* BH22 ....302 C5
 HEND SO30 ....250 C7
 HLER SO31 ....333 H1
Sherwood Cl
 CHCH/BSGR BH23 ....324 D8
 KBH RG22 ....89 N5
 LISS GU33 ....173 M8
 ROWN SO16 ....228 A9
Sherwood Dr *VWD* BH31 ....259 H4
Sherwood Gdns *HLER* SO31 ....216 E6
Sherwood Rd *CHFD* SO53 ....206 G4
 GPORT PO12 ....12 B2
Sherwood Ter *ALTN* GU34 * 132 C6
 TOTT SO40 ....245 H5
Shetland Cl *CHAM* PO6 ....275 H9
 TOTT SO40 ....245 H5
Shetland Ri *HLER* SO31 ....271 H4
Shetland Vw *VWD* BH31 ....258 C4
Shetland Wy *FLEETS* GU51 ....56 F9
Shildon Cl *LISS* GU33 ....59 J2
Shillinglee *WVILLE* PO7 ....275 N7
Shillingstone Dr
 MOOR/WNTN BH9 ....323 J3
Shillingstone Gdns
 BKME/WDN BH12 ....321 P5
Shillito Rd *BKME/WDN* BH12 ......321 M7
Shinewell Gdns *ROWN* SO16 ....247 J5
Shingle Bank Dr *LYMN* SO41 ....338 G2
Ship Aly *FARN* GU14 ....58 B5
Shipbuilding Rd *PSEA* PO1 ....316 B2
Shipcote La *BPWT* SO32 ....232 A2
Ship La *FARN* GU14 ....58 B7
Ship Leopard St *PSEA* PO1 ....18 C3
Shipley Cl *ALTN* GU34 ....132 C4
Shipley Ct *LIPH* GU30 ....175 J4
Shipley Rd *RWIN* SO21 ....184 A1
Shipton Wy *KBH* RG22 ....89 N1
Shire Av *FLEETS* GU51 ....74 F1
Shire Ct *ALDT* GU11 ....2 A3
Shires Cl *RGWD* BH24 ....282 E5
Shires Cps *SBNE* BH6 ....336 D3
Shires Md *VWD* BH31 ....258 C4
The Shires *HEND* SO30 ....250 A5
Shirley Av *WTLY* GU46 ....40 E8
Shirley Av *CFDH* BH17 ....321 K5
Shirley Av *ENEY* PO4 ....317 L4
 WSHM SO15 ....247 N3
Shirley Cl *CHCH/BSGR* BH23 ......305 M7
 FERN BH22 ....280 E7
Shirley High St *ROWN* SO16 ....247 M5
Shirley Holms *LYMN* SO41 ....308 F7
Shirley Park Rd *ROWN* SO16 ....247 M5

Shirley Rd BKME/WDN BH12 ....321 K6
  MOOR/WNTN BH9 ....322 C6
  SSEA PO5 ....316 C6
  WSHM SO15 ....247 N3
Shirley Towers WSHM SO15 * ..247 N5
Shoddesden La RAND SP11 ......80 A3
Shoe La ALDT GU11 ....75 P6
  BPWT SO32 ....209 M7
Sholing Ct HAV PO9 ....276 D4
Sholing Rd ITCH SO19 ....248 C7
Shooters Hill Cl ITCH SO19 ....249 K8
Shooters Wy BSTK RG21 ....7 G2
Shoot Hi WHAM PO17 ....253 P8
Shoot La LSOL/BMARY PO13 ...294 E9
Shop La HLER SO31 ....249 N8
  NWBY RG14 ....24 C1
Shore Av HSEA PO3 ....317 K2
Shore Cl LYMN SO41 * 338 G2
Shore Crs BPWT SO32 ....232 B5
Shorefield Crs LYMN SO41 .....338 F1
Shorefield Rd LYMN SO41 ......327 P9
  TOTT SO40 ....247 K9
Shorefield Wy LYMN SO41 .....338 F1
Shorehaven CHAM PO6 ....296 B1
Shore La BPWT SO32 ....232 B5
Shore Rd FAWY SO45 ....268 D6
  HLER SO31 ....270 C9
  PSTN BH14 ....333 L4
Shorewell HLER SO31 ....269 L5
Shorewood Cl HLER SO31 .....270 C9
Short Cl CHCH/BSGR BH23 ....324 C6
Short Dale Rd ALDT GU11 ......97 J5
Shortfield Rd RFNM GU10 ....116 C9
Shortheath Crest FNM GU9 ...115 P4
Shortheath La THLE RG7 ....26 F4
Shortheath Rd FNM GU9 ......116 A4
Short Hi RAND SP11 ....04 A4
Short La RAND SP11 ....101 N1
Short Rd FHAM/STUB PO14 ...293 N7
Short Row PSEA PO1 ....18 D1
Shorts Cl CHCH/BSGR BH23 ..324 C6
Shorts Rd ELGH SO50 ....230 B2
Short St ALDT GU11 ....142 F4
  RAND SP11 ....79 P1
Shortwood Cps DEAN RG23....89 K6
Shorwell HLER SO31 ....269 L3
Shotterfield Ter LISS GU33 ....192 D2
Shottermill Pk HASM GU27 * ..156 D6
Shotters Hill Cl HEND SO30 ...249 M2
Shotters La ALTN GU34 ....171 N1
Shottsford Rd FUL BH15 ......320 E7
Shotts La LYMN SO41 ....330 A3
Shraveshill Cl TOTT SO40 .....246 B2
The Shrave ALTN GU34 ....150 F4
Shrewsbury Ter NWBY RG14 * ..16 B5
Shrivenham Cl SHST GU47 .....41 L6
Shrubbery Cl
  FHAM/PORC PO16............295 N2
The Shrubbery FARN GU14 .....75 L1
  GPORT PO12 ....315 K1
Shrubb's La LYMN SO41 ......329 L3
Shrubbs Hill Gdns LYND SO43 .264 F6
Shrubbs Hill Rd LYND SO43 ...264 F6
Shrubbs La RFNM GU10 ......115 P6
Shrubland Cl WEND SO18 .....249 K3
Shyshack La TADY RG26 ....33 P5
Sian Cl FLEETS GU52 ....74 E7
Sibelius Cl KBH RG22 ....223 L2
Sibland Cl FHAM/STUB PO14 ..294 B1
Sickle Rd HASM GU27 ....156 E8
Sickles Rd BOR GU35 ....135 N5
Sidbury Circular Rd NTID SP9 ..78 F4
Sidbury Hts NTID SP9 * 78 G3
Sidbury Hill Av NTID SP9 ....78 F4
Siddal Cl ITCH SO19 ....249 L8
Sidestrand Rd ALDT GU11 .....75 M5
  NWBY RG14 ....24 A7
The Sidings ALDT GU11 ....3 H1
  HLER SO31 ....269 M5
  SSEA PO5 ....199 L5
Sidlaw Cl KBH RG22 ....208 D3
Sidlaws Rd FARN GU14 ....57 L6
Sidlesham Cl HSEA PO3 ....319 M6
Sidmouth Av HSEA PO3 ......297 J9
Sidmouth Rd AND SP10 ....5 H4
Silchester Cl AND SP10 ....82 C9
  WCLF BH2 ....8 C6
Silchester Rd HSEA PO3 ......317 K1
  TADY RG26 ....34 D5
  TADY RG26 ....51 H5
  TADY RG26 ....51 L2
Silkin Gdns TOTT SO40 ....246 B5
Silk Mill La OVTN RG25 ....85 J5
Silkstead La HAV PO9 ....276 F4
Silkstead La RWIN SO21 ......183 H9
Silkweavers Rd AND SP10 ....4 E3
Sillen La FBDG SP6 ....195 P6
Silver Birch Av
  FHAM/STUB PO14 ....10 A7
Silver Birch Cl
  BKME/WDN BH12 ....334 A2
  FLEETS GU52 ....74 C7
  LISS GU33 ....192 E2
Silver Birches HLER SO31 .....269 P2
Silverbirch Rd AND SP10 .....102 C2
Silverdale FLEETS GU52 ....74 D6
  NMIL/BTOS BH25 ....327 K8
Silverdale Cl BDST BH18 .....300 A9
Silverdale Crs FBDG SP6 ......239 N5
Silverdale Dr WVILLE PO7 ....275 N5
Silverdale Rd TADY RG26 ......34 C5
  WSHM SO15 ....248 A4
Silver Dr FRIM GU16 ....59 J2
Silverglades YTLY GU46 ....56 D1
Silver Hl SHST GU47 ....41 M6
Silver La THLE RG7 ....23 F5
Silverlock Cl NEND PO2 * 296 F9
Silverlock Pl EMRTH PO10 * ..277 P5
Silver Park Cl FLEETS GU52 ...74 E6
Silversands Gdns HISD PO11 ..319 H6
Silvers End FAWY SO45 ....268 C9
Silver St CHCH/BSGR BH23 ..324 F9
  LYMN SO41 ....327 P3
  LYND SO43 ....264 D5

SSEA PO5 ....19 F6
Silvers Wd TOTT SO40 ....246 A2
Silverthorne Wy WVILLE PO7 ..275 M2
Silvertrees EMRTH PO10 ....277 J8
  HLER SO31 ....270 E4
Silver Wy CHCH/BSGR BH23 ..326 A7
Silverweed Cl CHFD SO53 .....206 B6
Silverwood Ct FUFL SO22 .....183 M1
  WIMB BH21 ....300 F3
Silvester Cl BSTK RG21 ....7 H2
Silvester Rd HORN PO8 ....255 N9
Silvester Wy FLEETS GU52 .....74 B8
Silwood Cl FUFL SO22 ....164 E6
Simmonds Cl FAR BH15 ....320 F7
Simmondstone La
  RFNM GU10 ....136 D7
Simmons Cl HEND SO30 ....250 C3
Simmons On HISD PO11 ....319 J5
Simms Farm La THLE RG7 ......35 N2
Simnel St SHAM SO14 * 20 D6
Simonds Ct WINC SO23 ....165 H5
Simonds Rd RAND SP11 ....79 N1
Simons Cl CHIN RG24 ....70 A2
Simon Wy WEND SO18 ....249 N4
Simpson Cl FHAM/PORC PO16..295 N1
Simpson Rd NEND PO2 ....296 E8
Sims Cl TADY RG26 ....52 C3
Sinah La HISD PO11 ....318 C5
Sinclair Rd ROWN SO16 ....227 L7
Sine Cl FARN GU14 ....44 A6
Singleton Dr NBNE BH10 ......322 C5
Singleton Gdns HORN PO8 ....236 D8
Singleton Wy TOTT SO40 ......245 P3
Sinhurst Rd CBLY GU15 ....50 B1
Sir Christopher Cl FAWY SO45 ..268 D6
Sirdar Rd PTSW SO17 ....228 E9
Sir Galahad Rd CHFD SO53 ....206 B7
Sir George's Rd WSHM SO15 ..247 P5
Sir Lancelot Cl CHFD SO53 ....206 B7
Siskin Cl BPWT SO32 ....231 N4
  FERN BH22 ....302 B1
  ROWN SO16 ....227 L7
Siskin Gv WVILLE PO7 ....276 A4
Siskin Rd RAND SP11 ....317 L3
Sissinghurst Cl ITCH SO19 ....269 J1
Sissinghurst Rd
  FHAM/PORC PO16............295 M2
Six Oaks Rd RAND SP11 ....205 L8
Sixpenny Cl BKME/WDN BH12..321 P5
Sixth Av CHAM PO6 ....270 C9
Sixth St STHA RG19 ....51 L1
Sizer Wy FAWY SO45 ....267 N6
Skates La TADY RG26 ....34 E9
Skew Rd FHAM/PORC PO16....273 N8
  RAND SP11 ....100 B7
Skinner St PLE BH15 ....332 C2
Skipper Cl TOTT SO40 ....247 L8
Skipper Wy
  LSOL/BMARY PO13 ....314 D3
Skippetts La East BSTK RG21 ...90 E1
Skippetts La West BSTK RG21 ..90 E1
Skipton Cl BDST BH18 ....320 C2
Skipton Rd CHFD SO53 ....206 F9
Skye Cl CHAM PO6 ....275 H9
Sky End La LYMN SO41 ....328 A5
Skylark Cl DEAN RG23 ....98 A4
Skylark Mdw FHAM PO15......271 M5
Skylark Ri WHCH RG28 ....85 K5
Skylings NWBY RG14 ....24 C1
Skys Wood Rd CHFD SO53 ....206 C7
Slab La ROMY SO51 ....224 D1
  RSAL SP5 ....199 L6
Slade Cl LYMN SO41 ....328 A4
Slade La EPSF GU31 ....216 C1
Slades Farm Rd NBNE BH10 ...322 C6
Slades Hi FAWY SO45 ....291 H7
Slade's La NBNE BH10 ....322 C7
Slater Cl TOTT SO40 ....245 P3
Sleepbrook Cl VWD BH31 .....258 E4
Sleepers Delle Gdns FUFL SO22..22 A7
Sleepers Hl FUFL SO22 ....164 E9
Sleepers Hill Gdns
  FUFL SO22 * 164 E9
Slepe Crs BKME/WDN BH12 ...321 P4
Slessor Cl RAND SP11 ....101 P3
Slim Cl ALDT GU11 ....76 D5
Slindon Cl HORN PO8 ....236 D7
Slindon St PSEA PO1 ....19 E6
Slingsby Cl FHAM PO15 ....18 E6
Slinn Rd CHCH/BSGR BH23 ...325 J8
Slipper Ml EMRTH PO10 * 299 N2
Slipper Rd EMRTH PO10 ......299 N2
Slip Wy PLE BH15 ....332 D1
The Slipway CHAM PO6 * 296 C1
Sloane Av FAWY SO45 ....290 F5
Sloane Cl FAWY SO45 ....290 P5
Sloane Pk BPWT SO32 ....252 B4
Sloe Tree Cl HLER SO31 ....271 J8
Smallfield Dr HTWY RG27 ......72 B5
Smallridge KSCL RG20 ....30 B2
Smannell Rd AND SP10 ....82 F8
Smeaton Cl AND SP10 ....83 H5
Smay Down La MARL SN8......22 A7
Smeaton Rd AND SP10 * 81 P9
Smeeton Rd
  LSOL/BMARY PO13 ....314 D2
Smith Cl FAWY SO45 ....291 H7
Smithe Cl ELGH SO50 ....229 J1
Smith Gv HEND SO30 ....250 C3
Smith's Fld ROMY SO51 ......204 E4
Smiths La BPWT SO32 ....252 D3
Smith's Md OVTN RG25 ....108 D1
Smithson Cl
  BKME/WDN BH12 ....322 B7
Smith St GPORT PO12 ....12 B2
Smithy Cl ALTN GU34 ....133 K2
Smithy La BOR GU35 ....135 N7
The Smithy TADY RG26 ....52 A2
  WVILLE PO7 ....254 G7

Smugglers La NARL SO24 .....170 B5
  WIMB BH21 ....278 F6
Smugglers La North
  CHCH/BSGR BH23 ....325 N7
Smugglers La South
  CHCH/BSGR BH23 ....326 A7
Smugglers Wy RFNM GU10 ...117 L2
Smugglers Wood Rd
  CHCH/BSGR BH23 ....325 N6
Smythe Rd ITCH SO19 ....249 M8
Snailing La LISS GU33 ....172 C9
Snail's La RGWD BH24 ....266 C7
Snailslynch FNM GU9 ....96 C9
Snakemoor La BPWT SO32 ...230 E7
Snapdragon Cl HLER SO31 ....270 F8
Snape Cl LSOL/BMARY PO13 ..294 C9
Snellgrove Cl TOTT SO40 .....246 A1
Snellgrove Pl TOTT SO40 .....246 A1
Snoddington Rd RAND SP11 ...99 M3
Snode Hi ALTN GU34 ....132 A6
Snooks La LYMN SO41 ....329 P1
Snowberry Crs HAV PO9 ......277 H7
Snowdon Cl STHA RG19 ....25 N5
Snowdon Dr
  FHAM/STUB PO14 ....294 C1
Snowdon Rd FARN GU14 ......57 M6
  WBNE BH4 ....334 C2
Snowdrop Cl HLER SO31 .....270 F8
  KBH RG22 ....89 L3
Snowdrop Gdns
  CHCH/BSGR BH23 ....325 M6
Snowhill WHAM PO17 * 273 P4
Soake Rd WVILLE PO7 ....255 K8
Soalwood La PSF GU32 ....190 F5
Soames's La RAND SP11 ....169 P4
Sobers Sq AND SP10 ....82 C8
Soberton Rd CHAR BH8 ......328 K8
  HAV PO9 ....14 E3
Soke Hi ALTN GU34 ....149 P8
Soke Rd THLE RG7 ....34 F2
The Soke NARL SO24 ....148 A9
Solartron Rd FARN GU14 ......75 P1
Soby's Rd BSTK RG21 ....6 C6
Soldridge Cl HAV PO9 ....277 H4
Soldridge Rd ALTN GU34 .....149 P5
Solent Av ITCH SO19 ....249 N5
  LYMN SO41 ....329 M4
Solent Cl CHFD SO53 ....206 D7
  LYMN SO41 ....329 M4
Solent Dr FAWY SO45 ....268 B6
  HISD PO11 ....318 F6
  HLER SO31 ....292 D3
  KBH RG22 ....89 M4
  NMIL/BTOS BH25 ....327 J8
Solent Mdw HLER SO31 ......270 A9
Solent Rd CHAM PO6 ....297 L1
  CHCH/BSGR BH23 ....326 D5
  FAWY SO45 ....290 A1
  FHAM/STUB PO14 ....293 N8
  HAV PO9 ....14 E6
  SBNE BH6 ....336 E5
  WSHM SO15 ....20 A5
Solent Twentyseven
  CHAM PO6 * 287 L9
Solent Vw FHAM/PORC PO16 ..273 M9
Solent Wy BROC SO42 ....289 N4
  BROC SO42 ....311 M1
  EMRTH PO10 ....299 J2
  FHAM/STUB PO14 ....293 N8
  GPORT PO12 ....13 J4
  GPORT PO12 ....315 J5
  HAV PO9 ....15 H7
  HSEA PO3 ....317 M2
  LSOL/BMARY PO13 ....314 A5
  LYMN SO41 ....339 K5
Solly Cl BKME/WDN BH12 .....321 N5
Solomons La BPWT SO32 .....252 D1
Solona Cl CHFD SO53 ....207 H6
Somborne Dr HAV PO9 ....276 F5
Somborne Park Rd
  STOK SO20 ....141 P7
Somerby Rd PLE BH15 ....320 F6
Somerford Av
  CHCH/BSGR BH23 ....325 M7
Somerford Cl ITCH SO19 .....249 J5
Somerford Rd
  CHCH/BSGR BH23 ....325 K8
Somerford Wy
  CHCH/BSGR BH23 ....325 J8
Somerley Rd
  MOOR/WNTN BH9 ....322 G8
Somerley Vw RGWD BH24 ....282 E1
Somers Cl FUFL SO22 ....183 M1
Somerset Av CHAR BH8 ....328 G7
Somerset Crs CHFD SO53 .....228 E3
Somerset Rd
  CHCH/BSGR BH23 ....324 C8
  FARN GU14 ....76 B3
  LTON BH7 ....335 M1
  PTSW SO17 ....248 E1
  SSEA PO5 ....19 H5
Somers Rd North PSEA PO1 ...19 K3
Somerton Av WEND SO18 ....249 K4
Somerton Cl
  NMIL/BTOS BH25 ....327 M4
Somerton Gv STHA RG19 ......25 N5
Somervell Cl GPORT PO12 .....12 A7
Somervell Dr
  FHAM/PORC PO16............10 E2
Somerville Cl AND SP10 ....5 J7
Somerville Crs YTLY GU46 .....49 P7
Somerville Rd RGWD BH24 ...282 C1
  WCLF BH2 ....335 H4
Somme Rd RAND SP11 ....295 M3
Sonnet Wy WVILLE PO7 ......276 B2
Sonning Cl KBH RG22 ....89 K4
Sonninge Cl SHST GU47 ....41 M5
Soper Gv BSTK RG21 ....6 E3
Sopers La CFDH BH17 ....320 C5
  CHCH/BSGR BH23 ....324 E9
Sopers Rw CHIN RG24 * 70 B6

Sopley Cl NMIL/BTOS BH25 ..326 F7
Sopley Cl TOTT SO40 ....277 H4
Sopwith Cl CHCH/BSGR BH23..325 M9
  STOK SO20 ....161 M5
Sopwith Crs WIMB BH21 .....300 C3
Sopwith Pk AND SP10 ....101 P1
Sopwith Rd ELCH SO50 ......220 H1
Sopwith Wy BSTK RG21 ......270 E2
Sorrel Cl HLER SO31 ....24 C2
  THLE RG7 ....27 K4
  WVILLE PO7 ....276 A1
Sorrel Dr FHAM PO15 ....271 K5
Sorrel Gdns BDST BH18 ......320 B2
Sorrell Cl HLER SO31 ....270 F8
Sorrell's Cl CHIN RG24 ....70 A1
Sorrell Wy CHCH/BSGR BH23 ..325 M7
Sotherington La ALTN GU34 ..172 C1
Southampton Cl BLKW GU17...41 K8
Southampton Hl
  FHAM/STUB PO14 ....271 M9
Southampton Rd BROC SO42 ..308 G3
  CHAM PO6 ....296 B1
  ELGH SO50 ....229 J4
  FAWY SO45 ....268 F2
  FBDG SP6 ....240 F2
  FHAM PO15 ....271 J6
  FHAM/PORC PO16............11 G4
  LYMN SO41 ....329 K2
  LYND SO43 ....265 J4
  RGWD BH24 ....266 D5
  TOTT SO40 ....244 E3
Southampton St FARN GU14 ...76 A4
  WSHM SO15 ....248 B5
South Atlantic Dr ALDT GU11 ...3 H1
South Av FAWY SO45 ....290 C2
  FNM GU9 ....96 D5
  NEND PO2 ....296 G5
  NMIL/BTOS BH25 ....327 K5
South Baddesley Rd
  LYMN SO41 ....329 P3
South Bay EMRTH PO10 ....299 H8
South Beta Rd FARN GU14 ....76 A2
Southbourne Av CHAM PO6 ..297 K2
  EMRTH PO10 ....299 P1
  FAWY SO45 ....290 E5
Southbourne Coast Rd
  SBNE BH6 ....336 C5
  SBNE BH6 ....335 P2
Southbourne Overcliff Dr
  SBNE BH6 ....336 A3
Southbourne Rd LYMN SO41 ..329 J4
  SBNE BH6 ....335 P1
Southbrook Cl CFDH BH17 ...321 J2
  HAV PO9 ....298 F1
Southbrook Pl WEND SO18 ...126 C6
Southbrook Rd HAV PO9 .....298 F2
  WSHM SO15 ....20 A3
Southby Dr FLEETN GU51 .....74 E3
South Charford Dro
  FBDG SP6 ....198 B7
Southcliff LSOL/BMARY PO13..314 C1
Southcliffe Rd
  CHCH/BSGR BH23 ....325 M9
  SBNE BH6 ....326 F7
Southcliff Rd SHAM SO14 ....248 C4
South Cl GPORT PO12 ....315 K6
  HAV PO9 ....15 H7
  NARL SO24 ....167 N2
  ROMY SO51 ....204 C4
Southcote Rd BMTH BH1 ....9 H1
South Ct HLER SO31 ....269 N8
Southcroft Rd GPORT PO12 ..315 K3
South Cross St GPORT PO12 ...13 H2
Southdene Rd CHFD SO53 ....206 E8
Southdown Rd CHAM PO6 ....297 J1
  HORN PO8 ....256 C9
  STHA RG19 ....25 J4
  TADY RG26 ....34 B5
South Downs Wy BPWT SO32..187 H9
  BPWT SO32 ....211 L5
  NARL SO24 ....148 A7
  PSF GU32 ....217 G6
  PSF GU32 ....235 M1
  WINC SO23 ....23 H7
Southdown Vw WVILLE PO7 ..255 L9
Southdown Wy FERN BH22 ...280 F8
South Dr CHOB/PIR GU24 .....29 P7
  FERN BH22 ....303 H1
  FUFL SO22 ....164 B3
  NTID SP9 ....78 C7
  ROMY SO51 ....203 P2
South East Crs ITCH SO19 ....249 J7
South East Rd ITCH SO19 .....249 J7
Southend La RGWD BH24 .....25 M1
South End Cl RWIN SO21 .....182 D8
South End Rd BSTK RG21 ......6 C6
Southern Av FERN BH22 ......280 E6
Southern Gdns TOTT SO40 ...246 C4
Southern Haye HTWY RG27 ...55 H6
Southern La NMIL/BTOS BH25..327 H7
Southern Oaks
  NMIL/BTOS BH25 ....327 H6
Southern Rd BOR GU35 ....135 H4
  BSTK RG21 ....69 L8
  HEND SO30 ....249 M3
  LYMN SO41 ....329 K3
  SBNE BH6 ....336 A2
Southern Wy FARN GU14 .....116 C1
  FNM GU9 ....116 D1

Southgate Vls WINC SO23 * 22 D6
South Gv FLEETN GU51 ....75 M4
  LYMN SO41 ....329 M4
South Ham Rd KBH RG22 ......89 G3
South Hl BPWT SO32 ....233 L4
South Hurst GOR GU35 ....154 A7
Southill Av BKME/WDN BH12 ..321 L4
Southill Gdns
  MOOR/WNTN BH9 ....322 C6
Southill Rd BKME/WDN BH12 ..321 L6
  MOOR/WNTN BH9 ....322 C6
  NEND PO2 ....296 E5
Southington La OVTN RG25 ...86 E3
Southington Ct OVTN RG25 ...86 F3
South Kinson Dr BWD BH11 ..322 A3
Southlands CHIN RG24 ....329 J5
  LYMN SO41 ....329 J5
Southlands Av SBNE BH6 ....336 A2
  LSOL/BMARY PO13 ....314 D3
Southlands Rd ASHV GU12 ....97 N2
South La ASHV GU12 ....97 M2
  EPSF GU31 ....215 K9
  HORN PO8 ....236 B6
  HORN PO8 ....237 H9
  RSAL SP5 ....199 J6
  RSAL SP5 ....223 L5
Southlawns Wk
  NMIL/BTOS BH25 ....327 H6
Southlea Av SBNE BH6 ....336 D1
Southleigh Gv HISD PO11 ....318 E5
Southmead Rd EMRTH PO10 ..277 M7
  HAV PO9 ....15 K6
South Loading Rd
  GPORT PO12 * 13 L7
South Ldg FHAM PO15 ....13 M3
South Meadow CWTH RG45 ....41 L3
  FHAM PO15 ....272 B9
South Millers Dl CHFD SO53 ..206 F2
South Mill Rd WSHM SO15 ....247 K4
Southmoor La HAV PO9 ....298 D2
South Normandy PSEA PO1 ...18 D5
South Pde ENEY PO4 ....316 F7
South Park Rd
  BKME/WDN BH12 ....322 A7
South Pl LSOL/BMARY PO13 ..314 A4
South Rd ASHV GU12 ....76 B8
  BMTH BH1 ....335 L1
  CHAM PO6 ....297 M2
  CWTH RG45 ....41 M3
  HISD PO11 ....318 F5
  HORN PO8 ....256 C2
  KSCL RG20 ....48 D3
  LIPH GU30 ....175 K6
  NARL SO24 ....167 N2
  PSEA PO1 ....19 J1
  PTSW SO17 ....248 E3
  STOK SO20 ....140 B2
  WHAM PO17 ....274 C4
  WIMB BH21 ....300 C3
Southrope Gn OVTN RG25 ...111 L3
Southsea Ter SSEA PO5 ....19 F7
South Side PRTM GU10 ....97 M4
Southside Rd RAND SP11 ....104 D5
South Sp CHAM PO6 ....274 D8
South St AND SP10 ....4 D5
  ELGH SO50 ....229 J4
  EMRTH PO10 ....299 H1
  FARN GU14 ....76 D5
  FAWY SO45 ....268 C7
  FHAM/STUB PO14 ....293 M1
  FNM GU9 ....96 C9
  GPORT PO12 ....12 E3
  HAV PO9 ....15 G7
  LYMN SO41 ....329 J5
  NARL SO24 ....169 M3
  SSEA PO5 ....19 F6
South Sway La LYMN SO41 ...308 C2
South Ter PSEA PO1 ....18 C2
South Town Rd ALTN GU34 ..150 A2
South Trestle End FAWY SO45..291 L4
South Vw FUFL SO22 ....24 E8
South View Cots
  WHCH RG28 ....86 A1
Southview Gdns AND SP10 .....4 E6
South View Gdns
  NWBY RG14 ....24 E3
South View Pl WCLF BH2 ....8 B5
Southview Ri ALTN GU54 .....132 E5
Southview Rd BOR GU35 .....155 J3
South View Rd
  CHCH/BSGR BH23 ....324 E9
  FUFL SO22 ....183 N1
  WSHM SO15 ....247 P3
South View Ter RAND SP11 ....24 C3
Southville Rd BE/BOSC BH5 ...335 P1
Southwark Cl YTLY GU46 ......40 D8
South Wy AND SP10 ....83 J9
Southway CBLY GU15 ....49 J7
  FHAM PO15 ....271 L7
Southwater Rd
  PSTN BH14 ....333 K1
Southwick Av
  FHAM/PORC PO16............274 A9
Southwick Cl FUFL SO22 .....164 D3
Southwick Ct
  FHAM/STUB PO14 ....274 C9
Southwick Hill Rd CHAM PO6 ..274 C9
Southwick Pl SBNE BH6 ......336 A4
Southwick Rd CHAM PO6 .....274 E8
  WHAM PO17 ....274 E3
Southwood Av
  CHCH/BSGR BH23 ....326 C6
  SBNE BH6 ....336 A2
Southwood Cl
  CHCH/BSGR BH23 ....326 C6
  FERN BH22 ....302 D3
South Wood Gdns HLER SO31..270 F7

Southwood Gdns THLE RG7 ......27 J4
Southwood La FLEETN GU51 .....75 H1
Southwood Rd ALTN GU34 ....132 B1
  FARN GU14 ....56 F4
  FARN GU14 ....57 M9
  HISD PO11 ....519 J6
  NEND PO2 ....296 G5
Sovereign Av GPORT PO12 ....315 N1
Sovereign Cl LTDN BH7 ....323 M7
  TOTT SO40 ....245 P3
Sovereign Crs
  FHAM/STUB PO14 ......270 O9
Sovereign Dr ENEY PO4 ....317 L3
  HEND SO30 ....250 E5
Sovereign La WVILLE PO7 .....275 N7
Sovereign Wy ELGH SO50 .....207 H7
Sowcroft La ODIM RG29 ......112 C5
Sowden Cl HEND SO30 ....250 B4
Sowley La LYMN SO41 ....330 E2
Spackman Cl STHA RG19 ......25 N5
Spain La ALTN GU34 ....110 C7
The Spain PSF GU52 ....215 L2
Spalding Rd ITCH SO19 ....249 M6
Spa Meadow La STHA RG19 ....24 F7
Spaniard's La ROMY SO51 .....258 D5
Sparkford Cl FUFL SO22 ....22 B7
  LTDN BH7 ....525 P7
Sparkford Rd FUFL SO22 ......22 B7
Spa Rd SHAM SO14 ....20 D5
Sparrow Cl HORN PO8 ....255 P7
Sparrow Ct
  LSOL/BMARY PO13 .....314 D1
Sparrowgrove RWIN SO21 ....207 L1
Sparrowhawk Cl RFNM GU10 ..95 M3
Sparrow Sq ELGH SO50 ....228 F2
Sparshott Cl HAV PO9 ....276 C5
Sparshott Rd ITCH SO19 ......269 H2
  RWIN SO21 ....182 D3
Spartan Cl EMRTH PO10 ......299 N6
  FHAM/STUB PO14 ......294 A4
Spartina Dr LYMN SO41 ....329 L1
Sparvells HTWY RG27 ....39 P6
Spats La BOR GU35 ....135 P9
Speakers Corner Rbt
  SHAM SO14 ....20 E5
Spear Rd SHAM SO14 ....248 C3
Speckled Wood Rd CHIN RG24 ..69 L3
Specks La ENEY PO4 ....317 J4
Speedwell Cl HLER SO31 ......270 F8
Speedwell Dr
  CHCH/BSGR BH23 ......325 M7
Speen Hill Cl NWBY RG14 .....24 B3
Speen La NWBY RG14 ....24 B3
Speen Lodge Ct NWBY RG14 ..24 B3
Speen Pl NWBY RG14 ....24 B3
Speggs Wk HEND SO30 ....250 C5
Speltham Hl WVILLE PO7 .....254 F1
Spencer Cl ALTN GU34 ....150 C5
  FLEETS GU52 ....74 F7
  FRIM GU16 ....58 D7
  HISD PO11 ....518 G5
  TADY RG26 ....34 F5
Spencer Dr
  LSOL/BMARY PO13 .....314 D3
Spencer Gdns HORN PO8 .....256 F5
Spencer Rd BMTH BH1 ....335 J2
  CCLF BH15 ....333 N3
  ELGH SO50 ....228 C2
  EMRTH PO10 ....277 L6
  ENEY PO4 ....319 J3
  ITCH SO19 ....249 M5
  NMIL/BTOS BH25 ....327 J4
  NWBY RG14 ....24 B4
Spenlow Cl NEND PO2 ....296 F9
Spenser Cl ALTN GU34 ....150 C5
  HLER SO31 ....292 D1
Sperrin Cl KBH RG22 ....68 E9
Spetisbury Cl
  MOOR/WNTN BH9 .....323 H4
Spey Cl AND SP10 ....82 C9
Spicer La BWD BH11 ....301 N8
Spicers ALTN GU34 ....132 C6
Spicer St PSEA PO1 * 19 H1
Spicer's Wy TOTT SO40 ......246 C5
Spicewood FHAM PO15 ....10 A4
Spiers Cl TADY RG26 ....34 E6
Spiers La NARL SO24 ....129 J6
Spinacre NMIL/BTOS BH25 ....327 J7
Spindle Cl BDST BH18 ....320 B2
  HAV PO9 ....277 J7
Spindle Warren HAV PO9 .....277 J7
Spindlewood Cl
  NMIL/BTOS BH25 ....327 J6
  ROWN SO16 ....228 C6
Spindlewood Wy TOTT SO40 ..267 K2
Spinnaker Cl HISD PO11 ......518 H8
  LSOL/BMARY PO13 .....315 H1
Spinnaker Dr FARN GU14 .....296 F5
Spinnaker Gra HISD PO11 .....299 J5
Spinnaker Vw CHAM PO6 .....276 A9
Spinners Cl FERN BH22 ......280 E8
Spinney Cl HORN PO8 ....256 B3
  RGWD BH24 ....281 K5
Spinney Gv FAWY SO45 ......268 D8
Spinney Gdns FAWY SO45 ....268 D8
Spinneys La FERN BH22 ......302 D5
The Spinney ELGH SO50 ......230 A2
  FHAM/PORC PO16 .....273 K9
  FLEETS GU51 ....74 A4
  GSHT GU26 ....155 P4
  HASM GU27 * 156 C8
  HASM GU27 ....157 H5
  HORN PO8 ....256 A5
  HTWY RG27 ....71 P7
  LSOL/BMARY PO13 .....295 H8
  NARL SO24 ....187 N1
  RGWD BH24 ....281 M3
  ROWN BH24 ....228 B6
  RWIN SO21 ....183 L7
  TOTT SO40 ....246 A2
  WVILLE PO7 ....255 H8
  YTLY GU46 ....40 D7
Spinney Wk WEND SO18 ......229 H9

Spinney Wy NMIL/BTOS BH25 ..327 J1
Spitalfields Rd ALTN GU34 ....132 F5
Spitalhatch ALTN GU34 ....133 H6
Spitfire End WINC SO23 ......165 L1
Spitfire Loop ELGH SO50 .....229 H5
Spitfire Wy FARN GU14 ....75 M4
  HLER SO31 ....269 P8
Spithead Av GPORT PO12 ....315 N7
Spittlefields RGWD BH24 .....282 F2
Spoil La RFNM GU10 ....97 M4
Spokane Cl AND SP10 ....291 K6
Spouts La ROMY SO51 ....202 D7
Sprat's Hatch La ODIM RG29 ..73 J7
Spray Leaze RAND SP11 ......80 B1
Spriggs Cl STHA RG19 ....25 N5
Springbank Rd LTDN BH7 .....323 M7
Spring Cl CHIN RG24 ....68 C1
  CFDH BH17 ....320 C3
  ITCH SO19 ....249 H7
  VWD BH31 ....258 F5
Spring Crs PTSW SO17 ....248 D5
Springcroft
  LSOL/BMARY PO13 .....294 F4
Springcross Av BLKW GU17 ...57 L2
Springdale Av BDST BH18 ....300 B8
Springdale Gv WIMB BH21 ...300 A9
Springdale Rd WIMB BH21 ...300 C8
Springfarm Rd HASM GU27 ..156 D8
Springfield DEAN RG23 ....88 F1
Springfield Av
  CHCH/BSGR BH23 ......324 B5
  FAWY SO45 ....290 F5
  HTWY RG27 ....55 H6
  SBNE BH6 ....336 E2
Springfield Cl AND SP10 ......5 K4
  HAV PO9 ....276 B8
  LYMN SO41 ....329 N4
  VWD BH31 ....258 F5
  WHAM PO17 ....252 E7
Springfield Crs PSTN BH14 ...321 K8
  RSAL SP5 ....199 P8
Springfield Dr TOTT SO40 ....246 C5
Springfield Gdns
  NMIL/BTOS BH25 ......327 M5
Springfield Gv FAWY SO45 ...290 F5
Springfield La FLEETN GU51 ..74 B3
  NWBY RG14 ....24 D7
Springfield Pl CHIN RG24 * ...70 C5
Springfield Rd ASHV GU12 ...76 F7
  PSTN BH14 ....321 J7
  TADY RG26 ....34 F5
  VWD BH31 ....258 F5
Springfields WIMB BH21 .....278 G2
Springfields Cl RWIN SO21 ...207 P4
Springfield Wy
  FHAM/STUB PO14 .....294 A8
Springford Cl ROWN SO16 ...227 M3
Springford Crs ROWN SO16 ..227 M3
Springford Gdns ROWN SO16 .227 M8
Springford Rd ROWN SO16 ...227 M2
Spring Garden La GPORT PO12 .13 F1
Spring Gdns
  BKME/WDN BH12 ......321 M7
  EMRTH PO10 ....299 M1
  EWKG RG40 * 40 A1
  FARN GU14 ....50 A4
  NARL SO24 ....167 N3
  NBAD SO52 ....205 K6
  PSEA PO1 ....19 F3
Spring Gv HLER SO31 ....270 A1
Spring Hill La RAND SP11 ....84 B1
Springhill Rd CHFD SO53 ....206 E7
Spring Hills ITCH SO19 ......249 L7
Springhurst NWBY RG14 * ...24 E7
Springlakes Est ASHV GU12 * .76 D9
Spring La BPWT SO32 ....232 F8
  ELGH SO50 ....229 M1
  FNM GU9 ....96 A4
  KSCL RG20 ....30 E8
  NMIL/BTOS BH25 ......327 M5
  RWIN SO21 ....207 P4
  THLE RG7 ....27 J8
  THLE RG7 ....37 M3
Spring La West FNM GU9 .....96 A5
Spring Ms AND SP10 ....4 E2
Spring Pl ROMY SO51 ....204 C6
Spring Rd BMTH BH1 ....335 J1
  FAWY SO45 ....268 C6
  HLER SO31 ....270 F4
  ITCH SO19 ....249 H6
  LYMN SO41 ....329 N4
The Springs THLE RG7 ....36 C6
Spring St PSEA PO1 ....19 G2
The Spring WVILLE PO7 .....255 H8
Spring V BPWT SO32 ....232 F7
Springvale Av LTDN BH7 .....325 M7
  WINC SO23 ....165 J1
Springvale Rd WINC SO23 ...165 J2
Springwater Cl BWD BH11 ...322 A4
Spring Wy NARL SO24 ....167 P3
Springwell La HTWY RG27 ...322 E7
Springwood Av WVILLE PO7 ..275 P4
Spring Wood La THLE RG7 ....27 J5
Spring Woods FLEETS GU51 ..74 A4
  SHST GU47 ....41 K5
Spruce Av BOR GU35 ....153 N5
  WVILLE PO7 ....276 A3
Spruce Cl AND SP10 ....102 A3
  CFDH BH17 ....320 A3
  HLER SO31 ....292 D1
  RWIN SO21 ....148 F1
Spruce Dr ITCH SO19 ....249 N6
  TOTT SO40 ....245 P3
Spruce Wy FLEETN GU51 ....74 A3
Spur Cl WIMB BH21 ....279 L8
Spurcroft Rd STHA RG19 .....25 N5
Spurgeon Rd LTDN BH7 .....323 P9
Spur Hill Av PSTN BH14 .....321 M9
Spurlings Rd WHAM PO17 ...273 H6

Spur Rd CHAM PO6 ....297 H1
  PSTN BH14 ....321 M8
  WVILLE PO7 ....275 N1
Spurs Ct ALDT GU11 ....2 A3
The Spur GPORT PO12 ......315 K6
Spyglass Cl HLER SO31 .....269 H4
  WHAM PO17 ....252 E7
Spybush La NARL SO24 .....128 F6
Square Cl WIMB BH21 * 301 P2
Squarefield Gdns HTWY RG27 .72 B2
The Square BSTK RG21 * 7 H4
  EMRTH PO10 ....277 P7
  EPSF GU31 ....216 F9
  FAWY SO45 ....291 K4
  FERN BH22 * 281 H9
  GPORT PO12 ....295 M9
  HTWY RG27 ....52 C8
  LYMN SO41 ....329 J4
  PSF GU52 ....215 M2
  ROMY SO51 ....204 B4
  SHAM SO14 ....20 D5
  STHA RG19 ....31 M2
  STOK SO20 ....139 P2
  WHAM PO17 ....252 E8
  WINC SO23 ....22 E5
Squarey Cl RSAL SP5 ....199 L2
Squires Hill La RFNM GU10 ..117 J5
Squires Wk ITCH SO19 .....268 C1
Squirrel Cl ELGH SO50 ......229 P2
  FHAM PO15 ....271 J5
  SHST GU47 ....41 J6
Squirrel Dr DEAN RG23 .....88 C8
  ITCH SO19 ....249 J8
Squirrel La FARN GU14 .....57 P8
Squirrels Cl CHCH/BSGR BH23 .324 B5
Squirrels Drey CWTH RG45 ..40 C1
Squirrels Wk FAWY SO45 ....268 B8
Stable Cl FHAM/STUB PO14 ..271 K3
  HTWY RG27 ....71 N3
  THLE RG7 ....27 J4
Stable Ct WIMB BH21 ....24 E2
Stable Rd BOR GU35 ....153 P2
Stables Rd NTID SP9 ....78 G7
Stable Vw YTLY GU46 ......40 F7
Stacey Cl BKME/WDN BH12 ..321 L5
Stacey Ct HAV PO9 ....276 D3
Stacey Gdns CHAR BH8 .....323 M5
Stafford Rd BMTH BH1 .....9 G3
  PSF GU32 ....191 M9
  SSEA PO5 ....19 J7
  WSHM SO15 ....156 A2
Staff Ad ASHV GU12 * 3 J3
  ROMY SO51 ....179 P6
Stagbrake Cl FAWY SO45 ...290 D6
Stag Cl ELGH SO50 ....229 P2
  NMIL/BTOS BH25 .....328 C5
Stag Oak La CHIN RG24 ....51 P9
Stagshorn Rd HORN PO8 ...256 C4
Stags La WINC SO23 ....184 D9
Stagswood VWD BH31 ......258 D4
Stag Wy FHAM PO15 ....272 E5
Stainer Cl ITCH SO19 ......249 M8
Stainers La RWIN SO21 ....144 D4
Staith Cl ITCH SO19 ....249 L6
Stake La FARN GU14 ....57 P9
Stakes Hill Rd WVILLE PO7 ..275 N3
Stake's La BPWT SO32 .....256 D3
  PSF GU32 ....231 L2
Stakes Rd WVILLE PO7 .....275 M6
Stalbridge Dr FERN BH22 ...302 D4
Stalbridge Rd CFDH BH17 ...320 C5
Stalham Rd BKME/WDN BH12 .321 P6
Stallard Cl EMRTH PO10 ....277 L9
Stallards La RGWD BH24 ....280 C4
Stalybridge Cl HLER SO31 ...270 C4
Stamford Av RWIN SO21 ....58 E4
Stamford Rd SBNE BH6 .....336 B1
Stamford Wy ELGH SO50 ...228 D2
Stamshaw Rd NEND PO2 ...296 F8
Stanbridge Rd HAV PO9 ....15 K1
Stanbury Cl RAND SP11 ....100 E2
Stancombe Broad La
  ALTN GU34 ....149 M6
Stancombe La ALTN GU34 ..112 C9
  ALTN GU34 ....149 N5
Standard Wy
  FHAM/PORC PO16 ....11 K1
Standen Rd ROWN SO16 ...157 M5
Standford Hl BOR GU35 ....154 D7
Standford La BOR GU35 ....154 D5
Standford Rd SHAM SO14 ..21 H5
Standing Hl RSAL SP5 .....158 F7
Stanfield TADY RG26 ......34 C6
Stanfield Rd
  BKME/WDN BH12 .....321 M5
  FERN BH22 ....302 C2
  MOOR/WNTN BH9 ....322 E7
Stanford Cl CHAM PO6 ....296 F1
Stanford Ct HAV PO9 ......277 H5
Stanford Rd LYMN SO41 ...308 B6
Stanford Rd KBH RG22 ....89 N3
Stanham Cl RWIN SO21 ....144 E6
Stanhope Rd CBLY GU15 ...57 N1
  PSEA PO1 ....19 G2
Stanier Wy HEND SO30 ....250 C1
Stanley Av HISD PO11 .....299 K9
  GPORT PO12 ....295 L8
  VWD BH31 ....258 C5
Stanley Dr FARN GU14 ....75 K1
Stanley Green Rd PLE BH15 .320 E7
Stanley Hl CHOB/PIR GU24 ..59 P8
Stanley La ESSEA PO5 ......19 K5
Stanley Rd BMTH BH1 .....335 J1
  CHCH/BSGR BH23 ....326 C7
  EMRTH PO10 ....299 N1
  FAWY SO45 ....290 F5
  LYMN SO41 ....329 M5
  NEND PO2 ....296 E8
  NWBY RG14 ....17 G4
  PLE BH15 ....332 E2

PTSW SO17 ....248 E2
  TOTT SO40 ....246 B2
Stanley St SSEA PO5 ....316 E6
Stanmore Gdns THLE RG7 ..35 N1
Stanmore La FUFL SO22 ....164 D9
Stannington Cl
  NMIL/BTOS BH25 .....327 J5
Stannington Crs TOTT SO40 ..246 D3
Stannington Wy TOTT SO40 ..246 D3
Stanpit CHCH/BSGR BH23 ...337 J1
Stanstead Cl HAV PO9 .....257 J9
Stanstead Rd ELGH SO50 ...207 H9
Stansted Crs HAV PO9 .....277 K4
Stansted Rd SSEA PO5 .....19 K4
Stanswood Rd FAWY SO45 ..313 L3
  HAV PO9 ....276 D4
Stanton Dr FLEETN GU51 ...74 B4
Stanton Rd NBNE BH10 ....322 C5
  PSF GU32 ....215 L1
  WSHM SO15 ....247 K4
Stapehill Crs WIMB BH21 ...301 N3
Stapehill Rd WIMB BH21 ...301 N3
Staple Ash La PSF GU52 ...190 C7
Staple Cl WVILLE PO7 .....275 M1
Staple Close La PLE BH15 ..320 E6
Staple Cross WHAM PO17 ..273 M2
Staplecross La
  CHCH/BSGR BH23 ....325 H7
Stapleford Av FERN BH22 ..302 F2
Stapleford Cl ROMY SO51 ..204 F3
Stapleford Rd BPWT SO32 ..250 F7
Staple Gdns WINC SO23 ...22 D4
Staplehurst Cl ITCH SO19 ..269 J1
Staplers Reach
  LSOL/BMARY PO13 ....294 F8
Stapleton Rd HSEA PO3 ....297 J9
Stapley Cl NARL SO24 .....169 N5
Stares Cl LSOL/BMARY PO13 .314 C1
Star Hl HTWY RG27 ......55 L4
Star Hill Dr RFNM GU10 ...136 D6
Starina Gdns WVILLE PO7 ..276 B2
Star La ASHV GU12 ....97 M1
  KSCL RG20 ....29 N8
Starlight Farm Cl VWD BH31 .259 H3
Starling Cl BASS GU52 .....89 K3
Starling Gdns NWBY RG14 ..17 J5
The Starting Ga NWBY RG14 .82 C8
Statham Sq NTID SP9 ......78 G7
Station Ap ALTN GU34 .....150 C5
  AND SP10 ....4 A3
  BDST BH18 ....300 B8
  BLKW GU17 ....57 M1
  EMRTH PO10 * 277 M9
  NARL SO24 ....168 A2
  NWBY RG14 ....18 C5
  RAND SP11 ....119 P2
Station Cl RWIN SO21 .....166 D1
  WHAM PO17 ....252 E7
Station HI ELGH SO50 .....229 K1
  FNM GU9 ....96 C9
  HEND SO30 ....251 J4
  HLER SO31 ....270 D6
  OVTN RG25 ....87 H3
  RWIN SO21 ....166 D1
  WINC SO23 ....22 D3
Station La CHFD SO53 .....206 E7
Station Rd ALDT GU11 .....3 F3
  ALTN GU34 ....132 C5
  BOR GU35 ....153 P3
  BPWT SO32 ....232 D3
  BPWT SO32 ....233 N3
  CHAM PO6 ....324 E8
  CHCH/BSGR BH23 ...324 E8
  DEAN RG23 ....88 A9
  EPSF GU31 ....215 M1
  FARN GU14 ....3 A3
  FBDG SP6 ....239 M5
  FBDG SP6 ....239 N5
  FERN BH22 ....280 D7
  FHAM/PORC PO16 ...295 H1
  FRIM GU16 ....59 J5
  GPORT PO12 ....315 K1
  HISD PO11 ....518 D5
  HLER SO31 ....269 L4
  HTWY RG27 ....73 J5
  HTWY RG27 ....73 J3
  ITCH SO19 ....269 L1
  KSCL RG20 ....29 N4
  LIPH GU30 ....175 J5
  LISS GU33 ....192 D2
  LYMN SO41 ....308 B6
  NARL SO24 ....169 N5
  NTID SP9 ....79 H6
  NWBY RG14 ....16 E4
  NWBY RG14 ....24 A2
  OVTN RG25 ....87 H3
  OVTN RG25 ....90 D4
  PSF GU32 ....212 E1
  PSF GU32 ....215 K9
  PSTN BH14 ....321 K9
  RAND SP11 ....119 P2
  RFNM GU10 ....114 E6
  RGWD BH24 ....284 F9
  ROMY SO51 ....204 D5
  ROWN SO16 ....228 A1
  RWIN SO21 ....166 D1
  STOK SO20 ....123 K6
  THLE RG7 ....27 J5
  VWD BH31 ....258 D3
  WHAM PO17 ....273 H1
  WHCH RG28 ....85 L5
  WINC SO23 ....22 D3
  WSHM SO15 ....246 G3

Station Rd East ASHV GU12 ..76 E5
Station Rd North TOTT SO40 * .246 E4
Station Rd South TOTT SO40 * .246 E4
Station St LYMN SO41 .....329 M3
  PSEA PO1 ....19 G2
Station Ter WIMB BH21 ....300 F2
Staunton Av HISD PO11 ....318 D5
Staunton Rd HAV PO9 .....14 D5
Staunton St PSEA PO1 ....316 E2
Staunton Wy HAV PO9 ....14 D1
Stavedown Rd RWIN SO21 ..144 D4
Stead Cl HISD PO11 ....319 H5
Stedman Rd BOSC BH5 ....335 P1
Steele Cl CHFD SO53 .....206 F9
Steeles Rd ALDT GU11 ....76 A8
Steele's Dro FBDG SP6 ...221 J5
Steels La FBDG SP6 ....211 J8
Steep Cl FHAM/PORC PO16 * .273 N9
Steepdene PSTN BH14 .....321 K9
Steeple Cl CFDH BH17 ....320 F1
Steeple Dr ALTN GU34 ....132 E3
Stepleton Rd BDST BH18 ...320 B1
Steeple Wy FHAM/STUB PO14 .271 K7
Steerforth Cl NEND PO2 ...316 F1
Steerforth Copse SHST GU47 .41 J5
Steinbeck Cl FHAM PO15 ..271 J2
Steke La NMIL/BTOS BH25 ..327 J6
Stenbury Dr OVTN RG25 ...129 M1
Stenbury Wy HLER SO31 ...269 L3
Stenhurst Rd PLE BH15 ...320 G6
Stephen Cl HORN PO8 ....256 B9
Stephendale Rd FNM GU9 ..96 D7
Stephen Langton Dr
  BWD BH11 ....301 M8
Stephen Martin Gdns
  FBDG SP6 ....240 C1
Stephen Rd FHAM PO15 ...10 D5
Stephen's Cl THLE RG7 ...27 H9
Stephens Firs THLE RG7 ..26 G9
Stephenson Cl AND SP10 ..102 A1
  GPORT PO12 ....5 H2
  NTHA RG18 ....25 N3
Stephenson Rd BSTK RG21 ..69 H6
  FHAM PO15 ....271 L8
  TOTT SO40 ....246 B1
Stephenson Wy HEND SO30 .230 B9
Stephens Rd TADY RG26 ...34 D3
  THLE RG7 ....27 H9
Steplake Rd ROMY SO51 ...202 B2
Step Ter FUFL SO22 ....22 B4
Sterling Pk AND SP10 .....102 A1
Sterte Av PLE BH15 ....320 D8
Sterte Av West PLE BH15 ..320 D8
Sterte Cl PLE BH15 ....320 D8
Sterte Rd PLE BH15 ......320 D8
Steuart Rd WEND SO18 ...248 F4
Stevens Dro STOK SO20 ...160 G2
Stevens Gn RAND SP11 ...84 C2
Stevens Hl YTLY GU46 ....40 C6
Stevenson Crs PSTN BH14 ..321 M9
Stevenson Rd RWIN SO21 ..104 E8
  SBNE BH6 ....336 E5
Stevensons Cl WIMB BH21 ..308 C1
Stiles Dr AND SP10 ....149 L4
Stillions Cl ALTN GU34 ....132 G6
Stillmore Rd BWD BH11 ...321 M1
Stillwater Pk RGWD BH24 * .291 H8
Stilwell Cl YTLY GU46 ....40 F8
Stinchar Dr CHFD SO53 ...206 C8
Stinsford Cl
  MOOR/WNTN BH9 ....323 H3
Stinsford Rd CFDH BH17 ..320 F5
Stirling Av WVILLE PO7 ...275 P1
Stirling Cl ASHV GU12 ....76 E7
  FARN GU14 ....75 P1
  FRIM GU16 ....58 B6
  NMIL/BTOS BH25 ....327 K4
  TOTT SO40 ....246 E2
Stirling Crs HEND SO30 ..250 C2
  TOTT SO40 ....246 E3
Stirling Rd MOOR/WNTN BH9 .322 E8
Stirling St NEND PO2 ......296 F9
Stirling Wy CHCH/BSGR BH23 .325 M9
  FARN GU14 ....25 M5 (?)
  NTHA RG18 ....25 M3
Stirrup Cl WIMB BH21 .....279 L8
Stirrup Pightle NWBY RG14 ..24 E8
Stoatley Hollow HASM GU27 .156 F5
Stoatley Ri HASM GU27 ....156 F5
Stoatley River HASM GU27 ..156 F5
Stoborough Dr BDST BH18 ..319 L1
Stockbridge Cl CFDH BH17 ..321 K2
  CHIN RG24 ....69 K3
  HAV PO9 ....277 H5
Stockbridge Dr ALDT GU11 ..3 J7
Stockbridge Rd FUFL SO22 ..22 A2
  RAND SP11 ....121 N1
  ROMY SO51 ....180 A7
  RWIN SO21 ....125 L5
  RWIN SO21 ....143 K8
  STOK SO20 ....161 M4
Stockbridge Wy YTLY GU46 ..40 B6
Stocker Cl BSTK RG21 .....69 H6
Stocker Pl LSOL/BMARY PO13 .295 H7
Stockers Av FUFL SO22 ....164 G6
Stockheath La HAV PO9 ...14 D3
Stockheath Rd HAV PO9 ...276 F6
Stockheath Wy HAV PO9 ..276 F6
Stockholm Dr HEND SO30 .250 D7

Stock La RSAL SP5 ....201 L6
Stockley Cl FAWY SO45 ....290 E6
Stocks La ALTN GU34 ....189 J5
  BPWT SO32 ....211 N7
Stockton Av FLEETN GU51 ....74 C2
Stockton Cl HEND SO30 ....250 D4
Stockton Pk FLEETN GU51 ....74 C2
Stockwood Wy FNM GU9 ....96 F4
Stoddart Av STOV SO19 ....249 H5
Stodham La LISS GU33 ....192 C4
Stoke Charity Rd RWIN SO21 ....145 H5
Stoke Common Rd
  ELGH SO50 ....207 N8
Stoke Gdns GPORT PO12 ....12 E3
Stoke Hts ELGH SO50 ....230 B1
Stoke Hi RAND SP11 ....62 E9
Stoke Hills FNM GU9 ....96 C8
Stoke La RAND SP11 ....62 D7
Stoken La HTWY RG27 ....54 E6
Stoke Pde GPORT PO12 * 12 E3
Stoke Park Rd ELGH SO50 ....207 N9
Stoke Rd GPORT PO12 ....12 D6
  RAND SP11 ....62 C6
  RAND SP11 ....83 J4
  ROWN SO16 ....247 L2
  WINC SO23 ....165 H4
Stokes Av PLE BH15 ....320 E8
Stokesay Cl FAWY SO45 ....290 C1
Stoke Bay Rd GPORT PO12 ....315 H6
Stokes Ct WSHM SO15 * 248 A5
Stokes La STHA RG19 ....33 M5
Stokesway GPORT PO12 * 12 E3
Stoke Wood Cl ELGH SO50 ....230 B2
Stoke Wood Rd TWDS BH3 ....322 F8
Stonechat Cl EPSF GU31 ....146 C5
  FERN BH22 ....280 B9
Stonechat Dr TOTT SO40 ....245 P3
Stonechat Rd HORN PO8 ....256 A5
Stone Cl AND SP10 ....102 C4
  RSAL SP5 ....158 D1
Stonecrop Cl BDST BH18 ....320 A2
Stone Crop Cl ASHV GU12 ....270 E9
Stonedene Cl BOR GU35 ....155 J4
Stone Gdns CHAR BH8 ....323 N5
Stoneham Cemetery Rd
  WEND SO18 ....229 H8
Stoneham Cl PSF GU32 ....215 K1
  ROWN SO16 ....228 F7
Stoneham La ROWN SO16 ....228 F7
Stoneham Pk PSF GU32 ....215 K1
Stoneham Wy ELGH SO50 ....228 C7
Stonehill Pk BOR GU35 ....155 J4
Stonehill Rd BOR GU35 ....155 J4
Stonehills FAWY SO45 ....291 L7
Stonehouse Rd FRIM GU16 ....58 D4
Stonehouse Rd LIPH GU30 ....175 L3
Stone La GPORT PO12 ....12 D4
  WIMB BH21 ....278 C8
Stoneleigh Av LYMN SO41 ....327 P3
Stoneleigh Cl
  FHAM/PORC PO16 ....295 M1
Stoneleigh Ct FRIM GU16 ....58 E4
Stoners Cl LSOL/BMARY PO13 ....294 F6
Stone Sq HAV PO9 ....276 F6
Stone St SSEA PO5 ....19 G6
Stone Ter ELGH SO50 * 207 K4
Stoney Bottom GSHT GU26 ....156 B2
Stoney Cl YTLY GU46 ....56 E1
Stoney Ct FUFL SO22 ....164 F5
Stoney Cross RAND SP11 ....79 P1
Stoneyfields FNM GU9 ....116 E1
Stoneylas La ALTN GU34 ....134 C2
  FUFL SO22 ....164 F5
  NWBV RG14 ....24 C1
  STHA RG19 ....25 P4
Stony La CHCH/BSGR BH23 ....324 F5
  FBDC SP6 ....218 G8
  PSEA PO1 ....18 C1
Stony La South
  CHCH/BSGR BH23 ....324 G9
Stonymoor Cl FAWY SO45 ....290 E6
Stookes Wy YTLY GU46 ....56 C1
Stopples La LYMN SO41 ....327 H4
Storrington Rd HORN PO8 ....236 D7
Story La BDST PO18 ....300 D9
Stourbank Rd
  CHCH/BSGR BH23 ....324 E9
Stourcliffe Av SBNE BH6 ....336 A2
Stour Cl PSF GU32 ....215 L3
  WEND SO18 ....229 J9
  WIMB BH21 ....301 M1
Stourcroft Dr
  CHCH/BSGR BH23 ....324 B5
Stourfield Rd BOSC BH5 ....335 P2
Stourhead Cl AND SP10 ....102 D5
  FARN GU14 ....58 C9
Stourpaine Rd CFDH BH17 ....320 F2
Stour Pk NBNE BH10 ....322 E1
Stour Rd CHAR BH8 ....323 X9
  CHCH/BSGR BH23 ....324 E9
  DEAN BC23 ....88 F2
Stourvale Av
  CHCH/BSGR BH23 ....324 D7
Stourvale Gdns CHFD SO53 ....206 F8
Stourvale Pl BOSC BH5 ....335 P1
Stourvale Rd SBNE BH6 ....335 P1
Stour Valley Wy
  MOOR/WNTN BH9 ....323 J4
  SBNE BH6 ....324 C8
  WIMB BH21 ....300 A1
  WIMB BH21 ....301 J4
Stour View Gdns WIMB SO21 ....300 A4
Stour Wk CHAR BH8 ....323 K3
Stour Wy CHCH/BSGR BH23 ....324 B1
Stourwood Av SBNE BH6 ....336 A2
Stourwood Rd SBNE BH6 ....336 B2
Stouts La CHCH/BSGR BH23 ....305 M1
Stovold's Wy ALDT GU11 ....2 B6
Stowe Cl HEND SO30 ....250 D2
Stowe Rd ENEY PO4 ....317 K4
Stradbrook
  LSOL/BMARY PO13 ....294 F8
Stragwyne Cl NBAD SO52 ....205 J3
The Straight Mile ROMY SO51 ....205 J4
Strand SHAM SO14 ....20 E5

Strand St PLE BH15 ....332 D2
The Strand HISD PO11 ....319 J7
Stranding St ELGH SO50 ....229 H1
Strategic Pk HEND SO30 * 249 P4
Stratfield Av TADY RG26 ....34 C7
Stratfield Dr CHFD SO53 ....206 D4
Stratfield Pk WVILLE PO7 * 275 L2
Stratfield Pl NMIL/BTOS BH25 ....326 G4
Stratfield Rd BSTK RG21 ....69 L4
Stratford Dr LYMN SO41 * 36 B9
Stratford Pl ELCH SO50 ....329 K2
  LYMN SO41 ....329 K2
Stratford Rd ASHV GU12 ....274 A2
  WVILLE PO7 ....276 A2
Strathfield Rd AND SP10 ....102 D5
Strathmore Dr VWD BH31 ....258 C4
Strathmore Rd GPORT PO12 ....13 F2
  NBNE BH10 ....322 C3
Stratton Cl CHAM PO6 ....296 E1
  RWIN SO21 ....127 N5
Stratton La FARN GU14 ....57 P6
Stratton Pk KBH RG22 ....89 M1
Stratton Rd BSTK RG21 ....69 H8
  MOOR/WNTN BH9 ....323 J3
  WSHM SO15 ....23 H6
  WSHM SO15 ....247 N2
Stratton Wk FARN GU14 ....57 P6
Strauss Rd KBH RG22 ....90 C8
Stravinsky Rd KBH RG22 ....90 B5
Strawberry Cl FRIM GU16 ....59 J5
Strawberry Flds BROC SO42 ....311 H2
  HEND SO30 ....250 A5
  TADY RG26 ....52 A2
Strawberry Hi HLER SO31 ....270 F7
  NWBV RG14 ....24 C3
Strawberry Md ELGH SO50 ....230 B3
Stream Farm Cl RWIN GU10 ....116 D3
Streamleaze
  Streamside FLEETN GU51 ....74 D4
Stream Valley Rd RFNM GU10 ....116 C4
Street End HTWY RG27 ....205 M8
  NBAD SO52 ....205 M8
Streets La RGWD BH24 ....282 C5
The Street ALTN GU34 ....134 C2
  RDEN RG24 ....70 B6
  FLEETN GU51 ....74 B7
  HTWY RG27 ....53 M8
  ODIM RG29 ....92 F1
  ODIM RG29 ....93 K8
  RFNM GU10 ....97 M6
  RFNM GU10 ....115 N4
  RFNM GU10 ....115 N3
  RFNM GU10 ....136 C2
  RSAL SP5 ....201 J1
  RSAL SP5 ....201 P2
  TADY RG26 ....51 N3
  THLE RG7 ....36 A1
Streetway Rd RAND SP11 ....119 N3
Strete Mt CHCH/BSGR BH23 * 325 J8
Stride Av HSEA PO3 ....317 K2
Strides La RGWD BH24 ....282 D2
Strides Wy TOTT SO40 ....245 P4
Strode Gdns RGWD BH24 ....281 P4
Strode Rd NEND PO2 ....296 F7
Strokins Rd KSCL RG20 ....8 A4
Strongs Cl ROMY SO51 ....204 F5
Stroud Cl CHIN RG24 ....69 P2
  WIMB BH21 ....279 J8
Strouden Av CHAR BH8 ....323 P7
Strouden Ct HAV PO9 ....276 D3
Stroud End PSF GU32 ....215 H1
Strouden Rd
  MOOR/WNTN BH9 ....322 G6
Stroud Gdns
  CHCH/BSGR BH23 ....325 J9
Stroud Gn NWBV RG14 ....17 G5
Stroud Green La
  FHAM/STUB PO14 ....294 C4
Stroud La
  CHCH/BSGR BH23 ....325 J9
  FLEETN GU51 ....75 P7
Stroudley Av CHAM PO6 ....297 L3
Stroudley Rd CHIN RG24 ....69 P5
Stroudley Wy HEND SO30 ....250 D1
Stroud Park Av
  FHAM/STUB PO14 ....294 A6
Stroudwood La BPWT SO32 ....230 G1
  RWIN SO21 ....208 G8
Stroudwood Rd HAV PO9 ....15 H1
Struan Cl RGWD BH24 ....281 M3
Struan Dr RGWD BH24 ....281 M3
Struan Gdns RGWD BH24 ....281 M3
Stuart Cl FARN GU14 ....57 P8
Stuart Crs FUFL SO22 ....183 N1
Stuart Rd CHCH/BSGR BH23 ....326 D7
  NEND PO2 ....296 C8
Stubbington Gn
  FHAM/STUB PO14 ....294 A6
Stubbington La
  FHAM/STUB PO14 ....294 C4
Stubbington Wy ELGH SO50 ....230 D3
Stubbs Cl AND SP10 ....71 J2
Stubbs Dro HEND SO30 ....250 D4
Stubbs Folly SHST GU47 ....41 L7
Stubbs Moor Rd FARN GU14 ....57 N8
Stubbs Rd BSTK RG21 ....90 E1
  ITCH SO19 ....248 E6
Stuckton Rd FBDC SP6 ....240 E3
Studland Cl ROWN SO16 ....247 H2
Studland Dr LYMN SO41 ....338 C1
Studland Rd
  LSOL/BMARY PO13 ....314 C2
  ROWN SO16 ....247 H2
  WBNE BH4 ....334 B1
Studley Av FAWY SO45 ....290 E6
Studley Cl CHCH/BSGR BH23 ....325 J8
Studley Ct NMIL/BTOS BH25 ....326 F7
Stukeley Rd BSTK RG21 ....69 J8
Sturt Cl FRIM GU16 ....58 D4
Sturminster Rd
  MOOR/WNTN BH9 ....323 H3

Sturt Av HASM GU27 ....156 E8
Sturt Rd FNM GU9 ....96 B4
  FRIM GU16 ....58 E8
  HASM GU27 ....156 E8
Sudbury Rd CHAM PO6 ....296 F1
Suetts La BPWT SO32 ....232 D5
Suffolk Av CHCH/BSGR BH23 ....324 D5
  WSHM SO15 ....247 P4
Suffolk Cl CHFD SO53 ....228 E2
  NBAD SO52 ....279 L8
Suffolk Dr FRIM GU16 ....59 J5
Suffolk Gn CHFD SO53 ....228 E2
Suffolk Pl HAV PO15 ....271 H3
Suffolk Rd AND SP10 ....4 B5
  ENEY PO4 ....317 J5
  WCLF BH2 ....8 A3
Suffolk Rd South WBNE BH4 ....334 D2
Sulhamstead Hl THLE RG7 ....26 F5
Sulhamstead Rd THLE RG7 ....26 F5
Sullivan Cl CHAM PO6 ....296 A1
  FARN GU14 ....57 P9
Sullivan Rd CBLY GU15 ....49 H9
  ITCH SO19 ....249 H3
  KBH RG22 ....90 B3
Sultan Rd EMRTH PO10 ....277 M9
  NEND PO2 ....316 F1
Sumar Cl FHAM/STUB PO14 ....294 B4
Summercourt Wv FERN BH22 ....280 E6
Summer Down La TADY RG26 ....67 K7
Summer Fld WIMB BH21 ....301 K1
Summerfield Cl
  CHCH/BSGR BH23 ....324 C5
Summerfield Gdns
  ROWN SO16 ....228 F7
Summerfield La FARN GU14 ....116 A8
Summerfields CHIN RG24 ....52 B9
  FHAM/STUB PO14 ....271 H9
  LTDN BH7 ....323 M8
Summer Flds VWD BH31 ....258 C4
Summerhill Rd HORN PO8 ....255 P9
Summerlands Rd ELGH SO50 ....230 C2
Summerlands Wk HAV PO9 ....277 H5
Summer La BROC SO42 ....290 A8
Summerleaze Wk
  FHAM/STUB PO14 ....294 B4
Summerleg THLE RG7 ....35 P1
Summers Av BWD BH11 ....322 B1
Summers La
  CHCH/BSGR BH23 ....325 H6
Summers St SHAM SO14 ....248 D5
Summertrees Ct
  NMIL/BTOS BH25 ....327 M3
Summit Av FARN GU14 ....75 K1
Summit Wy WEND SO18 ....249 H2
Sumner Rd EPSF GU31 ....215 K8
  FNM GU9 ....96 C8
Sunbeam Wy GPORT PO12 ....12 C5
Sun Brow HASM GU27 ....156 E8
Sunbury Cl BOR GU35 ....154 B5
Sunbury Ct FHAM PO15 ....272 C6
Sunderland Dr
  CHCH/BSGR BH23 ....325 M8
Sunderland Pl NTHA RG18 ....25 M3
Sunderton La HAVN PO8 ....256 C8
Sundew Cl CHCH/BSGR BH23 ....325 N6
  NMIL/BTOS BH25 ....327 M3
Sundew Rd BDST BH18 ....320 A2
Sundridge Cl CHAM PO6 ....296 C1
Sunflower Cl KBH RG22 ....89 L4
Sun Gdns THLE RG7 ....27 J6
Sun Hill Crs NARL SO24 ....168 A3
Sun La NARL SO24 ....168 A3
  THLE RG7 ....37 N4
Sunley Cl NWBV RG14 ....24 A9
Sunningdale FAWY SO45 ....268 B8
Sunningdale Cl ELGH SO50 ....229 P2
  LSOL/BMARY PO13 ....294 G3
Sunningdale Crs NBNE BH10 ....322 C5
Sunningdale Gdns
  WEND SO18 ....249 K4
Sunningdale Rd
  FHAM/PORC PO16 ....295 P2
  HSEA PO3 ....317 J2
Sunnybank RAND SP11 ....101 L4
Sunnybank Rd FARN GU14 ....57 L7
  WIMB BH21 ....279 K8
Sunnyfield La AND SP10 * 116 A4
Sunnydown Rd FUFL SO22 ....183 J3
Sunnyfield Ri HLER SO31 ....270 A1
Sunnyfield Rd
  NMIL/BTOS BH25 ....327 J1
Sunnyheath HAV PO9 ....276 D6
Sunny Hill Rd ALDT GU11 ....46 B8
  BKME/WDN BH12 ....321 M7
Sunnyhill Rd SBNE BH6 ....335 P1
Sunnylands Av SBNE BH6 ....336 D2
Sunny Md DEAN RG25 ....48 H3
Sunnymead Dr DR WVILLE PO7 ....255 L9
Sunnymead Rd BWD BH11 ....322 A6
Sunnyside FLEETN GU51 ....74 B2
  KSCL RG20 * 7 M5
Sunnyside Cl AND SP10 * 82 B9
Sunnyside Rd
  BKME/WDN BH12 ....321 M6
  BOR GU35 ....155 J4
Sunny Vw ASHV GU12 ....13 J4
Sunny Wk PSEA PO1 ....18 E2
Sunny Wy TOTT SO40 ....246 D4
Sun Ray Est SHST GU47 ....41 J6
Sunridge Cl FAWY SO45 ....290 C1
Sunset Av TOTT SO40 ....246 C3
Sunset Rd TOTT SO40 ....246 C3
Sunshine Av HISD PO11 ....319 H6
Sun St PSEA PO1 ....18 D4
Suntrap Gdns HISD PO11 * 319 H4
Sunvale Av HASM GU27 ....156 C7
Sunvale Cl HASM GU27 ....156 C7
  ITCH SO19 ....13 J4
Sunwood Rd HAV PO9 ....276 D5
Surbiton Rd ELGH SO50 ....207 K8
Surrey Av CBLY GU15 ....57 P1
Surrey Cl CHCH/BSGR BH23 ....324 D5
  TOTT SO40 ....246 B6

Surrey Gdns WBNE BH4 ....334 C2
Surrey Rd BKME/WDN BH12 ....334 A1
  CHFD SO53 ....228 E1
  ITCH SO19 ....13 J4
Surrey Rd South WBNE BH4 ....334 C2
Surrey St PSEA PO1 ....19 G2
Sussex Border Pth
  EMRTH PO10 ....299 M6
  EPSF GU31 ....216 D8
  RFNM GU10 ....115 P6
Sussex Cl CHFD SO53 ....228 E1
Sussex Gdns EPSF GU31 ....215 M3
  FLEETN GU51 ....58 D3
Sussex Pl SSEA PO5 * 19 G7
Sussex Rd CHFD SO53 ....228 F1
  EPSF GU31 ....215 N3
  SHAM SO14 ....20 E4
  SSEA PO5 ....19 G7
Sussex St WINC SO23 ....22 F6
Sussex Ter SSEA PO5 * 19 G7
Sutcliffe Sq AND SP10 * 82 C8
Sutherland Av BDST BH18 ....300 A8
Sutherland Cl BOR GU35 ....154 A7
  ROMY SO51 ....204 F4
Sutherland Ct AND SP10 ....4 B1
Sutherland Rd ENEY PO4 ....316 G5
  ROMY SO51 ....227 K7
Sutherlands NWBV RG14 ....24 B8
Sutherlands Ct CHFD SO53 ....206 D6
Sutherlands Wy CHFD SO53 ....206 D6
Sutton Cl CFDH BH17 ....320 C7
  HORN PO8 ....255 M8
  HSEA PO3 ....297 K5
Sutton Fld BOR GU35 ....153 P7
Sutton Gdns WINC SO23 ....22 E4
Sutton Pl BROC SO42 ....286 G8
Sutton Rd BSTK RG21 ....69 J8
  HORN PO8 ....255 M8
  MOOR/WNTN BH9 ....323 H6
  NWBV RG14 ....24 A2
  TOTT SO40 ....246 B2
Sutton Wood La NARL SO24 ....149 H8
Swains Cl TADY RG26 ....34 C6
Swains Rd TADY RG26 ....34 C6
Swaledale Gdns FLEETN GU51 ....56 E9
Swale Dr CHFD SO53 ....206 C6
Swale Rd FARN GU14 ....57 L7
Swallow Cl ALTN GU34 ....132 C3
  CFDH BH17 ....320 B4
  FNM GU9 ....96 A4
  KBH RG22 ....89 K3
  NTID SP9 ....79 H5
  TOTT SO40 ....245 P5
  YTLY GU46 ....40 C8
Swallow Cl
  LSOL/BMARY PO13 ....314 D1
Swallow Dr LYMN SO41 ....339 J2
Swallowfields AND SP10 ....82 F9
Swallow Sq ELGH SO50 ....228 F2
Swallow Wy WIMB BH21 ....279 J6
Swallow Wd
  LSOL/BMARY PO13 ....314 C2
Swanage Cl ITCH SO19 ....248 G8
Swanage Rd
  LSOL/BMARY PO13 ....314 C2
Swan Barn Rd HASM GU27 ....157 J7
Swan Cl RFNM GU10 ....299 N2
  HLER SO31 ....270 E9
Swancote FHAM/PORC PO16 ....295 K1
Swan Ct AND SP10 ....4 E4
  HTWY RG27 ....55 J7
  NWBV RG14 * 16 D2
Swan La SHST GU47 ....41 J1
  WINC SO23 ....48 C8
Swanley Cl ELGH SO50 ....207 J8
Swanmore Av ITCH SO19 ....249 K8
Swanmore Cl FUFL SO22 ....164 D3
Swanmore Rd BPWT SO32 ....232 D5
  HAV PO9 ....276 D3
  LTDN BH7 ....323 P9
Swansbury Dr CHAR BH8 ....323 N5
Swan St KSCL RG20 ....48 B4
  PSF GU32 ....215 L2
Swans Wk HISD PO11 * 319 H5
Swanton Gdns CHFD SO53 * 206 D6
Swan Wy FLEETN GU51 ....74 A5
Swanwick La HLER SO31 ....270 E2
Swanwick Shore Rd
  HLER SO31 ....270 D3
Swanwick Cl BWD BH11 ....321 P3
Swarraton Rd HAV PO9 ....276 G6
Sway Ct HAV PO9 * 277 H5
Sway Gdns CHAR BH8 ....323 N5
Sway Rd BROC SO42 ....308 F1
  LYMN SO41 ....307 M9
  LYMN SO41 ....328 C2
  NMIL/BTOS BH25 ....327 K1
Swaything Rd HAV PO9 ....276 D6
  HEND SO30 ....249 K1
Swedish Houses TADY RG26 ....34 C6
The Sweep RGWD BH24 ....282 D2
Sweetbriar Gdns WVILLE PO7 ....275 P5
Sweethills Crs HLER SO31 ....271 H2
Sweetzer's Piece THLE RG7 ....26 G9
Swelling Hl ALTN GU34 ....170 B1
Sweyns Lease BROC SO42 ....310 G2
Swift Cl AND SP10 ....82 F9
  CFDH BH17 ....320 B4
  ELGH SO50 ....228 F2
  HORN PO8 ....255 M8
Swift Gdns ITCH SO19 ....268 F1
Swift Hollow ITCH SO19 ....268 F1
Swift Rd EMRTH PO10 ....299 N6
  FNM GU9 ....96 B4
  ITCH SO19 ....268 G1

Swift's Cl RFNM GU10 ....117 H1
Swinburn Gdns HORN PO8 ....255 P7
Swincombe Ri WEND SO18 ....249 K2
Swingate Rd FNM GU9 ....116 C2
Swing Swang La CHIN RG24 ....69 P5
Swiss Cl RFNM GU10 ....115 P6
Swiss Rd WVILLE PO7 ....275 N3
Switchback La RFNM GU10 ....115 P6
Swivelton La WHAM PO17 ....273 L7
Sword Ct GPORT PO12 ....315 J6
  HORN PO8 ....236 B7
Swordfish Dr
  CHCH/BSGR BH23 ....325 M8
Swordfish Wy FARN GU14 ....75 M5
Sword Sands Rd HSEA PO3 ....317 L1
Swordsman's Rd FARN GU14 ....59 J5
Sycamore Av CHFD SO53 ....206 E4
Sycamore Cl CFDH BH17 ....320 B3
  CHCH/BSGR BH23 ....324 B7
  FHAM/STUB PO14 ....271 J9
  FRIM GU16 ....58 D4
  HLER SO31 ....269 N8
  HORN PO8 ....255 N8
  LSOL/BMARY PO13 ....295 J8
  LYMN SO41 ....338 F1
  NBAD SO52 ....205 K8
  NTID SP9 ....79 J5
  RDCW/BURGH RG30 ....27 K2
  ROMY SO51 ....204 C7
  SHST GU47 ....41 J7
Sycamore Crs FLEETN GU51 ....74 B6
Sycamore Dr ASHV GU12 ....76 E5
  FAWY SO45 ....290 D4
  FRIM GU16 ....58 D5
  HISD PO11 ....318 E4
  RFNM GU10 ....117 J8
  WINC SO23 ....145 J8
Sycamore Pl WIMB BH21 ....279 M9
Sycamore Rd NWBV RG14 ....24 F1
Sycamore Rd BPWT SO32 ....232 C4
  FARN GU14 ....58 C2
  FAWY SO45 ....268 B7
  LYMN SO41 ....338 C3
  ROWN SO16 ....247 L1
The Sycamores BLKW GU17 ....41 H7
  FARN GU14 ....76 C1
Sycamore Wk AND SP10 ....102 B4
Sycamore Wy DEAN RG23 ....68 G3
Sydenham Ter PSEA PO1 ....19 G3
The Sydings NWBV RG14 ....24 A2
Sydling Cl CFDH BH17 ....321 K2
Sydmanton Cl ROMY SO51 ....204 E7
Sydmonton Ct HAV PO9 ....15 K6
Sydney Av HLER SO31 ....269 N7
Sydney Cl STHA RG19 ....25 P4
Sydney Loader Pl BLKW GU17 * 41 H8
Sydney Rd BDST BH18 ....320 C1
  BOR GU35 ....154 A5
  CHCH/BSGR BH23 ....324 C6
  ELGH SO50 ....207 M9
  GPORT PO12 ....12 D2
  WSHM SO15 ....247 M2
Sydney Smith Av FARN GU14 ....76 A3
Sylmor Gdns
  MOOR/WNTN BH9 ....322 G5
Sylvan Av ITCH SO19 ....249 L5
Sylvan Cl LYMN SO41 ....328 B5
  RGWD BH24 ....281 K5
Sylvan Dr NBAD SO52 ....205 K9
Sylvan La HLER SO31 ....270 A8
Sylvan Rdg SHST GU47 ....41 H5
Sylvan Rd BKME/WDN BH12 ....321 K6
The Sylvans FAWY SO45 ....267 P7
Sylvan Vw WVILLE PO7 ....275 P4
Sylvan Wy FLEETS GU52 ....74 B7
Sylvester Cl NWBV RG14 ....24 B2
Sylvia Cl BSTK RG21 ....69 K9
Sylvia Crs TOTT SO40 ....246 C2
Symes Rd PLE BH15 ....320 A8
  ROMY SO51 ....204 F6
Symonds Cl CHFD SO53 ....206 F9
Symonds St WINC SO23 ....22 E6
Sympson Rd TADY RG26 ....34 E5
Syon Pl FARN GU14 ....58 C9
Sywell Crs HSEA PO3 ....297 K5

T

Tadburn Cl CHFD SO53 ....206 F8
  ROMY SO51 ....204 E6
Tadburn Rd ROMY SO51 * 204 C7
Tadburn Rd ROMY SO51 ....204 E7
Tadden Wk BDST BH18 ....320 B2
Tadfield Rd ROMY SO51 ....204 E7
Tadham Pl STHA RG19 ....25 M5
Tadley Cl FLEETN GU51 ....56 B4
Tadley Common Rd
  TADY RG26 ....34 D5
Tadley Hi TADY RG26 ....34 C4
Tadpole La RFNM GU10 ....95 M2
Tagdell La HORN PO8 ....255 P5
Taeping St STOK SO20 ....120 C4
Tai Cl AND SP10 * 58 D5
Taplin Dr HEND SO30 ....250 A9
Tait Pl LSOL/BMARY PO13 ....295 H8
Talbot Av TWDS BH3 ....322 E8
Talbot Cl FRIM GU16 ....58 F3
  HAV PO9 ....14 A2
  NWBV RG14 ....16 E8
Talbot Ct NMIL/BTOS BH25 ....326 B6
Talbot Dr BKME/WDN BH12 ....322 B7
  CHCH/BSGR BH23 ....326 B5
Talbot Hill Rd
  MOOR/WNTN BH9 ....322 D7
Talbot Mdw
  BKME/WDN BH12 ....322 B7
Talbot Ms NBNE BH10 ....322 C6
Talbot Ri BKME/WDN BH12 ....322 C6
Talbot Rd ENEY PO4 ....316 G5
  FAWY SO45 ....267 P9
  FHAM PO15 ....271 L8

FNM GU9 116 B2
HAV PO9 14 B2
MOOR/WNTN BH9 322 E7
Talgarth Dr FARN GU14 76 C2
Talisman Cl CWTH RG45 40 E1
Talland Rd FHAM/STUB PO14 271 H9
Tallis Gdns KBH RG22 90 A2
Talmey Cl CHIN RG24 69 P1
Tamar Cl FERN BH22 302 G3
FHAM/PORC PO16 273 L9
Tamar Down WVILLE PO7 276 A3
Tamar Dr DEAN RG23 88 F2
Tamar Gv FAWY SO45 268 A7
Tamarisk Cl ENEY PO4 317 L5
FHAM/STUB PO14 294 A9
KBH RG22 89 N6
WVILLE PO7 276 A5
Tamarisk Gdns WEND SO18 248 G3
Tamarisk Rd HEND SO30 250 B4
Tamella Rd HEND SO30 250 E5
Tammys Turn
FHAM/STUB PO14 293 P1
Tamorisk Dr TOTT SO40 246 A5
Tamworth Dr FLEETN GU51 56 E9
Tamworth Pl GPORT PO12 12 D4
Tamworth Rd HSEA PO3 317 J2
LTDN BH7 335 M1
Tanfield La WHAM PO17 252 D8
Tanfield Pk WHAM PO17 252 D8
Tangier Ct ALDT GU11 2 B3
Tangier La BPWT SO32 231 N4
Tangier Rd HSEA PO3 317 J1
Tanglewood
FHAM/PORC PO16 10 E1
TOTT SO40 267 L1
Tanglewood Cl WVILLE PO7 275 L6
Tangley Wk HAV PO9 * 277 H5
Tangmere Cl
CHCH/BSGR BH23 325 M9
Tangmere Dr ROWN SO16 227 K8
Tangway CHIN RG24 52 A9
Tangyes Cl FHAM/STUB PO14 294 B6
Tanhouse Cl HEND SO30 250 C6
Tanhouse La ALTN GU34 132 E5
HEND SO30 250 D7
Tan Howse Cl LTDN BH7 323 P7
Tankerdale La PSF GU32 192 A6
Tanker Rd FARN GU14 76 A3
Tankerton Cl CHAM PO6 296 C1
Tankerville Rd ITCH SO19 248 F8
Tank Rd CBLY GU15 41 N9
The Tanneries
FHAM/STUB PO14 * 293 N1
HAV PO9 * 14 E6
Tanner's Brook Wy
WSHM SO15 247 K5
Tanners Cl THLE RG7 27 H6
Tanners La FBDG SP6 219 M9
FHAM/STUB PO14 294 C3
HASM GU27 157 H6
LYMN SO41 330 E3
ROMY SO51 203 K6
WVILLE PO7 255 H6
Tanner's Rdg WVILLE PO7 275 N7
Tanners Rd NBAD SO52 205 L9
The Tanners
FHAM/STUB PO14 293 J1
Tanner St WINC SO23 23 F5
Tanners Wy DEAN RG23 88 F1
Tansy Cl WVILLE PO7 276 A4
Tansy Meadow CHFD SO53 206 B9
The Tanyards CHFD SO53 206 D4
Taplin Dr HEND SO30 250 C3
Taplings Cl FUFL SO22 164 E4
Taplings Rd FUFL SO22 164 E4
Taplin's Farm La HTWY RG27 73 K1
Taranto Rd ROWN SO16 227 N8
Tarbat Ct SHST GU47 41 L6
Tarbery Crs HORN PO8 256 C4
Target Rd NEND PO2 296 E6
Tarius Cl LSOL/BMARY PO13 295 H7
Tarleton Rd CHAM PO6 274 D9
Tarn Cl FARN GU14 75 M2
Tarn Dr CFDH BH17 320 B3
Tarn Howes Cl STHA RG19 25 K4
Tarn La NWBY RG14 16 C7
Tarn Ri HORN PO8 256 C1
Tarn Rd GSHT GU26 156 C2
Tarragon Cl FARN GU14 57 K9
Tarragon Wy THLE RG7 27 K5
Tarrant Cl CFDH BH17 320 C2
Tarrant Gdns HAV PO9 14 C2
Tarrant Rd MOOR/WNTN BH9 323 H4
Taskers Dr RAND SP11 102 A5
Tasman Cl CHCH/BSGR BH23 324 D7
SHAM SO14 248 D9
Tasman Ct SHAM SO14 248 D9
Tasmania Cl CHIN RG24 69 M2
Taswell Rd SSEA PO5 316 F6
Tatchbury La TOTT SO40 245 M2
Tate Rd WSHM SO15 246 G3
Tate Sq AND SP10 * 82 G8
Tates Rd FAWY SO45 268 D8
Tatnam Rd PLE BH15 320 E8
Tattenham Rd BROC SO42 286 F9
Tattershall Crs
FHAM/PORC PO16 295 M2
Tatwin Cl ITCH SO19 249 M6
Tatwin Crs ITCH SO19 249 M6
Taunton Dr WEND SO18 249 K4
Tavells Cl TOTT SO40 267 J1
Tavell's La TOTT SO40 267 J1
Taverner Cl BSTK RG21 7 J2
PLE BH15 332 F2
Taverners Cl ITCH SO19 249 M8
Tavistock Cl ROMY SO51 204 F4
Tavistock Gdns FARN GU14 58 A6
HAV PO9 15 K6
Tavistock Rd FLEETN GU51 74 B4
Tavy Cl CHFD SO53 206 D7
Taw Dr CHFD SO53 206 D6
Tawny Gv ALTN GU34 150 B6
Tawny Owl Cl
FHAM/STUB PO14 293 P5
Tawny Rw SHST GU47 * 41 L6
Tay Cl FARN GU14 57 M7
Taylor Dr CHAR BH8 323 K3
TADY RG26 52 C3
Taylor's Buildings PLE BH15 332 E2
Taylors Cl BOR GU35 154 C3
Taylors La BOR GU35 154 C3
Taylor Wy VWD BH31 258 G4
Teachers Wy FAWY SO45 290 D5
Teal Cl FHAM/PORC PO16 295 K1
HISD PO11 319 H5
HORN PO8 256 A4
TOTT SO40 246 A4
Teal Crs KBH RG22 89 K4
Teasel Cl RAND SP11 79 P2
Teasel Wy FERN BH22 280 E8
Teazle Cl EPSF GU31 216 A3
Tebourba Dr GPORT PO12 12 A5
Tebourba Wy WSHM SO15 247 K4
Technology Rd CFDH BH17 320 C3
Tedder Cl BWD BH11 322 B4
RAND SP11 101 P3
Tedder Rd BWD BH11 322 B4
LSOL/BMARY PO13 295 H6
WEND SO18 249 J3
Tedder Wy TOTT SO40 246 B4
Teddington Rd ENEY PO4 317 J4
Tees Cl CHFD SO53 206 C6
FARN GU14 57 M7
Teg Down Meads FUFL SO22 164 C6
Tegg Down Rd NARL SO24 169 H4
Teignmouth Rd GPORT PO12 315 K1
HSEA PO3 297 J9
Tekels Av CBLY GU15 58 C1
Tekels Wy CBLY GU15 58 E2
Telconia Cl BOR GU35 155 K4
Telegraph La ALTN GU34 150 E5
Telegraph Rd HEND SO30 249 N3
Telegraph Wy RWIN SO21 166 A8
Telephone Rd ENEY PO4 316 G4
Telford Gdns HEND SO30 250 E1
Telford Rd BSTK RG21 69 H5
NEND PO2 296 G6
WIMB BH21 280 A9
Telford Wy FHAM PO15 271 J5
Teme Crs ROWN SO16 247 J3
Teme Rd ROWN SO16 247 J3
Tempest Av WVILLE PO7 276 B1
Templar Cl SHST GU47 41 H6
Templars Mede CHFD SO53 228 D1
Templars Wy CHFD SO53 206 B9
Templecombe Rd ELGH SO50 229 P3
Temple Gdns ITCH SO19 249 H9
Temple La PSF GU32 213 M5
Templemere
FHAM/STUB PO14 294 A2
Temple Ms BMTH BH1 * 323 K9
Templer Av FARN GU14 75 P3
Templer Cl BKME/WDN BH12 321 P3
Temple Rd ITCH SO19 249 H9
LISS GU33 173 M9
Temple's Cl RFNM GU10 117 J1
Temple St PSEA PO1 19 H1
Templeton Cl NEND PO2 * 296 G6
Tenby Cl WEND SO18 249 J3
Tenby Dr CHFD SO53 206 C9
Tenby Rd FRIM GU16 58 F5
Tench Wy ROMY SO51 204 D5
Tennyson Cl BPWT SO32 232 C4
FAWY SO45 290 D4
Tennyson Crs WVILLE PO7 275 M1
Tennyson Gdns
FHAM/PORC PO16 10 E4
Tennyson Rd ELGH SO50 229 H2
MOOR/WNTN BH9 322 F5
NEND PO2 297 H9
NTHA RG18 25 M3
PSTN BH14 321 J9
PTSW SO17 248 D3
TOTT SO40 246 B1
WIMB BH21 278 E8
Tennyson's La HASM GU27 157 K9
Tennyson Wy KBH RG22 69 H9
Tensing Cl FHAM/PORC PO16 10 E1
Tensing Rd CHCH/BSGR BH23 325 J8
Tenterton Av ITCH SO19 269 K1
Terence Av CFDH BH17 320 E3
Terminus Ter SHAM SO14 21 G7
Tern Cl FAWY SO45 268 D8
KBH RG22 89 K4
Tern Ct SBNE BH6 324 B9
Tern Wk ENEY PO4 317 K3
Terrace Rd WCLF BH2 8 C4
The Terrace CBLY GU15 41 N9
CWTH RG45 41 L1
FARN GU14 * 76 C1
Terrier Cl HEND SO30 230 C9
Terrington Av
CHCH/BSGR BH23 326 A6
Terriote Cl CHFD SO53 206 E6
Terry Cl DEAN RG23 89 K7
Tesimond Dr YTLY GU46 40 B9
Tess Farm Rd RWIN SO21 207 P5
Testbourne Av TOTT SO40 246 B4
Testbourne Cl TOTT SO40 246 B4
Testbourne Rd TOTT SO40 246 B4
Test Cl PSF GU32 215 L4
Testcombe Rd GPORT PO12 12 B5
Testlands Av ROWN SO16 227 H6
Test La ROWN SO16 226 F9
Test Ms WHCH RG28 85 L6
Test Mills ROMY SO51 * 204 B5
Test Ri STOK SO20 123 L6
Test Rd SHAM SO14 268 D2
WHCH RG28 85 L7
Test Wy BSTK RG21 7 J6
MARL SN8 43 K1
RAND SP11 84 A1
RAND SP11 84 C2
RAND SP11 104 B2
RAND SP11 104 B4
RAND SP11 123 K1
ROMY SO51 179 L3
ROMY SO51 203 N3
STOK SO20 161 H6
TOTT SO40 246 E2
Testwood Av TOTT SO40 246 C2
Testwood Crs TOTT SO40 246 B1
Testwood La TOTT SO40 246 D2
Testwood Pl TOTT SO40 246 E3
Testwood Rd HAV PO9 276 D5
WSHM SO15 247 M5
Tethering Dro FBDG SP6 221 P1
Tetney Cl ROWN SO16 227 J9
Teviot Rd CHFD SO53 206 C8
Tewkesbury Av FHAM PO15 272 A7
GPORT PO12 315 L1
Tewkesbury Cl CHIN RG24 69 L3
CHAM PO6 296 F1
Texas Dr FUFL SO22 183 K4
Thackeray Ml
FHAM/PORC PO16 11 J5
Thackeray Rd PTSW SO17 248 D3
Thackham's La HTWY RG27 54 E8
The Thakerays STHA RG19 25 N5
Thames Cl FARN GU14 57 M7
FERN BH22 302 G2
WEND SO18 249 K1
Thames Ct AND SP10 83 H9
BSTK RG21 7 K6
Thames Dr FHAM PO15 272 B6
Thamesmead Cl GPORT PO12 315 K1
Thames Ms PLE BH15 * 332 D2
Thames Rd NTHA RG18 25 L2
Thames St PLE BH15 332 D2
Thatched Cottage Pk
LYND SO43 * 265 H4
Thatchers La
CHCH/BSGR BH23 305 H7
LYMN SO41 310 D8
Theal Cl SHST GU47 41 L6
Theale Rd RDGW/BURGH RG30 27 K1
Theatre Ms SSEA PO5 316 F6
Theatre Rd FARN GU14 76 A4
Theobalds Wy FRIM GU16 59 H2
Theobold Rd
CHCH/BSGR BH23 303 N8
Theseus Rd
LSOL/BMARY PO13 314 B1
Thetchers Cl
NMIL/BTOS BH25 327 K2
Thetford Gdns CHFD SO53 206 C6
Thetford Rd
BKME/WDN BH12 321 P6
Thibet Rd SHST GU47 41 K6
The Thicket
FHAM/PORC PO16 273 K9
LSOL/BMARY PO13 295 J8
ROMY SO51 204 G7
SSEA PO5 * 19 J7
WVILLE PO7 275 M8
Third Av CHAM PO6 296 G1
HAV PO9 15 J4
WSHM SO15 247 K5
Third St East STHA RG19 31 M1
Thirlmere ELGH SO50 229 H2
Thirlmere Cl BOR GU35 154 A3
FARN GU14 57 M9
FHAM/STUB PO14 294 B5
Thirlmere Crs FLEETS GU52 74 B7
Thirlmere Rd ROWN SO16 247 J1
Thirlstane Firs CHFD SO53 206 D9
Thirsk Ct ASHV GU12 3 K2
Thirt Wy STOK SO20 123 N8
Thistlebarrow Rd LTDN BH7 323 L9
Thistledown HORN PO8 256 B6
Thistledown Cl AND SP10 102 C1
Thistledowne Gdns
EMRTH PO10 299 P1
Thistle Rd CHFD SO53 206 B8
HEND SO30 250 B5
Thomas Cl TOTT SO40 246 B5
Thomas Lewis Wy
PTSW SO17 248 E2
Thomas Merriman Ct
NWBY RG14 * 16 E3
Thomas Rd NBAD SO52 205 L9
Thompson Dr STHA RG19 25 P5
Thompson's La RWIN SO21 208 F6
WVILLE PO7 254 E6
Thorburn Cha SHST GU47 41 M8
Thoresby Ct NMIL/BTOS BH25 326 G4
Thornbrake Rd GPORT PO12 13 F4
Thornbury Av FAWY SO45 290 G9
WSHM SO15 248 A4
Thornbury Cl CWTH RG45 41 J1
FHAM/STUB PO14 294 A1
Thornbury Hts CHFD SO53 207 H4
Thornbury Rd SBNE BH6 336 E2
Thornbury Wd CHFD SO53 207 H4
Thorncliffe Cl NEND PO2 297 H5
Thorn Cl ELGH SO50 207 J8
EPSF GU31 216 A3
RFNM GU10 115 P6
Thorncombe Cl CFDH BH17 320 G3
Thorn Ct ALTN GU34 150 C6
Thorn Crs ALTN GU34 150 C6
Thorncroft Rd PSEA PO1 316 G3
Thorndike Cl ROWN SO16 247 L1
Thorn Dr ALTN GU34 150 C6
Thorne Cl VWD BH31 258 E3
Thorneley Rd KSCL RG20 48 C3
Thorness Cl ROWN SO16 246 G2
Thorney Cl FHAM/STUB PO14 294 B1
Thorney Rd EMRTH PO10 299 P4
Thorney Vw HISD PO11 * 299 J7
Thornfield STHA RG19 32 A3
Thornfield Dr
CHCH/BSGR BH23 326 B6
Thornfield Gn BLKW GU17 57 N2
Thornford Rd STHA RG19 31 N2
Thorngate RSAL SP5 * 159 H7
Thorngate Wy GPORT PO12 13 H2
Thornham La EMRTH PO10 299 P3
Thornham Rd
NMIL/BTOS BH25 327 M4
Thornhill Av ITCH SO19 249 M5
Thornhill Cl FAWY SO45 291 H7
Thornhill Park Rd
WEND SO18 249 M4
Thornhill Rd ALDT GU11 76 C8
FAWY SO45 291 H7
ROWN SO16 227 P8
Thornhill Vw GSHT GU26 * 156 C2
Thornhill Wy CHIN RG24 52 B9
Thorni Av FHAM PO15 272 A7
Thorn La ALTN GU34 150 D6
Thornleigh Rd ITCH SO19 248 G9
Thornley Rd NBNE BH10 322 D3
Thorn Rd CFDH BH17 320 E1
RFNM GU10 115 P6
Thorns La LYMN SO41 311 K9
Thornton Av HLER SO31 270 C9
Thornton Cl CHAM PO6 275 K8
TADY RG26 52 C3
Thornton End ALTN GU34 133 J3
Thornton Rd GPORT PO12 295 M9
Thornycroft Av ITCH SO19 248 F9
Thornycroft Rbt KBH RG22 69 H7
Thornyhurst Rd FRIM GU16 58 F9
Thorold Rd CHFD SO53 206 G4
FNM GU9 96 C8
WEND SO18 248 G2
Thorpe Gdns ALTN GU34 132 D5
Threadgill Wy NTID SP9 98 E3
Three Acre Dr
NMIL/BTOS BH25 327 H7
Three Acre Rd NWBY RG14 24 C7
Three Acres WVILLE PO7 255 J8
Three Castles Pth HTWY RG27 39 K9
NARL SO24 130 B3
NARL SO24 148 A1
ODIM RG29 92 F1
OVTN RG25 92 A2
RWIN SO21 147 H8
RWIN SO21 165 K3
Three Cross Rd WIMB BH21 280 E3
Threefield La SHAM SO14 21 F6
Three Firs Wy THLE RG7 26 G6
Three Gates La HASM GU27 157 J6
Three Horse Shoes La
ALTN GU34 188 G4
Three Oaks ITCH SO19 249 N6
Three Stiles Rd FNM GU9 95 P8
Three Tun Cl PSEA PO1 18 D3
Thresher Cl HORN PO8 276 C1
Threshers Cnr FLEETN GU51 56 F9
Throgmorton Rd YTLY GU46 40 B9
Throop Cl CHAR BH8 323 N5
Throop Rd CHAR BH8 323 L3
Throopside Av
MOOR/WNTN BH9 323 K3
Thrush Cl KBH RG22 89 K3
THLE RG7 27 K4
Thrush Rd BKME/WDN BH12 321 L3
Thrush Wk HORN PO8 255 N8
Thruxton Ct ITCH SO19 248 G6
Thruxton Rd HAV PO9 276 C5
Thuillier Rd RWIN SO21 104 F8
Thumwood CHIN RG24 70 A1
Thundery Hl RFNM GU10 97 M7
Thurbans Rd FNM GU9 116 A3
Thurbern Rd NEND PO2 296 G7
Thurmell Cl HEND SO30 250 C7
Thurmond Crs FUFL SO22 164 D9
Thurmond Rd FUFL SO22 164 D9
Thursby Rd CHCH/BSGR BH23 326 B5
Thursley Rd MFD/CHID GU8 137 P4
RFNM GU10 137 J6
Thurston Cl CHFD SO53 206 F6
Thurstons ALTN GU34 134 C3
Thwaite Rd BKME/WDN BH12 334 B1
Thyme Av FHAM PO15 271 K2
Thyme Cl CHIN RG24 52 B9
Thyme Ct FARN GU14 57 K8
Tiberius Cl DEAN RG23 68 F5
Tiberius Rd AND SP10 82 F8
Tichborne Cl BLKW GU17 41 L9
Tichborne Down NARL SO24 167 P4
Tichborne Gv HAV PO9 276 D5
Tichborne Pl ASHV GU12 3 K7
Tichborne Rd ELGH SO50 229 H4
WEND SO18 249 M3
Tichborne Wy
LSOL/BMARY PO13 295 H8
Tichbourne Cl FRIM GU16 58 E2
Tickleford Dr ITCH SO19 269 J2
Tickner Cl HEND SO30 250 E6
Ticonderoga Gdns ITCH SO19 268 G1
Tidemill Cl CHCH/BSGR BH23 324 F7
Tides Reach WEND SO18 248 F3
Tides Wy TOTT SO40 247 K9
Tideway Gdns ENEY PO4 317 L4
Tidworth Rd AMSY SP4 98 B4
HAV PO9 276 F6
RAND SP11 79 M2
Tiffany Cl LYMN SO41 327 P3
Tiffield Cl HSEA PO3 297 L5
Tiger Moth Cl
LSOL/BMARY PO13 314 E2
Tigwells Fld ODIM RG29 92 G7
Tilbrook Rd WSHM SO15 247 L3
Tilburg Rd CHCH/BSGR BH23 325 H8
Tilbury's Cl BOR GU35 154 A5
Tilden Rd RWIN SO21 183 L9
Tile Barn Cl FARN GU14 57 P7
Tilebarn La BROC SO42 308 G1
Tilford Rd FNM GU9 116 D1
HORN PO8 255 P5
RFNM GU10 117 J7
Tilford St RFNM GU10 117 J7
Tillington Gdns HORN PO8 236 D8
Tilmore Gdns PSF GU32 191 M9
Tilmore Rd PSF GU32 215 L1
Tilney Cl ALTN GU34 132 E5
Timber Bank FRIM GU16 58 F8
Timber Cl FNM GU9 * 96 B9
Timbercroft Cl ALTN GU34 150 B7
Timberlake Rd BSTK RG21 6 E6
Timberlane WVILLE PO7 275 M6
Timberley La RSAL SP5 200 C7
Timberley Pl CWTH RG45 40 F2
Timberly Cl FAWY SO45 290 E5
Timbermill Ct HASM GU27 156 E7
The Timbers FHAM PO15 272 A9
Timor Cl CHIN RG24 69 M3
HLER SO31 271 H2
Timothy Cl NBNE BH10 322 D2
Timpson Rd PSEA PO1 316 G2
Timsbury Crs HAV PO9 14 D2
Timsbury Dr ROWN SO16 247 K1
Timson Cl TOTT SO40 246 A5
Tincleton Gdns
MOOR/WNTN BH9 323 H3
Tindal Cl YTLY GU46 40 E8
Tindale Rd ROWN SO16 247 J1
Tinker Aly ELGH SO50 229 J5
Tinley Gdns ODIM RG29 72 E9
Tinneys Cl RSAL SP5 199 P9
Tintagel Cl AND SP10 82 E8
DEAN RG23 68 F6
Tintagel Dr FRIM GU16 58 E4
Tintagel Wy CHAM PO6 296 D2
Tintern Cl CHIN RG24 69 J4
CHAM PO6 274 B9
Tintern Gv WSHM SO15 20 A2
Tintern Rd GPORT PO12 12 B2
Tipner Gn NEND PO2 296 E6
Tipner La NEND PO2 296 E6
Tipner Rd NEND PO2 296 E7
Tippet Gdns KBH RG22 90 B3
Tiptoe Rd NMIL/BTOS BH25 307 L7
Tiptree Cl ELGH SO50 207 J8
Tisbury Cl FLEETN GU51 74 B1
Tisted Ct HAV PO9 * 277 H5
Titchfield Cl TADY RG26 34 D7
Titchfield Hl
FHAM/STUB PO14 293 N1
Titchfield La FHAM PO15 272 A2
Titchfield Park Rd
FHAM PO15 271 K7
Titchfield Rd
FHAM/STUB PO14 293 N2
Tithe Barn LYMN SO41 329 L2
Tithelands La NARL SO24 188 B2
Tithe Md ROMY SO51 204 D4
Tithe Meadow KBH RG22 89 N6
The Tithe WVILLE PO7 255 H8
Tithewood Cl CHFD SO53 206 D3
Tittymouse La RAND SP11 81 J9
Titus Gdns WVILLE PO7 276 A2
Tiverton Rd DEAN RG23 68 F7
Tivoli Cl CHFD SO53 207 H6
Toad La BLKW GU17 57 M1
Tobago Cl CHIN RG24 69 L3
Tobruk Cl RAND SP11 82 F4
Tobruk Rd RAND SP11 79 M5
Toby St PSEA PO1 19 G1
Todber Cl BWD BH11 321 M1
Todmore LISS GU33 173 L4
Tokar St ENEY PO4 317 J6
Tokio Rd HSEA PO3 297 J8
Toledo Gv AND SP10 5 G1
Tolefrey Gdns CHFD SO53 206 B7
Tollard Cl BKME/WDN BH12 321 N4
Tollbar Wy HEND SO30 250 A3
Tollerford Rd CFDH BH17 320 F2
Tollgate CHFD SO53 228 E2
Tollgate Cl DEAN RG23 67 N9
Tollgate Rd AND SP10 102 C1
HLER SO31 270 D2
Tollway CHIN RG24 70 B1
Tolpuddle Gdns
MOOR/WNTN BH9 323 H3
Tolpuddle Wy YTLY GU46 40 G9
Tolstoi Rd PSTN BH14 321 J6
Tomkyns Cl CHFD SO53 206 B7
Tomlin Cl STHA RG19 25 P5
Tomlins Av FRIM GU16 58 E3
Tomlins Cl TADY RG26 34 C7
Tomlinscote Wy FRIM GU16 58 F3
Tommy Green Wk ELGH SO15 229 H1
Toms La RGWD BH24 261 L2
Tonbridge St SSEA PO5 316 E6
Tonge Rd BWD BH11 322 B1
Tongham Mdw RFNM GU10 97 L4
Tongham Rd ASHV GU12 3 K7
Tonnant Cl FHAM/STUB PO14 294 B8
Toogoods Wy ROWN SO16 227 H7
Toomer Cl FAWY SO45 291 H7
Toomers Whf NWBY RG14 * 16 E2
Toothill Rd ROMY SO51 226 G3
Topaz Gv WVILLE PO7 276 B2
Topiary Gdns HLER SO31 271 H6
The Topiary CHIN RG24 70 B4
FARN GU14 75 M1
PSTN BH14 321 H7
Toplady Pl FNM GU9 96 C4
Top La RGWD BH24 282 E2
Top Terrace Rd FARN GU14 75 P4
Torbay Rd PSTN BH14 321 L9
Torberry Dr EPSF GU31 215 P3
Torch Cl ELGH SO50 230 B2
Tor Cl FHAM/PORC PO16 273 J9
WVILLE PO7 275 P7
Torcross Cl ITCH SO19 248 G9
Torfrida Ct ENEY PO4 317 L5
Tormead FAWY SO45 268 B7
Tornay Gv NBAD SO52 205 K9
Toronto Pl GPORT PO12 12 D1
Toronto Rd NEND PO2 316 G1
Torquay Av GPORT PO12 295 L9
WSHM SO15 247 N3
Torque Cl ITCH SO19 249 N7
Torre Cl ELGH SO50 207 J7
Torridge Gdns WEND SO18 229 K9
Torrington Cl BOR GU35 * 154 D3
ITCH SO19 249 J7
Torrington Rd NEND PO2 296 G6
Tor Rd FNM GU9 95 P9
Tortworth Cl
FHAM/STUB PO14 294 B1
Tor Wy EPSF GU31 215 N2
Torwood Gdns ELGH SO50 229 P2
Tosson Cl ROWN SO16 * 247 J3
Totland Cl FARN GU14 57 P7
ROWN SO16 247 J3
Totland Rd CHAM PO6 296 G2
LSOL/BMARY PO13 294 G7
Totmel Rd CFDH BH17 321 J2
Totnes Cl ELGH SO50 207 H8

Tottehale Cl NBAD SO52 ......227 K1
Tottenham Cl TADY RG26 ......52 A1
Tottenham Rd PSEA PO1 ......316 G2
Tottenham Wk SHST GU47 ......41 L5
Totterdown THLE RG7 ......71 H6
Totters La HTWY RG27 ......72 E3
Totton By-Pass TOTT SO40 ......246 E5
Tournai Cl ALDT GU11 ......76 D5
Tournerbury La HISD PO11 ......318 G4
Tourney Rd BWD BH11 ......301 M7
Tovey Cl AND SP11 ......5 K2
Tovey Pl WINC SO23 ......145 K8
Tower Cl AND SP10 ......82 B8
　　GPORT PO12 ......315 H5
Tower Gdns HAV PO9 ......298 F3
Tower Hl FARN GU14 ......76 F6
Tower La ELGH SO50 ......229 L2
　　WIMB BH21 ......278 F8
Tower Pl HEND SO30 ......249 M2
Tower Rd BMTH BH1 ......335 L1
　　CCLF BH13 ......334 B5
　　GSHT GU26 ......156 D1
　　LIPH GU30 ......175 J5
　　WINC SO23 ......22 D4
Tower Rd West CCLF BH13 ......334 A5
Towers Dr CWTH RG45 ......41 J2
Tower St ALTN GU34 ......132 E7
　　EMRTH PO10 ......299 N1
　　PSEA PO1 ......18 B6
　　WINC SO23 ......22 D4
Town Centre East Jct
　　CHIN RG24 ......69 P6
Town Cl NARL SO24 ......169 N3
Towngate Br PLE BH15 ......332 E1
Towngate Ms RGWD BH24 * 282 C3
Town Hall Rd HAV PO9 ......14 E5
Townhill Wy WEND SO18 ......249 J3
Town La EPSF SO21 ......191 P9
Town Mill La WHCH RG28 ......85 M6
Town Mills NWBY RG14 * 16 E2
Town Quay SHAM SO14 ......248 B9
Townsend Cl BSTK RG21 ......6 B7
　　BWD BH11 ......322 B1
Townsend La FBDC SP6 ......195 N5
Townsville Rd
　　MOOR/WNTN BH9 ......323 H5
Towpath Md ENEY PO4 ......317 L4
Toynbee Cl ELGH SO50 ......229 J1
Toynbee Rd ELGH SO50 ......229 J1
Tozer Cl BWD BH11 ......321 P2
Trade St KSCL RG20 ......29 L6
Trafalgar Cl CHFD SO53 ......206 D8
Trafalgar Ct
　　FHAM/STUB PO14 ......294 D2
　　FNM GU9 ......116 B1
Trafalgar Pl PSEA PO1 * 316 C2
Trafalgar Rd
　　MOOR/WNTN BH9 ......322 F8
　　WSHM SO15 ......247 N5
Trafalgar Sq GPORT PO12 ......315 M5
Trafalgar St WINC SO23 ......3 G5
Trafalgar Wy CBLY GU15 ......57 N1
　　FAWY SO45 ......268 D9
　　STOK SO20 ......141 L6
Trafford Rd FRIM GU16 ......58 C5
Trafford Wy ELGH SO50 ......230 B5
Trajan Wk AND SP10 ......82 B7
Trampers La WHAM PO17 ......273 L1
Tranby Rd ITCH SO19 ......248 C2
Tranmere Cl LYMN SO41 ......329 M5
Tranmere Rd ENEY PO4 ......317 K4
Transport Rd FARN GU14 ......76 A5
Travellers Cnr THLE RG7 * 35 M1
Travellers End FUFL SO22 ......164 E6
Travis La SHST GU47 ......41 L7
Treadwheel Rd HORN PO8 ......256 C5
Treagore Rd TOTT SO40 ......246 A2
Treaman Cl ROWN SO16 ......227 K7
Treble Cl FUFL SO22 ......183 K2
Trebor Av FNM GU9 ......116 D1
Tredegar Rd FARN GU14 ......76 B4
Tredenham Cl FARN GU14 ......76 B4
Tree Av HASM GU27 ......156 E5
Treeside
　　CHCH/BSGR BH23 ......325 H6
Treeside Av TOTT SO40 ......246 E4
Treeside Dr FNM GU9 ......96 C4
Treeside Rd WSHM SO15 ......247 N3
Tree Side Wy WVILLE PO7 ......275 N1
Trefoil Cl HTWY RG27 ......
　　WVILLE PO7 ......275 P3
Tregaron Av CHAM PO6 ......297 K2
Tregolls Dr FARN GU14 ......76 B1
Tregonwell Rd WCLF BH2 ......8 A3
Trellis Dr CHIN RG24 ......70 B4
Treloar Rd HISD PO11 ......319 M7
Treloyhan Cl CHFD SO53 ......206 F9
Tremayne Wk CBLY GU15 ......59 H1
Tremona Rd ROWN SO16 ......227 M9
Trenchard Rd RAND SP11 ......101 P5
Trenchmead Gdns CHIN RG24 ......68 A4
Trenley Cl FAWY SO45 ......290 E6
Trent Cl FAWY SO45 ......57 M7
　　WEND SO18 ......249 H2
Trentham Av LTDN BH7 ......324 E5
Trentham Cl LTDN BH7 ......323 P7
Trenton Cl FRIM GU16 ......58 F3
Trent Rd WEND SO18 ......249 H2
Trent Wy BSTK RG21 ......7 K6
　　FERN BH22 ......302 C2
　　NEND PO2 ......316 E1
Trent Cl LSOL/BMARY PO13 ......314 D3
Tresham Crs YTLY GU46 ......40 D8
Tresillian Gdns WEND SO18 ......229 K9
Tresillian Wy
　　CHCH/BSGR BH23 ......236 D5
Trevis Rd ENEY PO4 ......317 L4
Trevone Cl TOTT SO40 ......265 M6
Trevor Cl ENEY PO4 ......316 G5
Trevose Cl CHFD SO53 ......206 F9
　　LSOL/BMARY PO13 ......294 G8
Trevose Crs CHFD SO53 ......206 F9

Trevose Wy
　　FHAM/STUB PO14 ......271 H9
Triangle La FHAM/STUB PO14 ......293 L5
The Triangle
　　NMIL/BTOS BH25 * 326 E8
　　NWBY RG14 ......24 E8
　　RSAL SP5 ......201 K1
　　WCLF BH2 ......8 B3
　　WEND SO18 * 248 G2
Tribe Rd GPORT PO12 ......12 D1
Tricketts La FERN BH22 ......302 F2
Trigon Rd PLE BH15 ......320 F5
Trimaran Cl ALDT GU11 * 76 D5
Trimaran Rd HLER SO31 ......270 E9
Trimmers Cl FNM GU9 ......116 E1
Trimmers Fld FNM GU9 ......116 E1
Trimm's Dro FBDC SP6 ......221 J4
Trims Ct OVTN RG25 ......86 G3
Trinidad Cl CHIN RG24 ......69 L5
Trinidad Crs
　　BKME/WDN PO12 ......321 L4
Trinity SHST GU47 ......41 M4
Trinity Cl GPORT PO12 ......13 H5
Trinity Flds FNM GU9 ......96 A5
Trinity Gdns FHAM/PORC PO16 ......11 F5
Trinity Gn GPORT PO12 ......13 J3
Trinity Hl ALTN GU34 ......130 C9
　　FNM GU9 ......96 A5
Trinity Ri BWD BH11 ......81 M7
Trinity Rd ALTN GU34 ......130 G8
　　BMTH BH1 ......9 G3
Trinity St FHAM/PORC PO16 ......11 G5
Tristan Cl FAWY SO45 ......313 N1
Tristram Cl CHFD SO53 ......206 B9
Triumph Cl FHAM/STUB PO14 ......272 B8
Triumph Rd
　　FHAM/STUB PO14 ......294 D4
Troak Cl CHCH/BSGR BH23 ......325 J7
Trojan Wy WVILLE PO7 ......275 L8
Troon Crs CHAM PO6 ......275 L9
Troon Rd BDST BH18 ......300 C8
Trosnant Rd HAV PO9 ......14 D3
Trotsford Meadow
　　BLKW GU17 ......57 K1
Trotton Rd GPORT PO12 ......217 P5
Trotts La TOTT SO40 ......246 C7
Trotwood Cl SHST GU47 ......41 M4
Trout Rd HASM GU27 ......156 D7
Trout Wk NWBY RG14 ......24 E2
Trowbridge Cl ROWN SO16 ......228 E8
Trowe's La THLE RG7 ......37 J2
　　THLE RG7 ......38 A1
Trueman Sq AND SP10 * 82 G8
Truman Rd BWD BH11 ......322 B1
Trunk Rd FARN GU14 ......95 J1
Truro Ct HAV PO9 ......296 H1
Truscott Av
　　MOOR/WNTN BH9 ......322 G8
Trussell Cl FUFL SO22 ......164 E4
Trussell Crs FUFL SO22 ......164 E4
Trust Cl HTWY RG27 ......71 N3
Tryplets FLEETS GU52 ......74 A4
Tubb's La KSCL RG20 ......29 N8
　　TADY RG26 ......50 D5
Tuckers La PLE BH15 ......332 B2
Tucks Cl CHCH/BSGR BH23 ......305 L7
Tuckton Cl SBNE BH6 ......336 B2
Tuckton Rd SBNE BH6 ......336 C2
Tudor Av EMRTH PO10 ......277 L6
Tudor Cl FBDC SP6 ......239 N6
　　FHAM/PORC PO16 ......273 M9
　　GU26 ......156 C3
　　HISD PO11 ......318 F6
　　LSOL/BMARY PO13 ......295 J9
　　ROMY SO51 ......51 M3
　　TOTT SO40 ......246 A3
Tudor Ct FHAM/STUB PO14 * 294 D2
　　PLE BH15 ......320 C6
　　TADY RG26 ......34 C5
Tudor Crs CHAM PO6 ......297 H5
Tudor Dr YTLY GU46 ......56 E1
Tudor Gdns HEND SO30 ......250 A6
Tudor Rd BDST BH18 ......300 D9
　　NWBY RG14 ......17 F5
Tudor Wy FLEETS GU52 ......74 D8
Tukes Av LSOL/BMARY PO13 ......294 F5
Tuffin Cl ROWN SO16 ......226 G7
Tukes Cl LSOL/BMARY PO13 ......294 F5
Tulip Cl KBH RG22 ......89 L4
Tulip Gdns HAV PO9 ......276 C8
　　HLER SO31 ......270 F7
Tulip La ROWN SO16 ......228 E8
Tulls La BOR GU35 ......154 E6
Tull Wy NTHA RG18 ......25 J5
Tumbridge Crs LIPH GU30 ......175 J2
Tumbridge La LIPH GU30 ......175 J1
Tumulus Cl ITCH SO19 ......249 P7
Tunball La MARL SN8 ......42 B6
Tunbridge Crs LIPH GU30 ......175 J2
Tunbridge La LIPH GU30 ......175 J1
Tunnel Rd FARN GU14 ......75 M5
Tunstall Rd CHAM PO6 ......298 H9
　　ITCH SO19 ......249 N7
Tunworth Cl FLEETN GU51 ......56 B9
Tunworth Crt HAV PO9 ......277 H5
Tunworth Ms TADY RG26 ......34 D6
Tunworth Rd OVTN RG25 ......70 F8
Turbary Cl BKME/WDN PO12 ......321 N4
Turbary Gdns WIMB BH21 ......34 C5
Turbary Rd BKME/WDN BH12 ......321 M5
Turgis Rd FLEETN GU51 ......56 B9
Turin Ct AND SP10 ......82 F7
Turks La PSTN BH14 ......333 J1
　　THLE RG7 ......38 A5
Turk St ALTN GU34 ......132 F6
Turnberry Cl
　　CHCH/BSGR BH23 ......324 D9
Turnberry Dr DEAN RG23 ......88 L6
Turner Av LSOL/BMARY PO13 ......295 J9
Turner Cl BSTK RG21 ......69 P8
Turner Ct AND SP10 ......4 B1

U

Turner Pl SHST GU47 ......41 L8
Turner Rd PSEA PO1 ......316 F1
Turners Av FLEETN GU51 ......56 B9
Turners Dr STHA RG19 ......25 P4
Turners Farm Crs LYMN SO41 ......328 G5
Turner's Green La HTWY RG27 ......55 P9
Turners Wy FLEETN GU51 ......74 A1
The Turnery STHA RG19 ......25 N4
Turnfields STHA RG19 ......25 N4
Turnill Ct RAND SP11 * 82 F4
Turnpike Cots OVTN RG25 ......87 H3
Turnpike Down WINC SO23 ......23 K4
Turnpike Rd NTHA RG18 ......25 H3
　　NWBY RG14 ......24 C3
Turnpike Wy DEAN RG23 ......88 E1
　　HEND SO30 ......250 A5
Turnstone End YTLY GU46 ......40 C8
Turnstone Gdns ROWN SO16 ......227 M7
Turnworth Cl BDST BH18 ......320 E1
Turtle Cl FHAM/STUB PO14 ......293 P5
Tuscan Wk CHFD SO53 ......206 C7
Tuscany Wy WVILLE PO7 ......276 B2
　　YTLY GU46 ......56 D1
The Tussocks TOTT SO40 ......247 K9
Tutland Rd NBAD SO52 ......205 K9
Tutor Cl HLER SO31 ......269 P7
Tutts La ROMY SO51 ......202 E9
Tweedale Rd
　　MOOR/WNTN BH9 ......323 J4
Tweed Cl CHFD SO53 ......206 C6
　　FARN GU14 ......57 M7
Tweed La LYMN SO41 ......309 K8
Tweedsmuir Cl FARN GU14 ......75 L1
　　KBH RG22 ......88 C8
Twelve Acre Crs FARN GU14 ......57 L8
Twemlow Av PSTN BH14 ......333 H1
Tweseldown Rd FLEETS GU52 ......74 E3
Twiggs End Cl HLER SO31 ......270 F6
Twiggs La TOTT SO40 ......267 H4
Twiggs Lane End TOTT SO40 ......267 K4
Twinley La WHCH RG28 ......65 H8
Twin Oaks Cl BDST BH18 ......320 C1
Twisell Thorne FLEETS GU52 ......74 B4
Twittens Wy HAV PO9 ......15 C6
Two Gate La OVTN RG25 ......87 H4
Two Gate Meadow OVTN RG25 ......87 H5
Two Rivers Wy NWBY RG14 ......24 G4
Twyford Av NEND PO2 ......296 F6
　　WSHM SO15 ......247 H2
Twyford Cl CHAR BH8 ......323 K5
Twyford Dr
　　LSOL/BMARY PO13 ......314 D2
Twyford La RFNM GU10 ......116 B4
Twyford Rd ELGH SO50 ......207 K7
　　FHAM/PORC PO16 * 321 J2
Twynham Av
　　CHCH/BSGR BH23 ......324 E9
Twynham Cl RSAL SP5 ......199 K7
Twynham Rd SBNE BH6 ......336 D2
Twynhams Hl BPWT SO32 ......252 E3
Tydehams NWBY RG14 ......24 B8
Tyfield CHIN RG24 ......69 H1
Tylers Cl LYMN SO41 ......329 J7
The Tyleshades ROMY SO51 ......204 E7
Tylney Av PSEA PO1 ......17 M3
Tylney La HTWY RG27 * 71 H4
Tylston Meadow LIPH GU30 ......175 J2
Tyndalls CSHT GU26 ......156 C5
Tyne Cl CHFD SO53 ......206 C8
　　FARN GU14 ......57 M7
Tyne Ct AND SP10 ......82 C9
Tynedale Cl GPORT PO12 ......295 K9
　　MOOR/WNTN BH9 ......323 J3
Tyneham Av
　　BKME/WDN BH12 ......321 K4
Tyne Wy HEND SO30 ......249 N1
Tyrell Rd CHFD SO53 ......206 E6
Tyrells Crt AND SP10 ......5 G4
Tyrells La RGWD BH24 ......284 A5
Tyrrell Gdns CHAR BH8 ......323 N5
Tyrrells Ct CHCH/BSGR BH23 ......305 M7
Tyseley Rd SSEA PO5 ......19 H4
Tytherley Gn CHAR BH8 ......323 K5
Tytherley Rd RSAL SP5 ......158 D1
　　WEND SO18 ......249 L3

Ubsdell Cl NMIL/BTOS BH25 ......327 J4
Uddens Dr WIMB BH21 ......279 M6
Ufton Br THLE RG7 ......26 B1
Ullswater Av FARN GU14 ......75 M1
　　FNM GU9 ......96 A5
　　STHA RG19 ......25 K4
Ullswater Cl ASHV GU12 * 76 E7
Ullswater Gv NARL SO24 ......168 A3
Ullswater Rd ROWN SO16 ......228 E5
　　WIMB BH21 ......300 E3
Undercliff Cl BMTH BH1 ......9 G5
Undercliff Rd BOSC BH5 ......335 J3
Underdown Av WVILLE PO7 ......275 M8
Underhill La FNM GU9 ......96 A5
Undershore LYMN SO41 ......329 L1
Underwood Av ASHV GU12 ......97 L2
Underwood Cl CFDH BH17 ......300 B7
　　ROWN SO16 ......228 A8
Underwood Rd ELGH SO50 ......207 M9
　　ROWN SO16 ......228 A8
Unicorn Rd
　　LSOL/BMARY PO13 ......314 D1
　　PSEA PO1 ......19 G1
Union Cl SHST GU47 ......41 M4
Union Pl PSEA PO1 ......19 K1
Union Ri LISS GU33 ......174 A5
Union Rd HAV PO9 ......96 C9
　　FRIM GU16 ......59 J5

　　HAV PO9 ......14 E5
　　SHAM SO14 ......21 H1
Union St ALDT GU11 ......2 D5
　　CHOB/PIR GU24 ......59 M7
　　FARN GU14 ......57 P9
　　FHAM/PORC PO16 ......11 K6
　　PSEA PO1 ......18 D2
　　WINC SO23 ......23 G4
University Crs PTSW SO17 ......228 C8
University Pkwy ROWN SO16 ......227 N5
University Rd PTSW SO17 ......228 C9
Unwin Cl ITCH SO19 ......268 F1
Upfallow CHIN RG24 ......70 B5
Upham St BPWT SO32 ......209 J9
Uphill Rd FUFL SO22 ......164 B2
Upland La LISS GU33 ......172 F8
Uplands Av NMIL/BTOS BH25 ......327 J7
Uplands Cl FERN BH22 ......280 C9
　　HASM GU27 ......157 J5
　　SHST GU47 ......41 J6
Uplands Crs FHAM/PORC PO16 ......11 G3
Uplands La ALTN GU34 ......150 B7
Uplands Rd CHAM PO6 ......275 L9
　　CHAR BH8 ......323 J5
　　FERN BH22 ......280 C9
　　FNM GU9 ......116 E1
　　FUFL SO22 ......164 B2
　　HAV PO9 ......257 J9
　　WVILLE PO7 ......254 D5
Uplands Wy PTSW SO17 ......248 C7
Uplyme Cl CFDH BH17 ......321 J2
Upmill Cl WEND SO18 ......229 K9
Upnor Cl RAND SP11 ......79 M4
Upper Arundel St PSEA PO1 ......19 H2
Upper Banister St
　　WSHM SO15 ......248 B5
Upper Barn Copse ELGH SO50 ......230 B1
Upper Bere Wd WVILLE PO7 ......275 P4
Upper Bourne La RFNM GU10 ......116 A5
Upper Bourne Rd RFNM GU10 ......116 A5
Upper Broadmoor Rd
　　CWTH RG45 ......41 L1
Upper Brook Dr HLER SO31 ......270 E8
Upper Brook St WINC SO23 ......22 E4
Upper Brownhill Rd
　　ROWN SO16 ......227 K9
Upper Bugle St SHAM SO14 ......20 C6
Upper Chestnut Dr BSTK RG21 ......69 J9
Upper Chobham Rd
　　CBLY GU15 ......58 G1
Upper Church La FNM GU9 ......96 B9
Upper Church La RFNM GU10 ......116 A5
Upper Common Rd
　　LYMN SO41 ......328 F4
Upper Cornaway La
　　FHAM/PORC PO16 ......295 M1
Upper Crabbick La
　　WVILLE PO7 ......254 E6
Upper Crescent Rd
　　NBAD SO52 ......205 K9
Upper Deacon Rd ITCH SO19 ......249 K5
Upper Dro AND SP10 ......102 A2
Upper Elms Rd ALDT GU11 ......2 D4
Upper Froyle FNM GU9 ......88 F5
Upper Golf Links Rd
　　BDST BH18 ......300 D9
Upper Gordon Rd
　　CHCH/BSGR BH23 ......326 C6
Upper Grove Rd ALTN GU34 ......132 F7
Upper Hale Rd FNM GU9 ......116 C1
Upper Heyshott EPSF GU31 ......215 N2
Upper High St FUFL SO22 ......22 C3
Upper Hinton Rd BMTH BH1 ......8 E4
Upper House Ct WHAM PO17 ......252 E8
Upper Lamborough La
　　NARL SO24 ......148 C1
Upper Lanham La NARL SO24 ......148 C1
Upper Market St ELGH SO50 ......229 K1
Upper Mead Cl ELGH SO50 ......230 D2
Upper Moors Rd ELGH SO50 ......207 P5
Upper Mt HASM GU27 ......157 J4
Upper Mullin's La FAWY SO45 ......268 A7
Upper Neatham Mill La
　　ALTN GU34 ......133 J3
Upper New Rd HEND SO30 ......249 M2
Upper Northam Cl
　　HEND SO30 ......250 A5
Upper Northam Dr
　　HEND SO30 ......249 N5
Upper Northam Rd
　　HEND SO30 ......250 A5
Upper Norwood Rd WCLF BH2 ......8 A4
Upper Old Park La FNM GU9 ......95 P6
Upper Old St
　　FHAM/STUB PO14 ......293 P5
Upper Piece WVILLE PO7 ......255 J8
Upper Pinewood Rd
　　ASHV GU12 ......77 H9
Upper Rd BKME/WDN BH12 ......321 L6
Upper St Helens Rd
　　HEND SO30 ......250 B7
Upper St Michaels Gv
　　FHAM/STUB PO14 ......294 D1
Upper St Michael's Rd
　　ALDT GU11 ......3 F6
Upper School Dr HASM GU27 ......156 E8
Upper Shaftesbury Av
　　PTSW SO17 ......248 D1
Upper Shirley Av WSHM SO15 ......247 N2
Upper Soldridge Rd
　　ALTN GU34 ......149 N6
Upper South Vw FNM GU9 ......96 C8
Upper Spinney HLER SO31 ......292 C1
Upper St FLEETN GU51 ......74 C3
Upper Terrace Rd WCLF BH2 ......75 P4
　　WCLF BH2 ......8 C4
Upper Toothill Rd
　　ROWN SO16 ......227 J3
Upper Union St ALDT GU11 ......2 C3
Upper Union Ter ALDT GU11 ......2 D3
Upper Verran Rd CBLY GU15 ......58 C2
Upper Wardown EPSF GU31 ......215 P1
Upper Wy FNM GU9 ......116 B2
Upper Weston La ITCH SO19 ......249 J9
Upper Weybourne La
　　FNM GU9 ......96 D3
Upper Wht FHAM/PORC PO16 ......11 J7
Upper Wield Dr FLEETN GU51 ......56 B9
Uppleby Rd BKME/WDN BH12 ......321 L7
Upron Field Cl KBH RG22 ......89 M4
Up St OVTN RG25 ......108 C1
　　OVTN RG25 ......86 C1
Upton Cl FARN GU14 ......76 C1
　　HAV PO9 ......276 D3
Upton Crs BSTK RG21 ......6 D1
　　ROWN 226 G5
Upton Grey Cl FUFL SO22 ......164 E4
Upton Grey Rd ODIM RG29 ......92 E1
Upton La ROWN SO16 ......226 F7
Upton Rd CFDH BH17 ......320 B5
Upton Wy BDST BH18 ......320 B1
Upwey Av PLE BH15 ......320 A9
Urquhart Rd STHA RG19 ......25 N5
Usborne Cl
　　LSOL/BMARY PO13 ......314 D1
Utrecht Ct CHCH/BSGR BH23 ......325 H8
Uxbridge Cl HLER SO31 ......270 F4

V

Vadne Gdns GPORT PO12 * 315 M2
Vaggs La LYMN SO41 ......307 M9
Vale Cl RFNM GU10 ......116 C6
Vale Dr WEND SO18 ......249 H2
Vale Gv GPORT PO12 ......315 L1
Valencia Cl CHCH/BSGR BH23 ......324 B3
Valencia Wy AND SP10 ......5 F2
Valentine Av ITCH SO19 ......249 L8
Valentine Cl FHAM PO15 ......272 A7
Valentine Ct WVILLE PO7 ......275 H3
Valentine Rd FHAM PO15 ......271 M7
Valerian Cl ELGH SO50 ......230 C6
Valerian Rd HEND SO30 ......250 C5
Vale Rd ASHV GU12 ......76 F5
　　BMTH BH1 ......335 L2
　　CBLY GU15 ......57 P7
　　PSTN BH14 ......321 N8
　　RSAL SP5 ......199 P7
　　WINC SO23 ......23 J7
The Vale DEAN RG23 ......88 E2
　　FAWY SO45 ......268 B7
　　HASM GU27 ......157 H8
　　HORN PO8 ......256 C2
　　SSEA PO5 ......316 E6
Valetta Pk EMRTH PO10 ......299 L1
Valette Rd MOOR/WNTN BH9 ......322 G4
Vale View Dr THLE RG7 ......37 J1
Valiance Pk LYMN SO41 * 307 P9
Vale Wy WINC SO23 ......3 J7
Vale Wood Dr RFNM GU10 ......116 C6
Vale Wood La GSHT GU26 ......156 B1
Valewood Rd HASM GU27 ......157 H9
Valiant Gdns NEND PO2 ......296 F5
Valiant Rd CHCH/BSGR BH23 ......325 M8
　　FARN GU14 ......75 L4
Valley Cl CHCH/BSGR BH23 ......325 L4
　　FAWY SO45 ......268 B7
　　RSAL SP5 ......199 P7
　　RWIN SO21 ......207 P5
　　WVILLE PO7 ......254 E3
Valleydene FAWY SO45 ......268 B8
Valley Hl FUFL SO22 ......164 D2
Valley La CHCH/BSGR BH23 ......306 A4
Valley Md RAND SP11 ......102 A5
Valley Park Dr HORN PO8 ......256 D6
Valley Ri HLER SO31 ......270 E6
　　RAND SP11 ......102 C6
Valley Rd CHAR BH8 ......323 M4
　　CHFD SO53 ......206 E6
　　FRIM GU16 ......164 C2
　　FUFL SO22 ......164 C2
　　NWBY RG14 ......24 C7
　　THLE RG7 ......37 J4
　　TOTT SO40 ......246 D6
Valley Side RAND SP11 ......175 J2
The Valley FUFL SO22 ......164 E6
Valley Vw BMTH BH12 ......322 B8
Valley Wy TADY RG26 ......34 F5
Vallis Cl PLE BH15 ......332 F2
Valmeade Cl HTWY RG27 ......72 A3
Valsheba Dr
　　FHAM/STUB PO14 ......293 P8
Vampire Wy FARN GU14 ......75 M4
Vanburgh Gdns KBH RG22 ......89 M4
Vanburgh Wy CHFD SO53 ......206 D4
Van Dyck Cl BSTK RG21 ......69 P9
Vanguard Hl FUFL SO22 ......164 B2
Vanguard Rd CHAR BH8 ......323 L6
　　GPORT PO12 ......295 N9
　　PLE BH15 ......332 E1
　　WEND SO18 ......249 J3
Vanners La KSCL RG20 ......29 K9
Vanstone Rd
　　LSOL/BMARY PO13 ......295 H9
Vantage Wy BKME/WDN BH12 ......321 K2
Vardy Cl ITCH SO19 ......249 M8
Varna Rd BOR GU35 ......154 B5
　　WSHM SO15 ......247 N6
Varndell Rd HTWY RG27 ......71 J1
Varney Cl FARN GU14 ......57 M8
Varos Cl GPORT PO12 ......315 L2
Vaudrey Cl WSHM SO15 ......247 N2
Vaughan Cl ITCH SO19 ......249 N6
Vaughan Rd FAWY SO45 ......267 N6
Vaughan Wk ALDT GU34 ......132 C6
Vauxhall Wy PSF GU32 ......215 L2
Vear's La TOTT SO40 ......267 M3
Vear's La RWIN SO21 ......207 M3
Vecta Cl CHCH/BSGR BH23 ......325 N9
Vectis Cl ALTN GU34 ......150 C6

Vectis Rd GPORT PO12 .....315 J5
NMIL/BTOS BH25 .....326 F8
Vernon Dro CHAM PO6 .....297 H2
Velder Av ENEY PO4 .....317 K5
Velian Ct ROWN SO16 .....246 C2
Velmead Cl FLEETS GU52 .....74 E5
Velmead Rd FLEETS GU52 .....74 D5
Velmore Rd CHAM PO6 .....206 D9
Velmore Ct FAWY SO45 .....268 C5
Velvet Lawn Rd
NMIL/BTOS BH25 .....327 H3
Venator Pl WIMB BH21 .....278 E8
Venerable Rd
FHAM/STUB PO14 .....294 E4
Vengeance Rd
LSOL/BMARY PO13 .....314 C1
Venice Cl WVILLE PO7 .....276 A2
Venice Ct AND SP10 .....82 C8
Venison Ter STOK SO20 * 140 B2
Venning Av BWD BH11 .....301 N8
Ventnor Rd ENEY PO4 .....316 C4
LSOL/BMARY PO13 .....294 F6
Ventnor Ter ASHV GU12 .....3 H5
Ventnor Wy
FHAM/PORC PO16 .....273 J9
Ventry Cl CCLF BH13 .....321 P8
Venture Ct HSEA PO3 * 297 J4
Venture Rd ROWN SO16 .....227 P3
Venture Sidings ENEY PO4 * 316 C4
Verbena Crs HORN PO8 .....256 D7
Verbena Wy HEND SO30 .....250 C5
Verdi Cl KBH RG22 .....89 P3
Verdon Av HLER SO31 .....269 N7
Verdun Wy AND SP10 .....82 D8
Verger Cl FHAM/STUB PO14 .....271 J7
Verge Wk ALDT GU11 .....96 G4
Verity Crs CFDH BH17 .....321 J3
Vermont Cl ROWN SO16 .....228 B8
Vernalls Cl NBNE BH10 .....322 D1
Vernalls Ct NMIL/BTOS BH25 .....327 L2
Vernalls Gdns NBNE BH10 .....322 D2
Verner Cl BOR GU35 .....154 F4
Verne Rd VWD BH31 .....258 C5
The Verne FLEETS GU52 .....74 D7
Verney Cl BWD BH11 .....332 B4
Verney Rd BWD BH11 .....322 A4
Vernham Rd FUFL SO22 .....164 E5
Verno La CHCH/BSGR BH23 .....325 N5
Vernon Cl GPORT PO12 .....12 B1
Vernon Hl BPWT SO32 .....232 A2
Vernon Ms ENEY PO4 * 317 J3
Vernon Rd GPORT PO12 .....12 B1
HSEA PO3 .....297 J7

WVILLE PO7 .....275 K7
Victoria Cl HLER SO31 .....270 G9
Victoria Ca ABOT PO12 * 4 C5
Victoria Crs BKME/WDN BH12 .....321 M6
Victoria Dr BLKW GU17 .....57 K1
Victoria Gdns FBDG SP6 .....240 B2
FERN BH22 .....302 D2
FLEETN GU51 * 74 C3
NWBD BH24 .....282 E5
RGWD BH24 .....282 E5
Victoria Gld HLER SO31 .....269 L5
Victoria Gv SSEA PO5 .....19 K7
Victoria Hill Rd FLEETN GU51 .....74 B3
Victoria Ms FLEETN GU51 * 74 C5
LYMN SO41 * 329 M5
WHAM PO17 .....272 C5
Victoria Pde FLEETN GU51 * 74 C5
Victoria Park Rd
MOOR/WNTN BH9 .....322 E6
Victoria Pl BMTH BH1 .....335 J1
GPORT PO12 * 12 D5
KBH RG22 * 88 G8
LYMN SO41 .....329 L5
RAND SP11 * 62 B5
Victoria Rd ALDT GU11 .....2 E3
ALTN GU34 .....132 F5
BMTH BH12 .....335 J1
BPWT SO32 .....231 P4
CHCH/BSGR BH23 .....337 J1
ELGH SO50 .....207 K8
EMRTH PO10 .....272 F9
FARN GU14 .....57 P9
FBDG SP6 .....240 B2
FERN BH22 .....302 D2
FLEETN GU51 .....74 B3
FNM GU9 .....96 C9
HISD PO11 .....298 F7
HLER SO31 .....269 J4
ITCH SO19 .....268 E1
LYMN SO41 .....338 F2
PSEA PO1 .....316 B2
SHST GU47 .....41 M5
THLE RG7 .....27 H9
Victoria Rd East ALTN GU34 .....132 G5
Victoria Rd North SSEA PO5 .....19 K5
Victoria Rd South SSEA PO5 .....19 K7
Victoria Sq
LSOL/BMARY PO13 .....314 C2
Victoria St BSTK RG21 .....6 E1
GPORT PO12 .....12 E1
PSEA PO1 .....316 E1
SHAM SO14 .....21 J5
Victoria Ter CHAM PO6 * 297 H2
Victoria Ter ALDT GU11 * 75 L5
Victoria Wy LIPH GU30 .....175 J3
Victor Rd HSEA PO3 .....317 H1
STHA RG19 .....25 P4
Victor St WSHM SO15 .....247 N3
Victor Wy FARN GU14 .....75 P4
Victory Cl CHFD SO53 .....206 D8
WIMB BH21 .....281 H3
Victory Gn NEND PO2 .....296 E7
Victory Rd FHAM/STUB PO14 .....294 B7
PSEA PO1 .....18 C3
WSHM SO15 .....247 M5
Victory Rbt BSTK RG21 .....6 D5
Victory Sq WSHM SO15 .....247 M5
Vigo La YTLY GU46 .....40 D9
Vigo Rd AND SP10 .....5 J5
Viking Cl FAWY SO45 .....291 H9
FHAM/STUB PO14 .....295 P6
ROWN SO16 .....227 J7
The Vikings ROMY SO51 .....204 F6
Viking Wy AND SP10 .....82 F7
CHCH/BSGR BH23 .....338 D9
HORN PO8 .....236 C9
Villa Gdns WVILLE PO7 .....275 N2
Village Cl FHAM/STUB PO14 .....294 A7
Village Rd GPORT PO12 .....315 K6
Village Wy ALTN GU34 .....131 K4
The Village EWKG RG40 .....39 P3
Village Wy YTLY GU46 .....40 E7
Ville De Paris Rd
FHAM/PORC PO14 .....294 E4
Villette Cl CHCH/BSGR BH23 .....324 E6
Villiers Rd FAWY SO45 .....290 B1
SSEA PO5 .....316 F6
WSHM SO15 .....247 N4
Vimoutiers Ct FBDG SP6 .....240 C2
Vince Cl BWD BH11 .....321 M1
Vincent Av ROWN SO16 .....247 N1
Vincent Gv FHAM/PORC PO16 .....295 N2
Vincent Rd NMIL/BTOS BH25 .....327 H4
NTHA RG18 .....8 C5
WSHM SO15 .....247 N5
Vincent's Cv WSHM SO15 * 247 N5
Vincent's Wk SHAM SO14 .....20 E5
Vindomis Cl ALTN GU34 .....133 K2
Vine Bank WEND SO18 .....249 L3
Vine Cl ALDT GU11 * 75 M5
HLER SO31 .....270 D7
LTDN BH7 .....323 N8
Vine Hl WIMB BH21 .....278 A9
Vine House Cl FRIM GU16 .....76 F1
Vineries Cl WIMB BH21 .....279 H8

The Vineries WIMB BH21 .....279 H8
Vine Rd ROWN SO16 .....227 L9
Vinery Gdns ROWN SO16 .....247 M1
Vinery Rd ROWN SO16 .....247 N1
Vineside LSOL/BMARY PO13 .....295 J8
Vine St ALDT GU11 .....2 A2
Vine Tree Cl TADY RG26 .....34 E7
Vine Wy RFNM GU10 .....116 A5
Vineyard Ct ITCH SO19 .....248 F8
The Vineyards NBAD SO52 .....205 L9
Viney Av ROMY SO51 .....204 F5
Viney Rd LYMN SO41 .....329 L6
Vinnells La PSF GU32 .....188 F7
Vinneys Cl CHCH/BSGR BH23 .....324 C5
Vinns La OVTN RG25 .....86 F4
Vinson Rd LISS GU33 .....192 E2
Vintney St FLEETN GU51 .....74 A1
Violet Av FHAM/STUB PO14 .....293 P7
Violet Cl CHFD SO53 .....206 C7
KBH RG22 .....89 L4
Violet Gv NTHA RG18 .....25 P2
Violet La NMIL/BTOS BH25 .....327 J3
TADY RG26 .....33 M8
Violet Rd ROWN SO16 .....228 C8
Virginia Cl BKME/WDN BH12 .....321 L5
Virginia Gdns FARN GU14 .....76 B2
Virginia Park Rd GPORT PO12 .....315 K2
Viscount Dr CHCH/BSGR BH23 .....325 M9
Viscount Wk WIMB BH21 .....301 L8
Vita Rd NEND PO2 .....296 C6
Vitellius Gdns CHIN RG24 .....68 F4
Vitre Gdns LYMN SO41 .....329 L5
Vivaldi Cl KBH RG22 .....90 A4
Vivian Cl FLEETS GU52 .....74 E6
Vivian Rd BSTK RG21 .....7 H1
Vixen Cl FHAM/PORC PO14 .....293 P7
Vixen Wk NMIL/BTOS BH25 .....327 K2
Vockins Cl NTID SP9 .....78 F1
Vokes Cl ITCH SO19 .....249 K6
Vulcan Cl WSHM SO15 .....247 K5
Vulcan Rd WSHM SO15 .....247 K5
Vulcan Wy FARN GU14 .....75 K4
SHST GU47 .....41 H7
Vyne Cl ALTN GU34 .....132 F5
Vyne Meadow CHIN RG24 .....51 J9
Vyne Rd BSTK RG21 .....6 E5
CHIN RG24 .....51 J9
Vyse La SHAM SO14 * 20 D7

W

Wade Court Rd HAV PO9 .....15 H7
Wade La HAV PO9 .....298 D2
Wadham Cl HAV PO9 .....298 D2
Wadham Rd NEND PO2 .....296 F7
Wadhurst Gdns ITCH SO19 .....269 J2
Wadhurst Rd HEND SO30 .....250 C5
Wadmore Cl FAWY SO45 .....268 B6
Wadwick Bottom RAND SP11 .....63 J9
Waggoners Wy GSHT GU26 .....155 P5
Waggoners Wells Rd
GSHT GU26 .....155 P6
Wagner Cl KBH RG22 .....90 A3
Wagon La HTWY RG27 .....72 A2
Wagtail Dr NMIL/BTOS BH25 .....327 H5
Wagtail Rd HORN PO8 .....256 A5
Wagtail Wy
FHAM/PORC PO16 .....295 K1
Wainscott Rd ENEY PO4 .....317 J6
Wainsford Cl LYMN SO41 * 329 H4
Wainsford Plantation
LYMN SO41 .....328 E7
Wainsford Rd LYMN SO41 .....328 E5
Wainwright Cl CHAM PO6 .....297 L3
Wait End Rd WVILLE PO7 .....275 N4
Wakefield Av
FHAM/PORC PO16 .....10 D1
Wakefield Ct WEND SO18 .....249 J2
Wakefield Rd WEND SO18 .....249 J2
Wakeford Cl TADY RG26 .....34 F5
Wakeford Ct TADY RG26 * 34 F4
Wakefords Copse
FLEETS GU52 .....74 E9
Wakefords Pk FLEETS GU52 * 74 E8
Wakefords Pk FLEETS GU52 .....74 E9
Wakely Gdns BWD BH11 .....322 A2
Wakely Rd BWD BH11 .....322 B2
Walberton Av CHAM PO6 .....297 J7
Walburton Wy HORN PO8 .....236 D8
Walcott Av CHCH/BSGR BH23 .....324 D6
Waldegrave Cl ITCH SO19 .....268 F1
Waldegrave Pl NWBY RG14 * 16 E2
Walden Cots RGUW GU3 .....77 M9
Walden Gdns HORN PO8 .....256 B6
Walden Rd NEND PO2 .....296 F7
Waldie Rd WIMB BH21 .....278 C8
Waldon Gdns WEND SO18 .....249 K1
Waldorf Hts BLKW GU17 .....57 L1
Waldren Cl PLE BH15 .....332 F1
Wales St WINC SO23 .....2 E5
Walford Cl WIMB BH21 .....278 E8
Walford Gdns WIMB BH21 .....278 D8
Walford Rd CHAM PO6 .....296 F1
Walhampton Hl LYMN SO41 .....329 N2
Walker Gdns HEND SO30 .....250 C3
Walker Pl
LSOL/BMARY PO13 * 295 H4
Walker Rd NEND PO2 .....296 E7
Walkers Cl ELGH SO50 .....230 D2
Walkers La North FAWY SO45 .....291 H8
Walker's La South
FAWY SO45 .....313 H1
Walkford La NMIL/BTOS BH25 .....326 F4
Walkford Rd
CHCH/BSGR BH23 .....326 D6
Walkford Wy
CHCH/BSGR BH23 .....326 D6
Walking Field La PLE BH15 .....332 F1

The Walk FUFL SO22 * 183 N1
Walkwood Av LTDN BH7 .....323 P7
Wallace Ct KBH RG22 .....88 C5
Wallace La BROC SO42 .....310 G2
Wallace Rd BDST BH18 .....320 C1
ITCH SO19 .....269 H1
NEND PO2 .....297 H9
Wallace Wy ALDT GU11 .....3 G5
Walldown Rd BOR GU35 .....154 B7
The Walled Gdns ODIM RG29 * 92 C8
Walled Meadow AND SP10 .....5 F5
Waller Dr NTHA RG18 .....25 H2
Wallington Ct
FHAM/STUB PO14 .....294 D3
Wallington Dr CHFD SO53 .....206 C5
Wallington Hl
FHAM/PORC PO16 .....11 J4
Wallington Orch
FHAM/PORC PO16 * 273 H7
Wallington Rd NEND PO2 .....297 H8
Wallington Shore Rd
FHAM/PORC PO16 .....11 K4
Wallins Copse CHIN RG24 .....70 A2
Walliscott Rd BWD BH11 .....322 A6
Wallisdean Av
FHAM/STUB PO14 .....10 D7
HSEA PO3 .....317 K1
Wallisdown Rd
BKME/WDN BH12 .....321 N5
Wallis Dr TADY RG26 .....52 C3
Wallis Gdns WVILLE PO7 .....275 N1
Wallis Rd BSTK RG21 .....69 L9
NBNE BH10 .....322 D6
WVILLE PO7 .....275 N1
Wall La THLE RG7 .....35 K4
Wallop Dr KBH RG22 .....90 A3
Wallop Dro STOK SO20 .....139 L4
Wallop Rd STOK SO20 .....120 A5
Walmer Cl CWTH RG45 .....41 K1
ELGH SO50 .....207 J6
FRIM GU16 .....58 E6
Walmer Rd PSEA PO1 .....316 G3
Walnut Av WEND SO18 .....232 C1
Walnut Cl ALDT GU11 .....2 E7
ALTN GU34 .....132 C4
CHFD SO53 .....206 E3
NMIL/BTOS BH25 .....327 H4
ROWN SO16 .....246 F1
YTLY GU46 .....56 E1
Walnut Dr FUFL SO22 .....180 D6
ROWN SO16 .....247 K3
The Walnuts FLEETS GU52 .....74 F7
Walnut Tree Cl HISD PO11 .....318 F5
RWIN SO21 .....144 E4
Walnut Tree La AND SP10 .....4 A6
Walpole Gdns HEND SO30 .....250 C9
Walpole Cl HTWY RG27 .....55 J7
Walpole La HLER SO31 .....270 E3
Walpole Rd BMTH BH1 .....335 K1
FUFL SO22 .....183 J1
GPORT PO12 .....12 A3
Walrus Rd FARN GU14 .....75 K4
Walsall Rd HSEA PO3 .....317 J2
Walsford Rd WBNE BH4 .....334 C1
Walsingham Cl CHAM PO6 * 274 F9
Walsingham Dene LTDN BH7 .....323 K7
Walsingham Gdns
WEND SO18 .....228 G9
Waltham Cl BPWT SO32 .....233 L2
FHAM/PORC PO16 .....273 N8
SHST GU47 .....41 L5
Waltham Crs ROWN SO16 .....227 N8
Waltham La OVTN RG25 .....87 H5
Waltham La OVTN RG25 .....87 L7
Waltham Rd CHAM PO6 .....323 P8
OVTN RG25 .....87 J4
Waltham St SSEA PO5 .....19 F4
Walton Cl GPORT PO12 .....12 A5
WVILLE PO7 .....275 N5
Walton Ct FHAM PO15 .....272 B6
Walton Dr FUFL SO22 .....183 M1
Walton Rd CHAM PO6 .....296 F9
GPORT PO12 .....12 A5
ITCH SO19 .....249 M8
NBNE BH10 .....322 C5
PLE BH15 .....321 J6
Waltons Av FAWY SO45 .....290 F5
Walton Wy NWBY RG14 .....16 A4
Walworth Rbt AND SP10 .....83 H9
Walworth Rd AND SP10 .....83 H9
Wandesford Pl GPORT PO12 .....295 L8
Wandle Cl ASHV GU12 .....97 N2
Wangfield La BPWT SO32 .....251 J2
Wansbeck Cl CHFD SO53 .....206 B4
Wansey Gdns NWBY RG14 .....24 C2
Wanstead Cl WEND SO18 .....260 F9
Wantage Rd SHST GU47 .....41 L4
Wapiti Wy FARN GU14 .....75 L4
Warbler Cl HORN PO8 .....256 A4
Warburton Rd CFDH BH17 .....320 D6
ITCH SO19 .....249 M6
Ward Cl AND SP10 .....5 K3
Ward Crs EMRTH PO10 .....277 N7
Warden Cl HEND SO30 .....249 M2
Wardens Cl HISD PO11 .....318 F5
Warden Rd ELGH SO50 .....207 M6
Ward Rd ENEY PO4 .....316 E6
Wardroom Rd NEND PO2 .....296 D8
Warehouse Rd STHA RG19 .....31 L1
Warfield Av WVILLE PO7 .....275 N5
Warfield Crs WVILLE PO7 .....275 N3

Wargrove Dr SHST GU47 .....41 L6
Warland Wy WIMB BH21 .....300 A6
Warley Cl ITCH SO19 .....249 M8
Warlock Cl ITCH SO19 .....249 M8
Warnwell Cl CFDH BH17 .....321 H2
Warner Ct AND SP10 .....
Warner Ms HEND SO30 .....250 G4
Warnes La RGWD BH24 .....284 B7
Warnford Cl GPORT PO12 .....12 A3
Warnford Crs HAV PO9 .....276 D5
Warnford Rd BMTH BH1 .....253 N1
Warnford Prd BH7 .....323 P8
Warren Av CHCH/BSGR BH23 .....337 K1
CHFD SO53 .....206 G8
ENEY PO4 .....317 K3
ROWN SO16 .....247 M2
Warren Cl BOR GU35 .....153 M6
CHFD SO53 .....206 G8
FLEETS GU52 .....74 E5
HISD PO11 .....318 C4
HTWY RG27 .....55 J8
RGWD BH24 .....282 B4
Warren Cnr RFNM GU10 .....95 L4
Warren Crs ROWN SO16 .....247 L3
Warren Dr RAND SP11 .....101 M7
RGWD BH24 .....282 B4
Warren Edge Cl SBNE BH6 .....336 D5
Warren Edge Rd SBNE BH6 .....336 D5
Warren La BROC SO42 .....311 P8
EWKG RG40 .....39 N1
PSF GU32 .....191 J1
RGWD BH24 .....282 A4
RWIN SO21 .....185 L6
Warren Pk LYMN SO41 .....328 A9
Warren Pl TOTT SO40 .....246 A1
Warren Ri FRIM GU16 .....58 D2
Warren Rd LISS GU33 .....173 M8
LISS GU33 .....174 A1
NWBY RG14 .....24 A9
PSTN BH14 .....321 M8
WBNE BH4 .....334 B4
WINC SO23 .....23 K3
Warrens La RSAL SP5 .....199 J1
The Warren ALDT GU11 .....2 C4
FAWY SO45 .....290 D4
FNM GU9 .....96 E3
TADY RG26 .....34 B6
Warren Wk FERN BH22 .....302 B1
Warrington Ms ALDT GU11 .....96 E3
Warrior Cl CHFD SO53 .....206 D9
Warrys Cl FAWY SO45 .....290 C1
Warsash Cl HAV PO9 .....276 E4
Warsash Gv
LSOL/BMARY PO13 .....294 F7
Warsash Rd
FHAM/STUB PO14 .....271 L9
HLER SO31 .....270 E9
Warspite Cl NEND PO2 .....296 F5
Warton Cl BROC SO42 .....310 G2
Warton Rd BSTK RG21 .....7 G3
Warwick Av NMIL/BTOS BH25 .....327 K4
Warwick Cl ALDT GU11 .....
CBLY GU15 .....58 C2
CHFD SO53 .....206 C9
LSOL/BMARY PO13 .....314 G4
Warwick Crs SSEA PO5 .....19 H5
Warwick Dr NWBY RG14 .....17 H6
Warwick Rd ASHV GU12 .....76 E3
DEAN RG23 .....68 G6
FARN GU14 .....
LTDN BH7 .....335 N1
PSTN BH14 .....321 L9
TOTT SO40 .....246 D3
WSHM SO15 .....247 P1
Wash Brook HTWY RG27 .....71 P2
Washbrook Rd CHAM PO6 .....296 F1
Washford La BOR GU35 .....154 C4
Washington Av BMTH BH1 .....323 L3
Washington Rd EMRTH PO10 .....277 M9
NEND PO2 .....296 F9
Wash Water KSCL RG20 .....30 A3
Watchetts Dr CBLY GU15 .....58 B3
Watchetts Lake Cl CBLY 58 C2
Watchetts Rd CBLY GU15 .....58 A2
Watchmoor Point
CBLY GU15 * 58 A1
Watchmoor Rd CBLY GU15 .....57 P2
Watcombe Rd SBNE BH6 .....336 B1
Waterbeech Dr HEND SO30 .....250 C3
Waterberry Dr WVILLE PO7 .....275 L1
Watercress Meadow
NARL SO24 .....167 N3
Waterditch Rd
CHCH/BSGR BH23 .....325 K4
Water End La CHIN RG24 .....70 C5
Water End Pk CHIN RG24 .....
Waterford Cl LYMN SO41 .....329 M4
PSTN BH14 .....333 J1
Waterford Gdns
CHCH/BSGR BH23 .....326 C8
Waterford La LYMN SO41 .....329 M4
Waterford Pl
CHCH/BSGR BH23 .....326 C8
Waterford Rd
CHCH/BSGR BH23 .....326 D9
NMIL/BTOS BH25 .....327 L4
Waterhouse La WSHM SO15 .....247 M5
Waterhouse Wy WSHM SO15 .....247 L4
Wateridge Rd BSTK RG21 .....69 M4
Water La FARN GU14 .....57 P6
FAWY SO45 .....268 A8
FNM GU9 .....96 F7
NARL SO24 .....168 F3
NBAD SO52 .....205 L2
SBNE BH6 .....336 B6
STHA RG19 .....24 F8
TOTT SO40 .....246 B3
WINC SO23 .....23 G4
Waterlily Cl BSTK RG21 .....7 K6

Waterlock Gdns *ENEY* PO4 ....317 M4
Waterloo Av *DEAN* RG23 ....68 F5
Waterloo Cl *HORN* PO8 ....255 M8
Waterloo Ct *ALDT* SP10 ....4 D5
Waterloo Pl *CI CWTH* RG45 * 41 J2
Waterloo Rd *ASHV* GU12.........13 H5
CFDH BH17............................320 E4
CWTH RG45 ....41 H2
GPORT PO12..........................315 N7
HAV PO9 ....14 C4
LYMN SO41 ....329 M3
MOOR/WNTN BH9 ....322 F8
WSHM SO15 ....247 P5
Waterloo St *SSEA* PO5 ....19 H4
Waterloo Ter *WSHM* SO15 ......20 D1
Waterloo Wy *RGWD* BH24 ......282 E3
Waterman Rd *RGWD* BH24 ......305 N3
Waterman Cl *BOR* GU35 ....154 C6
Watermans La *FAWY* SO45 ......268 A9
The Watermeadows
AND SP10 ....102 D5
Watermead Rd *FAWY* PO6.......297 N2
Watermill Rd
CHCH/BSGR BH23 ....324 E7
Watermills Cl *AND* SP10.........102 D4
Water Rede *FLEETS* GU52.......74 B9
Water Ridges *DEAN* RG23 ......88 F3
Water's Edge *HEND* SO30.......250 B5
Waters Edge Gdns
EMRTH PO10........................299 M1
Watersedge Rd *CHAM* PO6......296 C1
Waters Gn *BROC* SO42 ....286 C7
Waters Green Ct *BROC* SO42 ...286 C7
Watership Dr *RGWD* BH24 ......283 H5
Waterside *CHCH/BSGR* BH23 ...337 K2
FAWY SO45 ....268 B5
RGWD BH24 ....260 F9
Waterside Ct *ALTN* GU34 ......132 C5
FLEETS GU51 ....74 E1
Waterside Gdns
FHAM/PORC PO16................273 H9
Waterside La
FHAM/PORC PO16................296 A3
Waterside Ms *FLEETS* GU51 ....74 E1
Waterside Rd *ROMY* SO51 ......204 E4
Watersmeet
FHAM/PORC PO16................294 F5
The Waters *WHAM* PO17........272 C5
Waterston Cl *CFDH* BH17 ....320 F3
Water Tower Rd *BDST* BH18 ...300 E4
Water Wy *BSTK* RG21 ....7 J2
Waterworks Rd *CHAM* PO6......297 M1
PSF GU32 ....191 N8
RWIN SO21 ....207 L1
Watery La *AND* SP10...................5 F1
CHCH/BSGR BH23 ....325 L6
FLEETS GU52 ....74 B9
RGUW SO21 ....28 C1
Watkin Rd *BOSC* BH5............335 M2
HEND SO30.............................250 E2
Watley Cl *ROWN* SO16 ....227 H7
Watley La *RWIN* SO21............163 N3
RWIN SO21............................184 C9
RWIN SO21............................208 D2
Watling End *KBH* RG22 ....6 A3
Watson Acre *AND* SP10 ....102 C2
Watson Wk *TOTT* SO40 ....246 A4
Watt Cl *AND* SP10 ....102 A1
Watton Cl *CHAR* BH8 ....323 J5
Watton La *BPWT* SO32 ....233 P2
Watton Rd *FAWY* SO45 ....290 E6
Watts Cl *ROWN* SO16 ....247 J1
Watts Common Rd *ALDT* GU11 ...75 M5
Watts Rd *FARN* GU14 ....57 N8
FBDG SP6 ....250 C4
PSEA PO1 ....316 F1
Wavecrest Cl *TOTT* SO40.......247 K8
Wavell Av *CFDH* BH17 ....320 C3
Wavell Cl *KBH* RG22 ....90 A1
Wavell Rd *BWD* BH11 ....322 B3
LSOL/BMARY PO13 ....295 H6
NTID SP9 8
WEND SO18 ....249 J4
Wavell Wy *FUFL* SO22...........183 L1
Wavendon Av
NMIL/BTOS BH25 ....326 G7
Waverley Cl
LSOL/BMARY PO13 ....314 D2
Waveney Gn *ROWN* SO16.......247 J2
Waverley Av *BSTK* RG21 ....90 C1
FLEETS GU51 ....74 C1
HLER SO31............................269 L4
Waverley Cl *CBLY* GU15 ....58 E1
FBDG SP6 ....220 D9
FNM GU9 ....89 J8
ODIM RG29 ....72 E9
ROMY SO51...........................204 F4
Waverley Ct *HLER* SO31.........269 L5
Waverley Crs *BLE* BH15 ....320 F7
Waverley Dr *ASHV* GU12........76 F6
RWIN SO21............................144 F4
Waverley Gdns *ALDT* GU12 .....76 F6
Waverley Gv *ENEY* PO4 ....316 G6
Waverley La *FNM* GU9 ....116 E1
RWIN SO21 ....117 J2
Waverley Rd *CHAM* PO6........297 L1
FARN GU14 ....57 J8
FBDG SP6 ....220 D9
NMIL/BTOS BH25 ....327 K5
SSEA PO5 ....316 G6
Waverley Wy *AND* SP10 ....247 P6
The Waverleys *NTHA* RG18......25 N5
Wayfarer Cl *ENEY* PO4 * 317 L5
HLER SO31.............................269 J5
Wayfarers Wk *BPWT* SO32 ....210 F5
Wayfarer's Wk *LSOL/BMARY* PO13....315 H1
BPWT SO32 ....233 M4
DEAN RG23 ....89 J8
EMRTH PO10 ....299 L2
HAV PO9 ....14 A4
KSCL RG20 ....28 C7
KSCL RG20 ....47 N7
NARL SO24 ....128 G5

NARL SO24 ....186 G8
OVTN RG25 ....88 C5
RAND SP11 ....44 C1
WVILLE PO7.............................275 H2
Wayground Rd *WIMB* BH21.....300 A4
Waylands Pl *HEND* SO30.........250 A7
Wayman Rd *FARN* GU14..........57 M5
Wayne Rd *BKME/WDN* BH12 ...321 K6
Waynflete Cl *BPWT* SO32 ......232 A4
Waynflete La *FHAM* GU9 ....95 P9
Waynflete Pl *FUFL* SO22 ....164 E9
Ways End *CBLY* GU15 ....58 D1
Wayside *HLER* SO31 ....270 D2
Wayside Cl *LYMN* SO41 ....338 C1
Wayside Rd *DEAN* RG23 ....68 E7
RGWD BH24 ....281 L8
SBNE BH6 ....336 C2
Wayte St *CHAM* PO6..............297 H2
Waytown Cl *CFDH* BH17.........320 F5
Weald Cl *AND* SP10 ....270 C6
Weale Ct *BSTK* RG21 ....6 E5
Weardale Rd *CHFD* SO53 ....206 F9
Weatherby Gdns *HTWY* RG27 ....55 J7
Weathermore La *CHAR* SO34 ...150 E6
Weaver Moss *SHST* GU47 ....41 J7
Weavers Cl *AND* SP10.................4 E3
FERN BH22 ....280 E8
Weavers Down *LIPH* GU30 * ...174 E4
Weavers Gdns *RFNM* GU10 .....115 P5
Weavers Gn *HAV* PO9 ....277 J7
Weavers Piece *HTWY* RG27 * 53 M8
Weavers Wk *NWBY* RG14 * 16 E1
Weavills Rd *ELGH* SO50 ....230 A2
Webb Cl *CHIN* RG24 ....69 P2
HISD PO11..............................318 G6
Webb La *HISD* PO11...............318 G6
Webb Rd *FHAM/PORC* PO16 ...295 P3
Webbs Cl *RGWD* BH24 ....281 K3
Webbs Farm Cl *WHCH* RG28 ...85 L8
Webbs Gn *BPWT* SO32 ....233 M9
Webburn Gdns *WEND* SO18 ....229 J9
Webster Rd *FUFL* SO22 ....164 C6
MOOR/WNTN BH9 ....322 C4
Wedderburn Av *BOSC* BH5......335 M2
Wedgewood Gv *FAWY* SO45 ...290 E5
Wedgewood Gdns
CHCH/BSGR BH23 ....305 N7
Wedgwood Wy *HORN* PO8 ......255 N8
Wedgwood Dr *PSTN* BH14 ......333 J1
Wedman's La *HTWY* RG27 ....53 N6
Wedmore Cl *FUFL* SO22 ....183 J3
Weeke Cl *RSAL* SP5 ....199 H6
Weeke Manor Cl *FUFL* SO22 ...164 E5
Weevil La *GPORT* PO12 ....315 P3
Weir Av *FARN* GU14 ....75 P1
Weir Cl *FARN* GU14 ....75 P1
Weir Rd *FARN* GU14 ....75 H2
HTWY RG27 ....54 C9
The Weirs *WINC* SO23 ....23 G6
The Weir *WHCH* RG28 ....85 L8
Welbeck Av *PTSW* SO17 ....248 D1
Welbeck Cl *FARN* GU14 ....57 N9
Welch Rd *ENEY* PO4 ....316 C6
GPORT PO12 ....315 L1
Welch Wy *ROWN* SO16 ....227 J7
Welchwood Cl *HORN* PO8 ....255 P5
Weldon Av *BWD* BH11 ....301 N8
Weldon Cl *FLEETS* GU52 ....74 E7
Welland Gdns *WEND* SO18 .....249 K1
Welland Gn *ROWN* SO16 ....247 J3
Welland Rd *WIMB* BH21 ....300 F1
Wellands Rd *LYND* SO43 ....264 C5
Wella Rd *KBH* RG22 ....90 B1
Wellbrooke Gdns *CHFD* SO53 ...206 D6
Wellburn Cl *SHST* GU47 ....41 J7
Well Cl *CBLY* GU15 ....58 A1
NMIL/BTOS BH25 ....327 H6
OVTN RG25 ....108 C1
Well Copse Cl *HORN* PO8 ....256 C2
Weller Dr *CBLY* GU15 ....58 B2
Wellers Cl *TOTT* SO40 ....245 P4
Wellesley Av
CHCH/BSGR BH23 ....325 M8
Wellesley Cl *ASHV* GU12 ....76 E5
WVILLE PO7.............................275 N5
Wellesley Dr *CWTH* RG45 ....40 F1
Wellesley Gdn *FNM* GU9..........89 J8
Wellesley Gv *AS4V* GU12 * 3 F4
Wellesley Rd *ALDT* SP10..........102 E4
FARN GU14 ....137 H3
RFNM GU10 ....137 H3
Welles Rd *CHFD* SO53 ....206 A7
Well House Cl *FBDC* SP6 ....219 P1
Well House La *FUFL* SO22 ......164 F2
HTWY RG27 ....38 E3
Wellhouse Rd *ALTN* GU34 ......131 P7
Wellington Av *ALDT* GU11 ....2 D2
BOR GU35 ....153 P6
CHCH/BSGR BH23 ....325 N8
FLEETS GU51 ....74 E2
WEND SO18 ....249 K4
Wellington Cl *FAWY* SO45 ......267 P9
HORN PO8 ....256 D5
NWBY RG14 ....16 A3
SHST GU47 ....41 K6
Wellington Ct *HEND* SO30 * 249 L1
Wellington Cts *TADY* RG26 ....33 N5
Wellington Gdns *ALDT* GU11 * 2 D4
Wellington Gv
FHAM/PORC PO16 ....295 N2
Wellingtonia Av *EWKG* RG40 ....40 C2
Wellington Gv *FNM* GU9 ....96 D4
Wellington Pk *HEND* SO30 ......250 A2
Wellington Pl *ASHV* GU12 ....76 E4
LYMN SO41 * 329 M3
Wellington Rd *AND* SP10 ....4 A2
CHAR BH8...............................334 D1
CWTH RG45 ....40 F1
PSTN BH14 ....321 L9
SHST GU47 ....41 J6
WEND SO18 ....248 F1
Wellington St *ALDT* GU11 ....2 E2
SSEA PO5 ....19 G4

Wellington Ter *DEAN* RG23 .....68 F5
SHST GU47 ....41 K6
Wellington Wy *FARN* GU14 ......75 L5
WVILLE PO7.............................275 N3
Well La *ALTN* GU34 ....113 P2
BPWT SO32 ....232 F5
FBDC SP6 ....241 J1
HASM GU27 ....157 J7
HLER SO31 ....270 A8
PLE BH15...............................320 E8
Wellmans Meadow
KSCL RG20 ....48 B2
Well Meadow *HAV* PO9 ....276 E4
NWBY RG14 ....14 E2
Wellowbrook Cl *CHFD* SO53 ...206 C7
Wellow Cl *HAV* PO9 ....14 C2
WEND SO18 ....249 L4
Wellow Dro *ROMY* SO51 ....202 E6
Wellow Gdns
FHAM/STUB PO14 ....271 J8
Wellow Wood Rd *ROMY* SO51 ...202 D5
Well Rd *RFNM* GU10 ....94 G5
Wells Cots *FNM* GU9 ....116 A3
Wells La *RGUW* GU3 ....158 C3
Wellsmoor *FHAM/STUB* PO14 ...271 J7
Wells Pl *ELGH* SO50 ....229 J2
Wells's La *WHCH* RG28 ....85 K7
Well St *KSCL* RG20 ....30 F8
Wellsworth La *HAV* PO9 ....257 J8
Wellsworth La *HAV* PO9 ....257 J8
Welsh La *THLE* RG7 ....37 M4
Welshman's Rd *THLE* RG7 ....35 J1
Welton Ct *BSTK* RG21 ....6 C5
Wembley Gv *CHAM* PO6..........297 K3
Wendan Rd *NWBY* RG14 ....16 D7
Wendover Cl
NMIL/BTOS BH25 ....327 H6
Wendover Dr *FRIM* GU16 ....59 H2
Wendover Rd *HAV* PO9 ....14 D4
Wendys Crs *FERN* BH22 * 302 F5
Wenlock Wy *STHA* SO34 ....25 N5
Wensley Gdns *EMRTH* PO10 ....277 M7
Wentwood Gdns
NMIL/BTOS BH25 ....327 M5
Wentworth Av *BOSC* BH5........335 N2
Wentworth Cl *ASHV* GU12 ....76 F5
BOSC BH5..............................335 N3
FNM GU9 ....89 L6
YTLY GU46 ....40 F9
Wentworth Ct *NWBY* RG14 .....17 C5
Wentworth Crs *ASHV* GU12 ....76 E5
DEAN RG23 ....89 L6
Wentworth Dr *BDST* BH18 .....300 C8
CHCH/BSGR BH23 ....306 B4
HORN PO8 ....256 B4
Wentworth Gdns *ALTN* GU34 ...132 E5
FAWY SO45 ....290 F7
ITCH SO19..............................269 K1
Wentworth Gra *FUFL* SO22 .....22 B7
Wentworth Gv *FAWY* SO45 .....290 F8
Wescott Wy *BWD* BH11..........301 N9
Wesermarsch Rd *HORN* PO8 ...256 A7
Wesley Cl *BMTH* BH1 ....335 J1
ITCH SO19 ....249 M7
Wesley Gv *HSEA* PO3..............297 H6
Wesley Rd *PSTN* BH14............321 L7
WIMB BH21 ....278 F9
WINC SO23 ....23 H5
Wessex Av *NMIL/BTOS* BH25 ...327 J5
ODIM RG29 ....93 K2
Wessex Cl *BSTK* RG21 ....69 K9
CHCH/BSGR BH23 ....325 N8
FAWY SO45.............................291 H8
LSOL/BMARY PO13 ....314 C2
Wessex Crs *ODIM* RG29...........93 K2
Wessex Dr *FUFL* SO22 ....164 F5
ODIM RG29 ....93 K2
Wessex Est *RGWD* BH24 ....282 F1
Wessex Gdns *AND* SP10 ....8 B3
FHAM/PORC PO16 ....295 M2
ROMY SO51...........................204 F6
Wessex Ga *CHAR* BH8 ....323 J9
Wessex La *WEND* SO18 ....228 F8
Wessex Pl *FNM* GU9 ....116 C1
Wessex Rd *HORN* PO8.............236 C9
PSTN BH14 ....321 J9
RGWD BH24 ....282 F1
Wessex Wy *CHAR* BH8 ....323 J9
RWIN SO21 ....208 A5
WBNE BH4 ....334 C2
WCLF BH2 ....8 D3
Wess Av *FNM* GU9 ....96 D5
WIMB BH21 ....280 D1

Westbury Cl *CHAM* PO6..........274 D9
CHCH/BSGR BH23 ....305 L9
FLEETS GU51 ....74 F4
NMIL/BTOS BH25 ....327 J7
Westbury Ct *HEND* SO30 ....250 C6
Westbury Gdns *FLEETS* GU51 ...74 G4
FNM GU9 ....96 E7
Westbury Rd
FHAM/PORC PO16 ....11 H5
RGWD BH24 ....282 F2
WSHM SO15 ....247 K4
Westbury Wy *ASHV* GU12 ....3 K2
West Butts St *PLE* BH15 ....332 D1
Westby Rd *BOSC* BH5 ....335 L2
Westcliff Cl
LSOL/BMARY PO13 ....314 C1
West Cliff Gdns *WCLF* BH2 .....8 B6
Westcliff Ms *ITCH* SO19.........248 F8
West Cliff Rd *WBNE* BH4 ....334 C4
WCLF BH2 ....8 C5
West Cl *FNM* GU9...................96 D4
LYMN SO41.............................329 H5
SBNE BH6 ....336 E2
West Common *FAWY* SO45 .....312 F2
Westcot Rd *FAWY* SO45 ....290 D6
Westcroft Pde
NMIL/BTOS BH25 ....327 K5
Westcroft Pk *BDST* BH18 ......300 E9
Westcroft Rd *GPORT* PO12 .....315 K3
Westdeane Ct *BSTK* RG21 ....6 E7
Westdown Rd *BWD* BH11........322 A2
West Downs Cl
FHAM/PORC PO16 ....272 C6
West Dr *ELGH* SO50 ....207 M9
West End *TADY* RG26 ....105 H1
West End Cl *BSTK* RG21 ....22 B4
West End Gv *FNM* GU9.............96 A9
West End La *ALTN* GU34 ....149 L4
RFNM GU10 ....115 N9
West End Rd *HEND* SO30 ....249 M2
HEND SO30.............................249 P7
THLE RG7 ....35 M1
WEND SO18 ....249 J3
West End Ter *FUFL* SO22 ....22 B4
Westerdale *STHA* RG19 ....25 M4
Westerham Cl *CHAM* PO6.......296 C1
Westerham Ct *CCLF* BH13 ......334 D5
Westering *ROMY* SO51 ....204 G5
Westerley Cl *HLER* SO31 * 270 E9
Western Av
AND SP10 ....4 C6
CCLF BH13 ....333 N1
EMRTH PO10 ....299 L1
NBNE BH10 ....322 D3
NWBY RG14 ....24 C3
WSHM SO15 ....247 J5
West End La ... (duplicate)
Western District Cut
WSHM SO15 ....247 P4
Western Esp *SHAM* SO14 ....20 B3
Western La *ODIM* RG29............93 K1
Western Pde *EMRTH* PO10 .....277 N8
ITCH SO19..............................268 C2
SSEA PO5 ....19 F7
Western Rd *ALDT* GU11 ....2 A4
AND SP10 ....4 C5
CCLF BH13 ....153 P7
CHAM PO6.............................296 C5
CHFD SO53 ....206 G8
FHAM/PORC PO16 ....11 G6
FUFL SO22 ....22 B3
HAV PO9 ....14 D4
HEND SO30.............................249 M2
LISS GU33 ....192 D2
NWBY RG14 ....24 C3
Western Wy
FHAM/PORC PO16 ....11 H6
GPORT PO12 ....315 J5
KBH RG22 ....89 P1
Westfield Av
FHAM/STUB PO14 ....294 D1
HISD PO11..............................318 E5
West Field Cl *TADY* RG26 ....34 E6
Westfield Cl *ELGH* SO50 ....230 C5
HLER SO31 ....269 N8
WIMB BH21 ....278 D9
Westfield Common
NWBY RG14.........................269 M8
Westfield Crs *CHFD* SO53 ....228 E1
NTHA RG18..............................25 L3
Westfield Dr *NARL* SO24 ....186 E6
Westfield Gdns
CHCH/BSGR BH23 ....325 M6
Westfield La *RFNM* GU10 ....115 N4
Westfield Rd *WINC* SO23 ....145 K8
Westfield Rd *BSTK* RG21.........69 K9
CBLY GU15 ....58 E3
CHFD SO53 ....228 E1
ENEY PO4 ....317 J5
FUFL SO22 ....164 C2
GPORT PO12 ....315 K3
WBNE BH4 ....334 B4
West Green Rd *HTWY* RG27 .....54 C7
Westgate *FBDC* SP6 ....240 C2
Westgrove Rd *BSTK* RG21 ....7 H2
Westham Cl *CFDH* BH17 ....320 G1

West Ham Cl *KBH* RG22 ....68 F8
West Ham La *KBH* RG22 ....68 G8
West Haye Rd *HISD* PO11.......319 K7
West Hayes *LYMN* SO41 ....329 M4
Westheath Rd *BDST* BH18 ......300 D9
West Heath Rd *FARN* GU14 .....57 N9
West Hill *FLEETS* GU52 * 82 B4
West Hill Dr *FAWY* SO45 ....268 B5
FUFL SO22 ....22 A4
West Hill Gdns *FLEETS* GU51 ...74 A2
West Hill Pk *FUFL* SO22 ....164 E7
West Hill Pl *WCLF* BH2 ....8 B4
West Hill Rd *WCLF* BH2 ....8 B5
West Hill Rd North
RWIN SO21 ....144 F3
West Hill Rd South
RWIN SO21 ....144 F4
West Hoe La *BPWT* SO32 ....232 D4
West Horton La *ELGH* SO50 ....229 P5
West Howe Cl *BWD* BH11 ....322 A3
The West Hundreds
FLEETN GU51 ....74 B1
Westland *NTHA* RG18..............25 L3
Westland Dr *WILLE* PO7 ....275 N6
Westland Gdns *GPORT* PO12 ...12 A5
Westlands Ct
CHCH/BSGR BH23 ....305 L8
Westlands Gv
FHAM/PORC PO16 ....295 N2
Westlands Rd *NWBY* RG14 ......17 F7
West La *HISD* PO11................318 E4
LYMN SO41.............................328 E6
NBAD SO52 ....205 J8
Westley Cl *FUFL* SO22 ....164 E6
Westley Gv *FHAM/STUB* PO14 ...10 D7
Westley La *RWIN* SO21 ....163 M3
Westlyn Rd *TADY* RG26 ....34 F5
Westmead *FARN* GU14 ....76 A1
West Md *FNM* GU9 * 96 B9
Westmead Ct *HISD* PO11.........318 D5
Westmead Dr *NWBY* RG14 ......24 C7
West Mills *NWBY* RG14 ....16 E2
West Mills Rd *NWBY* RG14 ......240 C2
West Mills Yd *NWBY* RG14 * 16 D2
Westminster Cl *LYMN* SO41 ....338 E2
KBH RG22 ....89 M4
Westminster Gdns
FHAM/STUB PO14 ....271 J7
Westminster Ga *FUFL* SO22 ....183 K1
Westminster Ct *CCLF* BH13 ....334 B5
Westminster Rd East
CCLF BH13 ....334 B5
West Moors Rd *FERN* BH22 ....302 E1
WIMB BH21 ....302 A2
Westmorland Dr *CBLY* GU15 ...58 G2
Westmorland Rd *CHFD* SO53 ...206 G8
Weston Av *ENEY* PO4..............317 K4
Weston Cl *ITCH* SO19..............269 H1
Weston Ct *RAND* SP11 ....92 E3
Weston Cres *ROWN* SO16 ....227 L1
Weston Down Rd *RWIN* SO21 ...126 E4
Weston Dr *BMTH* BH1 ....8 A4
Weston Grove Rd *ITCH* SO19 ...248 F9
Weston La *ITCH* SO19.............268 G2
PSF GU32 ....215 H5
ROWN SO16 ....268 E2
RSAL SP5 ....158 A2
Weston Rd *ELGH* SO50 ....229 J1
EPSF GU31 ....193 N2
OVTN RG25 ....92 A8
WIMB BH21 ....279 H7
West Overcliff Dr *WBNE* BH4 ...334 A5
Westover La *RGWD* BH24.......282 B3
Westover Rd *BMTH* BH1 ....8 E3
FLEETN GU51 ....74 E3
HSEA PO3 ....297 K9
LYMN SO41.............................338 G2
ROWN SO16 ....247 L1
West Pk *RAND* SP11 ....81 H5
West Park Cl *FBDC* SP6 ....219 K7
West Park La *FBDC* SP6 ....219 J7
West Park Rd *WSHM* SO15 .....20 C3
West Portway *AND* SP10 ....81 P9
West Quay Rd *PLE* BH15 ....332 D2
WSHM SO15 ....20 B4
Westray Cl *BSTK* RG21 ....7 J2
Westridge *KSCL* RG20............29 M9
West Rdg *RFNM* GU10 * 97 M6
West Ring *RFNM* GU10 ....248 D2
West Rd *BOSC* BH5................335 N1
CHCH/BSGR BH23 ....305 L8
EMRTH PO10 ....299 L1
FARN GU14 ....57 P5
FAWY SO45 ....267 P9
FAWY SO45 ....268 F9
HEND SO30 ....250 A7
ITCH SO19..............................338 D1
LYMN SO41.............................338 D1
RWIN SO21 ....208 A5
SHAM SO14 ....248 C9
WHAM PO17 ....272 B2
West Rw *WIMB* BH21 ....300 D1
Westrow Gdns *WSHM* SO15 ...248 A4
Westrow Rd *WSHM* SO15 ....248 A4
Westside *AMSY* SP5 ....118 A5
Westside Cl *KBH* RG22 ....67 P9
Westside La *WVILLE* PO7 ....275 L1
West St *AND* SP10 ....4 C4
BPWT SO32 ....233 M7
EMRTH PO10 ....299 M1
FAWY SO45 ....268 B5
FBDC SP6 ....240 C2
FHAM/PORC PO16 ....11 F6
FHAM/STUB PO14 ....293 M1
FNM GU9 ....115 P1
HASM GU27 ....157 H7
HAV PO9 ....14 C5
KSCL RG20 ....30 D9
NARL SO24 ....168 A1
NWBY RG14 ....16 D1
ODIM RG29 ....93 J3

PLE BH15 ....332 D1
PSEA PO11 ....18 B6
RGWD BH24 ....282 C2
SHAM SO14 ....20 D6
TADY RG26 ....34 E6
WHAM PO17 ....274 A4
WHAM BH21 ....300 D1
WVLLE PO7 ....254 E2
West Street Cl TADY RG26 ....34 D6
West Vw BOR GU35 * 153 N7
West View Dr STOK SO20 ....123 L6
Westview Gdns AND SP10 ....4 C6
West View Rd BOR GU35 ....155 K4
  CHCH/BSGR BH23 ....325 J9
  PLE BH15 ....320 E8
Westview Rd FUFL SO22 ....164 B5
Westward Rd HEND SO30 ....250 C3
West Wy AND SP10 ....5 K1
  BDST BH18 ....320 B1
  SHAM SO14 ....329 J5
  MOOR/WNTN BH9 ....323 H5
Westway FHAM PO15 ....271 L7
West Way Cl
  MOOR/WNTN BH9 ....323 H6
Westways CHAM PO6 ....299 P7
Westways Cl FHAM/STUB PO14 ....294 E7
Westways Ct BOR GU35 ....227 N7
Westwood Av FERN BH22 ....302 C2
Westwood Gdns CHFD SO53 ....206 G5
Westwood La RGUW GU3 ....77 M9
Westwood Pk
  NMIL/BTOS BH25 * 326 C2
  LYND SO43 ....264 F4
  NEND PO2 ....296 C5
  NWBY RG14 ....17 K9
  PTSW SO17 ....248 B3
Westwood Vw NARL SO24 ....187 J5
Wetherby La CFDH BH17 ....320 C2
Wetherby Gdns AND SP10 ....82 F3
  FARN GU14 ....76 B4
  TOTT SO40 ....246 A3
Wetherdown EPSF GU31 ....215 N2
Wey Bank ALTN GU34 ....114 C7
Weybank Cl FERN BH22 ....301 J2
Weybourne Rd FNM GU9 ....96 C8
Weybridge Cl HLER SO31 ....270 F4
Weybridge Md YTLY GU46 ....40 F7
Weybrook Ct TADY RG26 ....50 C9
Wey Cl ASHV GU12 ....97 M7
Weycombe Rd HASM GU27 ....157 H5
Weydon Farm La FNM GU9 * 116 B2
Weydon Hill Cl FNM GU9 ....116 B2
Weydon Hill Rd FNM GU9 ....116 B2
Weydon La FNM GU9 ....116 A2
Weydon Mill La FNM GU9 ....116 B1
Weydown Rd HASM GU27 ....156 C6
Wey Hl HASM GU27 ....156 F7
Weyhill Cl FHAM/PORC PO16 ....273 N9
  HAV PO9 ....276 D5
  TADY RG26 ....50 C9
Weyhill Gdns RAND SP11 ....81 K9
Weyhill Rd AND SP10 ....4 A5
  RAND SP11 ....81 K9
Weyland Cl LIPH GU30 ....175 K2
Wey Lodge Cl LIPH GU30 * 175 L3
Weyman's Av NBNE BH10 ....322 C1
Weymans Dr NBNE BH10 ....322 C1
Weymouth Av GPORT PO12 ....295 K9
Weymouth Rd NEND PO2 * 296 F8
  PSTN BH14 ....321 N6
Weyside Pk ALTN GU34 * 133 H4
Weysprings HASM GU27 ....156 E6
Weysprings Cl BSTK RG21 ....7 J5
Wey Valley Cl FNM GU9 ....96 F4
Weywood La FNM GU9 ....96 E4
Whaddon Cha
  FHAM/STUB PO14 ....293 P7
Whaddon Ct HAV PO9 ....256 G7
Whaddon La RWIN SO21 ....208 C5
Whale Island Wy NEND PO2 ....296 E8
Whalesmead Cl ELGH SO50 ....229 P3
Whalesmead Rd ELGH SO50 ....229 P3
Whaley Rd NEND PO2 ....296 D8
Wharf Cl BKME/WDN BH12 ....321 N6
Wharfdale Rd
  BKME/WDN BH12 ....321 M6
  WBNE BH4 ....334 C2
Wharfenden Wy FRIM GU16 ....58 E7
Wharf Hl WINC SO23 ....23 G7
Wharf Rd ASHV GU12 ....76 F8
  FARN GU16 ....58 D6
  ITCH SO19 ....248 F8
  NEND PO2 ....296 E9
  NWBY RG14 ....17 F2
Wharf St NWBY RG14 ....16 E2
The Wharf HAV PO9 * 17 F2
Wharf Wy FRIM GU16 ....58 E7
Wharncliffe Gdns
  CHCH/BSGR BH23 ....326 C8
Wharncliffe Rd BMTH BH1 ....335 K2
  CHCH/BSGR BH23 ....326 C8
  ITCH SO19 ....248 F8
Whartons La TOTT SO40 ....246 A7
Whatleigh Cl PLE BH15 ....332 E2
Wheat Cl CHFD SO53 ....206 B7
Wheatcroft Dr WEND SO18 ....249 K2
Wheatcroft Rd
  LSOL/BMARY PO13 ....314 D2
Wheatear Dr EPSF GU31 ....216 A3
Wheatears Dr ROMY SO51 ....224 E1
Wheatland Cl FUFL SO22 ....183 M1
Wheatlands
  FHAM/STUB PO14 ....271 J6
Wheatlands Av HISD PO11 ....319 L7
Wheatlands Crs HISD PO11 ....319 L7
Wheatley La ALTN GU34 ....134 E2
Wheatley Rd ALDT GU11 ....2 C2
Wheaton Rd LTDN BH7 ....335 N1
Wheatsheaf Cl HEND SO30 ....250 B5
Wheatsheaf Dr HORN PO8 ....255 M8
Wheatsheaf La NWBY RG14 ....24 E3
Wheatstone Rd ENEY PO4 ....316 C5
Wheeler Cl GPORT PO12 ....315 M2

THLE RG7 ....27 K4
WHCH RG28 ....85 M7
Wheelers Green Wy
  STHA RG19 ....25 P5
Wheelers Hl HTWY RG27 ....72 B3
Wheelers La BWD BH11 ....301 M7
Wheelers Wk FAWY SO45 ....290 G9
Wheelhouse Rd RWIN SO21 * 125 L5
Wheelhouse Pk NBAD SO52 * 206 C4
Wheelwrights La GSHT GU26 ....155 P4
Whernside Cl ROWN SO16 ....247 K3
Wherwell Cl HAV PO9 ....277 H5
Wherwell Rd FARN GU14 ....57 L8
Whichers Cl HAV PO9 ....277 H2
Whichers Gate Rd HAV PO9 ....277 H2
Whimbrel Cl ENEY PO4 ....317 L3
Whinchat Cl FHAM PO15 ....272 A6
  HTWY RG27 ....55 H6
Whincroft Cl FERN BH22 ....302 E1
Whincroft Dr FERN BH22 ....302 E2
Whinfield Rd FAWY SO45 ....268 A9
Whin Holt FLEETS SO22 ....74 D6
Whins Cl CBLY GU15 ....58 A1
Whins Dr CBLY GU15 ....58 A1
Whinwhistle Rd ROMY SO51 ....225 H2
Whistler Cl BSTK RG21 ....69 N9
Whistler Gv SHST GU47 ....41 L8
Whistler Rd ITCH SO19 ....249 L8
Whistlers Ct FNM GU9 ....305 M7
Whistlers La THLE RG7 ....35 J5
Whitaker Crs LYMN SO41 ....329 J4
Whitakers Ct NTHA RG18 ....25 L3
Whitby Av BDST BH18 ....320 C2
Whitby Cl CHCH/BSGR BH23 ....324 B3
  FARN GU14 ....76 D3
Whitby Crs BDST BH18 ....320 C2
Whitby Rd LYMN SO41 ....338 E2
Whitchurch Av BDST BH18 ....320 E1
Whitchurch Cl ALDT GU11 ....97 K5
Whitchurch Ct ITCH SO19 ....249 H8
Whitchurch Rd FLEETN GU51 ....74 A1
Whitcombe Cl TOTT SO40 ....246 C4
Whitcombe Gdns NEND PO2 ....297 H6
Whiteacres Cl GPORT PO12 ....315 M3
White Acres Rd FRIM GU16 ....58 E9
Whitebeam Cl LISS GU33 ....173 P5
White Barn Crs LYMN SO41 ....328 A4
Whitebeam Cl
  FHAM/STUB PO14 ....10 A7
  HORN PO8 ....256 C6
  RWIN SO21 ....208 A5
White Beam Ri HORN PO8 ....256 C7
Whitebeam Rd HEND SO30 ....250 D5
Whitebeams Gdns FARN GU14 ....75 K1
Whitebeam Wy NBAD SO52 ....205 L8
  VWD BH31 ....259 H5
Whitechimney Rw
  EMRTH PO10 ....277 P7
White City CWTH RG45 ....41 L1
Whitecliff Crs PSTN BH14 ....333 J1
Whitecliffe Av HASM GU27 ....317 J1
Whitecliff Rd PSTN BH14 ....333 H1
White Cliff Rd PSTN BH14 ....333 J1
White Cl PLE BH15 ....321 J5
White Cloud Pk ENEY PO4 ....317 H5
White Cottage Cl FNM GU9 ....96 D5
Whitecroft FAWY SO45 * 268 C8
Whitecross Cl CFDH BH17 ....320 C1
Whitecross Gdns NEND PO2 ....297 H6
Whitedell La WHAM PO17 ....273 H6
White Dirt La HORN PO8 ....256 B1
Whitedown ALTN GU34 ....132 C4
Whitedown La ALTN GU34 ....132 D7
Whitedown Rd TADY RG26 ....34 A4
White Farm Cl NBNE BH10 ....322 D7
Whitefield Rd FAWY SO45 ....290 E6
  NMIL/BTOS BH25 ....327 J4
  PSTN BH14 ....333 J1
White Gates BPWT SO32 ....231 H7
Whitehall CHCH/BSGR BH23 ....326 B5
Whitehall Rd STOK SO20 ....162 B1
Whitehart Flds RGWD BH24 ....282 G1
White Hart La BSTK RG21 ....7 G7
  FHAM/PORC PO16 ....295 M2
  TADY RG26 ....50 B5
  TOTT SO40 ....244 F3
White Hart Rd ELGH SO50 ....230 C3
  GPORT PO12 ....12 D4
  PSEA PO1 ....18 C6
Whitehaven
  FHAM/PORC PO16 ....295 M2
  HORN PO8 ....256 D5
Whitehayes Cl
  CHCH/BSGR BH23 ....325 H5
Whitehayes Rd
  CHCH/BSGR BH23 ....324 G6
Whitehead Cl CHIN RG24 ....69 H3
White Heather Ct FAWY SO45 ....268 C4
White Hl KSCL RG20 ....46 C3
Whitehill La NARL SO24 ....168 C3
Whitehill Rd BOR GU35 ....154 D7
Whitehorn Dr RSAL SP5 ....223 M4
White Horse Dr PLE BH15 ....320 E7
White Horse La EWKG RG40 ....39 M7
  WVLLE PO7 ....255 J5
Whitehouse Cl FARN GU14 ....58 A7
White House Cl KBH RG22 ....88 D8
Whitehouse Gdns PSF GU52 ....191 L9
White House Gdns
  WSHM SO15 ....247 L5
  YTLY GU46 ....40 D7
Whitehouse Rd WIMB BH21 ....300 F3
White House Wk FNM GU9 ....96 D4
White Knights
  NMIL/BTOS BH25 ....327 H8
White Ladies Cl HAV PO9 ....15 H6
Whitelands CHCH/BSGR BH23 ....305 P5
Whitelands Rd NTHA RG18 ....25 N3
White La OVTN RG25 ....92 D1
  RWIN SO21 ....184 A6
  TADY RG26 ....67 H4

Whitelaw Rd WSHM SO15 ....247 M4
Whiteleaf La WVLLE PO7 ....234 E5
Whitelegg Wy NBNE BH10 ....322 E2
Whiteley La FHAM PO15 ....271 J1
  HLER SO31 ....271 J3
Whiteley Wy FHAM PO15 ....271 L3
White Lion Wk GPORT PO12 ....13 H1
White Lion Wy YTLY GU46 ....40 E7
White Lodge Gdns
  FHAM/PORC PO16 ....272 C6
Whitemoor La TOTT SO40 ....225 L8
Whitemoor Rd BROC SO42 ....286 D7
Whitenap Cl ROMY SO51 ....204 G7
Whitenap La ROMY SO51 ....204 G7
White Oak Wy RAND SP11 ....102 A6
White Post La RFNM GU10 ....116 A6
White Rd CBLY GU15 ....41 N8
  ENEY PO4 ....317 J2
White Rose La FNM GU9 ....116 B5
Whites Cl HTWY RG27 ....71 N3
Whites Hl RWIN SO21 ....208 F1
  THLE RG7 ....26 G3
Whiteshoot RSAL SP5 ....200 B9
  STOK SO20 ....140 A9
Whiteshoot Hl RSAL SP5 ....200 B9
Whiteshute La WINC SO23 ....183 N2
Whites La FAWY SO45 ....291 K6
Whites Rd FARN GU14 ....76 D5
  ITCH SO19 ....249 J6
Whitestone Cl ROWN SO16 ....247 K3
Whitestones KBH RG22 ....89 N5
White Swan Rd PSEA PO1 ....19 F3
Whitethorn Cl ASHV GU12 ....97 P2
Whitethorn Rd HISD PO11 ....319 H5
Whitewater Rd ODIM RG29 ....72 B8
Whiteways WIMB BH21 ....278 G8
Whiteways Ms HLER SO31 ....270 D9
The White Wy BPWT SO32 ....211 L4
Whitewood CHIN RG24 ....70 A1
Whitfield Cl HASM GU27 ....157 H4
Whitfield Pk RGWD BH24 ....281 P4
Whitfield Rd HASM GU27 ....157 H5
Whitgift Cl DEAN RG23 ....89 M6
Whithedwood Av
  WSHM SO15 ....247 P3
Whithers La BROC SO42 ....310 C2
Whitlet Cl FNM GU9 ....116 B1
Whitley Cl EMRTH PO10 ....277 P5
  YTLY GU46 ....56 E1
Whitley Wy FARN GU14 ....75 M1
  NMIL/BTOS BH25 ....327 H8
Whitmarsh La CHIN RG24 ....70 C1
Whitmead La RFNM GU10 ....117 L5
Whitmoor Vale Rd
  GSHT GU26 ....155 N1
Whitmore Cl SHST GU47 ....41 L6
Whitmore Gn FNM GU9 ....96 E5
Whitmore La RFNM GU10 ....155 N2
Whitmore Vale Rd
  GSHT GU26 ....156 A1
Whitney Rd CHIN RG24 ....69 P5
Whitsbury Cl CHAR BH8 ....323 K5
Whitsbury Rd FBDG SP6 ....240 D1
  HAV PO9 ....276 C5
Whitstable Rd FHAM PO15 ....296 C1
Whittington Cl FAWY SO45 ....268 B8
Whittington Ct EMRTH PO10 ....299 M1
Whittle Av FHAM PO15 ....271 J5
Whittle Cl ASHV GU12 ....76 E7
  SHST GU47 ....41 N7
Whittle Crs FARN GU14 ....57 N6
Whittle Rd AND SP10 ....101 P1
  WIMB BH21 ....279 P7
Whittles Wy PLE BH15 ....332 D1
Whitwell HLER SO31 ....269 L3
Whitwell Rd ENEY PO4 ....316 G7
Whitworth Cl GPORT PO12 ....12 B2
Whitworth Crs WEND SO18 ....248 F3
  NEND PO2 ....297 H9
Whitworth Rd GPORT PO12 ....12 B2
  NEND PO2 ....297 H9
Whynot La AND SP10 ....248 F3
Whyte Av ASHV GU12 ....97 K4
Whyte Cl FAWY SO45 ....290 D6
Whyteways ELGH SO50 ....207 H9
Wick Dr NMIL/BTOS BH25 ....326 C5
Wicket Hl RFNM GU10 ....116 A4
Wicket La RFNM GU10 ....116 A4
The Wicket FAWY SO45 ....268 B8
Wickfield Av CHCH/BSGR BH23 ....324 F5
Wickfield Cl CHCH/BSGR BH23 ....324 F5
Wickham Cl ALTN GU34 ....132 D7
  FLEETS GU52 ....74 B7
  TADY RG26 ....50 C6
Wickham Rd BPWT SO32 ....233 L8
  FHAM/PORC PO16 ....11 G1
  FLEETS GU52 ....74 B6
  WHAM PO17 ....272 F5
Wickham St PSEA PO1 ....18 E3
Wick Hill La EWKG RG40 ....40 B1
Wicklea Rd SBNE BH6 ....336 F2
Wicklow Cl KBH RG22 ....88 E8
Wickmeads Rd SBNE BH6 ....336 E2
Wickor Cl EMRTH PO10 ....277 N8
Wickor Wy EMRTH PO10 ....277 M7
Wick Point Ms
  CHCH/BSGR BH23 ....336 F1
Wicor Mill La
  FHAM/PORC PO16 ....295 M3
Widbury Rd LYMN SO41 ....329 J5
Widden Cl LYMN SO41 ....308 B6
Widdicombe Av PSTN BH14 ....333 N1
Widecombe Dr FAWY SO45 ....268 A6
Wide Lane Cl BROC SO42 ....286 F8
Widgeon Cl GPORT PO12 ....315 M3

ROWN SO16 ....227 M6
Widgeons ALTN GU34 ....132 F4
Widget Cl BWD BH11 ....322 B5
Widlers La BPWT SO32 ....209 L7
Widley Ct FHAM/STUB PO14 ....294 D5
Widley Court Dr FHAM PO6 ....297 J2
Widley Gdns WVILLE PO7 ....275 M7
  NEND PO2 ....296 E7
Widley Rd FHAM PO6 ....297 J1
Widley Wk FHAM PO6 ....275 H8
Widworthy Dr BDST BH18 ....300 B8
Wield Cl HAV PO9 ....276 C6
Wield Rd ALTN GU34 ....130 D6
Wigan Crs HAV PO9 ....276 B8
Wigan Rd FARN GU14 ....75 P1
Wight Cl KBH RG22 ....89 M4
Wight Wk FERN BH22 ....302 E6
Wigmore Rd TADY RG26 ....34 A5
Wilberforce Cl FUFL SO22 ....164 D9
Wilberforce Rd GPORT PO12 ....315 N7
  SSEA PO5 ....18 E7
Wild Arum Wy CHFD SO53 ....206 B8
Wildburn Ct TOTT SO40 ....246 A1
Wild Cherry Wy CHFD SO53 ....206 C7
Wild Ridings DEAN RG23 ....88 A2
Wildern Cl HLER SO31 ....271 H3
Wildern Ct HEND SO30 ....249 L2
Wildern La HEND SO30 ....250 B3
Wilderness Rd FRIM GU16 ....58 D3
Wildern La HEND SO30 ....250 B3
Wilders Cl FRIM GU16 ....58 C3
Wilderton Rd CCLF BH13 ....321 P9
Wilderton Rd West
  CCLF BH13 ....321 P8
Wildfell Cl CHCH/BSGR BH23 ....324 E6
Wild Herons HTWY RG27 ....72 B3
Wildmoor La HTWY RG27 ....52 D7
Wildown Gdns SBNE BH6 ....336 D5
Wildown Rd SBNE BH6 ....336 E5
Wild Ridings
  FHAM/STUB PO14 ....293 P1
Wild Rose Crs HLER SO31 ....270 E8
Wildwood Dr TADY RG26 ....33 N5
Wildwood Gdns YTLY GU46 ....56 D1
Wilfred Rd BOSC BH5 ....335 M2
Wilkins Cl HORN PO8 ....256 B6
Wilkinson Dr CHAR BH8 ....323 N5
Wilks Cl ROWN SO16 ....226 C7
Willems Av ALDT GU11 ....2 B2
Willersley Cl CHAM PO6 ....274 E9
Willett Rd WIMB BH21 ....300 C3
Will Hall Cl ALTN GU34 ....132 D7
William Cl CHCH/BSGR BH23 ....326 C5
William Farthing Cl
  ALDT GU11 ....2 D3
William Macleod Wy
  ROWN SO16 ....247 L3
William Panter Ct
  ELGH SO50 ....229 J2
William Price Gdns
  FHAM/PORC PO16 ....11 G3
William Rd LTDN BH7 ....335 M2
  LYMN SO41 ....329 L2
Williams Cl FAWY SO45 ....290 F6
  LSOL/BMARY PO13 ....315 H1
Williamson Cl HASM GU27 ....157 L4
  RAND SP11 ....79 N1
Williams Rd HSEA PO3 ....297 K6
Williams St SHAM SO14 ....21 K2
Williams Wy FLEETN GU51 ....74 F3
William Wy ALTN GU34 ....132 G4
Willis Av NBAD SO52 ....205 M9
Willis La ALTN GU34 ....150 E7
Willis Rd GPORT PO12 ....13 F5
  PSEA PO1 ....19 G2
  ROWN SO16 ....228 F7
Willis Wy CFDH BH17 ....321 K1
Willis Waye WINC SO23 ....165 K2
Willoughby Cl ALTN GU34 ....132 D7
Willoughby Wy DEAN RG23 ....68 G6
Willow Av FBDG SP6 ....240 C1
Willow Cl BOR GU35 ....154 B5
  FRIM GU16 ....58 D9
  HAV PO9 ....15 H6
  HEND SO30 ....249 N1
  LIPH GU30 ....175 L4
  WIMB BH21 ....278 D8
Willow Crs FARN GU14 ....58 A6
Willowdale Cl HAV PO9 ....276 B6
Willow Dr RGWD BH24 ....282 E4
  TOTT SO40 ....267 K2
Willow Flds ASHV GU12 ....97 P2
Willowford YTLY GU46 ....40 E8
Willow Gdns EMRTH PO10 ....277 M7
  LIPH GU30 ....175 L4
  NBAD SO52 ....205 K8
Willow Gn AWIN SO21 ....207 N1
Willow Herb Cl HLER SO31 ....271 H3
Willow La BLKW GU17 ....57 L1
Willow Md CHAR BH8 ....323 K5
Willow Mede HAV PO9 ....276 B6
Willow Ms NTID SP9 * 79 J4
Willow Pk ASHV GU12 ....97 M1
  PSTN BH14 ....321 H9
Willow Pl GPORT PO12 ....315 M3
Willow Rd BPWT SO32 ....232 D2
  LISS GU33 ....192 D2
  RWIN SO21 ....127 H8
  STOK SO20 ....161 N4
  WHCH RG28 ....85 L8
Willows End SHST GU47 ....41 J6
The Willows AND SP10 ....4 A7

CHFD SO53 * 228 E1
NMIL/BTOS BH25 ....327 K7
RFNM GU10 ....254 C7
Willow Tree Av HORN PO8 ....256 B9
Willow Tree Gdns
  FHAM/STUB PO14 ....10 A7
Willow Tree Ri BWD BH11 ....322 B5
Willow Tree Wk ITCH SO19 ....249 K8
Willow Wk NMIL/BTOS BH25 ....327 K8
Willow Wy ASHV GU12 ....97 L3
  CHCH/BSGR BH23 ....336 F1
  DEAN RG23 ....68 G5
  FERN BH22 ....302 D1
  FNM GU9 ....96 D5
  HTWY RG27 ....55 H4
  SHST GU47 ....40 G5
  STOK SO20 ....121 H5
Willow Wood Rd HISD PO11 ....318 G5
Wills Rd PSTN BH14 ....321 P8
Wills Wy ROMY SO51 ....204 E7
Willwood Cl CFDH BH17 ....320 C2
Wilmer Rd ELGH SO50 ....229 J2
Wilmington Ct WEND SO18 ....229 H9
Wilmot Cl ELGH SO50 ....207 N8
Wilmott Ct GPORT PO12 ....315 K5
Wilmott La GPORT PO12 ....315 K5
Wilmott Wy DEAN RG23 ....68 E6
Wilmot Wy CBLY GU15 ....58 E2
Wilmur Crs PLE BH15 ....320 G6
Wilsom Cl ALTN GU34 ....132 G6
Wilsom Rd ALTN GU34 ....133 H6
Wilson Gv SSEA PO5 ....19 K6
Wilson Rd ASHV GU12 ....97 K3
  BMTH BH1 ....335 K1
  FARN GU14 ....75 N1
  NEND PO2 ....296 E7
  PSTN BH14 ....321 L8
Wilsons Rd BOR GU35 ....155 J3
Wilson St SHAM SO14 ....21 J2
Wilton Av WSHM SO15 ....248 A5
Wilton Cl CHCH/BSGR BH23 ....324 B6
Wilton Ct FARN GU14 ....76 C1
Wilton Crs WSHM SO15 ....247 P2
Wilton Dr HORN PO8 ....256 A6
Wilton Gdns NMIL/BTOS BH25 ....327 H4
  WSHM SO15 ....247 P2
Wilton Pl BSTK RG21 ....6 B6
  SSEA PO5 ....316 E6
Wiltshire Gdns
  CHCH/BSGR BH23 ....305 K8
Wiltshire Rd
  CHCH/BSGR BH23 ....305 K8
Wiltshire St SSEA PO5 ....228 F1
Wilverley Av CHAR BH8 ....323 M5
  HAV PO9 ....276 C6
Wilverley Pl FAWY SO45 ....290 G4
Wilverley Rd BROC SO42 ....286 F8
  CHCH/BSGR BH23 ....325 L7
Wimbledon Park Rd
  SSEA PO5 ....316 E6
Wimborne Rd BWD BH11 ....301 P7
  ENEY PO4 ....317 J4
  MOOR/WNTN BH9 ....322 F7
  PLE BH15 ....320 E6
  WCLF BH2 ....8 E1
  WIMB BH21 ....278 D8
  WIMB BH21 ....300 B3
Wimborne Rd East
  WIMB BH21 ....302 A2
Wimborne Rd West
  WIMB BH21 ....301 J1
Wimpole St ROWN SO16 ....19 K1
Wimpson Gdns ROWN SO16 ....247 K2
Wimpson La ROWN SO16 ....247 K2
Wincanton Cl ALTN GU34 ....132 G7
Wincanton Wy WVILLE PO7 ....276 B1
Winchcombe Cl FLEETN GU51 ....74 D3
Winchcombe Rd BSTK RG21 ....6 C7
  CHAM PO6 ....274 D9
  NWBY RG14 ....17 F3
Winchester By-Pass
  WINC SO23 ....165 K4
Winchester Cl HLER SO31 ....269 K4
Winchester Gdns AND SP10 ....102 E4
Winchester Hl ROMY SO51 ....204 F5
  RWIN SO21 ....125 J1
Winchester Rd ALTN GU34 ....132 E8
  ALTN GU34 ....150 E4
  AND SP10 ....4 E7
  ASHV GU12 ....76 F9
  BPWT SO32 ....230 B3
  BPWT SO32 ....231 K1
  BPWT SO32 ....232 C8
  BSTK RG21 ....6 A5
  CHFD SO53 ....206 F7
  DEAN RG23 ....68 A3
  ELGH SO50 ....208 C9
  KBH RG22 ....90 A1
  KBH RG22 ....6 C8
  KSCL RG20 ....48 B6
  NARL SO24 ....167 M2
  NEND PO2 ....296 F8
  NMIL/BTOS BH25 ....327 L2
  PSF GU52 ....190 B8
  PSF GU52 ....215 K1
  RAND SP11 ....123 H1
  RFNM GU10 ....137 H2
  ROMY SO51 ....204 E2
  RWIN SO21 ....127 H8
  STOK SO20 ....161 N4
  WHCH RG28 ....85 L8
Winchester Road Rbt
  KBH RG22 ....69 J9

Winchester St AND SP10 ....4 E5
  BSTK RG21 ....8 E7
  FARN GU14 ....76 B4
  HEND SO30 ....250 C3
  OVTN RG25 ....87 H5
  WHCH RG28 ....47 H2
  WSHM SO15 ....20 D1
Winchester Wy BLKW GU17 .....41 L8
  TOTT SO40 ....246 C5
Winchfield CI ITCH SO19 ....269 J2
Winchfield Ct HTWY RG27 ....73 M3
Winchfield Crs HAV PO9 ....276 C6
Winchfield Gdns TADY RG26 .....34 C7
Wincombe CI FERN BH22 ....302 C5
Wincombe Dr FERN BH22 ....302 D4
Windbury Rd ROWN SO16 ....247 J1
Windermere Av
  FHAM/STUB PO14 ....294 B5
  KBH RG22 ....89 L2
  ROWN SO16 ....247 J1
Windermere CI FARN GU14 ....75 L1
Windermere Ct ASHV GU12 * 76 E8
Windermere Gdns NARL SO24 ..168 A3
  TOTT SO40 ....246 C3
Windermere Rd BOR GU35 ....154 A3
  NEND PO2 ....297 H6
  TWDS BH3 ....322 C9
  WEND SO18 ....249 K2
Windermere Wy FNM GU9 ....96 A5
  STHA RG19 ....25 K4
Windfield Dr ROMY SO51 ....204 F5
Windham Rd BMTH BH1 ....335 J1
Winding Wood Dr CBLY GU15 ....58 C1
Windmill CI HORN PO8 ....236 C7
  LYMN SO41 ....338 Q1
  RCWD BH24 ....282 B5
Windmill Copse FAWY SO45 .....268 B9
Windmill Cnr THLE RG7 ....27 J9
Windmill Dr BOR GU35 ....155 J2
Windmill Fld WVILLE PO7 ....255 J7
Windmill Flds ALTN GU34 ....150 C5
Windmill Gv
  FHAM/PORC PO16 ....295 M3
Windmill HI ALTN GU34 ....132 C7
Windmill La HLER SO31 ....250 A9
  RAND SP11 ....61 P5
  RAND SP11 ....102 A6
  RCWD BH24 ....282 B5
Windmill Rd ASHV GU12 ....3 H4
  THLE RG7 ....27 J9
The Windmills ALTN GU34 * 132 F6
Windover CI ITCH SO19 ....249 L5
Windrush Gdns WVILLE PO7 .....275 M3
Windrush Hts SHST GU47 ....41 J6
Windrush Rd ROWN SO16 ....247 J1
Windrush Wy FAWY SO45 ....268 C7
Windsor CI ALTN GU34 ....132 D6
  FARN GU14 ....57 P9
  LYMN SO41 ....327 N5
  RCWD BH24 ....281 M4
Windsor Ct ELGH SO50 ....207 J7
  NWBY RG14 ....17 C2
Windsor Crs FNM GU9 ....96 B5
  KBH RG22 ....89 L5
Windsor Ga ELGH SO50 ....207 J7
Windsor Pk ALTN GU34 ....132 F7
Windsor Ride CBLY GU15 ....41 P6
Windsor Ri NWBY RG14 ....17 J7
Windsor Rd ALTN GU34 ....150 C4
  AND SP10 ....4 B4
  BOR GU35 ....154 C3
  BOSC BH5 ....335 L2
  CHAM PO6 ....297 H2
  CHCH/BSGR BH23 ....324 C7
  FARN GU14 ....75 L4
  FHAM/PORC PO16 ....295 P2
  GPORT PO12 ....13 J3
  NARL SO24 ....167 P3
  PSF GU32 ....215 M2
  PSTN BH14 ....321 K9
  WVILLE PO7 ....255 M9
Windsor Wk BOR GU35 ....154 C3
Windsor Wy ALDT GU11 ....3 G3
Windwhistle La RSAL SP5 ....176 B7
Winfield Wy EMRTH PO10 ....277 M6
Winfrith Crs
  BKME/WDN BH12 ....321 N4
Winfrith Wy ROWN SO16 ....227 H7
Wingate CI ALDT GU11 ....2 C2
Wingate Dr ITCH SO19 ....249 K6
Wingate Rd
  LSOL/BMARY PO13 ....295 K8
  ODIM RG29 ....93 K8
  TOTT SO40 ....246 B3
Wingfield Av
  CHCH/BSGR BH23 ....325 P6
  PLE BH15 ....320 F6
Wingfield Gdns FRIM GU16 .....59 J2
Wingfield St PSEA PO1 ....316 F1
Wingrove Rd TOTT SO40 ....246 A8
Wings CI FNM GU9 ....96 B5
Winifred CI ELGH SO50 ....230 C1
Winifred Rd PLE BH15 ....320 C7
  WVILLE PO7 ....275 N2
Winkfield Mw HORN PO8 ....236 C7
Winklebury Wy DEAN RG23 .....68 E7
Winkle St SHAM SO14 * Q8 G7
Winkton CI CHCH/BSGR BH23 ..324 C4
  HAV PO9 ....14 C2
Winkworth La THLE RG7 ....34 E4
Winkworth PI FARN GU14 ....96 C8
Winnall CI WINC SO23 ....23 J5
Winnall Manor Rd WINC SO23 ..23 K4
Winnall Valley Rd WINC SO23 ...23 J3
Winnards Pk FERN BH22 ....302 E6
Winnards Pk HLER SO31 ....270 D7
Winners Enclosure
  ELGH SO50 * 230 D5

Winnham Dr
  FHAM/PORC PO16 ....273 M1
Winnington CI FHAM PO15 ....272 B6
Winnington CI FHAM PO15 * 272 B6
Winnipeg CI LIPH GU30 ....175 K4
Winn Rd PTSW SO17 ....248 C3
Winscombe Av HORN PO8 ....256 A9
Winsford Av ELCH SO50 ....230 A3
Winsford CI
  CHCH/BSGR BH23 ....325 P6
  ELGH SO50 ....230 A3
Winsford Gdns ELGH SO50 ....230 A3
Winslade Rd FUFL SO22 ....164 D3
Winsley PI HAV PO9 ....276 D5
Winsley Av SBNE BH6 ....336 A2
Winsor CI HISD PO11 ....319 K7
Winsor La TOTT SO40 ....245 K3
Winsor Rd TOTT SO40 ....245 H4
  TOTT SO40 ....246 E5
Winspit CI PLE BH15 ....320 A9
Winstanley Rd NEND PO2 ....296 E8
  ROWN SO16 ....226 C7
Winston Av
  BKME/WDN BH12 ....322 B9
  TADY RG26 ....34 E7
Winston Churchill Av
  SSEA PO5 ....19 H4
Winston CI ELCH SO50 ....207 J9
  FRIM GU16 ....58 E7
  HISD PO11 ....318 E5
  ROWN SO16 ....247 K1
Winstone Crs NBAD SO52 ....227 L1
Winston Gdns
  BKME/WDN BH12 ....322 A9
Winston Ri ALTN GU34 ....150 C5
Winston Rd
  MOOR/WNTN BH9 ....322 C4
Winston Wk FNM GU10 ....116 C4
Winston Wy BLKW GU17 ....41 J9
Winston Wy BSTK RG21 ....6 D5
  STHA RG19 ....25 J3
Winterbourne Rd CHAM PO6 ..274 B9
  PLE BH15 ....320 F8
  ROMY SO51 ....204 C4
Winterdyne Ms AND SP10 ....4 A5
Winterhayes CI CFD SO53 ....321 F1
Winterhill Rd CHAM PO6 ....296 F1
Winter Rd ENEY PO4 ....317 J5
Winters CI FAWY SO45 ....290 F6
Winters Hill BPWT SO32 ....231 L4
Wintersiow Dr HAV PO9 ....276 E4
Winters Rd BPWT SO32 ....252 E3
Winterthur Wy BSTK RG21 ....6 D5
Winterton Dr NWBY RG14 ....24 A2
Winton Cha AND SP10 ....5 J4
Winton CI FUFL SO22 ....164 C5
  SHAM SO14 ....329 M4
  NTID SP9 ....79 H7
Winton Crs YTLY GU46 ....40 E9
Winton HI STOK SO20 ....141 M5
Winton Rd ALDT GU11 ....2 D5
  FNM GU9 * 96 D8
  NEND PO2 ....297 H7
  PSF GU32 ....215 M2
Winton Sq BSTK RG21 ....6 E7
Winton St SHAM SO14 ....21 F5
Winton Wy NBNE BH10 ....322 D6
  NMIL/BTOS BH25 ....327 K2
Wiremead La RAND SP11 ....100 C4
Wisbech Wy LYMN SO41 ....327 P4
Wisborough Rd SSEA PO5 ....316 F6
Wise's Firs THLE RG7 ....26 F4
Wishanger La BOR GU35 ....136 B7
Wishart Gdns
  MOOR/WNTN BH9 ....323 H2
Wish PI SSEA PO5 ....316 C5
Wisley Gdns FARN GU14 ....75 L2
Wisley Rd AND SP10 ....102 B3
Wisley Rd AND SP10 * 102 B3
Wisteria Ct AND SP10 ....35 G6
Wisteria La YTLY GU46 ....40 D9
Wisteria Dr BOR GU35 ....154 A6
  VWD BH31 ....259 J6
Wisteria Gdns HAV PO9 ....277 H6
Witan CI AND SP10 ....82 F7
Witan Ct WHCH RG28 ....85 K5
Witchampton CI HAV PO9 * 276 C5
Witchampton Rd BDST BH18 ...320 B2
Witham CI CHFD SO53 ....206 C7
Witherbed La FHAM PO15 ....271 L6
Withermoor Rd
  MOOR/WNTN BH9 ....322 E7
Wither Ri DEAN RG23 ....88 E1
Withies Rd
  LSOL/BMARY PO13 ....295 H9
The Withies RSAL SP5 ....159 H6
Withingham Rd CCLF SO53 ....321 P9
Withybed Wy NTHA RG18 ....25 P2
Withy CI ROMY SO51 ....204 D5
Withy Rd CFDH BH17 ....320 A3
Wittcomb Ter BOR GU35 * 153 P7
Wittenford La LYND SO43 ....244 C3
Wittering Rd HISD PO11 ....319 M6
  ROWN SO16 ....227 K7
Wittmead Rd FNM GU16 ....348 F8
Witton HI NARL SO24 ....167 P3
Witt Rd ELCH SO50 ....230 C2
  RSAL SP5 ....158 C1
Witts HI WEND SO18 ....249 J3
Wivelrod Rd ALTN GU34 ....131 L9
Wiverley CI LYMN SO41 ....329 H5
Woburn Av FARN GU14 ....58 C9
Woburn CI ELCH SO50 ....230 C1
  FRIM GU16 ....58 F4
Woburn Gdns KBH RG22 ....68 F9
Woburn Rd ROWN SO16 ....227 N7
Wode CI HORN PO8 ....236 C9
Wodehouse Rd ITCH SO19 ....248 G7
Wokefield Ev THLE RG7 ....27 M7
Wokingham Rd CFRH RG45 ....40 F3
Woking Rd PSTN BH14 ....321 L8
The Wolds RCWD BH24 ....68 E9
Wolfe CI CHCH/BSGR BH23 ......325 J8
  FUFL SO22 ....183 L1
Wolfe Rd ASHV GU12 ....3 J4
Wolfmere La LISS GU33 ....173 M5

Wolf's La ALTN GU34 ....132 E9
Wollaston Rd SBNE BH6 ....336 D3
Wollaton Rd FERN BH22 ....302 C5
Wollstonecraft Rd
  BOSC BH5 ....335 M3
Wolseley Rd ALDT GU11 ....2 E4
  BKME/WDN BH12 ....321 M6
  WSSM SO15 ....247 N4
Wolsey Wy LYMN SO41 ....338 C1
Wolsingham Wy STHA RG19 .....25 N5
Wolterton Rd
  BKME/WDN BH12 ....334 A1
Wolverley Ct ROWN SO16 ....247 P1
Wolversdene Cl AND SP10 ....5 G6
Wolversdene Gdns AND SP10 ....5 H6
Wolverdene Rd AND SP10 ....5 H6
Wolverton La TADY RG26 ....49 J4
Wolverton Rd HAV PO9 ....276 C5
  LTDN BH7 ....335 M1
  SHAM SO14 * 21 H2
  TADY RG26 ....49 H5
Wolverton Wy SHAM SO14 ....21 G2
Wolvesey PI CHFD SO53 ....206 C9
Wolvesey Ter WINC SO23 ....23 G7
Wonderholme Pde
  BWD BH11 * 322 B5
Wonston CI RWIN SO21 ....125 M6
Wonston La HAV PO9 ....277 J4
Wonston La RWIN SO21 ....144 D1
Wonston Rd ROWN SO16 ....227 N8
Woodacre Gdns FERN BH22 ....302 E4
Woodavon Gdns NTHA RG18 .....25 N2
Wood Barn Rd FHAM PO15 ....272 B9
The Woodbarn FNM GU9 ....116 C1
Woodberry La HAV PO9 ....277 K1
Woodbind Wk HLER SO31 ....270 F8
Woodbine CI SHST GU47 ....41 K7
Woodbine La KSCL RG20 ....30 E5
Woodbourne FNM GU9 ....96 A6
Woodbourne CI FHAM PO15 ....272 B9
  LISS GU33 ....192 E2
  YTLY GU46 ....40 E8
Woodbridge Rd BLKW GU17 ....301 N7
Woodbury Av CHAR BH8 ....323 M5
  HAV PO9 ....298 F1
  PSF GU32 ....191 L9
Woodbury CI
  CHCH/BSGR BH23 ....324 C4
Woodbury Gv HORN PO8 ....256 A6
Woodbury Rd KBH RG22 ....89 M5
Woodbury Wy PO15 ....249 L8
  KBH RG22 ....89 M5
Woodcock CI NTID SP9 ....79 H5
Woodcock La LYMN SO41 ....328 A4
Woodcocks Crs LTDN BH7 ....323 N8
Woodcot Crs HAV PO9 ....276 C4
Woodcote La FLEETN GU51 ....74 A4
Woodcote La BPWT SO32 ....209 N6
  FHAM/STUB PO14 ....294 C7
Woodcote Gdns FARN GU14 .....57 L9
Woodcott Ter ASHV GU12 * 3 K6
Woodcroft Rd HORN PO8 ....255 N7
Woodcut Rd FHAM PO15 ....115 P5
Wood End CHIN RG24 ....69 F1
  CWTH RG45 ....41 J3
Woodend FARN GU14 ....76 C1
Woodend Rd FRIM GU16 ....59 H6
  MOOR/WNTN BH9 ....322 E8
Wood End Rd RCWD BH24 ....283 J4
Wood End Wy CHFD SO53 ....206 C6
Wooden House La
  LYMN SO41 ....309 P6
Wooderson CI ELGH SO50 ....230 A4
Woodfern FBDG SP6 ....241 H1
Woodfield CI BOR GU35 ....154 F8
Woodfield Av CHAM PO6 ....297 H4
Wood Field CI CHIN GU34 * 133 N8
Woodfield Dr FUFL SO22 ....164 C9
Woodfield Gdns
  CHCH/BSGR BH23 ....325 P6
Woodfield Park Rd
  EMRTH PO10 ....277 P9
Woodfield Ri CHIN RG24 ....70 A1
Woodford BWD BH11 ....322 A2
Woodford CI RGWD BH24 ....282 F2
Woodford Rd BMTH BH1 ....9 K2
Woodgarston Dr KBH RG22 .....89 L5
Woodgason La HISD PO11 ....299 J8
Woodgate La FLEETN GU51 ....74 F1
Wood Glade Cl TOTT SO40 ....267 J1
Woodgreen Av HAV PO9 ....14 C3
Woodgreen Rd BMTH BH1 ....300 M9
Woodgreen Rd FUFL SO22 ....164 E3
Woodhall Wy FHAM PO15 ....10 B1
Woodhayes Av
  CHCH/BSGR BH23 ....326 A5
Wood Hill La ODIM RG29 ....93 K7
Woodhouse La HAV PO9 ....257 J7
  HEND SO30 ....250 E3
  HORN PO8 ....256 C5
  STHA RG19 ....33 H5
Woodhouse Rd HORN PO8 ....256 F4
Woodington CI HAV PO9 ....276 C4
Woodington Rd LYMN SO41 ....203 J7
Woodlake CI CFDH BH17 ....320 E3
Woodland Av HAV PO9 ....335 N2
Woodland CI ROMY SO51 ....204 E1
  VWD BH31 ....258 E3
  WEND SO18 ....249 M4
Woodland Crs FARN GU14 ....58 B7
Woodland Dr RFNM GU10 ....116 B4
  RSAL SP5 ....159 J1
  TADY RG26 ....52 C3
Woodland Dro RWIN SO21 ....208 A2
Woodland Ms HEND SO30 ....249 M2
Woodland RI FLEETS GU52 ....74 B7
Woodlands CHIN RG24 ....52 B9
  CWTH RG45 ....41 J3
  FHAM/PORC PO16 ....273 H8
  FLEETN GU51 ....74 C1
  KSCL RG20 ....30 C5
  OVTN RG25 ....86 C3
  YTLY GU46 ....56 D2

Woodlands Av EMRTH PO10 .....277 L7
  FNM GU9 ....96 F4
  HAV PO9 ....320 P9
  THLE RG7 ....27 P3
Woodlands CI ASHV GU12 ....76 F7
  CHCH/BSGR BH23 ....305 L8
  CHFD SO53 ....206 F3
  FARN GU14 ....57 M4
  FAWY SO45 ....290 C5
  HLER SO31 ....270 F4
  LSOL/BMARY PO13 ....314 C2
Woodlands Ct FAWY SO45 ....268 A9
  SHST GU47 ....41 H5
Woodlands Crs PLE BH15 ....320 A9
Woodlands Dr HLER SO31 ....269 M4
Woodlands Dro TOTT SO40 ....245 M8
Woodlands Gv WVILLE PO7 .....275 M5
Woodlands La HASM GU27 ....156 C6
  HISD PO11 ....318 C5
  LISS GU33 ....192 F4
Woodlands Rd BROC SO42 ....308 F1
  FARN GU14 ....57 M4
  NMIL/BTOS BH25 ....326 C8
  TADY RG26 ....33 N5
  TOTT SO40 ....245 L7
The Woodlands BOR GU35 ....154 A7
  WINC SO23 ....165 K1
Woodland St PSEA PO1 ....316 E3
Woodlands Wk FARN GU14 ....57 M4
Woodlands Wy AND SP10 ....5 G6
  HAV PO9 ....276 F6
  HLER SO31 ....269 P2
  NMIL/BTOS BH25 ....327 K1
  RCWD BH24 ....281 M5
  WSHM SO15 ....248 B3
Woodland Vw HLER SO31 ....269 P2
  HORN PO8 ....255 P5
Woodland Wy
  CHCH/BSGR BH23 ....325 P7
  LYMN SO41 ....338 F2
Wood La BWD BH11 ....301 N7
  FARN GU14 ....75 P1
  FLEETN GU51 ....74 A1
  HTWY RG27 ....71 K7
  LYMN SO41 ....338 F2
  NARL SO24 ....187 P1
  RFNM GU10 ....97 P7
  THLE RG7 ....37 K1
  WHAM PO17 ....271 J9
Woodlane CI NARL SO24 ....187 P1
Wood Lawn CI
  NMIL/BTOS BH25 ....327 H7
Woodlea CI FUFL SO22 ....164 F5
Woodlea Gdns HEND SO30 ....249 N2
Woodlea Wy ROMY SO51 ....206 B3
Woodleaze CI BDST BH18 ....300 D7
Woodleigh FLEETN GU51 ....74 D4
Woodleigh CI HAV PO9 ....277 J7
Woodley CI ROMY SO51 ....204 G5
Woodley La LYMN SO41 ....329 K2
Woodley La ROMY SO51 ....204 E4
  ITCH SO19 ....248 F8
Woodley Wy ROMY SO51 ....204 G5
Woodling Crs FBDG SP6 ....241 H1
Woodlinken Dr VWD BH31 ....259 J6
Woodlinken Wy VWD BH31 ....259 J6
Woodlinken Wy VWD BH31 ....259 J6
Wood Ldg TOTT SO40 ....245 P2
Woodmancote Rd
  ENEY PO4 ....317 J4
Woodman La RWIN SO21 ....165 N5
Woodman's La THLE RG7 ....27 H4
Woodmere Cft KBH RG22 ....89 K4
Woodmill La WEND SO18 ....228 F9
Wood Moor CHIN RG24 ....51 P3
Woodmoor CI TOTT SO40 ....267 L1
Woodpath SSEA PO5 ....19 H7
Woodpecker CI BOR GU35 ....154 A6
  HAV PO9 ....15 K5
  KBH RG22 ....89 K3
  RFNM GU10 ....95 M5
  VWD BH31 ....258 F5
Woodpecker Copse
  HLER SO31 ....271 H7
Woodpecker Dr CFDH BH17 ....320 A4
  TOTT SO40 ....267 J1
Woodpeckers Dr
  WVILLE PO7 ....204 ...
Woodpecker Wy
  ELGH SO50 ....228 F2
Wood Rdg NWBY RG14 ....24 B8
Wood Rd CBLY GU15 ....58 A4
  FNM GU9 ....96 C4
  TOTT SO40 ....245 P9
Woodrofe Dr KBH RG22 ....89 N2
Woodrow WVILLE PO7 ....254 C7
Woodruff CI
  CHCH/BSGR BH23 ....325 N7
Woodrush Crs HLER SO31 ....270 E8
Woodsedge WVILLE PO7 ....276 A5
Woodside ALTN GU34 ....151 H4
  LYMN SO41 ....329 L5
Woodside Pk BOR GU35 ....154 A5

Woodside Rd ALDT GU11 ....75 N5
  BOSC BH5 ....335 P2
  ELGH SO50 ....206 C9
  FERN BH22 ....280 C5
  FERN BH22 ....302 E2
  FNM GU9 ....96 E4
  NBAD SO52 ....205 M3
  PSTN BH14 ....321 L9
  PTSW SO17 ....248 D3
Woodside Wy HEND SO30 ....250 A6
Woods La OVTN RG25 ....90 B4
Woodstock Av HORN PO8 ....256 A6
Woodstock CI FHAM PO15 ....10 A5
  HEND SO30 ....250 D6
Woodstock Dr PTSW SO17 ....248 C2
Woodstock La RGWD BH24 ....282 E2
Woodstock Md KBH RG22 ....89 M5
Woodstock Rd
  CHCH/BSGR BH23 ....325 H5
  GPORT PO12 ....12 E3
  HAV PO9 ....14 A3
  SHST GU47 ....333 J1
Woodstocks FARN GU14 ....58 B7
Wood View Rd
  MOOR/WNTN BH9 ....322 D7
Woodthorpe Gdns
  HLER SO31 ....270 F4
Woodvale FHAM PO15 ....272 B8
Woodvale Gdns
  NMIL/BTOS BH25 ....327 L3
Wood Vw WIMB BH21 ....279 J6
Woodview CI ROWN SO16 ....228 C6
Woodville CI BLKW GU17 ....41 J9
Woodville Dr PSEA PO1 ....18 B6
Woodville Rd FAWY SO45 ....291 K6
  HAV PO9 ....276 B8
Woodward CI GPORT PO12 ....315 K4
Woofferton Rd CHAM PO6 ....274 C9
Woolbridge Crs ODIM RG29 .....93 J3
Woolfield La ALTN GU34 ....190 B5
Woolford CI FUFL SO22 ....164 D9
Woolfords La
  MFD/CHID GU8 ....137 N2
Woolford Wy DEAN RG23 ....68 G6
Wool Gv AND SP10 ....5 C5
Woollards Rd ASHV GU12 ....76 F8
Woolley Sq AND SP10 ....82 G8
Woolmead Rd FNM GU9 ....96 C9
The Woolmead FNM GU9 * 96 C9
Woolmer Ct HAV PO9 ....277 H5
Woolmer Hill Rd HASM GU27 ..155 K8
  RCWD BH24 ....260 D8
Woolmer Rd LISS GU33 ....173 N4
Woolmer St EMRTH PO10 ....277 L8
Woolmer Wy BOR GU35 ....155 P6
Woolmer Av CHAM PO6 * ....
  PSF GU32 ....215 M1
Wool Rd BKME/WDN BH12 ....321 K4
Wools Br RGWD BH24 ....281 J3
Woolslope CI FERN BH22 ....280 E8
Woolslope Gdns FERN BH22 ....280 F8
Woolslope Rd FERN BH22 ....280 E8
Woolston Rd HAV PO9 ....276 C4
  HLER SO31 ....269 K2
Woolton Lodge Gdns
  KSCL RG20 ....29 N4
Woolven CI PSTN BH14 ....321 J7
Woolwich CI HLER SO31 ....249 P9
Wooteys Wy ALTN GU34 ....132 F4
Wootton Rd
  LSOL/BMARY PO13 ....314 E4
  HLER SO31 ....269 L3
Wootton Farm Rd
  NMIL/BTOS BH25 ....306 G6
Wootton Gdns BMTH BH1 ....9 F3
Wootton Mt BMTH BH1 ....9 G3
Wootton Rough
  NMIL/BTOS BH25 ....307 K8
Wootton St CHAM PO6 ....297 H2
Worbarrow Gdns
  BKME/WDN BH12 ....321 L4
Worcester Av KBH RG22 ....89 M5
Worcester CI FARN GU14 ....58 A6
  SSEA PO5 ....19 H5
Worcester Ct
  LSOL/BMARY PO13 * 314 C2
  LYMN SO41 ....329 M5
Wordsworth Av CHAM PO6 ....274 A9
  CHAR BH8 ....323 L6
  YTLY GU46 ....56 C1
Wordsworth CI BPWT SO32 ....252 C4
  FARN GU14 ....69 M4
Wordsworth Rd NTHA RG18 .....25 M3
  ROWN SO16 ....227 N2
Worgret Rd PLE BH15 ....320 F5
Worksop CI LSOL/BMARY PO13 ..314 E7
Workman's La ALTN GU34 ....133 N8
Workshop Rd WVILLE PO7 ....274 C8
Worldham HI ALTN GU34 ....133 N8
Worley Wy FHAM BH22 * ....
Wormersley Rd STHA RG19 .....24 G8
Worner Dr BKME/WDN BH12 ....321 L4
Worrell Sq AND SP10 * 82 G8
Worsam Ct KBH RG22 ....68 E8
Worsley Rd FRIM GU16 ....58 E6
  SSEA PO5 ....19 H7
Worsley St ENEY PO4 ....317 J4
Worthing Av GPORT PO12 ....295 K9
Worthing Rd SSEA PO5 ....316 F6
Worthington Crs PSTN BH14 ...321 J9
Worthy CI HAV PO9 ....277 H5
Worthy La WINC SO23 ....23 D2
Worthy Rd NMIL/BTOS BH25 ....327 J4
  WINC SO23 ....165 H5
Wote St BSTK RG21 ....6 C5
  DEAN RG25 ....68 C8
Wortley Rd
  CHCH/BSGR BH23 ....326 C8
Wote St BSTK RG21 ....6 F7
Wouldham CI RAND SP11 ....79 M4

Wraxhall Cl *CFDH* BH17 ....**320** F3
Wraysbury Park Dr
 EMRTH PO10 ....**277** M6
Wrecclesham Hl
Wrecclesham Rd *FNM* GU9 ...**115** N5
Wrekin Cl *KBH* RG22 ....**68** E9
The Wrekin *FARN* GU14 ....**76** D3
Wren Cl *ALTN* GU34 ....**132** G4
 CHCH/BSGR BH23 ....**337** M1
 FUFL SO22 ....**183** M1
 NMIL/BTOS BH25 ....**327** H5
 RGWD BH24 ....**282** C3
 THLE RG7 ....**27** K4
 YTLY GU46 * **40** C8
Wren Crt *ASHV* GU12 ....**76** C9
Wren Crs *BKME/WDN* BH12 ...**334** B1
Wren Gdns *FBDG* SP6 ....**239** P5
Wren Rd *BOSC* BH5 ....**228** C3
Wren Wy *FARN* GU14 ....**57** N6
 FHAM/PORC PO16 * **295** K1
Wrexham Gv *HORN* PO8 ....**236** B9
Wright Cl *FHAM* PO15 ....**271** M4
Wrights Cl *RWIN* SO21 ....**124** F1
Wright's Hl *ITCH* SO19 ....**249** J9
Wrights Wk *KBH* RG21 ....**268** P7
Wrights Wy *RWIN* SO21 ....**144** E4
Wroxham Rd
 BKME/WDN BH12 ....**321** P7
Wryneck Cl *ROWN* SO16 ....**227** M6
Wulwyn Side *CWTH* RG45 ....**41** K1
Wyborn Cl *HISD* PO11 ....**318** G6
Wych La *LSOL/BMARY* PO13 ...**294** F5
Wychwood Cl *ASHV* GU12 ....**97** M1
 WCLF BH2 ....
Wychwood Dr *FAWY* SO45 .....**312** G1
 WCLF BH2 ....**334** F1
Wychwood Gv *CHFD* SO53 ......**206** G5
Wyck La *ALTN* GU34 ....**133** N4
 ALTN GU34 ....**134** C3
Wycliffe Rd
 MOOR/WNTN BH9 ....**322** F7
 WEND SO18 ....**249** J2
Wycote Rd
 LSOL/BMARY PO13 ....**294** F5
Wye Ct *AND* SP10 ....**82** G9
Wyeford Cl *HAV* PO9 ....**277** H4
Wyelands Av *WIMB* BH21 ....**279** M9
Wyke Av *ASHV* GU12 ....**77** J9

Wykeham Cl *CFDH* BH17 ....**320** G4
 ROWN SO16 ....**228** A8
Wykeham Ct *ODIM* RG29 ....**93** K3
Wykeham Dr *DEAN* RG23 ....**68** D8
Wykeham Rd *WHAM* PO17 .....**252** E8
Wykeham Pk *RWIN* SO21 * **166** B8
Wykeham Pl *FUFL* SO22 ....**183** M1
 LYMN SO41 ....**329** L4
Wykeham Rd *FNM* GU9 ....**96** G8
 NEND PO2 ....**296** G8
 NEND PO2 ....**296** G8
Wyke La *ASHV* GU12 ....**77** J9
Wykwood *LIPH* GU30 ....**175** L3
Wylde Green La *LISS* GU33 .....**192** E1
Wylds La *PSF* GU32 ....**215** J5
Willie Rd *NEND* PO2 ....**296** G5
Wylye Cl *WEND* SO18 ....**49** K3
Wylye Rd *NTID* SP9 ....**79** J4
Wymering CE *FARN* GU14 ....**76** C1
Wymering La *CHAM* PO6 ....**296** C1
Wymering Manor Cl
 CHAM PO6 ....**296** C1
Wymering Rd *NEND* PO2 ....**296** G9
Wyncombe Rd *BOSC* BH5 ....**335** P1
Wyndcliffe Rd *ENEY* PO4 ....**316** C5
Wynford Rd
 MOOR/WNTN BH9 ....**322** G3
 PSTN BH14 ....**321** J9
Wynne Cl *BDST* BH18 ....**300** B9
Wynne Gdns *FLEETS* GU52 .....**74** E7
Wynter Cl *LTDN* BH7 ....**323** M8
Wynter Rd *WEND* SO18 ....**249** K3
Wynyards Gap *NBAD* SO52 ....**205** K9
Wyre Cl *CHFD* SO53 ....**206** D7

Wyvern Cl *ASHV* GU12 * **76** E7
 BKME/WDN BH12 ....**321** M5
 CHFD SO53 ....**206** F7

Y

Yachtsman Cl *HLER* SO31 ....**270** B2
Yaldhurst Cl *HAV* PO9 ....**277** H4
Yaldhurst La *LYMN* SO41 ....**329** H3
Yale Cl *SHST* GU47 ....**41** N4
Yapton St *PSEA* PO1 ....**19** C2
Yarborough Rd *SSEA* PO5 ....**19** G7
Yardlea Cl *HAV* PO9 ....**277** H1
Yardley Cl *HSEA* PO3 ....**297** L5
Yardley Rd *HEND* SO30 ....**250** B6
Yarmley La *RSAL* SP5 ....**158** A1
Yarmouth Cl
 BKME/WDN BH12 ....**334** A1
Yarmouth Gdns *WSHM* SO15 ..**247** M2
Yarmouth Rd
 BKME/WDN BH12 ....**321** P6
Yarnhams Cl *ALTN* GU34 ....**150** C6
Yarrell Md *LYMN* SO41 ....**329** H3
Yarrow Cl *CHCH/BSGR* BH23 ..**325** M7
 NTHA RG18 ....**25** N2
Yarrow Rd *BKME/WDN* BH12 ..**321** J4
Yarrow Wy *HLER* SO31 ....**270** E8
Yateley Cl *HAV* PO9 ....**276** C5
Yateley Rd *YTLY* GU46 ....**40** C7
Yatesbury Cl *FARN* GU14 ....**57** J4
Yates Copse *NTHA* RG18 ....**25** H2
Yaverland *HLER* SO31 ....**269** L4
Yeatmister Rd *CFDH* BH17 ......**321** H2
Yellowhammer Rd *KBH* RG22 ...**89** K5
Yellowhammers *ALTN* GU34 ...**132** F3
Yelverton Av *FAWY* SO45 ....**268** C9
Yelverton Rd *WCLF* BH2 ....**8** D3
Yeo Ct *ENEY* PO4 ....**317** L5
Yeomans *HTWY* RG27 ....**39** P7
Yeomans Cl *FARN* GU14 ....**57** P8
 RFNM GU10 ....**97** M3
Yeomans La *KSCL* RG20 ....**30** F5
 LIPH GU30 ....**195** K1
Yeomans Pl *BOR* GU35 ....**154** F5
Yeomans Rd *CHAR* BH8 ....**323** L4
Yeomans Wy *CHAR* BH8 ....**323** M5

Yeovil Cha *WEND* SO18 ....**249** K3
Yeovil Cl *FARN* GU14 ....**76** C5
Yeovil Rd *SHST* GU47 ....**41** M5
Yeovilton Cl *LYMN* SO41 ....**328** E6
Yerville Gdns *LYMN* SO41 ......**327** P4
Yetminster Rd *FARN* GU14 ......**76** D2
Yew Cl *KSCL* RG20 ....**48** D5
Yew Ga *NWBY* RG14 ....**24** C1
Yew La *NMIL/BTOS* BH25 ......**327** L3
Yew Rd *WEND* SO18 ....**249** J3
Yewside
 LSOL/BMARY PO13 * **295** J8
The Yews *HORN* PO8 ....**256** D4
Yew Tree Cl *DEAN* RG23 ....**88** F5
 ELGH SO50 ....**230** C1
 FARN GU14 * **75** K1
 HEND SO30 ....**250** B5
 RAND SP11 ....**102** E9
 RSAL SP5 ....**158** A1
 TADY RG26 ....**52** E5
 WIMB BH21 ....**278** F9
Yewtree Cl *FAWY* SO45 ....**290** C1
Yew Tree Ct *SHOV* SO30 * **249** N2
Yew Tree Dr *FHAM* PO15 ....**271** J2
Yew Tree Gdns *WVILLE* PO7 ....**256** G7
Yew Tree La *OVTN* RG25 ....**108** C1
 RSAL SP5 ....**159** J4
Yewtree La *HORN* PO8 ....**202** E7
Yew Tree Pl *LISS* GU33 ....**192** E2
Yew Tree Rd *HISD* PO11 ....**298** C9
Yew Tree Wk *FRIM* GU16 ....**58** D4
Yockley Cl *CBLY* GU15 ....**59** J2
Yoells Crs *HORN* PO8 ....**255** P5
Yoells La *HORN* PO8 ....**255** P5
Yokesford Hl *ROMY* SO51 ....**180** C9
Yolland Cl *HORN* PO8 ....**96** C4
Yonge Cl *ELGH* SO50 ....**229** K1
York Av *NMIL/BTOS* BH25 ......**327** K4
York Buildings *SHAM* SO14 ......**20** E5
York Cl *BDST* BH18 ....**320** C2
 BOR GU35 ....**154** A6
 CHCH/BSGR BH23 ....**324** D8
 CHFD SO53 ....**206** B9
 ELGH SO50 ....**230** D5
 KBH RG22 ....**89** M3
 NWBY RG14 ....**17** G4
 PSF GU32 ....**215** K2
 SHAM SO14 ....**21** K1

York Crs *ALDT* GU11 ....**2** C5
 LSOL/BMARY PO13 ....**314** E4
Yorkdale *HLER* SO31 ....**270** C7
York Dro *RSAL* SP5 ....**223** L4
 WEND SO18 ....**249** K4
Yorke St *SSEA* PO5 ....**19** F5
York Gdns
 FHAM/PORC PO16 ....**295** P3
York Pl *LTDN* BH7 ....**335** N1
 PSEA PO1 ....**18** E1
York Rd *ALDT* GU11 ....**2** C5
 ASHV GU12 ....**76** F9
 BDST BH18 ....**320** C1
 BMTH BH1 ....**9** J1
 ELGH SO50 ....**229** J3
 FARN GU14 ....**75** N3
 FUGH BH18 ....**116** C2
 NWBY RG14 ....**17** G4
 WSHM SO15 ....**247** N4
York Terrace La *CBLY* GU15 * **41** P9
Yorktown Rd *SHST* GU47 ....**41** K7
York Wy *SHST* GU47 ....**41** K7
Yorkwood *LISS* GU33 ....**192** D2
Young Crs *STHA* RG19 ....**24** G7
Youngs Dr *ASHV* GU12 ....**97** M1
Youngs Paddock *RSAL* SP5 .....**158** B1
Youngs Rd *ALTN* GU34 ....**132** F5
 BWD BH11 ....**322** A2
Yves Ms *SSEA* PO5 ....**316** F6

Z

Zamek Cl *BWD* BH11 ....**322** A2
Zetland Rd *CHAM* PO6 ....**297** M2
 GPORT PO12 ....**12** C1
Zeus La *WVILLE* PO7 ....**275** P7
Zinnia Cl *KBH* RG22 ....**89** L5
 NBNE BH10 ....**322** E5
Zion Rd *RAND* SP11 ....**119** M4
Zouch Av *NTID* SP9 ....**78** G4
Zouch Cl *NTID* SP9 ....**78** G4
Zouch Farm Rd *NTID* SP9 ....**78** G4

Index - featured places

36 On the Quay Hotel
 EMRTH PO10 ....**299** M1
The AA-Fanum House
 BSTK RG21 ....**7** K4
Aaron Croham Hurst Hotel
 WCLF BH2 ....**8** A4
Abbey Business Park
 FNM GU9 ....**116** F2
Abbey Chiropractic Clinic
 ROMY SO51 ....**204** C6
Abbey House
 WINC SO23 ....**23** F5
The Abbey School
 FNM GU9 ....**116** D1
Abbotsford Farm Business
 Centre *ALTN* GU34 ....**150** D5
Abbotswood Road
 TOTT SO40 ....**246** B4
Abbotts Ann Primary School
 RAND SP11 ....**101** M6
ABC Cinema
 BMTH BH1 ....**8** E4
Abro Industrial Estate
 ALDT GU11 ....**76** C9
Acorn Business Centre
 BKME/WDN BH12 ....**321** K3
 CHAM PO6 ....**296** F1
Action Stations! Exhibition
 PSEA PO1 ....**18** C2
Ad Astra First School
 CFDH BH17 ....**321** H2
Addington Clinic
 BWD BH11 ....**322** B2
Admiral Lord Nelson School
 HSEA PO3 ....**297** K8
Adult Education Centre
 FNM GU9 ....**96** B9
AFC Bournemouth (Fitness
 First Stadium) *LTDN* BH7 .....**323** M9
AFC Newbury
 NWBY RG14 ....**17** G1
Airborne Forces Museum
 ALDT GU11 ....**75** P7
Airfield Industrial Estate
 CHCH/BSGR BH23 ....**325** K9
Albany Business Centre
 WHAM PO17 ....**272** F3
Albany Park Industrial Estate
 FRIM GU16 ....**58** A4
Alder Hills Industrial Park
 BKME/WDN BH12 ....**321** P5
The Alderman Quilley School
 ELGH SO50 ....**229** H3
Aldermoor Health Centre
 ROWN SO16 ....**227** N8
Alderney Community Hospital
 BKME/WDN BH12 ....**321** L3
Alderney Middle School
 BKME/WDN BH12 ....**321** M3
Aldershot & Farnham
 County Court *ALDT* GU11 ....**3** F3
Aldershot Health Centre
 ALDT GU11 ....**2** C2
Aldershot Military Museum
 ALDT GU11 ....**76** B5
Aldershot Military Stadium
 ALDT GU11 ....**76** B6

Aldershot Outpatients
 Department *ALDT* GU11 ....**3** F1
Aldershot Town FC
 ALDT GU11 ....**3** H3
Aldworth Science College
 KBH RG22 ....**89** P1
Alexander Barracks
 CHOB/PIR GU24 ....**59** N7
Alexander House
 Business Centre *ALDT* GU11 ....**3** F3
Alice in Wonderland Park
 CHCH/BSGR BH23 ....**303** L9
Allenbourn Middle School
 WIMB BH21 ....**278** E8
All Hallows RC Comprehensive
 School *FNM* GU9 ....**106** M1
Allington Manor
 Business Centre *ELGH* SO50 ..**229** N5
Allington Manor School
 ELGH SO50 ....**229** P5
All Saints CE Infant School
 RFNM GU10 ....**117** J7
All Saints CE Junior School
 FLEETS GU52 ....**74** A4
All Saints CE Primary School
 RSAL SP5 ....**201** K2
 WINC SO23 ....**23** H7
Alpha Business Park
 SHAM SO14 ....**248** D4
Alpine Snowsports
 Dry Ski Slope *ALDT* GU11 ....**76** B8
Airesford County Junior School
 NARL SO24 ....**168** A2
Airesford Golf Club
 NARL SO24 ....**167** P4
Alton Business Centre
 ALTN GU34 ....**133** H6
Alton College
 ALTN GU34 ....**132** F4
Alton Community Centre
 ALTN GU34 ....**132** F6
Alton Community Hospital
 ALTN GU34 ....**132** E6
Alton Convent School
 ALTN GU34 ....**132** G3
Alton County Infant School
 ALTN GU34 ....**132** G5
Alton Golf Club
 ALTN GU34 ....**112** E9
Alton Grange Hotel
 ALTN GU34 ....**133** H4
Alton Health Centre
 ALTN GU34 ....**132** G5
Alton House Hotel
 ALTN GU34 ....**132** G5
Alton Sports Centre
 ALTN GU34 ....**132** D8
Alton Town FC
 ALTN GU34 ....**133** H4
Alton Town RFC
 ALTN GU34 ....**133** H4
Alverstoke CE Junior School
 GPORT PO12 ....**12** A5
Alverstoke Infant School
 GPORT PO12 ....**12** A7
Ambassador Industrial Estate
 CHCH/BSGR BH23 ....**325** L9

Amery Hill Secondary School
 ALTN GU34 ....**132** F5
Amesbury School
 GSHT GU26 ....**156** D4
Amey Industrial Estate
 PSF GU32 ....**215** L2
AMF Bowling
 ITCH SO19 ....**249** J5
 PSEA PO1 ....**19** H2
Ampfield Par 3 Golf Club
 ROMY SO51 ....**205** N2
Ampfield Primary School
 ROMY SO51 ....**205** N1
Amport CE J & I School
 RAND SP11 ....**100** G5
Ampress Works Halt
 LYMN SO41 ....**329** K1
Anchor Business Centre
 CHFD SO53 ....**206** D7
Andover Athletics Club
 AND SP10 ....**82** A9
Andover CE Primary School
 AND SP10 ....**4** E5
Andover FC
 AND SP10 ....**82** A9
Andover Golf Club
 AND SP10 ....**102** E4
Andover Leisure Centre
 AND SP10 ....**4** D3
Andover Museum & The Museum
 of the Iron Age
 AND SP10 ....**4** E3
Andover Road Retail Park
 FUFL SO22 ....**22** C2
Andrews Endowed CE Primary
 School
 ALTN GU34 ....**133** J3
Annie Lawson School
 NWBY RG14 ....**16** B4
Ansells Farm Community Centre
 FLEETN GU51 ....**56** F9
Anstey County Junior School
 ALTN GU34 ....**132** F5
Anton County Infant School
 AND SP10 ....**102** E4
Anton Junior School
 AND SP10 ....**102** E4
Anton Trading Estate
 AND SP10 ....**4** C6
The Anvil Concert Hall
 BSTK RG21 ....**6** E5
Apollo Cinema
 FHAM/PORC PO16 ....**11** H5
Apollo Hotel
 CHIN RG24 ....**69** J4
Apple Industrial Estate
 FHAM PO15 ....**271** J5
Applemore College
 FAWY SO45 ....**267** N7
Applemore Recreation Centre
 FAWY SO45 ....**267** N7
Ardglen Industrial Estate
 WHCH RG28 ....**85** K6
Argyle Community Centre
 SHAM SO14 ....**21** F2
The Ark School
 THLE RG7 ....**26** B6

Arlington Hotel
 BMTH BH1 ....**8** E5
Army Golf Club
 ALDT GU11 ....**75** M6
Army Medical Services Museum
 FRIM GU16 ....**76** C3
Army Training Regiment
 CHOB/PIR GU24 ....**59** P7
Arndale Court Hotel
 PLE BH15 ....**320** E9
The Arnewood School
 NMIL/BTOS BH25 ....**327** H5
Arnhem Barracks
 ALDT GU11 ....**75** P9
Arrow Industrial Estate
 FARN GU14 ....**75** N2
The Arts Institute
 of Bournemouth
 BKME/WDN BH12 ....**322** C7
Arundel Court J & I School
 PSEA PO1 ....**19** K1
Arundel Tower
 AND SP10 ....**20** D5
Ashburn Hotel
 FBDG SP6 ....**240** C2
Ashdown County
 Secondary School
 CFDH BH17 ....**320** G3
Ashdown Leisure Centre
 CFDH BH17 ....**321** H3
Ashford Hill Primary School
 STHA RG19 ....**33** H5
Ash Grange CP School
 ASHV GU12 ....**97** P1
Ashley Heath
 Industrial Estate
 WIMB BH21 ....**281** J2
Ashley Infant School
 NWBY RG14 ....**327** M4
Ashley Junior School
 NMIL/BTOS BH25 ....**327** L4
Ash Manor School
 ASHV GU12 ....**97** M3
Ashurst Hospital
 TOTT SO40 ....**265** P1
Ash Vale Health Centre
 ASHV GU12 ....**76** G8
The Atherley School
 ROWN SO16 ....**226** F6
Audleys Wood Hotel
 OVTN RG25 ....**90** E3
Avenue Clinic
 WSHM SO15 ....**20** C1
The Avenue Shopping Centre
 WCLF BH2 ....**8** A3
Avington Park
 RWIN SO21 ....**166** D2
Avonbourne Girls School
 LTDN BH7 ....**323** N8
Avon Heath Country Park
 RGWD BH24 ....**281** N6
Avonlea School
 RGWD BH24 ....**282** F1
The Avonmouth Hotel
 CHCH/BSGR BH23 ....**337** L1
Avon Trading Park
 CHCH/BSGR BH23 ....**324** E7

Awbridge Primary School
 ROMY SO51 ....**179** K9
Baddesley Park Industrial
 Estate *NBAD* SO52 ....**205** M9
Baden Powell & St Peters
 CE Middle School
 PSTN BH14 ....**321** K9
Badshot Lea Village
 Infant School *FNM* GU9 ....**96** G5
Balksbury Hill Industrial Estate
 RAND SP11 ....**102** C5
The Balksbury J & I School
 AND SP10 ....**102** B4
Ballard College
 NMIL/BTOS BH25 ....**327** J3
Balmer Lawn Hotel
 BROC SO42 ....**286** G6
Banister Infant School
 WSHM SO15 ....**248** B4
The Banks Medical Centre
 TWDS BH5 ....**322** E8
Bar End Industrial Estate
 WINC SO23 ....**184** B1
Barfield School
 RFNM GU10 ....**97** H8
Bargate Museum
 SHAM SO14 ....**20** D5
Bargate Shopping Centre
 SHAM SO14 ....**20** E5
Barncroft Infant School
 HAV PO9 ....**14** B1
Barncroft Junior School
 HAV PO9 ....**276** C6
Barratt Industrial Park
 FHAM PO15 ....**271** J5
Bartley CE Junior School
 TOTT SO40 ....**245** H4
Bartley Lodge Hotel
 TOTT SO40 ....**244** F4
Bartley Wood Business Park
 HTWY RG27 ....**72** B4
Bartley Wood Business Park
 (West) *HTWY* RG27 ....**72** A4
Barton Industrial Estate
 NARL SO24 ....**130** B8
Barton-on-Sea Golf Club
 NMIL/BTOS BH25 ....**327** L8
Barton Peveril College
 ELGH SO50 ....**229** H3
Barton Stacey CE
 Primary School *RWIN* SO21 ..**124** C1
Basing House
 CHIN RG24 ....**70** B6
Basingstoke Aquadrome
 KBH RG22 ....**68** F7
Basingstoke Business Centre
 KBH RG22 ....**90** A1
Basingstoke College of
 Technology *BSTK* RG21 ....**6** C1
Basingstoke County Court
 BSTK RG21 ....**7** H5
Basingstoke Crematorium
 OVTN RG25 ....**108** A3
Basingstoke Golf Club
 DEAN RG23 ....**89** K6
Basingstoke Leisure Park
 KBH RG22 ....**68** F7

Basingstoke Planet Ice
KBH RG22 ....68 F7
Basingstoke RFC
KBH RG22 ....89 M2
Basingstoke Sports Centre
BSTK RG21 ....6 E5
Basingstoke Town FC
KBH RG22 ....90 A1
Bassett Green Primary School
SO16 ....228 D8
Baycroft School
FHAM/STUB PO14 ....294 B7
Bay House School
GPORT PO12 ....315 J6
Bay View Court Hotel
BMTH BH1 ....9 K4
BBC South TV & Radio Solent
WSHM SO15 ....20 C2
Bearwood CP School
WIMB BH21 ....301 L7
Bearwood Medical Centre
BWD BH11 ....301 M8
Beaucroft Foundation School
WIMB BH21 ....278 G8
The Beaufort Hotel
ENEY PO4 ....317 H6
Beaulieu Abbey
BROC SO42 ....289 K7
Beaulieu Hotel
BROC SO42 ....266 C9
Beaulieu:National Motor Museum *BROC* SO42 ....289 J7
Beaulieu Primary School
BROC SO42 ....289 K8
Beaumont County Junior School *ALDT* GU11 ....2 A3
Beaver Industrial Estate
CHCH/BSGR BH23 ....325 L9
LIPH GU30 ....175 K5
Bedales School
PSF GU32 ....191 L7
Bedenham Primary School
LSOL/BMARY PO13 ....294 C6
Beech Down Primary School
KBH RG22 ....89 P3
Beechleas Hotel & Restaurant
WIMB BH21 ....300 E1
Beechnut Industrial Estate
ALDT GU11 ....3 G4
Beechwood Junior School
WEND SO18 ....249 H4
Beggarwood Surgery
DEAN RG23 ....89 K6
Belbins Business Park
ROMY SO51 ....204 E2
Belgrave Industrial Estate
PTSW SO17 ....248 E1
Bellemoor Secondary School
ROWN SO16 ....247 P1
Bell Inn Hotel
LYND SO43 ....244 A2
Belvedere Hotel
BMTH BH1 ....9 F4
Benridge Business Park
CFDH BH17 ....320 C4
Bentley Industrial Centre
RFNM GU10 ....114 E6
Bentley Trimmings Business Park
RFNM GU10 ....114 F5
Bentworth CE (Aided) Primary School
ALTN GU34 ....131 J4
Berrywood Business Village
HEND SO30 ....230 B9
Berrywood Primary School
HEND SO30 ....250 D2
Bethany CE Junior School
BMTH BH1 ....335 K1
Bevois Town Primary School
SHAM SO14 ....248 C4
Bicknell Special School
LTDN BH7 ....323 N8
Bidbury J & I School
HAV PO9 ....14 B3
Bilton Industrial Estate
CHIN RG24 ....69 P3
Binsted CE Primary School
ALTN GU34 ....134 B2
Binswood View Business Centre *ALTN* GU34 ....153 J4
Birchwood Medical Centre
CFDH BH17 ....320 B4
Birdworld & Underwaterworld
RFNM GU10 ....115 L7
Bishop Challoner RC School
KBH RG22 ....68 F9
Bishop of Winchester Comprehensive School
CHAR BH8 ....323 K6
Bishops Palace
WINC SO23 ....23 F6
Bishop's Table Hotel
FNM GU9 ....96 B9
Bishops Waltham Infant School *BPWT* SO32 ....232 B4
Bishop's Waltham Palace
BPWT SO32 ....232 A5
Bishopswood Golf Club
TADY RG26 ....34 A7
Bishopswood J & I School
TADY RG26 ....34 C7
Bitterne CE (Controlled) Junior School *ITCH* SO19 ....249 H5
Bitterne CE Infant School
ITCH SO19 ....249 H5
Bitterne Health Centre
WEND SO18 ....249 J4
Bitterne Leisure Centre
WEND SO18 ....249 J4
Bitterne Manor Primary School
WEND SO18 ....248 F4
Bitterne Park Clinic
WEND SO18 ....248 G3
Bitterne Park J & I School
WEND SO18 ....248 G3

Bitterne Park Secondary School *WEND* SO18 ....248 G1
Blackbrook Business Park
FHAM PO15 ....10 A5
Blackbushe Airport
BLKW GU17 ....56 B5
Blackbushe Business Park
YTLY GU46 ....56 D1
Blackdown Barracks
FRIM GU16 ....59 J7
Blackdown Primary School
FRIM GU16 ....59 K5
Blackfield Health Centre
FAWY SO45 ....290 F7
Blackfield Infant School
FAWY SO45 ....290 G8
Blackfield Junior School
FAWY SO45 ....290 F8
Blackmoor Golf Club
BOR GU35 ....153 M7
Blackness Industrial Park
FAWY SO45 ....134 G1
Blackwater & Hawley Leisure Centre *BLKW* GU17 ....57 L2
Blackwater Industrial Estate
CBLY GU15 ....41 M9
Blackwater Trading Estate
ASHV GU12 ....97 K3
Bleach's Yard Industrial Estate
LIPH GU30 ....175 K5
Bohunt Community School
FHAM/PORC PO16 ....11 F7
Bohunt Manor
LIPH GU30 ....175 J3
Boldrewood Centre
ROWN SO16 ....228 B9
Bone Lane Industrial Area
NWBY RG14 ....17 K1
Bordon Infant School
BOR GU35 ....153 P4
Bordon Trading Estate
BOR GU35 ....153 M3
Boscombe Dental Health Centre *LTDN* BH7 ....335 M1
Boscombe Manor Medical Centre *BOSC* BH5 ....335 M2
Boscombe Pier
BOSC BH5 ....335 L4
Bosmere Junior School
HAV PO9 ....15 F6
Botleigh Grange Hotel
HEND SO30 ....250 D3
Botley CE Primary School
HEND SO30 ....250 F4
Botley Park Hotel, Golf & Country Club *BPWT* SO32 ....250 F1
Boundary Oak School
WVILLE PO17 ....272 C5
Bourne Hall Hotel
WCLF BH2 ....8 C6
Bourne Mill Industrial Estate
FNM GU9 ....96 E8
Bournemouth Aviation Museum *CHCH/BSGR* BH23 ....303 N4
Bournemouth Business Centre
BMTH BH1 ....9 H2
Bournemouth College
BMTH BH1 ....335 J2
Bournemouth Crematorium
CHAR BH8 ....323 J6
Bournemouth Crown & County Courts *LTDN* BH7 ....323 P6
Bournemouth International Airport *CHCH/BSGR* BH23 ....303 M8
Bournemouth International Centre & Leisure Pool
WCLF BH2 ....8 D6
Bournemouth Jewish Day School
BMTH BH1 ....9 F3
Bournemouth Learning Support Centre
NBNE BH10 ....322 C6
Bournemouth Magistrates Court *BMTH* BH1 ....9 G3
The Bournemouth Nuffield Hospital *CHAR* BH8 ....334 G1
Bournemouth Pier
WCLF BH2 ....8 E6
Bournemouth & Poole College
BMTH BH1 ....9 H1
PSTN BH14 ....321 H8
Bournemouth Sands Hotel
WCLF BH2 ....8 B6
Bournemouth School
CHAR BH8 ....323 J6
Bournemouth School for Girls
CHAR BH8 ....323 J5
Bournemouth Sports Club
CHCH/BSGR BH23 ....303 J1
Bournemouth University
BKME/WDN BH12 ....322 C7
BMTH BH1 ....9 J3
The Bourne School
FNM GU9 ....116 D3
Bourne Tennis Club
FNM GU9 ....116 C2
Bourne Valley Business Park
BKME/WDN BH12 ....334 A1
Bowlplex
KBH RG22 ....68 F7
Boyatt Shopping Centre
ELGH SO50 ....207 H9
Boyatt Wood Industrial Estate *ELGH* SO50 ....207 H9
Bradbury Centre
ROWN SO16 ....227 N8
Braishfield Primary School
ROMY SO51 ....181 H8
Brambles Farm Industrial Estate *WVILLE* PO7 ....275 M2
Bramley CE J & I School
TADY RG26 ....52 A1
Bramshaw Golf Club
LYND SO43 ....244 A2

Branksome Cemetery
BKME/WDN BH12 ....321 L5
Branksome Heath Middle School *BKME/WDN* BH12 ....321 L6
Bransgore CE Primary School
CHCH/BSGR BH23 ....305 N8
Bratley Arch
RGWD BH24 ....262 G3
Braxton Gardens
LYMN SO41 ....328 E7
Breamore CE Primary School
FBDG SP6 ....220 F4
Breamore House & Countryside Museum
FBDG SP6 ....220 E1
Briar Park Business Centre
CHCH/BSGR BH23 ....324 E8
Brickfield Trading Estate
CHFD SO53 ....206 D8
Brick Kiln Industrial Estate
TADY RG26 ....34 D5
Brickyards Industrial Estate
PSF GU32 ....191 N5
Bridgemary Community School
LSOL/BMARY PO13 ....294 C4
The Bridge Shopping Centre
PSEA PO1 ....19 K2
Brighton Hill Community College *KBH* RG22 ....89 P2
Brighton Hill Retail Park
KBH RG22 ....90 A1
Bristow Infant School
CBLY GU15 ....58 A3
British Gas Training Centre
CFDH BH17 ....320 A7
Broadlands House
ROMY SO51 ....204 C8
Broadmarsh Business & Innovation Centre *HAV* PO9 ....14 A7
Broadmoor CP School
CWTH RG45 ....41 L2
Broadmoor Hospital
CWTH RG45 ....41 M1
Broadstone Cemetery
BDST BH18 ....300 E8
Broadstone (Dorset) Golf Club
WIMB BH21 ....300 E7
Broadstone First School
BDST BH18 ....300 D9
Broadstone Leisure Centre
BDST BH18 ....300 C8
Broadstone Middle School
BDST BH18 ....300 E8
Brockenhurst CE Primary School *BROC* SO42 ....286 F9
Brockenhurst College
BROC SO42 ....286 C7
Brockhurst Infant School
GPORT PO12 ....315 K1
Brockhurst Junior School
GPORT PO12 ....315 K1
Brokenford Business Centre
TOTT SO40 ....246 D5
Brokenhurst Manor Golf Club
BROC SO42 ....308 E2
Brookes Hill Industrial Estate
TOTT SO40 ....225 P8
Brookfield Community School
HLER SO31 ....270 E6
Brookfield Hotel
EMRTH PO10 ....277 K9
Brookham School
LIPH GU30 ....175 M5
Brookway Industrial Estate
NWBY RG14 ....24 G5
Brookwood Industrial Estate
ELGH SO50 ....229 J1
Broughton Primary School
STOK SO20 ....140 A9
Browning Barracks
ALDT GU11 ....75 P7
Brownsea Island (NT)
CCLF BH13 ....333 G7
Brownsea Open Air Theatre
CCLF BH13 ....333 H7
Broxhead Trading Estate
BOR GU35 ....154 C2
Brune Park Community School
LSOL/BMARY PO13 ....295 J9
Buckholme Towers School
PSTN BH14 ....321 J9
Buckland Medical Centre
NEND PO2 ....296 F9
Bucklers Hard Village & Maritime Museum
BROC SO42 ....311 P4
Budds Lane Trading Estate
ROMY SO51 ....204 B4
The Burgate School & Sixth Form Centre *FBDG* SP6 ....220 C8
Burghclere Primary School
KSCL RG20 ....30 F8
Burghfield Health Centre
THLE RG7 ....27 K4
Burghfield St Marys Primary School
THLE RG7 ....27 L1
Buriton Business Park
EPSF GU31 ....215 J6
Buriton Primary School
EPSF GU31 ....215 K8
Burley Court Hotel
BMTH BH1 ....9 G4
Burley Golf Club
RGWD BH24 ....284 D7

Burley Manor Hotel
RGWD BH24 ....284 C5
Burley Primary School
RGWD BH24 ....284 C6
Burnham Copse J & I Schools
TADY RG26 ....34 B5
Burrfields Retail Park
CFDH BH17 ....297 L8
Burridge Social & Sports Club
HLER SO31 ....251 H9
Bursledon CE J & I School
HLER SO31 ....250 A9
Bursledon Windmill Museum
HLER SO31 ....250 A9
Burton CE Primary School
CHCH/BSGR BH23 ....324 C4
Burton Medical Centre
CHCH/BSGR BH23 ....325 H5
Buryfields Infant School
ODIM RG29 ....93 L1
Bury Hill
RAND SP11 ....102 B6
The Bush Hotel
FNM GU9 ....96 C9
Business Aviation Centre
ALDT GU11 ....75 N5
Busketts Lawn Hotel
TOTT SO40 ....245 L8
Butser Ancient Farm
HORN PO8 ....236 G7
The Butts CP School
ALTN GU34 ....132 D7
Byngs Business Park
WVILLE PO7 ....255 K9
Cabot Business Village
CFDH BH17 ....320 A7
Cadogan Hotel
WBNE BH4 ....334 D3
Calleva
THLE RG7 ....35 M4
Calleva Museum
THLE RG7 ....35 J5
Calmore Industrial Estate
TOTT SO40 ....246 C1
Calmore J & I School
TOTT SO40 ....246 A2
Calmore Sports Club
TOTT SO40 ....245 N1
Calshot Castle
FAWY SO45 ....292 B8
Calshot Spit Lightship
SHAM SO14 ....248 D9
Calthorpe Park School
FLEETN GU51 ....73 P4
Camberley CC
CBLY GU15 ....58 C2
Camberley Health Centre
CBLY GU15 ....58 A2
Camberley Heath Golf Club
CBLY GU15 ....58 B2
Camberley RFC
CBLY GU15 ....58 B2
Camberley Town FC
CBLY GU15 ....58 A2
Cameleon Theatre
FNM GU10 ....116 G1
Campbell Court Industrial Estate *TADY* RG26 ....52 B3
Camp Road Industrial Estate
FARN GU14 ....76 B4
Cams Hall Estate Golf Club
FHAM/PORC PO16 ....295 H2
Cams Hill School
FHAM/PORC PO16 ....295 J1
Canada House Business Centre *NMIL/BTOS* BH25 ....327 L5
Candlesticks Inn
RGWD BH24 ....282 D5
Canford Heath First School
CFDH BH17 ....320 C5
Canford Heath Middle School
CFDH BH17 ....320 F5
Canford Magna Golf Club
BWD BH11 ....301 M5
Canford School
WIMB BH21 ....301 J3
Cantell Secondary School
ROWN SO16 ....228 C8
Careys Manor Hotel
BROC SO42 ....286 C7
Carnegie Library
PSEA PO1 ....316 C2
Carnival Hall
BSTK RG21 ....69 G8
Carrington House Hotel
BMTH BH1 ....335 K2
Carter Community Sports College *PLE* BH15 ....332 B1
Carvers Trading Estate
RGWD BH24 ....282 C2
Carwarden House School
FRIM GU16 ....58 F2
Cascades Shopping Centre
PSEA PO1 ....19 G1
Castle CP School
FHAM/PORC PO16 ....295 P2
Castledown School
RAND SP11 ....79 L2
Castle Hill Infant School
DEAN RG23 ....88 E2
Castle Industrial Park
PSEA PO1 ....24 F2
Castlepoint Shopping Centre
CHAR BH8 ....323 L5
The Castle Special School
NWBY RG14 ....24 C1
Castle Trading Estate
FHAM/PORC PO16 ....296 A2
Catchcold Tower
SHAM SO14 ....20 D5

Cathedral Church of St Thomas of Canterbury *PSEA* PO1 ....18 C6
Cathedral Discovery Centre
PSEA PO1 ....19 F1
Catherine Corbett Clinic
HAV PO9 ....15 G5
Catherington CE Controlled Infant School *HORN* PO8 ....256 B2
Cedar School
ROWN SO16 ....227 J8
Cenotaph
WSHM SO15 ....20 C2
Central Estate
ALDT GU11 ....3 F4
Central Hall
SHAM SO14 ....21 G5
Central Health Clinic
WSHM SO15 ....20 E2
Central Industrial Estate
HAV PO9 ....14 E6
Central Trading Estate
SHAM SO14 ....21 H5
Centurion Industrial Park
SHAM SO14 ....248 E4
Chalcroft Distribution Park
HEND SO30 ....230 A7
Chalk Ridge Primary School
KBH RG22 ....90 A2
Chalwyn Industrial Estate
BKME/WDN BH12 ....321 J5
Chamberlayne Park School
ITCH SO19 ....269 J1
Chandler's Ford Industrial Estate *CHFD* SO53 ....206 E8
Chandler's Ford Infant School
CHFD SO53 ....206 F6
The Chantry Centre
AND SP10 ....4 D4
Chapel of St Johns Hospital
WINC SO23 ....23 F5
Charles Dickens' Birthplace Museum *PSEA* PO1 ....316 E1
Charles Dickens J & I School
PSEA PO1 ....316 F2
Charles Kingsleys CE Primary School *HTWY* RG27 ....39 M6
Charlton House School
WEND SO18 ....248 C4
Charlton Sports & Leisure Centre *AND* SP10 ....82 A9
Charris Camping & Caravan Park *WIMB* BH21 ....300 A3
Chase Community Hospital
BOR GU35 ....154 A6
Chaucer Business Centre
WINC SO23 ....165 K3
Chawton Primary School
ALTN GU34 ....151 L1
Cheam School
STHA RG19 ....32 A6
The Chequers Hotel
NWBY RG14 ....24 C3
Cherbourg Primary School
ELGH SO50 ....229 J3
The Cheriton Brewhouse
NARL SO24 ....187 G1
Cheriton Primary School
NARL SO24 ....167 P9
Cherry Wood Primary School
FARN GU14 ....57 P7
Chesil Theatre
WINC SO23 ....23 G6
Chevron Business Park
FAWY SO45 ....290 D3
Chewton Glen Hotel
NMIL/BTOS BH25 ....326 E7
Chilworth Golf Club
NBAD SO52 ....227 M1
Chilworth Manor Hotel
NBAD SO52 ....227 N3
Chineham Business Park
CHIN RG24 ....51 P9
Chineham Park Primary School
CHIN RG24 ....69 N4
Chineham Shopping Centre
CHIN RG24 ....70 A3
Chine Hotel
BOSC BH5 ....335 K3
Chinehurst Hotel
WBNE BH4 ....334 C5
Christchurch Castle & Norman House *CHCH/BSGR* BH23 ....324 G9
Christchurch Hospital
CHCH/BSGR BH23 ....324 D6
Christchurch J & I School
CHCH/BSGR BH23 ....324 E8
Christchurch Medical Centre
CHCH/BSGR BH23 ....325 J8
HAV PO9 ....277 J7
Christchurch Priory
CHCH/BSGR BH23 ....324 G9
Christchurch Rowing Club
CHCH/BSGR BH23 ....336 F1
Christchurch Ski & Leisure Centre *CHCH/BSGR* BH23 ....303 P5
Christ's Hospital
WINC SO23 ....22 D6
Christ the King Catholic Primary School *BWD* BH11 ....322 A2
Church Cottage
BSTK RG21 ....6 E6
Church Crookham Junior School *FLEETS* GU52 ....74 D8
Churchers College
EPSF GU31 ....215 N1
Churchers College Junior Department *PSF* GU32 ....215 L2
Church Grange & Bramblys Grange Health Centre
BSTK RG21 ....6 D7
Churchill Plaza
BSTK RG21 ....7 F5
Churchill Yard Industrial Estate *WVILLE* PO7 ....275 N1

City Business Centre WINC SO23 ...22 E3
City Grove Trading Estate ELGH SO50 ...206 C9
City Industrial Park WSHM SO15 ...20 A5
City Museum & Records Office PSEA PO1 ...18 E5
The City of Portsmouth Boys School NEND PO2 ...296 C5
City of Portsmouth Girls School PSEA PO1 ...316 C1
City of Portsmouth Sports Club NEND PO2 ...296 F6
Civic Gateway BSTK RG21 ...7 F7
Civil Service Sports Ground HSEA PO3 ...297 J6
NBNE BH10 ...302 C9
Clanfield Junior School HORN PO8 ...236 B5
Clarence Pier & Amusement Centre SSEA PO5 ...316 C6
Clarendon J & I School NTID SP9 ...79 H5
Clatford CE J & I School RAND SP11 ...102 E9
Clayfields Sports Centre FAWY SO45 ...267 P6
Clayton Barracks ALDT GU11 ...76 C8
The Clere School KSCL RG20 ...30 F7
Clewborough House School at Cheswycks FRIM GU16 ...58 G8
Cliddesden Primary School OVTN RG25 ...90 C6
Cliff Court Hotel WCLF BH2 ...8 A5
Cliffdale Primary School NEND PO2 ...297 H7
Cliffeside Hotel BMTH BH1 ...9 J4
Cloud Hotel BROC SO42 ...286 C7
The Club at Meyrick Park WCLF BH2 ...8 B1
Cluster Industrial Estate HSEA PO3 ...317 J5
The Coast Clinic FAWY SO45 ...291 K6
Cody Technology Park FARN GU14 ...75 K4
Cogdean Elms Industrial Estate WIMB BH21 ...300 A4
Colden Common Primary School RWIN SO21 ...207 P4
Colehill First School WIMB BH21 ...279 K7
Coliseum Business Centre CBLY GU15 ...57 P2
College Park Infant School NEND PO2 ...297 H7
College Town Infant & Nursery School SHST GU47 ...41 M6
Collingwood Business Park FHAM/STUB PO14 ...294 E3
Colthrop Business Park RG19 ...25 P4
Coltwood Business Centre ALDT GU11 ...3 F3
Commercial Business Centre CHFD SO53 ...206 E7
Common Marsh STOK SO20 ...141 K7
Community Centre Cinema LYMN SO41 ...329 L3
Compton Acres Gardens PSTN BH14 ...333 N3
Compton CE Primary School RWIN SO21 ...183 M6
Compton Place Business Centre CBLY GU15 ...57 P1
Concorde Club & Hotel ELGH SO50 ...228 C4
The Connaught Hotel WCLF BH2 ...8 B5
The Connaught School ASHV GU12 ...97 L4
Copnor Bridge Business Centre PSEA PO1 ...317 H1
Copnor J & I School HSEA PO3 ...297 J8
Copythorne CE Infant School TOTT SO40 ...245 H1
Corfe Hills School WIMB BH21 ...300 B7
Corhampton Golf Club BPWT SO32 ...211 J9
Corn Exchange NWBY RG14 ...16 E2
Corpus Christi Catholic Primary School BOSC BH5 ...335 M1
Corpus Christi RC (Aided) Primary School NEND PO2 ...296 F7
Corus Hotel CWTH RG45 ...41 H1
Cosham Health Centre CHAM PO6 ...297 H2
Costello Technical College BSTK RG21 ...7 H7
Cottage Grove Primary School SSEA PO5 ...19 H6
Courthill First School BWD BH14 ...321 M8
Court Lane J & I School CHAM PO6 ...297 J2
Court Moor School FLEETS GU52 ...74 C6
Cove CC FARN GU14 ...57 M9
Cove Infant School FARN GU14 ...57 M7
Cove Junior School FARN GU14 ...57 M8

Cove Secondary School FARN GU14 ...57 M8
Cowplain Community School WVILLE PO7 ...255 N9
Coxlease School LYND SO43 ...264 F8
Coxmoor Farm Light Industrial Estate RFNM GU10 ...94 F1
Cracknore Industrial Park TOTT SO40 ...247 M9
Cranbourne Secondary School BSTK RG21 ...69 J9
Craneswater Junior School ENEY PO4 ...317 H6
Crane Valley Golf Club WIMB BH21 ...258 B3
The Crescent Primary School ELGH SO50 ...229 J1
Crestwood College of Business & Enterprise ELGH SO50 ...207 H8
Cricklade College AND SP10 ...4 D3
Cricklade Theatre AND SP10 ...4 C3
Crofton Anne Dale J & I School FHAM/STUB PO14 ...294 A7
Crofton Hammond Infant School FHAM/STUB PO14 ...293 P7
Crofton School FHAM/STUB PO14 ...294 C7
Crondall Primary School RFNM GU10 ...95 H5
Crookham CE Infant School FLEETS GU52 ...74 C8
The Crookhorn Community School WVILLE PO7 ...275 P6
Cross Farm Infant School FRIM GU16 ...58 D7
Crow Arch Lane Industrial Estate RGWD BH24 ...282 F4
Crown Hotel LYND SO43 ...264 F5
Crowthorne CE Primary School CWTH RG45 ...41 J1
Cumberland Business Centre SSEA PO5 ...19 K3
Cumberland Hotel BMTH BH1 ...9 J4
Cumberland Infant School ENEY PO4 ...317 J5
Cupernham J & I School ROMY SO51 ...204 F4
Curdridge Primary School BPWT SO32 ...251 K2
Curtis Museum ALTN GU34 ...132 F6
Danebury Ring STOK SO20 ...121 L9
Daneshill East Industrial Estate CHIN RG24 ...69 P5
Daneshill House School HTWY RG27 ...53 L1
Daneshill West Industrial Estate CHIN RG24 ...69 N4
Danesmead Community Centre RSAL SP5 ...69 M4
David Hart Business Centre RSAL SP5 ...199 J5
Days Inn FLEETN GU51 ...56 A9
D-Day Museum & Overlord Embroidery SSEA PO5 ...316 E7
Deacon Trading Estate ELGH SO50 ...229 L2
Deanery Campus SHAM SO14 ...21 G6
The Deanery WINC SO23 ...22 E6
Deane's Almshouses BSTK RG21 ...69 L8
Dean Farm Estate RAND SP11 ...272 E5
Dean Farm Golf Club BOR GU35 ...134 F9
Deer Park Farm Industrial Estate ELGH SO50 ...230 E3
Delta Business Park FHAM/PORC PO16 ...294 F2
Denmark Road Medical Centre MOOR/WNTN BH9 ...322 F6
Denmead Health Centre WVILLE PO7 ...254 C6
Denmead Infant School WVILLE PO7 ...255 J7
Denmead Junior School WVILLE PO7 ...255 H7
Denvale Trading Park NWBY RG14 ...24 G5
Derry Down Health Clinic RAND SP11 ...84 C2
The Derwent Hospital LTDN BH7 ...323 P6
De Vere Grand Harbour Hotel SHAM SO14 ...20 C6
De Vere Royal Bath Hotel BMTH BH1 ...9 F5
Devonshire Infant School ENEY PO4 ...317 H4
Devon Towers Hotel WCLF BH2 ...8 C5
Dial House Hotel CWTH RG45 ...41 J1
Dibden Golf Centre FAWY SO45 ...267 N5
Dibles Park HLER SO31 ...270 E9
Ditcham Park School EPSF GU31 ...237 M4
Dockyard Apprentice Exhibition PSEA PO1 ...18 B2
Dogmersfield CE Primary School HTWY RG27 ...73 M5
The Dolphin Shopping Centre & Sports Centre PLE BH15 ...332 F1

Dolphin Swimming Pool PLE BH15 ...332 F1
The Donald Burrell Centre BWD BH11 ...88 C4
Dorset Heavy Horse Centre WIMB BH21 ...258 D9
Dorset Magistrates Court PLE BH15 ...320 F8
Dorset Medical Centre SHAM SO14 ...20 E3
Dorset Police Eastern Division HQ FERN BH22 ...280 B8
The Dorset Racquets & Health Club CFDH BH17 ...320 D4
Dove House School BSTK RG21 ...7 F2
Down Grange Athletics Track KBH RG22 ...89 M2
Down House RSAL SP5 ...199 P5
Downton CE Primary School RSAL SP5 ...199 J5
Downton Industrial Estate RSAL SP5 ...199 J5
Downton Secondary School RSAL SP5 ...199 J6
Drewitts Industrial Estate BWD BH11 ...321 N2
Droxford Junior School BPWT SO32 ...233 L3
Duck's Nest FBDG SP6 ...197 J8
Dudmoor Farm Golf Course CHCH/BSGR BH23 ...324 E3
Dudsbury Golf Club FERN BH22 ...302 C7
Dukes Mill ROMY SO51 ...204 C6
Dummer Golf Club OVTN RG25 ...89 J9
Dumpton School WIMB BH21 ...278 F6
Dunces Arch LYND SO43 ...265 J4
Dunhurst (Bedales Junior School) PSF GU32 ...191 L8
Dunston Park Infant School NTHA RG18 ...25 N3
Dunwood Manor Golf Club ROMY SO51 ...203 K3
Durley CE Primary School BPWT SO32 ...230 C6
Durley Grange Hotel WCLF BH2 ...8 B4
Durley Hall Hotel WBNE BH4 ...334 D4
Duriston Court School NMIL/BTOS BH25 ...327 J7
Eagle House School SHST GU47 ...41 H4
East Anglia Hotel BMTH BH2 ...8 A3
East Berkshire Golf Club CWTH RG45 ...40 F1
East Cemetery LTDN BH7 ...323 M9
East Cliff Lift BMTH BH1 ...9 H5
Eastern Industrial Centre CHAM PO6 ...297 L3
Eastleigh College ELGH SO50 ...229 J2
Eastleigh College of FE ELGH SO50 ...229 H2
Eastleigh FC ELGH SO50 ...228 G5
Eastleigh Health Centre ELGH SO50 ...229 J1
Eastleigh Museum ELGH SO50 ...229 J2
Eastleigh RFC ELGH SO50 ...229 L1
Eastney Beam Engine House ENEY PO4 ...317 L5
Eastney Health Centre ENEY PO4 ...317 J5
Eastney Swimming Baths ENEY PO4 ...317 L6
Easton Lane Business Park WINC SO23 ...23 J3
Eastrop Community Centre BSTK RG21 ...7 K5
East Shore School HSEA PO3 ...317 K2
East Street Shopping Centre SHAM SO14 ...21 F5
Ebblake Industrial Estate VWD BH31 ...259 J6
The Eddie Read Swimming & Diving Complex SHAM SO14 ...20 C6
Edgebarrow School CWTH RG45 ...41 J3
Edgebarrow Sports Centre CWTH RG45 ...41 K3
Edgeborough School RFNM GU10 ...116 C7
The Edge Sports Centre HASM GU27 ...156 C5
Education Other Than At School (EOTAS) GPORT PO12 ...13 H6
Eelmoor Road Depot Trading Estate FARN GU14 ...75 P2
Eggars School ALTN GU34 ...133 H3
Eling Infant School TOTT SO40 ...246 E5
Elizabeth Barracks CHOB/PIR GU24 ...59 M7
Elizabeth House Hotel WSHM SO15 ...248 B4
Elliott Industrial Park ASHV GU12 ...97 L1
Elmers Court Hotel LYMN SO41 ...329 P4

Elmhurst Business Park GPORT PO12 ...12 D2
Elmrise CP School BWD BH11 ...301 P9
Elson County Infant School GPORT PO12 ...295 L9
Elson County Junior School GPORT PO12 ...295 L9
Elstead Hotel BMTH BH1 ...9 J2
Embley Park Industrial Estate ROMY SO51 ...203 L6
Embley Park Junior School ROMY SO51 ...203 L6
Embley Park School ROMY SO51 ...203 L7
The Emmanuel CE VA Middle School VWD BH31 ...258 E5
Emsworth Museum EMRTH PO10 ...299 M1
Emsworth Primary School EMRTH PO10 ...277 L9
Enterprise Industrial Estate ASHV GU12 ...97 L1
HORN PO8 ...256 C3
Enterprise Park VWD BH31 ...259 J6
The Epiphany CE Primary School MOOR/WNTN BH9 ...323 H3
Essebornе Manor Hotel RAND SP11 ...62 F2
Eversley CC HTWY RG27 ...40 A6
Exbury Gardens & Railway FAWY SO45 ...312 C3
Exbury House FAWY SO45 ...312 C3
Experimental Horticulture Station LYMN SO41 ...328 G7
Explosion! Museum of Naval Firepower GPORT PO12 ...315 P1
Express by Holiday Inn HEND SO30 ...249 N2
PLE BH15 ...332 F1
ROWN SO16 ...226 C9
Fairfax Industrial Estate ASHV GU12 ...97 L1
Fairfield Infant School HAV PO9 ...15 H5
Fairfields Arts Centre BSTK RG21 ...69 L8
Fairfields Primary School BSTK RG21 ...69 L8
Fairisle Infant School ROWN SO16 ...227 J8
Fairisle Junior School ROWN SO16 ...227 J8
Fairlands Montessori School BPWT SO32 ...252 C4
Fair Oak Cemetery ELGH SO50 ...230 C3
Fair Oak Junior School ELGH SO50 ...230 C3
Fairway Business Centre HSEA PO3 ...297 L6
Falcon Hotel FARN GU14 ...76 B3
Falkland Memorial NWBY RG14 ...24 A9
Falkland Primary School NWBY RG14 ...24 A9
Fareham College FHAM/STUB PO14 ...10 C6
The Fareham Gallery FHAM/PORC PO16 ...11 G6
Fareham Leisure Centre FHAM/PORC PO16 ...11 F4
Fareham Megabowl FHAM/STUB PO14 ...294 F4
Fareham Shopping Centre FHAM/PORC PO16 ...11 J5
Farleigh School RAND SP11 ...121 P1
Farley Hill Primary School THLE RG7 ...38 F1
Farley Mount RWIN SO21 ...163 K7
Farnborough Aerospace Centre FARN GU14 ...75 N4
Farnborough Airport FARN GU14 ...75 N3
Farnborough Business Centre FARN GU14 ...75 N2
Farnborough College of Technology FARN GU14 ...76 A4
FARN GU14 ...76 B2
Farnborough Gate Retail Park FARN GU14 ...58 B6
Farnborough Hill School FARN GU14 ...58 B8
Farnborough Recreation Centre FARN GU14 ...76 A1
Farnborough RFC FARN GU14 ...57 P7
Farnborough Town FC FARN GU14 ...57 P5
Farnham Business Centre FNM GU9 ...96 C8
Farnham Business Park FNM GU9 ...116 A1
Farnham Castle Keep FNM GU9 ...96 B8
Farnham College FNM GU9 ...116 C1
Farnham Golf Club RFNM GU10 ...97 K9
Farnham Health Centre FNM GU9 ...96 C9
Farnham Heath End School FNM GU9 ...96 E5
Farnham Hospital FNM GU9 ...96 E8
Farnham House Hotel RFNM GU10 ...115 L2

Farnham Museum FNM GU9 ...96 A9
Farnham Park Golf Club FNM GU9 ...96 B7
Farnham Retail Park FNM GU9 ...96 E6
Farnham Trading Estate FNM GU9 ...96 F7
Farringdon Industrial Centre ALTN GU34 ...151 K6
Farringdon Industrial Estate ALTN GU34 ...151 K6
Fawley Business Centre FAWY SO45 ...291 J6
Fawley Infant School FAWY SO45 ...291 J6
Fenwick Hospital LYND SO43 ...264 E4
Ferndown First School FERN BH22 ...302 C3
Ferndown Forest Golf Club FERN BH22 ...280 C8
Ferndown Golf Club FERN BH22 ...302 E4
Ferndown Industrial Estate WIMB BH21 ...279 P8
Ferndown Medical Centre FERN BH22 ...302 C3
Ferndown Middle School FERN BH22 ...302 C3
Ferndown Sports Centre FERN BH22 ...302 B2
Ferndown Upper School FERN BH22 ...302 B2
Ferneham Hall FHAM/PORC PO16 ...11 H5
Fernhill Primary School FARN GU14 ...57 N4
Fernhill Secondary School FARN GU14 ...57 N4
Fernhurst Junior School ENEY PO4 ...317 H4
Fernside Business Park WIMB BH21 ...302 A1
Festival Place Shopping Centre BSTK RG21 ...6 E6
The Fieldgate Centre KSCL RG20 ...48 B3
Fifehead Manor Hotel STOK SO20 ...120 D9
Finchampstead CE Primary School EWKG RG40 ...39 P3
Finchampstead Sports Club EWKG RG40 ...39 P3
Finkley Down Farm Park RAND SP11 ...83 J8
Finns Industrial Park RFNM GU10 ...94 F1
Fircroft Hotel BOSC BH5 ...335 L2
Fir Tree Primary School LTDN BH7 ...25 H3
Fish Farm RSAL SP5 ...199 S2
Fish Market PSEA PO1 ...18 C5
Flanders Industrial Park HEND SO30 ...250 B3
Fleet Business Park FLEETS GU52 ...74 E9
Fleet Community Hospital FLEETS GU52 ...74 B2
Fleet CC FLEETN GU51 ...74 B4
Fleet Infant School FLEETS GU51 ...74 E5
Fleetsbridge Business Centre CFDH BH17 ...320 D5
Fleetspoint Business Centre PLE BH15 ...320 D7
Fleet Town FC FLEETN GU51 ...74 B4
Fleming Park Golf Club ELGH SO50 ...228 G1
Fleming Park Leisure Centre ELGH SO50 ...228 G1
Flying Bull Primary School NEND PO2 ...296 F9
Focus 503 Business Centre AND SP10 ...5 K1
Folly Farm Touring Caravan Park RWIN SO21 ...143 K9
Folly Hill Infant School FNM GU9 ...96 A5
Fordingbridge Business Park FBDG SP6 ...240 A2
Fordingbridge Hospital FBDG SP6 ...240 D2
Fordingbridge J & I School FBDG SP6 ...220 D9
Forest Edge Touring Park RGWD BH24 ...281 K7
Forest Lodge Hotel LYND SO43 ...264 F4
Forest Park Hotel BROC SO42 ...286 E7
The Forest Shopping Centre BOR GU35 ...154 B5
Forres Sandle Manor School FBDG SP6 ...240 B1
Fort Brockhurst LSOL/BMARY PO13 ...295 K8
Fort Cumberland ENEY PO4 ...317 N5
Fort Fareham FHAM/STUB PO14 ...294 E3
Fort Fareham Industrial Estate FHAM/STUB PO14 ...294 E3
Fort Hill Community School DEAN RG23 ...68 F6
Fort Monckton GPORT PO12 ...315 N8
Fort Nelson WHAM PO17 ...273 M7

Fort Purbrook
  CHAM PO6 ....275 M9
Fort Southwick
  WHAM PO17 ....274 B8
Fort Wallington Industrial
  Estate FHAM/PORC PO16 ....273 H8
Fort Widley
  CHAM PO6 ....275 H8
Fosters Business Park
  HTWY RG27 ....71 L5
Foundry Lane Primary School
  WSHM SO15 ....247 M4
Four Lanes Infant & Community
  Junior School CHIN RG24 ....70 A1
Foxhills Infant School
  TOTT SO40 ....246 B7
Foxhills Junior School
  TOTT SO40 ....246 A7
Francis Avenue Industrial
  Estate BWD BH11 ....321 M1
Francis Baily Primary School
  STHA RG19 ....25 P4
Fratton Community Centre
  PSEA PO1 ....316 G2
Fratton Industrial Estate
  ENEY PO4 ....317 H3
Fred Woolley House (Hospital)
  ELGH SO50 ....228 D4
Freegrounds County
  J & I School HEND SO30 ....250 D5
Freemantle Business Centre
  WSHM SO15 ....247 N6
Freemantle CE (Controlled)
  Infant School WSHM SO15 ....247 N5
Frensham Common &
  Country Park RFNM GU10 ....136 E3
Frensham Pond Hotel
  RFNM GU10 ....136 C5
Frensham Pond Sailing Club
  RFNM GU10 ....136 C4
Friarsgate Medical Centre
  WINC SO23 ....23 F5
Friends Meeting House
  WINC SO23 ....23 F6
Frimley Business Park
  FARN GU14 ....58 A5
Frimley CE Junior School
  FRIM GU16 ....58 D6
Frimley Green Medical Centre
  FRIM GU16 ....58 E7
Frimley Park Hospital
  FRIM GU16 ....58 C3
Frobisher Industrial Centre
  ROMY SO51 ....204 C4
Frogmore Community School
  BLKW GU17 ....40 C9
Frogmore County Infant School
  BLKW GU17 ....57 J1
Frogmore Junior School
  BLKW GU17 ....41 J9
Front Lawn Junior School
  HAV PO9 ....276 F5
Froxfield Endowed
  National School PSF GU32 ....190 E4
Fryern J & I School
  CHFD SO53 ....206 C7
Furzeley Golf Club
  WVILLE PO7 ....255 H9
Furzey Gardens
  LYND SO43 ....244 A8
Futcher School
  CHAM PO6 ....297 L1
Garderobe Tower
  SHAM SO14 ....20 C6
Garland Junior School
  THLE RG7 ....27 J4
Garrison Theatre
  NTID SP9 ....78 F5
Gaston's Wood
  Industrial Estate CHIN RG24 ....69 N3
Gatcombe Park Primary
  School NPND PO2 ....297 H5
The George Gale & Co Ltd
  Brewery HORN PO8 ....256 D4
The George Hotel
  ODIM RG29 ....72 D9
George Street School
  Branch Clinic PSEA PO1 ....317 H1
Georgian House Hotel
  HASM GU27 ....157 J6
Giant's Grave
  FBDC SP6 ....198 A8
Gilbert White's House & The
  Oates Museum ALTN GU34 ....152 C8
Gillies Health Centre
  KBH RG22 ....89 P3
Glenfield Infant School
  WEND SO18 ....249 H4
Glenhurst School
  HAV PO9 ....15 H5
Glenmoor Girls School
  NBNE BH10 ....322 D6
Glenwood School
  EMRTH PO10 ....277 L9
Goldsmith Infant School
  ENEY PO4 ....316 G4
Gomer Infant School
  GPORT PO12 ....315 J5
Goodway Sea School
  GPORT PO12 ....295 M9
Gordleton Industrial Estate
  LYMN SO41 ....328 F2
Gordleton Industrial Park
  LYMN SO41 ....328 G5
Gore Road Industrial Estate
  NMIL/BTOS BH25 ....326 G5
Gosport Airfield
  LSOL/BMARY PO13 ....294 C8
Gosport Health Centre
  GPORT PO12 ....12 A3
Gosport Museum
  GPORT PO12 ....13 G2
Gosport & Stokes Bay Golf Club
  GPORT PO12 ....315 N7
Gosport War Memorial Hospital
  GPORT PO12 ....12 A3

The Grange Comprehensive
  School CHCH/BSGR BH23 ....325 J8
Grange Community
  Junior School FARN GU14 ....57 N5
Grange Farm Business Park
  BPWT SO32 ....252 A3
Grange J & I School
  LSOL/BMARY PO13 ....314 G1
Grange Road Business Centre
  CHCH/BSGR BH23 ....325 L7
The Grange
  RAND SO24 ....147 K3
Grateley Business Park
  RAND SP11 ....119 N2
Grateley Primary School
  RAND SP11 ....120 B1
Gravatom Business Centre
  GSWT GU26 ....231 P4
Grayshott CE Primary School
  CSHT GU26 ....156 A1
Grayshott Clinic
  GSHT GU26 ....156 A1
Grayswood CE Infant School
  HASM GU27 ....157 L3
Great Binfields Primary School
  CHIN RG24 ....70 A3
Greatbridge Business Park
  ROMY SO51 ....204 B4
The Great Hall
  WINC SO23 ....22 D4
Greatham Primary School
  LISS GU33 ....173 L5
Greenfields Junior School
  ROMY SO51 ....55 H8
Greenham Road Retail Park
  NWBY RG14 ....17 F4
Greenhill Farm Camping &
  Caravan Park RSAL SP5 ....223 P2
Green Pastures Farm
  TOTT SO40 ....225 L8
The Gregg School
  WEND SO18 ....229 J9
Gresham Industrial Estate
  ASHV GU12 ....97 L1
Grey House Preparatory School
  HTWY RG27 ....55 J7
Greywell Shopping Centre
  HAV PO9 ....276 F5
Griffin Industrial Park
  TOTT SO40 ....226 B9
Grosvenor Casino
  WSHM SO15 ....20 B5
Grosvenor Hotel
  BMTH BH1 ....9 F4
Grovebell Industrial Estate
  RFNM GU10 ....115 P5
Grove CP School
  FNM GU16 ....58 D3
Grove Farm Meadow Holiday
  Caravan Park
  CHCH/BSGR BH23 ....324 A6
Grove House Business Centre
  CHIN RG24 ....70 A4
Groveley Business Centre
  CHCH/BSGR BH23 ....325 J9
Grove Park Industrial Estate
  ALTN GU34 ....133 H5
Grove Place Preparatory
  School ROWN SO16 ....226 F6
The Guard Room
  FUFL SO22 ....22 C4
Guildford Road Industrial Estate
  FNM GU9 ....96 D8
The Guildhall Gallery
  WINC SO23 ....23 F5
Guillemont County
  Junior School FARN GU14 ....57 K7
Gundrymoor Trading Estate
  WIMB BH21 ....280 E4
Gunwharf Quays Retail &
  Leisure Park PSEA PO1 ....18 C4
Gurkha Museum
  WINC SO23 ....22 C5
Hackwood House
  OVTN RG25 ....90 F5
Hackwood Medical Centre
  BSTK RG21 ....6 D6
Hale Primary School
  FBDG SP6 ....221 N1
The Hamble School
  FBDG SP6 ....96 B4
Halterworth Primary School
  ROMY SO51 ....204 C6
Hamble Community Sports
  College HLER SO31 ....269 N4
Hamble Court Business Park
  HLER SO31 ....269 N7
Hambledon CC
  WVILLE PO7 ....234 C7
Hambledon Infant School
  WVILLE PO7 ....234 F9
Hamble Primary School
  HLER SO31 ....269 N6
Hamilton Business Park
  NMIL/BTOS BH25 ....326 C5
Hammond Industrial Estate
  FHAM/STUB PO14 ....294 B8
Hammond Junior School
  FHAM/STUB PO14 ....294 A7
Hampreston CE First School
  WIMB BH21 ....301 N2
Hampshire Brewery
  ROMY SO51 ....204 C4
Hampshire CCC (The Rose Bowl)
  HEND SO30 ....249 P2
The Hampshire Centrecourt
  CHIN RG24 ....70 A3
Hampshire Clinic
  CHIN RG24 ....69 P6
Hampshire Golf Club
  RAND SP11 ....102 F8
Hampshire International
  Business Park CHIN RG24 ....51 P9
Hampshire Records Office
  WINC SO23 ....22 D3
Hampshire Tennis &
  Health Club HEND SO30 ....249 P3

Hamptworth Golf &
  Country Club RSAL SP5 ....201 J9
Hamworthy Community Clinic
  PLE BH15 ....320 A9
Hamworthy First School
  PLE BH15 ....332 B2
Hamworthy Middle School
  PLE BH15 ....332 B2
Handy Cross
  RGWD BH24 ....262 B7
Hankley Common Golf Club
  RFNM GU10 ....117 K9
Harbour Heights Hotel
  CCLF BH13 ....333 N5
Harbour Lights Picture House
  SHAM SO14 ....248 D9
Harbridge School
  RAND BH24 ....260 B2
The Hard Interchange
  PSEA PO1 ....18 B3
Hardley School & Sixth Form
  FAWY SO45 ....290 E4
Harefield Clinic
  WEND SO18 ....249 J4
Harefield Infant School
  WEND SO18 ....249 K3
Harefield Junior School
  WEND SO18 ....249 K3
Harestock Primary School
  FUFL SO22 ....164 E4
Harewood Forest Industrial
  Estate RAND SP11 ....104 A7
Harlington Centre
  FLEETN GU51 ....74 C4
Harrison Primary School
  FHAM/PORC PO16 ....11 H4
Harrow Way Community
  School AND SP10 ....82 B9
Harrow Wood Farm
  Caravan Park
  CHCH/BSGR BH23 ....305 N8
Hartley Park Farm Business
  Centre ALTN GU34 ....152 C4
Hartley Wintney CC
  HTWY RG27 ....55 J7
Hartley Wintney Golf Club
  HTWY RG27 ....55 K6
Hart Plain Infant School
  HORN PO8 ....255 N9
Hart Plain Junior School
  WVILLE PO7 ....255 N9
Hart Shopping Centre
  FLEETN GU51 ....74 C3
Hart Sports Centre
  FLEETN GU51 ....73 P4
Haselworth CP School
  GPORT PO12 ....12 D4
Haslemere Hall
  HASM GU27 ....157 H6
Haslemere Hospital &
  Health Centre
  HASM GU27 ....157 J6
Haslemere Museum
  HASM GU27 ....157 J6
Haslemere Preparatory School
  HASM GU27 ....157 J8
Hassocks Wood Industrial
  Estate CHIN RG24 ....69 P5
Hatch Warren Primary School
  KBH RG22 ....89 L4
Hatch Warren Retail Park
  KBH RG22 ....89 L5
Hatherden CE Primary School
  RAND SP11 ....82 A2
Havant Arts Centre
  HAV PO9 ....15 G6
Havant Business Centre
  HAV PO9 ....14 C7
Havant Leisure Centre
  HAV PO9 ....15 G3
Havant Museum
  HAV PO9 ....15 H6
Havant Retail Park
  HAV PO9 ....276 B9
Havant RFC
  HAV PO9 ....14 C3
Havant Sixth Form College
  HAV PO9 ....14 E2
Havant War Memorial Hospital
  HAV PO9 ....14 E4
Havant & Waterlooville FC
  HAV PO9 ....276 C5
Haveluck Community Centre
  ENEY PO4 ....316 C5
Haven Hotel
  CCLF BH13 ....333 K8
The Hawk Conservancy
  RAND SP11 ....100 G2
Hawley CP School
  BLKW GU17 ....57 M2
Hawley Lane Industrial Estate
  FARN GU14 ....58 A5
Hawley Place School
  BLKW GU17 ....57 M4
The Hawthorns School
  KBH RG22 ....89 N2
Hayesowood First School
  WIMB BH21 ....279 J8
Hayling Billy Business Centre
  HISD PO11 ....318 C4
Hayling Golf Club
  HISD PO11 ....317 P4
Hayling Island Health Centre
  HISD PO11 ....318 C5
The Hayling School
  HISD PO11 ....318 C3
Haymarket Theatre
  BSTK RG21 ....6 E7
Haymoor Middle School
  CFDH BH17 ....320 C3
Hayward Business Centre
  HAV PO9 ....15 K1
Hazel Wood Infant School
  TOTT SO40 ....246 A4
Headlands Business Park
  RGWD BH24 ....260 E8

  RCWD BH24 ....282 G1
Headley Park Country Club
  BOR GU35 ....135 M8
Health Club & Swimming Pool
  STHA RG19 ....24 G5
Heatherlands First School
  BKME/WDN BH12 ....321 M7
Heather Ridge County Infant
  School CBLY GU15 ....59 J1
Heatherside Schools
  FLEETS GU52 ....74 D5
Heatherview Medical Centre
  BKME/WDN BH12 ....322 A8
Heathfield Junior School
  ITCH SO19 ....249 L9
Heathfield School
  FHAM/STUB PO14 ....294 A1
Heathlands Hotel
  BMTH BH1 ....9 H4
Heathlands Primary School
  BWD BH11 ....322 A4
Hedge End Business Centre
  HEND SO30 ....250 B2
Hedge End Retail Park
  HEND SO30 ....250 A4
Helix Business Park
  CBLY GU15 ....58 A2
Henry Beaufort School
  FUFL SO22 ....164 F3
Henry Cort Community School
  FHAM PO15 ....272 A7
Henry Tyndale School
  FARN GU14 ....58 B7
Herbert Day Hospital
  HAM BH8 ....334 B4
Hermitage Hotel
  BMTH BH1 ....8 E5
The Herne Farm Leisure Centre
  EPSF GU31 ....215 N1
The Herne Junior School
  EPSF GU31 ....215 N1
The Herons Swimming &
  Fitness Centre HASM GU27 ....156 E7
Highbury College
  CHAM PO6 ....297 J4
Highbury College of
  Technology PSEA PO1 ....316 D2
Highbury Primary School
  CHAM PO6 ....297 J3
Highclere Castle & Gardens
  KSCL RG20 ....46 A3
Highclere Castle
  CHCH/BSGR BH23 ....326 A8
Highcliffe Castle Golf Club
  CHCH/BSGR BH23 ....326 C6
Highcliffe Medical Centre
  CHCH/BSGR BH23 ....326 B7
Highcliffe School
  CHCH/BSGR BH23 ....337 M1
Highcliffe School
  CHCH/BSGR BH23 ....325 P6
Highcliff Marriott Hotel
  WCLF BH2 ....8 C6
Highcroft Industrial Estate
  HORN PO8 ....256 C3
Highfield CE (Aided) Primary
  School PTSW SO17 ....228 C9
Highfield School
  LIPH GU30 ....175 M5
Highgrove Industrial Park
  FHAM PO15 ....272 B8
Hightown Industrial Estate
  RGWD BH24 ....282 F3
Hightown Primary School
  ITCH SO19 ....249 N7
Hillbourne Community
  First School CFDH BH17 ....320 D2
Hillbourne Middle School
  CFDH BH17 ....320 C2
Hill Farm Caravan Park
  ROMY SO51 ....202 F2
Hill Head Preparatory School
  FHAM/STUB PO14 ....293 P8
Hill House School
  LYMN SO41 ....309 K7
Hill Park Clinic
  FHAM PO15 ....10 B1
Hillside First School
  LYMN SO41 ....309 K7
Hillside Industrial Estate
  HORN PO8 ....256 C3
Hillview Business Centre
  NBNE BH10 ....322 E4
Hill View First School
  NBNE BH10 ....24 G5
Hilsea Lines Business Park
  HSEA PO3 ....297 J5
Hiltingbury County J & I
  School CHFD SO53 ....206 A4
Hilton Hotel
  BSTK RG21 ....7 K7
HM Prison
  FUFL SO22 ....22 C4
  HSEA PO3 ....317 H2
HMS Dolphin
  GPORT PO12 ....13 G4
HMS Nelson
  PSEA PO1 ....18 E1
HMS Temeraire
  PSEA PO1 ....18 E4
HMS Victory
  PSEA PO1 ....18 B3
HMS Warrior
  PSEA PO1 ....18 B3
Hoburne Bashley
  NMIL/BTOS BH25 ....307 K9
Hockley Golf Club
  RAND SO24 ....184 A4
Hogs Back Brewery
  RFNM GU10 ....97 M6
Holbrook Primary School
  LSOL/BMARY PO13 ....294 C6

Holbrook Recreation Centre
  LSOL/BMARY PO13 ....295 J8
Holbury J & I School
  FAWY SO45 ....290 E6
Holiday Inn
  BSTK RG21 ....90 E1
  ELGH SO50 ....228 G1
  FARN GU14 ....76 A5
  FHAM PO15 ....271 L8
  PSEA PO1 ....18 E7
  WSHM SO15 ....20 C6
Hollybrook Cemetery
  ROWN SO16 ....227 N9
Hollybrook Infant School
  ROWN SO16 ....227 P9
Hollybrook Junior School
  ROWN SO16 ....227 P9
Hollybush Industrial Park
  ALDT GU11 ....76 D7
Hollycombe Steam Collection
  LIPH GU30 ....175 M8
Holly Lodge Primary School
  ASHV GU12 ....76 E4
Holy Cross Hospital
  HASM GU27 ....156 E6
Holy Family RC (Aided) Primary
  School ROWN SO16 ....246 C1
Holy Ghost Chapel Ruins
  BSTK RG21 ....6 C4
Home Farm Business Centre
  RSAL SP5 ....178 E1
Homefield Preparatory School
  CHCH/BSGR BH23 ....324 G2
Hones Yard Business Park
  FNM GU9 ....96 D9
Hook Bowling Club
  HTWY RG27 ....71 N3
Hook Community Centre
  HTWY RG27 ....72 A3
Hook House Hotel
  HTWY RG27 ....72 B2
Hook J & I School
  HTWY RG27 ....72 A3
Hook with Warsash CE
  Primary School
  HLER SO31 ....292 D1
Hordle CE Primary School
  LYMN SO41 ....328 A4
Hordle House School
  LYMN SO41 ....338 C1
Hordle Walhampton School
  NWBY RG14 ....329 N1
Horizon West Industrial Estate
  NWBY RG14 ....24 C4
Horndean CE Junior School
  HORN PO8 ....256 C4
Horndean FC
  HORN PO8 ....256 C4
Horndean Health Centre
  HORN PO8 ....256 D4
Horndean Infant School
  HORN PO8 ....256 C4
Horndean Technology College
  HORN PO8 ....256 B4
Horris Hill School
  KSCL RG20 ....30 D3
Hoskins Place Industrial Estate
  CBLY GU15 ....58 A2
Hospital of St Cross
  WINC SO23 ....183 P2
Hotel Collingwood
  WCLF BH2 ....8 C5
Hotel du Vin
  WINC SO23 ....22 D5
Hotel Ibis
  WSHM SO15 ....19 G4
  WSHM SO15 ....20 B4
Hotel Miramar
  BMTH BH1 ....9 G4
Hotel Piccadilly
  BMTH BH1 ....9 G4
Houghton Lodge & Garden
  RAND SO20 ....141 H9
Houndmills Industrial Estate
  BSTK RG21 ....69 H6
Hounsdown Business Park
  TOTT SO40 ....246 D7
Hounsdown Secondary School
  TOTT SO40 ....246 D7
Household Waste
  Disposal Centre AND SP10 ....4 E2
Hughes Business Centre
  CHCH/BSGR BH23 ....325 L8
Hulbert Junior School
  WVILLE PO7 ....275 P4
Hurlands Business Centre
  FNM GU9 ....96 F7
Hurstbourne Tarrant CE
  J & I School RAND SP11 ....62 B9
Hurst Castle
  LYMN SO41 ....339 N6
The Hurst Community College
  TADY RG26 ....33 N5
Hurst Leisure Centre
  TADY RG26 ....33 N5
Hyde Primary School
  FBDG SP6 ....241 H6
Hythe Medical Centre
  FAWY SO45 ....268 B8
Hythe Primary School
  FAWY SO45 ....268 C6
Icknield School
  AND SP10 ....82 G9
Iford Bridge Golf Club
  CHCH/BSGR BH23 ....324 B7
IMAX Cinema
  BMTH BH2 ....8 E5
Indoor Bowls Centre
  HAV PO9 ....15 F3
Indoor Tennis Centre
  BSTK RG21 ....69 M9
  PSEA PO1 ....18 E4

Innkeeper's Lodge
 FLEETEN GU51 ....57 H9
 FRIM GU16 ....58 D2
 HAV PO9 ....277 H2
 NEND PO2 ....297 H5
Intec Business Park
 CHIN RG24 ....69 P4
Irish Centre
 BSTK RG21 ....69 L8
Isle of Wight Car Ferry Terminal
 PSEA PO1 ....18 B5
Itchen Abbas CP School
 RWIN SO21 ....166 E1
Itchen College
 ITCH SO19 ....249 J6
Itchen Valley Brewery
 NARL SO24 ....167 P3
Itchen Valley Country Park
 HEND SO30 ....229 L7
Jameson House
 CHIN RG24 ....70 A3
Jane Austen's House
 ALTN GU34 ....132 D9
 WINC SO23 ....22 E6
Jellicoe Theatre
 PSTN BH14 ....321 H7
The Jigsaw School
 FRIM GU16 ....76 D1
JML Trading Estate
 WSHM SO15 ....20 A3
John Arlott Pavilion
 BSTK RG21 ....69 M8
The John Hanson Secondary
 School AND SP10 ....102 B3
John Hunt of Everest School
 CHIN RG24 ....69 M3
John Nearne Swimming Pool
 PSTN BH14 ....321 K8
John Pounds Community
 Centre PSEA PO1 ....18 D2
John Rankin Infant School
 NWBY RG14 ....24 A7
John Rankin Junior School
 NWBY RG14 ....24 A7
Jubilee Business Centre
 WVILLE PO7 ....275 M2
Kanes Hill Primary School
 ITCH SO19 ....249 N5
Keble Memorial
 Primary School
 RWIN SO21 ....182 D8
Kempshott Infant School
 KBH RG22 ....89 L3
Kempshott Junior School
 KBH RG22 ....89 L3
Kemps Quay Industrial Park
 WEND SO18 ....248 F4
Kemp Welch Leisure Centre
 BKME/WDN BH12 ....321 M4
Kendall Court Business Park
 CBLY GU15 ....57 N1
Kennet Business Centre
 STHA RG19 ....25 P4
Kennet School
 STHA RG19 ....25 P4
Kenwood Business Centre
 HAV PO9 ....15 K2
The Kerridge Industrial Estate
 ALTN GU34 ....132 G5
Kimpton CE J & I School
 RAND SP11 ....100 D1
King Alfreds Statue
 WINC SO23 ....23 G5
King Edward VI School
 WSHM SO15 ....248 A3
Kingfisher Court Industrial
 Estate NWBY RG14 ....24 C4
King Richard Secondary
 School CHAM PO6 ....296 B1
The Kings Centre
 ALDT GU11 ....2 E2
Kingsclere CE Primary School
 KSCL RG20 ....48 C3
Kingsclere Health Centre
 KSCL RG20 ....48 B3
Kingsclere Park
 KSCL RG20 ....48 B2
Kings Copse Primary School
 HEND SO30 ....250 C6
Kings Court School
 HORN PO8 ....256 A2
Kings Furlong Infant School
 BSTK RG21 ....69 J9
Kings Furlong Junior School
 BSTK RG21 ....69 J9
Kingsgrove Industrial Estate
 FARN GU14 ....75 P1
Kings High School
 NBNE BH10 ....322 C4
Kings International College
 CBLY GU15 ....58 B3
Kingsland Centre
 STHA RG19 ....25 N4
Kingsland Industrial Estate
 CHIN RG24 ....69 P3
Kingsland Market
 SHAM SO14 ....21 F4
Kingsleigh Primary School
 NBNE BH10 ....322 C4
Kingsley Business Park
 BOR GU35 ....134 G8
Kingsmead Shopping Centre
 FARN GU14 ....76 A1
King's Park Athletics Centre
 LTDN BH7 ....323 M9
Kings Park Community
 Hospital LTDN BH7 ....323 M9
Kings Park Primary School
 BMTH BH1 ....323 L9
The Kings Primary School
 HEND SO30 ....229 M9
Kings Road Industrial Estate
 HASM GU27 ....156 F7
The King's Royal Hussars
 Regimental Museum
 WINC SO23 ....22 C4

Kings School
 BSTK RG21 ....6 D7
 FUFL SO22 ....164 C9
The Kings School Senior
 ELGH SO50 ....230 B4
Kings Somborne CE J & I
 School STOK SO20 ....161 L5
Kings Theatre
 SSEA PO5 ....19 K7
Kingston Cemetery
 PSEA PO1 ....317 H1
Kingston Great Common
 National Nature Reserve
 RGWD BH24 ....283 L7
Kingstons Industrial Estate
 ASHV GU12 ....97 L1
Kingsworthy Primary School
 WINC SO23 ....165 K1
Kin Hon Clinic
 SSEA PO5 ....19 F4
Kinson Cemetery
 BWD BH11 ....322 B3
Kinson Pottery Industrial
 Estate BWD BH11 ....321 J6
Kinson Primary School
 BWD BH11 ....322 B2
Kinson Road Medical Centre
 NBNE BH10 ....322 C1
Kinson Swimming Pool
 BWD BH11 ....322 B3
Knighton Heath Golf Club
 WIMB BH21 ....321 L1
Knighton Heath Industrial
 Estate BWD BH11 ....321 N1
Knights Enham Junior School
 AND SP10 ....82 E8
Knightwood Lodge
 LYND SO43 ....265 H4
Knightwood Primary School
 CHFD SO53 ....206 B6
Knoll Gardens & Nursery
 WIMB BH21 ....279 P9
Ladle Hill (Unfinished Hill Fort)
 WHCH RG28 ....46 C7
Lainston House Hotel
 RWIN SO21 ....163 P3
Lake Road Health Centre
 PSEA PO1 ....316 C2
Lakeside Business Park
 SHST GU47 ....41 H7
Lakeside Country Club
 FRIM GU16 ....58 F7
Lakeside International Hotel
 FRIM GU16 ....58 F7
Lakeside Primary School
 FRIM GU16 ....58 E4
Landford CE Primary School
 RSAL SP5 ....201 M9
Landport Community Centre
 PSEA PO1 ....19 J1
Land Registry
 PSEA PO1 ....19 F3
Langdown Infant School
 FAWY SO45 ....268 D8
Langdown Junior School
 FAWY SO45 ....268 D7
Langrish House Hotel
 PSF GU32 ....214 C2
Langrish Primary School
 PSF GU32 ....214 G2
Langside School
 BKME/WDN BH12 ....322 A7
Langstone Infant School
 HSEA PO3 ....317 J2
Langstone Junior School
 HSEA PO3 ....317 J1
Langtry Manor Lovenest of a
 King Hotel BMTH BH1 ....335 J2
Lankhills School
 WINC SO23 ....22 D1
Lansdowne Clinic
 BMTH BH1 ....334 G1
Lasham Airfield
 ALTN GU34 ....111 M7
Laverstoke Mill (Engineering
 Works) WHCH RG28 ....86 C5
Leckford Golf Club
 STOK SO20 ....141 N2
Lee On Solent Health Centre
 LSOL/BMARY PO13 ....11 K4
Lee-on-the-Solent Golf Club
 LSOL/BMARY PO13 ....294 E9
Lee-on-the-Solent
 Infant School
 LSOL/BMARY PO13 ....314 D5
Lee-on-the-Solent
 Junior School
 LSOL/BMARY PO13 ....314 D5
Leesland CE Infant School
 GPORT PO12 ....12 C2
Leesland CE Junior School
 GPORT PO12 ....12 C2
Leigh House Hospital
 CHFD SO53 ....206 D5
Lepe Country Park
 FAWY SO45 ....313 K6
Le Poussin at Parkhill Hotel
 LYND SO43 ....265 J7
Lido Sports Club
 FRIM GU16 ....22 E2
Lifeboat Museum
 PLE BH15 ....332 E2
The Lighthouse
 PLE BH15 ....320 F9
Lilliput CE First School
 PSTN BH14 ....333 L3
Limington House School
 KBH RG22 ....68 G9
Liners Industrial Estate
 WSHM SO15 ....247 N5
Linsford Business Park
 FRIM GU16 ....76 E1
Linwood School
 TWDS BH3 ....322 G8
Lion & Lamb Yard Shopping
 Centre FNM GU9 ....96 B8

Liphook CE Junior School
 LIPH GU30 ....175 H3
Liphook Golf Club
 LIPH GU30 ....175 H8
Liphook Infant School
 LIPH GU30 ....175 H3
Liss Business Centre
 LISS GU33 ....192 C1
Liss J & I School
 LISS GU33 ....192 E3
Littledown Leisure Centre
 LTDN BH7 ....323 N7
Local Education Office
 HAV PO9 ....15 H2
Lockerley CE J & I School
 ROMY SO51 ....178 G5
Locks Heath J & I School
 HLER SO31 ....270 G9
Loddon Business Centre
 CHIN RG24 ....70 A5
Loddon Centre
 CHIN RG24 ....69 P4
The Loddon School
 HTWY RG27 ....52 E8
London Road Industrial Estate
 NWBY RG14 ....17 G1
Longbridge Industrial Park
 SHAM SO14 ....21 J7
Long Meadow Industrial
 Estate WIMB BH21 ....280 F2
Longparish Primary School
 RAND SP11 ....104 D6
Longstone School
 CFDH BH17 ....320 F5
Long Sutton CE Primary School
 ODIM RG25 ....93 K8
Lord Wandsworth College
 ODIM RG29 ....93 M9
Lord Wilson School
 HLER SO31 ....270 F6
Lower William Street
 Industrial Estate
 SHAM SO14 ....248 F5
Lucia Foster Welch College
 SHAM SO14 ....21 G7
Ludgershall Castle Primary
 School RAND SP11 ....80 A1
Ludgershall Sports Club
 RAND SP11 ....79 N1
Ludlow Infant School
 ITCH SO19 ....248 G8
Ludlow Junior School
 ITCH SO19 ....248 G7
Ludshott Common (NT)
 GSHT GU26 ....155 M5
Lulworth Business Centre
 TOTT SO40 ....246 C1
Lydlynch Infant School
 TOTT SO40 ....246 C4
Lymington Barn Industrial
 Estate ALTN GU34 ....150 B5
Lymington Community
 Hospitals LYMN SO41 ....329 L3
Lymington Hospital
 LYMN SO41 ....329 K3
Lymington J & I School
 LYMN SO41 ....329 K3
Lymington RC Primary School
 LYMN SO41 ....329 M3
Lymington Recreation Centre
 LYMN SO41 ....329 J4
Lyndhurst Junior
 Foundation School
 NEND PO2 ....297 H8
Lyndhurst Park Hotel
 LYND SO43 ....264 G5
Lyon Way Industrial Estate
 FRIM GU16 ....58 B4
Lysses House Hotel
 FHAM/PORC PO16 ....11 K4
Lythe Hill Hotel & Spa
 HASM GU27 ....157 N8
Lytton Lawn Touring Park
 LYMN SO41 ....328 E8
Magpies Sports Club
 WIMB BH21 ....280 C1
Mainline Business Centre
 LISS GU33 ....192 D2
The Malls Shopping Centre
 BSTK RG21 ....7 F5
Malmesbury Park CP School
 CHAR BH8 ....323 H9
Malvern Business Centre
 ROWN SO16 ....247 P1
Mannings Heath Retail Park
 BKME/WDN BH12 ....321 J4
Manor Farm Business Centre
 RFNM GU10 ....97 M6
Manor Farm Country Park
 HAV PO9 ....3 H4
Manor Field J & I School
 KBH RG22 ....90 A4
Manor Infant School
 FAWY SO45 ....290 E4
 PSEA PO1 ....316 G1
Manor J & I School
 FARN GU14 ....57 N7
Manor Park Industrial Estate
 ASHV GU12 ....3 H4
Mansbridge Primary School
 WEND SO18 ....228 G8
Mansel Infant School
 ROWN SO16 ....246 G1
Mansel Junior School
 ROWN SO16 ....247 H1
Mansfield Business Park
 ALTN GU34 ....150 B5

Mansfield Hotel
 WCLF BH2 ....8 B6
Mansion House Hotel
 PLE BH15 ....332 D1
Maple Business Park
 WIMB BH21 ....279 P7
Maple Ridge School
 BSTK RG21 ....69 J7
Marchwood CE Infant School
 TOTT SO40 ....267 J2
Marchwood Industrial Park
 TOTT SO40 ....247 L8
Marchwood Junior School
 TOTT SO40 ....267 K1
Marchwood Priory Hospital
 TOTT SO40 ....267 J3
Market Quay
 FHAM/PORC PO16 ....11 H6
The Mark Way School
 AND SP10 ....5 H3
Marlands Shopping Centre
 SHAM SO14 ....20 D3
Marlborough Infant School ALDT GU11 ....76 B5
Marnel J & I Schools
 CHIN RG24 ....69 M3
Marriott Meon Valley Hotel &
 Country Club
 BPWT SO32 ....252 B3
Marsham Court Hotel
 BMTH BH1 ....9 G5
Marsh Farm Business Centre
 RFNM GU10 ....95 H2
Marwell Hotel
 RWIN SO21 ....208 E6
Marwell Zoological Park
 RWIN SO21 ....208 F5
Marycourt School
 GPORT PO12 ....315 L7
Mary Hare Primary School
 STHA RG19 ....25 H7
Mary Rose Exhibition
 PSEA PO1 ....18 B2
Mary Rose Ship Hall
 PSEA PO1 ....18 B1
Mason Moore Primary School
 ROWN SO16 ....247 J3
Master Builders House Hotel
 BROC SO42 ....311 P3
Matbro Industrial Estate
 HLER SO31 ....103 P7
Mayfield Avenue Industrial Park
 RAND SP11 ....80 G9
Mayfield School
 ALTN GU34 ....133 H4
Mayfield Secondary School
 NEND PO2 ....296 G7
Mayflower Memorial
 SHAM SO14 ....20 D7
Mayflower Theatre
 WSHM SO15 ....20 B2
Mayhill Junior School
 ODIM RG25 ....93 L1
May's Bounty (Basingstoke &
 North Hants CC)
 BSTK RG21 ....69 L9
Maytree Nursery & Infant
 School SHAM SO14 ....248 D5
Mayville High School
 SSEA PO5 ....316 F6
Meadowlands Infant School
 HORN PO8 ....255 N6
Meadowlands Junior School
 HORN PO8 ....255 N6
The Meadow School
 BOR GU35 ....154 D4
The Meadows Hospital
 HLER SO31 ....270 F5
The Meadows (Superstores)
 SHST GU47 ....41 M9
Medina Primary School
 CHAM PO6 ....296 G2
Megabowl
 BKME/WDN BH12 ....321 K3
Mengham Infant School
 HISD PO11 ....318 G4
Mengham Junior School
 HISD PO11 ....318 G4
Menzies Anglo-Swiss Hotel
 BMTH BH1 ....9 H5
Menzies Carlton Hotel
 BMTH BH1 ....9 H5
Menzies East Cliff Court Hotel
 BMTH BH1 ....9 J4
Meoncross School
 FHAM/STUB PO14 ....294 D3
Meon Junior School
 ENEY PO4 ....317 K4
Meon Junior School
 ENEY PO4 ....317 K3
Meonstoke CE School
 BPWT SO32 ....211 N9
Meon Valley Police Station
 BPWT SO32 ....232 B4
Merdon Junior School
 CHFD SO53 ....206 F6
Meredith Infant School
 NEND PO2 ....296 G9
Meridian Shopping Centre
 HAV PO9 ....15 F5
Meridian TV Studios
 SHAM SO14 ....248 E5
Merley Court Touring Park
 WIMB BH21 ....300 F4
Merley First School
 WIMB BH21 ....300 F4
Merton J & I School
 CHIN RG24 ....69 K4
Micheldever Primary School
 RWIN SO21 ....126 G6
Middle Hill Health Centre
 ALDT GU11 ....2 E1
Middle Park Medical Centre
 HAV PO9 ....276 C6
Middle Wallop Airfield
 STOK SO20 ....121 H7

Mid Hants Railway
 (Watercress Line)
 ALTN GU34 ....150 E4
 NARL SO24 ....168 B2
 NARL SO24 ....169 K1
Milestones Hampshire's Living
 History
 KBH RG22 ....69 H7
Milford CE Primary School
 LYMN SO41 ....328 E9
The Mill at Gordleton Hotel
 LYMN SO41 ....328 E2
Millbrook Clinic
 ROWN SO16 ....247 K5
Millbrook Community School
 ROWN SO16 ....227 J9
Millbrook Secondary School
 ROWN SO16 ....227 J9
Millbrook Trading Estate
 WSHM SO15 ....247 H4
Mill Chase Community School
 BOR GU35 ....154 C5
Mill House Business Centre
 ITCH SO19 ....248 F7
Mill Lane Industrial Estate
 ALTN GU34 ....133 H5
Mill Rythe J & I School
 HISD PO11 ....319 H2
Millstream Trading Estate
 HEAD 282 E4
Milton Business Centre
 NMIL/BTOS BH25 ....326 C5
Miltoncross Secondary School
 ENEY PO4 ....317 J3
Milton Park J & I School
 ENEY PO4 ....317 K4
MLS College
 BMTH BH1 ....8 D5
MN War Memorial
 SHAM SO14 ....20 E6
Moniton Trading Estate
 DEAN RG23 ....68 E8
Monks Brook Industrial Park
 CHFD SO53 ....206 D8
Montacute Special School
 KBH RG22 ....320 E2
Montagu Arms Hotel
 BROC SO42 ....289 K8
The Montague Hotel
 WCLF BH2 ....8 A5
Moordown Medical Centre
 MOOR/WNTN BH9 ....322 F4
Moorgreen Hospital
 HEND SO30 ....249 P1
Moorhill House Hotel
 RCWD BH24 ....284 C8
Moorings Way Infant School
 ENEY PO4 ....317 L2
Moorlands College
 CHCH/BSGR BH23 ....324 F1
Moorlands Infant School
 WEND SO18 ....249 J2
Moors Valley Country Park
 RCWD BH24 ....281 L2
Moors Valley Golf Course
 RCWD BH24 ....259 K9
Moortown Lodge Hotel
 RCWD BH24 ....282 E4
More House School
 RFNM GU10 ....116 C8
Morelands Primary School
 WVILLE PO7 ....275 N8
Morgans Vale & Woodfalls CE
 Primary School
 RSAL SP5 ....199 P6
Mortimer St John's
 Infant School THLE RG7 ....35 P1
Mortimer St Marys CE
 Primary School THLE RG7 ....36 C1
Mortimers Farm Industrial
 Estate ROMY SO51 ....225 L6
Mottisfont Club House
 ROMY SO51 ....179 L4
Mountbatten Business Centre
 WSHM SO15 ....247 P6
Mountbatten Business Park
 CHAM PO6 ....297 L3
Mountbatten Centre Athletics
 Track NEND PO2 ....296 F6
Mountbatten School
 ROMY SO51 ....204 G7
The Mount Hospital
 ELGH SO50 ....207 M8
Mount Pleasant Industrial
 Estate SHAM SO14 ....248 D4
Mount Pleasant Junior School
 SHAM SO14 ....248 D4
Mount Pleasant Touring Park
 CHCH/BSGR BH23 ....303 P5
Moyles Court School
 RCWD BH24 ....260 C4
Mrs Blands Infant School
 THLE RG7 ....27 H5
Mudeford Infant School
 CHCH/BSGR BH23 ....325 J9
Mudeford Junior School
 CHCH/BSGR BH23 ....325 K9
Murrell Green Business Park
 HTWY RG27 ....72 D2
Muscliff Primary School
 MOOR/WNTN BH9 ....323 J3
Museum of Archaeology
 SHAM SO14 ....21 G6
Museum of Army Flying
 STOK SO20 ....120 G6
Mylen Road Business Centre
 AND SP10 ....102 C2
Mytchett Primary School
 FRIM GU16 ....58 E2
Naked Man
 BROC SO42 ....285 K9
National Museum of Artillery
 WHAM PO17 ....273 M7
Natural History Museum &
 Butterfly House
 ENEY PO4 ....317 H9

Nelson Industrial Park
HEND SO30 ....250 B2
Nest Business Park
HAV PO9 ....277 H6
Nethercliffe Preparatory
School *FUFL* SO22 ....22 B2
Netley Abbey
HLER SO31 ....269 J4
Netley Abbey J & I School
HLER SO31 ....269 K3
Netley Court School
HLER SO31 ....269 J5
Netley Marsh CE Infant School
TOTT SO40 ....245 N4
Neville Lovett Community
School *FHAM/STUB* PO14 .....294 C1
Newbridge Junior School
NEND PO7 ....317 H1
Newbury Business Park
NWBY RG14 ....24 F3
Newbury Bus Station
NWBY RG14 ....16 E3
Newbury College
NWBY RG14 ....24 D8
Newbury Cricket & Hockey Club
NWBY RG14 ....16 C1
Newbury & Crookham Golf Club
STHA RG19 ....25 H8
Newbury Racecourse
STHA RG19 ....17 K4
Newbury Retail Park
NWBY RG14 ....24 E8
Newbury RFC
NWBY RG14 ....24 C9
New College Swimming Pool
WSHM SO15 ....248 B4
New Durley Dean Hotel
WCLF BH2 ....8 A6
New Fields Business Park
CFDH BH17 ....320 F4
New Forest Golf Club
LYND SO43 ....265 H4
New Forest Museum &
Visitor Centre *LYND* SO43 ...264 C5
The New Forest Otter, Owl &
Wildlife Park *TOTT* SO40 ....266 C2
New Greenham Park
STHA RG19 ....31 L1
New Greenham Park
Leisure Centre *STHA* RG19 ...31 M1
New Inn
HTWY RG27 ....38 A9
Newlands CP School
YTLY GU46 ....40 D9
The New Medical Centre
CHCH/BSGR BH23 ....305 L7
New Milton J & I School
NMIL/BTOS BH25 ....327 J6
New Milton Recreation Centre
NMIL/BTOS BH25 ....327 H5
New Milton Sports Club
NMIL/BTOS BH25 ....327 L4
New Park Manor Hotel
BROC SO42 ....286 F4
Newport Junior School
ASHV GU12 ....3 K5
New Scotland Hill Primary
School *SHST* GU47 ....41 H4
New Street RC
RAND SP11 ....82 B6
New Theatre Royal
PSEA PO1 ....19 F3
The Newton Health Clinic
SHAM SO14 ....248 C5
Newtown Tony CE
Primary School *AMSY* SP4 ...118 D4
Newtown Business Park
BKME/WDN BH12 ....321 K5
Newtown Soberton
Infant School
WHAM PO17 ....253 M5
New Westcliff Hotel
WCLF BH2 ....8 A5
The Nightingale Primary
School *ELGH* SO50 ....228 F5
Noadswood Comprehensive
School *FAWY* SO45 ....268 A8
Nomansland & Hamptworth CE
Primary School *RSAL* SP5 ...223 K4
Norfolk Lodge Hotel
CCLF BH15 ....333 N4
Norman Court Preparatory
School *RSAL* SP5 ....158 G5
Norman Gate School
AND SP10 ....5 H3
Northam Business Centre
SHAM SO14 ....248 E5
Northam Community Centre
SHAM SO14 ....21 J2
North Baddesley Infant School
NBAD SO52 ....205 M9
North Baddesley Junior School
NBAD SO52 ....205 M9
Northbrook Industrial Estate
ROWN SO16 ....247 N1
North Cemetery
CHAR BH8 ....323 J6
Northcroft Leisure Centre
NWBY RG14 ....16 B1
Northern County
J & I School
FHAM/PORC PO16 ....273 N9
Northern Parade Clinic
NEND PO2 ....296 G5
Northern Parade J & I School
NEND PO2 ....296 F6
North Farnborough County
Infant School *FARN* GU14 ...58 C8
North Hampshire Hospital
CHIN RG24 ....69 H4
North Hampshire Maternity
Hospital *CHIN* RG24 ....68 G4
North Hants Golf Club
FLEETN GU51 ....56 D9
North Lodge Industrial Park
LIPH GU30 ....175 L7

Northtown Trading Estate
ASHV GU12 ....97 L2
North Waltham Business Centre
OVTN RG25 ....88 F9
North Waltham Primary School
OVTN RG25 ....108 C1
Norwood Primary School
ELGH SO50 ....229 J1
Novotel
WSHM SO15 ....20 A4
Nuffield Centre University
of Portsmouth *PSEA* PO1 .....18 E4
Nuffield Industrial Estate
CFDH BH17 ....320 F3
Nuffield Theatre
PTSW SO17 ....228 C9
Nursling CE Primary School
ROWN SO16 ....227 H7
Nursling Industrial Estate
ROWN SO16 ....226 F7
Oakdale Middle School
PLE BH15 ....320 E7
Oakdene Forest Park
FERN BH22 ....303 H1
Oak Farm Community School
FARN GU14 ....57 P7
Oakfield Primary School
FERN BH22 ....280 F7
Oakhurst First School
FERN BH22 ....280 F7
Oaklands Catholic School
WVILLE PO7 ....275 P5
Oaklands Community School
ROWN SO16 ....27 J7
Oaklands Swimming Pool
ROWN SO16 ....227 K7
Oakley CE Junior School
DEAN RG23 ....88 E2
Oakley County Infant School
DEAN RG23 ....88 E2
Oakley Shopping Centre
WIMB BH21 ....300 G4
Oak Lodge School
FAWY SO45 ....267 N7
Oakmeadians RFC
WCLF BH1 ....334 E1
Oakmead School College
BWD BH11 ....301 P9
Oak Meadow Early Years &
Family Centre *FHAM* PO15 ...272 A7
Oak Meadow Primary School
FHAM PO15 ....272 A7
Oak Park Golf Club
RFNM GU10 ....95 J5
Oakridge Infant School
BSTK RG21 ....6 C1
Oakridge Junior School
BSTK RG21 ....6 C1
Oakridge West Community
Centre *BSTK* RG21 ....6 D1
Oakwood Infant School
HTWY RG27 ....55 J8
Oakwood Junior School
HTWY RG27 ....227 M7
Oakwood Junior School
ROWN SO16 ....227 M7
Oatlands House Health Clinic
ROWN SO16 ....247 N1
Oceanarium
WCLF BH2 ....8 E6
Ocean View Hotel
BMTH BH1 ....9 K4
Odeon Cinema
BMTH BH1 ....8 E4
CHAM PO6 ....297 H2
NEND PO2 ....296 F8
Odeon Leisure World
WSHM SO15 ....20 B5
Odiham Airfield
ODIM RG29 ....93 K4
Odiham Castle
ODIM RG29 ....72 A8
Odiham Cottage Hospital
ODIM RG29 ....93 L1
The Odiham Health Centre
HSEA PO3 ....72 C9
O Jays Industrial Park
HSEA PO3 ....297 J7
Old Basing Infant School
CHIN RG24 ....70 C6
Old Hambledonians CC
HORN PO8 ....235 N2
Old House Hotel
WHAM PO17 ....252 E8
Old Thorns Hotel, Golf &
Country Club *LIPH* GU30 ....174 E4
Old Town First School
PLE BH15 ....332 E1
Old Turnpike Business Park
FHAM/PORC PO16 ....11 H3
Olivers Battery Primary School
FUFL SO22 ....183 L3
The Omni Business Centre
ALTN GU34 ....133 H6
Open Golf Centres
LTDN BH7 ....324 A5
Orchard Infant School
FAWY SO45 ....268 A8
Orchard Lea Infant School
FHAM PO15 ....272 B6
Orchard Lea Junior School
FHAM PO15 ....272 C6
Ordnance Survey Office
ROWN SO16 ....247 K1
Oriel Business Park
ALTN GU34 ....133 H5
Orion Business Centre
WEND SO18 ....228 G7
Ormonde House Hotel
LYND SO43 ....265 H5
The Osborn Clinic
FHAM/PORC PO16 ....11 J5
Otterbourne CE Primary School
RWIN SO21 ....207 K3
Our Lady & St Joseph Catholic
Primary School
LYMN SO41 ....328 G3

Our Ladys Preparatory School
CWTH RG45 ....41 H1
Overton CE Primary School
OVTN RG25 ....86 F2
Overton Community Centre
OVTN RG25 ....86 G3
Owlsmoor Primary School
SHST GU47 ....41 M5
Owslebury CP School
RWIN SO21 ....208 C1
Padnell Infant School
HORN PO8 ....256 A8
Padnell Junior School
HORN PO8 ....256 B8
Padworth College
THLE RG7 ....26 A6
Palace House
BROC SO42 ....289 K7
Palmers Road Industrial Estate
EMRTH PO10 ....277 N9
Palmerston Business Park
FHAM/STUB PO14 ....294 E2
Pamphill First School
WIMB BH21 ....278 A8
Park Community School
HAV PO9 ....276 C5
Park Crematorium
ASHV GU12 ....97 K5
Park Farm Industrial Estate
FRIM GU16 ....58 B4
Park Gate Business Centre
HLER SO31 ....270 G4
Park Gate Primary School
HLER SO31 ....271 H5
Park House Primary School
HAV PO9 ....276 C5
Park House School
NWBY RG14 ....24 B9
Parklands Business Park
WVILLE PO7 ....255 H8
Parklands Hospital
CHIN RG24 ....68 G3
Park Lane Medical Centre
HAV PO9 ....14 B1
Park Primary School
GPORT GU11 ....97 J4
The Park School
CHAR BH8 ....323 K9
Parkstone Cemetery
PSTN BH14 ....333 K1
Parkstone Golf Club
PSTN BH14 ....333 M1
Parkstone Grammar (Girls)
School *CFDH* BH17 ....320 D3
Parkstone Health Centre
PSTN BH14 ....321 L7
Park View Infant School
KBH BH20 ....89 M1
Park View Junior School
KBH BH20 ....89 M1
Parkway Retail Park
BMTH BH1 ....9 J1
Parley First School
FERN BH22 ....302 D5
Parley Golf Course
CHCH/BSGR BH23 ....303 K9
Parley Sports Club
FERN BH22 ....302 F7
Parsons Down Infant School
STHA RG19 ....25 K4
Parsons Down Junior School
STHA RG19 ....25 K4
Passfield Mill Business Park
LIPH GU30 ....154 E7
Passford House Hotel
LYMN SO41 ....308 G8
Paulsgrove Industrial Centre
CHAM PO6 ....296 D1
Paulsgrove Primary School
CHAM PO6 ....296 D1
Paultons Golf Centre
ROMY SO51 ....225 L6
Paultons Park
ROMY SO51 ....225 K6
Pavilion Hotel
BMTH BH1 ....9 G3
Pavilion Theatre
BMTH BH1 ....8 E5
Peacock Trading Estate
ELGH SO50 ....206 G9
Peel Common Infant School &
Nursery *FHAM/STUB* PO14 ...294 E7
Peel Common Junior School
FHAM/STUB PO14 ....294 E7
Pegham Industrial Park
FHAM PO15 ....271 P4
Penhale Infant School
PSEA PO1 ....316 D3
Penn Hill Clinic
PSTN BH14 ....321 N9
Pennington J & I School
LYMN SO41 ....329 J4
Perins Community School
NARL SO24 ....167 P2
Petersfield Business Park
PSF GU32 ....215 K2
Petersfield Community
Hospital *PSF* GU32 ....215 L2
Petersfield Golf Club
PSF GU32 ....192 A6
Petersfield Golf Club
(Old Course) *EPSF* GU31 ....215 N4
Petersfield Infant School
PSF GU32 ....215 M2
Petersfield RFC
PSF GU31 ....216 B1
The Petersfield School
PSF GU32 ....215 L3
Petersfield Swimming Pool
EPSF GU31 ....215 N2
Petersfield Town FC
EPSF GU31 ....215 N1
Petersgate Infant School
HORN PO8 ....236 C8
Peter Symonds College
FUFL SO22 ....22 C1

Philip Green Memorial School
WIMB BH21 ....218 A9
The Phoenix Cinema
ROWN SO16 ....228 B9
Phoenix Industrial Park
ROWN RG25 ....229 L2
Pierreponte School
FNM GU10 ....116 E9
Pier Theatre
WCLF BH1 ....8 E7
The Pilgrims School
WINC SO23 ....23 F6
The Pilgrims Way Primary
School *FNM* GU9 ....116 B2
Pine Ridge Golf Club
FRIM GU16 ....59 J3
Pinewood Infant School
FARN GU14 ....57 L6
Pipers Wood Industrial Park
WVILLE PO7 ....275 L2
Pirbright Camp
CHOB/PIR GU24 ....59 N6
Pirbright First School
CHFD SO53 ....207 H5
The Plague Monument
FUFL SO22 ....22 C4
Planet Ice-Gosport
LSOL/BMARY PO13 ....295 J8
Plaza Theatre
ROMY SO51 ....204 D6
Pokesdown Primary School
BOSC BH5 ....335 P1
Polygon School
WSHM SO15 ....20 B1
Polymonds Tower
SHAM SO14 ....20 E5
The Pompey Centre
(Retail Park)
ENEY PO4 ....317 H3
Poole County Court Offices
PLE BH15 ....321 H9
Poole Crematorium
WIMB BH21 ....300 F8
Poole Freight Ferry Terminal
PLE BH15 ....332 D3
Poole Grammar (Boys) School
PLE BH15 ....320 F2
Poole High School
PLE BH15 ....320 E8
Poole Hospital NHS Trust
PLE BH15 ....320 F9
Poole Passenger Ferry
Terminal *PLE* BH15 ....332 D3
Poole Pottery
PLE BH15 ....332 E2
Poole Stadium (Speedway
Track & Football Stadium)
PLE BH15 ....320 E8
Popham Airfield
RWIN SO21 ....107 L5
Popham Beacons
RWIN SO21 ....107 J6
Popley Fields Community
Centre *CHIN* RG24 ....69 M2
Portcastrian RFC
SBNE BH6 ....324 C9
Portchester Boys School
LTDN BH7 ....323 N8
Portchester Castle
FHAM/PORC PO16 ....296 A3
Portchester Community
School *FHAM/PORC* PO16 .....295 N2
Portchester Crematorium
FHAM/PORC PO16 ....273 M9
Portchester Health Centre
FHAM/PORC PO16 ....295 P1
Portfield School
CHCH/BSGR BH23 ....303 H8
Portsdown Primary School
CHAM PO6 ....297 H1
Portsea Clinic
PSEA PO1 ....18 D3
Portsmouth College
HSEA PO3 ....317 L1
Portsmouth Continental
Ferry Port *NEND* PO2 ....296 E9
Portsmouth County Court
PSEA PO1 ....19 G3
Portsmouth Crown Court
PSEA PO1 ....19 G3
Portsmouth Deaf Association
Centre *PSEA* PO1 ....19 K2
Portsmouth FC (Fratton Park)
ENEY PO4 ....317 H3
Portsmouth Golf Club
WVILLE PO7 ....275 N8
Portsmouth Grammar Junior
School *PSEA* PO1 ....18 E5
Portsmouth Grammar School
PSEA PO1 ....18 D5
Portsmouth High School
SSEA PO5 ....316 E6
Portsmouth High School GDST
SSEA PO5 ....316 E6
Portsmouth Marriott Hotel
CHAM PO6 ....296 E2
Portsmouth Natural Health
Centre *SSEA* PO5 ....19 F5
Portsmouth RFC
HSEA PO3 ....297 J5
Portuguese Fireplace
LYND SO43 ....263 P6
Portway Industrial Estate
AND SP10 ....102 A1
Portway Infant School
AND SP10 ....102 A2
Portway Junior School
AND SP10 ....102 A2
Potley Hill CP School
BLKW GU17 ....41 H9
Potters Gate CE Primary School
FNM GU9 ....96 A9
The Potters Heron Hotel
ROMY SO51 ....206 A2

Potters Industrial Park
FLEETS GU52 ....74 F7
Potters International Hotel
ALDT GU11 ....75 N8
Poulner Junior School
RGWD BH24 ....260 G8
Premier Business Centre
FHAM/STUB PO14 ....294 F4
Premier Business Park
FHAM/STUB PO14 ....10 A7
Premier Inn
LDTN BH7 ....323 N6
Premier Lodge *CFDH* BH17 ...320 D4
ROWN SO16 ....108 D3
Preston Candover CE Primary
School *OVTN* RG25 ....129 M1
Preston House
ROWN RG25 ....109 M9
Preymead Industrial Estate
FNM GU10 ....97 H4
Pride of the Valley Hotel
RFNM GU10 ....137 H6
Priestlands School
LYMN SO41 ....329 K5
Priest's House Museum &
Garden *WIMB* BH21 ....300 E1
Prince Consort's Library
ALDT GU11 ....75 N9
Princes Hall
ALDT GU11 ....2 D2
Princes Mead School
RWIN SO21 ....165 M1
Princes Mead Shopping Centre
FARN GU14 ....76 A1
Princess Anne Hospital
ROWN SO16 ....227 M9
The Princess Royal Barracks
FRIM GU16 ....59 J6
The Priory CE VA Primary
School *CHCH/BSGR* BH23 ....324 F9
Priory College
SSEA PO5 ....316 G4
Priory Industrial Park
CHCH/BSGR BH23 ....325 M8
The Priory Primary School
TADY RG26 ....50 E4
Prospect Business Centre
NARL SO24 ....167 P3
Purbeck Pottery
PLE BH15 ....332 D2
Purbrook CC
WVILLE PO7 ....275 K6
Purbrook J & I School
WVILLE PO7 ....275 M5
Purbrook Park School
WVILLE PO7 ....275 M7
The Pyramids Leisure Centre
SSEA PO5 ....316 F7
The Quadrant Centre
BMTH BH1 ....8 E3
Quality Hotel
AND SP10 ....5 H6
BMTH BH1 ....9 G4
Quarley Hill
RAND SP11 ....99 N9
Quayside Educations Centre
GPORT PO12 ....315 N2
Queen Alexandra Hospital
CHAM PO6 ....275 H9
Queen Elizabeth Country Park
EPSF GU31 ....236 G1
Queen Elizabeth's Leisure
Centre *WIMB* BH21 ....278 B8
Queen Elizabeths School
WIMB BH21 ....278 B8
Queen Marys College
BSTK RG21 ....69 L9
Queen's Hotel
BMTH BH9 ....9 H4
SSEA PO5 ....316 D6
Queens Inclosure Primary
School *WVILLE* PO7 ....276 A1
Queen's Park Golf Club
CHAR BH8 ....323 K8
Queens Park Infant School
CHAR BH8 ....323 J6
Queens Park Junior School
CHAR BH8 ....323 H6
Raceview Business Centre
NWBY RG14 ....17 H3
Rachel Madocks School
HORN PO8 ....255 N7
Railway Triangle Industrial
Estate *CHAM* PO6 ....297 K3
Rake Business Park
LISS GU33 ....193 J2
Rake CE First School
LISS GU33 ....193 K1
Ranvilles Infant School
FHAM/STUB PO14 ....294 A1
Ranvilles Junior School
FHAM/STUB PO14 ....294 A1
Rare Breeds Farm
AMSY SP4 ....98 B9
Red Barn CP School
FHAM/PORC PO16 ....295 M1
Redbridge Community School
ROWN SO16 ....246 G3
Redbridge Primary School
ROWN SO16 ....247 H3
Redfields Business Park
FLEETS GU52 ....95 J1
Red Funnel Ferry Terminal
SHAM SO14 ....248 B9
Red House Museum & Gardens
CHCH/BSGR BH23 ....336 F1
Redlands Primary School
FHAM/PORC PO16 ....294 E2
Red Lion Hotel
BSTK RG16 ....7 F6
Red Lodge School
ROWN SO16 ....228 A8
Redlynch CE Primary School
RSAL SP5 ....200 B8
Red Shoot Brewery
RGWD BH24 ....261 M3

Redwood Park Secondary
School *CHAM* PO6 ....297 K3
Regency Park Hotel
NTHA RG18 ....25 L1
Regent Centre
CHCH/BSGR BH23 ....324 F9
Regents Park Girls School
ROWN SO16 ....247 L3
Rex Industrial Estate
CHFD SO53 ....206 E8
Rhinefield House Hotel
BROC SO42 ....285 P5
Richmond Court Business
Centre *CHAR* BH8 ....323 H9
Riders J & I School
HAV PO9 ....276 D5
Ridgemede Junior School
BPWT SO32 ....232 B4
The Ridgeway Centre
KBH RG22 ....68 E9
The Ridgeway Community
School *FNM* GU9 ....116 C3
Ridgeway House School
ITCH SO19 ....248 C6
Ringwood Brewery
RGWD BH24 ....282 E3
Ringwood CE Infant School
RGWD BH24 ....282 E2
Ringwood Junior School
RGWD BH24 ....282 E2
Ringwood Recreation Centre
RGWD BH24 ....282 E2
Ringwood Road Retail Park
BWD BH11 ....321 N1
Ringwood Secondary School
RGWD BH24 ....282 E2
Ringwood Trading Estate
RGWD BH24 ....282 E3
Riverpark Industrial Estate
NWBY RG14 ....17 J1
River Park Leisure Centre
WINC SO23 ....23 F2
Riverside Business Park
FNM GU9 ....96 C8
LYMN SO41 ....329 M3
Riverside Park
Industrial Estate *FNM* GU9 ..96 D8
Riverside School
WVILLE PO7 ....275 P7
Riverway Industrial Park
ALTN GU34 ....133 H5
The Riviera Hotel
WBNE BH4 ....334 C5
RNLI Headquarters
PLE BH15 ....332 D1
Robert Mays School
ODIM RG29 ....72 B9
Robert Sandilands
Primary School *NWBY* RG14 ..24 B3
Rockbourne Roman Villa
FBDG SP6 ....219 M5
Rogate CE Primary School
EPSF GU31 ....217 K1
Romans Business Park
FNM GU9 ....96 D8
Romans Country House Hotel
THLE RG7 ....35 J6
Roman Way Primary School
AND SP10 ....82 F7
Romsey Abbey CE (A) Primary
School *ROMY* SO51 ....204 B6
Romsey CC
ROMY SO51 ....204 C5
Romsey Golf Club
ROWN SO16 ....226 G5
Romsey Hospital
ROMY SO51 ....204 C6
Romsey Industrial Estate
ROMY SO51 ....204 C4
Romsey Infant School
ROMY SO51 ....204 D6
Romsey Junior School
ROMY SO51 ....204 C5
Romsey RFC
ROMY SO51 ....204 D7
The Romsey School
ROMY SO51 ....204 C5
Romsey Sports Centre
ROMY SO51 ....204 D7
Romsey Town FC
ROMY SO51 ....204 D7
Rookesbury Park School
WHAM PO17 ....253 H7
Rookwood School
AND SP10 ....102 C3
Rosemary Medical Centre
BKME/WDN BH12 ....321 K5
Rosewood School
ROWN SO16 ....227 N8
Rossmore Community College
BKME/WDN BH12 ....321 M4
Round Tower
PSEA PO1 ....18 B6
Rowland's Castle Golf Club
HAV PO9 ....257 H9
Rowledge CE (Controlled)
Primary School
RFNM GU10 ....115 M7
Rowner Health Centre
LSOL/BMARY PO13 ....294 G9
Rowner Infant School
LSOL/BMARY PO13 ....295 H8
Rowner Junior School
LSOL/BMARY PO13 ....295 H8
Rowner Swimming Centre
LSOL/BMARY PO13 ....314 G2
Rownhams House Industrial
Estate *ROWN* SO16 ....227 J6
Rownhams St Johns Primary
School *ROWN* SO16 ......227 J4
Royal Army Medical Corps
ALDT GU11 ....76 C8
Royal Beach Hotel
ENEY PO4 ....316 G7

Royal Bournemouth Hospital
LTDN BH7 ....323 P6
Royal Exeter Hotel
BMTH BH1 ....8 D5
Royal Hampshire County
Hospital *FUFL* SO22 ......164 E8
Royal Hampshire Regiment
Museum & Memorial Garden
WINC SO23 ....22 C5
Royal Hospital Haslar
GPORT PO12 ....13 H6
Royal Logistic Corps Museum
FRIM GU16 ....59 J5
The Royal Marines Museum
ENEY PO4 ....317 K6
Royal Military Academy
CBLY GU15 ....41 N8
Royal Naval Memorial
SSEA PO5 ....316 D6
Royal Naval Museum
PSEA PO1 ....18 A2
Royal Navy Submarine
Museum & HMS Alliance
GPORT PO12 ....13 J5
Royal Pier
SHAM SO14 ....248 B9
The Royal School for Girls
HASM GU27 ....156 F5
Royal South Hants Hospital
SHAM SO14 ....248 C5
Royal Victoria Country Park
HLER SO31 ....269 L6
Royal Winchester Golf Club
FUFL SO22 ....164 C8
RSPB Reserve
CHAM PO6 ....297 N3
Rucstall Comminity Centre
BSTK RG21 ....69 N9
Rucstall J & I School
BSTK RG21 ....69 N9
Rufus Stone
LYND SO43 ....244 A6
Rural Life Centre
RFNM GU10 ....116 F7
Rushington Business Park
TOTT SO40 ....246 C6
Russell Cotes Art Gallery &
Museum *BMTH* BH1 ....9 F5
Russell Court Hotel
BMTH BH1 ....9 F4
Russell Hicks & Temple
ROMY SO51 ....204 C6
St Albans CE Primary School
HAV PO9 ....15 J1
St Albans Medical Centre
CHAR BH8 ....323 H7
St Aldhelms CE Combined
School *BKME/WDN* BH12 ..322 A9
St Andrews CE Infant School
FNM GU9 ....96 B9
St Annes Catholic
Primary School *KBH* RG22 ..68 C9
St Annes Convent RC Girls
School *WSHM* SO15 ....248 B5
St Annes School
LSOL/BMARY PO13 ....314 C1
St Anns Hospital
CCLF BH13 ....333 N1
St Anthonys Catholic
Primary School
FHAM/STUB PO14 ....271 K9
St Barbe Museum &
Visitor Centre *LYMN* SO41 ..329 L3
St Bartholomews Primary
School *HASM* GU27 ....157 H5
St Bartholomews School
NWBY RG14 ....16 B5
St Bede CE Primary School
WINC SO23 ....23 F3
St Bedes Catholic Primary
School *CHIN* RG24 ....69 K3
St Bernadettes CP School
FARN GU14 ....57 P8
St Catherines RC Primary
School *WIMB* BH21 ....279 J8
St Catherines Road Junior
School *ELGH* SO50 ....207 J8
St Christophers Hospital
FHAM/PORC PO16 ....11 J2
St Clements CE Infant School
BMTH BH1 ....335 K1
St Denys Primary School
PTSW SO17 ....248 E2
St Edmunds Catholic
Secondary School *PSEA* PO1 ..19 J2
St Edmunds School
GSHT GU26 ....156 C2
St Edwards Comprehensive
School *PLE* BH15 ....321 H5
St Edwards School
ROMY SO51 ....202 A4
St Faiths CE Primary School
WINC SO23 ....183 P1
St Francis Primary School
CHFD SO53 ....206 C8
St Francis School
FHAM/STUB PO14 ....272 A9
St Gabriels School
KSCL RG20 ....24 E9
St George RC Boys School
ELGH SO50 ....228 F6
St Georges Business Centre
PSEA PO1 ....18 D4
St Georges CE Primary School
PSEA PO1 ....18 C2
St Georges Hospital
LYMN SO41 ....338 F2
St Georges Industrial Estate
CBLY GU15 ....58 A2
ENEY PO4 ....317 J3

St James CE First School
FBDG SP6 ....239 N5
St James CE Primary School
EMRTH PO10 ....277 M8
HEND SO30 ....249 P1
St James CE VA Primary
School *LTDN* BH7 ....323 P9
St James Hospital
ENEY PO4 ....317 K3
St Johns Almshouses
WINC SO23 ....23 G5
St Johns Cathedral
PSEA PO1 ....316 C2
St Johns Catholic Primary
School *PSEA* PO1 ....19 J2
St Johns CE First School
WIMB BH21 ....300 F1
St Johns CE Infant School
RFNM GU10 ....136 E8
St Johns CE Primary School
BSTK RG21 ....69 K9
GPORT PO12 ....315 M1
St Johns College
SSEA PO5 ....19 J7
St Johns cross
RAND SP11 ....101 N8
St Johns Infant School
SHAM SO14 ....20 D7
St Johns Primary School
Rowlands Castle *HAV* PO9 ..277 H2
St Johns RC Cathedral
PSEA PO1 ....19 F2
St John the Baptist CE Primary
School *BPWT* SO32 ....252 C1
FHAM/STUB PO14 ....271 J8
St John the Baptist RC
J & I School *AND* SP10 ..102 B3
St John the Evangelist Infant
School *NWBY* RG14 ....16 D7
St John VA CE Primary School
MOOR/WNTN BH9 ....322 F6
St Joseph RC Primary School
NWBY RG14 ....24 E3
St Josephs Catholic Primary
School *ALDT* GU11 ....2 E7
St Josephs Primary School
CHCH/BSGR BH23 ....325 L7
St Josephs RC Combined
School *BKME/WDN* BH12 ..321 N5
St Judes CE (Controlled)
Primary School *PSEA* PO1 ..18 E6
St Judes Primary School
FHAM/STUB PO14 ....10 B6
St Jude's Youth Centre
SSEA PO5 ....19 F6
St Katharines CE VA Primary
School *SBNE* BH6 ....336 F2
St Lawrence CE (Controlled)
Primary School *ALTN* GU34 ..132 E5
St Leonards Community
Hospital *RGWD* BH24 .....281 J8
St Lukes CE Primary School
HEND SO30 ....308 B6
St Lukes CE Secondary School
SSEA PO5 ....19 H3
St Lukes CE VA Primary School
MOOR/WNTN BH9 ....322 F7
St Marks CE Junior School
CHCH/BSGR BH23 ....326 B6
St Marks CE Junior School
WSHM SO15 ....247 P4
St Marks CE VA Primary School
FARN GU14 ....76 C4
St Marks Primary School
KBH RG22 ....89 M5
St Martins East Woodhay CE
Primary School
KSCL RG20 ....29 H7
St Martins School
TWDS BH3 ....322 F9
St Mary Bourne Primary School
RAND SP11 ....84 B1
St Mary Extra Cemetery
ITCH SO19 ....249 K9
St Mary Magdalen Almshouses
WINC SO23 ....23 G6
St Marys Catholic Combined
School *PLE* BH15 ....320 C2
St Marys CE Aided School
RFNM GU10 ....136 D2
St Marys CE (Controlled)
Primary School
SHAM SO14 ....21 G3
St Marys CE First School
FERN BH22 ....280 D6
St Marys CE Junior School
CHIN RG24 ....70 C6
NTHA RG18 ....25 N2
St Mary's Church Centre
BSTK RG21 ....7 C6
St Marys College
HEND SO30 ....248 G3
St Marys CP School
GPORT PO12 ....315 L3
St Marys Hospital
HSEA PO3 ....317 H3
St Michael & All Angels Infant
School *LYND* SO43 ....264 F5
St Michaels Abbey
FARN GU14 ....58 B8
St Michaels CE Infant School
ALDT GU11 ....3 H7
St Michaels CE Junior School
ALDT GU11 ....3 H7
St Michaels CE Middle School
WIMB BH21 ....278 C2
St Michaels CE Primary School
SHST GU47 ....40 F6
St Michaels CE VC Primary
School *WCLF* BH2 ....8 A4
St Michael's Hospice
CHIN RG24 ....69 H3
St Michaels School
KSCL RG20 ....30 E8

St Monica Infant School
ITCH SO19 ....249 J8
St Monica Junior School
ITCH SO19 ....249 J8
St Neots School
HTWY RG27 ....39 J6
St Nicholas School
FLEETS GU52 ....95 J1
St Nicolas CE Junior School
NWBY RG14 ....16 D4
St Omer Barracks
ALDT GU11 ....76 C8
St Patricks Catholic Primary
School *FARN* GU14 ....5B C9
ITCH SO19 ....288 G8
St Pauls Catholic VA Primary
School *CHAM* PO6 ....296 D1
St Pauls CE Infant School
RFNM GU10 ....97 N4
St Peters Catholic Primary
School *WVILLE* PO7 ....275 P5
St Peters CE (Aided) Primary
School *FNM* GU9 ....115 P3
St Peters CE Junior School
FARN GU14 ....5B B9
YTLY GU46 ....40 E8
St Peter's Church
BMTH BH1 ....8 E4
St Peters CE Primary School
RAND SP11 ....81 H4
St Peters RC Primary School
FUFL SO22 ....183 K1
St Peters School
LTDN BH7 ....323 P7
SBNE BH6 ....336 D2
St Polycarps Catholic Primary
School *FNM* GU9 ....58 D9
St Swithuns RC (Aided)
Primary School *SSEA* PO5 ..316 C6
St Swithuns School
RWIN SO21 ....165 L7
St Swithun upon Kingsgate
WINC SO23 ....22 E6
St Swithun Wells Primary
School *CHFD* SO53 ....206 F8
St Thomas Clinic
LYMN SO41 ....329 L4
St Thomas Infant School
KSCL RG20 ....29 M6
St Thomas Mores RC Primary
School *HAV* PO9 ....14 B2
St Vincent College
GPORT PO12 ....315 M3
St Walburgas RC Primary
School *MOOR/WNTN* BH9 ..323 H5
St Winifreds School
PTSW SO17 ....248 C2
Salesian College
FARN GU14 ....76 C3
Salterns Harbourside Hotel
PSTN BH14 ....333 K3
Salterns School
SSEA PO5 ....246 E3
Salto Gym Club
AND SP10 ....82 B9
Sammy Miller Motorcycle
Museum *NMIL/BTOS* BH25 ..326 C2
Sampson Business Park
CBLY GU15 ....5B A2
The Samuel Cody School
ALDT GU11 ....76 A5
Sandbanks Business Centre
CCLF BH13 ....333 K8
Sandbanks Hotel
CCLF BH13 ....333 N6
Sandford Springs Golf Club
TADY RG26 ....48 F3
Sandhurst School
SHST GU47 ....41 L5
Sandhurst Sports Club
SHST GU47 ....41 K7
Sandy Balls Holiday Centre
FBDG SP6 ....241 H1
Sarisbury CE Junior School
HLER SO31 ....270 E6
Sarisbury Infant School
HLER SO31 ....270 E6
Sarum Road Hospital
FUFL SO22 ....164 D8
Saxon Centre
CHCH/BSGR BH23 ....324 F8
Saxon Shore Infant School
CHAM PO6 ....296 A1
Saxon Square Shopping
Centre *CHCH/BSGR* BH23 ..324 F9
Saxon Wood School
DEAN RG23 ....68 E4
Scantabout Primary School
CHFD SO53 ....207 H6
Screen Cinema
WINC SO23 ....22 D6
Seacrest Hotel
SSEA PO5 ....316 F7
Sea Life Centre
SSEA PO5 ....316 E7
Seaview Business Centre
BKME/WDN BH12 ....322 A1
Sea Vixen Industrial Estate
CHCH/BSGR BH23 ....325 L8
Selborne Primary School
ALTN GU34 ....152 C8
Shakespeare Business Centre
ELGH SO50 ....207 K9
Shakespeare Infant School
ELGH SO50 ....207 J9
Shamba Holiday Park
RGWD BH24 ....281 J8
Shamblehurst Primary School
HEND SO30 ....250 C3
Sharps Copse Primary School
HAV PO9 ....277 H5
Shawcross Industrial Park
HSEA PO3 ....297 J4
Shaw Cum Donnington
Primary School
NWBY RG14 ....24 D1

Shawfield Primary School
ASHV GU12 ....76 F9
Sheet CP School
PSF GU32 ....191 P8
Shelling School
RGWD BH24 ....282 A3
Shelley Museum
BOSC BH5 ....335 M2
Shepherds Down Special
School *RWIN* SO21 ....183 L8
Sherborne St John CE Primary
School *CHIN* RG24 ....51 H9
Sherbourne House School
CHFD SO53 ....206 F5
Sherfield on Loddon CC
HTWY RG27 ....52 E5
Shipton Bellinger Primary
School *NTID* SP9 ....98 F2
Shirley Business Park
WSHM SO15 ....247 P5
The Shirley Health Centre
WSHM SO15 ....247 N3
Shirley J & I School
WSHM SO15 ....247 N2
Shirley Swimming Pool
WSHM SO15 ....247 N4
Shirley Warren Primary School
ROWN SO16 ....247 L1
Sholing J & I School
ITCH SO19 ....249 J6
Sholing Technology College
ITCH SO19 ....249 H7
Shottermill Infant School
HASM GU27 ....156 E6
Sidings Industrial Estate
HLER SO31 ....269 M5
Silchester CE Primary School
THLE RG7 ....35 J5
Silk Mill
WHCH RG28 ....85 L1
Silver Business Park
CHCH/BSGR BH23 ....325 K8
Simcoe Clinic
WSHM SO15 ....248 A4
Sinclair Primary School
ROWN SO16 ....227 L7
The Sir Harold Hillier Gardens
& Arboretum *ROMY* SO51 ..205 H1
Siskin Infant & Nursery School
LSOL/BMARY PO13 ....315 H2
The Sixth Form College
FARN GU14 ....5B A6
Skate Park
SSEA PO5 ....316 E7
Smannell & Enham CE Primary
School *RAND* SP11 ....83 H4
Solent Business Centre
WSHM SO15 ....247 M5
Solent Hotel & Spa
FHAM PO15 ....271 K3
Solent Industrial Centre
WSHM SO15 ....247 N4
Solent Industrial Estate
HEND SO30 ....250 B2
Solent Infant School
CHAM PO6 ....297 M1
Solent Junior School
CHAM PO6 ....297 M1
Solent Peoples Theatre
ITCH SO19 ....249 L8
Somerford Business Park
CHCH/BSGR BH23 ....325 L8
Somerford Primary &
Community School
CHCH/BSGR BH23 ....325 J8
Somers Park Primary School
SSEA PO5 ....19 J5
Somers Town Health Centre
SSEA PO5 ....19 J4
Sopley Primary School
CHCH/BSGR BH23 ....304 C2
Southampton Cemetery
WSHM SO15 ....248 A3
Southampton City Art Gallery
SHAM SO14 ....20 D2
Southampton City College
SHAM SO14 ....21 G5
Southampton FC (St Mary's
Stadium) *SHAM* SO14 ......21 H4
Southampton General Hospital
ROWN SO16 ....227 M9
Southampton Institute &
Millais Gallery *SHAM* SO14 ..20 E3
Southampton International
Airport *ELGH* SO50 ....229 H6
Southampton Magistrates
Court *WSHM* SO15 ....248 C5
Southampton Maritime
Museum *SHAM* SO14 ....20 D7
Southampton Municipal
Golf Course *ROWN* SO16 ..228 A6
Southampton & New Forest
Magistrates Courts
WSHM SO15 ....20 B2
Southampton Oceanography
Centre *SHAM* SO14 ......268 D1
Southampton Park Hotel
WSHM SO15 ....20 C1
Southampton Sports Centre
ROWN SO16 ....227 P8
Southampton Sports Club
ROWN SO16 ....227 P8
South Baddesley
Primary School *LYMN* SO41 ..330 B1
Southbourne Surgery
SBNE BH6 ....336 A1
South Downs College
WVILLE PO7 ....276 A7
Southdowns Country Hotel
EPSF GU31 ....217 N5
Southern Electric Museum
CHCH/BSGR BH23 ....324 F8
South Farnborough County
Junior School *FARN* GU14 ..76 C2
South Farnborough
Infant School *FARN* GU14 ..76 C4

South Farnham Middle School *FNM* GU9 ....116 E1
South Ham Medical Centre *KBH* RG22 ....68 F9
South Hampshire Industrial Park *TOTT* SO40 ....226 B9
South Hants Country Club *WHAM* PO17 ....273 L1
Southlands School *LYMN* SO41 ....309 L9
South Lawn Hotel *LYMN* SO41 ....328 E8
Southlea Golf Club & Great Salterns Public Club *HSEA* PO3 ....297 K8
South Parade Pier *ENEY* PO4 ....316 C7
Southsea Castle *THLE* RG7 ....316 E7
Southsea Community Centre *SSEA* PO5 ....19 F5
Southsea Hovercraft Terminal *SSEA* PO5 ....316 C6
Southsea Infant School *SSEA* PO5 ....316 C6
South View J & I School *BSTK* RG21 ....7 G1
Southwick Park Naval Recreation Centre *WHAM* PO17 ....274 C5
South Winchester Golf Club *FUFL* SO22 ....183 J2
South Wonston Primary School *RWIN* SO21 ....144 E4
Southwood Golf Club *FARN* GU14 ....75 M2
Sovereign Business Centre *PLE* BH15 ....320 D6
Sovereign Business Park *CFDH* BH17 ....320 D6
Sparsholt College *RWIN* SO21 ....163 K3
Sparshot CE Primary School *RWIN* SO21 ....163 N4
Spectrum Sports Club *SBNE* BH6 ....336 A2
Speenhamland Primary School *NWBY* RC14 ....24 C3
Spinnaker Tower *PSEA* PO1 ....18 B4
Spinners Garden & Nursery *LYMN* SO41 ....309 L7
Spitbank Fort *SSEA* PO5 ....316 D9
Springdale First School *BDST* BH18 ....300 A9
Springfield School *CHAM* PO6 ....297 L2
Springhill Catholic Primary *ASHV* GU12 ....248 A5
Springlake Country Club *ASHV* GU12 ....76 D8
Spurcroft Primary School *STHA* RG19 ....25 N1
Spurlings Industrial Estate *WHAM* PO17 ....273 H7
Square Tower *PSEA* PO1 ....18 B7
SS Shieldhall *SHAM* SO14 ....248 D9
Staffvale Business Centre *CHAM* PO6 ....297 H3
Stag Business Park *RGWD* BH24 ....282 E4
Stakes Hill Infant School *WVILLE* PO7 ....275 P4
Stamshaw Infant School *NEND* PO2 ....296 F7
Stamshaw Junior School *NEND* PO2 ....296 E6
Stamshaw & Tipner Leisure Centre *NEND* PO2 ....296 F7
Stanbridge Earls School *ROMY* SO51 ....203 P2
Stanley Casino *SHAM* SO14 ....21 G7
Stanley Green First School *PLE* BH15 ....320 E6
Stanley Green Industrial Estate *PLE* BH15 ....320 D7
Stanmore Primary School *FUFL* SO22 ....183 N1
Stanwell House Hotel *LYMN* SO41 ....329 M4
Stapehill Abbey, Crafts & Garden *WIMB* BH21 ....279 N9
Station Industrial Estate *FLEETN* GU51 ....74 E1
Station Theatre *HISD* PO11 ....318 D4
Staunton Country Park *HAV* PO9 ....256 E9
Staunton Park Community School *HAV* PO9 ....277 H3
Steep School *PSF* GU32 ....191 L7
Ster Century Cinema *BSTK* RG21 ....7 F6
Sterling Industrial Estate *NWBY* RC14 ....17 G3
Sterte Industrial Estate *PLE* BH15 ....320 D8
Stockbridge J & I School *STOK* SO20 ....141 M5
Stoke Park Infant School *ELGH* SO50 ....229 N1
Stoke Park Junior School *ELGH* SO50 ....229 N2
Stoneham Golf Club *ELGH* SO50 ....228 D6
Stone Lane Industrial Estate *WIMB* BH21 ....278 C8

Stourfield Junior School *SBNE* BH6 ....324 E9
Stratfield Saye *THLE* RG7 ....37 J7
String of Horses Country House Hotel *LYMN* SO41 ....308 A6
Strouden Park Medical Centre *CHAR* BH8 ....323 L6
The Stroud School *ROMY* SO51 ....205 J5
Stubbs Industrial Estate *LYMN* SO41 ....76 D7
Studland Industrial Estate *KSCL* RG20 ....29 J2
Sulhamstead & Ufton Nervet Primary School *THLE* RG7 ....26 E3
Suncliff Hotel *BMTH* BH1 ....9 J4
Sun Court Hotel *WCLF* BH2 ....8 B5
Sundridge School *HORN* PO8 ....255 P9
Sun Hill Infant School *NARL* SO24 ....168 A3
Sun Valley Business Park *FRIM* GU16 ....23 K2
Superbowl *BMTH* BH1 ....9 F3
Super Bowl *WSHM* SO15 ....247 K4
Surrey Institute of Art & Design *FNM* GU9 ....96 A9
Swan Centre *ELGH* SO50 ....229 K2
Swan Hotel *NARL* SO24 ....168 A1
Swanmore Business Park *BPWT* SO32 ....232 D7
Swanmore CE Primary School *BPWT* SO32 ....232 F6
Swanmore College of Technology *BPWT* SO32 ....232 E7
Swanwick Business Park *HLER* SO31 ....270 D3
Swanwick Lodge *HLER* SO31 ....270 F3
Sway Manor Restaurant & Hotel *LYMN* SO41 ....308 B7
Sway Park Industrial Estate *LYMN* SO41 ....308 A6
Swaything Clinic *PTSW* SO17 ....228 E9
Swaything Primary School *PTSW* SO17 ....228 D9
Sylvan First School *BKME* WDN BH12 ....321 K6
Tadley Community Primary School *TADY* RG26 ....34 C8
Tadley Swimming Pool *TADY* RG26 ....34 D7
Talavera Primary School *ALDT* GU11 ....2 E1
Talbot Combined School *WBNE* BH4 ....322 F7
Talbot Heath School *WBNE* BH4 ....334 C1
Talbot House Preparatory School *MOOR* WNTN BH9 ....322 E7
Talbot Medical Centre *BWD* BH11 ....322 A6
Talisman Business Centre *HLER* SO31 ....271 H4
The Tanneries Industrial Estate *HAV* PO9 ....14 E6
Tanners Brook J & I School *WSHM* SO15 ....247 K4
Taro Leisure Centre *EPSF* GU31 ....216 B2
Tatchbury Manor House *TOTT* SO40 ....245 M2
Tatchbury Mount Hospital *TOTT* SO40 ....245 N1
Tauntons College *WSHM* SO15 ....248 A2
Tavistock Infant School *FLEETN* GU51 ....74 A4
Tempus Business Centre *BSTK* RG21 ....6 A2
Tennis Centre *HASM* GU27 ....156 C6
Terminus Industrial Estate *PSEA* PO1 ....19 J3
Testbourne Community School *WHCH* RG28 ....85 M8
Test Valley Business Centre *ROWN* SO16 ....246 F1
Test Valley Business Park *NBAD* SO52 ....205 L7
Test Valley Golf Club *OVTN* RG25 ....107 H2
Testwood School *TOTT* SO40 ....246 D2
Thatcham Bowling Club *THLE* RG7 (The Vine *ELGH* SO50) 25 N3
Theatre Royal *WINC* SO23 ....22 E5
Thomson House *FARN* GU14 ....58 B8
Thornden School *CHFD* SO53 ....207 H5
Thorney Island Primary School *EMRTH* PO10 ....299 N6
Thornford Park Track *STHA* RG19 ....25 P9
Thorngate Hall *GPORT* PO12 ....12 A3
Thorngrove School *KSCL* RG20 ....29 M7
Thornhill Clinic *ITCH* SO19 ....249 M5
Thornhill Primary School *ITCH* SO19 ....249 L6

Thornycroft Industrial Estate *BSTK* RG21 ....69 H8
Three Legged Cross First School *WIMB* BH21 ....258 E9
Thruxton Aerodrome & Motor Racing Circuit *RAND* SP11 ....100 B2
Thruxton Industrial Estate *RAND* SP11 ....100 B3
Tidworth Garrison Golf Club *NTID* SP9 ....78 E7
Tidworth Leisure Centre *NTID* SP9 ....79 H5
Tidworth Military Cemetery *NTID* SP9 ....78 G1
Tiptoe Primary School *LYMN* SO41 ....307 M8
Titanic Memorial *WSHM* SO15 ....20 D2
Titchfield Abbey *FHAM* PO15 ....271 N8
Titchfield Primary School *FHAM* STUB PO14 ....271 M9
Tivoli Theatre *WBNE* BH2 ....278 D9
Tomlinscote School *FRIM* GU16 ....58 E3
Totton College *TOTT* SO40 ....246 B3
TOTT SO40 ....246 C6
Totton Recreation Centre *TOTT* SO40 ....246 A3
Tower Hill Primary School *FARN* GU14 ....75 N1
Tower Industrial Estate *BKME* WDN BH12 ....321 K3
Tower Park *BKME* WDN BH12 ....321 L2
Towngate Shopping Centre *PLE* BH15 ....332 E1
Townhill Infant School *WEND* SO18 ....249 J1
Townhill Junior School *WEND* SO18 ....249 J1
Townhill Park Health Clinic *WEND* SO18 ....249 J1
Town Quay *SHAM* SO14 ....248 B9
Townsend Primary School *CHAR* BH8 ....323 N5
Town Walls *PSEA* PO1 ....18 B6
Toynbee Further Education Centre *CHFD* SO53 ....206 F8
Travel Inn *ALDT* GU11 ....2 A2
CHCH BSGR BH23 ....324 D8
CHCH BSGR BH23 ....325 L7
ELGH SO50 ....228 C1
FARN GU14 ....75 M1
FERN BH22 ....302 F1
FHAM PO15 ....271 J6
HAV PO9 ....276 B9
KBH RG22 ....68 C7
PLE BH15 ....320 D6
ROMY SO51 ....227 K4
ROWN SO16 ....227 H7
SHAM SO14 ....21 F3
SHST GU47 ....41 L7
Travelodge *ALTN* GU34 ....150 A6
ELGH SO50 ....207 K7
EMRTH PO10 ....277 L8
KBH RG22 ....89 P2
KSCL RG20 ....30 D6
LIPH GU30 ....174 G2
LYND SO43 ....243 N7
NEND PO2 ....296 F9
RGWD BH24 ....281 L6
RWIN SO21 ....104 F8
RWIN SO21 ....125 L5
SHAM SO14 ....248 B4
Treadgolds Museum *PSEA* PO1 ....18 D2
Treloar College *ALTN* GU34 ....133 H2
Treloar School *ALTN* GU34 ....113 P8
Treloar Trust *ALTN* GU34 ....113 N8
Trilakes Country Park *SHST* GU47 ....40 G7
Trinidad First School *BKME* WDN BH12 ....321 L4
Trinity Business Centre *TOTT* SO40 ....246 C1
Trinity CE VA First School *VWD* BH31 ....258 F2
Trinity Church Hall *BSTK* RG21 ....6 E7
Trinity Industrial Estate *WIMB* BH21 ....300 C2
WSHM SO15 ....247 K4
Trinity School & Performing Arts College *ELGH* SO50 ....228 E5
Trojans Sports Club *ELGH* SO50 ....228 E5
Trosnant Primary & Infant School *HAV* PO9 ....14 E1
Trouville Hotel *WCLF* BH2 ....8 D5
Tudor House Museum *SHAM* SO14 ....20 D6
Tudor Merchants Hall *SHAM* SO14 ....20 D6
Tunworth House *OVTN* RG25 ....91 M3
Turbary Retail Park *BWD* BH11 ....321 M1
Turnpike Business Park *FHAM* PORC PO16 ....11 H3
Turnpike Industrial Estate *NWBY* RC14 ....24 G2
Tweseldown Infant School *FLEETS* GU52 ....74 E8

Twin Oaks Medical Centre *CHCH* BSGR BH23 ....305 M8
Two Riversmeet Leisure Centre *CHCH* BSGR BH23 ....324 C9
Twyford St Mary's CE Primary School *RWIN* SO21 ....183 P8
Twyford School *RWIN* SO21 ....184 A3
Twynam School *CHCH* BSGR BH23 ....324 C9
Tylney Hall Hotel *HTWY* RG27 ....71 L1
Tylney Park Golf Club *HTWY* RG27 ....53 L9
Tyrrells Ford Country House Hotel *CHCH* BSGR BH23 ....304 D4
UCI Cinema *BKME* WDN BH12 ....321 J3
ROWN SO16 ....296 C9
Uddens Trading Estate *WIMB* BH21 ....279 N8
UGC Cinema *SHAM* SO14 ....248 D9
Ullswater Hotel *WCLF* BH2 ....8 A6
Unicorn Trading Estate *HASM* GU27 ....156 C6
United Services RFC *PSEA* PO1 ....18 E3
United Services Sports Ground *PSEA* PO1 ....18 D4
University College Winchester *FUFL* SO22 ....164 E8
FUFL SO22 ....22 A6
University College of Winchester (Chute House) *BSTK* RG21 ....6 E5
University of Portsmouth *ENEY* PO4 ....317 H6
HISD PO11 ....317 H4
PSEA PO1 ....18 D2
PSEA PO1 ....19 K3
SSEA PO5 ....19 F4
SSEA PO5 ....19 H5
University of Southampton *PTSW* SO17 ....228 A2
PTSW SO17 ....248 B2
WSHM SO15 ....248 B3
University of Southampton (Winchester School of Art) *WINC* SO23 ....23 G3
Upham CE Primary School *BPWT* SO32 ....209 L8
Uplands CP School *SHST* GU47 ....41 J6
Uplands Primary School *FHAM* PORC PO16 ....10 E2
Uplands School *PSTN* BH14 ....321 L9
Upton Country Park *UPTN* BH16 ....320 A6
Upton Grey House *OVTN* RG25 ....92 A5
Velmead Community Centre *FLEETS* GU52 ....74 A8
Venture Industrial Park *HSEA* PO3 ....297 J4
LSOL BMARY PO13 ....295 H6
Vermont School *ROWN* SO16 ....228 A8
Vernham Dean School *RAND* SP11 ....43 H8
Verwood CE First School *VWD* BH31 ....258 E5
Verwood Industrial Estate *VWD* BH31 ....258 C4
Verwood Leisure Centre *VWD* BH31 ....258 F4
Viables Craft Centre *KBH* RG22 ....90 C2
Viables Industrial Estate *KBH* RG22 ....90 B3
Vicarage Farm Business Park *ELGH* SO50 ....208 C8
Vicarage Lane Clinic *HASM* GU27 ....156 E7
Vickers Business Centre *CHIN* RG24 ....69 H4
Victoria Cottage Hospital *EMRTH* PO10 ....299 M1
Victoria Park Swimming Centre *PSEA* PO1 ....19 F2
The Victoria School *CCLF* BH15 ....321 D9
Victoria Stadium *PSEA* PO1 ....18 E4
Victory Business Centre *PSEA* PO1 ....316 G3
Victory Retail Park *PSEA* PO1 ....316 E1
Victory Trading Estate *HSEA* PO3 ....297 K7
Vigo J & I School *AND* SP10 ....5 L2
The Vine School *BPWT* SO32 ....251 K3
Vinyard & Winepress *WVILLE* PO7 ....234 F8
Vistarama Balloon *BMTH* BH1 ....8 D4
VUE Cinema *KBH* RG22 ....68 C7
PSEA PO1 ....18 C4
The Vyne Community School *BSTK* RG21 ....6 E1
The Vyne (NT) *TADY* RG26 ....51 L7
Waite End Primary School *WVILLE* PO7 ....275 N4
Walford Mill Medical Centre *WIMB* BH21 ....278 D9
Wallisdean Junior School *FHAM* STUB PO14 ....10 C7

Wallop J & I School *STOK* SO20 ....120 F9
Walsh CE First & Middle School *ASHV* GU12 ....97 M2
Waltham Business Park *BPWT* SO32 ....232 E8
Walworth Road Industrial Estate *AND* SP10 ....83 H9
Warblington Secondary School *HAV* PO9 ....15 K5
War Memorial Hospital *AND* SP10 ....82 C9
Warren Avenue Industrial Estate *HSEA* PO3 ....317 K3
Warren Park Primary School *HAV* PO9 ....276 D3
Warrior Business Centre *PSEA* PO1 ....297 N2
The Watchetts Junior School *CBLY* GU15 ....58 B3
Waterford Lodge Hotel *CHCH* BSGR BH23 ....325 M9
Waterfront Business Park *FLEETN* GU51 ....74 E2
Waterfront Museum *PLE* BH15 ....332 D2
Waterloo Industrial Estate *HEND* SO30 ....250 B2
Waterloo School *WVILLE* PO7 ....275 N3
Waterlooville Golf Club *HORN* PO8 ....256 D9
Waterlooville Health Centre *WVILLE* PO7 ....255 M9
The Waterside Health Centre *FAWY* SO45 ....268 C3
Waterside Medical Centre *GPORT* PO12 ....13 H1
Waterside School *NEND* PO2 ....296 D6
Watersplash Hotel *BROC* SO42 ....286 F8
The Wavell Technology College *ALDT* GU11 ....76 A5
Waverley Abbey CE School *RFNM* GU10 ....117 J3
Waverley Abbey House *FNM* GU9 ....117 H2
WEA Clovelly Centre *SHAM* SO14 ....21 F1
Webb Peploe House Surgery *LYMN* SO41 ....329 L4
Weeke Primary School *FUFL* SO22 ....164 E5
Wellington Arms Hotel *HTWY* RG27 ....37 J9
Wellington Business Park *CWTH* RG45 ....40 F2
Wellington College *CWTH* RG45 ....41 H2
Wellington Country Park *THLE* RG7 ....38 C4
Wellington Monument (Arboretum) *CWTH* RG45 ....40 D2
Wellington Monument *HTWY* RG27 ....37 N6
Wellington Shopping Centre *ALDT* GU11 ....2 E3
Wellington Sports Centre *CWTH* RG45 ....40 G2
Wellington Sports Club *ELGH* SO50 ....228 F5
Wellow Golf Club *ROMY* SO51 ....203 L9
Wellow Primary School *ROMY* SO51 ....224 F1
Wentworth College *BOSC* BH5 ....335 N2
Wessex Complementary Medical Centre *SBNE* BH6 ....336 C1
Wessex Gate Retail Park *CFDH* BH17 ....320 D6
Wessex Hotel *WCLF* BH2 ....8 B5
The Wessex Hotel *WINC* SO23 ....22 E5
Wessex Nuffield Hospital *CHFD* SO53 ....207 H4
Wessex Road Surgery *PSTN* BH14 ....321 J9
Wessex Super Bowl *BKME* WDN BH12 ....321 P8
HAW PO9 ....276 B9
West Berkshire Community Hospital *NTHA* RG18 ....25 H3
West Berkshire Museum *NWBY* RC14 ....16 E2
Westbourne CP School *EMRTH* PO10 ....277 P6
Westbourne Medical Centre *WBNE* BH4 ....334 C2
West Canford Heath Medical Centre *CFDH* BH17 ....320 F3
West End Infant School *ALDT* GU11 ....2 C4
Western Community Hospital *ROWN* SO16 ....247 L2
Western Downland CE Primary School *FBDG* SP6 ....219 M3
Western Primary School *FUFL* SO22 ....164 E7
Westfield Hall Hotel *ENEY* PO4 ....317 N6
Westfield Industrial Estate *GPORT* PO12 ....12 A2
HORN PO8 ....256 D4
Westfield Junior School *CHAM* PO6 ....296 A1
Westfields Primary School *YTLY* GU46 ....40 C9
Westgate School *FUFL* SO22 ....164 E6
The Westgate *WINC* SO23 ....22 C4

West Hill Park School
  FHAM/STUB PO14 ....293 L1
West Howe Clinic
  BWD BH11 ....322 A4
West Howe Industrial Estate
  BWD BH11 ....321 N1
Westlands Medical Centre
  FHAM/PORC PO16 ....295 N2
West March Business Centre
  AND SP10 ....82 F9
West Moors Middle School
  FERN BH22 ....280 F8
Weston Park Boys School
  ITCH SO19 ....269 K1
Weston Park Infant School
  ITCH SO19 ....269 J1
Weston Park Junior School
  ITCH SO19 ....269 J1
Weston Shore Infant School
  ITCH SO19 ....269 H2
Westover Hall Hotel
  LYMN SO41 ....338 F2
Westover Primary School
  HSEA PO3 ....297 J9
West Point Business Park
  AND SP10 ....101 P1
  AND SP10 ....102 C2
West Portway Industrial Estate
  RAND SP11 ....101 N1
West Quay Retail Park
  WSHM SO15 ....20 B4
West Quay Shopping Centre
  SHAM SO14 ....20 C4
West Tytherley Primary School
  RSAL SP5 ....159 H7
Westwood Business Park
  TOTT SO40 ....246 D1
Weybourne County
  Infant School *FNM* GU9 ....96 E5
Weybrook Park Golf Club
  CHIN RG24 ....68 G3
Weydon County Secondary
  School *FNM* GU9 ....115 P3
Weydown Industrial Estate
  HASM GU27 ....157 H6
Weyford County Junior School
  BOR GU35 ....154 C4
Weyford Primary School
  BOR GU35 ....154 C4
Weyhill Business Park
  RAND SP11 ....81 H9
Wherwell J & I School
  RAND SP11 ....123 M2

Whitchurch CE Primary School
  WHCH RG28 ....85 M7
Whitchurch Medical Centre
  WHCH RG28 ....85 K6
Whitedown Special School
  ALTN GU34 ....132 D7
Whitehall Hotel
  BMTH BH1 ....8 D4
White Hart Industrial Estate
  BLKW GU17 ....41 M9
Whitehill Cemetery
  BOR GU35 ....154 D5
The White Horse Hotel
  ROMY SO51 ....204 C6
Whitelands Park Primary
  School *NTHA* RG18 ....25 M2
Whiteley Primary School
  FHAM PO15 ....271 J3
Whitewater CE Primary School
  HTWY RG27 ....53 M8
Whitley Ridge Country
  House Hotel *BROC* SO42 ....287 K7
Wick I Industrial Estate
  NMIL/BTOS BH25 ....326 C5
Wick 2 Industrial Estate
  NMIL/BTOS BH25 ....326 C5
Wickham CE Primary School
  WHAM PO17 ....252 E7
Wickham Park Golf Club
  WHAM PO17 ....252 C7
Wicor CP School
  FHAM/PORC PO16 ....295 L1
Wildern Clinic
  HEND SO30 ....250 C4
Wildern Secondary School
  HEND SO30 ....250 C3
Wildground Infant School
  FAWY SO45 ....268 B9
Wildground Junior School
  FAWY SO45 ....268 B9
Wilksworth Farm Caravan
  Park *WIMB* BH21 ....278 D6
William Cobbett Junior School
  FNM GU9 ....96 E5
William Gilpin CE
  Primary School
  LYMN SO41 ....309 M7
Williams Industrial Park
  NMIL/BTOS BH25 ....326 C5
Willink Leisure Centre
  THLE RG7 ....27 H5
Willink School
  THLE RG7 ....27 H5

Willis Museum
  BSTK RG21 ....7 F7
Willment Marine &
  Business Park *ITCH* SO19 ....248 F6
Wilverley Post
  BROC SO42 ....285 J8
Wimbledon Park Sports Centre
  SSEA PO5 ....316 F6
Wimborne First School
  WIMB BH21 ....278 D9
Wimborne Hospital
  WIMB BH21 ....278 C9
Wimborne Industrial Estate
  WIMB BH21 ....278 E9
Wimborne J & I School
  ENEY PO4 ....317 J4
Wimborne Market
  WIMB BH21 ....300 F1
Wimborne Minster
  WIMB BH21 ....300 D1
Wimborne RFC
  WIMB BH21 ....300 G1
Wimborne Town FC
  WIMB BH21 ....278 C9
Winchcombe J & I School
  NWBY RG14 ....24 D2
Winchelsea Special School
  BKME/WDN BH12 ....321 M3
Winchester Agricultural
  Museum *WINC* SO23 ....22 E2
Winchester Cathedral
  WINC SO23 ....22 E5
Winchester City Mill (NT)
  WINC SO23 ....23 G5
Winchester City FC
  WINC SO23 ....23 F1
Winchester City Museum
  WINC SO23 ....22 E5
Winchester College
  WINC SO23 ....22 E7
Winchester Lawn Tennis Club
  FUFL SO22 ....164 E5
Winchester RFC
  WINC SO23 ....23 G1
Winchester Road
  Industrial Estate
  KBH RG22 ....90 B1
The Winchester Royal Hotel
  WINC SO23 ....22 E4
Winklebury Centre
  DEAN RG23 ....68 F7
Winklebury J & I School
  DEAN RG23 ....68 G6

Winklebury Medical Centre
  DEAN RG23 ....68 F6
Winnall CP School
  WINC SO23 ....23 J4
Winnall Farm Industrial Estate
  WINC SO23 ....23 H3
Winnall Trading Estate
  WINC SO23 ....23 J2
Winter Gardens Theatre
  WCLF BH2 ....8 C5
Winterslow CE Primary School
  RSAL SP5 ....158 A1
Winton Primary School
  MOOR/WNTN BH9 ....322 E5
Winton School
  AND SP10 ....5 J3
  NBNE BH10 ....322 D6
Wispers School
  HASM GU27 ....157 H4
Wokefield Park Golf Club
  THLE RG7 ....27 N7
Wolverdene School
  AND SP10 ....5 F6
Wolvesey Castle
  WINC SO23 ....23 F6
Woodcote Primary School
  FHAM/STUB PO14 ....294 F5
Woodhill Preparatory School
  CHFD SO53 ....206 F6
  HEND SO30 ....250 F4
Woodlands Business Village
  BSTK RG21 ....7 J3
Woodlands Community School
  WEND SO18 ....249 L3
Woodlands Education Centre
  HORN PO8 ....255 N7
The Woodlands Lodge Hotel
  TOTT SO40 ....245 K8
Woodlea Primary School
  BOR GU35 ....154 A7
Woodlings Vineyard
  WHCH RG28 ....85 P2
Woolmer Hill Athletics Track
  HASM GU27 ....156 C5
Woolmer Hill Technology
  College *HASM* GU27 ....156 C6
Woolsbridge Industrial Estate
  WIMB BH21 ....281 H5
Woolsbridge Manor Farm
  Caravan Park
  WIMB BH21 ....281 H3
Woolsbridge Small Business
  Centre *WIMB* BH21 ....280 G3

Woolston Infant School
  ITCH SO19 ....248 G9
Woolton Hill Junior School
  KSCL RG20 ....29 M6
Wootey Primary School
  ALTN GU34 ....132 F3
Wordsworth House
  ROWN SO16 ....247 M1
Wordsworth Infant School
  WSHM SO15 ....247 M2
Works Industrial Estate
  FBDG SP6 ....240 B2
Worting County Infant School
  DEAN RG23 ....68 D8
Wyke CP School
  RGUW GU3 ....77 L8
Wykeham Gallery
  STOK SO20 ....141 L5
Wykeham House School
  FHAM/PORC PO16 ....11 K5
Wykeham Industrial Estate
  WINC SO23 ....23 J1
The Wykeham Industrial
  Estate *WINC* SO23 ....165 K5
Wynford Farm
  Industrial Estate
  ROMY SO51 ....204 D1
Wyvern Technology College
  ELCH SO50 ....230 C3
Yateley Common Country Park
  BLKW GU17 ....56 G2
Yateley Health Centre
  YTLY GU46 ....40 E8
Yateley Infant School
  YTLY GU46 ....40 E8
Yateley Manor Preparatory
  School *YTLY* GU46 ....40 E8
Yateley School & Sixth
  Form Centre *YTLY* GU46 ....40 D9
Yeoman Industrial Park
  ROWN SO16 ....246 F1
Yeomans Industrial Park
  CHAR BH8 ....323 L4
York Town Industrial Estate
  CBLY GU15 ....41 P9
Youngs Industrial Estate
  THLE RG7 ....34 A2
Yvs Business Park
  BKME/WDN BH12 ....321 L5
Zouch Primary School
  NTID SP9 ....78 F3

Acknowledgements

The Post Office is a registered trademark of Post Office Ltd. in the UK and other countries.

Schools address data provided by Education Direct.

Petrol station information supplied by Johnsons

One-way street data provided by © Tele Atlas N.V. Tele Atlas

Garden centre information provided by

Garden Centre Association  Britains best garden centres

Wyevale Garden Centres

The statement on the front cover of this atlas is sourced, selected and quoted
from a reader comment and feedback form received in 2004

AA **Street by Street** QUESTIONNAIRE

Dear Atlas User
Your comments, opinions and recommendations are very important to us.
So please help us to improve our street atlases by taking a few minutes
to complete this simple questionnaire.

You do not need a stamp (unless posted outside the UK). If you do not want to remove
this page from your street atlas, then photocopy it or write your answers on a plain sheet
of paper.

Send to: The Editor, AA Street by Street, FREEPOST SCE 4598,
Basingstoke RG21 4GY

ABOUT THE ATLAS...

Which city/town/county did you buy?
_____

Are there any features of the atlas or mapping that you find particularly useful?
_____
_____
_____

Is there anything we could have done better?
_____
_____
_____

Why did you choose an AA Street by Street atlas?
_____
_____
_____

Did it meet your expectations?

Exceeded ☐   **Met all** ☐   **Met most** ☐   **Fell below** ☐

Please give your reasons
_____
_____
_____
_____

ML011z

continued overleaf

Where did you buy it?

For what purpose? (please tick all applicable)

To use in your own local area ☐   **To use on business or at work** ☐

Visiting a strange place ☐   **In the car** ☐   **On foot** ☐

Other (please state)

LOCAL KNOWLEDGE...

Local knowledge is invaluable. Whilst every attempt has been made to make the information contained in this atlas as accurate as possible, should you notice any inaccuracies, please detail them below (if necessary, use a blank piece of paper) or e-mail us at *streetbystreet@theAA.com*

ABOUT YOU...

Name (Mr/Mrs/Ms)

Address

Postcode

Daytime tel no   **Mobile tel no**

E-mail address

Please only give us your e-mail address and mobile phone number if you wish to hear from us about other products and services from the AA and partners by e-mail or text or mms.

Which age group are you in?

Under 25 ☐   **25-34** ☐   **35-44** ☐   **45-54** ☐   **55-64** ☐   **65+** ☐

Are you an AA member?   YES ☐   **NO** ☐

Do you have Internet access?   YES ☐   **NO** ☐

The information we hold about you will be used to provide the product(s) and service(s) requested and for identification, account administration, analysis, and fraud/loss prevention purposes. More details about how that information is used is in our Privacy Statement, which you will find under the heading "Personal information" in our Terms and Conditions and on our website. Copies are available from us by post, by contacting our Data Protection Manager at AA, Fanum House, Basing View, Hampshire, Basingstoke RG21 4EA.

We may want to contact you about other products and services provided by us or our partners but please tick the box if you DO NOT wish to hear about such products and services from us by mail or telephone. ☐

Thank you for taking the time to complete this questionnaire. Please send it to us as soon as possible, and remember, you do not need a stamp (unless posted outside the UK).   ML